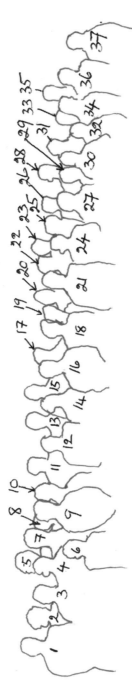

CONFERENCE PARTICIPANTS

(1) Claudio Mello (2) Franz Goller (3) Roderick Suthers (4) Clive Catchpole (5) David Clayton (6) Mei-Fang Cheng
(7) Michale Fee (8) Heather Williams (9) Daniel Margoliash (10) Ofer Tchernichovski (11) Gregory Ball (12) Mark Konishi
(13) Richard Mooney (14) Constance Scharff (15) John Kirn (16) Fernando Nottebohm (17) Michael Brainard
(18) Erich Jarvis (19) David Perkel (20) Linda Wilbrecht (21) Martin Wild (22) Steve Nowicki (23) Arthur Arnold
(24) Phil Zeigler (25) Manfred Gahr (26) Timothy Gentner (27) Kazuo Okanoya (28) David Vicario (29) Cheryl Harding
(30) Timothy DeVoogd (31) Peter Marler (32) Juli Wade (33) Sarah Woolley (34) Katherine Nordeen
(35) Frederic Theunissen (37) Sarah Bottjer

BEHAVIORAL NEUROBIOLOGY
OF BIRDSONG

ANNALS OF THE NEW YORK ACADEMY OF SCIENCES
Volume 1016

BEHAVIORAL NEUROBIOLOGY OF BIRDSONG

Edited by H. Philip Zeigler and Peter Marler

The New York Academy of Sciences
New York, New York
2004

Library of Congress Cataloging-in-Publication Data

Behavioral neurobiology of birdsong / edited by H. Philip Zeigler and Peter Marler.
   p. cm. — (Annals of the New York Academy of Sciences ; v. 1016)
   Includes bibliographical references (p.).
   ISBN 1-57331-472-2 (cloth : alk. paper) — ISBN 1-57331-473-0 (pbk. : alk.
paper) 1. Birds–Vocalization. 2. Birds—Nervous system. 3. Birdsongs. I.
Zeigler, H. Philip (Harris Philip), 1931– II. Marler, Peter. III. Series.
   Q11 .N5
   [QL698]
   500 s--dc22
   [598.15

                2004009704

GYAT / PCP
Printed in the United States of America
ISBN 1-57331-472-2 (cloth)
ISBN 1-57331-473-0 (paper)
ISSN 0077-8923

ANNALS OF THE NEW YORK ACADEMY OF SCIENCES

Volume 1016
June 2004

BEHAVIORAL NEUROBIOLOGY OF BIRDSONG

Editors
H. PHILIP ZEIGLER AND PETER MARLER

Conference Organizing Committee
H. PHILIP ZEIGLER, *CHAIR*, CHERYL HARDING,
RICHARD MOONEY, AND J. MARTIN WILD

This volume is the result of a conference entitled the Behavioral Neurobiology of Birdsong held December 12–14, 2002 at Hunter College, City University of New York. The conference was one of an annual symposium series sponsored by the Hunter College Gene Center.

CONTENTS

Financial assistance was received from:

- **NATIONAL INSTITUTE OF CHILD HEALTH AND HUMAN DEVELOPMENT, NIH**
- **NATIONAL INSTITUTE OF MENTAL HEALTH, NIH**
- **NATIONAL INSTITUTE OF NEUROLOGICAL DISEASES AND STROKE, NIH**
- **NATIONAL SCIENCE FOUNDATION**
- **RESEARCH PROGRAMS IN MINORITY INSTITUTIONS, NIH**

To the memory of WILLIAM H. THORPE

With gratitude to *Fringilla coelebs*, *Melospiza melodia*, *M. georgiana*, *Taeniopygia guttata* and *Serinus canarius* for their invaluable contributions to the scientific study of birdsong.

Acknowledgments

This Conference on the Behavioral Neurobiology of Birdsong was presented under the general auspices of The Center for Gene Structure and Function, Hunter College, City University of New York, which is supported by a grant from the Program for Research Centers in Minority Institutions of the NIH. We thank Professor Robert Dottin, Director of the Gene Center, for his support, and Mekbib Gemeda and Jeanne Waxman for indispensable help with conference arrangements. We gratefully acknowledge the specific assistance of the National Institutes of Health and the National Science Foundation whose generous conference grants made it possible to invite not only senior investigators, but also a large number of young birdsong researchers from many countries. Thanks to these various sources of support, the conference was able to bring together three generations of birdsong researchers, from the founders of the field to its present and future leaders. Thanks are also due to the organizing committee (Profs. Harding, Mooney, and Wild) and to the members of the birdsong community who responded with such enthusiasm to our initial invitation to participate and followed through with the contributions that have made this volume possible. Special thanks are also extended to Erich Jarvis for his help with the cover illustrations and the genealogy. Finally, I want to thank Professor Peter Marler for assuming the burden of co-editorship of this volume and sharing with its contributors the insights acquired over half a century of birdsong research.

— PHIL ZEIGLER

Genealogy of Birdsong Researchers

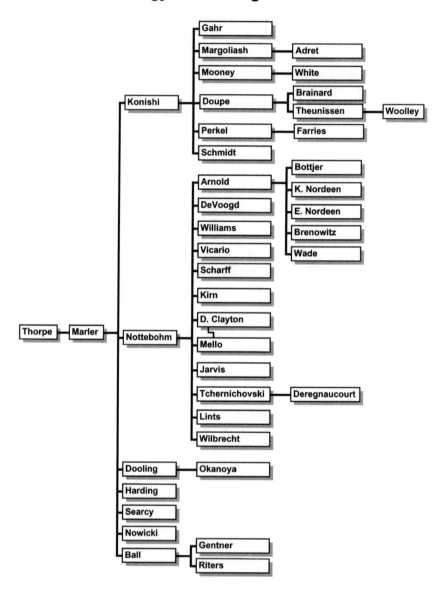

Introduction

H. PHILIP ZEIGLER

Department of Psychology, Hunter College, City University of New York,
New York, New York 10021, USA

The study of birdsong has a long past but a relatively short formal history. It was known to Chinese bird fanciers that many species of songbirds learn their song from their parents, and this was the impetus for a thriving trade in tutored birds. That song learning was familiar to Europeans as well is apparent from the report that George Henschel, a late 19th century English conductor, kept a highly trained bullfinch that sang "God Save the Queen." It was reported, perhaps apocryphally, that whenever the bullfinch paused too long in mid-melody, an untrained canary in the next room would pick up the tune and finish it off properly.

In addition to the fact that it is a highly noticeable and aesthetically striking feature of bird behavior, birdsong is of interest to biologists both because it is associated with reproductive behavior (and is therefore of interest to students of evolution) and because it is a learned behavior. Song learning became the subject of a long and productive series of studies by William Thorpe (1958) of Cambridge University, by his student Peter Marler, and by Marler's many associates and students (see Genealogy on facing page). Interest in the neurobiology of birdsong was quickened by two developments, one technical, the other neurobiological. The first was the development of the sound spectrogram, which provided a means for the preservation and objective analysis of bird songs (see the chapter by Tchernichovski and colleagues in this volume). The second was the report, by Nottebohm and his colleagues, that the vocalizations of songbirds reflected the operations of a definable collection of neural structures—a song circuit—originating in the bird's forebrain and capable of influencing the functioning of interneurons and motor neurons involved in the control of the bird's vocal organ.

Subsequent studies have identified many features of birdsong that have made it an increasingly fruitful model for research on a number of important problems in behavioral neurobiology. Among these features are (a) the reproducible and quantifiable nature of song behavior, (b) the many similarities between the acquisition of birdsong and of human speech, and (c) the identification and increasingly precise characterization of a central neural circuit dedicated to song. These features have engaged the attention of researchers on species-typical behavior, communication, behavioral development, memory systems, central sensory processing, motor learning, sensorimotor control, neurogenesis, and neuronal plasticity.

In the 25 years since the identification of a "song-circuit," birdsong researchers have shown that the structure of male brains differs from that of female brains; that

Address for correspondence: H. Philip Zeigler, Department of Psychology, Hunter College, city University of New York, New York, NY 10021. Voice: 212-772-5363; fax: 212-772-5629.
hzeigler@hunter.cuny.edu

Ann. N.Y. Acad. Sci. 1016: xv–xviii (2004). © 2004 New York Academy of Sciences.
doi: 10.1196/annals.1298.004

these structural differences correlated with differences in behavior; that the structure of adult brains and the songs they generate was much more plastic than had been thought, altering with changes in season and endocrine function; and, finally, that new neurons were born in the adult brain, migrated into position in brain areas involved in learning tasks, and became integrated into functional circuits. Subsequently, many features of the bird song system were found to apply to vertebrate brains in general, further increasing the utility of the model. These findings have had a major impact on neuroscience research and fundamentally altered our concepts of brain function. During the past decade there have been a number of new developments including (1) novel methods for the computer-assisted analysis of song learning; (2) techniques for the abolition or reversible disruption of auditory feedback from song; (3) techniques for the microanalysis of vocal tract activity from the syrinx to the beak; (4) the ability to monitor neural activity in the "song circuit" in awake, singing birds; (5) the identification of song circuit structures putatively homologous to basal ganglia structures implicated in human motor learning and movement disorders; (6) the molecular analysis of gene expression as a method for functional localization of song-related CNS structures; and (7) the continuing contribution of research on the avian song system to the study of neurogenesis in the adult brain.

The conference provided a venue for birdsong researchers to review substantive developments as well as to introduce the birdsong community to new methods in electrophysiology, genomics and the study of song development. Although its primary focus was on behavioral neurobiology, a number of participants were invited to review the interplay between neurobiological, ecological and evolutionary aspects of birdsong research. Almost all the formal participants at the conference have contributed reports, reviews, or essays to this volume. In addition, the editors have solicited chapters from a number of individuals to cover developments or issues for which even three very full days of presentations and discussions were not sufficient.

With some exceptions, the organization and content of this volume parallels that of the conference. One of those exceptions is the first section, **The Scientific Study of Birdsong**, which contains several chapters that provide background material designed to make subsequent chapters more accessible to the nonspecialist. They include a review of some important features of birdsong behavioral biology (Williams), a discussion of the utility of bird calls by Marler, an introduction to the important new area of birdsong genomics (Clayton), an introduction to issues of avian and mammalian brain homology (Farries), and an exposition of the recent revision of the classical nomenclature of avian brain structures that should help bring about a welcome rapprochement between avian and mammalian neuroscientists (Reiner et al.). Similarly, the chapter by Harding on hormones and singing behavior provides the nonspecialist with an introduction to the historical evidence for a critical contribution of neuroendocrine factors to the control of singing behavior.

The sections **Hearing the Song** and **Learning the Song** supplement the original conference presentations with reviews of novel (computer-assisted) methodologies for the quantitative analysis of auditory signal processing in the song system (Theunissen and colleagues) and the analysis of song development over both short-term and long-term time scales (Tchernichovski et al.). An important chapter by Adret reviews the history and current status of the "song template," a central construct in the study of birdsong. Two chapters are of unique historical interest. In one, Mark Konishi revisits his seminal work on the critical role of auditory feedback from the bird's own song, linking it to contemporary studies. In the other, Fernando Nottebohm provides an account of his pioneering studies of neurogenesis in the adult songbird brain. An innovative feature of the conference was a focus on the female's song preferences and their evolutionary and developmental implications (chapters by Gahr and by Nowicki and Searcy).

Professor Marler, the undoubted *doyen* of birdsong research was an observer rather than a formal participant at the conference. His contributions during the conference and his editorial comments on the chapters, many of them the work of former students, were notable for their breadth and incisiveness. They have enormously enriched this book.

Birdsong and Singing Behavior

HEATHER WILLIAMS

Biology Department, Williams College, Williamstown, Massachusetts 01267, USA

ABSTRACT: Birdsong provides neuroscientists with a uniquely powerful model for studying imitative vocal learning in a system where the brain structures responsible for song learning and production are well known. The 4,500+ species of songbirds provide a remarkable diversity of songs with a variety of tonal, structural, and learning characteristics, but most studies of the neural bases of learning have concentrated on two domesticated species, the canary and the zebra finch. Important differences in the songs of these two species provide useful properties for comparative studies, which could be expanded by using other species that demonstrate mimicry or action-based learning. Although the primary goal of most studies of the neural bases of song has been to define the mechanisms responsible for imitative learning during development, studies of adult crystallized song are important for two reasons. First, they define the endpoint of learning, and second, adult song shows interesting forms of variability in its performance. The degree of adult song variability itself varies among individuals and is influenced by the sources from which the song was learned, how the song was assembled during learning, behavioral responses of adult listeners, and levels of circulating sex steroids. In addition, song may be associated with coordinated visual displays, which also contribute to its communicative function. Thus the study of crystallized adult song is likely to provide insights into the neural control of facultative behavior as well as into the important question of how imitative learning takes place.

KEYWORDS: song; singing; zebra finch; canary; learning; untutored; crystallization; plasticity

Address for correspondence: Heather Williams, Biology Department, Williams College, Williamstown, Massachusetts 01267, USA. Voice: 413-597-3315; fax: 413-507-3495.
hwilliams@williams.edu; <http://www.williams.edu/Biology/hwilliams/>

Ann. N.Y. Acad. Sci. 1016: 1–30 (2004). © 2004 New York Academy of Sciences.
doi: 10.1196/annals.1298.029

The flowers appear on the earth;
the time of the singing of birds is come,
and the voice of the turtle dove is heard in our land.
—Song of Songs
Sumer is icumen in, Lhude sing cuccu!
—Anon
It was the nightingale, and not the lark,
That pierc'd the fearful hollow of thine ear;
Nightly she sings on yond pomegranate tree:
Believe me, love, it was the nightingale.
—Shakespeare

As these quotes indicate, birdsong has never lacked for admirers drawn by its purely aesthetic attributes. But to the naturalist, and increasingly to the contemporary neuroscientist, birdsong has two other aspects of interest. One is its role in reproduction. We now know that the voice of the turtle dove triggers hormonal changes in the producer and his mate that lead to successful breeding, and that the sweetly singing nightingale is not only trying to attract potential females, but is also displaying an auditory "no trespassing" sign, designed to repel intruders from his breeding area (see Nowicki and Searcy, this volume). Our understanding of its role in reproduction gradually led to a focus on the song itself, as a mode of communication, bringing with it the second important insight: that birdsong represents an unique form of vocal learning. Beginning in the early 1950s at Cambridge University, William Thorpe's and Peter Marler's work on song development and alarm calls led the way to a more systematic analysis of song behavior, yielding a bountiful harvest of insights into the stages of song learning, critical periods, the role of auditory models for song, and song dialects. As the understanding of the behavioral processes and nuances of birdsong deepened and grew richer, the next step was to begin to use experimental approaches to ask questions about the neural bases and correlates of song learning.

In some respects, work on the behavioral neurobiology of birdsong was both an exemplar and a departure from the trend towards the use of "simple" model systems for the study of neural mechanisms of behavior. As Chip Quinn put it, in a parody of the quest for the "ideal" model system,[1]

> The organism should have no more than three genes, a generation time of twelve hours, be able to play the cello or at least recite classical Greek, and learn these tasks with a nervous system containing only ten large, differently colored, and therefore easily recognizable neurons.

There is an important kernel of truth in this overdrawn picture: that simplicity of neural structure, while it may facilitate experimental investigation, constrains the complexity of the behavior to be modeled. For example, the "simpler systems" approach, exemplified by the use of the sea slug *Aplysia*, favors small nervous systems with few neurons and has proved to be a powerful and fruitful avenue for studying the neuronal mechanisms and circuits that underlie phenomena such as habituation and sensitization.[2,3] However, it has not added much to our understanding of the kinds of cognitive mechanisms involved in learning and playing a Beethoven piano sonata, or dancing *Swan Lake*. Similarly, organisms such as the fruit fly *Drosophila*, with well-studied genomes and short generation times, are ideal systems for studying the genetic basis and development of nervous systems.[4,5] But they have been of little assistance in understanding the complexities involved in the postnatal interactions of those systems with the environmental influences that shape complex adult behaviors.

Hence the appropriateness of Quinn's citation of "playing the cello" and "reciting classical Greek." Against this background, it is interesting that these two examples of complex learned behaviors, playing a musical instrument or speaking a language, both consist of learned motor sequences that produce auditory signals that communicate information about brain states of the human who is playing or speaking. Such behaviors represent the higher cognitive abilities that most fascinate us when we contemplate the question of what makes humans special. It is abilities such as these that have been the basis for arguments, by linguists such as Chomsky[6] and philosophers such as Dennett,[7] that humans have uniquely special capacities that are not accessible to study by a reductionist approach. For those of us who do not accept such arguments but instead see such highly developed cognitive skills as part of an evolutionary continuum, the utility of birdsong as a model for studying the neurobiology of complex behaviors is both attractive and important.

Songbirds (and their cousins, the parrots) offer neuroscientists several advantages. First is the nature of the song, as a vocal-auditory signal that is amenable to analysis, learned, and used in communication. Song is a complex and yet repeatable vocalization that is stereotyped in adults and can be readily recorded, quantified, and analyzed. It is learned with reference to an auditory model during a critical period. As a communication system, birdsong is a behavior that is affected by the conditions and social context the singer experiences, and in turn affects subsequent behaviors by conspecific listeners. Second is the fact that several songbird species have been domesticated and may be raised and studied in the laboratory; some species may produce three generations each year. Third is our increasing knowledge of the neural circuitry that mediates singing behavior (see articles by Wild, Mooney, Doupe, Brainard, and others, this volume) and our growing recognition that the avian brain is based on the same organizational schema as that of mammals (see articles by Farries, Perkel, and by Reiner and colleagues, this volume). Fourth is the rapid development of methods that harness the powerful tools of molecular biology for understanding genetic mechanisms involved in the acquisition and expression of singing behavior (see articles by Mello, Clayton, and Jarvis, this volume). Thus the birdsong system is currently the best, if not the only, model system that allows approaches that combine neural and genetic analyses with a complex natural behavior learned through imitation.

None of this might matter, were it not for the fact that vocal learning is rare among mammals. One primate species (humans), the cetaceans (whales and dolphins), and two bats account for all of the mammalian species that have been demonstrated to imitate vocal communication signals—a total of perhaps 300 species. In contrast, three large groups of birds are known to learn their vocalizations: parrots and their allies (350+ species), hummingbirds (300+ species), and oscine songbirds (4,500+ species). (The order Passeriformes, the perching birds, includes over 5,700 species,[8] which are divided into two main groups, the suboscines [~1,150 species], a primarily New World group that does not learn its songs or calls, and the oscines, or songbirds, [~4,580 species], which are distributed worldwide and do demonstrate vocal learning. The term "songbirds" includes both of these groups, but research on song learning is necessarily restricted to the oscine songbirds.)

Since many of these bird species are relatively easy to maintain in the lab (compared to cetaceans), sing readily, and are diurnal, the pre-eminence of singing behavior as an model system is understandable (see also articles by Scharff and White, and Jarvis, this volume).

BIRDSONG DIVERSITY

It is important to note at the outset that much of what we know about birdsong neurobiology is based upon the study of a very small subset of the relatively small number of species whose singing behavior has been studied in any detail. A recent survey of the literature (as indexed by PubMed, which omits many papers focusing solely on behavior) reveals that, among the oscine songbirds used as subjects of song studies, one species (the zebra finch, *Taeniopygia guttata*) accounts for approximately 51% of the total. The second most frequently mentioned species (the canary, *Serinus canaria*) represents a further 14%. Six additional species (starlings, *Sturnus vulgaris*; song sparrows, *Melospiza melodia*; white-crowned sparrows, *Zonotrichia leucophrys*; brown-headed cowbirds, *Molothrus ater*; swamp sparrows, *Melospiza georgiana*; and Bengalese finches, *Lonchura domestica*) account for a further 19% of the subject species. The remaining 16% were spread among 59 different species. Thus the study of brain correlates of vocal learning in songbirds has concentrated upon a very few species. Three domesticated species (zebra finches, canaries, and Bengalese finches) together account for more than two-thirds of all studies.

While some wild-caught birds [e.g., starlings and black-capped chickadees (*Parus atricapillus*)] may adapt quite readily to captivity, others may not unless they are captured as nestlings and hand-reared (a difficult, time-consuming process). Hence the choice of the primary species used for laboratory-based studies of vocal learning is, understandably, most often based upon criteria other than the properties of the song. Domesticated species are easy to breed in captivity and are not stressed by human presence and the laboratory environment, and so provide an easily accessible substrate for experimental manipulations of singing behavior.

This bias towards domesticated species, and, in particular, towards zebra finches, may in turn have affected our current view of vocal learning, since it is all too easy to generalize from zebra finches or canaries to "birds." Fortunately, the songs of the two most widely used species—the canary and the zebra finch—have different structures as well as different learning trajectories. While these two species' songs cannot begin to span the variety present among avian vocal learners, they nevertheless provide instructive examples of the important features of birdsong and their relation to vocal learning. However, these two species cannot between them represent the entire range of songbird vocal learning capacities. For example, mimicry, the ability to produce accurate imitations after hearing a single example of a sound [exemplified by species such as mockingbirds (*Mimus polyglottus)* and mynahs (*Gracula religiosa*)] is absent in zebra finches and canaries, both of which require an extended period of weeks or months to develop an accurate copy of a tutor's song. In addition, Peter Marler[9] has used the term "action-based learning" to describe the process of pruning inappropriate songs from the repertoire at the end of the song learning period; this pruning occurs very rapidly, in response to the actions of conspecifics. Including birds that are adept at mimicry and action-based learning among the species used for neuro-scientific studies of vocal learning might yield both new insights and new questions.

THE SONG LEARNING PROCESS

Since a primary impetus for studying birdsong is its value as a model for vocal learning (with parallels to human speech), it is worth considering how this process takes place. Song learning has several stages:[10] first, a sensory learning period, during which the young male listens to and memorizes the song of a socially salient tutor; second, a subsong stage, akin to the babbling of human infants, during which the young male produces sounds and listens to the results, calibrating his vocal instrument; the third stage, plastic song, during which the young male adjusts his song to approximate the memorized model; finally, crystallization, when the song is fixed in its adult form and the components of the song and the order in which they are sung become stereotyped. At the time of crystallization, birds of some species (e.g., song sparrows and swamp sparrows) prune material that was sung during plastic song to fix upon a particular subset of what was learned. These stages may be separate and distinct during development, or may overlap (particularly in the case of the first and second stages). In seasonally breeding birds, such as canaries and most temperate species, the stages of song learning usually begin in the summer, soon after fledging (when young birds leave the nest) and crystallization is completed in the following spring, when young males come into breeding condition for the first time.[11] In contrast, species that are not seasonal breeders may complete all of the stages of song learning during a very compressed period; zebra finches reach sexual maturity at about 90 days, and song crystallizes at that time.[12,13] Species also differ in whether song is fixed after it crystallizes during the first year (as in zebra finches and some seasonal breeders) or whether new songs are learned or old ones re-learned each year (as in canaries and some other seasonal breeders). Notwithstanding these species differences in the timing and repetition of song learning, the four classic stages (sensory learning, subsong, plastic song, and crystallization) are readily apparent in the developmental trajectories of commonly studied songbirds.

What material do young birds learn? Most often, it is the sounds and structure of the songs their parent(s) and neighbors sing. Some species, such as the canary and white-crowned sparrow (*Zonotrichia leucophrys*), will copy songs played through speakers. Others, such as the zebra finch, must have some interactive relationship with the song model, either in the form of an adult bird,[13] a key pecked to trigger a song playback,[14] or a visual model of the bird as well as an appropriate song triggered by key pecking.[15,16] In species that learn from tape recordings (such as the white-crowned sparrow), young males learn best from the adults with which they interact, even if they first encounter singing males well after the time they would normally have crystallized their songs.[17,18] A young bird's choice of which song model to copy is also guided by innate predispositions.[19] Hand-reared young male chaffinches exposed to recorded songs from a variety of species tend to copy only songs with conspecific properties,[20,21] and young male sparrows that are deafened or deprived of the opportunity to listen to any adult tutor (live or recorded) during song development develop songs that deviate from the normal pattern in a systematic fashion yet still retain some characteristics of the species-typical song.[22,23] Both the units of sound (syllables, notes, and elements) and the organization of those units within the song may influence the choice of model to be copied.[24,25] However, during development, young birds may occasionally alter a learned note or introduce what appear to be novel notes into their songs. Such notes are considered to be "improvised" or "invented," in that there is no specific example in the model song that was reproduced in the young male's song. Young birds may also rearrange the song notes they learn to generate a new order. Because of improvised or invented notes and rearrangement of copied notes, the learned song may not be an exact copy of a tutor's song, but it usually includes many notes that are near or exact matches of the material copied from one or more adult models. Thus the song material that is learned depends both upon genetic predispositions for certain acoustic and structural properties and the specific properties of the songs sung by socially salient conspecific birds—as well as some "creative" contributions when young birds improvise new song units or arrangements of those units.

Understanding the neural mechanisms that underlie imitative song learning is the holy grail of the field. To fully comprehend this phenomenon, studies focus upon two aspects of birdsongs: first, the neural basis for the production of stable, crystallized song, and second, the additional processes that are responsible for lability in song behavior—during development, during seasonal re-learning, or after inducing plasticity in adults. However, understanding either of these processes requires a comprehensive analysis of the endpoint of song learning, the adult crystallized song. The remainder of this article focuses upon the production of song by adults: what is sung,

---

FIGURE 1. Structure of zebra finch and canary song. The sonograms show recordings of a portion of one **zebra finch's song** (a) and a portion of one canary's song (b); expanded segments of each of these two songs are also shown. The dark bar along the 0 kHz line corresponds to 0.5 sec for the longer song segments and to 0.1 sec for the expanded sections of the song. Sound amplitude, in the form of an oscillogram, is shown along the 8 kHz (zebra finch) or 6 kHz (canary) line in the sonogram. The terminology for song structures differs slightly from some existing practices to ensure that similar units in the two species' songs have consistent labels. (a) In the zebra finch song, introductory notes (i) precede a series of motifs, some of which may be incomplete or truncated. A motif consists of a repeated sequence of unique notes. A note is defined as an uninterrupted sound; each note may include one or more elements. An element is defined as a unit of song that has a coherent time/frequency structure that distinguishes it from neighboring elements within a note. For example, notes 5 and 7 both have initial elements with strong frequency modulation, followed by elements that are held at constant frequency throughout most of their length. In these constant-frequency elements, the harmonic nature of zebra finch vocalizations can be clearly seen: element b from note 7 has a fundamental frequency of approximately 650 Hz, and eleven harmonics (integer multiples of the fundamental frequency) can be readily distinguished. NOTE: the song included five additional motifs that are not shown here. (b) Canary song consists of a string of phrases, each made up of many repeats of a single syllable (the term "syllable" is sometimes used to describe the unit called a "note" in zebra finch song, but a syllable is more properly defined as a song unit that is repeated to form a trill or phrase). A syllable may consist of a single note (as in phrase 6) or may be made up of two or more notes. The syllable that is repeated to form phrase 2 (see expanded version) is made up of two notes, an extended nearly constant-frequency note at approximately 2 kHz and a short higher-frequency note. The third mark on the sonogram, a short sound at approximately 4 kHz, is in fact the second harmonic from the loudest portion of note a and so does not represent a third note in this syllable. (The sonogram shown here was made from part of a recording provided by Dr. Fernando Nottebohm's laboratory.)

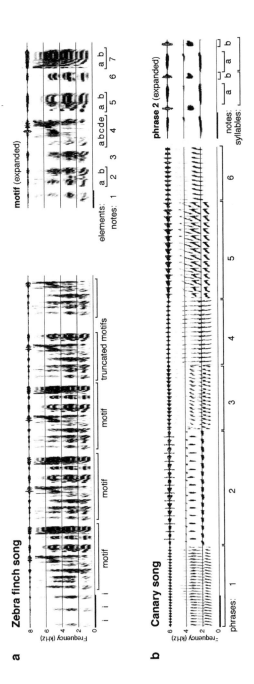

FIGURE 1. *See previous page for legend.*

how it is sung, and how the social context of singing affects song performance, with reference to the species most commonly used in laboratory studies of birdsong, the zebra finch.

CHARACTERISTICS OF ADULT SONG:
STEREOTYPY AND REPERTOIRES

The most salient feature of adult, crystallized song (for the human and, one presumes, the avian listener) is the stereotypy of delivery, both in the acoustic structure of the song syllables and the sequence in which syllables are sung. Accompanying the increase of stereotypy that marks crystallization is an increase in the volume and amount of singing, particularly for seasonal breeders that hold territories, such as canaries. This is not surprising, given that song is used for territory defense and advertisement in such species; a louder song is more effective in establishing a presence over a wide area. Since there is an energetic cost of frequent, loud singing,[26] softer singing outside the breeding season when song learning takes place presumably confers an energetic and thus a survival advantage. Some species do not show a marked increase in volume after crystallization; zebra finch song remains relatively quiet, most probably because the intended receivers are generally no more than a few meters from the singer. However, an increase in stereotypy of syllable structure and of the ordering of syllables does occur in zebra finches, and appears to be a universal characteristic of crystallized song.

An individual bird's crystallized song consists of a distinct repertoire, a set of elements, notes, syllables, phrases, motifs, or songs from which all instances of singing behavior are drawn. In some species the repertoire may be limited to a small set of syllables or notes that are each sung in nearly every utterance, so that a single 1–10 second song includes the entire repertoire; in others, recordings of many songs may be needed to define the large repertoire. A zebra finch's repertoire is quite small, ranging from 3 to 15 notes[27] (sometimes called elements or syllables). Each song opens with a series of identical repeated introductory notes followed by one or more repetitions of a "motif" that consists of most or all of the repertoire of song notes delivered in a fixed sequence, without repeating any individual notes. The majority of an individual zebra finch's song output usually consists of what is known as the "canonical" motif (sometimes called the canonical song), a note sequence that is repeated in a nearly invariant fashion (FIG. 1a). Other species, such as the canary[28] or starling,[29] may have a repertoire of dozens of such notes grouped into syllables that are repeated to form trills or phrases (FIG. 1b). Such songs, consisting of strings of trills or phrases, may continue for well over a minute, and phrases may be repeated within the song. Although transitions between phrases are highly predictable, with a given phrase accurately predicting its successor, the transitions are nevertheless somewhat variable and the sequence and number of phrases sung within a given song is only very rarely an exact replicate of the previous song. For this reason, it may be necessary to record several minutes of song from such species in order to accurately describe an individual's repertoire. Still other species (e.g., song sparrows and redwinged blackbirds) may have a repertoire consisting of several distinct song types, each of which is stereotyped and each of which differs from other song types in the repertoire.[30] Such species may sing with "immediate variety," moving to from song to song without repetition, or with "eventual variety," repeating songs several times before changing to another song in the repertoire.

Although the patterns of song behavior represented by the two most often studied species, domesticated zebra finches and canaries, do not span the entire range of songbird performance, they do represent relatively distant points within that spectrum. However, there are important aspects of song repertoires that are not well represented in studies of brain mechanisms for singing based on these two species in their domesticated forms: neither canaries nor zebra finches have repertoires with multiple song types or repertoires defined by dialects associated with specific geographical regions, nor do they mimic recently heard sounds or provide a clear example of action-based learning (the pruning of learned material based on the observed behaviors of conspecifics). Nevertheless, the two species have two different types of repertoires organized in different ways (an extended song consisting of syllabic trills in the canary as opposed to a short string of individual notes in the zebra finch) and learn their songs according to different schedules (canaries recapitulate song learning each year, singing crystallized song only during the breeding season, while zebra finches complete song learning once, crystallizing the song at 90 days and retaining that song for the entire lifespan). Despite these differences, the two species (like all songbirds except mimics) have song learning trajectories that culminate in a stereotyped and crystallized adult song. Although the salient characteristic of the crystallized song is its stereotypy, there does remain some potential for variation, and adults with similar song repertoires may vary their delivery of the material within the repertoire in dramatically different ways. The types and sources of this variability are interesting in their own right and also provide a potential bridge between studies of crystallized song and song learning.

ADULT SONG VARIABILITY

Crystallized zebra finch song is among the least variable songs, consisting of relatively few notes that are delivered in a fixed sequence. Yet even these songs have a limited form of variability: sequences of song notes can be omitted, with the song stopping short or skipping the initial syllables.[31,32] This kind of variability is akin to the variation in the order of delivery of phrases in canaries and of song types in birds with repertoires that include multiple types. In species that have been well studied, events associated with the development of song have a continuing impact on song performance in adults, most particularly on the ordering and packaging of notes or song types during adult song performance that can produce variability to the crystallized song.

One fundamental characteristic of vocal learning is that it results in the expression of a trait, the song, that is derived from conspecific antecedents—and these "song ancestors" differ from the sources of most phenotypic traits in that they are not limited to genetic ancestors of the singer. Although the father's song is often the only or most important source of material for the son's song, the evolution of vocal learning has made it possible for young birds to acquire song material from males other than their fathers, which presumably increases their ability to attract mates and to form dialect groups.[33] In the lab, however, song may often be learned exclusively from the father (as when offspring are raised in single-family cages), or from a song

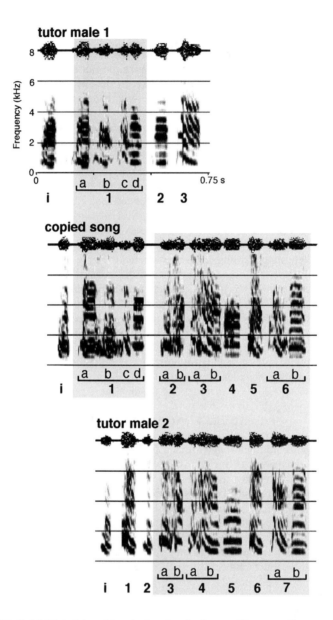

FIGURE 2. Multiple tutors for a single zebra finch song. The song of a young male zebra finch raised in an aviary with eight adult males was copied from two of those adults. The presumptive father of the young male sang the song denoted "tutor male 1," but because of the potential for extra pair copulations and egg dumping, paternity cannot be conclusively attributed to the adult in whose nest the young male hatched. The young male copied the first note (4 elements) from the social father, and copied the remainder of the song (5 notes made up of 8 elements) from a second male (tutor male 2). The young male's introductory note was not judged to be a copy of the introductory note sung by either tutor.

chosen by the researcher may be learned from a tape (canaries) or a dummy male who "sings" when a key is pecked (zebra finches). These environments are impoverished compared to the social and song environment encountered by wild populations, particularly in zebra finches, where a young male will interact with many adults within the colony after fledging. A breeding aviary with multiple pairs also exposes a young male zebra finch to multiple song models, and in such an environment young zebra finch males may copy song elements from more than one adult male (FIG. 2).[34]

Copying from more than one male and from males that are not the father is common in many species, particularly those in which young males have large repertoires and/or disperse before their first breeding season to an area where a different song dialect is sung. In such species, vocal elements associated with a specific tutor and sung by that tutor in a specific order tend to be associated. Nightingales (*Luscinia luscinia*) have repertoires of up to 100 songs and learn their songs as "packages," each consisting of approximately four songs sung by a single tutor.[35] As adults, they organize their songs so that songs within a package are sung in the same order the tutor used, and packages acquired from one tutor are likely to be sung in succession.[36,37] The structure of canary song, with its strings of repeated notes and predictable but not fixed transitions between notes, may represent a similarly "packaged" structure that reflects units of song learned from individual tutors. Zebra finches, with a much less complex song, nevertheless show a similar structure: "chunks" of notes (average length = 3) are learned as units and sung as units within the adult song, maintaining the original order as well as the acoustic structure of individual notes.[32] When multiple tutors provide source material for a male's song, the notes copied from each tutor are not intermixed in the new song, but rather chunks of notes from each song are sung in sequence. Even when a young male copies all of its song notes from a single tutor, the learned song may be novel because the chunks learned from the tutor's song have been rearranged (FIG. 3a). The performance of the song also reflects this chunked structure; if the singer truncates a motif, as sometimes happens in normal song production, the breaks in the normal sequence most often occur at chunk boundaries (FIG. 3b).

Thus, just as the repertoire of the nightingale is packaged, the adult song of the zebra finch has a hidden level of organization that reflects processes that occurred during development and that are apparent in truncated motifs, motifs that diverge from the canonical version.

INDIVIDUAL VARIATION IN THE STEREOTYPY OF ADULT SONG

Variability between individuals' songs is strikingly apparent to anyone working with songbirds. The most prominent source of this variability arises from song learning: both accuracy of song copying and final repertoire size varies among individuals tutored by the same adult singer. The accuracy of song copying is influenced by social cues in zebra finches,[38] and repertoire size is correlated with volumes of some forebrain song nuclei in both canaries[39] and zebra finches.[40,41] Beyond these sources of variability, there are also individual differences in how adults perform their learned songs, affecting several parameters of that performance. Some males sing

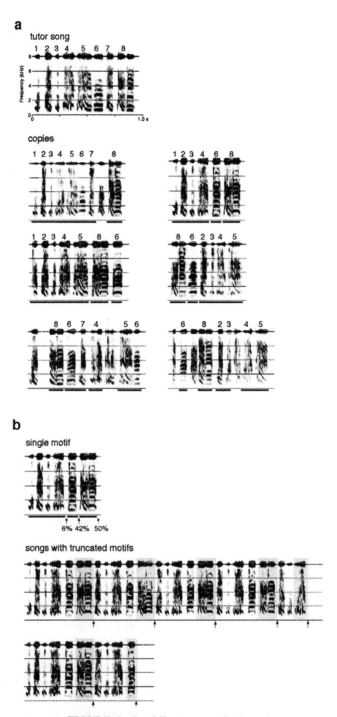

FIGURE 3. *See following page for legend.*

readily, others do not; some unmated male zebra finches sing only to specific females (or males), while others sing readily to all potential mates; some males sing extended songs or long bouts, while others may sing equal amounts of song in shorter segments; one male's song may vary between renditions, while another's will be more classically stereotyped; some male zebra finches sing several introductory notes before each song bout, while others may sing only one introductory note or forego these notes altogether. This variability in adult male performance of crystallized, stereotyped song, which is apparent even in critical-period learners such as zebra finches, has largely been ignored in studies of the neural basis of behavior (but see the article by Vicario on the variability in calling behavior in this volume), as it is the presence of a "canonical" song that is so useful in electrophysiological studies (the ability to examine neural patterns associated with multiple examples of the same complex behavior has proven to be very valuable). Variability in the note sequence within crystallized adult zebra finch song, which takes the form of alternative song motifs that lack particular notes (or added notes that are sung only occasionally) is more limited than the corresponding variability in canary and many other types of song, and hence is somewhat more tractable for analysis. One way to analyze individual variability in adult male zebra finch song is to use the formulas developed by Scharff,[42] which express stereotypy as a ratio of unusual syllable transitions to canonical syllable transitions:

(1) linearity is equal to the number of notes divided by the number of transitions;
(2) consistency is equal to the number of typical transitions divided by the number of total transitions; and
(3) stereotypy is equal to linearity plus consistency divided by 2.

Thus a song with a linear motif (having one transition for each note and no alternative forms) that is never truncated during delivery would receive a score of 1 for linearity, consistency and stereotypy, while the presence of any alternative motifs will reduce the linearity score, and more frequent singing of alternative motifs will reduce the consistency score (to determine these measures, approximately 100 consecutive motifs should be recorded and analyzed). Another measure uses the minimum number of different motif types that account for 85% of all song motifs sung (again within a sample of approximately 100 motifs). This measure demonstrates that there

---

FIGURE 3. Chunks of zebra finch notes are copied and sung as units. (**a**) The motif of an adult male zebra finch that was copied by many young males in an aviary environment (the same male's motif is shown as tutor male 2 in Fig. 2). Each note in the motif is numbered. The motifs of six young males that copied the adult are also shown; notes that were copied are numbered to correspond with the notes in the adult male's song. Notes that were not copied from the adult male's song are not labeled. Beneath each of the copied motifs, *bars* denote note sequences that were copied as continuous sequences, or chunks. (**b**) One of the copied song motifs shown in **a**, with *bars* indicating the extent of copied chunks. *Arrows* and associated percentages denote the proportion of motifs ending after each note during an extended series of recordings. Two songs including a total of seven motifs are shown; arrows denote the end of each motif. The final note in each motif is highlighted with gray shading. (In color figure published on-line, the final note in each motif is highlighted with color-coding that matches the system used for the standard, or canonical, motif.) Truncated motifs ended between chunks learned as units from the adult male's song, and not within chunks.

is substantial variability among normally reared males in song stereotypy (FIG. 4). Such individual differences in song variability may potentially provide a useful substrate for defining the neural mechanisms responsible for alternate sequences, which could then be applied to species with more complex syllable ordering. The fact that such variation in adult song exists, even in a species that sings one of the simplest and most stereotyped songs, indicates that it plays an important role in behavior. One possible reason for such variability in adult song is that it may allow the singer to tailor the song to a targeted listener, in a fashion similar to the way young birds' song development can be influenced by the responses of conspecific listeners.

THE INFLUENCE OF A LISTENER UPON SONG DEVELOPMENT

The song developed by a male raised without access to a song tutor or model is sometimes called "isolate song," as it is developed by males raised in isolation. However, song with similarly abnormal properties is also produced by males raised without a male tutor but in the company of females or of same-age conspecifics, and so the more accurate term is "untutored song." Untutored zebra finch song, though it retains many characteristics of normal song, is marked by unusual note structure, decreased stereotypy of that note structure, and decreased stereotypy of song structure.[13,43] In zebra finches, untutored birds are likely to have upsweeps as well as downsweeps in their songs (upsweeps are not seen in the songs of normally reared birds) and are likely to include larger numbers of high-frequency notes in their songs. The songs of untutored birds also show abnormalities in the assembly of notes into motifs and songs. Stereotypy of note order within a motif is reduced, and zebra finches raised without tutors may not have a canonical motif and may only rarely repeat any given sequence of notes. Untutored males' songs may also include repeated notes in a structure similar to the trills of canaries. It has been generally assumed that

---

FIGURE 4. Motif variation in tutored and untutored zebra finch song. (**a**) A continuous recording of 15 sec of song sung by an untutored male zebra finch. Compare this song to that of a young male raised with a song model (FIG. 1a). In the case of the untutored male, it is difficult to determine exactly which motif represents the standard, or "canonical," motif; in fact, none of the seven motifs sung in this segment are identical, and thus seven motif variants are represented within the recording. In comparison, FIGURE 1a shows five motifs from a song that included ten motifs and three motif variants. (**b**) Motif variability differs among normally reared birds, but is highest in untutored birds. The number of times each motif variant was sung within a recording of approximately 100 motifs was tabulated, and motif variants were ordered from most common to least common. This plot shows the cumulative proportion of the total number motifs sung that are included as each successive motif variant is added to the sample. For the bird shown with *diamonds*, the most common motif variant represented 64.4% of all motifs sung, the second most common 19% of all motifs—for a cumulative total 83.4%—and each successive motif variant added a smaller proportion to the total. The number of motif variants needed to generate 85% of all motifs sung (a level represented by the *dotted line*) can be used to describe the variability of an adult male's song. A typical pattern of motif variation for a normally reared male is shown by the *diamonds* (the 85% level is reached with 2.18 motif variants), the extreme for normally reared males by the *triangles* (8.69 motif variants were required to reach the 85% level), and a distribution seen only in untutored males by the *circles* (21.67 motifs were required to reach the 85% level).

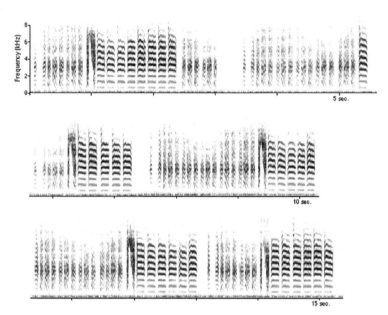

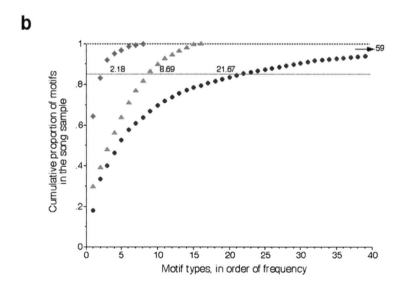

FIGURE 4. *See previous page for legend.*

these unusual properties of untutored song are due to the absence of a song model, but it is also possible that some features of untutored song arise in part because of absence of behavioral feedback from a conspecific listener.

Listening to conspecific song plays an obvious and crucial role during song development. A young male listens to the model song he will copy, and hearing that song is crucial to normal development. The importance of a listener for a young male singing plastic song is somewhat less obvious, as birds can develop normal song in the absence of conspecifics if they were earlier exposed to an appropriate song model. However, the listener's role in guiding song development can be powerful, as Meredith West and Andrew King have demonstrated in brown-headed cowbirds. A cowbird female listening to a young male's song efforts responds selectively to different versions of the plastic song, and so directs the course of song learning and strongly influences its outcome.[44] Although evidence for powerful listener effects in other species is not as compelling as for cowbirds (which are brood parasites and so do not hear appropriate song models until relatively late in development), the highly social colonial environment a young zebra finch experiences during song learning is likely to favor a function for listeners in song development. Some laboratory data support the possibility that listeners influence song development: males raised with deaf adult females sing more frequently than do males raised with hearing adult females, and the songs of males raised with deaf females are less stereotyped and include more atypical syllables than do the songs of males raised with hearing females (FIG. 5). Interactions with siblings may also contribute to the process of song learn-

---

FIGURE 5. Effect of an audience upon zebra finch song development. (**a**) Examples of songs generated by males reared with and without tutors (the untutored male was raised with a male sibling of the same age). Elements that are not similar to zebra finch calls are designated by gray shading. (In color figure published on-line, the elements that are similar to zebra finch calls are shown in black, and those that would not be found in calls are highlighted in red.) Non-call elements include high-frequency elements with few harmonics, upwardly modulated elements, and click trains. (**b**) The presence of a hearing female during development decreases the proportion of non-call elements incorporated into a young male's song. In recordings made after birds reached 90 days of age, males reared with at least one hearing companion (an adult male tutor, a hearing mother, or a hearing adult female companion) included significantly fewer non-call elements in their songs than did males that were housed alone or with deaf conspecifics (deaf mothers and deaf adult female companions; $P<0.001$). The condition of the mother is designated first, followed by the condition of the adult female companion; young males were housed with their mothers for the first four weeks after hatching, and then housed with the adult female companion until reaching at least 90 days of age. Whether a hearing female was present during early development (the mother) or after fledging (an adult female companion) had no effect on the learning of non-call elements, provided that one of the two was not deaf. (**c**) Males raised with an adult male song model sing their song elements in a highly stereotyped sequence: fewer than 5% of transitions between elements are atypical (typical transitions are those present in the canonical motif). In contrast, males raised with adult females sing a less stereotyped song with a significantly greater number of atypical transitions ($P<0.05$). The recordings from which these data were derived were made when untutored males were 200 days old, well after the age when song normally crystallizes (90 days); values for normal males are from recordings made at 150 days. (**d**) At ages between 60–75 days, when song learning is in progress, the singing rate of males housed with deaf females was significantly higher than that of males housed with hearing females ($P<0.001$). Singing rates were measured by tabulating the total amount of time spent singing during 30-min recording sessions.

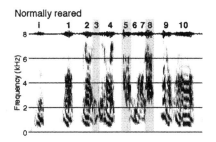

a

Normally reared

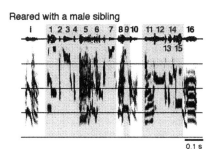

Reared with a male sibling

0.1 s

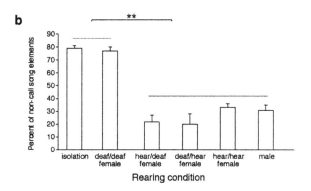

b

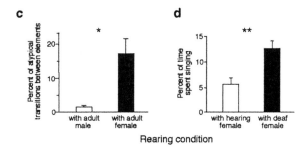

FIGURE 5. *See previous page for legend.*

ing, as exemplified by the demonstration that young males housed together converge on an abnormal song[45] and the finding that the differing pace of song development among a clutch of zebra finches affects the outcome of vocal learning.[38] Thus the presence of conspecifics during song learning provides two potential contributions to the development of a young male's's song: first, a model song to copy, and second, the presence of a listener that, by means of behavioral responses to what is sung, provides feedback about the content of the developing song. The relative importance of these two contributions may vary depending upon the species and the circumstances, but the potential role of a listener during song development should not be ignored.

THE INFLUENCE OF A LISTENER UPON
ADULT SONG PERFORMANCE

The delivery of crystallized adult song, which has two well-documented functions—territory defense and mate attraction—has evolved specifically to influence listeners' behavior. Thus it is not surprising that listeners' behaviors affect song performance in several ways. Species with large repertoires and flexible delivery patterns are the most likely to show obvious variations in the delivery patterns of adult stereotyped song. Species with multiple songs, such as the nightingale (and potentially those with multiple phrases, such as the canary or starling) may also have preferred song orders, but these too are strong statistical trends rather than invariant rules. Such preferences for delivery of notes, phrases, or songs in a particular order are affected by conspecifics' behavior. When a rival sings from an adjacent territory or as part of a territorial incursion, the delivery of a male's repertoire often shifts during this "countersinging." One type of shift in the preferred order of song delivery is known as "song matching," a form of song performance in which a male sings the song in his repertoire that best matches that being sung by the rival. Song matching has been observed in many species, including indigo buntings (*Passerina cyanea*),[46] meadowlarks (*Sturnella magna*),[47] nightingales, and song sparrows.[48] Other forms of variation in performance during countersinging may include the timing of song delivery so that it overlaps that of the other male (nightingale, chickadee), or shifting the pitch of the song so that it assumes a specific relationship to that of the other male (chickadee). Wild canaries, with their labile syllable order and large repertoires used in territorial advertisement and defense, may engage in countersinging (it is well known that domesticated males are more likely to sing in the presence of other singing males or similar sounds). Canaries may also perform a type of song matching by shifting the usual syllable sequence in order to best match the countersinging male. If shifts in syllable order could be triggered in response to specific playback tapes, canaries could provide a valuable model for studying the plasticity of crystallized behavioral sequences, a phenomenon that has not been examined at the level of neural mechanisms.

In contrast to songbirds that broadcast high-volume song from a large, defended territory that provides the male with access to resources needed for reproduction, zebra finches sing a low-volume song intended for listeners within a few meters.[27] This song takes two forms: a courtship song that is "directed" at a specific bird, and "undirected" song, which is sung without an obvious object.[31] These two forms of the song both consist of the same syllables given in the same order, but differ in the num-

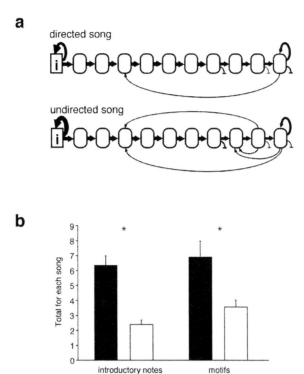

FIGURE 6. Differences between courtship and undirected song in the zebra finch. Courtship song is directed to a conspecific individual; the male orients himself and directs a courtship display, or dance, to that individual during song delivery. In contrast, a male singing undirected song does not orient towards an individual or perform a courtship display. Song stereotypy also differs in these two contexts. (**a**) The transitions between elements are less stereotyped during undirected song than during courtship song. Thicker lines in this diagram represent transitions that are more frequently observed. The box denoted "i" represents introductory notes. (After Sossinka and Böhner.[31]) (**b**) Males singing courtship song use more introductory notes ($P < 0.01$) and sing more motifs in each song ($P < 0.01$). (The data for this figure and analysis were drawn from Sossinka and Böhner.[31])

ber of introductory notes, which is higher for undirected song, and the stereotypy of the song motif. Birds singing undirected song have more sequence variability. They are more likely to truncate motifs, start in mid-motif, or use atypical transitions between notes than while singing directed song (FIG. 6). The differences in stereotypy between the two song forms is of considerable interest, especially since the discovery that the two forms are associated with differences in gene expression in the song basal ganglia circuitry.[49] In the case of zebra finches, song directed at a listener is less variable and activates the basal ganglia, while the more variable song that is not clearly directed at a conspecific does not. It is possible that other species that have alternate forms of their songs with different degrees of variability may also activate basal ganglia circuits while singing one form of the song but not the other. Although the role of social context in generating the two types of neural activation patterns and associated songs is not clear, it is of considerable interest because of the correlation with song variability.

The form of adult male song can also be affected by behavioral feedback from non-singing females. The classic example of this phenomenon is that of brown-headed cowbirds.[50,51] A male's adult song performance may change after the male observes the effect of his own song and other males' songs on female behavior. Such observations of female responses may cause an adult cowbird male to copy another male's song or to favor the use of portions of his own repertoire that are most effective. Female effects on the delivery of adult male song are not restricted to brood parasites (such as cowbirds), which have special circumstances surrounding song learning because the young are raised by other species. Zebra finch males' vocal behavior is affected by the behavior of females, which do not sing, in two ways. First, the probability that males will call in response to another individual's call is affected by the characteristics, and particularly the sexually dimorphic characteristics, of the heard call (see Vicario, this volume). Second, the probability that a male will sing a canonical motif is affected by calls the female gives while he sings (FIG. 7). A male is more likely to truncate his song motif if the female to which he sings calls during the song. Since individual females respond differently to a male's song, repeated exposure to a specific female may result in a shift in a male's canonical motif. A shift in the favored motif will have the result of changing the frequency with which certain notes are delivered within the repertoire are. Thus, even after an adult male has crystallized his song, he may shift its constituents in response to his observation of the listener's behavior.

VISUAL DISPLAYS ASSOCIATED WITH SONG

The especially attractive properties of birdsong as a model for studying the neural bases of imitative vocal learning and auditory-motor interactions can sometimes draw attention away from the fact that the acoustic signal may be part of a coordi-

---

FIGURE 7. Female calls affect male song performance in zebra finches. (a) Individual male and female zebra finches were placed so they could see but not hear each other through a lucite partition, and their vocalizations were recorded. By relaying the recording directly to a speaker, the experimenter controlled which bird could hear the other. In the example shown here, the female could not hear the male, but the female's vocalizations were played to the male through a speaker on his side of the partition (note the presence of the female's calls in the recording of the male). To highlight variation in motif structure, motifs and the sequence of notes are designated by bars and numbers under each sonogram. Calls are not numbered. (In the color figure published on-line, notes and chunks of notes within the male's song are shown by color-coded bars over the male's sonogram. Calls are not color coded.) The calls and unusual motif structure sung when the female first called were repeated for several motifs before the male returned to the more standard motif structure. (b) Female call rates were not affected by the male's ability to hear the calls, but were significantly higher ($P<0.05$) when the female could hear the male's vocalizations. (c) The number of non-standard motifs the male sang was not significantly affected by whether or not the male could hear the female. (d) When the male could hear the female's calls, non-standard motifs were more likely to overlap with female calls than were standard motifs, as reflected in the significantly higher ($P<0.05$) female call rate during non-standard motifs.

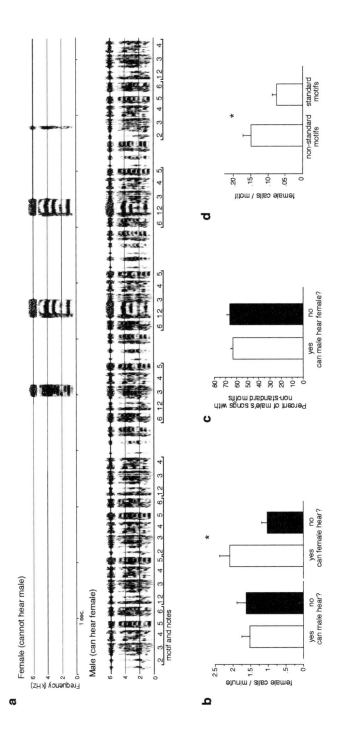

FIGURE 7. *See previous page for legend.*

nated display rather than the only component of song behavior. Many species do broadcast their song over a wide area from a hidden location, and such songs can be accurately represented as an auditory signal without visual correlates. However, visual stimuli are an important component of singing in many species. Such stimuli may include plumage displays (ranging from simply adjusting feather posture to complex demonstration of specialized plumes, as in birds of paradise) as well as stylized movements delivered by individuals or pairs. These displays may be delivered by individuals singing alone, or by groups of males performing at leks (a lek is a traditional display area consisting of a cluster of small territories occupied by courting males; lekking species include various types of grouse, the New Zealand parrot known as the kakapo, many birds of paradise, and several manakins). The more spectacular displays are not found among the species most often used as subjects of vocal learning studies. Canaries assume a specific song posture, with the head raised and the feathers of the throat loosely fluffed out. Zebra finches alter the position of feathers at the crest, giving the normally rounded head a flat top. As part of directed song, zebra finch males also perform a courtship dance oriented to a female.[52] This dance includes a set of hopping and bobbing movements as well as changes in beak aperture. Changes in gape have an important effect upon the sounds of song because opening and closing the beak changes the length of the vocal tract, thereby adjusting its resonance, and consequently changes the filtering of sounds generated by the vocal organ.[53,54] The effect upon the sounds being produced is consistent with a model in which a shorter vocal tract (open beak) emphasizes higher-frequency sounds. Changes in beak gape are tightly coupled to specific song syllables, and, although the primary function is to filter the sounds produced by the syrinx, beak movements are also clearly visible to a nearby observer. In a similar fashion, the inflation of the interclavicular air sacs that is a component of song respiratory behavior causes the feathers of the throat to be projected outwards. In many birds, the plumage in this area is of a color that contrasts with surrounding feathers, and the visual prominence of these feathers varies with changes in internal air pressure during singing. Beak gape and throat feather position thus provide visual correlates of some of the struc-

---

FIGURE 8. Coordination of zebra finch song with beak and "dance" movements. The song motifs of an adult male (song model, top) and a young male hatched in the adult's nest (copied song, bottom) are shown. The final note in the adult's motif was not copied, and a novel note was inserted into the young male's motif; these notes are shaded. (In the color figure published on-line, the portions of the motif that were copied are shown in red in the model song and in blue in the copy.) Only copied notes were included in the analysis of beak and body movements; the data from the copied song were shifted to the left to align notes to corresponding notes in the tutor's song (as indicated by *arrows* above the copied song). Videotapes of approximately 100 motifs were examined frame by frame, and the proportion of motifs that included beak movements (opening or closing) for each 33-msec segment within the motif was determined, as was the proportion of motifs that included the initiation of "dance," or body movements within each 33-msec segment. The location of beak movements was highly stereotyped within the motif, and there were also peaks in the initiation of dance movements. A comparison of the movement patterns in the song model and the copy showed a significant correlation between the patterns of the tutor and learned songs for both beak movements ($P<0.0001$) and for dance movements ($P<0.001$). This correlation was also seen in another father/son song pairing.[55]

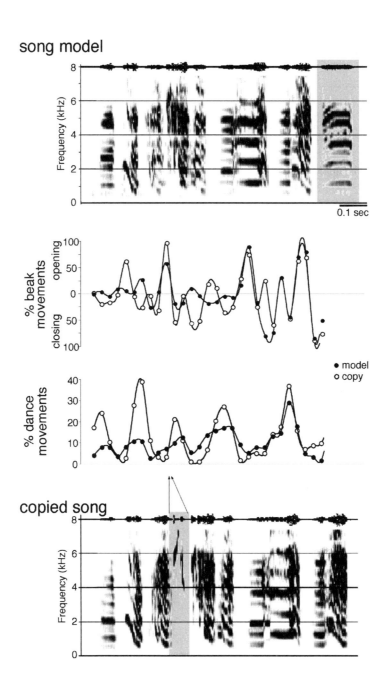

FIGURE 8. *See previous page for legend.*

tural features of song, and may accentuate those features for a nearby conspecific listener.

In contrast, dance movements may be distributed throughout the song and need not be as tightly coupled to specific notes or respiratory phases. In zebra finches, the patterns of dance movements in a male's song are very similar to the dance patterns of the birds that provided the auditory model for the song, as are the patterns of changes in beak gape (FIG. 8).[55] Thus these courtship dance patterns are closely co-ordinated with the rhythm of the learned song.

Although the primary function of such clearly visible movements as changes in gape and inflation of air sacs is likely to be directly related to sound production or filtering, such movements are prominently visible to any observer just as are the hops and head movements of a courtship dance. The reliable coupling of dance and beak movements to song suggests that the traditionally defined song circuitry also engages other motor patterns, perhaps using respiratory and extra-vocal pathways (Wild, this volume). It further suggests that listeners' responses to a particular song may be affected by the visual signals associated with the song as well as by the acoustic parameters of the song itself. Although the acoustic properties of song are far more tractable for analysis and for research into vocal learning and motor patterns, it is important to keep in mind that the biological function of the song may be difficult to separate from movements associated with the song that add visual signals to the display.

HORMONES, MOTIVATION, AND SONG PERFORMANCE

Much of the variation in adult song stereotypy might be attributable to differences in motivation, with song sung in low motivational states showing more variability than highly motivated song. As a behavior that is affected by day length, sex steroids, and the presence of specific individuals that are potential rivals or mates, crystallized song is presumably under the influence of emotional and motivational factors.[56–58] Although most considerations of the role of photoperiod and hormonal influences on song circuitry have tended to focus upon structures analogous or homologous to the mammalian cortex and basal ganglia and efferent pathways,[59–61] motivational influences upon song are most likely to be mediated by subcortical structures such as the hypothalamus and limbic system. The specific projections responsible for links between song circuitry and the hypothalamus and limbic system have not yet been fully defined, but are likely to be similar to those in non-songbird species such as the ring dove (Cheng and Durand, this volume).

The best characterized of the potential brain correlates of motivation are the sex steroids, testosterone (T) and its metabolites. In mammals, the effects of T upon the central nervous system and behavior are thought to be mediated by the areas where receptors for sex steroids are found: the hypothalamus, limbic system, and midbrain[62]—all of which are thought to affect motivational states. In addition to these areas, sex steroid receptors in songbirds are found in the cells of forebrain, midbrain, and hindbrain song circuit nuclei[63] (see articles by Ball and colleagues, Brenowitz, and Gahr, this volume). In open-ended learners, such as the canary, the seasonal modulation of song plasticity, volume, and stereotypy is associated with changes in day length and circulating T levels.[64,65] In the canary, T causes an in-

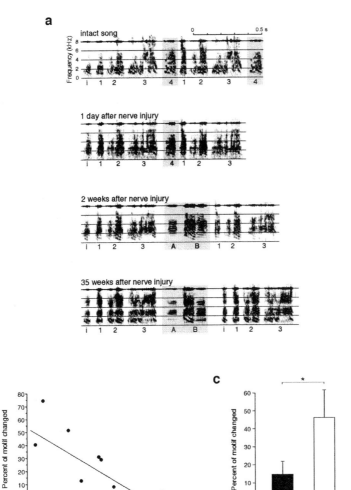

FIGURE 9. Testosterone reduces adult song plasticity in zebra finches. (**a**) An example of adult song plasticity. The original song motif included four distinct notes, all of which were retained (in a noisier form) in recordings made one day after one of the nerves serving the vocal organ was severed. Note 4 (highlighted by gray shading and in red in color figure published on-line) was not sung in any subsequent recordings, and thus was considered to be deleted. In a recording made two weeks after the nerve injury, two new notes, A and B (also highlighted by gray shading and highlighted in blue in color figure published on-line), were inserted at the end of the motif. These two new notes persisted in the same form and position during all subsequent recordings and thus were considered to have been added to the song. The total length of the deleted and added notes was measured and expressed as the percentage of the length of the original motif; this percentage was used as a measure of song

crease the volume of brain song nuclei,[66] and, within those nuclei, an increase in the length of dendrites,[67] an increase in the density of synapses,[68] and a change in the turnover of new neurons.[69] Sex steroids play an important role in mediating the rapid increase in stereotypy that defines crystallization. Artificially increasing T levels early in development can cause early crystallization of song in zebra finches.[70] Reducing testosterone levels or pharmacologically blocking testosterone activity delays song crystallization in sparrows.[57] In zebra finches and possibly some other critical period learners, T-associated fluctuations in song plasticity and stereotypy are not seen after crystallization at 90 days, but manipulating circulating testosterone levels does affect song performance.[56,71] Castrated male zebra finches sing less than do their intact counterparts, and supplementing testosterone by means of implanted silastic capsules is widely and effectively used to induce higher singing rates in intact adult males. High levels of circulating testosterone also affect adult zebra finch song by decreasing the potential for a latent form of song plasticity. This adult plasticity, which is usually only apparent over the course of several weeks, is revealed when auditory feedback is disrupted during song production by deafening[72] or introducing auditory interference,[73] causing adult males to lose song structure and stereotypy. Adult plasticity in the form of a reconfiguration of crystallized song also appears after disruption of the vocal output by syringeal nerve section,[74] muting,[75] or mechanical interference with phonation.[76] At least one form of adult plasticity is also sensitive to circulating testosterone; adult male zebra finches with high T levels are less likely to change their songs after syringeal nerve section (FIG. 9).[77] Thus testosterone's effects on adult song performance and plasticity in zebra finches are consistent with the better-understood role of T during development. Supplementing testosterone to increase singing should be used with care, as it has consequences for song and for song circuitry that extend beyond enhancing song rate.

The strong relationships between circulating testosterone and song rate, stereotypy, and the potential for adult plasticity all point to a role for T in reducing variability in song performance while increasing song production. If we view testosterone as a proxy for motivation, we are left, however, with the observation that testosterone levels do not account for all of the variation in song stereotypy and performance. Either factors other than motivation must account for some aspects of song variability, or brain mechanisms unrelated to testosterone contribute to motivational control of song variability. Given the variety of factors known to be related to variability in song performance, it is likely that the mechanisms that control this variability have some elements that are yet to be described.

---

plasticity. (**b**) The proportion of the song motif that was changed after nerve injury varied widely among males, and was significantly correlated with wet testis mass ($P<0.05$). Birds with larger testes were less likely to change their songs, leading to the prediction that high T levels would reduce song plasticity. (**c**) When circulating testosterone levels or responsiveness to T were manipulated by implanting T or a T receptor blocker (flutamide), differences in song plasticity resulted. Birds with T implants altered a smaller proportion of their song motifs than did birds with flutamide implants (one-tailed $P <0.05$).[77]

SUMMARY AND CONCLUSION

Because the primary impetus for studying birdsong is as a model for vocal learning, we sometimes forget that the endpoint of that process is the adult song. Adult song provides the reference that allows for retrospective understanding of the trajectory of song development, and manipulations that skew the outcome of the process, such as rearing young birds without a song model, allow for better understanding of what is required for appropriate song learning. But it is the normal adult song that plays the biologically important roles that have been shaped by natural and sexual selection—primarily territory defense and advertisement for a mate. Adult song, however much it represents a completed process in its crystallized and stereotyped form, is nevertheless variable and subject to a variety of influences, including steroid hormones, visual displays, conspecific listeners, and the sources for the elements of the song repertoire. Adult song variability may be normally limited to relatively few degrees of freedom, as in the restricted possibilities for delivering alternative motifs in the zebra finch, but this limited situational plasticity may nevertheless have important insights to offer. The original motivation for studying the neural bases of birdsong, its unique qualities as a model for a complex behavior that is acquired through imitative learning, is still of central importance to neuroscience. Birdsong has the potential to offer additional insights, in particular because of the opportunities it offers for examining the mechanisms responsible for conditional outcomes in a well-characterized, easily analyzed behavior.

REFERENCES

1. KANDEL, E.R. 1976. Cellular Basis of Behavior. 1976. W.H. Freeman and Co. San Francisco.
2. KANDEL, E.R. 2000. Cellular mechanisms of learning and the biological basis of individuality. *In* Principles of Neural Science. E.R. Kandel, J.H. Schwartz & T.M. Jessell, Eds.: 1247–1279. McGraw-Hill. New York.
3. LEONARD, J.L. 2001. Theodore H. Bullock and simpler systems in comparative and integrative neurobiology: an introduction to the Festschrift. Prog. Neurobiol. **63:** 365–370.
4. REICHERT, H. & G. BOYAN. 1997. Building a brain: developmental insights in insects. Trends Neurosci. **20:** 6258–6264.
5. YOSHIHARA, M., A.W. ENSMINGER & J.T. LITTLETON. 2001. Neurobiology and the *Drosophila* genome. Funct. Integr. Genomics **1:** 235–240.
6. CHOMSKY, N. 1972. Language and Mind. Harcourt Brace Jovanovich. New York.
7. DENNETT, D.C. 1998. Brainchildren: essays on designing minds. MIT Press. Cambridge, MA.
8. SIBLEY, C.G, & B.L. MONROE. 1990. Distribution and Taxonomy of Birds of the World. Yale University Press. New Haven, CT.
9. MARLER, P. 1997. Three models of song learning: evidence from behavior. J. Neurobiol. **33:** 501–516.
10. MARLER, P. 1981. Birdsong: the acquisition of a learned motor skill. Trends Neurosci. **4:** 88–94.
11. NOTTEBOHM, F., M.E. NOTTEBOHM & L. CRANE. 1986. Developmental and seasonal changes in canary song and their relation to changes in the anatomy of song-control nuclei. Behav. Neur. Biol. **46:** 445–471.
12. IMMELMANN, K. 1969. Song development in the zebra finch and other estrildid finches. *In* Bird Vocalizations. R.A. Hinde, Ed.: 61–74. Cambridge University Press. Cambridge.

13. PRICE, P. 1979. Developmental determinants of structure in zebra finch song. J. Comp. Physiol. Psychol. **93:** 260–277.
14. ADRET, P. 1993. Operant conditioning, song learning and imprinting to taped song in the zebra. Anim. Behav. **46:** 149–159.
15. BOLHUIS, J.J., D.P. VAN MIL & B.B. HOUX. 1999. Song learning with audiovisual compound stimuli in zebra finches. Anim. Behav. **58:** 1285–1292.
16. TCHERNICHOVSKI, O. *et al.* 2001. Dynamics of the vocal imitation process: how a zebra finch learns its song. Science **291:** 2564–2569.
17. PETRINOVICH, L. & L.F. BAPTISTA. 1987. Song development in the white-crowned sparrow: modification of learned song. Anim. Behav. **35:** 961–974.
18. NELSON, D.A. 1998. External validity and experimental design: the sensitive phase for song learning. Anim. Behav. **56:** 487–491.
19. MARLER, P. 1989. Learning by instinct: birdsong. Am. Sp.-Lang.-Hear. Assoc. **31:** 75–79.
20. THORPE, W.H. 1958. The learning of song patterns by birds, with especial reference to the song of the chaffinch, *Fringilla coelebs.* Ibis **100:** 535–570.
21. THORPE, W.H. 1961. Bird Song. Cambridge University Press. Cambridge.
22. MARLER, P. & V. SHERMAN. 1983. Song structure without auditory feedback: emendations of the auditory template hypothesis. J. Neurosci. **3:** 517–531.
23. MARLER, P. & V. SHERMAN. 1985. Innate differences in singing behavior of sparrows reared in isolation from adult conspecific song. Anim. Behav. **33:** 57–71.
24. MARLER, P. & S. PETERS. 1977. Selective vocal learning in a sparrow. Science **198:** 519–521.
25. MARLER, P. & S. PETERS. 1988. The role of song phonology and syntax in vocal learning preferences in the song sparrow, *Melospiza melodia.* Ethology **77:** 125–149.
26. OBERWEGER, K. & F. GOLLER. 2001. The metabolic cost of birdsong production. J. Exp. Biol. **204:** 3379–3388.
27. ZANN, R.A. 1996. The Zebra Finch: a synthesis of field and laboratory studies. Oxford University Press. New York.
28. NOTTEBOHM, F. & M. NOTTEBOHM. 1978. Relationship between song repertoire and age in the canary, *Serinus canarius.* Z. Tierpsychol. **46:** 298–305.
29. CHAIKEN, M., J. BOHNER & P. MARLER. 1993. Song acquisition in European starlings, *Sturnus vulgaris*: a comparison of the songs of live-tutored, tape-tutored, untutored, and wild-caught males. Anim. Behav. **46:** 1079–1090.
30. KROODSMA, D.E. 1982. Song repertoires: problems in their definition and use. *In* Acoustic Communication in Birds. Vol. 2. Song Learning and its Consequences. D.E. Kroodsma & E.H. Miller, Eds.: 125–146. Academic Press. New York, NY.
31. SOSSINKA, R. & J. BÖHNER. 1980. Song types in the zebra finch (*Poephila guttata castanotis*). Z. Tierpsychol. **53:** 123–132.
32. WILLIAMS, H. & K. STAPLES. 1992. Syllable chunking in zebra finch (*Taeniopygia guttata*) song. J. Comp. Psychol. **106:** 278–286.
33. NOTTEBOHM, F. 1972. The origins of vocal learning. Am. Nat. **106:** 116–140.
34. WILLIAMS, H. 1990. Models for song learning in the zebra finch: fathers or others? Anim. Behav. **39:** 745–757.
35. HULTSCH, H. & D. TODT. 1989. Memorization and reproduction of songs in nightingales: evidence for package formation. J. Comp. Physiol. A. **165:** 197–203.
36. HULTSCH, H. & D. TODT. 1989. Context memorization in the song-learning of birds. Naturwissenschaften **76:** 584–586.
37. HULTSCH, H. 1991. Early experience can modify singing styles: evidence from experiments with nightingales, *Luscinia megarhynchos.* Anim. Behav. **42:** 883–889.
38. TCHERNICHOVSKI, O. *et al.* 1999. Vocal imitation in zebra finches is inversely related to model abundance. Proc. Natl. Acad. Sci. USA **96:** 12901–12904.
39. NOTTEBOHM, F., S. KASPARIAN & C. PANDAZIS. 1981. Brain space for a learned task. Brain Res. **213:** 99–109.
40. WARD, B.C., E.J. NORDEEN & K.W. NORDEEN. 1998. Individual variation in neuron number predicts differences in the propensity for avian vocal imitation. Proc. Natl. Acad. Sci. USA **95:** 1277–1282.

41. AIREY, D.C. & T.J. DEVOOGD. 2000. Greater song complexity is associated with augmented song system anatomy in zebra finches. Neuroreport **11:** 2339–2344.
42. SCHARFF, C. & F. NOTTEBOHM. 1991. A comparative study of the behavioral deficits following lesions of various parts of the zebra finch song system: implications for vocal learning. J. Neurosci. **11:** 2896–2913.
43. WILLIAMS, H., K. KILANDER & M.L. SOTANSKI. 1993. Untutored song, reproductive success and song learning. Anim. Behav. **45:** 695–705.
44. WEST, M.J. & A.P. KING. 1988. Female visual displays affect the development of male song in the cowbird. Nature **334:** 244–246.
45. VOLMAN, S.F. & H. KHANNA. 1995. Convergence of untutored song in group-reared zebra finches (*Taeniopygia guttata*). J. Comp. Psychol. **109:** 211–221.
46. PAYNE, R.B. 1983. The social context of song mimicry: song-matching dialects in indigo buntings. Anim. Behav. **31:** 788–805.
47. FALLS, J.B. 1985. Song matching in western meadowlarks. Can. J. Zool. **63:** 2520–2524.
48. STODDARD, P.K., M.D. BEECHER & S.E. CAMPBELL. 1992. Song-type matching in the song sparrow. Can. J. Zool. **70:** 1440–1444.
49. JARVIS, E.D. *et al.* 1998. For whom the bird sings: context-dependent gene expression. Neuron **21:** 775–788.
50. KING, A.P. & M.J. WEST. 1983. Epigenesis of cowbird song—a joint endeavour of males and females. Nature **305:** 704–706.
51. KING, A.P. & M.J. WEST. 1989. The effect of female cowbirds on vocal imitation and improvisation in males. J. Comp. Psychol. **103:** 39–44.
52. MORRIS, D. 1954. The reproductive behaviour of the zebra finch (*Poephila guttata*) with special reference to pseudofemale behaviour and displacement activities. Behaviour **7:** 1–31.
53. WESTNEAT, M.W. *et al.* 1993. Kinematics of Birdsong: Functional correlation of cranial movements and acoustic features in sparrows. J. Exp. Biol. **182:** 147–171.
54. HOESE, W.H. *et al.* 2000. Vocal tract function in birdsong production: experimental manipulation of beak movements. J. Exp. Biol. **203:** 1845–1855.
55. WILLIAMS, H. 2001. Choreography of song, dance and beak movements in the zebra finch (*Taeniopygia guttata*). J Exp Biol. **204:** 3497–3506.
56. ARNOLD, A.P. 1975. The effects of castration and androgen replacement on song, courtship, and aggression in zebra finches (*Poephila guttata*). J. Exp. Zool. **191:** 309–326.
57. MARLER, P. *et al.* 1988. The role of sex steroids in the acquisition and production of birdsong. Nature **336:** 770–772.
58. NOWICKI, S. & G.F. BALL. 1989. Testosterone induction of song in photosensitive and photorefractory male sparrows. Horm. Behav. **23:** 514–525.
59. SMITH, G.T., E.A. BRENOWITZ & J.C. WINGFIELD. 1997. Roles of photoperiod and testosterone in seasonal plasticity of the avian song control system. J. Neurobiol. **32:** 426–442.
60. TRAMONTIN, A.D., J.C. WINGFIELD & E.A. BRENOWITZ. 1999. Contributions of social cues and photoperiod to seasonal plasticity in the adult avian song control system. J. Neurosci. **19:** 476–483.
61. BALL, G.F., L.V. RITERS & J. BALTHAZART. 2002. Neuroendocrinology of song behavior and avian brain plasticity: multiple sites of action of sex steroid hormones. Front. Neuroendocrinol. **23:** 137–178.
62. MCEWEN, B.S. *et al.* 1979. The brain as a target for steroid hormone action. Ann. Rev. Neurosci. **2:** 65–112.
63. ARNOLD, A.P., F. NOTTEBOHM & D.W. PFAFF. 1976. Hormone concentrating cells in vocal control and other areas of the brain of the zebra finch (*Poephila guttata*). J. Comp. Neurol. **165:** 487–512.
64. NOTTEBOHM, F. *et al.* 1987. Seasonal changes in gonadal hormone levels of adult male canaries and their relation to song. Behav. Neur. Biol. **47:** 197–211.
65. BERNARD, D.J. & G.F. BALL. 1997. Photoperiodic condition modulates the effects of testosterone on song control nuclei volumes in male European starlings. Gen. Comp. Endocrinol. **105:** 276–283.

66. NOTTEBOHM, F. 1980. Testosterone triggers growth of brain vocal control nuclei in adult female canaries. Brain Res. **189:** 429–437.
67. DEVOOGD, T.J. & F. NOTTEBOHM. 1981. Gonadal hormones induce dendritic growth in the adult avian brain. Science **214:** 202–204.
68. CANADY, R.A. *et al.* 1988. Effect of testosterone on input received by an identified neuron type of the canary song system: a Golgi/EM/ Degeneration study. J. Neurosci. **8:** 3770–3784.
69. RASIKA, S., F. NOTTEBOHM & A. ALVAREZ-BUYLLA. 1994. Testosterone increases the recruitment and/or survival of new high vocal center neurons in adult female canaries. Proc. Natl. Acad. Sci. USA **91:** 7854–7858.
70. KORSIA, S. & S.W. BOTTJER. 1991. Chronic testosterone treatment impairs vocal learning in male zebra finches during a restricted period of development. J. Neurosci. **11:** 2362–2371.
71. ADKINS-REGAN, E. & M. ASCENZI. 1987. Social and sexual behavior of male and female zebra finches treated with testosterone. Anim. Behav. **35:** 1100–1112.
72. NORDEEN, K.W. & E.J. NORDEEN. 1992. Auditory feedback is necessary for the maintenance of stereotyped song in adult zebra finches. Behav. Neur. Biol. **57:** 58–66.
73. LEONARDO, A. & M. KONISHI. 1999. Decrystallization of adult birdsong by perturbation of auditory feedback. Nature **399:** 466–470.
74. WILLIAMS, H. & J.R. MCKIBBEN. 1992. Changes in stereotyped central vocal motor patterns are induced by peripheral nerve injury. Behav. Neural Biol. **57:** 67–78.
75. PYTTE, C.L. & R.A. SUTHERS. 2000. Sensitive period for sensorimotor integration during vocal motor learning. J. Neurobiol. **42:** 172–189.
76. HOUGH, G.E. & S.F. VOLMAN. 2002. Short-term and long-term effects of vocal distortion on song maintenance in zebra finches. J. Neurosci. **22:** 1177–1186.
77. WILLIAMS, H., D.M. CONNOR & J.W. HILL. 2003. Testosterone decreases the potential for song plasticity in adult male zebra finches. Horm. Behav. **44:** 402–412.

Bird Calls

Their Potential for Behavioral Neurobiology

PETER MARLER

Department of Neurobiology, Physiology and Behavior, University of California, Davis, Davis, California 95616, USA

ABSTRACT: Birdsongs are always part of larger set of sound signals. Every bird uses a repertoire of calls for communication. Calls are shorter and simpler than songs, with a much larger range of functions. Whereas songs are specialized for application in reproduction and territoriality, calls also serve such functions as signaling about food, maintaining social cohesion, contact calls, synchronizing and coordinating flight, and the resolution of aggressive and sexual conflicts. Alarm calls of various kinds are a major component, including distress, mobbing, and hawk alarm calls. Call repertoires vary greatly in size, up to 20 or so distinct call types. Rough estimates for songbirds range between 5 and 10, but some birds, especially galliforms, may have twice as many. Call usage is often sexually dimorphic and commonly varies seasonally and with physiological state. Most calls appear to be innate, but more and more examples of developmental plasticity in bird calls are emerging. Some display well-defined local dialects. A case is made for the value to avian behavioral neurobiology of including bird calls in studies of the psychophysics and sensory physiology of signal perception. They may also help to extend the range of neurobiological investigations of the song system to include circuitry controlling such functionally related behaviors as aggression and reproduction.

KEYWORDS: calls; bird song; call repertoires; sexual dimorphism; alarm calls; food calls; contact calls; motivational rules; local dialects; learned bird calls

Bird calls are the neglected orphans of avian behavioral neurobiology. It is natural that the songs of birds have pride of place. They are the most elaborate and complex communication signals known to us from the animal kingdom. In a typical song, one second of singing requires scores of breathtakingly rapid neuromuscular events, orchestrated by the brain and executed by the syrinx with great precision (Suthers, this volume; Goller and Cooper, this volume). Songs are not random, disorderly concatenations of sound, but highly structured, stable patterns of motor activity, reproducible in detail from utterance to utterance. Patterns of airflow through the syrinx, changing from moment to moment, are coordinated with exquisitely timed shifts of muscular activity between right and left sides of the songbird syrinx, surely one of

Address for correspondence: Peter R. Marler, Animal Communication Laboratory, Department of Neurobiology, Physiology and Behavior, University of California, Davis, Davis, California 95616, USA. Fax: 530-752-8391.

prmarler@ucdavis.edu; <http://neuroscience2.ucdavis.edu/faculty/?PMarler>

Ann. N.Y. Acad. Sci. 1016: 31–44 (2004). © 2004 New York Academy of Sciences.
doi: 10.1196/annals.1298.034

the most extraordinary sound-producing instruments imaginable. Add the fact that songs are learned, and passed between generations as cultural traditions, and we can understand why the songbird brain, responsible for developing and maintaining this phenomenal behavior has so much fascination for behavioral biologists. It presents us with unique opportunities to investigate some of the most important issues confronting contemporary neuroscience.

This volume attests to the dramatic progress that has been made on many fronts. The ontogeny of a natural, highly complex, learned motor pattern has been documented in detail for the first time. We have a new understanding of the mechanisms by which the "fixed action patterns" of classical ethology are actually maintained, not just by static central motor programs, but by elaborate feedback networks, both internal and external (Konishi, this volume). In retrospect it seems clear that to adjust to changing circumstances and to compensate for the inevitable perturbations to which behavior is constantly subject, dynamic controls are the only way to ensure motor pattern stability. We have a deeper appreciation than ever before of how behaviors with a signal function, like song, are actually used in communication and how intricate and varied patterns of social interaction can be. But we often forget that songs are part of the larger repertoire of sound signals that birds employ to enable reproduction and survival and to provide essential underpinnings for the many complexities of avian societies. Along with song, all birds have a set of calls, much simpler acoustic signals, often innate, that in their way are as important as songs in maintaining the fabric of social life. They are worthy of more of our attention.

THE FUNCTIONS OF BIRD CALLS

Although the differences between songs and calls are occasionally blurred, most of the time they are clear and unequivocal. First, calls are usually structurally much simpler than songs, often monosyllabic. Some songs are relatively simple, but even then they can be distinguished from calls by other criteria. They are delivered differently. Singing is always a more formal affair. Despite the individuality and variability of song within and between populations, there is always an underlying stereotypy to adult song, encompassing not only the structure of notes, syllables, and phrases, but also the way in which songs and song repertoires are delivered. There is a predictable rhythmicity to singing, with underlying programs for uttering song sequences and for progression through song repertoires. The mode of delivery of calls is clearly different. Calling behavior is much more erratic and opportunistic, with highly variable patterns of production, changing from moment to moment dependent on the circumstances. The greater number of degrees of freedom in how calls are delivered adds to their communicative potential. Above all there are many functional differences. Those of song are focused on reproduction and territoriality and they are highly specialized for these purposes. In exchanges of song between rivals, there are often formalistic rules for varying signaling potency according to the degree of song matching and temporal overlap.[1,2] There are specializations for attracting and stimulating females. By comparison, the functions of calls, although often in their own way equally specialized, as a signal class are much more diverse, though playing some roles like those of songs. In practice there is usually little doubt about which side of the song/call boundary a given vocalization falls.

Maintaining the coherence of social groupings, whether a flock, family, or a mated pair, is one widespread function of calls. Almost all birds possess a contact call, often used to keep in touch while foraging. Contact calling is frequently contagious, usually employing sounds that are short, soft, and wide band, audible only at close range. Separation calls, given when a bird loses contact with companions, can be strident versions of the contact call, but are sometimes quite different, more structured, and sometimes individually distinctive, as well as being louder. Flight calls are another common category. The ability to fly puts a special burden on bird calls, given both before taking wing and during flight, helping to synchronize and coordinate movements. The distinctive flight calls of night migrants are a special case, coordinating activities in the dark.[3–5] In another context, a safe, sheltered roosting place to rest and sleep is a critical, year-round resource for many birds, sometimes a communal gathering place that is signaled by special roosting calls

To survive birds must find food. Many birds have special calls that attract others, induce them to feed, and in some cases announce readiness to share it.[6–10] Food calls are especially important in the social life of quail, pheasants, jungle fowl, and other galliforms. Roosters use them in courtship and in attracting chicks to food. In a complementary way, begging calls invite parental approach and the donation of food. Birds that nest colonially sometimes have distinctive begging calls, with individual signatures that parents learn to recognize and use to renew contact.[11,12] Call recognition between parents and young can be mutual, as has been confirmed in every colonial seabird in which it has been studied.[13–15] The potency of juvenile begging calls in eliciting food donation by adults is especially obvious in parasitic cuckoos, some of which mimic the calls of their hosts.[16]

Hostile interactions provide another context in which calls can serve an important function. The resolution of conflicts is facilitated in many birds by distinctive aggressive calls, usually harsh, buzzy, relatively low-pitched sounds. A possible link has been suggested between acoustic structure and function, embodied in the so-called "motivational rules" hypothesis; this posits direct relationships between call structure and physiological state, supposedly applying widely across taxa.[17–20]

Links between function and signal structure have been best explored in alarm calls, which dominate the vocal repertoire of many birds. There are many different types of alarm calls for different kinds of danger. Distress calls, often very similar across species, are loud, harsh, far-reaching sounds given repeatedly by birds in the grip of a predator.[21,22] Mobbing calls are also conspicuous, loud and repetitive, but much more structured and diverse.[23,24] They are given in response to a ground predator or a bird of prey perched nearby, and they attract others to join in harassing the predator, and encouraging it to hunt elsewhere.[25,26] When small birds see a flying hawk in the distance they give another very distinctive alarm call, a thin, high-pitched whistle, delivered infrequently, only audible near the caller, and difficult to locate.[27,28] Other alarm calls signal varying degrees of alarm, from uneasiness to outright panic. A given species may have several for use in different circumstances.

No doubt more functions for bird calls will be discovered as research continues, but we already have some notion of the wide range of situations in which distinctive calls are used. One species will typically focus on some subset of these functions, although as we will see, call repertoires are sometimes surprisingly large, with a wide functional range.

CALL REPERTOIRES AND SEXUAL DIMORPHISM

Defining a call repertoire is not easy. Some calls are relatively stereotyped; others vary greatly, and category boundaries are often blurred, making it difficult to determine where one ends and another begins. Nevertheless ornithologists have been listening long enough to give us an idea of how many distinct calls a bird uses during its daily life. Some estimates are quite consistent. Three independent studies con-

The Chaffinch Call Repertoire

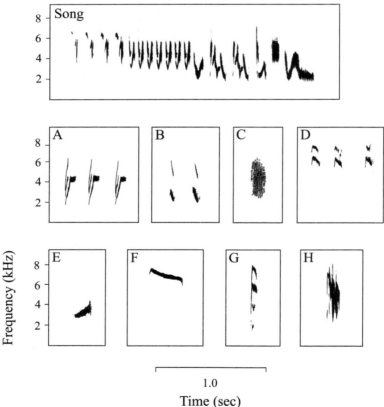

FIGURE 1. In addition to male song and its variants, the European chaffinch has an adult repertoire of eight calls. Two are used by both sexes year-round, a multi-purpose contact/mobbing/mild alarm call (**A**) and a flight call (**B**). The other six are all restricted to the breeding season. An aggressive buzz (**C**) is used by both sexes towards other birds close to the nest. Females have a copulation solicitation call (**D**). The four remaining male breeding season calls are two specialized alarm calls the "rain call" (**E**) and a hawk-alarm call (**F**) and two courtship signals given while interacting with the female (**G** and **H**). (Modified from Marler,[29] Poulsen,[30] and Bergmann.[32])

cluded that adult European chaffinches have a basic repertoire of eight call types (FIG. 1).[29-32] The two most common chaffinch calls are used throughout the year. One is a preflight "tupe" call, the other a multifunctional contact, mobbing and mild alarm call, familiar to birdwatchers as the chaffinch "chink." They are used by both males and females in a similar fashion, in both summer and winter. Most calls, six out of the eight, are used only in the breeding season. One breeding season call, an aggressive "buzz," is used by both sexes. One is a precopulatory signal used only by females. The other four are unique to reproductive males, which have two specialized alarm calls, and two courtship signals used in close interactions with females. Thus the chaffinch call repertoire is sexually dimorphic, and its usage is strongly influenced by seasonal changes in physiological state.

The chaffinch call repertoire is broadly representative of other songbirds. Some, like the zebra finch and other estrildines[33-35] have fewer call types, and others, like chickadees, have more.[36,37] In some other avian taxa call repertoires are much larger. Galliforms, like quail and jungle fowl, have twice as many call types as the chaffinch. Their calls have a wider range of functions, including signaling about food and various kinds of danger, maintaining group contact, resolving sexual and aggressive encounters, and communicating between parents and young.[38-40] As in songbirds, sexual differences in galliform call repertoires are common, and usage often varies with the season. In many of these the sexual differences are not subtle contrasts in the structure of the same basic call type, as in zebra finches (Vicario, this volume). Entire call categories may be absent in one sex, sometimes with interesting complications. Both the aerial alarm call and the food call of jungle fowl and domestic chickens are restricted to males, except for a brief period in the annual cycle when a female is broody, with newly hatched young, when she uses both—an inviting subject for study of the endocrine basis of avian call production.

There is thus ample evidence of sexual dimorphisms, some of which also vary with the season. Interest in this topic was kindled by Simpson and Vicario's zebra finch work, which revealed some of the insights into the brain mechanisms controlling vocal behavior that bird calls can provide.[41] The zebra finch contact call (also known as the "loud call") differs in males and females and is modifiable by learning in males but not in females.[42] The female contact call is innate and, unlike the male call is not dependent on the song system for its production (Vicario this volume). Simpson and Vicario[43,44] showed that contact call behavior is masculinized by estrogen and testosterone treatment early in life, but not later. Like song learning, call learning cannot be induced by steroid therapy in adult female zebra finches. There are other finches, like the canary, in which female singing is enhanced by testosterone therapy. Mundinger[45] reported that the contact call of domestic canaries is developmentally plastic, but the question of sexual dimorphism has not been addressed. We do know that singing of both wild and domestic canaries varies seasonally in harmony with changing testosterone titers.[46-48] Perhaps, like many of their cardueline finch relatives, male and maybe even female canaries will indeed prove to have learned calls. If so, a next question would be whether adult call learning is influenced by testosterone therapy in canaries, including females, though we should not forget that, although female singing is enhanced by testosterone therapy, and neurogenesis in the song system is increased, song learning has not yet been demonstrated in them (Wilbrecht and Kirn, this volume; Nottebohm, this volume).[49,50]

DIALECTS AND CALL LEARNING

Local dialects in song provided an early clue that it might be learned. Although many, and perhaps most, bird calls are geographically uniform, there are examples of local dialects. They have been well documented in southern Germany in the chaffinch "Regenruf" or "rain call."[32,51–53] Other examples are cowbird and ring-neck parrot flight calls, the gargle call of chickadees, and the contact calls of yellow-naped parrots and orange-chinned parakeets (FIG. 2).[54-65] Experimental studies confirm that, contrary to prevailing dogma, some bird calls are indeed learned

Some calls are modified by exposure to a tape or live tutor that calls differently. Hand-reared chaffinches learned the unusual rain call of Corsican birds when exposed to it.[66] Siskins, goldfinches, and other carduelines learned novel flight calls

Cowbird Flight Call Dialects in California

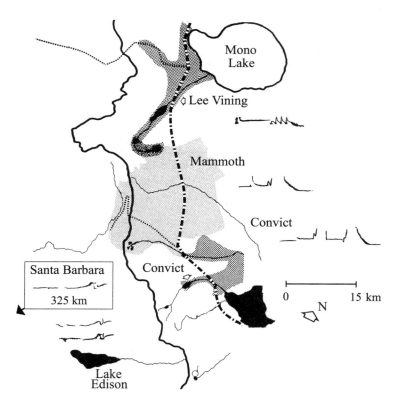

FIGURE 2. There are local dialects in the flight call of the brown-headed cowbird, mapped here in the Sierra Nevada, California. Sonograms are sketched of the major call types. (Modified from Rothstein and Fleischer.[55])

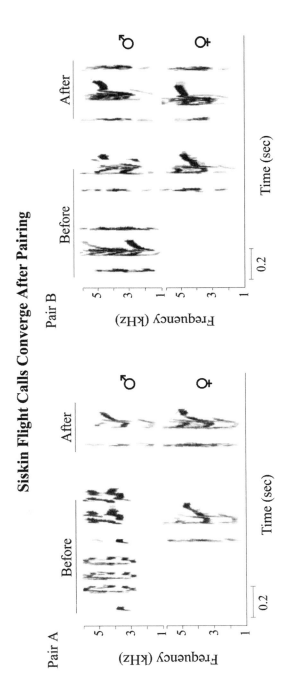

FIGURE 3. Convergence in the flight calls of two pairs of siskins after being caged together. (Modified from Mundinger.[45])

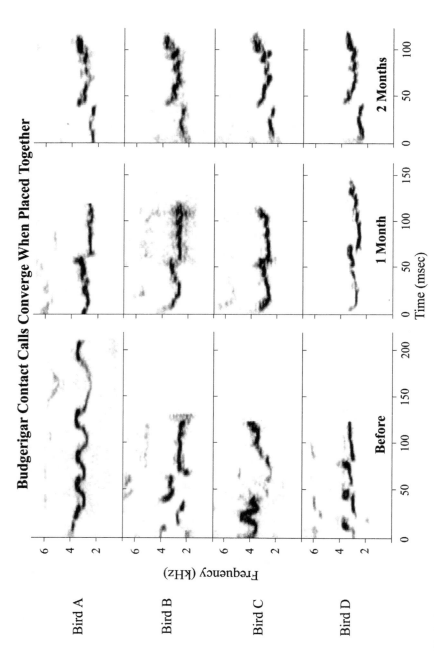

FIGURE 4. Contact calls of four budgerigars converging over a two-month period after being caged together. (Modified from Hile & Streidter.[89])

from companions when housed with them (FIG. 3).[45,67–69] Cross-fostered crossbills learn calls from their adopted parents.[70,71] In some species birds caged together or forming a new flock will converge on the same call variant, a process well-documented in both black-capped chickadees and budgerigars (FIG. 4).[72–78]

But although we know that call learning is a reality, study of the underlying processes is in its infancy. In some species it appears to be an open-ended process, in others there are suggestions of a single early sensitive period, but there have been no comprehensive studies. We do not know how far tutoring will carry a bird's call structure beyond the species-typical limits. The case of cross-fostered cockatoos in Australia learning some calls of galahs suggests that quite radical changes are sometimes possible, although interestingly some calls were unchanged.[79] But despite these cases of developmental plasticity, which may turn out to be more common in parrots than other birds, there is nevertheless little doubt that the acoustic structure of most bird calls is innate, though the ways in which they are used and the responses given to them may well be subject to learned modification.

CALLS AND THE NEUROBIOLOGIST

What are the prospects for the future if calls are brought more fully into focus by behavioral neurobiologists? A first question is will they be suitable for use as stimuli in the laboratory? The structure of most calls appears to be simple enough for comprehensive acoustical analysis; they lend themselves to experimental modification and synthesis. This should stand them in good stead for studying both perceptual processing and production. They have already been used productively in study of the psychophysics of signal perception. In a series of studies, birds proved to be more adept at discriminating individual differences between calls of their own species compared with those of others.[80] However the acoustic basis of the individual differences has not been established, and there may be surprises awaiting us as new methods are brought to bear on the fine-grained analysis of bird calls.

Another aspect of their tractability is the relative ease with which at least some calls can be elicited, by presenting stimuli such as live or videotaped predators,[81] or by call playback, often responded to in kind. Another advantage is that call playback often evokes distinctive non-vocal responses, providing a basis for judgments about call recognition.[82,83] We may get new perspectives on the species specificity of vocal behavior—whether recognition is based on subtle, as-yet-undescribed acoustic features that pervade all vocalizations of an individual or a species, as some have speculated, or whether there is a checklist of multiple features, as the data suggest is more likely.[84,85] Some calls form discrete categories; others intergrade, inviting studies of categorical perception, important in the processing of speech.[86]

What relevance do calls have for the sensory physiologist? Aside from the early work of Leppelsack[87] on starling calls, we know almost nothing about where and how calls are processed in the brain. There are potentially important issues at stake. Some calls are innate, others are learned. Are their auditory processing sites, and those for song, shared or separate? If there is overlap with sites for the perception of song, it will become necessary to include calls in the arrays of sounds used to explore responsiveness of brain sites to biologically significant stimuli, if confusion is to be avoided.

Another emerging theme in behavioral neurobiology is exploration of the links that must exist between vocal processing centers and parts of the brain that control activities with functional relationships to vocal behavior, like aggression, reproduction, escape behavior, and feeding (Ball, this volume). Perhaps the functional diversity of calls has potential value for the study of such connections, by aiding in the localization of brain areas activated by, say, playback of an alarm call or a food signal? If we could somehow register the production antecedents of aggressive or alarm calls, might they be helpful when, in some future enterprise, we think we have found where aggressive or alarm behavior originates in the brain? Are functional connections with the limbic system likely, perhaps with cognitive implications (Cheng, this volume)? The potential speculations are limitless!

ARE THERE CALLS WITH MEANING?

One of the most challenging issues for the future is mapping the pathways in the brain that are engaged when identified external stimuli give rise to appropriate action. When a predator elicits an alarm call, what is the underlying circuitry? Stimulus identification may be innate, learned, or most likely some mix of both. Once sensory registration and preliminary analysis is completed, there will surely be a need to consult internal representations of past encounters with predators. Then appropriate pathways must be activated, both to produce the appropriate alarm call and to launch the suite of escape behaviors appropriate for the particular predator class. These behaviors must in turn be modulated by the caller's awareness of its own circumstances—whether it is safe under cover or out in the open and vulnerable, whether it is alone or in the presence of companions, all of which we know have an influence on alarm-calling behavior.[88]

Something like this sequence of events must take place in a host of cases when a signal with a specific meaning is given and heard. To trace all of these steps on their way through the brain is a daunting undertaking, though I have no doubt that it will ultimately be achieved. It may be a benefit if experimenters of the future can use their knowledge of call circuitry to identify particular processing sites that mark the completion of steps in the functional sequence. If we can map the production circuitry for at least some of the important calls in the species repertoire, each with its own functional connotations, this could prove to be an asset in meeting some of the challenges of that will confront the next generation of avian behavioral neurobiologists.

REFERENCES

1. HULTSCH, H. & D. TODT. 1982. Temporal performance roles during vocal interactions in nightingales (*Luscinia megarhynchos B.*). Behav. Ecol. Sociobiol. **11:** 253–260.
2. TODT, D. & M. NAGUIB. 2000. Vocal interactions in birds: the use of song as a model in communication. Adv. Study Behav. **29:** 247–296.
3. TYLER, W.M. 1916. The call-notes of some nocturnal migrating birds. Auk **33:** 132–141.
4. HAMILTON, W.J. III. 1962. Evidence concerning the function of nocturnal call notes of migratory birds. Condor **64:** 390–401.
5. GRABER, R.R. & W.W. COCHRAN. 1960. Evaluation of an aural record of nocturnal bird migration. Wilson Bull. **72:** 253–273.

6. STOKES, A.W. 1971. Parental and courtship feeding in red jungle fowl. Auk **88:** 21–29.
7. MARLER, P., A. DUFTY & R. PICKERT. 1986. Vocal communication in the domestic chicken: I. Does a sender communicate information about the quality of a food referent to a receiver? Anim. Behav. **34:** 188–193.
8. MARLER, P., A. DUFTY & R. PICKERT. 1986. Vocal communication in the domestic chicken: II. Is a sender sensitive to the presence and nature of a receiver? Anim. Behav. **34:** 194–198.
9. GYGER, M. & P. MARLER. 1988. Food calling in the domestic fowl, *Gallus gallus*: the role of external referents and deception. Anim. Behav. **36:** 358–365.
10. EVANS, C.S. & P. MARLER. 1994. Food calling and audience effects in male chickens, *Gallus gallus*: their relationships to food availability, courtship and social facilitation. Anim. Behav. **47:** 1159–1170.
11. BEECHER, M.D. 1990. The evolution of parent-offspring recognition in swallows. *In* Contemporary Issues in Comparative Psychology. D.A. Dewsbury, Ed.: 360–380. Sinauer Associates. Sunderland, MA.
12. LOESCHE, P., P.K. STODDARD, B.J. HIGGINS & M.D. BEECHER. 1991. Signature vs. perceptual adaptations for individual vocal recognition in swallows. Behaviour **118:** 15–25.
13. TSCHANZ, B. 1965. Beobachtungen und Experimente zur Entstehung der 'persönlichen' Beziehung zwischen Jungvogel und Eltern bei Trottellummen. Verhandlungen Schweizerische Naturforschende Gesellschaft 1964: 211–216.
14. BEER, C.G. 1970. Individual recognition of voice in the social behavior of birds. *In* Advances in the Study of Behavior. D.S. Lehrman, R.A. Hinde & E. Shaw, Eds. **3:** 27–74. Academic Press. New York, NY.
15. WHITE, S.J., R.E.C. WHITE & W.H. THORPE. 1970. Acoustic basis for individual recognition in the gannet. Nature **225:** 1156–1158.
16. DAVIES, N.B. 2000. Cuckoos, Cowbirds and Other Cheats. Academic Press. London.
17. MORTON, E.S. 1977. On the occurrence and significance of motivation-structural rules in some bird and mammal sounds. Amer. Nat. **111:** 855–869.
18. MORTON, E.S. 1982. Grading, discreteness, redundancy, and motivation-structural rules. *In* Ecology and Evolution of Acoustic Communication in Birds. Vol. 1. Production, Perception, and Design Features of Sounds, D.E. Kroodsma & E.H. Miller, Eds.: 183–212. Academic Press. New York.
19. EISENBERG, J.F. 1974. The function and motivational basis of hystricomorph vocalizations. *In* The Biology of Hystricomorph Rodents. (Symposium no. 34), I.W. Rowlands & B. Weir, Eds.: 211–244. Zoological Society of London. London.
20. HAUSER, M.D. 1993. The evolution of nonhuman primate vocalizations: effects of phylogeny, body weight, and social context. Amer. Nat. **142:** 528–542
21. STEFANSKI, R.A. & J.B. FALLS. 1972. A study of distress calls of song, swamp, and white-throated sparrows (Aves: *Fringillidae*). I. Intraspecific responses and functions. Can. J. Zool **50:** 1501–1512.
22. STEFANSKI, R.A. & J.B. FALLS. 1972. A study of distress calls of song, swamp, and white-throated sparrows (Aves: *Fringillidae*). II. Interspecific responses and properties used in recognition. Can. J. Zool. **50:** 1513–1525.
23. JURISEVIC, M.A. & K.J. SANDERSON. 1994. Alarm vocalisations in Australian birds: Convergent characteristics and phylogenetic differences. Emu **94:** 69–77.
24. FICKEN, M.S. & J.W. POPP. 1996. A comparative analysis of passerine mobbing calls. Auk **113:** 370–380.
25. FLEUSTER, W. 1973. Versuche zur Reaktion freilebender Vögel auf Klangattrappen verschiedener Buchfinkenalarme. J. Ornithol. **114:** 417–428.
26. KRAMS, I. & T. KRAMS. 2002. Interspecific reciprocity explains mobbing behaviour of the breeding chaffinches, *Fringilla coelebs*. Proc. R. Soc. London B **269:** 2345–2350.
27. MARLER, P. 1955. Characteristics of some animal calls. Nature **176:** 6–8.
28. KLUMP, G.M. & M.D. SHALTER. 1984. Acoustic behaviour of birds and mammals in the predator context. I. Factors affecting the structure of alarm signals. II. The functional significance and evolution of alarm signals. Z. Tierpsychol. **66:** 189–226.
29. MARLER, P. 1956. The voice of the chaffinch and its function as a language. Ibis **98:** 231–261.

30. POULSEN, H. 1958. The calls of the chaffinch (*Fringilla coelebs* L.) in Denmark. Dansk Ornithologisk Forening Tidsskrift **52:** 89–105.
31. BERGMANN, H.-H. & H.-W. HELB. 1982. Stimmen der Vögel Europas. B.L.V. München.
32. BERGMANN, H.-H. 1993. Der Buchfink. AULA-Verlag. Wiesbaden.
33. GOODWIN, D. 1982. Estrildid finches of the world. Oxford University Press.
34. GÜTTINGER, H.R. 1970. Zur Evolution von Verhaltensweisen und Lautaüsserungen bei Prachtfinken (Estrildidae). Z. Tierpsychol. **27:** 1011–1075.
35. GÜTTINGER, H.-R. & J. NICOLAI. 1973. Struktur und Funktion der Rufe bei Prachtfinken (Estrildidae). Z. Tierpsychol. **33:** 319–334.
36. SMITH, S.T. 1972. Communication and other social behavior in *Parus carolinensis*. Nuttall Ornithological Club **11:** 1–125.
37. HAILMAN, J.P. & M.S. FICKEN. 1996. Comparative analysis of vocal repertoires, with reference to chickadees. *In* Ecology and Evolution of Acoustic Communication in Birds. D.E. Kroodsma & E.H. Miller, Eds.: 136–159. Cornell University Press. Ithaca, NY.
38. WILLIAMS, H.W. 1969. Vocal behavior of adult California Quail. Auk **86:** 631–659.
39. COLLIAS, N.E. 1987. The vocal repertoire of the red junglefowl: a spectrographic classification and the code of communication. Condor **89:** 510–524.
40. MARLER, P. 2004. Bird Calls: A cornucopia for communication. *In* Nature's Music: The Science of Birdsong. P. Marler & H. Slabbekoorn, Eds.: 135–180. Elsevier/Academic Press. San Diego, CA.
41. SIMPSON, H.B. & D.S. VICARIO. 1990. Brain pathways for learned and unlearned vocalizations differ in zebra finches. J. Neurosci. **10:** 1541–1556.
42. ZANN, R. 1985. Ontogeny of the zebra finch distance call: I. Effects of cross-fostering to Bengalese finches. Z. Tierpsychol. **68:** 1–23.
43. SIMPSON, H.B. & D.S. VICARIO. 1991. Exogenous estrogen treatment alone causes female zebra finches to produce learned, male-like vocalizations. J. Neurobiol. **22:** 755–776.
44. SIMPSON, H.B. & D.S. VICARIO. 1991. Early estrogen treatment of female zebra finches masculinizes the brain pathway for learned vocalizations. J. Neurobiol. **22:** 777–793.
45. MUNDINGER, P.C. 1970. Vocal imitation and individual recognition of finch calls. Science **168:** 480–482.
46. NOTTEBOHM, F., M.E. NOTTEBOHM & L.A. CRANE. 1986. Development and seasonal changes in canary song and their relation to changes in the anatomy of song control nuclei. Behav. Neur. Biol. **46:** 445–471.
47. FUSANI, L., T. VAN'T HOF, J.B. HUTCHISON & M. GAHR. 2000. Seasonal expression of androgen receptors, oestrogen receptors and aromatase in the canary brain in relation to circulating androgens and oestrogens. J. Neurobiol. **43:** 254–268.
48. LEITNER, S., C. VOIGT, L.M. GARCIA-SEGURA, *et al.* 2001. Seasonal activation and inactivation of song motor memories in free living canaries is not reflected in neuroanatomical changes of forebrain song areas. Horm. Behav. **40:** 160–168.
49. NOTTEBOHM, F. 1981. A brain for all seasons: cyclical anatomical changes in song control nuclei of the canary brain. Science **214:** 1368–1370.
50. NOTTEBOHM, F. 1993. The search for neural mechanisms that define the sensitive period for song learning in birds. Netherlands J. Zool. **43:** 193–234.
51. SICK, H. 1939. Über die Dialektbildung beim Regenruf des Buchfinken. J. Ornithol. **87:** 568–592.
52. DETERT, H. & H.-H. BERGMANN. 1984. Regenrufdialekte von Buchfinken (*Fringilla coelebs* L.): Untersuchungen an einer Population von Mischrufern. Ökologie der Vögel **6:** 101–118.
53. BAPTISTA, L.F. 1990. Dialectal variation in the raincall of the chaffinch (*Fringilla coelebs*). Die Vogelwarte **35:** 249–256.
54. ROTHSTEIN, S.I. & R.C. FLEISCHER. 1987. Vocal dialects and their possible relation to honest status signalling in the brown-headed cowbird. Condor **89:** 1–23.
55. ROTHSTEIN, S.I., D.A. YOKEL & R.C. FLEISCHER. 1986. Social dominance, mating and spacing systems, female fecundity, and vocal dialects in captive and free-ranging Brown-headed Cowbirds. *In* Current Ornithology. R.F. Johnston, Ed. 3: 127–185. Plenum Press. New York.

56. BAKER, M.C. 2000. Cultural diversification in the flight call of the ringneck parrot in Western Australia. Condor **102:** 905–910.
57. FICKEN, M.S., C.M. WEISE & J.A. REINARTZ. 1987. A complex vocalization of the black-capped chickadee. II. Repertoires, dominance and dialects. Condor **89:** 500–509.
58. HAILMAN, J.P. & C.K. GRISWOLD. 1996. Syntax of black-capped chickadee (*Parus atricapillus*) gargles sorts many types into few groups: Implications for geographic variation, dialect drift, and vocal learning. Bird Behav. **11:** 39–57.
59. MIYASATO, L.E. & M.C. BAKER. 1999. Black-capped chickadee call dialects along a continuous habitat corridor. Anim. Behav. **57:** 1311–1318.
60. BAKER, M.C., T.M HOWARD & P.W. SWEET. 2000. Microgeographic variation and sharing of the gargle vocalization and its component syllables in black-capped chickadee (Aves, Paridae, *Poecile atricapillus*) populations. Ethology **106:** 819–838.
61. WRIGHT, T.E. 1996. Regional dialects in the contact call of a parrot. Proc. R. Soc. London B **263:** 867–872.
62. WRIGHT, T.F. & M. DORIN. 2001. Pair duets in the yellow-naped amazon (*Amazona auropalliata*): responses to playbacks of different dialects. Ethology **107:** 111–124.
63. BRADBURY, J.W. 2003. Vocal communication in wild parrots. *In* Animal Social Complexity: Intelligence, Culture and Individualized Societies. F.B.M. DeWaal & P.L. Tyack, Eds.: 293–316. Harvard University Press. Cambridge, MA.
64. BRADBURY, J.W., K.A. CORTOPASSI & J.R. CLEMMONS. 2001. Geographical variation in the contact calls of orange-fronted parakeets. Auk **118:** 958–972.
65. VEHRENCAMP, S.L., A.F. RITTER, M. KEEVER & J.W. BRADBURY. 2003. Responses to playback of local vs. distant contact calls in the orange-fronted conure, *Aratinga canicularis*. Ethology **109:** 37–54.
66. RIEBEL, K. & P.J.B. SLATER. 1998. Male chaffinches (*Fringilla coelebs*) can copy calls from a tape tutor. J. Ornithol. **139:** 353–355.
67. MUNDINGER, P.C. 1979. Call learning in the *Carduelinae*: ethological and systematic considerations. System. Zool. **28:** 270–283.
68. MARLER, P. & P. MUNDINGER. 1971. Vocal learning in birds: *In* Ontogeny of Vertebrate Behavior. H. Moltz, Eds.: 389–450. Academic Press. New York.
69. MARLER, P. & P. MUNDINGER. 1975. Vocalizations, social organization and breeding biology of the twite, *Acanthus flavirostris*. Ibis **117:** 1–17.
70. GROTH, J.G. 1993. Evolutionary differentiation in morphology, vocalizations, and allozymes among nomadic sibling species in the North American red crossbill (*Loxia curvirostra*) complex. University of California Publications in Zoology **127:** 1–143.
71. GROTH, J.G. 1993. Call matching and positive assortative mating in red crossbills. Auk **110:** 398–401.
72. MAMMEN, D.L. & S. NOWICKI. 1981. Individual differences and within-flock convergence in chickadee calls. Behav. Ecol. Sociobiol. **9:** 179–186.
73. NOWICKI, S. 1983. Flock-specific recognition of chickadee calls. Behav. Ecol. Sociobiol. **12:** 317–320.
74. NOWICKI, S. 1989. Vocal plasticity in captive black-capped chickadees: the acoustic basis and rate of call convergence. Anim. Behav. **37:** 64–73.
75. HUGHES, M.S., S. NOWICKI & B. LOHR. 1998. Call learning in black-capped chickadees (*Parus atricapillus*): the role of experience in the development of 'chick-a-dee' calls. Ethology **104:** 232–249.
76. FARABAUGH, S.M., A. LINZENBOLD & R.J. DOOLING. 1994. Vocal plasticity in budgerigars (*Melopsittacus undulatus*): evidence for social factors in the learning of contact calls. J. Comp. Psychol. **108:** 81–92.
77. HILE, A.G., T.K. PLUMMER & G.F. STRIEDTER. 2000. Male vocal imitation produces call convergence during pair-bonding in budgerigars, *Melopsittacus undulatus*. Anim. Behav. **59:** 1209–1218.
78. BARTLETT, P. & P.J.B. SLATER. 1999. The effect of new recruits on the flock specific call of budgerigars (*Melopsittacus undulatus*). Ethol. Ecol. Evol. **11:** 139–147.
79. ROWLEY, I. & G. CHAPMAN. 1986. Cross-fostering, imprinting and learning in two sympatric species of cockatoo. Behaviour **96:** 1–16.

80. DOOLING, R.J., S.D. BROWN, G.M. KLUMP & K. OKANOYA. 1992. Auditory perception of conspecific and heterospecific vocalizations in birds: evidence for special processes. J. Comp. Psychol. **106:** 20–28.
81. EVANS, C.S. & P. MARLER. 1991. On the use of video images as social stimuli in birds: audience effects on alarm calling. Anim. Behav. **41:** 17–26.
82. GYGER, M., P. MARLER & R. PICKERT. 1987. Semantics of an avian alarm call system: The male domestic fowl, *Gallus domesticus*. Behaviour **102:** 15–40.
83. EVANS, C.S., L. EVANS & P. MARLER. 1993. On the meaning of alarm calls: functional reference in an avian vocal system. Anim. Behav. **46:** 23–38.
84. MARLER, P. & S. PETERS. 1989. Species differences in auditory responsiveness in early vocal learning. *In* The Comparative Psychology of Audition: Perceiving Complex Sounds. R. Dooling & S. Hulse, Eds.: 243–273. Lawrence Erlbaum Assoc. Hillsdale, NJ.
85. MARLER, P. 1997. Three models of song learning: evidence from behavior. J. Neurobiol. **33:** 501–516.
86. HARNAD, S. 1987. Categorical Perception: The Groundwork of Cognition. Cambridge University Press. Cambridge, England.
87. LEPPELSACK, H.-J. 1978. Unit responses to species-specific sounds in the auditory forebrain center of birds. Fed. Proc. **37:** 2336–2341
88. MARLER, P., S. KARAKASHIAN & M. GYGER. 1991. Do animals have the option of withholding signals when communication is inappropriate? The audience effect. *In* Cognitive Ethology: The Minds of Other Animals. C. Ristau, Ed.: 187–208. Lawrence Erlbaum, Hillsdale, NJ.
89. HILE, A.G. & G.F. STRIEDTER. 2000. Call convergence within groups of female budgerigars (*Melopsittacus undulatus*). Ethology **106:** 1105–1114.

Songbird Genomics

Methods, Mechanisms, Opportunities, and Pitfalls

DAVID F. CLAYTON

Cell and Structural Biology, Neuroscience and Bioengineering, Beckman Institute, University of Illinois, Urbana-Champaign, Illinois 61801, USA

ABSTRACT: The biology of songbirds poses fundamental questions about the interplay between gene, brain, and behavior. New tools of genomic analysis will be invaluable in pursuing answers to these questions. This review begins with a summary of the broad properties of the songbird genome and how songbird brain gene expression has been measured in past studies. Four key problems in songbird biology are then considered from a genomics perspective: What role does differential gene expression play in the development, maintenance, and functional organization of the song control circuit? Does gene regulation set boundaries on the process of juvenile song learning? What is the purpose of song-induced gene activity in the adult brain? How does the genome underlie the profound sexual differentiation of the song control circuit? Finally, the range of genomic technologies currently or soon to be available to songbird researchers is briefly reviewed. These technologies include online databases of expressed genes ("expressed sequence tags" or ESTs); a complete library of the zebra finch genome maintained as a bacterial artificial chromosome (BAC) library; DNA microarrays for simultaneous measurement of many genes in a single experiment; and techniques for gene manipulation in the organism. Collectively, these questions and techniques define the field of songbird neurogenomics.

KEYWORDS: gene; genome; genomics; songbird; birdsong; zebra finch; expressed sequence tag (EST); microarray; mRNA

INTRODUCTION

For anyone interested in the biological roots of behavior, nature has provided an extraordinary object lesson in the songbird. As Brenowitz has pointed out,[1] a single evolutionary lineage gave rise to literally thousands of different songbird species. These species are spread across the planet in diverse niches and their songs exhibit an enormous variety with respect to repertoire size (see Todt and Hultsch[2] on the nightingale) and song complexity (see the classic analysis of swamp and song sparrow song by Marler and Peters[3]). These heritable variations in behavior must reflect species differences in neural organization, which must arise from differences in the

Address for correspondence: David F. Clayton, Cell & Structural Biology, Neuroscience and Bioengineering, Beckman Institute, University of Illinois, Urbana, IL 61801, USA. Voice: 217-244-3668; fax: 217-244-1640.
dclayton@uiuc.edu; <http://www.life.uiuc.edu/clayton/default.html>

Ann. N.Y. Acad. Sci. 1016: 45–60 (2004). © 2004 New York Academy of Sciences.
doi: 10.1196/annals.1298.028

songbird genome. Not so long ago, the "genome" was an abstract concept; a genetic potential, whose properties could be inferred only indirectly from the inherited traits of organisms studied across many generations. During the past decade, however, this abstraction has increasingly been embodied in the concrete precision of ASCII text files and sequence databases. As an offshoot of the Human Genome Project, sophisticated facilities (high-throughput robotics, micro-scale laser optics, supercomputers) are now churning at breathtaking speed through the entire genomic legacies of organism upon organism. This new science of genomics has the potential to transform the way we approach and appreciate the rich natural diversity of songbird species.

Several aspects of songbird biology (in addition to monophyletic diversity) invite an aggressive application of molecular genetic methods and genomic perspectives. One is the general nuclear organization of the avian forebrain, which surely reaches a pinnacle of functional specificity in the song control circuit. Here we can trace the neurological root of a highly complex but accessible learned behavior. The development, expression, and modification of this behavior must involve actions of the genome, and we know where to look for these actions. Even the physical development of the song control circuit is unusually accessible, with the late, post-hatching formation (in the juvenile zebra finch) of the primary telencephalic connection for song control.[4,5] The profound effects of gender and hormones on the song control system also imply genomic mechanisms.[6] And the song-mediated social interactions of adult birds[7-10] present a terra incognita awaiting exploration with a functional genomics approach. This article will review current knowledge about genes and gene expression in the songbird brain, and consider the future opportunities and challenges of birdsong genomics.

FUNDAMENTALS OF SONGBIRD MOLECULAR BIOLOGY

The genome of a typical Passeriformes species comprises 1–2 billion base pairs (or 1,000–2,000 Mb) of DNA, spread across ~40 haploid chromosomes.[11] In comparison, the human and fruit fly genomes are ~3,000 Mb and ~200 Mb, respectively. As is true for all vertebrates, only a small fraction of the genomic DNA is believed to represent actual genes (where "gene" is defined as a coding and regulatory sequence necessary to produce a specific functional RNA; each RNA is then typically used as a template for the synthesis of a particular protein). Moreover, the profile of genes expressed varies by cell type and developmental stage, and not all genes are expressed in all tissues. The first step in the expression of any gene is the transcription of a specific RNA from the genomic template. Hence it is possible to estimate the number of genes expressed in a given tissue by analyzing the population of RNAs extracted from that tissue. Of most immediate interest to neurobiologists are the genes that are expressed in the nervous system. How many are there? What kinds of proteins do they encode?

The first attempt to estimate the number of genes expressed in a songbird brain used the technique of solution hybridization kinetics to model the population of RNAs extracted from the canary forebrain.[12] Although the initial estimate was close to 100,000 distinct gene products, many of them were very scarce and of doubtful physiological significance, leading the authors to adopt the figure of 30,000 as a conservative estimate of the number of genes expressed at significant levels in canary

TABLE 1. General profile of mRNAs in songbird brain

Abundance Class	Number of Different Transcripts	Abundance of Each Transcript (as % of all transcripts in forebrain)
I	60	0.2%
II	1,900	0.02%
III	6,700	0.003%
IV	At least 20,000	0.0001–0.001%

forebrain (TABLE 1). This resembles the estimate of genes expressed in the mammalian brain.[12] Gene products that are abundant in the brain as a whole (e.g., TABLE 1, Class I) are typically distributed widely in many or all cells of the nervous system. Most genes, however, give rise to transcripts that are present at much lower levels in the brain as a whole (e.g., Classes III and IV), and these are typically found in distinct subsets of cells and anatomical regions. For example, about 5,000 genes are expressed at higher levels in the forebrain than in the rest of the brain.[12] The technique of *in situ* hybridization is especially useful for localizing specific RNAs to specific cell types or brain regions. When it was applied to a small random sampling of genes expressed in the canary forebrain, *in situ* hybridization revealed many distinct but overlapping RNA distributions. This suggests that functional diversity is created within the songbird brain by varying the combination of gene products expressed in different cells, circuits, and systems.[13]

Identification and characterization of specific songbird genes was initially slow, but promises to accelerate rapidly with the recent application of high-throughput genomic techniques (see below). The first cloned songbird gene sequences were published in 1988, and a 1997 review documented accounts of 15 well-characterized gene products cloned from songbird brain.[13,14] In early 2002, a search of the National Center for Biotechnology Information (NCBI) nucleotide database for "canary" and "zebra finch" revealed 72 entries, contributed by 17 laboratories and representing 35 distinct gene/protein families (TABLE 2).

SURVEY OF PROCESSES WITH ESTABLISHED GENETIC ROOTS

Specific genes or patterns of gene regulation have now been associated with fundamental aspects of songbird neurobiology.

Organization of the Song Circuit

The discrete interconnected telencephalic nuclei that comprise the song control system are a unique specialization of the oscine brain.[1,15–17] The nuclei sit within more general avian brain pathways but may be distinguished by several criteria: cytological, neurochemical, and hodological (Farries, this volume).[18] At a most basic level, this raises two questions that immediately involve the genome. First, are these nuclei also distinguishable by their patterns of gene expression from the surrounding tissue from which they presumably evolved? Second, can we identify the evolutionary and ontogenic pathways that have produced this distinctive interconnected neu-

TABLE 2. Identified songbird genes in Genbank (2002)

Functional Category	Gene/Protein Name
Axon/dendrite	Synuclein (alpha)
	Canarigranin
	GAP-43
	Myelin basic protein
	Myelin proteolipid protein
Blood protein	Serum albumin
Cytoskeleton	Ankyrin
	Actin (beta)
	Neurofilament (medium MW)
Growth factor/receptor	BDNF
	IGF II
	trkB
Intermediary metabolism	Glyceraldehyde 3 phosphatase
Mitochondrial	ATP synthase (alpha subunit)
	Cytochrome *b*
Signal transduction	cAMP Phosphodiesterase
	MEK-1
	n-Chimaerin
	Neurocalcin
	Opsin
	rab 1a
	Rhodopsin
Steroid production/response	Aldehyde dehydrogenase
	Aromatase
	Androgen receptor
	Estrogen receptor
	Steroidogenic factor 1
Transcription factor	n-myc
	c-jun
	c-myc
	zenk
Transmitter/receptor systems	Glutamic acid decarboxylase
	Serotonin receptor, 5HT-7-like
	Cannabinoid receptor
	Glutamate receptor NR2B

ral network? The answer to the first is clear. As TABLE 3 indicates there are substantial differences in patterns of gene expression in the major telencephalic song control nuclei compared to the surrounding brain regions.

Foremost among these are genes involved in steroid signaling. Indeed, the molecular characterization of the song system began with the observation of differential steroid binding.[19] These studies followed upon the primary observations of robust sex and seasonal differences in singing behavior and song system neuroanatomy[20–22] and

TABLE 3. Differential gene expression in song nuclei

Gene	Function	Change in Development	References
A. Locally enriched in some song nuclei			
Androgen receptor	Steroid-regulated transcription	HVc, lMAN, RA	16, 19, 24, 72, 73
Aldehyde dehydrogenase	Retinoid acid production	RA	28
CBP	Transcription coactivator		26
SRC-1	Transcription coactivator	HVc	27
Adrenergic R (alpha2, beta)	Neuromodulator receptor		34
Muscarinic R	Cholinergic receptor		74, 75
NGF	Neurotrophin		76
TrkB	Neurotrophin receptor	HVc, lMAN, RA	77, 78
SNAg	Undefined antibody epitope		31
Parvalbumin, calbindin	Calcium buffering	HVC, RA	79
Melatonin R	Neuromodulator receptor	HVC	80
B. Locally impoverished in song nuclei			
BDNF	Neurotrophin	HVc	78, 81
NR1	NMDA receptor subunit	lMAN, Area X	82
NR2A	NMDA receptor subunit	lMAN, Area X	37
NR2B	NMDA receptor subunit	lMAN, Area X	82, 83
Synelfin/alpha-synuclein	Presynaptic modulator	lMAN	30, 38, 84
GAP-43	Axonal growth/signaling	RA	See [14]
MEK-1	Signal transduction kinase		See 14
n-Chimaerin	Signal transduction		85
C. Locally enriched in caudal nidopallium near HVc			
Aromatase	Steroid metabolism		16, 86, 87
Estrogen receptor-alpha	Steroid-regulated transcription	HVc	16, 86–88
Estrogen receptor-beta	Steroid-regulated transcription		73, 86

The references in this table establish examples of differential gene expression occurring within cells of the song system compared to adjacent brain regions, but do not include variations in content of afferent terminals that arise outside the song system.[89] Where developmental changes in expression have been documented, the anatomical locus of the effect is indicated. Most of the data referred to here were collected in studies of zebra finches, canaries, or European starlings. There may be significant species differences in patterns of regulations, as observed for example with SNag[31] and estrogen receptor alpha[15] in canaries versus zebra finches.

led ultimately to direct evidence of localized expression of the androgen receptor gene.[23–25] More recently, general advances in the understanding of transcriptional regulation and steroid hormone function have inspired demonstrations of differential expression of steroid receptor coactivator proteins in song nuclei.[26,27] These coactivators can modulate the effects of steroid hormones, and variations in their expression could contribute in novel ways to seasonal, developmental, and gender-specific variation in song system function. The song system also appears to be "special" with respect to other, non-gonadal steroids. A direct molecular screen for gene products enriched in song nucleus HVC identified an RNA encoding a form of aldehyde dehydrogenase, responsible for synthesis of retinoids (vitamin A and derivatives). Further experiments then showed that this enzymatic activity is necessary for normal song development.[28] Retinoids have profound organizational effects in the vertebrate embryo, but this was the first demonstration of a post-embryonic function in any brain for these steroids.

The song system is distinctive in other ways, too. Several of the nuclei contain notably high levels of (TrkB) receptors for neurotrophins as well as for neuromodulatory (adrenergic, muscarinic) signals. Interestingly, the adult song nuclei also contain notably reduced levels of several gene products, including some commonly associated with synaptic plasticity, such as BDNF, NMDA receptor subunits, GAP-43, and alpha-synuclein (TABLE 3). It is tempting to speculate that reduction in these gene products may support the overall stability of adult song, perhaps helping to restrict functional plasticity to particular seasons[29] or hormonal contexts,[30] or eliminating it altogether in the case of closed-ended learners like the zebra finch.

The fact that the song system is indeed set apart from other parts of the brain, not only anatomically but with respect to gene expression, raises the question of the system's evolutionary and developmental origins. Could the dispersed nuclei of the system share a common neurogenic root, a unique steroid-receptive precursor cell, whose progeny colonized the rest of the brain and then interconnected? Although attractive in its simplicity, this hypothesis does not account for the many observed differences among the various song nuclei (TABLE 3), nor for the fact that each nucleus generally shares the same profile of gene expression as the surrounding region in which it sits.[13] From this standpoint, it is apparent that the mystery of the song system is not so different from the mystery of the brain in general. Given the diversity of cell types and functions and anatomical domains, how is it that distributed circuits and coordinated phenotypes emerge to support conserved behavioral ends? The eventual answer to this question will require new directions in analysis and conceptualization to perceive how intracellular networks using a common pool of gene products can give rise to many different stable cellular phenotypes, how these many phenotypes can interact to produce distributed neural circuits, and how genomic variation in evolution can then produce selectable differences in the song system that define different species. The discovery of a monoclonal antibody that reacts with song nuclei in members of the Estrildidae family of songbirds, but not in canaries, suggests that there may be significant molecular variation in the song system across different songbird species.[31] With the new genomics technologies, it now becomes possible to imagine a complete catalog of all the genes expressed in the songbird brain, with a record of how these genes vary in their expression patterns across species and during development. The challenge for the future will be to make sense of the logic underlying global gene profiles and how they shift over evolutionary time.

Control of Vocal Learning and Plasticity

A central mystery of songbird behavior is how the singer acquires his particular song. Might differential changes in gene expression mark the different stages in learning? Are certain patterns of gene expression associated with periods of active song modification, and other patterns associated with the extraordinary stability of crystallized song? The clear effects of gonadal steroids on song development and plasticity[32] are especially suggestive of a mechanism that involves gene regulation, since gonadal steroids classically act through receptors that are themselves DNA-binding transcriptional regulators.

Indeed, there is abundant evidence for changes in gene regulation in sensorimotor control nuclei of the song system and the associated auditory/perceptual centers in the telencephalon during the period of song learning. A 1997 review charted 15 developmental changes in gene expression that are potentially associated with phases of song learning in the zebra finch.[14] Some genes are expressed primarily in the early phases of song learning (e.g., alpha-synuclein in lMAN, NO synthase and canarigranin in Area X, enhanced basal expression of ZENK in NCM). Others are expressed during the period of most active song rehearsal (GAP-43, zRALDH) while still others begin to increase toward the end of the critical period (parvalbumin, receptors for androgen and melatonin). Study of other species where the phases of song acquisition and production are even better separated might further clarify the links between specific gene function and song development.[33] Seasonal changes in song structure in seasonally breeding species may also provide a window onto the mechanisms that influence learning and plasticity. Seasonal changes in the NMDA receptor subunit NR2B correlate with seasonal plasticity in adult canaries.[29] Seasonal changes in alpha2-adrenergic receptor densities in HVc and RA correlate with seasonal changes in courtship song in male starlings.[34] Here, gene regulation may be the mechanism that links neuroendocrine signals to functional change in appropriate neural circuits and systems.

The critical issue here is to establish which of these molecular changes are necessary and/or sufficient for a step in the learning process, which are secondary consequences (resulting, for example, from different levels of neural activity at different learning stages), and which are simply developmental correlations with no relevance to song learning. Experiments to date have relied on the rather indirect strategy of altering the learning process via hormonal and social manipulations, and then testing whether there are concomitant effects on molecular expression. This approach has been used to question the putative association of NMDA receptor regulation[35–37] and synelfin (alpha-synuclein) gene expression[38] with progression of zebra finch song learning. Unfortunately, these experimental manipulations may act through non-physiological mechanisms or invoke compensatory processes that override the normal developmental mechanisms. Thus, while this approach has the power to prove that a particular molecular change is not both necessary and sufficient for the behavioral phenomenon, it cannot prove that the molecular event has no role in the normal development of the behavioral phenomenon. A more direct way to assess the functional consequences of specific gene regulation would be to selectively alter the expression of the molecule in question and test for effects on song learning. For example, would suppression of ZENK gene expression in juvenile NCM[39] disrupt the ability to form an auditory memory of tutor song? Molecular genetic interference techniques may soon allow such experiments in the songbird model (see below).

THE SOCIAL CONTEXT OF SONG PERCEPTION AND PERFORMANCE

Birds sing for many reasons. Song is used in territorial defense. Song is used in male-female courtship. The sound of her mate's song influences a female's nesting behavior. Song may also be used in the organization of larger group activities, such as colony formation, flocking, and foraging.[40,41]

At first sight, the social context of song might seem far removed from the genome and matters of gene regulation. Songbirds, however, have provided perhaps the best evidence yet that the genome is actively engaged by daily social experience. The sound of song triggers a genomic reaction in centers of the brain believed responsible for forming cognitive representations of sound.[42–46] The act of singing triggers gene expression in nuclei of the song control circuit.[39,47]

These genomic responses are not fixed and automatic but are malleable, and apparently sensitive to the immediate social context of the experience. The same song may or may not activate a gene response, depending upon when and where the bird has heard the song before.[48–52] The selectivity of the response changes not only with song experience, but also with the physiological state of the bird,[10] perhaps as a result of sensitivity to neuromodulatory signals.[53,54] The anatomical pattern of gene activation during singing also varies, depending upon the intended audience for the song.[8] Furthermore there is now abundant evidence linking brain gene activation to memory storage.[55] Gene expression can also provide a readout of the organism's cognitive processing: Is this experience novel and significant, or not?[7,49,56] A critical direction for future research will be to understand the mechanisms that underlie the changing categorical response of the genome to perceptual experience.

It is thus becoming clear that variations in gene expression may reflect variations in the location and function of brain activity as the animal moves through the world of experience. Monitoring patterns of gene expression in the awake behaving bird may provide a window onto the involvement of specific brain regions during changes of environment and social interactions. The concept of a "genomic action potential" has been proposed as an analogy between the integrative functions of electrophysiological activity, operating on a timescale of minutes, and of gene expression, operating on a timescale of minutes to hours.[57] Like the electrophysiological action potential, a "pulse" of gene expression may be decisive in channeling information transfer along neuronal circuits by transiently altering the protein composition and function at the synapse.

These findings from songbird research show that the genome is not just a passive blueprint for ontogeny, but plays a dynamic ongoing role in the response of adult animals to daily experience. Gene expression thus has its uses as a functional mapping tool in the brain.[43]

Brain Sex

Male and female brains are different, and the avian song control system is one of the most striking and profound illustrations of this difference. For years, neurobiologists have tended to look outside the brain for explanations, to the gonads and the endocrine system. Recent results in songbirds, however, are forcing a major reevaluation of the idea that brain is a *tabula rasa* to be acted upon by circulating sex hormones. Instead, compelling evidence now indicates that each songbird brain carries an intrinsic gender identity, determined apparently by its complement of sex chromosomes (Wade and Arnold, this volume).

By manipulating gonadal development with embryonic hormonal treatments, Wade and colleagues were able to show that normal testicular tissue is neither sufficient[58] nor required[59] for the male pattern of song system development. Rather, masculine development depends simply upon genetic sex of the brain. Holloway and Clayton[5] showed that brain slices containing song nuclei would develop according to their genetic sex, via a process that involves differential production of estrogen *de novo* (independent of endocrine support). Most recently, Agate and his colleagues[6] presented a fascinating analysis of a rare spontaneous gynandromorph, which had a different genetic sex on either half of the brain, and this despite the exposure of both sides to the same circulating endocrine environment. Here again, the song nuclei were seen to develop according to the intrinsic genetic sex of the tissue.

It follows that there must either be some sex-linked genes, and/or genes whose expression is sensitive to sex chromosome balance, that have direct roles in neural organization as late as the juvenile period, when male and female song control pathways diverge in the zebra finch. The tools of songbird genomics will be crucial in finding these genes, in determining how they are regulated and to what extent they are conserved in the evolutionary process.

GENOMICS: THE NEW FRONTIER

The discoveries and insights summarized in this review were mostly based on painstaking studies of one gene at a time. The last few years have seen a paradigm shift in how gene research is conducted, however—with the tools of modern genomics, literally thousands of genes can be studied simultaneously. Not only does this increase the rate of discovery, it also makes possible a new kind of observation, of multigenic interactions and gene networks. For the songbird community, the infrastructure for this new kind of research is just now being developed.

The *sine qua non* for genomics research is a comprehensive organized database of gene sequences. In the U.S., there are at least two organized efforts to produce large systematic collections of DNA sequences expressed in the zebra finch brain, one centered at Duke University (<http://ccis1599.duhs.duke.edu/jsp/songbird_new/public.jsp?>) and the other at the University of Illinois (<http://titan.biotec.uiuc.edu/songbird/>). Both follow the approach of producing "expressed sequence tags" (ESTs), rapid partial determinations of many gene sequences using high-throughput robotics[60–62] (FIG. 1). Virtually the entire process of EST sequencing—from cDNA library production to sequence database organization—can be automated using robotics and computers. This makes it quite feasible to obtain useful sequence information about most or all genes expressed in a given tissue in a matter of months, impossible just a few years ago. At an immediate practical level, EST information can be used to assess whether a particular protein sequence has been conserved in songbirds and whether detection reagents (e.g., antibodies) developed in other spe-

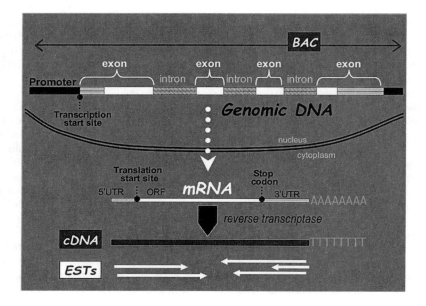

FIGURE 1. Fundamental elements of gene structure and genomic analysis. The central white dotted arrow represents the core process of gene expression: a gene is represented in the cell nucleus as a piece of genomic DNA; the gene's sequence is transcribed into an mRNA; the mRNA is transported from the cell nucleus to the cytoplasm, where it can be used as a template for translation of a specific protein. Additional detail labels the basic structural elements of a gene and its corresponding mRNA. Along the genomic DNA to the left is the gene's promoter; the promoter is not transcribed into RNA but it regulates the start of transcription, which proceeds to the right. The transcribed portion of the genomic DNA is shown as a series of alternating gray and white boxes. Only the white boxes (parts of exons) contain information that directly codes for a protein. A single contiguous protein-coding sequence ("open reading frame," ORF) is assembled in the RNA transcript by removing the non-coding introns and splicing together the exons. The mRNA still contains some non-coding sequence from the gene in two "untranslated regions" (UTR), on its left (5′) and right (3′) flanks. After its initial transcription, the mRNA is also modified by addition of a sequence of A residues to its 3′ end. These A residues ("poly-A tail") are useful in the laboratory production and purification of a cloned copy of the mRNA (cDNA, below). The three labeled boxes indicate experimental manipulations that allow isolation and analysis of a specific gene sequence. BAC: a large piece of intact genomic DNA (potentially containing several contiguous genes) can be copied, isolated and propagated in bacteria as a "bacterial artificial chromosome." A complete BAC library from an organism will contain many BAC clones, collectively comprising the entire genome. The availability of a BAC library simplifies the process of characterizing a gene's overall structure and regulatory sequences. cDNA: an individual mRNA can be copied into DNA (copy DNA) using the enzyme reverse transcriptase. This cDNA can then be cloned in bacteria, sequenced (to predict the protein sequence that would be produced by the process of mRNA translation), and used as a molecular probe to measure the amount and distribution of the corresponding mRNA in cells and tissues. A collection of many thousands of cDNA clones prepared from a particular source (such as brain RNA) is referred to as a cDNA library. ESTs: Modern sequence determination methods work inward from either end of a cloned cDNA (5′ or 3′) toward the mid-

cies should cross-react with songbird material. The ESTs themselves can be used to generate nucleic acid probes for measuring the specific mRNAs from which they were derived. Moreover, the ESTs can be used as a basis for microarray development, which allows measurement of literally thousands of mRNA simultaneously in a single experiment (below). The efforts now underway in the songbird research community should lead to the initial identification in the near future of ESTs representing most of the 30,000 genes expressed in the songbird brain (TABLE 1).

The EST strategy has its limitations: it does not necessarily obtain the complete sequence of any individual gene, nor is it capable of identifying the regulatory regions in the genomic DNA that flank the coding sequence (FIG. 1). However, EST sequencing is often sufficient to predict the identity of the protein encoded by a given gene. If the EST records are actively maintained in a curated sequence database, the quality and completeness of sequence information will improve over time as individual genes are studied in detail and the resulting information is used to update and annotate the database.

To obtain the complete genomic DNA sequence for a given gene, other approaches are needed. The complete sequence may not be important for investigators simply interested in knowing what proteins are expressed in their tissue of interest, or using microarrays to measure the amount of mRNA produced by various genes. However, to understand the mechanisms that regulate the expression of any gene, one must eventually consider the structure of its genomic DNA and the sequence of the gene's promoter (FIG. 1). This sort of analysis in songbirds has recently been facilitated by the construction of a zebra finch brain BAC (Bacterial Artificial Chromosome) library. BAC clones are large fragments of foreign chromosomal DNA maintained in a relatively stable form by bacteria (FIG. 1). Additional information about this resource may be found at <www.genome.arizona.edu>.

Another major tool in modern genomics is the DNA microarray, which allows measurement of expression levels for many genes simultaneously (the rich literature on this topic includes early examples[63,64] as well as detailed methodological reviews[65–68]). Using robotics, thousands of different DNA probes are arrayed on a single support the size of a standard microscope slide. RNAs extracted from tissues of interest are then labeled with fluorescent dyes and hybridized to the DNA probes on the glass slide, and the intensity of binding monitored by computerized optical methods. An explicit goal of the National Institutes of Health–funded initiative centered at Illinois (<http://titan.biotec.uiuc.edu/songbird/songbird.html>) is the production and distribution of songbird microarrays, with the first arrays expected in 2004.

For songbird researchers, microarrays have at least two broad uses: functional diagnostics and gene discovery. In functional diagnostics, the investigator uses pat-

---

dle, continuing for a length of 500–1000 nucleotides in a single process that can be entirely automated and performed very rapidly. The sequence obtained in a single such determination is called an "expressed sequence tag." Since the typical size of a brain mRNA is several thousand nucleotides, a single EST will usually represent only a portion of the original mRNA. However, because the sequencing process can be automated, many thousands of ESTs can be determined very quickly from a cDNA library. Computational methods can then be used to align overlapping ESTs that represent parts of the same mRNA/cDNA.

terns of gene expression known to be associated with a particular cell type or physiological state to assess the status of a biological sample. For example, a songbird researcher might want to monitor how gene profiles associated with neurogenesis or synaptic plasticity change across seasons or during the juvenile song acquisition period. The potential power of this sort of analysis is growing rapidly with the concerted development of various schemes for organizing gene expression data collected from many different species and experiments.[69] In gene discovery, an investigator compares tissues that differ in a specific functional property of interest and seeks to discover genes whose expression is correlated with that functional difference.

Microarray experiments do have drawbacks: they are expensive and interpretation of the large volumes of data they produce can challenge even the most sophisticated statistician.[65–68,70] DNA microarrays are uninformative about post-transcriptional processes, such as protein modification, trafficking, release and turnover, and will not necessarily detect RNA differences that involve alternative splicing of the target RNA, a very common occurrence in the brain.[71] Thus it is important to recognize that microarrays are just one technique in a larger arsenal of methods for measuring gene expression. A complete research program will probably involve concerted application of other complementary methods previously applied in songbird research such as *in situ* hybridization and immunochemical analysis.

A technical frontier with a longer horizon in songbird research is the development of genetic methods for direct manipulation of the genome. These include organized breeding programs to isolate distinct strains for conventional genetic mapping and gene transfer methods for targeted introduction of specific engineered gene sequences into the organism. Potential methods of gene transfer applicable to songbird research include variations on the "transgenic" approach (whereby a new gene sequence is stably integrated into the chromosomes of germ cells followed by breeding and rearing), and the "expression vector" approach (whereby a DNA or RNA sequence is delivered directly into targeted brain cells in the juvenile or adult organism). Such methods are central to research with mice, fruit flies, and several other common model organisms in biological science, but researchers are just beginning to explore their application in songbirds.

SONGBIRD NEUROGENOMICS

Although much remains to be done, the power of modern genomics technology is now being brought to bear on the unique biological problems and opportunities posed in the songbird model. In birdsong we see the intersection of the two master control systems in biology: the genome and the brain. A major frontier in all of science is to understand how these two control systems work together. The "songbird neurogenomics" of the future will teach us much about how genes and brains harmonize to produce rich, subtle behavioral diversity in nature.

REFERENCES

1. BRENOWITZ, E.A. 1997. Comparative approaches to the avian song system. J. Neurobiol. **33**: 517–531.

2. TODT, D. & H. HULTSCH. 1998. How songbirds deal with large amounts of serial information: retrieval rules suggest a hierarchical song memory. Biol. Cybernetics **79:** 487–500.

3. MARLER, P. & S. PETERS. 1977. Selective vocal learning in a sparrow. Science **198:** 519–527.

4. KONISHI, M. & E. AKUTAGAWA. 1985. Neuronal growth, atrophy and death in a sexually dimorphic song nucleus in the zebra finch. Nature **315:** 145–147.

5. HOLLOWAY, C.C. & D.F. CLAYTON. 2001. Estrogen synthesis in the male brain triggers development of the zebra finch song control circuit *in vitro.* Nat. Neurosci. **4:** 170–175.

6. AGATE, R.J. *et al.* 2003. Neural, not gonadal, origin of brain sex differences in a gynandromorphic finch. Proc. Natl. Acad. Sci. USA **100:** 4873–4878.

7. STRIPLING, R. *et al.* 2003. Rapidly learned song-discrimination without behavioral reinforcement in adult male zebra finches (*Taeniopygia guttata*). Neurobiol. Learn. Mem. **79:** 41–50.

8. JARVIS, E.D. *et al.* 1998. For whom the bird sings—context-dependent gene expression. Neuron **21:** 775–788.

9. LIPKIND, D. *et al.* 2002. Social change affects the survival of new neurons in the forebrain of adult songbirds. Behav. Brain Res. **133:** 31–43.

10. PARK, K.H. & D.F. CLAYTON. 2002. Influence of restraint and acute isolation on the selectivity of the adult zebra finch zenk gene response to acoustic stimuli. Behav. Brain Res. **136:** 185–191.

11. GREGORY, T.R. 2001. Animal Genome Size Database. <http://www.genomesize.com>.

12. CLAYTON, D.F. & M. HUECAS. 1990. Forebrain-enriched RNAs of the canary: a population analysis using hybridization kinetics. Mol. Brain Res. **7:** 23–30.

13. CLAYTON, D.F. *et al.* 1988. Probes for rare mRNAs reveal distributed cell subsets in canary brain. Neuron **1:** 249–261.

14. CLAYTON, D.F. 1997. Role of gene regulation in song circuit development and song learning. J. Neurobiol. **33:** 549–571.

15. GAHR, M., H.-R. GUTTINGER & D. KROODSMA. 1993. Estrogen receptors in the avian brain: survey reveals general distribution and forebrain areas unique to songbirds. J. Comp. Neurol. **327:** 112–122.

16. METZDORF, R., M. GAHR & L. FUSANI. 1999. Distribution of aromatase, estrogen receptor, and androgen receptor mRNA in the forebrain of songbirds and nonsongbirds. J. Comp. Neurol. **407:** 115–129.

17. NOTTEBOHM, F., T. STOKES & C.M. LEONARD. 1976. Central control of song in the canary. J. Comp. Neurol. **165:** 457–486.

18. FARRIES, M.A. 2001. The oscine song system considered in the context of the avian brain: lessons learned from comparative neurobiology. Brain Behav. Evol. **58:** 80–100.

19. ARNOLD, A.P., F. NOTTEBOHM & D.W. PFAFF. 1976. Hormone-concentrating cells in vocal control and other areas of the brain of the zebra finch. J. Comp. Neurol. **165:** 487–512.

20. NOTTEBOHM, F. & A. ARNOLD. 1976. Sexual dimorphism in vocal control areas of the songbird brain. Science **194:** 211–213.

21. NOTTEBOHM, F. 1980. Testosterone triggers growth of brain vocal control nuclei in adult female canaries. Brain Res. **189:** 429–436.

22. NOTTEBOHM, F. 1981. A brain for all seasons: cyclical anatomical changes in song control nuclei of the canary brain. Science **214:** 1368–1370.

23. BALTHAZART, J. *et al.* 1992. Immunocytochemical localization of androgen receptors in the male songbird and quail brain. J. Comp. Neurol. **317:** 407–420.

24. NASTIUK, K.L. & D.F. CLAYTON. 1995. The canary androgen receptor mRNA is localized in the song control nuclei of the brain and is rapidly regulated by testosterone. J. Neurobiol. **26:** 213–224.

25. GAHR, M. & J.M. WILD. 1997. Localization of androgen receptor mRNA-containing cells in avian respiratory-vocal nuclei—an *in situ* hybridization study. J. Neurobiol. **33:** 865–876.

26. AUGER, C.J. *et al.* 2002. Expression of cAMP response element binding protein-binding protein in the song control system and hypothalamus of adult European starlings (*Sturnus vulgaris*). J. Neuroendocrinol. **14:** 805–813.

27. CHARLIER, T.D., J. BALTHAZART & G.F. BALL. 2003. Sex differences in the distribution of the steroid receptor coactivator SRC-1 in the song control nuclei of male and female canaries. Brain Res. **959:** 263–274.
28. DENISENKO-NEHRBASS, N.I. *et al.* 2000. Site-specific retinoic acid production in the brain of adult songbirds. Neuron **27:** 359–370.
29. SINGH, T.D., *et al.* 2003. Seasonal regulation of NMDA receptor NR2B mRNA in the adult canary song system. J. Neurobiol. **54:** 593–603.
30. HARTMAN, V.N. *et al.* 2001. Testosterone regulates alpha-synuclein mRNA in the avian song system. Neuroreport **12:** 943–946.
31. AKUTAGAWA, E. & M. KONISHI. 2001. A monoclonal antibody specific to a song system nuclear antigen in estrildine finches. Neuron **31:** 545–556.
32. MARLER, P. *et al.* 1988. The role of sex steroids in the acquisition and production of birdsong. Nature **336:** 770–772.
33. MARLER, P. & S. PETERS. 1982. Long-term storage of learned bird songs prior to production. Anim. Behav. **30:** 479–482.
34. RITERS, L.V. *et al.* 2002. Seasonal changes in the densities of alpha(2) noradrenergic receptors are inversely related to changes in testosterone and the volumes of song control nuclei in male European starlings. J. Comp. Neurol. **444:** 63–74.
35. AAMODT, S.M., E.J. NORDEEN & K.W. NORDEEN. 1995. Early isolation from conspecific song does not affect the normal developmental decline of n-methyl-d-aspartate receptor binding in an avian song nucleus. J. Neurobiol. **27:** 76–84.
36. LIVINGSTON, F.S., S.A. WHITE & R. MOONEY. 2000. Slow NMDA-EPSCs at synapses critical for song development are not required for song learning in zebra finches. Nat. Neurosci. **3:** 482–488.
37. HEINRICH, J.E. *et al.* 2002. Developmental and hormonal regulation of NR2A mRNA in forebrain regions controlling avian vocal learning. J. Neurobiol. **51:** 149–159.
38. JIN, H. & D.F. CLAYTON. 1997. Synelfin regulation during the critical period for song learning in normal and isolated juvenile zebra finches. Neurobiol. Learn. Mem. **68:** 271–284.
39. JIN, H. & D.F. CLAYTON. 1997. Localized changes in immediate-early gene regulation during sensory and motor learning in zebra finches. Neuron **19:** 1049–1059.
40. ZANN, R.A. 1996. The Zebra Finch: A Synthesis of Field and Laboratory Studies. Oxford University Press. Oxford.
41. KROODSMA, D. E. & B. E. BYERS. 1991. The function(s) of birdsong. Am. Zool. **31:** 318–328.
42. MELLO, C.V., D.S. VICARIO & D.F. CLAYTON. 1992. Song presentation induces gene expression in the songbird forebrain. Proc. Natl. Acad. Sci. USA **89:** 6818–6822.
43. MELLO, C.V. 2002. Mapping vocal communication pathways in birds with inducible gene expression. J. Comp. Physiol. A Neuroethol. Sens. Neural Behav. Physiol. **188:** 943–959.
44. STRIPLING, R., A.A. KRUSE & D.F. CLAYTON. 2001. Development of song responses in the zebra finch caudomedial neostriatum: role of genomic and electrophysiological activities. J. Neurobiol. **48:** 163–80.
45. GENTNER, T.Q. *et al.* 2001. Response biases in auditory forebrain regions of female songbirds following exposure to sexually relevant variation in male song. J. Neurobiol. **46:** 48–58.
46. JARVIS, E.D. *et al.* 1997. Brain gene regulation by territorial singing behavior in freely ranging songbirds. Neuroreport **8:** 2073–2077.
47. JARVIS, E.D. & F. NOTTEBOHM. 1997. Motor-driven gene expression. Proc. Natl. Acad. Sci. USA **94:** 4097–4102.
48. SOCKMAN, K.W., T.Q. GENTNER & G.F. BALL. 2002. Recent experience modulates forebrain gene-expression in response to mate-choice cues in European starlings. Proc. R. Soc. Lond. B Biol. Sci. **269:** 2479–2485.
49. MELLO, C.V., F. NOTTEBOHM & D.F. CLAYTON. 1995. Repeated exposure to one song leads to a rapid and persistent decline in an immediate early gene's response to that song in zebra finch telencephalon. J. Neurosci. **15:** 6919–6925.
50. BOLHUIS, J.J. *et al.* 2000. Localized neuronal activation in the zebra finch brain is related to the strength of song learning. Proc. Natl. Acad. Sci. USA **97:** 2282–2285.

51. BOLHUIS, J.J. *et al.* 2001. Localized immediate early gene expression related to the strength of song learning in socially reared zebra finches. Eur. J. Neurosci. **13:** 2165–2170.
52. KRUSE, A.A. 2001. Dynamic modulation of an immediate-early gene in the songbird forebrain. University of Illinois. Urbana, IL.
53. CIRELLI, C. & G. TONONI. 2000. Differential expression of plasticity-related genes in waking and sleep and their regulation by the noradrenergic system. J. Neurosci. **20:** 9187–9194.
54. RIBEIRO, S. & C.V. MELLO. 2000. Gene expression and synaptic plasticity in the auditory forebrain of songbirds. Learning Memory **7:** 235–243.
55. TISCHMEYER, W. & R. GRIMM. 1999. Activation of immediate early genes and memory formation. Cell. Molec. Life Sci. **55:** 564–574.
56. JARVIS, E.D., C.V. MELLO & F. NOTTEBOHM. 1995. Associative learning and stimulus novelty influence the song-induced expression of an immediate early gene in the canary forebrain. Learning Memory **2:** 62–80.
57. CLAYTON, D.F. 2000. The genomic action potential. Neurobiol. Learn. Mem. **74:** 185–216.
58. WADE, J. & A.P. ARNOLD. 1996. Functional testicular tissue does not masculinize development of the zebra finch song system. Proc. Natl. Acad. Sci. USA **93:** 5264–5268.
59. WADE, J., A. GONG & A.P. ARNOLD. 1997. Effects of embryonic estrogen on differentiation of the gonads and secondary sexual characteristics of male zebra finches. J. Exp. Zool. **278:** 405–411.
60. GERHOLD, D. & C.T. CASKEY. 1996. It's the genes! EST access to human genome content. Bioessays **18:** 973–981.
61. PORCEL, B.M. *et al.* 2000. Gene survey of the pathogenic protozoan *Trypanosoma cruzi*. Genome Res. **10:** 1103–1107.
62. DIMOPOULOS, G. *et al.* 2000. *Anopheles gambiae* pilot gene discovery project: identification of mosquito innate immunity genes from expressed sequence tags generated from immune-competent cell lines. Proc. Natl. Acad. Sci. USA **97:** 6619–6624.
63. DERISI, J.L., V.R. IYER & P.O. BROWN. 1997. Exploring the metabolic and genetic control of gene expression on a genomic scale. Science **278:** 680–686.
64. SCHENA, M. *et al.* 1995. Quantitative monitoring of gene expression patterns with a complementary DNA microarray. Science **270:** 467–470.
65. YANG, Y. H. & T. SPEED. 2002. Design issues for cDNA microarray experiments. Nature Rev. Genet. **3:** 579–88.
66. NADON, R. & J. SHOEMAKER. 2002. Statistical issues with microarrays: processing and analysis. Trends Genet. **18:** 265–271.
67. SIMON, R.M. & K. DOBBIN. 2003. Experimental design of DNA microarray experiments. Biotechniques Suppl: 16–21.
68. CHURCHILL, G.A. 2002. Fundamentals of experimental design for cDNA microarrays. Nat. Genet. **32:** 490–495.
69. ASHBURNER, M. *et al.* 2000. Gene ontology: tool for the unification of biology. The Gene Ontology Consortium. Nat. Genet. **25:** 25–29.
70. KERR, M.K. & G.A. CHURCHILL. 2001. Experimental design for gene expression microarrays. Biostatistics **2:** 183–201.
71. BRETT, D. *et al.* 2000. EST comparison indicates 38% of human mRNAs contain possible alternative splice forms. FEBS Lett. **474:** 83–86.
72. PERLMAN, W.R., B. RAMACHANDRAN & A.P. ARNOLD. 2003. Expression of androgen receptor mRNA in the late embryonic and early posthatch zebra finch brain. J. Comp. Neurol. **455:** 513–530.
73. BERNARD, D.J. *et al.* 1999. Androgen receptor, estrogen receptor alpha, and estrogen receptor beta show distinct patterns of expression in forebrain song control nuclei of European starlings. Endocrinology **140:** 4633–4643.
74. BALL, G.F. *et al.* 1990. Muscarinic cholinergic receptors in the songbird and quail brain: a quantitative autoradiographic study. J. Comp. Neurol. **298:** 431–42.
75. RYAN, S. & A. ARNOLD. 1981. Evidence for cholinergic participation in the control of birdsong: acetylcholinesterase distribution and muscarinic receptor autoradiography in the zebra finch brain. J. Comp. Neurol. **202:** 211–219.

76. FIORE, M *et al.* 1999. Song behavior, NGF level and NPY distribution in the brain of adult male zebra finches. Behav. Brain Res. **101:** 85–92.
77. WADE, J. 2000. TrkB-like immunoreactivity in the song system of developing zebra finches. J. Chem. Neuroanat. **19:** 33–39.
78. DITTRICH, F *et al.* 1999. Estrogen-inducible, sex-specific expression of brain-derived neurotrophic factor mRNA in a forebrain song control nucleus of the juvenile zebra finch. Proc. Natl. Acad. Sci. USA **96:** 8241–8246.
79. BRAUN, K *et al.* 1991. Parvalbumin and calbindin-D28K immunoreactivity as developmental markers of auditory and vocal motor nuclei of the zebra finch. Neuroscience **40:** 853–869.
80. GAHR, M. & E. KOSAR. 1996. Identification, distribution and developmental changes of a melatonin-binding site in the song control system of the zebra finch. J. Comp. Neurol. **367:** 308–318.
81. JOHNSON, F., E. NORSTROM & K. SODERSTROM. 2000. Increased expression of endogenous biotin, but not BDNF, in telencephalic song regions during zebra finch vocal learning. Brain Res. Dev. Brain Res. **120:** 113–123.
82. SINGH, T.D *et al.* 2000. Early sensory and hormonal experience modulate age-related changes in NR2B mRNA within a forebrain region controlling avian vocal learning. J. Neurobiol. **44:** 82–94.
83. BASHAM, M.E *et al.* 1999. Developmental regulation of NMDA receptor 2B subunit mRNA and ifenprodil binding in the zebra finch anterior forebrain. J. Neurobiol. **39:** 155–167.
84. GEORGE, J.M *et al.* 1995. Characterization of a novel protein regulated during the critical period for song learning. Neuron **15:** 361–372.
85. GEORGE, J.M. & D.F. CLAYTON. 1992. Differential regulation in the avian song control circuit of an mRNA predicting a highly conserved protein related to protein kinase C and the bcr oncogene. Mol. Brain Res. **12:** 323–329.
86. PERLMAN, W.R. & A.P. ARNOLD. 2003. Expression of estrogen receptor and aromatase mRNAs in embryonic and posthatch zebra finch brain. J. Neurobiol. **55:** 204–219.
87. JACOBS, E.C., A.P. ARNOLD & A.T. CAMPAGNONI. 1999. Developmental regulation of the distribution of aromatase- and estrogen-receptor mRNA-expressing cells in the zebra finch brain. Dev. Neurosci. **21:** 453–472.
88. JACOBS, E.C., A.P. ARNOLD & A.T. CAMPAGNONI. 1996. Zebra finch estrogen receptor cDNA-cloning and mRNA expression. J. Steroid Biochem. Molec. Biol. **59:** 135–145.
89. BALL, G.F., L.V. RITERS & J. BALTHAZART. 2002. Neuroendocrinology of song behavior and avian brain plasticity: multiple sites of action of sex steroid hormones. Front. Neuroendocrinol. **23:** 137–178.

The Avian Song System in Comparative Perspective

MICHAEL A. FARRIES

Departments of Biology and Otolaryngology, University of Washington, Seattle, Washington 98195, USA

ABSTRACT: The song system of oscine birds has become a versatile model system that is used to study diverse problems in neurobiology. Because the song system is often studied with the intention of applying the results to mammalian systems, it is important to place song system brain nuclei in a broader context and to understand the relationships between these avian structures and regions of the mammalian brain. This task has been impeded by the distinctiveness of the song system and the vast apparent differences between the forebrains of birds and mammals. Fortunately, accumulating data on the development, histochemistry, and anatomical organization of avian and mammalian brains has begun to shed light on this issue. We now know that the forebrains of birds and mammals are more alike than they first appeared, even though many questions remain unanswered. Furthermore, the song system is not as singular as it seemed—it has much in common with other neural systems in birds and mammals. These data provide a firmer foundation for extrapolating knowledge of the song system to mammalian systems and suggest how the song system might have evolved.

KEYWORDS: song system; avian brain; evolution; vocal learning; telencephalon; pallium; oscine

INTRODUCTION

The last 50 years have seen the rise of the songbird vocal system from a curiosity studied by only a handful of neurobiologists to a major area of research in neuroscience. Birdsong has been proposed as a model system for the study of such diverse problems as communication, neural development, plasticity and learning, behavioral endocrinology, and motor control. For neuroscientists, birdsong is attractive as a model system because it is a naturally learned behavior that is easily recorded and quantified, and its neural substrate consists of discrete brain structures that appear to be functionally specific to song and are quite distinct from surrounding brain regions. Yet the very distinctiveness of the oscine (i.e., songbird) song system endangers its utility as a model system whose features can be readily generalized to neural systems in other vertebrate taxa, particularly mammals. If we are to make the most effective use of birdsong as a model system, we must understand how it is related to

Address for correspondence: Michael A. Farries, University of Washington Medical Center, Box 356515, Seattle, WA 98195-6515. Voice: 206-616-2582; fax: 206-543-5152.
farries@u.washington.edu

Ann. N.Y. Acad. Sci. 1016: 61–76 (2004). © 2004 New York Academy of Sciences.
doi: 10.1196/annals.1298.007

the avian brain as a whole and how that, in turn, compares to the organization of the mammalian brain. Fortunately, there is now a large body of comparative data that is beginning to clarify those relationships (see Reiner *et al.,* this volume).

This chapter provides an overview of avian song circuitry and its relationship to vertebrate brain organization. Comparisons between mammalian and avian fore-brains will provide a framework for understanding how the song system relates to the overall structure of the avian brain, and will suggest how data obtained in the song system can be applied to mammals (and vice versa). I will also compare song circuitry to structures in surrounding regions of the oscine forebrain and to corre-sponding regions in nonoscines, with a view toward clarifying the relation between the song system and other avian neural circuits. One aim of the chapter is to show how much of the organization of the song system can be accounted for simply by inheritance from the nonoscine structures from which it evolved. Its primary aim is to provide a firm comparative foundation for the continuing contribution of birdsong neurobiology to our understanding of brain function.

OVERVIEW OF THE BRAINS OF BIRDS AND MAMMALS

The central nervous systems (CNS) of all vertebrates share a common organiza-tional plan, consisting of four major subdivisions along the rostrocaudal axis. For three of these divisions, the basic vertebrate organization is highly conserved. The caudalmost division is the spinal cord, characterized by ventrally located motor neu-rons and motor nerve roots, and a dorsal sensory zone containing fibers of sensory neurons that enter the spinal cord through dorsal nerve roots and whose somata are located in the dorsal root ganglia. Immediately rostral to the spinal cord is the hind-brain, which resembles the spinal cord in many ways but has more specialized and elaborate motor and sensory systems associated with organs in the head, and has ma-jor viscerosensory and visceromotor centers. The rostrally adjacent midbrain re-ceives inputs from several sensory systems, including the retina, and can integrate these inputs to generate relatively complicated and well-coordinated behaviors. The midbrain also contains monoaminergic and cholinergic systems that innervate the rostralmost region of the CNS, the forebrain. It is when we reach the fourth division, the forebrain, that substantial differences between mammals and birds begin to ap-pear. The forebrain is divided into the telencephalon and diencephalon, and in both taxa the diencephalon contains regions labeled hypothalamus and thalamus. The avi-an diencephalon may contain structures comparable to all of the major divisions and nuclei known in mammals, but this is not immediately obvious on cursory inspec-tion. The differences only become more pronounced when one examines the telencephalon.

The vertebrate telencephalon consists of the olfactory bulb and two universally recognized subdivisions: a dorsally situated pallium containing mainly glutamater-gic projection neurons and a ventrally located subpallium containing mainly GABAergic and cholinergic projection neurons (FIG. 1). Although these subdivi-sions are presumed to exist in all vertebrates, identifying homologous regions within these broad divisions is problematic. Designation of structures in the avian and mammalian brain as "homologous" implies inheritance from a common ancestor. However, nervous systems leave no fossil record, so questions of homology must be

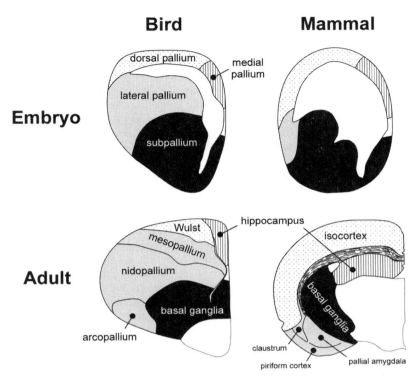

FIGURE 1. Schematic coronal sections through the telencephala of mammals and birds at embryonic and adult stages, illustrating their basic subdivisions. *Black areas* denote subpallium, while the *gray, stippled*, and *striped areas* are lateral, dorsal, and medial pallial areas, respectively. This figure presents only one view among several on the relationship between the embryonic pallial subdivisions and structures in the adult mammalian brain. In particular, some or all of the claustrum may be effectively a part of isocortex,[30] and thus would lie within the dorsal pallium in this scheme. Furthermore, some hypotheses hold that isocortex includes some lateral pallium, either through cell migration[43] or because the border between lateral and dorsal pallia in adults lies within the isocortex.[47]

resolved by comparing the brains of contemporary species using similarities in connectivity, location, and embryonic development. This task is complicated by the fact that telencephala of birds and mammals are quite different in their gross appearance: the mammalian telencephalon is dominated by a laminated isocortex (a major component of the mammalian pallium) that is clearly separated from the underlying basal ganglia (subpallium) by a thick band of myelinated axons ("white matter"), whereas the entire avian telencephalon has a pseudolaminar arrangement of wider cell masses that bear a superficial resemblance to the mammalian basal ganglia. Indeed, for many years the orthodox view held that most of the avian telencephalon actually *is* basal ganglia, with a comparatively tiny pallium.[1] This theory became untenable as more concrete information about the anatomy and histochemistry of the avian brain accumulated,[2-6] but homologizing many regions of the avian and mammalian telencephalon remains challenging and contentious.

Of the two major subdivisions of the telencephalon, the subpallium presents the fewest difficulties. The subpallium consists primarily of the basal ganglia and basal forebrain, which are now known to comprise only a modest proportion of the avian telencephalon, as they do in mammals. Modern tract-tracing and histochemical studies have shown that the organization of the subpallium is fairly well conserved across amniotes.[7] In both birds and mammals, the input structure of the basal ganglia, the striatum ("paleostriatum augmentatum" and "lobus parolfactorius" in the older avian nomenclature) receives topographic glutamatergic input from almost the entire pallium[8] and is heavily innervated by midbrain dopaminergic neurons[9] (I cite the primary literature on the basal ganglia for birds only—the vast mammalian literature is reviewed by Parent and Hazrati[10,11]). The striatum makes inhibitory, GABAergic projections to the globus pallidus ("paleostriatum primitivum" in the older avian nomenclature) and substantia nigra, the output structures of the basal ganglia.[4,12] These output structures then make GABAergic projections to parts of the thalamus and brainstem,[4,13,14] through which the basal ganglia influence the rest of the brain (the substantia nigra is actually a part of the midbrain, and also contains dopaminergic neurons that project far more widely). Unlike the avian globus pallidus, however, the mammalian pallidum is divided into "internal" and "external" segments with distinct connections and histochemical traits.[10,11] Both birds and mammals have a subthalamic nucleus ("anterior nucleus of the ansa lenticularis" in the old avian nomenclature) that is reciprocally connected with the globus pallidus.[12,15] In the basal forebrain, birds and mammals have a population of cholinergic neurons that project to the pallium; in songbirds, such neurons project to some song system nuclei.[16] Finally, the avian striatum contains all of the electrophysiologically identified cell types found in mammals,[17,18] and the basal ganglia as a whole have comparable histochemical cell types in mammals and birds.[5,19-25] Nevertheless, the basal ganglia of birds and mammals do differ in certain respects that are relevant to the song system. In particular, the striatum of at least some birds projects directly to the thalamus (a projection unknown in mammals), and these projection neurons appear to correspond to a cell type lacking in mammalian striatum.[18,26-29] The significance of this difference for the song system is discussed in detail by Perkel (this volume).

In contrast to the subpallium, the nature of homologies between the avian and mammalian pallia remains contentious. The difficulties in comparing the pallia of birds and mammals stem largely from the great disparity in their organization, at least at a superficial level. In most mammalian species, the pallium consists largely of a six-layered isocortex supplemented with the trilaminar hippocampus, piriform cortex (also of three layers), claustrum, and a group of small ventrolaterally located cell masses known as the amygdala (actually, the mammalian amygdala contains both pallial and subpallial elements[30]). The avian pallium, on the other hand, contains little that could readily be called "cortex." Birds do have a hippocampus, but the rest of their pallium consists of four major subdivisions known in the old nomenclature as "Wulst," "hyperstriatum ventrale," "neostriatum," and "archistriatum." The suffix "-striatum" in part reflects the old (incorrect) belief that these structures are comparable to the striatum of mammals; to remedy this, they have been renamed "hyperpallium," "mesopallium," "nidopallium," and "arcopallium," respectively (see Reiner *et al.*, this volume). None of these structures has a clear counterpart in the mammalian brain, and this uncertainty has given rise to several competing proposals on their homology to mammalian structures that are difficult to test based on adult anatomy and histochemistry alone.

Some difficulties can be mitigated by comparing the developmental precursors of the pallium because the embryonic telencephala of mammals and birds are much more alike than their adult forms.[1] However, this developmental comparison can resolve questions of adult homology only if the developmental primordia of adult structures are themselves readily identifiable, and this issue remains a matter of some debate. The vertebrate embryonic pallium is classically divided into three parts: dorsal, medial, and lateral (FIG. 1),[31] and recent studies using several new (and highly conserved) molecular markers of vertebrate telencephalic development suggest that these pallial domains can be reliably identified in the embryos of both mammals and birds.[32,33] Puelles *et al.*[33] has proposed that the classically defined lateral pallium contains another subdivision dubbed "ventral pallium," but since distinction is not critical for this review, I will use the old tripartite scheme. In mammals, a common view holds that the dorsal pallium develops into the isocortex, the medial pallium becomes the hippocampal formation, and the lateral pallium gives rise to the piriform (olfactory) cortex, parts of the amygdala, and perhaps the claustrum[33,34] (FIG. 1).

The avian dorsal pallium corresponds to the hyperpallium (Wulst) of adults, and resembles the mammalian isocortex in several respects.[35] For example, caudal hyperpallium receives visual input from a proposed avian homologue of the dorsal lateral geniculate nucleus[36] and is therefore anatomically, functionally, and topologically similar to mammalian visual cortex. The rostral hyperpallium, on the other hand, receives somatosensory input from the thalamus,[37–39] has descending projections to the brainstem and spinal cord,[40] and is reciprocally connected with the hypothalamus.[40] Based on these connections, the rostral hyperpallium seems to combine features of mammalian somatosensory, motor, and prefrontal cortices, further bolstering the impression that avian hyperpallium may be a simplified and relatively undifferentiated version of mammalian isocortex. All major proposals of avian-mammalian pallial homology agree that hyperpallium is homologous to at least a portion of mammalian isocortex. In contrast to mammalian isocortex, however, the hyperpallium in the best-studied avian species (pigeon, chicken, songbird, parrot) comprises a relatively small part of the avian pallium. The bulk of the pallium in these species is composed of the mesopallium, nidopallium, and arcopallium—structures that have been the source of the greatest disagreement among the various proposals of mammalian-avian pallial homology.

Developmental studies suggest that mesopallium, nidopallium, and arcopallium are derivatives of lateral pallium.[33,34,41,42] In the hypotheses of Striedter[41] and Puelles *et al.*,[33] this would make them collectively homologous to the piriform cortex, pallial amygdala, and claustrum of mammals. However, this conclusion depends on the proper identification of adult structures generated by these embryonic domains. One alternative hypothesis, proposed by Karten,[43] holds that parts of mammalian isocortex are actually a hybrid of dorsal pallium and lateral pallial neurons that have migrated to a more dorsal location, whereas in birds these cell populations remain physically segregated into adulthood. This hypothesis requires a large tangential migration of neurons from one part of the mammalian pallium to another, which has not been observed (some tangential migration has been demonstrated in the developing telencephalon, but these migratory neurons originate in the subpallium[44–46]). A third hypothesis, advanced by Butler and Molnár,[47] denies that the dorsal-lateral pallial border maps onto the adult boundary between isocortex and other pallial domains at all; rather, some parts of isocortex are regarded as purely lateral pallium while others are derived from dorsal pallium. Unfortunately, this proposal also suffers from the difficultly of confidently relating adult structures to their developmental precursors. The homologies between avian and mammalian pallial structures remain unresolved; nevertheless, the available evidence suggests that the large apparent differences between the pallia of mammals and birds could well reflect genuine and significant differences in organization and developmental origins. Whatever differences there may be between the pallia of mammals and birds, there appears to be much convergence of function between mammalian isocortex and avian pallium. Certainly, some of these regions appear to perform sensorimotor functions normally ascribed to isocortex in mammals. Specific regions in the avian nidopallium receive three major primary sensory inputs (FIG. 2): auditory input comes from a projection from the thalamic nucleus oviodalis to field L;[48] visual in-

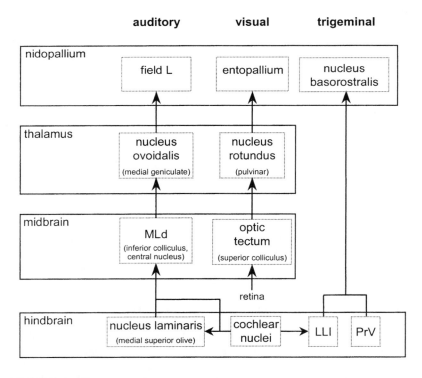

FIGURE 2. Direct ascending sensory pathways to the nidopallium. Possible mammalian homologues of each structure are indicated in parentheses, pallium excepted. *Abbreviations*: MLd, lateral mesencephalic nucleus; LLI, intermediate nucleus of the lateral lemniscus; PrV, principal trigeminal sensory nucleus.

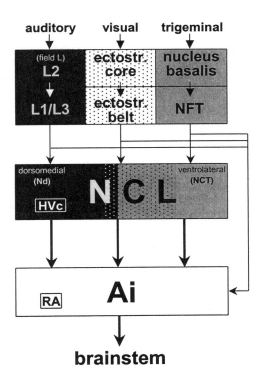

FIGURE 3. The "general motor pathway" of avian caudal pallium. The NCL-Ai-brainstem pathway consists of several independent circuits organized in parallel. The nonuniform distribution of sensory inputs to NCL is very schematically depicted by the shading in this figure. *Abbreviations*: NFT, trigeminal frontal nidopallium; NCT, trigeminal caudal nidopallium. Other abbreviations are given in the text.

put is provided by a projection from the thalamic nucleus rotundus to the entopallium;[49] and trigeminal somatosensory input arrives via a direct projection from the principal trigeminal sensory nucleus in the brainstem to the nidopallial nucleus basorostralis ("nucleus basalis" in the old nomenclature). The nucleus basorostralis also receives auditory input from the intermediate nucleus of the lateral lemniscus.[50–52] In addition to these sensory inputs, avian lateral pallium evidently has motor outputs: the arcopallium has major descending projections to the brainstem, including motor and premotor neuron pools.[53–56]

Naturally, the primary sensory regions of the nidopallium must somehow be linked to the motor outputs in the arcopallium. One such link is direct: the arcopallium receives direct input from sensory nidopallium in at least some cases.[51,57] An arguably more prominent link is indirect, via a circumscribed belt of caudolateral nidopallium (NCL), a structure that was first defined as a region of caudal nidopallium receiving dense dopaminergic input.[9] All three of the major sensory centers of the nidopallium (visual, auditory, and trigeminal) project to NCL, as do somatosensory and visual areas the hyperallium, providing NCL with a rich set of sensory inputs.[51,58–63] These sensory inputs are partially segregated within NCL, with field L (auditory) input concentrated in its dorsomedial sector, while the region surrounding the nucleus basalis (trigeminal) mainly innervates a ventrolateral region.[62,63] NCL, in turn, provides a dense topographic projection to a belt of "intermediate" arcopallium (Ai).[62,63] Thus, NCL and Ai together appear to form a sensorimotor pathway in the caudal part of the avian pallium (FIG. 3). This pathway may be closely related to parts of the song system, as argued below.

OVERVIEW OF THE OSCINE SONG SYSTEM

At the heart of the song system lies a motor pathway in the caudal telencephalon that innervates vocal and respiratory control centers in the brainstem (FIG. 4). This pathway begins with nucleus HVC in the caudal nidopallium (HVC is the name, not an abbreviation), which projects to the robust nucleus of the arcopallium (RA).[64] RA then projects to a variety of brainstem motor centers concerned with vocalization and respiration,[64,65] including a prominent projection to the motor neurons that innervate the syrinx, the principal vocal organ of songbirds (see Wild, this volume, for a detailed discussion of this pathway). Lesions of the motor pathway disrupt singing,[64] and microstimulation within this pathway can evoke vocalizations, but not full-fledged song, and can disrupt or modulate singing that is already under way.[66,67] Thus, the results of anatomical, lesion, and microstimulation studies all imply that HVC and RA function as the song system analogue of motor cortex, a claim that is further supported by the observation of motor-related neural activity in both nuclei during singing.[68–70] Auditory responses, often selective for the bird's own song, have also been recorded throughout the motor pathway in anesthetized birds[71–73] and are present in an attenuated form in the HVC of awake birds,[68,74,75] indicating that the motor pathway may also be an important site for sensory-motor integration.

The forebrain song system contains another major pathway, the anterior forebrain pathway (AFP; FIG. 4), that provides a second, indirect connection between HVC and RA. The AFP begins with a projection from HVC to area X,[64] a specialized region of the anteromedial striatum. Area X projects to the medial part of the dorsolateral anterior thalamic nucleus (DLM),[27,28] and this projection is GABAergic.[76,77] This is an example of a direct striatothalamic projection not found in mammals. DLM then projects to the lateral magnocellular nucleus of the anterior nidopallium (LMAN),[27,28] and LMAN projects to RA[78] and area X.[79,80] DLM also receives a small projection from RA.[65] The AFP is not absolutely required for singing, but is required for song learning[81–83] and adult song plasticity.[84,85] Neurons in the AFP often exhibit song-selective auditory responses, suggesting that the AFP is involved in processing song-related auditory information,[86,87] a hypothesis considered in more detail by Brainard (this volume).

In addition to these core components, there are several other forebrain nuclei associated with the song system whose functions are poorly understood. The nucleus interfacialis (NIf) is a nidopallial nucleus that projects to HVC;[78] it may transmit premotor signals[88] or auditory information.[89] Indeed, NIf may be the main conduit of auditory information to HVC[90] (see chapters by Konishi and Mooney, this vol-

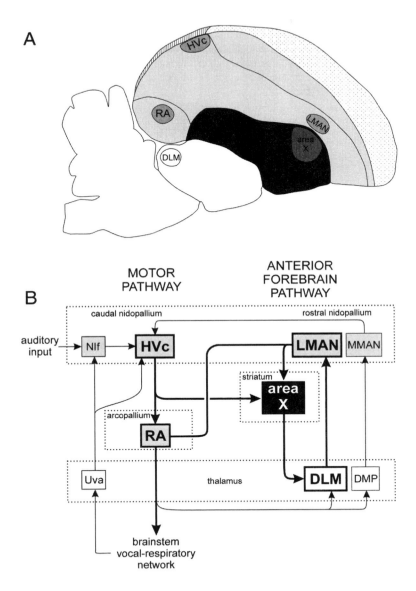

FIGURE 4. The oscine song system. **(A)** Schematic parasagittal section through the brain of a songbird showing the approximate location of the principal song system nuclei. The shading indicates the different subdivisions of the telencephalon, as in FIGURE 1. **(B)** Diagram of the connections among song system nuclei. *Thick arrows* show the connections of the "core" song system for emphasis; *thin arrows* do not necessarily symbolize weak projections.

ume). Both NIf and HVC receive input from the thalamic nucleus uvaeformis (UVA),[78] which in turn receives input from brainstem vocal and respiratory centers[91] in addition to some visual and somatosensory inputs.[92] Uva may be involved in co-ordinating song-related motor activity on both sides of the brain[93,94] (see Schmidt *et al.*, this volume). In the anterior forebrain, a nucleus adjacent to LMAN, the medial magnocellular nucleus of the anterior neostriatum (MMAN), projects to HVC[78] and receives input from the posterior nucleus of the dorsomedial thalamus (DMP), adja-cent to DLM.[95] DMP in turn receives input from the arcopallium (including part of RA) and the hypothalamus.[95] MMAN appears to play some role in song production and perhaps learning.[96]

THE PLACE OF THE SONG SYSTEM WITHIN THE OSCINE BRAIN

None of the pallial components of the song system (HVC, RA, NIf, LMAN, and MMAN) can be unequivocally regarded as homologues of mammalian isocortex. The hypotheses of Striedter[34] and Puelles *et al.*[33] would place these nuclei within regions homologous to the claustrum, piriform cortex, and pallial amygdala of mam-mals, although the hypotheses of Karten[43] and Butler and Molnár[47] suggest the pos-sibility of a closer relationship to isocortex. Regardless of their evolutionary relationship to isocortex, they can be regarded as functionally analogous to isocortex—their functions as currently understood are quintessentially sensorimo-tor. Some song system nuclei also resemble nonvocal neural pathways found in the pallium of non-osines, especially when one compares the song system motor path-way to the NCL-Ai pathway described in above.[97] In fact, the locations of HVC and RA in the caudal part of the pallium raise the possibility that they lie *within* the os-cine NCL-Ai complex. A detailed comparison of the song system motor pathway to these more general sensorimotor circuits should clarify the relationships between them.

The first issue to be addressed is precisely where the oscine NCL-Ai system is located relative to the song system motor pathway and specifically whether the NCL-Ai system is adjacent to or even engulfs these nuclei. This question is best an-swered by examining the connections of neural structures immediately surrounding HVC and RA. The nidopallium around HVC, called "HVC shelf," receives dense in-put from field L, although HVC itself receives sparse input at best.[90,98,99] In that re-spect, HVC shelf resembles the dorsomedial end of nonoscine NCL, generally called "dorsal nidopallium" (Nd). HVC shelf, like nonoscine Nd, projects to a medial re-gion of Ai;[90] in oscines this target is called "RA cup"' (a crescent of tissue rostro-ventrally adjacent to RA), while in nonoscines it is dorsomedial and ventromedial Ai (Aidm, Aivm).[59] The oscine RA cup and nonoscine Aidm/Aivm have very simi-lar descending projections: both project to the shell region of the nucleus ovoidalis, the intercollicular complex (ICo), and the interface between ICo and the lateral mes-encephalic nucleus.[59,90] These data argue that the oscine HVC shelf-RA cup circuit is homologous to the nonoscine Nd-Aidm/Aivm pathway,[90] and that HVC and RA are themselves a subdivision of this circuit specialized for vocal control.[97] The only major features that distinguish the song system motor pathway from the Nd-Aidm/ Aivm circuit of nonoscines are the direct projections from RA to brainstem vocal centers and a relative lack of direct projections from field L to HVC. Further confirmation of the song system motor pathway's position within a broader NCL-Ai circuit is provided by the work of Bottjer and co-workers,[100,101] who identified belts of nidopallium and arcopallium extending ventrolaterally from HVC and RA that appear to be more complete representatives of the full oscine NCL-Ai pathway.

If the song system motor pathway is a specialized subdivision of a circuit found in nonoscines, one must ask whether the same is true of the AFP. Unfortunately, comparatively little is known about the anatomy of the rostral telencephalon in nonoscines. Nevertheless, there is some evidence for a nonoscine AFP. Thalamic nuclei in a region comparable to DLM and DMP of the song system project to a zone of rostral nidopallium that might be related to oscine LMAN and MMAN.[26,102] However, these thalamic nuclei also project to the striatum, a projection that has not been found in oscine DLM. This rostral nidopallial area then projects to the underlying anteromedial striatum, mirroring the projection from LMAN to area X, and preliminary evidence indicates that it also projects to Ai and NCL (personal observations; see also Dubbeldam and Visser[103]), like the projections from LMAN to RA and MMAN to HVC. The existence of an "accessory AFP" in oscines, a set of structures surrounding the core AFP nuclei that share a similar pattern of projections, provides some indirect support for this point of view. The tissue around LMAN (LMAN shell) projects to oscine NCL, Ai, and the striatum surrounding area X, and receives input from a ventromedial segment of DLM.[100,101] Thus, the song system AFP, like the motor pathway, may be a specialized subdivision of a broader set of circuits found in both oscines and nonoscines. Only further comparative studies of oscines and nonoscines can definitively test this hypothesis.

CONCLUSION

The song system is a highly specialized set of neural structures, several of which appear to be almost exclusively devoted to the various sensory and motor aspects of one specific behavior—the production of learned vocalizations. Yet it evolved from neural circuits which are found in many other taxa and which perform many other functions. It may come as some surprise that the song system retains many of the organizational features of these ancestral circuits, in spite of its extreme specialization. This evolutionary conservatism by no means detracts from the song system's position as a uniquely valuable model system, however. Far from it—it provides an opportunity to apply what is discovered in the song system to other systems and to use what is known about other systems to generate testable hypotheses concerning the neural basis of birdsong. This is most true of circuits found in the forebrain of nonoscine birds, which may closely resemble the immediate evolutionary precursors of the song system. But it can also be true of neural systems found in other vertebrate classes, including mammals, so long as a careful consideration of comparative neurobiology is used to define the appropriate scope of such applications. As things stand now, there appear to be enough similarities between the pallial components of the song system and mammalian isocortex (whether from common inheritance or convergent evolution) to support a number of useful parallels between them, although the available data also argue for some circumspection in this area. In the basal ganglia, the parallels between the song system and mammalian neural systems can be stronger—the basal ganglia are well conserved across all amniotes, and comparisons to mammals have proven very fruitful in predicting the histochemical and physiological properties of neurons in area X, the song-related component of the oscine basal ganglia. Overall, comparative studies suggest that an understanding of the neural basis of singing and song learning would tell us much about the workings of neural systems in mammals, including humans.

REFERENCES

1. STRIEDTER, G.F. 1998. Progress in the study of brain evolution: from speculative theories to testable hypotheses. Anat. Rec. **253:** 105–112.
2. JUORIO, A.V. & M. VOGT. 1967. Monoamines and their metabolites in the avian brain. J. Physiol. **189:** 489–518.
3. KARTEN, H.J. 1969. The organization of the avian telencephalon and some speculations on the phylogeny of the amniote telencephalon. Ann. N.Y. Acad. Sci. **167:** 164–179.
4. KARTEN, H.J. & J.L. DUBBELDAM. 1973. The organization and projections of the paleostriatal complex in the pigeon (*Columba livia*). J. Comp. Neurol. **148:** 61–90.
5. MEDINA, L. & A. REINER. 1994. Distribution of choline acetyltransferase immunoreactivity in the pigeon brain. J. Comp. Neurol. **342:** 497–537.
6. VEENMAN, C.L. & A. REINER. 1994. The distribution of GABA-containing perikarya, fibers, and terminals in the forebrain and midbrain of pigeons, with particular reference to the basal ganglia and its projection targets. J. Comp. Neurol. **339:** 209–250.
7. MEDINA, L. & A. REINER. 1995. Neurotransmitter organization and connectivity of the basal ganglia in vertebrates: implications for the evolution of basal ganglia. Brain Behav. Evol. **46:** 235–258.
8. VEENMAN, C.L., J.M. WILD & A. REINER. 1995. Organization of the avian "corticostriatal" projection system: a retrograde and anterograde pathway tracing study in pigeons. J. Comp. Neurol. **354:** 87–126.
9. DURSTEWITZ, D., S. KRÖNER & O. GÜNTÜRKÜN. 1999. The dopaminergic innervation of the avian telencephalon. Prog. Neurobiol. **59:** 161–195.
10. PARENT, A. & L.-N. HAZRATI. 1995. Functional anatomy of the basal ganglia. I. The cortico-basal ganglia thalamo-cortical loop. Brain Res. Rev. **20:** 91–127.
11. PARENT, A. & L.-N. HAZRATI. 1995. Functional anatomy of the basal ganglia. II. The place of subthalamic nucleus and external pallidum in basal ganglia circuitry. Brain Res. Rev. **20:** 128–154.
12. BRAUTH, S.E., J.L. FERGUSON & C.A. KITT. 1978. Prosencephalic pathways related to the paleostriatum of the pigeon (*Columba livia*). Brain Res. **147:** 205–221.
13. KITT, C.A. & S.E. BRAUTH. 1981. Projections of the paleostriatum upon the midbrain tegmentum in the pigeon. Neuroscience **7:** 1551–1566.
14. MEDINA, L. & A. REINER. 1997. The efferent projections of the dorsal and ventral pallidal parts of the pigeon basal ganglia, studied with biotinylated dextran amine. Neuroscience **81:** 773–802.
15. JIAO, Y. *et al.* 2000. Identification of the anterior nucleus of the ansa lenticularis in birds as the homolog of the mammalian subthalamic nucleus. J. Neurosci.. **20:** 6998–7010.
16. LI, R. & H. SAKAGUCHI. 1997. Cholinergic innervation of song control nuclei by the ventral paleostriatum in the zebra finch: a double-labeling study with retrograde fluorescent tracers and choline acetyltransferase immunohistochemistry. Brain Res. **763:** 239–246.
17. FARRIES, M.A. & D.J. PERKEL. 2000. Electrophysiological properties of avian basal ganglia neurons recorded in vitro. J. Neurophysiol. **84:** 2502–2513.
18. FARRIES, M.A. & D.J. PERKEL. 2002. A telencephalic nucleus essential for song learning contains neurons with physiological characteristics of both striatum and globus pallidus. J. Neurosci. **22:** 3776–3787.
19. REINER, A., H.J. KARTEN & A.R. SOLINA. 1983. Substance P: localization within paleostriatal-tegmental pathways in the pigeon. Neuroscience **9:** 61-85.

20. REINER, A. *et al.* 1984. The distribution of enkephalin-like immunoreactivity in the telencephalon of the adult and developing domestic chicken. J. Comp. Neurol. **228:** 245–262.
21. REINER, A. & R.E. CARRAWAY. 1985. Phylogenetic conservatism in the presence of a neurotensin-related hexapeptide in neurons of globus pallidus. Brain Res. **341:** 365–371.
22. REINER, A. 1986. The co-occurence of substance P-like immunoreactivity and dynorphin-like immunoreactivity in striatopallidal and striatonigral projection neurons in birds and reptiles. Brain Res. **371:** 155–161.
23. ANDERSON, K.D. & A. REINER. 1991. Striatonigral projection neurons: a retrograde labeling study of the percentages that contain substance P or enkephalin in pigeons. J. Comp. Neurol. **303:** 658–673.
24. VEENMAN, C.L. & K.D. ANDERSON. 1993. Co-occurrence of γ-aminobutyric acid, parvalbumin and the neurotensin-related neuropeptide LANT6 in pallidal, nigral and striatal neurons in pigeons and monkeys. Brain Res. **624:** 317–325.
25. VON BARTHELD, C.S. & A. SCHOBER. 1997. Nitric oxide synthase in learning-relevant nuclei of the chick brain: morphology, distribution, and relation to transmitter phenotypes. J. Comp. Neurol. **383:** 135–152.
26. KITT, C.A. & S.E. BRAUTH. 1982. A paleostriatal-thalamic-telencephalic path in pigeons. Neuroscience **7:** 2735–2751.
27. OKUHATA, S. & N. SAITO. 1987. Synaptic connections of thalamo-cerebral vocal nuclei of the canary. Brain Res. Bull. **18:** 35–44.
28. BOTTJER, S.W. *et al.* 1989. Axonal connections of a forebrain nucleus involved with vocal learning in zebra finches. J. Comp. Neurol. **279:** 312–326.
29. SZÉKELY, A.D. *et al.* 1994. Connectivity of the lobus parolfactorius of the domestic chicken (*Gallus domesticus*): an anterograde and retrograde pathway tracing study. J. Comp. Neurol. **348:** 374–393.
30. SWANSON, L.W. & G.D. PETROVICH. 1998. What is the amygdala? Trends Neurosci. **21:** 323–331.
31. BUTLER, A.B. & W. HODOS. 1996. Comparative Vertebrate Neuroanatomy. Wiley-Liss. New York.
32. SMITH FERNANDEZ, A. *et al.* 1998. Expression of the *Emx-1* and *Dlx-1* homeobox genes define three molecularly distinct domains in the telencephalon of the mouse, chick, turtle, and frog embryos: implications for the evolution of telencephalic subdivisions in amniotes. Development **125:** 2099–2111.
33. PUELLES, L. *et al.* 2000. Pallial and subpallial derivatives in the embryonic chick and mouse telencephalon, traced by the expression of the genes Dlx-2, Emx-1, Nkx-2.1, Pax-6, and Tbr-1. J. Comp. Neurol. **424:** 409–438.
34. STRIEDTER, G.F. 1997. The telencephalon of tetrapods in evolution. Brain Behav. Evol. **49:** 179–213.
35. MEDINA, L. & A. REINER. 2000. Do birds possess homologues of mammalian primary visual, somatosensory and motor cortices? Trends in Neurosci. **23:** 1–12.
36. KARTEN, H.J. *et al.* 1973. Neural connections of the "visual Wulst" of the avian telencephalon. Experimental studies in the pigeon (*Columba livia*) and owl (*Speotyto cunicularia*). J. Comp. Neurol. **150:** 253–278.
37. FUNKE, K. 1989. Somatosensory area in the telencephalon of the pigeon I. Response characteristics. Exp. Brain Res. **76:** 603–619.
38. FUNKE, K. 1989. Somatosensory areas in the telencephalon of the pigeon II. Spinal pathways and afferent connections. Exp. Brain Res. **76:** 620–638.
39. WILD, J.M. 1989. Avian somatosensory system: II. Ascending projections of the dorsal column and external cuneate nuclei in the pigeon. J. Comp. Neurol. **287:** 1–18.
40. WILD, J.M. & M.N. WILLIAMS. 2000. Rostral Wulst in passerine birds. I. Origin, course and terminations of an avian pyramidal tract. J. Comp. Neurol. **416:** 429–450.
41. STRIEDTER, G.F. & S. BEYDLER. 1997. Distribution of radial glia in the developing telencephalon of chicks. J. Comp. Neurol. **387:** 399–420.
42. STRIEDTER, G.F., T.A. MARCHANT & S. BEYDLER. 1998. The "neostriatum" develops as part of the lateral pallium in birds. J. Neurosci. **18:** 5839–5849.
43. KARTEN, H.J. 1991. Homology and evolutionary origins of the 'neocortex'. Brain Behav. Evol. **38:** 264–272.

44. CARLOS, J.A.D., L. LÒPEZ-MASCARAQUE & F. VALVERDE. 1996. Dynamics of cell migration from the lateral ganglionic eminence in the rat. J. Neurosci. **16:** 6146–6156.
45. ANDERSON, S.A. *et al.* 1997. Interneuron migration from basal forebrain to neocortex: dependence on *Dlx* genes. Science **278:** 474–476.
46. COBOS, I., L. PUELLES & S. MARTÍNEZ. 2001. The avian telencephalic subpallium originates inhibitory neurons that invade tangetiallly the pallium (dorsal ventricular ridge and cortical areas). Dev. Biol. **239:** 30–45.
47. BUTLER, A.B. & Z. MOLNÁR. 2002. Development and evolution of the collopallium in amniotes: a new hypothesis of field homology. Brain Res. Bull. **57:** 475–479.
48. KARTEN, H.J. 1968. The organization of the ascending auditory pathway in the pigeon *(Columba livia)* II. Telencephalic projections of the nucleus oviodalis thalami. Brain Res. **11:** 134–154.
49. KARTEN, H.J. & W. HODOS. 1970. Telecephalic projections of the nucleus rotundus in the pigeon *(Columba livia)*. J. Comp. Neurol. **140:** 35–52.
50. DUBBELDAM, J.L., C.S.M. BRAUCH & A. DON. 1981. Studies on the somatotopy of the trigeminal system in the mallard, *Anas platyrhynchos* L. III. Afferents and organization of the nucleus basalis. J. Comp. Neurol. **196:** 391–405.
51. WILD, J.M., J.J.A. ARENDS & H.P. ZEIGLER. 1985. Telencephalic connections of the trigeminal system in the pigeon *(Columba livia)*: a trigeminal sensorimotor circuit. J. Comp. Neurol. **234:** 441–464.
52. WILD, J.M. & S.M. FARABAUGH. 1996. Organization of afferent and efferent projections of the nucleus basalis prosencephali in a passerine, *Taeniopygia guttata*. J. Comp. Neurol. **365:** 306–328.
53. ZEIER, H. & H.J. KARTEN. 1971. The archistriatum of the pigeon: organization of afferent and efferent connections. Brain Res. **31:** 313–326.
54. KNUDSEN, E.I., Y.E. COHEN & T. MASINO. 1995. Characterization of a forebrain gaze field in the archistriatum of the barn owl: microstimulation and anatomical connections. J. Neurosci. **15:** 5139–5151.
55. DAVIES, D.C. *et al.* 1997. Efferent connections of the domestic chick archistriatum: a Phaseolus lectin anterograde tracing study. J. Comp. Neurol. **389:** 679–693.
56. DUBBELDAM, J.L., A.M. DEN BOER-VISSER & R.G. BOUT. 1997. Organization and efferent connections of the archistriatum of the mallard, *Anas platyrhynchos* L.: an anterograde and retrograde tracing study. J. Comp. Neurol. **388:** 632–657.
57. HUSBAND, S.A. & T. SHIMIZU. 1999. Efferent projections of the ectostriatum in the pigeon *(Columba livia)*. J. Comp. Neurol. **406:** 329–345.
58. WILD, J.M. 1987. The avian somatosensory system: connections of regions of body representation in the forebrain of the pigeon. Brain Res. **412:** 205–223.
59. WILD, J.M., H.J. KARTEN & B.J. FROST. 1993. Connections of the auditory forebrain in the pigeon *(Columba livia)*. J. Comp. Neurol. **337:** 32–62.
60. SHIMIZU, T., K. COX & H.J. KARTEN. 1995. Intratelencephalic projections of the visual Wulst in pigeons *(Columba livia)*. J. Comp. Neurol. **359:** 551–572.
61. LEUTGEB, S. *et al.* 1996. Telencephalic afferents to the caudolateral neostriatum of the pigeon. Brain Res. **730:** 173–181.
62. METZGER, M., S. JIANG & K. BRAUN. 1998. Organization of the dorsocaudal neostriatal complex: a retrograde and anterograde tracing study in the domestic chick with special emphasis on pathways relevant to imprinting. J. Comp. Neurol. **395:** 380–404.
63. KRÖNER, S. & O. GÜNTÜRKÜN. 1999. Afferent and efferent connections of the caudolateral neostriatum in the pigeon *(Columba livia)*: a retro- and anterograde pathway tracing study. J. Comp. Neurol. **407:** 228–260.
64. NOTTEBOHM, F., T.M. STOKES & C.M. LEONARD. 1976. Central control of song in the canary, *Serinus canarius*. J. Comp. Neurol. **165:** 457–486.
65. WILD, J.M. 1993. Descending projections of the songbird nucleus robustus archistriatalis. J. Comp. Neurol. **338:** 225–241.
66. VU, E.T., M.E. MAZUREK & Y.-C. KUO. 1994. Identification of a forebrain motor programming network for the learned song of zebra finches. J. Neurosci. **14:** 6924–6934.
67. VICARIO, D.S. & H.B. SIMPSON. 1995. Electrical stimulation in forebrain nuclei elicits learned vocal patterns in songbirds. J. Neurophysiol. **73:** 2602–2607.

68. McCasland, J.S. & M. Konishi. 1981. Interaction between auditory and motor activities in an avian song control nucleus. Proc. Natl. Acad. Sci. USA **78:** 7815–7819.
69. Yu, A.C. & D. Margoliash. 1996. Temporal hierarchical control of singing in birds. Science **273:** 1871–1875.
70. Hahnloser, R.H.R., A.A. Kozhevnikov & M.S. Fee. 2002. An ultra-sparse code underlies the generation of neural sequences in a songbird. Nature **419:** 65–69.
71. Katz, L.C. & M.E. Gurney. 1981. Auditory responses in the zebra finch's motor system for song. Brain Res. **211:** 192–197.
72. Margoliash, D. 1986. Preference for autogenous song by auditory neurons in a song system nucleus of the white-crowned sparrow. J. Neurosci. **6:** 1643–1661.
73. Williams, H. 1989. Multiple representations and auditory-motor interactions in the avian song system. Ann. N.Y. Acad. Sci. **563:** 148–164.
74. Cardin, J.A. & M.F. Schmidt. 2003. Song system auditory responses are stable and highly tuned during sedation, rapidly modulated and unselective during wakefulness, and suppressed by arousal. J. Neurophysiol. **90:** 2884–2899.
75. Rauske, P.L., S.D. Shea & D. Margoliash. 2003. State and neuronal class-dependent reconfiguration in the avian song system. J. Neurophysiol. **89:** 1688–1701.
76. Luo, M. & D.J. Perkel. 1999. Long-range GABAergic projection in a circuit essential for vocal learning. J. Comp. Neurol. **403:** 68–84.
77. Luo, M. & D.J. Perkel. 1999. A GABAergic, strongly inhibitory projection to a thalamic nucleus in the zebra finch song system. J. Neurosci. **19:** 6700–6711.
78. Nottebohm, F., D.B. Kelley & J.A. Paton. 1982. Connections of vocal control nuclei in the canary telencephalon. J. Comp. Neurol. **207:** 344–357.
79. Nixdorf-Bergweiler, B.E., M.B. Lips & U. Heinemann. 1995. Electrophysiological and morphological evidence for a new projection of L-MAN neurons towards area X. Neuroreport **6:** 1729–1732.
80. Vates, G.E. & F. Nottebohm. 1995. Feedback circuitry within a song-learning pathway. Proc. Natl. Acad. Sci. USA **92:** 5139–5143.
81. Bottjer, S.W., E.A. Miesner & A.P. Arnold. 1984. Forebrain lesions disrupt development but not maintenance of song in passerine birds. Science **224:** 901–903.
82. Sohrabji, F., E.J. Nordeen & K.W. Nordeen. 1990. Selective impairment of song learning following lesions of a forebrain nucleus in juvenile zebra finches. Behav. Neural Biol. **53:** 51–63.
83. Scharff, C. & F. Nottebohm. 1991. A comparative study of the behavior deficits following lesions of various parts of the zebra finch song system: implications for vocal learning. J. Neurosci. **11:** 2896–2913.
84. Williams, H. & N. Mehta. 1999. Changes in adult zebra finch song require a forebrain nucleus that is not necessary for song production. J. Neurobiol. **39:** 14–28.
85. Brainard, M.S. & A.J. Doupe. 2001. Postlearning consolidation of birdsong: stabilizing effects of age and anterior forebrain lesions. J. Neurosci. **21:** 2501–2517.
86. Doupe, A.J. & M. Konishi. 1991. Song-selective auditory circuits in the vocal control system of the zebra finch. Proc. Natl. Acad. Sci. USA **88:** 11339–11343.
87. Doupe, A.J. 1997. Song- and order-selective neurons in the songbird anterior forebrain and their emergence during vocal development. J. Neurosci. **17:** 1147–1167.
88. McCasland, J.S. 1987. Neuronal control of bird song production. J. Neurosci. **7:** 23–39.
89. Janata, P. & D. Margoliash. 1999. Gradual emergence of song selectivity in sensorimotor structures of the male zebra finch song system. J. Neurosci. **19:** 5108–5118.
90. Vates, G. E.. et al. 1996. Auditory pathways of caudal telencephalon and their relation to the song system of adult male zebra finches. J. Comp. Neurol. **366:** 613–642.
91. Striedter, G.F. & E.T. Vu. 1998. Bilateral feedback projections to the forebrain in the premotor network for singing in zebra finches. J. Neurobiol. **34:** 27–40.
92. Wild, J.M. 1994. Visual and somatosensory inputs to the avian song system via nucleus uvaeformis (Uva) and a comparison with the projections of a similar thalamic nucleus in a nonsongbird, *Columba livia*. J. Comp. Neurol. **349:** 512–535.
93. Coleman, M.J., P.J. Sule & E.T. Vu. 1999. Recovery of impaired songs following unilateral but not bilateral lesions of nucleus uvaeformis of adult zebra finches. Soc. Neurosci. Abstr. **25:** 1367.

94. SCHMIDT, M.F. & M. KONISHI. 2000. Bilateral hemisphereic coordination of birdsong. *In* Proceedings of the 22nd International Ornithology Conference, Durban. N.J. Adams & R.H. Slotow, Eds.: 509–523. BirdLife South Africa. Johannesburg.
95. FOSTER, E.F., R.P. MEHTA & S.W. BOTTJER. 1997. Axonal connections of the medial magnocellular nucleus of the anterior neostriatum in zebra finches. J. Comp. Neurol. **382:** 364–381.
96. FOSTER, E.F. & S.W. BOTTJER. 2001. Lesions of a telencephalic nucleus in male zebra finches: influences on vocal behavior in juveniles and adults. J. Neurobiol. **46:** 142–165.
97. FARRIES, M.A. 2001. The oscine song system considered in the context of the avian brain: lessons learned from comparative neurobiology. Brain Behav. Evol. **58:** 80–100.
98. KELLEY, D.B. & F. NOTTEBOHM. 1979. Projections of a telencephalic auditory nucleus —field L—in the canary. J. Comp. Neurol. **183:** 455–470.
99. FORTUNE, E.S. & D. MARGOLIASH. 1995. Parallel pathways and convergence onto HVc and adjacent neostriatum of adult zebra finches *(Taeniopygia guttata)*. J. Comp. Neurol. **360:** 413–441.
100. JOHNSON, F., M.M. SABLAN & S.W. BOTTJER. 1995. Topographic organization of a forebrain pathway involved with vocal learning in zebra finches. J. Comp. Neurol. **358:** 260–278.
101. BOTTJER, S.W., J.D. BRADY & B. CRIBBS. 2000. Connections of a motor cortical region in zebra finches: relation to pathways for vocal learning. J. Comp. Neurol. **420:** 244-260.
102. WILD, J.M. 1987. Thalamic projections to the paleostriatum and neostriatum in the pigeon *(Columba livia)*. Neuroscience **20:** 305–327.
103. DUBBELDAM, J.L. & A.M. VISSER. 1987. The organization of the nucleus basalis-neostriatum complex of the mallard (*Anas platyrynchos* L.) and its connections with the archistriatum and the paleostriatal complex. Neuroscience **21:** 487–517.

Songbirds and the Revised Avian Brain Nomenclature

ANTON REINER,[a] DAVID J. PERKEL,[b] CLAUDIO V. MELLO,[c]
AND ERICH D. JARVIS[d]

[a]Department of Anatomy and Neurobiology, University of Tennessee Health Science
Center, Memphis, Tennessee 38163, USA

[b]Departments of Biology and Otolaryngology, University of Washington,
Seattle, Washington 98195-6515, USA

[c]Neurological Sciences Institute, Oregon Health and Science University,
Beaverton, Oregon 97006-3499, USA

[d]Department of Neurobiology, Duke University Medical Center, Box 3209,
Durham, North Carolina 27710, USA

ABSTRACT: It has become increasingly clear that the standard nomenclature
for many telencephalic and related brainstem structures of the avian brain is
based on flawed once-held assumptions of homology to mammalian brain
structures, greatly hindering functional comparisons between avian and mammalian brains. This has become especially problematic for those researchers
studying the neurobiology of birdsong, the largest single group within the avian
neuroscience community. To deal with the many communication problems this
has caused among researchers specializing in different vertebrate classes, the
Avian Brain Nomenclature Forum, held at Duke University from July 18–20,
2002, set out to develop a new terminology for the avian telencephalon and
some allied brainstem cell groups. In one major step, the erroneous conception
that the avian telencephalon consists mainly of a hypertrophied basal ganglia
has been purged from the telencephalic terminology, and the actual parts of the
basal ganglia and its brainstem afferent cell groups have been given new names
to reflect their now-evident homologies. The telencephalic regions that were incorrectly named to reflect presumed homology to mammalian basal ganglia
have been renamed as parts of the pallium. The prefixes used for the new names
for the pallial subdivisions have been retained most established abbreviations, in an
effort to maintain continuity with the pre-existing nomenclature. Here we
present a brief synopsis of the inaccuracies in the old nomenclature, a summary of the nomenclature changes, and details of changes for specific songbird vocal and auditory nuclei. We believe this new terminology will promote more
accurate understanding of the broader neurobiological implications of song
control mechanisms and facilitate the productive exchange of information between researchers studying avian and mammalian systems.

Address for correspondence: Anton Reiner, Department of Anatomy and Neurobiology, University of Tennessee Health Science Center, Memphis, Tennessee 38163, USA. Voice: 901-448-
8298; fax: 901-448-7193.
  areiner@utmem.edu; <http://cns.utmem.edu/faculty/Reiner/Reiner_cv.html>

Ann. N.Y. Acad. Sci. 1016: 77–108 (2004). © 2004 New York Academy of Sciences.
doi: 10.1196/annals.1298.013

KEYWORDS: archistriatum; paleostriatum; hyperstriatum; paleocortex; archicortex; neocortex; cerebrum; pallium; striatum; pallidum; arcopallium; nidopallium; hyperpallium

A BRIEF HISTORY OF AVIAN TELENCEPHALIC NOMENCLATURE

The advent of improved techniques for cutting and staining brain tissue resulted in a wealth of new knowledge on brain structure in various vertebrate species at the turn of the 19th century and the beginning of the 20th century.[1] Based on his interpretation of such material, Ludwig Edinger formulated a theory of cerebral evolution[2–4] that, as further developed by his colleague C.U. Ariëns-Kappers[5,6] and subsequently refined and widely promulgated in Ariëns-Kappers and colleagues,[7] became the dominant view, and led to an avian telencephalic nomenclature that has continued to be used into the early years of the 21st century (FIG. 1A). According to this view, birds and mammals inherited from their fish ancestors, via the fish to amphibian to reptile lineage, an old basal ganglia structure that was called the paleostriatum (old striatum; corresponding largely to the globus pallidus of mammals), and a newer structure from their reptilian ancestors that Ariëns-Kappers called the neostriatum (new striatum; including most of the caudate and putamen in mammals). Reptiles were thought to have elaborated the paleostriatum further into two distinct parts, one Ariëns-Kappers called the paleostriatum primitivum (comparable to a primitive mammalian globus pallidus) and another part he called the paleostriatum augmentatum (i.e., an augmentation of globus pallidus), and both subdivisions were assumed to have been passed onto birds. Similarly, the neostriatum was also thought to have become enlarged in birds and to have given rise to a novel overlying territory that Edinger and colleagues[3] and Ariëns-Kappers[5,6] called the hyperstriatum, in the be-

---

FIGURE 1. (A) Classical view of avian and mammalian brain relationships according to the historical nomenclature. Although past authors had differing opinions as to which brain regions are part of the pallium versus subpallium, the images are color-coded according to the meaning of the actual names given to these brain regions. *White lines* represent laminae, cell-sparse regions separating brain subdivisions. *Large white areas* in the human cerebrum are the fibers bundles making up the white matter. *Dashed lines* divide regions that differ by cytoarchitecture. The abbreviations PA and LPO designate regions as defined by Karten and Hodos,[16] while the spelled-out term paleostriatum augmentatum designates this entire area as defined by Ariëns-Kappers, Huber and Crosby.[7] (B) Modern view of avian and mammalian brain relationships according to the new nomenclature. In birds, the lateral ventricle is located in the dorsal part of the pallium, whereas in mammals much of the ventricle is located near the border of the pallium with the subpallium. ABBREVIATIONS, classical view: Ac=accumbens; Ap=posterior archistriatum; B=nucleus basalis; Cd=caudate nucleus; CDL=dorsal lateral corticoid area; E=ectostriatum; GP=globus pallidus (i=internal segment, e=external segment); HA=hyperstriatum accessorium; HIS=hyperstriatum intercalatum superior; HD=hyperstriatum dorsale; HV=hyperstriatum ventrale; L2=field L2, LPO=lobus parolfactorius, OB=olfactory bulb; PA=paleostriatum augmentatum; Pt=putamen; Tn=nucleus taeniae. ABBREVIATIONS, modern view where different from panel A: E=entopallium; B=basorostralis; HA=hyperpallium apicale; HI=hyperpallium intercalatum; HD=hyperpallium densocellulare; Hp=hippocampus; LSt=lateral striatum; MSt=medial striatum; PoA=posterior pallial amygdala; TnA=nucleus taeniae of the amygdala; SpA=subpallial amygdala. (Figure adapted from Jarvis and colleagues.[40])

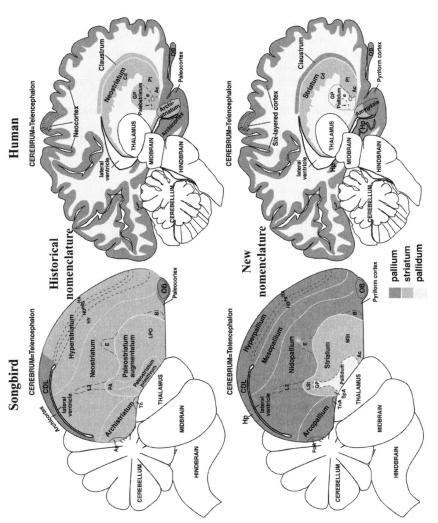

FIGURE 1. *See previous page for legend.*

lief that it was entirely "striatal" in nature and a hypertrophy of the neostriatum. Thus by this view, the avian telencephalon was thought to consist nearly entirely of an enlarged basal ganglia (i.e., what are now commonly called caudate, putamen, and globus pallidus in mammals; FIG. 1A). Finally, mammals, birds, and reptiles were also thought to have inherited an additional subcortical structure that Edinger and Ariëns-Kappers called the archistriatum (in the belief that it was also part of the basal ganglia) from their amphibian ancestors. This brain region in mammals is now called the amygdala, and it is no longer commonly regarded as part of the basal ganglia.

In contrast to the basal ganglia expansion thought to characterize birds, mammals were thought to have expanded the upper, outer part of the telencephalon (the pallium) into a six-layered cortex from a small dorsal cortical region present in the reptile ancestors of mammals.[2–6,8] The novel cortical region in mammals was referred to as neocortex, to distinguish it from the presumed older cortices represented by the olfactory cortex (which they called paleocortex) and hippocampus (which they called archicortex). Ariëns-Kappers and colleagues[7] slightly modified the position of Ariëns-Kappers' earlier works by concluding that a small upper part of the hyperstriatum (largely corresponding to what we now call the Wulst) provided birds with a meager pallial territory comparable to mammalian neocortex. Nonetheless, the view espoused by Ariëns-Kappers and colleagues[7] and by other influential authors[9–12] was that the avian telencephalon consisted mainly of greatly expanded basal ganglia. Except for a dissenting minority,[13–15] this accretionary theory of vertebrate brain evolution became the prevailing view for the first two-thirds of the 20th century. This led to the predominant use of the terms neostriatum, archistriatum, and hyperstriatum to refer to the major sectors of the avian telencephalon above the so-called paleostriatum. The Ariëns-Kappers terminology for the avian telencephalon was, thus, already the most commonly used at the time that Karten and Hodos constructed the first stereotaxic atlas of an avian brain.[16] Although they were aware of possible inaccuracies in this nomenclature, they felt compelled to adopt it because it was entrenched. As a consequence, the Ariëns-Kappers terminology became the standard telencephalic nomenclature for the avian telencephalon.

As neurobiologists have gained deeper insights into the evolution, development, and function of avian and mammalian brains, it has become clear that the accretionary theory of vertebrate telencephalic evolution is incorrect.[1,17–19] Being flawed, the homologies implied by the classical nomenclature have greatly hindered communication between avian and mammalian brain specialists by perpetuating the view that the telencephalon in birds differs qualitatively in structure and function from that in mammals. In particular, the presumed necessity of neocortex for adaptive behavior and higher order cognition[12] and the presumed absence of neocortex in birds have continued to make many believe that birds are incapable of such behavioral abilities. Since the basal ganglia were thought to control instinctive motor behavior and the avian telencephalon was thought to be largely a hypertrophied basal ganglia, all complex behavior in birds had widely been thought to be instinctive.[4,12] As a result of the misconceptions abetted by the Ariëns-Kappers–based terminology, the relevance of the many findings on the avian brain to understanding the functioning of the mammalian brain has been obscured. It is now, however, evident that birds are not uniformly impoverished in their adaptive learning skills. Songbirds, parrots, and hummingbirds show vocal learning abilities not paralleled by any mammals other than humans and cetaceans.[20–25] Crows, members of the oscine songbird family, show the ability to make and use tools,[26,27] and parrots are capable of learning to communicate with human words and show cognitive skills otherwise evident only in apes and cetaceans among nonhuman species.[23] In parallel with the growing awareness of avian behavioral sophistication, it has become clear that the neural substrate for such behavior is not a hypertrophied basal ganglia but the same general brain region used for such tasks as in mammals (i.e., the pallium), albeit without the laminar morphology characteristic of mammalian neocortex, in combination with a basal ganglia region of the same general size as in mammals.[25,28–35]

While research on all avian species was affected by the outdated terminology for the avian telencephalon, the confusion was especially acute for those studying songbirds, for two major reasons. First, researchers on song control mechanisms now constitute the largest single group within the avian brain research community. Secondly, several major cell groups involved in song perception, learning, or production are located within the part of the brain that in birds has been called the neostriatum. These findings have been habitually misinterpreted by researchers on the mammalian brain, for whom the term "neostriatum" refers to part of the basal ganglia, as pertaining to the functioning of the basal ganglia. This has been the case regardless of the efforts of songbird researchers to provide disclaimers about the use of the term "neostriatum" in birds. A revision in terminology thus is of particular importance for those studying the neural basis of song control.

To address the problems inherent to the old terminology, formal efforts to revise avian brain nomenclature were begun in 1997 by a small group of avian brain specialists, who then sought to involve a more broadly representative group of researchers than had participated in two previous attempts to standardize avian neuroanatomical terms.[36,37] This process culminated in an open Avian Brain Nomenclature Forum, held July 18–20, 2002 at Duke University in Durham, North Carolina, at which an international and multidisciplinary group of neuroscientists adopted a new terminology by consensus. This chapter presents a summary of the decisions made by the Forum, the basic rationale for the revision or retention of existing names (FIG. 1B), and the recommendations relevant to birdsong vocal and auditory nuclei (FIG. 2 and TABLE 1). In the new terminology, the Forum was attentive to the impact of a drastic change in names of pallial structures on continuity in the literature on song control and to the benefits accruing from a more homology-accurate nomenclature than has existed. A full account of the mechanics of the Forum, a description of all structures whose names have been changed, detailed discussions of the evidence, an explanation of the significance of the new nomenclature for understanding vertebrate brain evolution, and a summary of the implications for understanding brain mechanisms of cognition in birds are available[38–40] and a collection of satellite papers is in preparation.[41–47]

NOMENCLATURE AND THE PROBLEM OF HOMOLOGY

Several detailed reviews[18,48–51] address the theoretical issues surrounding the identification of homologous forebrain structures between birds and mammals. It is valuable for the current chapter to define what is meant by homology, and equally importantly, what is not meant. As commonly used in biology, structures in two or more species are considered to be homologous if they are thought to derive from the same antecedent structure in their common ancestor.[48] Major difficulties arise, however, in identifying homologous brain structures because brain, being a soft tissue, does not fossilize in sufficient detail to make it possible to use the fossil record to trace the natural history of given brain structures. The only remaining approach that can be taken is comparing a variety of features of the structures in question in extant species, including embryological origin, location within the adult brain, afferent and efferent connections, and neurochemical phenotype. In the simplest case, if candidate avian and mammalian homologues (to use sample groups of present interest) arise from the same developmental primordium and have similar adult features and if a similar structure is found in extant reptiles, then a convincing case can be made that the stem amniote common ancestor had an equivalent structure. If, on the other hand, the structures are dissimilar in birds and mammals and/or a comparable structure is not evident in living reptiles, then the compared structures in birds and mammals cannot be said to be demonstrably homologous. It also cannot be automatically said with authority, however, that two morphologically dissimilar structures in birds and mammals are not homologous, since homologous structures can evolve different morphologies.[48] Nonetheless, if the dissimilarities are numerous and living reptiles clearly lack a structure resembling either the compared structure in mammals or the compared structure in birds, then the conclusion that the compared structures in birds and mammals are not homologous is the most likely interpretation.

Terms, such as "analogous," "functionally analogous," or "functionally homologous" have also been used in comparing brain structures. The first two terms mean the same and refer to a circumstance in which structures in different species perform the same function (e.g., bird wings and insect wings), even if they are morphologically different and have evolved independently.[48,52–54] "Analogous" would be the appropriate word to use in this context, and some authors consider the term only to refer to structures of the same function that are independently evolved.[48,52] Note that bat wings and bird wings are analogous as wings but not homologous, since the wings subserve flight in both but the wingedness of the forelimbs was independently evolved. Nonetheless, the forelimbs of bats and birds are homologous as forelimbs, since both inherited their forelimbs from their stem amniote common ancestor. The term "functionally analogous" is redundant with the term "analogous," the latter already implying a functional comparison. The term "functionally homologous" can be ambiguous, meant either as a synonym for analogous (which would be an incorrect use of the word homologous) or to suggest a common origin of a function in two or more species from a function in the common ancestor. The latter misapplies a term commonly used to refer to common ancestry of a morphological entity, i.e., "homologous," to a functional context. The complexities of trying to identify homology at the functional level have been discussed by others.[53,55–57]

Two uses of the term homology by the nomenclature revision effort are one-to-one homology and field homology. In most instances, the term homology is applied to specific structures, such as the humerus of a mouse and the humerus of a chicken. Since they are both derived from the humerus of the stem amniote common ancestor, the humerus of a mouse and chicken would be said to show discrete, or one-to-one, homology.[48,58] This type of homology (which is the type most commonly implied by use of the word) is the type that the Forum required to rename a structure in avian brain with the term used for its mammalian homologue. A second type of homology is field homology. This term, when applied to brain, refers to a circumstance in

TABLE 1. New terminology relevant to songbird vocal and auditory areas

Old Term	Old Abbreviation	New Term	New Abbreviation
	BRAINSTEM		
Nucleus intermedius of the medulla	IM	Hypoglossal nucleus –the twelfth cranial nerve nucleus	nXII
Nucleus nervi hypoglossi the twelfth cranial nerve nucleus	nXII	Supraspinal nucleus	SSp
Area ventralis of Tsai	AVT	Ventral tegmental area or A10	VTA or A10
Nucleus tegmenti-pedunculopontinus, pars compacta	TPc	Substantia nigra, pars compacta or A9	SNc or A9
Anterior nucleus of ansa lenticularis	ALa	Subthalamic nucleus	STN
	SUBPALLIUM PART OF THE TELENCEPHALON		
	Striatal subdivision		
Lobus parolfactorius	LPO	Medial striatum	MSt
–Area X within songbird LPO	X	–Area X within songbird MSt	X
Paleostriatum augmentatum	PA	Lateral striatum	LSt
–Caudal paleostriatum (auditory region)	PC	–Caudal part of the lateral striatum (auditory region)	CSt
	Pallidal subdivision		
Paleostriatum primitivum	PP	Globus pallidus	GP
Ventral paleostriatum	VP	Ventral pallidum	VP
	PALLIUM PART OF THE TELENCEPHALON		
	Hyperpallium subdivision		
Hyperstriatum, Wulst regions	H	Hyperpallium	H
–Hyperstriatum accessorium	HA	–Hyperpallium apicale	HA
–Hyperstriatum intercalatum superior	HIS	–Hyperpallium intercalatum	HI
–Hyperstriatum dorsale	HD	–Hyperpallium dorsale	HD
	Mesopallium subdivision		
Hyperstriatum ventrale	HV	Mesopallium	M
–Nucleus avalanche	Av	–Nucleus avalanche	Av
–Oval nucleus of the hyperstriatum ventrale	HVo	–Oval nucleus of the mesopallium	MO
–Caudal medial hyperstriatum ventrale	CMHV	–Caudal medial mesopallium	CMM
–Caudal lateral hyperstriatum ventrale	CLHV	–Caudal lateral mesopallium	CLM

TABLE 1. (*continued*) New terminology relevant to songbird vocal and auditory

Old Term	Old Abbreviation	New Term	New Abbreviation
Nidopallium subdivision			
Neostriatum	N	Nidopallium	N
–Hyperstriatum ventrale, pars caudale, or high vocal center, or HVc (letter-based name)	HVC or HVc	–HVC (letter-based proper name)	HVC
–Lateral magnocellular nucleus of the anterior neostriatum	lMAN or LMAN	–Lateral magnocellular nucleus of the anterior nidopallium	LMAN
–Medial magnocellular nucleus of the anterior neostriatum	mMAN or MMAN	–Medial magnocellular nucleus of the anterior nidopallium	MMAN
–Interfacial nucleus	NIf	–Interfacial nucleus of the nidopallium	NIf
–Caudal medial neostriatum	NCM	Caudal medial nidopallium	NCM
–HVC shelf	HVC shelf	–HVC shelf (letter-based proper name)	HVC shelf
–Field L	L	–Field L	L
–Ectostriatum	E	–Entopallium	E
–Nucleus basalis	B or Bas	–Nucleus basorostralis	B or Bas
Arcopallium subdivisions			
Archistriatum	A	Arcopallium	A
–Robust nucleus of the archistriatum	RA	–Robust nucleus of the arcopallium	RA
–Cup of robust nucleus of the archistriatum	RA cup	–Cup of robust nucleus of the arcopallium	RA cup
–Ventromedial nucleus of the intermediate archistriatum	Aivm	–Ventromedial nucleus of the intermediate arcopallium	AIVM

which homologous parts of developing brain give rise to a set of adult brain structures in two or more species.[59] The adult brain structures would be said to be field homologues, even if the sets included different nuclei in different species.[57,59] This type of homology was of relevance to the efforts of the Forum to rename the subdivisions of the pallial sector of the avian telencephalon. The Forum required for all of its decisions that evidence for one-to-one or field homology be ample, including for the former multiple types of morphological data and the presence of a comparable structure in living reptiles. Since adoption of each new name for birds required 80% approval from the Forum attendees, any acceptance of a homology-based name was, in effect, based on at least 80% agreement on the homology. In cases in which there was not enough evidence to convince 80% or more of the participants of the existence of homology, new names were chosen that differed from those for any specific mammalian brain structure, but retained similarity to the outdated avian terms in abbreviation, syllabication, and/or phonetics.

A REVISED NOMENCLATURE OF THE AVIAN BRAIN: PRINCIPLES

The decisions of the Forum on the renaming of the cell groups in the avian telencephalon were based on current evidence showing that birds, as do mammals, possess a complex forebrain that contains a well-developed upper sector called the pallium and a smaller ventral sector called the subpallium. Pallium means mantle and the term refers to the upper part of the developing telencephalon and its adult derivatives.[51,60] In mammals, the embryonic pallium gives rise to the neocortex, hippocampal complex, piriform cortex, olfactory bulbs, claustrum, and part of the amygdala, while the embryonic subpallium gives rise to the basal ganglia and several additional basal telencephalic cell groups, including part of the amygdala.[51,60] The Forum concluded that developmental, topological, neurochemical, cellular, connectional, and functional data strongly support the conclusion that approximately the dorsal three-fourths of the avian telencephalon is pallial and in adults includes what has been termed the hyperstriatum, neostriatum, ectostriatum, and archistriatum (as defined by Karten and Hodos[16]), as well as nucleus basalis, hippocampus, piriform cortex, and olfactory bulb.[28,31,49,50,60–62] It is thus inappropriate that the root "-striatum" be present in the names of any of these structures. In contrast to the mammalian pallium, the avian pallium does not have a cortical organization, but rather is organized into a largely continuous field of nuclei.[28,31,63] Although these nuclei have similar connectivity and functional properties to those of the mammalian cortex, amygdala, and possibly the claustrum, their histological appearance is more like that of the basal ganglia, explaining, in part, the erroneous conclusions of many early comparative neuroanatomists.

In renaming avian pallial structures, the Forum confronted the issue of whether sufficient data were available to conclude safely and unequivocally that the structures that have been called the archistriatum, neostriatum, and hyperstriatum in birds possess one-to-one homologies with specific structures in adult mammals.[18,28,31,50,51,60,62,64–67] The Forum decided that the evidence was insufficient to conclusively identify one-to-one mammalian homologues for most pallial structures in birds. While it was agreed that the new names for these structures should include the word or root "pallium," several issues needed to be considered in renaming the pallial structures that possessed "-striatum" as a root word in their outdated name. One major issue was the extent to which choosing new names that allowed retention of existing abbreviations was desirable and could be achieved with esthetically pleasing new terms. Alternatively, the possibility had to be considered that a simple and new descriptive terminology that did not retain established abbreviations might be desirable by making the structures of the avian brain easier to learn and more broadly accessible to neuroscientists. In the end, new terms were selected that allowed abbreviations to be retained for the most intensely studied structures of the avian pallium, to provide easy linkage and clear continuity between the old and new terminologies. The accepted homologies of the avian and mammalian hippocampi, piriform cortices, and olfactory bulbs were not disputed, and it was agreed that there was no need to change the name for these regions.

The Forum further concluded that developmental, topological, neurochemical, cellular, connectional, and functional data strongly support the conclusion that the ventral one-fourth of the avian telencephalon is subpallial, and that the subpallial region lateral to the telencephalic ventricle in birds and reptiles contains homologues of the mammalian basal ganglia, while the subpallial region medial to the lateral ventricle in birds and reptiles contains homologues of the mammalian septum.[60,62,63,68–75] The region lateral to the telencephalic ventricle in birds includes what had been termed the paleostriatum primitivum, the paleostriatum augmentatum, and the lobus parolfactorius. Other subpallial cell groups in birds include the bed nucleus of the stria terminalis, the basal nucleus of Meynert, and the subpallial amygdala. For many subpallial structures, the Forum concluded that there was sufficient evidence to infer one-to-one homologies with mammals. In these instances, the Forum adopted for birds the same name as used for the homologous subpallial structure in mammals. The gain in communication and the already established familiarity of each new avian term, because of their prior use in mammals, were thought to far outweigh disadvantages inherent to abandoning the old names and abbreviations.

The Forum also focused attention on several brainstem cell groups connected with the subpallium or the song control system, for which the homology implied by the name was clearly incorrect, or at best obscure, and for which the true homologue had been amply demonstrated. Below we describe in detail the brainstem, subpallial, and pallial revisions that are relevant to the songbird vocal and auditory nuclei.

SUMMARY OF THE REVISED NOMENCLATURE: THE BRAINSTEM

Nucleus Intermedius (IM) → Hypoglossal Nucleus (nXII)

In the Karten and Hodos atlas[16] of the pigeon brain, a population of motoneurons located ventral to the dorsal motor nucleus of the vagus nerve and the nucleus intercalatus at levels straddling the obex was named the nucleus intermedius, following the practice of Ariëns-Kappers and colleagues.[7] A yet more ventral and somewhat larger population of motoneurons abutting the lateral edge of the medial longitudinal fasciculus was identified as the hypoglossal nucleus. While Ariëns-Kappers and colleagues[7] did suspect that IM innervates lingual and syringeal muscles via bifurcating branches of the twelfth nerve, this has now been demonstrated unambiguously in birds by more recent experimental studies of the innervation of the tongue, trachea and syrinx.[76–84] The IM of Karten and Hodos[16] was thus subsequently renamed the hypoglossal nucleus, or alternatively the 12th cranial nerve nucleus by Nottebohm,[77] and the Forum formally adopted this renaming. Because many investigators had already been using the correct name for this nucleus since 1976, there is no widespread need for investigators to change their customary usage for nXII in birds.

Nucleus Nervi Hypoglossi (nXII) → Supraspinal Nucleus (SSp)

Numerous retrograde labeling studies have demonstrated that the cell group identified by Karten and Hodos[16] as the hypoglossal nucleus actually innervates upper neck musculature (e.g., Mm. complexus, biventer cervicis, splenius capitis, and rectus capitis).[79,80,85–87] This nucleus was thus subsequently renamed supraspinalis,[78,79,88] and the Forum also formally adopted this renaming. It is important to reiterate that most work referring to the hypoglossal nucleus in songbirds has referred to the correct structure, so no change in the customary usage to supraspinalis is needed.

Area Ventralis of Tsai (AVT) → *Ventral Tegmental Area (VTA)*

The cell group named area ventralis of Tsai in the Karten and Hodos pigeon brain atlas is known to be homologous to the mammalian ventral tegmental area, which was also once commonly called the ventral tegmental area of Tsai[89] and is now also known as the A10 dopaminergic cell group.[90–92] As in mammals, this midbrain-diencephalic cell group sends a massive dopaminergic projection to the basal ganglia, mainly to the medial and ventral part of the region that had been called the lobus parolfactorius (LPO),[91,93–96] including to the song nucleus Area X.[93] To eliminate the eponym "Tsai" (since eponyms are no longer employed according to standard international rules of anatomical nomenclature)[37] and to emphasize the homology with mammals, the Forum renamed the avian area ventralis of Tsai to the ventral tegmental area, with the acceptable alternative name of the A10 dopaminergic cell group.

Nucleus Tegmenti Pedunculopontinus Pars Compacta (TPc) → *Substantia Nigra Pars Compacta (SNc)*

This cell field, laterally adjacent and continuous with VTA, contains a large population of dopaminergic neurons that send a massive dopaminergic innervation to the dorsal striatal part of the avian basal ganglia (the regions that have been called lobus parolfactorius and paleostriatum augmentatum, the latter including the auditory area PC)[90,91,94,96–99] and therefore is accepted as homologous to the substantia nigra pars compacta of other vertebrates.[71,72,75,92] The name applied to this region, however, incorrectly suggested homology with the pedunculopontine tegmental nucleus of mammals, located in rhombomere 1, which is characterized by cholinergic neurons, but no dopaminergic neurons.[92,100] Moreover, the actual avian pedunculopontine tegmental nucleus (PPT) homologue, which contains cholinergic neurons, has been identified in rhombomere 1 of pigeons.[100] To rectify these misnomers and avoid confusion, the Forum renamed what had been called the nucleus tegmenti pedunculopontinus pars compacta (TPc) in birds to the substantia nigra pars compacta (SNc), or the alternative name, the A9 dopaminergic cell group. While the dopaminergic field of neurons in the avian A9 is not as compact as it is in rodents or as pigmented as it is in humans, the A9 varies in its degree of compactness and blackness (i.e., pigmentedness) even among mammals. For this reason, and because of the gain in using a homology-based term for avian A9, the Forum decided that the descriptive inaccuracies of the terms "compacta" and "nigra" in the avian name for A9 were far outweighed by the benefits obtained in adopting the commonly used term SNc as the name for this structure.

Anterior Nucleus of the Ansa Lenticularis (ALa) → *Subthalamic Nucleus (STN)*

The avian anterior nucleus of the ansa lenticularis is an inconspicuous cell group located in and along the medial edge of the ansa lenticularis (a fiber bundle interconnecting the basal ganglia with various brainstem cell groups) at rostral diencephalic levels.[68] Based upon its function, the neurochemistry of its inputs and outputs, its developmental profile, its position in the diencephalon, and its apparent presence in reptiles, the ALa is homologous to the subthalamic nucleus (STN) of mammals.[75,101] The Forum therefore renamed the avian ALa as the subthalamic nucleus.

It remains to be determined whether the song nucleus Area X of the basal ganglia is connected with the avian STN.

SUMMARY OF THE REVISED NOMENCLATURE: THE SUBPALLIUM

The basal ganglia in mammals forms within a ventral part of the developing telencephalon called the subpallium. The subpallium, which contains the septal nuclei and several other nuclei in addition to those of the basal ganglia, is notably distinct from the overlying telencephalic region called the pallium in its neurochemistry, in the genes that regulate its development,[102,103] and in its connectivity.[75] Developmental, topological, neurochemical, cellular, connectional, and functional data now strongly support the conclusion that the subpallial region lateral to the telencephalic ventricle in birds and reptiles contains homologues of the mammalian basal ganglia, while the subpallial region medial to the lateral ventricle in birds and reptiles contains the homologue of the mammalian septum.[60,62,63,68-75]

Embryological and developmental molecular studies in both birds and mammals show that the developing avian and mammalian subpallium consists of two separate radially oriented histogenetic zones, a dorsally situated zone that in mammals corresponds to the lateral ganglionic eminence and a ventrally situated zone that in mammals corresponds to the medial ganglionic eminence.[60,104,105,157] Among the derivatives of the lateral ganglionic eminence are the various striatal cell groups, which in mammals make up the dorsal striatum (i.e., the caudate and putamen), the ventral striatum (nucleus accumbens and olfactory tubercle), and the lateral septum. Among the derivatives of the medial ganglionic eminence are the various pallidal cell groups, which in mammals make up the dorsal pallidum (or globus pallidus), the ventral pallidum, and the medial septum. The Forum thus sought to rename the various parts of the avian subpallium so as to more accurately reflect their homologues in mammals. The revisions to the subdivisions that contain vocal and auditory regions are as follows.

Lobus Parolfactorius (LPO), Excluding Its Rostral Ventromedial Part → Medial Striatum (MSt)

Neurochemical, hodological, and developmental evidence indicate that the LPO has striatal traits. The neurochemical and hodological evidence includes a prominent dopaminergic input from the substantia nigra pars compacta and ventral tegmental area, an enrichment in dopamine receptors, a projection back to the SNc/A9 and VTA cell groups, an acetylcholine-rich and cholinesterase-rich neuropil, an enrichment in GABAergic neurons that either contain SP/DYN or enkephalin, and a glutamate receptor pattern very similar to that of the mammalian striatum.[65,72,75,91,93-95,106-111] Developmental evidence includes the finding that the major part of LPO develops from a part of the telencephalic neuroepithelium that expresses the transcription factors *Dlx1* and *Dlx2*, but not the transcription factor *Nkx2.1*, as does the mammalian lateral ganglionic eminence.[60,62] For these and additional reasons summarized by Reiner and colleagues,[75] the Forum replaced the arcane name lobus parolfactorius (meaning lobe next to the olfactory bulb) with the term medial striatum (FIG. 1A,B).

While we recommend that LPO now be called medial striatum in birds, it is also important to note that we do not mean to imply one-to-one homology to the medial part of the mammalian striatum, i.e., the caudate nucleus, and the available evidence seems to be against such a homology. Principal among the reasons against such a notion is that although the avian medial striatum projects predominantly to the substantia nigra, it does not appear to target the pallidal part of the basal ganglia.[68,112,113] By contrast, the caudate nucleus in mammals contains both striatonigral and striatopallidal projection neurons.[75,106,114,115] A second argument against this notion is that the medial striatum in at least some avian species contains pallidal neurons, while such a trait has not been demonstrated for mammalian caudate. These pallidal neurons were first discovered in the specialized song nucleus called Area X within songbird MSt.[116–118] Although the majority of Area X cell types resemble those typical of mammalian striatum in physiology, dendritic morphology, and neurotransmitter features,[108,110,117,118] this sparse but important cell type appears to be pallidal in its aspiny morphology, its probable input from spiny striatal neurons, its GABAergic, inhibitory projection to the thalamus, its neurochemistry, and its physiological features.[110,113,117–119] Compelling evidence now exists showing that the lateral part of MSt outside of Area X and the lateral part of MSt of avian species lacking an Area X also contains pallidal-type neurons.[118–121] Consistent with these observations, developmental studies have suggested that ventrolateral parts of the chicken medial striatum abutting the pallidum may ontogenetically be a pallidal territory that is heavily invaded by striatal cells during development and thereby becomes predominantly striatal in its cell type composition.[60,122] If further study shows such striatal-pallidal neuron mixing in medial striatum to be a general avian trait absent from mammals, it might be advisable to recognize some unique striato-pallidal subdivision within medial striatum and attach to it a suitable name. The Forum concluded, however, that sufficient data were not yet available on the location of this region, on the prevalence of striatal and pallidal cell mixing as an avian trait, and on its absence from mammals. It was also clear to the Forum that what has been called LPO has predominantly striatal cellular traits,[75,91] and so it is appropriate for now to simply rename LPO as the medial striatum, and emphasize the evidence against one-to-one homology with mammalian caudate.

Paleostriatum Augmentatum (PA) → Lateral Striatum (LSt)

Similar lines of evidence demonstrate that PA also has striatal traits and together with MSt makes up the avian dorsal striatum. These traits in PA include a prominent dopaminergic input from the substantia nigra pars compacta, an enrichment in dopamine receptors, an acetylcholine-rich and cholinesterase-rich neuropil, an enrichment in GABAergic neurons that either contain SP/DYN or enkephalin, projections to the paleostriatum primitivum (now to be called the globus pallidus), and a glutamate receptor pattern very similar to that of the mammalian striatum.[28,60,65,72,75,91,93–95,106,107,109,111,121] Additionally, the PA develops from the *Dlx1/2*-rich and *Nkx2.1*-poor neuroepithelial zone corresponding to the mammalian lateral ganglionic eminence.[60,62] For these reasons, and additional ones summarized by Reiner and colleagues,[75] the Forum replaced the name paleostriatum augmentatum with the term lateral striatum (FIG. 1A,B). Similar to LPO, this change is attended by the qualification that there is no compelling evidence that the lateral striatum of birds is homologous in a one-to-one manner with the lateral part of the mammalian striatum, namely the putamen. Principal among the reasons against such a notion is that avian lateral striatum projects predominantly to the pallidal part of the basal ganglia and very little to the substantia nigra.[68,73,123-125] By contrast, the putamen in mammals contains both striatonigral and striatopallidal projection neurons.[75,106,114,115]

Area X → Area X

While Area X of songbirds resides within the avian medial striatum,[29,113] its own name is unaffected by the change of the name of LPO to medial striatum. Thus, the Forum recommended that Area X retain its name (FIG. 2A). A change to nucleus X was proposed, to reflect the clear boundaries of this structure; after discussion, the Forum took no position on whether Area X should be called nucleus X.

Caudal Paleostriatum (PC) → Caudal Striatum (CSt)

The Forum did not discuss renaming of the PC, an auditory region of the caudal lateral striatum. This region possibly receives auditory input from the thalamus and pallium,[126,127] and it shows audition-related gene expression and electrophysiological activity.[25,128,129] Here, we suggest renaming the caudal paleostriatum (PC) to the caudal part of the lateral striatum or more simply the caudal striatum (FIG. 2B). We have not included the letter L for lateral, to simplify the abbreviation.

Ventromedial Rostral LPO → Nucleus Accumbens (Ac)

Although there are no known auditory or vocal regions within the avian nucleus accumbens, a revision to the location of nucleus accumbens relative to LPO, and thus

---

FIGURE 2. Vocal and auditory pathways of the songbird brain within the context of the new avian brain nomenclature. Only the most prominent and/or most studied projections are indicated. For the vocal pathways (**A**), *black arrows* show connections of the components (*dark grey*) of the posterior vocal pathway, *white arrows* show connections of the components (*white*) of the anterior forebrain pathway, and *dashed lines* connections between the two pathways. For the auditory pathway (**B**), most of the hindbrain connectivity is extrapolated from non-songbird species. For clarity, only the lateral part of the anterior vocal pathway is shown, and the connection from Uva to HVC and reciprocal connections in the pallial auditory areas are not indicated. Note that the NCM and CMM are shown for schematic purposes, as they actually lie in a sagittal plane medial to that depicted, and the pathway from NCM to CMM is not depicted. ABBREVIATIONS: Av=avalanche; CLM=caudal lateral mesopallium; CMM=caudal medial mesopallium; CN=cochlear nucleus; CSt=caudal striatum; DM=dorsal medial nucleus; DLM=dorsal lateral nucleus of the medial thalamus; E, entopallium; B=basorostralis; HVC (no formal name other than HVC); LLD=lateral lemniscus, dorsal nucleus; LLI=lateral lemniscus, intermediate nucleus; LLV=lateral lemniscus, ventral nucleus; MLd=dorsal lateral nucleus of the mesencephalon; LMAN=lateral magnocellular nucleus of the anterior nidopallium; Area X=Area X of the medial striatum; MO=oval nucleus of the mesopallium; NCM= caudal medial nidopallium; NIf= nucleus interface of the nidopallium; nXIIts=nucleus XII, tracheosyringeal part; Ov=ovoidalis; PAm=paraambiguus; RAm=retroambiguus; RA=robust nucleus of the arcopallium; SO=superior olive; Uva=nucleus uvaeformis. (Figure adapted from Jarvis and colleagues.[40])

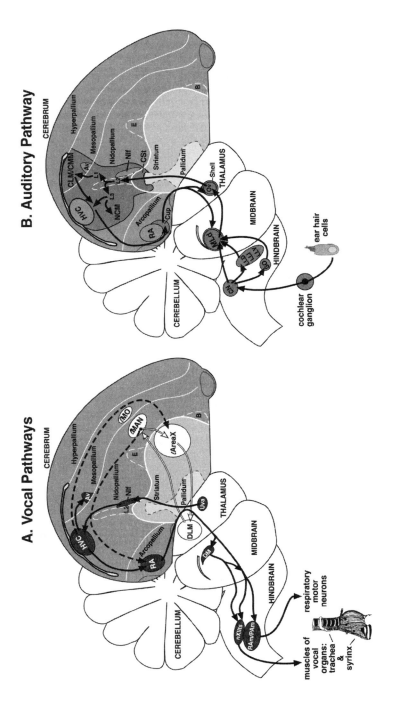

FIGURE 2. *See previous page for legend.*

to Area X within MSt is of relevance. In the Karten and Hodos atlas,[16] nucleus accumbens was identified as a small bulge at the ventral tip of the lateral ventricle extending several millimeters rostral from the level of the anterior commissure. However, based on compelling evidence,[130] the Forum concluded that this region instead is homologous to the lateral part of the mammalian bed nucleus of the stria terminalis (BNST). The Forum further concluded that the region surrounding the tip of the lateral ventricle, at the ventromedial margin of the rostral pole of what has been called LPO in birds possesses the same topographic, hodological, and neurochemical traits as the nucleus accumbens of mammals.[106,124,131–138] This includes for both birds and mammals preferential reciprocal connections with the ventral tegmental area, afferent input from limbic pallial regions (such as the hippocampal complex, amygdala, and cingulate cortex, as well as from frontal pallium), and the frequent co-localization of substance P and enkephalin in spiny projection neurons. By contrast, much of the remainder of what has been called LPO in birds and caudatoputamen in mammals is reciprocally connected with the substantia nigra pars compacta, receives pallial input from somatosensory and somatomotor areas of the pallium, and shows little co-localization of SP and enkephalin in spiny striatal projection neurons.[63,106,112,123–125,131,132,135–137,139] Moreover, a topographically, hodologically, and neurochemically similar cell group has been identified as nucleus accumbens in turtles, lizards, and snakes.[71,106,132,140–143] For these reasons, the Forum recognized and recommended that the rostral ventromedial part of the former LPO of birds be called nucleus accumbens and that the term medial striatum be only used to refer to the remainder of LPO. As in mammals, however, a precise cytoarchitectonic border between the dorsal striatum and nucleus accumbens is not evident, and a neurochemical criterion by which to unambiguously distinguish the two fields has not been identified. Additionally, while the nucleus accumbens of mammals possesses core and shell subdivisions, comparable subdivisions of nucleus accumbens in birds have not been conclusively identified.[135,136]

Paleostriatum Primitivum (PP) → Globus Pallidus (GP)

Although there are no described auditory or vocal nuclei within avian pallidal regions, it is important to be acquainted with the renaming of pallidal subdivisions within the context of subpallial nomenclature revisions. Diverse lines of evidence indicate that the avian PP is derived from the avian equivalent of the medial ganglionic eminence and has traits comparable to those of the dorsal pallidum (globus pallidus) in mammals.[60,63,68,74,75,91,122,131,144–149] In both birds and mammals, the projection neurons of these regions possess large cell bodies and smooth dendrites, derive from an *Nkx2.1*-expressing neuroepithelium, and give rise to the motor output projections of the basal ganglia. In birds and mammals, these neurons are also GABAergic, contain the neuropeptide LANT6, receive inputs with a woolly fiber morphology from either SP/DYN-containing or ENK-containing striatal neurons, receive a prominent glutamatergic input from the subthalamic nucleus, and share similar electrophysiological properties.[75,101,121,150] Thus, the Forum renamed the avian paleostriatum primitivum as the globus pallidus (FIG. 1A,B). This term is appropriate for descriptive reasons, as the avian GP and its mammalian counterpart are pale. Nonetheless, there are some differences between avian GP and mammalian GP. Avian GP neurons, for example, migrate farther laterally than do mammalian pallidal neurons, with the result that avian GP is more laterally situated than adult mammalian GP.[60,122] The GP in mammals is separated into two segments, the internal and external, with distinct connectivity and neurochemistry, whereas in birds the neuronal types of the two segments are intermingled.[75] The avian globus pallidus as a cell field is also not as globular in shape as the comparable cell field is in mammals, but different mammalian species show variation in the shape of the GP as well. Thus, the Forum concluded that despite any differences, the advantages in the use of the homology-based term globus pallidus as the new name for PP in birds outweighed any slightly misleading implications as to its shape or organization.

Ventral Paleostriatum (VP) → Ventral Pallidum (VP)

A group of GABAergic neurons within the medial forebrain bundle (MFP; also called the fasciculus prosencephali medialis, FPM) has been demonstrated in birds. This cell group has also been called the ventral paleostriatum.[151] It has the cellular neurochemistry, receives the ventral striatal inputs (including from nucleus accumbens), and has the outputs characteristic of the ventral pallidum of mammals.[106,135,144–146] Its glutamate receptor expression profile is identical to that of GP of both birds and mammals.[65] In addition, in both mammals and birds, the neurons of this region arise from the same *Nkx2.1*-expressing histogenetic subpallial neuroepithelium as the GP.[60] A comparable cell group is present in turtles, crocodilians, and lizards.[69,140,141,145,152,153] The Forum thus renamed this cell group as the avian ventral pallidum (TABLE 1). The word ventral is used because it provides the VP with a positional term that distinguishes it from its more dorsal somatic counterpart, the GP, which has also alternatively been termed the dorsal pallidum. Note that the ventral pallidum in birds overlaps a field of cholinergic neurons that spans the medial and lateral forebrain bundles. These cholinergic neurons send diffuse projections into the pallium, including the pallial song control nuclei.[154,155] Since the ventral pallidum in mammals also overlaps a similar field of cholinergic neurons with projections to the pallium,[156] the Forum recommended these neurons in birds be given a name similar to those in mammals, the basal magnocellular cholinergic nucleus (NBM).

SUMMARY OF THE REVISED NOMENCLATURE: THE PALLIUM

The structures constituting the pallium in adult birds and mammals derive from a large histogenetic zone located dorsal to the subpallium and distinguishable from the subpallium in the developmentally regulated genes it expresses.[60,157] Owing to the flawed identification of brain regions by Edinger and his followers, the major pallial sectors of the lateral telencephalic wall in birds have the incorrect root word "-striatum" in their names (hyperstriatum, neostriatum, ectostriatum, archistriatum), and in some cases possess prefixes with questionable evolutionary implications (e.g., "neo-" and "archi-"). The perceived need to correct these errors was the main driving force behind the Forum. The reasoning used by the Forum in selecting the new names is briefly reviewed below (FIG. 1B), followed by specific recommendations of the Forum for vocal and auditory areas (FIG. 2; TABLE 1).

Rationale for New Names for Hyperstriatum, Neostriatum, Ectostriatum, and Archistriatum

Hyperstriatum

In revising the terminology for the hyperstriatum, a guiding consideration was that the hyperstriatum ventrale (HV) should have a name distinct from that for the hyperstriatal subdivisions composing the Wulst [i.e., the hyperstriatum accessorium, (HA), the hyperstriatum intercalatus superior (HIS), and the hyperstriatum dorsale (HD) in the outdated nomenclature]. It has been apparent for some time, from developmental, hodological, neurochemical, and functional studies, that HV and the Wulst are distinct telencephalic subdivisions.[15,50,65,111,158–164] After consideration of various possibilities, the Forum decided to replace the term "hyperstriatum" in HA, HIS, and HD with hyperpallium, replacing the secondary terms of accessorium with apicale, intercalatus superior with intercalatum, and dorsale with densocellulare, and replacing HV with mesopallium (FIG. 1A,B; TABLE 1). Since the prefix "hyper-" refers to an enlarged entity, "hyper-" in hyperpallium was considered acceptable, as the Wulst is an enlarged (bulging) structure at the upper aspect of the pallium. In addition, "hyper" possesses the merits that it is a commonly employed neuroanatomical term, already having been used in the names for the subregions of the Wulst, and it offers easy linking of the new term to the old, with abbreviations retained. "Meso-" as a prefix is descriptive of the location of this region (the former hyperstriatum ventrale) between the hyperpallium and the subdivision below it (the former neostriatum). Of course, the use of mesopallium as a replacement for hyperstriatum ventrale means that abbreviations for this region must change. The Forum did not consider this a serious disadvantage, since relatively few subregions have been named in the literature on the mesopallium.

Neostriatum and Ectostriatum

In revising the terminology for the neostriatum, a guiding principle was to devise a suitable and acceptable prefix that is descriptive of the region and that maintains abbreviations with the past literature. The Forum decided that the prefix "nido-," derived from the Latin word for nest (nidus) met these requirements, resulting in the new term nidopallium as a replacement for neostriatum (FIG. 1A,B). The prefix "nido-" is apt for the neostriatum, since it is the pallial structure in which the overlying pallial structures are nested. Moreover, the prefix "nido-" offers an aural link to the existing prefix for this region (i.e., "neo-"), and allows abbreviation retention. In revising the term ectostriatum, the Forum noted that the term ectostriatum, broken into its prefix and root word, means "outside the striatum." as the striatum is now recognized in birds, and is therefore semantically appropriate. Thus, ectostriatum could have been retained without any erroneous denotation. Nonetheless, the term ectostriatum was linked to the set of incorrect names for the avian pallium by the root word "-striatum", and could be misconstrued as being part of the striatum. For this reason, the name for the ectostriatum was changed to the entopallium, which means "within (ento-) the pallium". This new term also retains existing abbreviations for this region and possesses an aural linkage to the term ectostriatum.

Archistriatum

In revising the terminology for the archistriatum, a number of issues had to be considered. These included defining the boundaries of the archistriatum, as different reports had set different boundaries,[16,165] and coming to consensus on any homologies between the avian archistriatum (or its parts) with cell groups of the mammalian telencephalon. The avian archistriatum has been thought to be, at least in part, homologous to the mammalian amygdala,[3,4,7,60,64,165] a structure that itself is now known to possess both pallial and subpallial portions.[103] In revising the terminology for the avian archistriatum, the relationship of its subfields (including nucleus taeniae, also known as the taenia) to the pallial and subpallial parts of the mammalian amygdala needed to be addressed. Based on neurochemical and developmental data, the Forum concluded that the evidence overwhelmingly indicates that all parts of the avian archistriatum, i.e., structures with archistriatum in their names in the pigeon and chicken brain atlases,[16,151] are pallial.[65,166,167] As part of the discussion on the pallial versus subpallial nature of the archistriatum, the Forum concluded that the taenia has typically been regarded as a part of the archistriatal complex, although this was not reflected in its name,[165,168–170] but that much or all of it is subpallial.[104,170,171] Thus, the conclusion that the structures with archistriatum in their name, as their limits have been traditionally defined (excluding the taenia), are entirely pallial, made it appropriate that the new name for the archistriatum and its subdivisions have "-pallium" as part of the name.

Given the desirability of retaining existing abbreviations for the archistriatum, the Forum considered a number of possible prefixes beginning with the letter "A". "Archi-" was ruled out because of its questionable evolutionary implications. Consideration was given to the idea that "amygdalo-" be used, based on the interpretation that all of the archistriatum was amygdaloid in developmental origin and homologous as a field to all or part of the amygdala in mammals.[60,64] The Forum concluded that while the evidence for an amygdaloid nature of the taeniae and the posterior archistriatum was supported by hodological, developmental, neurochemical, and behavioral evidence,[60,123,135,165,170,172] the anterior, the intermediate, and at least parts of the medial archistriatum appeared to have largely somatic features, making them unlike the amygdala.[65,123,165,166,173,174] While it was further acknowledged that perhaps these regions were homologous to some parts of the mammalian amygdala and had evolved divergently in birds, the Forum concluded that this had not been demonstrated unequivocally. In addition, even if such an evolutionary relationship were established, the concern was expressed that it would be misleading and inappropriate to attach a name with viscerolimbic functional implications (i.e., the term "amygdala") to a field with somatic functional traits.[175–177] In the end, the Forum decided that only the posterior archistriatum and taenia warranted the designation of amygdala (PoA and TnA, FIG. 1B). For the remaining parts of the archistriatum, the Forum decided to replace archistriatum with the term arcopallium, with the prefix "arco-" referring to the arched contour of the upper boundary of the field (FIG. 1B). This choice does not foreclose the future option of replacing "arco-" with "amygdalo-" for specific arcopallial subdivisions if the evidence for this homology becomes more convincing. The subpallial region inferior to the globus pallidus was renamed the subpallial amygdala (SpA, FIG.1B).

Vocal and Auditory Regions of the Mesopallium

Nucleus Avalanche (Av)→ Nucleus Avalanche (Av)

This is a little-studied vocal nucleus in the old named HV that receives a projection from HVC[178] (FIG. 2A) and shows vocalization-associated gene expression.[179] A similar mesopallial nucleus has been identified by vocalization-associated gene expression in budgerigars and hummingbirds.[25,34] Because the name given to this nucleus in songbirds did not have hyperstriatum ventrale in it, no name change is necessary.

Oval Nucleus of the Hyperstriatum Ventrale (HVo) → Oval Nucleus of the Mesopallium (MO)

First described in parrots,[32,33] a similarly positioned, oval-shaped nucleus in the anterior part of songbird HV that shows vocalization-associated gene expression has been noted.[180] With the renaming of the HV, the Forum recommended renaming this nucleus to the oval nucleus of the mesopallium (MO, FIG. 2A). Here the abbreviation for "oval" is capitalized, as the Forum decided to capitalize the letters representing the main words of each name, with only subordinate letters or words in lowercase.

Caudal Medial Hyperstriatum Ventrale (CMHV) →
Caudal Medial Mesopallium (CMM)

The caudal medial HV is a distinct region that is part of the telencephalic auditory pathway and that shows auditory-induced gene expression and neural activity.[25,127–129,181–185] With the renaming of the HV, this region becomes the caudal medial mesopallium (CMM, TABLE 1). CMM also has a lateral auditory counterpart that was called the caudal lateral hyperstriatum ventrale (CLHV).[127] This becomes the caudal lateral mesopallium (CLM, FIG. 2B).

Vocal and Auditory Regions of the Nidopallium

HVC (Higher Vocal Center) or HVc → HVC

This nucleus was the first identified part of the telencephalic song control circuit.[29] It was thought to occupy the caudal-most part of the hyperstriatum ventrale, and was thus named the hyperstriatum ventrale, pars caudale, and abbreviated HVc. Subsequent work, however, recognized that this region is in actuality located within the pallial field that had been called the neostriatum[30] (FIG. 2A). To retain the abbreviation, which had already become entrenched, but eliminate the inaccurate location implied by its name, Nottebohm[186] suggested calling this region the higher vocal center, and abbreviating it with all capital letters HVC. Subsequently, the concern was raised that HVC was arguably not the apex of a hierarchy of vocal centers of the brain, making the name unwarranted.[187] Thus, Fortune and Margoliash[188] and Brenowitz and colleagues[189] recommended use of "HVc" as a letter-based proper name for the nucleus. However, the use of "high (or higher) vocal center" has persisted in published reports by some investigators, while "HVc" used as a proper name has been employed by others. In order to unify the field behind a single name, the Forum solicited feedback from the songbird research community, who overwhelmingly supported using HVC as the proper name (i.e., letter-based name only, all caps) and recommended against using HVc or any form of the term "higher vocal center."

Lateral and Medial Magnocellular Nucleus of the Anterior Neostriatum
(lMAN and mMAN) → Lateral and Medial Magnocellular Nucleus
of the Anterior Nidopallium (LMAN and MMAN)

The magnocellular nucleus of the anterior neostriatum (MAN) is a vocal nucleus of the anterior telencephalon that is necessary for song learning[113,190–192] and is active during singing.[179,193] This nucleus has two named subdivisions, the lateral and medial (typically abbreviated lMAN and mMAN). With the renaming of the neostriatum, the name for each of these is altered by substituting nidopallium for neostriatum; the established abbreviations remain the same (FIG. 2A; TABLE 1). Based upon feedback from songbird researchers, the Forum recognized that using the lowercase letter "l" for the word "lateral" in the abbreviation for the lateral magnocellular nucleus of the anterior nidopallium causes confusion due to the resemblance of the lowercase letter "l" to the number "1" or to the capital letter "I." Using all capital letters in this case (LMAN and MMAN) eliminates this confusion.

Nucleus Interface (NIf) → Nucleus Interface of the Nidopallium (NIf)

The nucleus interface (NIf) is a telencephalic constituent of the song control circuit that projects to HVC[178] (FIG. 2A), and shows singing-associated neural activity and gene expression.[180,194] While this nucleus is located in what has been called the neostriatum, the word neostriatum does not appear in the established name for NIf. To emphasize its location, the Forum adopted the official name nucleus interface of the nidopallium (or its Latin equivalent), and its abbreviation remains the same (TABLE 1).

Caudal Medial Neostriatum (NCM) → Caudal Medial Nidopallium (NCM)

The caudal medial neostriatum is a large and well-studied region of the avian auditory circuit, subjacent to the caudal medial mesopallium (CMM). It shows specialized auditory processing properties in response to species-specific sounds.[128,195–199] With the renaming of the neostriatum, the name is altered to caudal medial nidopallium (NCM), and the established abbreviation remains the same (FIG. 2B; TABLE 1).

HVC (or HVc) Shelf → HVC Shelf

The HVC shelf is an auditory region continuous with NCM dorsally, and is located immediately ventral to HVC[126,128,174] (FIG. 2B). Because the word neostriatum is not in the name, there is no change. However, due to the Forum recommendation that HVC serve as a proper name, it is similarly recommended that the HVC part of the term "HVC shelf" be a letter-based proper name.

Field L → Field L

The nidopallial region containing the primary auditory thalamo-recipient zone was not recognized as a distinct region in the Karten and Hodos atlas[16] and was not assigned a name. However, the experimental work of Karten[200] established that this zone largely coincided with the cytoarchitectonic region named Field L by Rose,[13] and this name subsequently became entrenched in the literature on this region.[126,127,181,183,201–203] Given its identification as Field L in a large number of studies, and given that the term has no erroneous evolutionary implications, the existing name was retained. The Forum recognized, however, that an inconsistency exists in the literature in the extent of the territory to which the term Field L is applied. In many studies, Field L is taken to mean the region in the caudal medial neostriatum (now nidopallium) defined by Rose[13] and identified by Karten[200] as receiving a prominent input from nucleus ovoidalis (Ov, FIG. 2B). The work of Scheich and colleagues[183,204,205] led to the recognition that the auditory field in the caudal medial nidopallium was actually larger than the ovoidalis-recipient Field L alone. Thus, the main ovoidalis thalamo-recipient zone was named L2, and the regions immediately adjacent to L2, which receive L2 input as well as a smaller amount of thalamic input from the ovoidalis shell region, were named L1 and L3 (FIG. 2B). As a consequence of the presence of subfields, the term "Field L" has come to have two different definitions in the recent literature, one in which it refers to L2 alone and one in which it refers to L1, L2, and L3 together. Similar problems exist for what the Forum has renamed the entopallium,[161,206–209] and for the nucleus basalis (renamed nucleus basorostralis by the Forum).[78,210–212] The Forum concluded that it would be desirable to develop a uniform and consistent terminology for core and shell subdivisions of these three sensory fields in the nidopallium, and will make recommendations in a separate publication devoted to this issue.[46]

Vocal and Auditory Regions of the Arcopallium

Robust Nucleus of the Archistriatum (RA) →
Robust Nucleus of the Arcopallium (RA)

The robust nucleus of the arcopallium (RA) is a specialized nucleus within the intermediate archistriatum of songbirds, required for and active during the production of learned song.[29,177,179,213] With the renaming of the archistriatum, the name for this nucleus becomes the robust nucleus of the arcopallium (RA), and the existing abbreviation is retained (FIG. 2A).

Cup of the Robust Nucleus of the Archistriatum (RA cup) →
Cup of the Robust Nucleus of the Arcopallium (RA cup)

The RA cup is a region within the songbird auditory pathway located immediately rostroventral to the vocal nucleus RA[126,128,174,180] (FIG. 2B). A similar region has been found in the intermediate arcopallium of other vocal learning birds, as well as in vocal non-learning birds.[25,34,181] In pigeons, this region has been called the ventromedial nucleus of the intermediate archistriatum (AIVM).[181] With the new nomenclature, archistriatum in these names is replaced by arcopallium, and the existing abbreviations are retained (TABLE 1).

CONCLUSIONS

The understanding of avian brain organization and function has advanced enormously in the past one hundred years.[3,5–7,12,13,18,28,31,38,40,60,75] The facts that have emerged have shown the existing terminology for the avian telencephalon and many brainstem cell groups related to it to be erroneous. These errors perpetuated misconceptions about birds and the avian brain. The Avian Brain Nomenclature Forum was the culmination of a growing awareness of how these errors have affected the understanding of the avian brain and of the communication problems caused by the faulty and outdated terminology. The Forum thus sought to devise a new terminology that is free of errors and promotes accurate understanding of avian brain organization and evolution. The Forum was scrupulous in its renaming efforts to use names implying homology only when it was confident that the names would not later prove to be in error. We believe the nomenclature we have devised can serve the field well, and we thus urge all avian brain researchers, birdsong neurobiologists included, to adopt the new nomenclature. Further information and avian brain images depicting this new nomenclature are available in our related papers[39,40,167] and on the Avian Brain Nomenclature Exchange website (<http://avianbrain.org>).

ACKNOWLEDGMENTS

In addition to the authors of this chapter, the Forum participants included Laura L. Bruce, Ann B. Butler, András Csillag, Wayne Kuenzel, Loreta Medina, George Paxinos, Toru Shimizu, Georg Striedter, Martin Wild as the core committee, and Gregory F. Ball, Sarah Durand, Onur Güntürkün, Diane Lee, Alice Powers, Stephanie A. White, Gerald Hough, Lubica Kubikova, Tom V. Smulders, Kazuhiro Wada, Jennifer Dugas-Ford, Scott Husband, Keiko Yamamoto, Jing Yu, and Connie Siang as other faculty and student participants. Preparation for the Forum, the Forum itself, and the dissemination of the conclusions are supported by grants from the National Science Foundation (IBN-0110894) and the National Institutes of Health (1R13-MH-64400-01). We thank Drs. Carol van Hartesveldt and Christopher Platt of National Science Foundation and Israel Lederhendler of National Institute of Mental Health for their support in securing funding and for their encouragement of the Forum enterprise.

REFERENCES

1. NORTHCUTT, R.G. 2001. Changing views of brain evolution. Brain Res. Bull. **55:** 663–674.
2. EDINGER, L. 1885. The Anatomy of the Central Nervous System of Man and of Vertebrates in General: 1896 Fifth German edition, English published 1899; Translators, W.S. Hall, P.L. Holland, E.P. Carlton. F.A. Davis Company. Philadelphia.
3. EDINGER, L., A. WALLENBERG & G.M. HOLMES. 1903. Untersuchungen über die vergleichende Anatomie des Gehirns. Das Vorderhirn der Vögel. Abhandlungen der Senckenbergischen naturforschenden Gesellschaft. **20:** 343–426.
4. EDINGER, L. 1908. The relations of comparative anatomy to comparative psychology. Comp. Neurol. Psychol. **18:** 437–457.
5. ARIËNS-KAPPERS, C. 1922. The ontogenetic development of the corpus striatum in birds and a comparison with mammals and man. Proc. Kon. Akad. v. Wetens. te Amsterdam. **26:** 135–158.
6. ARIËNS-KAPPERS, C. 1928. Three lectures on neurobiotaxis and other subjects delivered at the University of Copenhagen. Leven and Munksgaard. Copenhagen.
7. ARIËNS-KAPPERS, C.U., C.G. HUBER & E.C. CROSBY. 1936. Comparative Anatomy of the Nervous System of Vertebrates, Including Man. Reprinted 1960, Hafner. New York.

8. ARIËNS-KAPPERS, C. 1909. The phylogenesis of the paleo-cortex and archi-cortex compared with the evolution of the visual neo-cortex. Arch. Neurol. Psychiat. **4:** 161–173.
9. JOHNSTON, J.B. 1923. Further contributions to the study of the evolution of the forebrain. J. Comp. Neurol. **35:** 337–481.
10. CRAIGIE, E.H. 1932. The cell structure of the cerebral hemisphere of the humming bird. J. Comp. Neurol. **56:** 135–168.
11. HERRICK, C.J. 1948. The Brain of the Tiger Salamander. The University of Chicago Press. Chicago, IL.
12. HERRICK, C.J. 1956. The Evolution of Human Nature. University of Texas Press. Austin, TX.
13. ROSE, M. 1914. Uber die cytoarchitektonische gliederung des vorderhirns der vogel. J. f. Psychol. Neurol. **21**(suppl. 1): 278–352.
14. KUHLENBECK, H. 1938. The ontogenetic development and phylogenetic significance of the cortex telencephali in the chick. J. Comp. Neurol. **69:** 273–301.
15. KÄLLÉN, B. 1953. On the nuclear differentiation during the embryogenesis in the avian forebrain and some notes on the amniote strio-amygdaloid complex. Avata. Anat. (Basel) **17:** 72–84.
16. KARTEN, H.J. & W. HODOS. 1967. A Stereotaxic Atlas of the Brain of the Pigeon (*Columba livia*). Johns Hopkins University Press. Baltimore.
17. PARENT, A. 1997. The brain in evolution and involution. Biochem. Cell Biol. **75:** 651–667.
18. STRIEDTER, G.F. 1997. The telencephalon of tetrapods in evolution. Brain Behav. Evol. **49:** 179–213.
19. SWANSON, L.W. 2000. Cerebral hemisphere regulation of motivated behavior. Brain Res. **886:** 113–164.
20. THORPE, W.H. 1951. The learning abilities of birds. Ibis **93:** 1–52, 252–296.
21. MARLER, P. 1970. Birdsong and speech development: could there be parallels? Am. Sci. **58:** 669–673.
22. BAPTISTA, L.F. & K.L. SCHUCHMANN. 1990. Song learning in the anna hummingbird (*Calypte anna*). Ethology **84:** 15–26.
23. PEPPERBERG, I.M. 2002. In search of King Solomon's ring: cognitive and communicative studies of grey parrots (*Psittacus erithacus*). Brain Behav. Evol. **59:** 54–67.
24. HILE, A.G., T.K. PLUMMER & G.F. STRIEDTER. 2000. Male vocal imitation produces call convergence during pair bonding in budgerigars, *Melopsittacus undulatus*. Anim. Behav. **59:** 1209–1218.
25. JARVIS, E.D. et al. 2000. Behaviourally driven gene expression reveals song nuclei in hummingbird brain. Nature **406:** 628–632.
26. WEIR, A.A., J. CHAPPELL & A. KACELNIK. 2002. Shaping of hooks in New Caledonian crows. Science **297:** 981.
27. HUNT, G.R. & R.D. GRAY. 2003. Diversification and cumulative evolution in New Caledonian crow tool manufacture. Proc. R. Soc. Lond. B Biol. Sci. **270:** 867–874.
28. KARTEN, H.J. 1969. The organization of the avian telencephalon and some speculations on the phylogeny of the amniote telencephalon. *In* Comparative and Evolutionary Aspects of the Vertebrate Central Nervous System, Vol. 167. J. Pertras, Ed.: 164–179.
29. NOTTEBOHM, F., T.M. STOKES & C.M. LEONARD. 1976. Central control of song in the canary, *Serinus canarius*. J. Comp. Neurol. **165:** 457–486.
30. PATON, J.A., K.R. MANOGUE & F. NOTTEBOHM. 1981. Bilateral organization of the vocal control pathway in the budgerigar, *Melopsittacus undulatus*. J. Neurosci. **1:** 1279–1288.
31. KARTEN, H.J. 1991. Homology and evolutionary origins of the "neocortex." Brain Behav. Evol. **38:** 264–272.
32. STRIEDTER, G.F. 1994. The vocal control pathways in budgerigars differ from those in songbirds. J. Comp. Neurol. **343:** 35–56.
33. DURAND, S.E. et al. 1997. Vocal control pathways through the anterior forebrain of a parrot (*Melopsittacus undulatus*). J. Comp. Neurol. **377:** 179–206.
34. JARVIS, E.D. & C.V. MELLO. 2000. Molecular mapping of brain areas involved in parrot vocal communication. J. Comp. Neurol. 419: 1–31.

35. GAHR, M. 2000. Neural song control system of hummingbirds: comparison to swifts, vocal learning (songbirds) and nonlearning (suboscines) passerines, and vocal learning (budgerigars) and nonlearning (dove, owl, gull, quail, chicken) nonpasserines. J. Comp. Neurol. **426:** 182–196.

36. BAUMEL, J.J. 1979. Nomina Anatomica Avium: An Annotated Anatomical Dictionary of Birds. Academic Press. London, New York.

37. BAUMEL, J.J. 1993. Handbook of Avian Anatomy: Aomina anatomica avium. Nuttall Ornithological Club. Cambridge, MA.

38. REINER, A. *et al.* 2004. Revised nomenclature for avian telencephalon and some related brainstem nuclei. J. Comp. Neurol. In press.

39. REINER, A. *et al.* 2004. The Avian Brain Nomenclature Forum: A New Century in Comparative Neuroanatomy. J. Comp. Neurol. In press.

40. JARVIS, E.D. *et al.* A paradigm shift in understanding the organization, evolution and function of the avian brain. (Submitted for publication.)

41. WILD, M., L. MEDINA & A. REINER. Homologies for some avian and mammalian brainstem cell groups. Brain Behav. Evol. (Manuscript in preparation.)

42. JARVIS, E.D. *et al.* The Avian Brain Nomenclature Forum: a new century in comparative neuroanatomy II. Brain Behav. Evol. (Manuscript in preparation.)

43. KUENZEL, W. *et al.* The avian basal ganglia and other subpallial cell groups. Brain Behav. Evol. (Manuscript in preparation.)

44. BRUCE, L. *et al.* The avian arcopallium and amygdala. Brain Behav. Evol. (Manuscript in preparation).

45. MEDINA, L. *et al.* The new avian brain nomenclature in the context of telencephalic homology among amniotes. Brain Behav. Evol. (Manuscript in preparation).

46. JARVIS, E.D. *et al.* The avian nidopallium and mesopallium. Brain Behav. Evol. (Manuscript in preparation).

47. SHIMIZU, T.V. *et al.* The avian hyperpallium. Brain Behav. Evol. (Manuscript in preparation).

48. CAMPBELL, C.B. & W. Hodos. 1970. The concept of homology and the evolution of the nervous system. Brain Behav. Evol. **3:** 353–367.

49. BUTLER, A.B. 1994. The evolution of the dorsal pallium in the telencephalon of amniotes: cladistic analysis and a new hypothesis. Brain Res. Brain Res. Rev. **19:** 66–101.

50. MEDINA, L. & A. REINER. 2000. Do birds possess homologues of mammalian primary visual, somatosensory and motor cortices? Trends Neurosci. **23:** 1–12.

51. REINER, A.J. 2000. A hypothesis as to the organization of cerebral cortex in the common amniote ancestor of modern reptiles and mammals. Novartis Found Symp. **228:** 83–102; discussion 102–113.

52. CARCRAFT, J. 1967. Comments on homology and analogy. Syst. Zool. **16:** 356–359.

53. LAUDER, G.V. 1986. Homology, analogy, and the evolution of behavior. *In* Evolution of Animal Behavior. M.H. Nitecki & J.A. Kitchell, Eds.: 9–40. Oxford University Press. NY.

54. SCHMITT, M. 1995. The homology concept—still alive. *In* The Nervous System of Invertebrates: An Evolutionary and Comparative Approach. O. Briedbach & W. Kutsch, Eds.: 425–438. Birkhauser Verlag. Basel, Switzerland.

55. HODOS, W. 1974. The comparative study of brain–behavior relationships. *In* Birds: Brain and Behavior. I.J. Goodman & M.W. Schein, Eds.: 15–25. Academic Press. NY.

56. HODOS, W. 1976. The concept of homology and the evolution of behavior. *In* Evolution, Brain and Behavior: Persistent Problems. R.B. Masterton, W. Hodos & H. Jerison, Eds.: 153–167. L. Erlbaum Associates. Hillsdale, NJ.

57. STRIEDTER, G.F. & R.G. NORTHCUTT. 1991. Biological hierarchies and the concept of homology. Brain Behav. Evol. **38:** 177–189.

58. SMITH, H. 1967. Biological similarities and homologies. System. Zool. **16:** 101–102.

59. PUELLES, L. & L. MEDINA. 2002. Field homology as a way to reconcile genetic and developmental variability with adult homology. Brain Res. Bull. **57:** 243–255.

60. PUELLES, L. *et al.* 2000. Pallial and subpallial derivatives in the embryonic chick and mouse telencephalon, traced by the expression of the genes *Dlx-2*, *Emx-1*, *Nkx-2.1*, *Pax-6*, and *Tbr-1*. J. Comp. Neurol. **424:** 409–438.

61. GÜNTÜRKÜN, O. 1991. The functional organization of the avian visual system. *In* Neural and Behavioral Plasticity. R.J. Andrew, Ed.: 92–105. Oxford University Press. Oxford.
62. SMITH-FERNANDEZ, A.S. *et al.* 1998. Expression of the *Emx-1* and *Dlx-1* homeobox genes define three molecularly distinct domains in the telencephalon of mouse, chick, turtle and frog embryos: implications for the evolution of telencephalic subdivisions in amniotes. Development **125:** 2099–2111.
63. REINER, A., S.E. BRAUTH & H.J. KARTEN. 1984. Evolution of the amniote basal ganglia. Trends Neurosci. **7:** 320–325.
64. BRUCE, L.L. & T.J. NEARY. 1995. The limbic system of tretopods: a comparative analysis of cortical and amygdalar populations. Brain Behav. Evol. **46:** 224–234.
65. WADA, K., H. SAKAGUCHI & E. JARVIS. 2001. Brain evolution revealed through glutamate receptor expression profiles. Soc. Neurosci. **27:** 1425.
66. MOLNAR, Z. & A.B. BUTLER. 2002. Neuronal changes during forebrain evolution in amniotes: an evolutionary developmental perspective. Prog. Brain Res. **136:** 21–38.
67. BUTLER, A.B., Z. MOLNAR & P.R. MANGER. 2002. Apparent absence of claustrum in monotremes: implications for forebrain evolution in amniotes. Brain Behav. Evol. **60:** 230–240.
68. KARTEN, H.J. & J.L. DUBBELDAM. 1973. The organization and projections of the paleostriatal complex in the pigeon (*Columba livia*). J. Comp. Neurol. **148:** 61–90.
69. Brauth, S.E. & C.A. Kitt. 1980. The paleostriatal system of *Caiman crocodilus*. J. Comp. Neurol. **189:** 437–465.
70. BRAUTH, S.E., *et al.* 1983. The substance P-containing striatotegmental path in reptiles: an immunohistochemical study. J. Comp. Neurol. **219:** 305–327.
71. SMEETS, W.J.A.J. 1994. Catecholamines in the CNS of reptiles: structure and functional considerations. *In* Phylogeny and Development of Catecholamine Systems in the CNS of Vertebrates. W.J.A.J. Smeets, Ed.: 103–133. Cambridge University Press. Cambridge, England.
72. MEDINA, L. & A. REINER. 1995. Neurotransmitter organization and connectivity of the basal ganglia in vertebrates: implications for the evolution of basal ganglia. Brain Behav. Evol. **46:** 235–258.
73. MEDINA, L., C.L. VEENMAN & A. REINER. 1997. Evidence for a possible avian dorsal thalamic region comparable to the mammalian ventral anterior, ventral lateral, and oral ventroposterolateral nuclei. J. Comp. Neurol. **384:** 86–108.
74. MEDINA, L. & A. REINER. 1997. The efferent projections of the dorsal and ventral pallidal parts of the pigeon basal ganglia, studied with biotinylated dextran amine. Neuroscience **81:** 773–802.
75. REINER, A., L. MEDINA & C.L. VEENMAN. 1998. Structural and functional evolution of the basal ganglia in vertebrates. Brain Res. Brain. Res. Rev. **28:** 235–285.
76. HILLEBRAND, A. 1971. Experimental and descriptive study of the hypoglossal nerve nucleus in the turkey and the goose (in Romanian). Lucrari Stiintifice. Seria C **XIV:** 45–55.
77. NOTTEBOHM, F. 1976. Vocal tract and brain: a search for evolutionary bottlenecks. Ann. NY Acad. Sci. **280:** 643–649.
78. WILD, J.M. & H.P. ZEIGLER. 1980. Central representation and somatotopic organization of the jaw muscles within the facial and trigeminal nuclei of the pigeon (*Columba livia*). J. Comp. Neurol. **192:** 175–201.
79. WILD, J.M. 1981. Identification and localization of the motor nuclei and sensory projections of the glossopharyngeal, vagus, and hypoglossal nerves of the cockatoo (*Cacatua roseicapilla*), Cacatuidae. J. Comp. Neurol. **203:** 351–377.
80. EDEN, A.R. & M.J. CORREIA. 1982. An autoradiographic and HRP study of vestibulocollic pathways in the pigeon. J. Comp. Neurol. **211:** 432–440.
81. YOUNGREN, O.M. & R.E. PHILLIPS. 1983. Location and distribution of tracheosyringeal motorneuron somata in the fowl. J. Comp. Neurol. **213:** 86–93.
82. VICARIO, D.S. & F. NOTTEBOHM. 1988. Organization of the zebra finch song control system: I. Representation of syringeal muscles in the hypoglossal nucleus. J. Comp. Neurol. **271:** 346–354.
83. WILD, J.M. 1990. Peripheral and central terminations of hypoglossal afferents innervating lingual tactile mechanoreceptor complexes in *Fringillidae*. J. Comp. Neurol. **298:** 157–171.

84. DUBBELDAM, J.L. & R.G. BOUT. 1990. The identification of the motor nuclei innervating the tongue muscles in the mallard (*Anas platyrhynchos*); an HRP study. Neurosci. Lett. **119:** 223–227.
85. WATANABE, T. & Y. OHMORI. 1988. Location of motoneurons supplying upper neck muscles in the chicken studied by means of horseradish peroxidase. J. Comp. Neurol. **270:** 271–278.
86. HORSTER, W., A. FRANCHINI & S. DANIEL. 1990. Organization of neck muscle motoneurons in the cervical spinal cord of the pigeon. Neuroreport. **1:** 93–96.
87. ZILJSTRA, C. & J.L. DUBBELDAM. 1994. Organization of the motor innervation of craniocervical muscles in the mallard, *Anas platyrhynchos*. J. Hirnforsch. **35:** 425–440.
88. HILLEBRAND, A. 1975. An experimental study concerning the accessory nerve in the chicken and turkey. Anatomischer Anzeiger. **137:** 296–302.
89. CROSBY, E.C., T. HUMPHREY & E.W. LAUER. 1962. Correlative Anatomy of the Nervous System. Macmillan. New York.
90. BAILHACHE, T. & J. BALTHAZART. 1993. The catecholaminergic system of the quail brain: immunocytochemical studies of dopamine beta-hydroxylase and tyrosine hydroxylase. J. Comp. Neurol. **329:** 230–256.
91. REINER, A. *et al.* 1994. Catecholaminergic perikarya and fibers in the avian nervous system. *In* Phylogeny and Development of Catecholaminergic Systems in the CNS of Vertebrates. W.J.A.J. Smeets & A. Reiner, Eds.: 135–181. Cambridge University Press. Cambridge, England.
92. PUELLES, L. & L. MEDINA. 1994. Development of neurons expressing tyrosine hydroxylase and dopamine in the ckicken brain: a comparative segmental analysis. *In* Phylogeny and Development of Catecholaminergic Systems in the CNS of Vertebrates. W.J.A.J. Smeets & A. Reiner, Eds.: 381–404. Cambridge University Press. Cambridge, England.
93. LEWIS, J.W. *et al.* 1981. Evidence for a catecholaminergic projection to area X in the zebra finch. J. Comp. Neurol. **196:** 347–354.
94. KITT, C.A. & S.E. BRAUTH. 1986. Telencephalic projections from midbrain and isthmal cell groups in the pigeon. II. The nigral complex. J. Comp. Neurol. **247:** 92–110.
95. BOTTJER, S.W. 1993. The distribution of tyrosine hydroxylase immunoreactivity in the brains of male and female zebra finches. J. Neurobiol. **24:** 51–69.
96. SZEKELY, A.D. *et al.* 1994. Connectivity of the lobus parolfactorius of the domestic chicken (*Gallus domesticus*): an anterograde and retrograde pathway tracing study. J. Comp. Neurol. **348:** 374–393.
97. KARLE, E.J. *et al.* 1996. Light and electron microscopic immunohistochemical study of dopaminergic terminals in the striatal portion of the pigeon basal ganglia using antisera against tyrosine hydroxylase and dopamine. J. Comp. Neurol. **369:** 109–124.
98. METZGER, M. *et al.* 1996. Organization of the dopaminergic innervation of forebrain areas relevant to learning: a combined immunohistochemical/retrograde tracing study in the domestic chick. J. Comp. Neurol. **376:** 1–27.
99. DURSTEWITZ, D., S. KRONER & O. GÜNTÜRKÜN. 1999. The dopaminergic innervation of the avian telencephalon. Prog. Neurobiol. **59:** 161–195.
100. MEDINA, L. & A. REINER. 1994. Distribution of choline acetyltransferase immunoreactivity in the pigeon brain. J. Comp. Neurol. **342:** 497–537.
101. JIAO, Y. *et al.* 2000. Identification of the anterior nucleus of the ansa lenticularis in birds as the homologue of the mammalian subthalamic nucleus. J. Neurosci. **20:** 6998–7010.
102. RUBENSTEIN, J.L. *et al.* 1994. The embryonic vertebrate forebrain: the prosomeric model. Science **266:** 578–580.
103. SWANSON, L.W. & G.D. PETROVICH. 1998. What is the amygdala? Trends Neurosci. **21:** 323–331.
104. COBOS, I. *et al.* 2001. Fate map of the avian anterior forebrain at the four-somite stage, based on the analysis of quail-chick chimeras. Dev. Biol. **239:** 46–67.
105. REDIES, C., L. MEDINA & L. PUELLES. 2001. Cadherin expression by embryonic divisions and derived gray matter structures in the telencephalon of the chicken. J. Comp. Neurol. **438:** 253–285.
106. REINER, A. & K.D. ANDERSON. 1990. The patterns of neurotransmitter and neuropeptide co-occurrence among striatal projection neurons: conclusions based on recent findings. Brain Res. Brain Res. Rev. **15:** 251–265.

107. CASTO, J.M. & G.F. BALL. 1994. Characterization and localization of D1 dopamine receptors in the sexually dimorphic vocal control nucleus, area X, and the basal ganglia of European starlings. J. Neurobiol. **25:** 767–780.
108. GRISHAM, W. & A.P. ARNOLD. 1994. Distribution of GABA-like immunoreactivity in the song system of the zebra finch. Brain Res. **651:** 115–122.
109. SOHA, J.A., T. SHIMIZU & A.J. DOUPE. 1996. Development of the catecholaminergic innervation of the song system of the male zebra finch. J. Neurobiol. **29:** 473–489.
110. LUO, M. & D.J. PERKEL. 1999. A GABAergic, strongly inhibitory projection to a thalamic nucleus in the zebra finch song system. J. Neurosci. **19:** 6700–6711.
111. SUN, Z. & A. REINER. 2000. Localization of dopamine D1A and D1B receptor mRNAs in the forebrain and midbrain of the domestic chick. J. Chem. Neuroanat. **19:** 211–224.
112. REINER, A., H. J. KARTEN & A. R. SOLINA. 1983. Substance P: localization within paleostriatal-tegmental pathways in the pigeon. Neuroscience **9:** 61–85.
113. BOTTJER, S.W. *et al.* 1989. Axonal connections of a forebrain nucleus involved with vocal learning in zebra finches. J. Comp. Neurol. **279:** 312–326.
114. BECKSTEAD, R.M. & C.J. CRUZ. 1986. Striatal axons to the globus pallidus, entopeduncular nucleus and substantia nigra come mainly from separate cell populations in cat. Neuroscience **19:** 147–158.
115. SELEMON, L.D. & P.S. GOLDMAN-RAKIC. 1990. Topographic intermingling of striatonigral and striatopallidal neurons in the rhesus monkey. J. Comp. Neurol. **297:** 359–376.
116. BOTTJER, S.W. & F. JOHNSON. 1997. Circuits, hormones, and learning: vocal behavior in songbirds. J. Neurobiol. **33:** 602–618.
117. LUO, M. & D.J. PERKEL. 1999. Long-range GABAergic projection in a circuit essential for vocal learning. J. Comp. Neurol. **403:** 68–84.
118. FARRIES, M.A. & D.J. PERKEL. 2002. Pallidum-like elements in the avian "striatum" outside of specialized vocal structures project directly to the thalamus. Soc. Neuro. Abs. 680.618.
119. REINER, A. *et al.* 2004. An immunohistochemical and pathway tracing study of the striatopallidal organization of Area X in the zebra finch. J. Comp. Neurol. In press.
120. IYENGAR, S., S.S. VISWANATHAN & S.W. BOTTJER. 1999. Development of topography within song control circuitry of zebra finches during the sensitive period for song learning. J. Neurosci. **19:** 6037–6057.
121. FARRIES, M. & D.J. PERKEL. 2000. Electrophysiological properties of avian basal ganglia neurons recorded *in vitro.* J. Neurophysiol. **84:** 2502–2513.
122. COBOS, I., L. PUELLES & S. MARTINEZ. 2001. The avian telencephalic subpallium originates inhibitory neurons that invade tangentially the pallium (dorsal ventricular ridge and cortical areas). Dev. Biol. **239:** 30–45.
123. VEENMAN, C.L., J.M. WILD & A. REINER. 1995. Organization of the avian "corticostriatal" projection system: a retrograde and anterograde pathway tracing study in pigeons. J. Comp. Neurol. **354:** 87–126.
124. MEZEY, S. & A. CSILLAG. 2002. Selective striatal connections of midbrain dopaminergic nuclei in the chick (*Gallus domesticus*). Cell Tissue Res. **308:** 35–46.
125. ANDERSON, K.D. & A. REINER. 1991. Striatonigral projection neurons: a retrograde labeling study of the percentages that contain substance P or enkephalin in pigeons. J. Comp. Neurol. **303:** 658–673.
126. KELLEY, D.B. & F. NOTTEBOHM. 1979. Projections of a telencephalic auditory nucleus-field L-in the canary. J. Comp. Neurol. **183:** 455–469.
127. VATES, G.E. *et al.* 1996. Auditory pathways of caudal telencephalon and their relation to the song system of adult male zebra finches. J. Comp. Neurol. **366:** 613–642.
128. MELLO, C.V. & D.F. CLAYTON. 1994. Song-induced ZENK gene expression in auditory pathways of songbird brain and its relation to the song control system. J. Neurosci. **14:** 6652–6666.
129. JARVIS, E.D. *et al.* 2002. A framework for integrating the songbird brain. J. Comp. Physiol. A Neuroethol. Sens. Neural. Behav. Physiol. **188:** 961–980.
130. ASTE, N. *et al.* 1998. Anatomical and neurochemical definition of the nucleus of the stria terminalis in Japanese quail (*Coturnix japonica*). J. Comp. Neurol. **396:** 141–157.

131. BRAUTH, S.E., J.L. FERGUSON & C.A. KITT. 1978. Prosencephalic pathways related to the paleostriatum of the pigeon (*Columba livia*). Brain Res. **147:** 205–221.
132. ANDERSON, K.D. & A. REINER. 1990. Extensive co-occurrence of substance P and dynorphin in striatal projection neurons: an evolutionarily conserved feature of basal ganglia organization. J. Comp. Neurol. **295:** 339–369.
133. ANDERSON, K.D. & A. REINER. 1991. Immunohistochemical localization of DARPP-32 in striatal projection neurons and striatal interneurons: implications for the localization of D1-like dopamine receptors on different types of striatal neurons. Brain Res. **568:** 235–243.
134. VEENMAN, C.L. *et al.* 1995. Thalamostriatal projection neurons in birds utilize LANT6 and neurotensin: a light and electron microscopic double-labeling study. J Chem. Neuroanat. **9:** 1–16.
135. ROBERTS, T.F., W.S. HALL & S.E. BRAUTH. 2002. Organization of the avian basal forebrain: chemical anatomy in the parrot (*Melopsittacus undulatus*). J. Comp. Neurol. **454:** 383–408.
136. HEIMER, L. *et al.* 1997. The accumbens: beyond the core-shell dichotomy. J. Neuropsychiatr. Clin. Neurosci. **9:** 354–381.
137. HEIMER, L., G.F. ALHEID & L. ZABORSZKY. 1985. Basal ganglia. *In* The Rat Nervous System. G. Paxinos, Ed.: 37–86. Academic Press. Orlando.
138. PAXINOS, G. & C. WATSON. 1998. The Rat Brain in Stereotaxic Coordinates. Academic Press. San Diego, California.
139. REINER, A. *et al.* 1984. The distribution of enkephalinlike immunoreactivity in the telencephalon of the adult and developing domestic chicken. J. Comp. Neurol. **228:** 245–262.
140. RUSSCHEN, F.T., W.J. SMEETS & P.V. HOOGLAND. 1987. Histochemical identification of pallidal and striatal structures in the lizard *Gekko gecko*: evidence for compartmentalization. J. Comp. Neurol. **256:** 329–341.
141. RUSSCHEN, F.T. & A.J. JONKER. 1988. Efferent connections of the striatum and the nucleus accumbens in the lizard *Gekko gecko*. J. Comp. Neurol. **276:** 61–80.
142. GUIRADO, S. *et al.* 1999. Nucleus accumbens in the lizard *Psammodromus algirus*: chemoarchitecture and cortical afferent connections. J. Comp. Neurol. **405:** 15–31.
143. SMEETS, W.J., J.M. LOPEZ & A. GONZALEZ. 2001. Immunohistochemical localization of DARPP-32 in the brain of the lizard, *Gekko gecko*: co-occurrence with tyrosine hydroxylase. J. Comp. Neurol. **435:** 194–210.
144. KITT, C.A. & S. E. BRAUTH. 1981. Projections of the paleostriatum upon the midbrain tegmentum in the pigeon. Neuroscience **6:** 1551–1566.
145. REINER, A. & R.E. CARRAWAY. 1987. Immunohistochemical and biochemical studies on Lys8-Asn9-neurotensin8-13 (LANT6)-related peptides in the basal ganglia of pigeons, turtles, and hamsters. J. Comp. Neurol. **257:** 453–476.
146. VEENMAN, C.L. & A. REINER. 1994. The distribution of GABA-containing perikarya, fibers, and terminals in the forebrain and midbrain of pigeons, with particular reference to the basal ganglia and its projection targets. J. Comp. Neurol. **339:** 209–250.
147. MARIN, O., W.J. SMEETS & A. GONZALEZ. 1998. Evolution of the basal ganglia in tetrapods: a new perspective based on recent studies in amphibians. Trends Neurosci. **21:** 487–494.
148. BROX, A. *et al.* 2003. Expression of the genes GAD67 and Distal-less-4 in the forebrain of *Xenopus laevis* confirms a common pattern in tetrapods. J. Comp. Neurol. **461:** 370–393.
149. GONZALEZ, A. *et al.* 2002. Regional expression of the homeobox gene NKX2-1 defines pallidal and interneuronal populations in the basal ganglia of amphibians. Neuroscience **114:** 567–575.
150. REINER, A., L. MEDINA & S.N. HABER. 1999. The distribution of dynorphinergic terminals in striatal target regions in comparison to the distribution of substance P-containing and enkephalinergic terminals in monkeys and humans. Neuroscience **88:** 775–793.
151. KUENZEL, W.J. & M. MASSON. 1988. A Stereotaxic Atlas of the Brain of the Chick (*Gallus domesticus*). The Johns Hopkins University Press. Baltimore.

152. BRAUTH, S.E. 1984. Enkephalin-like immunoreactivity within the telencephalon of the reptile *Caiman crocodilus*. Neuroscience **11**: 345–358.
153. REINER, A. 1987. The distribution of proenkephalin-derived peptides in the central nervous system of turtles. J. Comp. Neurol. **259**: 65–91.
154. LI, R. & H. SAKAGUCHI. 1997. Cholinergic innervation of the song control nuclei by the ventral paleostriatum in the zebra finch: a double-labeling study with retrograde fluorescent tracers and choline acetyltransferase immunohistochemistry. Brain Res. **763**: 239–246.
155. LI, R., M.X. ZUO & H. SAKAGUCHI. 1999. Auditory-vocal cholinergic pathway in zebra finch brain. Neuroreport **10**: 165–169.
156. MAYO, W. *et al.* 1984. Cortical cholinergic projections from the basal forebrain of the rat, with special reference to the prefrontal cortex innervation. Neurosci. Lett. **47**: 149–154.
157. MARIN, O. & J. L. RUBENSTEIN. 2001. A long, remarkable journey: tangential migration in the telencephalon. Nat. Rev. Neurosci. **2**: 780–790.
158. BRAUTH, S.E. *et al.* 1986. Neurotensin binding sites in the forebrain and midbrain of the pigeon. J. Comp. Neurol. **253**: 358–373.
159. WACHTLER, K. & P. EBINGER. 1989. The pattern of muscarinic acetylcholine receptor binding in the avian forebrain. J. Hirnforsch. **30**: 409–414.
160. CSILLAG, A. *et al.* 1993. Quantitative autoradiographic demonstration of changes in binding to delta opioid, but not mu or kappa receptors, in chick forebrain 30 minutes after passive avoidance training. Brain Res. **613**: 96–105.
161. HUSBAND, S.A. & T. SHIMIZU. 1999. Efferent projections of the ectostriatum in the pigeon (*Columba livia*). J. Comp. Neurol. **406**: 329–345.
162. DENISENKO-NEHRBASS, N.I. *et al.* 2000. Site-specific retinoic acid production in the brain of adult songbirds. Neuron **27**: 359–370.
163. HODOS, W. 1993. The visual capabilities of birds. *In* Vision, Brain, and Behavior in Birds. H. Zeigler & H.-J. Bischof, Eds.: 63–76. The MIT Press. Cambridge, MA.
164. SHIMIZU, T., K. COX & H.J. KARTEN. 1995. Intratelencephalic projections of the visual wulst in pigeons (*Columba livia*). J. Comp. Neurol. **359**: 551–572.
165. ZEIER, H. & H.J. KARTEN. 1971. The archistriatum of the pigeon: organization of afferent and efferent connections. Brain Res. **31**: 313–326.
166. REINER, A., K. Yamamoto & B.S. Kristal. 2002. A multivariate statistical approach to the study of brain homology and development. Soc. Neuro. Abs.87.15.
167. SUN, Z. *et al.* 2003. The distribution and cellular localization of glutamic acid decarboxlyase (GAD65) mRNA in the forebrain and midbrain of domestic chick. Soc. Neuro. Abs.
168. THOMPSON, R.R., *et al.* 1998. Role of the archistriatal nucleus taeniae in the sexual behavior of male Japanese quail (*Coturnix japonica*): a comparison of function with the medial nucleus of the amygdala in mammals. Brain Behav. Evol. **51**: 215–229.
169. CHENG, M. *et al.* 1999. Nucleus taenia of the amygdala of birds: anatomical and functional studies in ring doves (*Streptopelia risoria*) and European starlings (*Sturnus vulgaris*). Brain Behav. Evol. **53**: 243–270.
170. ABSIL, P. *et al.* 2002. Effects of lesions of nucleus taeniae on appetitive and consummatory aspects of male sexual behavior in Japanese quail. Brain Behav. Evol. **60**: 13–35.
171. FOIDART, A. *et al.* 1999. Estrogen receptor-beta in quail: cloning, tissue expression and neuroanatomical distribution. J. Neurobiol. **40**: 327–342.
172. LANUZA, E. *et al.* 2000. Distribution of CGRP-like immunoreactivity in the chick and quail brain. J. Comp. Neurol. **421**: 515–532.
173. DAVIES, D.C. *et al.* 1997. Efferent connections of the domestic chick archistriatum: a phaseolus lectin anterograde tracing study. J. Comp. Neurol. **389**: 679–693.
174. MELLO, C.V. *et al.* 1998. Descending auditory pathways in the adult male zebra finch (*Taeniopygia guttata*). J. Comp. Neurol. **395**: 137–160.
175. WILD, J.M. 1993. Descending projections of the songbird nucleus robustus archistriatalis. J. Comp. Neurol. **338**: 225–241.
176. KNUDSEN, E.I. & P.F. KNUDSEN. 1996. Disruption of auditory spatial working memory by inactivation of the forebrain archistriatum in barn owls. Nature **383**: 428–431.

177. MARGOLIASH, D. 1997. Functional organization of forebrain pathways for song production and perception. J. Neurobiol. **33:** 671–693.
178. NOTTEBOHM, F., D.B. KELLEY & J.A. PATON. 1982. Connections of vocal control nuclei in the canary telencephalon. J. Comp. Neurol. **207:** 344–357.
179. JARVIS, E.D. & F. NOTTEBOHM. 1997. Motor-driven gene expression. Proc. Natl. Acad. Sci. USA **94:** 4097–4102.
180. JARVIS, E.D. *et al.* 1998. For whom the bird sings: context-dependent gene expression. Neuron **21:** 775–788.
181. WILD, J.M., H.J. KARTEN & B.J. FROST. 1993. Connections of the auditory forebrain in the pigeon (*Columba livia*). J. Comp. Neurol. **337:** 32–62.
182. GENTNER, T.Q. & D. MARGOLIASH. 2003. Neuronal populations and single cells representing learned auditory objects. Nature **424:** 669–674.
183. BONKE, B.A., D. BONKE & H. SCHEICH. 1979. Connectivity of the auditory forebrain nuclei in the guinea fowl (*Numida meleagris*). Cell Tissue Res. **200:** 101–121.
184. HEIL, P. & H. SCHEICH. 1991. Functional organization of the avian auditory cortex analogue. II. Topographic distribution of latency. Brain Res. **539:** 121–125.
185. HEIL, P. & H. SCHEICH. 1991. Functional organization of the avian auditory cortex analogue. I. Topographic representation of isointensity bandwidth. Brain Res. **539:** 110–120.
186. NOTTEBOHM, F. 1987. Birdsong. *In* Encyclopedia of Neuroscience. G. Edelman, Ed.: 133–136. Birkhauser Boston. Boston.
187. MARGOLIASH, D. *et al.* 1994. Distributed representation in the song system of oscines: evolutionary implications and functional consequences. Brain Behav. Evol. **44:** 247–264.
188. FORTUNE, E.S. & D. MARGOLIASH. 1995. Parallel pathways converge onto HVc and adjacent neostriatum of adult male zebra finches (*Taeniopygia guttata*). J. Comp. Neurol. **360:** 413–441.
189. BRENOWITZ, E.A., D. MARGOLIASH & K.W. NORDEEN. 1997. An introduction to birdsong and the avian song system. J. Neurobiol. **33:** 495–500.
190. SOHRABJI, F., E.J. NORDEEN & K.W. NORDEEN. 1990. Selective impairment of song learning following lesions of a forebrain nucleus in the juvenile zebra finch. Behav. Neural Biol. **53:** 51–63.
191. SCHARFF, C. & F. NOTTEBOHM. 1991. A comparative study of the behavioral deficits following lesions of various parts of the zebra finch song system: implications for vocal learning. J. Neurosci. **11:** 2896–2913.
192. FOSTER, E.F. & S.W. BOTTJER. 2001. Lesions of a telencephalic nucleus in male zebra finches: influences on vocal behavior in juveniles and adults. J. Neurobiol. **46:** 142–165.
193. HESSLER, N. A. & A.J. DOUPE. 1999. Singing-related neural activity in a dorsal forebrain-basal ganglia circuit of adult zebra finches. J. Neurosci. **19:** 10461–10481.
194. MCCASLAND, J.S. 1987. Neuronal control of bird song production. J. Neurosci. **7:** 23–39.
195. MELLO, C.V., D.S. VICARIO & D.F. CLAYTON. 1992. Song presentation induces gene expression in the songbird forebrain. Proc. Natl. Acad. Sci. USA **89:** 6818–6822.
196. CHEW, S.J. *et al.* 1995. Decrements in auditory responses to a repeated conspecific song are long-lasting and require two periods of protein synthesis in the songbird forebrain. Proc. Natl. Acad. Sci. USA **92:** 3406–3410.
197. RIBEIRO, S. *et al.* 1998. Toward a song code: evidence for a syllabic representation in the canary brain. Neuron **21:** 359–371.
198. STRIPLING, R., S.F. VOLMAN & D.F. CLAYTON. 1997. Response modulation in the zebra finch neostriatum: relationship to nuclear gene regulation. J. Neurosci. **17:** 3883–3893.
199. BOLHUIS, J.J. *et al.* 2001. Localized immediate early gene expression related to the strength of song learning in socially reared zebra finches. Eur. J. Neurosci. **13:** 2165–2170.
200. KARTEN, J.H. 1968. The ascending auditory pathway in the pigeon (*Columba livia*) II. Telencephalic projections of the nucleus ovoidalis thalami. Brain Res. **11:** 134–153.
201. BRAUTH, S.E. & C.M. MCHALE. 1988. Auditory pathways in the budgerigar. II. Intratelencephalic pathways. Brain Behav. Evol. **32:** 193–207.

202. FORTUNE, E.S. & D. MARGOLIASH. 1992. Cytoarchitectonic organization and morphology of cells of the field L complex in male zebra finches (*Taenopygia guttata*). J. Comp. Neurol. **325:** 388–404.
203. BRAUTH, S.E. *et al.* 1987. Auditory pathways in the budgerigar. I. Thalamo-telencephalic projections. Brain Behav. Evol. **30:** 174–199.
204. MULLER, S.C. & H. SCHEICH. 1985. Functional organization of the avian auditory field L. J. Comp. Physiol. **156:** 1–12.
205. BONKE, B.A., H. SCHEICH & G. LANGNER. 1979. Responsiveness of units in the auditory neostriatum of the guinea fowl (*Numida meleagris*) to species-specific calls and synthetics stimuli. I. Tonotopy and functional zones of Field L. J. Comp. Physiol.**132:** 243–255.
206. KARTEN, H.J. & A.M. REZVIN. 1966. Rostral projections of the optic tectum and nucleus rotundus in the pigeon. Brain Res. **3:** 264–276.
207. KARTEN, H.J. & W. HODOS. 1970. Telencephalic projections of the nucleus rotundus in the pigeon (*Columba livia*). J. Comp. Neurol. **140:** 35–51.
208. BENOWITZ, L. 1980. Functional organization of the avian telencephalon. *In* Comparative Neurology of the Telencephalon. S.O.E. Ebbesson, Ed.: 389–421. Plenum Publishing Corporation.
209. NIXDORF, B.E. & H.J. BISCHOF. 1982. Afferent connections of the ectostriatum and visual wulst in the zebra finch (*Taeniopygia guttata castanotis Gould*)—an HRP study. Brain Res. **248:** 9–17.
210. WILD, J.M., J.J. ARENDS & H.P. ZEIGLER. 1985. Telencephalic connections of the trigeminal system in the pigeon (*Columba livia*): a trigeminal sensorimotor circuit. J. Comp. Neurol. **234:** 441–464.
211. VEENMAN, C.L. & K.M. GOTTSCHALDT. 1986. The nucleus basalis-neostriatum complex in the goose (*Anser anser L.*). Adv. Anat. Embryol. Cell Biol. **96:** 1–85.
212. DUBBELDAM, J.L. & A.M. VISSER. 1987. The organization of the nucleus basalis-neostriatum complex of the mallard (*Anas platyrhynchos L.*) and its connections with the archistriatum and the paleostriatum complex. Neuroscience **21:** 487–517.
213. SIMPSON, H.B. & D.S. VICARIO. 1990. Brain pathways for learned and unlearned vocalizations differ in zebra finches. J. Neurosci. **10:** 1541–1556.

Producing Song

The Vocal Apparatus

RODERICK A. SUTHERS[a–c] AND SUE ANNE ZOLLINGER[c]

[a]Medical Sciences, [b]Program for Neural Science, [c]Department of Biology,
Indiana University, Bloomington, Indiana 47405, USA

ABSTRACT: In order to achieve the goal of understanding the neurobiology of birdsong, it is necessary to understand the peripheral mechanisms by which song is produced. This paper reviews recent advances in the understanding of syringeal and respiratory motor control and how birds utilize these systems to create their species-typical sounds. Songbirds have a relatively homogeneous duplex vocal organ in which sound is generated by oscillation of a pair of thickened labia on either side of the syrinx. Multiple pairs of syringeal muscles provide flexible, independent control of sound frequency and amplitude, and each side of the syrinx exhibits a degree of acoustic specialization. This is in contrast to many non-songbirds, including vocal learners such as parrots, which have fewer syringeal muscles and use syringeal membranes to generate sound. In doves, at least, these membranes generate a harmonic signal in which the fundamental frequency is regulated by respiratory pressure in the air sac surrounding the syrinx and the overtones are filtered out by the vocal tract. The songs of adult songbirds are generally accompanied by precisely coordinated respiratory and syringeal motor patterns that, despite their relative stereotypy, are modulated in real time by somatosensory feedback. Comparative studies indicate songbirds have evolved species-specific motor patterns that utilize the two sides of the syrinx in specific ways and enhance the particular acoustic effects characterizing the species song. A vocal mimic tutored with heterospecific song uses the same motor pattern as the tutor species when he accurately copies the song, suggesting that physical or physiological constraints on sound production have had a prominent role in the evolution of species-specific motor patterns. An understanding of the relationship between the central processing and peripheral performance of song motor programs is essential for an understanding of the development, function, and evolution of these complex vocal signals.

KEYWORDS: birdsong; syrinx; sound production; motor control; vocalization

THE AVIAN VOCAL ORGAN

The vocal organ, or syrinx, of birds is located in the interclavicular air sac where the primary bronchi join to form the trachea. Its location deep in the thorax, close to

Address for correspondence: Roderick A. Suthers, Medical Sciences, Indiana University, Bloomington, Indiana 47405, USA. Voice: 812-855-8353; fax: 812-855-4436.
suthers@indiana.edu; <http://www.indiana.edu/~neurosci/suthers.html>;
<http://www.bio.indiana.edu/facultyresearch/Suthers.html>

Ann. N.Y. Acad. Sci. 1016: 109–129 (2004). © 2004 New York Academy of Sciences.
doi: 10.1196/annals.1298.041

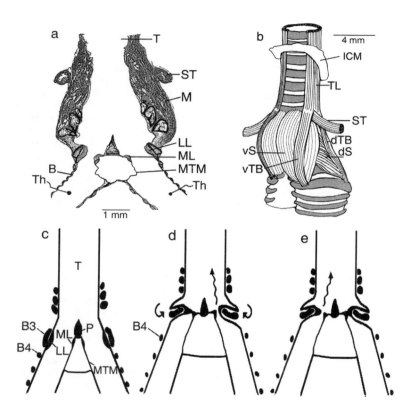

FIGURE 1. The songbird syrinx is a bipartite structure located at tracheobronchial junction. (**a**) Frontal section through the syrinx of a mockingbird, showing the dual nature of the vocal organ and placement of microbead thermistors (Th) for recording airflow. (**b**) ventrolateral external view of syrinx illustrating syringeal musculature. (**c–e**) Schematic ventral views of songbird syrinx during quiet respiration (**c**); phonation on the left side with labial valve closed on right side (**d**); phonation of right side with left side closed (**e**). In preparation for phonation the syrinx moves rostrad. Contraction of the ipsilateral dorsal syringeal muscles (dS and dTB) rotates the bronchial cartilages (*curved arrows*) into the syringeal lumen, moving the labia into the air stream, where they are set into vibration, producing sound (*wavy arrows*). Phonation may be bilateral (not shown) or unilateral (shown). ABBREVIATIONS: T, trachea; M, syringeal muscle; ML, medial labium; LL, lateral labium; MTM, medial typaniform membrane; B, bronchus; ICM, membrane of the interclavicular air sac; TL, m. tracheolateralis; ST, m. sternotrachealis; vS, m. syringealis ventralis; vTB, m. tracheobronchialis ventralis; dTB, m. tracheobronchialis dorsalis; dS, m. syringealis dorsalis; B3 and B4, third and fourth bronchial cartilages; P, pessulus. (**c–e**, Modified from Suthers and Goller[63]).

the heart, poses challenges for those who attempt to study its function, but an understanding of how vocal motor patterns are converted into sound is an important piece in the neuroethological puzzle of birdsong.

Syrinxes vary in their anatomical design across different avian taxa. Some are located in the trachea and a few are in the primary bronchi. The most common type of syrinx, however, lies at the junction between these structures. Although a tracheobronchial syrinx is also present in many non-songbirds it is most highly developed in songbirds, which are the principal focus of this article.

The songbird (suborder Passeri or Oscine in the Passeriformes) syrinx consists of modified cartilages at the cranial end of each bronchus and the caudal end of the trachea together with six bilaterally paired syringeal muscles, including the tracheolateralis and sternotrachealis muscles (FIG. 1).[1] All of these muscles are innervated by the tracheosyringeal branch of the ipsilateral hypoglossal nerve. One of their important actions is to control the movement, and probably the tension, of a pair of small connective tissue pads, the medial (ML) and lateral (LL) labia, located at the cranial end of each bronchus. The medial labium is intimately associated with a thin medial tympaniform membrane (MTM) that is continuous with its caudal edge.[1]

The syringeal structure and physical mechanism responsible for producing sound long remained controversial. The MTM was for some time the leading candidate for this important function, based mainly on Miskimen's [2] observation that when air was drawn in an expiratory direction through the syrinx of an anesthetized house sparrow (*Passer domesticus*) a "chirping noise" was produced and the MTM could be seen to vibrate.

Endoscopic observations by Goller and Larsen,[3] of labial motion during spontaneous vocalizations by a crow (*Corvus brachyrhynchos*) and vocalizations elicited by brain stimulation in northern cardinals (*Cardinalis cardinalis*) and brown thrashers (*Toxostoma rufum*) show that during phonation the medial and lateral labia are adducted into the bronchial lumen to form a slit and vibrate. The destruction of both MTM's in zebra finches (*Taeniopygia guttata*) and cardinals had only a small effect on their song, involving syllable fine structure and harmonic emphasis.[3] These direct observations indicate that the medial and lateral labia are the primary sound source in the songbird syrinx and vindicate the intuition of Setterwall,[4] who a century earlier named them the inner and outer vocal cords.

In other experiments, Larsen and Goller[5] used an optical vibration sensor to measure the average motion of the labia in an anesthetized hill myna (*Gracula religiosa*) and the motion of the lateral tympaniform membrane (LTM) in pigeons (*Columba livia*) and cockatiels (*Nymphicus hollandicus*) during sounds elicited by brain stimulation. They found that the dominant frequency of vibration matched that in the sound being produced.

Theories of sound generation by vibrating structures have been challenged to account for the presence in birdsong of tonal elements with only low level overtones and also for the presence of harmonic sounds. It was argued that edge-clamped membranes like the MTM would not produce such sounds. Furthermore, if the oscillating structures touch each other and close the airway during each cycle, like a vibrating valve, their motion will not be sinusoidal and there should be prominent overtones present at the syrinx. Since the suppression of source-generated harmonics by a vocal tract filter in birds was considered unlikely,[6] one of the alternative hypotheses put forth to resolve this dilemma[7-10] proposed that tonal and harmonic vocalizations were generated aerodynamically in the manner of a hole tone whistle, as air flowed at high velocity through a constriction in the syrinx, obviating the need for a vibrating acoustic source. The whistle hypothesis of birdsong, however, has so far failed to receive experimental support, e.g., Ballintijin and ten Cate.[11]

Subsequent light gas experiments by Nowicki[12] indicated vocal tract resonance was more important in modulating the syringeally generated sound than previously thought. When songbirds sing in a light gas mixture, the speed of sound is increased. To the extent that vocal tract resonance is important, the acoustic energy shifts from the fundamental to the second harmonic.[12] As Nowicki pointed out, the relative increase in harmonic levels in light gas could be caused by either of two mechanisms. The vocal tract resonance in air might be tuned to the fundamental frequency and produce a tonal vocalization by filtering out overtones present at the syrinx. This source-filter mechanism is present in human speech.[13] Alternatively, vocal tract resonance in air might generate a non-linear feedback within the vocal tract onto the labia that supports vibration at the fundamental frequency while suppressing it at harmonic frequencies, to produce a tonal sound at the syrinx.[14] This technique is used in some soprano singing.[15]

In an experiment designed to discriminate between these models, Beckers and colleagues[16] found that sound recorded near the syringeal source in the interclavicular air sac and trachea of awake, spontaneously cooing streptopelid doves has prominent overtones, not present in the emitted vocalization. This is not predicted by the soprano model and supports the source-filter model. The sinusoidal motion of the pigeon's LTM observed by Larsen and Goller might be due to differences between sounds produced spontaneously versus those elicited by brain stimulation or to the fact that the integrity of the vocal tract was compromised by opening the trachea to insert the optical fiber of the angioscope. Experiments are needed to determine if a similar source-filter mechanism is present in songbirds.

MOTOR CONTROL OF SONG IN THE DUPLEX SYRINX

The muscular control of birds singing spontaneously with both sides of their syrinx functionally intact has been investigated by placing a heated microbead thermistor in each primary bronchus to measure the rate of airflow through each side of the syrinx, while also measuring the subsyringeal or tracheal pressure and recording song.[17] In some experiments, electromyograms (EMGs) of syringeal or respiratory muscles were also recorded. Signals from these transducers were transmitted from a small backpack worn by the bird via a flexible tether of fine wires connected to conditioning and recording instruments outside the bird's cage.

The results of these experiments show that during song bouts, the songbird labia tend to operate in one of three different functional modes, depending on the changing vocal and respiratory demands associated with singing. These three labial motor actions are associated with inspiration, phonation, and muting, respectively. During inspiration (FIG. 1c) the labia are withdrawn from the air stream, reducing the resistance to airflow and facilitating rapid replacement of air exhaled during vocalization. Phonation is initiated by adducting the labia into the syringeal lumen at the beginning of expiration (FIG. 1d right and 1e left). The adductive force is opposed by the positive subsyringeal expiratory pressure which tends to push the labia apart. The balance between these forces is important in maintaining the labia in a phonatory position where airflow can sustain oscillation.

The labia also serve as pneumantic valves that control airflow, and hence phonation, independently on each side of the syrinx. If the adductive force on the labia exceeds that abducting them or pushing them apart, they will close the syringeal lumen and mute that side of the syrinx by preventing air from flowing through it (FIG. 1d left and 1e right). The duplex structure of the songbird syrinx in combination with independent motor control of each side make it possible for the bird to mute one side of the syrinx while phonating on the other side, to switch phonation from one side to the other, or to produce a different sound on each side at the same time. The two sides of the syrinx can potentially function independently of each other within the constraints of the respiratory rhythm.

Electromyographic recordings of syringeal muscles during song show that the activity of the dorsal syringeal muscles and dorsal tracheobronchialis muscles increases with increasing syringeal resistance, indicating that they play an important role in adducting the labia for phonation or to mute one side of the syrinx. Direct observation of the biomechanical effects in response to electrical stimulation of individual syringeal muscles in anesthetized brown thrashers and cardinals[18] supports the inferences based on electromyography. In addition, observation suggests separate roles for the two dorsal muscles with the medial portion of the dorsal syringeal muscle controlling the adduction of the ML and the dorsal tracheobronchialis muscle adducting LL. The ventral tracheobronchialis muscle plays a role in opening the syringeal lumen by abducting the LL. Recent data (see Goller and Cooper, this volume) suggest that the lateral portion of the ventral syringeal muscles may also participate in labial adduction. These muscles are thus primarily responsible for determining when each side of the syrinx produces sound during a song bout.

Just as the timing of phonation within the appropriate phase of the respiratory cycle is primarily controlled by dorsal syringeal muscles, the ventral syringeal muscles are primarily responsible for controlling the fundamental frequency of labial oscillation, which they presumably do by varying the tension they exert on the labia. The EMG amplitude of these muscles increases exponentially with the fundamental frequency of the ipsilateral sound ($R^2 = 0.71$ to 0.95) (FIG. 2).[19,20] Electrical stimulation of this muscle does not adduct the labia, but does cause a change in the reflection of light from the ML, which is consistent with a change of tension.[18] The activity of other syringeal muscles also tends to increase with sound frequency and the ventral tracheobronchial and sternotrachealis muscles may also assist in frequency regulation, but the correlation of EMG activity with sound frequency is much lower than it is for the ventral syringeal muscles.[19,20]

Studies on mimic thrushes indicate that during song, ventral muscles on both sides of the syrinx are active, even though one side may be fully adducted and mute. It appears that each side of the brain continues to send a song motor program to the ipsilateral side of the syrinx regardless of whether its labia are in a phonating or muting configuration. Lateralization of song production is determined by the motor program or sub-program to the dorsal muscles. Strong activation of these muscles on one side silences it by closing the labial valve and prevents the ongoing ipsilateral song motor program from being converted into an acoustic signal.[20,21] The lateralization of birdsong thus involves peripheral gating of central motor programs, which is fundamentally different than the left hemisphere dominance of human speech.[22]

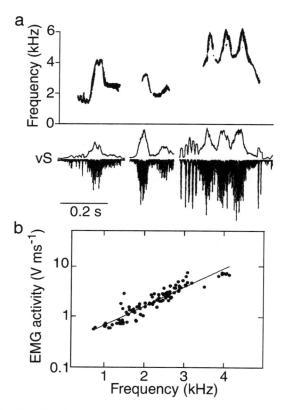

FIGURE 2. The role of ventral syringeal muscles in the control of sound frequency in the brown thrasher. (**a**) EMG amplitude of ipsilateral ventral syringeal muscle (vS) is positively correlated with frequency modulation of sounds generated on the ipsilateral side. EMG is shown integrated envelope (upward, time constant 5 msec) and rectified (downward). (**b**) Amplitude of EMG activity is correlated exponentially with fundamental frequency of ipsilaterally produced sounds. EMG activity was averaged over segments of syllables having a relatively constant frequency. (Modified from Goller and Suthers.[19])

SYRINGEAL MECHANISMS IN PARROTS: A DIFFERENT VOCAL LEARNER

Parrots, like oscine songbirds, are vocal learners but the vocal apparatus of these two groups is quite different. The syrinx of parrots is in the base of the trachea (FIG. 3). There are only two intrinsic syringeal muscles and no labia—sound is produced by vibration of the LTMs.[5] Whereas the elaboration of intrinsic syringeal muscles in songbirds has made it possible to control sound frequency largely independently from subsyringeal pressure, the control of vocal frequency in parrots appears to be more complex and not strongly correlated with the activity of a particular syringeal muscle (Davis, Banta, and Suthers, unpublished data).[18,23]

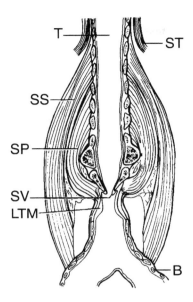

FIGURE 3. Frontal section of monk parakeet syrinx showing tracheal location. B, first bronchial cartilage; T, trachea; SS, superficial syringeal muscle; SP, deep syringeal muscle; ST, sternotrachealis muscle; SV, syringeal valve; LTM, lateral tympaniform membrane. (Modified from King.[1])

Experiments on doves,[24] which like parrots have a tracheal syrinx in which sound is produced by the LTMs,[5,25] have revealed an alternative mechanism for controlling fundamental frequency. In ring doves (*Streptopelia risoria*), fundamental frequency is highly correlated with the pressure in the interclavicular air sac that surrounds the syrinx, but not with the pressure in the cranial thoracic air sacs. The lateral ("outer") surface of the LTM is exposed to pressure fluctuations in the interclavicular air sac that may stretch these membranes and vary their resonant frequency.[24] Whether a similar mechanism of frequency regulation is used by parrots is not known, but deserves investigation in view of similarities with doves in key aspects of their vocal anatomy.

RESPIRATORY ADJUSTMENTS FOR SINGING

Song requires major adjustments in respiratory ventilation, which must continue to meet the needs for pulmonary gas exchange while at the same time providing appropriate rates and patterns of syringeal airflow required for phonation. The body cavity of birds is not divided by a muscular diaphragm as it is in mammals.[26] A thin post-hepatic septum anterior to the abdominal air sacs separates the coelomic cavity into two compartments, but this septum has few muscle fibers and appears to play

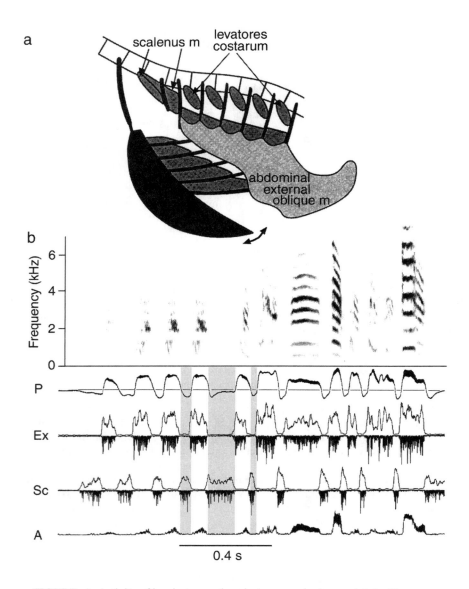

FIGURE 4. Activity of inspiratory and expiratory muscles is correlated with song production. (**a**) Some of the inspiratory and one of the four abdominal expiratory muscles. (**b**) EMG activity of inspiratory and expiratory muscles during zebra finch song, showing that inspiratory muscle EMG activity occurs only during inspiration and does not overlap temporally with expiratory muscle EMG activity. *Shaded bars* mark inspirations. P, pressure; Sc, EMG activity in m. scalenus; Ex, EMG activity in abdominal expiratory muscles. A, rectified and integrated sound amplitude (time constant 2 msec). See legend for FIGURE 2. (**a**, Modified from Wild[64]; **b**, Modified from Wild and colleagues.[31])

no significant role in silent respiration. Inspiratory muscles expand the air sacs by moving the sternum ventrally and cranially (FIG. 4a). This motion is reversed by expiratory muscles, which compress the air sacs.[27] In the absence of song, peak expiratory air sac pressure is only +0.5 to +3.0 cm H_2O in the canary, but increases about an order of magnitude during song, often reaching 10 to 15 cm H_2O in the anterior thoracic air sac and peaking at about 30 cm H_2O for some syllables.[28] Nearly all song is produced during expiratory airflow. Two known exceptions are occasional inspiratory syllables in the songs of some zebra finches[29] and an inspiratory "wah" sound associated with coos of doves.[9]

During song the respiratory motor pattern has to be coordinated with that of the syrinx. This can potentially involve up to eleven principal respiratory muscles that participate in normal breathing, plus eight additional muscles that become active during labored breathing.[30] Electromyograms during singing have been recorded from only a few abdominal expiratory muscles (primarily the external oblique and transverse abdominal muscles) and from two thoracic inspiratory muscles, the scalenus and levatores costarum (FIG. 4a). The role of the other respiratory muscles in singing is not known. In zebra finches, cowbirds, and cardinals the amplitude of the EMG in the muscles studied increases 5- to 12-fold during singing, compared to quiet respiration, presumably reflecting the recruitment of additional motor units.[31–33] Electrical activity in expiratory and inspiratory muscles does not overlap in time (FIG. 4b).[31] The activity of expiratory muscles is not lateralized. The similar timing and amplitude of EMG's on both sides, regardless of which side of the syrinx is producing sound, suggest bilateral motor control. Expiratory muscles modulate their activity in the same way on both sides when generating syllable-specific patterns of pressure and airflow, even though phonation is unilateral.[34]

The temporal pattern of respiration changes markedly during song and sets the song's basic tempo.[35] Depending on syllable repetition rate, songbirds use one of two basically different respiratory motor patterns. At moderate syllable repetition rates a brief inspiratory minibreath[36] is taken after each syllable to replace the volume of air exhaled to produce the sound[28] (FIG. 5). Syllable duration generally has an inverse relationship to repetition rate. Since long syllables use more air, the minibreaths must also be larger. In waterschlager canaries, for example, a syllable 119 msec long, sung at a repetition rate of 6.5 sec^{-1} required 0.25 mL of air to produce, which was also the volume of its associated minibreath. The corresponding volumes for an 11 msec syllable sung 30 times per second were about 0.04 mL.[28]

By using minibreaths, a bird in theory could maintain an almost constant respiratory volume throughout its song. This might provide important advantages in producing precision, stereotyped respiratory movements needed during vocalization, since the inspiratory and expiratory muscles could always operate near their resting length and with predictable forces of thoracic elastic recoil. The direction of elastic recoil reverses on either side of the neutral position of the sternum at rest. At smaller air sac volumes, elastic recoil supplements inspiratory muscle effort returning the sternum toward its neutral point, but at larger volumes elastic recoil force is in the opposite direction and supplements expiratory effort. A constant respiratory volume during song could allow the sternum to oscillate around its neutral point so that elastic recoil forces supplement the action of both expiratory and inspiratory muscles in reversing the respiratory phase, perhaps permitting faster minibreaths and higher syllable repetition rates.

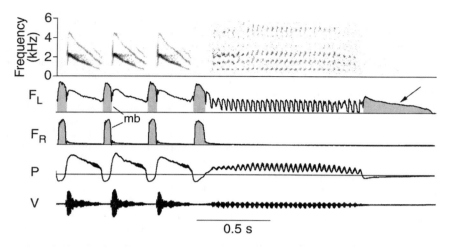

FIGURE 5. Songbirds use different respiratory motor patterns during song, depending on syllable repetition rate. This segment of cardinal song includes the last three syllables of a phrase sung at about two syllables sec^{-1} using a minibreath (mb) after each syllable. Note that both sides open for each minibreath during negative air sac pressure. These low frequency syllables are sung entirely on the left side with the right side closed. This is followed by a trill at 30 syllables sec^{-1} produced by pulsatile expiration in which the left side of the syrinx is repetitively opened while the right side remains closed and air sac pressure is positive during the entire phrase. Cardinals switch from a minibreath to a pulsatile pattern at about 16 syllables sec^{-1}. Note the longer inspiration immediately following the pulsatile *(arrow)* portion of the trill. F_L and F_R, rate of airflow through left and right sides of syrinx, airflow associated with positive pressure is expiratory; *shaded flow* is inspiratory (corresponds with negative pressure). P, pressure in cranial thoracic air sac. V, oscillograph of vocalizations. *Horizontal lines* indicate zero airflow and ambient pressure.

It is also possible that the syntax of a song may be partially dictated by respiratory needs. At high syllable repetition rates the minibreath volume is smaller than the tracheal dead space.[28] It is not known if these minibreaths provide oxygen to the lungs. A bird could conceivably adjust the syntax of its song to meet its respiratory needs, without interrupting song for a large breath, by periodically inserting a phrase of low repetition rate, long syllables with correspondingly large minibreaths that ventilate its lungs.

A different respiratory motor pattern of pulsatile expiration is used during phrases sung at very high syllable repetition rates (FIG. 5). The rate is increased by eliminating minibreaths at the cost of placing an upper limit on phrase duration as either the air reserve or oxygen is exhausted. During a phrase produced by pulsatile expiration, the subsyringeal air sac pressure is maintained at a positive level by expiratory muscle activity. Typically, one side of the syrinx is closed during the entire phrase and the other side opens periodically to release a puff of air that produces the syllable.[28,32] Rarely, both sides of the syrinx contribute to the syllable. The repetition rate at which a bird switches from minibreath to pulsatile respiratory pattern decreases with increasing body size, being about 30 syllables sec^{-1} in an 18-g

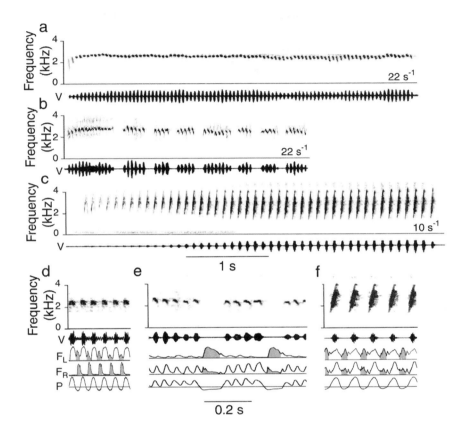

FIGURE 6. Long duration trills produced by canaries and mockingbirds. The canary tutor song (**a**; expanded view in **d**) is an uninterrupted trill lasting four seconds. At this repetition rate (22 sec^{-1}), the canary uses a minibreath respiratory pattern (**d**). The much larger mockingbird cannot achieve the canary syllable repetition rate using minibreaths, but instead broke the trill into short segments each containing several syllables (**b**; expanded view in **e**). Each segment was produced using a pulsatile expiratory pattern. Within each segment the mockingbird accurately copied the repetition rate of the tutor song (22 sec^{-1}), but without minibreaths to replenish the air supply, was forced to periodically interrupt the trill by opening the non-phonating side for a breath (**e**). The overall duration of the interrupted trill is one second shorter than that of the tutor. At lower repetition rates (below 11 sec^{-1}), mockingbirds were able to use a minibreath respiratory pattern (**c**; expanded view in **f**) and, like canaries, were able to sing longer uninterrupted trills (up to 9 sec). Bars above the oscillographic traces of the mockingbird vocalizations indicate portion shown in expanded views (**e** and **f**). Inspiratory airflow is *shaded*. Syllable repetition rates are indicated in the lower right hand corner of each spectrogram (**a–c**). Abbreviations as in FIGURE 5. (**a**, top and middle panel and **d** modified from Zollinger and Suthers.[37])

waterslager canary (*Serinus canaria*) and 10 sec^{-1} in a 50-g mockingbird. This inverse relationship with body mass is most likely due to the increased mass and inertia of the thoracic and abdominal body wall that must oscillate at the respiratory frequency.

Zollinger and Suthers[37] tested this hypothesis by tutoring a vocal mimic, the northern mockingbird (*Mimus polyglottos*), with high repetition rate trills sung by a canary using minibreaths. Although the mockingbird copied the canary's repetition rate of 22 syllables sec^{-1} (Fig. 6a and d), he could not take a minibreath between syllables. Instead he divided the trill into groups of syllables. Each group was sung using pulsatile expiration with a pause between groups for an inspiration (Fig. 6b and e). At lower syllable repetition rates (<11 sec^{-1}) there is a longer interval between syllables and the mockingbird can sing minibreath trills rivaling canary trills in length (Fig. 6c and f).

MOTOR STEREOTYPY AND SENSORY FEEDBACK

In the songbirds studied, each syllable type in the adult repertoire is always produced in a similar way, as judged by stereotyped temporal patterns of syringeal airflow, air sac pressure, and the contribution each side of the syrinx makes to the vocalization. The time-varying pattern of airflow and pressure on each side of the syrinx reflects the combined activity pattern of respiratory muscles driving airflow and syringeal muscles controlling the resistance on each side due to constriction at the labia. In brown-headed cowbirds (*Molothrus ater*), different song types in an individual's repertoire have characteristic patterns of pressure and airflow that are repeated with each repetition of the song.[38] Even in open-ended learners, such as brown thrashers, the repetition of a syllable, either immediately to produce a "couplet" or after an intervening period of song composed of different syllables, is accompanied by a similar motor pattern characteristic of that syllable.[39] When juvenile zebra finches copy song syllables from adult male tutors they usually also copy the air sac pressure pattern used by the tutor to produce the syllable. If a strobe flash is used to interrupt zebra finch song, the bird normally stops singing at the end of an expiratory pressure pulse suggesting that these pulses represent units of motor production in which the syllable is the smallest unit.[40]

This motor stereotypy is consistent with the hypothesis that each syllable type in the crystallized song repertoire is represented by a central motor program.[41–44] But, even during adult song, sensory feedback continues to influence the motor output. Various experiments have shown that auditory feedback is necessary for long-term maintenance of song.[45–47] Somatosensory feedback also modulates, in real time, the activity of expiratory and syringeal muscles during song. Both deaf and hearing adult cardinals adjust the contraction of their abdominal expiratory muscles to compensate for unpredictable changes in respiratory pressure caused by injection of a small volume of air into an air sac. Small increases in air sac pressure are followed, after a latency of about 50 msec, by a reduction in the amplitude of the abdominal expiratory EMG, which tends to stabilize expiratory airflow during the remainder of the song syllable (Fig. 7).[33] Syringeal muscles also respond to the injection of air into an air sac during a syllable by increasing their contraction, presumably to maintain an appropriate sound frequency in the presence of an unpredicted change in

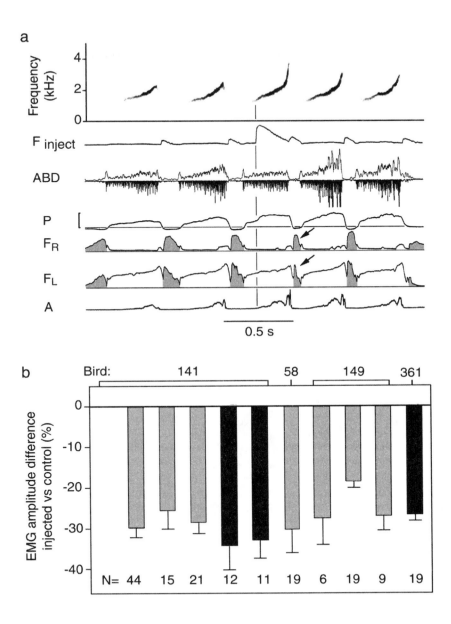

FIGURE 7. Real-time somatosensory feedback of perturbation in air sac pressure to abdominal expiratory muscles aids birds in precise ventilatory control necessary for song. (a) A puff of air injected into the air sac during the third syllable in this northern cardinal song results in a compensatory reduction in EMG amplitude in the abdominal expiratory muscle. The air sac pressure increases as a result of the injection and the following mini-breath inspiration (*arrows*) is smaller than normal, presumably because the of the added vol-

pressure and airflow.[48] As juveniles learn to sing with the aid of auditory feedback, they may also learn to use the proprioceptive or mechanoreceptive feedback associated with each syllable. In addition to adjusting the central motor pattern for changing conditions at the vocal and respiratory periphery, somatosensory feedback might enable the bird to achieve the correct motor configuration for a syllable prior to the onset of phonation or more quickly during phonation than would be possible using auditory feedback.

BILATERAL MOTOR SKILLS AND VOCAL COMPLEXITY

Songbirds have taken advantage of their duplex vocal organ in several ways to increase their vocal versatility. In species studied to date, the left side of the syrinx has a lower frequency range than the right side, although there is usually considerable overlap between sides in mid-range frequencies.[37,49] The presence of lateral specializations for producing low or high frequencies increases the range of frequencies that can be included when both sides of the syrinx contribute to song. In brown thrashers and catbirds, the right side of the syrinx is responsible for more of the frequency modulation and amplitude modulation, particularly rapid AM, than the left side (FIG. 8).[50] This functional lateralization creates a division of labor that allows lateral specialization of vocal skills and increases the acoustic diversity of sounds that can be produced using both sides of the syrinx.

Borror and Reese[51] and Greenewalt[6] were among the first to demonstrate that the songs of many birds contain two simultaneous, independently modulated frequencies. They suggested the components of these two-voice syllables originated on opposite sides of the syrinx. This view received further support from experiments on chaffinches (*Fringilla coelebs*),[52,53] canaries, and white-crowned sparrows (*Zonotrichia leucophrys*),[54] which showed that disabling either side of the syrinx by section of the ipsilateral tracheosyringeal nerve caused the loss of certain song elements. In these and subsequent similar experiments by other investigators, reviewed by Suthers,[55] denervating the left side of the syrinx resulted in more syllables being lost or altered than when the right side was denervated. This lateralization of song production was most prominent in the waterslager strain of canaries, bred selectively for their song. About 90% of the waterslager song repertoire is lost after disabling the left side of the syrinx, but only about 10% is eliminated if the right side is disabled.[54,56] This extreme left dominance of song production is not a universal char-

---

ume of air. (**b**) Reduction in mean amplitude of the abdominal expiratory muscle EMG, compared to control, after injection of air puffs. Seven different syllable types in hearing birds (*grey bars*), and three syllable types from deafened birds (*black bars*) are shown. Mean ± SE. Syllables sung by hearing birds: $P < 0.013$; syllables sung by deaf birds: $P < 0.001$; paired t test. F_{inject}, rate of airflow through the injection cannula from the picospritzer. The large upward inflection in the flow rate indicates the time course of the injected air puff. ABD, abdominal expiratory muscle EMG activity shown rectified (time constant 0.1 msec) and integrated (time constant 5 msec) (upward) and rectified (downward); P, subsyringeal air sac pressure (bracket = 10 cm H_2O). A, sound amplitude rectified (time constant 0.1 msec) and integrated (time constant 1 msec). Other abbreviations as in FIGURE 5. (Modified from Suthers and colleagues.[33] Copyright 2002, National Academy of Sciences.)

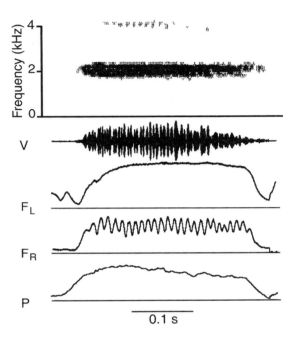

FIGURE 8. Rapid, cyclical amplitude modulation in brown thrasher song produced by modulating airflow through right side of syrinx. Abbreviations in legend of FIGURE 5. (Modified from Suthers and colleagues.[50])

acteristic of the species, however. The conspecific outbred domestic canary strain produces about an equal number of notes on each side.[57] In similar experiments on zebra finches, in which one side of the syrinx was disabled, one study[58] found a modest right-side dominance for some song parameters, but another[59] reported a left dominance. New direct measures from zebra finches with a bilaterally intact vocal system reveal complex bilateral contributions with little lateralization except for a right-side dominance in some calls (see Goller and Cooper, this volume).

Songbirds have also exploited their ability to independently control sound production on each side of the syrinx in ways that enhance particular acoustic effects characteristic of their species-specific songs.[49,55] The brown thrasher, for example, includes many two-voice syllables to which independently modulated simultaneous contributions from each side add a dissonant quality (FIG. 9a). The songs of brown-headed cowbirds begin with two or three note clusters separated by a brief inspiration, followed by a high frequency "whistle." The first note in each note cluster is very low frequency sung on the left side of the syrinx. Subsequent notes are produced in rapid succession on alternate sides with successive notes on each side starting at a higher frequency than the previous one (FIG. 9c). Northern cardinal song includes many frequency modulated sweeps spanning a broad range of frequencies. The portion of each sweep that extends above about 3.5 kHz is generated by the right

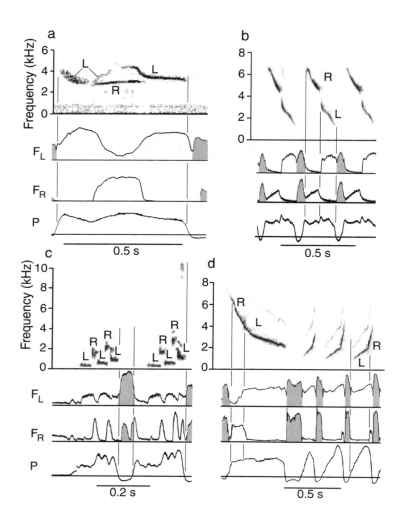

FIGURE 9. Species differences in patterns of syringeal lateralization. (**a**) Independently modulated, simultaneous contributions from the right and left sides of the syrinx in brown thrasher song (two-voice). (**b**) Domestic canary syllables which, like cardinal FM sweeps, are produced by sequential contributions from the right and left sides of the syrinx, but unlike the cardinal, the notes are not connected to form a continuous sweep. (**c**) Brown-headed cowbird song note clusters are produced by rapid alternation between phonation on the right and left sides, giving rise to abrupt frequency steps between notes. Final whistle at end of song (not shown) is sung on the right side. (**d**) Broadband, frequency-modulated (FM) sweeps by northern cardinals are produced by sequential coordinated contributions of the right and left sides. Frequencies higher than ~3.5 kHz are generated on the right side, lower frequencies are produced by the left side. Most cardinal syllables are formed by coordinated switches mid-syllable between sides. (**a**, modified from Suthers and colleagues[39]; **b**, modified from Suthers and colleagues[57]; **c**, modified from Allen and Suthers.[38])

side of the syrinx and the portion below this frequency is generated by the left syrinx. In most syllables the two sides are coordinated so that their combined output forms a single continuous sweep (FIG. 9d). Domestic canaries also use both sides of their syrinx to produce about one-third of their repertoire. Each side of the syrinx contributes distinct, unconnected notes that are sung sequentially, not simultaneously. Even in syllables where the two sides sweep over complementary frequency bands, the notes are not connected, as they are in cardinal song, but remain temporally distinct (FIG. 9b).[57] It thus appears that the distinctive acoustic features that characterize each species' song depend on similarly distinctive species-specific vocal motor patterns.

Did the vocal motor patterns in these species diverge as a way to increase the complexity of their songs despite constraints on how sounds can be produced, or did

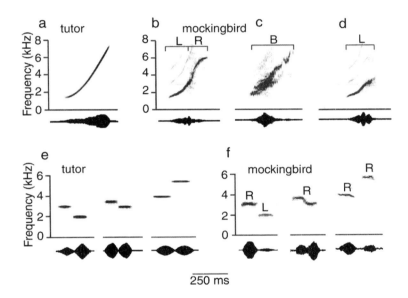

FIGURE 10. Mockingbird copies of synthesized tutor sounds. When copying cardinal-like synthesized FM sweeps (**a**), mockingbirds were able to reproduce both the tonal quality and wide bandwidth of the sweep only when they used a cardinal-like motor pattern, switching smoothly mid-syllable from the left to right side of the syrinx (**b**). If mockingbirds attempted to sing the sweep with both sides of the syrinx open, the resulting copies were not tonal (**c**). If sweeps were produced using only one side of the syrinx (**d**), the bandwidth of the sweep was greatly reduced (mean BW unilateral=2.96±0.715 kHz, mean bilateral=4.7±0.52 kHz. t=8.761, df=38, P<0.001, N=198 sweeps). Abrupt, step-like frequency jumps (**e**) were only accurately copied by mockingbirds that used a cowbird-like alternating phonation pattern, switching between sides to produce successive tones (first tone pair in **f**). If mockingbirds did not switch between sides, they could either retain the immediate onset of the second frequency, but introduce a slur between tones (center tone pair in **f**), or insert a short silent interval between tones (last tone pair **f**), preserving the spectral contrast between tones, but altering the temporal pattern. (Modified from Zollinger and Suthers.[37])

they arise through developmental or evolutionary pressures unrelated to acoustic production? To answer this question juvenile northern mockingbirds, which are vocal mimics, were tutored with heterospecific song and the motor pattern they used to copy that song when they became adults was compared to the motor pattern of the tutor. If the tutor species' motor pattern has become specialized through selection to produce the salient acoustic features of that song then the mockingbird's success in copying the song should depend on the accuracy with which he reproduces the tutor's vocal motor pattern. If, on the other hand, there is not an obligatory relationship between a particular motor pattern and a certain acoustic output then, in the process of trial-and-error motor learning, the mockingbird should sometimes develop a different motor pattern for copying the tutor's song.

Mockingbirds tutored with cardinal or cowbird song generally used the same motor pattern as the tutor when they copied his song or acoustically similar computer synthesized sounds. When the mockingbird's motor pattern differed from that used by the tutor, the vocalization was also a less accurate copy (FIG. 10).[37] It is particularly interesting that the mockingbird seemed to have the most difficulty reproducing the "special" acoustic features of other species' songs, such as the cardinals smoothly coordinated switch from one side of the syrinx to the other in the middle of its frequency sweep or copying the frequency jumps between cowbird notes without either connecting the notes with a slurred sweep or introducing a silent interval between them (FIG. 10).[37] The developmental convergence of model and mimic onto the same motor patterns for production of the similar sounds suggests that song motor patterns have evolved through selection for increased diversity by pushing the envelope of performance limits in a particular direction for each species. Each species has become an acoustic specialist for producing its style of song with a skill that the mockingbird, as a vocal generalist, has difficulty equalling.

PERIPHERAL MECHANISMS AND CENTRAL PROCESSING

Studies on the peripheral mechanisms of song production raise a variety of questions that depend for answers on studies of central processing.[60] Coordination of the various motor subsystems that contribute to song seems to pose a daunting challenge in motor control. The variety and complexity that are now apparent in patterns of song lateralization employed by different species emphasize the need to better understand central mechanisms of bilateral motor coordination, especially at high syllable repetition rates. How is each side of the brain kept informed of contralateral motor actions? How are respiratory and syringeal pattern generators coordinated and what are the pathways by which somatosensory feedback modulates motor control? To what extent do the acoustic specializations of the left and right sides of the syrinx reflect central, as opposed to peripheral, lateralization of function? Are limitations in vocal performance imposed at central or peripheral levels or both? The importance of understanding the relationship between neural processing in the song control system and peripheral motor function is apparent in a recent model of song production that indicates much of the diversity observed in song could be achieved by simply varying the temporal relationship between respiratory pressure and the tension of the labia, as indicated by the activity of syringeal muscles.[61,62] Brain mechanisms and peripheral effectors for singing have evolved together under the selective forces shaping vocal communication. They are intimately related, complementary approaches to understanding the neuroethology of birdsong.

ACKNOWLEDGMENTS

Research of the authors was supported by National Institutes of Health–National Institute of Neurological Disorders and Stroke NS029467 (R.A.S.) and National Institutes of Health–National Institute on Deafness and other Communication Disorders DC00012 (S.A.Z.). We thank Phil Zeigler and Peter Marler for their comments that improved this manuscript and the opportunity to participate in this symposium.

REFERENCES

1. KING, A.S. 1989. Functional anatomy of the syrinx. *In* Form and Function in Birds, A.S. King & J. McLelland, Eds. **4:** 105–192. Academic Press. London.
2. MISKIMEN, M. 1951. Sound production in passerine birds. Auk **68:** 493–504.
3. GOLLER, F. & O.N. LARSEN. 1997. A new mechanism of sound generation in songbirds. Proc. Natl. Acad. Sci. USA **94:** 14787–14791.
4. SETTERWALL, C.G. 1901. Studies öfver syrinx hos polymyoda passeres. Ph.D. dissertation, University of Lund.
5. LARSEN, O.N. & F. GOLLER. 1999. Role of syringeal vibrations in bird vocalizations. Proc. R. Soc. London B **266:** 1609–1615.
6. GREENEWALT, C.H. 1968. Bird Song: Acoustics and Physiology. Smithsonian Institution Press. Washington, D.C.
7. NOTTEBOHM, F. 1976. Phonation in the orange-winged Amazon Parrot, *Amazona amazonica*. J. Comp. Physiol. **108:** 157–170.
8. GAUNT, A.S. 1983. An hypothesis concerning the relationship of syringeal structure to vocal abilities. Auk **100:** 853–862.
9. GAUNT, A.S., S.L.L. GAUNT & R.M. CASEY. 1982. Syringeal mechanics reassessed: evidence from *Streptopelia*. Auk **99:** 474–494.
10. CASEY, R.M. & A.S. GAUNT. 1985. Theoretical models of the avian syrinx. J. Theor. Biol. **116:** 45–64.
11. BALLINTIJN, M.R. & C. TEN CATE. 1998. Sound production in the collared dove: a test of the "whistle" hypothesis. J. Exp. Biol. **201:** 1637–1649.
12. NOWICKI, S. 1987. Vocal tract resonances in oscine bird sound production: evidence from birdsongs in a helium atmosphere. Nature **325:** 53–55.
13. FANT, G. 1970. Acoustic Theory of Speech Production. Mouton. The Hague.
14. GAUNT, A.S. & S. NOWICKI. 1998. Sound production in birds: acoustics and physiology revisited. *In* Animal Acoustic Communication. Sound analysis and research methods. S.L. Hopp, M.J. Owren & C.S. Evans, Eds.: 291–321. Springer-Verlag. Berlin.
15. ROTHENBERG, M. 1981. Acoustic interaction between the glottal source and the vocal tract. *In* Vocal Fold Physiology. K.N. Stevens & M. Hirano, Eds.: 305–328. University of Tokyo Press. Tokyo.
16. BECKERS, G.J.L., R.A. SUTHERS & C. TEN CATE. 2003. Pure-tone birdsong by resonance filtering of harmonic overtones. Proc. Natl. Acad. Sci. USA **100:** 7372–7376.
17. SUTHERS, R.A. 1990. Contributions to birdsong from the left and right sides of the intact syrinx. Nature **347:** 473–477.
18. LARSEN, O.N. & F. GOLLER. 2002. Direct observation of syringeal muscle function in songbirds and a parrot. J. Exp. Biol. **205:** 25–35.
19. GOLLER, F. & R.A. SUTHERS. 1996. Role of syringeal muscles in controlling the phonology of bird song. J. Neurophysiol. **76:** 287–300.

20. GOLLER, F. & R.A. SUTHERS. 1995. Implications for lateralization of bird song from unilateral gating of bilateral motor patterns. Nature 373: 63–66.
21. GOLLER, F. & R.A. SUTHERS. 1996. Role of syringeal muscles in gating airflow and sound production in singing brown thrashers. J. Neurophysiol. 75: 867–876.
22. BROCA, P. 1861. Remarques sur le siege da la faculte du language articule, suive d'une observation d'aphemie. (Transl. J. Kann, 1950). J. Speech Hearing Disorders 15: 16–20.
23. GAUNT, A.S. & S.L.L. GAUNT. 1985. Electromyographic studies of the syrinx in parrots (Aves, Psittacidae). Zoomorph. 105: 1–11.
24. BECKERS, G.J.L., R.A. SUTHERS & C. TEN CATE. 2003. Mechanisms of frequency and amplitude modulation in ring dove song. J. Exp. Biol. 206: 1833–1843.
25. GOLLER, F. & O.N. LARSEN. 1997. In situ biomechanics of the syrinx and sound generation in pigeons. J. Exp. Biol. 200: 2165–2176.
26. SCHEID, P. & J. PIIPER. 1989. Respiratory mechanics and air flow in birds. In Form and Function in Birds. A.S. King & J. McLelland, Eds. 4: 369–392. Academic Press. London.
27. KING, A.S. & V. MOLONY. 1971. The anatomy of respiration. In Physiology and Biochemistry of the Domestic Fowl. D.J. Bell & B.M. Freeman, Eds. 1: 93–169. Academic Press. London.
28. HARTLEY, R.S. & R.A. SUTHERS. 1989. Airflow and pressure during canary song: evidence for mini-breaths. J. Comp. Physiol. A. 165: 15–26.
29. GOLLER, F. & M.A. DALEY. 2001. Novel motor gestures for phonation during inspiration enhance the acoustic complexity of birdsong. Proc. R. Soc. London B 268: 2301–2305.
30. FEDDE, M.R. 1987. Respiratory muscles. In Bird Respiration. T.J. Seller, Ed. 1: 3–37. CRC Press. Boca Raton.
31. WILD, J.M., F. GOLLER & R.A. SUTHERS. 1998. Inspiratory muscle activity during birdsong. J. Neurobiol. 36: 441–453.
32. HARTLEY, R.S. 1990. Expiratory muscle activity during song production in the canary. Respir. Physiol. 81: 177–187.
33. SUTHERS, R.A., F. GOLLER & J.M. WILD. 2002. Somatosensory feedback modulates the respiratory motor program of crystallized birdsong. Proc. Natl. Acad. Sci. USA 99: 5680–5685.
34. GOLLER, F. & R.A. SUTHERS. 1999. Bilaterally symmetrical respiratory activity during lateralized birdsong. J. Neurobiol. 41: 513–523.
35. VICARIO, D.S. 1991. Neural mechanisms of vocal production in songbirds. Curr. Opin. Neurobiol. 1: 595–600.
36. CALDER, W.A. 1970. Respiration during song in the canary (Serinus canaria). Comp. Biochem. Physiol. 32: 251–258.
37. ZOLLINGER, S.A. & R.A. SUTHERS. 2004. Motor mechanisms of a vocal mimic: implications for birdsong production. Proc. R. Soc. London B. 271: 483–491.
38. ALLAN, S.E. & R.A. SUTHERS. 1994. Lateralization and motor stereotypy of song production in the brown-headed cowbird. J. Neurobiol. 25: 1154–1166.
39. SUTHERS, R.A., F. GOLLER & R.S. HARTLEY. 1996. Motor stereotypy and diversity in songs of mimic thrushes. J. Neurobiol. 30: 231–245.
40. FRANZ, M. & F. GOLLER. 2002. Respiratory units of motor production and song imitation in the zebra finch. J. Neurobiol. 51: 129–141.
41. KONISHI, M. 1994. Pattern generation in birdsong. Curr. Opin. Neurobiol. 4: 827–831.
42. KONISHI, M. 1965. The role of auditory feedback in the control of vocalization in the white-crowned sparrow. Z. Tierpsychol. 22: 770–783.
43. KONISHI, M. 1985. Birdsong: from behavior to neuron. Annu. Rev. Neurosci. 8: 125–170.
44. VU, E.T., M.E. MAZUREK & Y.-C. KUO. 1994. Identification of a forebrain motor programming network for the learned song of zebra finches. J. Neurosci. 14: 6924–6934.
45. LEONARDO, A. & M. KONISHI. 1999. Decrystallization of adult birdsong by perturbation of auditory feedback. Nature. 399: 466–470.

46. OKANOYA, K. & A. YAMAGUCHI. 1997. Adult bengalese finches (*Lonchura striata* var. *domestica*) require real-time auditory feedback to produce normal song syntax. J. Neurobiol. **33:** 343–356.
47. NORDEEN, K.W. & E.J. NORDEEN. 1992. Auditory feedback is necessary for the maintenance of stereotyped song in adult zebra finches. Behav. Neural Biol. **57:** 58–66.
48. SUTHERS, R.A. & J.M. WILD. 2000. Real-time modulation of the syringeal motor program in response to externally imposed respiratory perturbations in adult songbirds. Soc. Neurosci. Abst. 26.
49. SUTHERS, R.A. 1999. The motor basis of vocal performance in songbirds. *In* The Design of Animal Communication. M. Hauser & M. Konishi, Eds.: 37–62. MIT Press. Cambridge, MA.
50. SUTHERS, R.A., F. GOLLER & R. S. HARTLEY. 1994. Motor dynamics of song production by mimic thrushes. J. Neurobiol. **25:** 917–936.
51. BORROR, D.J. & C.R. REESE. 1956. Vocal gymnastics in wood thrush songs. Ohio J. Sci. **56:** 177–182.
52. NOTTEBOHM, F. 1971. Neural lateralization of vocal control in a passerine bird I. Song. J. Exp. Zool. **177:** 229–262.
53. NOTTEBOHM, F. 1971. Neural lateralization of vocal control in a passerine bird II. Subsong, calls, and a theory of vocal learning. J. Exp. Zool. **179:** 35–50.
54. NOTTEBOHM, F. & M. E. NOTTEBOHM. 1976. Left hypoglossal dominance in the control of canary and white-crowned sparrow song. J. Comp. Physiol. **108:** 171–192.
55. SUTHERS, R.A. 1997. Peripheral control and lateralization of birdsong. J. Neurobiol. **33:** 632–652.
56. HARTLEY, R.S. & R.A. SUTHERS. 1990. Lateralization of syringeal function during song production in the canary. J. Neurobiol. **21:** 1236–1248.
57. SUTHERS, R.A., E.M. VALLET, A. TANVEZ & M. KREUTZER. 2004. Bilateral song production in domestic canaries. J. Neurobiol. (In press.)
58. WILLIAMS, H., L.A. CRANE, T.K. HALE, *et al.* 1992. Right-side dominance for song control in the zebra finch. J. Neurobiol. **23:** 1006–1020.
59. FLOODY, O.R. 1997. Song lateralization in the zebra finch. Horm. Behav. **31:** 25–34.
60. SUTHERS, R.A. & D. MARGOLIASH. 2002. Motor control of birdsong. Curr. Opin. Neurobiol. **12:** 684–690.
61. MINDLIN, G.B., T.J. GARDNER, F. GOLLER & R.A. SUTHERS. 2003. Experimental support for a model of birdsong production. Phys. Rev. E. **68:** 041908.
62. GARDNER, T., G. CECCHI, M. MAGNASCO, *et al.* 2001. Simple motor gestures for birdsongs. Phys. Rev. Lett. **87:** art. no.-208101.
63. SUTHERS, R.A. & F. GOLLER. 1997. Motor correlates of vocal diversity in songbirds. Curr. Ornithol. **14:** 235–288.
64. WILD, J.M. 1997. Neural pathways for the control of birdsong production. J. Neurobiol. **33:** 653–670.

Peripheral Motor Dynamics of Song Production in the Zebra Finch

FRANZ GOLLER AND BRENTON G. COOPER

Department of Biology, University of Utah, Salt Lake City, Utah 84112, USA

ABSTRACT: Singing behavior in songbirds is a model system for motor control of learned behavior. The target organs of its central motor programs are the various muscle systems involved in sound generation. Investigation of these peripheral motor mechanisms of song production is the first step toward an understanding of how different motor systems are coordinated. Here we review physiological studies of all major motor systems that are involved in song production and modification in the zebra finch (*Taeniopygia guttata*). Acoustic syllables of zebra finch song are produced by a characteristic air sac pressure pattern. Electromyographic (EMG) and sonomicrometric recording of expiratory muscle activity reveals that respiratory motor control is tightly coordinated with syringeal gating of airflow. Recordings of bronchial airflow demonstrate that most of the song syllables are composed of simultaneous independent contributions from the two sides of the syrinx. Sounds generated in the syrinx can be modified by the resonance properties of the upper vocal tract. Tracheal length affects resonance, but dynamic changes of tracheal length are unlikely to make a substantial contribution to sound modification. However, beak movements during song contribute to sound modification and, possibly, affect the vibratory behavior of the labia. Rapid beak aperture changes were associated with nonlinear transitions in the acoustic structure of individual syllables. The synergy between respiratory and syringeal motor systems, and the unique bilateral, simultaneous, and independent sound production, combined with dynamic modification of the acoustic structure of song, make the zebra finch an excellent model system for exploring mechanisms of sensorimotor integration underlying a complex learned behavior.

KEYWORDS: respiration; syringeal dynamics; tracheal resonance; beak; motor coordination

INTRODUCTION

Singing behavior in songbirds involves translation of a central song motor program into the coordinated peripheral muscle activity of various motor systems. Because many aspects of its *central* motor control have been explored in detail in the zebra finch, *Taeniopygia guttata* (see, for example, chapters by Wild and Mooney, this volume), the present review of mechanisms of *peripheral* motor control summa-

Address for correspondence: Franz Goller, Department of Biology, University of Utah, Salt Lake City, UT 84112.

goller@biology.utah.edu; <http://www.biology.utah.edu/faculty2.php?inum=17>

Ann. N.Y. Acad. Sci. 1016: 130–152 (2004). © 2004 New York Academy of Sciences.
doi: 10.1196/annals.1298.009

rizes knowledge on all major motor systems involved in sound production in that species. It is intended to provide a foundation for future studies of motor integration.

Song in the zebra finch consists of a sequence of 3–8 acoustically distinct syllables (motif; for a detailed discussion of sound classification and terminology see Williams, this volume), which can be repeated a variable number of times during a song bout (e.g., refs. 1 and 2). The acoustic character of syllables is somewhat unusual for a small songbird. The lowest frequency present in many syllables is 500–800 Hz; these syllables display a dense harmonic structure, and peak energy is typically found at higher frequencies (3–6 kHz). This type of syllable contrasts with the mostly tonal and higher-frequency sounds of songs in many songbird species. Individual zebra finch syllables vary in duration. Longer syllables are often composed of different acoustic elements (notes), and some transitions between notes are sudden without any silent gap.

The two main motor systems of sound generation are the respiratory system and the muscles of the syrinx (e.g., for review, see ref. 3; Suthers, this volume). The songbird syrinx contains two sound sources, which are independently controlled by two sets of six syringeal muscles on each side. In addition to the respiratory and syringeal motor systems, structures and motor systems of the upper vocal tract may modify the generated sound.[4] Movements of the beak, tongue, larynx, or trachea may cause changes in resonance properties of the upper vocal tract or change the acoustic impedance for radiation of sound.[5]

Motor control of song production requires coordination between syringeal motor tasks and respiratory movements, as well as between the two syringeal sound generators;[3] however, respiratory-syringeal integration is still poorly understood. The degree to which the respiratory muscles contribute to the fine control of pressure and airflow conditions is not known. Respiratory muscles might simply provide pulses of pressure, which are then modulated by syringeal gating activity. Alternatively, the two motor systems might simultaneously contribute to modulations of pressure and airflow, giving rise to a need for intricate coordination between them.

Similarly, the interaction between upper vocal tract movements and other vocal motor gestures is of great interest. Although there is good evidence that beak movements play a role in upper vocal tract filtering,[6,7] little is known about how they are coordinated with syringeal and respiratory movements. Our aim here is to provide a synthesis of current information on the peripheral motor patterns of song production in the zebra finch and to attempt to address motor integration at each level of song production and modification.

SYRINGEAL FUNCTION AND SOUND PRODUCTION

In songbirds, sound is generated by vibration of the lateral and medial labia (see Suthers, this volume). These labia also comprise the syringeal valve and can be actively moved into and out of the syringeal lumen. Labial vibrations are induced by the interplay of Bernoulli and elastic recoil forces as air flows past the partially constricted syrinx. Indirect evidence also suggests that the labia are the main sound-generating structures in the intact zebra finch syrinx. Surgical destruction of the medial tympaniform membranes does not remove the ability to generate sound.[8,9] Studies of the vibratory behavior of an excised syrinx preparation confirm that there are labial vibrations and provide further insight into the physical mechanisms of sound production.[10,11] Sound generation was induced by pulling air through one side of the syrinx while the contralateral side was sealed. Sounds generated by this method display characteristics of typical zebra finch vocalizations, including a dense harmonic structure with lowest-frequency components around 600 Hz and nonlinear transitions. In excised syrinx preparations, the left and right medial labia have resonance peaks at 575 and 830 Hz respectively.[11] These vibrational modes are consistent with the lowest frequency observed in zebra finch song syllables and calls. Furthermore, the difference between left and right sides of the syrinx suggests a possible difference in frequency range of sounds emanating from the two sides as has been found in most other investigated species[12,13] (and Suthers, this volume). In such cases, the left side of the syrinx consistently contributes sounds with lower fundamental frequency than those generated by the right side. This lateralization of function between the two sides can be accompanied by strongly asymmetric sound production in some species, such as the Waterslager canary (*Serinus canaria*).[14–16] In zebra finches, the changes in song syllables induced by unilateral tracheosyringeal nerve cuts suggested a right-side dominance in song production in one study,[17] but not in another.[18] The complex harmonic structure of many zebra finch song syllables can make the effects of denervation difficult to interpret. Direct determination of the respective contributions of the two syringeal sound generators to the song of intact birds is needed to address the question of syringeal lateralization during phonation.

DIFFERENCES IN ACTIVITY ON THE TWO SIDES OF THE SYRINX

To determine the relative contributions of the two syringeal sound generators to sound production, we recorded bilateral airflow through the syrinx using microbead thermistors as flow sensors.[19,20] To record bronchial flow, custom-built flow probes can be inserted into the lumen of the primary bronchi, using a feedback circuit designed to regulate current such that the thermistor bead is maintained at a constant temperature. However, because of the small size of the zebra finch syrinx and bronchi, song generation may be impaired in some subjects. To insure that we are approximating normal singing, we gathered data only from males that were still able to generate most of their motifs with flow probes in place.

Airflow was registered on the right side of the syrinx during production of all syllables. Airflow on the left side ranged from 58 to 100% (avg = 86%) of the expiratory duration of the motif (FIG. 1). Notes that were generated entirely on the right side were either high-frequency syllables (5 of 7 cases), ranging from 2 to 6 kHz, or constant-frequency harmonic stacks with the lowest-frequency components near 750 Hz (2 of 7 cases). In the 6 individuals, we found no notes that were generated only on the left side of the syrinx.

Although most syllables were accompanied by airflow through both sides, the sound generated by them was rarely the same (FIG. 1). In most birds the flow recordings were good enough to determine contributions of each side by high-pass filtering. Frequently, the flow probe on one side also registered the sound produced on the contralateral side, but at a reduced amplitude. In a few cases, we could not determine conclusively on which side a particular sound was generated. The right side generated sounds with significantly higher average frequency than the left side (avg ± SEM: $937 ± 66.8$ Hz; $n = 15$ vs. $651 ± 32.7$ Hz; $n = 14$; $t_{28} = 3.84$, $P = 0.0006$). In 4 of the 19 notes with bilateral airflow, only one sound was registered on both flow probes, suggesting that both sides generated the same note. In two cases, the right side generated a frequency that was close to the second harmonic of the sound gen-

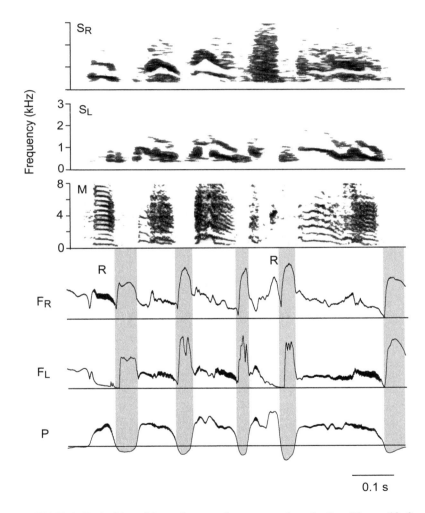

FIGURE 1. Both sides of the syrinx contribute to sound production. The motif of a zebra finch is displayed spectrographically (M), together with air sac pressure (P, horizontal line indicates atmospheric pressure), airflow through the left (F_L) and right (F_R) bronchi. The *top spectrograms* were calculated after the left and right airflow recordings were highpass filtered (>400 Hz) and represent the left (S_L) and right (S_R) sound. *Grey bars* mark inspirations. Whereas most notes are produced by bilateral contributions, some notes are generated only on the right side (R).

erated on the left side. In most cases the left and right side produced acoustically independent sounds with different frequency modulation patterns. Evidently, the combination of the two independent contributions can give rise to very complex sounds.

Contact calls of the zebra finch are generated with pronounced right-side dominance. During calling, there was airflow through the right side of the syrinx for the entire duration (FIG. 2). The left side was closed with the exception of one bird, in which the left side contributed a low-frequency sound at the beginning of the contact call and then closed (FIG. 2b). Contact call-like syllables are frequently part of the song, posing the question as to whether they are generated with the same right-side dominance during the song. Because none of the song motifs of the six individuals in this study included contact call-like syllables, this question awaits further clarification.

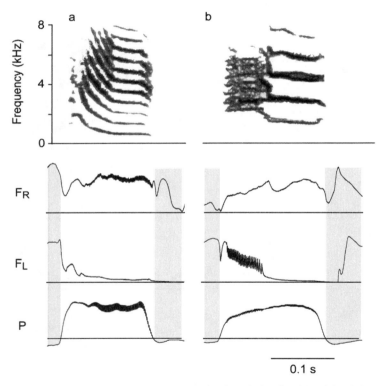

FIGURE 2. Contact calls are generated predominantly by the right side of the syrinx. Two contact calls (**a, b**) from two male zebra finches are displayed spectrographically (*top*) together with air sac pressure (P) and airflow through the left (F_L) and right (F_R) side of the syrinx. In one bird (**a**), the contact call is generated on the right side with left airflow near zero. The second bird (**b**) initially generates a two-voice segment with the left side, contributing a low-frequency sound (approx. 480 Hz; note the vibration on the airflow signal), which is only manifested on the spectrogram in its interaction with the right-side–generated sound at higher harmonic frequencies. The left side then closes (zero airflow) and the remainder of the call is produced on the right side only.

IS THERE A DOMINANT SIDE IN THE ZEBRA FINCH SYRINX?

The bilateral airflow data indicate clearly that there is no strong dominance of either side in song production in the zebra finch. But production of contact calls is strongly lateralized. These physiological results may help resolve the conflict between studies using unilateral denervation to assess the respective contributions of the two syringeal halves.[17,18] More frequent use of high-frequency syllables in one zebra finch colony, generated only on the right side of the syrinx, might result in more pronounced right-side dominance.

Lateralization of song production in zebra finches differs from that of other species in that there is almost continuous simultaneous production of independent sounds on both sides of the syrinx.[12,13] Simultaneous production of different sounds creates the potential for complex bilateral interactions, which characterize many syllables of zebra finch song and may, in part, explain why zebra finches can produce songs with acoustic characteristics so different from those of most small songbirds.

NEUROMUSCULAR CONTROL OF THE SYRINX

The two syringeal sound sources are independently controlled by a set of six syringeal muscles. The electrical activation of muscles involved in sound production has been monitored with electromyography.[21-24] To record EMG activity, small bipolar wire electrodes are inserted into the respective muscle. Vicario[21] presented the first data on activity of the intrinsic muscles of a spontaneously singing zebra finch. The activity of the main ventral muscle, m. syringealis ventralis (vS), and the dorsal muscle was recorded. Of the dorsal muscles, only the lateral portion is accessible for electrode placement. It is therefore likely that Vicario's recordings were made in m. tracheobronchialis dorsalis (dTB) and the lateral part of m. syringealis dorsalis (dS) (cf., Larsen and Goller[25]). Activity of the ventral muscle was most prominent only at the end of syllables. The dorsal muscle was active during syllables, and the pattern of activity in both muscles was stereotyped for repeated calls. Whereas the dorsal muscle activity was consistent with shaping the acoustic structure of syllables, the alignment of bursts in the ventral muscle with the end of syllables suggested a role in sound termination.[21]

The small size of the syringeal muscles in zebra finch constrains precise electrode localization. We have therefore studied syringeal muscle activity in larger species, combining the EMG monitoring with bilateral airflow and air-sac pressure recordings. These studies showed that the vS muscle activity is closely correlated with the ipsilaterally generated fundamental frequency.[23] Activity of the m. tracheobronchialis ventralis (vTB) was associated with syringeal abduction, and dTB and lateral dS activity were correlated with syringeal adduction.[22,25] We therefore suggest that the recordings in Vicario[21] illustrate abductive action by the lateral ventral muscles, although the precise electrode placement was not specified. We are now starting to investigate lateralized activity in the syringeal muscles with fine steel electrodes (Cooper and Goller, unpublished data). Initial recordings from the medial portions of vS do not indicate bursts of activity at the end of syllables (FIG. 3), but the activity is consistent with a possible role in tension control, as has been found in other spe-

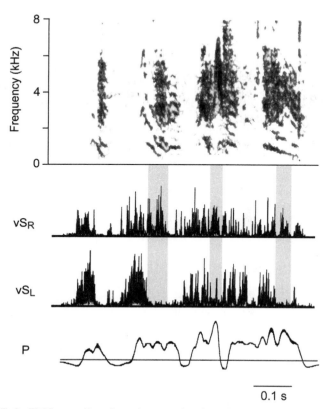

FIGURE 3. EMG recordings from the ventral syringeal muscles indicate lateralized activation patterns. Left (vS_L) and right (vS_R) EMG activity is displayed (rectified, time constant 0.1 ms) together with subsyringeal air sac pressure (P, horizontal line is ambient pressure) and spectrographic representation of the microphone recording of song. Segments with pronounced lateralized activity are marked with *grey bars*.

cies. We suggest that the bursts of activity observed at the end of syllables[21] may have been related to abductive action by lateral ventral muscles.

RESPIRATORY MOTOR PATTERNS DURING SONG

Analysis of respiratory patterns was based, in part, upon measurements of air sac pressure, which involved insertion of a small flexible cannula into one of the thoracic air sacs. Pressure changes are transduced by a miniature pressure sensor whose output voltage is linearly related to pressure. Note that while pressure recordings in the air sac system provide instantaneous information about the driving pressure, they do not reveal precise contributions of respiratory muscles to the generation of pressure.[26]

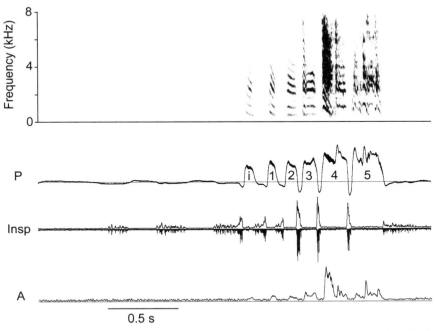

FIGURE 4. The regular respiratory pattern of quiet breathing changes to a less rhythmic pattern within the motif. One motif of a zebra finch is displayed spectrographically (*top*) with the corresponding air sac pressure (P; horizontal line marks ambient pressure, air sac pressure below this line is inspiratory and above expiratory, respectively), the electromyographic activity of the m. scalenus, an inspiratory muscle (Insp; rectified original trace downward and integrated upward), and the rectified and integrated sound amplitude (A). Individual syllables of the motif are marked by numbers (1–5) and are preceded by one introductory note (i). Modified from Wild *et al.*[24]

During quiet breathing, there is regular switching between inspiration and expiration; both respiratory phases having similar duration and amplitude. During zebra finch song, this regular pattern is changed dramatically (FIG. 4). Expirations during song typically have a longer duration (75–300 ms) than inspirations (range 15–100 ms), which are considerably shorter than those during quiet respiration (200–300 ms). The amplitude of air sac pressure pulses is increased severalfold over quiet respiration; expiration increases 6–20-fold and inspirations 4–10-fold.[20] A given motif is characterized by a particular alternating pattern of expiratory and short inspiratory pressure pulses, or minibreaths (FIG. 4). Typically, sound is generated during expiration and most minibreaths are silent. However, some high-frequency sounds are generated during inspiration.[20] The coarse temporal structure of song, with its characteristic pattern of sound and silent periods, is therefore a result of the respiratory activity. When males repeat the motif, each pulse is generated with high stereotypy and the air sac pressure pattern is as characteristic of syllables as the sound itself.[26]

Because there tends to be a one-to-one correspondence between respiratory pulses and acoustically defined song syllables, Franz and Goller[26] hypothesized that individual respiratory pulses may be the fundamental units of motor production in the
zebra finch. Supporting evidence for this hypothesis was derived from experiments
in which the song was interrupted with stroboscopic light flashes. When songs were
interrupted, they were terminated at the end of an expiratory pulse,[26] confirming earlier behavioral evidence.[27] In cases where different individuals sang similar song
syllables, details of the air sac pressure patterns were more similar than these accompanying different song syllables. It appears that particular patterns of air sac pressure
are required for the production of certain sounds, placing a potential physical constraint on the range of sounds that can be produced.

The expiratory muscles (abdominal muscle sheet, mainly, m. obliquus externus
abdominis and m. transversus abdominis) and inspiratory muscles (m. scalenus) act
in alternation, in harmony with the appropriate respiratory phase (FIGS. 4 and 5).[24]
Because each muscle group was always inactive during the other respiratory phase,

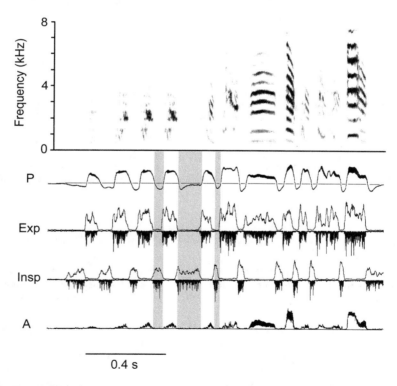

FIGURE 5. The activity of inspiratory and expiratory muscles is restricted to their respective respiratory phase and therefore alternates with no temporal overlap between them.
The song is depicted spectrographically (*top*) with corresponding air sac pressure (P), expiratory muscle activity (Exp, m. obliquus externus abdominis), inspiratory muscle activity
(Insp; m. scalenus), and sound amplitude. Modified from Wild *et al.*[24]

it is unlikely that antagonistic action of either muscle is used for fine control of air sac pressure.

INTEGRATION BETWEEN EXPIRATION AND SYRINGEAL ACTIVITY

EMG data confirm that the respiratory system plays a major role in determining the temporal structure of song. However, it remains unclear to what degree respiratory muscles are also involved in the fine control of air sac pressure. Expiratory activity might be contributing to pressure modulations, or fine regulation may only be the result of gating of airflow at the syringeal valves (adjusting the syringeal resistance).

To complement information gained from EMG recordings of expiratory muscles, we used the technique of soniomicrometry to monitor muscle length in order to carry out an analysis of the fine control of expiratory muscle activity (FIG. 6). Sonomicrometry was only performed on the abdominal expiratory muscle sheet. Two crystals are inserted into the muscle sheet approximately 3 mm apart following the fiber

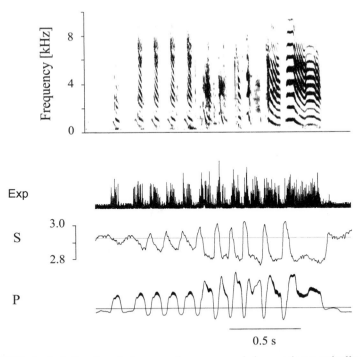

FIGURE 6. Activity of expiratory muscles was recorded sonomicrometrically as muscle length changes in the abdominal muscle sheet (S, distance between crystals in mm) and electromyographically (Exp, rectified with time constant 0.1 ms), together with the resulting air sac pressure pattern (P) and the song (*spectrogram, top*). Muscle-length changes correspond to the EMG activity and air sac pressure. Note that inspiratory activity causes a lengthening of the abdominal muscle sheet beyond resting length (*dotted line*).

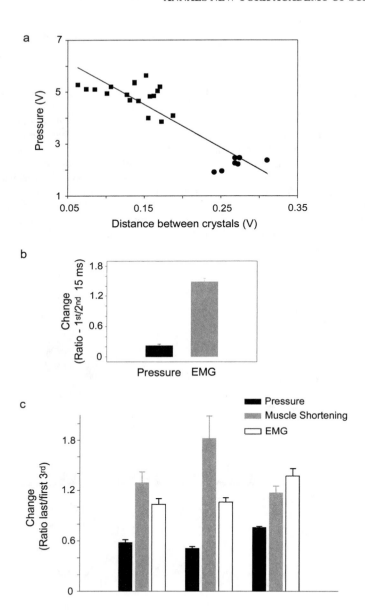

FIGURE 7. (a) Representative example of the relationship between muscle length (expressed as relative voltage indicating distance between the sonomicrometry crystals) and the resulting air sac pressure. Increased muscle shortening results in higher air sac pressure. It is likely that the variability is partly a result of changes in syringeal resistance to airflow during sound production. Data points represent peak pressure and the corresponding muscle shortening for individual syllables (*circles*, introductory notes; *squares,* syllables of the motif). (b) Mean ratio ± 1 SEM between measurements of air sac pressure and expiratory EMG activity for the first 15 ms of a syllable and the second 15 ms bin ($n = 12$; data are from 3

direction of the outermost layer of the muscle sheet (m. obliquus externus abdominis).[28] One of the crystals functions as the sender of an ultrasonic signal, which is received by the second crystal. From the time delay between sending and receiving a distance is calculated based on the sound velocity in muscle tissue (approx. 1525 m·s^{-1} at 40°C). Any length changes in the muscle sheet are translated into crystal movement, which can be monitored with a spatial resolution of 0.025 mm and a temporal resolution of 600 Hz.[29]

We found that EMG activity at the onset of an expiratory pressure pulse is disproportionately high when compared to the activity during later stages of the pressure pulse (FIGS. 6 and 7). This increased activity may reflect increased effort to overcome rapidly elastic components in the body wall. EMG activity at the end of longer pressure pulses is higher than it is during the first third of the pulse. Greater muscle shortening at the end of pressure pulses, corresponding to this increased EMG activity, results, however, in lower air sac pressure (FIG. 7). A possible interpretation of these data is that the volume of air sacs decreases during a long expiratory pulse, such that, toward the end, more shortening of the expiratory muscles is needed even for generating lower air sac pressure. This volume effect may be accompanied by a change in biomechanical efficiency caused by the decreasing length of the abdominal muscle sheet. Syringeal gating changes may also contribute to the observed changes. Assuming that different acoustic characteristics are associated with different syringeal resistance, acoustic changes might contribute to the modification of respiratory effort as well. This latter possibility, however, is unlikely to be the sole cause of the modulation of expiratory effort. It seems more likely that the consistently increased effort with resulting lower pressure is related to the decrease of the volume of air in the air sac system over the course of a long expiration.

These findings illustrate that even a simple maintenance of air sac pressure for 150–250 ms requires adjustments in expiratory effort. The presence of air sac pressure modulations during many expiratory pulses suggests that more rapid modulation may take place as well. Sonomicrometric data show a correlation of pressure modulations with consistent changes in muscle length as well as pressure modulations without muscle length changes (FIG. 8). These data provide direct evidence that the activity of expiratory muscles is rapidly modulated to effect changes in air sac pressure. They also illustrate that syringeal gating activity plays a role in effecting pressure modulations, though it is not possible to determine precisely to what degree each motor system contributes to the modulation.

---

individuals). These data illustrate that at the onset of expiratory pressure pulses EMG activity is greater than for the second 15-ms bin, but results in lower amplitude of the air sac pressure pulse. The EMG activity precedes pressure generation by 8–12 ms; we used a 10-ms shift of EMG activity to align it with the air sac pressure. (c) At the end of syllables, increased EMG activity and increased muscle shortening result in lower air sac pressure, presumably because the volume of air is reduced in the air sac. The change in all three parameters is expressed as the ratio of the respective mean for the last third divided by the mean for the first third of a given syllable ($n = 5$; data from the longest syllable of each individual; duration varied between 120–250 ms).

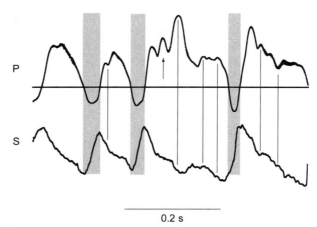

0.2 s

FIGURE 8. Many modulations of air sac pressure (P) are paralleled by appropriate length changes in the abdominal expiratory muscle sheet (recorded with sonomicrometry, S; increasing length is upward) as displayed by the motif of one zebra finch. The most pronounced modulations in pressure that show concurrent muscle length change are marked by *lines*. Only one pressure peak was not clearly accompanied by a decrease in muscle length (*arrow*).

MOTOR SYSTEMS OF THE UPPER VOCAL TRACT

To explore the resonance properties of the upper vocal tract in the zebra finch, we have investigated two properties: tracheal length and beak movements. Tracheal length affects resonance characteristics,[5,30] and birds might be able to dynamically change the length with an extrinsic syringeal muscle. Also, beak movements are a striking feature of singing songbirds, including zebra finches,[7] and are thought to influence upper vocal tract resonance properties either by adjusting effective tube length or by changing acoustic impedance.[6]

To explore this question, tracheal length was monitored with sonomicrometry.[29] Because of the small size of the crystals, only a short segment (<1 cm) of the trachea can be monitored for length changes. We chose the basal end of the trachea, above the point where the interclavicular air sac membrane is attached, as a likely place to reveal active shortening of the trachea via contraction of the tracheolateral muscle. This muscle is most developed at the basal end and thins considerably at higher portions of the trachea. During song, the segment at the base shortened in a stereotyped pattern. At the onset of the song motif, a shortening step occurred, which was sustained throughout the song bout. During the motif, the tracheal segment shortened with each expiratory pulse and lengthened with each minibreath (FIG. 9). Bilateral sectioning of the tracheosyringeal nerve eliminated the tracheal shortening at the onset of the song bout, but left the pattern of tracheal shortening and lengthening during the motif intact (FIG. 10). Together, these data suggest that active tracheal length change is occurring at the beginning of song, but that subsequent modulation of tracheal length is predominantly driven by pressure changes in the interclavicular air

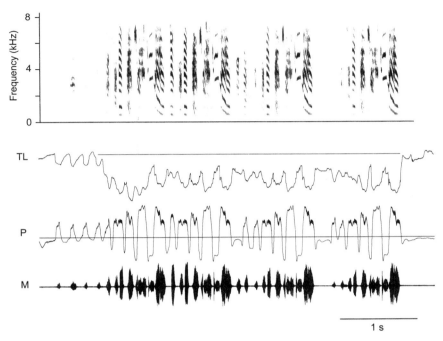

FIGURE 9. Tracheal-length changes accompany song production in the zebra finch. At the beginning of the first motif of the bout, there is a sustained shortening of the trachea (TL; relative voltage changes indicate distance between the sonomicrometry crystals where downward indicates shortening). The air sac pressure pulses (P) are paralleled by length changes in the trachea, with expiration corresponding to shortening and inspiration to lengthening, respectively. The vocalizations are displayed oscillographically (M) and spectrographically (*top*). From Daley and Goller.[29]

sac and translated to tracheal movement by the tracheal attachment of the membrane craniad to the syrinx.

The extent of the change of length is very small (maximally 0.2 mm), constituting no more than a maximum of a 3% change in the length of the monitored segment. If this strain is assumed to be uniformly applied to the whole trachea (3.3 cm), a 3% length change would result in a 1-mm length change. If equations for resonance in a uniform tube are used to calculate the shift in resonance properties resulting from this length change, resonance changes would amount to 78 Hz for a tube stopped at one end and 168 Hz for a tube stopped at both ends. This is a relatively insubstantial shift in relation to the harmonic spacing of 500–800 Hz in most harmonic stacks of zebra finch song. Furthermore, the assumption that the strain is uniform along the whole trachea may be incorrect. In fact, slight head turning caused a length change at the base of the trachea that was equal to or greater than that observed during song, suggesting that other behavior may influence tracheal length more than changes that are pressure-mediated or mediated by syringeal muscles. Because zebra finch males

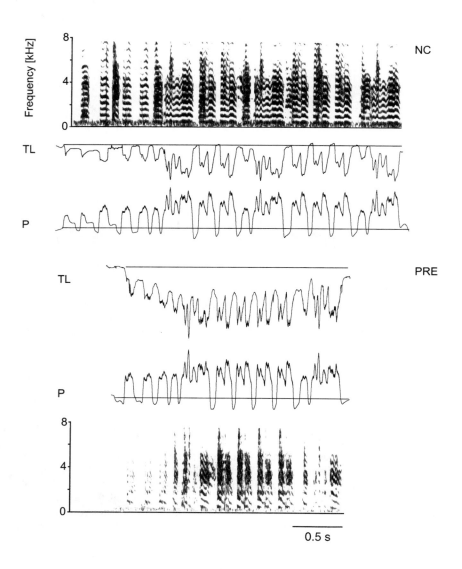

FIGURE 10. A bilateral cut of the tracheosyringeal branch of the hypoglossal nerves eliminates the initial shortening of the trachea, but leaves the length changes with pressure pulses intact. The intact song (PRE) and the post-nerve cut song (NC) are displayed with corresponding air sac pressure and tracheal length. From Daley and Goller.[29]

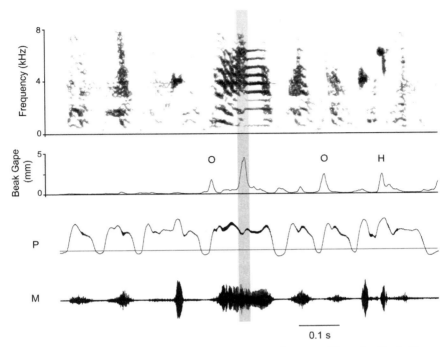

FIGURE 11. Distinct beak movements accompany the song of the zebra finch. The vocalizations are displayed oscillographically (M) and spectrographically (*top*), together with air sac pressure (P) and calibrated beak opening (values refer to the distance between the tips of upper and lower beak). Whereas beak gape is small throughout most of the song, there are pronounced peaks at the onset of syllables (O), at one high-frequency syllable (H) and at a rapid acoustic transition (*grey bar*). From Goller *et al.*[32]

perform a "dance" display while singing, head turning may be important. However, head movements are not strongly stereotyped[7] and depend on the spatial relationship of the male relative to the female to which the song is directed.

Beak movements during song were studied by videotaping singing males.[7] To improve the temporal resolution of beak movement records, we modified a method developed by Zeigler[31] that provides a continuous record by fixing a magnetosensitive transducer on the upper mandible and a small magnet to the lower beak.[32]). Zebra finch males change beak aperture during song in a stereotyped manner (FIG. 11).[7,32] A positive correlation emerged for the motifs of most males (7 of 8), when beak aperture for all syllable types was related to fundamental frequency (determined as the lowest frequency in harmonic stacks). This correlation was mostly driven by a few high-frequency syllables, which were accompanied by a wide beak gape. For harmonic stack syllables, however, there was no longer a significant relationship between fundamental frequency and beak aperture. Beak gape increased with increasing peak frequency, measured as the harmonic with highest relative amplitude. This relationship suggests that beak aperture modifies upper vocal tract filter

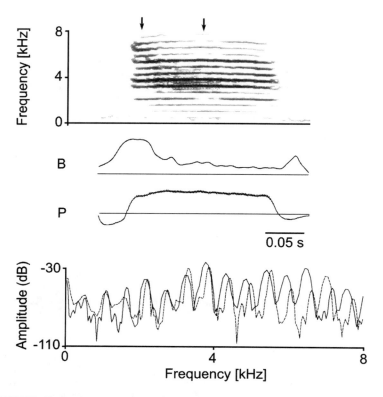

FIGURE 12. During a syllable of nearly constant frequency (*spectrogram, top*), beak aperture was higher at the beginning than during most of the syllable (B, uncalibrated voltage output; upward indicates a more open beak). As illustrated by the power spectra (*bottom panel*), the change in beak aperture was accompanied by a shift in harmonic emphasis from high frequency (*solid line*) for wider beak opening (15 ms centered around *first arrow*) to lower frequency (*stippled*) for a more closed beak (*second arrow*). From Goller *et al.*[32]

properties to shift harmonic emphasis. In support of this notion, strong qualitative evidence was found by looking closely at syllables in which beak gape varied, but frequency remained constant (FIG. 12). The segment with the greater beak aperture displayed a higher peak frequency than the segment with a more closed beak.

We also tested the hypothesis that beak aperture adjusts upper vocal tract resonance by fixing the beak either in an almost closed position (<1 mm) or in a more open position (6 mm). Although in some syllables the almost-closed position caused a lower peak frequency than the unmanipulated control (FIG. 13), there was no overall difference compared to the unmanipulated condition if all syllables were pooled. On the other hand, with the open beak there was a significant shift to higher peak frequency bands (FIG. 14). The lack of a consistent effect for the nearly closed beak treatment can be attributed to the small beak aperture during most of the harmonic stack syllables.

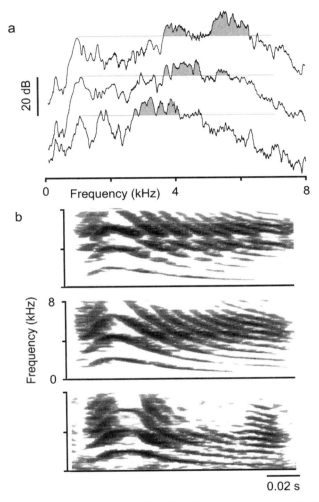

FIGURE 13. Fixing beak aperture affected the harmonic emphasis of syllables. Power spectra (*top panel*, **a**) show an upward shift in harmonic content for the open beak condition (*top trace* and *top spectrogram*, **b**) and a downward shift for the closed beak condition (*bottom trace* and *spectrogram*) as compared to the unmanipulated control (*middle trace* and *spectrogram*). From Goller *et al.*[32]

Although the pooled data indicate a positive correlation between beak aperture and sound amplitude, this multisyllable comparison may not indicate a causal relationship between beak gape and amplitude. Syllables with higher amplitude are typically generated with higher subsyringeal air sac pressure. Because sound amplitude for individual syllables does not vary substantially between different renditions of the motif, we shifted focus to contact calls with varying sound amplitude that we could compare quantitatively.[32] Although beak aperture was positively related to

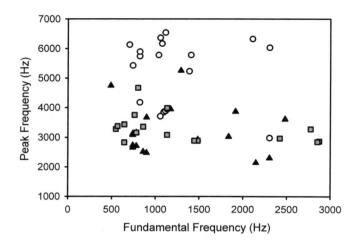

FIGURE 14. The effects of fixing the beak in open and closed condition are quantified for all notes of the motif of one bird. An increase in peak frequency (frequency with highest amplitude) compared to when the beak could be moved freely (*grey squares*) occurs in the open beak condition (*open circles*), whereas the peak frequency in the closed beak condition (*black triangles*) did not systematically differ from that of the syllables sung with no manipulation. From Goller et al.[32]

amplitude, this relationship was confounded by simultaneous relationships between beak aperture and air sac pressure and amplitude and air sac pressure. When these confounding relationships were controlled by using residuals, beak aperture and sound amplitude were no longer significantly related.[32]

With the exception of high-frequency syllables, beak apertures were small (approx. 1 mm) for most of the motifs. However, rapid beak opening and closing movements occurred during the motifs of all males, lasting typically between 30–40 ms. These dynamic changes of beak aperture were frequently associated with syllable onset and occurred during short parts of syllables with low-frequency components, but were rarely associated with the end of syllables. Dynamic beak movements during syllables were associated with rapid acoustic changes (FIG. 11). All individuals with such acoustic transitions in their syllables also had rapid beak movements accompanying the switch. If the beak was fixed at a very small aperture, rapid transitions in the sound were no longer present, whereas the open beak manipulation did not affect the acoustic switching. This suggests that dynamic beak movements influence the vibrational behavior of the labia. There might be a feedback mechanism, with the impedance changes reflecting back onto the labia, inducing a nonlinear behavior of the vibrating labia.[33]

We rarely hear mention of the possibility that singing activity could have implications for respiratory mechanisms and gas exchange. Song requires radical modifications of the rhythmic respiratory pattern seen during quiet breathing, which could affect gas exchange. Zebra finch males can sing long song bouts that last between 5–10 s. The modified respiratory pattern of song still enables males to maintain sufficient air supply,[20] as minibreaths replenish air expelled during the phonatory expirations. However, even if the volume of air sacs is maintained during the song, gas exchange in the lungs may still be compromised. We approached this question indirectly by measuring oxygen consumption in singing zebra finches with high temporal resolution.[34] Measurements of oxygen uptake throughout long bouts of song demonstrated that the altered respiratory patterns still allow a singing male to meet its oxygen requirements. Some males underwent significant periods of apnea after a song bout, suggesting that hyperventilation occurred during the song and may be a factor limiting song-bout duration. Thus, the temporal pattern of song may be constrained by respiratory demands. Sensory information, peripheral or central, about the oxygen/CO_2 balance may play a significant role in how the respiratory pattern of song develops. Thus, the integration of singing behavior with other, ongoing physiological activity may prove to be an important factor in the evolution of song complexity.

CONCLUSIONS AND FUTURE DIRECTIONS

The experimental evidence we have presented illustrates qualitatively that song requires complex adjustments to respiration, such as volume changes in air sacs, elastic properties of body wall, and biomechanical effects, but also calls for fine control of pressure conditions associated with the coordinated activity of respiratory and syringeal muscles. The generation of certain acoustic properties appears to require particular physical conditions of airflow and air sac pressure. Subtle changes in driving pressure can give rise to complex acoustic effects.[10] This interpretation is also supported by the observation that if different males sing the same song syllables, they tend to generate similar pressure patterns including modulations in air sac pressure.[26] However, it remains unclear whether this requirement for particular pressure conditions also leads to similarity in the motor gestures that generate it. Theoretically, the same physiological targets of pressure and airflow could be generated by different patterns of syringeal–respiratory interaction within and between males (see also refs. 35 and 36). One question for the future is whether morphological and physiological constraints influence the development of motor gestures, an issue that is important for our understanding of song development and evolution of singing behavior.

The frequent simultaneous use of both sound generators in zebra finches opens up possibilities for the study of interactions between the two sources. The complex acoustic structure of many zebra finch syllables clearly indicates that such interactions play an important role. It has been suggested that increments in acoustic complexity might arise from "simple" changes in motor gestures.[10] Behavioral complexity may thus in some degree be the result of peripheral biomechanical aspects and interactions and simple neural adjustments in their control. Along these lines, changes in coordination of the motor systems of the two syringeal sound generators could have major repercussions for song production. The advances being made in the investigation of neural activity in motor control nuclei of the zebra finch brain[37–39] have the potential to link central control and hemispheric coordination to the peripheral target systems.

We have presented evidence for a possible causal relationship between beak opening movements and rapid acoustic transitions in song syllables. It is possible that labial vibrations are affected by feedback mechanisms. Although more data are needed, we propose that there may be a role for upper vocal tract movements that goes beyond simple modification of sounds generated in the syrinx. It has been suggested that the correlation between beak opening and sound amplitude in contact calls may be indirect, actually reflecting a relationship between beak opening and the amplitude of the expiratory pressure pulse.[32] The possibility that there is coordination between beak movements, on the one hand, and syringeal and respiratory movements, on the other, emphasizes the importance of exploring the involvement of the mandibular motor systems in motor control of song production. There is a particular need for further research into the neuroanatomical and functional aspects of mechanisms underlying integration of the joint and finely coordinated activities of the motor systems of respiration, the syrinx, and the beak.

This sophisticated coordination of motor systems suggests that feedback mechanisms might play a role in song production. There is good evidence that auditory feedback is important for song maintenance (zebra finch).[40–42] We know very little, however, about the existence or role of non-auditory feedback (Wild, this volume). A somatosensory feedback mechanism in songbirds was illustrated by experimental perturbation of air sac pressure during song in the cardinal, *Cardinalis cardinalis*.[43] Singing birds modified expiratory effort, as measured by EMG activity, in response to the induced change in air sac pressure, but the precise sensory mechanism remains unknown (Wild, this volume). A similar feedback mechanism may also be present in brown-headed cowbirds (*Molothrus ater*). Respiratory effort was modified depending upon the presence, or absence, of the visual display. The biomechanical effects of the visual display presumably affect expiration, which was indicated by lower expiratory EMG activity. This reduced effort nevertheless produced the same amplitude of air sac pressure pulses as was present during song without display.[44] Somatosensory monitoring of respiratory variables, such as air sac pressure and airflow, may be a general phenomenon in songbirds including the zebra finch. In addition, intrapulmonary chemoreceptors may provide a mechanism that also affects respiratory patterns during song.[34] However, as the above examples illustrate, feedback mechanisms may contribute to song production largely unnoticed once song learning is completed and the respiratory patterns have become stereotyped. Experimental manipulation and developmental studies are required to reveal feedback mechanisms. Their investigation at the level of all peripheral motor systems of song production will be necessary to understand how integration of this complex vocal behavior is achieved centrally.

ACKNOWLEDGMENTS

The research of the authors is supported by grants NIH DC 04390 (F.G.) and NIH DC 05722 (B.G.C.). We thank Phil Zeigler and Peter Marler for their help in improving this chapter and for the opportunity to participate in the symposium.

REFERENCES

1. ZANN, R.A. 1993. Variation in song structure within and among populations of Australian zebra finches. Auk **110:**716–726.
2. ZANN, R.A. 1996. The Zebra Finch. A Synthesis of Field and Laboratory Studies. Oxford University Press. Oxford, UK.
3. SUTHERS, R.A., F. GOLLER & C. PYTTE. 1999. The neuromuscular control of birdsong. Phil. Trans. R. Soc. Lond. B **354:** 927–939.
4. GAUNT, A.S. & S. NOWICKI. 1998. Birdsong: acoustics and physiology revisited. *In* Animal Acoustic Communication. S.L. Hopp, M.J. Owren & C.S. Evans, Eds.: 291–321. Springer-Verlag. Heidelberg.
5. FLETCHER N.H. & A. TARNOPOLSKY. 1999. Acoustics of the avian vocal tract. J. Acoust. Soc. Am. **105:** 35–49.
6. HOESE, W.J., J. PODOS, N.C. BOETTICHER & S. NOWICKI. 2000. Vocal tract function in birdsong production: experimental manipulation of beak movements. J. Exp. Biol. **203:** 1845–1855.
7. WILLIAMS, H. 2001. Choreography of song, dance and beak movements in the zebra finch (*Taeniopygia guttata*). J. Exp. Biol. **204:** 3497–3506.
8. GOLLER F. & O.N. LARSEN. 1997. A new mechanism of sound generation in songbirds. Proc. Natl. Acad. Sci. USA **94:** 14787–14791.
9. GOLLER, F. & O.N. LARSEN. 2002. New perspectives on mechanisms of sound generation in songbirds. J. Comp. Physiol. A **188:** 841–850.
10. FEE, M.S., B. SHRAIMAN, B. PESARAN & P.P. MITRA. 1998. The role of nonlinear dynamics of the syrinx in the vocalizations of a songbird. Nature **395:** 67–71.
11. FEE, M.S. 2002. Measurement of the linear and nonlinear mechanical properties of the oscine syrinx: implications for function. J. Comp. Physiol. A **188:** 829–839.
12. SUTHERS, R.A. & F. GOLLER. 1997. Motor correlates of vocal diversity in songbirds. *In* Current Ornithology, Vol. 14. V. Nolan, Jr., E.D. Ketterson & C.F. Thompson, Eds.: 235–288. Plenum. New York.
13. SUTHERS, R.A. 1999. The motor basis of vocal performance in songbirds. *In* The Design of Animal Communication. M.D. Hauser & M. Konsihi, Eds.: 37–62. MIT Press, Cambridge, MA.
14. NOTTEBOHM, F. 1971. Neural lateralization of vocal control in a passerine bird. I: song. J. Exp. Zool. **177:** 229–262.
15. NOTTEBOHM, F. & M.E. NOTTEBOHM. 1976. Left hypoglossal dominance in the control of canary and white-crowned sparrow song. J. Comp. Physiol. **108:** 171–192.
16. HARTLEY, R.S. & R.A. SUTHERS. 1990. Lateralization of syringeal function during song production in the canary. J. Neurobiol. **21:** 1236–1248.
17. WILLIAMS, H., L.A. CRANE, T.K. HALE, M.A. ESPOSITO & F. NOTTEBOHM. 1992. Right-side dominance for song control in the zebra finch. J. Neurobiol. **23:**1006–1020.
18. FLOODY, O.R. & A.P. ARNOLD. 1997. Song lateralization in the zebra finch. Horm. Behav. **31:** 25–34.
19. SUTHERS, R.A., F. GOLLER & R.S. HARTLEY. 1994. Motor dynamics of song production by mimic thrushes. J. Neurobiol. **25:** 917–936.
20. GOLLER, F. & M. DALEY. 2001. Novel motor gestures for phonation during inspiration enhance the acoustic complexity of birdsong. Proc. R. Soc. Lond. B **268:** 2301–2305.
21. VICARIO, D.S. 1991. Contributions of syringeal muscles to respiration and vocalization in the zebra finch. J. Neurobiol. **22:** 63–73.
22. GOLLER, F. & R.A. SUTHERS. 1996a. The role of syringeal muscles in gating airflow and sound production in singing brown thrashers. J. Neurophysiol. **75:** 867–876.
23. GOLLER, F. & R.A. SUTHERS. 1996b. The role of syringeal muscles in controlling the phonology of bird song. J. Neurophysiol. **76:** 287–300.
24. WILD, J.M., F. GOLLER & R.A. SUTHERS. 1998. Inspiratory muscle activity during bird song. J. Neurobiol. **36:** 441–453.
25. LARSEN O.N. & F. GOLLER. 2002. Direct observation of syringeal muscle function in songbirds and a parrot. J. Exp. Biol. **205:** 25–35.
26. FRANZ, M. & F. GOLLER. 2002. Respiratory units of motor production and song imitation in the zebra finch. J. Neurobiol. **51:** 129–141.

27. CYNX, J. 1990. Experimental determination of a unit of song production in the zebra finch (*Taeniopygia guttata*). J. Comp. Psychol. **104:** 3–10.
28. FEDDE, M.R. 1987. Respiratory muscles. *In* Bird Respiration, Vol. I. T.J. Seller, Ed.: 995–1004. CRC Press. Boca Raton, FL.
29. DALEY, M. & F. GOLLER. 2004. Tracheal length changes during zebra finch song and their possible role in upper vocal tract filtering. J. Neurobiol. **59:** 319–330.
30. NOWICKI, S. & P. MARLER. 1988. How do birds sing? Music Percept. **5:** 391–426.
31. DEICH, J.D., D. HOUBEN & H.P. ZEIGLER. 1985. On-line monitoring of jaw movements in the pigeon. Physiol. Behav. **35:** 307–312.
32. GOLLER, F., M.J. MALLINCKRODT & S.D. TORTI. 2004. Beak gape dynamics during song in the zebra finch. J. Neurobiol. **59:** 289–303.
33. LAJE, R., T. GARDNER & G.B. MINDLIN. 2001. Continuous model for vocal fold oscillations to study the effect of feedback. Phys. Rev. **E64:** 056201.
34. FRANZ, M. & F. GOLLER. 2003. Respiratory patterns and oxygen consumption in singing zebra finches. J. Exp. Biol. **206:** 967–978.
35. LAJE, R. & G.B. MINDLIN. 2002. Neuromuscular control of vocalizations in bird song: a model. Phys. Rev. **E65:** 051921.
36. SUTHERS, R.A. & D. MARGOLIASH. 2002. Motor control of birdsong. Curr. Opin. Neurobiol. **12:** 684–690.
37. YU, A.C. & D. MARGOLIASH. 1996. Temporal hierarchical control of singing in birds. Science **273:** 1871–1875.
38. HAHNLOSER, R.H., A.A. KOZHEVNIKOW & M.S. FEE. 2002. An ultra-sparse code underlies the generation of neural sequences in a songbird. Nature **419:** 65–70.
39. SCHMIDT, M.F. 2003. Pattern of interhemispheric synchronization in HVc during singing correlates with key transitions in the song pattern. J. Neurophysiol. **90:** 3931–3949.
40. NORDEEN, K.W. & E.J. NORDEEN. 1992. Auditory feedback is necessary for the maintenance of stereotyped song in adult zebra finches. Behav. Neural Biol. **57:** 58–66.
41. LEONARDO, A. & M. KONISHI. 1999. Decrystallization of adult birdsong by perturbation of auditory feedback. Nature **399:** 466–470.
42. LOMBARDINO, A. & F. NOTTEBOHM. 2000. Age at deafening affects the stability of learned song in adult male zebra finches. J. Neurosci. **20:** 5054–5064.
43. SUTHERS, R.A., F. GOLLER & J.M WILD. 2002. Somatosensory feedback modulates the respiratory motor program of crystallized birdsong. Proc. Natl. Acad. Sci. USA **99:** 5680–5685.
44. COOPER, B.G. & F. GOLLER. 2004. Multi-modal signals: enhancement and constraint of song by visual display. Science **303:** 544–546.

Neural Mechanisms of Vocal Sequence Generation in the Songbird

MICHALE S. FEE, ALEXAY A. KOZHEVNIKOV, AND
RICHARD H.R. HAHNLOSER[a]

*McGovern Institute for Brain Research, Department of Brain and Cognitive Sciences,
Massachusetts Institute of Technology, Cambridge, Massachusetts 02139, USA*

ABSTRACT: Little is known about the biophysical and neuronal circuit mechanisms underlying the generation and learning of behavioral sequences. Songbirds provide a marvelous animal model in which to study these phenomena. By use of a motorized microdrive to record the activity of single neurons in the singing bird, we are beginning to understand the circuits that generate complex vocal sequences. We describe recent experiments elucidating the role of premotor song-control nucleus HVC in the production of song. We find that HVC neurons projecting to premotor nucleus RA each generate a single burst of spikes at a particular time in the song and may form a sparse representation of temporal order. We incorporate this observation into a working hypothesis for the generation of vocal sequences in the songbird, and examine some implications for song learning.

KEYWORDS: temporal order; premotor nucleus RA; vocal sequence generation; HVC neurons

TEMPORAL SEQUENCES IN THE ORGANIZATION OF BIRDSONG

Temporal structure plays a fundamental role in all aspects of brain function—not only in sensory systems[1-4]—but at a motor and cognitive level as well.[5,6] For example, when we learn the alphabet, we do not learn twenty-six uncorrelated symbols; we really learn a cognitive and motor sequence. Most of us can say the letters of the alphabet in just a few seconds, but only if we say them in one particular order—the order in which we learned them. This ability of the brain to step rapidly through a learned sequence of states underlies not only our ability to say the alphabet, but also our ability to speak, to perform music and athletic feats, and perhaps our ability to think and plan as well. Despite the fundamental importance of temporal order to brain function, little is known about the biophysical and circuit mechanisms that underlie the generation and learning of temporal sequences.

[a]Present affiliation: Institute for Neuroinformatics, UNIZH/ETHZ, Zurich, Switzerland.
Address for correspondence: Michale S. Fee, McGovern Institute for Brain Research, Department of Brain and Cognitive Sciences, Massachusetts Institute of Technology, Cambridge, MA 02139. Voice: 617-324-0173; fax: 617-324-0258.
fee@mit.edu; <http://web.mit.edu/feelab>

Ann. N.Y. Acad. Sci. 1016: 153–170 (2004). © 2004 New York Academy of Sciences.
doi: 10.1196/annals.1298.022

The songbird is a remarkable model system in which to study learned sequence generation. Songbirds, such as the zebra finch, generate complex learned vocal sequences to convey identity and attract mates (see Williams, this volume). The zebra finch sings a repeated song element called a song motif. The motif, typically of 0.5 to 1 s in duration, is composed of 3–7 smaller vocal gestures called song syllables.[7,8]

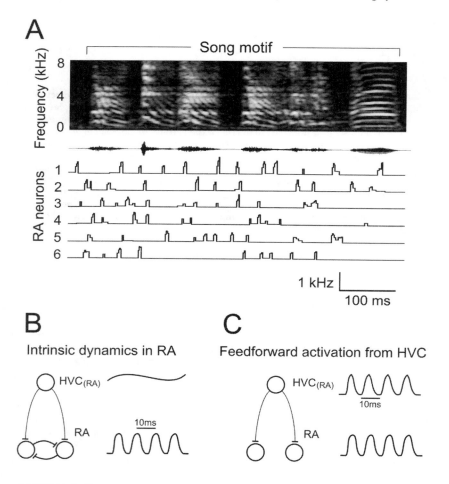

FIGURE 1. Burst sequences in RA of the singing zebra finch and two models of the generation of these sequences. (**A**) Instantaneous firing rate of six RA neurons recorded sequentially in one zebra finch during singing. Each RA neuron generates a complex sequence of roughly 10 brief bursts (~10 ms average duration). The bursts are distributed throughout the song such that on average 12% of RA neurons are active at each time. At top is shown the spectrogram of one song motif, to which neural activities have been aligned. (**B**) A cartoon model of burst sequence generation in RA in which circuitry within nucleus RA generates the short (~10 ms) timescale structure in RA firing patterns. (**C**) A cartoon model of RA sequence generation in which short timescale structure in RA is driven directly from premotor nucleus HVC.

One useful property of zebra finch song, particularly for the study of a motor system, is that the motifs are highly stereotyped. That is, each time the zebra finch sings its song motif, the pattern of acoustic signals may be nearly identical.

The generation of these vocal sequences is under the control of a small number of premotor brain areas. Muscles of the vocal organ, or syrinx, are innervated by motorneurons of the hypoglossal nucleus (nXIIts).[9,10] The motor neurons receive synaptic inputs from a forebrain nucleus RA, which in turn receives a predominant premotor input from another forebrain nucleus HVC[11–13] (see chapters by Suthers and Wild, this volume). In the present chapter, we describe some recent results on the mechanism by which HVC and RA generate the complex sequences of motor commands that produce learned vocal behavior in the songbird.

During singing, RA neurons generate a complex sequence of high-frequency bursts of spikes, the pattern of which is precisely reproduced each time the bird sings a song motif.[14] By recording large numbers of RA neurons in the singing bird, we have recently found that each RA neuron, on average, produces roughly 12 bursts of ~10 ms in duration. In addition, each RA neuron has a fairly unique pattern of bursts. Thus, as a population, RA neurons are active throughout the song vocalization, and at each moment in the song roughly 12% of the RA neuron population is active (FIG. 1A).

How are the complex burst sequences of RA neurons generated? Several recent models of vocal sequence generation have suggested that short-timescale temporal patterning is produced by circuitry within the premotor nucleus RA itself[14–17] (FIG. 1B). In this view, each burst in an RA neuron is perhaps driven by bursts in a temporally preceding group of RA neurons. Alternatively, the bursts patterns of RA neurons may be directly driven by inputs from a brain area afferent to RA, for example, from HVC (FIG. 1C). In this view, each burst in an RA neuron is driven by activity in some population of HVC neurons. Can we distinguish between these two views of sequence generation in RA? This is a central issue we wish to address in this chapter.

How do we discriminate between a model in which the rapidly evolving ~10 ms-long burst patterns of RA neurons result from circuitry within RA, and a model in which this activity is directly driven from HVC? A reasonable approach is to record from HVC neurons that project to RA ($HVC_{(RA)}$ neurons). If RA bursts are driven directly from HVC, one might expect to observe bursts of spikes in $HVC_{(RA)}$ neurons precisely time-locked to bursts in RA and to the song vocalization. In contrast, if $HVC_{(RA)}$ neurons are not involved in driving RA bursts, one might not expect to find precisely time-locked bursting activity in HVC. In fact, this latter view was supported by recordings of HVC neurons in the singing bird that generate rather noisy trains of spikes at a high rate throughout the song vocalization, in striking contrast to the sparse bursting spike patterns of RA neurons.[14]

MODELS OF SEQUENCE GENERATION—EXPERIMENTAL ANALYSIS

To test these alternative hypotheses, we set out to record specifically from the population of HVC neurons that project to RA. HVC contains at least three distinct classes of neurons[18,19,47] (see also Mooney, this volume): neurons projecting to area-X ($HVC_{(X)}$), neurons projecting to RA ($HVC_{(RA)}$), and at least one class of local interneurons ($HVC_{(I)}$). Because we were unable to distinguish these classes of neurons on the basis of their spike waveform, we used antidromic stimulation[20,21] to identify these neurons. By placing bipolar electrodes in RA and in X, we can stimulate the axon terminals of an HVC neuron that projects to either of these brain areas.[22] We found that stimulation in X by a single biphasic pulse (0.2-ms duration) activates $HVC_{(X)}$ neurons and $HVC_{(I)}$ neurons, but not $HVC_{(RA)}$ neurons. Likewise, stimulation in RA activates $HVC_{(RA)}$ neurons and $HVC_{(I)}$ neurons, but not $HVC_{(X)}$ neurons. The projection neurons (of either type) were easily distinguished from interneurons by examining the variability in latency from stimulus to spike response. Projection neurons produced the first spike with a timing jitter less than 50 µs, whereas putative interneurons produced the first spike with a timing jitter more than 500 µs.[b]

Recording single neurons in singing birds poses several technical challenges. First, singing is a natural social behavior and zebra finches will sing only while relatively unrestrained, necessitating the use of a small device, or microdrive, mounted on the head to hold and position electrodes in the brain. The microdrive allows an extracellular recording electrode to be advanced and retracted to isolate the electrical signal from a single neuron; electrode positioning may be accomplished by holding the animal and manually turning a small screw on the microdrive. Unfortunately, handling a zebra finch in order to operate the microdrive greatly reduces the likelihood that the bird will sing once a neuron is isolated and the bird is released. We have solved this problem using a motorized microdrive. This microdrive permits us to remotely and independently position up to three electrodes and has resulted in an increase by a factor of 50 in the per-animal yield of neurons recorded during singing,[23] as compared to results from an earlier nonmotorized version of the microdrive.[24] Once an HVC neuron is isolated using the microdrive and identified using antidromic stimulation, the bird is induced to sing by presenting a female zebra finch. After the bird sings several tens of song motifs, or after the neuron signal is lost, the electrode is advanced until another neuron is isolated and identified. The process can be repeated many times, building up a data set of firing patterns in a single bird.

In carrying out our experiments in HVC of singing birds, we found that antidromic activation is essential not so much to distinguish different HVC neuron types, but to avoid the tremendous selection bias associated with differences in spontaneous firing rates in the different classes of HVC neurons. $HVC_{(I)}$ neurons have

---

[b]Antidromic responses in HVC were characterized in two stages: First, we characterized the distribution of latencies and latency variability of each HVC neuron type to stimulation in RA and X in awake and sleeping birds. The responses were found to fall into four clear categories based on (1) site of stimulation (RA or X) and (2) latency variability (< 50 µs or > 500 µs). Second, in a separate set of experiments, we used the spike collision test to verify the identity of a subset of neurons in each category.[21] These experiments were done in sleeping birds, in which all HVC neuron types exhibit significant spontaneous rates. By this test, all neurons responding to RA stimulation with a latency variability < 50 µs exhibited spike collision; all neurons responding to X stimulation with a latency variability < 50 µs exhibited spike collision; finally, no putative interneurons (those neurons responding to RA or X stimulation with latency variability > 500 µs) exhibited spike collision. We concluded that identification on the basis of stimulation site (RA or X) and latency variability is unambiguous. All neurons recorded in the singing bird were identified solely on the basis of stimulation site and latency variability. Spike collision tests were not carried out in these recordings because of the extremely low rates of spontaneous activity of projection neurons in the awake adult bird.

relatively high spontaneous rates in the awake nonsinging bird (2–40 Hz). In contrast, HVC projection neurons have very low rates of spontaneous activity: $HVC_{(X)}$ neurons generate spontaneous spikes at <1 Hz, and we have not yet observed a spontaneous spike in an $HVC_{(RA)}$ neuron in an awake adult zebra finch. As a result, by simply searching for neurons in HVC with an extracellular recording electrode, one is most likely to find an interneuron. For the same reason, $HVC_{(RA)}$ neurons cannot be found by searching for spontaneous activity in an awake nonsinging bird (the birds do not sing often enough to search for these neurons during singing). We have

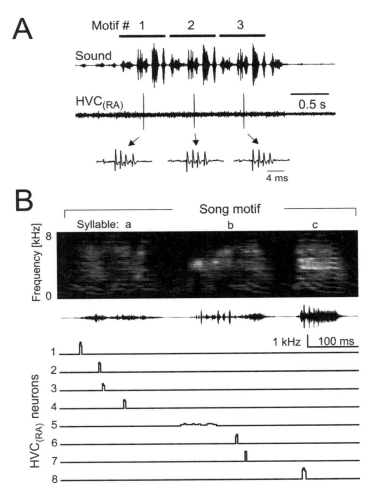

FIGURE 2. Spike activity of identified HVC neurons in the singing zebra finch. (**A**) Extracellular recording of one antidromically identified RA-projecting HVC neuron during three renditions of the song motif. (**B**) Instantaneous firing rate of 8 RA-projecting HVC neurons recorded in the same bird. These neurons generated a single burst of high-frequency firing, each at a different time in the song.

avoided this source of selection bias by searching for antidromically activated spikes during ongoing stimulation (1 Hz) in RA and/or X. Even with this approach, $HVC_{(RA)}$ neurons are still difficult to isolate because of their small size; we find them at a rate far lower than expected from their relative abundance (50–80% of the HVC neuronal population[25]).

Using antidromic identification, we were able to record from RA-projecting neurons during singing and to test our hypotheses as to the origin of the complex burst sequences in RA. FIGURE 2A shows the extracellular signal from an isolated $HVC_{(RA)}$ neuron during three sequential song motifs. Most $HVC_{(RA)}$ neurons generated a single burst of 3–4 spikes during each song motif.[22] The firing rate during bursts of song-related $HVC_{(RA)}$ neurons was 680 ± 138 Hz (not including one outlier that generated a 50- Hz burst, see FIG. 2B). The bursts generated by a single neuron were highly stereotyped across song motifs, as determined from the alignment of burst onset to vocal output (0.66 ms rms jitter), the number of spikes per burst (± 1), and interspike intervals within a burst (0.13 ms rms jitter).

Most $HVC_{(RA)}$ neurons were active during vocalizations—either songs or calls. Roughly 16% (3/18) of vocal-related $HVC_{(RA)}$ neurons burst during calls, but not during song. Another 11% (2/18) of vocal-related neurons burst during introductory notes, but not during the song motif. An additional seven units were identified by antidromic stimulation as $HVC_{(RA)}$ neurons, but these were not spontaneously active, nor were they active during singing nor during any calls that could be elicited. Because spikes were only observed from these neurons during antidromic stimulation, there is less certainty about the classification of these units. However, if these are assumed to be $HVC_{(RA)}$ neurons, then up to half of antidromically activated $HVC_{(RA)}$ neurons in our data set were not active during song motifs, consistent with previous observations that only half of $HVC_{(RA)}$ neurons showed elevated ZENK expression during singing.[26]

To display the behavior of the population of $HVC_{(RA)}$ neurons, we show the firing patterns of all song-related $HVC_{(RA)}$ neurons aligned to the song. Because the song is highly stereotyped, we chose one song motif as a template and lined up all motifs (sung by the same bird) to the template motif; alignment can be done with submillisecond timing precision. Because the song and the neural signals were recorded simultaneously, we can display the firing patterns of all neurons recorded in the same bird, aligned to the template motif (FIG. 2B). All $HVC_{(RA)}$ neurons recorded in this bird burst at different times in the song, with no apparent relation to syllable onsets or offsets.

It is clear that $HVC_{(RA)}$ neurons generate sparse patterns of bursts precisely time-locked to the song vocalization. How does this observation relate to our two initial hypotheses about the generation in burst sequences in RA? As we have argued above, the presence of precisely song-locked bursts in $HVC_{(RA)}$ neurons is consistent with the view that bursts in RA neurons are directly driven by inputs from HVC. In fact, our observations suggest an interesting possible model for the generation of RA burst sequences. We hypothesize that at each moment in the song a small ensemble of $HVC_{(RA)}$ is active. We further hypothesize that the effect of a burst of activity in a population of $HVC_{(RA)}$ neurons is to drive a single burst of activity in an ensemble of RA neurons with a short latency (~4.5 ms) and a short duration (~10 ms). Thus, at each moment in the song, the ensemble of active RA neurons is driven by a small subpopulation of $HVC_{(RA)}$ neurons. Our working hypothesis for the generation of RA burst sequences is summarized in FIGURE 3A.

In the framework of this model, we can estimate the number of $HVC_{(RA)}$ neurons coactive at each time in the song. A typical motif duration is (roughly speaking) 600 ms and the average burst duration of $HVC_{(RA)}$ neurons is 6 ms. Each song-related $HVC_{(RA)}$ neuron is therefore active for ~1% of the duration of the motif. Assuming that song-related $HVC_{(RA)}$ neurons are active at random times, uniformly and independently distributed across the motif, then on average 1% of song-related $HVC_{(RA)}$ neurons should be coactive at any given time. Thus, of the total ~40,000 $HVC_{(RA)}$

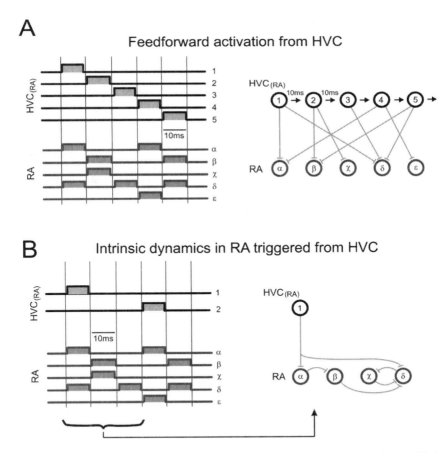

FIGURE 3. Two possible models for RA burst sequence generation consistent with the firing patterns of RA-projecting HVC neurons. (**A**) At each time in the sequence, an ensemble of HVC neurons activates an ensemble of RA neurons to which it is synaptically connected. Conversely, each burst in RA is driven by a synaptically connected ensemble of HVC neurons. (**B**) Bursts in HVC trigger short self-propagating sequences in the RA circuitry.

neurons in each hemisphere,[25] of which ~20,000 may be song-related, we estimate that ~200 $HVC_{(RA)}$ neurons are coactive at each moment in the song motif.

The hypothesis that a subpopulation of $HVC_{(RA)}$ neurons is active at each moment in the song motif is based on our previous finding that, at any time in the song, roughly 10% of RA neurons are active (Leonardo and Fee, unpublished data). However, based solely on our recordings of $HVC_{(RA)}$ neurons in the singing bird, we cannot exclude the possibility that the population of $HVC_{(RA)}$ neurons is active at only a few discrete times in the motif, each time triggering some sequence-generating circuitry intrinsic to RA (FIG. 3B). We were not able to record from enough $HVC_{(RA)}$ neurons in a single bird to demonstrate that there is at least one of these neurons active at each moment in the song. (Given the 6-ms burst width of $HVC_{(RA)}$ neurons, this would require many $HVC_{(RA)}$ neurons to be recorded in the same animal.) How then is it possible to discriminate between the two different models shown in FIGURE 3?

The question is essentially one of causality: Is every burst (in a coactive ensemble of neurons) in RA driven by an immediately preceding burst in a population of $HVC_{(RA)}$ neurons? To address the issue of causality between HVC and RA requires recording simultaneously in these brain areas and manipulating these circuits to tease apart the role of both the intrinsic circuitry in RA and the input to RA. Unfortunately, these are very difficult experiments, particularly in an unrestrained singing bird. Fortunately, there is an alternative approach—to use the sleeping bird.

It has recently been shown that when a zebra finch sleeps, neurons in nucleus RA generate patterns of bursts.[27] The sleep-related patterns of an individual RA neuron can be compared to the burst patterns generated by the same neuron during singing. Remarkably, the burst patterns observed during sleep can be nearly identical to those observed during singing, suggesting that during sleep the motor pathway can "replay" the patterns it generates for singing (FIG. 4A). Such replay of neural activity patterns is reminiscent of that seen in rat hippocampus during sleep after the animal explores a novel environment, and may be involved in learning—specifically in the transfer of short-term memories into long-term memories.[28] The significance of sleep replay in song learning is still unresolved, but we have used the phenomenon of sleep replay as a sort of "fictive singing" (i.e., motor output without movement[29]) to study the circuitry that underlies the generation of burst sequences.

To address the generative mechanism of RA burst sequences, we have performed paired recordings from $HVC_{(RA)}$ neurons and from RA neurons in the sleeping bird. The $HVC_{(RA)}$ neurons burst only rarely during sleep, roughly once every 18 s. (Bursts were defined as events where the instantaneous firing rate continuously exceeds 100 Hz). In contrast, RA neurons exhibited ongoing dense patterns of bursting, on average one burst every 1.2 s. Interestingly, the ratio of burst densities in RA neurons and $HVC_{(RA)}$ neurons during sleep was roughly the same as during singing. If RA sequences are driven by HVC, then by aligning the RA neuron activity to the bursts of the simultaneously recorded $HVC_{(RA)}$ neuron, we should expect to see a coherent pattern. In fact, for most RA-$HVC_{(RA)}$ neuron pairs, the RA neurons exhibited a statistically significant pattern of bursts aligned to the $HVC_{(RA)}$ neuron burst (FIG. 4B). The RA burst sequences often extended over a range of several hundred milliseconds before and after an $HVC_{(RA)}$ burst.

Do $HVC_{(RA)}$ neurons also burst sequentially during sleep? Simultaneous recordings of pairs of $HVC_{(RA)}$ neurons in the sleeping bird showed this to be the case in

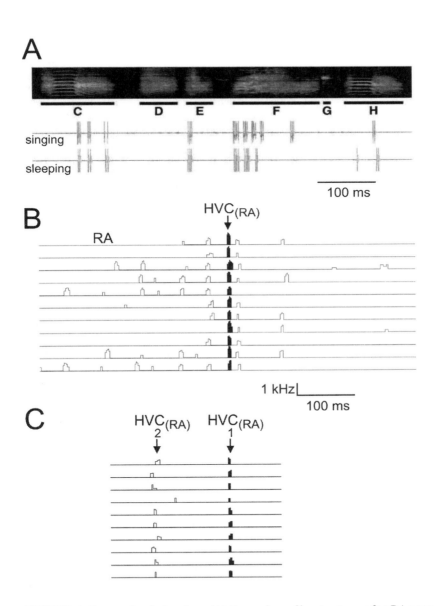

FIGURE 4. Song replay during sleep. (**A**) Comparison of burst patterns of an RA neuron during singing (*top trace*) with a burst pattern during sleep (*bottom trace*). Adapted from Dave and Margoliash,[27] with permission. Burst patterns during sleep can closely resemble burst patterns during singing. (**B**) Simultaneous extracellular recording from an HVC$_{(RA)}$ neuron (*filled trace*) and an RA neuron (*empty trace*) during sleep. Plotted is the instantaneous firing rate of the RA neuron aligned to the onset of the sparse bursts of the HVC$_{(RA)}$ neuron. (**C**) Simultaneous recording of two sequentially-bursting HVC$_{(RA)}$ neurons, during sleep.

about one-third of recorded pairs (FIG. 4C). Thus, during sleep, just as during singing, RA neurons generate complex sequences of bursts that are temporally locked to sparse sequences in HVC.

In contrast to $HVC_{(RA)}$ neurons, HVC interneurons ($HVC_{(I)}$) burst densely during sleep and were highly synchronized to each other. Simultaneous recordings of $HVC_{(I)}$ neuron pairs showed that on average 74% of the bursts in one neuron were synchronized with a burst in the other neuron (within a 10-ms window). Similarly, paired recordings of $HVC_{(RA)}$ and $HVC_{(I)}$ neurons showed that on average 61% of bursts in an $HVC_{(RA)}$ neuron were synchronized with a burst in the $HVC_{(I)}$ neuron. Thus, a single $HVC_{(I)}$ neuron can serve as a "read-out" of activity in the population of $HVC_{(RA)}$ neurons.

Let us now return to the question of whether each step of the RA burst sequence is driven directly from HVC. There is one feature that clearly differentiates the two models in FIGURE 3. If activity in HVC drives every burst in RA (FIG. 3A), then every burst in RA should be immediately preceded by a burst of activity in HVC. If, on the other hand, HVC triggers an autonomous sequence in RA, then a large proportion of RA bursts will not be immediately preceded by a burst in HVC (FIG. 3B). Is there a way to estimate the fraction of RA sleep bursts that are preceded (by a small latency) by a burst in the population of $HVC_{(RA)}$ neurons?

Given the sparseness of $HVC_{(RA)}$ bursts, it would seem that one would have to record from many $HVC_{(RA)}$ neurons to estimate this fraction. However, because a single $HVC_{(I)}$ neuron can serve as a read-out of activity in the population of $HVC_{(RA)}$ neurons, we can answer this question by examining the relation between RA bursts and $HVC_{(I)}$ bursts. Simultaneous recordings of RA neurons and $HVC_{(I)}$ neurons showed that bursts in the RA neuron were preceded with high probability by a burst in the $HVC_{(I)}$ neuron (FIG. 5A). The probability that an $HVC_{(I)}$ burst fell within a window 0 ms to 10 ms preceding an RA neuron burst was on average 0.58 for all RA-$HVC_{(I)}$ pairs recorded (35 pairs). This number is highly significant because the probability that an $HVC_{(I)}$ burst fell in any random 10-ms window was only 0.05 (FIG. 5C). Because on average 58% of RA bursts were preceded by an HVC interneuron burst, and 61% of $HVC_{(RA)}$ bursts were synchronized with an HVC interneuron burst, our results are consistent with the possibility that every RA burst is driven by $HVC_{(RA)}$ neurons. In other words, if every RA burst is driven from HVC, it is expected that an $HVC_{(I)}$ neuron will not be active before roughly 40% of bursts in an RA neuron, because this $HVC_{(I)}$ neuron fails to read-out ~40% of the $HVC_{(RA)}$ bursts.

Of course, the analysis given here is correlative and cannot completely exclude the unlikely possibility that burst sequences in $HVC_{(I)}$ neurons and burst sequences in RA neurons are each generated by independent, but precisely timed, circuitry within HVC and RA. In this way, the strong correlation between $HVC_{(I)}$ bursts and RA bursts would not result from a causal link between $HVC_{(RA)}$ and RA neurons. Strong synchrony in HVC and RA could in principle also be produced by common drive from another brain area. However, there are no known inputs common to HVC and RA likely to produce such correlations.

Our observations suggest that, during sleep, the large majority of sleep-replay bursts in RA are directly driven by immediately preceding bursts in a subpopulation of $HVC_{(RA)}$ neurons, as depicted in FIGURE 3A. Of course, we cannot naively assume that the same mechanisms are operating in the singing bird. In particular, we cannot yet rule out the possibility that RA burst sequences in the singing bird may be generated largely by circuitry intrinsic to RA, and that this circuitry is simply being "tickled" into action (i.e., raised above some threshold level) by inputs from HVC. However, given the similarity of sleep-related and singing-related burst sequences in both HVC and RA, and the strongly bursting nature of HVC inputs to RA, the simplest explanation is that burst sequences in RA, during sleep and singing, are driven by direct feedforward input from HVC.

What is the role of the recurrent excitatory and inhibitory connections observed within RA? Although no recurrent excitatory EPSPs have been observed between pairs of RA projection neurons, strong inhibitory interactions within RA have been demonstrated.[30] While our observations suggest that, at least during sleep, RA burst sequences are driven from HVC, recurrent connections in RA could still play an important role in shaping the patterns of RA activity. For example, inhibition could temporally or spatially sharpen RA activity patterns. The role of recurrent circuitry

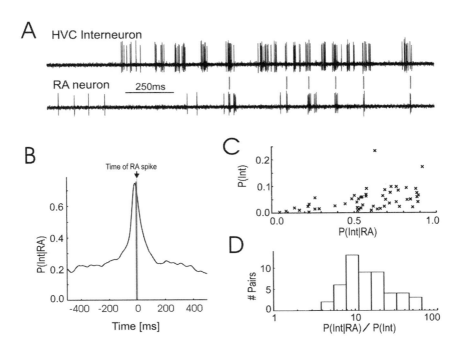

FIGURE 5. During sleep, most bursts in RA are preceded by bursts in HVC interneurons. (**A**) Simultaneous recording from an RA neuron and an HVC interneuron during sleep. (**B**) Probability as a function of time that the HVC interneuron generated a spike relative to the time at which the RA neuron spiked, calculated for the neuron pair in **A**. (**C**) Probability that the HVC interneuron generated a spike in a window 0–10 ms preceding the RA spike, P(Int|RA) (x-axis) versus the probability that the HVC interneuron generated a spike in any random time window, P(Int), for all HVC$_{(I)}$–RA pairs recorded. Each point represents a different pair. (**D**) Distribution of probability ratios P(Int|RA)/P(Int) over all the neuron pairs. The ratio represents how much more likely the HVC interneuron was to spike, given the presence of a following RA spike.

in RA could be addressed experimentally in the sleeping bird by comparing intracellular recordings of subthreshold patterns of synaptic input to an RA neuron before and during the suppression of recurrent circuitry in RA with GABA injection.

RA EFFERENCE AND THE GENERATION OF MOTOR SEQUENCES DURING SINGING

Let us turn now from the origin of burst patterns in RA, to the effect of RA bursts in the downstream motor pathway. What is the basic unit of signaling from RA neurons to brainstem vocal nuclei? During singing, RA neurons generate exquisitely stereotyped bursts. That is, the intervals between spikes within a given burst can be reproduced with less than 50 µs jitter each time the bird sings the song motif.[14] The spike timing precision in RA has led to the suggestion that RA forms a temporal code for song; that is, the vocal output is specified by the precise timing of individual spikes within the bursts of one or more RA neurons [31]. We consider the simpler hypothesis that RA neurons converge onto downstream targets, such as brainstem motor neurons, in which motor control signals are derived from a weighted sum of synaptic currents from RA neurons. In this view, the precise timing of RA spikes could play a role in reducing motif-to-motif variability in motor output, but would not constitute a temporal code for motor output, in the usual sense of the term. The precise spike timing in RA may be simply a consequence of the mechanism by which RA bursts are generated, i.e., that they are directly driven by highly stereotyped bursts in $HVC_{(RA)}$ neurons. We may speculate as to why $HVC_{(RA)}$ neurons generate highly stereotyped bursts in the first place. One possibility is that precisely timed spikes within $HVC_{(RA)}$ bursts reflect the biophysical mechanisms involved in the generation of the precisely timed temporal sequences observed in HVC. In other words, the stereotypy of bursts of RA and $HVC_{(RA)}$ neurons is related, not to a specialized neural code, but to the demands of producing a stereotyped and precisely timed motor behavior.

Another question that naturally arises is that of the timescale on which RA bursts affect vocal output. Evidence that RA activity has a brief transient effect on vocal output is provided by experiments to measure the latency and duration of vocal perturbations induced by brief electrical stimulation in RA (see also ref. 32). We carried out preliminary measurements in two birds in which bipolar stimulating electrodes were previously implanted in RA for antidromic identification of $HVC_{(RA)}$ neurons. The song of each of these birds contained a long harmonic stack syllable (>50-ms duration). A computer was used to trigger a brief (0.2 ms) electrical stimulation in RA 10 ms after the onset of the harmonic stack syllable. Recordings of the song vocalization show that RA stimulation induced a brief increase in the pitch of the vocalization, with a duration (full width at half-maximum) of ~15 ms and a latency of ~15 ms between the stimulation and the peak of the perturbation (FIG. 6). These results suggest that RA activity is integrated on a short timescale by downstream motor circuitry and that it has a similarly brief effect on vocal output.

At present, little is known about the role of brainstem motor and respiratory circuits downstream from RA. However, a reasonable starting point for thinking about motor control in the songbird is that each RA neuron contributes transiently with some effective weight to the activity of the syringeal muscles,[17] as has also been pro-

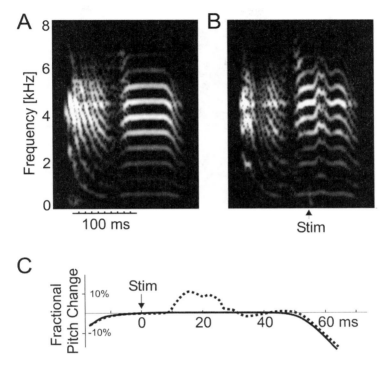

FIGURE 6. Effect of brief electrical stimulation in RA during singing. (**A**) Zebra finch song syllable containing a harmonic stack. (**B**) A single 0.2-ms pulse (~300 µA) in RA produces a brief transient perturbation in the vocal output. (**C**) Pitch of stimulated song syllable (*dashed*) and unstimulated song syllable (*solid*). Note the transient pitch change with 15-ms latency to the peak and 15-ms duration (full width at half-maximum deviation).

posed for cortical control of arm movement in primates.[33] The total force produced by a muscle, including that required to overcome inertia, damping, and spring forces, can be expressed as a linear weighted sum of instantaneous activities of higher premotor neurons.[34] (Consistent with this approach, recent recordings from syringeal motor neurons reveal a linear firing rate change in response to somatic current injection.[35]) Of course, syringeal muscle forces are related in a complex manner to vocal output,[36–38] but in further discussion here we will neglect muscle dynamics (i.e., inertia, and damping) and syringeal dynamics, and will adopt the simplified view that vocal acoustic parameters such as pitch are given directly by the summed weighted contributions of RA neuron activity.

SIMPLE HYPOTHESIS FOR SONG GENERATION AND LEARNING

We can now put our picture of sequence generation in RA into a working hypothesis of vocal sequence generation and learning (FIG. 7): that is, HVC$_{(RA)}$ neurons are

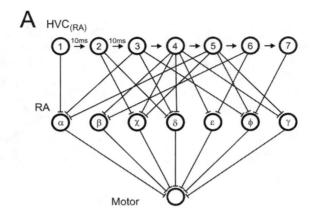

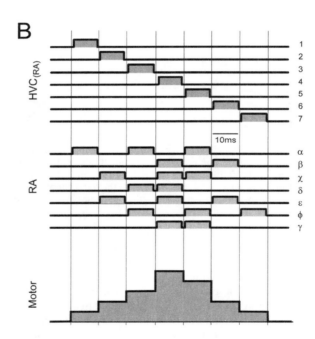

FIGURE 7. Working hypothesis of vocal sequence generation in the zebra finch song control system. (**A**) $HVC_{(RA)}$ neurons burst at a single time in the song motif. At each time in the song, a coactive population of ~200 $HVC_{(RA)}$ neurons activates ~10% of RA neurons, which in turn converge (through motor neurons) to produce a motor control signal (e.g., muscle activation). (**B**) Representation of firing rate of each population of neurons during a brief sequence (~70-ms duration, corresponding roughly to a short song syllable). NOTE: The alignment of burst onsets and offsets is only for artistic clarity; at present we have no conclusive evidence for such alignment.

each active at only one particular moment in the song motif. Furthermore, each moment in the song motif is associated with a unique population of coactive $HVC_{(RA)}$ neurons. These neurons drive a brief (~10 ms) burst of activity in a small fraction (~10%) of RA neurons. The ensemble of neurons activated is determined by the pattern of synaptic connections from HVC to RA. In this model, the effect of RA on vocal output is of short duration and is produced by the convergence of RA neurons, with a set of fixed synaptic weights, onto a single neuron representing motor output.[17] One might think of this motor output as controlling a particular vocal parameter, such as pitch. The sequence of motor, or muscle, configurations is thus driven at each time step by activity in $HVC_{(RA)}$ neurons, where both the activity of $HVC_{(RA)}$ neurons and their effects downstream are highly localized in time.

How would song learning proceed in the model presented above? The convergence of the anterior forebrain pathway, a circuit necessary for song learning and maintenance,[39–41] onto RA in the song motor-control pathway, suggests that song learning is mediated by plasticity in RA, either in the recurrent synaptic connections within RA or in the input to RA.[42,43] In our model, the pattern of activity in RA, and thus the vocal output, is determined by the pattern of $HVC_{(RA)}$-to-RA synapses; in this view, vocal learning is controlled by synaptic plasticity at these synapses. Song learning is then simply the process of modulating the effective connectivity from sparsely active HVC neurons to downstream motor neurons such that, at each moment, the correct motor output is produced: RA serves as a switchboard on which $HVC_{(RA)}$ neurons are wired up to the correct motor output.

At present it is unclear when in the ontogeny of the zebra finch sparse $HVC_{(RA)}$ sequences arise. If sensorimotor learning is the process of mapping the sparse sequence in $HVC_{(RA)}$ to motor output, it seems plausible that the sparse $HVC_{(RA)}$ sequence develops before the onset of sensorimotor learning. Learning the mapping from HVC to RA would be most efficiently carried out after the sparse HVC sequence is established. Note that, in principle, $HVC_{(RA)}$ sequences are universal; that is, for every zebra finch song of a given length, $HVC_{(RA)}$ activity can be plotted as an diagonal band equivalent to that in FIGURE 7B, regardless of the vocal content of the song. Thus, auditory/vocal experience may not be necessary in the development of sparse sequences in HVC, consistent with the possibility that HVC sequences form spontaneously before the developmental onset of sensorimotor learning.

We have hypothesized that each unique 5–10-ms interval in the zebra finch vocal repertoire is associated, one-to-one, with a small ensemble of coactive $HVC_{(RA)}$ neurons. Our hypothesis implies that the number of coactive $HVC_{(RA)}$ ensembles may scale with total duration of unique song repertoire of the bird. In other words, if we can think of each coactive $HVC_{(RA)}$ ensemble as a piece of "tape" in the bird's "tape player," then birds with a longer repertoire should have more tape. If the number of $HVC_{(RA)}$ neurons in each coactive ensemble (i.e., ~200 neurons in the zebra finch) is roughly constant across birds, and the burst duration of each ensemble is roughly constant across birds, then we would expect the number of $HVC_{(RA)}$ neurons to vary linearly with the duration of the unique vocal repertoire. In fact, HVC volume, and thus possibly the number of $HVC_{(RA)}$ neurons, correlates positively with repertoire size and phrase duration in zebra finches.[44] Likewise, large differences in HVC volume between male and female songbirds are reflected in large differences in song repertoire size, within individual songbird species.[45] Additionally, it has been found that across many species of songbirds, total song repertoire size is correlated with HVC volume (see DeVoogd, this volume).[46] Note that repertoire size is typically quantified as the number of different song types produced by an individual. It would be interesting to compare directly across many species the number of $HVC_{(RA)}$ neurons with the repertoire duration, as defined by the total duration of all unique vocal elements produced by an individual. Deviations from a linear relation could indicate that, in some birds, $HVC_{(RA)}$ neurons are shared across different parts of the vocal repertoire, or could suggest interspecies variations in the $HVC_{(RA)}$ burst duration, or variations in the number of neurons within coactive $HVC_{(RA)}$ ensembles.

The sparse representation of temporal order in HVC has interesting implications for vocal learning. For example, if there is an error in the vocal output at one particular time in the song, synaptic outputs need only be modified for the subpopulation of the $HVC_{(RA)}$ neurons that were active at that time (or preceding by synaptic and axonal latency of ~20 ms). If $HVC_{(RA)}$ neurons were active multiple times in the song, then correcting an error at one time would introduce errors at other times in the song. Because $HVC_{(RA)}$ neurons are active very sparsely, the learning process at different times becomes uncoupled, thus allowing learning to occur at a faster rate. Recent theoretical work confirms that the time required to learn motor sequences in simple feedforward network models of HVC and RA is minimized when $HVC_{(RA)}$ neurons burst exactly once per song motif.[48] Thus, the sparse code observed in HVC hints at possible evolutionary pressures for optimizing the premotor neural machinery for the task of song learning.

Our observations also raise the question of how the sparse $HVC_{(RA)}$ sequences are generated. Using the same logic we applied to the origin of RA burst sequences (FIG. 1B and C), we can ask whether sparse sequences arise from circuitry intrinsic to HVC, or whether they are directly driven from nuclei that project to HVC, such as nucleus Interface (NIf) or nucleus Uvaeformis (Uva). We expect that a combination of the techniques described, in both the singing and sleeping bird, will continue to be useful as we pursue an understanding of the circuits that underlie the generation and learning of temporal sequences in the brain.

ACKNOWLEDGMENTS

Recordings of RA neurons in the singing bird were carried out in collaboration with A. Leonardo. The work described here was supported in part by the National Science Foundation.

REFERENCES

1. CARR, C.E. 1993. Processing of temporal information in the brain. Annu. Rev. Neurosci. **16:** 223–243.
2. CASSEDAY, J.H., D. EHRLICH & E. COVEY. 1994. Neural tuning for sound duration: role of inhibitory mechanisms in the inferior colliculus. Science **264:** 847–850.
3. BUONOMANO, D.V. 2000. Decoding temporal information: a model based on short-term synaptic plasticity. J. Neurosci. **20:** 1129–1141.
4. TALLAL, P. 1994. *In* Temporal Coding in the Brain. G. Buzsaki, R. Llinas, W. Singer, A. Berthoz & Y. Christen, Eds.: 291–299. Springer. Berlin.
5. IVRY, R. 1996. The representation of temporal information in perception and motor control. Curr. Opin. Neurobiol. **6:** 851–857.

6. GALLISTEL, C.R. 1980. The Organization of Action: A New Synthesis. Lawrence Erlbaum Associates. Hillsdale, NJ.
7. IMMELMANN, K. 1969. *In* Bird Vocalizations. R.A. Hinde, Ed.: 61–74. Cambridge University Press. New York.
8. PRICE, P.H. 1979. Developmental determinants of structure in zebra finch song. J. Comp. Physiol. Psychol. **93:** 268–277.
9. VICARIO, D.S. & F. NOTTEBOHM. 1988. Organization of the zebra finch song control system: I. Representation of syringeal muscles in the hypoglossal nucleus. J. Comp. Neurol. **271:** 346–354.
10. WILD, J.M. 1993. Descending projections of the songbird nucleus Robustus archistriatalis. J. Comp. Neurol. **338:** 225–241.
11. NOTTEBOHM, F., D.B. KELLEY & J.A. PATON. 1982. Connections of vocal control nuclei in the canary telencephalon. J. Comp. Neurol. **207:** 344–357.
12. WILD, J.M. 1997. Neural pathways for the control of birdsong production. J. Neurobiol. **33:** 653–670.
13. VICARIO, D.S. 1991. Organization of the zebra finch song control system: II. Functional organization of outputs from nucleus Robustus archistriatalis. J. Comp. Neurol. **309:** 486–494.
14. YU, A.C. & D. MARGOLIASH. 1996. Temporal hierarchical control of singing in birds. Science **273:** 1871–1875.
15. LAJE, R. & G.B. MINDLIN. 2002. Diversity within a birdsong. Phys. Rev. Lett. **89:** 288102.
16. TROYER, T.W. & A.J. DOUPE. 2000. An associational model of birdsong sensorimotor learning. I. Efference copy and the learning of song syllables. J. Neurophysiol. **84:** 1204–1223.
17. DOYA, K. & T.J. SEJNOWSKI. 1998. *In* Central Auditory Processing and Neural Modeling. P.W.F. Poon & J.F. Brugge, Eds.: 77–88. Plenum. New York.
18. DUTAR, P., H.M. VU & D.J. PERKEL. 1998. Multiple cell types distinguished by physiological, pharmacological, and anatomic properties in nucleus HVc of the adult zebra finch. J. Neurophysiol. **80:** 1828–1838.
19. MOONEY, R. 2000. Different subthreshold mechanisms underlie song selectivity in identified HVc neurons of the zebra finch. J. Neurosci. **201:** 5420–5436.
20. SWADLOW, H. 1998. Neocortical efferent neurons with very slowly conducting axons: strategies for reliable antidromic identification. J. Neurosci. Methods **79:** 131–141.
21. FULLER, J.H. & J.D. SCHLAG. 1976. Determination of antidromic activation by the collision test: problems of interpretation. Brain Res. **112:** 283–298.
22. HAHNLOSER, R.H.R., A.A. KOZHEVNIKOV & M.S. FEE. 2002. An ultra-sparse code underlies the generation of neural sequences in a songbird. Nature **419:** 65–70.
23. FEE, M.S. & A. LEONARDO. 2001. Miniature motorized microdrive and commutator system for chronic neural recordings in small animals. J. Neurosci. Methods **112:** 83–94.
24. VENKATACHALAM, S., M.S. FEE & D. KLEINFELD. 1999. Ultra-miniature headstage with 6-channel drive and vacuum-assisted microwire implantation for chronic recording from the neocortex. J. Neurosci. Methods **90:** 37–46.
25. WANG, N., P. HURLEY, C. PYTTE & J.R. KIRN. 2002. Vocal control neuron incorporation decreases with age in the adult zebra finch. J. Neurosci. **22:** 10864–10870.
26. JARVIS, E.D., C. SCHARFF, M.R. GROSSMAN, *et al.* 1998. For whom the bird sings: context-dependent gene expression. Neuron **21:** 775–788.
27. DAVE, A.S. & D. MARGOLIASH. 2000. Song replay during sleep and computational rules for sensorimotor vocal learning. Science **290:** 812–816.
28. LOUIE, K. & M.A. WILSON. 2001. Temporally structured replay of awake hippocampal ensemble activity during rapid eye movement sleep. Neuron **29:** 145–156.
29. WALLEN, P., S. GRILLNER, J.L. FELDMAN & S. BERGELT. 1985. Dorsal and ventral myotome motoneurons and their input during fictive locomotion in lamprey. J. Neurosci. **5:** 654–661.
30. SPIRO, J.E., M.B. DALVA & R. MOONEY. 1999. Long-range inhibition within the zebra finch song nucleus RA can coordinate the firing of multiple projection neurons. J. Neurophysiol. **81:** 3007–3020.

31. CHI, Z. & D. MARGOLIASH. 2001. Temporal precision and temporal drift in brain and behavior of zebra finch song. Neuron **32:** 899–910.
32. VU, E.T., M.E. MAZUREK & Y. KUO. 1994. Identification of a forebrain motor programming network for the learned song of zebra finches. J. Neurosci. **14:** 6924–6934.
33. FETZ, E.E. & P.D. CHENEY. 1980. Postspike facilitation of forelimb muscle activity by primate corticomotoneuronal cells. J. Neurophysiol. **44:** 751–772.
34. TODOROV, E. 2000. Direct cortical control of muscle activation in voluntary arm movements: a model. Nat. Neurosci. **3:** 391–398.
35. STURDY, C.B., J.M. WILD & R. MOONEY. 2003. Respiratory and telencephalic modulation of vocal motor neurons in the zebra finch. J. Neurosci. **23:** 1072–1086.
36. SUTHERS, R.A., F. GOLLER & C. PYTTE. 1999. The neuromuscular control of birdsong. Philos. Trans. R. Soc. Lond. B Biol. Sci. **354:** 927–939.
37. FEE, M.S., B. SHRAIMAN, B. PESARAN & P.P. MITRA. 1998. The role of nonlinear dynamics of the syrinx in the vocalizations of a songbird. Nature **395:** 67–71.
38. GARDNER, T., G. CECCHI, M. MAGNASCO, *et al.* 2001. Simple gestures for birdsongs. Phys. Rev. Lett. **87:** 208101.
39. BOTTJER, S.W., E.A. MIESNER & A.P. ARNOLD. 1984. Forebrain lesions disrupt development but not maintenance of song in passerine birds. Science **224:** 901–903.
40. BOTTJER, S.W., K.A. HALSEMA, S.A. BROWN & E.A. MIESNER. 1989. Axonal connections of a forebrain nucleus involved with vocal learning in zebra finches. J. Comp. Neurol. **279:** 312–326.
41. BRAINARD, M.S. & A.J. DOUPE. 2000. Interruption of a basal ganglia-forebrain circuit prevents plasticity of learned vocalizations. Nature **404:** 762–766.
42. STARK, L.L. & D.J. PERKEL. 1999. Two-stage, input-specific synaptic maturation in a nucleus essential for vocal production in the zebra finch. J. Neurosci. **19:** 9107–9116.
43. MOONEY, R. 1992. Synaptic basis for developmental plasticity in a birdsong nucleus. J. Neurosci. **12:** 2464–2477.
44. AIREY, D.C. & T.J. DEVOOGD. 2000. Greater song complexity is associated with augmented song system anatomy in zebra finches. Neuroreport **11:** 2339–2344.
45. BRENOWITZ, E.A. 1997. Comparative approaches to the avian song system. J. Neurobiol. **33:** 517–531.
46. DEVOOGD, T.J., J.R. KREBS, S.D. HEALY & A. PURVIS. 1993. Relations between song repertoire size and the volume of brain nuclei related to song: comparative evolutionary analyses amongst oscine birds. Proc. R. Soc. Lond. B **254:** 75–82.
47. KUBOTA, M. & I. TANIGUCHI. 1998. Electrophysiological characteristics of classes of neurons in HVC of the zebra finch. J. Neurophysiol. **80:** 914–923.
48. FIETE, I.R., R.H.R. HAHNLOSER, M.S. FEE & H.S. SEUNG. 2004. Temporal sparseness of the premotor drive is important for rapid learning in a neural network model of birdsong. J. Neurophysiol. In press.

Bilateral Control and Interhemispheric Coordination in the Avian Song Motor System

MARC F. SCHMIDT,[a,b] ROBIN C. ASHMORE,[a] AND ERIC T. VU[c]

[a]*Neuroscience Graduate Group and* [b]*Department of Biology, University of Pennsylvania, Philadelphia, Pennsylvania 19104, USA*

[c]*Division of Neurobiology, Barrow Neurological Institute, Phoenix, Arizona 85013, USA*

ABSTRACT: Birdsong is a complex learned motor behavior controlled by an interconnected network of vocal control nuclei that are present in both cerebral hemispheres. Unilateral lesions of song nuclei in the left or the right hemisphere result in different effects on song structure, suggesting that normal song output results from the activation of two parallel but functionally different motor pathways. Because each syringeal half is innervated primarily by ipsilateral motor structures and activity in both halves is tightly coordinated during singing, motor commands originating from both hemispheres must be tightly coordinated to produce the appropriate vocal output. This coordination occurs despite the absence of direct interhemispheric connections between song control nuclei. In this article, we discuss how motor commands in nucleus HVC, a key forebrain song control region, are coordinated by precisely timed inputs that act to synchronize premotor activity in both hemispheres. Synchronizing inputs are tightly linked to syllable and note onset, which suggests that bilaterally organized circuits in the midbrain or brainstem act in specifying higher-order song features, such as duration, order, and possibly even structure of individual song syllables. The challenge ahead lies in identifying the networks that generate the synchronizing timing inputs and to determine how these inputs specify the motor commands in HVC. Resolving these issues will help us gain a better understanding of how pattern-generating networks in the midbrain/brainstem interface with forebrain circuits to produce complex learned behaviors.

KEYWORDS: motor control; interhemispheric coordination; birdsong; HVC

INTRODUCTION

Song production results primarily from the combined action of the muscles that control the syrinx (the avian vocal organ) and respiration.[1–3] The precision with which vocalizations are produced requires that the motor commands that control these muscles be highly coordinated.[4,5] Because the left and right halves of the

Address for correspondence: Marc F. Schmidt, Department of Biology, 312 Leidy Laboratories, University of Pennsylvania, Philadelphia, PA 19104-6018. Voice: 215-898-9375; fax: 215-898-8780.

marcschm@sas.upenn.edu; <http://www.bio.upenn.edu/faculty/schmidt/marc/index.html>

Ann. N.Y. Acad. Sci. 1016: 171–186 (2004). © 2004 New York Academy of Sciences.
doi: 10.1196/annals.1298.014

syrinx can be independently controlled to produce separate sounds,[1,4,6] exquisite coordination is also required between the syringeal motor commands that control each side. The neural commands that control these respiratory and syringeal muscles during song originate in a complex network of interconnected forebrain nuclei[7,8] collectively known as the song system. This system is bilaterally organized and is anatomically symmetrical across hemispheres.[7] Because each syringeal half receives the majority of its neural inputs from song nuclei on the ipsilateral side[3] (however see Wild and colleagues[9]), motor commands originating from song nuclei in one hemisphere are assumed to control mainly the ipsilateral half of the syrinx. Given this assumption, precise and rapid coordination between both syringeal halves is likely to require that song commands in each hemisphere be tightly coordinated with one another, despite the absence of direct connections between forebrain song nuclei across the midline.

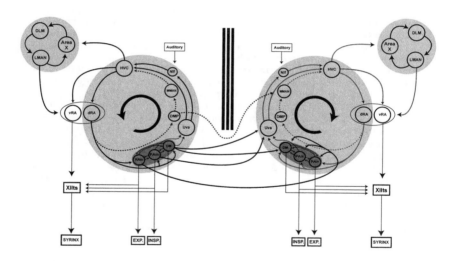

FIGURE 1. Anatomical organization of the song system highlighting its bilateral organization as well as three known pathways that originate in RA and project indirectly back to HVC. All three pathways project back to HVC via the intermediary of thalamic nuclei Uva (*solid line*) or DMP (*dotted line*). This depiction of the song system emphasizes its "recursive" nature where no single structure serves as the "top" of the hierarchy. For clarity, sparse bilateral projections between brainstem structures controlling the syrinx and respiration are not illustrated. Anatomical names: DLM, dorsal lateral nucleus of the medial thalamus; DM, dorsomedial nucleus of the intercollicular complex; DMP, dorsomedial posterior nucleus of thalamus; HVC, acronym is used as name; LMAN, lateral magnocellular nucleus of the anterior nidopallium; NIf, nucleus interfacialis of the nidopallium; MMAN, medial magnocellular nucleus of anterior nidopallium; PAm, nucleus paraambigualis; dRA, dorsal portion of the robust nucleus of the arcopallium; vRA, ventral portion of the robust nucleus of the arcopallium; RAm, nucleus retroambigualis; Uva, nucleus uvaeformis; nXIIts, tracheosyringeal part of the hypoglossal nucleus; Area X. Area X of the medial striatum. The abbreviations INSP and EXP represent, respectively, the muscles that control inspiration and expiration.

BILATERAL ORGANIZATION OF THE SONG MOTOR SYSTEM

In many simplified representations of the song system, nuclei are diagrammed linearly as a descending motor pathway that starts with the forebrain nucleus HVC and ends at the brainstem nuclei that control the syrinx (tracheosyringeal part of the hypoglossal nucleus) and the muscles of respiration (medullary respiratory nuclei). Representation in this way encourages the biased view that HVC lies at the top of a hierarchically organized motor pathway; it also fails to show the song system as a bilaterally organized network. A better understanding of the organization of the system may be gained by examination of FIGURE 1 which incorporates most of the anatomical connections known to be involved in vocal production and highlights the existence of multiple pathways from the midbrain and brainstem to HVC.[10–12] As this figure makes clear, the song system is best represented as a circular network, with many recurrent connections, where no single structure serves as the "top" of the hierarchy.

Highlighted in this representation of the song system are three independent projections to HVC on both the ipsilateral as well as the contralateral side. These projections provide the only known pathways by which song commands from one hemisphere can be shared with their anatomical counterparts in the contralateral hemisphere. They are therefore positioned to play a crucial role in coordinating and synchronizing motor commands across hemispheres. This chapter discusses the specific contribution of each of these pathways in coordinating song motor commands between hemispheres.

HEMISPHERIC SPECIALIZATION OF SONG CONTROL

The existence of two parallel song control systems raises the possibility that each hemisphere may make different contributions to song production through independent instructions to each half of the syrinx. Support for this idea comes from studies where unilateral lesions of forebrain song structures, such as HVC, cause song deficits that are specific to the side in which the lesion is made.[7,13,14] The most dramatic example of such lateralization of function has been described in the Waterschlager canary (*Serinus canarius*) by Nottebohm and colleagues.[7] In this species, left hemisphere lesions of HVC cause significant deterioration of the song while right hemisphere lesions produce much less pronounced song deficits (FIG. 2). This lateralization of function at the level of HVC parallels what is observed at the periphery.[15,16] Cutting the syringeal nerve (nXIIts) on the left side causes greater than 80% of the syllables of the bird's song to be severely distorted or silenced. In contrast, severing the right nerve causes only minor changes in song output.[15]

In zebra finches (*Taeniopygia guttata*), the effects of left and right HVC lesions differ more subtly even though these effects do appear to be lateralized, with lesions in the right hemisphere producing more pronounced effects.[14] The effect of HVC lesions parallel what is observed at the periphery since unilateral XIIts nerve cuts cause a spectral deterioration of the song but the greatest effect is observed following nerve cuts on the right side.[14,17] The overall similarity of the effects produced by central and peripheral manipulations in the zebra finch suggests that motor commands originating from each hemisphere may exhibit more functional overlap than

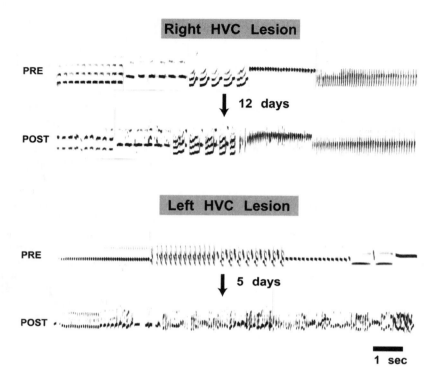

FIGURE 2. Evidence for the differential contribution of HVC to song production. The top half of the figure depicts song recorded from a Waterschlager canary before (PRE) and after (POST) HVC was lesioned in the right hemisphere. Right HVC lesions caused little effect on song structure. In contrast (bottom half of the figure), lesioning HVC in the left hemisphere caused nearly complete deterioration of the bird's song. (Modified from Figure 12 in Nottebohm and colleagues.[7])

in the canary. While both species described above show a parallel between central and peripheral lateralization, this need not always be the case. In the domestic canary, a strain distinct from the Waterschlager canary described earlier,[7,15] the effect of HVC lesions is strongly dependent on the side of the lesion even though the effect of XIIts nerve cuts is not.[13] While motor commands to the syrinx are primarily ipsilateral in nature in the zebra finch, it has recently been shown that the amount of anatomical projection between sides, both between RA and brainstem vocal structures as well as between respiratory nuclei, varies across songbird species.[9] Although individual hemispheres might generate distinct motor commands, denser contralateral projections from RA in some species but not others might explain why lateralization at the level of HVC does not always translate into peripheral lateralization.

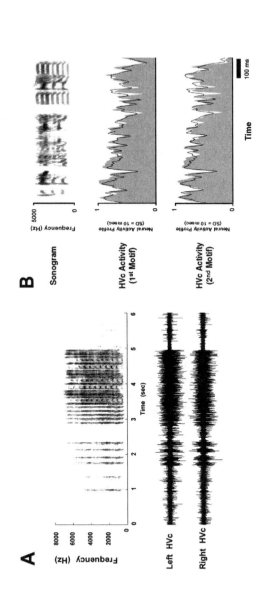

FIGURE 3. Similarity of HVC premotor activity in both hemispheres. (**A**) Simultaneous recording of premotor activity in left and right HVC during singing of an adult zebra finch. This example of raw neural traces reveals that premotor activity obtained from multiunit electrodes is generally elevated in both hemispheres during the song bout. Premotor bursts prior to the song can be observed during production of short calls and introductory notes. (**B**) Comparison of premotor activity patterns across hemispheres and across motifs. (*Top*) Spectrogram of the first motif of a canonical song used as a reference to compute profiles of song premotor activity. (*Middle and bottom*) Average neural activity levels (Neural Activity Profile) shown for the first motif from neural traces recorded simultaneously in left (*gray line*) and right (*black line*) HVC. Each Neural Activity Profile has been smoothed with a wide gaussian filter (S.D. = 10 msec) and normalized to the maximum firing rate. This figure illustrates the similarity in the smoothed neural pattern across hemispheres as well as motifs. (Reproduced with permission from Schmidt.[23]

NEURAL CORRELATES OF HEMISPHERIC LATERALIZATION

Understanding the neural basis for the observed functional differences between HVC across hemispheres will require a detailed understanding of the motor commands generated in each structure. HVC contains at least three distinct populations of neurons[18–20] and motor output appears to be carried by a single class of neurons, known as the RA-projecting neurons.[21] Interestingly, in the zebra finch at least, the premotor discharge pattern of this population of neurons is very sparse, in that individual RA-projecting neurons produce only a single, precisely timed, burst of action potentials during a given motif with different neurons being activated at different times in the song motif[22] (Fee and colleagues, this volume). Because of the sparseness of motor output of single HVC neurons, it will be difficult to examine similarities and differences in the nature of HVC motor commands generated by each hemisphere until we are able to record simultaneously from many single-units in each hemisphere.

Although information concerning single neurons is lost, an alternative approach to investigating functional differences between hemispheres is to record motor output from multi-unit clusters in HVC with the assumption that the recorded neural activity reflects something about the population motor output of each hemisphere.[23–25] Using this approach in zebra finches, multi-unit recordings in HVC during singing reveal that the slowly varying premotor activity pattern (i.e., smoothed activity) is nearly identical in both hemispheres (FIG. 3). This slowly varying premotor pattern is modulated during the song, is highly stereotyped across renditions of the bird's song (FIG. 3b), and shows the same modulated firing pattern at all locations within HVC.[23] The high correlation in premotor activity patterns between hemispheres suggests, in zebra finches at least, that certain features of the motor command generated by each hemisphere are shared. This may explain why the effects of left and right HVC lesions on the song of the zebra finch differ so little.

The similarity in premotor activity, however, should not be taken as evidence that there is no hemispheric lateralization of function. Assessment of similarity of non-smoothed neural activity reveals that correlations between electrode sites are much lower. In fact, with the exception of a few short segments in the premotor trace (see below), rapidly modulated events in the premotor trace are quite different in the two hemispheres.[23] Both hemispheres might therefore be modulated by a common input that determines the general shape of the overall premotor activity pattern, while the details of the motor trace (i.e., the rapidly varying firing patterns), are unique to each hemisphere and in fact to each spatial location within HVC.[23] Interestingly, preliminary recordings from the song sparrow (*Melospiza melodia*) suggest that there may be species differences in the extent to which the slowly varying song premotor patterns show hemispheric differences. Unlike the zebra finch, multiunit recordings from HVC in song sparrows can show significant differences in the slowly varying premotor patterns in each hemisphere during specific portions of the song.[26] It is intriguing to speculate that hemispheric differences in neural activity reflects hemispheric specialization. If so, one would predict differential effects of unilateral HVC lesions in this species.

INTERHEMISPHERIC COORDINATION OF
SONG PREMOTOR ACTIVITY

Whether or not each hemisphere encodes different features of the bird's song, the requirement remains that motor commands generated in each hemisphere must somehow be coordinated to produce the intended acoustic signal. A lack of such coordination, with one hemisphere drifting in time with respect to the other, would result in temporally misaligned motor commands in the periphery and highly abnormal

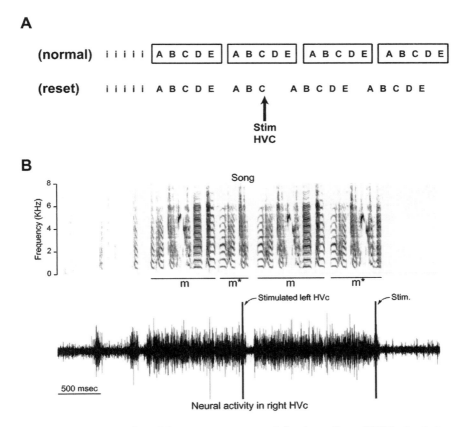

FIGURE 4. Resetting of the song motor pattern following unilateral HVC stimulation. (**A**) Schematic diagram of effect of stimulation on song patterning. Under normal conditions (*top row*), zebra finch song consists of several introductory notes, which are followed by a stereotyped sequence of syllables, known as motifs. Motifs are repeated several times throughout a given song bout. Stimulation of HVC during singing (*bottom row*) causes the ongoing syllable to truncate, which then results in termination of the ongoing motif. In this example, the terminated motif is followed by the initiation of several new motifs. (**B**) Unilateral stimulation of HVC causes suppression of HVC premotor activity in the contralateral side (*bottom trace*). This suppression of activity is followed by cessation of the ongoing motif. In this example, stimulation was delivered in the left HVC and activity recorded in the right HVC. (**B** is reproduced with permission from Vu and colleagues.[25])

vocal output. The minimal requirement for such interhemispheric coordination would be a common timing source to song nuclei in both hemispheres.

Insights into how premotor activity might be coordinated were obtained in zebra finches by experiments in which HVC activity in one hemisphere was perturbed with brief electrical stimulation while the bird was singing.[25] Stimulation on either side, even in the absence of auditory feedback, was shown to cause cessation of song premotor activity in the contralateral HVC approximately 35 msec after stimulation onset. Suppression of HVC activity was followed after a short delay by cessation of the ongoing syllable. In some cases, within a short but variable delay of 100–200 msec, one or more new motifs were initiated (FIG. 4). The ability of perturbations in one hemisphere to reset premotor patterns in the contralateral hemisphere hinted at the existence of a common timing source that could coordinate premotor output in both hemispheres.[25]

Mechanistically, song resetting following HVC stimulation in one hemisphere could be thought of as a two-stage process. In a first stage, unilateral perturbation of ongoing premotor activity in HVC causes a cessation of sound production. Typically, individual syllables become truncated 40–60 msec after the stimulus is delivered. Syllable truncation occurs independently of when the stimulus is delivered in the ongoing motif[27] or ongoing syllable.[28] In a second stage, HVC premotor activity is reinitiated in both hemispheres and results in the production of a new motif.

One possible mechanism by which HVC stimulation in one hemisphere might cause a suppression of the ongoing syllable is that perturbation of premotor activity interrupts a putative circuit that drives premotor activity in both hemispheres. Interruption of such a "timing-signal generator" would then lead to suppression of HVC activity in both hemispheres. We have previously proposed that a circuit might exist that monitors the motor output from both hemispheres and that a mismatch in motor output between hemispheres, such as the one caused by stimulation in HVC, would interrupt this timing generating circuit.[25] However, preliminary evidence obtained from birds forced to sing with only one hemisphere suggests that comparing motor output between hemispheres is not a necessary requirement for resetting the song pattern.[28] In these birds, perturbation of HVC premotor activity in one hemisphere is still able to interrupt the song pattern despite the absence of premotor output from the contralateral hemisphere. These results suggest that activity of this putative "timing-signal generator" depends directly on motor commands originating from HVC and that any significant distortion in HVC motor output leads to its interruption and ultimately to the suppression of HVC premotor activity in both hemispheres. Because suppression of the ongoing syllable closely follows any distortion in HVC motor output no matter when in the song the distortion occurred, these results suggest that the putative "timing-signal generator" monitors HVC motor output relatively frequently and that bilateral timing signals to both hemispheres are updated frequently, certainly more than once per motif and perhaps even at a sub-syllabic interval.

EVIDENCE FOR SYNCHRONIZATION OF HVC PREMOTOR ACTIVITY ACROSS HEMISPHERES

If a common timing source is required for the coordination of song motor activity between hemispheres, careful analysis of the temporal pattern obtained from simul-

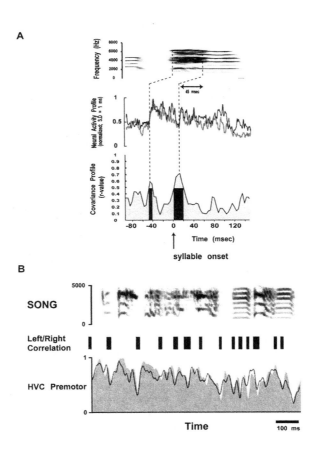

FIGURE 5. Evidence for synchronization of premotor activity across hemispheres during short segments of the song trace (**A**) Simultaneous recording in left and right HVC during production of a two-note syllable (*top panel*). In this representative example, premotor activity (*middle panel*) in both left (*gray*) and right (*black*) HVC is elevated but highly modulated during the entire syllable. The onset of premotor activity occurs approximately 45 msec prior to the acoustic onset of the syllable. Using sliding window cross-covariance analysis (*lower panel*), premotor activity is shown to be highly correlated (r > 0.5) across hemispheres during two short periods of the motor trace. The black bars highlight these periods. When shifted by a 45-msec premotor delay time, the first period of correlated activity corresponds to the acoustic onset of the syllable and the second period to the transition between the first and second note of the syllable. (**B**) Pattern of synchronized activity during production of a song motif. Using the same criteria as described above, periods of correlated activity across hemispheres are represented as *black bars* and their distribution during the production of an entire song motif is shown in the *middle panel*. For reference, the slowly varying premotor trace is shown in the *bottom panel*. (**A** is reproduced with permission from Schmidt.[23])

taneous bilateral HVC recordings should provide evidence for synchronous initiation of premotor activity in both hemispheres. Simultaneous recordings from HVC in both hemispheres reveal that neural activity is highly correlated during short segments of the song, and that these segments are observed many times during a given song, occurring at precisely the same song transition points from one rendition to the next.[23] Many of these segments of synchronized premotor activity occur 40–50 msec prior to the acoustic onset of syllables and notes suggesting that they are intimately linked to the acoustic onset of individual song elements (FIG. 5). Because there exist no known direct connections between the left and right HVC, the observed synchronization of activity in both hemispheres suggests the existence of a bilaterally organized network that sends precisely synchronized timing inputs to both hemispheres that help to specify syllable and note onset. This network could serve as the hypothesized "timing-signal generator" described in the previous section. In addition to the tight association with acoustic onset, precisely synchronized bursts of neural activity are also linked to periods in the song that are associated with the inter-syllable silent interval. The significance of these bursts is not known, but they may play a role in specifying the duration[29] or amplitude of the inspiratory breath that define these silent intervals.[30]

While synchronization between hemispheres may result from common timing inputs into both left and right HVC, some of the observed synchrony may stem from intrinsic network patterns in HVC initiated by common inputs to both hemispheres.[31] Thus one possibility is that HVC premotor activity is initially synchronized and that the remainder of the song pattern is generated by intrinsic pattern-generating networks in each hemisphere. Alternatively, HVC might be resynchronized by frequent, but separate and brief input timing signals. Because a mechanism based largely on intrinsic mechanisms would cause the observed synchronization between hemispheres to drift with time, it is likely that HVC receives timing inputs relatively frequently. Depending on the frequency with which timing signals are generated, the putative synchronizing structures might not only specify the timing with which syllables are produced within the song but also the order and identity of the syllables within the song motif.

POSSIBLE SUBSTRATES FOR INTERHEMISPHERIC SYNCHRONIZATION

There exist at least three different anatomical pathways that could serve the function of synchronizing premotor activity in both hemispheres (FIG. 1b).[10–12] All three pathways originate in the dorsal part of RA (dRA) and project back to HVC via the thalamus. The first of these [dRA → DM → Uva → (NIf) → HVC] projects back to HVC via the midbrain nucleus DM, a structure whose stimulation is known to generate unlearned vocalizations in both passerines[32] and nonpasserine birds.[33–35] The second pathway [dRA → PAm → Uva → (NIf) → HVC] projects back to HVC via the medullary nucleus paraambigualis (PAm), a structure known to contain inspiratory bulbospinal neurons.[3,36] The third pathway [dRA → DMP →MMAN → HVC] does not use Uva as a relay but instead projects back to HVC via the thalamic nucleus dorsomedialis posterior (DMP).

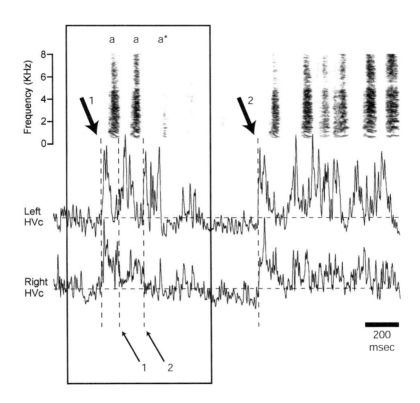

FIGURE 6. Unilateral lesion in Uva leads to uncorrelated HVC premotor activity across hemispheres. Premotor activity was recorded simultaneously in both left and right HVC while the bird attempted to sing (*top trace*). As is typical for birds recorded shortly after unilateral Uva lesion, singing attempts typically result in stuttered iterations of a few introductory notes or syllables. In the sequence of syllables highlighted by the box, the bird produces two identical song elements (**a**) followed by a truncated version of a third element (**a***). In this example, where premotor activity was recorded 19 days after Uva was lesioned in the right hemisphere, HVC premotor activity in the intact left hemisphere shows distinct bursts of premotor activity that precede individual syllable elements by approximately 45 msec. Premotor onset is shown by the dotted lines. HVC premotor activity in the lesioned right HVC shows an initial premotor burst during production of the first syllable that is tightly correlated with the onset of the premotor burst in the contralateral hemisphere (*thick arrow #1*). A similar correlation is observed during a second attempt to sing (*thick arrow #2*). In contrast, however, the second burst (*small arrow #1*) is temporally delayed relative to the premotor pattern recorded on the intact contralateral side. The expected third burst (*small arrow #2*) on the lesioned side never occurs. This uncorrelated pattern of premotor activity across hemispheres is never observed in intact birds. In this example, neural activity has been rectified and smoothed with a wide gaussian filter (S.D. = 10 msec) and normalized to the maximum firing rate. (Figure adapted from Coleman and Vu.[39])

As shown in FIGURE 1, these three feedback pathways include bilateral projections from DM to Uva, from PAm to Uva, and from DMP to MMAN. Thus, only two song nuclei in the forebrain, MMAN and Uva, relay bilateral ascending inputs from other song nuclei back to HVC. Although both of these structures could potentially play an important role in interhemispheric synchronization, complete bilateral lesions of MMAN have little or no effect on adult zebra finch song.[45] In contrast, bilateral lesions of Uva have rather severe and permanent effects on song.[37,38] Taken together, the lesion studies suggest that Uva is necessary for any interhemispheric coordination, whereas MMAN normally plays a comparatively minor role.

Unilateral Uva lesions on either side produce immediate and severe song deficits that recover substantially after less than 15 days.[38] If Uva plays a critical role in interhemispheric coordination, then lesioning it should result in a reduction or loss in synchrony of song premotor activity across hemispheres. Preliminary findings suggest that unilateral Uva lesions in zebra finches lead to a mismatch in HVC activity patterns between hemispheres during singing attempts[39] (FIG. 6). Interestingly, however, the onset of premotor activity associated with the first syllable of the bird's distorted song (*thick arrow*) remains synchronized between hemispheres. This observation raises the possibility that MMAN inputs, at least in birds with unilateral Uva lesions, may be involved in initially synchronizing premotor activity in both hemispheres.

If unilateral lesions of Uva impair interhemispheric coordination, then the intriguing question arises as to how this coordination is restored following song recovery. Preliminary results indicate that MMAN plays a critical role in this recovery.[40] Adult zebra finches that sustain a unilateral Uva lesion combined with either unilateral or bilateral MMAN lesions do not recover their song. Furthermore, the recovered song of birds with unilateral Uva lesions is re-impaired by a subsequent MMAN lesion, with no recovery occurring after the second lesion. Because MMAN is the only other known forebrain song nucleus to receive bilateral inputs, the possibility thus arises that after song recovery from unilateral Uva lesion, MMAN might play a significant role in interhemispheric coordination, a role for which it normally is not necessary.

INSIGHTS INTO THE NEURAL MECHANISMS OF SONG CONTROL

The findings described in this review pertain directly to the issue of coordination of motor commands across hemispheres. Many of the mechanisms involved in hemispheric coordination, however, are also central to general issues of song motor control. In this last section, we propose a model of song production that is consistent with the work presented above.

The timing signals that synchronize HVC activity in both hemispheres must play a key role in coordinating the motor commands in each hemisphere and are therefore likely to ensure that sound-producing structures in the periphery are highly synchronized. In addition to this role, these synchronizing inputs, by determining when the acoustic onset of syllables and notes will occur, may also establish the tempo and possibly even the sequence order of the bird's song. Properly timed inputs could serve to activate intrinsic circuits within HVC that translate this timing information into motor commands that define the appropriate acoustic morphology of each syllable. Whether these timing inputs simply act to initiate premotor activity in HVC or whether they also play a role in specifying the identity of syllables is an open question. The proposition that structures upstream from HVC act as "timing-signal generators" implies that different features of the bird's song might be specified at different anatomical levels within the song motor network. It has already been suggested that nuclei HVC and RA encode features that are, respectively, specific to syllables and notes within a song motif.[24] It seems reasonable that structures upstream from HVC might therefore encode higher-order features, such as syllable sequencing, motif duration, and song length.[41]

The ability of short perturbations in HVC to reset the entire song pattern, irrespective of when it is delivered in the song, suggests that the putative bilateral timing source requires input from HVC in order to generate the next timing signal in the sequence. Failure to receive the correct input would result either in cessation of the song (i.e., the "timing-signal generator" does not send a synchronizing input to HVC) or resetting the motif (i.e., the "timing-signal generator" resets to the default state and sends a timing signal that specifies the first syllable of a new motif). Given the anatomical organization of the song system (Fig. 1), the only pathway by which HVC could directly affect the putative "timing-signal generating" structure(s) is by way of nucleus RA. While this might seem inconsistent with previous work suggesting that stimulation in RA fails to reset the song pattern,[27] it should be recalled that RA is made up of two functionally distinct regions,[42,43] only one of which, the dorsal region (dRA), projects to the three structures that connect bilaterally back to HVC. If dRA in fact relays such a signal from HVC, it is predicted that brief perturbation of activity in dRA should reset the song pattern.[44] Preliminary findings suggest that this may be the case (Ashmore and Schmidt, unpublished observations).

CONCLUSIONS AND FUTURE DIRECTIONS

The avian song system offers a powerful model of how the two hemispheres of a brain can each make different contributions to the production of a complex, learned behavior, and how those distinct contributions can be integrated to produce coordinated output. The studies we have reviewed in this article highlight these two related issues, and provide a framework for understanding the overall functional organization of song motor control. They also suggest three important areas of investigation for future research.

First, there is still little understanding of the differential contribution of each hemisphere to song production. As exemplified by the dramatic degradation of song in the canary following left, but not right, HVC lesion, the nature of the motor commands in each hemisphere are likely to be quite different. Analysis of the neural mechanisms that underlie these differences will be important in understanding the differential contribution of each hemisphere to song output. It should be possible to capitalize on the similarities and differences of the neural output in each hemisphere to extract some of the underlying principles of how motor commands are encoded in HVC. Because most studies are performed in the zebra finch, a species in which both hemispheres contribute more or less equally to song production, results such as those obtained in the canary underline the importance of the comparative approach in studying the neural mechanisms of vocal production.[26]

Second, the finding that left and right HVC are synchronized by a common timing signal suggests that a network of bilaterally connected structures in the brainstem, midbrain, or thalamus is responsible for generating these timing signals. The identification of this network will be an important step in understanding the hierarchical organization of the song motor system and may help determine where higher order song features are encoded.

Finally, it will be of great interest to understand the nature of the timing signal that reaches HVC. Does this input simply activate and synchronize HVC circuits in both hemispheres or does it also specify the spatio-temporal activation pattern of these circuits? In other words, do these inputs play a role in specifying some of the variables that determine the duration and acoustic morphology of individual syllables? Taken together, these unresolved issues and future directions highlight the value of using the bilateral organization of the song control system as a venue for understanding the neural mechanisms of vocal motor production.

REFERENCES

1. SUTHERS, R.A. 1997. Peripheral control and lateralization of song. J. Neurobiol. **33:** 632–652.
2. GOLLER, F. & R.A. SUTHERS. 1995. Implications for lateralization of bird song from unilateral gating of bilateral motor patterns. Nature **373:** 63–66.
3. WILD, J.M. 1997. Neural pathways for the control of birdsong production. J. Neurobiol. **33:** 653–670.
4. GOLLER, F. & R.A. SUTHERS. 1996. Role of syringeal muscles in gating airflow and sound production in singing brown thrashers. J. Neurophysiol. **75:** 867–876.
5. GOLLER, F. & R.A. SUTHERS. 1996. Role of syringeal muscles in controlling the phonology of bird song. J. Neurophysiol. **76:** 287–300.
6. GOLLER, F. & R.A. SUTHERS. 1999. Bilaterally symmetrical respiratory activity during lateralized birdsong. J. Neurobiol. **41:** 513–523.
7. NOTTEBOHM, F., T.M. STOKES & C.M. LEONARD. 1976. Central control of song in the canary, *Serinus canarius*. J. Comp. Neurol. **165:** 457–486.
8. NOTTEBOHM, F., D.B. KELLEY & J.A. PATON. 1982. Connections of vocal control nuclei in the canary telencephalon. J. Comp. Neurol. **207:** 344–-357.
9. WILD, J.M., M.N. WILLIAMS & R.A. SUTHERS. 2000. Neural pathways for bilateral vocal control in songbirds. J. Comp. Neurol. **423:** 413–426.
10. VATES, G.E., D.S. VICARIO & F. NOTTEBOHM. 1997. Reafferent thalamo-"cortical" loops in the song system of oscine songbirds. J. Comp. Neurol. **380:** 275–290.
11. STRIEDTER, G.F. & E.T. VU. 1998. Bilateral feedback projections to the forebrain in the premotor network for singing in zebra finches. J. Neurobiol. **34:** 27–40.
12. REINKE, H. & J.M. WILD. 1998. Identification and connections of inspiratory premotor neurons in songbirds and budgerigar. J. Comp. Neurol. **391:** 147–163.
13. HALLE, F., M. GAHR & M. KREUTZER. 2003. Effects of unilateral lesions of HVC on song patterns of male domesticated canaries. J. Neurobiol. **56:** 303–314.
14. WILLIAMS, H. *et al.* 1992. Right-side dominance for song control in the zebra finch. J. Neurobiol. **23:** 1006–1020.
15. NOTTEBOHM, F. & M.E. NOTTEBOHM. 1976. Left hypoglossal dominance in the control of canary and white-crowned sparrow song. J. Comp. Physiol. A. **108:** 171–192.
16. HARTLEY, R.S. & R.A. SUTHERS. 1990. Lateralization of syringeal function during song production in the canary. J. Neurobiol. **21:** 1236–1248.
17. FLOODY, O.R. & A.P. ARNOLD. 1997. Song lateralization in the zebra finch. Horm. Behav. **31:** 25–34.

18. DUTAR, P., H.M. VU & D.J. PERKEL. 1998. Multiple cell types distinguished by physiological, pharmacological, and anatomic properties in nucleus HVc of the adult zebra finch. J. Neurophysiol. **80:** 1828–1838.
19. KUBOTA, M. & I. TANIGUCHI. 1998. Electrophysiological characteristics of classes of neurons in the HVc of the zebra finch. J. Neurophysiol. **80:** 914–923.
20. NIXDORF, B.E., S.S. DAVIS & T.J. DEVOOGD. 1989. Morphology of Golgi-impregnated neurons in hyperstriatum ventralis, pars caudalis in adult male and female canaries. J. Comp. Neurol. **284:** 337–349.
21. SCHARFF, C. *et al.* 2000. Targeted neuronal death affects neuronal replacement and vocal behavior in adult songbirds. Neuron **25:** 481–492.
22. HAHNLOSER, R.H.R., A.A. KOZHEVNIKOV & M.S. FEE. 2002. An ultra-sparse code underlies the generation of neural sequences in a songbird. Nature **419:** 65–70.
23. SCHMIDT, M.F. 2003. Pattern of interhemispheric synchronization in HVc during singing correlates with key transitions in the song pattern. J. Neurophysiol. **90:** 3931–3949.
24. YU, A.C. & D. MARGOLIASH. 1996. Temporal hierarchical control of singing in birds. Science **273:** 1871–1875.
25. VU, E. T., M. F. SCHMIDT & M. E. MAZUREK. 1998. Interhemispheric coordination of premotor neural activity during singing in adult zebra finches. J. Neurosci. **18:** 9088–9098.
26. NEALEN, P.M. & M.F. SCHMIDT. 2002. Comparative approaches to avian song system function: insights into auditory and motor processing. J. Comp. Physiol. **188:** 929–941.
27. VU, E. T., M. E. MAZUREK & Y.-C. KUO. 1994. Identification of a forebrain motor programming network for the learned song of zebra finches. J. Neurosci. **14:** 6924–6934.
28. ASHMORE, R.C., P.M. NEALEN & M.F. SCHMIDT. 2003. Disruption of song production from microstimulation in HVC of finches with unilateral lesions of RA. Soc. Neurosci. Abstract 942.9.
29. VICARIO, D.S. & J.N. RAKSIN. 2000. Possible roles for GABAergic inhibition in the vocal control system of the zebra finch. Neuroreport **11:** 3631–3635.
30. GOLLER, F. & M.A. DALEY. 2001. Novel motor gestures for phonation during inspiration enhance the acoustic complexity of birdsong. Proc. R. Soc. Lond. B Biol. Sci. **268:** 2301–2305.
31. SOLIS, M.M. & D.J. PERKEL. 2002. Induction of discrete, repetitive synaptic events in the forebrain nucleus HVc in vitro. Soc. Neurosci. Abstract 680.17.
32. VICARIO, D.S. & H.B. SIMPSON. 1995. Electrical-stimulation in forebrain nuclei elicits learned vocal patterns in songbirds. J. Neurophysiol. **73:** 2602–2607.
33. SELLER, T.J. 1981. Midbrain vocalization centers in birds. Trends Neurosci. **12:** 301–303.
34. SHAW, B.K. 2000. Involvement of a midbrain vocal nucleus in the production of both acoustic and postural components of crowing behavior in the Japanese quail. J. Comp. Physiol. **186:** 747–757.
35. POTASH, L.M. 1970. Vocalizations elicited by brain stimulation in *Coturnix coturnix Japonica*. Behavior **36:** 149–167.
36. WILD, J.M., F. GOLLER & R.A. SUTHERS. 1998. Inspiratory muscle activity during bird song. J. Neurobiol. **36:** 441–453.
37. WILLIAMS, H. & D.S. VICARIO. 1993. Temporal patterning of song production: participation of nucleus uvaeformis of the thalamus. J. Neurobiol. **24:** 903–912.
38. COLEMAN, M.J., P.J. SULE & E.T. VU. 1999. Recovery of impaired songs following unilateral but not bilateral lesions of nucleus uvaeformis of adult zebra finches. Soc. Neurosci. Abstract **25:** 1367.
39. COLEMAN, M.J. & E.T. VU. 2000. Neural activity in HVc of adult zebra finches during the song recovery following unilateral lesions of nucleus uvaformis. Soc. Neurosci. Abstract **26:** 2031.
40. VU, E.T. & M.J. COLEMAN. 2001. Song recovery by adult zebra finches following unilateral Uva lesion requires nucleus mMAN. Soc. Neurosci. Abstract 538.13.
41. HOSINO, T. & K. OKANOYA. 2000. Lesion of a higher-order song nucleus disrupts phrase level complexity in Bengalese finches. Neuroreport **11:** 2091–2095.

42. VICARIO, D.S. 1991. Organization of the zebra finch song control system: II. Functional organization of outputs from nucleus robustus archistriatalis. J. Comp. Neurol. **309:** 486–494.
43. VICARIO, D.S. & F. NOTTEBOHM. 1988. Organization of the zebra finch song control system: I. Representation of syringeal muscles in the hypoglossal nucleus. J. Comp. Neurol. **271:** 346–354.
44. SUTHERS, R.A. & D. MARGOLIASH. 2002. Motor control of birdsong. Curr. Opin. Neurobiol. **12:** 684–690.
45. FOSTER, E.F. & S.W. BOTTJER. 2001. Lesions of a telencephalic nucleus in male zebra finches: influences on vocal behavior in juveniles and adults. J. Neurobiol. **46:** 142–165.

Methods for the Analysis of Auditory Processing in the Brain

FRÉDÉRIC E. THEUNISSEN, SARAH M.N. WOOLLEY, ANNE HSU, AND THANE FREMOUW

Department of Psychology and Neurosciences Institute, University of California Berkeley, Berkeley, California 94720-1650, USA

ABSTRACT: Understanding song perception and singing behavior in birds requires the study of auditory processing of complex sounds throughout the avian brain. We can divide the basics of auditory perception into two general processes: (1) encoding, the process whereby sound is transformed into neural activity and (2) decoding, the process whereby patterns of neural activity take on perceptual meaning and therefore guide behavioral responses to sounds. In birdsong research, most studies have focused on the decoding process: What are the responses of the specialized auditory neurons in the song control system? and What do they mean for the bird? Recently, new techniques addressing both encoding and decoding have been developed for use in songbirds. Here, we first describe some powerful methods for analyzing what acoustical aspects of complex sounds like songs are encoded by auditory processing neurons in songbird brain. These methods include the estimation and analysis of spectro-temporal receptive fields (STRFs) for auditory neurons. Then we discuss the decoding methods that have been used to understand how songbird neurons may discriminate among different songs and other sounds based on mean spike-count rates.

KEYWORDS: spectro-temporal receptive fields; amplitude modulation tuning; song-selective neurons; reverse correlation; modulation transfer function

INTRODUCTION

Much of the methodology that is used to study neural encoding and decoding of sensory information is applicable to auditory information processing in songbirds.[1] Songbirds are particularly well suited to the study of auditory processing because their brains contain a large number of auditory processing centers (see Fig. 1 in Theunissen *et al.*, Song Selectivity in the Song System and in the Auditory Forebrain, this volume) and because they have the extraordinary ability to learn acoustically complex songs. In this chapter, we summarize some of the methods that have been used to quantify neuronal firing patterns during the processing of songs and we de-

Address for correspondence: Frédéric E Theunissen, Department of Psychology and Neuroscience Institute, 3210 Tolman Hall, Berkeley, California 94720-1650, USA. Fax: 510-642-5293.

fet@socrates.berkeley.edu;
<http://psychology.berkeley.edu/directories/facultypages/theunissenresearch.html>

Ann. N.Y. Acad. Sci. 1016: 187–207 (2004). © 2004 New York Academy of Sciences.
doi: 10.1196/annals.1298.020

scribe a new generation of analysis techniques for studying how auditory neurons encode song and other sounds. These newer techniques have only recently been adapted for use with biologically meaningful sounds such as songs.

Neural encoding in the auditory system is the process whereby sounds presented at the ear are transformed into neuronal firing patterns in the auditory processing regions of the brain. Neuronal firing patterns can be analyzed as sequences of action potentials occurring over time, or spike trains. Songs are presented at the ear, and neurons produce spike trains in response. Different songs produce different spike trains, and spike trains in response to the same song differ across different brain regions. Thus, for the birdsong researcher, the encoding goal is to understand how complex sounds, such as songs, are transformed into spike trains, and what aspects of songs are important for producing spike trains and shaping spike train patterns, such as changes in spike rate over time. By studying auditory encoding mechanisms, one hopes to understand and describe how the representation of a meaningful sound like a song changes at different stages of sensory processing, eventually (with the added step of decoding the neural signal) resulting in perception.

Neural decoding is the process whereby the meaning of spike trains is deciphered. Perception is the end result of neural decoding. But, in order to understand how spike trains lead to perception, we must determine what information is carried by the spike trains. Studying sensory decoding entails the analysis of spike rates in response to sounds, how spike rates vary over time and in response to particular sounds, and what kinds of information are carried in spike trains. Much of this type of analysis has been used to understand neural responses to songs and other sounds in the song control system. But the variability, dynamic range, temporal patterning, and efficiency of spike trains have yet to be examined in detail. Here, we describe some methods for analyzing these aspects of spike trains and what we may learn from the application of such methods to the study of birdsong.

This chapter is organized in two sections. First, we describe methods for analyzing how sounds are transformed into spike trains: encoding. These methods examine the tuning properties of auditory neurons in hierarchically organized auditory processing centers. Second, we describe some of the widely used and historically important methods for analyzing how spike trains confer meaning (such as the discrimination and identification of songs), i.e., decoding. These methods examine decoding in terms of mean spike-count rates in response to sounds.

1. NEURAL ENCODING: MEASURING THE TUNING PROPERTIES OF AUDITORY NEURONS

1a. Describing The Time/Frequency Tuning Properties of Neurons using Spectro-Temporal Receptive Fields (STRFs)

Neurons carry information about the identity of particular songs. Simple visual inspection of neural responses to songs (see Figure 2 in Theunissen and colleagues, this volume) shows that auditory neurons in the songbird auditory system phase lock reliably to specific acoustic features found in the spectrogram of each song. The time scale of these acoustic features is much shorter than that for neurons in the song system. Therefore, the encoding of the identity of song in these auditory processing regions may be found in the joint, precise spike patterns obtained from ensembles of neurons. Since auditory processing begins with the initial frequency/amplitude decomposition of sound in the inner ear, the response of many higher-level auditory neurons can be, in part, characterized by their static frequency tuning.[2] In addition, auditory neurons in the auditory midbrain and forebrain acquire novel dynamic and cross-frequency channel properties that are not observed at the lower levels of auditory processing stream.[3] For this reason, the characterization of the response properties of higher level auditory neurons has included their response to amplitude-modulated tones,[4,5] spectrally modulated sounds,[6,7] and, more recently, complex spectro-temporal stimuli, which are used to extract the joint spectro-temporal tuning of neurons.[8–12]

The particular aspects of a complex sound that any one neuron is encoding can be described by estimating the spectro-temporal receptive field (STRF) for that neuron's response to that stimulus. The STRF is a method for visualizing and quantifying the linear relationship between the presentation sounds of particular frequencies at particular times, and the increase or decrease in the probability of spiking. The STRF is an informative and efficient tool because it can show visually and give measures of: (1) frequency tuning bandwidth (the range of frequencies to which a neuron responds) for both excitation and inhibition; (2) the spike latencies for excitation and their complex relationships with individual frequencies, such as sensitivity to frequency sweeps; (3) latencies for spike inhibition; (4) how time-locked the relationship between a sound and the neural response is; and (5) what temporal and spectral modulations best drive a neuron. Perhaps most importantly, the STRF describes the basic tuning of the neuron during the processing of complex sounds such as song. Classical analysis methods used in auditory physiology can only determine the basic tuning properties of neurons during the processing of relatively simple sounds such as tones and noise. As we are now learning through the use of STRFs (see Theunissen and colleagues, this volume), the basic tuning properties of auditory neurons can differ based on the stimulus to which they are responding, making our current understanding of auditory tuning much more dynamic than was previously thought.

The STRF can explain what aspects of songs and other complex sounds are encoded by individual neurons in different auditory processing regions. While this is a powerful tool, it is important to understand that the STRF describes the linear response of a neuron. Therefore, the STRF does not perfectly explain the response of a neuron to a stimulus because auditory responses are the result of both linear and nonlinear tuning properties. However, the STRF can be used to measure how much of a neural response is linear versus how much is nonlinear by computing how well the STRF explains the observed response to a sound. Below, we describe (1) how STRFs are estimated; (2) how to "validate" an STRF or measure how well it has captured the neural response; and (3) what STRFs can tell us about neural encoding of complex sounds in the songbird brain.

1b. Estimating STRFs from Neural Responses to Sound

STRFs were, until recently, used only with sounds that did not contain correlations in frequency and time, such as white noise. White noise is essentially a random sound. For example, the frequency composition of the sound occurring at one time is not related to the sounds preceding or following it. Similarly, at any point in time, the sound frequencies at which power is concentrated are not related. Using white noise as the sound stimulus, an STRF can be estimated directly from the correlation between the stimulus and the response. When the response consists of spike trains, this correlation is in turn simply given by the spike-triggered average (STA) stimulus. Every time a spike occurs, the sounds that preceded it (up to several hundred milliseconds before it) are averaged with the sounds that preceded earlier and later spikes. Eventually, all the sounds except the ones that occur consistently before a spike average out to zero. But the sounds that are consistently correlated with an increase or decrease in spiking build up. This methodology is known as the reverse-correlation and was first used in neuroscience to characterize the tuning curves of auditory nerve fibers.[13,14] An example of an STRF calculated from the STA is shown in FIGURE 1A. Here the stimulus is the spectrogram of a white noise sound that is band limited in its amplitude and spectral modulations. The STRF shows the sound frequencies that reliably occurred at a certain time lag before increases in spiking (red/black) and the sound frequencies that reliable occurred at a certain time lag before decreases in spiking (blue/white). Green/grey represents the overall mean spike rate, with no systematic relationships among time, frequency, and changes in spike rate. The STRF reversed in time (flipped to appear as a mirror image) can be thought of as a spectrogram showing the "best" stimulus for driving that neuron.

The use of white-noise and the reverse-correlation method has been successfully applied at "lower" stages of sensory processing both in vision[15] and in audition.[16] However, in the case of songbirds, there are two problems with using white noise to measure the time/frequency tuning of auditory neurons with STRFs. First, in "higher" sensory processing regions like those in the songbird auditory forebrain, many neurons don't respond well to white noise and the STRF generated using white noise fails to match with responses to other stimuli.[10,17,18] Second, we are interested in how these neurons process song and other complex sounds that contain correlations in time and frequency, rather than white noise. But, when sounds contain correlations in time and frequency (are non-stationary), problems with the simple reverse-correlation technique for estimating STRFs arise. For complex stimuli, different frequencies within the stimulus will be correlated and the STA will reflect not only the response properties of the neuron but also the structure (correlations) in the stimulus. For example, what if a neuron is only responsive to sound frequencies around 2 kHz, and the complex sound we are interested in contains sounds around 6 kHz, which are correlated with the 2 kHz sounds in time. An example of such frequency correlations in time would be the harmonic stacks that are observed in zebra finch song and many other animal vocalizations (see spectrogram in FIG. 1B).[19] The STRF estimated using the simple reverse correlation will then falsely show that the neuron in question responds to sounds around 6 kHz as well as 2kHz. A solution that removes the impact of the correlations in time and frequency inherent to complex, structured sounds is needed. Recently, this solution, with special reference to birdsong, has been developed.[10,20,21] We have shown how the correlated STA can be normalized to take into account the statistical structure (correlations among frequencies and across time) in the stimulus. The solution requires the calculation of the stimulus autocorrelation, which gives values for how correlated certain frequencies are and the time course of such correlations.

The mathematics involved in the removal of the stimulus autocorrelations are described in detail in Theunissen and colleagues.[20] The steps in that normalization are

A. Reverse correlation: Spike-triggered average with ripple-noise yields the STRF

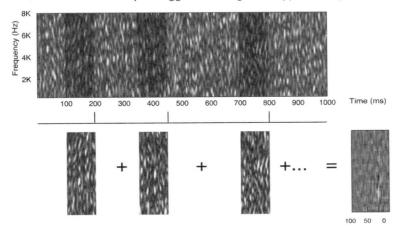

B. Spike-triggered average with song does not recover the STRF

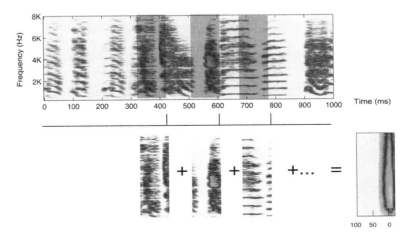

FIGURE 1. Estimating the STRF using the spike-triggered averaged spectrogram. (**A**) The STRF can be estimated from the spike triggered average (STA) when the stimulus is white noise. This estimation method is called **reverse correlation**. The equivalent of band-limited white-noise in the space of spectrograms is called modulation-limited-noise or ripple noise. (**B**) The result of the **spike-triggered average operation** for the same hypothetical neuron, when zebra finch song is used as a stimulus. In this case, the correlations in time and frequency in the stimulus lead to a much broader STA and the STRF can only be estimated with further processing as explained in the text and illustrated in FIGURE 3.

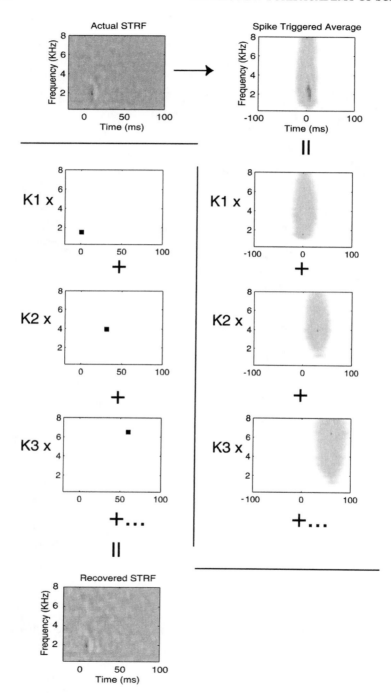

FIGURE 2. *See following page for legend.*

illustrated in FIGURE 2. Using a model STRF shown in the top left panel ("Actual STRF"), we generate artificial spike trains in response to an ensemble of zebra finch songs. As mentioned above, because zebra finch song has correlations in time and in frequency, the spike-triggered average (STA) obtained by the reverse-correlation procedure does not match the actual STRF. The STA is shown on the right column next to the actual STRF. Based on the STRF, we expect the STA to show just an area of energy localized around 2 kHz and 10 msec but instead a much larger region of activity is found. This is because sound energy in the 2 kHz band in zebra finch song is correlated with energy at other frequencies. For zebra finch song, which contains broadband harmonic and noisy sounds (see spectrogram of zebra finch song in Fig. 1B), the correlation occupies most of the frequency range of the song spectrum. Similarly, sound energy at one particular point in time is correlated with sound energy at previous and later times because zebra finch syllables have an average duration. To eliminate these correlations and get an STRF, we calculate the STAs that would be obtained if the STRFs had values of one at particular points in time and frequency and a value of zero everywhere else (known in mathematical terms as a delta function). These elemental STRFs are shown in the left column below the actual STRF with their corresponding spike-triggered averages in the right column. The STA for each elemental STRF can be estimated from model spike trains but is also given by the correlations in the stimulus between the point where the elemental STRFs show energy and all the other points in time-frequency. To recover the actual STRF, we find the particular combination of weights (k1, k2, etc.) of the STA obtained from the elemental STRFs such that their weighed sum is equal to the STA for the real neuron. Finally, the weighted sum of the elemental STRFs obtained with these same weights is the recovered STRF.

One final consideration when estimating STRFs during the processing of complex stimuli like songs is that the STRF can only show correlations (or the lack there of) between spikes and sounds that are contained in the stimulus; the STRF is limited by the sounds used to estimate it. Therefore, when estimating STRFs, it is best to use stimuli that cover the "sound space" well, meaning that they represent a wide range of frequencies, occurring in many different combinations at any one point in time (spectral modulations) and containing a high degree of variation in frequency and amplitude over time (temporal modulations). An example of a good complex stimulus is zebra finch song because it covers a wide range of time/frequency relation-

---

FIGURE 2. Normalization of the spike-triggered average to obtain the STRF. The spike-triggered average (STA) obtained from responses to zebra finch song for a model linear neuron that has an actual STRF shown on the *upper left panel*, is shown on the *upper right panel*. This STA is a broad version of the STRF due to the correlations in time and frequency of the stimulus. To estimate the effect of these correlations, STAs can be calculated for hypothetical elemental STRFs that have zero gain everywhere except at a single point in time-frequency where they have a gain of one (shown with a red pixel [color in online version] on the figure). The STAs for these elemental STRFs are the auto-correlations of the stimulus around that single point. To recover the STRF, the STA obtained from the neuron is written as a weighted sum of the STAs obtained for all the elemental STRFs as shown on the right column. The weights on the figure are written as K1, K2, etc. The recovered STRF is then the weighted sum of the elemental STRFs using these exact same weights as shown on the left column (excluding the *top panel*). As shown on the figure, the model STRF is very well recovered by this procedure.

ships. A song like that of the white-crowned sparrow is more tricky to use because the STRF is limited by the more narrow range of frequencies and modulations present in that more tonal song.

1c. How Well Does an STRF Describe the Neural Response?

Once an STRF has been estimated, how well it has captured the response of the neuron to the stimulus must be determined. This process is called validation and it is crucial to the value of the STRF as an analysis tool in sensory processing. To validate an STRF, a "prediction" is generated. This process is illustrated in FIGURE 3. The prediction takes the form of an estimated PSTH (red/or black dashed), which is made by convolving the STRF with the spectrograph of the stimulus. This convolution is the cross-product between the STRF reversed in time and the spectrogram (FIG. 3). The estimated PSTH (red) is then compared to the actual PSTH (black) by calculating the correlation coefficient between the two waveforms. How well the real and estimated PSTHs match demonstrates how well the STRF captures the real neural response. There are additional, more in depth, methods for further validation of the STRF described in detail in Theunissen and colleagues[20] and in Hsu and Theunissen.[40]

How well do STRFs actually capture the neural responses of auditory neurons? For a discussion of this issue in songbirds specifically, see chapter on song selectivity by Theunissen and colleagues in this volume. Generally speaking, the current results are mixed. Although the STRF-generated predictions can explain a large fraction of the neural responses of auditory forebrain neurons both in mammals[22,23] and in birds,[10] a fraction remains unexplained. Thus, the linear STRF model is limited. Nevertheless, it can be used as a starting point both for more complex models of auditory encoding that include non-linear processing and for other models that include auditory processing occurring at longer time scales. For example, a dynamic STRF could be used to model stimulus-specific adaptation[24] or other learning dynamics.

A set of Matlab routines that implement all the calculations including a user-friendly graphical interface has been developed in our laboratory and is available for downloading by the neuroscience community at large (<http://strfpak.berkeley.edu>).

1d. What Can Be Learned from the STRF? Frequency Tuning, Temporal Tuning, and Modulation Tuning

As mentioned above, the STRF is a powerful descriptor of the response properties of neurons because many classical characterizations of responses of auditory neurons can be extracted from the STRF. As illustrated in FIGURE 4, the relationships among frequency, time, excitation, and suppression can be measured using the STRF. Slices can be made through the STRF (FIG. 4A), cutting across frequency at one point in time (FIG. 4B) or cutting across time at any one frequency (FIG. 4C). Often these slices are taken by cutting through the peak excitation (red/black) frequency and time. The slice-through frequency shows the "spectral profile" of the STRF, providing measures of excitatory bandwidth (BW), characteristic frequency (CF) and gain of the excitatory response. This same sequence of measures can be made for the inhibitory response (blue/white) by taking a slice through the peak inhibition frequency and time. Considering the patterns of excitation and inhibition to-

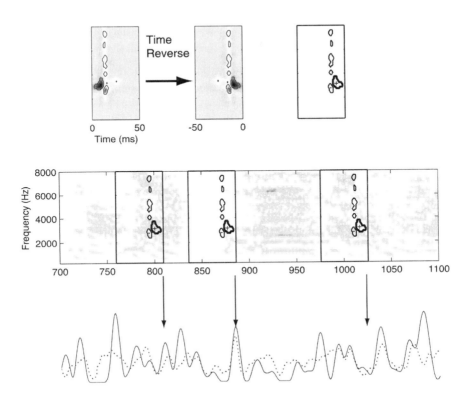

FIGURE 3. The convolution between the spectro-temporal receptive field (STRF) and the spectrogram gives an estimate of the time-varying firing rate of the neuron (a PSTH). The STRF obtained for a neuron in field L is shown on the *upper left graph* where it is displayed with the traditional convention in dynamical systems analysis as an impulse response: time zero would correspond to the time of a very brief pure tone sound at a particular frequency and the colors in the STRF to increase (red [color in online version]) or decrease (blue [color in online version]) in probability of firing as a function of latency (time) and frequency of the tone. To obtain the predicted mean response, the STRF is convolved with a spectrogram. This operation is illustrated on the other panels. The STRF is first reversed in time so that it can now be interpreted as the feature in the spectrogram that would elicit the maximum firing at time *t*=0. This particular neuron was responsive to sounds around 3 kHz, in particular when that sound immediately followed a section of sound that lacked energy around 2.5 kHz as well as other frequencies. To show the match between the STRF and the spectrogram, the time-reversed STRF is shown with contour lines: a *bold line* surrounds the excitatory region and a *solid line* surrounds the inhibitory regions. The predicted response, shown as dashed line or red in online version on the *bottom panel*, is obtained by overlaying the time-reversed STRF on the spectrogram and calculating the match. This calculation is shown at three points in time for a section of a zebra finch song. The *leftmost arrow* illustrates a point in the middle of a syllable that had high energy around 3 kHz while the preceding point in time lacked power in the frequencies surrounded by the inhibitory areas. The *middle arrow* illustrates a point in time that corresponds to the onset of a sound that has energy in the excitatory region

gether within a moment in time reveals tuning characteristics such as the presence or absence of inhibitory sidebands.

The slice through one frequency shows the "temporal profile" of the STRF and describes the timing of the response so that the latencies of the excitatory and inhibitory responses can be measured (Fig. 4C). The gains of the excitatory and inhibitory responses can also be measured. For example, the STRF in FIGURE 4 shows that this neuron's excitatory response was more powerful than it inhibitory response. Additionally, how tightly locked in time the occurrence of certain frequencies and the excitation or inhibition of the neurons are can be examined by measuring the bandwidth of the signal on the temporal profile. The temporal profile can also be used to estimate the best temporal modulation (BTM). The BTM is classically determined using sinusoidally amplitude-modulated (SAM) tones at the CF. The temporal profile of the STRF shows the filter that would be applied to the amplitude envelopes of sound at the CF. Finally, the spectral and temporal profiles can also be obtained by finding the pair of spectral and temporal functions that best approximate the STRF when they are multiplied together. These "average" spectral and temporal profiles are called the separable parts of the STRF. Although both methods lead to similar estimates of CF, BW, latency, and BTM, it has been argued that the second method is more complete because it takes into account the response at all frequencies and time and not at two particular slices in time and frequency.[23]

The STRF can also be analyzed to show the neuron's tuning for spectral modulations, such as harmonic stacks, and temporal modulations, such as the peaks and valleys of sound amplitude over time that are typical of bird song. This analysis entails doing a two-dimensional (2D) Fourier transform of the STRF (FIG. 5). The resultant plot is called a modulation transfer function (MTF) and it shows the combined spectral and temporal modulations to which the neuron with the given STRF will respond best. In other words, it shows the modulation tuning of the neuron's linear response. (FIG. 5B and D).

1e. Matching Modulation Tuning and the Modulations Composing Sounds: The Modulation Spectrum of Song and Ensemble Modulation Transfer Functions

One of the most interesting aspects of determining the modulation tuning of a neuron is that it can be compared to the modulations that compose certain sounds of interest. For example, does the modulation tuning observed in neurons in the songbird auditory processing regions match the modulations that are in songs? This and related questions can be addressed by first measuring the modulations that are in song and then comparing those to the neurons' MTFs.

---

of the receptive field. The *rightmost arrow* shows a section found in the middle of a syllable that lacked energy at 3 kHz and that therefore led to a depressed predicted response. By mentally sliding the contour lines of the STRF, the reader can attempt to predict other points in time. The *black line* is the actual time-varying responses obtained from the PSTH smoothed with a 30 msec hanning window. This particular song was not used in the estimation of the STRF.

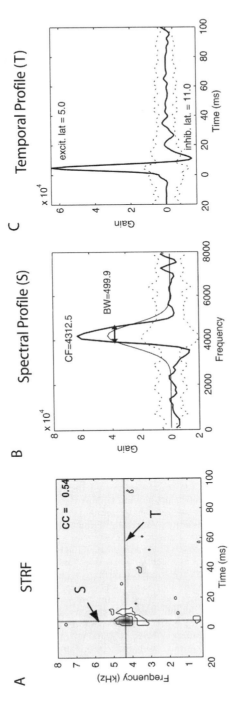

FIGURE 4. Obtaining tuning properties from the STRF. The STRF of a neuron in the auditory nidopallium is shown on the *right panel*. A vertical slice of the STRF that crosses its peak excitatory response (S for Spectral profile) can be used as a tuning curve and is shown on the *middle panel*. The neuron's best frequency (BF) and tuning bandwidth (BW) can be extracted from this spectral profile. Similarly a horizontal slice of the STRF that crosses the same peak excitatory response (T for Temporal profile) can be used to describe the dynamics of the response and is shown on the *right panel*. The neurons excitatory and inhibitory latency can be obtained from this temporal profile. In panels **B** and **C**, the dotted lines (shown in red and green in the online version) correspond to the noise level in the estimate.

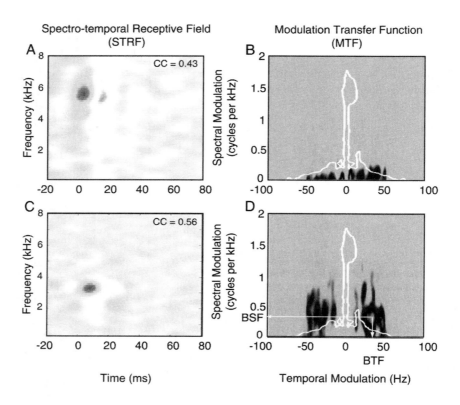

FIGURE 5. The STRF and it corresponding modulation transfer function (MTF). The 2D Fourier transform of the STRF can be calculated to show the spectral and temporal modulation frequencies that best drive the neuron. On this figure, an example STRF and its corresponding MTF is shown for two neurons: a neuron in the auditory midbrain area MLd (**A** and **B**) and a neuron in the auditory forebrain region field L (**C** and **D**). These particular STRFs are not necessarily characteristic of these two areas since each area contains a heterogeneous population of neurons. The neuron whose STRF and MTF are shown in **A** and **B** has low-pass tuning properties to spectral modulations and band pass properties to temporal modulations. Its MTF is also fairly symmetrical along the y axis, reflecting the lack of strong sensitivity to directional modulations such as FM sweeps. The neuron whose STRF and MTF are shown in **C** and **D** has band-pass tuning properties along both the temporal and spectral dimension, with a preference for temporal modulations around 40 Hz (the best temporal modulation or BTF) and a preference for spectral modulations around 0.4 cycles per kHz (the best spectral modulation or BSF). The MTF of this neuron is also asymmetrical, illustrating the fact that this neuron will respond more strongly to frequency down-sweeps that up-sweeps. The *black solid contour line* on the MTF plots surrounds the regions of the modulation spectrum that contains 80% of the energy found in zebra finch song (see text and FIGURE 6).

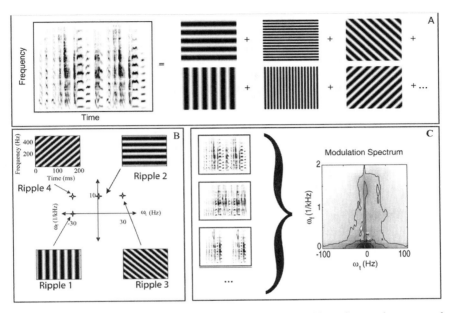

FIGURE 6. Modulation spectrum of sound. (**A**) Decomposition of a sound represented by its spectrogram into its Fourier components: a sum of spectrally and temporally sinusoidal amplitude modulated sounds (called a ripple sound), which can be thought of as the acoustic analog of visual gratings. Each sub-figure on the right side of the equation is the spectrogram of a single ripple sound component. The sound shown is a zebra finch song. (**B**) Ripples are characterized by their temporal modulation, ω_t (Hz), their spectral modulations, ω_f (1/Hz or 1/octave), and their phase (R1, R2, R3, R4, linked to sound online). A single point in a two-dimensional Cartesian plot can be used to represent the ripple sound components of a given spectral and temporal modulation, irrespective of phase. (**C**) To calculate the modulation spectrum, a representative group of sounds is decomposed into its ripple components and the power density of each ripple is estimated and plotted on the two-dimensional Cartesian plot. For the modulation spectrum shown in **C**, we used 20 zebra finch songs of approximately 2 seconds each. (Modified from Figure 1 in Singh and Theunissen.[19])

The modulations present in certain types of sounds, such as zebra finch songs, can be measured by creating a modulation power spectrum, or modulation spectrum. Just as a sound waveform can be broken down into the sine waves that compose it, or its Fourier components using a Fourier transform, a spectrogram of a sound can be transformed in two dimensions to show the spectral and temporal modulations that compose that sound (FIG. 6A). This two-dimensional plot is called the modulation spectrum of the sound.[19]

The modulation spectrum of zebra finch song is shown in FIGURE 6C. The modulation spectrum of zebra finch song has most of its energy at low spectral and temporal frequencies. In addition, most of the higher spectral modulation is only found at the lowest temporal frequencies. To determine whether a particular auditory neuron is tuned to modulations present in particular complex sounds, the MTF corresponding to its STRF can be directly compared to the modulation spectra of a characteristic ensemble of such sounds. For example FIGURE 5 (B and D) show the MTF plots of two example neurons. The black contour line seen on those plots surrounds 80% of the modulation energy in zebra finch song. This contour line is the same as the one shown on the zebra finch song modulation spectrum in FIGURE 6 (C). The energy in the MTF for the example neuron in the midbrain is found almost completely within this contour line. This match suggests that this neuron will respond to the fast temporal modulations that are present in zebra finch song. Indeed, this neuron responds to the onsets of all song syllables; it shows broadband onset responses. On the other hand, the energy in the MTF for the example neuron in FIGURE 5 (C and D) shows power mostly outside the contour line. This particular neuron will respond to acoustical features that are rare in zebra finch song: rapid down-sweep from ~4 kHz to ~2.5 kHz. It is possible, however, that this rare feature could still be essential for the discrimination of two different songs.

The MTF and modulation spectrum can also be used to determine whether a group of neurons taken as an ensemble are tuned to song. Auditory neurons in the avian forebrain have a heterogeneous set of STRFs, reflecting the fact that, individually, the neurons are tuned to many different sounds.[21] But how do they encode sounds as an ensemble? And how do ensembles of neurons in different auditory processing regions encode sounds differently (see Theunissen *et al.*, Song Selectivity in the Song System and in the Auditory Forebrain, this volume)? For this purpose, it does not make sense to obtain an ensemble STRF because the different latencies in time and shifts in frequency would lead to the canceling of individual STRFs as well as a blurring of the spectral and temporal features being encoded. The MTF, however, is insensitive to these phase shifts. Therefore, we can average the MTFs for individual cells and get an ensemble MTF (eMTF), which reflects how responsive an ensemble of neurons (as measured by the ensemble firing rates) would be to specific spectral and temporal modulations found in song. In FIGURE 7, we show the eMTF obtained for an ensemble of neurons in the avian auditory midbrain area (MLd). The contour line that surrounds 80% of the energy of zebra finch song is also shown. In this example, the MLd neurons as an ensemble are tuned to the modulation spectrum of zebra finch song in the sense that the power in the eMTF falls mainly within this 80% contour line of the song modulation spectrum.

2. NEURAL DECODING: MEASURES OF SONG DISCRIMINATION BASED ON MEAN RATES

One of the persistent problems of research on birdsong is the degree to which auditory or song system structures are selectively responsive to sounds that may have functional significance to the bird. For example, how does the nervous system discriminate between the bird's own song and those of conspecifics? Addressing this question means presenting a variety of sounds to the bird and asking whether some properties of the neuronal responses vary with the properties of the sound. One very straightforward way of looking at such differences in responses is to measure whether the response to one sound is "stronger" or more probable than the response to another sound. Addressing this question requires finding a good quantitative measure of response strength and ensuring that quantitative comparisons are not confounded by inherent differences in the spiking behavior of the neurons in question.

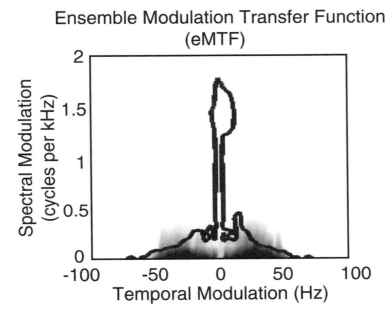

FIGURE 7. The ensemble modulation transfer function (eMTF). The average modulation transfer function for an ensemble of neurons can be obtained by averaging the individual MTFs of the neurons in the ensemble. The figure shows the average MTF for a population of neurons in the auditory midbrain region MLd. In this case, the individual STRFs and MTFs of the neurons where obtained from their responses to modulation-limited noise. By comparing the eMTF to the modulation spectrum of different sound ensembles, the tuning of auditory areas to these specific sound ensembles can be evaluated. As in FIGURE 5, the *black contour line* circles the region that includes 80% of the power in the modulation spectrum of zebra finch song.

The most immediate quantifier of the neural response strength to a complex stimulus such as birdsong is its spike-count rate taken over the duration of the stimulus. The spike-count rate, in spikes/sec, is measured by counting the number of spikes that occur during the presentation of a sound and dividing that number by the duration of the sound. Comparing the stimulus-driven spike-count rate to the spontaneous spike rate provides a measure of response strength. Similarly, to determine whether the response of a neuron is selective to one stimulus over another, the differences in spike-count rates obtained in response to the two stimuli can be computed. For intracellular potential recordings[25] or for extra-cellular waveform recordings,[26] the spike-count rate can be replaced by the integral of the voltage recording divided by the duration of the stimulus.

For birdsong research, rate comparisons have been used to determine the response selectivity of neurons for different classes of song: bird's own song (BOS) versus conspecific song (CON), BOS versus reverse-BOS, etc. To minimize confounding factors, meaningful rate comparisons require that the two stimuli have similar duration and equal power. If the stimuli have different lengths, adaptation could lead to a negative bias for the longer stimulus. If the stimuli have different power, these intensity level differences could also affect the neural response. Finally, the common acoustic properties of the two sound ensembles must be clearly defined so that specific conclusions about the significance of the result can be made. For example, for birdsong researchers interested in high level selectivity, the two (or more) stimuli being compared should share a similar frequency range and power spectrum. Otherwise, simple frequency filtering at the periphery could be responsible for spike-count rate differences observed in higher level auditory neurons.

Rate comparisons are well suited to the comparison of forward song versus reverse or reverse-order song. In reverse song the sound is played backwards and in reverse-order song the syllables are played in reverse order (last syllable first) but with each syllable played forward. In these comparisons, the length, overall power, and power spectrum are identical. Differences in spike-count rate can therefore only be explained by selectivity for the structure of the sound that determines the identity of the song. Spike-count rate differences can also be used to compare responses to the BOS with CON using a statistical approach. As long as the mean duration and the mean power of the ensemble of BOS and CON are similar, the comparison of the mean response, measured by averaging over many birds and many neurons, to each sound type will be valid. These types of comparisons have been made extensively in both the song system[25,26–30] and in other auditory forebrain areas[31–33] (see Theunissen and colleagues in this volume for a review of these and other studies).

Comparing spike-count rates to conspecific versus heterospecific vocalizations is more complicated because of the potential for substantial differences in acoustic properties (as mentioned above). If the songs from the two species are significantly different in duration, frequency range, and/or power spectrum, then spike-count differences could be explained by simpler tuning properties of the neurons and not by higher-order tuning for particular spectro-temporal sound structure that would be characteristic of the species vocalizations. In this case, strong conclusions can only be made in a comparative study where the neural responses to conspecific and heterospecific songs are measured in two or more species.

The raw spike-count rate or the time normalized integral of the voltage recording gives the strength of the response in absolute units. These values are important because they give a sense of the absolute magnitude of the effect and can directly be related to the biophysical properties of the neurons. However, it is difficult to compare raw spike-count rates (or potentials) across neurons that might have different rates of spontaneous activity (or resting potential) and different dynamic ranges. For example, a response of 5 spikes/sec above a background rate of 30 spikes/sec and a dynamic range of 10 spikes/sec to 100 spikes/sec would be different from a response of 5 spikes/sec for a neuron with no spontaneous firing and with a maximum firing rate of 10 spikes/sec. For that reason, the mean rate during background is usually subtracted from the response yielding what has been called the response strength. This measure isolates response differences from inherent differences in the firing properties of the neurons so that the response differences among many neurons can be averaged. Ultimately, analyses that consider both the response and spontaneous firing properties of neurons should be used to fully understand the spiking behavior of neurons (see section 3 below).

To compare the relative responses to two stimuli, a normalized measure of selectivity can be obtained by dividing the response strength to one stimulus by the sum of the two responses[26,28,30]

$$SI_{A-B} = \frac{\mu_A - \mu_{BG}}{(\mu_A - \mu_{BG}) + (\mu_B - \mu_{BG})}$$

where μ_A is the mean response during stimulus A, μ_B is the mean response during stimulus B, and μ_{BG} is the mean response during the background. This measure is called the selectivity index and is a number between 0 and 1 as long as both responses are excitatory. A selectivity index of 0 indicates a complete preference for stimulus B over A, a SI of 0.5 indicates no preference, and a selectivity index of 1 indicates a complete selectivity for stimulus A over B.

Similarly a relative response strength measure, called response strength index, can be obtained by normalizing the response strength by the sum of the background and stimulus-driven mean spike-count rates [34]:

$$RSI = \frac{\mu_S - \mu_{BG}}{\mu_S + \mu_{BG}}$$

For positive measures of response rate, the relative stimulus response strength is a number between −1 and 1.

These normalized measures do not take into account the variability in the responses and therefore cannot definitively provide a measure of neural discriminability, which is the goal of the neural decoding approach. For that purpose, measures from signal detection theory can be used.[1,35] A measure including mean responses and their variances is needed. If the distribution of spike-count rates during stimulus and background are assumed to be normal and the variance in the spike count rates during background and during stimulus presentation are assumed to be the same, then the distributions can be fully characterized by their means and averaged variances.

The response strength measure is then replaced by a Z score given by:

$$Z = \frac{\mu_S - \mu_{BG}}{\sqrt{\sigma_S^2 + \sigma_{BG}^2 - 2\mathrm{Cov}(S, BG)}}$$

where, σ_S^2 is the variance of the response during the stimulus, σ_{BG}^2 the variance of the response during baseline and $Cov(S,BG)$ the covariance between the stimulus and the response. The Z score is unit-less but unbounded. It measures the response in terms of standard deviations above background: a Z score of 1 implies that the mean spike count during the stimulus is one standard deviation above background. Similarly a Z score of −1, would be found for an inhibitory response that is one standard deviation below background. If the distributions satisfy the normal assumptions, then Z scores can be translated into probability of signal detection. For a Z value of 1 or −1, the ideal observer would be able to determine from a single trial whether silence versus sound was presented with a probability of correct detection of ~85%.

Along the same lines, to take into account the variability in the responses, the selectivity index measure can be substituted by the d' of signal detection theory for a two-alternative forced choice test (2AFC):

$$d'_{A-B} = \frac{2(\mu_A - \mu_B)}{\sqrt{\sigma_A^2 + \sigma_B^2}}$$

where μ_A and μ_B are the mean responses to stimulus A and B, respectively, and σ^2 is the variance of the response. This d' quantifies the performance of the ideal observer in the 2AFC test where the neuron would be presented successively but in random order with stimulus A and B. The ideal observer would have to decide given the two spike trials the order of the stimulus presentation. In the expression for d', the estimate of the average variance is

$$\frac{\sigma_A^2 + \sigma_B^2}{2}$$

but, because the observer is presented with two trials, there is an additional noise reduction of $\sqrt{2}$ resulting in the factor of 2 in the numerator. As with the Z score, the d' value can be translated into the probability of correct answers: for normal probabilities, a d' value of 1 corresponds to a probability of correct discrimination of ~85%.

The measure of d' has recently been used to quantify neural selectivity both in the song system and auditory forebrain[29,33,36,37] and can also be used with mean voltage traces obtained in intracellular recordings.[25] Although the use of d' has facilitated the comparison of neural selectivity across different types of neurons (Theunissen and colleagues, this volume) it has not yet been used to correlate neural and behavioral performance of songbirds. Such analysis has been performed with the visual system[38] and could also be done in the songbird system by combining recent techniques in chronic recordings with behavioral experiments. These types of experiments and analyses are needed in order to determine which songbird brain areas encode sufficient information about the identity of the sound to be able to explain behavioral performance.

SUMMARY AND CONCLUSIONS

The processing of sounds in the songbird auditory system is an important issue because song perception undoubtedly depends on how sounds are encoded in those brain regions. In the auditory system, neurons are not tuned to the "identity" of an entire song but, instead, respond to acoustical features on a much shorter time scale. Estimating the spectro-temporal receptive fields (STRFs) of the neurons from their responses to sounds including ensembles of songs provides a visual and quantitative method for determining the time/frequency responses of single neurons. From the STRF, many important tuning properties of a neuron such as CF, bandwidth, spike latency, temporal response pattern, and modulation tuning can be extracted. Although the STRF model is limited because it can only tell us about a neuron's linear tuning, it is useful as an initial representation of what features of sound are being encoded by single neurons and by ensembles of neurons.

Most of the research that has examined high-level auditory decoding in song birds has relied on measuring the spike count rates for responses to song. For sensory neurons with long integration times such as those found in song nuclei, these measures are appropriate and have led to a quantitative description of song-selective neurons. The methods used suggest that song-selective neurons in the song system encode the identity of the feedback of the bird's own song by their spike-count rate obtained over a long integration time. This neural activity can be used to discriminate effectively between the birds own song and other stimuli. It is not known, however, whether this neural discrimination matches the perceptual behavioral discrimination. In addition, if the role of the auditory responses in the song system is to provide feedback during song learning and/or maintenance, the measures of neural discrimination will have to be applied to stimuli that are relevant for this particular behavior, such as good and poor renditions of the bird's own song. This type of analysis has yet to be done. It will require a better understanding of the type of sounds produced during song learning (Tchernichovski and colleagues, this volume) and, optimally, chronic awake recordings in young birds (Fee and colleagues, this volume). Once these techniques are developed, we can expect to see great progress in this area in the near future.

Birdsong researchers have also not explored decoding measures that take into account either the time varying mean rate or precise temporal spike patterns in the neural response. Recently, information theoretic measures that do not make any assumptions on what is being encoded nor how it is being encoded have been developed.[39] These methods have been applied successfully to the study of invertebrate sensory systems but require very large amounts of data. Since both experimental methods allowing for the acquisition of large data sets and simplified calculation methods for the information theoretic values are being developed,[40] we also expect that in the near future, the quantification of neural decoding to different stimuli will include the role of precise spike timing.

The study of how auditory stimuli are represented in the brain of songbirds and how neural responses can be decoded to quantify neural discriminability is a challenging enterprise that requires methods borrowed from statistics, signal detection theory, information theory, and systems analysis. Although these methods have been developed for some time and are common in the engineering community, they are just starting to be used extensively by sensory physiologists. The neural study of auditory coding in birdsong provides particular challenges because it focuses on some of the highest levels of auditory processing and is interested in describing how complex, behaviorally relevant natural sounds are represented. On the other hand, for behavioral or computational neuroscientists interested in the development of methodological approaches, these additional challenges are an opportunity to develop unique analyses that will be of use to sensory physiologists interested in the sensory processing of natural stimuli. For example, the methods first developed to estimate the auditory STRF from birdsong[10] were then generalized to estimate visual spatio-temporal receptive fields from natural scenes.[20] As the study of the songbird auditory system matures, we expect that it will provide both methodological and empirical contributions to our understanding of the processing of complex sensory stimuli.

REFERENCES

1. DAYAN, P. & L.F. ABBOTT. 2001. Computational and Mathematical Modeling of Neural Systems. MIT Press. Cambridge, MA.
2. ZARETSKY, M.D. & M. KONISHI. 1976. Tonotopic organization in the avian telencephalon. Brain Res. **111:** 167–171.
3. POPPER, A.N. & R.R. FAY. 1992. The mammalian auditory pathway: neurophysiology. Springer-Verlag. New York.
4. PHILLIPS, D.P. & S.E. HALL. 1987. Responses of single neurons in cat auditory cortex to time-varying stimuli: linear amplitude modulations. Exp. Brain Res. **67:** 479–492.
5. EGGERMONT, J.J. 2002. Temporal modulation transfer functions in cat primary auditory cortex: separating stimulus effects from neural mechanisms. J. Neurophysiol. **87:** 305–321.
6. CALHOUN, B. & C. SCHREINER. 1998. Spectral envelope coding in cat primary auditory cortex: linear and non-linear effects of stimulus characteristics. Eur. J. Neurosci. **10:** 926–940.
7. SCHREINER, C.E. & B.M. CALHOUN. 1994. Spectral envelope coding in cat primary auditory cortex: properties of ripple transfer functions. Auditory Neurosci. **1:** 39–61.
8. EGGERMONT, J.J., A.M. AERTSEN & P.I. JOHANNESMA. 1983. Quantitative characterisation procedure for auditory neurons based on the spectro-temporal receptive field. Hear Res. **10:** 167–190.
9. DECHARMS, R.C., D.T. BLAKE & M.M. MERZENICH. 1998. Optimizing sound features for cortical neurons. Science. **280:** 1439–1443.
10. THEUNISSEN, F.E., K. SEN & A.J. DOUPE. 2000. Spectral-temporal receptive fields of nonlinear auditory neurons obtained using natural sounds. J. Neurosci. **20:** 2315–2331.
11. DEPIREUX, D.A. et al. 2001. Spectro-temporal response field characterization with dynamic ripples in ferret primary auditory cortex. J. Neurophysiol. **85:** 1220–1234.
12. ESCABI, M.A. & C.E. SCHREINER. 2002. Nonlinear spectrotemporal sound analysis by neurons in the auditory midbrain. J. Neurosci. **22:** 4114–4131.
13. DE BOER, E. & P. KUYPER. 1968. Triggered correlation. IEEE Trans. Biomed. Eng. **15:** 159–179.
14. DE BOER, E. 1967. Correlation studies applied to the frequency resolution of the cochlea. J. Auditory Res. **7:** 209–217.
15. DAN, Y., J.J. ATICK & R.C. REID. 1996. Efficient coding of natural scenes in the lateral geniculate nucleus: experimental test of a computational theory. J. Neurosci. **16:** 3351–3362.
16. EGGERMONT, J.J., P.M. JOHANNESMA & A.M. AERTSEN. 1983. Reverse-correlation methods in auditory research. Q. Rev. Biophys. **16:** 341–414.
17. AERTSEN, A.M.H.J. & P.I.M. JOHANNESMA. 1981. A comparison of the spectro-temporal sensitivity of auditory neurons to tonal and natural stimuli. Biol. Cybernetics **42:** 145–156.
18. NELKEN, I. & E.D. YOUNG. 1997. Linear and nonlinear spectral integration in type IV neurons of the dorsal cochlear nucleus. I. Regions of linear interaction. J. Neurophysiol. **78:** 790–799.
19. SINGH, N.C. & F.E. THEUNISSEN. 2003. Modulation spectra of natural sounds and ethological theories of auditory processing. J. Acoust. Soc. Am. **114:** 3394–3411.
20. THEUNISSEN, F.E. et al. 2001. Estimating spatio-temporal receptive fields of auditory and visual neurons from their responses to natural stimuli. Network: Comp. Neural Syst. **12:** 1–28.
21. SEN, K., F.E. THEUNISSEN & A.J. DOUPE. 2001. Feature analysis of natural sounds in the songbird auditory forebrain. J. Neurophysiol. **86:** 1445–1458.
22. KOWALSKI, N., D.A. DEPIREUX & S.A. SHAMMA. 1996. Analysis of dynamic spectra in ferret primary auditory cortex. II. Prediction of unit responses to arbitrary dynamic spectra. J. Neurophysiol. **76:** 3524–3534.
23. LINDEN, J.F. et al. 2003. Spectrotemporal structure of receptive fields in areas AI and AAF of mouse auditory cortex. J. Neurophysiol. **18:** 18.

24. ULANOVSKY, N., L. LAS & I. NELKEN. 2003. Processing of low-probability sounds by cortical neurons. Nat. Neurosci. **6:** 391–398.
25. MOONEY, R. 2000. Different subthreshold mechanisms underlie song selectivity in identified HVc neurons of the zebra finch. J. Neurosci. **20:** 5420–5436.
26. VOLMAN, S.F. 1996. Quantitative assessment of song-selectivity in the zebra finch "high vocal center." J. Comp. Physiol. A **178:** 849–862.
27. MARGOLIASH, D. 1983. Acoustic parameters underlying the responses of song-specific neurons in the white-crowned sparrow. J. Neurosci. **3:** 1039–1057.
28. MARGOLIASH, D. 1986. Preference for autogenous song by auditory neurons in a song system nucleus of the white-crowned sparrow. J. Neurosci. **6:** 1643–1661.
29. THEUNISSEN, F.E. & A.J. DOUPE. 1998. Temporal and spectral sensitivity of complex auditory neurons in the nucleus HVc of male zebra finches. J. Neurosci. **18:** 3786–802.
30. DOUPE, A.J. 1997. Song- and order-selective neurons in the songbird anterior forebrain and their emergence during vocal development. J. Neurosci. **17:** 1147–1167.
31. LEWICKI, M.S. & B.J. ARTHUR. 1996. Hierarchical organization of auditory temporal context sensitivity. J. Neurosci. **16:** 6987–6998.
32. STRIPLING, R., S. VOLMAN & D. CLAYTON. 1997. Response modulation in the zebra finch caudal neostriatum: relationship to nuclear gene regulation. J. Neurosci. **17:** 3883–3893.
33. JANATA, P. & D. MARGOLIASH. 1999. Gradual emergence of song selectivity in sensorimotor structures of the male zebra finch song system. J. Neurosci. **19:** 5108–5118.
34. CARDIN, J.A. & M.F. SCHMIDT. 2003. Song system auditory responses are stable and highly tuned during sedation, rapidly modulated and unselective during wakefulness, and suppressed by arousal. J. Neurophysiol. **90:** 2884–2899. Epub 2003 Jul 23.
35. GREEN, D.M. & J.A. SWETS. 1966. Signal Detection and Psychophysics. Peninsula Publishing. Los Altos, CA.
36. SOLIS, M.M. & A.J. DOUPE. 1997. Anterior forebrain neurons develop selectivity by an intermediate stage of birdsong learning. J. Neurosci. **17:** 6447–6462.
37. GRACE, J.A. *et al.* 2003. Selectivity for conspecific song in the zebra finch auditory forebrain. J. Neurophysiol. **89:** 472–487.
38. BRITTEN, K. *et al.* 1992. The analysis of visual motion: a comparison of neuronal and psychophysical performance. J. Neurosci. **12:** 4745–4765.
39. STRONG, S.P. *et al.* 1998. Entropy and information in neural spike trains. Phys. Rev. Lett. **80:** 197–200.
40. HSU, A., A. BORST & F.E. THEUNISSEN. 2004. Quantifying variability in neural responses and its application for the validation of model predictions. Network: Comput. Neural Syst. **15:** 91–109.

Auditory Experience and Adult Song Plasticity

SARAH M. N. WOOLLEY

University of California, Berkeley, Department of Psychology,
3210 Tolman Hall, Berkeley, California 94720, USA

ABSTRACT: Adults Bengalese finches normally sing stereotyped songs, which do not change under the influence of auditory experience. If deafened, however, adult birds sing significantly degraded songs that are characterized by a lack of stereotypy of syllable order and the deterioration of syllable structure. We studied the importance of auditory feedback for maintenance of normal adult song. Auditory feedback can be partially or completely removed by eliminating auditory hair cells, the sensory receptor cells for hearing. The effects are reversible because birds regenerate new hair cells when original cells are lost. Limiting the frequency range of auditory feedback available to birds using partial hair cell lesions indicated that low-frequency information (1500 Hz) is necessary and sufficient for the maintenance of normal adult song. Reversible deafening experiments using hair cell loss and regeneration indicated that adult Bengalese finches store memories of their own songs, which can be used to guide vocal behavior. Additionally, destabilizing song behavior by removing auditory feedback leads to renewed song plasticity, and some adults can be induced to learn new song. These studies suggest that Bengalese finches maintain normal song by comparing ongoing vocal output to stored models of their own stable songs and that neural circuitry for song learning persists beyond the sensitive period for song learning.

KEYWORDS: auditory feedback; songbird; sensory-motor integration; vocalization; hair cell; regeneration; plasticity

SENSORY-MOTOR INTEGRATION IN THE BRAIN

Songbirds offer a unique opportunity to study how sensory feedback guides learned, complex motor behavior. In adult birds of some but not all species,[1] normal song behavior requires ongoing auditory feedback. In these birds, if auditory feedback is removed, singing behavior degrades. For example, the normally stereotyped songs of adult zebra finches and Bengalese finches show acoustic deterioration following surgical deafening.[2–6] Therefore, in adults of these species, the auditory system and the vocal motor system are continually exchanging information; auditory cues guide vocal output well beyond the age at which song is learned. Because much of the circuitry involved in the control of song production has been described and given that changes in song behavior can be well quantified, the songbird makes an ideal model for investigating the control of complex motor behavior by sensory feedback.

Address for correspondence: Sarah M. N. Woolley, Department of Psychology, 3210 Tolman Hall, University of California, Berkeley, Berkeley, CA 94720. Voice: 510-643-1531; fax: 510-642-5293.

swoolley@socrates.berkeley.edu

Ann. N.Y. Acad. Sci. 1016: 208–221 (2004). © 2004 New York Academy of Sciences.
doi: 10.1196/annals.1298.017

In this chapter, two topics will be addressed: (1) *what* components of auditory feedback are used to maintain normal adult song patterns; and (2) *how* is auditory feedback used to control adult song behavior. The first topic concerns the specific acoustic cues from a bird's own voice that are crucial for maintaining normal singing. The second topic addresses how sensory feedback and motor commands meet and interact in the brain. This topic is also addressed by Mark Konishi (this volume).

HEARING AND SONG PRODUCTION IN ADULT BIRDS

Bengalese finches are social (nonterritorial), domesticated finches with Southeast Asian ancestry.[7] Only males sing; each individual sings a stereotyped sequence of syllables called a motif (FIG. 1A), which he repeats over and over again in a singing bout. With respect to repertoire size, the organization of song, body posturing, and the conditions under which song is elicited, Bengalese finches are similar to zebra finches. Bengalese finch song and zebra finch song share the same acoustic frequency range (~250–8000 kHz) and some structural characteristics such as the frequent occurrence of harmonic stacks. But Bengalese finch song contains trills which are composed of rapid, repeated sequences of short song elements or notes, and are not found in zebra finch song (FIG. 1A).

Like zebra finches, Bengalese finches are excellent for studies in which the acoustic composition of songs must be carefully quantified because: (1) they will readily sing in the laboratory; (2) each male sings one song type; and (3) as adults, they normally sing highly stereotyped, stable songs that are not influenced by expo-

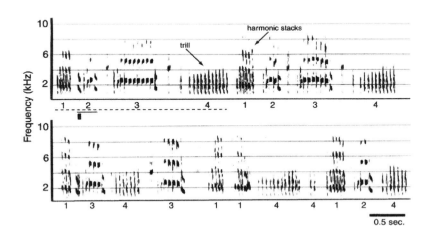

FIGURE 1. Normal Bengalese finch song is composed of stereotyped sequences of syllables (motifs) which are repeated in a singing bout. (**A**) A spectrogram of two normal song motifs. (**B**) The same bird as in **A** but recorded one week after deafening. The syllable order does not match that of the original song and is no longer stereotyped. Syllable types are labeled with numbers below the time axis. The *dashed line* indicates a motif. The *solid line* indicates a syllable, and the *black box* indicates a note.

sure to other birds.[7–11] During song learning, a young bird memorizes the song of an adult tutor (usually the father). This memorization is followed by a period of vocal practice during which the juvenile uses the auditory feedback of his own singing to gradually match his vocal output with the stored memory of his tutor's song. As is true with the zebra finch,[12] some improvisation is involved. Therefore, at the time of sexual maturity (~90 days of age), each young adult male stabilizes or "crystallizes" his own unique version of the tutor's song.

Bengalese finches depend heavily on auditory feedback for the maintenance of **normal adult song**, which degrades if they are **deafened**.[3,4,13,14] Zebra finches also show this effect of deafening, but the changes in song occur more slowly.[2,6,15,16] In zebra finches, the dependence of adult song on hearing appears to vary depending on the bird's age at deafening. Older birds maintain normal song patterns longer than younger birds after deafening, suggesting that the motor circuitry for song production becomes more fixed and less dependent on sensory feedback as adults age.[5]

The quantification of changes in syllable order (sequencing) and syllable structure in deafened Bengalese finches has suggested that there may be at least two different organizational mechanisms involved in the use of auditory feedback to control song production. One mechanism may control syllable order, while another may control syllable structure. The evidence for this idea comes from the different onset times and time frames of the degradation of syllable ordering and syllable structure following deafening.[4] Normal syllable ordering is described by the production of syllables in a fixed temporal order. For example, a bird with four-syllable types will sing 1-2-3-4-1-2-3-4-1-2-3-4 (FIG. 1A). Within one week of deafening, however, the syllable sequencing becomes nearly random so that the bird may sing 1-3-4-4-4-4-3-2-1-3-2-2 (FIG. 1B). The syllable order changes from song bout to song bout such that no stereotypy over time remains. Most singing bouts still begin with introductory notes followed by the first syllable from the normal song, suggesting that initiating a song bout can occur normally without feedback but the production of the next "correct" syllable (#2) requires auditory feedback of the first syllable. Thus, a significant change in syllable order is seen early after deafening. The deterioration of syllable structure begins to occur after the changes in syllable order. Spectrographic cross-correlations between predeafening and postdeafening syllables showed that the degradation of syllable structure was significant two weeks after surgical deafening and gradually worsened over time.[4] This pattern of degradation is quite different from that of syllable ordering and suggests that the precision of the motor commands coding syllable structure can persist without feedback for a couple of weeks but then are slowly lost in the continued absence of auditory feedback. The differences between the changes in syllable order and syllable structure after auditory feedback removal suggest that these two aspects of song organization may depend on auditory feedback in different ways.

MANIPULATING AUDITORY FEEDBACK

Two techniques involving auditory hair cells were developed for manipulating auditory feedback: (1) partial deafening in which feedback of some but not all frequencies is removed; and (2) reversible deafening in which profound hearing loss across all frequencies is induced but later reverses so that hearing is restored. In both

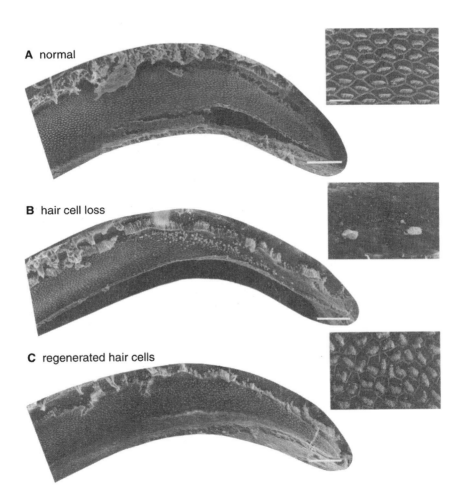

FIGURE 2. Auditory hair cells in the Bengalese finch regenerate after original cells are lost. (**A**) A scanning electron photomicrograph montage of a normal basilar papilla (avian cochlea). The basal (high frequency) half of the papilla is shown. A high-magnification photomicrograph shows the sensory epithelium which is composed of hair cells and support cells. Note the highly organized array of stereocilia bundles on neighboring cells. (**B**) A basilar papilla from a bird that has been treated with the ototoxic drug, Amikacin. Hair cells in the basal end of the epithelium (*right*) have been killed. A high-magnification view shows that the epithelial surface has been denuded of hair cells except for two dead cells lying on the surface. (**C**) A basilar papilla from a bird that recovered from hair cell loss for 12 weeks. The epithelium is populated with regenerated hair cells. A high-magnification view shows the surface structure of regenerated hair cells. The array of regenerated hair cells is less well organized than an array of original hair cells (see **A**). Scale bars indicate 100 μm on montages and 10 μm on high-magnification images.

methods, hair cells, the sensory receptor cells for hearing in the basilar papilla (avian cochlea) are eliminated (FIG. 2). The basilar papilla is tonotopically organized such that high-frequency sounds are encoded by hair cells lying in the base of the sensory epithelium and low-frequency sounds in the apex or distal end of the epithelium. Accordingly, mid-frequencies are encoded by hair cells in the midregion of the epithelium. Hair cells are vulnerable to mechanical and chemical stimuli, particularly a class of antibiotics called aminoglycosides. When the avian ear is exposed to toxic levels of aminoglycosides, hair cells in the base of the sensory epithelium, the high frequency cells, die and are extruded from the epithelium (FIG. 2B). With increased dose and duration of exposure to these ototoxic drugs, cells in progressively more apical (lower frequency) regions of the epithelium also die. The exact pattern and extent of hair cell loss and consequent hearing loss depend on which drug is used, in what dose, and for how long. Hair cells can also be killed by exposure to loud sound, essentially by overstimulation. The hair cell death and hearing loss caused by this type of stimulus depends on the intensity, frequency, and duration of the sound. But, again, the high-frequency cells in the base of the inner ear are most sensitive. High-frequency sound will kill hair cells in the base and spare the others. Midfrequency sound will kill both basal and midregion hair cells. Low-frequency sound alone creates patches of hair cell loss which are highly variable in location and extent of damage[17,18] (Woolley, unpublished observations). If treatment with ototoxic drugs and sound exposure are combined, they appear to have a synergistic effect, causing more hair cell loss than either stimulus alone.[19–21]

Avian and mammalian hair cells differ in that birds can regenerate new hair cells once the original cells have died.[22–25] In Bengalese finches, even when nearly all original hair cells have been lost, a new population of cells will grow and cover the

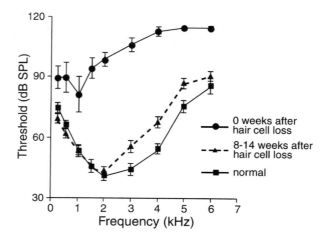

FIGURE 3. Hearing thresholds show profound shifts after original hair cells are killed. They recover to normal (lower frequencies) and near normal (higher frequencies) levels after hair cell regeneration. Auditory thresholds are shown for birds that are normal, birds with profound hearing loss, and those that have recovered for 8 or 14 weeks. Error bars represent ± SEM.

epithelial surface thoroughly by 8 weeks after the loss of original hair cells.[14] An array of regenerated hair cells can always be distinguished from the original hair cell array because it is less precisely organized (compare FIG. 2A and C). Most importantly, regenerated hair cells become innervated by the brain and restore hearing.[14,26–29] Thus, the hearing loss caused by hair cell loss can be reversed. In Bengalese finches, new hair cells grow mostly over the first 4 weeks after loss of the original cells, and the recovery of auditory response thresholds accompanies this regeneration[29] (FIG. 3). The functional recovery is remarkably good but not perfect. Hearing thresholds in mid- and low frequencies recover to match normal hearing thresholds. But, when hair cell loss is extensive, the recovery of high-frequency hearing sensitivity suffers; threshold shifts in the higher hearing frequencies persist after hair cell regeneration is complete[26,27,29] (FIG. 3). Thus, the tonotopic specificity of hair cell damage and the ability of birds to regenerate hair cells make it possible to eliminate auditory feedback, selectively and reversibly.

WHAT COMPONENTS OF AUDITORY FEEDBACK REGULATE SONG PRODUCTION?

We used selective hair cell loss to address the question of what kind of auditory feedback is necessary for the maintenance of normal adult song behavior. With either ototoxic drugs alone or drugs combined with sound exposures, we created hair cell lesions such that the amount and location of hair cell death could be specified.[13] Using this approach, we studied the effects of frequency-specific hearing losses on song. In some birds, high-frequency feedback was removed by killing the hair cells in the basal one-half of the basilar papilla. In others, hair cells encoding high- and midfrequency sounds were killed; only low-frequency feedback was preserved. And in some birds, all auditory feedback was removed by killing hair cells across the entire length of the basilar papilla. Birds with only high-frequency hearing were not included because it is not possible to eliminate only low- and midfrequency hair cells (see above). Songs of these three groups of birds were analyzed for any changes that resulted from hearing loss. We found that birds with normal hearing below 1500 Hz maintained normal song patterns. The birds without those low-frequency hair cells, those with the largest amount of hair cell loss, showed song degradation similar to that of surgical deafening. Therefore, the preservation of apical hair cells encoding only low-frequency auditory feedback (1500 Hz and below) was sufficient to maintain normal song, even though the frequency range of song goes up to at least 8000 Hz.

The finding that low-frequency feedback is sufficient for normal singing behavior in adults suggests that either the temporal pattern of the song which can be obtained from low-frequency feedback or the spectral information carried by low frequencies in song is the crucial auditory feedback used to maintain normal singing. Thus, even though birds normally hear feedback of the entire song, only a portion of the information in the song may be necessary and sufficient to control song production. Understanding the components of auditory feedback that are crucial for normal singing in adults may be helpful for investigating the neural mechanisms of auditory-vocal integration.

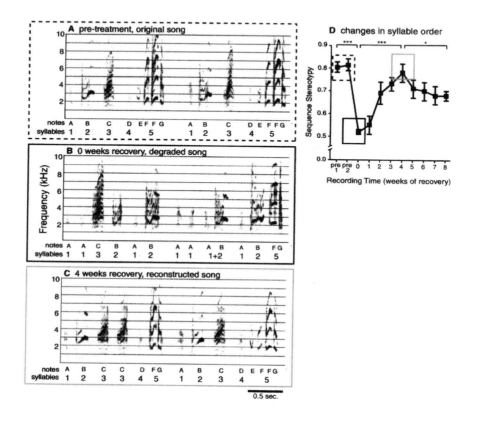

FIGURE 4. Birds with profound hearing loss showed degraded song. Syllable sequences returned to the original, pretreatment order, and some aspects of syllable structure recovered toward that of the original song by 4 weeks after treatment. (**A**) **Spectrogram** of two song motifs recorded before treatment. (**B**) Song from the **same bird** as in **A** but one day after the end of treatment. Comparison of **A** and **B** shows that syllable order is changed and the acoustic structure of syllables is degraded. (**C**) Two **song motifs** from the same bird as in **A** and **B** recorded 4 weeks after treatment. The song recorded after 4 weeks of recovery appears similar to the pretreatment song and dissimilar to the song recorded immediately after treatment. Individual syllables are labeled with numbers, and notes are labeled with letters below the x-axis. (**D**) Sequence stereotypy scores [expressed as:(# syllables types per bout / # transition types per bout) + (sum typical transitions / sum total transitions per bout)/2; transitions are defined as the progression from one syllable to the next—typical transitions are those that occur in the normal song] for birds singing degraded song after hair cell loss decreased significantly by one day after treatment. By 4 weeks after treatment, scores had increased significantly and were no longer different from pretreatment scores. Between 4 and 8 weeks after treatment, scores decreased again (see FIG. 6). *$P < 0.05$, ***$P < 0.001$.

HOW AUDITORY FEEDBACK REGULATES SONG PRODUCTION

The ability to reversibly deafen songbirds allows us to ask several questions that permanent deafening cannot address. Do adult songbirds store memories of their own songs? If so, are these memories stable in the brain no matter what the bird is actually singing? Can they be used to shape song production? And, finally, if disrupting sensory-motor integration can destabilize the circuitry for song production, can new plasticity and maybe even new song learning result from the restoration of sensory-motor integration?

Birds with profound hearing loss due to hair cell loss show song degradation within a week.[13,14] Syllable sequences become nearly random immediately after the completion of a one-week treatment to cause hair cell loss (FIG. 4), while syllable structure significantly degrades by one week after the end of treatment (FIG. 5). But most important is what happens to the songs during and after the recovery of hearing, as hair cells regenerate. We analyzed the songs of birds recovering from extensive hair cell loss. As hair cells regenerated over the four weeks following treatment, syllable order gradually returned toward the ordering in the original, pretreatment songs (FIG. 4). By the end of four weeks, the syllable sequences matched those of the original songs. Syllable structure also recovered significantly, but more slowly and less completely (FIG. 5). Some syllables recovered better than others, perhaps because some acoustic elements are more difficult to produce than others. This recovery of the original song indicated that the birds that had undergone loss of hair cells and hearing retained a neural representation of their own normal songs even though they were unable to produce those songs for a time. Once feedback was restored, they were able to reconstruct their original songs. Therefore, song memories can be used to shape vocal output once access to them becomes available with the restoration of hearing. These findings suggest that adult birds may normally use auditory feedback to compare their own vocal output with a stored model of the "normal" song in a process that is similar to the sensory-motor integration between the tutor song model and vocal output during development.

Evidence that adult birds store memories of their own songs has been demonstrated in adult zebra finches using a delayed feedback paradigm.[30] Singing birds received delayed feedback of their songs through a computer-controlled speaker so that they heard their own feedback both in real time and with an artificial delay. Under these conditions, songs degraded significantly by six weeks after the onset of the feedback delay. When normal feedback was restored, birds' songs gradually recovered their original forms, suggesting that zebra finches, like Bengalese finches, retain stored models of their normal songs despite singing degraded songs.

These studies seem to imply that there is a stored set of instructions for adult song that *should* be produced and another for the motor commands that actually produce the song, and that they can be decoupled. If we consider the motor commands that produce degraded song to contain errors, then the stored song model in the adult brain could be considered a set of stable circuits that are upstream from those commands. This leads to the question of the physical representation of a song memory. Is this a stored sensory model, similar to the stored representation of the tutor song that is formed and used as a template in the juvenile brain? Perhaps the tutor song model becomes the model of the bird's own song as a young adult stabilizes his learned song at sexual maturity.[31,32] The adult song memory may be a separate rep-

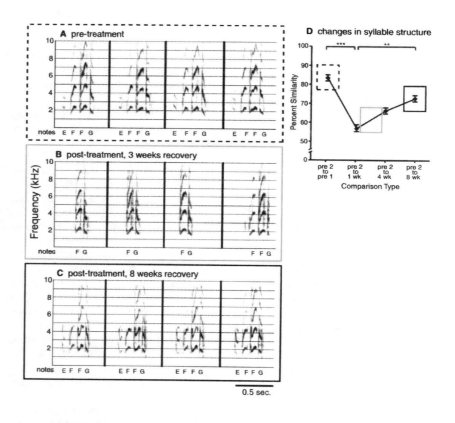

FIGURE 5. Most syllables that degraded after hearing loss returned to match their original structure. By 8 weeks, syllable structure was more similar to pretreatment song than to song recorded earlier in recovery. (**A**) Spectrograms of the first four iterations of the same syllable type taken from one randomly selected song bout in pretreatment records. The variability of several iterations of the same syllable type in normal song can be seen. (**B**) Spectrograms of the first four iterations of the same syllable type from the same bird as in **A** taken from one randomly selected song bout recorded after 3 weeks of recovery. (**C**) The first four iterations of the same syllable type from the same bird as in **A** and **B** taken from one randomly selected bout recorded after 8 weeks of recovery. **A** and **C** are more similar than **B** is to either **A** or **C**. Notes are labeled with letters below each syllable. (**D**) Average acoustic similarity [measured using Sound Analysis softwar;[34] pitch, spectral continuity, frequency modulation and Wiener entropy are calculated and compared between two sounds (e.g., syllables) to indicate the acoustic similarity between sounds] between pretreatment syllables and between pretreatment syllables and syllables recorded after treatment show that syllables significantly deteriorated by one week after treatment. Acoustic similarity between syllables from pretreatment recordings and recordings made 8 weeks after recovery was significantly improved. *Pre 1* indicates the first pretreatment recording, and *pre 2* indicates the second pretreatment recording. 1 wk indicates one week after treatment. Error bars represent ± SEM; **$P < 0.01$, ***$P < 0.001$.

resentation that is stored in sensory, motor, or sensory-motor brain regions. Or, it may be a stored set of motor commands that are separate from vocal motor commands that actually produce the song but can instruct those commands. In this case, removing auditory feedback could sever the connection between the stored motor commands representing the normal song and the vocal motor commands producing the song. Under these circumstances, vocal motor commands are no longer instructed by the stored song representation, and vocal output degrades.

The above hypotheses on how song memory is represented in the brain need to be addressed with physiological and behavioral studies. First, a greater understanding is needed of how the songbird's ascending auditory regions that are presynaptic to the song system process song. Currently, we have little knowledge of what song feedback information reaches the sensory/motor structures of the song control system (but see the chapters by Theunissen). Second, the interactions between sensory activity in the ascending auditory system and motor activity in the vocal motor system should be examined. For example, if the activity of the vocal motor system and the processing of feedback in the auditory system are physiologically monitored at the same time during singing, a functional relationship between auditory feedback and vocal control may be established. Third, the relationship between song-specific neurons and adult song production should be examined using reversible paradigms for induced plasticity in adult songs. For example, does response selectivity in song-specific neurons change when the song changes? If so, then the song selectivity exhibited by these neurons may be susceptible to training through auditory experience that occurs after the sensitive period for song development, and potentially throughout a bird's life. This is best approached using a delayed feedback[30] or noise masking[33] paradigm because normal hearing can be restored soon after song has degraded. Finally, the location(s) of a song memory in the brain must be investigated. Lesion studies combined with manipulations to auditory feedback similar to those designed by Brainard and Doupe[16] could be successful in identifying candidate brain regions for memory storage and retrieval. Once some idea of where to look has been attained, the organization of neuron ensembles that represent the memory coding of a complex and learned behavior can be approached. This will be an exciting opportunity and one that demonstrates how understanding song production in birds can contribute to the basic question of how a memory is represented in the brain.

SONG PLASTICITY: ADULTS CAN BE INDUCED TO LEARN

Reversible deafening experiments are advantageous for testing the potential plasticity of the adult songbird brain. Could adult birds that do not normally learn new song in adulthood be induced to learn by causing a disruption in normal singing? If so, this would imply that the circuitry required for new song acquisition is present in the adult brain. To address this issue, birds were treated with a combination of ototoxic drugs and sound exposure to cause extensive hair cell loss and profound hearing loss.[14] Then birds were housed in two social conditions while they were regenerating hair cells and undergoing hearing restoration. One group of birds was housed together. In the other group, each recovering male was isolated with one untreated cagemate who was singing normal song, serving as a potential tutor. All birds recovered their original songs initially, with no apparent differences between social conditions. However, after that song recovery was completed, some (3 of 7) birds from both groups changed their songs away from a match with their original songs. Changes included deleting notes from within syllables, structurally modifying notes into new notes and rearranging those notes to form new syllables (FIG. 6). Often, modified/new notes and new syllables were sung at the end of a motif. When we analyzed these changes, we found that the modified/new notes and syllables matched the notes and syllables of the cagemates' songs. As the match between notes of the recovering birds and the original versions gradually and significantly decreased, between 4 and 8 weeks after hair cell loss (see ref. 34; FIG. 6D), the match between those same notes and the cagemates' notes increased significantly. After 8 weeks of recovery, these notes were significantly more similar to the cagemates' notes than to their original versions (FIG. 6D). We interpreted these results as evidence that the birds with regenerated hair cells had copied the notes and syllables of the songs of their cagemates, implying that these adult birds had been induced to learn. This copying process is not the same as the learning that occurs during normal song development. The new notes that adults acquire are the result of incremental modification of existing notes over time, and the new syllables result from the assembly of those notes into patterns that match the cagemate's song, but do not match the original song. Thus, revising and rearranging previously existing song material forms the new material in adult songs. In contrast, juveniles develop highly structured copies of their tutors' songs with a previous vocal repertoire of simple begging calls only. Therefore, the song learning exhibited by adults appears to be constrained in comparison to song acquisition that is accomplished by juvenile birds.

If song learning, which normally occurs only during a sensitive period, can be induced long after the end of that period, albeit in a limited way, then at least some song learning circuits are retained past the age at which the sensitive period closes. There is evidence that the sensitive period for song learning can be extending by withholding the appropriate sensory input. Young Bengalese and zebra finches that do not get an appropriate song model will continue to be able to learn for several weeks after the normal close of the sensitive period, until an acceptable model can be copied.[9,35] This suggests that the timing of the sensitive period can be manipulated. However, the extension of juvenile song learning is quite different from inducing birds with formerly stable songs to learn new notes and syllables, and it is possible that different neural circuitry in involved in each process. It will be interesting to discover whether this learning effect can be replicated in other species and whether methods of auditory feedback manipulation other than hair cell regeneration can be used.

The value of demonstrating that adult birds can be induced to learn lies in its support of two ideas: (1) circuitry that is required for song motor learning is present in the adult brain; (2) a behavior may change more readily after it has been destabilized. Forms of song learning which are more subtle than the classical memorization process that is bounded by a sensitive period may exist.[36] Similar to Marler and Nelson's "action-based learning" theory, adult learning in Bengalese finches occurs during a period of vocal plasticity such that experimentation is possible and may be a prerequisite for learning. And, adult learning may be subject to social reinforcement through interactions with another bird from which the new song elements are learned. Additionally, different forms of song learning may employ different neural circuits. It is possible that the circuitry required for adult song learning does not

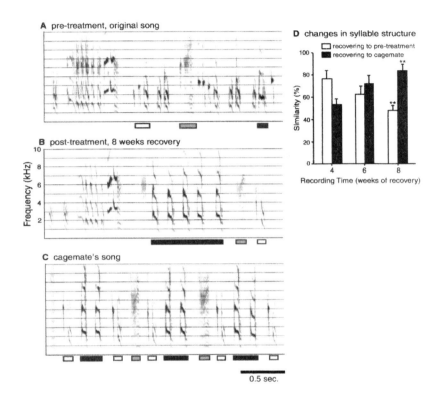

FIGURE 6. An example of song modification that occurs after initial song recovery. (**A**) One pretreatment motif. (**B**) One motif from the **same bird** as in **A** after 8 weeks of recovery; the introductory note and the first syllable recovered to their original structures, but the following notes were modified such that they do not match their original structures. [Listeners (online) should pay special attention to the five repeated notes that are sung after the first sound and that are underlined by the black bar in the figure.] These modified notes immediately follow the first syllable, and the rest of the original motif is skipped. (**C**) **Song** from the cagemate of the bird shown in **A** and **B**. The similarities between **B** and **C** are stronger than between **A** and **B**. [Listeners (online) should pay special attention to the two repeated notes that are intermittently sung and that are underlined by the black bars in the figure. These are the notes shared with the learner in 6**B**.] Bars below the x-axis indicate the similar song portions among **A**, **B**, and **C**. (**D**) Acoustic similarity between modified notes and their original versions (*open bars*) decreased significantly between 4 and 8 weeks after treatment. Similarity between modified notes and the cagemate's notes (*filled bars*) increased significantly between 4 and 8 weeks of recovery. Similarities are higher at 4 weeks than would be expected on the basis of data shown in FIGURE 5 because notes deleted from syllables during song modification could not be included in this analysis. **P < 0.01.

function in that capacity until normal song behavior is destabilized. Neural activity during singing in birds with normal, stable song and in birds with abnormal, destabilized song may differ in ways that can offer clues as to how sensory and motor circuits interact to accomplish song learning.

Study of a songbird that depends on auditory feedback for the maintenance of normal adult song has provided us with several insights as to how song may be represented in the brain. First, only a subset of the auditory feedback cues available to a bird appears to be necessary for maintaining normal song behavior. Second, adult finches appear to store memories of their own songs that can be used to instruct vocal behavior. This conclusion prompts the pursuit of where and how that memory is represented in the adult brain. Third, limited song learning can be induced in adults who normally learn only during a sensitive developmental period. This indicates that the adult songbird brain is capable of greater plasticity than previously believed.

REFERENCES

1. KONISHI, M. 1965. The role of auditory feedback in the control of vocalization in the white-crowned sparrow. Z. Tierpsychol. **22:** 770–783.
2. NORDEEN, K.W. & E.J. NORDEEN. 1992. Auditory feedback is necessary for the maintenance of stereotyped song in adult zebra finches. Behav. Neural Biol. **57:** 58–66.
3. OKANOYA, K. & A. YAMAGUCHI. 1997. Adult Bengalese finches (*Lonchura striata* var. *domestica*) require real-time auditory feedback to produce normal song syntax. J. Neurobiol. **33:** 343–356.
4. WOOLLEY, S.M.N. & E.W. RUBEL. 1997. Bengalese Finches *Lonchura striata domestica* depend upon auditory feedback for the maintenance of adult song. J. Neurosci. **17:** 6380–6390.
5. LOMBARDINO, A.J. & F. NOTTEBOHM. 2000. Age at deafening affects the stability of learned song in adult male zebra finches. J. Neurosci. **20:** 5054–5064.
6. SCOTT, L L., E.J. NORDEEN & K.W. NORDEEN. 2000. The relationship between rates of HVc neuron addition and vocal plasticity in adult songbirds. J. Neurobiol. **43:** 79–88.
7. IMMELMANN, K. 1969. Song development in the zebra finch and other estrildid finches. *In* Bird Vocalizations: Their Relations to Current Problems in Biology and Psychology: Essays Presented by W.H. Thorpe. R.A. Hinde, Ed.: 61–74. Cambridge Umiversity Press. London, England.
8. DIETRICH, K. 1980. Model choice in the song development of young male Bengalese finches. Z. Tierpsychol. **52:** 57–76.
9. CLAYTON, N.S. 1987. Song learning in Bengalese finches: a comparison with zebra finches. Ethology **76:** 247–255.
10. CLAYTON, N.S. 1988. Song tutor choice in zebra finches and bengalese finches: the relative importance of visual and vocal cues. Behaviour **104:** 281–299.
11. CLAYTON, N.S. 1989. The effects of cross-fostering on selective song learning in estrildid finches. Behaviour **109:** 163–175.
12. WARD, B.C., E.J. NORDEEN & K.W. NORDEEN. 1998. Individual variation in neuron number predicts differences in the propensity for vocal imitation. Proc. Natl. Acad. Sci. USA **95:** 1277–1282.
13. WOOLLEY, S.M.N. & E.W. RUBEL. 1999. High-frequency auditory feedback is not required for adult song maintenance in Bengalese finches. J. Neurosci. **19:** 358–371.
14. WOOLLEY, S.M.N. & E.W. RUBEL. 2002. Vocal memory and learning in adult Bengalese finches with regenerated hair cells. J. Neurosci. **22:** 7774–7787.
15. NORDEEN, K.W. & E.J. NORDEEN. 1993. Long-term maintenance of song in adult zebra finches is not affected by lesions of a forebrain region involved in song learning. Behav. Neural Biol. **59:** 79–82.
16. BRAINARD, M. & A.J. DOUPE. 2000. Interruption of a basal ganglia-forebrain circuit prevents plasticity of learned vocalizations. Nature **404:** 762–766.

17. RYALS, B.M. & E.W. RUBEL. 1982. Patterns of hair cell loss in chick basilar papilla after intense auditory stimulation. Frequency organization. Acta Otolarynol. **93:** 205–210.

18. COTANCHE, D.A. *et al.* 1994. Hair cell regeneration in the bird cochlea following noise damage or ototoxic drug damage. Anat. Embryol. **189:** 1–18.

19. BONE, R.C. & A.F. RYAN. 1978. Audiometric and histologic correlates of the interaction between kanamycin and subtraumatic levels of noise in the chinchilla. Otolaryngology **86:** 400–404.

20. COLLINS, P.W. 1988. Synergistic interactions of gentamicin and pure tones causing cochlear hair cell loss in pigmented guinea pigs. Hear. Res. **36:** 249–259.

21. BRUMMETT, R.E., K.E. FOX & J.B. KEMPTON. 1992. Quantitative relationships of the interaction between sound and kanamycin. Arch. Otolaryngol. Head Neck Surg. **118:** 498–500.

22. COTANCHE, D.A. 1987. Regeneration of hair cell stereociliary bundles in the chick cochlea following severe acoustic trauma. Hear. Res. **30:** 181–195.

23. CRUZ, R.M., P.R. LAMBERT & E.W. RUBEL. 1987. Light microscopic evidence of hair cell regeneration after gentamicin toxicity in chick cochlea. Arch. Otolaryngol. Head Neck Surg. **113:** 1058–1062.

24. CORWIN, J.T. & D.A. COTANCHE. 1988. Regeneration of sensory hair cells after acoustic trauma. Science **240:** 1772–1774.

25. RYALS, B.M. & E.W. RUBEL. 1988. Hair cell regeneration after acoustic trauma in adult Coturnix quail. Science **240:** 1774–1776.

26. TUCCI, D.L. & E.W. RUBEL. 1990. Physiologic status of regenerated hair cells in the avian inner ear following aminoglycoside ototoxicity. Otolaryngol. Head Neck Surg. **103:** 443–450.

27. MAREAN, G.C. *et al.* 1993. Hair cell regeneration in the European starling (*Sturnus vulgaris*): recovery of pure-tone detection thresholds. Hear. Res. **71:** 125–126.

28. MAREAN, G.C. *et al.* 1995. Regenerated hair cells in the European starling: are they more resistant to kanamycin ototoxicity than original hair cells? Hear. Res. **82:** 267–276.

29. WOOLLEY, S.M.N., A.M. WISSMANN & E.W. RUBEL. 2001. Hair cell regeneration and recovery of auditory thresholds following aminoglycoside ototoxicity in Bengalese finches. Hear. Res. **153:** 181–195.

30. LEONARDO, A. & M. KONISHI. 1999. Decrystallization of adult birdsong by perturbation of auditory feedback. Nature **399:** 466–470.

31. VOLMAN, S. 1993. Development of neural selectivity for birdsong during vocal learning. J. Neurosci. **13:** 4737–4747.

32. DOUPE, A.J. 1997. Song- and order-selective neurons in the songbird anterior forebrain and their emergence during vocal development. J. Neurosci. **17:** 1147–67.

33. ZEVIN, J.D., M.S. SEIDENBERG & S.W. BOTTJER. 2000. Song plasticity in adult zebra finches exposed to white noise. Soc. Neurosci. Abstr. **26:** 723.

34. TCHERNICHOVSKI, O. *et al.* 2000. A procedure for an automated measurement of song similarity. Anim. Behav. **59:** 1167–1176.

35. EALES, L.A. 1985. Song learning in zebra finches: some effects of song model availability on what is learnt and when. Anim. Behav. **33:** 1293–1300.

36. MARLER, P. 1997. Three models of song learning: evidence from behavior. J. Neurobiol. **33:** 501–516.

Song Selectivity in the Song System and in the Auditory Forebrain

FRÉDÉRIC E. THEUNISSEN, NOOPUR AMIN, SARITA S. SHAEVITZ,
SARAH M. N. WOOLLEY, THANE FREMOUW, AND MARK E. HAUBER

Department of Psychology and Neuroscience Institute, University of California Berkeley, Berkeley, California 94720-1650, USA

ABSTRACT: The sensorimotor neurons found in the song-system nuclei are responsive to the sounds of the bird's own song. This selectivity emerges during vocal learning and appears to follow the development of the bird's song vocalization in two ways: at each stage, the neurons are most selective for the bird's current vocalizations and this selectivity increases as the bird learns to produce a stable adult song. Also, because of their location in the sensori-vocal pathway and because their physiological properties are correlated with the motor program, it is postulated that these neurons play a crucial role in interpreting the auditory feedback during song to preserve a desirable vocal output. The neurons found in presynaptic auditory areas lack this selectivity for the bird's own song. Auditory neurons in the secondary auditory areas caudal nidopallium and caudal mesopallium show specific responses to familiar songs or behaviorally relevant songs. These auditory areas might therefore be involved in perceptual tasks. Neurons in the primary forebrain auditory area are selective for the spectrotemporal modulations that are common in song, yielding an efficient neural representation of those sounds. Neurons that are particularly selective for the tutor song at the end of the sensory period have not yet been described in any areas. Although these three levels of selectivity found in the primary auditory forebrain areas, the secondary auditory forebrain areas, and the song system suggest a form of hierarchical sensory processing, the functional connectivity between these areas and the mechanisms generating the specific selectivity for songs that are behaviorally relevant or crucial in song learning and production have yet to be revealed.

KEYWORDS: natural sounds; vocalizations; auditory cortex

INTRODUCTION: BRAIN MECHANISMS, AUDITORY PROCESSING, AND PERCEPTUAL BEHAVIORS

Auditory perception is crucial for reproductive success in both male and female songbirds (see Nowicki and Searcy, this volume). However, the neural mechanisms mediating song perception and recognition are not well understood. This article reviews song behavior involving song perception and then compares the auditory re-

Address for correspondence: Frédéric E Theunissen, Department of Psychology and Neuroscience Institute, 3210 Tolman Hall, Berkeley California 94720-1650, USA. Fax: 510-642-5293.
fet@socrates.berkeley.edu
<http://psychology.berkeley.edu/directories/facultypages/theunissenresearch.html>

Ann. N.Y. Acad. Sci. 1016: 222–245 (2004). © 2004 New York Academy of Sciences.
doi: 10.1196/annals.1298.023

sponses in the song nuclei with those found in the auditory forebrain. This approach is top-down and reflects the historical progression of research in this field. Shortly after the song nuclei were characterized[1] and their role in song production and learning was verified by lesion studies,[1,2] much of the auditory research on the neurobiology of birdsong focused on the auditory responses found in the song system. The discovery of neurons that were selective to the sound of the bird's own song (BOS)[3,4] made this line of research very appealing, and as a result, there was an explosion in the generation of hypotheses on how these selective responses could participate in both vocal learning and in song perception. At the same time, the research on sound processing in the general auditory areas did not seem to provide many answers about how the tutor song was recognized and stored, or more generally, about how overall song perception was mediated.[5] That original picture has changed. As our knowledge of the properties of neurons in the song system has increased, it has become clear that the perception of familiar conspecific songs and the storage of the tutor song must either exclusively or additionally involve brain areas other than the song system. It has also become clear that to understand how the selectivity for the BOS found in the song system is generated, the representations in auditory areas that are presynaptic to the song nuclei and the circuitry between these auditory areas and the song system must be understood. This article will review both the historic and more recent work that has taken us on this path.

THE AUDITORY SYSTEM OF SONGBIRDS AND ITS CONNECTIVITY WITH THE SONG SYSTEM

FIGURE 1 shows the ascending auditory system and its known connections with the song system. The avian auditory system shares many similarities with that of mammals in terms of the number of auditory nuclei and the pattern of feed-forward connections from the cochlear nucleus to the forebrain. As shown in FIGURE 1, afferents from the auditory medulla converge in nucleus MLd in the midbrain, which is analogous to the inferior colliculus in mammals. As in mammals, the auditory midbrain projects to a nucleus in the thalamus (Ov), which in turn sends projections to the primary auditory forebrain area in the nidopallium, field L.[6] Field L has been divided into subregions (L, L1, L2a, L2b, L3) based on differences in cytoarchitecture and connectivity.[7,8] This primary auditory region has bidirectional connections with secondary auditory areas in the caudal nidopallium (NCM) and caudal mesopallium (CM). The song nuclei, shown in gray in FIGURE 1, are specialized brain areas for song production and learning that are only found in songbirds that learn to sing.[9] The connectivity pattern in the song nuclei is mostly unidirectional: nucleus NIf (in the nidopallium) and Uva (in the thalamus) project to HVC. HVC projects to RA via two distinct pathways, and RA projects to vocal and respiratory motor nuclei (see introduction). Note that for the purpose of classification in this article, NIf has been classified as part of the sensorimotor song system and not the general auditory forebrain system.

The exact flow of information from the auditory system to the song system is not well understood. NIf shows robust auditory responses and, as demonstrated both anatomically[8,10] and functionally,[11] projects strongly to HVC. NIf receives input from the secondary auditory area CM[8] and potentially directly from ovoidalis (see

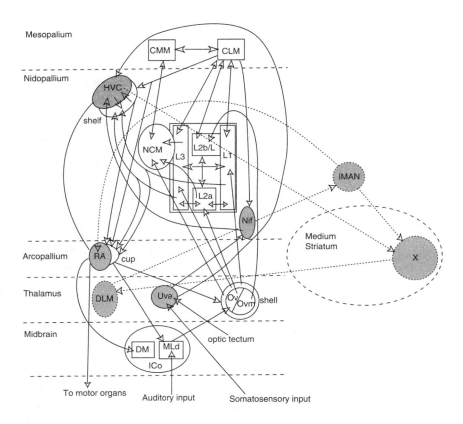

FIGURE 1. The ascending auditory system and its connectivity with the song system. Song nuclei are shown in *gray*. The *dashed* song nuclei and connections comprise the anterior forebrain pathway.

Wild, this volume). NIf is therefore a good candidate for auditory input to the song system. On the other hand, the shelf region of both HVC and RA receive auditory projections from auditory forebrain areas (in this case from L1, L3, and CM) and input from the shelf region of HVC might enter the nucleus proper. Moreover, direct sparse projections from L1 and L3 to HVC have been described anatomically.[10] The relative importance of these two (one direct and one indirect) routes for sensory input into the song system is not known. In addition, nucleus Uva (in the thalamus) is known to project to both HVC and NIf[12] and appears to play a functional role in initiating and terminating neural activity in HVC and correspondingly in song output.[13] The responses of Uva neurons to complex song stimuli have not yet been investigated, but given its afferent connections from sensory areas,[12] a thorough exploration of its sensory properties seems warranted. Such an investigation could provide valuable information about Uva's potential position in the sensorimotor hierarchy.

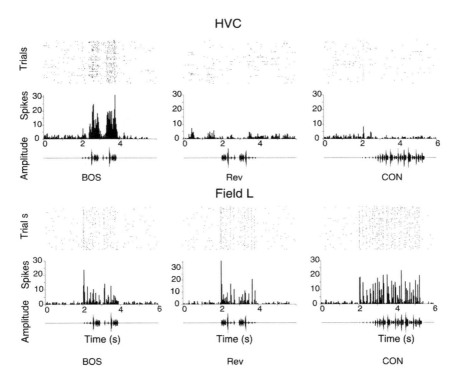

FIGURE 2. Example of neural responses to the bird's own song (**BOS**), the BOS played in reverse (**Rev**) and conspecific song (**CON**) in the song system (HVC) and in the primary auditory forebrain (field L). These recordings were obtained in urethane-anesthetized adult male zebra finches. The recordings in HVC and field L were obtained simultaneously in a double-electrode experiment. Fifty trials to each stimulus were acquired. The figure shows the spike raster on the top line (Trials), the PSTH in the middle line (Spikes) and the oscillogram of the stimulus (Amplitude) on the bottom line.

AUDITORY RESPONSES IN THE SONG SYSTEM

Selectivity for the Bird's Own Song

The auditory properties of neurons in the song system, particularly in HVC, have been studied extensively in playback experiments. A striking property of neurons in the song system of adult male songbirds is their selective responses to the sound of the bird's own song (BOS) over the BOS played in reverse (BOS-Rev) or other conspecific songs (BOS-CON). The differences in responses between these three stimuli can be drastic as seen in the example recording from HVC neurons in an adult male zebra finch shown in the top panel of FIGURE 2. In this example, there is a strong response to the bird's own song and a lack of response to the song played in reverse or to a conspecific song. This response property has been labeled "song selectivity." The use of that phrase is somewhat misleading since sensory neurons in the song system are in fact selective for one particular song, the BOS, as compared to other conspecific songs. Moreover, as we will describe below, a more general form of song selectivity is found in the forebrain auditory areas where selective responses are found to familiar conspecific song relative to non-familiar conspecific songs or to conspecific song relative to matched synthetic sounds. We will therefore refer to the auditory property of neurons in the song system as BOS selectivity.

BOS selectivity was first observed in awake restrained songbirds (canary, white-crowned sparrow, and zebra finch) using a chronic recording technique that allowed the comparison of sensory and motor responses in HVC.[3] The specificity of the BOS-selective response in HVC was then explored in detail in awake restrained or urethane-anesthetized white-crowned sparrows and zebra finches by Margoliash and his collaborators.[4,14–17] These studies clearly demonstrated the specificity of the selectivity to the BOS and highlighted some of the acoustical features responsible for the selective responses. The auditory responses in HVC were shown to be sensitive to the particular temporal and spectral combinations of sounds found in the BOS. Theunissen and Doupe quantified this selectivity and found it to be extremely sensitive to the temporal and spectral structure of the natural sound. More specifically, the spectrotemporal amplitude envelope of the bird's own song had to be preserved at a 98% level to obtain neural responses that were indistinguishable from those of the original sound.[18] The presence of sensory responses in the song nuclei confirmed both their place as a center for sensorimotor integration and their role in song learning and maintenance. However, the specific role of BOS-selective responses in song learning or song perception remains unclear. Some of the additional properties of BOS selectivity and the implications that such properties might have for their role in sensory-motor learning and auditory perceptual behavior will be briefly discussed.

The Development of BOS Selectivity and the Tutor Template

The remarkable BOS selectivity observed in adult songbirds leads quite naturally to the hypothesis that these BOS-selective neurons might play a role in the storage of the tutor template during learning. Experiments that followed the development of BOS selectivity in song nuclei during the two phases of song learning (Williams, this volume) refuted that hypothesis, at least in its strongest form. In effect, the selectivity for the BOS in neurons of the song nuclei emerges during the vocal practice phase of song learning[19,20] and is absent at an earlier time when the young bird has not begun to sing but has been exposed sufficiently to the tutor song for model matching.[21] Moreover, the development of the response properties of the BOS-selective neurons in the song system appears to follow the vocal output of the young birds such that the neurons become selective for the plastic song that the bird is producing (TABLE 1),[20] even when this song is highly distorted and quite distinct from the tutor song.[22] The nature and development of the majority of BOS-selective neurons is therefore inconsistent with early memory storage of the tutor song. If the tutor song is in fact stored in the song system, this storage would have to be in a minority of neurons[22] or in a form that is not revealed by single unit recordings in the anesthetized songbirds.

The selectivity of auditory responses in the song nuclei appears to follow the development of the vocal motor program: the largest response is obtained for the song

TABLE 1. Song selectivity for the bird's own song in song-system nuclei

Area	Stimuli	Neuron Type	d′	N	Comment	Reference
NIf	BOS-CON	Unknown	1.5	15	14/15>0	11
HVC	BOS-CON	Unknown	2.3	54	98%>0	18
	BOS-Rev	Unknown	1.7	63	99%>0	
HVC	BOS-Rev	RA-projecting	1.3	10	Intracellular recording	42
		X-projecting	1.3	16		
		Interneuron	3.0	11		
		X-projecting	1.0	15	Inhibitory potential	
HVC	BOS-Rev	Interneuron	3.5	9	Sleeping bird	33
		(Putative)	2.2	21	Awake bird	
			2.3	13	Urethane	
HVC	BOS-Rev	Unknown	−0.5		Awake/aroused	34
			2.7		Awake/sedated	
X	BOS-CON	Unknown	1.0	28		19
	BOS-Rev		1.3	21		
X	BOS-CON	Unknown	0.6	47	60-day-old birds; BOS	20
	BOS-Rev		0.9	40	is plastic song; CON is adult song	
LMAN	BOS-CON	Unknown	1.3	48		19
	BOS-Rev		1.3	41		
LMAN	BOS-CON	Unknown	1.0	47	60-day-old birds; BOS	20
	BOS-Rev		1.1	47	is plastic song; CON is adult song	

Mean selectivity for the bird's own song (BOS) measured in song system nuclei for male zebra finches. The selectivity is quantified by calculating the d′ obtained by comparing the neural responses to the BOS with responses to conspecific song (CON) or the BOS played in reverse (Rev).

that the bird is currently producing. This selectivity can therefore be interpreted as a memory for the produced vocalization; a sensorimotor template for the current song output. If the auditory feedback deviates from the currently produced song, a lack of response could be used to modify the motor program in order to re-establish the previously learned output. Such a mechanism could be used for the continuous evaluation of the produced BOS in the adult bird, which has been shown behaviorally. Alteration of auditory feedback leads to song changes that can be reversed once normal feedback is restored (see articles by Brainard and Woolley *et al.*, this volume).[23,24] The same mechanism could be also used in young birds during song learning in order to stabilize the motor program that has already been learned. Additional factors would then be involved in guiding the plastic output of the young birds towards a tutor-like song. For example, the degree of BOS selectivity has been shown to be correlated with the quality of the produced BOS relative to the tutor song both in young birds (TABLE 1)[20] and in adult birds that sing a distorted song.[25] Thus, in a situation where the current motor output is not particularly desirable, the reduced BOS selectivity would allow for greater motor plasticity. In other words, the degree of BOS selectivity, both in adult birds with poor song or in young birds who are learning to sing, could be a marker of the goodness of fit of the vocal output with a desired model. In young birds, deviations of vocal output in the direction of the tutor template would then be favorably reinforced by an additional signal. The neural basis of such a reinforcement signal, of the comparison between the vocal output and the tutor template, and of storage of the tutor song (which must precede the sensory-motor template in the song system) remains to be seen.

The Similarity between Motor and Sensory Responses in the Song System and Sensorimotor Integration

A second striking property of the auditory responses in the song system is their similarity with the motor response. In the song nucleus of RA in the adult bird, the temporal pattern of the sensory responses to the playback of the BOS has been shown to be similar to the pattern of motor activity produced by the same neuron during singing.[26] This striking property provides further evidence that BOS-selective neurons in the song system may play a crucial role in integrating auditory feedback information with the motor circuitry for vocal learning and maintenance.[27–29] The detailed analysis of this particular response property and its role in song learning and maintenance either on-line or off-line during sleep is covered in more detail in the articles by Konishi, Mooney, and Doupe in this volume.

The Modulation of BOS-Selective Responses

Most of the original recordings of auditory responses in the song system were performed in anesthetized or awake but restrained songbirds. More recent work has shown convincingly that the auditory responses in the song system are sensitive to the arousal state of the animal. In particular, in the zebra finch, strong sensory responses are only observed in urethane-anesthetized animals or in sleeping animals.[30–32] Weaker and less selective responses are found in the awake bird for a subclass of interneurons in HVC[33] and these awake responses are modulated by the arousal state of the animal where a higher arousal state leads to a suppression of the sensory responses (TABLE 1).[34] BOS-selective responses in awake birds have also been observed in the song nuclei X and LMAN of the anterior forebrain pathway.[28,35] The modulation of neural activity in HVC and in the song system in general might be mediated by neuromodulators, such as acetylcholine and norepinephrine, implicated in arousal and attention. Both NIf and HVC receive cholinergic and noradrenergic innervation[36–39] and injections of norepinephrine into HVC, mimicking the presumed noradrenergic modulation observed in awake aroused animals, eliminates auditory responses in RA under anesthesia.[31]

BOS-selective responses are observed to some extent both in the awake (non-aroused) and in the sleeping bird. It is therefore possible that these auditory responses play a role both in on-line and off-line feedback for song maintenance and learning (Konishi, this volume). In addition, the decrease in selectivity of sensory responses observed during a calm awake state relative to a sleeping state might be a desired feature. The high degree of selectivity of auditory responses makes them poor candidates for mediating conspecific song recognition other than their own song. It has, however, been argued that a decrease in selectivity observed in awake recordings would allow the song system circuitry to participate in the perception of songs in general.[33,34]

BOS Selectivity in Different Neuronal Types and Different Nuclei

BOS selectivity appears to be ubiquitous in the song system. The selective response for the BOS has been observed in all of the nuclei of the song system[40,41] and, in particular, it is present in the two song nuclei, HVC and NIf, that receive input from the non-specialized auditory system of birds[11] (FIG. 1). Since the auditory afferent areas to HVC and NIf are not selective for the BOS relative to CON (as discussed below), BOS selectivity seems to be a characteristic of the song system and must initially appear in one processing stage at the interface between the auditory system and the song system.

The degree of selectivity of single neurons can be quantified by the signal detection measure of d', a normalized measure of the difference in responses to two stimuli (see the methods article by Theunissen and colleagues, this volume). TABLE 1 shows a summary of mean d' values obtained for the BOS-CON or BOS-rev comparison in a series of studies from different groups. Unless specified, the data are from urethane-anesthetized adult male zebra finches.

Two somewhat contradictory conclusions can be made from these studies. First, at a gross level there seems to be little or no hierarchical processing of song across the different nuclei in the song system. As shown in FIGURE 1 and TABLE 1, the feedforward flow of processing is from NIf to HVC to X and LMAN. The d' values for NIf are smaller than those for interneurons in HVC, but are similar to the projection neurons in HVC and also of the same order as the neurons recorded in the song nuclei of the anterior forebrain pathway (X and LMAN). Based on that analysis, it would be difficult to argue that one role of the song system circuitry is to process auditory information with the purpose of increasing the selectivity for BOS relative to other sounds. By contrast, BOS selectivity differs across different neurons within HVC and auditory response properties are clearly different across different song nuclei. Within HVC, the projection neurons to RA and X appear to have different sign: the RA-projecting neurons are depolarized and fire action potentials during the presentation of song. The X-projecting neurons are mostly hyperpolarized during song and fire action potentials at the offset of sound.[42] The spike output of both RA-projecting and X-projecting neurons is selective for song but at different temporal phases. The inhibitory interneurons in HVC have the highest firing rates and are the most selective in the zebra finch (TABLE 1).[42] Blocking the inhibition results in both an increase in the selectivity of X-projecting neurons and a drastic change in the temporal properties of the response.[43] In addition, in a study involving a songbird that sings multiple song types, the interneurons responded to many exemplars of the bird's own songs while the projection neurons responded selectively to one or two of the songs in the repertoire. In that case, there was a refinement of selectivity within nucleus HVC.[44] Therefore, the circuitry within HVC plays a crucial role in shaping the neural representation of BOS and these different representations are potentially mediating different roles in error correcting (see Mooney, this volume).

Although the intrinsic circuitry and corresponding physiology of other song-system nuclei have not been examined to the same extent, it is clear that the neurons have different auditory response properties. Auditory neurons in area X have high firing rates and will respond to non-song sounds, such as white-noise or pure tones, albeit with lower rates than those in response to BOS. Auditory neurons in LMAN have low spontaneous rates and respond much less frequently to sounds other than the BOS.[19] Just like the responses in the different neuron types in HVC, the different representation of sounds in X and LMAN might play a significant role in vocal learning.

BOS Selectivity and Activity-Induced Gene Expression

Activity-dependent immediate early genes (IEG) have also been used to measure brain activity and, indirectly, neural plasticity in the birdsong forebrain (see Mello, this volume). Although robust gene-expression of ZENK and c-fos is seen in the song system nuclei following singing, no significant activity has been measured after passive hearing of song.[45,46] This lack of gene expression correlates with the greatly reduced auditory responses observed in song nuclei in the awake and aroused bird.

BOS Selectivity in Song System Nuclei and Perception of Conspecific Song

Besides their potential role in vocal learning, the second postulated role of the BOS-selective responses has been to underlie conspecific song perception. It has been proposed that the BOS-selective responses of song nuclei neurons could mediate such purely perceptual tasks by using the BOS as a reference point.[15,47] The support for this hypothesis comes principally from a series of lesion studies that have implicated song system nuclei HVC and LMAN in acoustical discrimination experiments both in male and female birds.[48–51]

However, the properties of BOS selectivity measured in electrophysiological recordings, IEG studies, and the anatomy of the sexually dimorphic song system raise some questions. First, the extreme selectivity for the BOS and the typical lack of spiking response to many conspecific songs[15,18,44] do not appear to provide enough information for discriminating among songs other than the BOS. Second, auditory responses in the song nuclei are greatly reduced in the awake bird and further reduced in the awake aroused bird, which is presumably a more attentive state. In agreement with the neurophysiological recordings, there is also a lack of IEG activation in song system nuclei following passive exposure to conspecific song. Third, the output of the song system drives almost exclusively vocal control areas and not more general motor areas.[52] It is therefore unclear how behavioral responses other than singing could be triggered by a neural recognition of song in song system nuclei. Finally, the song system in female songbirds that do not sing atrophies during development but females can discriminate song as well or better than males.

As mentioned above and proposed by others,[33,34] there might be answers to some of these objections. Since there are different neuron types in HVC with different degrees of selectivity, a subpopulation of these might be involved in perception. Also there are some neurons in HVC, LMAN, and X that preserve their auditory responses in the awake bird.[28,33–35] The decrease in selectivity observed in awake animals would then provide the needed dynamic range for discrimination. Although these explanations are plausible, they lack simplicity and are contrary to what has been found in high-level sensory areas in the mammal where attention shrinks the receptive field[53] and increases firing rates.[54]

A stronger correlation between the auditory responses of neurons in the song nuclei and auditory discrimination could be achieved in experiments combining awake neurophysiological recordings with discrimination tasks (see article by Theunissen and colleagues on methods, this volume). The selectivity of individual neurons or ensembles of neurons as measured by their d′ could then be compared to behavioral performance. Such experiments as well as further research in the flow of auditory information through the song system nuclei and beyond will be necessary to demonstrate the role of the song system in auditory perception not related to song learning.

AUDITORY RESPONSES IN THE AUDITORY FOREBRAIN

The auditory forebrain consists of the auditory thalamus, nucleus ovoidalis (Ov); the primary recipients of the Ov in the nidopallium, areas L2a and L2b of field L; the neighboring secondary auditory areas in field L, namely, L1, L3, and L; the caudal medial auditory nidopallium (NCM); and the caudal mesopallium (CM). This review focuses on responses in field L, NCM, and CM because there are few neurophysiological studies of Ov.[55] Most of the recent data from the auditory forebrain in songbirds has been obtained from urethane-anesthetized adult male zebra finches. Although anesthesia is known to affect the temporal profile of auditory responses in field L,[56] the large modulation of responses across states of deep anesthesia, sleep, sedation, and wakefulness observed in the song system is absent in the auditory forebrain.[34] IEG studies to song playback also show strong activation in all auditory forebrain areas mentioned above, except for Ov and L2.[57]

Absence of BOS Selectivity in the Auditory Forebrain

In contrast to song system nuclei, auditory neurons in field L and CM are not selective for the BOS relative to conspecific song. The lower panel in FIGURE 2 shows the responses of a single unit in field L in response to BOS, conspecific song, and the BOS played in reverse. This response can be compared to the simultaneous recording that was obtained from multi-units in HVC shown in the above panels. The neuron in field L responded strongly to all three stimuli, whereas the neurons in HVC responded strongly only to the BOS. The auditory responses in field L compared to HVC were also more consistent across trials.

The lack of selectivity for BOS in field L was first observed in the white-crowned sparrow[15] and later verified in a second study in zebra finches.[11,58] We performed a more extensive study of the selectivity for BOS or tutor song in field L areas that included substantial sampling in all subareas of field L and also of the secondary area CM (647 recording sites in 24 birds).[59] One goal of that study was to determine whether particular anatomically or functionally defined subregions of field L would show intermediate levels of selectivity for BOS supporting a hierarchical emergence of BOS selectivity. A second goal of that study was to examine the selectivity for BOS or tutor song in CM since no previous studies had yet attempted to do this. Using neural tracers, CM has been shown to be an intermediate processing stage between the auditory system and the song system (FIG. 1). In addition, studies using

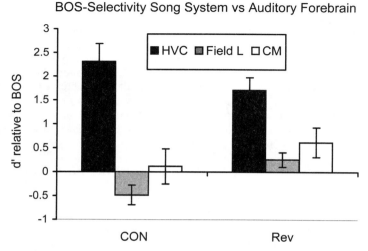

FIGURE 3. Average d' values for the BOS-CON comparison and the BOS-Rev comparison for neurons in HVC, field L, and CM in adult male zebra finches. The data for HVC are from Theunissen and Doupe.[18] The data for field L and CM are from Amin and colleagues.[59]

immediate early gene expression,[60] electrolytic lesions,[61] and awake behaving neural recordings[62] have implicated CM in the perception of conspecific songs. Secondary auditory area CM was therefore thought to be a good candidate for the selective neural representation of the tutor song or the BOS.

We found little evidence that the subregions of field L or CM were selective for BOS. The average d' values for the BOS-CON and BOS-Rev comparisons for neurons in field L and in CM are shown in FIGURE 3, where it is contrasted to the selectivity that we had measured in HVC as part of a previous study.[18] In contrast to the d' values for the song system (TABLE 1), we found that field L and CM neurons show on average no positive selectivity for the BOS: the mean or median d' values are very close to zero and actually slightly negative in field L. Although the effect is small, we have shown that it is highly significant and not due to stimulus adaptation during the course of the experiment.[59] The depressed response to BOS in field L could be due to a long-term adaptation to familiar song. This result needs to be verified by other groups and its behavioral significance tested in experiments combining chronic recordings with perceptual experiments. Our results also show a small preference for BOS over reverse BOS both in field L and in CM. These results in field L are consistent with those of Lewicki[58] and Janata and Margoliash.[11] We also found that the preference for BOS over reverse BOS is of a similar magnitude in CM. As will be explained in detail below, we interpret this effect as a preference for natural spectral-temporal structure found in natural sounds and particularly in conspecific song. The intermediate selectivity for BOS over reverse BOS is therefore not a sign of an intermediate stage of processing for BOS selectivity.

We also found an absence of selectivity for the tutor song. If, as suggested above, the development of BOS selectivity in the song system requires both crystallized song production and a match with a tutor song, then the neural circuits that lead to BOS selectivity must somehow interact with circuitry involved in storing the tutor template. The nature of this neural trace for the tutor song and of the underlying putative circuitry remains unknown.

Thus, our data suggest that there are no intermediate stages of selectivity for BOS over conspecific song prior to NIf. If the auditory input enters the song system via field L and/or CM, how might the selectivity in the song system initially arise? One possibility is that some auditory neurons in CM or field L exhibit stronger responses to certain syllables present in the BOS and selectively project to NIf or HVC. To test this hypothesis, simultaneous recordings of CM or field L neurons and NIf or HVC neurons could be performed to assess functional connectivity and sensory selectivity in the same experiment. Further selectivity could then be generated within NIf or HVC by temporally and non-linearly integrating this selective input.[63] This hypothesis is not blind to the fact that additional processing has been shown to occur in HVC leading to different song representations, all selective for BOS, which might be crucial for different aspects of vocal production and learning (as explained above); however, a quantal leap between selective and non-selective BOS responses would occur in one step at the interface of the auditory system and the song system. Alternatively, NIf or HVC could also receive auditory input from an auditory region other than CM or field L, which might show intermediate selectivity for BOS. Auditory information could also affect the neural responses of the song nucleus Uva, which is known to project to both NIf and HVC.[12]

Selectivity for Familiar Songs in Secondary Auditory Areas NCM and CM

Although the neurons in the auditory forebrain areas are not selective for the BOS, recent experiments have shown selectivity for particular songs among conspecific songs in secondary areas NCM and CM. In particular, IEG expression in NCM has been shown to be the largest for songs that have greater behavioral significance.[60,64] IEG expression in NCM also adapts to repeated presentation of the same conspecific song.[65] Similarly, neural recordings in NCM show rapid and long-lasting adaptation to the repeated presentation of the same song. The degree of adaptation is correlated with song familiarity.[66–68] The IEG and electrophysiological experiments are consistent with the idea that NCM is involved in the discrimination of familiar songs relative to novel songs. Theses studies and their implications are reviewed in more detail in the Mello article in this volume.

Similarly, IEG studies have implicated secondary auditory area CM in perception of conspecific song.[60] A lesion study in female zebra finches showed that CM but not HVC was important for song discrimination for mate choice.[61] More recently, Gentner and Margoliash[62] have combined behavior and chronic recordings to demonstrate that single neurons and the ensemble of neurons in CM become more responsive to conspecific song that is being learned in a perceptual discrimination task. These experiments and the role of CM in conspecific song perception are reviewed in greater detail in the Gentner article in this volume.

Selectivity for Conspecific Songs over Synthetic Sounds

Although the primary auditory forebrain of songbirds does not appear to be tuned to particular conspecific songs, many studies have shown that it is sensitive to the spectral and temporal structure commonly found in natural sounds, particularly to the spectral and temporal structure found in conspecific song or calls.

As mentioned above, multiple studies have shown in zebra finches that neurons in field L and CM show a small preference for the BOS played forward versus played in reverse.[11,58,59] Since there is no selectivity for the BOS over CON we would predict that the same preference would be observed for any unfamiliar conspecific song relative to the same sound played in reverse. We interpret this selectivity as a tuning for the particular spectral and temporal structure found in the natural song. Since there is little or no difference between the response to the song played forward and the response to the song with the order of the syllables reversed (reverse-order song)[11,58,59] it appears that for most neurons the order of syllables does not play an important role in the response. One can therefore conclude that it is the order of the temporal and spectral modulations within a single syllable of song that determines the selectivity for forward song over reverse. A statistical analysis of the spectral and temporal modulations of sound in a 300-msec time scale shows that zebra finch song was asymmetrical with more down-sweeps than up-sweeps.[69] In other words, neurons tuned for down-sweeps will be on average more excited by the syllables of the zebra finch song played in the natural order than the reverse order.

It has also been shown in many neurophysiological studies that subsets of neurons in field L do not respond well to simple sounds but will respond selectively to particular conspecific vocalizations.[70–73] These observations are reminiscent of the selectivity for vocalizations that is also found in subsets of neurons in the mammalian auditory cortex.[74–76] In these studies, the responses to vocalizations are compared to the responses to pure tones, tone complexes, or white noise. It was shown that the response to simple tones cannot be used to predict the response to natural sounds and that there is a population of neurons that fail to respond to synthetic sounds, but do respond to natural conspecific vocalizations. Although these results are intriguing, it can be argued that the described selectivity for the animal's vocalizations is simply a consequence of more selective tuning as one moves up in the auditory processing stream. At higher levels of auditory processing, auditory neurons become responsive to more and more complex spectrotemporal combinations of sounds. If these sound structures are often found in complex vocalizations but not in simple tones or white noise, one will observe a preference for natural sounds. A careful comparison of acoustical properties of natural and synthetic sounds and of the response properties of the neurons to these sounds must be performed to make a stronger statement about the specificity of the tuning of the neurons to conspecific vocalizations.[77] In the next three paragraphs we describe two studies where a comparison between responses to conspecific sounds and matched synthetic sounds was performed.

The first study used IEG expression in NCM to show that the neural representation of the whistle syllables found in canary song was drastically different than the representation of synthetic whistles or guitar notes that were matched in intensity and pitch.[78] The representation of the natural syllables in NCM was significantly more clustered suggesting that these natural sounds were better discriminated than the synthetic sounds or the guitar notes. The second study came from our laboratory.[79] We designed synthetic stimuli that had identical power spectra and similar amplitude modulation spectra as the zebra finch song. The synthetic sounds consisted of a train of tone pips ("pips"), combination tones ("tones"), and harmonic stacks ("stacks"). The tone pips and the combination tones had the same frequency spectrum and amplitude modulation in each frequency band as song. The harmonic stacks consisted of fundamental frequencies taken from the distribution of frequencies found in song. In addition, the duration of each stack and inter-stack interval was matched to the duration of zebra finch syllable and inter-syllable silence. If the neuron's response could be explained by their frequency tuning and their amplitude modulation tuning, then similar responses would be found for these matched synthetic sounds and for conspecific song. The results showed that neural responses were greater for the natural song (FIG. 4). A second result from that study was that the synthetic sounds that elicited the highest responses had a joint spectrotemporal modulation spectrum that was the most similar to the modulation spectrum of song.[79] As explained in our article on methods in this volume, the modulation spectrum of a sound ensemble characterizes the power in the amplitude envelopes of the sound both across time (amplitude modulation), frequency (spectral modulation), and jointly for the spectrotemporal patterns of the envelopes. This second result suggested that at least part of the selectivity for natural sounds could potentially be explained by linear tuning of neurons to the joint spectrotemporal modulations found in song. To test this hypothesis, we estimated the spectrotemporal receptive fields of auditory neurons in field L and compared the ensemble tuning to the modulation spectrum of zebra finch song. The results from that study are described in the following section.

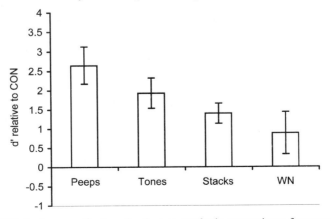

FIGURE 4. Average d′ values for the con-synthetic comparisons for neurons in field L and CM. The synthetic sounds consisted of a train of random tone pips constructed to have the same power spectrum and pip duration as song (pips), random combinations of sums of tone pip trains (tones), synthetic harmonic stacks (stacks), and white noise (WN). The data are from Grace and colleagues.[79]

Spectrotemporal Receptive Fields of Auditory Neurons in Field L and CM

To analyze and describe the precise response properties of auditory neurons, we estimate the spectrotemporal receptive fields (STRFs) of auditory neurons. The STRF is an estimate of the best linear transfer function between the set of amplitude envelopes of the sound stimulus obtained from a spectrographic representation and the neural response. In other words, the time-reversed STRF can be thought of as the spectrogram of the sound that drives the neuron to it maximal firing rate. The STRF model then predicts that a neuron will respond with a fraction of this maximal rate for any other sounds. The fraction is given by the overlap between the time-reversed STRF and the spectrogram of the sound being played to the animal. We have developed a methodology that allows us to estimate the STRFs of neurons in higher level auditory areas from their responses to natural and synthetic sounds (see Theunissen and colleagues article on methods, this volume).[80]

We initially used that methodology to estimate the STRFs of neurons in field L and CM from their responses to conspecific song and tone pips.[81,82] We found that auditory neurons in field L and CM make a heterogeneous ensemble: some had STRFs that were sharply tuned in frequency and others that were tuned to frequency edges, frequency sweeps, or combinations of frequencies. We had proposed that these STRFs make an appropriate basis set to represent sounds that are present in zebra finch song, such as the combination of frequencies that could be found within a syllable or even across two neighboring syllables. We did not, however, explicitly test the specificity of such a basis set for the representation of sound. We also found that the STRFs obtained from random tone pips and the STRFs obtained from conspecific song were significantly different for most neurons. Also, the STRFs obtained from the natural ensemble gave poor predictions for responses to the synthetic ensemble and vice versa. The fact that the STRF does not generalize across stimulus ensembles is a consequence of non-linear response properties of the neurons that are not captured by their STRF. We hypothesize that some of these non-linear tuning properties will also play a significant role in selectively shaping responses for conspecific song.

More recently, we attempted to test directly whether the ensemble linear response tuning of neurons in field L is indeed tuned to conspecific song. As shown in FIGURE 5, we designed a synthetic stimulus that covers all the spectral and temporal modulations commonly found in zebra finch song as described by the song modulation spectrum. We call this type of sound modulation-limited noise. It is the equivalent to band-limited white noise in the spectrographic representation of sound. The advantage of using modulation-limited sounds to characterize high level auditory neurons is twofold. First, we can limit the range of amplitude modulations and spectral modulations to those that are biologically relevant. Second, many neurons in higher level auditory areas do not respond in a reliable fashion to white noise but do respond reliably to the modulation-limited sounds by phase-locking to particular modulations in the spectrotemporal envelope of the sound.

We estimated STRFs for single neurons in field L from the responses to modulation-limited noise and conspecific song. As illustrated in FIGURE 6, we found five major classes of STRFs in response to conspecific song ($N = 119$). Twenty-one percent of the neurons had broadband excitatory frequency tuning followed by broadband inhibitory tuning. These neurons were responsive to the onset of most

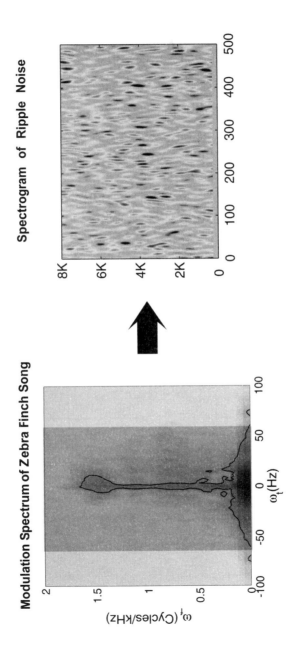

FIGURE 5. Modulation spectrum of zebra finch song and spectrogram of modulation-limited noise designed to cover all modulations present in song. (*Left*) The modulation spectrum of zebra song. The modulation spectrum quantifies the spectrotemporal structure that is present in an ensemble of sounds (see article by Theunissen and colleagues on methods, this volume).[69] The *bold contour line* surrounds 80% of the energy of the total modulation energy in zebra finch song. The *grey box* superimposed on the modulation spectrum shows the area of acoustic space that was sampled uniformly to generate modulation-limited noise sounds. (*Right*) A **spectrogram** of 500 msec of such modulation-limited noise.

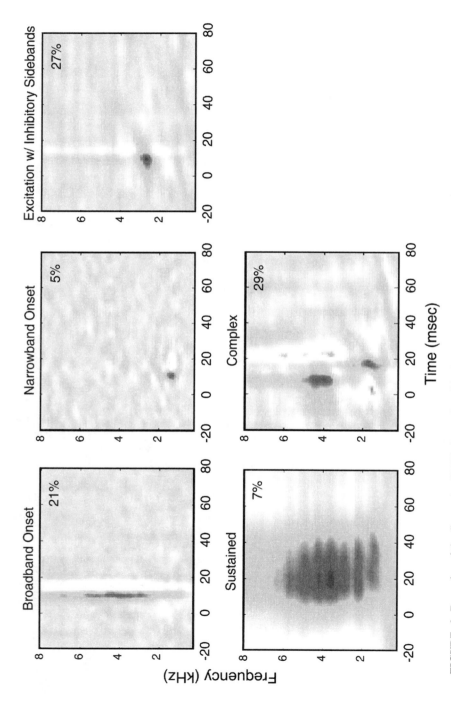

FIGURE 6. Examples of the five major STRF classes found in the zebra finch auditory forebrain region, field L. Classes are defined by both spectral tuning (e.g. broadband versus narrowband) and temporal tuning (e.g. onset versus sustained responses). The majority of cells (131 of 146 total; 90%) fit into one of these classes.

syllables or more generally for fast amplitude modulations in the sound (~50 Hz). A second class of neurons (5%), had sharp frequency tuning followed by sharp inhibitory tuning, not necessarily at the same frequency. These neurons have phasic responses and are sensitive to particular frequencies or fast frequency sweeps within song. A third category consisted of a group that was made for neurons with an excitatory area flanked by inhibitory regions (27%). The response of an ensemble of such neurons can be used to detect particular spectral modulations. A fourth group of neurons (7%) had STRFs that had only excitatory areas. These neurons are characterized by their tonic response to sound. A fifth group of neurons (29%) had STRFs with multiple excitatory and inhibitory regions. These neurons respond to more complex features in the sound and require particular spectral temporal combinations of sound for maximal response.

As we did in our previous analysis,[81] we propose that this heterogeneous set of response properties can be used to represent the acoustic structure in song efficiently. We are testing this hypothesis directly by calculating the ensemble modulation transfer function (eMTF) of field L neurons from their STRFs obtained in response to the modulation-limited noise. The eMTF shows the temporal and spectral modulations

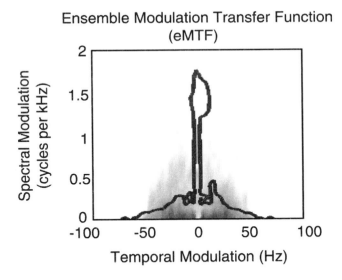

FIGURE 7. Ensemble modulation transfer function (eMTF) for STRFs calculated from responses to modulation-limited noise in the zebra finch field L. The online *red areas* (dark areas in print) indicate power in terms of what spectral and temporal modulations best drive the population of field L neurons. *Dark blue areas* (white in print version) indicate zero power, showing the spectral and temporal modulations that do not drive the field L population. The *black contour line* indicates the range of spectral and temporal modulations that are found in zebra finch song. The majority of the power in song (80%) shows modulations that fall inside the contour line, indicating that those modulations are well represented in zebra finch song. Modulations found outside of the contour are rarely or never present in the song. A match between the lower portion of the contour line and the modulation tuning of the field L population is observed.

that are represented by the ensemble neural response. The eMTF is estimated by first calculating the MTF for each neuron and then performing an average over all MTFs. The MTF of a neuron is defined by the amplitude of the 2D Fourier transform of its STRF. The eMTF can then be compared to the modulation spectrum of song (see Theunissen and colleagues article on methods, this volume). FIGURE 7 shows the eMTF for field L neurons in response to modulation-limited noise compared to the modulation spectrum of zebra finch song shown in contour lines. As is evident in the figure, the eMTF is matched to the modulation spectrum found in song in the sense that field L neurons mostly emphasize spectrotemporal modulations that are common in song. This is in stark contrast to the spectrotemporal modulations that exist in modulation-limited noise as shown in FIGURE 5. A more detailed description of the nature and quality of this match including the degree of specificity to zebra finch song relative to other animal vocalizations or other natural sounds will be presented in a future publication.

Tonotopy and Other Classical Characterizations of Response Properties in the Auditory Forebrain

The response properties of auditory forebrain neurons have also been characterized via more classical techniques. One of the principal results from those studies is the preservation of tonotopy in the auditory caudal nidopallium, as characterized by the measurement of the frequency of best response (BF) to pure tone stimuli. In sub-area L2 and in the neighboring auditory nidopallium and mesopallium, the frequency axis runs along the dorsal-caudal (low frequencies) rostral-ventral (high frequency) directions.[6,73,83] The tonotopy in the auditory forebrain of songbirds follows the same organization as in other avian species.[84,85] In a more recent study, this simple tonotopic picture of the caudal auditory neostriatum was questioned: Gehr and colleagues[86] found multiple functional areas in the neostriatum of the male zebra finch each with their own tonotopic gradient. These functional areas overlapped only loosely with anatomically defined subareas of field L. The tonotopic organization in field L and neighboring areas will have to be revisited.

The temporal and spectral response properties have also been characterized using sinusoidal amplitude modulation and sinusoidal frequency modulation of pure tones, band-passed Gaussian white-noise, and other pseudo-random stimuli.[73,87] As is the case in the mammalian auditory cortex, there is a significant fraction of neurons in the auditory forebrain of songbirds that do not respond to pure tones but do respond to sounds with frequency or amplitude modulation. The best modulation frequency (BMF) appears to be higher in birds than in mammals and, in the starling, frequency modulation is a more effective stimulus than amplitude modulation. The comparison between the response properties obtained in these studies and those that can be extracted from STRFs has begun,[77] but will require further analysis and classification. Ultimately, it will be desirable to understand the distribution of neuron types defined by their functional properties obtained both by classical methods and with the STRF methodology. To further understand the underlying circuitry mediating this auditory processing, it will then be important to assess whether these different neuron types are topographically organized in the auditory nidopallium and/or whether they can be correlated with different anatomically defined neuron types.

CONCLUSION

There appear to be three gross levels of auditory selectivity in the songbird fore-brain. First, at the highest level, sensorimotor neurons in the song system are selective for the current song that the bird is producing. The development of this selectivity during song learning and the striking similarity between the motor and sensory responses for the BOS-selective neurons strongly suggest that these responses can be used to evaluate the auditory feedback of the bird's vocalization for comparison with what the bird has been singing in the recent past. The role of the song system in perceptual learning, in our opinion, is more problematic. At the second level of selectivity, one finds neurons in NCM and CM that are tuned to behaviorally specific complex natural sounds, such as songs to which the bird has been exposed recently or which have particular behavioral relevance. These neurons are potentially involved in perceptual tasks requiring the recognition of familiar or recently heard song. Finally, in primary auditory areas, such as field L, neurons, as an ensemble, appear to be tuned to the spectrotemporal sounds that are found frequently in conspecific song. The result of this tuning is a preference for conspecific song over synthetic stimuli that lack this characteristic spectrotemporal structure but that are otherwise matched acoustically. These response properties suggest that complex natural sounds, such as conspecific song, and perhaps heterospecific songs with similar acoustical structure, are preferentially represented in the neural activity of the auditory forebrain relative to other background sounds that are commonly present in the bird's environment.

These three levels of selectivity are suggestive of a coarse hierarchical processing of auditory information. Conspecific song and other similar sounds are efficiently encoded in the primary auditory forebrain, field L. In the secondary forebrain areas of NCM and CM, the effect of recent experience becomes crucial and neurons can be selective for particular familiar songs or sounds. Finally, among those specific songs, the bird's own song plays a very special role and is selectively represented in the song nuclei. There are significant gaps in this picture. A major gap is our lack of understanding of the mechanisms that generate these different levels of selectivity, and the link between these different auditory areas and the song system. In this respect, further experiments that look at both the anatomical and functional connectivity between all these areas are very much needed. A second gap in our understanding is the nature of the reward or reinforcement signal that is involved in both the perceptual learning of arbitrary conspecific song and in the memorization of the tutor song. It is not known how the auditory information in field L is combined with a reward or recognition signal that leads to song-specific neural recognition in NCM or CM. It is also not known how the BOS-selective neurons in the song system obtain their selectivity and whether or not this processing involves the secondary areas NCM and CM or is achieved via a separate pathway. A third gap is an actual neural substrate for the tutor template. How the tutor template and the feedback of the young bird's vocalizations interact to progressively generate BOS-selective neurons in the song system, and how this information is then used to guide vocal learning and ultimately produce adult song remain a mystery. Aspiring birdsong researchers can look forward to solving these exciting puzzles.

REFERENCES

1. NOTTEBOHM, F., T.M. STOKES & C.M. LEONARD. 1976. Central control of song in the canary, *Serinus canarius*. J. Comp. Neurol. **165:** 457–486.
2. BOTTJER, S.W., E.A. MIESNER & A.P. ARNOLD. 1984. Forebrain lesions disrupt development but not maintenance of song in passerine birds. Science **224:** 901–903.
3. MCCASLAND, J.S. & M. KONISHI. 1981. Interactions between auditory and motor activities in an avian song control nucleus. Proc. Natl. Acad. Sci. USA **78:** 7815–7819.
4. MARGOLIASH, D. & M. KONISHI. 1985. Auditory representation of autogenous song in the song system of white-crowned sparrows. Proc. Natl. Acad. Sci. USA **82:** 5997–6000.
5. SACHS, M.B., N.G. WOOLF & J.M. SINNOTT. 1980. Response properties of neurons in the avian auditory system: comparisons with mammalian homologues and consideration of the neural encoding of complex stimuli. *In* Comparative Studies of Hearing in Vertebrates. A.N. Popper & R.R. Fay, Eds.: 323–353. Springer. Berlin.
6. ZARETSKY, M.D. & M. KONISHI. 1976. Tonotopic organization in the avian telencephalon. Brain Res. **111:** 167–171.
7. FORTUNE, E.S. & D. MARGOLIASH. 1992. Cytoarchitectonic organization and morphology of cells of the field L complex in male zebra finches (*Taeniopygia guttata*). J. Comp. Neurol. **325:** 388–404.
8. VATES, G.E. *et al.* 1996. Auditory pathways of caudal telencephalon and their relation to the song system of adult male zebra finches (*Taeniopygia guttata*). J. Comp. Neurol. **366:** 613–642.
9. KROODSMA, D.E. & M. KONISHI. 1991. A suboscine bird (eastern phoebe, *Sayornis phoebe*) develops normal song without auditory feedback. Anim. Behav. **42:** 477–487.
10. FORTUNE, E.S. & D. MARGOLIASH. 1995. Parallel pathways and convergence onto HVc and adjacent neostriatum of adult zebra finches (*Taeniopygia guttata*). J. Comp. Neurol. **360:** 413–441.
11. JANATA, P. & D. MARGOLIASH. 1999. Gradual emergence of song selectivity in sensorimotor structures of the male zebra finch song system. J. Neurosci. **19:** 5108–5118.
12. WILD, J.M. 1994. Visual and somatosensory inputs to the avian song system via nucleus uvaeformis (Uva) and a comparison with the projections of a similar thalamic nucleus in a nonsongbird, *Columba livia*. J. Comp. Neurol. **349:** 512–535.
13. WILLIAMS, H. & D.S. VICARIO. 1993. Temporal patterning of song production: participation of nucleus uvaeformis of the thalamus. J. Neurobiol. **24:** 903–912.
14. MARGOLIASH, D. 1983. Acoustic parameters underlying the responses of song-specific neurons in the white-crowned sparrow. J. Neurosci. **3:** 1039–1057.
15. MARGOLIASH, D. 1986. Preference for autogenous song by auditory neurons in a song system nucleus of the white-crowned sparrow. J. Neurosci. **6:** 1643–1661.
16. MARGOLIASH, D. & E.S. FORTUNE. 1992. Temporal and harmonic combination-sensitive neurons in the zebra finch's HVc. J. Neurosci. **12:** 4309–4326.
17. SUTTER, M.L. & D. MARGOLIASH. 1994. Global synchronous response to autogenous song in zebra finch HVc. J. Neurophysiol. **72:** 2105–2123.
18. THEUNISSEN, F.E. & A.J. DOUPE. 1998. Temporal and spectral sensitivity of complex auditory neurons in the nucleus HVc of male zebra finches. J. Neurosci. **18:** 3786–3802.
19. DOUPE, A.J. 1997. Song- and order-selective neurons in the songbird anterior forebrain and their emergence during vocal development. J. Neurosci. **17:** 1147–1167.
20. SOLIS, M.M. & A.J. DOUPE. 1997. Anterior forebrain neurons develop selectivity by an intermediate stage of birdsong learning. J. Neurosci. **17:** 6447–6462.
21. VOLMAN, S.F. 1993. Development of neural selectivity for birdsong during vocal learning. J. Neurosci. **13:** 4737–47.
22. SOLIS, M.M. & A.J. DOUPE. 1999. Contributions of tutor and bird's own song experience to neural selectivity in the songbird anterior forebrain. J. Neurosci. **19:** 4559–84.
23. LEONARDO, A. & M. KONISHI. 1999. Decrystallization of adult birdsong by perturbation of auditory feedback. Nature **399:** 466–470.

24. BRAINARD, M.S. & A.J. DOUPE. 2000. Auditory feedback in learning and maintenance of vocal behaviour. Nat. Rev. Neurosci. **1:** 31–40.
25. SOLIS, M.M. & A.J. DOUPE. 2000. Compromised neural selectivity for song in birds with impaired sensorimotor learning. Neuron **25:** 109–121.
26. DAVE, A.S. & D. MARGOLIASH. 2000. Song replay during sleep and computational rules for sensorimotor vocal learning. Science **290:** 812–816.
27. TROYER, T.W. & A.J. DOUPE. 2000. An associational model of birdsong sensorimotor learning I. Efference copy and the learning of song syllables. J. Neurophysiol. **84:** 1204–1223.
28. MARGOLIASH, D. 2002. Evaluating theories of bird song learning: implications for future directions. J. Comp. Physiol. A Neuroethol. Sens. Neural Behav. Physiol. **188:** 851–866.
29. MOONEY, R., M.J. ROSEN & C.B. STURDY. 2002. A bird's eye view: top down intracellular analyses of auditory selectivity for learned vocalizations. J. Comp. Physiol. A Neuroethol. Sens. Neural Behav. Physiol. **188:** 879–895.
30. SCHMIDT, M.F. & M. KONISHI. 1998. Gating of auditory responses in the vocal control system of awake songbirds. Nat. Neurosci. **1:** 513–518.
31. DAVE, A.S., A.C. YU & D. MARGOLIASH. 1998. Behavioral state modulation of auditory activity in a vocal motor system. Science **282:** 2250–2254.
32. NICK, T.A. & M. KONISHI. 2001. Dynamic control of auditory activity during sleep: correlation between song response and EEG. Proc. Natl. Acad. Sci. USA **98:** 14012–14016.
33. RAUSKE, P.L., S.D. SHEA & D. MARGOLIASH. 2003. State and neuronal class-dependent reconfiguration in the avian song system. J. Neurophysiol. **89:** 1688–1701.
34. CARDIN, J.A. & M.F. SCHMIDT. 2004. Song system auditory responses are stable and highly tuned during sedation, rapidly modulated and unselective during wakefulness, and suppressed by arousal. J. Neurophysiol. In press.
35. HESSLER, N.A. & A.J. DOUPE. 1999. Singing-related neural activity in a dorsal forebrain-basal ganglia circuit of adult zebra finches. J. Neurosci. **19:** 10461–10481.
36. RYAN, S.M. & A.P. ARNOLD. 1981. Evidence for cholinergic participation in the control of bird song: acetylcholinesterase distribution and muscarinic receptor autoradiography in the zebra finch brain. J. Comp. Neurol. **202:** 211–219.
37. BOTTJER, S.W. 1993. The distribution of tyrosine hydroxylase immunoreactivity in the brains of male and female zebra finches. J. Neurobiol. **24:** 51–69.
38. SOHA, J.A., T. SHIMIZU & A.J. DOUPE. 1996. Development of the catecholaminergic innervation of the song system of the male zebra finch. J. Neurobiol. **29:** 473–489.
39. MELLO, C.V., R. PINAUD & S. RIBEIRO. 1998. Noradrenergic system of the zebra finch brain: immunocytochemical study of dopamine-beta-hydroxylase. J. Comp. Neurol. **400:** 207–228.
40. WILLIAMS, H. & F. NOTTEBOHM. 1985. Auditory responses in avian vocal motor neurons: A motor theory for song perception in birds. Science **229:** 279–282.
41. DOUPE, A.J. & M. KONISHI. 1991. Song-selective auditory circuits in the vocal control system of the zebra finch. Proc. Natl. Acad. Sci. USA **88:** 11339–11343.
42. MOONEY, R. 2000. Different subthreshold mechanisms underlie song selectivity in identified HVc neurons of the zebra finch. J. Neurosci. **20:** 5420–5436.
43. ROSEN, M.J. & R. MOONEY. 2003. Inhibitory and excitatory mechanisms underlying auditory responses to learned vocalizations in the songbird nucleus HVC. Neuron **39:** 177–194.
44. MOONEY, R., W. HOESE & S. NOWICKI. 2001. Auditory representation of the vocal repertoire in a songbird with multiple song types. Proc. Natl. Acad. Sci. USA **98:** 12778–12783.
45. MELLO, C.V. & D.F. CLAYTON. 1994. Song-induced ZENK gene expression in auditory pathways of songbird brain and its relation to the song control system. J. Neurosci. **14:** 6652–6666.
46. KIMPO, R.R. & A.J. DOUPE. 1997. FOS is induced by singing in distinct neuronal populations in a motor network. Neuron **18:** 315–325.
47. NOTTEBOHM, F. *et al.* 1990. Song learning in birds: the relation between perception and production. Phil. Trans. R. Soc. Lond. B Biol. Sci. **329:** 115–124.

48. BRENOWITZ, E.A. 1991. Altered perception of species-specific song by female birds after lesions of a forebrain nucleus. Science **251:** 303–305.
49. SCHARFF, C., F. NOTTEBOHM & J. CYNX. 1998. Conspecific and heterospecific song discrimination in male zebra finches with lesions in the anterior forebrain pathway. J. Neurobiol. **36:** 81–90.
50. BURT, J.M. *et al.* 2000. Lesions of the anterior forebrain song control pathway in female canaries affect song perception in an operant task. J. Neurobiol. **42:** 487.
51. GENTNER, T.Q. *et al.* 2000. Individual vocal recognition and the effect of partial lesions to HVc on discrimination, learning, and categorization of conspecific song in adult songbirds. J. Neurobiol. **42:** 117–133.
52. WILD, J.M. 1993. Descending projections of the songbird nucleus robustus archistriatalis. J. Comp. Neurol. **338:** 225–241.
53. MORAN, J. & R. DESIMONE. 1985. Selective attention gates visual processing in the extrastriate cortex. Science **229:** 782–784.
54. MCADAMS, C.J. & J.H. MAUNSELL. 1999. Effects of attention on orientation-tuning functions of single neurons in macaque cortical area V4. J. Neurosci. **19:** 431–441.
55. BIGALKE-KUNZ, B., R. RUBSAMEN & G.J. DORRSCHEIDT. 1987. Tonotopic organization and functional characterization of the auditory thalamus in a songbird, the European starling. J. Comp. Physiol. A **161:** 255–265.
56. CAPSIUS, B. & H.J. LEPPELSACK. 1996. Influence of urethane anesthesia on neural processing in the auditory cortex analogue of a songbird. Hearing Res. **96:** 59–70.
57. MELLO, C.V. 2002. Mapping vocal communication pathways in birds with inducible gene expression. J. Comp. Physiol. A Neuroethol. Sens. Neural Behav. Physiol. **188:** 943–959.
58. LEWICKI, M.S. & B.J. ARTHUR. 1996. Hierarchical organization of auditory temporal context sensitivity. J. Neurosci. **16:** 6987–6998.
59. AMIN, N., J.A. GRACE & F.E. THEUNISSEN. 2004. Neural response to bird's own song and tutor song in the avian auditory forebrain. J. Comp. Physiol. A Neuroethol. Sens. Neural Behav. Physiol. In press.
60. GENTNER, T.Q. *et al.* 2001. Response biases in auditory forebrain regions of female songbirds following exposure to sexually relevant variation in male song. J. Neurobiol. **46:** 48–58.
61. MACDOUGALL-SHACKLETON, S.A., S.H. HULSE & G.F. BALL. 1998. Neural bases of song preferences in female zebra finches (*Taeniopygia guttata*). Neuroreport **9:** 3047–3052.
62. GENTNER, T.Q. & D. MARGOLIASH. 2003. Neuronal populations and single cells representing learned auditory objects. Nature **424:** 669–674.
63. LEWICKI, M.S. & M. KONISHI. 1995. Mechanisms underlying the sensitivity of songbird forebrain neurons to temporal order. Proc. Natl. Acad. Sci. USA **92:** 5582–5586.
64. MELLO, C.V., D.S. VICARIO & D.F. CLAYTON. 1992. Song presentation induces gene expression in the songbird forebrain. Proc. Natl. Acad. Sci. USA **89:** 6818–6822.
65. MELLO, C., F. NOTTEBOHM & D. CLAYTON. 1995. Repeated exposure to one song leads to a rapid and persistent decline in an immediate early gene's response to that song in zebra finch telencephalon. J. Neurosci. **15:** 6919–6925.
66. CHEW, S.J. *et al.* 1995. Decrements in auditory responses to a repeated conspecific song are long-lasting and require two periods of protein synthesis in the songbird forebrain. Proc. Natl. Acad. Sci. USA **92:** 3406–3410.
67. CHEW, S.J., D.S. VICARIO & F. NOTTEBOHM. 1996. A large-capacity memory system that recognizes the calls and songs of individual birds. Proc. Natl. Acad. Sci. USA **93:** 1950–1955.
68. STRIPLING, R., S. VOLMAN & D. CLAYTON. 1997. Response modulation in the zebra finch caudal neostriatum: relationship to nuclear gene regulation. J. Neurosci. **17:** 3883–3893.
69. SINGH, N.C. & F.E. THEUNISSEN. 2003. Modulation spectra of natural sounds and ethological theories of auditory processing. J. Acoust. Soc. Am. **114:** 3394–3411.
70. LEPPELSACK, H. 1978. Unit responses to species-specific sounds in the auditory forebrain center of birds. Fed. Proc. **37:** 2236–2241.

71. LEPPELSACK, H.J. 1983. Analysis of song in the auditory pathway of song-birds. *In* Advances in Vertebrate Neuroethology. J.P. Ewert, Ed.: 783–800. Plenum. New York.

72. LEPPELSACK, H.J. & M. VOGT. 1976. Responses of auditory neurons in the forebrain of a songbird to stimulation with species-specific sounds. J. Comp. Neurol. **107:** 263–274.

73. MULLER, C.M. & H.J. LEPPELSACK. 1985. Feature extraction and tonotopic organization in the avian auditory forebrain. Exp. Brain Res. **59:** 587–599.

74. NEWMAN, J. & Z. WOLLBERG. 1978. Multiple coding of species-specific vocalizations in the auditory cortex of squirrel monkeys. Brain Res. **54:** 287–304.

75. RAUSCHECKER, J.P., B. TIAN & M. HAUSER. 1995. Processing of complex sounds in the macaque nonprimary auditory cortex. Science **268:** 111–114.

76. WANG, X. *et al.* 1995. Representation of a species-specific vocalization in the primary auditory cortex of the common marmoset: temporal and spectral characteristics. J. Neurophysiol. **74:** 2685–2706.

77. SCHAFER, M. *et al.* 1992. Setting complex tasks to single units in the avian auditory forebrain. II. Do we really need natural stimuli to describe neuronal response characteristics? Hear Res. **57:** 231–244.

78. RIBEIRO, S. *et al.* 1998. Toward a song code: evidence for a syllabic representation in the canary brain. Neuron **21:** 359–371.

79. GRACE, J.A. *et al.* 2003. Selectivity for conspecific song in the zebra finch auditory forebrain. J. Neurophysiol. **89:** 472–487.

80. THEUNISSEN, F.E. *et al.* 2001. Estimating spatio-temporal receptive fields of auditory and visual neurons from their responses to natural stimuli. Network: Comp. Neural Syst. **12:** 1–28.

81. SEN, K., F.E. THEUNISSEN & A.J. DOUPE. 2001. Feature analysis of natural sounds in the songbird auditory forebrain. J. Neurophysiol. **86:** 1445–1458.

82. THEUNISSEN, F.E., K. SEN & A.J. DOUPE. 2000. Spectral-temporal receptive fields of nonlinear auditory neurons obtained using natural sounds. J. Neurosci. **20:** 2315–2331.

83. RUBSAMEN, R. & G. DORRSCHEIDT. 1986. Tonotopic organization of the auditory forebrain in a songbird, the European starling. J. Comp. Physiol. A Sens. Neural Behav. Physiol. **158:** 639–646.

84. BONKE, D., H. SCHEICH & G. LANGNER. 1979. Responsiveness of units in the auditory neostriatum of the guinea fowl (*Numida meleagris*) to species-specific calls and synthetic stimuli. I. Tonotopy and functional zones of field L. J. Comp. Physiol. **132:** 243–255.

85. HEIL, P. & H. SCHEICH. 1985. Quantitative analysis and two-dimensional reconstruction of the tonotopic organization of the auditory field L in the chick from 2-deoxyglucose data. Exp. Brain Res. **58:** 532–543.

86. GEHR, D.D. *et al.* 1999. Functional organisation of the field-L-complex of adult male zebra finches. Neuroreport **10:** 375–380.

87. KNIPSCHILD, M., G.J. DORRSCHEIDT & R. RUBSAMEN. 1992. Setting complex tasks to single units in the avian auditory forebrain. I: Processing of complex artificial stimuli. Hear Res. **57:** 216–230.

Using Learned Calls to Study Sensory-Motor Integration in Songbirds

DAVID S. VICARIO

Psychology Department, Rutgers University, Piscataway, New Jersey 08854, USA

ABSTRACT: Communicating songbirds produce calls as well as song and some of these are learned. One of these—the long call in zebra finches—is used by both sexes in similar behavioral contexts, but is learned in males and not in females. The male long call includes learned spectral and temporal features. In several studies, the learned long call has been used as a tool to study sensory-motor integration and vocal learning in a way that complements the use of song. Lesion studies showed that production of the male-typical call features requires an intact nucleus RA, the sexually dimorphic source of the telencephalic projection to brainstem vocal effectors. Behavioral studies that quantified zebra finch calling in response to long call playbacks showed that adult males have a categorical preference, absent in females, for the long calls of females over those of males. By using synthetic call stimuli, it was found that males use both spectral and temporal information to classify long call stimuli by gender, but that females use only temporal information. In juvenile males, the emergence of categorical preference occurs during the same period when RA matures anatomically (40–50 days) and the first male-typical vocalizations are produced. Adult males with RA lesions lost the categorical preference for female long calls, suggesting that RA could also play a role in long call discrimination. Preliminary analysis of recordings from neurons in NCM—a telencephalic auditory area (see Mello and colleagues, this volume)—suggests a pattern of responses to the spectral features of synthetic call stimuli that parallels the behavioral responses they elicit.

KEYWORDS: vocalization; sexual dimorphism; brain lesions; auditory processing; sensorimotor integration

Intraspecific signaling in social animals takes a wide variety of forms adapted to particular communication needs and constraints (see Genter, this volume). Songbirds are prominent in their use of the vocal-acoustic modality for communication. They use a set of complex and relatively arbitrary signals that are matched between sender and receiver through a process of learning constrained by innate predispositions.[1] Songbirds not only vocalize by singing, but also produce a variety of communication calls (see Marler, this volume). In everyday usage, "song" and "call" may be nearly synonymous but, as technical terms, they denote distinct types of intraspecific communication signals. Songs are typically multi-part sounds, usually produced only by

Address for correspondence: David S. Vicario, Psychology Department, Rutgers University, 152 Frelinghuysen Road, Piscataway, New Jersey 08854, USA. Voice: 732-445-2907; fax: 732-445-2263.

vicario@rci.rutgers.edu; <http://www.rci.rutgers.edu/~vicario/>

Ann. N.Y. Acad. Sci. 1016: 246–262 (2004). © 2004 New York Academy of Sciences.
doi: 10.1196/annals.1298.040

adult males, whereas calls are usually short, often monosyllabic sounds produced by all ages and both sexes, although certain call types may only be used by a particular sex or age group. In contrast to song, which is used in territorial and reproductive contexts, calls are used for general communication on a daily basis. Distinct calls send particular messages, e.g., food begging, alarm, presence of food, contact, etc.

There is a major focus in behavioral and neurobiological studies on the avian vocalization known as "song," and this approach has come to define the field of birdsong research. A major reason for this focus is that in oscine birds song is learned.[2] Vocal learning is rare in animals, so birdsong has come to be used not only to study the neural mechanisms of learning in birds, but also to provide the most tractable system for studying human speech learning.[3,4] Some songbird calls are learned through a process of vocal imitation similar to that for song and depend on the same neural substrate. These calls can be used to study sensory-motor integration and learning in ways that complement the use of song and even provide advantages for certain experimental questions. Calls generally do not depend on reproductive or seasonal cycles in the same way as song and thus are readily elicited in the laboratory. Typically, even learned calls are acoustically simpler than most songs, and thus easier to analyze and synthesize. In addition, because both males and females produce at least some calls in similar behavioral contexts, the vocal behavior of females can be studied in species where females do not sing. Moreover, calls provide an opportunity to study the perceptual side of vocal communication, which is often neglected. Calls are vocal signals that are often exchanged between individuals, and the behavioral response to a call is often another call, not a more covert behavioral or hormonal response.[5] This enables us to study the sensory processing associated with call discrimination. Furthermore, the tendency of some calls to be used in vocal exchanges that depend on perceptual as well as motor processing enables us to study the auditory side of vocal communication in a more naturalistic way. Because birds must hear, discriminate, and remember the vocal sounds that they will subsequently imitate, a better understanding of perceptual processing is useful not only for studying communication, but also for studying vocal imitation. In addition, the vocal learning that accompanies practice in young birds also depends on auditory discrimination.

When a young bird engages in vocal learning, it must first select a tutor, based at least in part on a species-specific bias, then memorize the auditory image, and use it to shape its own vocalizations. To do that it must memorize and use particular acoustic features in a way that can ultimately shape patterns of motor output. The ability to use calls to probe perceptual as well as motor processes makes them a useful tool in exploring the neural basis of this process.

LEARNED FEATURES OF THE SEXUALLY DIMORPHIC ZEBRA FINCH LONG CALL

Zebra finches exchange calls incessantly when they can hear each other and it is hard to discern a pattern in the relatively chaotic exchange of several call types. One of these calls, the "long" call, is used by both sexes in similar behavioral contexts, but is learned in males but not in females.[6] The long calls of females are relatively simple harmonic stacks with low fundamental frequencies, typically around 450 or 500 Hz, near the natural frequency of air passing through the zebra finch vocal tract,

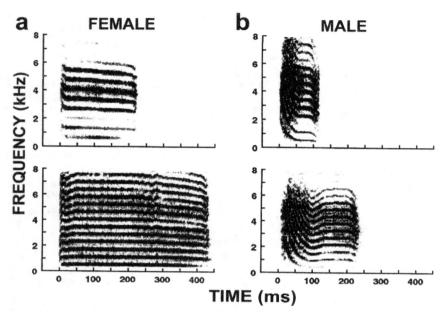

FIGURE 1. Sound spectrograms of representative female (**A**) and male (**B**) long calls from the stimulus set display the constituent frequencies of each call as a function of time. Male LCs differ from female LCs in one or more of the following ways: shorter duration, higher fundamental frequency, and presence of fast frequency modulations (see text). Males learn these acoustic features during development and male LCs resemble song syllables. The simpler LCs of females are unlearned. (Modified from Vicario et al.[14])

although some females call at slightly higher fundamental frequencies (FIG. 1). Female long calls are usually >200 msec in duration, with substantial individual variation within and between females. In contrast, each male has a stereotyped call with one or more of three male-typical features, as originally described by Zann.[7] Call duration is shorter (usually <200 msec) and much less variable than in females. Calls may have two spectral features: (1) a fast frequency modulation, typically at the end in wild birds, but at the beginning in domestic American stock and (2) a period of elevated fundamental frequency above 500 Hz. The male call is similar to a stereotyped song syllable and in fact long calls appear as syllables in the songs of many males.

THE VOCAL CONTROL PATHWAY CONTRIBUTES TO LEARNED FEATURES OF THE LONG CALL

In zebra finches, the telencephalic vocal control pathway[8] is sexually dimorphic.[9] The telencephalic nuclei HVC and the robust nucleus of the arcopallium (RA) are dramatically larger in males than in females, and the projection from HVC to RA appears not to be present in females.[10] The projection from RA to areas of the brain-

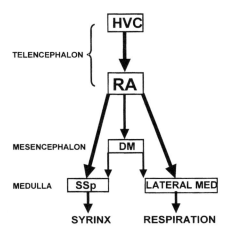

FIGURE 2. Schematic of vocal motor projections. Nerve sections interrupted neural control of the syrinx by bilaterally cutting the tracheo-syringeal nerve that runs from SSp to the syringeal muscles. Bilateral Lesions of RA interrupted telencepahlic control of both SSp and the lateral medulla involved in respiration.

stem that control respiratory and syringeal vocal effectors is known to be the final common output pathway from the telencephalon for song production, as shown schematically in FIGURE 2 (see also Wild, this volume). It should be emphasized that RA not only projects to tracheo-syringeal motor neurons in the supraspinal nucleus (SSp) but also to areas in the lateral medulla involved in the control of respiration. To examine its contribution to long call production, we lesioned the RA pathway at various levels in both males and females.[11]

When the tracheo-syringeal nerve that innervates the vocal organ was cut bilaterally, there was essentially no change in the female call. The example in FIGURE 3A shows a small shift in harmonic emphasis, but this wasn't consistent across birds. In females, active control of the syringeal musculature does not seem to be needed for normal long call production. In contrast, in lesioned males, the characteristic fast frequency modulation at the start of the call disappeared, as did the period of elevated fundamental frequency, although duration control remained intact. Thus, the nerve cut affects the male-typical spectral features but not the temporal feature of duration control. Comparable effects on the spectral and temporal features of song were observed in these males.[12,13]

When central lesions were made bilaterally at the level of RA, a different picture emerged. These lesions not only interrupted descending signals to the syrinx, but also signals that might influence respiration via RA's projection to the lateral medulla. Female zebra finches do not sing, and their calls were unaffected by these lesions (FIG. 3B). In males, song was abolished, as expected from earlier work. However, although the learned long call was not abolished, its acoustic structure was dramatically affected.[11] Males with bilateral lesions of RA continued to produce long calls in the correct behavioral context, but, as in the nerve-sectioned birds, these calls no longer possessed male-typical spectral features; i.e., they lost the initial fast frequen-

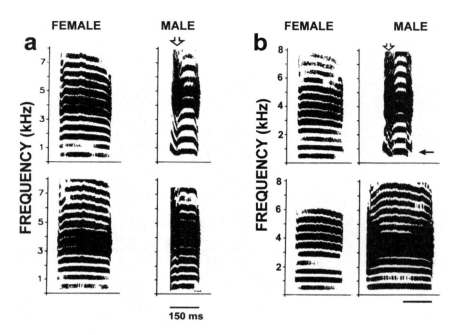

FIGURE 3. Effect of lesions on female and male long calls. (**A**) (*Left*) Long calls of one female before (*top*) and after (*bottom*) bilateral syringeal nerve section, showing no change in the call. (*Right*) Long calls of one male before (*top*) and after (*bottom*) bilateral syringeal nerve section, showing loss of the fast frequency modulation (*open arrow*) and the lowered fundamental frequency. (**B**) (*Left*) Long calls of one female before (*top*) and after (*bottom*) bilateral RA lesion, showing no change in the call. (*Right*) Long calls of one male before (*top*) and after (*bottom*) bilateral RA lesion, showing loss of the fast frequency modulation (*open arrow*), the lowered fundamental frequency (*solid arrow*), and the increase in duration. Time bar: 150 msec. (Modified from Simpson & Vicario.[11])

cy modulation and the period of elevated fundamental frequency. Moreover, their duration became as long and variable as that of female calls. The long calls of males with large bilateral lesions lost their male-typical spectral and temporal features and became indistinguishable from those of females. Similar effects were obtained when HVC was lesioned bilaterally.

Because calls, unlike song, continue to be produced in the lesioned birds, these results provide an additional insight into the original observation that RA and HVC are essential for production of learned song. They show that RA is making contributions to both the syringeal pattern of vocalization (responsible for spectral features) and the respiratory pattern (responsible for duration control), consistent with its anatomical projections. A further conclusion is that the learned long call in males may be assembled by adding complex features to a simpler unlearned call that is shared with females. Thus, a careful analysis of the features of the call suggests a general idea about motor learning: that a "learned" behavior may be constructed by modulating a previously existing motor pattern that itself may be unlearned.

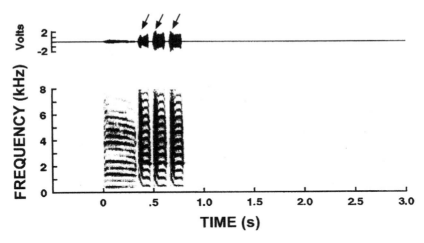

FIGURE 4. Example of stimulus presentation and LC responses: A female stimulus call (at time zero) elicits three LC responses from a male subject. *Arrows* indicate the amplitude peak associated with the fast frequency modulation on each response call in this subject. Upper traces show the recorded amplitude waveform and lower traces show the sound spectrogram for each trial. The latencies and durations of all responsive calls in the first 3 sec after stimulus onset were measured. (Modified from Vicario *et al.*[14])

USING CALL RESPONSE BEHAVIOR TO ASSESS CALL DISCRIMINATION IN ADULT MALES AND FEMALES

When a zebra finch is visually isolated and hears the long call of a conspecific, he or she is likely to call back in response. This behavior was incorporated into a laboratory paradigm in which the subject bird is isolated overnight, then hears a playback of a variety of long call stimuli in the morning. In the basic experiment, the stimuli consist of 10 repeats of the calls of 12 individual female and 12 individual male zebra finches, for a total of 240 calls presented in pseudo-random order. The bird's vocal responses to these stimuli are recorded and analyzed to assess the probability and quantity of responding to each individual call stimulus. A representative trial is shown in FIGURE 4. The responses were analyzed as a function of sex of the subject and the gender and acoustic features of each stimulus.[14]

In this paradigm, both male and female subjects call more in response to the calls of females than of males (FIG. 5A), with a preference ratio of about 1.2 in females and 2.4 in males. This quantitative difference turns out to be a qualitative difference when the responses to each of the individual call stimuli are considered separately. When the responses of female subjects are analyzed as a function of the stimulus duration for each of the 24 stimulus calls, there is a linear relationship with duration with the same regression slope for both male and female calls (FIG. 5C). In contrast, although the responses of males also are correlated with stimulus duration (FIG. 5B), something else is going on: there is an additional increase in the level of responding to all female calls over all male calls, even in the region where male and female stimuli overlap in duration. In addition, the regression for female calls in male subjects

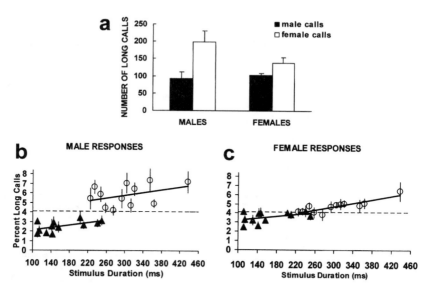

FIGURE 5. Responses to natural male and female long call stimuli in male and female subjects. (**A**) Total number of long calls produced by male and female subjects in response to hearing the standard stimulus set of 12 male and 12 female long calls each repeated ten times in a pseudorandom order. (**B**) Mean %Long calls (± standard error) as a function of stimulus duration for male (*solid triangles*) and female (*open circles*) stimuli in male subjects. (**C**) Mean %Long calls as a function of stimulus duration for responses in female subjects. If all 24 stimulus calls had received equal responses, the response percentage for each stimulus would have been 4.17 (1/24), indicated by the *dashed line*. (Modified from Vicario et al.[14])

is a trend that does not reach statistical significance; other factors seem to be at play. These observations led to attempts to determine the source of variation in this regression in further experiments that used a variety of manipulations of the natural call stimuli that were presented. Ultimately, the picture became clear with the use of completely synthetic calls that enabled the contribution of specific acoustic features of male and female calls to be probed parametrically.

RESPONSES TO SPECTRAL AND TEMPORAL FEATURES OF SYNTHETIC LONG CALL STIMULI

Birds were tested in the call response paradigm using synthetic call stimuli that differed parametrically in duration, fundamental frequency, and degree of initial fast frequency modulation (FIG. 6A–C). These stimuli elicited call responses from zebra finches at rates comparable to natural calls with similar parameters. Analysis of responses to an ensemble of all of these different stimulus types shows that, for both males and females, stimulus duration is a determining factor (FIG. 6D).

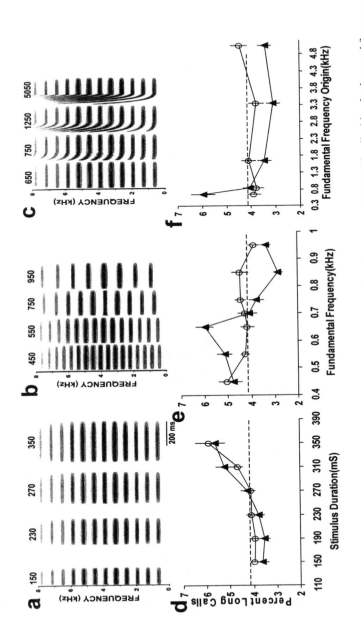

FIGURE 6. Spectrograms of representative schematic stimuli and response functions (Experiment 3). (**A**) Stimuli with a fundamental frequency (FF) of 650 Hz that varied in DUR (indicated above in msec). (**B**) Stimuli with DUR of 230 msec that varied in FF (indicated above in Hz). (**C**) Stimuli with FF of 650Hz and DUR of 230 msec that varied in FFM0 (indicated above in Hz). (**D**) Mean responses (%Long calls) for males (*solid triangles*) and females (*open circles*) to all FFs plotted as a function of stimulus DUR. (**E**) Mean responses (%Long calls) to all DURs plotted as a function of FF. (**F**) Mean responses (%Long calls) to all DURs plotted as a function of FFM0. (Modified from Vicario et al.[14])

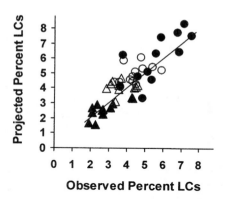

FIGURE 7. Comparison of predicted and observed responses. Scatterplot of predicted vs. observed responses to male (*triangles*) and female (*circles*) stimuli for males (*solid symbols*) and females (*open symbols*). The identity line is plotted at 45 degrees. (Modified from Vicario *et al.*[14])

In contrast, the spectral parameters (fundamental frequency and fast frequency modulation) elicited markedly different response patterns from the two sexes. Females respond more weakly as fundamental frequency increases, but males show a non-linear response that gets stronger for frequencies up to 650 Hz, then abruptly decreases for stimuli at 700 Hz and above (FIG. 6E). Females don't seem to discriminate different degrees of fast frequency modulation, but males, who respond strongly to a simple harmonic stack at the optimal frequency, respond much more weakly if even the slightest frequency modulation is present (FIG. 6F). When behavioral response levels to synthetic calls were used to predict the responses to natural calls with the same acoustic characteristics, there was an excellent correlation with the actual responses measured for the natural calls (FIG. 7). The correlation between predicted and observed responses for the stimuli was very high in male subjects ($P<0.001$) and good ($P=0.02$) in female subjects. This implies that the analysis of the behavioral effects of the acoustic parameters in the synthetic calls captures most of the salient features that distinguish the natural calls, at least in males.

Responses in male and female subjects can be summarized and compared by constructing three-dimensional diagrams that show the response to stimulus duration and fundamental frequency as the height of a surface (FIG. 8). In female subjects, the surface was quite flat, although there is an overall slope upward with duration as expected. In males there is also a general slope upward with duration, but the surface has a much more dramatic topography. There is a very pronounced ridge structure defined by the strong response to fundamental frequencies of 550–650 Hz, especially for longer stimulus calls. Long calls of females typically have long durations and lower fundamental frequencies. The lowest responses are observed in the opposite quadrant, which represents higher fundamental frequencies and shorter calls that are typical of male long calls. In effect, by attending to both spectral and duration parameters in calls, males can perfectly categorize the calls that they hear as belonging

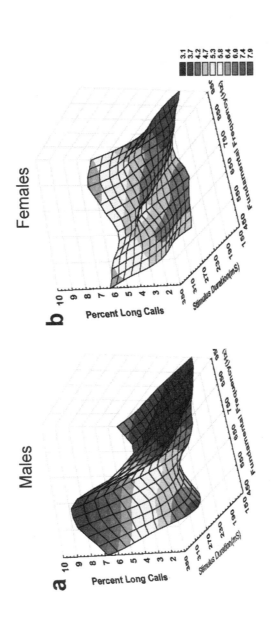

FIGURE 8. Response surfaces in male and female subjects hearing schematic calls. The strength of the vocal response to each stimulus (%Long calls) is plotted as a function of the fundamental frequency (FF) and duration (DUR) of the stimulus. The response surfaces display a composite least squares fit to the data (Statistica). (**A**) Males (*N*=10) show a prominent response peak for lower FF and longer DUR and a deep valley in the opposite quadrant. (**B**) Females (*N*=10) respond more to stimuli with longer DUR but have an almost flat response surface in the FF dimension. Data from multiple sessions have been combined and renormalized as necessary, using fiduciary stimuli included in each set. Color legends indicate the minimum response value (%Long calls) coded by each color (color figures appear online). (Modified from Vicario *et al.*[14])

to males or females, whereas the females seem to rely only on duration and do not make that categorical discrimination. It is not clear whether these experimental results reflect differences in the auditory capacities of males and females, or simply that females are not motivated to respond differentially to spectral features of the call stimuli. Evidence from operant studies suggests that even motivated females take longer than males to learn to discriminate songs, consistent with a difference in auditory capacity.[15]

EMERGENCE OF SEX DIFFERENCES IN LONG CALL RESPONSES DURING DEVELOPMENT

Behavioral testing with the same call response paradigm was carried out in young birds of different ages, enabling us to test when, during development, these sex differences arise. To do this, a simple preference ratio was computed by totaling all the responses to the female calls and dividing by all the responses to the male calls. We used this ratio to construct a time course for young male and female subjects (FIG. 9). In young males and females at 25–35 days of age, there is almost no difference between the responses to male calls and female calls. Both sexes start out with a very small bias toward female calls, a ratio of 1.1–1.2. During development, young females increase their bias slightly to the adult level, whereas young males increase that bias dramatically. By 45–55 days of age, young males show a response profile that is recognizably similar that seen for adult males, although a bit messier. When examined in detail, this developmental change is associated with the emergence in juvenile males of the spectrally selective responses seen in adults.[16]

During this same time period, young male zebra finches are beginning to imitate a tutor call and to produce a long call with male-typical features, as well as to pro-

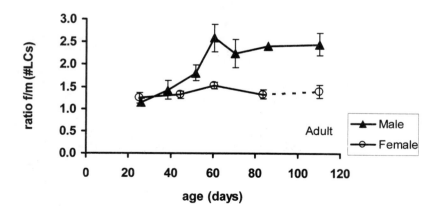

FIGURE 9. Call preference ratios for juvenile zebra finches as a function of age. Mean preference ratios ± S.E. for different age cohorts of males (*solid circles*) and females (*open circles*). Ratios for adults have been plotted arbitrarily over the point for 110 days of age (Modified from Vicario *et al.*[16])

duce the first song-like vocalizations.[17] For example, the emergence of spectral selectivity in call responses coincides with the appearance of fast frequency
modulations in the young males call (at 40–45 days of age) and a dramatic drop in
call duration from the longer form shared with females. This is also the time when
the projection from HVC to RA matures and RA reaches its maximum volume.[18]
These correlations may mean only that this is a time of active development at both
the brain and behavioral levels. Nonetheless, it is intriguing that the time when
young males are receptive to male models as the source for their calls, and when they
begin to introduce male-typical acoustic features into their vocalizations, is also the
time when long call discrimination and preference based on spectral features
emerge.[19,20]

RA LESIONS AFFECT LONG CALL DISCRIMINATION
BEHAVIOR IN ADULT MALES

A possible mediating factor in these results is the vocal motor nucleus RA. Males
show a much stronger call preference based on spectral cues than do females and
have a much larger RA. Developing males have a weak call preference and an immature RA. This suggested an experiment that assessed call discrimination in adult
males with RA lesions. After lesioning, birds were housed individually and behavioral testing occurred within two weeks of the lesion. The lesions did not affect the
probability of calling or the latency of calling, but the lesioned birds showed a drop
in call preference based on spectral cues.[21] The preference ratio dropped to the female level and the degree of change in preference ratio was correlated with the size
of the bilateral RA lesions for the larger, but not the smaller lesions in the dataset.
This implies that a minimum percentage of RA had to be damaged before a clear effect could be detected. The behavioral outcome is summarized in a set of three-dimensional graphs (FIG. 10). These experiments were done with natural calls, so the
response topography in these intact males before they received the RA lesion is a little bit different from FIGURE 8 (results obtained with synthetic calls), but the basic
topography is similar, e.g., the peak structure at 550–650 Hz. Female controls in this
experiment (FIG. 10B) show the slope upward with duration, but no sensitivity as a
function of fundamental frequency. In males with small RA lesions (FIG. 10C), the
topography begins to flatten. When the RA lesions exceed 50% on both sides
(FIG. 10D), male responses have the female pattern: the spectral topography is lost
while the relationship to stimulus duration remains.

Taken together with the observation that, at least under some conditions, RA neurons have auditory responses that are selective for the bird's own vocalizations,[20,22,23] this result could be interpreted as evidence for perceptual processing in
RA, a vocal motor nucleus with direct connections to brainstem motor regions. It
should be recalled that these lesioned birds also have feminized long calls (FIG. 3B).
One may speculate that the same neural processing hardware plays a perceptual role
in discriminating the very sounds that it is responsible for producing, and that both
functions are affected when it is damaged. However, these results could also be interpreted as evidence for a vocal learning process, in which acoustic feedback about
vocal output of male-typical features is fed back onto the premotor cells in RA.
These lesioned birds do continue to produce long calls, although they are feminized

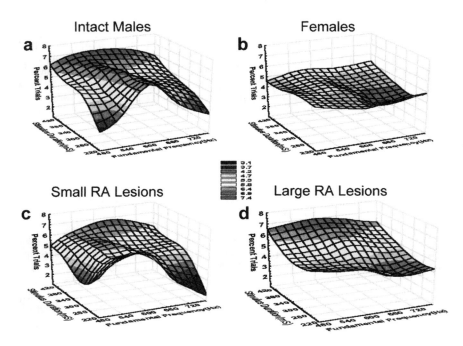

FIGURE 10. Response surfaces showing response probability in intact and lesioned male birds and female birds hearing conspecific long calls. The normalized probability of a LC response to each stimulus (%TRS) is plotted as a function of the fundamental frequency (FF) and duration (DUR) of the stimulus. The response surfaces represent composite least squares fits to the data (Statistica). (**A**) Intact males ($N=14$) show a prominent response ridge for intermediate FF and longer DUR. (**B**) Female subjects ($N=10$) respond more to longer stimuli but show almost no variation in the FF dimension. (**C**) After RA lesion, males with < 40% mean lesion ($N=5$) yield a surface qualitatively similar to that of pre-lesion males, but the FF and DUR slopes are less pronounced. (**D**) After RA lesion, males with >40% mean lesion ($N=9$) have a response surface similar to that of females, with no preferred FF and a gradually higher probability of response to stimuli as DUR increases. Color scale as in FIGURE 8. (Modified from Vicario et al.[21])

in morphology, and continue to produce more of those calls when the stimulus call duration is longer. Apparently, in these animals, information about the stimulus call duration manages to reach the putative call generation mechanism, which does not require RA. In contrast, in intact birds, spectral information about the stimulus reaches RA and influences the amount of calling. This suggests that the spectral and temporal parameters of the stimulus call are somehow channeled through the brain in different ways and arrive independently at the learned call generation mechanism (that includes RA in males) and the unlearned call generation mechanism (present in both sexes).

SELECTIVE AUDITORY RESPONSES FOR LONG CALLS IN NCM

Recently, we have begun to explore auditory structures in a search for neural selectivity that may contribute to the behavioral call selectivity seen to depend on spectral information, e.g., fundamental frequency. Neurophysiological responses to the same stimuli used in the behavioral experiments have been collected in an auditory area, NCM (see Mello and colleagues, this volume), in awake, restrained birds. Neurons in NCM respond to complex auditory stimuli, but the response habituates to repeated presentations of the same stimulus.[24] This makes conventional testing difficult and requires simultaneous recordings from multiple electrodes. Responses can be characterized by the rate at which they habituate (the habituation slope), which varies depending on the acoustic features and the familiarity of the stimulus. When synthetic long call stimuli of constant duration (270 msec) but with different fundamental frequencies (FIG. 6, top middle) were presented to NCM neurons in a male bird, habituation slopes showed a non-linear relationship to the frequency parameter (FIG. 11). This relationship was similar to that observed for these same stimuli in the behavioral paradigm in male subjects, also plotted in FIGURE 11 for comparison. Habituation slopes are less steep (i.e., habituation is slower) for the same stimuli that elicit a stronger behavioral response. This correspondence suggests the possibility that there already exists a response bias towards the behaviorally

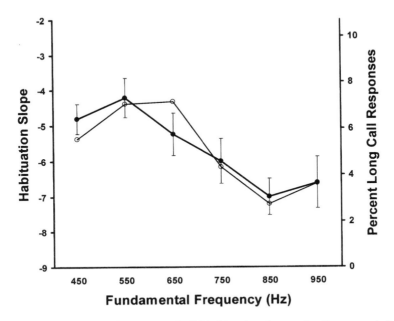

FIGURE 11. Relationship between NCM habituation slope and call response behavior in males. The habituation slope (mean ± SEM, *solid symbols*, left vertical axis) is computed as the percentage decrease in neural response per trial over multiple presentations for synthetic stimuli at different fundamental frequencies. Overlaid is the behavioral call response profile (*open symbols*, right vertical axis) for these same stimuli.

preferred call frequencies at the stage of auditory processing represented by NCM. These experiments, which are being conducted on birds of both sexes, should help identify neural mechanisms that mediate the qualitative sex difference in behavioral responses to spectral parameters of call stimuli.

SUMMARY AND CONCLUSIONS

(1) The learned long call in males seems to be assembled from a simpler un-learned form (shared with females) by modifying at least three acoustic features: duration, fundamental frequency, and frequency modulation. These complex features depend on RA's modulatory input to the brainstem vocal system responsible for producing the simpler calls seen in females and in males with RA lesions. More generally, the evolution of the telencephalic vocal control nuclei in songbirds may reflect the emergence of this modulatory capability, which we call "vocal learning." Moreover, vocal learning may well have begun with the modification of calls because they are simpler and produced by non-oscine birds. In zebra finches, it has been suggested that songs may be assembled from call elements.[25] In non-oscines, e.g., seabirds, un-learned differences in call morphology are used in individual identification (Marler, this volume); a learning process that exaggerated acoustic features might have made such calls more discriminable, with positive effects on survival.

(2) In a behavioral paradigm based on natural responsive calling, males utilize all three types of acoustic features to discriminate long calls. In contrast, the responses of females only reflect long call duration, but not spectral cues. Males call back vigorously to female-typical stimuli and tend to be silent when they hear male-typical sounds. As a result, they effectively categorize calls by gender, and their behavior tends to initiate a dialog with a female caller and avoid contact with a male caller.

(3) Sex differences in long call discrimination emerge during the same period (40–50 days of age) when young males produce the first recognizable male acoustic features in their calls (as well as their first song syllables), suggesting a possible relationship between perceptual and vocal development. This is the same post-natal period when the vocal control pathway rapidly matures.

(4) Sex differences in long call discrimination are abolished by lesions of the vocal motor pathway at the level of RA in adults, suggesting that information about the spectral features of the stimulus selectively reaches RA to modulate long call production. The vocal motor pathway thus could play some role in perceptual processing related to vocal production, at least in the behavioral situation studied. In development, the emergence of male-typical call features (cf. Conclusion 1) and male-typical discrimination behavior (cf. Conclusion 3) may reflect a common factor: the maturation of the vocal control pathway.

(5) In males, there is evidence of a pattern of spectral selectivity in the auditory area NCM that is similar to that observed in the behavioral responses, suggesting that there is already a sensory bias at this stage of auditory processing that contributes to the behavioral selectivity observed. Because we know that young males do not show the behavioral discrimination before a certain age, we are currently examining the influence of experiential factors on the development of this sensory bias.

The ensemble of results obtained in these studies of call perception and production is compatible with the following speculative scenario. In early ontogeny, young male and female zebra finches produce calls of several types and lengths, including a female-like long call. By 35–40 days of age , the vocal pathway matures in young males: RA increases in volume and becomes fully innervated by HVC. RA's projections then can modulate the simpler sounds so that male features begin to emerge. Song syllables begin to differentiate from the simpler sounds as well (Tchernichovski and colleagues, this volume). In birds that have heard a tutor, this differentiation proceeds in the direction of vocal imitation, but it occurs even in isolated birds that have only heard themselves. We may speculate that the auditory system comes with certain sensitivities but is also biased by auditory experience including experience of the bird's own vocalizations, beginning with calls.[26] The acoustic features of self-produced calls are fed back to the call generation pathway, including RA. In males, but not females, exposure to their own calling trains the neural system to associate differentiated patterns of motor output with the resulting patterns of auditory feedback. This self-training may bias subsequent tutor choice on the perceptual level and provide a basis set of output-input relationships that make the system capable of imitating an external model for the long call or for song.

REFERENCES

1. MARLER, P. & S. PETERS. 1988. Sensitive periods for song acquisition from tape recordings and live tutors in the swamp sparrow, *Melospiza georgiana*. Ethology **77**: 76–84.
2. MARLER, P. & M. TAMURA. 1964. Culturally transmitted patterns of vocal behavior in sparrows. Science **146**: 1483–1486.
3. DOUPE, A.J. & P.K. KUHL. 1999. Birdsong and human speech: common themes and mechanisms. Ann. Rev. Neurosci. **22**: 567–631.
4. WILBRECHT, L. & F. NOTTEBOHM. 2003. Vocal learning in birds and humans. Ment. Retard. Dev. Disabil. Res. Rev. **9**: 135–48.
5. MARLER, P. & C. EVANS. 1996. Bird calls: just emotional displays or something more? Ibis **138**: 26–33.
6. ZANN, R. 1985. Ontogeny of the zebra finch distance call: I. Effects of cross-fostering to bengalese finches. Z. Tierpsychol. **68**: 1–23.
7. ZANN, R. 1984. Structural variation in the zebra finch distance call. Z. Tierpsychol. **66**: 328–345.
8. NOTTEBOHM, F., T.M. STOKES & C.M. LEONARD. 1976. Central control of song in the canary, *Serinus canarius*. J. Comp. Neurol. **165**: 457–486.
9. NOTTEBOHM, F. & A.P. ARNOLD. 1976. Sexual dimorphism in vocal control areas of the songbird brain. Science **194**: 211–213.
10. SIMPSON, H.B. & D.S. VICARIO. 1991. Early estrogen treatment of female zebra finches masculinizes the brain pathway for learned vocalizations. J. Neurobiol. **22**: 777–793.
11. SIMPSON, H.B. & D.S. VICARIO. 1990. Brain pathways for learned and unlearned vocalizations differ in zebra finches. J. Neurosci. **10**: 1541–1556.
12. VICARIO, D.S. 1991. Contributions of syringeal muscles to respiration and vocalization in the zebra finch. J. Neurobiol. **22**: 63–73.
13. WILLIAMS, H. & J.R. McKIBBEN. 1992. Changes in stereotyped central motor patterns controlling vocalization are induced by peripheral nerve injury. Behav. Neurol. Biol. **57**: 67–78.
14. VICARIO, D.S., N.H. NAQVI & J.N. RAKSIN. 2001. Sex differences in discrimination of vocal communication signals in a songbird. Anim. Behav. **61**: 805–817.
15. CYNX, J. & F. NOTTEBOHM. 1992. Role of gender, season, and familiarity in discrimination of conspecific song by zebra finches (Taeniopygia-Guttata). Proc. Natl. Acad. Sci. USA **89**: 1368–1371.

16. VICARIO, D.S. *et al.* 2002. The relationship between perception and production in song-bird vocal imitation: what learned calls can teach us. J. Comp. Physiol. A Neuroethol. Sens. Neural Behav. Physiol. **188:** 897–908.
17. TCHERNICHOVSKI, O. & P.P. MITRA. 2002. Towards quantification of vocal imitation in the zebra finch. J. Comp. Physiol. A Neuroethol. Sens. Neural Behav. Physiol. **188:** 867–878.
18. BOTTJER, S.W., S.L. GLAESSNER & A.P. ARNOLD. 1985. Ontogeny of brain nuclei controlling song learning and behavior in zebra finches. J. Neurosci. **5:** 1556–1562.
19. VICARIO, D.S. 1994. Motor mechanisms relevant to auditory-vocal interactions in songbirds. Brain Behav. Evol. **44:** 265–278.
20. MARGOLIASH, D. 1997. Functional organization of forebrain pathways for song production and perception. J. Neurobiol. **33:** 671–693.
21. VICARIO, D.S., N.H. NAQVI & J.N. RAKSIN. 2001. Behavioral discrimination of sexually dimorphic calls by male zebra finches requires an intact vocal motor pathway. J. Neurobiol. **47:** 109–120.
22. VICARIO, D.S. & K.H. YOHAY. 1993. Song-selective auditory input to a forebrain vocal control nucleus in the zebra finch. J. Neurobiol. **24:** 488–505.
23. DOUPE, A.J. & M. KONISHI. 1991. Song-selective auditory circuits in the vocal control system of the zebra finch. Proc. Natl. Acad. Sci. USA **88:** 11339–11343.
24. CHEW, S.J. *et al.* 1995. Decrements in auditory responses to a repeated conspecific song are long-lasting and require two periods of protein synthesis in the songbird forebrain. Proc. Natl. Acad. Sci. USA **92:** 3406–3410.
25. ZANN, R. 1993. Structure, sequence and evolution of song elements in wild australian zebra finches. Auk **110:** 702–715.
26. NOTTEBOHM, F. 1972. Neural lateralization of vocal control in a passerine bird. II. Subsong, calls, and a theory of vocal learning. J. Exp. Zool. **179:** 35–50.

Song-Induced Gene Expression

A Window on Song Auditory Processing and Perception

CLAUDIO V. MELLO, TARCISO A.F. VELHO, AND RAPHAEL PINAUD

Laboratory of Vocal and Auditory Learning, Neurological Sciences Institute, Oregon Health and Science University, Beaverton, Oregon 97006, USA

ABSTRACT: We review here evidence that a large portion of the caudomedial telencephalon of songbirds, distinct from the song control circuit, is involved in the perceptual processing of birdsong. When songbirds hear song, a number of caudomedial pallial areas are activated, as revealed by expression of the activity-dependent gene *zenk*. These areas, which include field L subfields L1 and L3, as well as the adjacent caudomedial nidopallium (NCM) and caudomedial mesopallium (CMM), are part of the central auditory pathway and constitute a lobule in the caudomedial aspect of the telencephalon. Several lines of evidence indicate that the neural circuits integrating this lobule are capable of performing the auditory processing of song based on fine acoustic features. Thus, this lobule is well positioned to mediate song perceptual processing and discrimination, which are required for vocal communication and vocal learning. Importantly, the *zenk* gene encodes a transcription factor linked to synaptic plasticity, and it regulates the expression of target genes associated with specific neuronal cell functions. The induction of *zenk* likely represents a key regulatory event in a gene cascade triggered by song and leading to neuronal plasticity. Thus, *zenk* may be linked to molecular and cellular mechanisms underlying experience-dependent modification of song-responsive circuits. In summary, songbirds possess an elaborate system for song perceptual processing and discrimination that potentially also subserves song-induced neuronal plasticity and song memory formation. The continued use of a multidisciplinary approach that integrates molecular, anatomical, physiological and behavioral methodologies has the potential to provide further significant insights into the underlying neurobiology of the perceptual aspects of vocal communication and learning.

KEYWORDS: auditory; zebra finch; canary; immediate-early gene; *zenk*

PERCEPTUAL PROCESSING OF AUDITORY STIMULI: IN SEARCH OF A NEURAL SUBSTRATE

The ability to discriminate among songs and to memorize specific songs are essential aspects of vocal communication and vocal learning in songbirds.[1–3] Based

Address for correspondence: Claudio V. Mello, Neurological Sciences Institute, Oregon Health & Science University, 505 NW 185th Avenue, West Campus, Bldg. 1, Beaverton, OR 97006.Voice: 503-418-2650; fax: 503-418-2501.

melloc@ohsu.edu; <www.ohsu.edu/ngp/facultypages/mello_claudio.html >

Ann. N.Y. Acad. Sci. 1016: 263–281 (2004). © 2004 New York Academy of Sciences.
doi: 10.1196/annals.1298.021

upon anatomical, physiological and lesion/behavior studies, candidate structures mediating the perceptual processing of song stimuli include telencephalic areas involved in auditory processing and central telencephalic circuits implicated in song production. The focus of this chapter is on the auditory areas. As discussed below, evidence from electrophysiological and lesion studies have suggested that song control nuclei might also play a role in song auditory processing and perception, but this evidence is not conclusive.

Because normal hearing is required for the learning and maintenance of song,[4–7] it is often assumed that auditory information must reach the song control system to provide the auditory feedback needed for sensorimotor integration (for reviews, see refs. 8–10). Indeed, evoked electrophysiological responses to song stimulation can be recorded, in anesthetized birds, within all the nuclei of the song system, down to the motoneurons that innervate the syrinx.[11] These responses typically have high selectivity for the bird's own song (BOS)[11–16] and are shaped by exposure to song during development,[17,18] thereby likely reflecting the role of the song control nuclei during vocal learning. Studies on selective responses to BOS have helped clarify how auditory input modulates activity in the song control system[19,20] (and see Theunissen et al., this volume). However, because the auditory responses evoked by song in song nuclei are mostly seen under anesthesia or during sleep, and are weaker or absent during wakefulness[21–23] (but see also refs. 24, 25), their role in perceptual processing is unclear.

Lesion studies have also implicated the song control nuclei in the perceptual processing of song. Females are of special interest in this respect. They perform song discrimination and recognition,[26–28] even though their song nuclei and projections are often small or absent.[29,30] suggesting the involvement of structures other than the song control system.[31] Interestingly, lesions targeted at song control nuclei reportedly affect song-related auditory discrimination in both males and females.[32–34] In addition, a correlation has been identified between the size of song nuclei in females and the repertoire size of males.[35,36] Such results could be taken as evidence for a role of the song control system in sensory processing, although there are alternative explanations. For example, the lesions have often been large, encroaching upon auditory processing areas adjacent to song nuclei. This issue is acute for females, where song nuclei are small. Indeed, in some cases a similar disruption of perception can be obtained by targeting the lesions at the auditory structures.[37] Even the reported effects of small lesions to song nucleus HVC (high vocal center)[38] could reflect disruption of auditory processing by damage to fibers from L1 and/or L3 en route to the shelf area.[39] Moreover, because the lesion studies have used operant discrimination paradigms, the results may reflect lesion effects on associative capacities required for such tasks (for example, releasing copulatory behavior based on an auditory cue) rather than on auditory processing or perception per se. Finally, some of the contradictory results in lesion studies may reflect significant species-specific differences.

It should also be noted that the pathways by which song stimuli reach the song control system are not conclusively established. It is clear that HVC originates the main pathways and is the source of evoked auditory responses within the song control system.[15,40] However, a direct robust projection from a primary auditory area to HVC (or to other song nuclei) has not yet been identified.[39,41,42] Although the shelf area adjacent to HVC may provide some auditory input to HVC,[39,43] such input would at best be limited (see discussion in ref. 44). Currently, NIf (interfacial nucleus of the nidopallium) is the best candidate source of auditory input to the song system. It receives a direct projection from CM, a central auditory area,[39] and it projects robustly to HVC. In addition, NIf shows evoked responses to song stimulation in anesthetized birds,[45] but the contribution of NIf to song auditory processing and perception in awake birds is still unknown.

IMMEDIATE-EARLY GENE EXPRESSION AS A TOOL FOR THE STUDY OF SONG PERCEPTUAL PROCESSING

The study of activity-dependent immediate-early genes (IEG) has brought a new perspective to the identification of song-responsive brain areas. IEGs are activity-dependent genes whose expression in neurons is typically very low in the absence of stimulation, but increases rapidly and transiently in response to stimulation leading to neuronal depolarization.[46–48] Thus, IEGs are often sensitive indicators of neuronal activation[49,50] and analysis of their expression can reveal patterns of brain activation in response to specific stimuli or behavioral contexts.[49] In general, the expression of inducible activity-dependent genes in a given neuron can be taken as evidence of the previous activation of that cell by the stimulus under study; the expression of such genes typically does not occur in the absence of depolarization in mature neurons.[51] The relation between electrical activation and ensuing patterns of inducible gene expression is not a simple one, however. While both processes reflect membrane depolarization, gene expression is critically dependent on calcium entry and on the activation of calcium-dependent signaling pathways that ultimately control gene expression.[48,52] Regional differences in the components of these signaling pathways may help explain why various brain areas differ in their levels of inducible gene expression, as well as why some specific brain areas undergo activation without a concomitant gene expression response (reviewed in refs. 53 and 51). But used with caution and in combination with tract-tracing, electrophysiology and behavioral manipulations, gene expression analysis can yield significant insights, particularly regarding the spatial organization of the brain's response to stimulation.

In songbirds, most attention has focused on *zenk* (a.k.a. *zif-268*, *egr-1*, NGFI-A or *krox-24*[54–59]). This gene encodes a transcriptional regulator and its expression is highly sensitive to membrane depolarization.[54,60,61] When songbirds hear conspecific song, a rapid, robust and transient increase in *zenk* expression occurs in several discrete telencephalic and mesencephalic areas.[62,63] The ensuing *zenk* expression patterns can be analyzed by *in situ* hybridization (for mRNA) or immunocytochemistry (for protein) in serial brain sections,[62,64] yielding global maps of the brain's response to song.[65] In contrast, when songbirds engage in singing behavior,[66] *zenk* expression is induced in song control nuclei. *zenk* expression analysis has, thus, been very useful in generating detailed maps of brain activation associated with both perceptual and motor aspects of vocal communication (reviewed in refs. 67 and 68). This approach has been used to refine the mapping of vocal communication areas in songbirds and parrots, as well as to identify the brain areas involved in hearing and singing behavior in hummingbirds.[69]

The use of song-induced *zenk* expression as a marker of the brain's response to birdsong has helped in the identification of areas likely to be involved in song auditory processing, song perception, and the formation of song auditory memories. Two important characteristics of this analysis are its single cell resolution, permitting the identification of individual song-responsive neurons, and the fact that it is conducted on awake unrestrained birds, without any interference with their natural behavioral response to song (reviewed in refs. 67,68,70). Moreover, because the *zenk* gene encodes a transcription factor,[60,71] ZENK (we use *zenk* for the gene and ZENK for the protein), and has been linked to neuronal plasticity in the mammalian brain,[61,72–74] *zenk* induction may represent an early event in a gene regulatory cascade linking neuronal cell activation to long-lasting cellular and synaptic changes in the activated neuronal cells.[48,67,68,75] It is possible, therefore, that the songbird brain areas that express *zenk* in response to song stimulation are those that undergo experience-dependent plasticity in response to that stimulation.[70] More specifically, by modifying the expression of target genes related to neuronal and synaptic function, the transcription factor ZENK could orchestrate long-lasting changes in the characteristics of song-responsive neurons. Such changes could include, for example, modifications in neuronal morphology and/or synaptic physiology that would translate into changes in neuronal excitability and responsiveness to song stimulation. ZENK induction could, thus, serve to modify the neuronal circuits that process birdsong as an auditory stimulus, thereby potentially contributing to song auditory memories.

AUDITORY PROCESSING AREAS IN THE AVIAN TELENCEPHALON

Songbirds and other avian groups possess an ascending pathway along which auditory information can reach the telencephalon[41,76-78] (see also Theunissen *et al,* Song Selectivity..., this volume). Although some features of this pathway may be specific to certain avian groups (for instance, a lemniscal projection to the anterior telencephalon that bypasses the auditory thalamus in parrots), its general features appear to have been evolutionarily conserved among birds, and possibly among vertebrates in general.[79] The main telencephalic target of the auditory thalamus is field L, a complex region with subdomains that in songbirds can be distinguished based on cytoarchitectonics,[80] connectivity[39,42] and gene expression.[63] Field L2 is the subdomain that receives most of the auditory projections from the thalamus, whereas L1 and L3 send projections from field L to its telencephalic targets.[39,41–43] The main projections from field L are to the caudomedial mesopallium (CMM), the caudomedial nidopallium (NCM), the nidopallial shelf area adjacent to song nucleus HVC, and the arcopallial cup area adjacent to song nucleus RA (robust nucleus of the acropallium).[39,41–43] FIGURE 1 indicates, schematically, the connections among structures known to be involved in auditory processing and indicates some known relationships between auditory and song control nuclei in the caudomedial telencephalon.

Electrophysiological recordings in various birds have shown that field L and adjacent areas respond robustly to auditory stimulation.[81–84] The latencies are shortest in field L, in accordance with the known connectivity, and increase as one moves away from the field L core (subfield L2) to L1 and L3, and then to the adjacent CMM and NCM. In parallel, selectivity for complex stimuli including birdsong increases as one moves away from field L2 in the rostral and caudal directions, towards CMM and NCM. Recent evidence indicates that training with birdsong in operant conditioning paradigms can affect the response properties of neuronal cells in CM, the

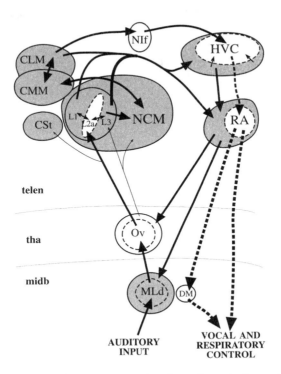

FIGURE 1. Schematic diagram representing the main projections of auditory structures and of some song control nuclei. *Gray areas* represent regions where the *zenk* gene is induced in response to conspecific song presentation; thick solid arrows represent auditory pathways and broken arrows represent connections of the motor pathway for song production. *Thin solid arrows* represent minor or to-be-confirmed projections. ABBREVIATIONS: CMM and CLM, medial and lateral portions of the caudomedial mesopallium; DM, dorsomedial nucleus of the intercollicular complex; L1, L2a, L2b and L3, subdivisions of field L; midb, midbrain; MLd, nucleus mesencephalicus lateralis, pars dorsalis; NCM, caudomedial nidopallium; NIf, nucleus interfacialis; Ov, nucleus ovoidalis; CSt, caudal striatum; RA, nucleus robustus arcopaliallis; telen, telencephalon, tha, thalamus.

area that comprises CMM.[85] More specifically, a significant number of units in CM appear to selectively respond to familiar songs that trained birds learned to discriminate, as opposed to unfamiliar songs (see Gentner, this volume). Taken together with the anatomical data, these observations suggest the existence of an auditory processing system with multiple parallel pathways and a hierarchical organization, although the precise role of each of the areas involved remains to be determined.

GENE EXPRESSION IN TELENCEPHALIC AUDITORY STRUCTURES

Comparison between birds exposed to conspecific song versus unstimulated controls reveals that several areas in the caudomedial telencephalon show a significant *zenk* induction response to song.[62–64] These areas, which are located in the pallial portion of the telencephalon, consist of subregions L1 and L3 within field L, as well as several field L targets, namely NCM, CMM, the shelf region adjacent to HVC and the cup region adjacent to RA. In addition, the caudodorsal part of the lateral striatum (CSt) and the MLd in the ascending auditory pathway (the latter equivalent to the inferior colliculus in mammals) show a significant *zenk* induction response to song (data from lower levels of the auditory system are not yet available). Song-induced *zenk* expression in all the areas above is elicited in birds that do not sing in response to song stimulation, and it also occurs in females, who normally do not sing. Furthermore, deafening abolishes *zenk* induction in these same areas.[66] Thus, song-induced *zenk* expression in these areas is correlated not with singing behavior, but rather with the experience of hearing birdsong. While our focus here is on *zenk* expression, *c-fos* and *c-jun*, two other IEGs that normally comprise the AP-1 transcriptional regulator and that are usually co-induced in mammalian cells,[86] are also induced by birdsong in patterns similar to that of *zenk*.[92] The *zenk* induction response to song occurs in similar brain areas in several species, including zebra finches, canaries, starlings and song sparrows, as well as in non-oscines such as chicks, doves, parrots and hummingbirds[62,69,87–90] (also Mello and Jarvis, unpublished observations).

In contrast, *zenk* is not induced in response to song stimulation either in the nuclei of the direct motor pathway or of the anterior forebrain pathway in the song control system.[63,66] This is paradoxical given the reported electrophysiological activation of song control nuclei by song stimulation (reviewed in ref. 44). It is important to note, however, that *zenk* expression studies are carried out in awake, unrestrained birds. The data obtained are consistent with the more recent findings from electrophysiological studies of awake birds with chronically implanted electrodes,[21,22,24,25] which have revealed that the activation of song nuclei by song auditory stimuli is either absent or much weaker in awake than in anesthetized birds. In addition, *c-fos* and *c-jun* are also not induced in song control nuclei by song auditory stimulation.[91,92] The fact that *zenk* (and *c-fos*) can be induced within the song control nuclei during active singing behavior[64,66,89,91] argues that *zenk* is not simply turned off or uncoupled from electrophysiological activity within the song system. Rather, to the extent that the expression of *zenk* and other IEGs reflects the brain activation that follows song stimulation, the most likely explanation for the lack of induction of *zenk* and other IEGs in song nuclei during song auditory stimulation is that relatively little electrophysiological activation occurs in the song control system in that situation. In this sense, the gene expression data argue against a prominent role for song control nuclei in song auditory processing and/or perception.

As diagrammed in FIGURE 1, tract-tracing studies have revealed that *zenk*-expressing areas are connected by a series of intricate projections.[39,43] Several projections within the telencephalon originate from field L, and several field L targets are interconnected. Some projections reach the shelf region adjacent to HVC. The shelf's most prominent projection is to the cup region adjacent to song nucleus RA, onto which other intratelencephalic projections also converge. From the cup region there is a long descending projection that terminates upon various nuclei of the ascending auditory pathway. The connectivity of the cup region suggests that it corresponds to Aivm and Aidm, the arcopallial auditory nuclei that originate descending projections in non-oscines.[93] Thus, the several *zenk*-expressing telencephalic nuclei and their projections form an interconnected circuitry that closely resembles the central auditory pathways in non-oscines, as has been best detailed in the pigeon.[39,43,93] This circuitry arguably constitutes a central auditory processing system that is conserved in birds, shares some general features with central auditory pathways in mammals, and likely plays a prominent role in song auditory processing.

Interestingly, some of these auditory areas in the caudomedial telencephalon, namely field L and the adjacent CMM and NCM, form a large semi-spherical bulge that protrudes into the ventricle. This structure constitutes what might be considered a caudomedial auditory lobule, and it can be easily visualized by dissecting out the

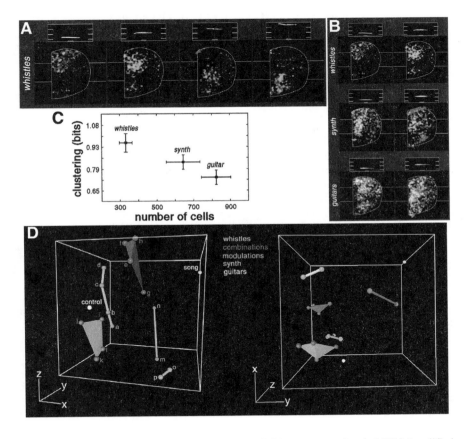

FIGURE 2. ZENK expression analysis of syllabic representation in NCM (modified from ref. 87). **A**–ZENK expression maps in NCM of adult female canaries resulting from the presentation of natural canary song whistles. The respective frequencies (*left to right*) are 1.4, 2.2, 2.8 and 3.5 kHz, as shown in the sonograms (*top*). **B**–The maps for natural whistles and artificial stimuli (synthetic tones and digitized guitar notes) of same frequencies differ markedly. **C**–Patterns elicited by natural whistles and artificial stimuli can be clearly separated by quantifying total cell number and spatial clustering. **D**–PCA analysis of ZENK expression maps in NCM. The first three components (*plotted on the x, y and z axes*) provide for a clear separation of the ZENK patterns that accords to the various groups of stimuli in this study. For further detail, see refs. 65, 87. [This figure was designed in color and is less clear in black and white; the color version can be viewed online.]

overlying hippocampus or by 3D reconstruction of the caudomedial telencephalon from serial parasagittal sections (Mello, unpublished observations). This auditory lobule occupies a considerable portion of the songbird telencephalon. As discussed next, the circuits that compose these caudomedial auditory areas are capable of fine discrimination based on the analysis of acoustic features of the stimuli, and present properties that could contribute mechanistically to fine auditory analysis and discrimination.

THE ORGANIZATION AND FUNCTION OF NCM

As the brain area that shows the most robust *zenk* response to song, both at the level of mRNA and protein,[63,64] NCM has been a major focus of attention. Although early neuroanatomical and electrophysiological studies had been conducted on auditory areas in the caudomedial telencephalon of starlings,[82] NCM had not been directly implicated in the brain's response to song. NCM consists of a relatively large expanse of the caudomedial nidopallidum, forming the bulk of a caudomedial lobule. Its dorsal, ventral and caudal boundaries, which are most clearly seen in parasagittal sections, are formed by the ventricular zone, but it lacks a distinct lateral boundary. Rostrally, NCM is contiguous with the medial portions of field L, and is separated from CMM by the lamina hyperstriatica. NCM's main inputs originate from the auditory thalamus, field L and CMM.[39] Based on its connectivity and on comparisons between the avian pallium and mammalian cortical areas (ref. 94 and see Farries, this volume), NCM seems to occupy a position in the auditory pathways comparable to that of superficial (supragranular) layers of the mammalian primary auditory cortex.

In awake birds, NCM neurons show a vigorous electrophysiological response to several auditory stimuli, including conspecific song, confirming their participation in auditory processing of song. These responses are of longer latency and appear to show higher selectivity for complex stimuli than those recorded in the primary area field L.[95–100] In contrast to the responses seen in song control nuclei of anesthetized birds,[12,13,16] though, NCM responses do not seem to be selective for BOS or conspecific song. NCM may thus represent an intermediate auditory station between field L and other song-responsive brain areas.

Studies of *zenk* expression in NCM have been instrumental in determining the internal organization of this brain area and its functional role in song processing. For instance, densitometric analysis of the relative levels of *zenk* mRNA revealed that song-induced *zenk* expression in NCM is most robust for conspecific song, followed by heterospecific song and non-song auditory stimuli.[62] In addition, the *zenk* response decreases upon repeated presentations of the same conspecific song, and is reinstated upon presentation of a novel song stimulus.[101] Repeated auditory stimulation with the same song also leads to a rapid and long-lasting decrease, or habituation, of the electrophysiological responses of NCM neurons in awake birds.[95–98,100] This habituation is song-specific, since the responses in habituated birds are restored upon presentation of a novel conspecific song. Thus, NCM neurons, either individually or acting as ensembles of units, appear to be able to discriminate between different conspecific songs, a property that is required for perceptual song discrimination. In addition, the habituation rates derived from the habituation curves can be interpreted as an indication of whether a song is "remembered" or not by neuronal cells or neuronal circuits.[95–97]

Stimulation with whole songs induces widespread *zenk* expression, making it difficult to use such stimuli to infer the rules of auditory representation in NCM. One approach to this problem has been to carry out the analysis using canary song, because it can be dissected into phrases containing individual component syllables that are much simpler in their acoustic structure than a whole song.[65,87] These studies showed that the topographical patterns of *zenk* expression in canary NCM correlate with acoustic features of the stimulus. Presentation of the prominent whistle component of canary song resulted in clusters of *zenk*-expressing cells whose position along the dorso-ventral axis of rostral NCM varies as a function of frequency, whereas caudal NCM showed little *zenk* expression (FIG. 2). In addition, combinations of whistles elicited *zenk* expression patterns that were not the sum of the patterns resulting from the individual component whistles. Instead, different whistle combinations resulted in patterns that differed both in the distribution and labeling intensities of *zenk* positive cells.[87] Thus, the neuronal activation patterns in response to complex stimuli cannot be predicted from responses to individual components of the stimulus. Similarly, the response to natural stimuli could not be predicted from the response to equivalent, but somewhat modified, synthetic stimuli, suggesting that NCM neurons may be tuned to quite subtle features of the natural stimulus. Overall, these observations indicate that, whether or not they are utilized by the bird, the activation patterns in NCM contain enough information to discriminate among the various song components used as stimuli.

Further evidence that *zenk* expression patterns in NCM correlate with acoustic features present in the song stimulus comes from experiments in female starlings.[88] Greater ZENK expression within a subdomain in NCM was observed when females were exposed to their preferred songs, i.e. long song stimuli, as compared to short ones. Importantly, long song stimuli are likely to contain more complex acoustic features due to the substantially larger motif repertoire size compared with short song stimuli. Thus, consistent with the work in canaries, local variations in ZENK expression in NCM of starlings also appear to depend on features present in the song stimulus.

HABITUATION, INHIBITION AND DISCRIMINATIVE FUNCTIONS OF NCM

We have noted that presentation of conspecific song in NCM may result in song-specific habituation of neural responses in this region. The paradigm of habituation of *zenk* expression was utilized in an attempt to differentiate the *zenk* expression pattern elicited in NCM by a given complex stimulus (a combination of whistles) from the response elicited by the individual components of that stimulus. The intent was to suppress the response to the individual components by their repetitive presentation, followed by the presentation of the combined stimulus, in order to reveal combination-selective units. *zenk* re-induction did occur under these conditions but, surprisingly, instead of revealing a subset of the units responding to the complex stimulus, the *zenk*-expressing area was now located outside the region where the individual component whistles elicited a *zenk* response in non-habituated birds.[87]

One possible explanation of this puzzling finding is that the patterns of neuronal activation and, consequently, of *zenk* expression may reflect both excitatory and inhibitory mechanisms in NCM. For example, the activation of GABAergic neurons might allow for neuronal activation in response to a given song stimulus to be restricted to certain subdomains within NCM. In fact, it has been previously demonstrated that GABAergic neurons play an important role in shaping tuning curve properties at different levels of the ascending auditory pathway. For example, antagonism of the GABA-A receptor in the inferior colliculus, medial geniculate nucleus, and cortical regions of bats leads to broadening of tuning curves in these regions.[102–104] While these circuit properties appear to arise from local inhibition, they may also be conferred upon the target region by inhibitory projection neurons. Blockade of GABA-A receptors leads to receptive field expansion in the visual and somatosensory systems, indicating that GABA plays a role in sharpening the receptive fields of central sensory units.[105–107] Thus, inhibitory mechanisms are likely to be involved in the sharpening of excitatory connections through local inhibition in various sensory modalities.

To determine whether similar mechanisms operate in songbirds, we have studied the anatomical distribution of GABAergic neurons and their participation in the brain's response to song. Using immunocytochemistry with an anti-GABA antibody, we have shown that NCM contains a high number of GABAergic cells. In addition, a large proportion of these cells co-express ZENK in song-stimulated birds and can, thus, be considered song-responsive.[108] Using patch-clamp recordings in NCM slices, we have isolated miniature post-synaptic currents and determined that these currents are mediated by the GABA-A receptor.[108] Thus, GABAergic cells and synapses are active in NCM and may play a pivotal role in NCM's physiology. This role could be exerted by regulating how the auditory input from the ascending pathway, or from auditory areas reciprocally connected to NCM, affects the activation of NCM neurons. Song-responsive GABAergic cells could also mediate stimulus-induced changes in synaptic transmission and receptive field properties that might determine perceptual and/or memory capabilities.

The phenomenon of habituation has also provided significant clues as to the differential contribution of NCM populations and/or individual neurons to discriminative processing of songs and song elements. *Zenk* expression data have shown that a high percentage of NCM cells participate in the brain representation of a given song. In addition, the habituation study suggested some degree of overlap in the neuronal populations that respond to different song stimuli.[101] This may not be surprising since, if completely non-overlapping populations were involved, just a few songs would saturate the capability of NCM to respond to different songs.[101] Our observations imply, however, that individual neurons can participate in the brain's response to two or more songs. Another implication is that a neuron that shows habituation of the *zenk* response to a given song can still show a *zenk* response to another song, or even to multiple songs. However, conclusive evidence for multiple song responses in single neurons[101] requires a method that assesses the *zenk* responses to multiple song stimuli in the same animal.

With current methods, *zenk* expression can be analyzed for only one stimulus per animal. A partial solution to this problem is the development, by Guzowski and colleagues,[109] working with rodent hippocampal place cells, of a technique called cellular compartment analysis of temporal activity by fluorescence *in-situ* hybridization (catFISH). The FISH method allows the localization of mRNAs of

IEGs such as *arc* and *zenk* at their transcription sites in the nucleus after a short post-stimulation interval, or at the site of translation in the cytoplasm after a longer post-stimulation period. By using catFISH, one can identify in the same animal the neuronal populations that respond to two stimuli presented at different times.[110]

We are currently using a two-epoch song stimulation protocol combined with catFISH analysis to further address auditory representations of birdsong in NCM. This analysis is facilitated by the following: a) basal *zenk* expression levels in auditory areas are very low; b) *zenk* is highly induced upon song presentation; and c) the time course of *zenk* induction is well known. We have already determined that NCM neurons in zebra finches show nuclear or cytoplasmic *zenk* distribution after a short or long survival following song presentation (Velho, Pinaud & Mello, unpublished observations). We now plan to present birds with two distinct songs and then determine the proportions of cells with nuclear, cytoplasmic, or both kinds of labeling, in an attempt to identify neurons that respond specifically to each of the two stimuli, or to both. Such analysis, focusing on the comparison between similar song elements or even between whole songs that differ in one or few discrete elements, should provide valuable information about the ability of NCM circuits to perform song categorization and discrimination.

SONG STIMULATION, GENE EXPRESSION AND NEURONAL PLASTICITY

As we have seen, songbirds have evolved an elaborate telencephalic auditory system consisting of intricate circuitry and involved in the analysis of acoustic features of birdsong. Such a system is arguably well-suited to perform the fine processing required for discriminating behaviorally relevant song stimuli. It may, thus, play an important role in the birds' ability to recognize the song of a neighbor or a familiar mate, and to discriminate it from the song of intruders (see reviews in refs. 1, 3). It is tempting to speculate that the same auditory processing system would be ideally suited to perform some of the computations required to determine whether a vocalization emitted by the bird matches that bird's expectation based on an internalized auditory memory of song. Such a comparison between song auditory feedback and a song auditory memory is generally thought to provide a basis for the perceptual aspects of song learning in juvenile songbirds,[111–114] as well as for the maintenance of learned songs during adulthood.[5–7] However, the identification of a neural substrate for auditory memories, and of the mechanisms involved in comparing an emitted song with an internal expectation have been elusive issues (see chapters by Adret, Konishi, and Mooney, this volume).

There is a well-established link between *zenk* expression and certain forms of long-term neuronal plasticity and memory in mammals.[61,72–74,115] By analogy, the brain areas revealed through *zenk* expression to respond to birdsong[63] may also be undergoing neuronal plasticity in response to that stimulation. If so, these same areas may be sites for the formation and/or storage of the auditory memories for song, a requisite for both vocal learning and vocal communication (see also discussions in refs. 67, 70, 116). Indeed, a growing body of evidence is consistent with the hypothesis that NCM representations are experience-dependent and may, to some extent, reflect the previous exposure history of the birds to song auditory stimuli. For example, the initiation of song-induced *zenk* expression in NCM coincides with the beginning of the song learning period in zebra finches.[100,117] In addition, adult *zenk* responses to a given song stimulus correlate with the degree to which the birds copied that song earlier during the song learning period.[118–120] In female starlings, the ZENK response to song in NCM can be influenced by previous exposure to short or long song stimuli.[121] Thus, as a result of early (or prolonged) exposure to conspecific song, NCM units and/or circuits may become more tuned to the acoustic features of that song.

Importantly, the long-term maintenance of the habituation of NCM responses to song depends on local gene regulatory processes, as it is blocked by the local injection of RNA or protein synthesis inhibitors during the post-stimulation period.[95] Song-induced *zenk* expression occurs within this same post-stimulation period and, thus, could be linked to NCM's habituation to song. More generally, we have hypothesized that song stimulation triggers a cascade of gene expression that leads to long-term changes in the properties of song-responsive neurons (FIG. 3).[64,70] *Zenk* encodes a zinc-finger DNA-binding protein, ZENK, that can regulate the expression of target genes containing the canonical ZENK-binding domain in their promoters.[60,122–124] ZENK action can be stimulatory or inhibitory,[125] and can occur in association with other transcription factors such as c-jun.[127] Although current knowledge on actual ZENK targets in neuronal cells is limited, the transcription of

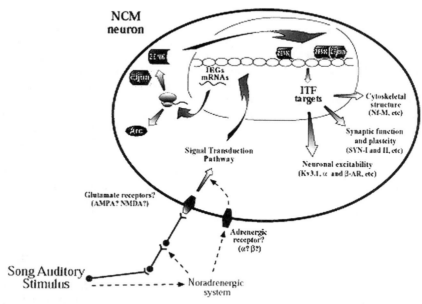

FIGURE 3. Schematic representation of the gene induction response to song in a given NCM neuron. Indicated is the flow of activity triggered by song exposure and leading to the activation of NCM neurons, followed by the induction of early activity-dependent genes and subsequently of their transcriptional targets. *zenk* and its candidate targets (based on the identification of genes with a ZENK-binding motif in their promoter region through Gen-Bank searches) are depicted as a representative example. Arc is depicted as a candidate song-regulated early effector gene.

genes controlling certain basic neuronal functions (e.g., cytoskeletal elements, components of the synaptic vesicle release machinery such as synapsins and synaptobrevin, neurotransmitter-gated ion channels, and catabolic enzymes) has been shown to be dependent on zif268/egr1 (mammalian ZENK homologues) in *in vitro* systems.[122–124,127–129] In addition, through Genbank searches, we have found that at least a few hundred genes, several of which linked to synaptic function and plasticity, contain a ZENK binding motif in their promoters (Velho & Mello, unpublished observations). Importantly, the ZENK protein is likely to bind the same DNA motif and to regulate the same genes in different species, since the aminoacid sequence of its DNA-binding domain is 100% identical[58] among birds and various other vertebrates. ZENK could thus represent an early key regulator in our postulated cascade.

The presence of the ZENK binding site in the promoter region is not proof that a given gene is regulated by ZENK. Our strategy to test our general hypothesis has been to clone the zebra finch homologues of selected candidate ZENK targets and determine whether their expression in NCM is regulated by song stimulation protocols that induce robust ZENK expression. Preliminary results suggest that *synII* is upregulated in NCM upon sustained song presentation,[130] with a time-course consistent with its regulation by ZENK or another early transcriptional regulator. Because synapsin function is associated with vesicle release mechanisms, its regulation by song could potentially link song stimulation to changes in synaptic physiology. A conclusive demonstration of a causal link between song-induced regulation of *zenk* (and of its targets) to neuronal plasticity and song memory formation, however, will require the ability to locally and specifically disrupt *zenk* expression in the songbird brain during song stimulation.

ACKNOWLEDGMENTS

The work discussed in the present review was supported by the NIH/NIDCD.

REFERENCES

1. CATCHPOLE, C.K. & P.J.B. SLATER. 1995. Bird Song: Biological Themes and Variations. Cambridge University Press. Cambridge, UK.
2. KROODSMA, D.E. & E.H. MILLER. 1982. Acoustic Communication in Birds. Academic Press. New York.
3. KROODSMA, D.E. & E.H. MILLER. 1996. Ecology and Evolution of Acoustic Communication in Birds. Cornell University Press. Ithaca, NY.
4. KONISHI, M. 1965. Effects of deafening on song development in American robins and black- headed grosbeaks. Z. Tierpsychol. **22:** 584–599.
5. NORDEEN, K.W. & E.J. NORDEEN. 1992. Auditory feedback is necessary for the maintenance of stereotyped song in adult zebra finches. Behav. Neural Biol. **57:** 58–66.
6. LEONARDO, A. & M. KONISHI. 1999. Decrystallization of adult birdsong by perturbation of auditory feedback. Nature **399:** 466–470.
7. WOOLLEY, S M. & E.W. RUBEL. 2002. Vocal memory and learning in adult Bengalese Finches with regenerated hair cells. J. Neurosci. **22:** 7774–7787.
8. KOPPL, C., G.A. MANLEY & M. KONISHI. 2000. Auditory processing in birds. Curr. Opin. Neurobiol. **10:** 474–481.
9. MARLER, P. & A.J. DOUPE. 2000. Singing in the brain. Proc. Natl. Acad. Sci. USA **97:** 2965–2967.

10. NOTTEBOHM, F. 1999. The anatomy and timing of vocal learning in birds. *In* The Design of Animal Communication. M. Konishi, Ed.: 63–110. MIT Press. Cambridge, MA.
11. WILLIAMS, H. & F. NOTTEBOHM. 1985. Auditory responses in avian vocal motor neurons: a motor theory for song perception in birds. Science **229:** 279–282.
12. MARGOLIASH, D. 1983. Acoustic parameters underlying the responses of song-specific neurons in the white-crowned sparrow. J. Neurosci. **3:** 1039–1057.
13. MARGOLIASH, D. 1986. Preference for autogenous song by auditory neurons in a song system nucleus of the white-crowned sparrow. J. Neurosci. **6:** 1643–1661.
14. DOUPE, A.J. & M. KONISHI. 1991. Song-selective auditory circuits in the vocal control system of the zebra finch. Proc. Natl. Acad. Sci. USA **88:** 11339–11343.
15. VICARIO, D.S. & K.H. YOHAY. 1993. Song-selective auditory input to a forebrain vocal control nucleus in the zebra finch. J. Neurobiol. **24:** 488–505.
16. VOLMAN, S.F. 1996. Quantitative assessment of song-selectivity in the zebra finch "high vocal center". J. Comp. Physiol. [A]. **178:** 849–862.
17. SOLIS, M.M. & A.J. DOUPE. 1997. Anterior forebrain neurons develop selectivity by an intermediate stage of birdsong learning. J. Neurosci. **17:** 6447–6462.
18. SOLIS, M.M. & A.J. DOUPE. 1999. Contributions of tutor and bird's own song experience to neural selectivity in the songbird anterior forebrain. J. Neurosci. **19:** 4559–4584.
19. MOONEY, R. 2000. Different subthreshold mechanisms underlie song selectivity in identified HVc neurons of the zebra finch [published erratum appears in J. Neurosci. 2000 Aug 1;**20**(15):following table of contents]. J. Neurosci. **20:** 5420–5436.
20. ROSEN, M.J. & R. MOONEY. 2000. Intrinsic and extrinsic contributions to auditory selectivity in a song nucleus critical for vocal plasticity. J. Neurosci. **20:** 5437–5448.
21. SCHMIDT, M.F. & M. KONISHI. 1998. Gating of auditory responses in the vocal control system of awake songbirds. Nature Neurosci. **1:** 513–518.
22. DAVE, A.S., A.C. YU & D. MARGOLIASH. 1998. Behavioral state modulation of auditory activity in a vocal motor system. Science **282:** 2250–2254.
23. DAVE, A.S. & D. MARGOLIASH. 2000. Song replay during sleep and computational rules for sensorimotor vocal learning. Science **290:** 812–816.
24. CARDIN, J.A. & M.F. SCHMIDT. 2003. Song system auditory responses are stable and highly tuned during sedation, rapidly modulated and unselective during wakefulness, and suppressed by arousal. J. Neurophysiol. **90:** 2884–2899.
25. RAUSKE, P.L., S.D. SHEA & D. MARGOLIASH. 2003. State and neuronal class-dependent reconfiguration in the avian song system. J. Neurophysiol. **89:** 1688–1701.
26. RATCLIFFE, L. & K. OTTER. 1996. Sex differences in song recognition. *In* Ecology and Evolution of Acoustic Communication in Birds. E.H. Miller, Ed.: 340–355. Cornell University Press. Ithaca, NY.
27. SEARCY, W.A. & K. YASUKAWA. 1996. Song and female choice. *In* Ecology and Evolution of Acoustic Communication in Birds. E.H. Miller, , Ed.: 455–473. Cornell University Press. Ithaca, NY.
28. GENTNER, T.Q. & S.H. HULSE. 2000. Female european starling preference and choice for variation in conspecific male song. Anim. Behav. **59:** 443–458.
29. NOTTEBOHM, F. & A.P. ARNOLD. 1976. Sexual dimorphism in vocal control areas of the songbird brain. Science **194:** 211–213.
30. ARNOLD, A.P., *et al.* 1986. Sexual dimorphisms in the neural vocal control system in song birds: ontogeny and phylogeny. Brain Behav. Evol. **28:** 22–31.
31. WILLIAMS, H. 1985. Sexual dimorphism of auditory activity in the zebra finch song system. Behav. Neural Biol. **44:** 470–484.
32. BRENOWITZ, E.A. 1991. Altered perception of species-specific song by female birds after lesions of a forebrain nucleus. Science **251:** 303–305.
33. SCHARFF, C., F. NOTTEBOHM & J. CYNX. 1998. Conspecific and heterospecific song discrimination in male zebra finches with lesions in the anterior forebrain pathway. J. Neurobiol. **36:** 81–90.
34. GENTNER, T.Q., *et al.* 2000. Individual vocal recognition and the effect of partial lesions to HVc on discrimination, learning, and categorization of conspecific song in adult songbirds. J. Neurobiol. **42:** 117–133.

35. DeVoogd, T.J. 1994. Interactions between endocrinology and learning in the avian song system. Ann. N.Y. Acad. Sci. **743:** 19–41; discussion 41–43.

36. Leitner, S. & C.K. Catchpole. 2002. Female canaries that respond and discriminate more between male songs of different quality have a larger song control nucleus (HVC) in the brain. J. Neurobiol. **52:** 294–301.

37. MacDougall-Shackleton, S.A., S.H. Hulse & G.F. Ball. 1998. Neural bases of song preferences in female zebra finches (*Taeniopygia guttata*). Neuroreport **9:** 3047–3052.

38. Del Negro, C. *et al.* 1998. The selectivity of sexual responses to song displays: effects of partial chemical lesion of the HVC in female canaries. Behav. Brain Res. **96:** 151–159.

39. Vates, G.E. *et al.* 1996. Auditory pathways of caudal telencephalon and their relation to the song system of adult male zebra finches. J. Comp. Neurol. **366:** 613–642.

40. Nottebohm, F., D.B. Kelley & J.A. Paton. 1982. Connections of vocal control nuclei in the canary telencephalon. J. Comp. Neurol. **207:** 344–357.

41. Kelley, D.B. & F. Nottebohm. 1979. Projections of a telencephalic auditory nucleus-field L-in the canary. J. Comp. Neurol. **183:** 455–469.

42. Fortune, E.S. & D. Margoliash. 1995. Parallel pathways and convergence onto HVc and adjacent neostriatum of adult zebra finches (*Taeniopygia guttata*). J. Comp. Neurol. **360:** 413–441.

43. Mello, C.V. *et al.* 1998. Descending auditory pathways in the adult male zebra finch (*Taeniopygia guttata*). J. Comp. Neurol. **395:** 137–60.

44. Margoliash, D. 1997. Functional organization of forebrain pathways for song production and perception. J. Neurobiol. **33:** 671–693.

45. Janata, P. & D. Margoliash. 1999. Gradual emergence of song selectivity in sensorimotor structures of the male zebra finch song system. J. Neurosci. **19:** 5108–5118.

46. Sagar, S.M., F.R. Sharp & T. Curran. 1988. Expression of c-fos protein in brain: metabolic mapping at the cellular level. Science **240:** 1328–1331.

47. Morgan, J.I. & T. Curran. 1989. Stimulus-transcription coupling in neurons: role of cellular immediate-early genes. Trends Neurosci. **12:** 459–462.

48. Sheng, M. & M.E. Greenberg. 1990. The regulation and function of c-fos and other immediate early genes in the nervous system. Neuron **4:** 477–485.

49. Chaudhuri, A. 1997. Neural activity mapping with inducible transcription factors. Neuroreport **8:** iii–vii.

50. Tischmeyer, W. & R. Grimm. 1999. Activation of immediate early genes and memory formation. Cell. Mol. Life Sci.. **55:** 564–574.

51. Ziólkowska, B.P. *et al.* 2002. Methods used in inducible transcription factor studies: focus on mRNA. *In* Handbook of Chemical Neuroanatomy, volume 19: Immediate Early Genes and Inducible Transcription Factors in Mapping of the Central Nervous System Function and Dysfunction. L.R. Kaczmarek & H.J. Robertson, Eds.: 1–38. Elsevier Science B.V. Amsterdam.

52. Bading, H., D.D. Ginty & M.E. Greenberg. 1993. Regulation of gene expression in hippocampal neurons by distinct calcium signaling pathways. Science **260:** 181–186.

53. Leah, J.W. *et al.* 2002. The Egr transcription factors and their utility in mapping brain functioning. *In* Handbook of Chemical Neuroanatomy, volume 19: Immediate Early Genes and Inducible Transcription Factors in Mapping of the Central Nervous System Function and Dysfunction. L.R. Kaczmarek & H. J. Robertson, Eds.: 309–328. Elsevier Science B.V. Amsterdam.

54. Milbrandt, J. 1987. A nerve growth factor-induced gene encodes a possible transcriptional regulatory factor. Science **238:** 797–799.

55. Christy, B.A., L.F. Lau & D. Nathans. 1988. A gene activated in mouse 3T3 cells by serum growth factors encodes a protein with "zinc finger" sequences. Proc. Natl. Acad. Sci. USA **85:** 7857–7861.

56. Lemaire, P. *et al.* 1988. Two mouse genes encoding potential transcription factors with identical DNA-binding domains are activated by growth factors in cultured cells. Proc. Natl. Acad. Sci. USA **85:** 4691–4695.

57. Sukhatme, V.P. *et al.* 1988. A zinc finger-encoding gene coregulated with c-fos during growth and differentiation, and after cellular depolarization. Cell **53:** 37–43.

58. MELLO, C.V. 1993. Analysis of immediate early gene expression in the songbird brain following song presentation, The Rockefeller University. New York.
59. LONG, K.D. & J.M. SALBAUM. 1998. Evolutionary conservation of the immediate-early gene ZENK. Mol. Biol. Evol. **15:** 284–292.
60. CHRISTY, B. & D. NATHANS. 1989. DNA binding site of the growth factor-inducible protein Zif268. Proc. Natl. Acad. Sci. USA **86:** 8737–8741.
61. JONES, M.W. *et al.* 2001. A requirement for the immediate early gene Zif268 in the expression of late LTP and long-term memories. Nature Neurosci. **4:** 289–296.
62. MELLO, C.V., D.S. VICARIO & D.F. CLAYTON. 1992. Song presentation induces gene expression in the songbird forebrain. Proc. Natl. Acad. Sci. USA **89:** 6818–6822.
63. MELLO, C.V. & D.F. CLAYTON. 1994. Song-induced ZENK gene expression in auditory pathways of songbird brain and its relation to the song control system. J. Neurosci. **14:** 6652–6666.
64. MELLO, C.V. & S. RIBEIRO. 1998. ZENK protein regulation by song in the brain of songbirds. J. Comp. Neurol. **393:** 426–438.
65. CECCHI, G.A., *et al.* 1999. An automated system for the mapping and quantitative analysis of immunocytochemistry of an inducible nuclear protein. J. Neurosci. Methods **87:** 147–158.
66. JARVIS, E.D. & F. NOTTEBOHM. 1997. Motor-driven gene expression. Proc. Natl. Acad. Sci. USA **94:** 4097–4102.
67. CLAYTON, D.F. 2000. The genomic action potential. Neurobiol. Learning Memory **74:** 185–216.
68. MELLO, C. 2002. Immediate early gene (IEG) expression mapping of vocal communication areas in the avian brain. *In* Handbook of Chemical Neuroanatomy, volume 19: Immediate Early Genes and Inducible Transcription Factors in Mapping of the Central Nervous System Function and Dysfunction. L.R. Kaczmarek & H. J. Robertson, Eds.: 59–101. Elsevier Science B.V. Amsterdam
69. JARVIS, E.D. *et al.* 2000. Behaviourally driven gene expression reveals song nuclei in hummingbird brain. Nature **406:** 628–632.
70. MELLO, C.V. 2002. Mapping vocal communication pathways in birds with inducible gene expression. J. Comp. Physiol. A Neuroethol. Sens. Neural Behav. Physiol. **188:** 943–959.
71. PAVLETICH, N.P. & C.O. PABO. 1991. Zinc finger-DNA recognition: crystal structure of a Zif268-DNA complex at 2.1 A. Science **252:** 809–817.
72. COLE, A.J. *et al.* 1989. Rapid increase of an immediate early gene messenger RNA in hippocampal neurons by synaptic NMDA receptor activation. Nature **340:** 474–476.
73. WISDEN, W. *et al.* 1990. Differential expression of immediate early genes in the hippocampus and spinal cord. Neuron **4:** 603–614.
74. WALLACE, C.S. *et al.* 1995. Correspondence between sites of NGFI-A induction and sites of morphological plasticity following exposure to environmental complexity. Mol. Brain Res. **32:** 211–220.
75. GOELET, P. *et al.* 1986. The long and the short of long-term memory—a molecular framework. Nature **322:** 419–422.
76. KARTEN, H.J. 1967. The organization of the ascending auditory pathway in the pigeon (*Columba livia*). I. Diencephalic projections of the inferior colliculus (nucleus mesencephali lateralis, pars dorsalis). Brain Res. **6:** 409–427.
77. KARTEN, H.J. 1968. The ascending auditory pathway in the pigeon (*Columba livia*). II. Telencephalic projections of the nucleus ovoidalis thalami. Brain Res. **11:** 134–153.
78. BRAUTH, S.E. *et al.* 1987. Auditory pathways in the budgerigar. I. Thalamo-telencephalic projections. Brain Behav. Evol. **30:** 174–199.
79. BUTLER, A.B. & W. HODOS. 1996. Comparative Vertebrate Neuroanatomy: Evolution and Adaptation. Wiley-Liss. New York, NY.
80. FORTUNE, E.S. & D. MARGOLIASH. 1992. Cytoarchitectonic organization and morphology of cells of the field L complex in male zebra finches (*Taenopygia guttata*). J. Comp. Neurol. **325:** 388–404.
81. BONKE, B.A., H. SCHEICH & G. LANGNEr. 1979. Responsiveness of units in the auditory neostriatum of the guinea fowl (*Numida meleagris*) to species-specific calls and syn-

thetic stimuli. I. Tonotopy and functional zones of field L. J. Comp. Physiol. **132:** 243–255.

82. MULLER, C.M. & H.J. LEPPELSACK. 1985. Feature extraction and tonotopic organization in the avian auditory forebrain. Exp. Brain Res. **59:** 587–599.
83. HEIL, P. & H. SCHEICH. 1991. Functional organization of the avian auditory cortex analogue. II. Topographic distribution of latency. Brain Res. **539:** 121–125.
84. SEN, K., F.E. THEUNISSEN & A.J. DOUPE. 2001. Feature analysis of natural sounds in the songbird auditory forebrain. J. Neurophysiol. **86:** 1445–1458.
85. GENTNER, T.Q. & D. MARGOLIASH. 2003. Neuronal populations and single cells representing learned auditory objects. Nature **424:** 669–674.
86. HERDEGEN, T. & J.D. LEAH. 1998. Inducible and constitutive transcription factors in the mammalian nervous system: control of gene expression by Jun, Fos and Krox, and CREB/ATF proteins. Brain Res. Brain Res. Rev. **28:** 370–490.
87. RIBEIRO, S. *et al.* 1998. Toward a song code: evidence for a syllabic representation in the canary brain. Neuron **21:** 359–371.
88. GENTNER, T.Q. *et al.* 2001. Response biases in auditory forebrain regions of female songbirds following exposure to sexually relevant variation in male song. J. Neurobiol. **46:** 48–58.
89. JARVIS, E.D. *et al.* 1998. For whom the bird sings: context-dependent gene expression. Neuron **21:** 775–788.
90. JARVIS, E.D. & C.V. MELLO. 2000. Molecular mapping of brain areas involved in parrot vocal communication. J. Comp. Neurol. **419:** 1–31.
91. KIMPO, R.R. & A.J. DOUPE. 1997. FOS is induced by singing in distinct neuronal populations in a motor network. Neuron **18:** 315–325.
92. NASTIUK, K.L. *et al.* 1994. Immediate-early gene responses in the avian song control system: cloning and expression analysis of the canary c-jun cDNA. Mol. Brain Res. **27:** 299–309.
93. WILD, J.M., H.J. KARTEN & B.J. FROST. 1993. Connections of the auditory forebrain in the pigeon (*Columba livia*). J. Comp. Neurol. **337:** 32–62.
94. KARTEN, H.J. 1991. Homology and evolutionary origins of the 'neocortex'. Brain Behav. Evol. **38:** 264–272.
95. CHEW, S.J. *et al.* 1995. Decrements in auditory responses to a repeated conspecific song are long-lasting and require two periods of protein synthesis in the songbird forebrain. Proc. Natl. Acad. Sci.USA **92:** 3406–3410.
96. CHEW, S.J., D.S. VICARIO & F. NOTTEBOHM. 1996. A large-capacity memory system that recognizes the calls and songs of individual birds. Proc. Natl. Acad.Sci. USA **93:** 1950–1955.
97. CHEW, S.J., D.S. VICARIO & F. NOTTEBOHM. 1996. Quantal duration of auditory memories. Science **274:** 1909–1914.
98. STRIPLING, R., S.F. VOLMAN & D.F. CLAYTON. 1997. Response modulation in the zebra finch neostriatum: relationship to nuclear gene regulation. J. Neurosci. **17:** 3883–3893.
99. ANG, CW-Y. 2001. Emerging Auditory Selectivity in the Caudomedial Neostriatum of the Zebra Finch Songbird. Ph.D. thesis, The Rockefeller University, New York.
100. STRIPLING, R., A.A. KRUSE & D.F. CLAYTON. 2001. Development of song responses in the zebra finch caudomedial neostriatum: role of genomic and electrophysiological activities. J. Neurobiol. **48:** 163–180.
101. MELLO, C.V., F. NOTTEBOHM & D.F. CLAYTON. 1995. Repeated exposure to one song leads to a rapid and persistent decline in an immediate early gene's response to that song in zebra finch telencephalon. J. Neurosci. **15:** 6919–6925.
102. SUGA, N., Y. ZHANG & J. YAN. 1997. Sharpening of frequency tuning by inhibition in the thalamic auditory nucleus of the mustached bat. J. Neurophysiol. **77:** 2098–2114.
103. WANG, J., D. CASPARY & R.J. SALVI. 2000. GABA-A antagonist causes dramatic expansion of tuning in primary auditory cortex. Neuroreport **11:** 1137–1140.
104. YANG, L., G.D. POLLAK & C. RESLER. 1992. GABAergic circuits sharpen tuning curves and modify response properties in the mustache bat inferior colliculus. J. Neurophysiol. **68:** 1760–1774.

105. SILLITO, A.M. 1975. The contribution of inhibitory mechanisms to the receptive field properties of neurones in the striate cortex of the cat. J. Physiol. **250:** 305–329.
106. DYKES, R.W. et al. 1984. Functional role of GABA in cat primary somatosensory cortex: shaping receptive fields of cortical neurons. J. Neurophysiol. **52:** 1066–1093.
107. TREMERE, L., T.P. HICKS & D.D. RASMUSSON. 2001. Expansion of receptive fields in raccoon somatosensory cortex in vivo by GABA(A) receptor antagonism: implications for cortical reorganization. Exp Brain Res. **136:** 447–455.
108. PINAUD, R. et al. 2003. Identification and characterization of inhibitory neurons in auditory processing areas of the zebra finch brain. 33rd Annual Meeting of the Society for Neuroscience. **29:** 294.1.
109. GUZOWSKI, J.F. et al. 1999. Environment-specific expression of the immediate-early gene Arc in hippocampal neuronal ensembles. Nature Neurosci. **2:** 1120–1124.
110. GUZOWSKI, J.F. et al. 2001. Imaging neural activity with temporal and cellular resolution using FISH. Curr. Opin. Neurobiol. **11:** 579–584.
111. KONISHI, M. 1965. The role of auditory feedback in the control of vocalization in the white-crowned sparrow. Z. Tierpsychol. **22:** 770–783.
112. NOTTEBOHM, F. 1969. The critical period of song learning. Ibis. **111:** 386–387.
113. MARLER, P. 1970. Birdsong and speech development: could there be parallels? Am. Sci. **58:** 669–673.
114. MARLER, P. & S. PETERS. 1977. Selective vocal learning in a sparrow. Science. **198:** 519–521.
115. PINAUD, R. et al. 2002. Complexity of sensory environment drives the expression of candidate-plasticity gene, nerve growth factor induced-A. Neuroscience **112:** 573–582.
116. MELLO, C.V. 1998. Auditory experience, gene regulation and auditory memories in songbirds. J. Braz. Assoc. Advance. Sci. **50:** 189–196.
117. JIN, H. & D.F. CLAYTON. 1997. Localized changes in immediate-early gene regulation during sensory and motor learning in zebra finches. Neuron. **19:** 1049–1059.
118. BOLHUIS, J.J. et al. 2000. Localized neuronal activation in the zebra finch brain is related to the strength of song learning. Proc. Natl. Acad. Sci. USA **97:** 2282–2285.
119. BOLHUIS, J.J. et al. 2001. Localized immediate early gene expression related to the strength of song learning in socially reared zebra finches. Eur. J. Neurosci. **13:** 2165–2170.
120. BOLHUIS, J.J. & H. EDA-FUJIWARA. 2003. Bird brains and songs: neural mechanisms of birdsong perception and memory. Animal Biol. **53:** 129–145.
121. SOCKMAN, K.W., T.Q. GENTNER & G.F. BALL. 2002. Recent experience modulates forebrain gene-expression in response to mate-choice cues in European starlings. Proc. R Soc. Lond. B Biol. Sci. **269:** 2479–2485.
122. THIEL, G., S. SCHOCH & D. PETERSOHN. 1994. Regulation of synapsin I gene expression by the zinc finger transcription factor zif268/egr-1. J. Biol. Chem. **269:** 15294–301.
123. PETERSOHN, D. & G. THIEL. 1996. Role of zinc-finger proteins Sp1 and zif268/egr-1 in transcriptional regulation of the human synaptobrevin II gene. Eur. J. Biochem. **239:** 827–834.
124. CARRASCO-SERRANO, C. et al. 2000. Phorbol ester activation of the neuronal nicotinic acetylcholine receptor alpha7 subunit gene: involvement of transcription factor Egr-1. J. Neurochem. **74:** 932–939.
125. GASHLER, A.L., S. SWAMINATHAN & V.P. SUKHATME. 1993. A novel repression module, an extensive activation domain, and a bipartite nuclear localization signal defined in the immediate-early transcription factor Egr-1. Mol Cell Biol. **13:** 4556–4571.
126. LEVKOVITZ, Y. & J.M. BARABAN. 2002. A dominant negative Egr inhibitor blocks nerve growth factor-induced neurite outgrowth by suppressing c-Jun activation: role of an Egr/c-Jun complex. J. Neurosci. **22:** 3845–3854.
127. POSPELOV, V.A., T.V. POSPELOVA & J.P. JULIEN. 1994. AP-1 and Krox-24 transcription factors activate the neurofilament light gene promoter in P19 embryonal carcinoma cells. Cell Growth Differ. **5:** 187–196.

128. PETERSOHN, D. *et al.* 1995. The human synapsin II gene promoter. Possible role for the transcription factor zif268/egr-1, polyoma enhancer activator 3, and AP2. J. Biol. Chem. **270:** 24361–24369.
129. WONG, W.K. *et al.* 2002. Activation of human monoamine oxidase B gene expression by a protein kinase C MAPK signal transduction pathway involves c-Jun and Egr-1. J. Biol. Chem. **277:** 22222–22230.
130. VELHO, T., R. PINAUD & C.V. MELLO. 2002. Synapsin II, a candidate ZENK target, is regulated by song in the NCM of songbirds. 32nd Annual Meeting of the Society for Neuroscience **28:** 382.5.

Neural Systems for Individual Song Recognition in Adult Birds

T.Q. GENTNER

Department of Organismal Biology and Anatomy, University of Chicago, Chicago, Illinois, USA

ABSTRACT: The songbird auditory system is an excellent model for neuroethological studies of the mechanisms that govern the perception and cognition of natural stimuli (i.e., song), and the translation of corresponding representations into natural behaviors. One common songbird behavior is the learned recognition of individual conspecific songs. This chapter summarizes the research effort to identify the brain regions and mechanisms mediating individual song recognition in European starlings, a species of songbird. The results of laboratory behavioral studies are reviewed, which show that when adult starlings learn to recognize other individual's songs, they do so by memorizing large sets of song elements, called motifs. Recent data from single neurons in the caudal medial portion of the mesopallium are then reviewed, showing that song recognition learning leads to explicit representation of acoustic features that correspond closely to specific motifs, but only to motifs in the songs that birds have learned to recognize. This suggests that the strength and tuning of high-level auditory object representations, of the sort that presumably underlie many forms of vocal communication, are shaped by each animal's unique experience.

KEYWORDS: audition; perception; representational plasticity; animal communication; neural coding; object recognition; adult learning

Recent research on the neurobiology of birdsong has focused so consistently and successfully on song acquisition and production that the communication function of song is sometimes overlooked. Like other communication signals, the adaptive function of birdsong is to control or influence the behavior of others, usually conspecifics.[1] Implicit in this function is the notion that communication signals transmit information between the sender of the signal and the receivers. The success of this transmission rests on predictability. When a singer produces a specific pattern of acoustic energy, it does so under the expectation that it will be perceived in a predictable way—that is, that it will elicit the intended behavior in the receiver. Without the predictable correspondence between production and perception, signals would lose their functionality. Conversely, a functional signal implies a reliable correspondence between production and perception.

Address for correspondence: T.Q. Gentner, Department of Organismal Biology and Anatomy, University of Chicago, 1027 E. 57th Street, Chicago, IL 60637. Voice: 773-702-8090.
t-gentner@uchicago.edu

Ann. N.Y. Acad. Sci. 1016: 282–302 (2004). © 2004 New York Academy of Sciences.
doi: 10.1196/annals.1298.008

In the case of birdsong, functions differ with the sex of the recipient. To other males, a bird's song may make a statement about the singer's species, sex, and territoriality. To females, male song may announce the singer's species, its readiness to mate, and/or convey important information about the singer's fitness. These functions, or rather the production/perception correspondences they require, constrain the acoustic structure of the signal and thereby limit the universe of functional signals that a sender may produce. For the receiver, these functions imply corresponding constraints in the form of (1) a sensory apparatus selectively tuned to signal properties, (2) perceptual mechanisms for the classification of the signals, and (3) cognitive (i.e., sensorimotor) mechanisms for the translation of perception into action.[2] These constraints provide starting points for neuroethological studies of the mechanisms governing the processing of natural communication signals.

Studies of the song recognition system require clarity both with respect to evolutionary constraints on the system and to the perceptual/cognitive operations that the system governs directly. One such operation, common to many species of songbirds, is the recognition of individuals based on their vocalizations.[3,4] Indeed, song recognition, i.e., the ability to associate specific songs with specific singers or other referents, is a prerequisite for many of the decisions involved in such elaborate social behaviors as female choice, female preferences, kin recognition, and territoriality (see ref. 5). Our ultimate goal is the identification of the brain regions and mechanisms mediating song recognition; namely, those structures where learned representations of songs are localized and whose differential activation is correlated with a behaviorally defined recognition process. This chapter summarizes my research strategy, describes some of the recent findings, and suggests directions for future research.

DECONSTRUCTING SONG RECOGNITION BEHAVIOR: THE "MEANING" OF SOUNDS

Learned (in contrast to innate) song recognition may be conceptualized as a sequence of subprocesses, beginning with the discrimination of a to-be-recognized "target" sound from noise and other potentially relevant sounds. The target sound must then be classified or associated with some specific referent (e.g., a mate or an intruder), and the association retained until the sound's next occurrence. Recognition of this form can thus be seen as a classification problem in associative learning and memory. This is true whether one considers the elementary "recognition" of a sound as novel vs. familiar, or the more complex associations that form between a specific sound and a specific individual, motivational state, location in space, etc. Importantly, these associations can vary within and between species depending on the behavioral context in which song recognition occurs, as, for example, when songs are used to recognize different individuals, kin, dialects, or species. The functional plurality of song probably reflects the coding of information at multiple levels within song and, as noted above, is also likely to evoke selection pressures on different perceptual and cognitive mechanisms. For my present purposes, I focus on mechanisms of "individual vocal recognition" of same-species members—so-called conspecifics—in which songs are associated with individuals or groups of individual conspecifics.

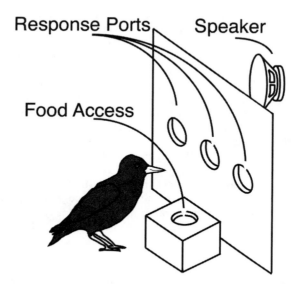

FIGURE 1. Schematic of operant training apparatus. Birds were given access to a metal panel housing three response buttons, and a feeder. Pressing the center button triggered playback of a training song. For the two-alternative choice procedure (see text), subjects had to peck the left button after hearing one-half of the training songs, and the right button after hearing the other half to receive a food reward. For the go/nogo procedure (see text), subjects had to peck the center button after hearing one-half of the training songs ("go" response, S+ stimulus), and had to withhold responses altogether after hearing the other half ("nogo" response, S– stimulus). Only "go" responses to the S+ stimuli were reinforced with food.

To study individual vocal recognition, one first needs to understand the behavioral schemes that birds use to classify and organize the songs of conspecific singers. Because the ultimate goal is to study the neural mechanism, I sought an operational definition of song recognition that permitted direct laboratory study, such that the "meaning" of a sound could be experimentally manipulated and the behavioral consequences of its presentation assessed. To do this, we used a set of operant conditioning techniques that required subjects to make one response to the songs of a specific bird and a different response to the songs of one or more other birds.[6,7] Typically, the birds are first trained to obtain food by pecking buttons on a panel mounted on the side of their cage (FIG. 1). They are then reinforced with food for pecking one button, say the left, every time they hear a song from male "A", and for pecking another button, in this case the right, every time they hear a song from male "B". Tasks such as this, in which two sets of stimuli (songs) are associated with similar operantly reinforced behaviors (peck right/ peck left) are called two-alternative choice tasks (2AC). In a close variant, the so-called go/nogo procedure, behavioral responses to only one set of stimuli are reinforced, leading the subject to cease responding to the nonreinforced stimuli. With both training procedures, subjects become proficient at recognizing stimuli in each class, and there are innumerable ways that both the task and the stimuli can be varied to ask specific questions about the

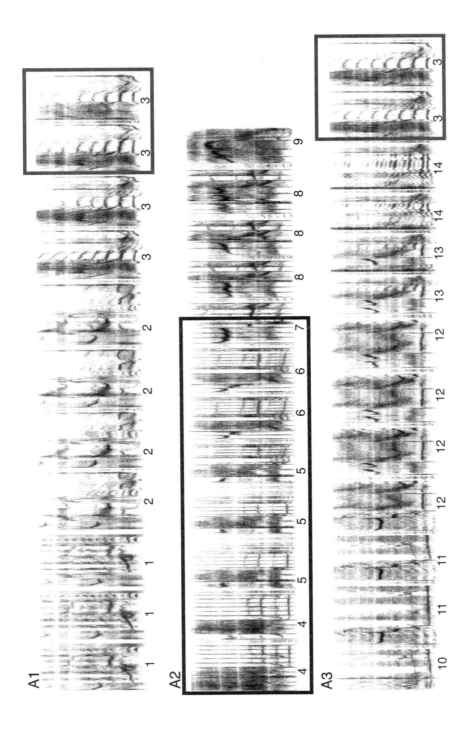

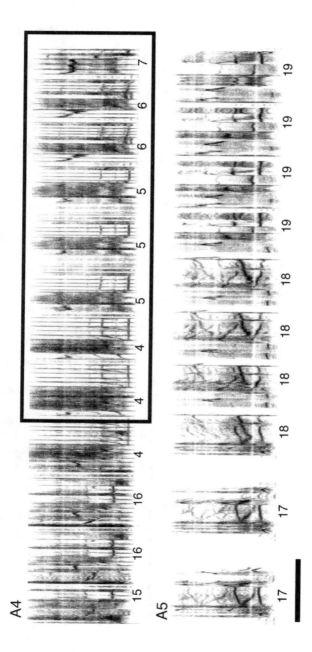

FIGURE 2. Starling song stimuli. Sonograms of typical stimulus exemplars used for operant training of song recognition. Each row shows a different (~10 s) sample of song. All samples shown were drawn from the songs of a single male starling. Unique motifs are labeled with different numbers along the bottom of each sonogram. The boxes outline similar motif sequences in different exemplars (i.e., songs). Note the high motif variability across song exemplars, the repetitive motif sequencing with songs, and the stereotyped note structure within similar motifs. Scale bars show 1 s. Frequency range 0–10 kHz.

acoustic features, as well as associative processes such as generalization and categorization, that guide song recognition.

Subjects in these experiments were European **starlings** (*Sturnus vulgaris*). Male starlings tend to sing in long continuous episodes (i.e., *bouts*). Song bouts, in turn, are composed of much smaller acoustic units referred to as *motifs*[8,9] (FIG. 2), and these, in turn, are composed of still smaller units called *notes*. Notes can be broadly classified by the presence of continuous energy in their spectrotemporal representations. Although a motif may consist of several notes, the note pattern within a motif is usually relatively stereotyped between successive renditions of that motif. Commonly, each motif is repeated two or more times before the next one is sung. Thus, starling song appears (acoustically) as a sequence of changing motifs, where each motif is an acoustically complex event (FIG. 2). Different motifs can vary in duration from roughly 200 to 1,000 ms, and the number of unique motifs that a male starling can sing (i.e., his repertoire size) can be very large. Consequently, different song bouts from the same male are not necessarily composed of the same set of motifs. Over time, however, the songs of a specific male can be characterized by a set of motifs typical of that male. Although some sharing of motifs does occur among captive males,[10,11] the motif repertoires of different males living in the wild are generally unique.[7–9,12,13] Thus, learning which males sing which motifs can provide a diagnostic cue for song recognition.

The results of our behavioral studies support the idea that individual song recognition operates at the level of the motif. Starlings trained to recognize sets of songs from different conspecific individuals can correctly recognize sets of novel song bouts from the same singers[7,14] (FIG. 3). One class of acoustic cues that could permit the recognition of novel song bouts are those resulting from idiosyncratic source and/or filter properties of each individual's vocal apparatus (i.e., "voice" characteristics). The use of voice characteristics (e.g., vocal timbre, the frequency of glottal pulsation, and spectral contours imparted by laryngeal morphology) is well documented for individual talker recognition in humans (e.g., ref. 15). The hypothesis that recognition is based at the level of the motif was tested by asking the birds to recognize novel song bouts that have *no* motifs in common with the training songs (FIG. 3). The hypothetical role of voice characteristics was tested by training birds to recognize isolated motifs shared by two different males (e.g., bird A singing motif 1 and bird B singing motif 2), and then watching recognition after *switching the motif but not the singer* (i.e., bird A singing motif 2 and bird B singing motif 1). In both cases, recognition falls to chance levels, suggesting the importance of motifs and eliminating a critical role for voice characteristics.

The most reasonable alternative hypothesis is that starlings learn to recognize the songs of individual conspecifics by memorizing sets of motifs that are associated with individual singers. If this is true, then once recognition is learned, it should be possible to control it systematically by varying the proportions of motifs in a "target" bout that come from two vocally familiar males. If subjects memorize a large set of motifs from each singer, recognition behavior should be correlated with the relative proportions of familiar motifs from different males independent of the specific motifs comprising a given song. If they attend to the presence (or absence) of a single motif or a small set of motifs, recognition should not follow relative motif proportions, and should not generalize between songs in which different motifs from the same singer make up similar proportions. To test these ideas, I again trained starlings to recognize sets of songs from different individual males, and then watched as subjects classified novel song bouts in which motifs from the training songs were combined in several different ways.[16] Consistent with the motif memorization hypothesis, we observed an approximately linear relationship between song classification and the relative proportions of familiar motifs from different singers composing each bout (FIG. 3). This suggests that when starlings are compelled to classify individual conspecific songs, they do so by memorizing large numbers of unique

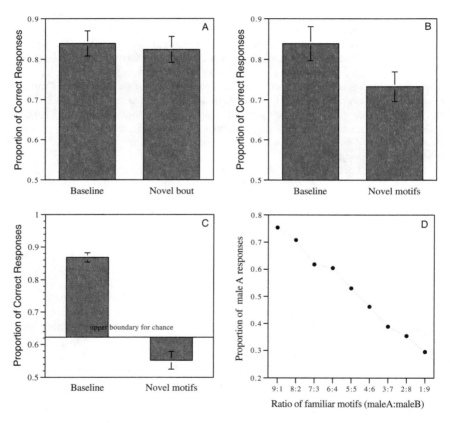

FIGURE 3. Individual song recognition behavior in European starlings. (**A**) Mean (± SEM) proportion of correct responses given during asymptotic performance on an operant recognition task (Baseline) and during initial transfer to novel songs containing familiar motifs (Novel bout). (**B** and **C**) Mean (± SEM) proportion of correct responses during transfer from the baseline training to novel songs from the same singers composed of novel motifs. Data in **B** show the transfer when the subjects were exposed to the training and test songs outside of the operant apparatus. Data in **C** show the results for the same transfer after controlling for this experience. Note that in **C** recognition of the novel motifs falls below chance. (**D**) Data showing the responses to chimeric songs composed of familiar motifs from two different singers. Note the close and approximately linear relationship between the ratio of familiar motifs from each singer and the subjects' recognition response.

song components (i.e., motifs) and then organizing subsets of these motifs into separate classes. From a human perspective, this might seem a suboptimal strategy to solve this vocal recognition problem. However, classifying songs according to their component structure represents a functionally parsimonious method of organizing these complex, but phonologically disjoint, sets of acoustic signals. Since individual starlings tend to possess unique motif repertoires, it is likely that, under natural conditions, these disjoint sets and the associated perceptual classes will correspond to individual identity.

NEURAL SUBSTRATES OF SONG RECOGNITION

From an operational standpoint, we consider individual recognition as a function that matches two representations—that of the incoming "to-be-recognized" ("target") sensory signal, and that of the memory (or memories) of similar, recognizable signals. The behavioral data suggest strongly that in starlings these representations should correspond to the functional components of songs, i.e., motifs. Moreover, because song recognition is an associative process, mnemonic representations may reflect the acoustics of the signal *and* the reward contingencies associated with specific signals. As a first step in understanding the neural substrates of song recognition, we attempted to localize these representations in the starling brain, and describe their form with respect to behaviorally relevant variation in conspecific songs.

Several lines of earlier work suggested auditory regions in the forebrain as likely locations in which one might observe neural correlates to individual vocal recognition in starlings. The large-scale architecture and general pattern of connectivity within the starling auditory forebrain appears to be similar to that observed for other songbird species[17] (and see Theunissen et al., Song Selectivity..., this volume). The field L complex is the primary telencephalic target for auditory information arriving via parallel pathways from the thalamus; interconnected subregions of field L project to the caudal medial nidopallium (NCM) and reciprocally to the lateral portion of the caudal mesopallium (clM). The NCM and clM share reciprocal connections with the caudal medial portion of the mesopallium (cmM), and projections from clM to Nif and the HVC shelf provide the likely source of auditory input to the classic "song control" system (Theunissen et al., Song Selectivity..., this volume). Thus, within the sensory hierarchy, NCM and the caudal mesopallial structures (clM, cmM) sit in positions analogous to secondary auditory cortices in mammals and, by extension, then are likely to be involved in the processing of behaviorally relevant complex stimuli such as conspecific song. This reasoning is supported by a number of studies.

In European starlings, neurons throughout the auditory telencephalon show complex patterns of tonotopic organization[18,19] that can be differentiated on the basis of the direction of the tonotopic gradient and tuning curve bandwidth,[20,21] and these patterns appear to respect the anatomical boundaries of the field L complex. Neurons in L1 and L3 subregions of field L have lower response rates to tone bursts than those in L2 and show greater selectivity to species-specific vocalizations.[22–25] This selectivity is borne out by the complexity of the spectrotemporal receptive fields (STRFs) for many neurons within field L. Indeed, more reliable estimates of the STRF are derived from responses to conspecific vocalizations than from tone pips[26] (cf. ref. 27).

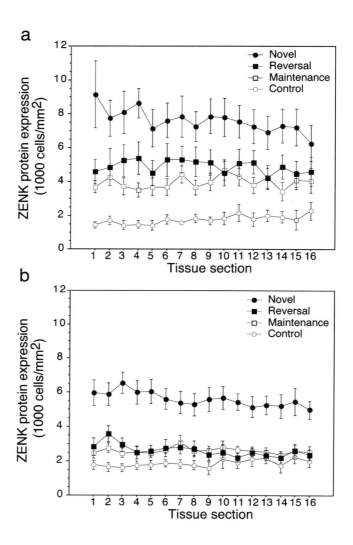

FIGURE 4. IEG *zenk* expression during vocal recognition. Zenk protein expression density in (**a**) NCM and (**b**) cmM following exposure to conspecific song under three different (see text) operant training regimes. In NCM, the response to novel songs is significantly elevated above that for all other groups. In cmM, expression was elevated in all three groups of operantly trained, and was higher still in the birds that heard novel songs. The 16 most medial tissue sections (40 μm) are shown (1, most medial; 16, most lateral) with the data collapsed across hemispheres.

The general pattern of increasing response selectivity along the sensory hierarchy areas continues into NCM and cM,[24] suggesting that these regions are involved in the extraction of complex features. Early data from white-crowned sparrows are consistent with this in identifying a small subset of NCM neurons that are selective for the direction of frequency modulation in particular elements of conspecific song.[28] More extensive studies using complex stimuli demonstrate that both cM and NCM are broadly tuned, i.e., selectively responsive, to conspecific songs,[29] with a hierarchy of increasingly nonlinear components driving neural responses from field L to cM respectively.[30] A similar sensitivity to complex acoustic features characteristic of conspecific songs is apparent in NCM. Repeated presentation of the same conspecific song gives rise to song-specific habituation of the NCM response,[31,32] suggesting that NCM plays an important role in vocal recognition.[33]

The second line of research supporting the role of NCM and cM in the processing of conspecific song comes from studies of stimulus-driven expression of the immediate-early-gene (IEG) *zenk*, a putative marker for song-induced experience-dependent plasticity.[34] Both NCM and cM show a rapid upregulation of the IEG *zenk* in response to the presentation of conspecific songs compared to a variety of other acoustic stimuli[35] (and see Mello, this volume). The *zenk* response is tuned to the acoustics of particular conspecific song syllables,[36] and habituates to the repeated presentation of the same conspecific song[37] on a time scale that mirrors the song-specific modulation of NCM neuron firing rates. In addition, pairing the presentation of song with an aversive stimulus leads to increased expression relative to controls in which song is unpaired, suggesting that associative mechanisms may mediate at least a portion of the NCM IEG response.[38]

To explore this idea in the context of individual vocal recognition, I trained starlings to recognize sets of conspecific songs using the operant two-alternative choice procedure. Once they had learned to recognize the baseline set of songs I transferred one-third of them to novel songs from different singers, kept one-third on the training songs, and reversed the response contingencies of the training songs for the final third. Following these transfer sessions Zenk expression was visualized in NCM and cM. The IEG response in NCM was consistent with the habituation and novelty responses described above. The density of Zenk protein expression in NCM was elevated *only* in the birds required to classify the novel songs; expression in the other two groups was no different than in control birds that heard no song but worked the apparatus for food. The pattern of expression in cmM, however, was qualitatively different, with all three groups showing significantly elevated levels of Zenk protein expression relative to the silent controls and birds in the novel song condition showing still higher levels relative to the other two groups of birds (FIG. 4). Thus, in addition to the effect of song novelty, Zenk protein expression in cmM also appeared to correlate with the ongoing recognition of familiar songs.

LEARNED REPRESENTATIONS OF SONGS IN CM

To examine the role of cmM in the representation of learned conspecific song in adult birds, I again trained starlings to recognize two sets of conspecific songs, using both two-alternative choice (2AC) and go/nogo (GNG) operant procedures (see FIG. 1). Both procedures teach the subject to recognize all the training songs, but for

the 2AC procedure the songs in both sets are associated with similar positively reinforced behaviors (pecks to two different buttons), and for the GNG procedure only
one set of songs is associated with a positively reinforced behavior. Regardless, in
both training regimens, subjects learned very accurate recognition of the training
songs. Once asymptotic behavior was attained, I anesthetized each subject with urethane and recorded the extracellular responses of single neurons in the cmM to an
ensemble of acoustic stimuli. The stimulus ensemble comprised the same song stimuli used during operant recognition training (termed "familiar" songs), a balanced
number of novel conspecific song stimuli (termed "unfamiliar" songs), and two synthetic stimuli. I used three sets of songs recorded from three different males. Each of
the different song stimulus exemplars was a 10-s sample of continuous singing, tak-
en from a single bout of a given male's song. Two sets of songs served as training
stimuli for each subject, and the third set was used as the novel song stimuli. Thus,
the stimulus ensemble was similar for each subject, except that the familiarity or
novelty of any given song varied systematically. Neurons were tested with 33 to 77
unique song motifs (73 to 178 total motifs), depending on the exact set of familiar
songs used to train each animal and the set of unfamiliar songs used during testing.[39]

As a *population*, cmM neurons responded selectively to the class of familiar
songs. The mean response strength, which reflects the cell's mean spike rate and
variance,[39] was strongly and significantly biased toward familiar (i.e., training)
songs compared with unfamiliar songs. The strong response bias for familiar songs
was consistent in animals trained under both the two-alternative choice and go/nogo
operant regimes (FIG. 5). Thus, in this paradigm song recognition learning shapes the
responses of cmM neurons.

The observed plasticity in cmM could result from either "bottom-up" or "top-
down" processes, or both. By bottom-up, I mean that the response is driven in a predictable way by patterns of acoustic variation in the stimulus. In the extreme case,
all the information represented by the cell's response is present in the acoustic variation of the signal. Thus, plasticity may result simply from exposure to a given set
of songs. In contrast, top-down processes refer to the attentional, motivational, and/
or reward mechanisms that might also shape a cell's response, but which are largely
independent of any particular signal acoustics. Our associative model of individual
song recognition requires both top-down and bottom processes.

Consistent with the associative model, and thus the important role of associative
learning in individual song recognition, a significant portion of the response tuning
in cmM appears to be under the control of different reinforcement signals. Whereas
the subjects trained using the two-alternative choice procedure showed no reliable
difference between response strengths associated with the two sets of training songs,
those trained with the go/nogo procedure did. That is, songs associated with positive
reinforcement (S+ stimuli) elicited significantly stronger responses than those associated with no reinforcement (S– stimuli; FIG. 5). Importantly, this difference was
not the result of overall failure to respond to the S– stimulus, because the S– stimuli
elicited stronger responses than unfamiliar songs. Thus, although animals in both
operant regimes learned to discriminate equally well between the sets of training
songs, the stimulus reinforcement contingencies specific to the training regime (see
FIG. 1) had differential effects on the distributions of neuronal responses. These task-
specific effects may reflect the use of different behavioral strategies to solve each
task, or perhaps the differential cost of incorrect responses under each regime. In the

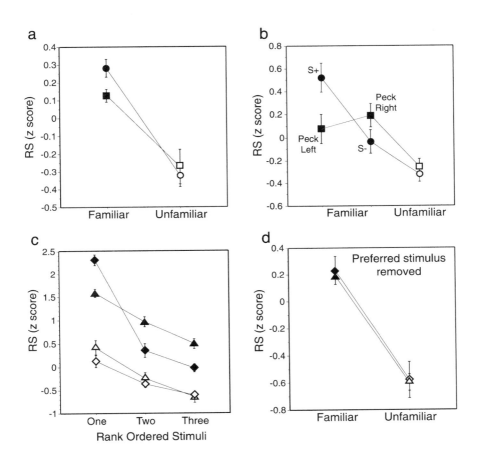

FIGURE 5. cmM neural responses. (**a**) Normalized response strength (z-scores) for familiar (*filled symbols*) and unfamiliar (*open symbols*) songs, split by training regime (two-alternative choice: ■, □; go/nogo: ●, ○). (**b**) Response strength as in **a**, but with the two sets of training stimuli and their accompanying responses labeled separately. (**c**) Rank-ordered response strength (z-scores) for the three most potent familiar (*filled symbols*) and unfamiliar (*open symbols*) songs for song-selective (◆, ◇) and nonselective neurons (▲, △). The interaction between stimulus rank-order and response selectivity among the familiar songs is significant, showing the strong bias in the song-selective cells for a single stimulus. The difference between the curves for the *filled* and *open symbols* shows the population-level bias for familiar songs. (**d**) Response strength z-scores for song-selective (◆, ◇) and nonselective neurons (▲, △) neurons, with the response to the preferred stimulus (the stimulus that elicited the strongest response) removed from the analysis. The differences are significant. All values are reported as means ± SEM.

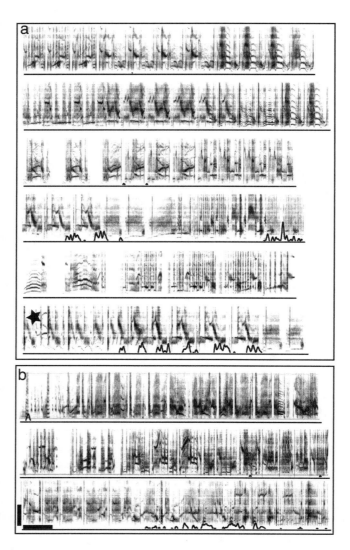

FIGURE 6. Typical single neuron responses in the cmM. (**a,b**) Response of a selective cmM unit to nine different song stimuli. Familiar songs are outlined in panel **a**, unfamiliar in panel **b**. The peristimulus time histogram (PSTH) of the response is superimposed over the sonogram of each stimulus. (**c**) Detailed view of the response of the unit in (**a**) and (**b**) to the song stimulus denoted by the black star. Traces from top to bottom show the raw spike waveform for a single stimulus presentation showing excellent single unit isolation, the

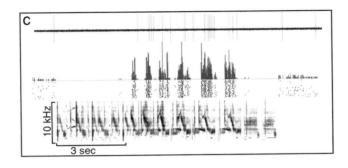

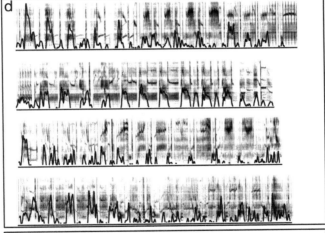

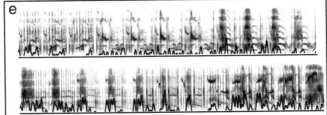

FIGURE 6. *Continued.*

PSTH, spike raster plots for several stimulus repetitions showing the reliability of the response, and the stimulus sonogram. (**d,e**) Example of another, very marginally selective, cmM neuron responding to four familiar songs (**d**) and two unfamiliar songs (**e**). Horizontal and vertical scale bars show 5 kHz and 1 s, respectively.

go/nogo condition, the failure to recognize an S+ stimulus meant a missed opportunity for food, whereas the failure to recognize an S– stimulus cost only a slight increase in the already present delay to reinforcement following the next S+ stimulus. Regardless of the specific behavioral strategies underlying differences between the two-alternative choice and go/nogo procedures, it is clear that bottom-up (i.e., stimulus-driven) mechanisms alone cannot account for the shaping of song representations in cmM. If the absolute or relative levels of stimulus activation were the only forces shaping cmM responses, then the response strength associated with the S+ and S– stimulus would not have been significantly different. Additional top-down mechanisms such as those governing attention, motivation or associative processing, etc., must also play a role.

Response Selectivity

The strong population response bias for familiar songs obviously indicates that cmM neurons did not respond equally to all songs in the test ensemble. To examine this bias in more detail, I developed a selectivity index (SI) score, in which a neuron's strongest response to a test stimulus is compared to that cell's response to all test stimuli.[39] An SI score close to one indicates that the cell responded to only one stimulus, while smaller SI scores indicate responses more evenly distributed across all stimuli. If the SI score for a cell was significantly different from a random distribution of SI scores, the cell was termed "song-selective" for the song that elicited the maximum response. The remaining cells were termed "nonselective." By this definition, roughly 64% of the cells in the cmM gave a selective response to one of the test stimuli; of these cells, a significant proportion (93%) preferred one of the training songs (FIG. 5). For nonselective cells, the song that elicited the strongest response was not significantly more likely to be either familiar or unfamiliar.

To our surprise, the population-level difference between the mean responses to the familiar and unfamiliar songs was not wholly dependent on the response to the preferred song. Even when the preferred song was removed from the comparison, the mean response strength associated with the familiar songs remained significantly greater than that for the unfamiliar songs (FIG. 5). This was observed for nonselective as well as selective cells (FIG. 5), demonstrating that as a population cmM neurons evince selectivity for the class (or a non-singleton subset) of familiar songs. The strong bias in the selectivity of single neurons for familiar songs resembles biases seen in the song control system for a bird's own song.[40,41] Here, however, I am describing neuronal selectivity for conspecific songs that adults have learned to recognize, in neurons outside of the song control system.

Motif Selectivity

Both song-selective and nonselective cells could respond with phasic or tonic patterns of activity, and with high or low spontaneous rates, but on average the song-selective cells had more phasic responses and lower spontaneous firing rates than nonselective cells. Thus, most cells with near-zero spontaneous firing rates and highly phasic responses were selective (FIGS. 6 and 7). For many of the song-selective cells, responses were restricted to one or a small number of repeated motifs within one or a few songs, typically with suppression of background activity for all other motifs. Be-a

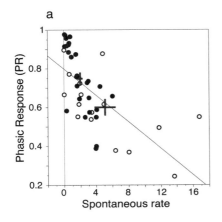

b

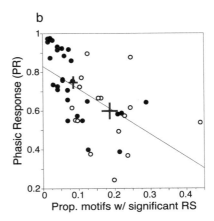

FIGURE 7. Response scattergrams. (**a**) Scatter plot showing the distribution of phasic responses (PR[39]) across the population of selective (*filled symbols*) and nonselective (*open symbols*) cmM neurons, as a function of spontaneous firing rate (spikes/s). The means (± SEM) for each class are shown as the gray crosses. The line shows the significant linear regression. (**b**) As in **a**, but with PR plotted as a function of the proportion of motifs that elicited significant responses. The line shows the significant linear regression.

cause these responses appeared to be driven by acoustic variation at the level of the motif, we simply counted the number of motifs that elicited a significant response (i.e., an increase in firing rate relative to spontaneous activity) from each cell. Consistent with their tendency toward phasic response patterns, the song-selective cells responded to on average about 8 motifs, whereas nonselective cells were driven by significantly more motifs, roughly 20, on average.

To quantify the relationship between motif features and each neuron's spike response, we used a multiple linear regression between the response strength associated with each motif in a given cell's test ensemble and the coefficients from a two-dimensional wavelet decomposition of the sonogram for each motif. (Wavelet decomposition is a very efficient data compression technique that allows us to characterize the high-dimension acoustic space of each motif by a relatively small list of weighted features, i.e., coefficients. To the extent that variation among the wavelet coefficients is correlated with variation in the spike rate of a single neuron, one can say that the neuron codes for those features represented by the significant regression coefficients. Thus, we are concerned primarily with two measures: the mean R^2 values across cells, which provide us with an estimate of the overall quality of the regressions, and the proportions of cells within different classes that show a significant regression with the wavelets). The mean R^2 value for regressions with the song-selective cells was significantly greater than that for the nonselective cells, indicating that acoustic features in individual motifs predicted the responses of the song-selective cells better than those of nonselective cells. In addition, the regressions were significant for roughly 60% of the song-selective cells, but only about 18% of the nonselective cells. This suggests strongly that the "song" selectivity we have described in this population of cmM neurons is derived from selective tuning for spectrotemporal features centered at the level of the motif.

Characterizing these critical spectrotemporal features in any detail is a complex task. Because of its emphasis on data compression, the wavelet decomposition technique tends to yield only arbitrary characterizations of the features driving each response. It was very difficult to reconstruct a spectrotemporal image of the relevant features that drove a cell using only the significant wavelets. What can be said is that the cells do not appear to be tuned in a linear way to relatively "simple" acoustic features, such as a sound at a given frequency or repetition rate. Consistent with the observation of others,[30] the cmM neurons we describe here are poorly modeled by spectrotemporal receptive fields (STRFs). Since STRF techniques provide an estimate of the optimal *linear* combination of spectrotemporal features that maximally drive a given cell (see Theunissen *et al.*, Methods..., this volume), the observation that STRFs provide poor predictions of a cell's response to a stimulus indicate a predominantly nonlinear response. Thus, neurons in cmM are driven by relatively complex acoustic features corresponding to specific motifs. We cannot yet say what those features are precisely. Nonetheless, I have demonstrated the selective neural representations for acoustic features diagnostic of individual or small sets of motifs. Such representation could obviously contribute to assessing the proportion of familiar motifs within a given song, which our earlier behavioral work has shown is important for learned recognition of individual conspecific songs in starlings.[17]

CONCLUSIONS

I have described a population of neurons selective for individually distinct conspecific songs that starlings that have been operantly trained to recognize—neurons that are, in other words, tuned to learned communication signals in adult animals. The neuronal population is found in a nonprimary forebrain auditory region, exhibits increased responses to the set of learned songs compared to novel songs, and exhibits differential responses to categories of learned songs based on recognition training contingencies. Within the population, many cells respond highly selectively to a subset of specific motifs present only in one individual's songs. Since behavioral recognition of individual songs is also driven by motif acoustics, one may infer that the experience-dependent neuronal selectivity shown here contributes substantially to individual song recognition behavior in this species. Data from lesion studies and preliminary recordings in awake, behaving starlings (Gentner and Margoliash, unpublished data) are consistent with this inference.

The behavioral strategy for individual vocal recognition used by starlings suggests that the upper boundary for accurate recognition is set by the memory capacity of the system for specific motifs. To this end, both the acoustic complexity and the sheer numbers of to-be-remembered motifs are likely to pose significant challenges to the representational system's capacity (cf. ref. 42). Although some coding efficiency is likely gained through adaptive sensory system specializations that lead to innate representational mappings, the idiosyncratic acoustic microenvironments encountered by any given individual are very hard to predict, and thus require representational plasticity mechanisms that operate on ontogenetic time scales. The observations of experience-dependent mechanisms that work to shape neural representations of unique sets of behaviorally relevant auditory objects (motifs) demonstrate exactly this sort of coding efficiency, and suggest the hypothesis that long-term memory constraints derive directly from the perceptual mechanisms for coding complex stimuli.

While the explicit spectrotemporal parameters underlying the selectivity of cmM neurons have not been described, the acoustic features of recognized motifs (as represented by the wavelet coefficients) were correlated with the response strength of many cmM neurons. Yet, a purely acoustic account of cmM responses, involving putative "feature detectors" is unlikely to be convincing. The distribution of cmM response properties depends not only on the spectrotemporal patterns of motifs in familiar (and unfamiliar) stimuli, but also on the specifics of the conditioning paradigm. This sensitivity to conditioning context may reflect seemingly subtle differences in the reward contingencies in the two training regimes. Because song recognition mediates a variety of behaviors in both agonistic and antagonistic contexts, different forms of learning under more natural conditions may act on the recognition system to produce a variety of top-down effects on auditory response properties.[43,44] The presence of these contextual influences on representational plasticity complicates the search for neural correlates in the absence of well-controlled behavior, and may account for the few reports of such neurons in sensory systems.

Even with the large stimulus repertoires that animals were trained to recognize, I estimate that less than 50% of the neurons responded to the test stimuli. The unresponsive neurons may not have been auditory, or may have been responding to other songs that these wild-caught birds had previously learned. Since we find almost no cells selectively tuned to the motifs in *unfamiliar* songs, the data argue that subpopulations of cmM neurons are selected from a pool composed primarily of neurons that have already been shaped by the animal's prior experiences with conspecific songs, rather than from a large pool of unselective neurons. cmM neurons were more selective than those observed in the Field L of starlings, where cells commonly respond to numerous novel conspecific vocalizations.[22] Response biases for species-specific vocalizations have been reported in Field L[22,45] and cM of birds,[29] and in mammalian primary and secondary auditory cortex.[46,47] Within this context, it is important to note that although cmM evinces a strong selectivity for familiar songs, the responses are not entirely exclusive. With the exception of the roughly 20% or so of cells that showed high phasic and selective responses, many of the cells were driven above spontaneous response levels by both familiar and unfamiliar songs. Thus, despite the prevalent bias for familiar songs, it does not appear that all information about unfamiliar songs is excluded from the system. Response to novel songs observed as modulations NCM neural firing rates,[31,32] and IEG *zenk* responses,[37] may reflect the incorporation of novel information that under appropriate conditions is consolidated into longer-term representations in cmM. Obviously, for learning to take place, some novel information must be available.

Experience-dependent representational plasticity, reported in a variety of animals and sensory systems,[48] is typified by shifts in the topography of primary cortical receptive fields.[49–52] In the auditory system, this plasticity leads to overrepresentation of the spectral and temporal properties of a learned stimulus.[43] Thus, in a hierarchical scheme of sensory processing, plasticity at primary levels should influence higher-order regions, such as cmM, so that the neuronal response properties and organization are expressly determined by an animal's unique experience in behaviorally relevant tasks. These higher-order regions could contribute to recognition of individual conspecific vocalizations, and could influence motor tasks such as countersinging and vocal learning in juveniles.

Neural correlates to learned object recognition have also been reported in extrastriate visual cortex where cells are broadly tuned,[53,54] and in prefrontal cortex[55] where selectivity for familiar objects is generally evidenced by a decrease in the numbers of neurons responding to a given object—an effect taken to indicate sharpening of the tuning for such objects.[56] In contrast, the proportion of cmM cells selective for familiar songs was much larger than that for unfamiliar songs, and many cells were sharply tuned. For vocal recognition, the predictability imparted by species-specific characteristics of vocalizations, and the constraints imposed by evolutionary history and experience, is likely to have produced a population of neurons predisposed to represent those vocalizations. I argue that the response properties of cmM neurons are elaborated continuously toward new functional representations depending upon the specific songs and behavioral contingencies an animal encounters. As in juvenile song learning,[57] the rules by which functional representations arise from biased populations may be complex, and are not likely to be well predicted by simple spectrotemporal similarities between the target songs and the initial representations of cmM neurons. The availability of "acquired neural representations" of auditory objects provides starlings, and perhaps other higher vertebrates, with an efficient mechanism for recognizing a wide and changing array of behaviorally important natural stimuli.

REFERENCES

1. KROODSMA, D.E. & E.H. MILLER. 1996. Ecology and Evolution of Acoustic Communication in Birds. Cornell University Press. Ithaca, NY.
2. MILNER, A.D. & M.A. GOODALE. 1995. The Visual Brain in Action. Oxford University Press. Oxford, UK.
3. FALLS, J.B. 1982. Individual recognition by sound in birds. In Acoustic Communication in Birds. D.E. Kroodsma & E.H. Miller, Eds.: 237–278. Academic Press. New York.
4. STODDARD, P.K. 1996. Vocal recognition of neighbors by territorial passerines. In Ecology and Evolution of Acoustic Communication in Birds. D.E. Kroodsma & E.H. Miller, Eds.: 356–374. Cornell University Press, Ithaca, NY.
5. GENTNER, T.Q. & D. MARGOLIASH. 2002. Neuroethology of vocal communication: perception and cognition. In Acoustic Communication. A.M. Simmons, A.N. Popper & R.R. Fay, Eds.: 324–386. Springer-Verlag. New York.
6. HULSE, S.H. 1995. The discrimination-transfer procedure for studying auditory perception and perceptual invariance in animals. In Methods in Comparative Psychoacoustics, Vol. 10. G.M. Klump, R.J. Dooling, R.R. Fay & W.C. Stebbins, Eds.: 319–330. Birkhäuser Verlag. Basel.
7. GENTNER, T.Q. & S.H. HULSE. 1998. Perceptual mechanisms for individual vocal recognition in European starlings, Sturnus vulgaris. Anim. Behav. 56: 579–594.
8. ADRET-HAUSBERGER, M. & P.F. JENKINS. 1988. Complex organization of the warbling song in starlings. Behav. 107: 138–156.
9. EENS, M., M. PINXTEN & R.F. VERHEYEN. 1991. Organization of song in the European starling: species-specificity and individual differences. Belg. J. Zool. 121: 257–278.
10. HAUSBERGER, M. & H. COUSILLAS. 1995. Categorization in birdsong: from behavioural to neuronal responses. Behav. Process. 35: 83–91.
11. HAUSBERGER, M. 1997. Social influences on song acquisition and sharing in the European starling (Sturnus vulgaris). In Social Influences on Vocal Development. C. Snowden & M. Hausberger, Eds.: 128–156. Cambridge University Press. Cambridge, UK.

12. EENS, M., M. PINXTEN & R.F. VERHEYEN. 1989. Temporal and sequential organization of song bouts in the European starling. Ardea 77: 75–86.
13. CHAIKEN, M., J. BÖHNER & P. MARLER. 1993. Song acquisition in European starlings, *Sturnus vulgaris*: a comparison of the songs of live-tutored, tape-tutored, untutored, and wild-caught males. Anim. Behav. 46: 1079–1090.
14. GENTNER, T.Q., S.H. HULSE, G.E. BENTLEY & G.F. BALL. 2000. Individual vocal recognition and the effect of partial lesions to HVc on discrimination, learning, and categorization of conspecific song in adult songbirds. J. Neurobiol. 42: 117–133.
15. BRICKER, P.D. & S. PRUZANSKY. 1976. Speaker recognition. *In* Contemporary Issues in Experimental Phonetics. N.J. Lass, Ed.: 295–326. Academic Press. New York.
16. GENTNER, T.Q. & S.H. HULSE. 2000. Perceptual classification based on the component structure of song in European starlings. J. Acoust. Soc. Am. 107: 3369–3381.
17. VATES, G.E., B.M. BROOME, C.V. MELLO & F. NOTTEBOHM. 1996. Auditory pathways of caudal telencephalon and their relation to the song system of adult male zebra finches. J. Comp. Neurol. 366: 613–642.
18. LEPPELSACK, H.J. & J. SCHWARTZKOPFF. 1972. Properties of acoustic neurons in the caudal neostriatum of birds. J. Comp. Physiol. A 80: 137–140.
19. RUBSAMEN, R. & G.J. DORRSCHEIDT. 1986. Tonotopic organization of the auditory forebrain in a songbird, the European starling. J. Comp. Physiol. A 158: 639–646.
20. HAÜSLER, U. 1996. Measurement of short-time spatial activity patterns during auditory stimulation in the starling. *In* Acoustical Signal Processing in the Central Auditory System. J. Syka, Ed.: 85–91. Plenum Press. New York.
21. CAPSIUS, B. & H.J. LEPPELSACK. 1999. Response patterns and their relationship to frequency analysis in auditory forebrain centers of a songbird. Hear. Res. 136: 91–99.
22. LEPPELSACK, H.J. & M. VOGT. 1976. Responses of auditory neurons in forebrain of a songbird to stimulation with species-specific sounds. J. Comp. Physiol. A 107: 263–274.
23. BONKE, D., H. SCHEICH & G. LANGNER. 1979. Responsiveness of units in the auditory neostriatum of the Guinea fowl (*Numida meleagris*) to species-specific calls and synthetic stimuli. I. Tonotopy and functional zones. J. Comp. Physiol. A 132: 243–255.
24. MÜLLER, C.M. & H.J. LEPPELSACK. 1985. Feature extraction and tonotopic organization in the avian forebrain. Exp. Brain Res. 59: 587–599.
25. THEUNISSEN, F.E. & A.J. DOUPE. 1998. Temporal and spectral sensitivity of complex auditory neurons in the nucleus HVc of male zebra finches. J. Neurosci. 18: 3786–3802.
26. THEUNISSEN, F.E., K. SEN & A.J. DOUPE. 2000. Spectral-temporal receptive fields of nonlinear auditory neurons obtained using natural sounds. J. Neurosci. 20: 2315–2331.
27. SCHÄFER, M., R. RUBSAMEN, G.J. DORRSCHEIDT & M. KNIPSCHILD. 1992. Setting complex tasks to single units in the avian auditory forebrain. II. Do we really need natural stimuli to describe neuronal response characteristics? Hear. Res. 57: 231–244.
28. LEPPELSACK, H.J. 1983. Analysis of song in the auditory pathway of songbirds. *In* Advances in Vertebrate Neuroethology. J.P. Evert, B.R. Capranica & D.J. Ingle, Eds.: 783–799. Plenum Press. New York.
29. GRACE, J.A., N. AMIN, N.C. SINGH & F.E. THEUNISSEN. 2003. Selectivity for conspecific song in the zebra finch auditory forebrain. J. Neurophys. 89: 472–487.
30. SEN, K., F.E. THEUNISSEN & A.J. DOUPE. 2001. Feature analysis of natural sounds in the songbird auditory forebrain. J. Neurophysiol. 86: 1445–1458.
31. CHEW, S. J., C.V. MELLO, F. NOTTEBOHM, *et al.* 1995. Decrements in auditory responses to a repeated conspecific song are long lasting and require two periods of protein synthesis in the songbird forebrain. Proc. Natl. Acad. Sci. USA 92: 3406–3410.
32. STRIPLING, R., S.F. VOLMAN & D.F. CLAYTON. 1997. Response modulation in the zebra finch neostriatum: relationship to nuclear gene expression. J. Neurosci. 17: 3883–3893.
33. CHEW, S.J., D.S. VICARIO & F. NOTTEBOHM. 1996. A large-capacity memory system that recognizes the calls and songs of conspecifics. Proc. Natl. Acad. Sci. USA 93: 1950–1955.
34. JONES, M.W., M.L. ERRINGTON, P.J. FRENCH, *et al.* 2001. A requirement for the immediate early gene Zif-268 in the expression of late LTP and long-term memories. Nat. Neurosci. 4: 289–296.

35. MELLO, C.V., D.S. VICARIO & D.F. CLAYTON. 1992. Song presentation induces gene expression in the songbird forebrain. Proc. Natl. Acad. Sci. USA **89:** 6818–6822.
36. RIBEIRO, S., G.A. CECCHI, M.O. MAGNASCO & C.V. MELLO. 1998. Toward a song code: evidence for a syllabic representation in the canary brain. Neuron **21:** 359–371.
37. MELLO, C.V., F. NOTTEBOHM & D. CLAYTON. 1995. Repeated exposure to one song leads to a rapid and persistent decline in an immediate early gene's response to that song in zebra finch telencephalon. J. Neurosci. **15:** 6919–6925.
38. JARVIS, E.D., C.V. MELLO & F. NOTTEBOHM. 1995. Associative learning and stimulus novelty influence the song-induced expression of an immediate early gene in the canary forebrain. Learn.Memory **2:** 62–80.
39. GENTNER, T.Q. & D. MARGOLIASH. 2003. Neuronal populations and single cells representing learned auditory objects. Nature **424:** 669–674.
40. MARGOLIASH, D. 1983. Acoustic parameters underlying the responses of song-specific neurons in the white-crowned sparrow. J. Neurosci. **3:** 1039–1057.
41. MARGOLIASH, D. 1986. Preference for autogenous song by auditory neurons in a song system nucleus of the white-crowned sparrow. J. Neurosci. **6:** 1643–1661.
42. STODDARD, P.K., M.D. BEECHER, P. LOESCHE & S.E. CAMPBELL. 1992. Memory does not constrain individual recognition in a bird with song repertoires. Behaviour **122:** 274–287.
43. KILGARD, M.P. & M.M. MERZENICH. 1998. Plasticity of temporal information processing in the primary auditory cortex. Nat. Neurosci. **1:** 727–731.
44. BAO, S., V.T. CHAN & M.M. MERZENICH. 2001. Cortical remodeling induced by activity of ventral tegmental dopamine neurons. Nature **412:** 79–83.
45. SCHEICH, H., G. LANGNER & D. BONKE. 1979. Responsiveness of units in the auditory neostriatum of the guinea fowl (numida-meleagris) to species-specific calls and synthetic stimuli. 2. discrimination of iambus-like calls. J. Comp. Physiol. A **132:** 257–276.
46. WANG, X. & S.C. KADIA. 2001. Differential representation of species-specific primate vocalizations in the auditory cortices of marmoset and cat. J. Neurophysiol. **86:** 2616–2620.
47. RAUSCHECKER, J.P., B. TIAN & M. HAUSER. 1995. Processing of complex sounds in the macaque nonprimary auditory cortex. Science **268:** 111–114.
48. GILBERT, C.D., M. SIGMAN & R.E. CRIST. 2001. The neural basis of perceptual learning. Neuron **31:** 681–697.
49. BAKIN, J.S. & N.M. WEINBERGER. 1990. Classical conditioning induces CS-specific receptive field plasticity in the auditory cortex of the guinea pig. Brain Res. **536:** 271–286.
50. RECANZONE, G.H., C.E. SCHREINER & M.M. MERZENICH. 1993. Plasticity in the frequency representation of primary auditory cortex following discrimination training in adult owl monkeys. J. Neurosci. **13:** 87–103.
51. KILGARD, M.P. & M.M. MERZENICH. 2002. Order-sensitive plasticity in adult primary auditory cortex. Proc. Natl. Acad. Sci. USA **99:** 3205–3209.
52. KAY, L.M. & G. LAURENT. 1999. Odor- and context-dependent modulation of mitral cell activity in behaving rats. Nat. Neurosci. **11:** 1003–1009.
53. Logothetis, N.K., J. Pauls & T. Poggio. 1995. Shape representation in the inferior temporal cortex of monkeys. Curr. Biol. **5:** 552–563.
54. KOBATAKE, E., G. WANG & K. TANAKA. 1998. Effects of shape-discrimination training on the selectivity of inferotemporal cells in adult monkeys. J. Neurophysiol. **80:** 324–330.
55. RAINER, G., W.F. ASAAD & E.K. MILLER. 1998. Selective representation of relevant information by neurons in the primate prefrontal cortex. Nature **393:** 577–579.
56. RAINER, G. & E.K. MILLER. 2000. Effects of visual experience on the representation of objects in the prefrontal cortex. Neuron **27:** 179 – 189.
57. TCHERNICHOVSKI, O., P.P. MITRA, T. LINTS & F. NOTTEBOHM. 2001. Dynamics of the vocal imitation process: how a zebra finch learns its song. Science **291:** 2564–2569.

In Search of the Song Template

PATRICE ADRET

Department of Organismal Biology & Anatomy, University of Chicago,
Chicago, Illinois 60637, USA

ABSTRACT: The auditory template theory—the conversion of memorized song to produced song using feedback as an error-correction mechanism—is central to neurobiological studies of birdsong learning. The essence of the theory is the construction of a complex sound replica based on a set of both genetic and environmental instructions. These premises, as yet unchallenged, have stimulated much research on the process of vocal imitation. Two somewhat distinct, but closely related streams of research have emerged. One seeks to determine the neural mechanisms that underlie the formation, storage, and retrieval of vocal memories as a consequence of experience during a sensitive phase—the template concept in its purest form. The other aims at establishing an explanatory basis for genetically based species differences in auditory responsiveness; here, the prime focus is on innately specified templates that guide learning preferences in young, naïve birds. The chapter begins with an historical overview of conceptual issues. Then recent progress in the attempt to characterize template properties is reviewed, focusing on selected studies of sparrows, nightingales, and zebra finches. The chapter concludes with a discussion of research strategy and tactics, including suggestions for criteria that must be met in identifying neural substrates for template specification and localization. The chapter is intended to provide a conceptual framework for further progress in this critical area.

KEYWORDS: vocal learning; memory; songbirds; auditory feedback; sensitive phase

Template: A gauge, pattern or mold, commonly
a thin plate or board, used as a guide to the
form of the work to be executed.
Webster's New International Dictionary, 1900

"It is conceivable that we will never be able to
point at one part of a complex brain and say: that
is where this particular memory is stored."
—F. Nottebohm, August 1992, letter to the author.

Address for correspondence: Patrice Adret, Department of Organismal Biology & Anatomy, The University of Chicago, 1027 E. 57th St., Chicago, IL 60637. Voice: 773-702-8090; fax: 773-702-0037.
 patrice@drozd.uchicago.edu
 http://pondside.uchicago.edu/oba/faculty/Margoliash/lab/people.html

Ann. N.Y. Acad. Sci. 1016: 303–324 (2004). © 2004 New York Academy of Sciences.
doi: 10.1196/annals.1298.005

INTRODUCTION

Konishi[1] (and this volume) first formulated the concept of an acquired auditory template as a general principle of imitative learning in oscine songbirds, a skill song-birds share with only few other avian and mammal taxa, including humans.[2] He showed that young birds first listen to and memorize an external model and, subsequently, use the memory trace (the "engram") as a template with which to match their own vocalizations. Almost 40 years later, despite much progress in understanding the neural basis of vocal learning, the search for a neural representation of the particular memory that is used as a reference for the song-learning process remains elusive.

This chapter will review some of the conceptual issues involved, reevaluate them in light of recent behavioral and physiological studies of birdsong learning, and suggest how future research might illuminate issues of memory specification and localization in the songbird brain.

THE TWO FACES OF THE TEMPLATE CONCEPT

Rooted in classical ethology, the notion of auditory templates[3] originated in the pioneering studies of bird song learning carried out in the 1950s by W.H. Thorpe of Cambridge University. He showed that naïve young male chaffinches, *Fringilla coelebs*, kept in isolation developed atypical song patterns, lacking many species-specific features. However, when given the opportunity to hear normal conspecific song at appropriate times during development, the young birds imitated the model, thereby producing songs that conformed to those of wild chaffinches.[4] He found that young birds were reluctant to acquire alien sounds and that they favored conspecific over heterospecific songs.[5] He attributed this perceptual bias to an endogenous "blueprint." By blueprint he meant an inherited sensory mechanism with filtering properties that enable a young bird to focus its attention on species-typical sounds and are capable of guiding song development. The blueprint idea, though a useful first step, is inadequate to convey concretely the complexity of the song development process, which involves, for example, the transformation—based on a set of both genetic and environmental instructions—of an internal representation of a song into a motor output (vocalization).

Thorpe's blueprint evolved into the conception of song templates advanced later by Marler,[3] who pointed out the need to distinguish between "motor programs" and "auditory templates" as potential mechanisms for the production of inherited vocalizations; Marler also envisioned a role for auditory feedback in the development and maintenance of learned vocalizations, thus stimulating experimental work on two of the central problems of birdsong research.

Templates for Instructional Models of Learning

Acquired Auditory Template

The concept of an "acquired" auditory template was developed by Konishi on the basis of a pioneering series of deafening experiments on several different avian species.[1,6] In nonpasserines (e.g., domestic fowl, *Gallus gallus*), bilateral extirpation of the cochlea immediately after hatching had no apparent effect on vocal development. In these birds, acquisition of a normal repertoire seems to be largely independent of auditory experience. In contrast, early deafening in oscine passerines (songbirds) had a dramatic effect on song development. Konishi[1] demonstrated that white-crowned sparrows, *Zonotrichia leucophrys*, that were operated upon prior to song production produced highly abnormal song patterns, while those deafened after song crystallization maintained a stable song. Moreover, songs of early-deafened birds were highly degraded regardless of the amount of prior auditory exposure to conspecific models, suggesting that (1) central motor programs are not sufficient for fully normal song development and (2) self-generated auditory feedback is essential for the conversion of memorized songs into produced songs.[1] Subsequent deafening experiments on chaffinches showed that the extent of song deterioration varied if the bird had even a little singing experience beforehand. The extent of the degradation depended critically on the developmental stage of song development at the time of deafening: the more practiced the bird was, the more structured the final song,[7] perhaps explaining why some of Konishi's later-deafened birds retained a degree of species-typical structure. It was thus predicted that deafening at an earlier age in these species would remove all remnants of species-specificity from their song.[8] This prediction led Marler and Sherman[9] to reexamine the auditory template hypothesis in a comparative framework. Two closely related species with sharply contrasting song patterns, swamp sparrows, *Melospiza georgiana*, and song sparrows, *Melospiza melodia*, were surgically deafened prior to any sign of subsong. Surprisingly, despite the loss of many acoustic features, their highly degraded songs still retained a number of species-specific *differences*, mostly apparent in the degree of song segmentation. This observation implied the operation of a central motor program sufficient to generate rudimentary songs with at least some degree of acoustic specificity, superimposed on a high degree of within- and between-individual variation.[9] The degree of species-specificity is minimal, however, and because of their lack of content the playback of such songs is without effect on conspecific receivers.[10]

Innate Auditory Template

Like Thorpe's chaffinches, many oscine songbirds reared in isolation with hearing intact develop songs that depart, to varying degrees, from their wild-type songs. For instance, while many species-specific features are lost in the isolate songs of white-crowned sparrows, many are retained in those of song sparrows. Thus, for normal song development, white-crowned sparrows rely more heavily on appropriate external stimulation than do song sparrows. In both species, however, early deafening results in highly degraded songs as described above. It was the obvious differences between the relatively impoverished songs of deafened birds and the more elaborate structure of isolate songs that gave rise to the notion of innate auditory templates. Isolate songs exhibit a high degree of variation both between and within individuals, which suggests that the innate song template specifies only "crude" instructions to the vocal motor pathway. Hence, the term crude template sometimes applied in the bird song literature.[11] In its original interpretation, the learned auditory template was viewed as a modified innate template.[1]

Templates for Learning Preferences

At an early stage of development, the young bird's attention is directed toward the detection and recognition of species-specific models. Both physiological and behavioral assays have shown that, beginning in the sensitive phase of song learning, or even earlier, newly fledged white-crowned sparrows and zebra finches, *Taeniopygia guttata*, as well as nestlings of brown-headed cowbirds, *Molothrus ater*, respond more strongly to conspecific than to heterospecific song.[12–15] These findings support the view that song acquisition involves rapid early learning and that songbirds are responsive to many details about their own species' vocalizations. Newly fledged sparrows will respond with more begging calls to first exposure to conspecific song (relative to foreign song), but after 10 days' exposure to such song, not only will they chirp more in response to familiar than novel conspecific song but, as adults, they will also reproduce these songs from memory.[16]

In many songbirds, there is an overproduction of syllables in the plastic song stage of development, which is then subject to a culling process just prior to song crystallization. This process was first documented in male swamp sparrows,[17] but also occurs in other emberizine species. Field and laboratory studies attest to the profound influence of social interactions on this attrition process. Marler[18] coined the term action-based learning for this form of protracted vocal plasticity. It differs from more traditional song learning in three ways: (1) learning can occur at a time when acquisition of novel songs is no longer possible; (2) an association between experience and vocal practice provides opportunity for selective reinforcement; and (3) the learning proceeds more slowly. When birds engage in countersinging, for example, young males retain in their repertoire those matched song types that closely resemble the song of a rival male. Another form of social interaction takes place when inexperienced male cowbirds "assess" their vocal competence while courting a female. During song performance, attention to a subtle wing-stroke display from a recipient female encourages them to retain those song types that prove more potent to the receiver.[19] It should be noted that song material discarded from the larger, preexisting repertoire is not necessarily forgotten but may reappear either spontaneously[20] or in a transient fashion when birds are experimentally challenged by means of interactive song playback.[21] Evidently, memory traces of songs may persist, even after they are discarded from the mature repertoire.

Of course, in addition to laying the groundwork for song learning, templates may encode auditory representations of heterospecific and other environmental sounds. Although Thorpe[5] pointed out the resistance of his chaffinches to acquiring alien songs, some aspects were clearly learned by the young birds, emerging as part of the plastic song repertoire. But they were subsequently rejected at the stage of song crystallization. A similar process of syllable deletion, when not subject to matched external stimulation, has been reported for nightingales, *Luscinia megarhynchos*,[22] and sparrows.[23] If auditory templates are involved in this late-stage deletion process, they must operate at a slower pace, requiring more time and effort, than those that guide vocal imitation. Templates employed in this way may be equivalent to those that underlie responsiveness to environmental sounds in general, which are also likely to prevail in species such as starlings, *Sturnus vulgaris*, mockingbirds, and other mimics.

Marler and Nelson[24] propose that song templates could serve as "flagging" devices, enabling the memorization of song components temporally associated with other species-specific cues and worthy of attention. For instance, the presence of a whistle in the song of white-crowned sparrows appears to facilitate acquisition of the entire song, even including heterospecific material, irrespective of its placement in the songs.[25] The "chatter" vocalization of cowbirds has been found to have similar "attentional" consequences for the nestlings.[15]

So over time, the two uses of the template concept have emerged: one in which the representation develops as a consequence of auditory experience,[1,8] and one in which the representation arises from an inborn predisposition of young, naïve birds to attend selectively to conspecific song.[26] In both cases, the template concept serves the same basic functions: (1) to mediate in the memorization of songs heard and (2) to engage the memory trace(s) in guiding vocal development. Heuristically, the template construct provides researchers with a useful framework for investigating the physiological underpinnings of song learning. For instance, we may ask, What song features does the template store? How and where does it store them? How are they retrieved? How, in the singing bird, does the template "guide the form of the work to be executed"—the production of a species-typical song.

WHAT IS ENCODED—DISTINGUISHING THE DANCER FROM THE DANCE

Recent advances in computerized methods of sound analysis[27] now allow researchers to achieve a fine-grain analysis of the imitation process (see Tchernichovski, this volume). The development of the bird's own song (BOS) reflects the interaction of auditory feedback and information encoded in the template. But how does one distinguish between what is encoded in the template and what is produced by the bird? One way is to attempt to identify the critical acoustic features selected by young birds for model imitation. Another is to assess, prior to song production, the perceptual biases that guide the acquisition process, using behavioral assays such as those based on phonotaxic[28] or vocal responses.[13]

Marler and Peters[29,30] examined song development in two sympatric and closely related sparrows with strikingly different songs. Young male swamp and song sparrows were presented with an array of synthetic songs, constructed from normal swamp or song sparrow syllables, embedded in the syntax of the other species. Swamp sparrows rejected foreign syllables, but imitated the conspecific ones regardless of the syntax in which they were embedded. Song sparrows were more ready to accept heterospecific syllables when they were embedded in multipartite songs compared to one-phrase songs. The authors suggest that swamp sparrows rely on phonological cues (note morphology) to select a tutor song, whereas song sparrows rely on both phonological and syntactical (phrase structure) cues, but the question remains whether these predispositions represent species differences as a sensory bias or as a production bias.

White-crowned sparrows, too, acquire song according to both phonological and syntactical rules. The introductory whistle qualifies as a species universal, prevailing in the song of all five known subspecies and emerging as the only syllable type to develop in the song of all young isolates.[31] Experiments in which young fledglings of the *oriantha* subspecies were tutored with an array of modified songs point to the whistle as a conspecific marker "facilitating the learning of phrases of other species' song when these are presented in the syntax of normal white-crowned sparrow song."[25] Pupils did not learn conspecific songs in which the introductory whistle had been removed but acquired heterospecific material (e.g., alarm calls of a Belding's ground squirrel, *Spermophilus beldingi*) with a whistle added at the beginning.[25] They even imitated sounds of unusual tonal quality from the song of a sympatric species, the hermit thrush (*Catharus guttatus*), which also begins with a whistle. A predisposition for segmenting song was revealed by exposing young sparrows to a rotating regime of model songs in which cues for segmentation had been erased.[32] Although birds were found to develop fewer phrases than were present in normal songs, they produced significantly more than the one repeated phrase (whistle, trill, or buzz) of model songs. Consistent with the species' syntactical rules of song production, a whistle almost always preceded other types of syllables.

As an index of song preference, the vocal response assay[13] has proved useful in (1) identifying aspects of what is encoded, even prior to any sign of song production, and (2) predicting what young males will learn.[16] Young birds vary the frequency of begging and other calls in response to song stimulation. These and other studies[33] have established a clear preference of newly fledged sparrows for conspecific songs. Moreover, given appropriate training, young sparrows will rapidly come to prefer tutor songs over novel ones.[16] Initially, newly fledged *oriantha* sparrows do not distinguish between song dialects but will do so with further tutoring.[34] The introductory whistle of white-crowned songs plays a special role. To examine this role Soha and Marler[23] subjected fledglings of the *nuttalli* subspecies to a set of modified songs in which the syllable was removed (conspecific song) or added either at the beginning or at the end of heterospecific song. Birds tested prior to the sensitive phase responded more strongly but indiscriminately to conspecific songs, regardless of the presence and placement of a whistle. In previous work,[33] fledglings were also found to respond initially indiscriminately to one-phrase (whistle, trill, or buzz) songs of their own species. Thus, conspecific phonology, not syntax, is the primary cue on which young sparrows focus their attention prior to the memorization phase. Soha and Marler's studies[23,25] implicate changes in template properties early in development: it appears that pre-encoded auditory mechanisms (templates) for the recognition of phonological cues are subsequently modified and supplemented so as to ensure that, at a later stage, the detection of syntactical features will also help to guide the learning process.

In the European nightingale, with an individual repertoire of up to 200 song types, a typical singing episode consists of a sequence (string) of distinct song types produced at about 4-s intervals and separated from the next string by a longer (> 5 min) silent period. Young males memorize with ease long stretches of song models (master strings) heard only a few times over the first 3 months of life.[22] Song is rehearsed during a sensory-motor phase starting several weeks after the sensory phase has ended. Detailed analyses of songs acquired from carefully controlled training programs revealed three levels of syntactical organization (FIG. 1). First, males produce imitations acquired from the same string as sequentially associated song types; these are segregated from imitations acquired from other strings, a manifestation of what is called the context effect. These superunits or "context groups" do not emerge when master strings are separated by an interval of less than five minutes. Second, during performance of context groups, smaller subsets of sequentially associated song types (packages) can be discerned. These song packages are self-induced in

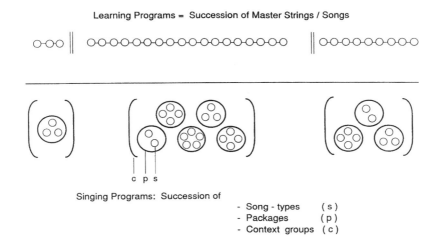

FIGURE 1. Diagram illustrating the two hierarchical levels of song segmentation (packages and context groups) thought to be encoded by young nightingales during the memorization phase and retrieved, after an interval of several weeks, during the production phase (from Hultsch et al. 1999, used with permission from W. de Gruyter.[22]).

that both their formation and mode of segmentation vary across individuals. More importantly, package formation does not emerge in isolates. The evidence suggests that the package effect is not a retrieval-based process but, instead, is generated during the acquisition phase.

These laboratory studies have revealed an acquisition process based on hierarchical rules of song segmentation, with context groups and song types respectively, at the top and bottom of the hierarchy: songs are acquired serially and stored as packages that are themselves parts of "context groups." Hultsch et al.[22] propose a scenario in which songs heard for the first time are committed to short-term memory and then translated as a package to a submemory for long-term storage. Each song type is categorized as novel or familiar, and assigned to a package or a context group by something like a "store" function. Thus, an internalized familiar song would be moved from short-term memory to its appropriate package where the existing information would be updated or consolidated. To account for context groups, a link must be established between the various packages that were stored during the same learning context. Thus, package formation in nightingales has much in common with the chunking of information in human memory research.[35]

In this review of stimulus properties that songbirds use to focus on songs heard early in life, I have highlighted contrasting modes of sensory acquisition in two oscine taxa. These and other data[26] call for experimental work to pin down the physiological mechanisms underlying the establishment of memories to guide song production mechanisms, which are likely to differ across species.

DEFINING THE TIME SCALE FOR SONG ACQUISITION

In most songbirds, the sensory phase for song learning usually starts after fledging,[11] suggesting that the internal representation of song models is not fully in place prior to that time. However, the post-fledging time span during which learning occurs varies widely across different species. "Age-limited" learners acquire their song early in life, normally with no further change past the stage of song crystallization. Among them are species in which the sensory and sensory-motor phases are well separated in time (nightingale), while in others both phases may overlap substantially (zebra finch). "Open-ended" learners such as the canary, *Serinus canaria*, can learn new songs as adults, varying them each season or retrieving unused song material acquired early in life.[36]

Within these broadly defined periods of heightened sensitivity to song exposure, we may ask whether learning is a continuous process or not, whether it varies with the frequency of exposure to the model, and whether learning is influenced by any nonacoustic factors. Evidence as to continuity is best revealed using a sequential tutoring paradigm in which young males are exposed to a series of models during song acquisition. Nightingales will learn equally well throughout the sensitive phase,[22] while other songbirds may exhibit several peaks of sensitivity.[37] A role for "recency" effects was found by Slater *et al.*[38] Zebra finches acquired song from several consecutive tutors, copying mostly from the one encountered last during the sensitive phase. It was suggested that learning might have resulted from an "overwriting" process (old memories replaced by new ones) or, else, from an "updating" process involving modification of stored representations that match best the song of the most recent tutor.[38]

In white-crowned sparrows, the sensitive phase for learning could be substantially extended by exposing naïve young birds to a live tutor between 50 and 200 days of age,[39] but this was not true for tape-tutored birds. This contrasting outcome may reflect important differences in the circumstances under which the two groups acquired their songs. As Nelson[40] pointed out, live-tutored pupils were able to engage in matched countersinging with their tutor during the course of song acquisition. This was not the case for tape-tutored birds, which were trained until 100 days of age, prior to onset of song production. Consequently, the live-tutored birds might have been able to match variants of their "already-learned" song as a consequence of a social influence.[40] Subsequent research has provided support for a contribution by such social factors.[39]

The sensitive period may also be extended in birds denied access to a song model early in life.[41] As a consequence, effects of auditory experience can, to some extent, be separated from developmental processes, making it possible to detect neural changes associated with delayed closure of a sensitive period for song memorization (see Nordeen & Nordeen and Bottjer, this volume). Finally, recent studies suggest that specific song components may be acquired at different times during development[32,42] and that learning is facilitated under spaced training programs. In fact, too much exposure can inhibit the learning process (see Tchernichovski *et al.*, this volume).

TEMPLATES: DISTRIBUTED OR LOCALIZED?

In discussing this issue it is useful to distinguish between two types of memory— (1) production memory (PM), in which the song template is used to guide the motor development of song during relatively brief developmental period and (2) recognition memory (RM),[43] which may operate throughout the entire lifespan of an individual.[44] The neural representations for these two types of memory are likely to differ. Within the category of production memory, we may distinguish two different types: sensory templates used for vocal learning during development (PM$_{TEM}$), a form of declarative memory, and sensory-motor templates used for song maintenance after crystallization (PM$_{MAI}$), a form of procedural memory.

A large body of evidence points to synaptic processes as the neural substrate for the mechanisms mediating storage of song-related memory, but provides few clues as to the brain regions involved. In theory, we are faced with a continuum of hypothetical representations. At one extreme, one could envision a template anatomically reduced to a single cell (a "grandmother" cell) or, more realistically, restricted to a network of a few "cardinal" cells having highly specialized response properties.[45] Auditory information, filtered at lower levels of brain processing, would then converge onto these high-order specialized (template) cells. Such cells would be expected to show selectivity—increased firing rates—in response to tutor songs relative to other songs (FIG. 2). At the other extreme, template functions could be mediated by a mosaic of large assemblies of widely distributed but highly interconnected neurons. Each neuron would be tuned to distinct acoustic features, but specialized templates would reflect integrated activity of a specific subset of cell assemblies.

Neither hypothesis is instructive with respect to memory localization. In fact, three plausible alternatives present themselves. First, because we are looking for an "auditory" template, i.e., one involving the selective responsiveness of neurons to sound, we might predict the involvement of central auditory structures, especially those at some distance from the primary ascending pathways, including mesopallial and nidopallial forebrain structures such as caudal mesopallium (CM) and caudal medial nidopallium (NCM), respectively (for a new nomenclature of the avian brain, see Reiner and Jarvis, this volume).[46] Second, because of the presence of neurons exhibiting a dual selectivity for BOS *and* tutor song within nuclei of the anterior forebrain pathway (AFP)[47] (see Perkel, this volume), the song system itself is a prime research target (see Mooney; Konishi; and Doupe , this volume). Finally, given the functional significance of song acquisition, we might expect songbirds to have evolved brain structures uniquely dedicated to song learning (e.g., HVC shelf [letter-based proper name], robust nucleus of the arcopallium cup [RAcup], see Farries, this volume), but linked to both receptive and sensory-motor circuitry. Current evidence implicates the first and second of these alternatives in song-template representation in early phases of song development.

SONG REPRESENTATIONS AND THE AUDITORY FOREBRAIN

At a gross level of organization, central auditory pathways appear to embody an hierarchical scheme of sensory processing that conveys different streams of acoustic information in parallel pathways from low- to high-level brain regions (see Theunis-

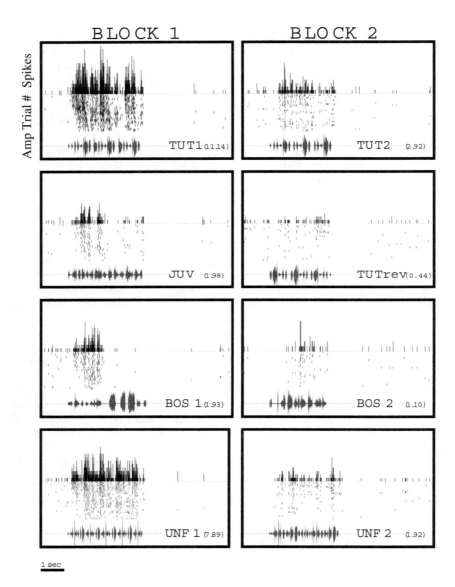

FIGURE 2. One example of a "template cell" recorded under anesthesia in the caudal nidostriatum of a 50-day-old male zebra finch raised by both parents until the age of 39 days. Each panel shows a peristimulus time histogram (*top*), a raster plot of spike occurrences (*middle*), and the amplitude envelope of song stimulus (*bottom*). Stimuli were presented in two blocks. In each block, 30 repetitions of four stimuli were played back (70 dB) in a pseudorandom fashion (except BOS2: 20 repetitions). The strength of the neuron response is shown in parentheses for each stimulus. Compared to all other stimuli in the same block, the unit fired maximally in response to different versions of tutor song (TUT1 and TUT2). Note the strong preference for tutor song played forward (TUT2) over the same song played back-

sen *et al.*, Methods...., this volume). Moving upward in the auditory system, one finds a substantial increase, in the incidence of neurons having low spontaneous rates, longer response latency, and more phasic discharges to stimulation. Such "listening" cells may be well suited to respond to specific features within a stimulus. Concomitantly, high-order brain regions include cells having complex selective properties, including time and frequency combination sensitivity.[48] The principle of reentry, involving reciprocal connections between different maps may prove to be an important component in encoding and decoding mechanisms of template information. Robust descending projections are known to connect the RA cup to regions surrounding thalamic and midbrain auditory nuclei.[49] Such (reentrant) feedback projections could in turn potentially alter the filtering properties of auditory neurons at sub-cortical levels. These aspects of auditory processing have been poorly studied.

A functional dissociation between auditory structures that are afferent to the song system and the classical song nuclei themselves is suggested by contrasting patterns of immediate-early gene (IEG) expression in these regions following exposure to conspecific song (see Clayton; Mello; and Jarvis, this volume). These gene activation markers (*zenk* and *c-fos* expression) are *not* expressed in any of the song nuclei when birds listen to song, but light up to varying extents when birds sing.[50] In contrast, presentation of conspecific song produces robust gene activation in most telencephalic auditory areas lying outside the song system. That deafening reduces or abolishes *zenk* expression in auditory pathways afferent to the song system, but not in the song nuclei of singing deaf birds,[51] supports such a distinction. Various lines of evidence in both mammalian and avian brains suggest that these IEGs could provide molecular markers of perceptual memories.[52]

Primary Forebrain Auditory Area (Field L)

Adret and Slater[53] found that juvenile zebra finches tutored with their father over the first 40 days of life exhibited significantly higher 2-deoxyglucose (2DG) uptake to presentation of familiar song on day 51 post-hatch compared with subjects similarly tutored but subsequently exposed to unfamiliar song (FIG. 3). The metabolic response in the latter group was comparable to that obtained from mother-reared young males first exposed to adult song on day 51 post-hatch. The increased metabolic activity was restricted to the caudal region of Field L (FIG. 4) with corresponding changes in both midbrain (dorsal lateral nucleus of the mesencephalon, MLD) and thalamic (ovoid nucleus, Ov) auditory structures. If the strength of the metabolic response could be shown to relate with some behavioral measure of tutor song preference *prior to* the onset of song production,[16] it would implicate this region in storage of template-related information.

---

ward (TUTrev). Evoked responses became weaker during the second block of stimulus presentation. JUV: plastic song of an age-matched juvenile; BOS1 and BOS2: two different versions of the bird's own plastic song; UNF1 and UNF2: unfamiliar songs recorded from two different males. Cell coordinates were 0.0 mm to the bifurcation of the central sinus, 1 mm from the midline and 1,250 mm deep (Adret and Margoliash unpublished data).

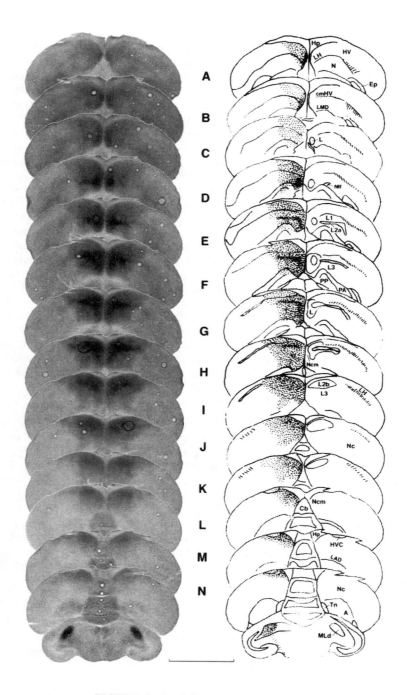

FIGURE 3. *See following page for caption.*

Caudal Medial Nidopallium (NCM)

IEG induction in response to playback of conspecific song is at its highest in NCM; in contrast, heterospecific song induces only moderate gene expression, and presentation of simple tone stimuli or white noise has little or no effect in NCM. Typically, the genomic response fades away with prolonged exposure to the same song and is rekindled with presentation of a novel song.[50] In finches, a nonselective song-induced *zenk* response was found to develop somewhere between day 20 and 30 post-hatch.[54,55] Because the gene induction was independent of whether juveniles had been raised by both parents or by the mother only, it cannot be linked, at that age, to song memorization. Interestingly, juveniles that had been raised singly, only with the mother, failed to develop the genomic response on both days 30 and 40 post-hatch.[54] Thus, in the absence both of father and siblings, the *zenk* gene was down-regulated in NCM, whereas the presence of siblings alone was sufficient for its up-regulation.

Neurons that signal stimulus familiarity have been found in the caudal part of NCM. In adult birds, these units adapt rapidly upon repetition of the same song stimulus, and a brisk response is reinstated by presentation of a novel song.[56] This form of neuronal habituation—known to mediate RM in monkeys[57]—is regulated by well-defined time windows requiring mRNA and protein synthesis, each of which generates a certain quantum of auditory memory.[58] Compared with adults, a much slower decremental response was found in both 20- and 30-day-old birds,[55] perhaps reflecting greater persistence of attention by juveniles.

Bolhuis and his colleagues tackled the issue of template localization explicitly, using IEG markers in developmental studies of imitative learning in songbirds.[59] Mother-reared young male zebra finches were either tape-tutored or exposed to the father as a live tutor during the sensitive phase, and songs developed at crystallization were visually inspected for the incidence of model imitations. Then as adults, subjects either received a 30-min exposure to tutor song or remained in silence as controls. Within the NCM of experimental birds, but not in the controls, the density of immunoreactive cells (Fos and Zenk protein products) increased with the strength of learning. These IEG studies are the first to implicate a brain region lying outside of the conventional song system in song template representation. However, the nidopallial region sampled in this work lies more laterally than the previously described NCM region.[50] Furthermore, and as a note of caution, it remains to be

---

FIGURE 3. Autoradiograms prepared from a juvenile zebra finch brain (coronal sections) and showing incorporation of radiolabeled 2-DG (*left*) following 45 min of tutor song presentation. Data were obtained from a 50-day-old male raised by both parents until the age of 40 days and subsequently exposed in the dark to a tape recording of his father's song after 10 days in isolation. The region where increased metabolic activity was found (experimental birds) overlaps autoradiograms G–N. The input layer L2a can be seen as a darker horizontal band on autoradiograms D–H. Corresponding anatomy (*right hemisphere* on sketches) was derived from Nissl-stained sections at 180-mm intervals and from alternate sections reacted for cytochrome oxidase. Rostral is up. Bar: 5 mm (from Adret and Slater unpublished).

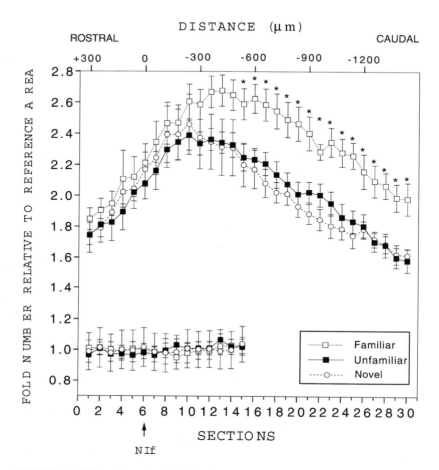

FIGURE 4. Change in optical density (means ± SE) along the rostrocaudal axis of the field L. Compared with unfamiliar and novel songs, the familiar song (father's: *n*=6) induced higher metabolic response in the caudal part of field L (asterisks: *P* < .05). A similar profile was found in juvenile birds that had been raised by both parents (unfamiliar: *n*=6) or by the mother alone (novel: *n*=7). For quantitative analysis, the interface nucleus (NIf) was used to align brain sections across individuals. An optical density ratio was derived by dividing the peak values measured in field L with the mean value obtained from a reference area within the lateral striatum and exhibiting low and stable metabolic activity (*lightest region* on autoradiograms **A–G** shown in FIG. 3).

determined which of the two subtypes of production memory (see above) was revealed by these techniques, i.e., whether the data reflect the mapping of the song model encoded in sensory coordinates (memory trace) or a representation of the BOS encoded in sensory-motor coordinates (matching process). Higher gene induction in the NCM of good learners would be expected as a result of a closer match between tutor song and the BOS.[60]

Caudal Mesopallium (CM)

Within this high-order auditory area, gene activation studies found elevated neuronal activation to playback of conspecific song[50] (see Mello, this volume), and lesions there abolished a preference for that stimulus in estradiol-treated female finches.[61] A relation between gene induction and song length, but not with the strength of learning, has also been reported.[59] More importantly, work in starlings[62] suggests a role in RM for the caudal medial mesopallium (see Gentner, this volume). Interestingly, this structure is reciprocally connected both with NCM and with the caudal lateral mesopallium, which in turn projects directly to the song system.[63] As such, CM might provide a neural substrate for auditory feedback to access and retrieve—via reentrant maps—putative template information stored elsewhere (e.g., NCM).

Nucleus LMAN of the Anterior Forebrain Pathway

Evidence for a direct involvement of the AFP in model acquisition comes from experiments aiming to block N-methyl-D-aspartate receptors (NMDARs) in the lateral magnocellular nucleus of the anterior nidopallium (LMAN) during sensory learning (Nordeen and Nordeen, this volume). For instance, when NMDARs were blocked by infusion of the NMDA receptor antagonist amino-5-phosphonopentanoic acid (AP5) into LMAN, zebra finches learned significantly less when treated on tutoring days than on nontutoring days.[64] Importantly, birds treated in LMAN on nontutoring days did not differ in their learning score from other controls treated on tutoring days with either saline in LMAN or AP5 into the cerebellum. In fact, infusions of AP5 into LMAN did not prevent the birds from discriminating zebra finch from canary song.[64] These experiments strongly suggest that aspects of sensory acquisition, rather than auditory perception in general, were selectively impaired by NMDARs blockade. Paradoxically, the effects of NMDARs antagonists on sensory acquisition occur at an age when 30–45-day-old LMAN neurons are known to respond indiscriminately to conspecific song stimuli, including tutor song.[47] If LMAN were to represent a store for song model representation, one would expect to find units selective for tutor song during early stages of sensory learning. Instead, such properties were found to emerge later, at 55–65 days post-hatch, in a small fraction of units dominated by a population of cells that were tuned to the BOS.[47]

The Quest for Innate Representations

An interesting dissociation between behavioral and physiological markers of response selectivity is seen in the case of the white-crowned sparrow. In this species, the introductory whistle appears as a conspecific marker for song memorization by innately specified auditory circuits.[23,25] Fledglings showed a clear preference for conspecific over heterospecific songs, responding equally to both isolate, normal, and modified songs.[33] In tests with *zenk*-mRNA markers, the HVC shelf shows high expression in response to playback of conspecific song.[50] Moreover, units recorded from HVC-shelf region of fledgling sparrows demonstrated vigorous responses to each category of conspecific song (normal, isolate, and modified). But, in contrast with the evidence from behavior, alien and conspecific songs were equally effective in driving HVC-shelf units.[33] However, despite this lack of selectivity, many shelf units behaved as "phrase detectors," exhibiting strong excitatory or inhibitory responses to distinct sections of a song. Whistles were quite effective in driving shelf units. Indeed, one class of "time-integrating" neurons responded to synthetic tones only when stimulus duration fell within the normal range of natural white-crown whistles. Such neurons may well be part of a circuitry holding pre-encoded species-specific information.

IN SEARCH OF THE "ENGRAM": RESEARCH STRATEGY AND TACTICS

Although we appear to have come a long way since Konishi's[1] elaboration of auditory template theory, we have in fact merely laid the groundwork for future investigations—refining the template construct and identifying some of the tools available for analysis of its neural substrate, including electrophysiology, lesions, genomics, and behavior. We have tentatively identified parts of the songbird brain that may function as repositories of vocal memories. While we have little understanding of their potential contributions to the song learning process, we do have specific and testable hypotheses of mechanisms of memory specification, localization, and function. However, at this point it may be useful to pause and consider what kinds of experiments and what sorts of evidence could be used to test such hypotheses. How will we know a song template (PM_{TEM}) when we see one? Put more concretely, what types of experimental designs and what kinds of data would allow one to conclude that a particular region functioned as PM_{TEM}—and to dismiss alternative interpretations of the data.

Identification of a brain region as a participating component of PM_{TEM} will be most convincingly made (1) by experimenting early in development when auditory templates first operate (2) by using converging evidence about that structure from more than a single method. This may include data on its connectivity, on the effects of lesions and pharmacological treatments, the electrophysiological properties of its constituent cells, and the mapping of neuronal activity in the behaving animal, combined with suitable tests of perception and discrimination. Above all, neurobiological research must be closely linked to behavioral studies of vocal development, making full use of new techniques for the analysis of large corpora of highly variable vocalizations (see Tchernichovski, this volume). Each of these approaches will require its own sets of controls to allow us to move from correlation to causation.

Future experiments should be designed so as to test alternate accounts of the phenomena under study. If the template construct is to be useful, many variables that confound our interpretation ought to be considered. We need to separate specific from such nonspecific effects as arousal and motivational factors that could account for changes detected in brain activity subsequent to song exposure. Similarly, in dealing with lesions or other forms of disruption, we need to control for such factors as impairments in hearing or perception (disruptions in attention, altered emotional reaction to a pleasurable stimulus) before concluding that we are dealing with template mechanisms.

Since the template concept does not refer to a unitary process, it presumably has no unitary anatomical representation. Different parts of the brain may participate in the perception, memorization, and production of different parts of the song, and may or may not be used at the same time. With carefully designed experiments, we hope to identify at least some of its components. One strategy, for instance, may be to look for "hotspots," that is, regions of the neuropil contacted by axonal terminations that undergo retraction subsequent to sensory acquisition.[65] According to this view, afferent neurons, unselective prior to learning, would become progressively more selective during acquisition, exhibiting less divergent axon arbors (synaptic selection) after learning.[66] Hotspots have been found at high level of brain organization, in visual pathways mediating the transformation of a percept into a memory trace, a critical step in signal encoding.[67] Impaired sensory acquisition following hotspot lesions or pharmacological blockade of biochemical pathways essential to learning would provide a further indication that hotspots encode critical features of a learned stimulus (tutor song). However, such disruptive effects could do no more than implicate the hotspot as a locus for memory storage. It still remains a challenge to distinguish mechanisms for memorization from mechanisms for production, especially in birds in which the phases of vocal development overlap. To work as a component of PM_{TEM}, one would expect a hotspot to be uniquely linked to both the sensory *and* motor sides of the circuit such that information encoded in a hotspot would be accessed by auditory feedback during sensory-motor learning, either directly in a feedforward fashion, or via reentrant maps between highly interconnected brain areas.[68] Thus, efferent projections from multiple hotspots would be expected to connect with the song system for the purpose of retrieving template information, a process involving three steps: (1) auditory feedback provides a mechanism for accessing to the template (see Konishi, this volume); (2) a "comparator" evaluates the match between actual (BOS) and intended (memorized tutor song) vocal output (see Mooney, this volume), and generates an error signal (see Brainard, this volume); and (3) an error-correction mechanism enables the modification of vocal output toward the desired target (see Doupe, this volume).

Indeed, the AFP does appear to carry an error signal to the motor pathway[69] where presumptive changes in neural patterns of activity can provide a substrate for vocal plasticity.[70] Song practice in developing birds generates, within the song system, a representation of BOS (PM_{DEV}) best reflected in the emerging selectivity, during sensory-motor learning, of neural responses to playbacks of that stimulus.[47,71] PM_{DEV} would be updated on a day-to-day basis by song-related feedback such that playback of the current BOS, relative to earlier versions of that motor pattern, would elicit a stronger auditory response (Adret and Margoliash, unpublished observation).[72] Such a process would give rise to a stable production memory used for song maintenance (PM_{MAI}) at crystallization. Song maintenance in adulthood may be viewed as the conversion of PM_{MAI} to a stereotyped motor program, a form of procedural memory. However, we currently have few clues as to how this sensory-to-motor conversion (which is another of the key issues in birdsong research) is accomplished.

Are the two subtypes of production memory—PM_{TEM} and PM_{MAI}—distinct neural entities or is PM_{TEM} translated into sensory-motor coordinates, giving rise ultimately to PM_{MAI}? Maintenance of stable song in the absence of PM_{TEM} would be congruent with a mnemonic dissociation but currently, unless we localize PM_{TEM}, this hypothesis cannot be tested. A translation mechanism is indeed plausible. In recent work, PM_{MAI} was prevented from developing normally by exposing cross-fostered zebra finches to continuous masking noise *after* song memorization. Opening the feedback loop in this manner resulted in birds producing deaf-like songs in adulthood. Remarkably, upon cessation of noise, subjects rapidly acquired good phonological replicas of Bengalese finch (*Lonchura striata*) songs with which they had been tutored early in life, thus demonstrating long-term retention of PM_{TEM}.[42] Intriguingly, the effect on the acquisition of the song syntax, not song phonology, was sensitive to the extent of acoustic perturbation. That is, only those birds released from the noise before 80 days of age successfully imitated the temporal order of heterospecific song syllables.[42] As to the other males, which were maintained under prolonged noise exposure (> 100 days), the challenge remains to ascertain whether their failure to recall the correct syntax reflected a sudden degradation of that mnemonic component or resulted from a dysfunction in retrieval mechanisms. Another approach to studying disruption of these processes is reversible deafening by antibiotically induced hair cell lesions (see Woolley, this volume).[73] When performed on adult Bengalese finches, such treatment transiently deactivated PM_{MAI}, resulting in birds producing degraded songs. Restoration of hearing after hair-cell regeneration led to recovery of original songs suggesting reenactment of sensory-motor processes. Interestingly, the reconstructed songs reverted to plastic songs in some of the birds, enabling them to acquire new notes from cage mates. This form of vocal plasticity, reminiscent of action-based learning,[18] offers a unique opportunity for exploring ways in which vocal memories are "updated" in the songbird brain.

Identifying neural substrates mediating PM_{TEM} will require electrophysiological investigation in the brain of freely moving juvenile songbirds. Although studies of sedated birds are the main source of our current information about such substrates, the use of anesthesia is incompatible with the detection of those behavioral state-dependent changes that are known to gate auditory activity in the awake animal.[74] While chronic records from juvenile birds present formidable technical problems, some progress has already been made (see Fee *et al.*, this volume). In fact, preliminary work suggests a striking behavioral state-dependent activation of HVC neurons early in the sensory-motor phase of song learning. That is, multiunit recordings from the young male zebra finch's HVC revealed a selective response of the neurons for the BOS during sleep, with their preference shifting toward the tutor song during wakefulness.[72] Although this important finding still awaits confirmation, it suggests a representation of PM_{TEM} arising, as a result of tutor song exposure, within HVC itself or in concert with other brain areas afferent to HVC. It will be fascinating to discover whether the two stimulus classes (tutor song and BOS) are represented in distinct populations of HVC cells or whether HVC neurons exhibit a selectivity which is modulated according to the behavioral state of the animal. The author found—inconsistent with the recent demonstration of a long memory[42]—the neural response to tutor song to weaken at fixed recording sites in older birds.[72] This latter result could either reflect a labile representation of the engram within HVC or be a direct consequence of the conversion of memorized song into produced song. Put in a broader perspective, work along these lines may help bridge the gap between song learning and the neuronal turnover that is known to take place in HVC during vocal development (see Nottebohm, this volume).[75] Obtaining simultaneous recordings from several carefully chosen hotspot neurons during song acquisition would represent a major advance in our understanding of PM_{TEM}.

Finally, the possibility that song learning preferences may be switched between species by tissue transfers early in life, once a researcher's fantasy, now has some experimental support. Recent reports of brain transplant experiments offer an intriguing but quite preliminary set of possibilities for identifying neural regions critical for the expression of inborn auditory predispositions in precocial avian species.[76]

CONCLUSIONS

It has long been accepted that mechanisms functioning as auditory templates for song acquisition and maintenance are a feature of the songbird brain. They are assumed to specify sets of both genetic and environmental instructions that guide vocal learning during critical periods of development. They have the heuristic value of focusing our research efforts on specific issues: how and where do the auditory mechanisms underlying selective song perception operate in young, naïve birds? Where are song memory traces stored? Are they moved around in the brain, as is known to take place in visual imprinting[77] and, if so, is the pattern of movement predetermined or influenced by whether or not memorization has occurred? Are we dealing with a multiprocess memory system, as has been found in mammals?[78,79]

At the moment templates (innate or acquired) represent constructs, rather than mechanisms. Giving them "a local habitation and a name" has been and will continue to be a daunting task. Despite the many issues outstanding, the template concept will continue to be a heuristically useful model of the song-learning process.

ACKNOWLEDGMENTS

I am most indebted to Phil Zeigler and Peter Marler for both their guidance and their penetrating comments during the preparation of this chapter. I also thank Dan Margoliash for continued support and stimulating discussions over the years.

REFERENCES

1. KONISHI, M. 1965. The role of auditory feedback in the control of vocalization in the white-crowned sparrow. Z. Tierpsychol. **22:** 770–783.
2. DOUPE, A.J. & P.K. KUHL. 1999. Birdsong and human speech. Common themes and mechanisms. Annu. Rev. Neurosci. **22:** 567–631.
3. MARLER, P. 1963. Inheritance and learning in the development of animal vocalizations. *In* Acoustic Behavior of Animals. R.G. Busnel, Ed.: 228–243. Elsevier. Amsterdam.
4. THORPE, W.H. 1961. Bird Song. The Biology of Vocal Communication and Expression in Birds. Cambridge University Press. Cambridge.
5. THORPE, W.H. 1958. The learning of song patterns by birds with special reference to the song of the chaffinch, *Fringilla coelebs*. Ibis **100:** 535–570.
6. KONISHI, M. 1978. Auditory environment and vocal development in birds. *In* Perception and Experience. R.D. Walk & H.L.J. Pick, Eds.: 105–118. Plenum. New York.
7. NOTTEBOHM, F. 1968. Auditory experience and song development in the chaffinch. Ibis **110:** 549–568.
8. KONISHI, M. & F. NOTTEBOHM. 1969. Experimental studies in the ontogeny of avian vocalizations. *In* Bird Vocalizations. Their Relations to Current Problems in Biology and Psychology. R.A. Hinde, Ed.: 29–48. Cambridge University Press. Cambridge.
9. MARLER, P. & V. SHERMAN. 1983. Song structure without auditory feedback: emendations of the auditory template hypothesis. J. Neurosci. **3:** 517–531.

10. SEARCY, W.A. & P. MARLER. 1987. Response of sparrows to songs of isolation-reared and deafened males: further evidence for innate auditory templates. Dev. Psychobiol. **3:** 509–519.
11. CATCHPOLE, C.K. & P.J.B. SLATER. 1995. Bird Song. Biological Themes and Variations. Cambridge University Press. Cambridge.
12. DOOLING, R. & M. SEARCY. 1980. Early perceptual selectivity in the swamp sparrow. Dev. Psychobiol. **13:** 499–506.
13. NELSON, D. & P. MARLER. 1993. Innate recognition of song in white-crowned sparrows: a role in selective vocal learning? Anim. Behav. **46:** 806–808.
14. BRAATEN, R.F. & K. REYNOLDS. 1999. Auditory preference for conspecific song in isolation-reared zebra finches. Anim. Behav. **58:** 105–111.
15. HAUBER, M.E., S.A. RUSSO & P.W. SHERMAN. 2001. A password for species recognition in a brood-parasitic bird. Proc. R. Soc. Lond. (Ser. B). **268:** 1041–1048.
16. NELSON, D.A. *et al.* 1997. The timing of song memorization differs in males and females: a new assay for avian vocal learning. Anim. Behav. **54:** 587–597.
17. MARLER, P. & S. PETERS. 1981. Sparrows learn adult song and more from memory. Science. **213:** 780–782.
18. MARLER, P. 1990. Song learning: the interface between behaviour and neuroethology. Phil. Trans. R. Soc. Lond. B **329:** 109–114.
19. WEST, M.J. & A.P. KING. 1988. Female visual displays affect the development of male song in the cowbird. Nature **334:** 244–246.
20. HOUGH II, G.E., D.A. NELSON & S.F. VOLMAN. 2000. Re-expression of songs deleted during vocal development in white-crowned sparrows, *Zonotrichia leucophrys.* Anim. Behav. **60:** 279–287.
21. GEBERZAHN, N., H. HULTSCH & D. TODT. 2002. Latent song type memories are accessible through auditory stimulation in a hand-reared songbird. Anim. Behav. **64:** 783–790.
22. HULTSCH, H., R. MUNDRY & D. TODT. 1999. Learning, representation and retrieval of rule-related knowledge in the song system of birds. *In* Learning Rule Extraction and Representation. A.D. Friederici & R. Menzel, Eds.: 89–115. W. de Gruyter. Berlin.
23. SOHA, J.A. & P. MARLER. 2001. Cues for early discrimination of conspecific song in the white-crowned sparrow (*Zonotrichia leucophrys*). Ethology **107:** 813–826.
24. MARLER, P. & D. NELSON. 1992. Neuroselection and song learning in birds: species universals in a culturally transmitted behavior. Semin. Neurosci. **4:** 415–423.
25. SOHA, J. A. & P. MARLER. 2000. A species-specific acoustic cue for selective song learning in the white-crowned sparrow. Anim. Behav. **60:** 297–306.
26. MARLER, P. 1997. Three models of song learning: evidence from behavior. J. Neurobiol. **33:** 501–516.
27. TCHERNICHOVSKI, O. *et al.* 2000. A procedure for an automated measurement of song similarity. Anim. Behav. **59:** 1167–1176.
28. PYTTE, C.L. & R.A. SUTHERS. 1999. A bird's own song contributes to conspecific song perception. NeuroReport **10:** 1773–1778.
29. MARLER, P. & S. PETERS. 1977. Selective vocal learning in a sparrow. Science **198:** 519–521.
30. MARLER, P. & S. PETERS. 1988. The role of song phonology and syntax in vocal learning preferences in the song sparrow, *Melospiza melodia.* Ethology **77:** 125–149.
31. MARLER, P. 1970. A comparative approach to vocal learning: song development in white-crowned sparrows. J. Comp. Physiol. Psychol. Monogr. **71:** 1–25.
32. SOHA, J.A. & P. MARLER. 2001. Vocal syntax development in the white-crowned sparrow. J. Comp. Psychol. **115:** 172–180.
33. WHALING, C.S. *et al.* 1997. Acoustic and neural bases for innate recognition of song. Proc. Natl. Acad. Sci. USA **94:** 12694–12698.
34. NELSON, D.A. 2000. Preference for own-subspecies' song guides vocal learning in a song bird. Proc. Natl. Acad. Sci. USA **97:** 13348–13353.
35. GOBET, F. *et al.* 2001. Chunking mechanisms in human learning. Trends Cognit. Sci. **5:** 236–243.
36. NOTTEBOHM, F. 1999. The anatomy and timing of vocal learning in birds. *In* The Design of Animal Communication. M.D. Hauser & M. Konishi, Eds.: 63–110. The MIT Press. Cambridge, MA.

37. KROODSMA, D.E. 1978. Aspects of learning in the ontogeny of bird song: where, from whom, when, how many, which, and how accurately. *In* The Development of Behavior. G.M. Burghardt & M. Bekoff, Eds.: 215–230. Garland STPM Press. New York.

38. SLATER, P.J.B., C. RICHARDS & N.I. MANN. 1991. Song learning in zebra finches exposed to a series of tutors during the sensitive phase. Ethology **88:** 163–171.

39. BAPTISTA, L.F. & S.L.L. GAUNT. 1997. Social interaction and vocal development in birds. *In* Social Influences on Vocal Development. C.T. Snodown & M. Hausberger, Eds.: 23–40. Social Influences on Vocal Development. Cambridge University Press. Cambridge.

40. NELSON, D. 1997. Social interaction and sensitive phases for song learning: a critical review. *In* Social Influences on Vocal Development. C.T. Snodown & M. Hausberger, Eds.: 7–22. Cambridge University Press. Cambridge.

41. JONES, A.E., C. TEN CATE & P.J.B. SLATER. 1996. Early experience and plasticity of song in adult male zebra finches (*Taeniopygia guttata*). J. Comp. Psychol. **110:** 354–369.

42. FUNABIKI, Y. & M. KONISHI. 2003. Long memory in song learning by zebra finches. J. Neurosci. **23:** 6928–6935

43. GENTNER, T.Q. & D. MARGOLIASH. 2002. The neuroethology of vocal communication: perception and cognition. *In* Acoustic Communication. A. Megela-Simmons, A.N. Popper & R.R. Fay, Eds.: 324–386. Springer. Berlin.

44. STODDARD, P.K. 1996. Vocal recognition of neighbors by territorial passerines. *In* Ecology and Evolution of Acoustic Communication in Birds. D.E. Kroodsma & E.H. Miller, Eds.: 356–376. Comstock. Ithaca, NY.

45. BARLOW, H. 1995. The neuron doctrine in perception. *In* The Cognitive Neurosciences. M. Gazzaniga, Ed.: 415–435. The MIT Press. Cambridge, MA.

46. REINER, A. *et al.* Revised nomenclature for avian telencephalon and some related brainstem nuclei. J. Comp. Neurol. In press.

47. DOUPE, A.J. & M.M. SOLIS. 1999. Song- and order-selective auditory responses emerge in neurons of the songbird anterior forebrain during vocal learning. *In* The Design of Animal Communication. M.D. Hauser & M. Konishi, Eds.: 343–368. The MIT Press. Cambridge, MA.

48. MARGOLIASH, D. & E.S. FORTUNE. 1992. Temporal and harmonic combination sensitive neurons in the zebra finch's HVc. J. Neurosci. **12:** 4309–4326.

49. MELLO, C.V. *et al.* 1998. Descending auditory pathways in the adult male zebra finch (*Taeniopygia guttata*). J. Comp. Neurol. **395:** 137–160.

50. MELLO, C.V. 2002. Mapping vocal communication pathways in birds with inducible gene expression. J. Comp. Physiol. A **188:** 943–959.

51. JARVIS, E.D. & F. NOTTEBOHM. 1997. Motor-driven gene expression. Proc. Natl. Acad. Sci. USA **94:** 4097–4102.

52. CLAYTON, D.F. 2000. The genomic action potential. Neurobiol. Learn. Mem. **74:** 185–216.

53. ADRET, P. & P.J.B. SLATER. 1995. Song presentation leads to changes in metabolic activity in the forebrain of zebra finches: effects of age and experience [abstract]. *In* Nervous System and Behaviour. M. Burrows *et al.*, Eds.: 315. Thieme Medical Publishers. New York.

54. JIN, H. & D.F. CLAYTON. 1997. Localized changes in immediate-early gene regulation during sensory and motor learning in zebra finches. Neuron **19:** 1049–1059.

55. STRIPLING, R., A.A. KRUSE & D.F. CLAYTON. 2001. Development of song responses in the zebra finch caudomedial neostriatum: role of genomic and electrophysiological activities. J. Neurobiol. **48:** 163–180.

56. CHEW, S.J. *et al.* 1995. Decrements in auditory responses to a repeated conspecific song are long-lasting and require two periods of protein synthesis in the songbird forebrain. Proc. Natl. Acad. Sci. USA **92:** 3406–3410.

57. BROWN, M.W. 2000. Neuronal correlates of recognition memory. *In* Brain, Perception, Memory. Advances in Cognitive Neuroscience. J.J. Bolhuis, Ed.: 185–208. Oxford University Press. Oxford.

58. CHEW, S.J., D.S. VICARIO & F. NOTTEBOHM. 1996a. Quantal duration of auditory memories. Science **274:** 1909–1914.

59. BOLHUIS, J.J. & H. EDA-FUJIWARA. 2003. Bird brains and songs: neural mechanisms of birdsong perception and memory. Anim. Biol. **53:** 129–145.
60. MARLER, P. & A.J. DOUPE. 2000. Singing in the brain. Proc. Natl. Acad. Sci. USA **97:** 2965–2967.
61. MACDOUGALL-SHACKLETON, S.A., S.H. HULSE & G.F. BALL. 1998. Neural bases of song preferences in female zebra finches (*Taeniopygia guttata*). NeuroReport **9:** 3047–3052.
62. GENTNER, T.Q. & D. MARGOLIASH. 2003. Neuronal populations and single cells representing learned auditory objects. Nature **424:** 669–674.
63. VATES, G.E. *et al.* 1996. Auditory pathways of caudal telencephalon and their relation to the song system of adult male zebra finches (*Taeniopygia guttata*). J. Comp. Neurol. **366:** 613–642.
64. BASHAM, M.E., E.J. NORDEEN & K.W. NORDEEN. 1996. Blockade of NMDA receptors in the anterior forebrain impairs sensory acquisition in the zebra finch (*Poephila guttata*). Neurobiol. Learn. Mem. **66:** 295–304.
65. IYENGAR, S. & S.W. BOTTJER. 2002. Development of individual axon arbors in a thalamocortical circuit necessary for song learning in zebra finches. J. Neurosci. **22:** 901–911.
66. YOSHIDA, M., Y. NAYA & Y. MIYASHITA. 2003. Anatomical organization of forward fiber projections from area TE to perirhinal neurons representing visual long-term memory in monkeys. Proc. Natl. Acad. Sci. USA **100:** 4257–4262.
67. MIYASHITA, Y. & T. HAYASHI. 2000. Neural representation of visual objects: encoding and top-down activation. Curr. Opin. Neurobiol. **10:** 187–194.
68. NAYA, Y., M. YOSHIDA & Y. MIYASHITA. 2003. Forward processing of long-term associative memory in monkey inferotemporal cortex. J. Neurosci. **23:** 2861–2871.
69. BRAINARD, M.S. & A.J. DOUPE. 2000. Interruption of a basal ganglia-forebrain circuit prevents plasticity of learned vocalizations. Nature **404:** 762–766.
70. MARGOLIASH, D. 2002. Evaluating theories of bird song learning: implications for future directions. J. Comp. Physiol. A **188:** 851–866.
71. VOLMAN, S.F. 1993. Development of neural selectivity for birdsong during vocal learning. J. Neurosci. **13:** 4737–4747.
72. NICK, T.A. 2003. Response bias: neural correlates of memory in the birdsong system [abstract]. Soc. Neurosci.: 294.2.
73. WOOLLEY, S.M.N. & E.W. RUBEL. 2002. Vocal memory and learning in adult Bengalese finches with regenerated hair cells. J. Neurosci. **22:** 7774–7787.
74. DAVE, A. S., A. C. YU & D. MARGOLIASH. 1998. Behavioral state modulation of auditory activity in a vocal motor system. Science **282:** 2250–2254.
75. WILBRECHT, L., A. CRIONAS & F. NOTTEBOHM. 2002. Experience affects recruitment of new neurons but not adult neuron number. J. Neurosci. **22:** 825–831.
76. LONG, K.D., G. KENNEDY & E. BALABAN. 2001. Transferring an inborn auditory perceptual predisposition with interspecies brain transplants. Proc. Natl. Acad. Sci. USA **98:** 5862–5867.
77. HORN, G. 2000. In memory. *In* Brain, Perception, Memory. Advances in Cognitive Neuroscience. J.J. Bolhuis, Ed.: 329–363. Oxford University Press. Oxford.
78. EICHENBAUM, H. & N. J. COHEN. 2001. From Conditioning to Conscious Recollection. Memory Systems of the Brain. Oxford University Press. Oxford.
79. SQUIRE, L.R. & E.R. KANDEL. 1999. Memory. From Mind to Molecules. Scientific American Library. New York.

Genetic Components of Vocal Learning

CONSTANCE SCHARFF[a] AND STEPHANIE A. WHITE[b]

[a]Max Planck Institute for Molecular Genetics, Ihnestrasse 73, 14195 Berlin, Germany

[b]Department of Physiological Science, University of California, 621 Charles E. Young Drive South, Los Angeles, California 90095-1606, USA

ABSTRACT: Vocal learning is a rare trait. Humans depend on vocal learning to acquire spoken language, but most species that communicate acoustically have an innate repertoire of sounds that they use for information exchange. Among the few non-human species that also rely on vocal learning, songbirds have provided by far the most information for understanding this process. This article concentrates on the genetic components of vocal learning in humans and birds. We summarize the existing evidence for a genetic predisposition towards acquiring the species-specific human and avian vocal repertoires. We describe the approaches used for finding genes involved in shaping the neural circuitry required for vocal learning or in mediating the learning process itself. Special attention is given to a particular gene, *FOXP2*, which has been implicated in a human speech and language disorder. We have studied *FoxP2* in avian vocal learners and non-learners and review evidence that links both the molecule and its close homologue *FoxP1* to the development of brain regions implicated in vocal learning and to their function. *FoxP2* has a characteristic expression pattern in a brain structure uniquely associated with learned vocal communication, Area X in songbirds, or its analogue in parrots and hummingbirds. In both avian song learners and non-learners *FoxP2* expression predominates in sensory and sensory-motor circuits. These latter regions also express *FoxP2* in mammals and reptiles. We conclude that *FoxP2* is important for the building and function of brain pathways including, but not limited to, those essential for learned vocal communication.

KEYWORDS: zebra finch; seasonal; hummingbird; parrot; budgerigar; transcription factor; basal ganglia

LANGUAGE: THE BALANCE BETWEEN NATURE AND NURTURE

Human language is unique in its capacity to express infinite meaning through combining a finite number of words or signs. Also characteristic for human language is the use of vocal signals to refer to things or concepts, a feature that, despite intense scrutiny, has been found only rarely in other animals.[1] What humans do share with a select group of other animals (songbirds,[2,3] hummingbirds,[4] parrots,[5] bats,[6] whales,[7] seals,[8] and dolphins[9,10]) is the need to learn their vocal repertoire by imi-

Address for correspondence: Constance Scharff, Max Planck Institute for Molecular Genetics, Ihnestrasse 73, 14195 Berlin, Germany. Voice: 49-30-8413-1214; fax 49-30-8413-1383.
scharff@molgen.mpg.de; <http://www.molgen.mpg.de/~abt_rop/neurobiology/>

Ann. N.Y. Acad. Sci. 1016: 325–347 (2004). © 2004 New York Academy of Sciences.
doi: 10.1196/annals.1298.032

tation. While many other species also communicate with vocal signals, they apparently do not need to learn them.

Yet the fact that language is learned does not imply the absence of a genetic bias towards this learning. Indeed, already Darwin suspected that language acquisition is an "instinct," and since then Chomsky and colleagues have collected convincing evidence for this view.[11] One of the central arguments is that despite the plethora of different languages in the world, all of them follow an intrinsic hierarchical logic termed "universal grammar" by Chomsky.[1] This suggests the existence of a common neural "hardware" that constrains how language is built. The same "predisposed" hardware is also assumed to account for the astonishing speed, ease, and autonomy with which children master the theoretically formidable task of learning thousands of words and understanding the rules of grammar that govern how they can be combined into meaningful sentences.

LANGUAGE GENES?

What then might be the genes involved in building language-ready brains. Should we expect to find one set for "constructing" the language circuitry and others involved in mediating the actual learning? The evidence, while admittedly fragmentary, points definitely towards some generalist and perhaps some specialist genes.

Before speculating about genetic mechanisms, we review evidence for the existence of "language-specialized" neural structures. That such structures exist in humans is indisputable. Damage to the regions around the left Sylvian fissure usually leads to problems with perception and/or production of language, recall of particular classes of words, and understanding or using grammar. Often, only particular domains of language are affected, such as difficulty with recalling objects,[11,12] or fluent grammatical speech devoid of clear meaning.[13] These observations have led to the assumption that different components of language are processed in discrete brain areas (Broca, production; Wernicke, perception; etc.), but this turns out to be a rough approximation at best. Rather, language is supported by distributed neural networks connecting populations of neurons in cortical and subcortical regions throughout the brain, including basal ganglia and cerebellar pathways.[14,15] Thus, the reason that dysfunction of a particular area tends to be associated with impairment of a particular language domain could reflect that this area is itself involved in processing of that particular language domain and/or that it presents a bottleneck for information flow passing through it, from and to other areas of the brain. While this makes it less likely that there are specific genes dedicated solely to construction and function of "language regions," the fact is that some genes might also serve as bottlenecks. Without them, language does not function properly. Although their discovery might not bring us immediately closer to understanding the neural "essence" of language, it might provide us with insights into the molecular machinery involved.

The search for language genes has focused on inherited language impairments, where deficits in language are dissociable from other mental functions.[16] This approach has not been easy, for two reasons.[17,18] First, only a handful of such conditions are known. Among those are verbal apraxia (also called verbal dyspraxia), i.e., the difficulty coordinating mouth and speech movements, developmental speech delay, and stuttering. Second, honing in on mutations causally related to disease is methodologically far easier for conditions in which a single gene causes the dysfunction than when a number of genes are involved.[19] Essentially, the association of a particular mutation with a particular phenotype is achieved by correlating the trait (i.e., language impairment) with a known DNA marker sequence. In affected individuals, the marker will segregate differently than in unaffected individuals, thus allowing geneticists to zero in on the chromosomal region that is characteristic for the affected individuals. Unfortunately, most hereditary diseases are suspected to be caused by dysfunction of more than one gene, and the elucidation of multigenic diseases has been notoriously difficult.[20]

So far, the search for genes associated with language impairments has yielded a number of linkage associations with chromosomal regions containing large numbers of genes. For instance, specific language impairment (SLI), which has an inherited component that is most evident from twin and adoption studies, is associated with regions on chromosome 7, 13, 16, and 19.[21–23] In the case of linkage to chromosome 7, analysis of the genomic DNA of three generations in the KE family, about half of whose members have impaired speech and language skills,[21] indicated that the affected gene was located among 70 genes on the long arm of chromosome 7. Discovery of the exact location of the mutation, which is inherited in a dominant manner, was facilitated by the identification and investigation of an unrelated individual that suffered from a remarkably similar language disorder and had a balanced translocation between chromosomes 7 and 5. This means that chromosomes 5 and 7 had both "broken" at a certain point along their lengths and that a piece of each had swapped places with the other. One of the breakpoints interrupted the gene *FOXP2*, which is normally located on chromosome 7. (For FoxP2 nomenclature we follow the convention proposed by the Nomenclature Committee for the Forkhead family of genes, i.e., FOXP2 in *Homo*, Foxp2 in *Mus*, and FoxP2 in all other species, proteins in roman type, genes and RNA in italics.[24]) Reexamination of chromosome 7 in the KE family revealed a point mutation in a stretch of the *FOXP2* DNA, which is crucial for the function of the protein. This mutation occurred in all affected family members but in none of the healthy individuals that were investigated. Thus the unlikely scenario described earlier, that a mutation within a single gene leads to dysfunction in a complex behavior, has arisen with the discovery that *FOXP2* is the monogenetic locus for a severe speech and language disorder.[25]

THE *FOXP2* GENE IN HUMANS

Human Behavioral Phenotype

The complex behavioral phenotype of the KE family has been extensively studied since 1990.[26,27] Individuals with the *FOXP2* mutation have difficulty in correctly articulating speech, which has been argued to be a consequence of impaired execution of sequenced movements of the orofacial musculature in general. In fact, affected members of the KE family do perform worse in executing commands like "bite your lip" than unaffected individuals, but perform normally for individual simple oral movements and limb movements, such as the use of a key or brushing one's hair.[28]

In addition, affected family members perform significantly worse than their unaffected relatives on a battery of tests that assess receptive and grammatical language. The deficit includes the inability to correctly inflect words (i.e., change tense or number), to match sentences describing subtle relationships between objects with the corresponding pictures, and to distinguish between words and non-words. The low scores on these kind of tests are not paralleled by test scores assessing non-verbal IQ. Even though as a group, the affected individuals score slightly but significantly lower on a non-verbal IQ test than non-affected individuals, there is considerable overlap between the groups.[29–31] Because there is much less overlap in scores for the language-related tasks, it is unlikely that the deficit in language skills is simply a reflection of overall slightly impaired cognitive function.

These findings suggest that the primary deficit in the affected KE family members might reflect a disruption of the sensorimotor mechanisms mediating the selection, control, and sequencing of fine learned movements involving the mouth and face. While it seems improbable that all of the linguistic deficits are symptoms of the articulation problems, it is formally possible that they are a developmental consequence. This interpretation is also compatible with the motor theory of speech perception,[15] which posits that decoding of speech involves part of the motor-production neural machinery. Recent human studies support this idea.[32,33]

Human Structural and Functional Abnormalities

To begin to determine the neural sites that are impacted by a mutation in *FOXP2*, imaging studies were used to examine the gross anatomical morphology of the KE family brains. Brain images from unaffected family members served as the reference point for discerning changes in the affected family members' brains. Across studies, the most consistent finding was a bilateral reduction in the grey matter density of a region of the basal ganglia called the caudate nucleus.[30,34–36] The basal ganglia are composed of striatal regions (caudate and putamen) and pallidal regions (globus pallidus pars externa and pars interna) and are critical for motor planning, sequencing, and cognitive function. Thus, the reduced caudate area observed in the affected family members is generally consistent with their impaired ability to perform motor tasks involving sequential movements, but isn't specifically indicative of orofacial impairments per se.

In addition to those in basal ganglia, cortical abnormalities were observed. In regions that are critical for speech perception (the posterior superior temporal gyrus), speech production (the dorsal inferior frontal and the precentral gyrus), or semantic processing (the angular gyrus) the amount of grey matter differed between affected and unaffected family members. Affected members also had less grey matter in the ventral cerebellum.[34] While structural deficits appear to be bilateral, functional studies revealed more lateralized disturbances. Positron emission tomography activation was lower in the left sensorimotor and supplementary face and mouth region of cortex of affected family members than normal controls during the performance of word repetition tasks.[30] The same subjects showed overactivation of the left caudate nucleus and the left premotor cortex, extending into Broca's area. These latter two areas are needed to generate words fluently.

Two studies used magnetic resonance to image the brains of unaffected versus affected family members during tasks of covert and overt speech.[36,37] In both studies, the left inferior frontal gyrus and the left putamen were consistently less active in affected members. In summary, the *FOXP2* mutation leads to both structural and functional neural deficits in a corticostriatal network that participates in speech and language. These anatomical findings fit well with the behavioral abnormalities described above. One idea is that the abnormal motor structures, which are bilateral, could represent a "core deficit" that inhibits speech production, which, according to the motor theory of speech perception,[15] could secondarily influence language and cognitive development evidenced by the functional abnormalities on the left side of the brain. As an alternative to the notion of a cascade of deficits over time, the gene could act simultaneously to influence motor, linguistic, and cognitive networks. In either case, the striking difficulty in executing orofacial movements on command, coupled with structural and functional abnormalities of the basal ganglia, suggest a major impairment within the corticostriatal circuitry controlling the sequencing of voluntary, fine, orofacial movements used in speech.

Evolution of FOXP2

Since humans are vocal learners and non-human primates are not, the discovery of the *FOXP2* mutation being causally linked to a language deficit raised the question of whether *FOXP2* might have undergone positive selection in the human lineage. Three studies indicate that this is indeed the case,[38–40] raising the provocative hypothesis that changes in FOXP2 amino acid composition were pivotal for the evolution of learned vocal communication in hominids.

The FOX Gene Family

Can information about the characteristics of FOXP2 protein provide clues about its role in the above described morphological, neural, and behavioral deficits? FOXP2 is a member of the Forkhead (FOX) family of proteins,[25] one of at least 40 that exist in humans. They act as transcriptional regulators, capable of either repressing (decreasing) or activating (increasing) the production of mRNA of a specific suite of molecules. This is achieved by structurally specialized regions, the DNA-binding domains of the protein that contact the promoters of target genes. In all FOX proteins, this domain comprises 80 to 100 highly conserved amino acids. The name "forkhead winged-helix (FOX) domain" stems from the fork-like head structure on *Drosophila* embryos in which the first FOX protein mutant was discovered, and the winged helix refers to the shape of the tertiary structure of this protein domain.[41] It is this FOX DNA binding domain that harbors the point mutation, which causes the language deficit in the KE family; at amino acid position 553 a histidine replaces an arginine.[25]

Within the FOX family there are subfamilies, clusters of proteins that show higher homology to one another than to other such clusters. Those are distinguished by letters, FOXA through (currently) FOXQ. The FOXP subfamily has four members (FOXP1-FOXP4), which, in addition to the FOX domain possess a DNA-binding dependent N-terminal transcriptional repression domain encompassing both a zinc finger and a leucine zipper motif (FIG. 1).[42–44] FOX proteins are involved in a wide variety of biological processes, and mutations in their genes lead to diverse developmental disorders.[26,41] Foxp1 and Foxp2 were initially investigated for their role in lung development. Based on their developmental expression pattern, they appear to coregulate proximal versus distal epithelial lung cell phenotypes.[42] Foxp1 is the

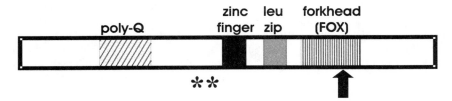

FIGURE 1. Schematic of FoxP2 primary structure. The forkhead/winged helix DNA-binding domain (*vertical stripe*) is common to all forkhead/winged helix (FOX) proteins. The FoxP subfamily is further characterized by a unique forkhead/DNA-binding domain and an N-terminal repression domain that contains a zinc finger and leucine zipper (*black and grey boxes*, respectively). FoxP2 additionally has a polyglutamine tract (*diagonal hatch*).[42,44] *Asterisks* indicate residues 303 and 325 which, among primates, are unique to humans.[25] *Arrow* points to arginine 553, which when mutated to histidine is linked to a rare speech and language abnormality in humans.[38]

closest Forkhead family member to Foxp2, shares a similar N-terminal domain whereby it represses transcription of genes that are also affected by Foxp2, and can dimerize with other Foxp subfamily members.[42,44,45] These findings raise the possibility that FOXP1 could interact with FOXP2 in other tissues, including the brain in regions where both are expressed.

Indeed, while other members of the Forkhead family of transcription factors are thought to function as monomers,[41] recent *in vitro* work demonstrates that Foxp subfamily members require either homo- or hetero-dimerization with each other or other regulatory proteins in order to bind DNA and affect transcription.[44] These functions are mediated by regions within the N-termini of the proteins, called *subdomains 1 and 2*. Within *subdomain 1*, the leucine zipper motif is essential for binding and repression. *Subdomain 2* interacts with a co-repressor protein known as C-terminal binding protein 1 to repress transcription. Foxp1 and Foxp2 possess both subdomains, which may be functionally redundant, while Foxp4 has only the first. These multiple opportunities for interaction may provide a dynamic range of transcriptional control, dependent upon the levels and types of Foxp proteins within a given cell.

SONG LEARNING IN BIRDS AS A MODEL
FOR HUMAN SPEECH LEARNING

In view of the relative intractability of studying the cellular and molecular mechanisms of human language learning, birds that learn their songs are an obvious choice as models of vocal learning. The ability to modify innate vocalizations in order to correctly imitate the sounds that constitute the vocal repertoire is essential for both human speech and learned birdsong. In both humans and avian vocal learners, this "learning to play the instrument" proceeds through characteristic stages and relies on the interaction of auditory and motor centers. If the learning does not occur within a "critical period," usually before puberty, imitation is incomplete, as for instance evidenced by people's accents in languages acquired as adults. Similarities between human and songbird vocal learning also exist with respect to social influences on the behavior.[46,47] Apparently, vocal learning evolved three times independently in the avian lineage, namely in songbirds, parrots, and hummingbirds (see also Jarvis, this volume).[4] Each of these groups of birds needs to learn at least one aspect of their communication sounds by imitating the adult vocalizations of other members of their species. The fact that not all birds are vocal learners provides ready-made control subjects for such studies.

Like human language learning, song learning has the quality of an "instinct"[48,49] and is the product of the interaction of genetic and epigenetic factors. Many of the initial song learning studies were in fact addressing the balance between genetic versus social and cultural influences in different species of songbirds. Evidence for the importance of the genetic background on vocal development comes from a wide range of experimental approaches trying to dissociate the genetic variables from the epigenetic. This may involve rearing different genetic populations of the same species in identical conditions, or mixing genetic backgrounds while keeping auditory input constant (hybrid breeding), or by keeping genetic background constant while changing auditory input. Among the manipulations that alter auditory input are deafening, rearing in white noise, isolation, or presenting different tutors (crossfostering) or tutor tapes. Using these approaches, genetic influences have been found on acoustic characteristics of song, repertoire size, preference for tutor song types, and speed of song development.[50] Probably because vocal learning is such a rare trait and one that is so central to human existence, most studies of birdsong have focused on the mechanism of vocal imitation itself. Thus, much progress has been made in elucidation of the neural circuits involved, their role in behavior, and increasingly their function at the cellular and molecular level.

CANDIDATE MOLECULES: PRIOR STUDIES IN BIRDS

How does one go about identifying genetic mechanisms that might be important for the rare trait of vocal learning? Since the initial observation of specialized nuclei within the telencephalon of song learners,[51] two general strategies have been employed to isolate and characterize functionally significant molecules, i.e., any molecule (gene, protein) that contributes to the formation or function of the vocal learning pathway. The first strategy focuses solely on songbird anatomy and hypothesizes (perhaps naively) that important molecules are those that are more abundant within song nuclei than in surrounding tissue. For a given molecule, abundance (i.e., level of expression) within song areas can be compared to (1) the most adjacent region of the brain that does not subserve song learning; (2) regions of female brain at similar anatomical positions to the song nuclei of males, in species in which only males learn song; and (3) similar coordinates in non-songbirds that do not learn song (e.g., suboscines). Once a molecule is selected, a demonstration that altered molecular expression specifically affects song development and/or production provides the most convincing evidence that the candidate molecule is indeed important for vocal learning.

The second strategy is based on the critical role played by information storage in the song system. Educated guesses at candidate molecules for vocal learning are based on studies of learning and memory in other species, typically rodents. Reagents are developed to identify the avian forms of these molecules (oligonucleotide probes for detection of gene expression, antibodies for immunohistochemical detection of protein, electrophysiological measures to detect synaptic function). Expression of these putative "memory" molecules within the song circuit is thereby tested, and, as with the first approach, correlations with brain regions, sex, and/or species, as well as aspects of song development are made. Causality is then inferred by the functional effects of manipulations of molecular expression on song behavior. The songbird system thus provides a powerful model allowing analysis of the role of molecules within a functional circuit and facilitating comparisons across brain area, sex, and species.

Molecules Studied Based on Heightened Levels of Expression within Song Nuclei

A classic example of the first approach was the discovery of the unique expression of sex steroid receptors within the telencephalon of songbirds in comparison to non-oscines, in and around song circuit nuclei (see also articles by Harding; Gahr; Brenowitz; and Ball and colleagues, this volume).[52] This unique pattern fits with the general "steroid hypothesis" that sex steroids cause the sexual differentiation of the brain and, specifically, the differentiation of the song circuit in songbirds.[53] Sex steroids strongly regulate the size and function of song control nuclei. However, detailed examination has clarified the contribution of hormonal versus genetic mechanisms to sexual differentiation and has refuted the strictest interpretation of the steroid hypothesis in both songbirds and mammals (see article by Wade and Arnold in this volume). These recent findings illustrate how crossfertilization between observations made in birds and mammals can reveal mechanisms common to both. Further, they raise the interesting question of which gene(s) act(s) in a hormone-independent manner to achieve full sexual differentiation of the song circuit.

The first systematic exploration of relatively abundant molecules in songbird telencephalon[54] did not find any gene expressed selectively in song nuclei. This indicated that song circuit–specific genes, if existent at all, are rare.[55] Subsequently, candidate molecules have been identified by virtue of being more concentrated in song nuclei and some are currently being probed for their potential role in song. For example, insulin-like-growth factor (IGF)-II is strongly expressed in the telencephalic song nucleus HVC, but only in those neurons that project to Area X. Accumulation of the protein in the HVC neurons that project to Area X implies a paracrine mode of action. In canaries, seasonal changes in IGF-II expression covary with changes in adult neurogenesis.[56] Another molecule that is expressed in a highly restricted fashion is an as-yet-unidentified antigen, detected using a monoclonal antibody raised against homogenates of microdissected tissue from song nucleus RA.[57] This antigen is expressed almost exclusively within the song circuit nuclei of the family of estrildine finches, including the zebra finch, and can be induced in female zebra finches upon treatment with masculinizing hormones. Based on its remarkable expression pattern, this single antigen promises to be a "molecular signature" of a functional neural circuit, although its role therein remains to be elucidated.

Differential and subtractive hybridization approaches using songbird brain have also been fruitful in identifying molecules that, while not limited to song nuclei, are expressed at relatively high levels in a subset of them, often during critical stages of song learning. One of these, synelfin, is a homolog to the mammalian protein known as α-synuclein. This protein is thought to play a role in Parkinson's and Alzheimer's diseases in humans and, in songbirds, is regulated in song nuclei during song learning.[58] Together, these mammalian and songbird studies implicate the protein in memory functions.

Another candidate molecule is retinoic acid, classically known for its role in embryogenesis, now recognized as a necessary protein within the HVC of juvenile songbirds for normal song development.[59,60] Retinoic acid is a ligand for receptor molecules that are potent transcription factors. Targets of retinoid regulation include growth factors and their receptors. Thus, these results suggest that processes of neuron growth, survival, and differentiation continue post-embryogenesis to affect neural plasticity within the developing song circuit (see Mello, this volume).

Molecules Investigated Based on Roles in Mammalian Learning and Memory

A second approach for identifying candidate genes for vocal learning has been to test molecules implicated in synaptic plasticity in rodent learning and memory for their role in songbird song learning. One such molecule is the N-methyl D-aspartate (NMDA) subtype of glutamate receptor, which has been fruitfully characterized in both rodent learning and songbird song circuitry (see Nordeen and Nordeen, this volume). Additional candidate molecules identified in mammals and examined in songbird brain include the endocannabinoids. In rodents, these molecules facilitate the induction of long-term potentiation (LTP) (see Nordeen and Nordeen, this volume) in the hippocampus. Perhaps more relevant to song circuitry, in the rodent striatum they are critical to another form of synaptic plasticity, long-term depression. In zebra finches, endocannabinoids are expressed in the song system where their activation appears to influence sensory-motor learning and perceptual/mnemonic processes without concomitant changes is measures of auditory input.[61–64] Another class of molecules are the immediate early genes c-fos[65] and ZENK (acronym for zif286, egr-1, ngfl-a, krox-24)[55] (see Clayton, this volume). While these molecules are not limited to song circuitry, their abundance and distinct activation patterns have been extremely useful to probe neural activation pattern involved in song behavior,[66] to map functional vocal learning circuitry across avian evolution,[67,68] and to gain insights into auditory processing of song and calls in females and males[69] (see Theunissen and colleagues, this volume). This list is not meant to be exhaustive, but rather illustrative of the principle of testing candidate learning and memory molecules across model systems. Increasingly, avian and mammalian models offer complementary insights as evidenced by experiments addressing the relationship of critical periods and the maturation of NMDA receptor–mediated synaptic currents.[70,71] Other areas where avian models have stimulated mammalian research are adult neurogenesis,[72–74] and the role of the basal ganglia for vocal learning and production (see Farries; and Perkel, this volume).[75]

FoxP2 AND FoxP1 IN BIRDS

Although the function of FOXP2 in language and speech remains open, progress has been made in demonstrating its localization in rodent and human embryos. As pointed out above, structural and functional brain anomalies of affected individuals carrying *FOXP2* mutations consistently implicate the basal ganglia as one of the key affected brain regions.[34,35] The striatum, a component of the basal ganglia, is also the site of high *FOXP2* expression in developing human and rodent brain.[76–79] Since vocal learning in songbirds depends in part on the specialized pathway through the basal ganglia, including striatal vocal nucleus Area X,[80–82] we were motivated to ask the following questions: (1) Does zebra finch *FoxP2* (*zfFoxP2*) bear molecular similarities to human *FOXP2* (*hFOXP2*)? (2) Is *FoxP2* differentially expressed in the brains of avian vocal learners and non-learners? Birds that have only innate vocalizations lack specialized telencephalic "song circuitry" but vocalize via a set of sub-telencephalic nuclei common to both vocal learners and non-learners.[83] (3) How do *FoxP2* and *FoxP1* expression in birds compare to that in mammals, including humans? To address these questions we cloned the *FoxP2* and *FoxP1* genes of a commonly studied vocal learner, the zebra finch, and evaluated expression patterns in brains of eight species of avian "vocal learners," two species of avian "vocal non-learners," a crocodilian, the closest living non-avian relative,[84] and humans.

Cloning of Zebra Finch FoxP2 and FoxP1

We identified the mRNA containing the entire open reading frame encoding *zfFoxP2* as well as some untranslated sequences on either side of it.[79,85] As with mammalian *FoxP2* transcripts, there are multiple isoforms in the zebra finch (FIG. 2). Four isoforms exist that differ based on the presence or absence of two DNA segments, called *splice1* (71 bp) and *splice2* (60 bp), each different at the 5′ end of the gene. *Splice1* introduces a stop codon at position 261 (relative to the first start codon) resulting in predicted protein isoforms III and IV that miss the first 92 amino acids (AA), also reported for human FOXP2.[86] *Splice2* introduces 20 additional AA in-frame into the predicted protein isoforms I and III, not reported in human or mouse. In adult zebra finch brain and lung, four mRNA transcripts are evident, of approximately 9.0 kb, 6.5 kb, 3.5 kb, and 2.5 kb, respectively, some of which correspond in size to the transcripts found in mouse and human.[25,42] The large size of the transcripts relative to the size of the predicted coding region suggests that they contain large amounts of regulatory sequence, perhaps to precisely regulate *zfFoxP2* translation, mRNA location, and/or mRNA stability.

In zebra finch brain, one or both of the long isoforms (I and II) predominate. The zfFoxP2 protein (Isoform I) shares 98.2% identity with human and 98.7% identity with mouse Foxp2, respectively. This emphasizes the remarkable degree of conservation of the *FoxP2* gene[38,39] as ~320 million years ago is the latest time at which modern birds and mammals had a common ancestor.[87] At five AA positions that are identical in mice and human, zfFoxP2 differs from all FoxP2 sequences currently known. At three additional positions, the mouse and zebra finch sequence are identical but the human sequence diverges. Of these three AAs, one also exists in carnivores,[39] one is common to primates, and one is unique to humans. In an analysis of *FOXP2* molecular evolution, the latter has been suggested to result from positive selection during recent primate evolution indicating that hFOXP2 might have been pivotal for the development of human language.[38] Although zfFoxP2 lacks this human-specific AA change, one cannot exclude the possibility that other sequence differences exist between avian vocal learners and non-learners that result from positive se-

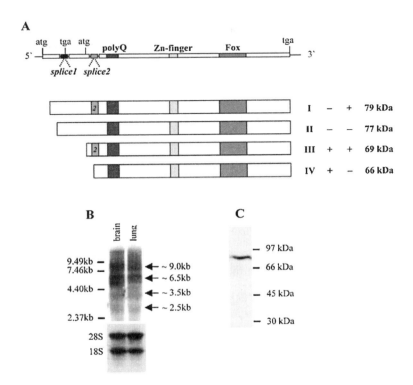

FIGURE 2. Identification of the zebra finch *FoxP2* mRNA (*zfFoxP2*). (**A**) Schematic representation of *zfFoxP2* mRNA structure and its four predicted protein isoforms (I–IV). Positions of start (atg) and stop (tga) codons, the polyglutamine tract (polyQ), zinc-finger (Zn-finger), and forkhead box (Fox) DNA binding domains are shown. Two mRNA segments (*splice1* and *splice2*) are subject to alternative splicing. Presence (+) or absence (–) of splice1 and splice2 leads to variation in length of open reading frames (ORF). *Splice1* contains a stop codon that shifts the frame so that the ORF begins at the second atg, *splice2* inserts 60 base pairs (bp) in-frame into the coding region. The four predicted protein isoforms are shown. For the calculation of their theoretical molecular weight we used Peptide Mass (http://www.expasy.org/tools/peptide-mass.html). (**B**) Northern blot analysis of 20 μg total RNA from adult zebra finch brain and lung was carried out with a ^{32}P-labeled DNA fragment spanning bp 114–959 (relative to first start codon). Ethidium bromide staining of 18S and 28S ribosomal bands demonstrates equal RNA loading. The different *zfFoxP2* transcripts are indicated with *arrows*. (**C**) Western blot analysis of 50 μg brain nuclear protein extract from a 40-day-old male zebra finch reveals a zfFoxP2 protein corresponding in size to either isoform I or II, recognized by a polyclonal antibody raised against amino acids 613–715 of mouse Foxp2.[85]

lection during avian evolution, as proposed for primates. The fact that zebra finches, in contrast to mouse, have a 6.5 kb transcript that corresponds in size to the human transcript also raises the possibility that selection acted on the regulatory sequence.

Expression Pattern of zfFoxP2

Within zebra finch brain, *FoxP2* shows differential expression over development in the song nucleus Area X—a part of the special basal ganglia-like forebrain network required for vocal learning that non-learners do not possess. *FoxP2* expression in Area X stands out, slightly but consistently, from its expression in the surrounding striatum only during the time when young zebra finches learn to imitate song.[85] Comparison of *FoxP2* expression pattern in Area X of adult canaries, zebra finches, bengalese finches, strawberry finches, song sparrows, and in the equivalent regions of Area X in parrots (MMSt) and hummingbirds (VAS) revealed interesting differences. In some species, we found expression in Area X to be higher than in the surrounding striatum, in others it was similar in both regions or lower in Area X compared to the surrounding striatum.[85] Investigating the variables that could account for these differences in *FoxP2* expression in adult Area X, we could rule out singing activity (see Mello, this volume) and song stereotypy. In contrast, a seasonal comparison in canaries, a species with seasonal variation in song plasticity, showed elevated *FoxP2* expression in Area X during the months of the year when song became plastic and less expression during months when song was highly stereotyped (FIG. 3). The differences in *FoxP2* expression within Area X of the other species were also roughly correlated with the likely state of song plasticity at the time of sacrifice.

Both juvenile and adult Area X expression patterns are compatible with a role for FoxP2 in learned vocalization, particularly during development, but also in adulthood even though the function of Area X is more enigmatic in adult songbirds than in juveniles. Experimentally induced lesions of Area X in adult zebra finches that have finished learning their song hardly affect normal song production.[80–82] Yet Area X in adult zebra finches has song-specific motor activity, which is modulated by social context.[66,88] This apparent paradox is reminiscent of the situation in the human basal ganglia, where the absence of striatal regions (e.g., due to stroke) may have less severe functional consequences than disruption of its function (e.g., in Parkinson's and Huntington's diseases). It is thought that Area X in adulthood monitors adult song production and is involved with correction of errors.[89,90] (see articles by Brainard; and Konishi, this volume) Since adult song is less error-prone than developing song, particularly in zebra finches, lesions of Area X might have less apparent effects. Consistent with this hypothesis is the observation that songbirds with different amounts of adult song plasticity apparently rely on Area X for their adult song production to different extents.[81,82,91–93] The differential *FoxP2* expression among avian species might be related to this.

FoxP2 is also expressed in non-vocal striatal regions outside of Area X/VAS/MMSt of all eleven bird species examined, regardless of whether or not they learn their vocalizations. Both vocal learners and vocal non-learners had similar developmental onset of *FoxP2* expression in comparable brain regions and equivalent expression pattern in adults. The strongest signal was consistently observed in the basal ganglia, the dorsal thalamus, the inferior olive, and the Purkinje cells of the

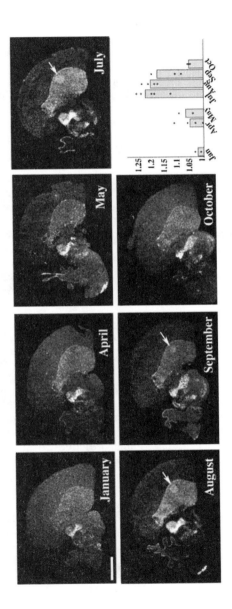

FIGURE 3. *FoxP2* expression in Area X of adult canaries varies seasonally. Area X expressed noticeably more *FoxP2* than the surrounding striatum only during the months of July, August, and September, resulting in higher ratios of Area X to striatum expression. Bar graph shows mean ratios for each month; superimposed points represent values for individual birds.[85]

cerebellum. Less intense but consistent expression was observed in various nuclei related to these regions. In all brain regions that expressed *FoxP2* (as observed by *in situ* hybridization) a Foxp2-specific antibody (used for immunohistochemistry) also recognized strongly labeled nuclei, as is expected for a transcription factor.[85]

Consistent with the reports from developing human and mouse brain,[42,77,78] we saw *FoxP2* expression in the embryonic zebra finch brain as early as stage 23.[85,94,95] The highest expression was in the striatum and dorsal thalamus. In older animals, the dorsal thalamic zone (DTZ),[96] located dorsomedially in the avian diencephalon exhibits distinct subregional labeling.[79] The DTZ is homologous to the mammalian intralaminar, midline and mediodorsal thalamic nuclear complex (IMMC).[96] It consists of multiple nuclei whose boundaries likely underlie the pattern of *FoxP2* expression. For example, nucleus dorsolateralis anterior thalami, pars medialis (DLM), part of the song circuit, expresses *FoxP2* mRNA, while the nucleus dorsolateralis anterior thalami, pars lateralis (DLL) does not. In the vicinity of, but histologically distinct from, the DTZ is the ventrointermediate area (VIA), a region described in pigeons as comparable to the motor part of the mammalian ventral tier.[97] In the zebra finch, *FoxP2* signals are visible in this region just medial to nucleus rotundus.

Striatal and dorsal thalamic expression patterns persist throughout development and adulthood. Expression levels in the striatum decrease slightly with age, but are always higher than in pallial regions, i.e., those dorsal to the striatum, that are low throughout development and in adulthood. The prominent expression in the striatum and caudal dorsal thalamus is common to all species investigated, regardless of sex and of song learning ability. And it is also seen in a crocodile, the closest non-avian relative of birds.[85]

Cellular Identity of zfFoxP2-Expressing Cells

In adult zebra finch striatum, FoxP2 immunoreactivity is characteristically seen in medium or small cells that are uniformly distributed throughout, except for one peculiarity.[85] Small FoxP2-positive cells form distinct, evenly spaced clusters in the lateral striatum (LSt), that abut the pallial-subpallial lamina (PSL, previously called LMD) which separates the pallium from subpallium. In pigeon striatum, similarly arranged patches contain dense choline acetyltransferase (ChAT)–immunoreactive fibers.[98] In zebra finch, these FoxP2-immunoreactive cell clusters are also innervated by ChAT. All FoxP2-immunoreactive brain cells are neurons, some of which also express the polysialylated neural cell adhesion molecule (PSA-NCAM), a marker for cellular plasticity and migration.[34]

To identify the types of striatal neurons expressing FoxP2, we used markers for the three classes of striatal interneurons[99] in conjunction with FoxP2 immunohistochemistry. We used ChAT to detect the large, aspiny cholinergic interneurons, nitric oxide synthase (nNOS) to detect the medium-sized aspiny interneurons that also contain somatostatin, and neuropeptide Y and the calcium binding protein parvalbumin to detect another population of medium-sized aspiny interneurons that also contain GABA and the neurotensin-related hexapeptide LANT6.[99] Neither ChAT, nor nNOS, nor parvalbumin are expressed in the same neurons as FoxP2, suggesting that the striatal neurons that express zfFoxP2 are projection neurons rather than interneurons. The striatal projection neurons in birds, as in mammals, are the site of convergent nigral dopaminergic and cortical (i.e., pallial in birds) glutamatergic input.[99] The adenosine-3′,5′–monophosphate (cAMP)-regulated phosphoprotein of M_R 32,000 (DARPP 32) is thought to serve as a critical integrator of these two inputs onto the striatal projection neurons.[100] Concordant with our expectation that zfFoxP2 is expressed in striatal projection neurons, we found two indicators of dopaminergic innervation: FoxP2-immunoreactive striatal neurons co-expressed DARPP32, which is indicative of the presence of dopamine D1 receptor, and immunoreactivity for tyrosine hydroxylase (TH), the synthetic enzyme for biogenic amines, was detected around perikarya of neurons with FoxP2 immunoreactive nuclei.

ZfFoxP2 Expression in Subtelencephalic Brain Regions

We also found prominent *zfFoxP2* expression in many subtelencephalic structures. Among these structures there were regions that project to the basal ganglia, such as the substantia nigra/ventral tegmental area and the DTZ. In addition, *zfFoxP2* is expressed in many regions that are involved in relaying and integrating ascending sensory information, including auditory regions (e.g., midbrain nucleus MLd and thalamic nucleus ovoidalis), visual regions (e.g., afferent upper layers of midbrain optic tectum, and thalamic nucleus rotundus), multimodal regions (e.g., layers 10 and 11 of optic tectum,) and somatosensory regions (e.g., sensory trigeminal). In addition, prominent *FoxP2* expression was observed in the Purkinje cells of the cerebellum and the inferior olive, which gives rise to all the climbing fibers innervating the Purkinje cells.[79,85] All species tested, regardless of sex and song learning ability, expressed *zfFoxP2* in these regions. In contrast, *zfFoxP2* expression was not found in midbrain and brainstem motor control areas, such as the vocal nucleus DM, the hypoglossal vocal and tongue nucleus, nXII, nor in most other cranial motor nuclei.[85]

ZfFoxP1 Expression

We also investigated *FoxP1* because studies in mouse lung and *in vitro* demonstrate that Foxp1 (1) is the closest forkhead family member to Foxp2; (2) shares similar N-terminal domains whereby it represses transcription of genes that are also affected by Foxp2; and (3) can dimerize with other Foxp subfamily members.[42,44,45] These features suggest that FoxP1 could interact with FoxP2 within the brain in regions where both are expressed. As with mammalian sequences, zfFoxP2 and zfFoxP1 AA sequences are highly similar and differ mainly by the fact that the longest *zfFoxP1* transcript that we isolated misses the region encoding the polyglutamine stretch and 100 AA on the N-terminus.[85] For human FOXP1, an isoform that lacks the first 100 AA is reported,[101] suggesting that we found a short zfFoxP1 isoform.

Within the zebra finch brain, *FoxP1* exhibited a striking sexual dimorphism, nearly concordant with the sexual dimorphism of the song circuit (FIG. 4).[78,84] Unlike *FoxP2*, *FoxP1* was expressed in the striatal vocal nucleus Area X of all songbirds tested. Also unlike *FoxP2*, within the pallium, *FoxP1* was consistently and prominently expressed in the mesopallium in all species.[85] Interestingly, for the three main songbird pallial vocal nuclei, lMAN, HVC, and RA, *FoxP1* expression differed notably from the expression of the subdivisions in which these nuclei are embedded. HVC and RA strongly expressed *FoxP1,* whereas the surrounding territories did not.

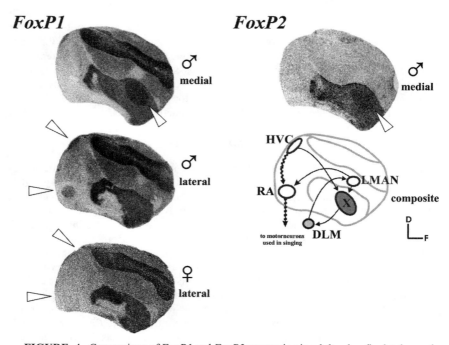

FIGURE 4. Comparison of *FoxP1* and *FoxP2* expression in adult zebra finch telenceph-alon. *In situ* hybridization of ^{32}P-labeled zebra finch *FoxP1* (*right*) versus FoxP2 (*left*) ribo-probes with sagittal sections of adult zebra finch brain reveal areas of overlap, as well as distinct regions of expression. (*Top*) Neural expression of *FoxP1* includes pallial (*top dark diagonal band* of signal) and striatal (*lower band*) regions. *Arrowhead* indicates Area X within the songbird striatum in a medial section from adult male brain. (*Middle*) In a more lateral section, two *arrowheads* point to HVC and RA. (*Bottom*) Section is taken from an adult female at approximately the same plane. *Arrowheads* here are for comparison to above section and indicate the lack of increased signal in regions of sexually dimorphic FoxP1 ex-pression. (*Right*) Top section shows striatal *FoxP2* expression in the same male as on the left. *Arrowhead* points to Area X, which is faintly discernible in this section, consistent with Nissl staining (data not shown). Beneath, composite schematic shows part of the song con-trol circuitry for reference, including the vocal control pathway (*stippled arrows*) and the anterior forebrain pathway (*smooth arrows*).[79]

The reverse was true for lMAN, which did not express *FoxP1*, while the region around it did. This was consistent across songbird species. The parrot pallial ana-logue of HVC, the central nucleus of the nidopallium, had noticeably higher levels than the surrounding nidopallium. *FoxP1* was expressed at high levels in the striatum and in the dorsal thalamus of zebra finches and other birds. A telencephalic expres-sion pattern remarkably similar to the avian brain was found in crocodile, which in-cluded high expression in striatal-like and mesopallium-like regions.[85] This suggests that the general *FoxP1* expression pattern in birds was inherited from their common reptilian ancestor.

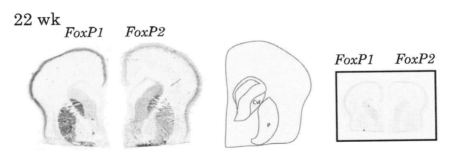

FIGURE 5. *FOXP1* and *FOXP2* expression in human embryonic brain. Coronal sections from 22-week embryo (*left*) show that expression of the two genes overlaps in regions of the striatum, as indicated by the schematic (*middle*), including in the ventrolateral caudate (Cvl) and the putamen (P). In cortex, *FOXP1* is expressed slightly more superficially than *FOXP2*. *Boxed inset* shows sense controls. (Images courtesy of Lili C. Kudo and Daniel H. Geschwind.[79])

FOXP Expression in Humans

The human language phenotype that arises from a mutation in *FOXP2* coupled with the overlapping expression of *FoxP2* with *FoxP1* in the striatum and thalamus of the zebra finch hints at a combinatorial role for these genes in the development of vocal control circuitry. This hypothesis would be supported by a similar overlap in the developing human brain. Thus, *in situ* hybridization analysis was performed on human embryonic brains between 19 and 22 weeks gestation,[79] when subcortical neurogenesis and migration is largely complete and cortical neurogenesis is ongoing.

In cortex, a complementary pattern of *FOXP* gene expression occurs in human embryos, with *FOXP1* localized to more superficial layers than *FOXP2*. Within the striatum, *FOXP1* and *FOXP2* are expressed in highly similar patterns, in the head and tail of nucleus caudatus and putamen where the intensity of *FOXP* label is reminiscent of the enhanced *FoxP* signals within Area X of the songbird striatum (FIG. 5). Interestingly, *FOXP2* shows restricted expression within the globus pallidus (GP) of the basal ganglia.[79] High levels of *FOXP2* expression occur in the GP pars interna, which provides the principal source of output from the basal ganglia to nucleus centrum medianum thalami (CM) and the major motor relay nuclei of the thalamus. As in the zebra finch, human *FOXP1* and *FOXP2* expression overlaps in the thalamus, with *FOXP2* revealing more extensive expression, specifically in CM and nucleus medialis dorsalis thalami, both regions with homologues in the avian DTZ,[96] and in the ventrobasal complex comprised of nucleus ventralis posterior lateralis/medialis thalami. More moderate signals arise from nuclei anterior thalami, dorsal and ventral, and nucleus parafascicularis thalami (Pf). Similar to VIA in the zebra finch,[97] the ventral tier of the human thalamus exhibited strong *FOXP2* expression, including nuclei ventralis anterior, lateralis, and nucleus ventralis posterior lateralis, pars oralis. These thalamic nuclei have strong motor and premotor cortex connectivity.[102] Both genes also demonstrated significant expression in nucleus subthalamicus bilaterally. Additionally, *FOXP2* is strongly expressed in nucleus ruber. The human brain regions of *FOXP* expression are key relays in essential motor control circuitry involved in motor planning and execution. This pattern of expression in specific subcortical structures for both *FOXP1* and *FOXP2* is entirely consistent with the putative role of these genes in pathways of sensorimotor integration that subserve vocalization and other complex learned motor movements. Note, however that in no case was lateralization of *FoxP* gene expression observed. Given the observations of lateralization in both humans and finch vocal systems, this finding may indicate (1) that expression was measured prior to the time of lateralization in humans; (2) that asymmetric expression was missed due to its occurrence in tissue outside of our samples; (3) that asymmetric differences in *FoxP* expression exist but were undetected by our current methods (e.g., there could be post-translational differences, the cumulative level of all neurally expressed FoxP proteins could be lateralized, quantitation by emulsion autoradiography may be required); and (4) that mechanisms downstream of FOXP account for lateralization; among other possibilities.

CONCLUSIONS

The striking conservation of the *FoxP2* gene sequence and overall brain expression pattern in reptilian and mammalian brains and in the brains of both song-learning and non-song-learning birds indicates that *FoxP2* has a more general role than to specifically enable vocal learning. FoxP2 could be an ancient transcription factor primarily involved in setting up and maintaining subtelencephalic and striatal sensory and sensory-motor circuits, creating a permissive environment upon which vocal learning can evolve if other circumstances/factors come into play. Given the prominent role of many other forkhead transcription factors in early development, this is a likely scenario.[41] Support of this notion also stems from the fact that regions where *FoxP2* is first expressed in the avian embryo are sources of inductive signals that organize adjacent neuroepithelium and neuronal migration during early development. The differences in cortical/pallial *FoxP2* expression between mammals and birds are harder to interpret since direct homologies between avian and mammalian pallial areas remain unresolved.[99]

The common expression pattern of *FoxP2* in birds and humans might provide valuable clues about what constitutes a "permissive environment" for vocal communication and evolution of vocal learning. Learning to imitate acoustic signals requires integration of sensory information with the desired motor output. The basal ganglia as well as the cerebellum in all vertebrates integrate afferent sensory information with descending motor commands and thus participate in the precise control of temporally sequenced muscle movements.[103] Both innate and learned avian and human vocalizations depend on such control,[104] as do many other complex learned behaviors. Anatomical evidence suggests that the specialized regions for vocal learning in birds were elaborated from already modularly connected forebrain regions translating ascending auditory, somatosensory, and visual information into motor commands. Consistent with this, an AFP-like circuit apparently also exists in vocal non-learners.[105] In humans, the basal ganglia and the cerebellum have attracted far less attention than the cortical speech and language areas, but there is increasing awareness that the basal ganglia and cerebellum are not only essential for the execution but might also be required for the acquisition of human vocal behavior.[75,106]

It has been suggested that the speech and language pathology in humans with *FOXP2* mutations consists of an orofacial dyspraxia core deficit.[26] This could be primarily due to a lack of central control over the peripheral muscles associated with the speech apparatus. However, our data suggest that in birds *FoxP2* is expressed in afferent sensory pathways, and in the striatal projection neurons, which are the site of convergence for both pallial and subpallial projections. Takahashi and colleagues[78] also argue that in rats FoxP2-positive striatal neurons are projection neurons. Expression in these sensory and sensorimotor integration areas makes sense, if *FoxP2* expression indeed highlights a "permissive environment" for vocal learning. Further, many sites of *FoxP2* expression, such as the inferior olive-Purkinje cell pathway, the optic tectum, and the striatum, are known substrates for experience-dependent plasticity.[103,107,108] This highlights the need for more studies investigating the role of ascending visual, auditory, and somatosensory information in complex learned motor skills such as birdsong and human speech.

ACKNOWLEDGMENTS

Constance Scharff and Stephanie A. White gratefully acknowledge our collaborators Erich Jarvis, Kaz Wada, Ed Morrisey, and Thierry Lints, and Lili Kudo and Dan Geschwind, respectively, as well as the members of our labs for contributing to the work presented here.

REFERENCES

1. HAUSER, M.D., N. CHOMSKY & W.T. FITCH. 2002. The faculty of language: what is it, who has it, and how did it evolve? Science **298:** 1569–1579.
2. THORPE, W.H. 1958. The learning of song patterns by birds, with especial reference to the song of the chaffinch *Fringilla coelebs*. Ibis **100:** 535–570.
3. KROODSMA, D.E. & J.R. BAYLIS. 1982. A world survey of evidence for vocal learning in birds. Academic Press. New York.
4. BAPTISTA, L.F. & K.L. SCHUCHMANN. 1990. Song learning in the anna hummingbird (*Calypte anna*). Ethology **84:** 15–26.
5. HALL, W.S. *et al.* 1997. Audio-vocal learning in budgerigars. Ann. N.Y. Acad. Sci. **807:** 352–367.
6. ESSER, K.H. 1994. Audio-vocal learning in a non-human mammal: the lesser spearnosed bat *Phyllostomus discolor*. Neuroreport **5:** 1718–1720.
7. PAYNE, R.S. & S. McVAY. 1971. Songs of humpback whales. Science **173:** 585–597.
8. RALLS, K., P. FIORELLI & S. GISH. 1985. Vocalizations and vocal mimicry in captive harbor seals, Phoca vitulina. Can. J. Zool. **63:** 1050–1056.
9. HERMAN, L.M., D.G. RICHARDS & J.P. WOLZ. 1984. Comprehension of sentences by bottlenosed dolphins. Cognition **16:** 129–219.
10. JANIK, V.M. 2000. Whistle matching in wild bottlenose dolphins (*Tursiops truncatus*). Science **289:** 1355–1357,1352.
11. PINKER, S. 1994. The Language Instinct. William Morrow and Co. New York.
12. LYONS, F., J.R. HANLEY & J. KAY. 2002. Anomia for common names and geographical names with preserved retrieval of names of people: a semantic memory disorder. Cortex **38:** 23–35.
13. WISE, R.J. 2003. Language systems in normal and aphasic human subjects: functional imaging studies and inferences from animal studies. Br. Med. Bull. **65:** 95–119.
14. BLANK, S.C. *et al.* 2002. Speech production: Wernicke, Broca and beyond. Brain **125:** 1829–1838.

15. LIBERMAN, A.M. & I.G. MATTINGLY. 1985. The motor theory of speech perception revised. Cognition 21: 1–36.
16. TROUTON, A., F.M. SPINATH & R. PLOMIN. 2002. Twins early development study (TEDS): a multivariate, longitudinal genetic investigation of language, cognition and behavior problems in childhood. Twin Res. 5: 444–448.
17. FELSENFELD, S. 2002. Finding susceptibility genes for developmental disorders of speech: the long and winding road. J. Commun. Disord. 35: 329–345.
18. PLOMIN, R. et al. 2002. Associations between behaviour problems and verbal and nonverbal cognitive abilities and disabilities in early childhood. J. Child Psychol. Psychiatr. 43: 619–633.
19. LEHESJOKI, A.E. & R.M. GARDINER. 2000. Genetics of disease: away from the beaten track. Curr. Opin. Genet. Dev. 10: 247–251.
20. COLHOUN, H.M., P.M. MCKEIGUE & G.D. SMITH. 2003. Problems of reporting genetic associations with complex outcomes. Lancet 361: 865–872.
21. FISHER, S.E., et al. 1998. Localisation of a gene implicated in a severe speech and language disorder. Nat. Genet. 18: 168–170.
22. S.L.I. CONSORTIUM. 2002. A genomewide scan identifies two novel loci involved in specific language impairment. Am. J. Hum. Genet. 70: 384–398.
23. BARTLETT, C.W. et al. 2002. A major susceptibility locus for specific language impairment is located on 13q21. Am. J. Hum. Genet. 71: 45–55.
24. KAESTNER, K.H., W. KNOCHEL & D.E. MARTINEZ. 2000. Unified nomenclature for the winged helix/forkhead transcription factors. Genes Dev. 14: 142–146.
25. LAI, C.S.L. et al. 2001. A forkhead-domain gene is mutated in a severe speech and language disorder. Nature 413: 519–523.
26. MARCUS, G.F. & S.E. FISHER. 2003. FOXP2 in focus: what can genes tell us about speech and language? Trends Cogn. Sci. 7: 257–262.
27. FISHER, S.E., C.S. LAI & A.P. MONACO. 2003. Deciphering the genetic basis of speech and language disorders. Annu. Rev. Neurosci. 26: 57–80.
28. VARGHA-KHADEM, F. et al. 1995. Praxic and nonverbal cognitive deficits in a large family with a genetically transmitted speech and language disorder. Proc. Natl. Acad. Sci. USA 92: 930–933.
29. ALCOCK, K.J. et al. 2000. Oral dyspraxia in inherited speech and language impairment and acquired dysphasia. Brain Lang. 75: 17–33.
30. VARGHA-KHADEM, F. et al. 1998. Neural basis of an inherited speech and language disorder. Proc. Natl. Acad. Sci. USA 95: 12695–12700.
31. WATKINS, K.E., N.F. DRONKERS & F. VARGHA-KHADEM. 2002. Behavioural analysis of an inherited speech and language disorder: comparison with acquired aphasia. Brain 125: 452–464.
32. FADIGA, L. et al. 2002. Speech listening specifically modulates the excitability of tongue muscles: a TMS study. Eur. J. Neurosci. 15: 399–402.
33. WATKINS, K.E., A.P. STRAFELLA & T. PAUS. 2003. Seeing and hearing speech excites the motor system involved in speech production. Neuropsychologia 41: 989–994.
34. BELTON, E. et al. 2003. Bilateral brain abnormalities associated with dominantly inherited verbal and orofacial dyspraxia. Hum. Brain Mapp. 18: 194–200.
35. WATKINS, K.E., D.G. GADIAN & F. VARGHA-KHADEM. 1999. Functional and structural brain abnormalities associated with a genetic disorder of speech and language. Am. J. Hum. Genet. 65: 1215–1221.
36. WATKINS, K.E. et al. 2002. MRI analysis of an inherited speech and language disorder: structural brain abnormalities. Brain 125: 465–478.
37. LIEGEOIS, F. et al. 2003. Language fMRI abnormalities associated with FOXP2 gene mutation. Nat. Neurosci. 6: 1230–1237.
38. ENARD, W. et al. 2002. Molecular evolution of FOXP2, a gene involved in speech and language. Nature (London) 418: 869–872.
39. ZHANG, J., D.M. WEBB & O. PODLAHA. 2002. Accelerated protein evolution and origins of human-specific features: Foxp2 as an example. Genetics 162: 1825–1835.
40. CLARK, A.G. et al. 2003. Inferring nonneutral evolution from human-chimp-mouse orthologous gene trios. Science 302: 1960–1963.

41. CARLSSON, P. & M. MAHLAPUU. 2002. Forkhead transcription factors: key players in development and metabolism. Dev. Biol. **250:** 1–23.
42. SHU, W.G. *et al.* 2001. Characterization of a new subfamily of winged-helix/forkhead (Fox) genes that are expressed in the lung and act as transcriptional repressors. J. Biol. Chem. **276:** 27488–27497.
43. LU, M.M. *et al.* 2002. Foxp4: a novel member of the Foxp subfamily of winged-helix genes co-expressed with Foxp1 and Foxp2 in pulmonary and gut tissues. Gene Expr. Patterns **2:** 223–228.
44. LI, S., J. WEIDENFELD & E.E. MORRISEY. 2004. Transcriptional and DNA binding activity of the Foxp1/2/4 family is modulated by heterotypic and homotypic protein interactions. Molec. Cell. Biol. **24:** 809–822.
45. WANG, B. *et al.* 2003. Multiple domains define the expression and regulatory properties of Foxp1 forkhead transcriptional repressors. J. Biol. Chem. **278:** 24259–24268.
46. KUHL, P.K. 2003. Human speech and birdsong: communication and the social brain. Proc. Natl. Acad. Sci. USA **100:** 9645–9646.
47. GOLDSTEIN, M.H., A.P. KING & M.J. WEST. 2003. Social interaction shapes babbling: testing parallels between birdsong and speech. Proc. Natl. Acad. Sci. USA **100:** 8030–8035.
48. GOULD, J.L. & P. MARLER. 1987. Learning by instinct. Sci. Am. **256:** 74–85.
49. MARLER, P. 1991. Song-learning behavior: the interface with neuroethology. Trends Neurosci. **14:** 199–206.
50. FREEBERG, T.M. *et al.* 2002. Cultures, genes, and neurons in the development of song and singing in brown-headed cowbirds (*Molothrus ater*). J. Comp. Physiol. A Neuroethol. Sens. Neural Behav. Physiol. **188:** 993–1002.
51. NOTTEBOHM, F. & A.P. ARNOLD. 1976. Sexual dimorphism in vocal control areas of the songbird brain. Science **194:** 211–213.
52. SCHLINGER, B.A. 1997. Sex steroids and their actions on the birdsong system. J. Neurobiol. **33:** 619–631.
53. ARNOLD, A.P. 1997. Sexual differentiation of the zebra finch song system: positive evidence, negative evidence, null hypotheses, and a paradigm shift. J. Neurobiol. **33:** 572–584.
54. CLAYTON, D.F. *et al.* 1988. Probes for rare mRNAs reveal distributed cell subsets in canary brain. Neuron **1:** 249–261.
55. CLAYTON, D.F. 1997. Role of gene regulation in song circuit development and song learning. J. Neurobiol. **33:** 549–571.
56. HOLZENBERGER, M. *et al.* 1997. Selective expression of insulin-like growth factor II in the songbird brain. J. NeuroSci. **17:** 6974–6987.
57. AKUTAGAWA, E. & M. KONISHI. 2001. A monoclonal antibody specific to a song system nuclear antigen in estrildine finches. Neuron **31:** 545–556.
58. CLAYTON, D.F. & J.M. GEORGE. 1999. Synucleins in synaptic plasticity and neurodegenerative disorders. J. Neurosci. Res. **58:** 120–129.
59. DENISENKO-NEHRBASS, N.I. *et al.* 2000. Site-specific retinoic acid production in the brain of adult songbirds. Neuron **27:** 359–370.
60. DENISENKO-NEHRBASS, N.I. & C.V. MELLO. 2001. Molecular targets of disulfiram action on song maturation in zebra finches. Brain Res. Mol. Brain Res. **87:** 246–250.
61. WHITNEY, O., K. SODERSTROM & F. JOHNSON. 2003. CB1 cannabinoid receptor activation inhibits a neural correlate of song recognition in an auditory/perceptual region of the zebra finch telencephalon. J. Neurobiol. **56:** 266–274.
62. SODERSTROM, K. & F. JOHNSON. 2003. Cannabinoid exposure alters learning of zebra finch vocal patterns. Brain Res. Dev. Brain Res. **142:** 215–217.
63. SODERSTROM, K. & F. JOHNSON. 2001. Zebra finch CB1 cannabinoid receptor: pharmacology and in vivo and in vitro effects of activation. J. Pharmacol. Exp. Ther. **297:** 189–197.
64. SODERSTROM, K. & F. JOHNSON. 2000. CB1 cannabinoid receptor expression in brain regions associated with zebra finch song control. Brain Res. **857:** 151–157.
65. KIMPO, R.R. & A.J. DOUPE. 1997. FOS is induced by singing in distinct neuronal populations in a motor network. Neuron **18:** 315–325.

66. JARVIS, E.D. *et al.* 1998. For whom the bird sings: context-dependent gene expression. Neuron **21:** 775–788.
67. JARVIS, E.D. & C.V. MELLO. 2000. Molecular mapping of brain areas involved in parrot vocal communication. J. Comp. Neurol. **419:** 1–31.
68. JARVIS, E.D. *et al.* 2000. Behaviourally driven gene expression reveals song nuclei in hummingbird brain. Nature **406:** 628–632.
69. MELLO, C.V. 2002. Mapping vocal communication pathways in birds with inducible gene expression. J. Comp. Physiol. A Neuroethol. Sens. Neural Behav. Physiol. **188:** 943–959.
70. LIVINGSTON, F.S., S.A. WHITE & R. MOONEY. 2000. Slow NMDA-EPSCs at synapses critical for song development are not required for song learning in zebra finches. Nat. Neurosci. **3:** 482–488.
71. LU, H.C., E. GONZALEZ & M.C. CRAIR. 2001. Barrel cortex critical period plasticity is independent of changes in NMDA receptor subunit composition. Neuron **32:** 619–634.
72. DOETSCH, F. & C. SCHARFF. 2001. Challenges for brain repair: insights from adult neurogenesis in birds and mammals. Brain Behav. Evol. **58:** 306–322.
73. NOTTEBOHM, F. 2002. Neuronal replacement in adult brain. Brain Res Bull. **57:** 737–749.
74. GAGE, F.H. 2002. Neurogenesis in the adult brain. J. Neurosci. **22:** 612–613.
75. LIEBERMAN, P. 2002. On the nature and evolution of the neural bases of human language. Am. J. Phys. Anthropol. Suppl. **35:** 36–62.
76. FERLAND, R.J. *et al.* 2003. Characterization of Foxp2 and Foxp1 mRNA and protein in the developing and mature brain. J. Comp. Neurol. **460:** 266–279.
77. LAI, C.S. *et al.* 2003. FOXP2 expression during brain development coincides with adult sites of pathology in a severe speech and language disorder. Brain **126:** 2455–2466.
78. TAKAHASHI, K. *et al.* 2003. Expression of Foxp2, a gene involved in speech and language, in the developing and adult striatum. J. Neurosci. Res. **73:** 61–72.
79. TERAMITSU, I. *et al.* 2004. Parallel *FoxP1* and *FoxP2* expression in human and songbird brain predicts functional interaction. J. Neurosci. **24:** 3152–3163.
80. BOTTJER, S.W., E.A. MIESNER & A.P. ARNOLD. 1984. Forebrain lesions disrupt development but not maintenance of song in passerine birds. Science **224:** 901–903.
81. SOHRABJI, F., E.J. NORDEEN & K.W. NORDEEN. 1990. Selective impairment of song learning following lesions of a forebrain nucleus in the juvenile zebra finch. Behav. Neural Biol. **53:** 51–63.
82. SCHARFF, C. & F. NOTTEBOHM. 1991. A comparative study of the behavioral deficits following lesions of various parts of the zebra finch song system: implications for vocal learning. J. Neurosci. **11:** 2896–2913.
83. WILD, J.M. 1997. Functional anatomy of neural pathways contributing to the control of song production in birds. Eur. J. Morphol. **35:** 303–325.
84. MEYER, A. & R. ZARDOYA. 2003. Recent advances in the molecular phylogeny of vertebrates. Annu. Rev. Ecol. Evol. Syst. **34:** 311–338.
85. HAESLER, S. *et al.* 2004. FoxP2 expression in avian vocal learners and non-learners. J. Neuroscience. J. Neurosci. **24:** 3164–3175.
86. BRUCE, H.A. & R.L. MARGOLIS. 2002. FOXP2: novel exons, splice variants, and CAG repeat length stability. Hum. Genet. **111:** 136–144.
87. EVANS, S. 2002. General Discussion II: Amniote Evolution. John Wiley & Sons, Ltd. Chichester.
88. HESSLER, N.A. & A.J. DOUPE. 1999. Social context modulates singing in the songbird forebrain. Nat.Neurosci. **2:** 209–211.
89. WILLIAMS, H. & N. MEHTA. 1999. Changes in adult zebra finch song require a forebrain nucleus that is not necessary for song production. J. Neurobiol. **39:** 14–28.
90. BRAINARD, M.S. & A.J. DOUPE. 2000. Interruption of a basal ganglia-forebrain circuit prevents plasticity of learned vocalizations. Nature **404:** 762–766.
91. NOTTEBOHM, F. *et al.* 1990. Song learning in birds: the relation between perception and production. Phil. Trans. R. Soc London B Biol. Sci. **329:** 115–124.
92. BENTON, S. *et al.* 1998. Anterior forebrain pathway is needed for stable song expression in adult male white-crowned sparrows (*Zonotrichia leucophrys*). Behav. Brain Res. **96:** 135–150.

93. KOBAYASHI, K., H. UNO & K. OKANOYA. 2001. Partial lesions in the anterior forebrain pathway affect song production in adult bengalese finches. Neuroreport **12:** 353–358.
94. HAMBURGER, V. & G.S. HAMILTON. 1951. A series of normal stages in the development of the chick embryo. J. Morphol. **88:** 49–92.
95. BUTLER, H. & B.H.J. JUURLINK. 1987. An atlas for staging mammalian and chick embryos. CRC Press. Florida.
96. VEENMAN, C.L., L. MEDINA & A. REINER. 1997. Avian homologues of mammalian intralaminar, mediodorsal and midline thalamic nuclei: immunohistochemical and hodological evidence. Brain Behav. Evol. **49:** 78–98.
97. MEDINA, L., C.L. VEENMAN & A. REINER. 1997. Evidence for a possible avian dorsal thalamic region comparable to the mammalian ventral anterior, ventral lateral, and oral ventroposterolateral nuclei. J. Comp. Neurol. **384:** 86–108.
98. MEDINA, L. & A. REINER. 1994. Distribution of choline acetyltransferase immunoreactivity in the pigeon brain. J. Comp. Neurol. **342:** 497–537.
99. REINER, A., L. MEDINA & C.L. VEENMAN. 1998. Structural and functional evolution of the basal ganglia in vertebrates. Brain Res. Brain Res. Rev. **28:** 235–285.
100. HEMMINGS, H.C. *et al.* 1995. Signal Transduction in the Striatum: DARPP32, a Molecular Integrator of Multiple Signaling Pathways. Springer. Heidelberg.
101. BANHAM, A.H. *et al.* 2001. The FOXP1 winged helix transcription factor is a novel candidate tumor suppressor gene on chromosome 3p. Cancer Res. **61:** 8820–8829.
102. OLSZEWSKI, J. 1952. The Thalamus of the *Macaca mulatta*: An Atlas for Use with the Stereotaxic Instrument. S. Karger. New York.
103. DOYON, J., V. PENHUNE & L.G. UNGERLEIDER. 2003. Distinct contribution of the cortico-striatal and cortico-cerebellar systems to motor skill learning. Neuropsychologia **41:** 252–262.
104. DOUPE, A.J. & P.K. KUHL. 1999. Birdsong and human speech: common themes and mechanisms. Annu. Rev. Neurosci. **22:** 567–631.
105. FARRIES, M.A. 2001. The oscine song system considered in the context of the avian brain: lessons learned from comparative neurobiology. Brain Behav. Evol. **58:** 80–100.
106. MARIEN, P. *et al.* 2001. The lateralized linguistic cerebellum: a review and a new hypothesis. Brain Lang. **79:** 580–600.
107. KRUPA, D.J. & R.F. THOMPSON. 1997. Reversible inactivation of the cerebellar interpositus nucleus completely prevents acquisition of the classically conditioned eyeblink response. Learn Mem. **3:** 545–556.
108. HYDE, P.S. & E.I. KNUDSEN. 2000. Topographic projection from the optic tectum to the auditory space map in the inferior colliculus of the barn owl. J. Comp. Neurol. **421:** 146–160.

Studying the Song Development Process

Rationale and Methods

O. TCHERNICHOVSKI,[a] T. J. LINTS,[a] S. DERÉGNAUCOURT,[a] A. CIMENSER,[b] AND P.P. MITRA[c]

[a]Department of Biology, City College of the City University of New York, New York, New York, USA

[b]Columbia University, New York, New York, USA

[c]Cold Spring Harbor Laboratories, Cold Spring, New York, USA

ABSTRACT: Current technology makes it possible to measure song development continuously throughout a vocal ontogeny. Here we briefly review some of the problems involved and describe experimental and analytic methods for automatic tracing of vocal changes. These techniques make it possible to characterize the specific methods the bird uses to imitate sounds: an automated song recognition procedure allows continuous song recording, followed by automated sound analysis that partition the song to syllables, extract acoustic features of each syllable, and summarize the entire song development process over time into a single database. The entire song development is then presentable in the form of images or movie clips. These Dynamic Vocal Development (DVD) maps show how each syllable type emerges, and how the bird manipulates syllable features to eventually approximate the model song. Most of the experimental and analytic methods described here have been organized into a software package, which also allows combined neural and sound recording to monitor changes in brain activity as vocal learning occurs. The software is available at http://ofer.sci.ccny.cuny.edu.

KEYWORDS: song development; Dynamic Vocal Development (DVD) maps; sound spectrogram; sound analysis

HISTORICAL PERSPECTIVE: FROM THE SOUND SPECTROGRAM TO AUTOMATED SOUND ANALYSIS

When listening to birdsong, it is immediately apparent that each song has a distinct rhythmic and sometimes even melodic structure. Songs of individual birds in a flock sound similar to each other and differ from those of other flocks. As early as the 18th century, Barrington noted that the songs of cross-fostered birds differed from the species-typical song, suggesting a role for vocal learning.[1] However, until

Address for correspondence: O. Tchernichovski, Department of Biology, City College, CUNY, New York, NY 10031. Voice: 212-650-8540; fax: 212-650-8959.

ofer@ccny.cuny.edu

Software and techniques presented are available at <http://ofer.sci.ccny.cuny.edu>; they can be used freely for basic research on animal communication.

Ann. N.Y. Acad. Sci. 1016: 348–363 (2004). © 2004 New York Academy of Sciences.
doi: 10.1196/annals.1298.031

the late 1950s, there had been no objective way of confirming these observations by physical measurements of the songs themselves. The invention of the sound spectrograph (sonogram) at Bell Laboratories was a significant breakthrough for quantitative investigation of animal vocal behavior.[2] The sonogram transforms a transient stream of sound into a simple static visual image (much like a single frame of film or video) revealing the time-frequency structure of each song syllable. Sonogram images can be measured, analyzed, and compared with one another. This allows the researcher to quantify the degree of similarity between different songs by inspecting (or cross-correlating) sonograms and categorizing song syllables into distinct types. Each song is then treated as a string of symbols, corresponding to syllable types, e.g., a, b, c, d..., and song similarity is estimated by the proportion of shared syllable types across the sonograms of the two songs. The procedure is equally useful in comparing the songs of different birds and that of the same bird at different ages or after control and experimental treatments.

The sonogram has played an essential role in facilitating the mechanistic analysis of birdsong. Much of the pioneering work on song development[3] and on the functional anatomy of the song system[4] relied on sonogram analysis. Indeed, few of the findings in this volume could have been discovered without the invention of the sound spectrogram. Nevertheless, the sonogram has its limitations.

First, the spectral image does not provide simple metrics for characterizing similarity between sounds (except from pure tones). Second, the most prominent features of the sonogram image are not necessarily the most important ones functionally. For example, when observing a spectrogram of human speech, the most apparent features are the harmonic structure and the distinct syllables. However, it is the formants,[d] rather than the harmonic structure, that carry information most important to speech, and it is the language-specific rules, rather than syllable boundaries, that determine the phrasing of words. The raw sound spectrogram is no longer used for analyzing human speech. Instead, modern time-frequency techniques are used to extract perceptually meaningful features that are then further analyzed. In the case of birdsong, however, we usually do not know what the perceptually relevant acoustic features are.

Finally, like the single frame of video, which it resembles, the sonogram presents a static representation of a dynamic process. The sonogram can only capture short-term changes in sound (over time scales of milliseconds), whereas song development is a process occurring over time scales of vocal change ranging from minutes to weeks. The study of that process requires the ability (a) to store large amounts of vocal data, (b) to analyze that data, and (c) to display the results of that analysis as visual representations that highlight key features of the development process as they occur over time. The availability of digital recording and the low cost of digital data storage have now made it possible to meet these requirements.

---

[d]A formant is a peak of frequencies in the spectrum of speech that is caused by the resonance of the vocal track, which enhance some frequencies and dump others. Speech articulation (e.g., moving the tongue or the lips) can change the length of the vocal track, hence, changing the resonance: this is how we produce different vowel sounds (aaa, iii, etc.). (Fucci, D.J. & N.J. Lass. 1999. Fundamentals of Speech Science, 1st edition. Allyn & Bacon. Boston, MA.)

A brief review of some of the techniques developed during the last 20 years to address those limitations is available at <http://ofer.sci.ccny.cuny.edu>, whereas here we present a specific solution that we implemented.

Articulation-based analysis. In human speech, it is possible to extract features of known perceptual function. Such features differ across languages—for example, pitch has phonetic meaning in Chinese, but only prosodic meaning in English. In birdsong, where perception is not well understood, it has been proposed to use articulation-based analysis to extract features with simple relation to production mechanism.[5,6] When considering the motion of an oscillating membrane such as a vocal fold, the most obvious features are the period (pitch) of oscillation and regularity (entropy) of oscillation. These features are also reflected in the sound and can be estimated by calculating pitch and Wiener entropy, respectively. Since sound progresses with time, it also makes sense to measure how pitch changes with time (frequency modulation). Analyzing sounds in terms of such simple features is relatively easy to perform, and the results often suggest an intuitive mechanistic hypothesis (in contrast to spectrographic cross correlation (SCC) and neural-network classification methods).[7–10] In sum, the advantage of our approach is simplicity and interpretability, and its most significant weakness is that the features (and metric system) are "ad hoc," so that some important information about the sound might have been excluded.

AN INTEGRATED SYSTEM FOR STUDYING VOCAL LEARNING

Computation and digital storage cost has decreased tremendously, and with that so have the cost and the efforts involved in collecting and analyzing sound data. A single PC can now handle the recording and the analysis of the entire vocal ontogeny of several birds simultaneously, functioning as a configurable multichannel recorder that recognizes and records songs to digital media and for on-line high-quality analysis of individual songs. However, the design of song storage and analysis systems is a formidable and labor-intensive task, and very few laboratories have been able to invest the time and effort required to design signal analysis tools appropriate to their needs.

There are now several software packages available that can be used for song recognition, sound and brain activity recording, training with operant song playbacks, sound analysis, and song database management. For example, AviSoft (<http://www.avisoft.info/>) is a wonderful integrated recording and analysis application. Other software packages such as Signal (<http://www.engdes.com/>) provide a variety of command-line functions, and Raven (<http://birds.cornell.edu/brp/Raven/>) provides a variety of recording and sound measurement toolboxes. Nevertheless, we found that each software package provides only some of the functions required for managing our vocal learning experiments, and that combining functionality across different software packages is often difficult or impossible (in general, commercial developers do not allow access to their source code). For this reason we decided to develop a new, open code, and noncommercial system designed specifically for the needs of vocal learning experiments—it recognizes and records songs, allows simultaneous recording of neural signal, analyzes features of each sound produced in nearly real-time, trains the birds with operant or passive playbacks, and manages a comprehensive database that allow on-line detection of vocal changes in each bird. This is achieved by constructing descriptive models of song development that show (e.g., as a movie clip) how song features changes, hence complementing the static representations provided by the traditional sonogram with a dynamic representation of vocal output over an extended time scale. Those representations, called Dynamic Vocal Development (DVD) maps stand in relation to the sonogram as a single frame of film does to a motion picture. This system can be easily generalized to support different experimental requirements. The present chapter has two goals. First, we describe the mechanism of automated song recording and sound-analysis technologies that makes it feasible to record the entire vocal ontogeny of an individual bird and to analyze and classify the features of every song syllable produced during song development. Second, because such intensive sampling and analysis of vocal output may seem excessive, we explain the methodological and heuristic advantages that such an approach offers not only to students of song development but for other areas of behavioral neuroscience.

Automated Maintenance of Song Development Experiments

The current version of our recording and analysis system is based upon an experimental unit consisting of a single PC connected to four custom-built soundproof training boxes (FIG. 1A, see <http://ofer.sci.ccny.cuny.edu>). The training regimen for each bird is fully automated and song playbacks are delivered in response to key-pecks (FIG. 1C). Once the bird is placed in the training box, the system records its vocalizations continuously. A song recognition procedure (FIG. 1D) detects and saves the recorded songs, discarding isolated calls and cage noises (for details, see the Sound Analysis user manual at <http://ofer.sci.ccny.cuny.edu>). A few milliseconds later, each recorded song bout is partitioned into syllables (FIG. 1E), then each syllable is analyzed and its time-frequency structure summarized by a set of simple features, such as duration, mean pitch, frequency modulation, etc. These features are promptly saved to a single database file (typically 1–2 million syllables per bird, FIG. 1F).

The Sound Analysis (SA) system (hardware and software) is based on integrating four core functions (FIG. 2): automated multichannel recording, automated operant training regiment, nearly on-line sound analysis, and comprehensive database management. Those core functions are hidden from the user, but they interact with each other at the background—for example, the song detector "knows" when the bird pecked on a key to trigger a playback (and avoid recording it, if so desired).

The function of *training control* is to monitor behaviors and respond appropriately. For example, it responds to a key-peck by delivering a song playback if the training regimen so indicates and registers the key-pecking event to the database. The data card provides many channels and only a few of them are currently in use. The open source-code makes it inexpensive to use those channels as automated on/off switches—for example, to activate a lamp or a buzzer in response to a song syllable, to detect and monitor motion, etc.

Recording control is the most computationally demanding task. It records continuously from four training boxes and, based on song recognition procedures, makes real-time decisions about which recording intervals should be saved for analysis and which should be discarded. The algorithm is based on generic (not bird-specific)

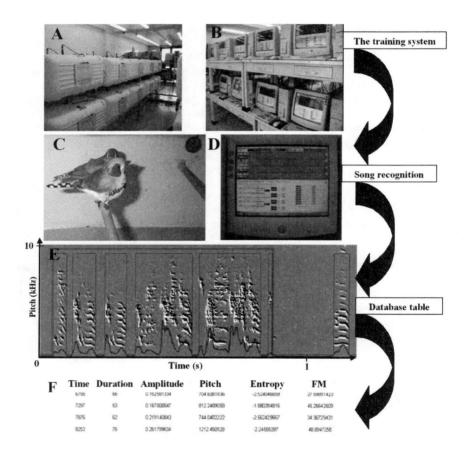

FIGURE 1. The training system. (**A**) Training box configuration (40 boxes). (**B**) Training and recording are fully automated by a network of computers. (**C**) A bird and a plastic model in the training box. (**D**) Each computer controls four training boxes and automatically detects singing. (**E**) Spectral derivatives of an early developmental version of a zebra finch song. Spectral derivatives provide a representation of song that is similar but superior to the traditional sound spectrogram. Instead of power spectrum versus time, we present directional derivatives (changes of power) on a gray scale so that the detection of frequency contours is locally optimized. This is particularly useful for the analysis of juvenile song. Songs are automatically analyzed and partitioned to syllables (green outlines) and bouts (red outlines). (**F**) The acoustic features of each syllable are saved in a database table; each row summarizes features of one syllable.

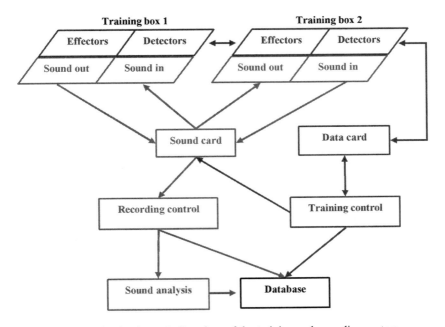

FIGURE 2. A schematic flowchart of the training and recording system.

considerations and works very well for detecting songs during all developmental stages. Each song bout is saved to a separate sound file and attributed with a serial number, bird ID, date, and time-stamps. *Recording control* can also interact with *training control* to cue responses to recorded vocalizations, in nearly real-time, although a highly precise response (such as a delayed auditory feedback) might require additional programming to bypass constraints imposed by the Microsoft Windows® operating system. In principle, a single computer can record and process sound from at least eight sound channels, but we are currently only handling four. Additional channels could be used to control more training boxes or, alternatively, to simultaneously record neural or peripheral data from the same bird. For this purpose, recording channels can be set to trigger each other—for example, a singing event can trigger simultaneous recording from both auditory and neural channels (which are "slaved" to the sound-recording channel).

The function of *Sound Analysis* is to perform on-line measurements to allow song detection and subsequent measurements for parsing the stream of sound to syllables and computing acoustic features of each syllable. The function of the *database* component is to provide easy access to data, including pointers to raw sound data, tables of syllable features, and key-pecking activity, the training protocol and the hatching date of birds, and so forth. We use the mySQL® database server, which is free, opencode application. Several measures, including the amount of daily singing, accumulated key pecking, and DVD-maps (see below) are presented as graphs and are updated in nearly real-time.

Hardware requirements of the system are modest, consisting of a standard PC (~$1,000), a multichannel soundcard (~$400), and an optional data card (~$100). Training boxes are custom designed from coolers and include an airflow system, a microphone, a plastic bird model equipped with a speaker and two keys.[11] A detailed description of how to build the hardware (including the training boxes) and how to use the software is available at <http://ofer.sci.ccny.cuny.edu>. The purpose of the documentation below is to provide a simple description of how hardware and software interact in our system, which is of particular interest to readers who might wish to extend it, e.g., to the processing of neural data.

DYNAMIC VOCAL DEVELOPMENT MAPS

With the entire vocal ontogeny of a bird on file, tracing vocal changes over time becomes straightforward, because we can visualize the raw data of an entire vocal ontogeny in a single image. To demonstrate the power of this approach, we implemented a method suggested by Janata[9] to examine the distribution of syllable durations during song development. An adult zebra finch song is composed of several different syllables; in some cases, each different song syllable has a unique duration. Therefore, plotting a histogram of durations for all syllables produced during a day (about 50,000 syllables) reveals several peaks. Although the histogram is constructed blindly for all sounds produced, it is easy to associate each peak with a specific syllable (FIG. 3A). For instance, syllable 2 is about 140-ms long, so we will consider all sounds around this peak as renditions of syllable 2. How can we know this for sure? We can examine other features such as mean pitch and verify that all sounds that are about 140-ms long have similar pitch, similar frequency modulation, etc. We will elaborate on that shortly, but let us first present a song development image based on syllable duration alone by revealingly plotting duration histograms throughout ontogeny.

Each row in FIGURE 3B presents a daily histogram of syllable durations produced by the same bird, for every day from day 35 until day 90. Overall, this bird produced over a million syllables during its development and all of them are used to construct FIGURE 3B. As shown, every peak presented in FIGURE 3A has turned into a portion of a ridge that can easily be traced back in time. Starting with syllable 1, we can see that the ridge that corresponds to this syllable can be traced back until day 44. Note that training started on day 43, so we can conclude that this syllable type emerged within a single day (this bird was a good learner). The ridge that corresponds to syllable 3 can also be traced and, as shown on about day 55, it takes a turn to the right (when traced bottom-up). This turn indicates a smooth increase in duration, demonstrating a vocal change (time warping) that occurred for this syllable. Finally, examining the ridges from day 35 onward shows that there is no apparent continuity between ridges that appear prior to training and those that appear after training starts.

It is easy to see how additional features, such as mean pitch, can be added to the development map shown in FIGURE 3B, which is the simplest example of a Dynamic Vocal Development (DVD) map. DVD-maps are generated automatically from the syllable database and can be updated in real time, as vocal learning occurs. The representation is robust because it is built on a very large amount of data. Even though parsing the emerging song is not 100% accurate, histograms based on this amount of

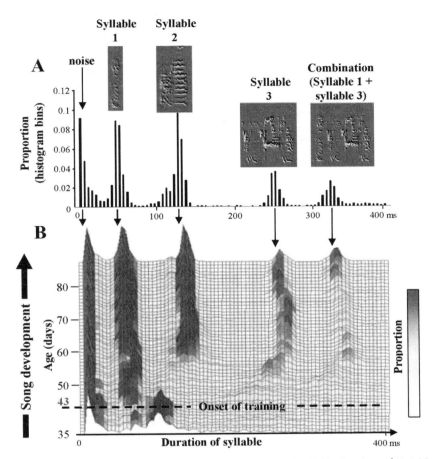

FIGURE 3. Dynamic Vocal Development (DVD) map of syllable durations. (**A**) A histogram of syllable durations in an adult bird. Each peak can be associated with a syllable type of unique duration. (**B**) To trace the evolution of these syllables during song development, we plot histograms of the entire vocal ontogeny. Each row represents the histogram of syllable durations during one developmental day. We can trace each syllable type to an early stage of song development since syllable duration has changed smoothly during song development.

data are insensitive to moderate levels of measurement noise. Inaccuracy in parsing sometimes results in two, partially overlapping versions of syllable boundaries. For example, for a song with three syllables [a, b, c], parsing may occasionally fail to separate syllable a from b, forming joint cluster [a,b] instead of [a] and [b]. Such combined clusters are easy to identify and one can then parse and reanalyze them.

Extending the DVD-map to include more features requires additional dimensions, but FIGURE 3B is already a three-dimensional (3-D) surface. There are several means of adding features to an image without additional spatial dimensions, e.g., using time as a dimension to turn the still image into a movie. To describe how such a movie is constructed, we start with an illustrative two-dimensional (2D) representation of the sounds produced by the same adult male shown in FIGURE 3. Each point displayed in FIGURE 4A plots the duration versus the mean frequency modulation of all syllables produced by the bird during day 90 posthatching. The peaks we observed in the duration histogram shown in FIGURE 3A are presented as *clusters* in FIGURE 4A. Those clusters can be detected automatically by means of cluster analysis (FIG. 4B). Note that the blue and green clusters [shown in color online] are of different frequency modulation (FM) but of similar duration; hence, the ridge in FIGURE 3B that corresponded to syllable 2 was contaminated with another cluster. We can now observe the residuals (FIG. 4C) to see that no additional clusters are available and can examine other features of the clusters (FIG. 4D–G). As shown, we still find the same number of clusters, but on the y axis we can see that the distance between clusters has changed. Some clusters are now more distant from each other

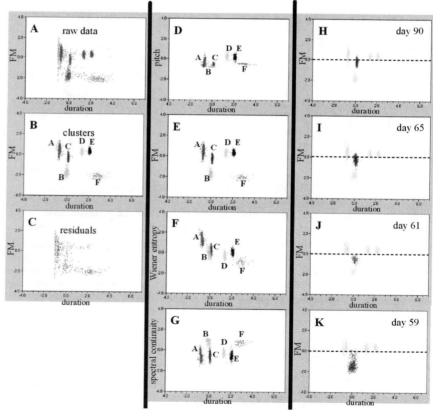

FIGURE 4. (A) A plot of duration versus FM, for each syllable produced during day 90 in a bird; (B) 10-dimensional cluster analysis of the same data, each color (color shown online) stands for a cluster; (C) the leftover residuals of unclustered data; (D–G) different projections of the same clusters; (H–K) tracking a single cluster.

(e.g., G and F), and other clusters are closer to each other (e.g., B and D). Thus, FIG-URE 4D–E can be thought of as different rotations of the high-dimensional image of the clusters. All the projections are consistent with the categorization to six clusters, and it seems reasonable to assume that each cluster represents a distinct type of sound. Nevertheless, the blue and green clusters are close to each other—are they perhaps related? To examine this question, we will have to examine how the image of clusters evolved in time.

The clusters produced from stereotyped adult zebra finch male songs are stably located in these 2D images. Playing a sequence of histogram snapshots, where each

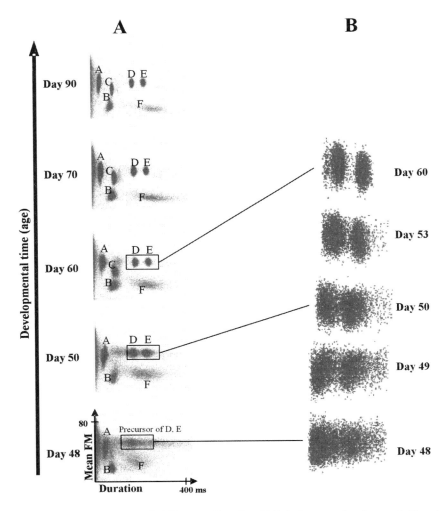

FIGURE 5. Snapshots of DVD-maps (duration, FM) during song development. Six syllable clusters are identified on day 90.

frame corresponds to a narrow time-window, therefore produces a rather static movie clip of sounds produced by the mature bird. When applied to vocal development data, however, such movie clips display very interesting dynamics, revealing the emergence of clusters corresponding to sounds of an imitation. Snapshots of an illustrative movie are presented in FIGURE 4H–K; in those snapshots, the automated cluster analysis routine is attempting to trace the blue cluster only. As shown, the blue and green clusters indeed emerged from the same prototype cluster. FIGURE 5 shows additional snapshots showing how syllables D and E also emerged from the same raw material (the entire movie available at <http://ofer.sci.ccny.cuny.edu>). Finally, we can see the emergence of song-syntax by plotting trajectories that connect one syllable to the next (FIG. 6). In most birds, we observed rapid changes in syntax between days 60 and 70 posthatch.

Overall, clusters emerge, divide, and "move" during song development. Since the features we use are simple, it is easy to interpret such events. For example, by observing DVD-maps of different features, we may detect that a syllable became longer, higher in pitch, or lower in frequency modulation. Each one of these vocal changes can be measured to assess the rate and extent of that change. Based on this type of DVD-map representation, it is possible to examine possible dependencies between different types of vocal change and how many different vocal changes the bird can manage, simultaneously and sequentially, during the imitation process.

DVD-maps represent song development using two complementary approaches: the formal approach involves performing cluster analysis across song development, taking all features into account, whereas the informal—yet equally important approach—is the graphic display in the form of movie clips. None of those approaches would have worked unless we had the entire song development on file. For example, we need about 500 syllables to generate a frame of a DVD-map, but because during each day the bird produces tens of thousands of syllables, each frame is very close in time to the next one. Therefore, each frame is very similar to the former one, obtaining a smooth trajectory of cluster evolution. The DVD movie clips are used to detect vocal changes in real time and to validate, by visual inspection, that the automated procedure did indeed trace the same cluster. A detailed account of this will be presented elsewhere (see <http://ofer.sci.ccny.cuny.edu>), but this chapter will be incomplete without some further elaboration on using a variety of graphic methods to explore changes in syllable morphology and song-syntax development with DVD-maps.

FIGURE 7 [color shown online] presents an example where color has been used to represent the progress of developmental time, with earlier-produced sounds represented by blue dots and later produced sounds by red dots. Over time, the cluster became shorter and higher in pitch. A similar sort of graphic approach can be used to display the history of cluster emergence over longer time frames by using colors to represent different time scales. For example, in FIGURE 8A [color shown online], the feature values of previously produced sounds are plotted in yellow, providing a long-term memory of cluster position. Overlaying this, the momentary production of sounds (in a user-specified window of time) is plotted in red. Therefore, the image in FIGURE 8A (a movie snapshot) provides both the history and momentary state of a cluster. In the case of FIGURE 8A, the momentary state shown is near the end of vocal ontogeny (at 90 days), and so the red dots fall on the clusters that have developed by this time. This type of movie may also be played in reverse, keeping the memory on. In this case, the yellow dots now represent the final target state that clus-

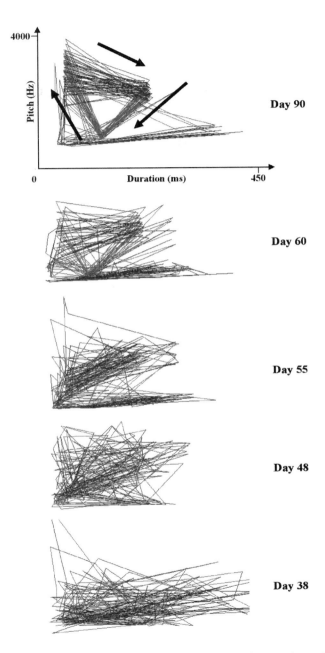

FIGURE 6. Snapshots of DVD-maps showing syntax development in one bird. Instead of plotting the clusters, we plot the trajectories that connect them to illustrate the sequential order of syllables within the song bout. Trajectories to the right (a sequence of a shorter-duration syllable followed by a longer-duration syllable) are denoted by blue lines and trajectories to the left by red lines (color shown online).

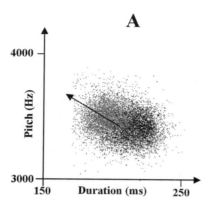

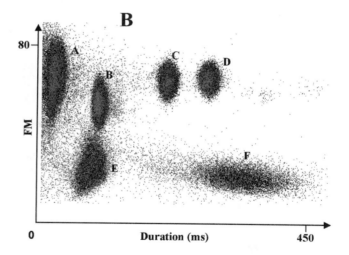

FIGURE 7. Color coding time in DVD-maps [color shown online]. Earlier-produced sounds are represented by blue dots and later-produced sounds by red dots. (**A**) Color representation of developmental time. The *arrow* indicates the direction of the movement of the cluster during one week of song development. (**B**) Color representation of circadian time: syllables denoted by red color occurred during the morning, whereas the blue dots stand for syllables produced during noon time of the same day.

ters will achieve, and the red dots represent sounds produced during an earlier window of time. In FIGURE 8B the yellow cluster on the left represents a sound that has not yet formed. By viewing this DVD-map movie, running the window of momentary state forward or backward in time, it is possible to see when, and how quickly, this time-warping occurred.

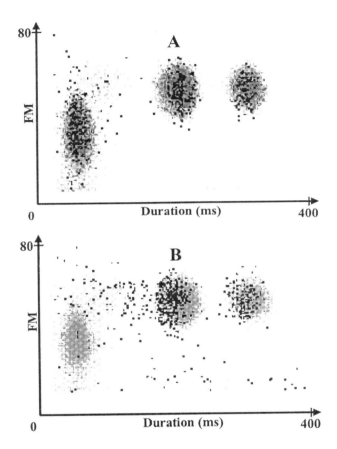

FIGURE 8. Representing different time scales on DVD-maps [color shown online]. **(A)** The feature values of previously produced sounds are plotted in yellow, providing a long-term memory of cluster position; the momentary production of sounds is plotted in red. **(B)** The yellow cluster on the left represents a sound that has not yet formed. The red dots (showing the momentary state at 60 days) indicate that the other two clusters have already been generated by 60 days, although the position of the red dots is displaced to the left, indicating that a time warping occurred for these sounds between day 60 and day 90.

CONCLUSIONS

Understanding the rules that govern development—whether of cells, circuits, or songs—using only static images is like trying to intuit the rules of soccer from examination of hundreds of snapshots taken at different times during different games. Developmental biologists are now using filming techniques to study the dynamic processes underlying such events as axonal path finding and synapse formation. As one investigator put it, "humans can take in lots of visual information at once and extract patterns from it; complex images and movies provide such information."[12]

We have applied an analogous strategy to the study of song development, creating sets of graphic representations that can be used to present song data from an entire vocal ontogeny. The methods we used are based on simple features of sound and so provide intuitive ways of exploring vocal changes in a large data set. Our system uses the sonogram image, which is much more detailed, to further explore the details of vocal changes, once DVD-maps have captured and characterized them.[14] With the approaches presented here, detecting vocal changes is now much easier and one can follow, more or less in real time, how learning progresses throughout each day. While our approach has focused on song development, its utility for other aspects of birdsong research is readily apparent. For example, most studies on the effects of experimental manipulations, such as lesions, upon stereotyped adult song production have used only sporadic sampling of the effect of an experimental treatment, for example, before and after comparisons, using a limited number of endpoints. The approach outlined in this chapter would allow the experimenter to follow the unfolding of changes in song structures from its initial disruption to its eventual recovery—shedding light on both processes. DVD-maps updated in real time could be particularly useful in the context of neural recording or molecular experiments, where data or tissue collection must be timed to coincide with particular events during the vocal learning process. Extending these tools further, one could attempt to generalize the DVD-maps to integrate, within a single accessible display, correlated data on song structures, neural firing, and behavioral state. The methods described in this chapter should facilitate the extension of such approaches to a wide range of problems in birdsong neurobiology.

ACKNOWLEDGMENT

This work was supported by a Public Health Service Grant DC004722-05 to O.T. and by a National Institutes of Health RCMI grant to CCNY.

REFERENCES

1. BARRINGTON, D. 1773. Experiments and observations on the singing of birds. Phil. Trans. R. Soc. Lond. **63:** 249–291.
2. THORPE, W.H. 1958. The learning of song patterns by birds, with especial reference to the song of the chaffinch *Fringilla coelebs*. Ibis **100:** 535–570.
3. CATCHPOLE, C.K. & P.J.B. SLATER. 1995. Bird Song: Biological Themes and Variations. Cambridge University Press. Cambridge.
4. HAUSER, M. & M. KONISHI. 1999. The Design of Animal Communication. MIT Press. Cambridge, MA.
5. HO, C.E., B. PESARAN, M.S. FEE & P.P. MITRA. 1998. Characterization of the structure and variability of zebra finch song elements. Proc. Joint Symp. Neural Computat. **5:** 76–83.
6. TCHERNICHOVSKI, O., F. NOTTEBOHM, C.E. HO, *et al.* 2000. A procedure for an automated measurement of song similarity. Anim. Behav. **59:** 1167–1176.
7. BAKER, M.C. & D.M. LOGUE. 2003. Population differentiation in a complex bird sound: a comparison of three bioacoustical analysis procedures. Ethology **109:** 223–242.

8. CORTOPASSI, K.A. & J.W. BRADBURY. 2000. The comparison of harmonically rich sounds using spectrographic cross-correlation and principal coordinates analysis. Bioacoustics **11:** 89–127.
9. JANATA, P. 2001. Quantitative assessment of vocal development in the zebra finch using self-organizing neural networks. J. Acoust. Soc. Am. **110:** 2593–2603.
10. DERÉGNAUCOURT, S., J.C. GUYOMARC'H & V. RICHARD. 2001. Classification of hybrid crows in quail using artificial neural networks. Behav. Process **56:** 103–112.
11. TCHERNICHOVSKI, O., T. LINTS, P.P MITRA & F. NOTTEBOHM. 1999. Vocal imitation in zebra finches is inversely related to model abundance. Proc. Natl. Acad. Sci. USA **96:** 12901–12904.
12. BECKMAN, M. 2003. Play-by-play imaging rewrites cells' rules. Science **300:** 76–77.

Song Development: In Search of the Error-Signal

S. DERÉGNAUCOURT,[a] P.P. MITRA,[b] O. FEHÉR,[a] K.K. MAUL,[a] T.J. LINTS,[a] AND O. TCHERNICHOVSKI[a]

[a]Department of Biology, City College, City University of New York, New York, New York 10031, USA

[b]Cold Spring Harbor Laboratories, Cold Spring Harbor, New York 11724, USA

ABSTRACT: Song development provides an opportunity to study the mechanisms of vocal learning dynamically at molecular, cellular and systems levels, and across time scales ranging from minutes to months. To exploit these opportunities one needs to identify appropriate units, types and time scales of vocal change in nearly real time. The previous chapter by Tchernikovski *et al.* in this volume described techniques that make this research strategy feasible by allowing us to observe the song learning process through a "temporal microscope" with variable degrees of resolution. In this chapter we summarize some of the new observations and raise hypotheses about the learning strategy of the bird. We focus on inferences that can be drawn from behavioral observations to the nature and complexity of the instructive signal that guides the vocal change (error-signal). We examine two effects: i) the emergence of syllable types and ii) changes in features within a syllable type. We found that different features of the same syllable change during different and sometimes disjointed developmental windows. We discuss the possibility that song imitation is achieved by correcting partial errors, and that features of those partial errors change adaptively during development, perhaps concurrently with changes in perception and in motor proficiency. Those hypotheses can be best examined by across levels investigation, starting from identifying critical moments in song development and recording of articulatory dynamics and neural patterns when only a few features of specific syllables undergo rapid changes. Such investigation could relate behavioral events to brain mechanisms that guide song learning from moment-to-moment and across extended periods.

KEYWORDS: song development; vocal production; auditory perception

INTRODUCTION

Vocal learning proceeds in two (sometimes overlapping) phases.[1] First, the bird memorizes a song it has heard (sensory learning) and then it modifies its vocal out-

Address for correspondence: S. Derégnaucourt, Department of Biology, City College, City University of New York, 138th Street and Convent Avenue, New York, NY 10031. Voice: 212-650-8608; fax: 212-650-8959.

sderegna@sci.ccny.cuny.edu; <http://ofer.sci.ccny.cuny.edu>

Ann. N.Y. Acad. Sci. 1016: 364–376 (2004). © 2004 New York Academy of Sciences.
doi: 10.1196/annals.1298.036

put to gradually approximate the remembered song model (sensorimotor learning).[2] Some songbirds are age-limited learners,[3] that is, vocal learning occurs more readily during specific stages of development.[1,4] In the zebra finch, the sensory phase of the sensitive period occurs from day 25–65 post hatch and the sensory-motor sensitive period for song learning occurs between days 30–90.[5] Immelmann made careful observations of zebra finch song development and found that at about day 30, the young bird produces its first subsong, with sounds that appear vague, without a distinct frequency structure of the syllables. About two weeks later, the bird starts producing structured syllables (with identifiable spectral structure); some are already similar to syllables of the "tutor" bird, although, the order of syllables is not yet similar to that of the tutor song. Finally, between days 70–90, the order of syllable (song syntax) becomes stereotyped and the song motif fully crystallizes. Thereafter, the zebra finch rarely changes its song motif.[5]

Some features of song development appear to be relatively independent of sensory guidance. For example, birds that are kept socially isolated go through subsong and plastic song stages.[6] Nevertheless, the timing and the outcome of song development are strongly affected by hearing,[2,7] social factors,[8] hormonal state[9] and nutrition.[10] Even the end of the sensitive period is not determined solely by age, but may be influenced by hormones and experience.[11] For example, castration [1] or withholding exposure to the song model[12–14] can delay the closure of the sensitive period for song learning.

Until recently, it has been sufficient to describe song development in terms of qualitative stages as summarized above. However, recent observations of fine-tuned neural activity during song, including the description of a temporal code for song generation,[15] the "rehearsal" of song during sleep,[16] and the analysis of dynamic changes in auditory responses to songs[17,18] require a correspondingly finely tuned analysis of the developmental process. For example, in the adult zebra finch, the activity of premotor HVC neurons resemble an array of accurate clocks, with each neuron "ticking" only once per song motif.[15] Song-time is thought to be explicitly encoded by the sparse propagation of ticks across those neurons (as in a music box), but how does this clock function during song development? What happens to it when song syntax changes, or when motif duration gradually increases? Being able to identify (or even trigger) the appropriate vocal changes and then trace the progression of such changes during short time scales is a prerequisite for answering such questions and for understanding the role of HVC in song learning.

More generally, studying how the neural code evolves during vocal learning requires dynamic measurements of song development, identifying moment-to-moment changes in vocal activity and simultaneous monitoring of correlated neural signals. Furthermore, one of the most important open questions in vocal learning is how sensory-motor conversion is achieved, namely, what are the features of the instructive (error) signal that guides vocal changes toward the model? At the motor end, measurements of vocal changes and of the articulatory and neural patterns that give rise to those changes are essential, but not yet fully explored. In this chapter we discuss the problem of identifying momentary instances of vocal changes and of relating such events to the overall process of matching a song model. We attempt to relate this methodological problem to the nature of error correction (via auditory feedback).

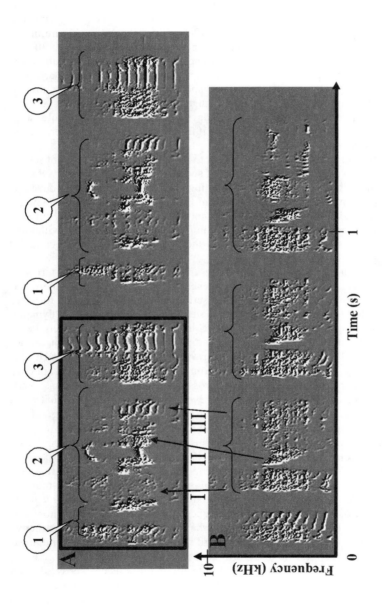

FIGURE 1. A: Spectral derivatives of the mature song of a bird, which is a close copy of the model song broadcast. Numerals show syllable boundaries. *Black rectangle* indicates the boundaries of the motif unit. **B:** the song of the same bird on training day 4 (when 47 days old). The brackets show the correspondence between early prototype sounds and the final structure of syllable 2. Note that the last rendition differs from the other two.

EVALUATING THE ACOUSTIC ERROR

During the sensory-motor phase of song learning the bird compares some memory of the song model to the auditory feedback of its own emerging song. Detection and reduction of acoustic differences can then be achieved,[19,20] but what are the specific song features that are being compared?

FIGURE 1A presents the mature song (day 100 post hatch) of a bird that achieved a perfect copy of a song model. FIGURE 1B presents an earlier version of the song of the same bird when 47 days old, 4 days after the onset of training with song playbacks.[21,22] As shown, the young bird already produces frequent back-to-back renditions of a statistically stable syllable type (we define "type" as an identifiable cluster in the distribution of syllable features, as elaborated in the methods chapter by Tchernichovski *et al.* in this volume). Tracking the imitation trajectory of this syllable from training day 4 to the conclusion of song development (as documented in the methods chapter) confirmed that it gave rise to a copy of model syllable 2. How can we estimate the acoustic error (in reference to the target syllable morphology) on training day 4? Comparing the prototype to the target, we can say that i) the first high-pitch sound of the song model is not present in the prototype (FIG. 1, arrow I), ii) the second high-pitch sound in the prototype (arrow II) is much too short with a down-sweep instead of a stable tone, iii) the last part of the prototype (arrow III) is still unstructured and iv) the duration of some of the prototypes is too short. We could continue to list mismatches, but is this useful? Do vocal changes occur by computing a global account of all acoustic differences between two complex sounds? Alternatively, are only "partial errors" corrected at any given time? If so, what could be the units, references, and features of such partial error estimates?

Obviously, it does not make sense to list mismatches arbitrarily as we did above, but experimentally we can examine what parts and what features of the song the bird changes at any given time during song development. Although we do not know how the features that we measure might correspond to those perceived and manipulated by the bird, we can hope that if the error-signal is indeed complex (e.g., including several partial error estimates), our features will capture some of this complexity, and detect natural time scales of different vocal changes that might be "hidden" in the imitation trajectory. Alternatively, if the error-signal is simple, we should not be able to detect a hidden structure in the developmental trajectory by looking at different features.

TIME SCALES OF VOCAL CHANGES

We now examine how different song features change during development, attempting to reveal the scope of vocal changes in song-time and in developmental-time.[23] We present vocal changes in units of daily change, but the same techniques can be used to explore finer time scales (down to several minutes).

The techniques of tracking clusters are described in the methods chapter (Tchernichovski *et al.*, this volume). Briefly: we record the entire song development, partition the sound to syllable units and calculate simple features (such as mean pitch and frequency modulation) of each syllable. We then examine imitation trajectories by identifying clusters (types) of syllables and tracing each cluster back throughout

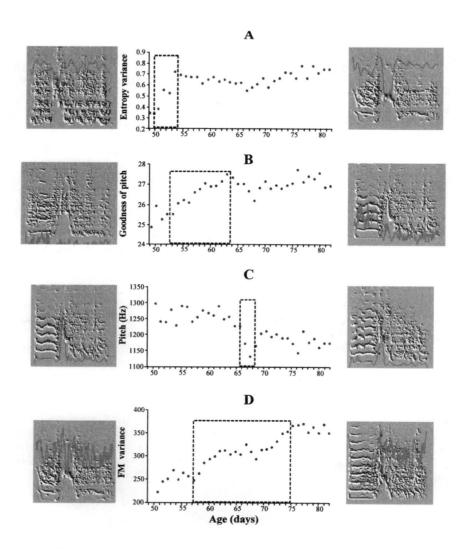

FIGURE 2. Time scales of vocal changes within one syllable type during song development: the middle panel show the mean daily value of syllable features. The dotted rectangle encloses the shortest developmental time that spans 80% of the overall change. Spectral derivatives of the syllable prior to change are shown on the left, and spectral derivatives of the syllable after the change are shown on the right. The curves show the actual values of the feature during a syllable. Note that each dot in the middle panel is an average obtained across all syllables produced during a day (typically 20-60 thousand). **A:** changes in Wiener entropy variance; **B:** changes of goodness of pitch; **C:** changes of pitch; **D:** changes of frequency modulation. (Color version of this figure appears online.)

song development. All those steps are performed automatically, with the exception of cluster analysis, which is also done automatically but under visual supervision (for details see Sound Analysis Pro, User Manual <http://ofer.sci.ccny.cuny.edu>). We study the evolution of each cluster by plotting mean daily values of acoustic features. Those daily values are calculated by averaging all of the syllables of that cluster produced during each given day (usually ranging between 1,000–5,000). We can now examine the curve of feature values and find the shortest developmental window that spans a large portion (say 80%) of the overall developmental change. This provides an estimate of the beginning and conclusion of a change in the value of a specific feature of a particular syllable.

FIGURE 2A (middle panel) presents daily values of a feature called "Wiener entropy variance". The dotted rectangle encloses the shortest interval that captures 80% of the change. As shown, the mean value of this feature increased rapidly between days 52–55 and changed little thereafter. How can we interpret this change? The variance of Wiener entropy captures the intra-syllabic transitions from tonal to broadband sounds. Such transitions often become more pronounced as the syllable matures. To see what exactly happened between days 52–55, we examine sonograms of this syllable just before the change, on day 51 (left panel), and compare those to sonograms obtained just after the change, on day 55 (right panel). As shown, the range (variance) of Wiener entropy increased because the first part of the syllable (particularly high-pitch note) became more tonal, causing a drop of Wiener entropy values only during the first part of this syllable.

FIGURE 2B shows how a different feature of the same syllable changes with time. *Goodness of pitch* captures the transition to harmonic frequency structure. The significant observation is that the time scale of this vocal change is very different and much longer (days 53–64) than that of Wiener entropy variance. Note also that the change can be seen throughout the syllable (the entire curve appears higher on the right panel). The next feature, *pitch*, shows rapid changes—but much later—from days 67–69 (FIG. 2C), whereas *FM* (FIG. 2D) changes very slowly (days 58–75).

Preliminary analysis of daily feature curves in 12 birds suggests to us that the example shown above is representative. Although the features we use are not orthogonal, we see in every single syllable a few uncorrelated curves that can be related to distinctive vocal changes such as time-warping, insertion of stop,[23] period-doubling[22] et cetera. Some of those changes are very rapid, whereas others are slow. Different vocal changes occur during different developmental times, and they are confined to specific parts of the song. That is, we observed no tight correlation between the occurrences of different vocal changes within a syllable, or between the occurrences of similar vocal changes across syllables.

Overall, our findings support the model of partial errors, but not conclusively. An additional question is whether different trajectories arise from a differential effect of motor development on the features that we measure. For example, as motor proficiency develops, the bird can better stabilize the frequency structure of harmonic stacks, but this should not indicate that something has changed in the error-signal. However, as a minimum, motor proficiency imposes constraints on the sounds that a bird can produce at a certain developmental stage. Behavioral observations alone cannot tell us if the error-signal succumbs to those constraints, but the ability to identify such events is only a first step, and a handle for further articulatory and brain-level investigations of the sensory-motor conversion.

Zebra Finch

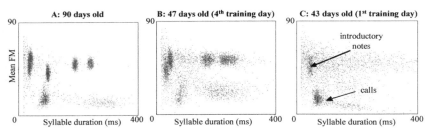

Human

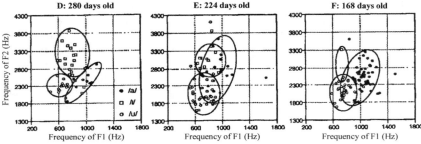

FIGURE 3. A–C: snapshots of DVD-maps [duration, FM] during song development. The production space of the subsong is continuous with only one or two vague clusters of simple calls, whereas song-like syllables do not form clusters. Within a few days after the onset of training, the production space takes the form of clusters. Note that even the very early clusters correspond to those of the mature song. **D–F:** categorical perception of speech in formant frequency space. (Reprinted with permission from Kuhl and Meltzoff.[25] Copyright 1996, Acoustical Society of America.) The speech sounds fill up the space rather smoothly, but biases in perceptual sensitivity create virtual boundaries between categories. (Color version of this figure appears online.)

PERCEPTUAL PLASTICITY AND MOTOR PROFICIENCY

We started this chapter by asking how an early version of the song can be compared to the target song model (FIG. 1) and showed that song development can tell us the parts and features of the song that change during a specific "moment" of song development. We now ask more generally: what does it take for the bird to compare its own song (BOS) to the target song model during different developmental stages? In the example of BOS on day 4 (FIG. 1), the bird already produces repeated prototypes. Those prototypes are entities, on the production level, that the bird can potentially compare to the target. To quantify this notion, we plot the distribution of syllable features in the mature song (when a nearly-perfect model match has been achieved) and compare it to the distribution of syllable features on training day 4 (FIG. 3A–B). As shown, even the distribution of two features (*duration* versus *FM*) show robust clusters (or types) in the mature song (FIG. 3A). On training day 4 (FIG. 3B), we also see clusters, albeit sparser, and those clusters are clearly related to those of the mature song. We therefore conclude that on training day 4, it should be possible for the bird to compare features of its prototype syllable types to those of the target syllable types. However, this is no longer the case on training day 1 (FIG. 3C), on which BOS syllables are unstable and show no distinct types (except for calls), but sparse and continuous distribution. We only plot two features, but we see a similar effect across all features we can measure. Since aside from simple calls, we cannot detect any statistically stable clusters of sounds, we wonder how the bird can compare its sounds to those of the model.

In essence, what we see in FIGURE 3B–C is a transition from what has been traditionally called a subsong, to a plastic song structure.[4] This transition has remarkable dynamics that can be observed in nearly real-time using Dynamic Vocal Development (DVD)-maps (see Tchernichovski *et al.*, this volume), and we often see its progression on time scales of several minutes. The vast majority (and often all) of the clusters observed early on will evolve into copies of song-model syllables, that is, there are only few dead-ends. This observation is still preliminary, but it does suggest that the appearance of any one cluster indicates a significant commitment the bird is making during the very early stages of song learning, and that clusters (as entities) are not subject to major pruning. As noted, once the bird can produce sounds of distinct and stable types, it is easy to imagine how it may compare features of each type to those of model (template) syllables, but it is less clear how the bird can evaluate its performance prior to the emergence of distinct types.

Interestingly, changing motor patterns of vocal production for better approximation of an acoustic target is reminiscent of another example of vocal learning, that of speech learning and language emergence in humans.[24] FIGURE 3D–F present developmental changes in the distribution of formant frequencies in human infants.[25] As shown, both vocal learners, songbirds and humans, express a progression from generally unstructured, indistinct sounds to highly structured, acoustically complex, and motorically difficult sounds.[24] Despite many gross differences between human speech and birdsong, in the crudest behavioral description, development of vocal production appears to follow a basic principle of organization, from unclustered to a clustered distribution. How can we explain this transition? In human speech, there are interesting correlates on both motor and perceptual levels: in the human infant, vocal production before 6–8 months is severely limited by maturation of the vocal tract and articulators, that is, physical and peripheral constraints restrict accurate production, but the difficulty of obtaining detailed recording in early stages of speech development limits the progress of research in this area. Much more is known at the perceptual level: in a nutshell, during the first year of life infants become perceptually "tuned" to their linguistic environment.[26] The degree of coupling between dynamic changes in perceptions and production of speech is not yet known, but song development provides an opportunity to test, in a simple and more traceable system, how perceptual changes might guide vocal development as elaborated below.

The practicality of matching specific model syllables to the unstable and unclustered sounds of the subsong suggests that computing a complex error signal is not very useful at the very early stage of song learning. Indeed, even a while after global syllable features (first and second order statistics, as shown in the feature distribution map in FIG. 3) had stabilized, the fine-grained syllable morphology (as shown in the sonogram) is highly variable, suggesting that the early clusters are a very rough approximation of model sounds. We therefore suggest that for generating

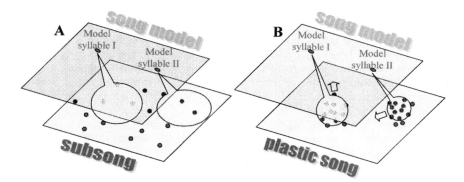

FIGURE 4. Comparing features of template sounds to features of the bird's own song during **A:** subsong stage where distribution of features is sparse and "search space" for even rough similarity must be broad, and **B:** during plastic song, where features of sounds that belong to distinct types can be compared to features of model syllables. The bird might then attribute error terms (*arrows*) for each cluster. Features are shown arbitrarily on a plane (we do not know what are the units and dimensionality of perceived sounds). Color version of this figure appears online.)

clusters, the bird needs to have broad perceptual tuning, perhaps centered on some global features (e.g., duration) of specific model sounds (FIG. 4A). Clusters can then emerge as a result of simple reinforcement learning, making sounds that are grossly similar to model syllables more likely.[27,28] Once the bird established clusters, the perceptual requirements are likely to change (FIG. 4B): now the bird can start "moving" each cluster, using increasingly sharper perceptual tuning, to match the fine details of model syllable features.

Although FIGURE 4 is purely speculative, judging by overwhelming evidences from a variety of sensory-motor systems,[29–31] it seems likely that development,[32] auditory experience,[33,34] and motor proficiency affect song perception, which can then affect the features of the error-signal. There is indirect evidence for perceptual plasticity during song learning: Nick has recently showed that auditory HVC activity is tuned to the song model in the awake bird, and to the BOS during sleep.[35] Remarkably, the tuning to the BOS changes dynamically during development to match the current versions of BOS.[17,18,36] Interesting clues for an effect of early experience on the metrics of song perception were recently obtained from EEG measurements of auditory evoked responses to playbacks of song syllables. Auditory evoked responses to song syllables have distinct patterns, those patterns vary across syllable types so that the pattern of the evoked response can tell us what syllable the bird has heard. Comparing patterns of evoked responses across birds showed that birds trained by the same tutor have similar auditory responses to playbacks of the same syllables, whereas birds trained by different tutors show much more variable responses to playbacks of the same sounds (those are all unfamiliar syllables).[33,34] This finding suggests that early auditory experience has a major role in shaping auditory perception. It will be interesting to see if critical moments of song development, (e.g., when clusters emerge), is also the time when the effect of experience on auditory perception comes about.

MOTOR CONTROL AND SONG LEARNING

The error signal is only useful to the extent that it can be converted to an appropriate motor action (articulatory gesture) that addresses the error. This is obviously an issue during the subsong stage (as we discussed above), but also later on, after the bird had achieved some motor proficiency. The bird's vocal organ (syrinx) is a complicated device, and when the bird performs a gentle articulatory gesture, it might experience abrupt and unexpected changes in sound structure.[37] Such nonlinear effects might sustain beyond the boundaries of the sound that the bird attempts to change.[38] The flip side of this argument is that a single articulatory gesture can, in principle, result in a series of sounds (just as throwing a ball may result in a series of events when the ball bounces on the floor). In other words, peripheral nonlinearities are a mixed blessing, allowing rapid transitions, sometimes at the cost of increasing control efforts. In the context of song learning, however, there is an additional problem that brings us back to the subject of perceptual tuning: if the bird hears two back-to-back sounds, it might be difficult for the bird to imitate them separately if productions mechanism of those two sounds are not distinct, namely, units of perception and units of production might be incompatible. We do not know what perceptual biases the bird might have prior to vocal experience, but as the bird acquires motor proficiency, it might be able to identify instances of nonlinearities in its own production mechanisms, and adjust its perceptual units accordingly. Evidence suggests that peripheral nonlinearities are taken into account during song learning.[22]

VARIABILITY ACROSS TIME SCALES OF VOCAL LEARNING

Early studies of song development showed that in contrast to the highly structured and stereotyped song of the adult bird, the young bird produces highly variable sounds.[5] What is the role (or the consequences) of this variability on the vocal learning process? Based on variability observed in sonograms of early songs, it seems as if song development is a messy, erratic process. Observing song development by means of DVD-maps however, (see examples at <http://ofer.sci.ccny.cuny.edu>) gives the impression of a structured and smooth process. This contrast is due to different time scales of the two representations: the sonogram presents dynamics on millisecond time scale whereas a single frame of a DVD-map is a summary (distribution of first and second order statistics) of a few minutes of singing (about 5 orders of magnitude higher). The stability of the DVD-map is therefore an indication that the short-term variability in syllable morphology is constrained, and that song development is a structured process. The role of this short-term variability in song development is obscure, it might reflect the lack of subtle control on the vocal instrument or it could reflect a random-search strategy of guiding the imitation trajectory towards the target model.[39] How can one distinguish between the two? If the variability is a mean of reaching a target, we would expect that once a target state is reached variability in the production of that sound should decrease abruptly. Since different features might reach their target during different developmental windows (as in FIG. 2), we should expect that the decrease of variability will correspond to those time scales. To the best of our knowledge, this hypothesis has not yet been tested.

SUMMARY

We started by asking how we can estimate the acoustic error between the bird's current song and the song model (FIG. 1). To the extent that we can infer about the internal state from the actions the bird takes, measurements of song development suggest that the error-signal is neither simple nor stationary. Nevertheless, during any particular window of song development, we can identify distinct events of vocal change. Early events are the emergence of stable syllable types that are only roughly similar to some model sounds. Later events are changes in specific features of a particular syllable type. Some vocal changes progress rapidly, within hours or days, and other vocal changes progress slowly within weeks. Therefore, when attempting to interpret brain measures of a learning bird, one can distinguish between features of the acoustic error that the bird is currently engaged with, and other features of the same sound, that are currently "ignored" by the bird.

The technical feasibility of measuring song development should further encourage the interdisciplinary approach in the field of birdsong neurobiology. In particular, one should avoid reductionism when thinking about concepts such as error-signal, since any view that ignores the roles of development, perception plasticity and motor proficiency is likely to be unrealistic (FIG. 5). Unfortunately, we do not

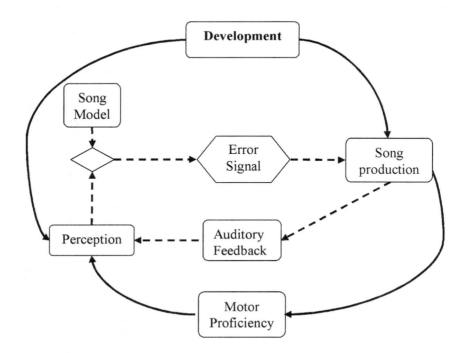

FIGURE 5. Perception plasticity and song learning. The *dashed arrows* show propagation of the feedback loop from moment-to-moment. *Plain arrows* show effects that occur on long time scales during development.

have the means to judge what are the most difficult challenges that the birds encounter while mastering a song. If singing were like riding a bike, we could infer, after some observations, that balancing the bike is important, but it is much more difficult to appreciate (without ever riding a bike), the fundamental relations between speed and balance, and that it is the most proficient rider that can keep the bike balanced at a very low speed (indeed, learning to ride a bike can be very difficult at low speeds). By this metaphor we mean to say that interpreting brain activity during song learning should become much easier if we understood more about the nature of the task, and much can be achieved by performing perceptual or articulatory measurements during song learning, and by attempting to control the syrinx in-vitro so as to actually experience some of the challenges of song learning. Other non-acoustic factors such as social interactions can profoundly influence song learning. Measuring their contribution with the same accuracy as those achieved now with the mechanisms of vocal production is another challenge for the study of birdsong.

ACKNOWLEDGMENTS

Work reported here was supported by US Public Health Services (PHS) grant DC04722-04 to O.T., by Fondation Fyssen grant to S.D., and by the National Institutes of Health RCMI grant to CCNY.

REFERENCES

1. NOTTEBOHM, F. 1993. The search for neural mechanisms that define the sensitive period for song learning in birds. Neth. J. Zool. **43:** 193–234.
2. KONISHI, M. 1965. The role of auditory feedback in the control of vocalization in the white-crowned sparrow. Z. Tierpsychol. **22:** 770–783.
3. MARLER, P. 1970. A comparative approach to vocal learning song development in white-crowned sparrows. J. Comp. Physiol. Psychol. **71:** 1–25.
4. THORPE, W.H. 1961. Bird Song. Cambridge University Press. Cambridge, UK.
5. IMMELMANN, K. 1969. Song development in the zebra finch and other estrildid finches. *In* Bird Vocalizations. RA Hinde, Ed.: 61–74. Cambridge University Press. Cambridge, UK.
6. PRICE, P. 1979. Developmental determinants of structure in zebra finch song. J. Comp. Physiol. Psychol. **93:** 260–277.
7. LEONARDO, A. & M. KONISHI. 1999. Decrystalization of adult birdsong by perturbation of auditory feedback. Nature **399:** 466–470.
8. KROODSMA, D. & R. PICKERT. 1984. Sensitive phases for song learning: effects of social interaction and individual variation. Anim. Behav. **32:** 389–394.
9. ARNOLD, A.P. 1975. The effects of castration on song development in zebra finches (*Poephila guttata*). J. Exp. Zool. **191:** 261–278.
10. NOWICKI, S., W.A. SEARCY & S. PETERS. 2002. Brain development, song learning and mate choice in birds: a review and experimental test of the "nutritional stress hypothesis". J Comp Physiol A. **188:** 1003–1014.
11. BAPTISTA, L.F. 1996. Nature and its nurturing in avian vocal development. *In* Ecology and Evolution of Acoustic Communication in Birds. D.E. Kroodsma & E.H. Miller, Eds.: 39–60. Cornell University Press. Ithaca, NY.
12. EALES, L. 1985. Song learning in zebra finches: some effects of song model availability on what is learnt and when. Anim. Behav. **33:** 1293–1300.
13. MORRISON, R. & F. NOTTEBOHM. 1993. Role of a telencephalic nucleus in the delayed song learning of socially isolated zebra finches. J. Neurobiol. **24:** 1045–1064.

14. JONES, A., C. TEN CATE & P.J.B. SLATER. 1996. Early experience and plasticity of song in adult male zebra finches (*Taenyopygia guttata*). J. Comp. Psychol. **110:** 354–369.
15. HAHNLOSER, R.H., A.A. KOZHEVNIKOV & M.S. FEE. 2002. An ultra-sparse code underlies the generation of neural sequences in a songbird. Nature **419:** 65–70.
16. DAVE, A.S. & D. MARGOLIASH. 2000. Song replay during sleep and computational rules for sensorimotor vocal learning. Science **290:** 812–816.
17. SOLIS, M.M. & A.J. DOUPE.1999. Contributions of tutor and bird's own song experience to neural selectivity in the songbird anterior forebrain. J. Neurosci. **19:** 4559–4584.
18. MOONEY, R. 2000. Different sub threshold mechanisms underlie song-selectivity in identified HVc neurons of the zebra finch. J. Neurosci. **20:** 5420–5436.
19. BRAINARD, M.S. & A.J. DOUPE. 2000. Interruption of a basal ganglia-forebrain circuit prevents plasticity of learned vocalizations. Nature **404:** 762–766.
20. BRAINARD, M.S. & A.J. DOUPE. 2001. Post-learning consolidation of birdsong: stabilizing effects of age and anterior forebrain lesions. J. Neurosci. **21:** 2501–2517.
21. ADRET, P. 1993. Operant conditioning, song learning and imprinting to taped song in the zebra finch. Anim. Behav. **46:** 159–159.
22. TCHERNICHOVSKI, O., P.P. MITRA, T. LINTS & F. NOTTEBOHM. 2001. Dynamics of the vocal imitation process: how a zebra finch learns its song. Science **291:** 2564–2569.
23. TCHERNICHOVSKI, O. & P.P. MITRA. 2002. Towards quantification of vocal imitation in the zebra finch. J. Comp. Physiol. A **188:** 867–878.
24. DOUPE, A.S. & P.K. KUHL. 1999. Birdsong and human speech: common themes and mechanisms. Annu. Rev. Neurosci. **22:** 567–631.
25. KUHL, P.K, & A.N. MELTZOFF. 1996. Infant vocalizations in response to speech: vocal imitation and developmental change. J. Acoust. Soc. Am. **100:** 2425–2438.
26. JUSCZYK, P.W. 1997. The Discovery of Spoken Language. MIT Press. Cambridge, MA.
27. TROYER, T.W. & A.J. DOUPE. 2000. An associational model of birdsong sensorimotor learning II. Temporal hierarchies and the learning of song sequence. J. Neurophysiol. **84:** 1224–1239.
28. TROYER, T.W. & A.J. DOUPE. 2000. An associational model of birdsong sensorimotor learning I. Efference copy and the learning of song syllables. J. Neurophysiol. **84:**1204–1223.
29. ELBERT, T., C. PANTEV, C. WIENBRUCH, *et al.* 1995. Increased cortical representation of the fingers of the left hand in string players. Science **270:** 305–307.
30. MÜHLNICKEL, W., T. ELBERT, E. TAUB & H. FLOR. 1998. Reorganization of auditory cortex in tinnitus. Proc. Natl. Acad. Sci. USA **95:** 10340–10343.
31. KNUDSEN, E.I. 1999. Early experience and critical periods. *In* Fundamental Neuroscience. M.J. Zigmond, F.E. Bloom, S.C. Landis, *et al.*, Eds.: 637–654. Academic Press. New York.
32. BRITTAN-POWELL, E. F. & R. J. DOOLING. Development of auditory sensitivity in budgerigars (*Melopsittacus undulatus*). J. Acoust. Soc. Am. In press.
33. ESPINO, G. G., C. LEWIS, D.B. ROSENFIELD & S. A. HELEKAR. 2003. Modulation of theta/alpha frequency profiles of slow auditory evoked responses in the songbird zebra finch. Neuroscience **122:** 521–529.
34. ESPINO, G.G., D.B. ROSENFIELD & S.A. HELEKAR. 2003. Similarities in neural correlates of song discrimination in zebra finches with similar song. Program No. 942.8. Abstract Viewer and Itinerary Planner. Society for Neuroscience. Washington, DC. Online.
35. NICK, T.A. 2003. Response bias: neural correlates of memory in the birdsong system. Program No. 294.2. 2003 Abstract Viewer and Itinerary Planner. Society for Neuroscience. Washington, DC. Online.
36. RIBEIRO, S., G.A. CECCHI, M.O. MAGNASCO & C.V. MELLO. 1998. Toward a song code: evidence for a syllabic representation in the canary brain. Neuron **21:** 359–371.
37. FEE, M.S., B. SHRAIMAN, B. PESARAN & P.P. MITRA. 1998. The role of nonlinear dynamics of the syrinx in the vocalizations of a songbird. Nature **395:** 67–71.
38. GARDNER, T, CECCHI, M. MAGNASCO, *et al.* 2001. Simple motor gestures for birdsongs. Phys. Rev. Lett. **87:** 208101.
39. NELSON, D.A. & P. MARLER. 1994. Selection-based learning in bird song development. Proc. Natl Acad. Sci. U S A. **91:** 10498–10501.

Contributions of the Anterior Forebrain Pathway to Vocal Plasticity

MICHAEL S. BRAINARD

Departments of Physiology and Psychiatry, Keck Center for Integrative Neuroscience, University of California San Francisco, San Francisco, California 94143-0444, USA

ABSTRACT: The anterior forebrain pathway (AFP) is a basal ganglia–dorsal forebrain circuit that is prominent specifically in birds that learn to sing. This circuit is interconnected with the song motor pathway, is active during song production, and contains neurons that are selective for the sound of the bird's own song, suggesting an important role for the AFP in vocal behavior. However, interruption of the AFP by lesions in adult birds has little overt effect on the production of learned song. In contrast, lesions in juvenile birds prevent the normal progression of song learning. Moreover, lesions in adults, while not disrupting production, can prevent experience-dependent plasticity of song. Such data implicate the AFP specifically in song learning and vocal plasticity. This chapter reviews some of the experimental evidence supporting a role for the AFP in these processes and discusses potential instructive and permissive functions of the AFP in vocal plasticity.

KEYWORDS: auditory feedback; vocal learning; sensorimotor integration; basal ganglia; birdsong

EVIDENCE FOR A ROLE OF THE AFP IN VOCAL PLASTICITY

The principal evidence suggesting a specific role for the AFP in vocal learning derives from lesion studies in zebra finches (FIG. 1). In adult birds with stable, crystallized songs, lesions of the AFP have no overt disruptive effect on song,[1–4] indicating that the AFP is not critical to the pre-motor pattern generation that underlies the production of the bird's learned song (FIG. 1A). However, in juvenile birds, lesions of the AFP prevent the normal progression of song learning and result in adult birds with songs that have highly abnormal features (FIG. 1B–D).[1–3] These data indicate that the AFP plays a key role during song learning in establishing the normal, learned patterns of connectivity within the song motor pathway.

Studies in adult birds provide further support for a dissociation between AFP lesion effects on song production and song plasticity. Normally, adult zebra finch song remains stable over time. However, manipulations of auditory and/or proprioceptive feedback in adults, such as deafening or tracheosyringeal nerve section, can produce

Address for correspondence: Michael S. Brainard, Departments of Physiology and Psychiatry, Keck Center for Integrative Neuroscience, University of California San Francisco, San Francisco, CA 94143-0444, USA.
msb@phy.ucsf.edu; <http://www.ucsf.edu/neurosc/faculty/neuro_brainard.html>

Ann. N.Y. Acad. Sci. 1016: 377–394 (2004). © 2004 New York Academy of Sciences.
doi: 10.1196/annals.1298.042

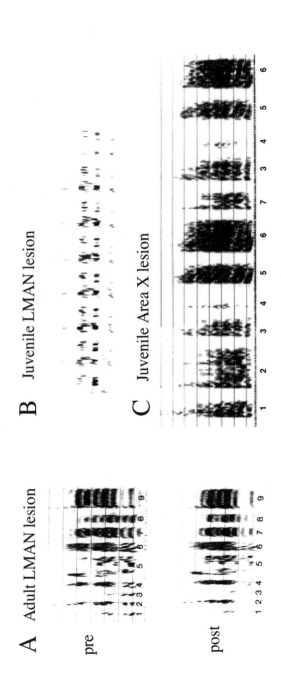

FIGURE 1. LMAN lesions disrupt normal song learning, but not song maintenance. (**A**) In adult zebra finches, learned song normally remains stable over time, and lesions of the AFP have little overt effect on song.[1–4] The *top panel* shows the learned song motif of a normal adult zebra finch. This bird's motif was composed of 9 distinct syllables (numbered 1–9) that were repeatedly produced in the stereotyped sequence illustrated here. The bottom panel shows the motif produced by the same bird 16 weeks following large bilateral lesions of LMAN. Lesions had no apparent effect on the bird's song. (Data are from Nordeen and Nordeen.[4]) (**B**) In juvenile zebra finches, lesions of the AFP disrupt song learning. The *top panel* shows the adult song produced by a zebra finch that received bilateral lesions of LMAN at 35 days of age. The individual syllables of song are atypical for adult zebra finches. Moreover, the number of syllables is reduced relative to normal, and these syllables are repeated in an abnormally long string. These features are typical of the adult songs that result from juvenile lesions of LMAN.[1,3] (Data are from Botjer and colleagues.[1]). The bottom panel shows the adult song produced by a zebra finch that received bilateral lesions of Area X at 31 days of age. Although the number of distinct syllables produced by this bird is typical of zebra finch song, the syllables are abnormally "noisy." In addition, both the structure of individual syllables and their sequencing are more variable from one song to the next than is normal for adult zebra finch song. These features are typical of the adult songs that result from juvenile lesions of Area X.[2,3] (Data are from Scharff and Nottebohm.[3])

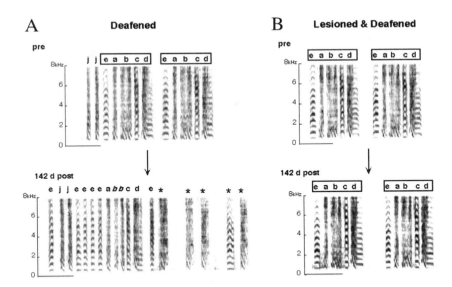

FIGURE 2. LMAN lesions prevent deafening-induced changes to adult song. (**A**) Disruption of auditory feedback normally causes a gradual deterioration of adult zebra finch song.[5] Here, the song of a normal adult zebra finch is shown before (*top*), and 142 days after (*bottom*) removal of auditory feedback by deafening. The bird's stereotyped motif (boxed: "eabcd") has degraded both with respect to individual syllables and with respect to the temporal pattern of the song. *Asterisks* (*) indicate strings of syllables not observed prior to deafening. (**B**) The song of a second adult zebra finch before (*top*) and 142 days after (*bottom*) a combination of deafening and bilateral lesions of LMAN. This bird was a brother to the bird pictured in **A**, and initially had a similar song motif (boxed: "eabcd"), due to shared tutor experience. In this lesioned bird, song remained unchanged following deafening. Horizontal scale bar = 500 msec. (Data are from Brainard and Doupe.[9])

plasticity in otherwise stable song.[5–7] Lesions of the AFP output nucleus LMAN prevent these experience-dependent changes to adult song (FIG. 2).[8,9] Additionally, in zebra finches that have been raised under conditions (isolation) that enable adult song learning, this learning also is prevented by lesions of LMAN.[10] Collectively, the data from lesion studies implicate the AFP in enabling vocal plasticity in both juvenile and adult birds.

INSTRUCTIVE VERSUS PERMISSIVE CONTRIBUTIONS TO VOCAL PLASTICITY

The various processes that are thought to contribute to sensorimotor learning of song are schematized in FIGURE 3. They include (1) the premotor control of song production ("motor structures"), (2) the encoding and transmission of information about the quality of the bird's own song ("auditory feedback"), (3) the evaluation of auditory feedback relative to a previously memorized song "template," and (4) the

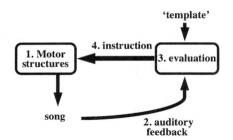

FIGURE 3. Schematic of processes underlying song learning and plasticity.[83] (1) Vocal motor structures produce song, (2) auditory feedback from the bird's own song is conveyed to the CNS, and (3) evaluated relative to a previously stored song "template." (4) A mismatch between experienced feedback and the template is presumed to give rise to instructive signals that actively guide changes in the song motor pathway. In juvenile birds, such a mismatch is naturally present during the period of sensorimotor learning, and instructive signals guide improvement in developing song, In adult birds, such a mismatch can be experimentally introduced either by altering or removing feedback. Here, evaluation mechanisms may interpret the altered feedback as an error of production, leading to the generation of aberrant instructive signals that actively drive song deterioration.

generation of instructive signals that impinge on motor structures and drive adaptive changes in song. Given these processes and the lesion data presented above, the AFP might play either an "instructive" or a "permissive" role in vocal plasticity.

Instructive Model

According to an "instructive" model, the AFP is part of the system schematized in FIGURE 3 that participates in evaluation of feedback from the bird's own vocalizations and the generation of instructive signals that guide adaptive changes in the motor pathway so that song progresses towards a better match to the template. Such signals could simply reflect the degree to which the song deviates from the template (i.e., scalar "reinforcement" or "punishment" signals). Alternatively, the information conveyed could be "parameterized," reflecting the direction of deviation of the current song from the template.

In this account, the deficits that follow AFP lesions in juvenile birds arise from aberrant or absent instructive input to the motor pathway. In lesioned juvenile birds, there is no guidance to drive song towards a good match with the tutor song. In contrast, for normal adults, after song learning has progressed to completion, the motor pathway is autonomously capable of producing the bird's learned song, and there is no longer a requirement for instructive input to guide changes to song. Hence, lesions in adults have no immediate effect on song. However, in adult birds subjected to manipulations such as deafening, the mechanisms that evaluate auditory feedback interpret the absence of feedback as an error of motor production, leading to the generation of aberrant instructive signals that actively drive deterioration of song. If the changes to adult song that occur following experimental manipulations are actively driven by mechanisms of feedback evaluation, then lesions of the AFP, if they do in-

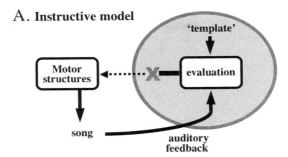

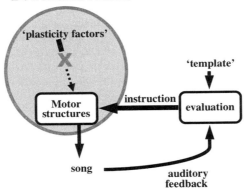

FIGURE 4. Instructive and permissive models of AFP function in vocal plasticity. (**A**) According to an instructive model, AFP lesions may prevent changes to song by interrupting or eliminating feedback-based instructive signals that normally drive song changes. (**B**) According to a permissive model, AFP lesions may remove neural or trophic factors that are required for the motor pathway to change in response to instructive input that potentially arises from elsewhere.

deed interrupt instructive input to the motor pathway, should prevent these attendant experience-dependent changes to adult song (FIG. 4a).

Permissive Model

According to a "permissive" model, the AFP provides "plasticity factors" that are required for change in the song motor pathway without directly providing signals that guide such change. In this account, the effects of AFP lesions in both juveniles and adults can be understood simply as arising from the removal of those factors necessary for changing functional connectivity in the motor pathway (FIG. 4b); song remains stable despite the presence of signals that would otherwise drive song learning (juveniles) or song deterioration (e.g., deafened adults).

One version of the permissive model suggests that abnormalities of song learning in juvenile birds following lesions of LMAN derive directly from "damage" to the motor pathway. This hypothesis is consistent with the observation that the AFP is necessary for normal development and physiological function of the song motor pathway, even prior to the initiation of song learning. Lesions of LMAN in juvenile birds cause atrophy of the motor nucleus RA, including extensive cell death.[11,12] However, since lesions of LMAN in adult birds have much less effect on RA neurons, and almost no effect on song, the effects of LMAN lesions on song plasticity in adults are dissociated from gross effects on the normal functioning of the motor pathway in song production.[1,4,8,13]

Nevertheless, despite grossly normal functioning of the motor pathway with respect to song production in lesioned adult birds, lesions may produce more subtle changes to physiological properties of RA that could impact plasticity. LMAN projections to RA are known to be glutamatergic and to rely principally on NMDA receptors.[14,15] Furthermore, these projections synapse on dendrites of RA neurons that also receive excitatory synapses intrinsic to the motor pathway[16] and that likely form a key part of the connectivity responsible for producing song. Lesions of LMAN, by physically removing one set of glutamatergic synapses onto RA neurons, might interfere with putative plasticity mechanisms within RA, such as LTP.

Similarly, lesions of LMAN may remove trophic factors from the motor pathway that normally support plasticity. A variety of evidence suggests that the AFP may provide BDNF or other neurotrophins to the motor pathway. The cell death within RA that is normally caused by lesions of LMAN can be rescued by infusion of BDNF.[17] Moreover, exogenous BDNF supplied to adult RA results in plasticity within the motor pathway and overt changes to song.[18] These results are consistent with the possibility that AFP-derived neurotrophins normally regulate the functioning of motor pathway neurons, and that lesions of the AFP may interfere with vocal plasticity by eliminating factors required for structural and functional reorganization.

A related possibility for mediating permissive effects is that the AFP provides inputs that, while not themselves critical to plasticity mechanisms (i.e., LTP or subsequent structural changes) do provide a necessary substrate for those mechanisms. For example, in addition to synaptic sprouting, BDNF has been linked to neurogenesis in the song system.[19,20] It has been suggested that new neurons might form a substrate for the formation of new "memories" and attendant plasticity of song, without providing signals that direct the nature of that plasticity.[19-23] If, in this case, the birth of new neurons requires trophic inputs from the AFP, then removal of those inputs could prevent the normal incorporation of new neurons and thereby block plasticity.

Current data do not clearly discriminate between instructive and permissive roles of the AFP. Indeed, these two models are not mutually exclusive, and it is possible that the AFP contributes to both kinds of processes. The following sections present observations about AFP function that provide evidence consistent with one or both models, and that ultimately must be incorporated in any comprehensive account of AFP function.

POSSIBLE ROLE OF THE AFP IN DEVELOPMENTAL REGULATION OF PLASTICITY

Since lesions of the AFP have a conspicuous effect on the plasticity of song, it is of course possible that regulation of plasticity is one of the normal functions of this pathway. In support of this idea, there are a number of developmental events both within the AFP and in its connections to the motor pathway that parallel at a gross level a developmental decline in song plasticity. In zebra finches, the AFP and its connection to RA undergo numerous changes by 60 days of age, when the critical period for zebra finch sensory learning closes. Strikingly, many of the changes are regressive in nature. The synapses from LMAN to the motor pathway, which are mediated largely by glutamate receptors of the NMDA type,[14,15,24] decrease in number when HVc innervates RA,[16] suggestive of synaptic elimination, and the initially coarse topographic projection from LMAN to RA undergoes refinement.[25] Pruning of connections is also prominent within the AFP itself: LMAN neuron spine density decreases between 25 and 55–60 days of age in zebra finches.[26] This is accompanied by decreased NMDA receptors in LMAN,[27,28] faster NMDA currents at the synapses from thalamus to LMAN,[29] pruning of thalamic arbors in LMAN,[30] and loss of activity-dependent synaptic potentiation and depression at synapses within LMAN.[31]

Lesions of LMAN, by removing the projection from the AFP to the motor pathway, directly mimic a process similar to the normal developmental decline in the strength of connections between LMAN and RA. In juvenile birds, LMAN lesions also appear to cause the premature appearance of adult-like properties in the motor pathway. This includes both a loss of dendritic spines within RA and an increase in the speed of synaptic currents at HVC to RA synapses.[13] These observations suggest that neural or trophic inputs from LMAN may normally serve to maintain the motor pathway in a juvenile, plastic state.[13] Lesions of the AFP may then mimic the normal developmental decline in these inputs, resulting in a prematurely crystallized song.

In this context, it is worth noting that the nature of song abnormalities that result from AFP lesions depend on where the pathway is disrupted (FIG. 1B–D). While lesions of the AFP output nucleus, LMAN, arrest song development in a manner that is suggestive of a premature crystallization of song,[1,3] lesions of the input nucleus, Area X, seem to have the opposite effect. Area X lesions prevent the normal progression of the juvenile song towards a good match with the tutor song. However, they appear to leave song in a perpetually variable state; song syllables and overall song structure do not improve, but continue to change from one rendition to the next.[2,3]

Given the known connectivity and physiology of the AFP, different effects of LMAN and Area X lesions are not entirely surprising. Lesions of LMAN necessarily remove the connections from the AFP to RA and any associated neural or trophic factors provided by these inputs. In contrast, lesions of Area X leave synapses from LMAN to RA intact. Moreover, because Area X sends an inhibitory projection to DLM (which in turn most likely excites LMAN), the net effect of Area X lesions may be to increase activity within LMAN.[32] In this case, Area X lesions may lead to a superabundance of those factors that enable or drive plasticity within the motor pathway.

In regulating vocal plasticity, a key function of the AFP may be to introduce variability into the patterns of activity within the motor pathway. Variability of motor output is a requisite component of reinforcement-based learning; in order for song to change in response to a feedback-based reinforcement signal, song must vary at least somewhat from rendition to rendition. Such variation is required so that evaluation mechanisms can differentially reinforce patterns of motor activity that give rise to better songs (i.e., renditions closer to the tutor song) and/or "punish" patterns that give rise to worse songs.

The AFP could potentially influence such variability within the motor pathway on more than one timescale. On a slow timescale, neurotrophins from the AFP might introduce song variability by promoting synaptogenesis or the incorporation of new neurons into the motor pathway.[3,13,17,19,20] On a faster timescale, neural activity from the AFP has the potential to modulate ongoing patterns of activity within the song motor pathway. Preliminary experiments directly examining the influence of LMAN activity on song structure are consistent with this possibility. Microstimulation of LMAN during singing can alter song structure on a moment-by-moment basis.[33] Moreover, removal of signals from the AFP, by lesioning LMAN, reduces the moment-by-moment variability present in song, suggesting that song variability is normally regulated in part by signals arising from the AFP.[34]

For efficient reinforcement learning, variability should be regulated over time in relation to the current status of motor performance. When song is far from the desired target, high variability is appropriate in order to coarsely search for changes that lead to improvement. In contrast, as the desired target is approached, low variability ensures that each rendition is near that target; once song is learned, only a low degree of residual variability should be required to maintain the song. Given the potential importance of motor variability or "exploration" to motor learning, it may be that a normal developmental decline in those factors from the AFP that promote variability is a central component of song crystallization.

Synaptic and morphological changes in the connections from LMAN to RA and within the motor pathway are most dramatic in zebra finches up to 60–90 days of age, with little overt change observed subsequently.[13,15,16] Likewise, the plasticity of song in response to manipulations of sensory experience (such as deafening) progressively declines over this period. Although song plasticity in response to deafening is comparatively attenuated in birds beyond 90 days of age, there is nevertheless a significant residual degree of song plasticity, which further declines over a period of months following the nominal crystallization of song.[35,36] It is unknown whether this decline in adult plasticity is paralleled by further, subtle regressive events in the connections of LMAN to RA. However, if this is the case, then LMAN lesions in adult birds may precipitate a stabilization of song (in response to manipulations such as deafening) by accentuating these events. Such lesions might, in effect, create a "hyper-crystallized" song.

SONG SELECTIVITY IN THE AFP AND A POSSIBLE ROLE OF THE AFP IN SENSORY LEARNING

Neural responses to song stimuli have been characterized in several parts of the song system and provide some insights into what mechanisms may contribute to representing the tutor song and feedback of the bird's own song. One intriguing property is "song selectivity," first described in HVc,[37–40] but now shown to exist throughout the song system, including the AFP.[41–44] Song-selective neurons respond more strongly to playback of the bird's own song and, in some cases, the tutor song, than to conspecific songs. Such neurons potentially are well suited to process auditory feedback of the bird's own song and to participate in evaluating the similarity of that song to the tutor song. For example, neurons that respond selectively to the tutor song would presumably fire more strongly to the extent that auditory feedback of the bird's own song resembles the tutor song, and hence could contribute to a signal indicating degree of match.

Although this article focuses on the importance of the AFP to song plasticity, the presence of song selectivity in many song nuclei suggests that mechanisms involved in song memorization and feedback evaluation could be highly distributed or reside elsewhere in the song system. Indeed, some of the specialized auditory processing that subserves song learning may occur in auditory areas that are afferent to the song system. Consistent with this possibility, neurons in the high level auditory areas NCM and cHV exhibit some aspects of song selectivity.[45–51] For each area exhibiting song selectivity, it will ultimately be important to investigate the extent to which this property reflects sensory learning of the tutor song versus acoustic experience of feedback from the bird's own song during sensorimotor learning.

Lesion studies are problematic for testing a specific role of brain regions in the sensory phase of song learning. This is because the main assay for what a bird has memorized is the song that the bird ultimately produces; any song abnormalities arising from lesions are therefore difficult to attribute to disruption of sensory learning as opposed to disruption of subsequent sensorimotor learning or song production. To circumvent this problem, reversible inactivation of LMAN has been used to disrupt AFP activity specifically during tutoring sessions but not during subsequent sensorimotor rehearsal.[52] Song learning in experimental birds was significantly reduced relative to controls. This intriguing experiment provides the most direct evidence to date of involvement of a brain area in memorization of tutor song. It is difficult to account for this result in the context of an exclusively permissive model of AFP function, and further experiments along these lines, in which AFP function is manipulated in a temporally and/or mechanistically controlled fashion, seem likely to provide important insights.

Another way in which sensory versus sensorimotor functions of the AFP can be dissociated is to study the effects of lesions in purely perceptual tasks, outside the context of vocal production. Although such studies have not addressed the issue of tutor song memorization, they have found that lesions of song nuclei, including HVc and LMAN, interfere with the performance of birds in tasks that require song memorization and discrimination.[53–55]

The regressive developmental changes within the AFP could potentially underlie an experience-dependent narrowing of song responsiveness as birds encode a particular tutor song memory. In zebra finches, however, the period of sensory learning also overlaps with the onset of vigorous singing, sensorimotor rehearsal, and refinement of auditory selectivity for BOS, making it difficult to specifically attribute any changes to sensory learning. Several manipulations, such as isolate rearing and hormonal treatments, have been used to alter the time-course of song learning in an attempt to test the correlation between physiological events and learning (as opposed to learning-independent developmental changes). Thus far, only a small number of observations have been tested and found to correlate with learning rather than developmental age. For example, the elimination of spines normally seen in LMAN of zebra finches by day 55 does not occur in birds raised without tutors[26] (but see also ref. 56). Thus, spine loss in LMAN may be a cellular consequence of sensory experience and learning. In contrast, although isolation rearing enables late learning, it delays, but does not prevent shortening of NMDA receptor kinetics within the AFP.[29,57,58] The ability of isolates to learn new songs indicates that changes in NMDA receptor kinetics do not prevent song learning in the way that closure of the sensitive period does.

SENSORIMOTOR ACTIVITY IN THE AFP AND A POSSIBLE ROLE IN FEEDBACK EVALUATION

Song-selective neurons have primarily been characterized in anesthetized birds presented with recorded stimuli. In awake birds, some neurons in the song system continue to respond to the presentation of song stimuli.[37,59,60] However, responses in awake birds are generally weaker than in anesthetized or sleeping birds, and in

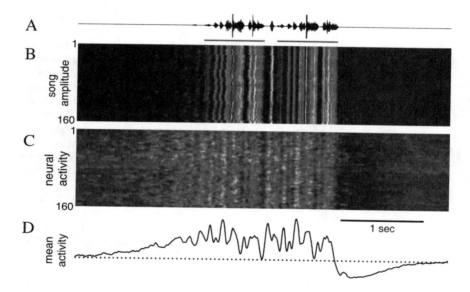

FIGURE 5. Neural activity in LMAN during singing. (**A**) Amplitude waveform of a typical song produced by an adult zebra finch. The song usually contained two motifs (indicated by black lines) sung in close succession. (**B**) Representation of the amplitude waveform for 160 song renditions that matched this pattern. Each horizontal line corresponds to a single rendition. Rendition number is indicated on the vertical axis. Waveforms are vertically aligned by the onset of the second motif. (**C**) Neural activity recorded in LMAN during song production. For each of the 160 renditions of song, corresponding multiunit neural activity was recorded with a chronically implanted electrode. Neural waveforms were rectified and smoothed to yield a representation of the level of neural activity. Each horizontal line indicates the level of neural activity recorded in LMAN during the corresponding song indicated in **B**. (**D**) Mean level of neural activity recorded in LMAN during a song rendition. The mean trace was calculated by averaging the 160 vertically aligned traces in **C**. The horizontal line indicates the average baseline level of activity recorded when the bird was not singing. There is a conspicuous, patterned increase in activity during song. Moreover, activity begins to increase prior to the onset of vocalizations. This indicates that at least a component of the activity present in LMAN reflects premotor activity relayed to the AFP from HVC. (Data are from Hessler and Doupe.[60])

some cases entirely absent.[59,61] Thus, the strength, and perhaps the nature, of responses to sounds are "gated" by the behavioral state of the bird. In other systems, sensory responses related to a behavior are "gated" by the motor activity that generates the behavior.[62] For songbirds, auditory feedback of the bird's own song is only available, and only relevant, when the bird is actually singing. This raises the possibility that the effects of anesthesia or sleep may be to artificially open a gate that normally is operated by the act of singing. These results also reiterate that an understanding of the mechanisms that participate in the evaluation of auditory feedback may require recording neural activity when that feedback is relevant, namely during the production of song.

Recordings from the AFP of adult birds that are singing and listening to their own songs indeed reveal that neural activity during singing is strikingly different from that elicited by playback of the bird's own song (FIG. 5).[60] In particular, the level of activity is much greater during singing than during playback, and a significant portion of this activity appears to correlate with motor production rather than sensory feedback. Activity such as this, which may reflect premotor commands without actually being required for motor production, is sometimes referred to as "corollary discharge" or "efference copy." Such activity may inform sensorimotor structures about the timing and nature of impending movements.[63] Hence, one possible role for corollary discharge in the song system could be to "gate" or otherwise inform the processing of auditory feedback.

The presence of corollary discharge during singing complicates the investigation of how auditory feedback is processed in the AFP, since sensory and motor-related activity may be intermingled. The most direct way to identify and characterize sensory components of AFP activity would be to alter auditory feedback during singing and look for correlated changes in neural activity. For humans, this technique has revealed that Wernicke's and other high-level speech processing areas are more active when auditory feedback of the subject's own voice is altered than when it is heard normally, indicating that such areas may participate in the evaluation of feedback.[64,65] For zebra finches, an approach to detecting signals related to processing of auditory feedback has been to assess the effects of deafening on singing-related activity in the AFP. At closely related sites in LMAN, the activity during singing was very similar before and 1–3 days after deafening (FIG. 6).[60] Similarly, preliminary reports suggest little change in the firing of AFP neurons in response to acute alterations of auditory feedback.[66] Thus, the hypothesis that deafening elicits a large and immediate change in AFP activity seems doubtful. It remains possible, however, that acute changes in activity elicited by deafening are small or present only in a minority of neurons, especially in adult zebra finches, in which deterioration after deafening is slow.

An alternative hypothesis about the effects of deafening on the AFP is suggested by the presence of corollary discharge activity in this pathway. In other systems, such activity may serve to provide information about the expected sensory consequences of motor commands.[63] Thus, rather than directly evaluating auditory feedback, the AFP may receive a prediction of expected feedback, perhaps created by the association of premotor signals and auditory feedback in HVc.[67,68] One advantage of such a model is that it potentially shortens the delay between premotor activity and evaluation of its sensory consequences. If the AFP receives a predictive signal from HVc, this signal may change only slowly, after consistently altered feedback

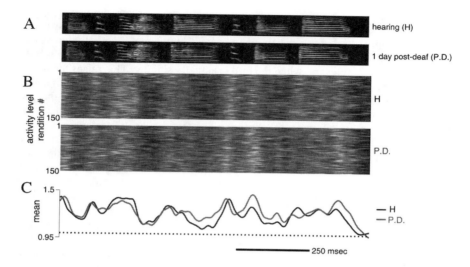

FIGURE 6. Effect of deafening on singing-related neural activity in LMAN. (**A**) Spectrograms of the song motif produced by an adult zebra finch before (*top*) and 1 day after (*bottom*) removal of auditory feedback by deafening. There was no apparent change in song structure, consistent with the slow time-course for song deterioration following removal of auditory feedback. (**B**) Multiunit neural activity level recorded in LMAN during 150 song renditions when the bird could hear (*top*) and post-deafening (*bottom*). The level of activity is plotted with a color scale where brighter colors indicate greater activity. (**C**) The mean activity level for 300 renditions of the motif prior to deafening (*black*) and 161 renditions following deafening (*red*). Activity level was normalized by the average background level. Deafening did not elicit a gross change in the overall level of activity in LMAN. Moreover, the pattern of activity changed only subtly, and this change was of comparable magnitude to that observed between control recording sessions without a change in auditory feedback 60. These data indicate that a significant portion of the singing-related activity in LMAN is independent of auditory feedback. (Data are from Hessler and Doupe.[60])

changes the pattern of association between motor commands and auditory feedback. In this case, the gradual deterioration of song following deafening might not reflect the time required to drive plastic changes in the motor pathway, but rather (or in addition) the time necessary to update an efference copy prediction.

POSSIBLE ATTENTIONAL AND MOTIVATIONAL FUNCTIONS OF THE AFP

In addition to hearing, it is clear that social interactions contribute to directing and modulating song learning. Social factors can influence which song models are memorized during sensory learning and which of a developing bird's song variants are retained during late stages of sensorimotor learning.[69–71] Moreover, in adult birds that have completed song learning, there continues to be an influence of social factors on song production; in many species, birds produce more song when singing to others, in courtship or territorial contexts ("directed" song) than when singing alone ("undirected" song). Subtle aspects of song structure may also vary between these two conditions.[72]

The AFP may contribute to mediating the effects of these non-auditory factors on vocal learning and production. In adult zebra finches, it has been shown that neural activity in the AFP varies between directed and undirected song (FIG. 7).[73,74] This raises the possibility that signals related to social interactions might also have access to the AFP during development, and that this circuit might mediate the influence of such signals on sensory and sensorimotor learning. Possible sources of such signals include midbrain dopaminergic neurons which are thought to participate in reward and reinforcement learning in all vertebrates. In songbirds, dopaminergic neurons project heavily to the song system,[75] especially Area X, and are thus well situated to provide signals to the AFP that could modulate or guide song learning.

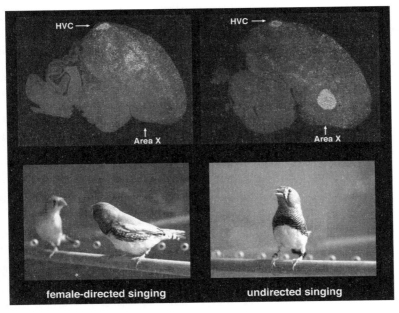

FIGURE 7. Singing-induced expression of the immediate early gene ZENK differs in a context-dependent manner. The top panels show the pattern of ZENK expression from the brain of two male zebra finches following 30 min of female-directed song (*left*) or 30 min of undirected song (*right*). Both birds sang approximately 90 bouts of song during the 30-min period. The levels of ZENK expression in the motor nucleus HVC were elevated and comparable between the two conditions. However, in Area X and LMAN ZENK expression was elevated only in the undirected condition. These data are consistent with a strong modulation of singing-related neural activity in the AFP between directed and undirected conditions, and indicate that social context strongly modulates the AFP. (Data are from Jarvis and colleagues.[73])

PARALLELS WITH MAMMALIAN CORTICO-BASAL GANGLIA CIRCUITS

The AFP shares homology with mammalian cortical-basal ganglia circuits based on numerous anatomical and physiological considerations.[75–77] Evidence in support of such homology is reviewed in the chapters by Farries, Jarvis, and Perkel in this volume. Here we briefly consider functional parallels between the avian AFP and cortico-basal ganglia circuits in other vertebrates.

Cortical-basal ganglia circuits in mammals are critical for motor control and for motor and reinforcement learning.[78,79] Moreover, as in adult zebra finches, the contribution of such circuitry to motor function in humans and monkeys can be more pronounced during conditions of learning and error correction than during previously learned performance.[78,80,81] However, one conspicuous difference between effects associated with basal ganglia damage in mammalian systems and AFP lesions in songbirds is that the former are typically associated with overt disruptions of motor performance, as in Huntington's and Parkinson's diseases. This contrasts with the minimal effects of AFP lesions on learned song in zebra finches. While this may reflect real phylogenetic and functional differences, it is also possible that the specificity of deficits in zebra finches reflects in part the extremely stereotyped and "overlearned" nature of adult song in this species. In the Bengalese finch, a related species with similar song ontogeny but more variable adult song, lesions of the AFP nucleus, Area X, have subtle but significant effects on production of learned song.[82] This suggests that it may be instructive to examine the functioning of the AFP in a greater diversity of species in order to more fully understand the contribution of this pathway to vocal motor control as well as vocal plasticity. Because the AFP is a specialized basal ganglia pathway involved in the learning of a stereotyped motor output, it may prove a particularly tractable system for revealing basic principles of basal ganglia function in motor control and learning.

REFERENCES

1. BOTTJER, S.W., E.A. MIESNER & A.P. ARNOLD. 1984. Forebrain lesions disrupt development but not maintenance of song in passerine birds. Science 224: 901–903.
2. SOHRABJI, F., E.J. NORDEEN & K.W. NORDEEN. 1990. Selective impairment of song learning following lesions of a forebrain nucleus in the juvenile zebra finch. Behav. Neural Biol. 53: 51–63.
3. SCHARFF, C. & F. NOTTEBOHM. 1991. A comparative study of the behavioral deficits following lesions of various parts of the zebra finch song system: implications for vocal learning. J. Neurosci. 11: 2896–2913.
4. NORDEEN, K.W. & E.J. NORDEEN. 1993. Long-term maintenance of song in adult zebra finches is not affected by lesions of a forebrain region involved in song learning. Behav. Neural Biol. 59: 79–82.
5. NORDEEN, K.W. & E.J. NORDEEN. 1992. Auditory feedback is necessary for the maintenance of stereotyped song in adult zebra finches. Behav. Neural Biol. 57: 58–66.
6. WILLIAMS, H. & J.R. MCKIBBEN. 1992. Changes in stereotyped central motor patterns controlling vocalization are induced by peripheral nerve injury. Behav. Neural Biol. 57: 67–78.
7. LEONARDO, A. & M. KONISHI. 1999. Decrystallization of adult birdsong by perturbation of auditory feedback. Nature 399: 466–470.
8. WILLIAMS, H. & N. MEHTA. 1999. Changes in adult zebra finch song require a forebrain nucleus that is not necessary for song production. J. Neurobiol. 39: 14–28.

9. BRAINARD, M.S. & A.J. DOUPE. 2000. Interruption of a basal ganglia-forebrain circuit prevents plasticity of learned vocalizations. Nature 404: 762–766.
10. MORRISON, R.G. & F. NOTTEBOHM. 1993. Role of a telencephalic nucleus in the delayed song learning of socially isolated zebra finches. J. Neurobiol. 24: 1045–1064.
11. AKUTAGAWA, E. & M. KONISHI. 1994. Two separate areas of the brain differentially guide the development of a song control nucleus in the zebra finch. Proc. Natl. Acad. Sci. USA 91: 12413–12417.
12. JOHNSON, F. & S.W. BOTTJER. 1994. Afferent influences on cell death and birth during development of a cortical nucleus necessary for learned vocal behavior in zebra finches. Development 120: 13–24.
13. KITTELBERGER, J.M. & R. MOONEY. 1999. Lesions of an avian forebrain nucleus that disrupt song development alter synaptic connectivity and transmission in the vocal premotor pathway. J. Neurosci. 19: 9385–9398.
14. MOONEY, R. 1992. Synaptic basis for developmental plasticity in a birdsong nucleus. J. Neurosci. 12: 2464–2477.
15. STARK, L L. & D.J. PERKEL. 1999. Two-stage, input-specific synaptic maturation in a nucleus essential for vocal production in the zebra finch. J. Neurosci. 19: 9107–9116.
16. HERRMANN, K. & A.P. ARNOLD. 1991. The development of afferent projections to the robust archistriatal nucleus in male zebra finches: a quantitative electron microscopic study. J. Neurosci. 11: 2063–2074.
17. JOHNSON, F., S.E. HOHMANN, P.S. DISTEFANO & S.W. BOTTJER. 1997. Neurotrophins suppress apoptosis induced by deafferentation of an avian motor-cortical region. J. Neurosci. 17: 2101–2111.
18. KITTELBERGER, J.M. & R. MOONEY. 2001. Acute BDNF injections that reversibly disrupt adult birdsong stability induce a rapid decrease in TRK receptor phosphorylation. Soc. Neurosci. Abstr. 27: 538.7.
19. RASIKA, S., A. ALVAREZ-BUYLLA & F. NOTTEBOHM. 1999. BDNF mediates the effects of testosterone on the survival of new neurons in an adult brain. Neuron 22: 53–62.
20. LI, X.-C., E.D. JARVIS, B. ALVAREZ-BORDA, et al. 2000. A relationship between behavior, neurotrophin expression, and new neuron survival. Proc. Natl. Acad. Sci. USA 97: 8584–8589.
21. GOLDMAN, S.A. & F. NOTTEBOHM. 1983. Neuronal production, migration, and differentiation in a vocal control nucleus in the adult female canary brain. Proc. Natl. Acad. Sci. USA 80: 2390–2394.
22. NOTTEBOHM, F. 2002. Why are some neurons replaced in adult brain? J. Neurosci. 22: 624–628.
23. NORDEEN, K.W. & E.J. NORDEEN. 1988. Projection neurons within a vocal motor pathway are born during song learning in zebra finches. Nature 334: 149–151.
24. KUBOTA, M. & N. SAITO. 1991. NMDA receptors participate differentially in two different synaptic inputs in neurons of the zebra finch robust nucleus of the archistriatum in vitro. Neurosci. Lett. 125: 107–109.
25. IYENGAR, S., S.S. VISWANATHAN & S.W. BOTTJER. 1999. Development of topography within song control circuitry of zebra finches during the sensitive period for song learning. J. Neurosci. 19: 6037–6057.
26. WALLHAUSSER-FRANKE, E., B.E. NIXDORF-BERGWEILER & T.J. DEVOOGD. 1995. Song isolation is associated with maintaining high spine frequencies on zebra finch LMAN neurons. Neurobiol. Learn. Mem. 64: 25–35.
27. AAMODT, S.M., M.R. KOZLOWSKI, E.J. NORDEEN & K.W. NORDEEN. 1992. Distribution and developmental change in [3H]MK-801 binding within zebra finch song nuclei. J. Neurobiol. 23: 997–1005.
28. BASHAM, M.E., F. SOHRABJI, T.D. SINGH, et al. 1999. Developmental regulation of NMDA receptor 2B subunit mRNA and ifenprodil binding in the zebra finch anterior forebrain. J. Neurobiol. 39: 155–167.
29. LIVINGSTON, F.S., S.A. WHITE & R. MOONEY. 2000. Slow NMDA-EPSCs at synapses critical for song development are not required for song learning in zebra finches. Nat. Neurosci. 3: 482–488.

30. IYENGAR, S. & S.W. BOTTJER. 2002. Development of individual axon arbors in a thalamocortical circuit necessary for song learning in zebra finches. J. Neurosci. **22:** 901–911.
31. BOETTIGER, C.A. & A.J. DOUPE. 2001. Developmentally restricted synaptic plasticity in a songbird nucleus required for song learning. Neuron **31:** 809–818.
32. LUO, M. & D.J. PERKEL. 1999. A GABAergic, strongly inhibitory projection to a thalamic nucleus in the zebra finch song system. J. Neurosci. **19:** 6700–6711.
33. KAO, M.H., A.J. DOUPE & M.S. BRAINARD. 2002. Activity in a basal ganglia-forebrain circuit modulates song output. Soc. Neurosci. Abstr. **28:** 680.4.
34. KAO, M.H., A.J. DOUPE & M.S. BRAINARD. 2003. Lesions of LMAN prevent context-dependent changes to song variability. Soc. Neurosci. Abstr. **29:** 522.10.
35. BRAINARD, M.S. & A.J. DOUPE. 2001. Postlearning consolidation of birdsong: Stabilizing effects of age and anterior forebrain lesions. J. Neurosci. **21:** 2501–2517.
36. LOMBARDINO, A.J. & F. NOTTEBOHM. 2000. Age at deafening affects the stability of learned song in adult male zebra finches. J. Neurosci. **20:** 5054–5064.
37. MCCASLAND, J.S. & M. KONISHI. 1981. Interactions between auditory and motor activities in an avian song control nucleus. Proc. Natl. Acad. Sci. USA **78:** 7815–7819.
38. MARGOLIASH, D. 1983. Acoustic parameters underlying the responses of song-specific neurons in the white-crowned sparrow. J. Neurosci. **3:** 1039–1057.
39. MARGOLIASH, D. & E.S. FORTUNE. 1992. Temporal and harmonic combination-sensitive neurons in the zebra finch's HVc. J. Neurosci. **12:** 4309–4326.
40. MOONEY, R. 2000. Different subthreshold mechanisms underlie song selectivity in identified HVc neurons of the zebra finch. J. Neurosci. **20:** 5420–5436.
41. DOUPE, A.J. 1997. Song- and order-selective neurons in the songbird anterior forebrain and their emergence during vocal development. J. Neurosci. **17:** 1147–1167.
42. JANATA, P. & D. MARGOLIASH. 1999. Gradual emergence of song selectivity in sensorimotor structures of the male zebra finch song system. J. Neurosci. **19:** 5108–5118.
43. SOLIS, M.M. & A.J. DOUPE. 1997. Anterior forebrain neurons develop selectivity by an intermediate stage of birdsong learning. J. Neurosci. **17:** 6447–6462.
44. SOLIS, M.M. & A.J. DOUPE. 1999. Contributions of tutor and bird's own song experience to neural selectivity in the songbird anterior forebrain. J. Neurosci. **19:** 4559–4584.
45. MELLO, C.V., D.S. VICARIO & D.F. CLAYTON. 1992. Song presentation induces gene expression in the songbird forebrain. Proc. Natl. Acad. Sci. USA **89:** 6818–6822.
46. CHEW, S.J., D.S. VICARIO & F. NOTTEBOHM. 1996. A large-capacity memory system that recognizes the calls and songs of individual birds. Proc. Natl. Acad. Sci. USA **93:** 1950–1955.
47. STRIPLING, R., S.F. VOLMAN & D.F. CLAYTON. 1997. Response modulation in the zebra finch neostriatum: relationship to nuclear gene regulation. J. Neurosci. **17:** 3883–3893.
48. JIN, H. & D.F. CLAYTON. 1997. Localized changes in immediate-early gene regulation during sensory and motor learning in zebra finches. Neuron **19:** 1049–1059.
49. MELLO, C.V. & S. RIBEIRO. 1998. ZENK protein regulation by song in the brain of songbirds. J. Comp. Neurol. **393:** 426–438.
50. BOLHUIS, J.J., G.G. ZIJLSTRA, A.M. DEN BOER-VISSER & E.A. VAN DER ZEE. 2000. Localized neuronal activation in the zebra finch brain is related to the strength of song learning. Proc. Natl. Acad. Sci. USA **97:** 2282–2285.
51. GENTNER, T.Q. & D. MARGOLIASH. 2003. Neuronal populations and single cells representing learned auditory objects. Nature **424:** 669–674.
52. BASHAM, M.E., E.J. NORDEEN & K.W. NORDEEN. 1996. Blockade of NMDA receptors in the anterior forebrain impairs sensory acquisition in the zebra finch. Neurobiol. Learning Mem. **66:** 295–304.
53. BRENOWITZ, E.A. 1991. Altered perception of species-specific song by female birds after lesions of a forebrain nucleus. Science **251:** 303–305.
54. SCHARFF, C., F. NOTTEBOHM & J. CYNX. 1998. Conspecific and heterospecific song discrimination in male zebra finches with lesions in the anterior forebrain pathway. J. Neurobiol. **36:** 81–90.

55. GENTNER, T.Q., S.H. HULSE, G.E. BENTLEY & G.F. BALL. 2000. Individual vocal recognition and the effect of partial lesions to HVc on discrimination, learning, and categorization of conspecific song in adult songbirds. J. Neurobiol. **42:** 117–133.
56. HEINRICH, J.E., E.J. NORDEEN & K.W. NORDEEN. 2003. Delayed spine loss in LMAN is not necessary for extended song acquisition in zebra finches. Soc. Neurosci. Abstr. **294:** 7.
57. LIVINGSTON, F.S. & R. MOONEY. 2001. Androgens and isolation from adult tutors differentially affect the development of songbird neurons critical to vocal plasticity. J. Neurophysiol. **85:** 34–42.
58. HEINRICH, J.E., T.D. SINGH, F. SOHRABJI, et al. 2002. Developmental and hormonal regulation of NR2A mRNA in forebrain regions controlling avian vocal learning. J. Neurobiol. **51:** 149–159.
59. DAVE, A.S., A.C. YU & D. MARGOLIASH. 1998. Behavioral state modulation of auditory activity in a vocal motor system. Science **282:** 2250–2254.
60. HESSLER, N.A. & A.J. DOUPE. 1999. Singing-related neural activity in a dorsal forebrain-basal ganglia circuit of adult zebra finches. J. Neurosci. **19:** 10461–10481.
61. SCHMIDT, M.F. & M. KONISHI. 1998. Gating of auditory responses in the vocal control system of awake songbirds. Nat. Neurosci. **1:** 513–518.
62. PEARSON, K.G. 1993. Common principles of motor control in vertebrates and invertebrates. Annu. Rev. Neurosci. **16:** 265–297.
63. JORDAN, M.I. 1995. Computational motor control. In The Cognitive Neurosciences. M. Gazzaniga, Ed.: 567–610. MIT Press. Cambridge, MA.
64. HIRANO, S., H. KOJIMA, Y. NAITO, et al. 1997. Cortical processing mechanism for vocalization with auditory verbal feedback. Neuroreport **8:** 2379–2382.
65. MCGUIRE, P.K., D.A. SILBERSWEIG & C.D. FRITH. 1996. Functional neuroanatomy of verbal self-monitoring. Brain **119:** 907–917.
66. LEONARDO, A., T.A. NICK & M. KONISHI. 2002. An efference copy may be used to maintain the stability of adult birdsong. Soc. Neurosci. Abstr. **28:** 680.15.
67. TROYER, T. & A.J. DOUPE. 2000. An associational model of birdsong sensorimotor learning. I. Efference copy and the learning of song syllables. J. Neurophys. **84:** 1204–1223.
68. TROYER, T. & A.J. DOUPE. 2000. An associational model of birdsong sensorimotor learning. II. Temporal hierarchies and the learning of song sequence. J. Neurophys. **84:** 1224–1239.
69. WEST, M.J. & A.P. KING. 1988. Female visual displays affect the development of male song in the cowbird. Nature **334:** 244–246.
70. NELSON, D.A. & P. MARLER. 1994. Selection-based learning in bird song development. Proc. Natl. Acad. Sci. USA **91:** 10498–10501.
71. MARLER, P. & S. PETERS. 1982. Developmental overproduction and selective attrition: new processes in the epigenesis of birdsong. Dev. Psychobiol. **15:** 369–378.
72. SOSSINKA, R. & J. BOHNER. 1980. Song types in the zebra finch Poephila guttata castanotis. Z. Tierpsychol. **53:** 123–132.
73. JARVIS, E.D., C. SCHARFF, M.R. GROSSMAN, et al. 1998. For whom the bird sings: context-dependent gene expression. Neuron **21:** 775–788.
74. HESSLER, N.A. & A.J. DOUPE. 1999. Social context modulates singing-related neural activity in the songbird forebrain. Nat. Neurosci. **2:** 209–211.
75. BOTTJER, S.W. & F. JOHNSON. 1997. Circuits, hormones, and learning: vocal behavior in songbirds. J. Neurobiol. **33:** 602–618.
76. LUO, M. & D.J. PERKEL. 1999. Long-range GABAergic projection in a circuit essential for vocal learning. J. Comp. Neurol. **403:** 68–84.
77. REINER, A., L. MEDINA & C.L. VEENMAN. 1998. Structural and functional evolution of the basal ganglia in vertebrates. Brain Res. Brain Res. Rev. **28:** 235–285.
78. GRAYBIEL, A.M., T. AOSAKI, A.W. FLAHERTY & M. KIMURA. 1994. The basal ganglia and adaptive motor control. Science **265:** 1826–1831.
79. HOUK, J.C., J.L. DAVIS & D.G. BEISER. 1994. Models of information processing in the basal ganglia. p. 382. MIT Press. Cambridge, MA.
80. SMITH, M.A., J. BRANDT & R. SHADMEHR. 2000. Motor disorder in Huntington's disease begins as a dysfunction in error feedback control. Nature **403:** 544–549.

81. NAKAMURA, K., K. SAKAI & O. HIKOSAKA. 1999. Effects of local inactivation of monkey medial frontal cortex in learning of sequential procedures. J. Neurophys. **82:** 1063–1068.

82. KOBAYASHI, K., H. UNO & K. OKANOYA. 2001. Partial lesions in the anterior forebrain pathway affect song production in adult Bengalese finches. Neuroreport **12:** 353–358.

83. KONISHI, M. 1965. The role of auditory feedback in the control of vocalization in the white-crowned sparrow. Z. Tierpsychol. **22:** 770–783.

Developmental Regulation of Basal Ganglia Circuitry during the Sensitive Period for Vocal Learning in Songbirds

SARAH W. BOTTJER

Department of Biology, University of Southern California,
Los Angeles, California 90089-2520, USA

ABSTRACT: A hallmark of sensitive periods of development is an enhanced capacity for learning, such that experience exerts a profound effect on the brain resulting in the establishment of behaviors and underlying neural circuitry that can last a lifetime. Songbirds, like humans, have a sensitive period for vocal learning: they acquire the sounds used for vocal communication during a restricted period of development. In principle, any organism that undertakes vocal learning is faced with the same challenge: to form some representation of target vocal sounds based on auditory experience, and then to translate that auditory target into a motor program that reproduces the sound. Both birds and humans achieve this translation by using auditory (and other) feedback resulting from incipient vocalizations ("babbling" in humans, "subsong" in birds) to adjust motor commands until vocal output produces a good copy of the target sounds. Similarities between vocal learning in birds and humans suggest that many aspects of the learning process have evolved to meet demands imposed by vocal communication. Thus songbirds provide a valuable animal model in which to study the physiological basis of learned vocal communication and the nature of sensitive periods in general. In this article, I describe aspects of both behavioral and neural frameworks that currently inform our thinking about mechanisms underlying vocal learning and behavior in songbirds, and highlight ideas that may need re-examination.

KEYWORDS: zebra finch; song system; sensorimotor integration; NMDA receptor; silent synapses; postsynaptic potentials; axon pruning; topography; corollary discharge

IDEAS ABOUT BEHAVIORAL MECHANISMS

Behavioral studies of vocal learning have suggested some important processes that must be accounted for by neural encoding, including the formation of an auditory representation of song, and sensorimotor integration based on song-related feedback. Classic studies of temperate, seasonally breeding species, such as white-crowned sparrows, song sparrows, and swamp sparrows showed that birds can form long-term stable representations of the acoustic structure of song.[1] For example,

Address for correspondence: Sarah W. Bottjer, Department of Biology, HNB 218, 3641 Watt Way, University of Southern California, Los Angeles, California 90089-2520, USA. Voice: 213-740-9183; fax: 213-740-5687.
bottjer@usc.edu; <http://www-rcf.usc.edu/~bottjer/>

Ann. N.Y. Acad. Sci. 1016: 395–415 (2004). © 2004 New York Academy of Sciences.
doi: 10.1196/annals.1298.037

swamp sparrows exposed to songs of adult tutors as juveniles produce accurate imitations eight months later with no intervening rehearsal.[2,3] This result shows that birds can form a detailed memory ("template") of song based on auditory experience. Deafening sparrows following template formation prevents the development of normal vocal behavior, showing that feedback of self-produced vocalizations is necessary for the translation of the template into a motor program.[4]

These data led to a behavioral framework in which it is thought that song learning consists of two separate stages: a distinct process of auditory learning resulting in a stable neural representation of a specific song pattern (the template), followed by a phase of auditory-motor integration in which auditory feedback is used to detect the degree of error between the template and what is actually produced (but see ref. 5). One important prediction derived from the idea that birds are forming a stable auditory memory of the tutor song pattern is that activity of neurons in one or more brain regions should show evidence for auditory tuning to sounds of a specific tutor song. Physiological evidence for a template has been sparse thus far based on examination of individual brain regions (but see below and ref. 6), although it should be stressed that negative results carry little weight in this situation.

However, mechanisms of vocal learning may vary by species according to ecological aspects of behavior. A behavioral framework emphasizing a stable auditory template might not apply fully to zebra finches, the species that has become the workhorse of neural studies of song learning. Unlike sparrows, zebra finches complete the process of vocal learning in ~2–3 months, and the time during which zebra finches learn tutor songs overlaps largely with the time when they begin to vocalize themselves and engage in sensorimotor integration. Thus, it seems possible that zebra finches never form a long-term auditory memory of song (but see ref. 7). An alternate possibility is that they use some type of short-term or working memory of auditory sounds that are gradually transformed into auditory-motor representations. The latter idea could be tested by preventing birds from singing during times when they hear tutors. If hearing song must coincide with producing song in zebra finches, then the behavior of such birds should be abnormal.

Another caveat is that a simple two-phase model of vocal learning may be insufficient to describe the full complexity of vocal learning in general. For example, a potential requirement for a basic mapping between articulatory gestures, vocal output, and auditory feedback may need to be achieved prior to learning tutor sounds or a motor program for a complex song sequence. In general, we need a better understanding of the precise aspects and timing of behavioral processes of vocal learning in order to correlate behavioral functions with known developmental changes in the neural substrate for song learning (see articles in this volume).[8] Detailed knowledge of behavioral development is an essential prerequisite to formulating precise hypotheses regarding mechanisms within the neural substrate for song control.

THE NEURAL ROADMAP: KNOWING THE CIRCUITRY UNDERLYING VOCAL LEARNING

Introduction: Functional Aspects of Basic Song-Control Circuitry

The projection from HVC to RA and thence to hindbrain vocal motor circuitry is largely constructed during the sensitive period for vocal learning,[9,10] and is a major repository of the engram for a learned song pattern in adult birds.[11–14] Although there is a sparse axonal projection from HVC to RA in 20-day-old birds at the onset of song learning,[15] many newly generated neurons migrate into HVC and extend axons to RA thereafter, such that the major efferent cortical limb subserving control of acquired vocalizations is created during the learning process. HVC may also be the sole gateway by which auditory information enters song-control circuitry.[16,17]

Interestingly, recordings in anesthetized sparrows (which are known to form an auditory memory of song) have shown that HVC neurons do not appear to develop selective auditory tuning to the tutor song during early stages of song learning.[18] However, HVC neurons show pronounced selective tuning to the bird's own song (BOS) by the time birds have learned to produce a fairly good copy of the tutor song.[19] This pattern of results suggests that the emergence of selective tuning to BOS in HVC reflects a process of auditory-motor integration rather than auditory learning of a specific tutor song, and is consistent with the idea that it may be possible to acquire a sensorimotor program rather than storing a long-term auditory template and translating it (see above).

Obvious alternative ideas are that the template is not stored in HVC, or that gating mechanisms make it difficult to detect responses to tutor sounds.[20,21] In zebra finches, some neurons in lMAN develop auditory tuning to tutor sounds that are distinct from BOS, suggesting that lMAN may contain a template of tutor sounds.[6] Interestingly, birds with a lesion that are prevented from matching their vocal output to the tutor song (via lesion of the vocal motor nerve) show lower levels of selective tuning to BOS in Area X compared to birds that do successfully mimic tutor song.[22] This result argues that the development of BOS selectivity in Area X is a reflection of the learning process and may represent a neural signature of matching the bird's own vocal output to the tutor song.

A distinct group of HVC neurons project to the basal ganglia (Area X) and, unlike the late-developing HVC→RA projection, the pathway to Area X is generated early in development.[23,24] Area X contains both striatal and pallidal neurons;[25,26] and the latter make a strong projection onto the dorsal thalamus (DLM) and thence to lMAN. Lesions in the X-DLM-lMAN pathway greatly disrupt vocal production in juvenile birds, but not in older juvenile or adult birds.[27,28] The time course of effectiveness of lesions roughly parallels the emergence of a stable temporal sequence of notes in juvenile zebra finches, although the stereotypy of individual notes is still fairly variable at the time when lesions fail to produce substantial disruption of behavior.[29] The decreased disruptive effect of lMAN lesions also appears to parallel the emergence of auditory tuning to BOS in lMAN,[19] suggesting that the role of the X-DLM-lMAN circuit may change as a function of the development of auditory tuning and/ or the state of sensory-motor integration.

Lateral MAN: Parallel Pathways and Feedback/Feedforward Loops

Full knowledge of the neural pathways underlying song behavior is essential for generating hypotheses regarding specific functions for different circuits. In this section I summarize some recent findings regarding the organization and axonal connections of lMAN within the AFP (anterior forebrain pathway). One key discovery was that lMAN actually consists of two subregions, a magnocellular core and a surrounding shell comprised of both magnocellular and parvocellular neurons

(FIG. 1).[30] These subregions form the basis of highly topographic, parallel connections to and from lMAN: different subgroups of thalamic neurons in DLM project to core versus shell; in turn lMAN$_{core}$ projects to RA (in motor cortex) and Area X (in basal ganglia), and lMAN$_{shell}$ projects to an adjacent region of motor cortex (Ad) and to LPO in basal ganglia adjacent to Area X.[31,32]

Core and Shell Parallel Projections to RA and Ad

Thus, core and shell regions of lMAN make one set of parallel projections to motor cortex (RA and Ad, respectively). Unlike RA, Ad does not project directly to vocal motor circuitry, but rather makes a variety of efferent projections, many of which may contribute to feedback and feedforward connections in the song-control sys-

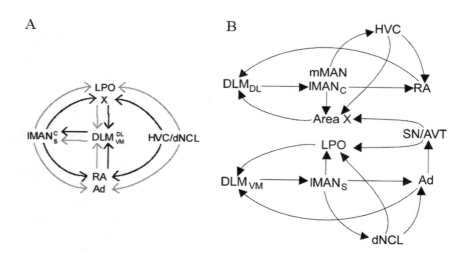

FIGURE 1. Two separate schematics of some of the neural circuits that control song learning and behavior. Both emphasize the fact that core and shell subregions of lMAN participate in parallel pathways that contribute to feedback and feedforward loops. (**A**) All roads lead to DLM. One idea emphasized in the text is that the lMAN$_{shell}$ pathway (*gray*) makes a substantial contribution to feedback and feedforward loops via the projection of Ad to a dorsal thalamic zone that includes both DLM and DMP, whereas the lMAN$_{core}$ pathway (*black*) contributes to feedback and feedforward loops mostly via the projection of Area X to the dorsal thalamic zone. An interesting contrast is that HVC sends separate projections to RA and X, whereas core and shell each send single (collateral) projections to RA/X and Ad/LPO, respectively. Not shown here is that lMAN$_{shell}$ sends a separate (direct) projection to dNCL, a cortical area caudolateral to HVC that has been implicated in imprinting in chicks. Dorsal NCL makes a strong projection onto Ad, so lMAN$_{shell}$ makes both monosynaptic and multisynaptic inputs onto Ad, suggesting that Ad may serve an important integrative function. (**B**) Core (*top*) and shell (*bottom*) pathways have a highly parallel organization, reflected here as mirror images. Medial MAN appears to be part of a larger MAN complex (see text), but its connections from DMP are omitted for the sake of simplicity.

tem.[32-36] Importantly, Ad neurons project to a dorsal thalamic zone that includes both DLM and DMP, potentially forming feedback loops to lMAN and feedforward pathways to mMAN-HVC (FIG. 1). Thus, an lMAN$_{shell}$→Ad→DLM/DMP pathway may serve as an important source of integration of song-related information via the dorsal thalamus. The projection to RA from lMAN$_{core}$ also gives rise to potential feedback and feedforward pathways. However, the main efferent projection of RA is onto hindbrain vocal motor and respiratory circuitry;[37] only the dorsal region of RA, which subserves a respiratory function, makes a sparse projection to the dorsal thalamic zone including DMP and DLM.[33,38,39] Thus, the contribution of lMAN$_{core}$ to feedback pathways via RA and the dorsal thalamus in adult birds may be relatively modest.

Core and Shell Parallel Projections to Area X and LPO

Core and shell regions of lMAN also make parallel projections to the basal ganglia (Area X and LPO, respectively), and X and LPO also project to the dorsal thalamic zone containing DLM and DMP, thereby completing additional potential feedback loops (FIG. 1). Individual projection neurons in lMAN$_{core}$ send axon collaterals to both RA and Area X, whereas those in lMAN$_{shell}$ send collaterals to both Ad and LPO. Thus, information emanating from lMAN is relayed to both motor cortex (RA and Ad) and basal ganglia (X and LPO), and then converges in the dorsal thalamic zone that includes DLM and DMP, suggesting this zone as an important region for exchange of information across functionally distinct pathways. Furthermore, the pattern of efferent projections from dorsal thalamus reveals an overall spatial organization in which adjacent nuclei DMP and DLM send separate, parallel projections to neighboring cortical song-control nuclei (mMAN, lMAN$_{core}$, and lMAN$_{shell}$, respectively) suggesting that these pathways may operate as a larger functional complex in which the dorsal thalamus serves as a nexus for feedback pathways that compare actual vocal output with desired or predicted output, as well as feedforward pathways that convey the results of such comparisons to HVC. The projection from lMAN$_{core}$ to Area X is robust (in terms of intensity and extent of anterogradely labeled axons), whereas that of lMAN$_{shell}$ to LPO is sparse,[36] suggesting that a feedback pathway from lMAN$_{core}$→Area X→DLM→lMAN$_{core}$ is stronger than the parallel one made by lMAN$_{shell}$→LPO→DLM→ lMAN$_{shell}$.

In summary, lMAN$_{shell}$ may signal feedback more strongly through an Ad→dorsal thalamus pathway, whereas lMAN$_{core}$ may signal feedback more strongly through an Area X→dorsal thalamus pathway. This asymmetry may indicate distinct functions of these two pathways, and it will be important to determine the precise kinds of information conveyed by each of these projections. Interestingly, viewing the dorsal thalamic zone of DLM and DMP as an important nexus of integration may help solve the problem of delay between premotor activity and resultant song-related feedback (see article by Konishi, this volume). For example, auditory activity being conveyed from HVC to basal ganglia (Area X) and motor cortex (RA) might converge in DLM, and enter feedback and feedforward loops into lMAN and mMAN emanating from DLM/DMP (FIG. 1A). Thus, working out temporal relationships of song-related activity in each relay of these circuits is also of paramount importance.[40,41]

FUNCTIONAL ASPECTS OF CIRCUITRY UNDERLYING VOCAL LEARNING: MAN HYPOTHESES

Functions of Lateral MAN: Core versus Shell

Although it is frequently claimed that lMAN does not contribute directly to motor production of song, this is a hypothesis that has not been tested directly. It seems clear that lMAN neurons are not on the main motor pathway in adult birds, since lesions of lMAN in normal adults have little or no effect on vocal motor output.[14,42–44] However, it is possible that $lMAN_{core}$ neurons are directly involved in producing vocal motor output in juvenile birds. The circumstantial evidence consistent with this hypothesis includes the following: (1) $lMAN_{core}$ neurons project directly to motor cortex (RA), bind androgens, and produce CGRP,[45,46] characteristics frequently associated with motor and pre-motor neurons; and (2) lesions of lMAN (that have included both core and shell regions) produce highly disrupted and precociously stereotyped vocal motor output within 24 hours post-lesion (the soonest that vocal behavior can be recorded following surgery).

One direct test of this idea would be to record chronic activity of $lMAN_{core}$ neurons in awake singing juvenile birds, and reversibly inactivate $lMAN_{core}$ neurons to test the resultant effects on behavior. Immediate disruption of vocal behavior due to inactivation of core neurons would argue that they are involved in on-line programming of vocalizations. Because core neurons make collateral projections to RA and Area X (see above), one hypothesis is that efference copy of motor commands generated in $lMAN_{core}$ is sent to Area X, where it could potentially integrate with auditory feedback being conveyed from HVC (see below). Interestingly, firing patterns of lMAN and Area X in awake singing adult birds show a pattern of activity that correlates with motor production of song, even in deaf birds,[47] which is consistent with the idea that $lMAN_{core}$ generates or relays some form of motor corollary discharge. However, core neurons are unlikely to be purely "motor" in function, as Rosen and Mooney[48] have shown that individual $lMAN_{core}$ neurons that project to RA (and X) respond briskly to BOS, suggesting that some type of auditory and motor integration occurs within core neurons themselves.

Thus, one hypothesis is that incipient vocalizations in young birds are programmed, at least in part, by $lMAN_{core}$ neurons. In contrast, $lMAN_{shell}$ neurons may be more important for evaluation and adjustment of the resulting vocal output. This division of different functions to core versus shell circuitry incorporates the idea that lMAN pathways subserve some "error detection" function that evaluates the match between real and desired vocal output (see Mooney, this volume),[49,50] but assigns this function primarily to shell circuitry while raising the possibility that core neurons may participate in programming motor behavior and also generating a copy of efferent commands that is relayed to other regions (such as Area X). Within this hypothetical framework, an important nexus that could help to carry out a comparison of actual versus desired vocal output, perhaps by integrating information across parallel pathways, is the dorsal thalamic zone that includes DLM and DMP, which may serve both as a site of convergence and integration, as well as a source of feedback and feedforward pathways (see above text and FIG. 1).[51] An initial test of this "division of labor" hypothesis for lMAN will be to separately lesion or inactivate the shell pathway and assess the behavioral result. If $lMAN_{shell}$ makes no direct contribution to vocal motor production, then inactivation of shell neurons should not produce any immediate behavioral disruption. However, if shell neurons are necessary for assisting in the matching (error detection) process that results in modification of vocal output, then lesions of $IMAN_{shell}$ should prevent the emergence of a stable copy of the tutor song.

FUNCTIONS OF MEDIAL MAN VERSUS LATERAL MAN

What about the rest of the MAN "complex"? The projection from the dorsal thalamus (DMP) to mMAN could also participate in both feedback and feedforward pathways. Lesions of mMAN cause substantial disruption of song behavior in young birds, but the pattern is different from that caused by lMAN lesions.[52] Juvenile birds with lMAN lesions are barely able to produce vocal sounds at all: the morphology of individual syllables is highly abnormal, the vocal pattern is prematurely stereotyped, and the amplitude of sounds produced is very low, suggesting that they have difficulty activating downstream motor circuitry. In contrast, juvenile birds with lesions of mMAN produce song syllables with some normal features, although they tend to produce multi-note syllables of unusually long duration, and the temporal sequence of syllables lacks stereotypy. Interestingly, juvenile ("plastic") song is similar in control and mMAN-lesioned birds; however, lesioned birds continue to produce highly unstereotyped song patterns even after 80 days of age, by which time control birds produce stereotyped vocal patterns with stable syllable sequences. This pattern also contrasts with lMAN-lesioned juvenile birds, in which vocal behavior is completely disrupted as soon as birds can be recorded post-surgery (~24 h). The overall pattern of results suggests that mMAN may participate in learning to parse sounds into distinct syllables and to produce a stable sequence of notes as juveniles are learning a specific vocal pattern.

Lesions of mMAN also cause mild disruption of stable adult song patterns, including slight increases in variability of vocal production, particularly at the onset of singing.[52] Thus, mMAN may mediate behavioral consistency in the initiation of a learned stereotyped vocal motor sequence in adult birds. Once again, this pattern stands in contrast to lesions of lMAN, which induce little or no change in normal adult song patterns.

The contrasting behavioral pattern following lesions of medial and lateral MAN suggests that these two brain regions may have opposing functions. That is, lMAN may contribute to behavioral variation during the process of song learning (since lesions of lMAN in juveniles abolish song variability prematurely), whereas mMAN may contribute to song stability (since lesions of mMAN in juveniles prevent behavioral stereotypy from developing). If, as suggested above, $IMAN_{core}$ has some direct function in producing vocalizations, then it may be that core neurons act primarily to generate "raw material" during early stages of vocal learning. For example, activity in $IMAN_{core}$ could lead to production of genetically specified vocal output, such as species-specific universals that are not based on auditory experience.[5] Such species-typical unlearned vocal output could provide an initial basis for vocally triggered, learning-based evaluation and adjustment at the onset of the sensitive period.

The idea that lMAN (core) may contribute to song variability accords well with the notion that lMAN (shell) is involved in detecting a discrepancy between auditory feedback of vocal output and tutor sounds in juvenile birds. As indicated above, the decline in effectiveness of lMAN lesions correlates with the emergence of tuning to BOS by neurons in lMAN, suggesting that congruence between motor production of BOS and auditory responsivity to this acoustic pattern may represent the absence or decline of an error signal, which curtails the ability of lMAN lesions to promote changes in vocal behavior. Thus, BOS tuning in lMAN neurons may represent a decline in an error signal, which removes the driving force for promoting variation in vocal behavior (and possibly permits or enhances the ability of mMAN to promote stereotypy). This is the situation that obtains in adult birds, unless an error signal is re-introduced (e.g., by motor nerve lesions or deafening[44,53]). A general caveat regarding "error signals" is that multiple types of comparisons, and hence multiple types of error signals, may be generated in different song-control circuits. All known brain regions involved with song learning and behavior contain neurons that respond to each bird's own song,[54] making every song-control region a potential site of comparison and error detection. For example, both classes of projection neurons in HVC (to RA and X), as well as lMAN$_{core}$ neurons that project to RA and X, are selectively responsive to BOS, and as suggested here both HVC→RA and lMAN$_{core}$→RA may serve some motor function. Thus, questions regarding structure-function relationships in the song-control system might profit by focusing on the nature and number of comparisons being made between actual and predicted vocal output, as opposed to where a single primary comparator function might be localized.

DEVELOPMENTAL CHANGES IN NEURAL CIRCUITS AND THEIR FUNCTION: STABILITY VERSUS PLASTICITY

Stability in Adult Song Patterns: A Central Motor Program?

Zebra finches develop a specific motor pattern of song during development, and under normal circumstances maintain that vocal pattern in a highly stereotyped fashion throughout adulthood. One interpretation of this apparent lack of adult plasticity is that vocal learning in such species entails the development of neural circuitry encoding a central motor program, such that adult birds are incapable of altering that pattern or learning novel ones. Traditionally, central motor programs have been thought to operate independently of peripheral feedback, but recent ideas incorporate the idea that sensorimotor feedback acts to fine-tune or adjust central pattern generators.[55] Study of the role of feedback in the song system can fairly be said to be in its infancy. Removal of song-related sensorimotor feedback does not exert any immediate effects on stereotyped vocal production in adult birds. For example, no short-term effects of deafening or of lesioning peripheral sensory nerves from the vocal organ have been observed in zebra finches.[27,56–58] But long-term consequences of removing or persistently altering auditory feedback include profound deterioration of song (see Woolley, this volume), especially for birds in whom stable song patterns are less engrained by extended practice.[59–62]

However, altering somatosensory feedback has an immediate effect on motor patterns during song production (Goller and Cooper, this volume):[63] perturbing respiratory pressure via a brief injection of air during song elicits an adaptive, compensatory change in activity of expiratory and vocal muscles in both hearing and deaf adult cardinals. Whether somatosensory feedback contributes to real-time adjustments to stable song to a greater degree than does auditory feedback (perhaps due to the need for adjustments in air pressure due to body movement during song, for example) remains to be determined. It is also not known whether long-term alterations in either auditory or motor feedback produce permanent changes in stereotyped song patterns, nor whether such changes could lead to new normal patterns of vocal motor output in adult birds.[62,64]

A related issue is the extent to which maintenance of stable adult songs represents an active process. Adult birds require an intact lMAN in order for song to be perturbed by deafening,[44,53] suggesting that lMAN is necessary for plasticity in adult song behavior. Lateral MAN circuitry may continue to subserve an error-detection function in adult birds, which could act to prevent drift in stable songs of normal birds. Remarkably however, deafened adult birds maintain their normal stereotyped song patterns for over a year when lMAN is lesioned.[65] This latter result raises the possibility that the HVC→RA pathway includes a central motor program that can maintain stable behavioral output in the absence of active maintenance from lMAN inputs (but does not rule out the possibility of an alternate source of error correction to the HVC→RA pathway that could serve to prevent behavioral drift). An alternate interpretation is that the HVC→RA pathway encodes a central motor program that is essentially incapable of change in the absence of input from lMAN.

Plasticity in Juvenile Song Behavior: Unique Mechanisms?

Another important question pertains to what extent mechanisms used for acquiring vocal patterns during development may be exercised in adult birds. There are several reasons to think that the emergence of stability in vocal behavior is accompanied by a reduction in the capacity for plasticity. First, although young birds that are maintained in social and acoustic isolation can learn to copy syllables from a tutor at a later date (as adults), the ability to learn new syllables is greatly decreased relative to juvenile birds within the timing of the normal sensitive period. Second, and possibly related, the neural substrate for vocal behavior undergoes extensive and permanent changes during development. For example, $lMAN_{shell}$ more than doubles in size during early stages of song learning (20 to 35 days of age), and this expansion represents both the area encompassed by postsynaptic cell bodies as well as by incoming thalamic presynaptic axons from DLM (FIG. 2).[30,31] The volume of $lMAN_{shell}$ (both pre- and postsynaptic elements) then undergoes substantial regression by adulthood. The density of neurons in $lMAN_{shell}$ does not appear to change during vocal development, suggesting a large increase (due to neurogenesis) and then decrease (due to cell death) in total number of neurons in this region. In addition, individual DLM axon arbors in $lMAN_{shell}$ undergo dramatic pruning, accompanied by a substantial decrease in number and density of synapses.[66,67]

Interestingly, the time course of this growth and regression in $lMAN_{shell}$ seems to parallel both the ability of lMAN lesions to disrupt vocal behavior and the development of auditory tuning to BOS in lMAN (see above). That is, the size of $lMAN_{shell}$ is very large when lesions of lMAN (including both core and shell) are highly effective and auditory selectivity is developing, and is regressing by the time lesions are relatively ineffective and auditory tuning to BOS is fairly well established. Given that nervous systems tend to increase neural processing capacity when they are do-

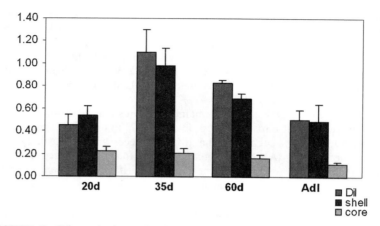

FIGURE 2. Changes in the total volume of core and shell regions of lMAN at different ages during vocal development. The core region was measured as the distribution of magnocellular neurons in Nissl-stained tissue (*light gray bars*); there is a small but significant regression in the size of $lMAN_{core}$ during the course of vocal learning. The shell region was measured as the distribution of magnocellular and parvocellular neurons surrounding core in Nissl-stained tissue (*dark gray bars*),[31] and as the distribution of labeled thalamic arbors following injections of the anterograde tracer DiI into DLM (*red bars*). The size of $lMAN_{shell}$ is large when lesions of lMAN are highly effective and auditory selectivity for BOS is undeveloped, and has started to regress by the time lesions are relatively ineffective and auditory tuning is emerging. Changes in the volume of shell (but not core) likely reflect large changes in neuronal number (see text).

ing something important like learning a specific representation or behavior,[68,69] it seems likely that the growth of $lMAN_{shell}$ could indicate a necessary role in particular functions essential to vocal learning. Such functions could include the establishment of basic associations between articulatory gestures and the sounds they produce, acquiring representations of the acoustic and/or motor structure of tutor song, and/or evaluating the degree to which vocal motor output matches the tutor song. In contrast, decreases in the absolute volume of brain space devoted to song-control circuitry presumably curtail the capacity for associated functions, suggesting in this case that regression of $lMAN_{shell}$ may preclude the ability to engage in one or more aspects of vocal learning. Thus, the developmental pattern of $lMAN_{shell}$ fits well with the hypothesis that some processes unique to development contribute to the stabilization of a specific behavioral pattern, and thereby "close the window" of the sensitive period during which the capacity for vocal learning is greatly enhanced.

DEVELOPMENT OF SPECIFICITY OF WIRING IN SONG-CONTROL CIRCUITS

Refinement of Axonal Connectivity during Song Learning

As indicated above, axon terminals of individual DLM neurons in $lMAN_{shell}$ undergo substantial retraction during early stages of song learning[66] and dendritic

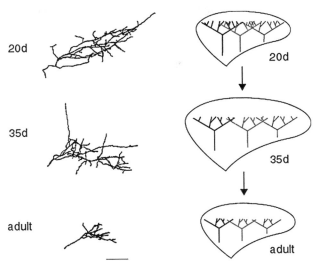

FIGURE 3. (*Left*) Reconstructions of individual DLM axon arbors in IMAN$_{shell}$ at different ages during vocal development.[66] The number of branches and total length of DLM arbors is highest at 20 days of age and lowest in adults indicating that these arbors undergo substantial retraction between 20 days of age and adulthood. Scale bar = 200 μm. (*Right*) Schematic diagram showing that pruning of DLM arbors between 20 and 35 days of age occurs as their post-synaptic target (IMAN$_{shell}$) increases in size, suggesting a decrease in overlap among DLM axon arbors and a consequent refinement in the topographic map during early stages of song learning.

spine frequencies and synaptic number and density decrease as well.[67,70] The most pronounced pruning of DLM axons occurs within IMAN$_{shell}$, which is growing in size, suggesting a significant decrease in overlap between individual axon arbors and a concomitant increase in the specificity of the topographic organization of the shell pathway around the height of the period for learning syllables from a tutor (FIG. 3). An even more pronounced example of refinement of axonal connectivity occurs in the projection from IMAN$_{core}$ to RA, which is almost completely lacking in topographic specificity at the onset of song learning (FIG. 4).[36] A substantial regression and remodeling of the IMAN$_{core}$→RA projection occurs during early stages of song learning, and this remodeling is prevented in birds that are deafened or exposed to loud white noise to prevent auditory feedback.[71] Thus, the rearrangement of this pathway is experience dependent, suggesting that it reflects one or more aspects of learning.

These changes suggest a dramatic remodeling of patterns of synaptic connectivity within the DLM→IMAN→RA pathway, and it is interesting that they occur primarily during early song development (from 20 to 35 days of age). This early reorganization of axonal connectivity raises the possibility that refinement of topographic specificity in this circuit may represent some type of learning that precedes syllable copying (perhaps contributing to a basic auditory-motor mapping of learned articulatory patterns and the sounds they represent).[72] However, it is also possible that such remodeling reflects one or more aspects of learning based on tutor-song exposure. Because $lMAN_{core}$ projects topographically onto RA, which contains a myotopic map of vocal muscles,[38] it seems possible that refinement of the connectivity within $lMAN_{shell}$ may serve to instruct or evaluate the development of higher-order information regarding specific articulatory gestures in core neurons. In addition, the development of pronounced auditory selectivity in lMAN neurons for self-produced sounds as song learning progresses suggests that specific acoustic information (or auditory-motor integrations) are also encoded in this circuitry as highly precise patterns of synaptic connectivity form.[6,19] One interesting test of whether shell circuitry "instructs" the core pathway would be to test whether selective lesions of the shell pathway prevent the experience-dependent refinement of topographic specificity normally seen in the $lMAN_{core} \rightarrow RA$ projection.

Signaling Molecules and Synapses: NMDA Receptors

Changes in signaling molecules also occur as neural circuits for song learning are being re-modeled. The incidence of NMDARs in lMAN is high at the onset of song development, but is gradually downregulated as indicated by a decrease in binding of the ligand MK-801 (see Nordeen and Nordeen, this volume).[73] Binding of an NR2B-specific ligand also decreases within lMAN (developmental changes in NR2A levels have not been studied),[74] and NMDAR-mediated currents attain mature (faster) speeds by ~40–45 days of age at DLM→lMAN synapses.[75,76] Auditory isolation of juvenile birds both prolongs the sensitive period for learning from a tutor and delays the shortening of NMDAR currents at DLM→lMAN synapses (but not lMAN→RA synapses;).[77,78] However, the transition to fast currents occurs by 65 days of age even in isolated birds, despite which these birds learn new song syllables when exposed to tutors starting at 65 days of age.

The ability to learn new tutor syllables with fast NMDA currents at DLM→lMAN synapses might be expected, since normal 40-day-old birds have already undergone most of the change to fast kinetics yet are able to learn tutor syllables around this time. Thus, the longer NMDAR currents seen in normal juveniles at this synapse during early song learning are not necessary for at least some types of learning to occur. Rather, the transition to faster NMDAR EPSCs might actually signify the onset of learning model syllables from a tutor.[79] Another possibility is that slower DLM→lMAN synaptic currents in young birds at the onset of song learning could subserve some early (unknown) aspect of learning that is necessary for later song development.[50] For example, longer NMDAR currents might facilitate the ability of young birds to learn an association between specific articulatory gestures and the vocal sounds they produce (i.e., some type of basic sensory-motor mapping, as suggested above). Consistent with this idea, precocious increases in serum testosterone levels cause premature maturation of NMDAR kinetics and disrupt song learning.[76,78,80]

A large proportion of DLM→lMAN synapses are post-synaptically "silent" in juvenile birds (FIG. 5).[81] Silent synapses express only NMDARs, but not AMPARs, and therefore do not detect neurotransmitter release at resting, hyperpolarized potentials due to the voltage-dependent Mg^{2+} blockade of NMDARs.[82–85] Conversion of silent (NMDAR-only) synapses to a functional state in hippocampus and tectum is due to the rapid addition of AMPARs, with a consequent decrease in the relative contribution of NMDARs to synaptic currents. However, the relative contribution of

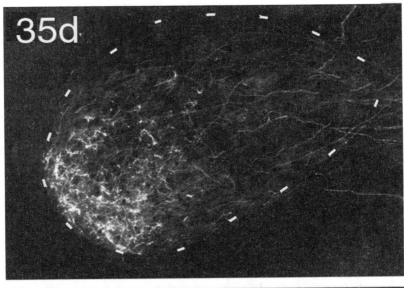

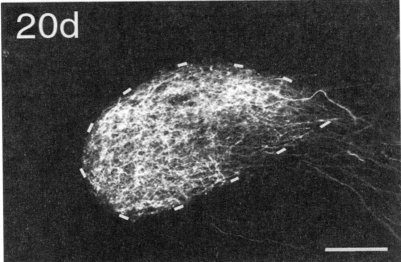

FIGURE 4. Cross-sections of RA showing labeled axons from IMAN$_{core}$ at 35 days of age (*top panel*) and 20 days of age (*bottom panel*).[36] Small injections of an anterograde tracer into IMAN$_{core}$ at 20 days of age produce labeled axons throughout most of RA; thus, topographic specificity is lacking at the onset of the sensitive period for vocal learning. In contrast, small injections into core at 35d produce a restricted, topographic pattern of label that matches the adult pattern. Interestingly, injections into IMAN$_{core}$ at 20 days of age produce "exuberant" label only in RA, but not in Area X, despite the fact that individual core neurons send collateral branches to both RA and X. This pattern suggests differential expression of some postsynaptic factors in RA versus Area X that cause (or are permissive for) exuberant growth only in the former axon branches.

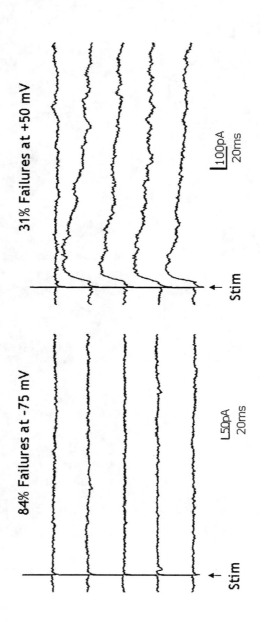

FIGURE 5. Whole-cell recordings from lMAN neurons in juvenile (20-day-old) zebra finches showing EPSCs at DLM→lMAN synapses at a holding potential of −75 mV (*left panel*) or +50 mV (*right panel*). The strength of stimulation to DLM axons ("Stim") was lowered to achieve a high failure rate at −75 mV, and then the holding potential was switched to +50 mV in order to test whether synapses containing only NMDA receptors could be unmasked. In this cell, the failure rate dropped to 31% (from 84%) once the cell was depolarized, thereby removing the Mg^{2+} blockade of NMDA receptors and allowing NMDAR-only synapses that are post-synaptically silent at hyperpolarized potentials to become activated. The incidence of synaptic failures decreases substantially at depolarized holding potentials only in normal solution, but not in the presence of drugs that block NMDA receptors (data not shown).

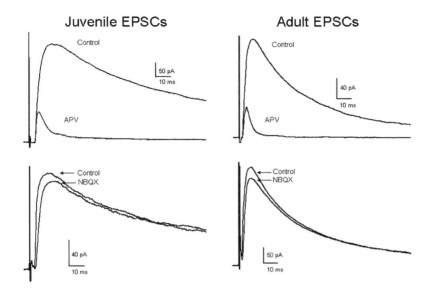

FIGURE 6. Pharmacological analysis of EPSCs at DLM→lMAN synapses reveals a very large contribution of NMDARs to total synaptic currents in both juvenile (20-day-old) and adult birds. (*Upper panels*) The total synaptic current at DLM→lMAN synapses is greatly reduced by APV, which blocks NMDA receptors selectively, revealing the AMPA receptor component; this effect is seen in both juvenile (*left*) and adult cells (*right*). Although lMAN neurons clearly show a brisk AMPAR-mediated synaptic response, the proportion of total synaptic current carried via AMPARs is less than 5%. (*Bottom panels*) As expected, blocking AMPA receptors with NBQX produces only a modest reduction in synaptic current at both ages. The kinetics of NMDARs are slow in juvenile cells, and mature to faster adult levels by ~40 days (see Nordeen and Nordeen, this volume).[89]

NMDARs remains high at DLM→lMAN synapses (FIG. 6), suggesting that both NMDA and AMPA receptors are added to silent synapses as vocal learning progresses or that a high incidence of NMDAR-only synapses continues to be maintained. In any case, it is also possible that NMDAR-only synapses are not post-synaptically silent in lMAN neurons, but that they are capable of transmitting current *in vivo*. The high proportion of total synaptic current carried by NMDARs at depolarized potentials *in vitro* in both juvenile and adult birds (FIG. 6) does not agree well with the finding that binding of the NMDAR ligand MK-801 declines substantially during song learning[73]; either this decline represents a loss of extra-synaptic NMDARs, or perhaps NMDARs decrease at some other subpopulation of lMAN synapses (e.g., intrinsic synapses).

Thus far there is no clear evidence that developmental changes in synaptic communication or plasticity correlate with important aspects of vocal learning (but see refs. 86–88). It will be important to determine the precise age course of potential changes in the incidence of NMDAR-only synapses in lMAN, since a decrease in silent synapses could represent an important mechanism for curtailing plasticity. Given the high proportion of synaptic current carried by NMDA receptors in the DLM→lMAN→RA pathway, it seems likely that correlated neural activity based on experience-driven inputs is selectively transmitted through these circuits, which could thereby contribute to song learning by regulating synaptic strength and thus the remodeling of individual axonal connectivity.[89] In particular, silent synapses could act as a filtering mechanism to gate only highly correlated convergent patterns of song-related feedback. One possibility is that a high incidence of silent synapses would enable experientially induced patterns of activity to selectively strengthen NMDAR-only synapses that are successfully activated; a low incidence of silent synapses would preclude opportunities for correlated patterns of activity to select and preserve such synapses. This scenario is reminiscent of remodeling of patterns of axonal connectivity in barn owls during re-learning of an association between visual and auditory cues in which NMDARs make an enhanced contribution to synaptic transmission.[90]

KNOW THE CODE: NEURAL CODING MECHANISMS
FOR LEARNED VOCAL PATTERNS

Understanding neural coding mechanisms in adult birds once they have learned to produce a stereotyped song is essential, since that constrains what mechanisms must be established during the sensitive period. The recent discovery that the engram of the motor program for song in HVC appears to use a timing-based population code in RA-projecting neurons is exciting.[14] Interestingly, the efferent projections from HVC to RA and Area X are not topographic, which contrasts markedly with the topographic organization in the axonal connections of lMAN.[31,32,35,36,91] The lack of topography in RA-projecting HVC neurons makes sense in the context of a timing-based population code in HVC. Because RA contains a myotopic map of vocal muscles,[38] and activity in most vocal muscles is probably required to produce the combinations of airflow and vocal tract configuration unique to each vocalization,[92] one prediction is that individual RA-projecting neurons in HVC should be selectively connected to different subsets of RA neurons that help drive specific configurations of muscle activity associated with production of particular sound types.

The development of functional patterns of synaptic connectivity in RA presumably represents the end product of whatever processing is carried out elsewhere by song-control circuitry. In adulthood, activity of single RA neurons in awake singing birds always precedes specific subsyllabic elements of song production, such that the pre-motor activity pattern in an individual RA neuron is predictive of sounds that will be made.[93] During vocal learning, there may be a hierarchy of instruction that results in specific patterns of synaptic activity developing in RA. For example, if one function of shell circuitry is to instruct core circuitry, and thereby contribute to the refinement of the lMAN$_{core}$→RA pathway (see above), then lMAN$_{core}$ inputs to RA may subsequently serve as a source of instruction for the large numbers of HVC axons growing into RA at later stages of song learning. That is, one important function of lMAN$_{core}$ inputs to RA could be to selectively strengthen patterns of HVC synaptic inputs to RA that correspond to specific sounds, thereby helping to establish the synaptic specificity of HVC-to-RA connections during learning.[94]

Individual RA neurons receive synaptic input from both $IMAN_{core}$ and HVC; the $IMAN_{core} \rightarrow RA$ projection is mediated almost wholly by NMDARs, whereas the HVC→RA projection uses both NMDA and AMPA receptors.[86,95] In order for $IMAN_{core}$ inputs to instruct HVC inputs in RA, one prediction is that neural activity should arrive approximately simultaneously from HVC and $IMAN_{core}$. Simultaneous activation of specific inputs from IMAN and HVC could provide sufficient depolarization to activate NMDARs, and thereby strengthen the activated synapses. If the high proportion of synaptic current carried by NMDARs in the DLM-$IMAN_{core}$-RA pathway serves as a filtering mechanism such that only activity corresponding to tutor sounds is gated through to RA (see above), then corresponding HVC→RA synapses for those sounds could be reinforced. Once HVC synapses are stabilized in RA, the need for input from $IMAN_{core}$ would presumably be diminished, as reflected in the substantial loss of synapses made by IMAN axons in RA.[96]

Whatever mechanisms are used to refine the patterns of synaptic inputs to RA will have to be compatible with a second type of neural coding in adult birds reported by Dave and Margoliash.[72] They made chronic recordings of individual RA neurons and showed that playback of BOS elicited bursts of neural activity that were temporally aligned with premotor bursts that occur during singing. They also reported that BOS-elicited bursts depended on the prior sequence of sounds in the song pattern, suggesting the possibility that auditory feedback of prior syllables may ultimately activate circuitry that recruits neural networks in RA necessary for production of subsequent syllables. An alternate possibility is that the activity evoked in RA neurons by hearing BOS does not represent a prediction, per se, of other syllables. For example, perhaps auditory feedback of a prior syllable reaches HVC and is relayed to the X-DLM-IMAN pathway for evaluation of a match to tutor sounds. The matching process, which may be integrated over time, would result in an output signal from IMAN only in the case of a correct match, and the resulting activity in RA (from IMAN) would be used purely as a reinforcement signal (possibly for subsequent syllables), but would not carry specific information concerning representations of sounds or articulatory gestures.[50] According to this hypothesis, whatever HVC inputs are simultaneously active with IMAN inputs at individual RA neurons would be maintained (strengthened), assuming that coincidence of activity in these two inputs as the mechanism mediating synaptic efficacy. Simultaneous activity would occur only for correct matches (since otherwise there is no output signal from IMAN).

It would be extremely interesting to determine when the matched BOS-elicited and premotor activity patterns emerge in juvenile birds during the song learning process, and whether different types of coincidence of premotor and auditory-evoked activity occur during plastic song. A major challenge for the future is to devise testable hypotheses that further test current theoretical frameworks and to ascribe specific functions necessary for different aspects of vocal learning to different subsets of neural circuits.

REFERENCES

1. MARLER, P. 1970. A comparative approach to vocal learning: song development in white-crowned sparrows. J. Comp. Physiol. Psychol. **71**: 1–25.

2. MARLER, P. & S. PETERS. 1981. Sparrow learn adult song and more from memory. Science **213**: 780–782.
3. MARLER, P. & S. PETERS. 1982. Long-term storage of learned birdsongs prior to production. Anim. Behav. **30**: 479–482.
4. KONISHI, M. 1965. Effects of deafening on song development in American robins and black-headed grosbeaks. Z. Tierpsychol. **22**: 584–599.
5. MARLER, P. 1997. Three models of song learning: evidence from behavior. J. Neurobiol. **33**: 501–516.
6. SOLIS, M.M. & A.J. DOUPE. 1999. Contributions of tutor and bird's own song experience to neural selectivity in the songbird anterior forebrain. J. Neurosci. **19**: 4559–4584.
7. FUNABIKI, Y. & M. KONISHI. 2003. Long memory in song learning by zebra finches. J. Neurosci. **23**: 6928–6935.
8. TCHERNICHOVSKI, O., P.P. MITRA, T. LINTS & F. NOTTEBOHM. 2001. Dynamics of the vocal imitation process: how a zebra finch learns its song. Science **291**: 2564–2569.
9. KONISHI, M. & E. AKUTAGAWA. 1985. Neuronal growth, atrophy and death in a sexually dimorphic song nucleus in the zebra finch brain. Nature **315**: 145–147.
10. NORDEEN, K.W. & E.J. NORDEEN. 1988. Projection neurons within a vocal motor pathway are born during song learning in zebra finches. Nature **334**: 149–151.
11. NOTTEBOHM, F., T.M. STOKES & C.M. LEONARD. 1976. Central control of song in the canary, *Serinus canarius*. J. Comp. Neurol. **165**: 457–486.
12. VU, E.T., M.E. MAZUREK & Y.C. KUO. 1994. Identification of a forebrain motor programming network for the learned song of zebra finches. J. Neurosci. **14**: 6924–6934.
13. YU, A.C. & D. MARGOLIASH. 1996. Temporal hierarchical control of singing in birds [see comments]. Science **273**: 1871–1875.
14. HAHNLOSER, R.H., A.A. KOZHEVNIKOV & M.S. FEE. 2002. An ultra-sparse code underlies the generation of neural sequences in a songbird. Nature **419**: 65–70.
15. FOSTER, E.F. & S.W. BOTTJER. 1998. Axonal connections of the high vocal center and surrounding cortical regions in juvenile and adult male zebra finches. J. Comp. Neurol. **397**: 118–138.
16. DOUPE, A.J. & M. KONISHI. 1991. Song-selective auditory circuits in the vocal control system of the zebra finch. Proc. Natl. Acad. Sci. USA **88**: 11339–11343.
17. VICARIO, D.S. & K.H. YOHAY. 1993. Song-selective auditory input to a forebrain vocal control nucleus in the zebra finch. J. Neurobiol. **24**: 488–505.
18. VOLMAN, S.F. 1993. Development of neural selectivity for birdsong during vocal learning. J. Neurosci. **13**: 4737–4747.
19. SOLIS, M.M. & A.J. DOUPE. 1997. Anterior forebrain neurons develop selectivity by an intermediate stage of birdsong learning. J. Neurosci. **17**: 6447–6462.
20. RAUSKE, P.L., S.D. SHEA & D. MARGOLIASH. 2003. State and neuronal class-dependent reconfiguration in the avian song system. J. Neurophysiol. **89**: 1688–1701.
21. CARDIN, J.A. & M.F. SCHMIDT. 2003. Auditory responses in multiple sensorimotor song system nuclei are co-modulated by behavioral state. J. Neurophysiol. **90**: 2884–2899.
22. SOLIS, M.M. & A.J. DOUPE. 2000. Compromised neural selectivity for song in birds with impaired sensorimotor learning. Neuron **25**: 109–121.
23. ALVAREZ-BUYLLA, A., M. THEELEN & F. NOTTEBOHM. 1988. Birth of projection neurons in the higher vocal center of the canary forebrain before, during, and after song learning. Proc. Natl. Acad. Sci. USA **85**: 8722–8726.
24. MOONEY, R. & M. RAO. 1994. Waiting periods versus early innervation: the development of axonal connections in the zebra finch song system. J. Neurosci. **14**: 6532–6543.
25. FARRIES, M.A. & D.J. PERKEL. 2002. A telencephalic nucleus essential for song learning contains neurons with physiological characteristics of both striatum and globus pallidus. J. Neurosci. **22**: 3776–3787.
26. REINER, A., A.V. LAVERGHETTA, C.A. MEADE, *et al.* 2004. An immunohistochemical and pathway tracing study of the striatopallidal organization of area X in the male zebra finch. J. Comp. Neurol. **469**: 239–261.

27. BOTTJER, S.W. & A.P. ARNOLD. 1984. The role of feedback from the vocal organ. I. Maintenance of stereotypical vocalizations by adult zebra finches. J. Neurosci. **4:** 2387–2396.
28. SCHARFF, C. & F. NOTTEBOHM. 1991. A comparative study of the behavioral deficits following lesions of various parts of the zebra finch song system: implications for vocal learning. J. Neurosci. **11:** 2896–2913.
29. BOTTJER, S.W. & A.P. ARNOLD. 1986. Handbook of Behavioral Neurobiology: Dev. Proc. Psychobiol. Neurobiol.: 129–161.
30. JOHNSON, F. & S.W. BOTTJER. 1992. Growth and regression of thalamic efferents in the song-control system of male zebra finches. J. Comp. Neurol. **326:** 442–450.
31. JOHNSON, F., M.M. SABLAN & S.W. BOTTJER. 1995. Topographic organization of a forebrain pathway involved with vocal learning in zebra finches. J. Comp. Neurol. **358:** 260–278.
32. BOTTJER, S.W., J.D. BRADY & B. CRIBBS. 2000. Connections of a motor cortical region in zebra finches: relation to pathways for vocal learning. J. Comp. Neurol. **420:** 244–260.
33. FOSTER, E.F., R.P. MEHTA & S.W. BOTTJER. 1997. Axonal connections of the medial magnocellular nucleus of the anterior neostriatum in zebra finches. J. Comp. Neurol. **382:** 364–381.
34. VATES, G.E. & F. NOTTEBOHM. 1995. Feedback circuitry within a song-learning pathway. Proc. Natl. Acad. Sci. USA **92:** 5139–5143.
35. VATES, G.E., D.S. VICARIO & F. NOTTEBOHM. 1997. Reafferent thalamo-"cortical" loops in the song system of oscine songbirds. J. Comp. Neurol. **380:** 275–290.
36. IYENGAR, S., S.S. VISWANATHAN & S.W. BOTTJER. 1999. Development of topography within song control circuitry of zebra finches during the sensitive period for song learning. J. Neurosci. **19:** 6037–6057.
37. WILD, J.M. 1997. Neural pathways for the control of birdsong production. J. Neurobiol. **33:** 653–670.
38. VICARIO, D.S. 1991. Neural mechanisms of vocal production in songbirds. Curr. Opin. Neurobiol. **1:** 595–600.
39. WILD, J.M. 1993. Descending projections of the songbird nucleus robustus archistriatalis. J. Comp. Neurol. **338:** 225–241.
40. LUO, M. & D.J. PERKEL. 1999. A GABAergic, strongly inhibitory projection to a thalamic nucleus in the zebra finch song system. J. Neurosci. **19:** 6700–6711.
41. MOONEY, R., M.J. ROSEN & C.B. STURDY. 2002. A bird's eye view: top down intracellular analyses of auditory selectivity for learned vocalizations. J. Comp. Physiol. A Neuroethol. Sens. Neural Behav. Physiol. **188:** 879–895.
42. BOTTJER, S.W., E.A. MIESNER & A.P. ARNOLD. 1984. Forebrain lesions disrupt development but not maintenance of song in passerine birds. Science **224:** 901–903.
43. NORDEEN, K.W. & E.J. NORDEEN. 1993. Long-term maintenance of song in adult zebra finches is not affected by lesions of a forebrain region involved in song learning. Behav. Neural Biol. **59:** 79–82.
44. WILLIAMS, H. & N. MEHTA. 1999. Changes in adult zebra finch song require a forebrain nucleus that is not necessary for song production. J. Neurobiol. **39:** 14–28.
45. KORSIA, S. & S.W. BOTTJER. 1989. Developmental changes in the cellular composition of a brain nucleus involved with song learning in zebra finches. Neuron **3:** 451–460.
46. BOTTJER, S.W., H. ROSELINSKY & N.B. TRAN. 1997. Sex differences in neuropeptide staining of song-control nuclei in zebra finch brains. Brain Behav. Evol. **50:** 284–303.
47. HESSLER, N.A. & A.J. DOUPE. 1999. Singing-related neural activity in a dorsal forebrain-basal ganglia circuit of adult zebra finches. J. Neurosci. **19:** 10461–10481.
48. ROSEN, M.J. & R. MOONEY. 2000. Intrinsic and extrinsic contributions to auditory selectivity in a song nucleus critical for vocal plasticity. J. Neurosci. **20:** 5437–5448.
49. BRAINARD, M.S. & A.J. DOUPE. 2000. Auditory feedback in learning and maintenance of vocal behaviour. Nat. Rev. Neurosci. **1:** 31–40.
50. TROYER, T.W. & S.W. BOTTJER. 2001. Birdsong: models and mechanisms. Curr. Opin. Neurobiol. **11:** 721–726.

51. GUILLERY, R.W. & S.M. SHERMAN. 2002. Thalamic relay functions and their role in corticocortical communication: generalizations from the visual system. Neuron **33:** 163–175.

52. FOSTER, E.F. & S.W. BOTTJER. 2001. Lesions of a telencephalic nucleus in male zebra finches: influences on vocal behavior in juveniles and adults. J. Neurobiol. **46:** 142–165.

53. BRAINARD, M.S. & A.J. DOUPE. 2000. Interruption of a basal ganglia-forebrain circuit prevents plasticity of learned vocalizations. Nature **404:** 762–766.

54. WILLIAMS, H. & F. NOTTEBOHM. 1985. Auditory responses in avian vocal motor neurons: a motor theory for song perception in birds. Science **229:** 279–282.

55. PEARSON, K. 2000. Motor systems. Curr. Opin. Neurobiol. **10:** 649–654.

56. PRICE, P.H. 1979. Developmental determinants of structure in zebra finch song. J. Comp. Physiol. Psychol. **93:** 260–277.

57. OKANOYA, K. & A. YAMAGUCHI. 1997. Adult Bengalese finches (*Lonchura striata* var. *domestica*) require real-time auditory feedback to produce normal song syntax. J. Neurobiol. **33:** 343–356.

58. WOOLLEY, S.M. & E.W. RUBEL. 1997. Bengalese finches *Lonchura striata domestica* depend upon auditory feedback for the maintenance of adult song. J. Neurosci. **17:** 6380–6390.

59. NORDEEN, K.W. & E.J. NORDEEN. 1992. Auditory feedback is necessary for the maintenance of stereotyped song in adult zebra finches. Behav. Neural Biol. **57:** 58–66.

60. LEONARDO, A. & M. KONISHI. 1999. Decrystallization of adult birdsong by perturbation of auditory feedback. Nature **399:** 466–470.

61. LOMBARDINO, A.J. & F. NOTTEBOHM. 2000. Age at deafening affects the stability of learned song in adult male zebra finches. J. Neurosci. **20:** 5054–5064.

62. ZEVIN, J.D., M.S. SEIDENBER & S.W. BOTTJER. 2004. Limits on reacquisition of song learning in adult zebra finches exposed to white noise. J. Neurosci. In press.

63. SUTHERS, R.A., F. GOLLER & J.M. WILD. 2002. Somatosensory feedback modulates the respiratory motor program of crystallized birdsong. Proc. Natl. Acad. Sci. USA **99:** 5680–5685.

64. WOOLLEY, S.M. & E.W. RUBEL. 2002. Vocal memory and learning in adult Bengalese finches with regenerated hair cells. J. Neurosci. **22:** 7774–7787.

65. BRAINARD, M.S. & A.J. DOUPE. 2001. Postlearning consolidation of birdsong: stabilizing effects of age and anterior forebrain lesions. J. Neurosci. **21:** 2501–2517.

66. IYENGAR, S. & S.W. BOTTJER. 2002. Development of individual axon arbors in a thalamocortical circuit necessary for song learning in zebra finches. J. Neurosci. **22:** 901–911.

67. NIXDORF-BERGWEILER, B.E. 2001. Lateral magnocellular nucleus of the anterior neostriatum (LMAN) in the zebra finch: neuronal connectivity and the emergence of sex differences in cell morphology. Microsc. Res. Tech. **54:** 335–353.

68. NOTTEBOHM, F., S. KASPARIAN & C. PANDAZIS. 981. Brain space for a learned task. Brain Res. **213:** 99–109.

69. WEINBERGER, N.M. 1995. Dynamic regulation of receptive fields and maps in the adult sensory cortex. Annu. Rev. Neurosci. **18:** 129–158.

70. NIXDORF-BERGWEILER, B.E., E. WALLHAUSSER-FRANKE & T.J. DEVOOGD. 1995. Regressive development in neuronal structure during song learning in birds. J. Neurobiol. **27:** 204–215.

71. IYENGAR, S. & S.W. BOTTJER. 2002. The role of auditory experience in the formation of neural circuits underlying vocal learning in zebra finches. J. Neurosci. **22:** 946–958.

72. DAVE, A.S. & D. MARGOLIASH. 2000. Song replay during sleep and computational rules for sensorimotor vocal learning. Science **290:** 812–816.

73. AAMODT, S.M., E.J. NORDEEN & K.W. NORDEEN. 1995. Early isolation from conspecific song does not affect the normal developmental decline of N-methyl-D-aspartate receptor binding in an avian song nucleus. J. Neurobiol. **27:** 76–84.

74. BASHAM, M.E., F. SOHRABJI, T.D. SINGH, *et al.* 1999. Developmental regulation of NMDA receptor 2B subunit mRNA and ifenprodil binding in the zebra finch anterior forebrain. J. Neurobiol. **39:** 155–167.

75. LIVINGSTON, F.S. & R. MOONEY. 1997. Development of intrinsic and synaptic properties in a forebrain nucleus essential to avian song learning. J. Neurosci. **17:** 8997–9009.
76. WHITE, S.A., F.S. LIVINGSTON & R. MOONEY. 1999. Androgens modulate NMDA receptor-mediated EPSCs in the zebra finch song system. J. Neurophysiol. **82:** 2221–2234.
77. LIVINGSTON, F.S., S.A. WHITE & R. MOONEY. 2000. Slow NMDA-EPSCs at synapses critical for song development are not required for song learning in zebra finches. Nat. Neurosci. **3:** 482–488.
78. SINGH, T.D., M.E. BASHAM, E.J. NORDEEN & K.W. NORDEEN. 2000. Early sensory and hormonal experience modulate age-related changes in NR2B mRNA within a forebrain region controlling avian vocal learning. J. Neurobiol. **44:** 82–94.
79. ROBERTS, E.B. & A.S. RAMOA. 1999. Enhanced NR2A subunit expression and decreased NMDA receptor decay time at the onset of ocular dominance plasticity in the ferret. J. Neurophysiol. **81:** 2587–2591.
80. KORSIA, S. & S.W. BOTTJER. 1991. Chronic testosterone treatment impairs vocal learning in male zebra finches during a restricted period of development. J. Neurosci. **11:** 2362–2371.
81. GRAMMER, M.K. & S.W. BOTTJER. 2001. Silent synapses at neural substrates important for song learning in zebra finches. Soc. Neurosci. Abstr. **27:** 1424.
82. LIAO, D., N.A. HESSLER & R. MALINOW. 1995. Activation of postsynaptically silent synapses during pairing-induced LTP in CA1 region of hippocampal slice. Nature **375:** 400–404.
83. ISAAC, J.T., R.A. NICOLL & R.C. MALENKA. 1995. Evidence for silent synapses: implications for the expression of LTP. Neuron **15:** 427–434.
84. DURAND, G.M., Y. KOVALCHUK & A. KONNERTH. 1996. Long-term potentiation and functional synapse induction in developing hippocampus. Nature **381:** 71–75.
85. WU, G., R. MALINOW & H.T. CLINE. 1996. Maturation of a central glutamatergic synapse. Science **274:** 972–976.
86. STARK, L.L. & D.J. PERKEL. 1999. Two-stage, input-specific synaptic maturation in a nucleus essential for vocal production in the zebra finch. J. Neurosci. **19:** 9107–9116.
87. BOETTIGER, C.A. & A.J. DOUPE. 2001. Developmentally restricted synaptic plasticity in a songbird nucleus required for song learning. Neuron **31:** 809–818.
88. DING, L. & D.J. PERKEL. 2004. Long-term potentiation in an avian basal ganglia nucleus essential for vocal learning. J. Neurosci. **24:** 488–494.
89. BOTTJER, S.W. 2002. Neural strategies for learning during sensitive periods of development. J. Comp. Physiol. A Neuroethol. Sens. Neural Behav. Physiol. **188:** 917–928.
90. FELDMAN, D.E., M.S. BRAINARD & E.I. KNUDSEN. 1996. Newly learned auditory responses mediated by NMDA receptors in the owl inferior colliculus. Science **271:** 525–528.
91. FORTUNE, E.S. & D. MARGOLIASH. 1995. Parallel pathways and convergence onto HVc and adjacent neostriatum of adult zebra finches (*Taeniopygia guttata*). J. Comp. Neurol. **360:** 413–441.
92. SUTHERS, R.A. & D. MARGOLIASH. 2002. Motor control of birdsong. Curr. Opin. Neurobiol. **12:** 684–690.
93. CHI, Z. & D. MARGOLIASH. 2001. Temporal precision and temporal drift in brain and behavior of zebra finch song. Neuron **32:** 899–910.
94. KITTELBERGER, J.M. & R. MOONEY. 1999. Lesions of an avian forebrain nucleus that disrupt song development alter synaptic connectivity and transmission in the vocal premotor pathway. J. Neurosci. **19:** 9385–9398.
95. MOONEY, R. 1992. Synaptic basis for developmental plasticity in a birdsong nucleus. J. Neurosci. **12:** 2464–2477.
96. HERRMANN, K. & A.P. ARNOLD. 1991. The development of afferent projections to the robust archistriatal nucleus in male zebra finches: a quantitative electron microscopic study. J. Neurosci. **11:** 2063–2074.

Synaptic and Molecular Mechanisms Regulating Plasticity during Early Learning

KATHY W. NORDEEN AND ERNEST J. NORDEEN

Departments of Brain & Cognitive Science and Neurobiology & Anatomy,
University of Rochester, Rochester, New York 14627-0268, USA

ABSTRACT: Many behaviors are learned most easily during a discrete developmental period, and it is generally agreed that these "sensitive periods" for learning reflect the developmental regulation of molecular or synaptic properties that underlie experience-dependent changes in neural organization and function. Avian song learning provides one example of such temporally restricted learning, and several features of this behavior and its underlying neural circuitry make it a powerful model for studying how early experience sculpts neural and behavioral organization. Here we describe evidence that within the basal ganglia–thalamocortical loop implicated in vocal learning, song acquisition engages N-methyl-D-aspartate receptors (NMDARs), as well as signal transduction cascades strongly implicated in other instances of learning. Furthermore, NMDAR phenotype changes in parallel with developmental and seasonal periods for vocal plasticity. We also review recent studies in the avian song system that challenge the popular notion that sensitive periods for learning reflect developmental changes in the NMDAR that alter thresholds for synaptic plasticity.

KEYWORDS: NMDA receptor; development; sensitive period; learning; birdsong

Many behaviors are shaped by specific sensory and/or hormonal events that occur during "sensitive" periods in life. For example, avian song learning, human language acquisition, the development of normal sensory function, sexual differentiation, and imprinting all exhibit periods when experience has a particularly profound effect on brain organization and behavior. It is generally assumed that sensitive periods arise because experience affects the outcome of specific cellular and synaptic changes that occur uniquely, or are at least exaggerated, during neural development. In some cases, those aspects of neural development that may constrain sensitive periods are obvious. For instance, the onset of a sensitive period depends minimally upon the establishment of circuitry competent to convey the learning stimulus, the presence of modulatory pathways or molecules that enable learning mechanisms, and the expression of the intracellular machinery that produces lasting neural and behavioral

Address for correspondence: Kathy W. Nordeen, Departments of Brain & Cognitive Science, University of Rochester, Rochester, NY 14627-0268. Voice: 585-275-8452; fax: 585-442-9216.
knordeen@bcs.rochester.edu
<http://www.bcs.rochester.edu/people/knordeen/knordeen.html>
<http://www.bcs.rochester.edu/people/ernie/ernie.html>

Ann. N.Y. Acad. Sci. 1016: 416–437 (2004). © 2004 New York Academy of Sciences.
doi: 10.1196/annals.1298.018

change. Also, in at least some cases, closure of a sensitive period is relatively straightforward. For example, during sexual differentiation, the sensitive period for some aspects of hormone-induced masculinization is limited by the time course of naturally occurring cell death, because in some regions hormones rescue cells that would otherwise die.[1,2] However, with regard to sensory development and early learning, the complexity of synaptic and intracellular mechanisms that promote change in neural and behavioral organization create a considerable challenge for identifying neural events that regulate the onset and termination of sensitive periods. Significant progress in understanding the neurobiology of sensitive periods has come from studies of the developing visual system. This literature has provided strong evidence that specific forms of sensory input early in life permanently shape neural circuits by driving an activity-dependent process of synaptic strengthening, sprouting, weakening, and elimination.[3–5] Such experience-dependent synaptic re-arrangement also is evident during imprinting[6–8] and likely exploits forms of synaptic plasticity that have been implicated in adult learning. Thus, research directed toward understanding sensitive periods has focused on characterizing age-related changes in the thresholds for inducing synaptic plasticity. However, changes in synaptic strength entail multiple interacting biochemical cascades and are subject to a myriad of modulatory influences. Thus, while this review focuses on a narrow set of changes in the molecular machinery that could directly have an impact on synaptic transmission and plasticity, it is important to recognize that multiple aspects of neural development affect thresholds for plasticity, and that the consequence of one developmental change will interact with the state of other relevant influences. In addition, synaptic strengthening and weakening is apt to have a more enduring affect on neural circuitry at times of rapid synaptogenesis and synapse elimination. Undoubtedly, sensitive periods are defined by the interaction of many events, and it is certainly possible (indeed likely) that no single aspect of development will prove sufficient to explain the timing of a given sensitive period.

RESEARCH STRATEGY AND TACTICS

Notwithstanding these complexities, a realistic hope is that certain developmental events produce powerful enough effects on synaptic plasticity so as to be able to measure their contribution to regulation of a sensitive period. From among the mix of events that overlap with any particular sensitive period, one can ask: which are necessary, and are any sufficient, to dampen plasticity? Generally, these questions are approached by first identifying the cellular mechanisms mediating a specific instance of developmental plasticity. There is an underlying prescription that the proposed cellular/molecular processes should be localizable and measurable in relevant brain regions during periods of learning. Moreover, if the candidate process is indeed necessary for the learning process, interfering with its function should impair behavioral indices of learning. Genetic or pharmacological manipulations are generally employed to test function, but their interpretation can be difficult because frequently they lack adequate specificity and may activate compensatory processes that can obscure the normal physiological role of a particular process. Despite these limitations, such studies add critical information because correlative studies alone are not sufficient to determine what processes are indeed necessary for learning. Only after a specific cellular, synaptic, or molecular change has been directly implicated in learning can one assess whether qualitative or quantitative changes in its expression modulate plasticity. And, of course, regulation of plasticity can occur through changes in any aspect of the biological cascade that transduces sensory experience into lasting neural and behavioral change: (1) upstream circuitry that provides information to the learning mechanism (e.g., balance of inhibitory and excitatory inputs or neuromodulatory pathways), (2) the molecular machinery that provokes synaptic plasticity (e.g., receptors, intracellular signaling molecules, trophic factors), or (3) downstream events involved in expression of those plasticity cascades (e.g. , specific patterns of gene expression, synapse formation or elimination). Thus, several criteria are needed to evaluate whether any particular developmental change results in a sensitive period for learning. We need to ask (1) whether the developmental regulation coincides with the timing of the sensitive period, (2) whether variables that regulate the timing of the sensitive period regulate, in parallel, the expression of the candidate mechanism, and (3) whether manipulations that alter the time course of the candidate mechanism predictably alter the temporal profile of the sensitive period.

Over the past 10–15 years, the N-methyl-D-aspartate subtype of glutamate receptor (NMDAR) has come under close scrutiny as one potential regulator of sensitive periods. Attention has focused on NMDARs both because they are critical for many forms of learning and synaptic plasticity and because they are developmentally regulated in ways that seem to alter thresholds for plasticity. Here, we review evidence that avian vocal plasticity involves NMDAR-mediated forms of synaptic plasticity, with special emphasis on experiments that have investigated whether changes in NMDAR phenotype constrain the timing of this learning.

THE N-METHYL-D-ASPARTATE RECEPTOR AND SYNAPTIC PLASTICITY

There is general agreement that experience is stored in the brain as a consequence of an activity-dependent process of synaptic strengthening and weakening, governed in turn by the relationships between presynaptic activity and postsynaptic firing. Synaptic strengthening (manifest as long-term potentiation, LTP) and stabilization occurs preferentially at sites where presynaptic activity consistently contributes to firing the postsynaptic cell ("Hebbian" modification). In contrast, synaptic weakening (manifest as long-term depression, LTD) occurs when such correlations in pre- and postsynaptic activity are sparse or absent. In both young and adult animals, NMDARs participate in many such forms of bidirectional synaptic plasticity[9–11] and learning.[12–16] NMDARs are uniquely suited to detect such correlations in pre- and postsynaptic activity patterns because their channel is fully activated only when presynaptic release of glutamate coincides with significant postsynaptic depolarization.

The chemical and electrical gating that characterizes NMDARs is illustrated schematically in FIGURE 1. At resting potential, presynaptic release of glutamate opens the channel but does not result in significant current flow because the NMDAR channel is subject to a voltage-gated Mg^{2+} block. However, when the postsynaptic membrane is sufficiently depolarized, the Mg^{2+} dissociates from its binding site within the channel, and if glutamate is still bound when this occurs then the channel is fully activated. NMDARs often are expressed at synapses also containing another

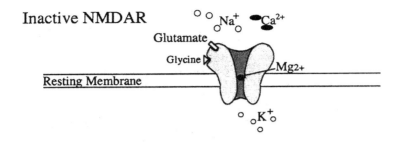

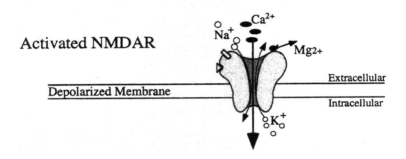

FIGURE 1. Voltage dependency of NMDAR function as compared to voltage-independent property of AMPAR function. Glutamate is the endogenous ligand for both receptor subtypes; NMDARs also contain several other binding sites (only glycine is shown here) that regulate channel function. NMDARs often coexist at synapses containing AMPARs, which mediate most of the initial depolarization from resting potential. As membrane depolarization increases, NMDARs become activated and can therefore contribute to late phases of the EPSP. See text for further details.

glutamate receptor subtype, alpha-amino-3-hydroxy-5-methyl-4-isoxazolepropionic acid receptors (AMPARs), which mediate most of the postsynaptic depolarization when membranes are close to resting potential. An additional critical feature of the NMDAR channel is that it is permeable to Ca^{2+} (as well as to Na^+ and K^+).

Changes in intracellular Ca^{2+} regulate a variety of biochemical cascades important for long-term changes in synaptic function, and Ca^{2+} entry through NMDARs appears to be a critical trigger for many forms of synaptic plasticity.[17–20] Importantly, most synapses that express LTP also express LTD, and Ca^{2+} influx via NMDARs has been linked to both of these forms of synaptic plasticity. Among the multiple factors that can have an impact on the magnitude and sign of synaptic change, the amplitude and duration of the Ca^{2+} signal are important. Because of differential effects on protein kinase and phosphatase cascades that generally act in opposition to one another, a relatively large sustained rise in $[Ca^{2+}]$ increases the probability of synaptic strengthening while a more modest rise may instead facilitate synaptic weakening.[21–23] Importantly, the crossover point between LTD and LTP (the LTD/LTP modification threshold) can itself change as a function of the recent history of activity at the synapse. As average activity increases, the threshold for inducing LTP is raised while the probability of inducing LTD is increased, resulting in a form of "metaplasticity."[24]

In the developing nervous system, the various forms of NMDAR-mediated plasticity may help shape key patterns of neural organization (such as topographic mapping), through the competitive, activity-driven rearrangement of synapses.[25,26] Given their importance to early learning and plasticity, attempts to account for the timing of "sensitive periods" have focused on the regulation of molecules that could impact thresholds for NMDAR-mediated LTP or LTD. First among such molecules is the NMDAR itself: studies in a variety of neural systems have revealed robust developmental regulation of NMDAR structure and function that generally coincides with sensitive periods for neural and behavioral plasticity.[27–31] Moreover, it is well established that changes in the expression of specific NMDAR subunits alter NMDAR current duration[32,33] and modify interactions with intracellular proteins,[34–36] either of which could modulate selective synapse stabilization.

AVIAN SONG LEARNING—A MODEL OF DEVELOPMENTALLY REGULATED LEARNING

Developmental studies of the visual system have yielded tremendous insights into the neurobiology of critical periods for sensory/perceptual development, but it is not yet clear whether similar formulations apply to more complex instances of developmentally regulated learning. Neuroethological studies have described several instances of learning that exhibit well-defined sensitive periods, and avian song learning in particular has several features that make it a powerful paradigm for investigating cellular substrates of learning and their developmental/temporal regulation. First, birdsong is mediated by a well-characterized neural circuit, discrete portions of which are implicated specifically in vocal learning and behavior. Second, many birds exhibit strong stimulus biases in song learning (see Adret, this volume). Third, while many songbirds can only imitate songs heard during a distinct developmental period, there is tremendous species diversity both in the timing, and even the existence of, sensitive periods for avian vocal learning. And, even in "age-limited" vocal learners, the timing of the sensitive period can be extended by early isolation from conspecific song,[37–39] allowing one to dissociate chronological age from the system's ability to support vocal learning. These natural stimuli and temporal constraints, which are rarely available in more traditional paradigms of learning and memory, provide powerful tools for discriminating between cellular events specifically related to learning and those involved in more general aspects of sensory processing, motor activity, or maturation. Current evidence is consistent with the hypothesis that at least some aspects of avian song learning engage experience-dependent forms of NMDAR-mediated synaptic change that have been associated with other instances of developmental plasticity and learning.

CELLULAR AND BIOCHEMICAL SUBSTRATES

Brain regions mediating vocal learning in songbirds form two intimately related circuits (see Fig. 2 in Reiner *et al.*, this volume); one pathway is necessary for song production, and the other is more specifically involved in song development and plasticity. Both of these circuits likely are involved in auditory-based vocal learning because they both contain auditory-sensitive neurons whose response selectivity reflects learned features of song, and both exhibit motor activity related to song production.[40,41] The "motor pathway" consists of several hierarchically organized neural regions (Uva-Nif-HVC-RA-motoneurons) that are necessary for song production (see Wild, this volume); damaging or stimulating this circuitry immediately disrupts song behavior in adult birds.[41,42] Importantly, this motor pathway provides a major input to, and receives the major output from, the other song-related circuit, the anterior forebrain pathway (AFP). Regions of the AFP form a basal ganglia-thalamocortical loop that has been implicated directly in song learning (see chapters by Bottjer, Brainard, and Perkel, this volume). This loop indirectly connects HVC to RA, and it consists of Area X, DLM, and lMAN. Area X, which is an avian homologue of the mammalian basal ganglia, also receives a large dopaminergic projection from the ventral tegmental area.[43,44]

Several observations indicate a role for AFP structures in song memorization (sensory acquisition) and/or sensorimotor learning (vocal practice). In zebra finches (*Taeniopygia guttata*), lesions of Area X,[45,46] DLM,[47] or the lMAN[46,48,49] do not disrupt the production of stable song behavior in adults, but permanently impair the development of song in young males. In fact, even extended learning, as occurs in isolation-reared birds, depends upon an intact lMAN.[50] Recently, a model of AFP function has been postulated in which the AFP circuit provides a permissive or instructive "error signal" that promotes behavioral change when a mismatch is detected between expected auditory feedback and the stored song template.[51] This model is consistent with the fact that both motor and auditory information is available to the AFP, and that lesions of the lMAN prevent the vocal change that occurs in adult zebra finches when auditory feedback is eliminated or distorted.[52,53]

A possible contribution of NMDARs to avian song behavior was first suggested by descriptions of regional NMDAR expression patterns and physiological characteristics within the song system of zebra finches. NMDARs were first identified at the lMAN–RA synapse, where they mediate the majority of the synaptic current in both young and adult males.[54] Shortly thereafter, receptor binding studies revealed the presence of NMDARs in other song-related brain regions, including expression in HVc, Area X, and lMAN.[55] Notably, developmental regulation of overall binding (using the noncompetitive NMDAR antagonist, MK-801) was detected only within the lMAN. Males still within the sensitive period for song learning exhibited elevated MK-801 binding in this region, and normal song development was associated with a gradual decrease in the number of lMAN NMDARs and an increase in their affinity for MK-801.[56]

Evidence of age-related changes in NMDAR expression within the lMAN was particularly interesting both because this region is critical for normal song development and because synapses here dramatically reorganize in response to experience during the sensitive period for song acquisition. That is, glutamatergic inputs arising from DLM expand greatly in young zebra finches between 20 and 35 days posthatch and then steeply reduce their terminal fields.[57,58] These anatomical modifications in zebra finches overlap with both sensory acquisition (occurring between ~25–60 days posthatch), and sensorimotor learning (occurring between ~35–120 days posthatch). As the DLM terminals are pruned within lMAN, there is a corresponding reduction in the density of dendritic spines (postsynaptic specializations) on lMAN neurons.[59] Furthermore, this pruning of dendritic spines is delayed in young birds isolated from conspecific song.[60] Given the involvement of NMDARs in many forms of learning, as well as the relationship between memory formation and the loss, addition, and modification of spines,[8,61,62] it was a logical step to test directly whether NMDAR activation is necessary for normal song development.

NMDARs AND SONG ACQUISITION

We used a pharmacological approach to test whether NMDARs are critical for sensory acquisition. First, we found that systemic blockade of NMDARs impairs song learning when it overlaps with restricted periods of song tutoring, but not when it occurs on nontutoring days.[63] Birds injected with the NMDAR antagonist just prior to tutoring developed songs that resembled those of birds never exposed to a song model. Subsequently, we found that song learning is compromised when NMDARs are blocked specifically within the AFP during periods of song exposure.[12] As shown in FIGURE 2, birds receiving infusions of the NMDAR antagonist AP5 directly into lMAN immediately prior to tutoring sessions ultimately reproduced significantly less of the tutor's song than did various different control groups, including birds that received identical infusions of AP5 on nontutoring days.

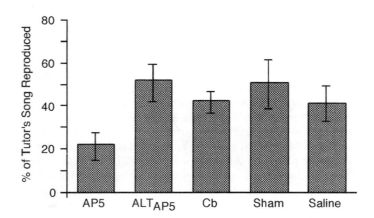

FIGURE 2. Percentage of tutor's song reproduced in five groups of 90-day-old zebra finches. Two groups received bilateral injections of the NMDA receptor antagonist AP5 into the lMAN either 10 min prior to tutoring (AP5) or on nontutoring days (ALT$_{AP5}$). Other birds received injections of either AP5 into the cerebellum (Cb) or saline into the lMAN (Saline) 10 min prior to tutoring, or were left uninjected (Sham). Tutoring sessions (90 min) occurred every other day from posthatch day 32–52. (From Basham et al.[12])

These data suggest that NMDAR activation in the AFP is necessary for normal song learning, perhaps because they mediate processes involved directly in encoding and/or storing the song template. Other interpretations are possible, however. The behavioral deficits could reflect impairments of vocal practice (*sensorimotor learning*) as opposed to acquisition, because both of these phases of song learning overlapped with our AP5 treatments. However, because birds experiencing NMDAR blockade on nontutoring days produced normal songs, this interpretation requires the added presumption that normal vocal learning requires periods when vocal practice actually coincides with tutor exposure. While this opportunity does normally exist for zebra finches, a high level of tutor imitation can be achieved in this species even when exposure to conspecific song terminates before, or shortly after, the onset of vocal practice.[64,65] Moreover, in other songbird species, sensory acquisition and the onset of sensorimotor learning can be separated by many weeks or months.[66] Thus, the most parsimonious interpretation is that NMDAR activation within the AFP is critical to template encoding, in addition to any role these regions (and NMDARs) also may play in sensorimotor learning.

Another consideration is that NMDAR blockade within the AFP may disrupt acquisition by interfering with fast excitatory transmission, rather than NMDAR-mediated synaptic plasticity *per se*.[67] While this possibility is difficult to rule out, *in vitro* recordings from lMAN neurons suggest that significant synaptic transmission persists even in the presence of NMDAR antagonists. That is, AP5 produces only a small reduction (~13%) in the peak amplitude of EPSPs evoked by DLM stimulation, but a somewhat larger peak amplitude reduction (~25%) of EPSPs evoked by stimulation of lMAN recurrent axon collaterals.[68-70] Importantly, several additional observations also support the idea that NMDARs within the AFP mediate synaptic plasticity during song learning. First, NMDAR-mediated LTP has been documented in both lMAN and Area X.[71,72] In lMAN, NMDAR-mediated LTP induced at the recurrent collaterals of lMAN neurons is accompanied by synaptic weakening at the DLM synapses,[72] and both of these forms of plasticity can be induced only during the sensitive period for song memorization. Because synaptic weakening at the DLM–lMAN synapse only occurs when the DLM input is inactive during postsynaptic activation, the authors suggest that the LTD may ultimately lead to the pruning of ineffective DLM afferents. As noted before, song learning is accompanied by both pruning of DLM afferents to lMAN[57,58] and elimination of dendritic spines on lMAN neurons that is modulated by exposure to conspecific song.[59,60]

Additional evidence that song exposure during the sensitive period may involve NMDAR-mediated plasticity within the AFP comes from recent biochemical studies we have initiated to investigate whether calcium-calmodulin–dependent protein kinase II (CaMKII) is critically involved in song learning. The activation of this protein is an event that is downstream of NMDAR activation: CaMKII is abundant in the postsynaptic compartment, it is activated (phosphorylated) by synaptically driven Ca^{2+} elevations, and CaMKII activity is critical for the induction of NMDAR-dependent LTP, as well as certain forms of learning and developmentally regulated synaptic plasticity.[73] In young zebra finches previously denied access to conspecific song, two hours of song exposure increases levels of phosphorylated CaMKII (pCaMKII) within Area X of the AFP.[74] Moreover, in juveniles exposed to song only until posthatch day 30, two hours of reexposure to familiar song promotes a robust elevation in pCaMKII within this region (unpublished observations). As noted earlier, Area X is essential for normal song development, and is a part of the avian basal ganglia that receives a major input from both HVC and lMAN. While this region exhibits both auditory and motor-related activity, the pCaMKII signal detected is not a reflection of vocal practice since it occurs even in the absence of juvenile song production. Remarkably, in birds exposed to song until day 30, exposure to an *unfamiliar* song does not elicit an elevation in pCaMKII. While the reasons for the differential effects of familiar versis unfamiliar song are not yet clear, one possibility is that it relates to modifications in synaptic strength resulting from earlier exposure to a particular song. Song exposure only until posthatch day 30 is sufficient to selectively tune neurons within the AFP to song patterns previously heard,[75] and this tuning presumably reflects the selective strengthening of pathways activated by that prior song exposure. Thus, exposure to familiar song should reactivate potentiated pathways and thus be optimal for activating CaMKII, whereas unfamiliar song would activate nonpotentiated or weakened pathways and thereby may produce insufficient postsynaptic activation to elicit a detectable pCaMKII signal. While we have not yet tested directly whether NMDAR activation is necessary for this pCaMKII signaling, or whether the pCaMKII signal is essential for normal song learning, these are important future directions for research.

CHANGES IN THE COMPOSITION AND FUNCTION OF NMDA RECEPTORS DURING SONG LEARNING—A SUBSTRATE FOR THE SENSITIVE PERIOD?

Developmental studies in a variety of vertebrate neural systems support the view that sensitive periods for plasticity are characterized by heightened susceptibility to Hebbian-like forms of synaptic change.[31,76] Likewise, constraints on the timing of song learning suggest that neural function is modified by development or season so as to affect the ability of auditory experience to shape song circuits. This suggestion is consistent with the observation that the ability to induce LTP and LTD at synapses within the lMAN normally declines in juvenile zebra finches as development proceeds.[72] In fact, the same stimulus parameters that induce LTP in young birds elicit LTD in adults, suggesting that the LTD/LTP modification threshold has shifted in favor of LTD. One of the many factors (e.g., see refs. 77 and 78) that can regulate thresholds for synaptic change is experience-driven, developmental change in NMDAR composition and physiology.[29,30,79–82] In fact, over the past 10–15 years, change in NMDAR subunit expression has been proposed as a leading mechanism for curtailing plasticity as sensitive periods close.

Native NMDARs consist of the NR1 subunit, essential for channel activity, and one or more modulatory subunits (NR2A–E) that determine the biophysical properties of the receptor channel.[32,83,84] During the sensitive period for song learning, NR1 mRNA levels within lMAN decline,[85] thus downregulation of gene transcription likely drives the developmental decrease in MK-801 binding sites. Similarly, in mammalian visual cortex, several investigators have reported a decline in NR1 expression and MK-801 binding as NMDAR-mediated plasticity wanes.[79,86,87] While these quantitative changes in overall NMDAR expression correlate with reduced plasticity at the close of sensitive periods, they do not themselves curtail plasticity. That is, they are insensitive to experiential manipulations that extend the sensitive period for either avian song learning or plasticity in the mammalian visual system.[56,85-88]

In contrast, some of the developmental changes in the NMDAR modulatory subunits and physiology are regulated by experience. NR2A and NR2B are the most prevalent modulatory subunits in vertebrate forebrain, and many regions express high levels of NR2B early in development and then gradually replace or augment these with NR2A subunits.[89,90] There are at least two distinct ways in which changes in NMDAR composition could affect thresholds for synaptic change. First, an increase in the NR2A:2B ratio decreases the decay time of NMDAR currents, thereby reducing the time course of NMDAR-mediated increases in postsynaptic Ca^{2+}.[32,33]

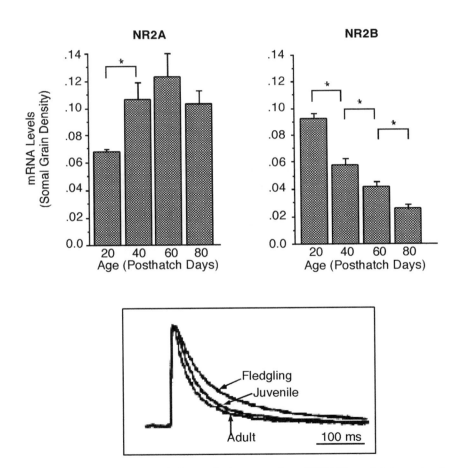

FIGURE 3. Developmental changes in the expression of NMDAR modulatory subunits NR2A and NR2B mRNA (*top*; modified from Singh *et al.*[85] and Heinrich *et al.*[95]) and physiology (*bottom*; modified from White *et al.*[93]) within the lMAN. As the NR2A:2B ratio increases, NMDAR currents within the lMAN become faster.

Second, NR2A and NR2B subunits associate differentially with various intracellular molecules that are involved with receptor localization and/or signaling cascades that regulate synaptic function.[35,91] Thus, changes in the expression of NMDAR modulatory subunits can affect the probability and outcomes of initiating specific signal transduction cascades involved in synaptic plasticity.

Within the avian song system, HVC, RA, Area X, and lMAN all exhibit a developmental increase in NR2A transcripts that accompanies a decrease in NR2B transcripts.[85,92] While the amplitude and timing of these changes vary somewhat across regions, the pattern in lMAN (FIG. 3, top) exemplifies the developmental regulation of these subunits within song regions. NR2A transcripts in lMAN increase relatively early in song development, while a reciprocal decline in NR2B mRNA tends to be more protracted. As noted earlier, an increase in the NR2A:2B ratio shortens NMDAR currents, and in both RA and lMAN (other regions have not been explored), the expected decrease in NMDAR current durations have been confirmed (FIG. 3, bottom).[68,72,93,94]

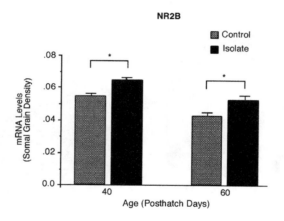

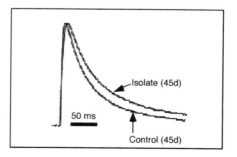

FIGURE 4. Early isolation delays the developmental decline in NR2B mRNA expression within lMAN (*top;* modified from Singh *et al.*[85]). Correspondingly, this manipulation also delays the developmental decline in the duration of NMDAR currents within the lMAN (*bottom*; modified from Livingston *et al.*[99]).

The hypothesis that developmental changes in NMDAR subunit composition limit sensitive periods for experience-dependent plasticity grew primarily out of studies on visual system development. Here, not only does the sensitive period for monocular deprivation coincide with changes in the NR2A:2B ratio and NMDAR current durations, but manipulations that extend this sensitive period also delay the developmental increase in NR2A subunit expression and the shortening of NMDAR currents.[29,96–98] Several years ago, it also was shown that within the lMAN of the avian song system, maturational changes in NMDAR expression and physiology are affected by manipulations that alter the timing of the sensitive period for vocal imitation. That is, early isolation from song delays the decrease in NR2B mRNA expression[85] and delays the developmental decrease in NMDAR current durations within this region.[99] These observations are illustrated in FIGURE 4: at both 40 days and 60 days posthatch, NR2B transcripts in lMAN are elevated in isolates relative to controls, and at 45 days isolates have slower NMDAR currents in lMAN than do age-matched controls. Interestingly, these effects of early experience are quite targeted—isolation does not alter NR2B mRNA expression in other song regions, nor does it affect NR2A mRNA expression in any region examined (lMAN, Area X, HVC, or RA).

Developmental changes in the NR2A:NR2B ratio and NMDAR physiology in lMAN also are regulated by hormones. They are accelerated by early testosterone treatment,[85,95,100] which impairs song development in zebra finches[101] and can both accelerate and disrupt learning in other age-regulated learners.[102] In fact, changes in NMDAR composition within the lMAN even map onto seasonally recurring periods of song plasticity in adult canaries. NR2B mRNA levels within the lMAN are higher during short-day photoperiod conditions when testosterone levels are low and song is being actively remodeled, than when measured under long-day conditions when testosterone levels are elevated and song structure is stable.[103] In contrast, NR2A mRNA expression in lMAN is similar under short- and long-day photoperiods.

While these intriguing brain/behavior relationships fueled the hypothesis that declining NR2B expression may contribute significantly to sensitive period closure, recent studies directly testing this idea have failed to confirm the hypothesis. As previously noted, early isolation from conspecific song delays developmental changes in the expression of NR2B mRNA within the lMAN, while also extending the sensitive period for learning. However, recently we found that either limited exposure (up until day 30) to a tutor's song, or brief exposure (day 24–30) to testosterone, restores in isolates a normal time course to these developmental changes in NMDAR gene expression within lMAN *without compromising extended learning.*[104] As shown in FIGURE 5, NR2B mRNA levels at 65 days were at, or even somewhat below, normal levels in these experimental groups. And yet both imitated the song of a tutor first encountered at 65 days while control birds did not. Although it is possible that the sensitive period remains open in these experimental birds due to post-transcriptional changes that enable high levels of synaptic NR2B protein despite depressed mRNA levels,[105] it should be noted that closure of the sensitive period for song acquisition also has been dissociated from developmental changes in lMAN NMDAR physiology. That is, T-treated isolate zebra finches can acquire new song material even well after NMDAR currents within lMAN have matured to their adult duration.[99]

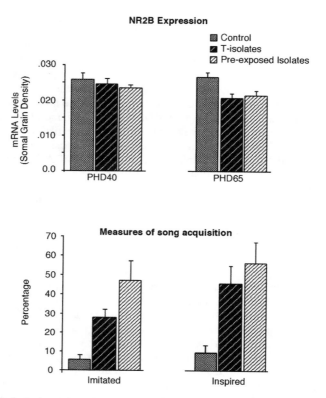

FIGURE 5. Isolate birds that are either treated with testosterone from days 24–30 (T-treated isolates), or exposed to song only until 30 days posthatch (preexposed isolates) have NR2B transcript levels within lMAN that are at, or below, the normal range of age-matched controls (*upper panel*). Yet, these two groups of isolates remain capable of imitating a significant amount of song first heard after day 65, while control birds are not (*lower panel*). "Imitated" reflects the amount of Tutor song reproduced by the pupil; "Inspired" reflects the amount of pupil song scored as learned (modified from Heinrich *et al.*[104]).

Although it is now clear that developmental regulation of NMDARs cannot account for the close of the sensitive period for vocal imitation, it would be premature to conclude that such regulation normally does not impact vocal learning. That is, our measures of how much song was imitated after a protracted period of tutoring are relatively crude, and it is entirely possible that small, but nevertheless important changes in learning propensity have gone undetected. Also, our studies do not address whether NMDAR maturation is a *necessary* component of sensitive period regulation. Investigations of developmental plasticity in the developing somatosensory and visual cortex clarify this distinction. By employing genetic knockouts, these studies have shown that deletion of the NR2A subunit does not impact the normal time-course of the sensitive period for monocular deprivation[106] or for synaptic and anatomical plasticity in barrel cortex.[107] Thus, the maturational increase in NR2A and the shortening of NMDAR currents are neither necessary nor sufficient for the opening and closing of these sensitive periods. However, the NR2A deletion does weaken overall sensitivity to monocular deprivation, and also impacts the timing of the sensitive period for development of orientation selectivity in visual cortex.[106] These observations bring into sharp focus the diversity of sensitive periods and emphasize the need to independently establish for any particular sensitive period the unique set of determinants that dictate responsiveness to specific patterns of input.

CONCLUSIONS AND FUTURE DIRECTIONS

While the last decade has seen most emphasis placed on the hypothesis that higher NR2A:NR2B ratios and faster NMDAR currents should reduce plasticity and curtail sensitive periods,[29,108–111] other evidence favors the hypothesis that these early changes in NMDAR phenotype actually may contribute to *opening* the sensitive period. In both ferret and rat visual systems, the NR2A:NR2B ratio increases and receptor currents quicken at the *onset* of the sensitive period, just as visual experience begins patterning synaptic organization.[112,113] Furthermore, while exposing dark-reared animals to light rapidly increases the NR2A:2B ratio and shortens NMDAR currents,[96,97] these changes clearly do not close the sensitive period, because dark-reared animals are sensitive to the effects of monocular deprivation for many days after first exposure to light. Finally, postponing NMDAR maturation by dark-rearing delays not only closure but also the *onset* of the sensitive period for visual cortical plasticity.[114]

In the song system as well, the most precipitous change in the NR2A:NR2B ratio and NMDA current duration in lMAN occurs between posthatch days 20–40, near the onset of the sensitive period for sensory acquisition and vocal motor practice. Because an increase in neural activity can facilitate maturation of NMDAR subunit expression,[96–98,115] the increased circuit activation associated with either phase of song learning could drive changes in NMDAR composition and physiology which, in turn, may raise the LTD/LTP modification threshold. This could help ensure that only precisely correlated activity patterns trigger NMDAR-mediated synaptic stabilization. Thus, initial exposure to song may "prepare" neural circuitry for encoding the rich temporal and acoustic structure of song, by fostering a period of rapid, experience-driven synapse elimination that is the hallmark of other sensitive periods. This view predicts that manipulations of the early auditory and endocrine environment that delay changes in NMDAR expression and function should likewise delay the *onset*, as well as the closure of the sensitive period for learning.

As noted earlier, the myriad of factors that can affect neural plasticity make it improbable that any single maturational change is responsible for limiting the timing of avian vocal learning. Yet, while the biology accounting for sensitive periods remains elusive, the established role of NMDAR activation in song learning, coupled with the insight provided by work on a variety of other instances of developmental plasticity, suggests two broad avenues for future research. The first of these should continue to investigate age-regulated processes that could modify thresholds for those forms of activity-dependent synaptic change most commonly thought to underlie learning and experience-dependent plasticity. For example, developmental changes in inhibitory circuitry could regulate sensitive periods by enabling and then constraining LTP/LTD-mediated synaptic change. Data from mammalian visual cortex suggest that a certain threshold level of inhibition may be permissive for sensitive period plasticity, but subsequent increases in inhibitory (relative to excitatory) transmission can reduce plasticity.[116] Developmental changes in parameters of inhibition within the song system have not been well characterized with respect to the timing of the sensitive period. Calecholaminergic and cholinergic systems also can modulate plasticity,[78,117] and within song nuclei there are striking developmental changes in the expression of these neurotransmitter systems that could modulate synaptic plasticity within the AFP or elsewhere.[118–121] And further work on NMDAR-linked biochemical cascades activated during sensory acquisition may reveal maturational changes in synaptic or nuclear signaling enzymes that could limit learning. For example, CaMKII,[122] extracellular signal-related kinase,[123] and protein kinase A[124] activation have all been associated with plasticity in the visual cortex of developing mammals. Alternatively, the regulation of molecules associated with forgetting or suppressing learning and memory,[125,126] could interfere with forming new representation of song. More specifically, their action could curtail the "rewritability" of song circuitry tuned to a particular song, and thus contribute to the end of the sensitive period for acquisition.

A second line of research should probe how cellular processes unique to (or at least exaggerated in) the developing brain might alter the impact of synaptic plasticity on circuit organization. For example, the normal overlap between sensory acquisition and synaptic pruning in lMAN may facilitate information storage (but see ref. 127) as suggested by recent studies of visual imprinting.[8,128] Another likely substrate for synaptic plasticity is the potential for novel synapse formation, or the formation, modification, and elimination of dendritic spines that do not necessarily result in a net gain or loss in synapse number. The rate of dendritic spine turnover in visual cortex is significantly higher throughout the sensitive periods for plasticity than it is in adulthood.[129] Yet, when portions of the extracellular matrix known to restrict dendritic spine motility are artificially decomposed, sensitivity to monocular deprivation is reinstated in adults.[125] Also, in layer 2/3 of whisker barrel cortex where experience-dependent plasticity can persist into adulthood, a physiological response to whisker manipulation is correlated with an increase in the rate of dendritic spine turnover.[130] Finally, in virtually every developing neural systems where NMDAR-dependent LTP occurs (including the avian song system), many glutamatergic synapses are functionally "silent" (NMDAR only, therefore generating no response at resting potential), and the incidence of these silent synapses declines with age.[131,132] Moreover, a growing body of evidence suggests that NMDAR activation can convert these silent synapses into functional excitatory connections by promoting the insertion of AMPA receptors into postsynaptic sites (see ref. 132 for review). The ability for activity related to the processing of song stimuli to recruit subthreshold synapses into functional ones could be essential for auditory experience to shape song circuitry.

In exploring these hypotheses it will continue to be important to move beyond purely correlative studies. Identifying relevant maturational events whose time course can be manipulated in parallel with the sensitive period will, of course, remain a valuable approach. But developmental investigations of NMDAR composition and physiology emphasize the need for manipulations that alter the timing of song learning while minimizing gross effects on system maturation. The early auditory, visual, social, and endocrine experiences so important to vocal learning undoubtedly also have an impact upon a variety of developmental processes not specifically involved in regulating early learning. When these stimuli are withheld completely, a host of maturational consequences can be expected, only some of which may contribute to sensitive period regulation. One useful approach exemplified by our recent studies is to employ gentler manipulations of early input so as to alter the timing of learning without necessarily altering all developmental changes that depend on that input. This will at least narrow the field of processes identified as candidate mechanisms for closing the sensitive period. Finally, as this approach uncovers developmentally regulated molecular changes that *reliably* parallel the sensitive period, emerging techniques for molecular and/or genetic manipulation can target these changes directly and individually in order to assess their contribution to sensitive period regulation.

ACKNOWLEDGMENTS

This work was supported by National Institutes of Health Grant MH45096, National Science Foundation Grant IBN-9983338, and the Schmitt Foundation.

The authors gratefully acknowledge Sandra Aamodt, Mark Basham, Tryambak Singh, Julie Heinrich, Luisa Scott, and Ann-Marie Wissman, who carried out much of the work described here. We also are grateful to our collaborators Drs. Farida Sohrabji and Eliot Brenowitz.

REFERENCES

1. BREEDLOVE, S.M. 1992. Sexual dimorphism in the vertebrate nervous system. J. Neurosci. **12:** 4133–4142.
2. NORDEEN, E.J. & K.W. NORDEEN. 1994. Hormonally-regulated neuron death in the avian brain. Semin. Neurosci. **6:** 299–306.
3. NIKONENKO, I. *et al.* 2002. Activity-induced changes of spine morphology. Hippocampus **12:** 585–591.
4. MALETIC-SAVATIC, M., R. MALINOW & K. SVOBODA. 1999. Rapid dendritic morphogenesis in CA1 hippocampal dendrites induced by synaptic activity. Science **283:** 1923–1927.
5. ENGERT, F. & T. BONHOEFFER. 1999. Dendritic spine changes associated with hippocampal long-term synaptic plasticity. Nature **399:** 66–70.
6. BUFFELLI, M. *et al.* 2003. Genetic evidence that relative synaptic efficacy biases the outcome of synaptic competition. Nature **424:** 430–434.
7. HORN, G. 1985. Memory, Imprinting, and the Brain. An Inquiry into Mechanisms. Clarendon Press. Oxford, UK.
8. BOCK, J. & K. BRAUN. 1999. Filial imprinting in domestic chicks is associated with spine pruning in the associative area, dorsocaudal neostriatum. Eur. J. Neurosci. **11:** 2566–2570.
9. LISMAN, J. 2003. Long-term potentiation: outstanding questions and attempted synthesis. Philos. Trans. R. Soc. Lond. B Biol. Sci. **358:** 829–842.
10. COTMAN, C.W., D.T. MONAGHAN & A.H. GANONG. 1988. Excitatory amino acid neurotransmission: NMDA receptors and Hebb-type synaptic plasticity. Annu. Rev. Neurosci. **11:** 61–80.

11. ROBERTS, E.B., M.A. MEREDITH & A.S. RAMOA. 1998. Suppression of NMDA receptor function using antisense DNA block ocular dominance plasticity while preserving visual responses. J. Neurophysiol. **80:** 1021–1032.

12. BASHAM, M.E., E.J. NORDEEN & K.W. NORDEEN. 1996. Blockade of NMDA receptors in the anterior forebrain impairs sensory acquisition in the zebra finch (*Poephila guttata*). Neurobiol. Learn. Mem. **66:** 295–304.

13. BRENNAN, P.A. 1994. The effects of local inhibition of N-methyl-D-aspartate and AMPA/kainate receptors in the accessory olfactory bulb on the formation of an olfactory memory in mice. Neuroscience **60:** 701–708.

14. BURCHULADZE, R. & S.P.R. ROSE. 1992. Memory formation in day-old chicks requires NMDA but not non-NMDA glutamate receptors. Eur. J. Neurosci. **4:** 535–538.

15. DAVIS, S., S.P. BUTCHER & R.G. MORRIS. 1992. The NMDA receptor antagonist D-2-amino-5-phosphonopentanoate (D-AP5) impairs spatial learning and LTP in vivo at intracerebral concentrations comparable to those that block LTP in vitro. J. Neurosci. **12:** 21–34.

16. KIM, M. & J.L. MCGAUGH. 1992. Effects of intra-amygdala injections of NMDA receptor antagonists on acquisition and retention of inhibitory avoidance. Brain Res. **585:** 35–48.

17. MORRIS, R.G.M. 1990. The role of NMDA receptors in certain kinds of learning and memory. *In* The Biology of Memory. L.R. Squire & E. Lindenlaub, Eds.: 299–318. F.K. Schattauer Verlag. Stuttgart, Germany.

18. BLISS, T.V. & G.L. COLLINGRIDGE. 1993. A synaptic model of memory: long-term potentiation in the hippocampus. Nature **361:** 31–39.

19. FIELDS, R.D., C. YU & P.G. NELSON. 1991. Calcium, network activity, and the role of NMDA channels in synaptic plasticity in vitro. J. Neurosci. **11:** 134–146.

20. CASTELLANI, G.C. *et al.* 2001. A biophysical model of bidirectional synaptic plasticity: dependence on AMPA and NMDA receptors. Proc. Natl. Acad. Sci. USA **98:** 12772–12777.

21. GHOSH, A. & M.E. GREENBERG. 1995. Calcium signaling in neurons: molecular mechanisms and cellular consequences. Science **268:** 239–247.

22. COUSSENS, C.M. & T.J. TEYLER. 1996. Protein kinase and phosphatase activity regulate the form of synaptic plasticity expressed. Synapse **24:** 97–103.

23. KIRKWOOD, A. & M.F. BEAR. 1994. Homosynaptic long-term depression in the visual cortex. J. Neurosci. **14:** 3404–3412.

24. BEAR, M.F. 2003. Bidirectional synaptic plasticity: from theory to reality. Philos. Trans. R. Soc. Lond. B Biol. Sci. **358:** 649–655.

25. CONSTANTINE-PATON, M., H.T. CLINE & E. DEBSKI. 1990. Patterned activity, synaptic convergence, and the NMDA receptor in developing visual pathways. Annu. Rev. Neurosci. **13:** 129–154.

26. SHATZ, C.J. 1996. Emergence of order in visual system development. Proc. Natl. Acad. Sci. USA **93:** 602–608.

27. HOFER, M., G.T. PRUSKY & M. CONSTANTINE-PATON. 1994. Regulation of NMDA receptor mRNA during visual map formation and after receptor blockade. J. Neurochem. **62:** 2300–2307.

28. FOX, K. & N.W. DAW. 1993. Do NMDA receptors have a critical function in visual cortical plasticity? Trends Neurosci. **16:** 116–122.

29. CARMIGNOTO, G. & S. VICINI. 1992. Activity-dependent decrease in NMDA receptor responses during development of the visual cortex. Science **258:** 1007–1011.

30. HESTRIN, S. 1992. Developmental regulation of NMDA receptor-mediated synaptic currents at a central synapse. Nature **357:** 686–689.

31. CRAIR, M.C. & R.C. MALENKA. 1995. A critical period for long-term potentiation at thalamocortical synapses. Nature **375:** 325–328.

32. MONYER, H. *et al.* 1992. Heteromeric NMDA receptors: molecular and functional distinction of subtypes. Science **256:** 1217–1221.

33. FLINT, A.C. *et al.* 1997. NR2A subunit expression shortens NMDA receptor synaptic currents in developing neocortex. J. Neurosci. **17:** 2469–2476.

34. BAYER, K.U. *et al.* 2001. Interaction with the NMDA receptor locks CaMKII in an active conformation. Nature **411:** 801–805.

35. SANS, N. *et al.* 2000. A developmental change in NMDA receptor-associated proteins at hippocampal synapses. J. Neurosci. **20:** 1260–1271.
36. HUSI, H. *et al.* 2000. Proteomic analysis of NMDA receptor-adhesion protein signaling complexes. Nat. Neurosci. **3:** 661–669.
37. KROODSMA, D. & R. PICKERT. 1980. Environmentally dependent sensitive periods for avian vocal learning. Nature **288:** 477–479.
38. EALES, L.A. 1985. Song learning in zebra finches: some effects of song model availability on what is learnt and when. Anim. Behav. **33:** 1293–1300.
39. EALES, L.A. 1987. Song learning in female-raised zebra finches: another look at the sensitive phase. Anim. Behav. **35:** 1356–1365.
40. BRAINARD, M.S. & A.J. DOUPE. 2002. What songbirds teach us about learning. Nature **417:** 351–358.
41. MARGOLIASH, D. 1997. Functional organization of forebrain pathways for song production and perception. J. Neurobiol. **33:** 671–93.
42. NOTTEBOHM, F., T.M. STOKES & C.M. LEONARD. 1976. Central control of song in the canary, Serinus canarius. J. Comp. Neurol. **165:** 457–86.
43. LEWIS, J.W. *et al.* 1981. Evidence for a catecholaminergic projection to area X in the zebra finch. J. Comp. Neurol. **196:** 347–354.
44. MELLO, C.V., R. PINAUD & S. RIBEIRO. 1998. Noradrenergic system of the zebra finch brain: immunocytochemical study of dopamine-beta-hydroxylase. J. Comp. Neurol. **400:** 207–228.
45. SOHRABJI, F., E.J. NORDEEN & K.W. NORDEEN. 1990. Selective impairment of song learning following lesions of a forebrain nucleus in the juvenile zebra finch. Behav. Neural Biol. **53:** 51–63.
46. SCHARFF, C. & F. NOTTEBOHM. 1991. A comparative study of the behavioral deficits following lesions of various parts of the zebra finch song system: implications for vocal learning. J. Neurosci. **11:** 2896–2913.
47. HALSEMA, K.A. & S.W. BOTTJER. 1992. Chemical lesions of a thalamic nucleus disrupt song development in male zebra finches. Soc. Neurosci. Abstr. **18:** 529.
48. BOTTJER, S.W., E.A. MIESNER & A.P. ARNOLD. 1984. Forebrain lesions disrupt development but not maintenance of song in passerine birds. Science **224:** 901–903.
49. NORDEEN, K.W. & E.J. NORDEEN. 1993. Long-term maintenance of song in adult zebra finches is not affected by lesions of a forebrain region involved in song learning. Behav. Neural Biol. **59:** 79–82.
50. MORRISON, R.G. & F. NOTTEBOHM. 1993. Role of a telencephalic nucleus in the delayed song learning of socially isolated zebra finches. J. Neurobiol. **24:** 1045–1064.
51. TROYER, T.W. & A.J. DOUPE. 2000. An associational model of birdsong sensorimotor learning. II. Temporal hierarchies and the learning of song sequence [In Process Citation]. J. Neurophysiol. **84:** 1224–1239.
52. WILLIAMS, H. & N. MEHTA. 1999. Changes in adult zebra finch song require a forebrain nucleus that is not necessary for song production. J. Neurobiol. **39:** 14–28.
53. BRAINARD, M.S. & A.J. DOUPE. 2000. Interruption of a basal ganglia-forebrain circuit prevents plasticity of learned vocalizations. Nature **404:** 762–766.
54. MOONEY, R. & M. KONISHI. 1991. Two distinct inputs to an avian song nucleus activate different glutamate receptor subtypes on individual neurons. Proc. Natl. Acad. Sci. USA **88:** 4075–4079.
55. AAMODT, S.M. *et al.* 1992. Distribution and developmental change in [^{3}H]MK-801 binding within zebra finch song nuclei. J. Neurobiol. **23:** 997–1005.
56. AAMODT, S.M., E.J. NORDEEN & K.W. NORDEEN. 1995. Early isolation from conspecific song does not affect the normal developmental decline of N-methyl-D-aspartate receptor binding in an avian song nucleus. J. Neurobiol. **27:** 76–84.
57. IYENGAR, S. & S.W. BOTTJER. 2002. Development of individual axon arbors in a thalamocortical circuit necessary for song learning in zebra finches. J. Neurosci. **22:** 901–911.
58. JOHNSON, F. & S.W. BOTTJER. 1992. Growth and regression of thalamic efferents in the song-control system of male zebra finches. J. Comp. Neurol. **326:** 442–450.
59. NIXDORF-BERGWEILER, B.E., E. WALLHAUSSER-FRANKE & T.J. DEVOOGD. 1995. Regressive development in neuronal structure during song learning in birds. J. Neurobiol. **27:** 204–215.

60. WALLHAUSSER-FRANKE, E., B.E. NIXDORF-BERGWEILER & T.J. DEVOOGD. 1995. Song isolation is associated with maintaining high spine frequencies on zebra finch lMAN neurons. Neurobiol. Learn. Mem. **64:** 25–35.

61. GOLDIN, M., M. SEGAL & E. AVIGNONE. 2001. Functional plasticity triggers formation and pruning of dendritic spines in cultured hippocampal networks. J. Neurosci. **21:** 186–193.

62. LUSCHER, C. et al. 2000. Synaptic plasticity and dynamic modulation of the postsynaptic membrane. Nat. Neurosci. **3:** 545–550.

63. AAMODT, S.M., E.J. NORDEEN & K.W. NORDEEN. 1996. Blockade of NMDA receptors during song model exposure impairs song development in juvenile zebra finches. Neurobiol. Learn. Mem. **65:** 91–98.

64. IMMELMANN, K. 1969. Song development in the zebra finch and other estrildid finches. In Bird Vocalizations. R.A. Hinde, Ed.: 61–77. Cambridge University Press. Cambridge.

65. BÖHNER, J. 1990. Early acquisition of song in the zebra finch, Taeniopygia guttata. Anim. Behav. **39:** 369–374.

66. MARLER, P. 1987. Sensitive periods and the roles of specific and general sensory stimulation in birdsong learning. In Imprinting and Cortical Plasticity. J.P. Rauschecker, & P. Marler, Eds.: 99–135. J. Wiley and Sons. New York.

67. DAW, N.W., P.S. STEIN & K. FOX. 1993. The role of NMDA receptors in information processing. Annu. Rev. Neurosci. **16:** 207–222.

68. LIVINGSTON, F.S. & R. MOONEY. 1997. Development of intrinsic and synaptic properties in a forebrain nucleus essential to avian song learning. J. Neurosci. **17:** 8997–9009.

69. BOETTIGER, C.A. & A.J. DOUPE. 1998. Intrinsic and thalamic excitatory inputs onto songbird LMAN neurons differ in their pharmacological and temporal properties. J. Neurophysiol. **79:** 2615–2628.

70. BOTTJER, S.W., J.D. BRADY & J.P. WALSH. 1998. Intrinsic and synaptic properties of neurons in the vocal-control nucleus lMAN from in vitro slice preparations of juvenile and adult zebra finches. J. Neurobiol. **37:** 642–658.

71. DING, L. & D.J. PERKEL. 2004. Long-term potentiation in an avian basal ganglia nucleus essential for vocal learning. J. Neurosci. **24:** 488–494.

72. BOETTIGER, C.A. & A.J. DOUPE. 2001. Developmentally restricted synaptic plasticity in a songbird nucleus required for song learning. Neuron **31:** 809–818.

73. LISMAN, J., H. SCHULMAN & H. CLINE. 2002. The molecular basis of CaMKII function in synaptic and behavioural memory. Nat. Rev. Neurosci. **3:** 175–190.

74. SINGH, T.D., E.J. NORDEEN & K.W. NORDEEN. 2002. Brief song exposure alters CaMKII expression and activation within the developing zebra finch song system. Abstract Viewer/Itinerary Planner. Program No. 382.8. Society for Neuroscience. Washington, DC.

75. YAZAKI-SUGIYAMA, Y. & R.D. MOONEY. 2002. Extended sensory acquisition and re-writable song-selective neurons in the zebra finch lMAN. Society for Neuroscience, Abstract. Program No. 588.6. Society for Neuroscience. Washington, DC.

76. KIRKWOOD, A., H.K. LEE & M.F. BEAR. 1995. Co-regulation of long-term potentiation and experience-dependent synaptic plasticity in visual cortex by age and experience. Nature **375:** 328–331.

77. IZQUIERDO, I. & J.H. MEDINA. 1997. Memory formation: the sequence of biochemical events in the hippocampus and its connection to activity in other brain structures. Neurobiol. Learn. Mem. **68:** 285–316.

78. BAILEY, C.H. et al. 2000. Is heterosynaptic modulation essential for stabilizing Hebbian plasticity and memory? Nat. Rev. Neurosci. **1:** 11–20.

79. BODE-GREUEL, K.M. & W. SINGER. 1989. The development of N-methyl-D-aspartate receptors in cat visual cortex. Brain Res. Dev. Brain Res. **46:** 197–204.

80. FOX, K. et al. 1992. The effect of visual experience on development of NMDA receptor synaptic transmission in kitten visual cortex. J. Neurosci. **12:** 2672–2684.

81. FOX, K. 1992. A critical period for experience-dependent synaptic plasticity in rat barrel cortex. J. Neurosci. **12:** 1826–1838.

82. HOFER, M. & M. CONSTANTINE-PATON. 1994. Regulation of N-methyl-D-aspartate (NMDA) receptor function during the rearrangement of developing neuronal connections. Prog. Brain Res. **102:** 277–285.
83. CULL-CANDY, S., S. BRICKLEY & M. FARRANT. 2001. NMDA receptor subunits: diversity, development and disease. Curr. Opin. Neurobiol. **11:** 327–335.
84. BULLER, A.L. *et al.* 1994. The molecular basis of NMDA receptor subtypes: native receptor diversity is predicted by subunit composition. J. Neurosci. **14:** 5471–5484.
85. SINGH, T.D. *et al.* 2000. Early sensory and hormonal experience modulate age-related changes in NR2B mRNA within a forebrain region controlling avian vocal learning. J. Neurobiol. **44:** 82–94.
86. GORDON, B., N. DAW & D. PARKINSON. 1991. The effect of age on binding of MK-801 in the cat visual cortex. Brain Res. Dev. Brain Res. **62:** 61–67.
87. REYNOLDS, I.J. & M.F. BEAR. 1991. Effects of age and visual experience on [3H] MK801 binding to NMDA receptors in the kitten visual cortex. Exp. Brain Res. **85:** 611–615.
88. CATALANO, S.M., C.K. CHANG & C.J. SHATZ. 1997. Activity-dependent regulation of NMDAR1 immunoreactivity in the developing visual cortex. J. Neurosci. **17:** 8376–8390.
89. MONYER, H. *et al.* 1994. Developmental and regional expression in the rat brain and functional properties of four NMDA receptors. Neuron **12:** 529–540.
90. SHENG, M. *et al.* 1994. Changing subunit composition of heteromeric NMDA receptors during development of rat cortex. Nature **368:** 144–147.
91. STRACK, S. & R.J. COLBRAN. 1998. Autophosphorylation-dependent targeting of calcium/calmodulin-dependent protein kinase II by the NR2B subunit of the N-methyl-D-aspartate receptor. J. Biol. Chem. **273:** 20689–20692.
92. SCOTT, L.L. *et al.* 2004. Developmental patterns of NMDAR expression within the song system do not recur during adult vocal plasticity in zebra finches. J. Neurobiol. **58:** 442–454.
93. WHITE, S.A., F.S. LIVINGSTON & R. MOONEY. 1999. Androgens modulate NMDA receptor-mediated EPSCs in the zebra finch song system. J. Neurophysiol. **82:** 2221–2234.
94. STARK, L.L. & D.J. PERKEL. 1999. Two-stage, input-specific synaptic maturation in a nucleus essential for vocal production in the zebra finch. J. Neurosci. **19:** 9107–9116.
95. HEINRICH, J.E. *et al.* 2002. Developmental and hormonal regulation of NR2A mRNA in forebrain regions controlling avian vocal learning. J. Neurobiol. **51:** 149–159.
96. PHILPOT, B.D. *et al.* 2001. Visual experience and deprivation bidirectionally modify the composition and function of NMDA receptors in visual cortex. Neuron **29:** 157–169.
97. QUINLAN, E.M. *et al.* 1999. Rapid, experience-dependent expression of synaptic NMDA receptors in visual cortex in vivo. Nat. Neurosci. **2:** 352–357.
98. QUINLAN, E.M., D.H. OLSTEIN & M.F. BEAR. 1999. Bidirectional, experience-dependent regulation of N-methyl-D-aspartate receptor subunit composition in the rat visual cortex during postnatal development. Proc. Natl. Acad. Sci. USA **96:** 12876–12880.
99. LIVINGSTON, F.S., S.A. WHITE & R. MOONEY. 2000. Slow NMDA-EPSCs at synapses critical for song development are not required for song learning in zebra finches. Nat. Neurosci. **3:** 482–488.
100. LIVINGSTON, F.S., S.A. WHITE & R. MOONEY. 1998. NMDA receptor-mediated EPSCs within two song nuclei are testosterone sensitive during early song development. Neurosci. Abstr. **24:** 191.
101. KORSIA, S. & S.W. BOTTJER. 1991. Chronic testosterone treatment impairs vocal learning in male zebra finches during a restricted period of development. J. Neurosci. **11:** 2362–2371.
102. WHALING, C.S., D.A. NELSON & P. MARLER. 1995. Testosterone-induced shortening of the storage phase of song development in birds interferes with vocal learning. Dev. Psychobiol. **28:** 367–376.

103. SINGH, T.D. *et al.* 2003. Seasonal regulation of NMDA receptor NR2B mRNA in the adult canary song system. J. Neurobiol. **54:** 593–603.
104. HEINRICH, J.E. *et al.* 2003. NR2B downregulation in a forebrain region required for avian vocal learning is not sufficient to close the sensitive period for song learning. Neurobiol. Learn. Mem. **79:** 99–108.
105. ERISIR, A. & J.L. HARRIS. 2003. Decline of the critical period of visual plasticity is concurrent with the reduction of NR2B subunit of the synaptic NMDA receptor in layer 4. J. Neurosci. **23:** 5208–5218.
106. FAGIOLINI, M. *et al.* 2003. Separable features of visual cortical plasticity revealed by N-methyl-D-aspartate receptor 2A signaling. Proc. Natl. Acad. Sci. USA **100:** 2854–2859.
107. LU, H.C., E. GONZALEZ & M.C. CRAIR. 2001. Barrel cortex critical period plasticity is independent of changes in NMDA receptor subunit composition. Neuron **32:** 619–634.
108. NASE, G. *et al.* 1999. Genetic and epigenetic regulation of NMDA receptor expression in the rat visual cortex. Eur. J. Neurosci. **11:** 4320–4326.
109. RAMOA, A.S. & G. PRUSKY. 1997. Retinal activity regulates developmental switches in functional properties and ifenprodil sensitivity of NMDA receptors in the lateral geniculate nucleus. Brain Res. Dev. Brain Res. **101:** 165–175.
110. BARTH, A.L. & R.C. MALENKA. 2001. NMDAR EPSC kinetics do not regulate the critical period for LTP at thalamocortical synapses. Nat. Neurosci. **4:** 235–236.
111. TANG, Y.P. *et al.* 1999. Genetic enhancement of learning and memory in mice. Nature **401:** 63–69.
112. CAO, Z. *et al.* 2000. Development of NR1, NR2A and NR2B mRNA in NR1 immunoreactive cells of rat visual cortex. Brain Res. **868:** 296–305.
113. ROBERTS, E.B. & A.S. RAMOA. 1999. Enhanced NR2A subunit expression and decreased NMDA receptor decay time at the onset of ocular dominance plasticity in the ferret. J. Neurophysiol. **81:** 2587–2591.
114. MOWER, G.D. 1991. The effect of dark rearing on the time course of the critical period in cat visual cortex. Brain Res. Dev. Brain Res. **58:** 151–158.
115. HOFFMANN, H. *et al.* 2000. Synaptic activity-dependent developmental regulation of NMDA receptor subunit expression in cultured neocortical neurons. J. Neurochem. **75:** 1590–1599.
116. FAGIOLINI, M. & T.K. HENSCH. 2000. Inhibitory threshold for critical-period activation in primary visual cortex. Nature **404:** 183–186.
117. BEAR, M.F. & W. SINGER. 1986. Modulation of visual cortical plasticity by acetylcholine and noradrenaline. Nature **320:** 172–176.
118. HARDING, C.F., S.R. BARCLAY & S.A. WATERMAN. 1998. Changes in catecholamine levels and turnover rates in hypothalamic, vocal control, and auditory nuclei in male zebra finches during development. J. Neurobiol. **34:** 329–346.
119. SOHA, J.A., T. SHIMIZU & A.J. DOUPE. 1996. Development of the catecholaminergic innervation of the song system of the male zebra finch. J. Neurobiol. **29:** 473–489.
120. SAKAGUCHI, H. & N. SAITO. 1989. The acetylcholine and catecholamine contents in song control nuclei of zebra finch during song ontogeny. Brain Res. Dev. Brain Res. **47:** 313–317.
121. SAKAGUCHI, H. & N. SAITO. 1991. Developmental change of cholinergic activity in the forebrain of the zebra finch during song learning. Brain Res. Dev. Brain Res. **62:** 223–228.
122. TAHA, S. *et al.* 2002. Autophosphorylation of alphaCaMKII is required for ocular dominance plasticity. Neuron **36:** 483–491.
123. DI CRISTO, G. *et al.* 2001. Requirement of ERK activation for visual cortical plasticity. Science **292:** 2337–2340.
124. BEAVER, C.J. *et al.* 2001. Cyclic AMP-dependent protein kinase mediates ocular dominance shifts in cat visual cortex. Nat. Neurosci. **4:** 159–163.
125. PIZZORUSSO, T. *et al.* 2002. Reactivation of ocular dominance plasticity in the adult visual cortex. Science **298:** 1248–1251.
126. GENOUX, D. *et al.* 2002. Protein phosphatase 1 is a molecular constraint on learning and memory. Nature **418:** 970–975.

127. HEINRICH, J., E.J. NORDEEN & K.W. NORDEEN. 2003. Delayed spine loss in lMAN is not necessary for extended song acquisition in zebra finches. Abstract Viewer/Itinerary Planner. Program No. 294.7. Society for Neuroscience. Washington, DC.

128. BISCHOF, H.J., E. GEISSLER & A. ROLLENHAGEN. 2002. Limitations of the sensitive period for sexual imprinting: neuroanatomical and behavioral experiments in the zebra finch (*Taeniopygia guttata*). Behav. Brain Res. **133:** 317–322.

129. GRUTZENDLER, J., N. KASTHURI & W.B. GAN. 2002. Long-term dendritic spine stability in the adult cortex. Nature **420:** 812–816.

130. STERN, E.A., M. MARAVALL & K. SVOBODA. 2001. Rapid development and plasticity of layer 2/3 maps in rat barrel cortex in vivo. Neuron **31:** 305–315.

131. GRAMMER, M.K. & S.W. BOTTJER. 2001. Silent synapses at neural substrates important for song learning in zebra finches. Soc. Neurosci. Abstr. **27.**

132. MALINOW, R., Z.F. MAINEN & Y. HAYASHI. 2000. LTP mechanisms: from silence to four-lane traffic. Curr. Opin. Neurobiol. **10:** 352–357.

Functional Neuroanatomy of the Sensorimotor Control of Singing

J. MARTIN WILD

*Department of Anatomy, Faculty of Medical and Health Sciences,
University of Auckland, Auckland, New Zealand*

ABSTRACT: Reviews of the songbird vocal control system frequently begin by describing the forebrain nuclei and pathways that form anterior and posterior circuits involved in song learning and song production, respectively. They then describe extratelencephalic projections upon the brainstem respiratory-vocal system in a manner suggesting, quite erroneously, that this system is itself well understood. One aim of this chapter is to demonstrate how limited is our understanding of that system. I begin with an overview of the neural network for the motor control of song production, with a particular emphasis on brainstem structures, including the tracheosyringeal motor nucleus (XIIts), which innervates the syrinx, and nucleus retroambigualis (RAm), which projects upon XIIts and upon spinal motor neurons innervating expiratory muscles. I describe the sources of afferent projections to XIIts and RAm and discuss their probable role in coordinating the bilateral activity of respiratory and syringeal muscles during singing. I then consider the routes by which sensory feedback, which could arise from numerous structures involved in singing, might access the song system to guide song learning, maintain accurate song production, and inform the song system of the requirements for air. I describe possible routes of access of auditory feedback, which is known to be necessary for song learning and maintenance, and identify potential sites of interaction with somatosensory and visceral feedback that could arise from the syrinx, the lungs and air sacs, and the upper vocal tract, including the jaw. I conclude that the incorporation of brainstem-based respiratory-vocal variables is likely to be a necessary next step in the construction of more sophisticated models of the control of vocalization.

KEYWORDS: song control system; brainstem; respiration; feedback

INTRODUCTION

Vocalization in general and singing in particular require the control and coordination of at least three sets of muscles, namely those acting on the vocal organ itself (the syrinx in birds), those of the respiratory system, and those acting on the structures of the upper vocal tract (trachea, larynx, pharynx, tongue, and beaks). The nuclei and pathways that mediate the neural control of the syrinx, from the

Address for correspondence: Department of Anatomy, Faculty of Medical and Health Sciences, University of Auckland, PB 92019, Auckland, New Zealand. Voice: 64-9-3737599; fax: 64-9-3737484.
jm.wild@auckland.ac.nz
<http://www.health.auckland.ac.nz/anatomy/staff/martin_wild.html>

Ann. N.Y. Acad. Sci. 1016: 438–462 (2004). © 2004 New York Academy of Sciences.
doi: 10.1196/annals.1298.016

telencephalon to the vocal (syringeal) motor neurons, have been known for many years.[1] Also known, at least in outline form, are the nuclei and pathways that mediate control of breathing, and, to a lesser extent, those that mediate control of upper vocal tract structures.[2] What is much less well known, however, is how the diverse sets of muscles involved in singing are coordinated, i.e., how the different neural control systems interact for the purposes of vocal production. In addition, there is little hard evidence about the sensory feedback that might be involved in the control of singing, apart from auditory feedback, that is. Here I first describe the various groups of motor neurons belonging to the three systems—vocal, respiratory, and upper vocal tract—and some of their premotor neurons, in so far as these are known. The descending pathways that act on these motor and premotor neurons are then outlined, followed by a focus on a nucleus in the caudal medulla called retroambigualis (RAm), which is hypothesized to play a significant role in the coordination of the different groups of motor neurons innervating syringeal and respiratory muscles, and possibly upper vocal tract muscles as well (in particular those of the jaw). I conclude with a brief survey of what we know about the various forms of sensory feedback and the routes of access of this feedback to the song system. The respiratory-vocal nuclei and pathways of the brainstem, their interconnections, and their afferent and efferent projections are schematically illustrated in FIGURE 1, which will serve to guide the reader through the complex anatomical connectivity to be discussed.

1. MOTOR OUTPUT

1a. The Vocal Motor Nucleus (XIIts)

Birds are apparently unique in the animal kingdom in having a vocal organ, the syrinx, situated deep in the chest at the confluence of the two primary bronchi at the distal end of the trachea, rather than at the proximal end of the trachea where the mammalian larynx is situated. Despite some recently discovered distinct similarities between the avian syrinx and the mammalian larynx in terms of their phonatory mechanisms,[3–6] the two structures are not homologous as vocal organs. Birds have their own larynx at the proximal end of the trachea, but it plays no part in phonation, although it may play some, as yet undiscovered, role either in modulation of the sounds produced by the syrinx or in the respiratory aspects of vocalization. Avian laryngeal muscles, unlike mammalian laryngeal muscles, are innervated by the glossopharyngeal nerve (CN IX), but the syringeal muscles are innervated by the hypoglossal nerve (CN XII). This innervation pattern suggests that the syringeal muscles, like those of the tongue, are developmental derivatives of occipital myotomes and thus share the same cranial nerve nucleus.

The role of the tongue in songbird vocalizations is unknown. Birds in general and songbirds in particular do not articulate their vocal sounds, as we do, for they have no lips or teeth, and their beaks are non-deformable, as appears to be true of their tongue in large part (except in parrots). Thus, despite the fact that lingual and syringeal motor neurons form part of the same nucleus, they are present as distinct subnuclei, reflecting their functional separation. In songbirds, lingual muscles are innervated by motor neurons occupying approximately the rostral third of the hypoglossal nucleus, and tracheal and syringeal muscles are innervated by motor neurons occupying approximately the caudal two-thirds of the nucleus. The lingual motor neurons slightly overlap the syringeal motor neurons in the rostrocaudal direction and are displaced slightly ventral to them (see figure 7 in Wild[7]). Their functional and physical separation from the tracheosyringeal (ts) motor neurons is reflected in the fact that, unlike the latter, they do not receive descending projections directly from the telencephalic and mesencephalic respiratory-vocal control nuclei, except in parrots.[7–9] The somata of the hypoglossal motor neurons are typical, polygonal alpha motor neurons. In the transverse plane, those of the ts portion form a small, dorsoventrally flattened oval cluster at caudal levels of the nucleus, but a larger, more circular cluster at rostral levels. The nucleus is surrounded by relatively cell-free neuropil, especially dorsally and dorsomedially, a region we have called "suprahypoglossal" and noted as a site of particularly concentrated terminations from descending axons of song control nuclei.[2,7]

The different pairs of syringeal muscles in songbirds have different functions in the respiratory-vocal mechanism, especially those located dorsally versus those located ventrally.[6,10–12] A simplified view of these differences is that dorsal muscles are separately concerned with adduction of the syringeal labia, and hence phonation on each side of the syrinx, i.e., the dorsal muscles are functionally lateralized; the tracheobronchialis ventralis functions as an abductor; and the largest ventral muscle (M. syringealis ventralis) is probably concerned with control of fundamental frequency and is not functionally lateralized. These fundamental differences are reflected in the organization of the vocal motor neurons, such that those innervating ventral muscles are located rostrally in XIIts whereas those supplying dorsal muscles are located caudally in XIIts.[13,14] Consistent with this myotopic organization of the vocal motor nucleus is the fact that the premotor nucleus, RA, is also organized functionally such that distinct parts of it separately innervate these two functional groups of motor neurons (see further below).[15]

The axons of the hypoglossal motor neurons exit the medulla ventrally in three roots.[a] The most rostral root carries lingual efferents, while the caudal two roots carry most, if not all, the tracheosyringeal efferents. The caudal roots also carry fibers that originate in nucleus supraspinalis (SSp), which lies ventral to XIIts, adjacent to the medial longitudinal fasciculus, and innervates craniocervical muscles of the upper neck.[18–22] This nucleus in the past has legitimately been called the ventral hypoglossal nucleus by some authors, but to avoid confusion with the vocal motor nucleus (which might otherwise be called the dorsal hypoglossal nucleus or nucleus intermedius[23]) the name supraspinalis is preferred.[22,24] Although SSp and XIIts share the same cranial nerve, the two nuclei are not usually thought to have any kind of functional association. It is interesting to note, however, that head extension (and open beak) is a common attitude adopted by the singing bird, suggesting that head

---

[a]Cambronero and Puelles[16] have speculated that the tracheosyringeal motor nucleus in birds corresponds to the medullary component of the accessory spinal nerve that innervates the larynx in mammals. If this were so one would expect the axons of these cells to exit the brainstem laterally, as do all the axons of motor neurons belonging either to the cranial or the spinal components of the accessory nerve. But they don't, they exit ventrally, like the axons of typical somatic efferent ventral horn motor neurons. In addition, birds have a medullary component of the accessory nerve of their own, the axons of which exit the brainstem laterally to innervate the cephalic part of M. cutaneous colli lateralis, known as M. cucullaris.[17,18] Furthermore, the avian larynx is innervated by a separate group of motor neurons in nucleus ambiguus.[7]

and neck extensor muscles (and beak muscles) may be under partial control of certain parts of the song system during singing.

After the fibers to the neck muscles are given off, the three hypoglossal roots merge, form an anastamosis with the vagus nerve, and then proceed as a single main nerve to the trachea. Here the nerve divides, with the lingual branch turning rostrally to the tongue and the ts nerve caudally to proceed down the neck to innervate the tracheolateralis muscle and the intrinsic syringeal muscles. In songbirds that husk their seeds, such as finches, the lingual branch of NXII (NXIII) is much larger than the ts branch, even though the intrinsic lingual muscles innervated by XIII are much smaller than the syringeal muscles. The reason for this is that the lingual branch in seed-husking birds carries a massive afferent component,[25] while the ts branch carries only a small afferent component.[26] The ts nerves in songbirds are paired, one on each side, and they do not anastamose with each other as they do in many non-songbirds. They are therefore strictly ipsilateral, even within the syrinx itself (Wild, unpublished observation). Therefore, bilateral coordination of the syrinx must involve crossed connections above the level of XIIts.

1b. Respiratory Motor and Premotor Nuclei

Because the respiratory system of birds is very different from that of mammals, a brief description of the avian system is in order. Unlike mammals, birds possess neither a diaphragm nor expandable lungs. It is the air sacs that inflate and deflate during breathing and singing, not the lungs. Inspiration is effected by the intercostal, scalene, and other muscles, which act on the ribs to assist thoracic recoil, expand the thorax, and fill the air sacs under negative pressure.[27] Also unlike mammals, expiration is an active process in birds, which is effected by abdominal and intercostal muscles compressing the thoracic and abdominal air sacs. Although these air sacs are independent, paired structures on either side of the body, they communicate across the midline with the rest of the air sac system and, in contrast to the distinctly lateralized function of the syrinx,[12] for which they supply the pressure head, they are compressed by the abdominal expiratory muscles during singing apparently in a bilaterally symmetrical way.[28]

Although a complete study of the spinal cord location and distribution of motor neurons innervating the respiratory muscles in birds has not been published, the information available suggests that they occupy a consistent location in the ventral horn throughout their rostrocaudal extent. In the absence of a phrenic nucleus, motor neurons innervating inspiratory muscles (e.g., Mm. scalenus and levatores costarum) are located in medial lamina IX at lower brachial levels and at the tip of the ventral horn at upper thoracic levels. Motor neurons innervating abdominal expiratory muscles occupy a similar position at the tip of the ventral horn at lower thoracic and upper lumbar levels.[29–31] All these motor neurons have two sets of very extensive dendrites, one extending dorsolaterally into the white matter, and another extending dorsomedially toward the central canal and column of Terni (which houses the avian sympathetic preganglionic neurons). The significance of the separation of the dendrites is not clear. Although it might suggest differential access to descending pathways, both sets appear to receive projections from the same premotor nucleus in the medulla.[29–31]

Apart from the lack of a phrenic nucleus, the organization of the premotor nuclei for respiratory control appears basically similar to that in mammals.[2,30,31] A ventral respiratory group (VRG) occupies the ventrolateral medulla and is made up of nucleus retroambigualis (RAm) situated most caudally, with neurons that fire in phase with expiration, and a more rostral nucleus parambigualis (PAm), whose neurons fire in phase with inspiration. A further description of RAm will be given later in this chapter, but for now we can note that the neurons of both RAm and PAm occupy a narrow arc that extends ventrolaterally from XIIts and widens as it approaches the lateral edge of the medulla. RAm and PAm both project to the cord bilaterally, with a contralateral predominance. This is in contrast to the predominantly ipsilateral projections of RA to all the respiratory-vocal nuclei of the brainstem.[7,32] The axons of RAm and PAm travel in the dorsolateral funiculus, apparently immediately under the pia, until they reach their level of termination where they turn ventromedially and begin to "run down" the dorsolaterally directed dendrites of the respiratory motor neurons. In pigeons the contacts appear to be largely in relation to the dendrites, but in songbirds the contacts clearly approximate the cell bodies. Although only light microscopic examination of these contacts has thus far been performed, they give every indication of being monosynaptic.[31]

1c. Laryngeal, Tongue, and Jaw Motor Neurons

Laryngeal motor neurons are located in the nucleus ambiguus, caudal to the obex, as they are in mammals, and lie dorsomedial to neurons of nucleus parambigualis (PAm).[7,33] Unlike the case in mammals, however, their axons travel to the laryngeal muscles in the glossopharyngeal nerve and not the vagus. A myotopic analysis has not been performed, but it could be that the adductors and abductors have their separate motor representation.

As we note above, the role of the avian tongue in singing is unknown, but it seems unlikely to be of great significance, in and of itself, because it is relatively stiff and not used for articulation in the way of the human tongue. In songbirds, the intrinsic lingual muscles are very small and restricted to the caudal part of the tongue and, to this writer's knowledge, their specific role in lingual manipulation has never been determined. Nevertheless, because the tongue is an integral component of the hyoid apparatus—the central (paraglossale) bone of the hyoid being actually situated within the structure of the tongue—it could be involved in a complex mechanism related to vocal modulation. This is because the hyoid, by virtue of the flexibility of its movements in the both the antero-posterior and mediolateral directions, may play a significant part in changing the shape and size of the oro-pharynx during singing. It is important to consider, therefore, how the tongue and hyoid are moved. In all birds the tongue as a whole is moved by extrinsic muscles that are attached to the hyoid horns rather than to the tongue itself. The tongue is protracted by M. geniohyoideus that attaches proximally to the lower jaw and distally and more caudally to the hyoid horn. This muscle is innervated by the glossopharyngeal nerve and its motor neurons are situated in the ventrolateral pons.[24,34] Retraction of the tongue is brought about by the actions of Mm. serpihyoideus and stylohyoideus, which also attach to the lower jaw and hyoid horns, but their rostrocaudal attachments are opposite to those of M. geniohyoideus, thus reversing the action. They are innervated by the facial nerve and their motor neurons are located ventromedially to the superior olive, anterior to those of M. geniohyoideus. Other movements of the hyoid apparatus and the muscles that act upon its different parts require further functional analysis.

Although jaw movements during singing are probably only part of a more complex oro-pharyngeal modulation of sound production, beak gape (distance between upper and lower beak) is to some extent correlated with the acoustic frequency of the sound emitted, such that higher or peak frequencies—up to about 3–4 kHz—are produced with wider gapes.[35–42] It is possible, therefore, that jaw motor neurons may be influenced by the telencephalic song control circuitry. The myotopic organization of jaw muscles within the trigeminal and facial nuclei in the pons has been worked out only for pigeons and ducks,[24,43] but not for songbirds. In pigeons and ducks the beak-opener muscles, M. depressor mandibulae and M. protractor quadratus are innervated by a composite subnucleus consisting of facial and trigeminal motor neurons, respectively, while the several beak-closer muscles are innervated by other subnuclei of the trigeminal complex. The jaw closers, but not the openers, have abundant spindles, which receive their sensory innervation from neurons in the mesencephalic trigeminal nucleus.[44,45] Presumably, they also receive a motor innervation from gamma motor neurons in or near the trigeminal motor nucleus.

1d. Nucleus Robustus Arcopallialis (RA), the Telencephalic Premotor Respiratory-Vocal Control Nucleus

In adult songbirds RA is a sexually dimorphic, spherical-to-oval, semi-encapsulated nucleus in the medial part of the arcopallium, comprising projection neurons and interneurons.[46,47] It is not present in non-songbirds, including suboscines.[48] The great majority of RA projection neurons project to subtelencephalic targets in the thalamus, midbrain, and rhombencephalon as far as upper C1, but it is not known whether any single neuron projects to more than one target. In males, but not in females, all the descending projection neurons, their axons and terminations express parvalbumin, a marker that can therefore be used to define the respiratory-vocal control pathway.[47] A very small proportion of RA neurons situated at the dorsocaudal edge of the nucleus project dorsally, probably to HVC (Wild, unpublished observation), which is one of RA's major sources of input (LMAN being the other[49]). RA interneurons are GABAergic and they probably also express one or both of the calcium binding proteins parvalbumin and calbindin.[46,47,50,51] They provide for long-range inhibition in RA and can synchronize the firing of RA projections neurons in vitro.[46] Therefore, various RA projections neurons with distinct respiratory and vocal targets may be coordinated by RA interneurons.

Songbirds are not only unique amongst avian species, but apparently also unique amongst all animal species, in having a single telencephalic nucleus that directly controls both the vocal motor nucleus and the respiratory premotor nuclei for the production of learned vocalizations, as in singing. RA's role in the control of song was discovered by Nottebohm and colleagues[52] in canaries. These authors showed that RA sends projections, via the occipitomesencephalic tract (OM), to the dorsomedial nucleus of the intercollicular complex (DM) and to the vocal motor neurons making up the tracheosyringeal portion of the hypoglossal nucleus in the medulla (XIIts). The authors immediately recognized the significance of this projection, both in terms of its role in song control and in terms of its anatomical uniqueness as a telencephalic projection directly to a cranial nerve nucleus, previously thought to exist only in humans. In terms of song control, Vicario[15] then showed in zebra finches that RA is organized functionally, such that projections to DM arise from a dorsal "cap" of neurons, whereas projections to XIIts arise from the remainder of the nucleus (see Vates and colleagues[53] for similar, but not identical, results in canaries). Vicario[15] also found that projections to syringeal motor neurons innervating either dorsal or ventral syringeal muscles arise from largely separate horizontal slabs of RA: ventral RA projects to caudal XIIts where motor neurons innervating dorsal syringeal muscles are located, while middle RA projects to rostral XIIts where motor neurons innervating ventral syringeal muscles are located.[13] Further analyses of RA projections found them to be considerably more extensive than previously thought, to be similarly distributed in both males and females, and, in some species, such as the canary, to have an appreciable contralateral component.[7,32,47,54] Thus, in addition to projections to DM and the vocal motor neurons in XIIts, RA was found to project to dorsal thalamic nuclei that project back upon nuclei of the anterior forebrain pathway [dorsolateral regions of the dorsolateral medial nucleus (DLM), and the dorsomedial posterior nucleus (DMP)][7,53,55] and to a series of nuclei in the ventrolateral rhombencephalon, including laryngeal motor neurons and the respiratory premotor nuclei parambigualis (PAm) and retroambigualis (RAm).[2,31] These latter findings showed how it might be possible for RA to coordinate respiratory and syringeal muscle activity in the service of vocal production, although the cellular and pharmacological analysis of this coordination has only just begun.[56] How the jaw and tongue muscle motor neurons might be controlled during singing is considered in *Section 1g* but for now we can note that RA axons do not appear to terminate on jaw or tongue motor neurons during their trajectory through the brainstem.[7]

1e. The Dorsomedial Nucleus of the Intercollicular Complex (DM), the Ventrolateral Parabrachial Nucleus (PBvl), and the Descending Cascade

Although it has long been recognized that in all birds there is component of the vocal control system that lies close to the inferior colliculus at mesencephalic levels,[52,57] the specific role of the nucleus called DM in singing has still not been determined. DM has sometimes been called a respiratory nucleus, but, like RA, its neurons do not appear to have a respiratory-related firing pattern (Wild, unpublished observations), at least when the bird is not singing or calling. Stimulation of DM with trains of electrical currents as low as 2 μA, with saline, or even with mechanical stimuli such as the presence of the stimulating electrode itself, can drive vocalizations accompanied by what appears to be a full-blown respiratory pattern.[8,58] The nucleus has descending projections and brainstem targets that mimic those of RA, i.e., DM projects upon RAm, PAm, and XIIts in both songbirds and non-songbirds,[8] although it is not known whether DM and RA terminate on the same parts of the same neurons or even on the same neurons. In songbirds—which have both an RA and a DM and in which RA projects upon DM—it is not know whether DM neurons have firing patterns during singing that are correlated with the temporal or acoustic aspects of syllabic production, or, if they do, whether they contribute to the control of vocal output in way different from that of RA. If DM is specifically removed bilaterally (by lesioning only that small part of the intercollicular complex that projects upon XIIts, etc.), is vocal output in any way different than in the intact bird?

In other words, is DM essential for singing, or not?[52] A cautionary note in this regard is that DM projects back upon nucleus uvaeformis of the posterior thalamus, which is a key source of input to the song control circuitry.[31,59] From the comparative and hodological points of view, DM seems very much akin to lateral regions of the periaqueductal grey (PAG) in mammals that are involved in vocal control by their projections upon nucleus retroambiguus.[60–63]

The ventrolateral parabrachial nucleus (PBvl) in the lateral pons is thought to be the avian equivalent of the mammalian Köllicker-Fuse nucleus.[64] PBvl receives ascending projections from a part of nucleus tractus solitarius (nTS)[65,66] that, in turn, receives a primary afferent input from the lung;[67] and, like RA and DM, PBvl projects to all the respiratory-vocal nuclei located more caudally in the brainstem.[64,65] It is thus ideally suited to play a role in the temporally regulated aspects of vocalization by mediating signals related to the inspiratory phase of respiration.

There are two other nuclei in the ventrolateral rhombencephalon that are also thought to be part of the respiratory-vocal control complex. One is a nucleus located between the superior olive and the spinal lemniscus (IOS), and the other (RVL) is located rostral to PAm. Almost nothing is known about these nuclei, although on the basis of their relative positions and some of their connections, it is possible that IOS is similar to the retrotrapezoid nucleus and RVL to the pre-Bötzinger complex of mammals. Both IOS and RVL receive projections from all the more rostral components of the respiratory-vocal control complex and project to each of the more caudal components of the complex, including XIIts.[2,68] There is thus what has been called a descending cascade of descending projections upon the medullary respiratory-vocal nuclei,[68] defined by both parallel and serial pathways (FIG. 1). The discovery of the way in which these pathways interact for the purposes of vocal control represents an ambitious goal for the future.

1f. Nucleus Retroambigualis (RAm): A Nucleus that Coordinates Respiration and Vocalization?

In mammals nucleus retroambiguus in the caudal medulla has been regarded as a nexus for the integration and distribution of vocal control signals emanating from the midbrain periaqueductal grey (PAG) to all the nuclei involved in vocalization, such as the laryngeal, peri-oral, and respiratory motor nuclei.[60] A very similar situation holds for the avian nucleus retroambigualis, which may be homologous with nucleus retroambiguus on the basis of its relative position, connections, and function. However, RAm in birds not only receives direct descending projections from the telencephalon (i.e., RA), in addition to the midbrain, but it also has a much greater mediolateral extent than retroambiguus in mammals, stretching in an arc from XIIts medially almost to the lateral edge of the medulla. Prior to the discovery of RAm as a respiratory premotor nucleus,[29] the region containing RAm was known simply as the dorsocentral medulla (Cnd in the atlas of the pigeon brain by Karten and Hodos[23]). RAm can be seen in the Nissl-stained photographs of that atlas in Plates P3.75–P4.5, although it is misidentified as the lateral cervical nucleus (CL) in Plate P4.5. (In reality, CL lies between RAm and the dorsal horn). The borders of the nucleus are not unambiguous in Nissl-stained material, although the nucleus as a whole can readily be delineated by labeling the terminal fields of RA either with a neural tracer, such as biotinylated dextran amine or cholera toxin subunit B, or with an anti-

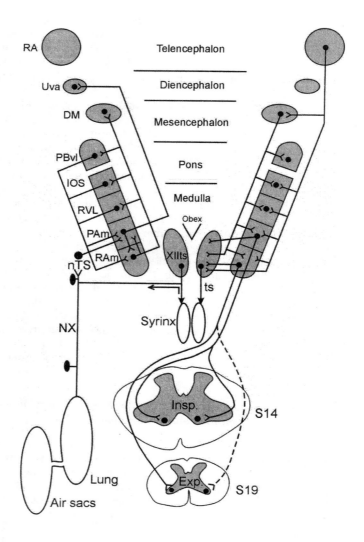

FIGURE 1. Nuclei and some of the interconnections of the respiratory-vocal system in a songbird. The system is shown from RA in the telencephalon to the respiratory motor neurons in the thoracic and lumbar spinal cord. A more or less continuous series of nuclei occupy the ventrolateral pons and medulla, with XIIts located dorsomedially in the medulla and projecting ipsilaterally to the bipartite syrinx. *Dots* represent cell bodies and *inverted arrows* terminations. The two sides are symmetrical, of course, but for clarity the projections of RA and DM to all the nuclei in the ventrolateral pons and medulla, as well as to XIIts, are shown on the right, and the cascade of descending projections is shown on the left, as are the ascending, feedback pathways from RAm and PAm. RAm projects upon expiratory motor neurons in the lower thoracic and upper lumbar spinal cord, while PAm projects upon inspiratory motor neurons in the lower brachial and upper thoracic spinal cord, both with a contralateral predominance (ipsilateral projections indicated by dashed lines). Note the sy-

parvalbumin antibody.[7,47] The delineation of RAm and XIIts by RA axon terminals points to the prime importance of telencephalic influence on the patterning and co-ordination of respiratory and vocal activity during singing in songbirds.

RAm is composed of several different types of projection neurons and possibly intrinsic neurons, although it is not yet clear whether all the different types of projection neurons project to separate targets. Projection neurons include: (1) bulbospinal neurons that project to motor neurons innervating abdominal expiratory muscles[29] and probably to those innervating expiratory intercostal muscles; (2) a separate group of XIIts-projection neurons, some of which project bilaterally, but most ipsilaterally, and provide a dense, largely glycinergic (inhibitory) innervation of the vocal motor nucleus;[32,56,69] (2a) a second group of XIIts-projecting cells that are excitatory;[56] (3) a group of large, multipolar, vagal neurons in the more ventrolateral parts of RAm, the specific peripheral target(s) of which are presently unknown, but may include respiratory structures; and (4) neurons that project in an ascending fashion to more rostral components of the respiratory-vocal network, viz. PAm, IOS, RVL, PBvl, and DM (Wild, unpublished observation). These ascending projections are bilateral with an ipsilateral predominance.

Extracellular single unit and multi-unit recordings from RAm in anesthetized birds establish the presence of a respiratory rhythm that is in phase with expiration. Each burst of action potentials commences approximately 30–50 msec before the start of EMGs recorded simultaneously from abdominal expiratory muscles and ceases with the commencement of inspiration,[29,68] consistent with the idea that these neurons are expiratory premotor in nature. Since bulbospinal RAm neurons are presumably part of an oscillating respiratory network, their rhythmicity is likely to be a function of network properties, and not simply due to intrinsic membrane potential oscillations. Such rhythmic activity may also be expressed by XIIts-projecting RAm cells; in fact it is this type of cell that is thought to account for the rhythmical activity of XIIts neurons that fire in phase with expiration.[29,56,70,71] A direct test of this notion is as yet lacking, but inactivating the XIIts-projecting RAm neurons should silence expiratory activity in XIIts, if this view is correct—although whether this needs to be done bilaterally is a moot point. Ultimately, this model suggests that the non-glycinergic, excitatory type of XIIts-projecting RAm cells are responsible for the XIIts expiratory-related rhythm recorded during quiet breathing.

Despite the unequivocal evidence of robust excitatory expiratory drive, XIIts neurons do not appear to be inhibited during inspiration,[56] so the glycinergic, inhibitory input to XIIts from RAm must serve another purpose, probably to do with shaping

---

ringeal and pulmonary afferents projecting to the nucleus of the tractus solitarius (nTS) via the vagus nerve (NX), which then projects onto the region containing PAm (syringeal afferents are indicated by the *bent arrow* beside the left tracheosyringeal (ts) nerve. DM, dorsomedial nucleus of the intercollicular complex; IOS, nucleus infra-olivarus superior; PAm, nucleus parambigualis; PBvl, ventrolateral nucleus of the parabrachial complex; RA, nucleus robustus arcopallialis; RAm, nucleus retroambigualis; RVL: rostroventrolateral medulla; S14 and S19, segments 14 and 19 of the spinal cord; Uva, nucleus uvaeformis. (Adapted from Reinke and Wild.[31])

XIIts motor-neuronal discharge during singing. Although speculative, it seems likely that these RAm neurons play a significant part in modulating the activity of XIIts motor neurons during song, since inhibitory influences on highly dynamic and phasic, muscle-specific motor neurons are intuitively required to rapidly sculpt discharge envelopes appropriate to the acoustic and temporal properties of the notes produced. When the bird sings, the intrinsic respiratory rhythm of quiet breathing is rapidly changed to one which supports syllabic production, frequently on the basis of one expiration to one syllable or even part-syllable, unless the syllable repetition rate is too high, and then pulsatile respiration takes over.[72] Interspersed during the phrase are minibreaths, making for a highly dynamic respiratory pattern that is intricately coordinated with syringeal activity and hence vocal output.[73,74] The telencephalic song premotor nucleus RA is likely to be the dominant forebrain structure that engages the RAm-XIIts network to achieve such exquisite coordination. Probably, different RA neurons project to XIIts and to RAm, enabling RA to exert influence on both XIIts motor neurons and RAm neurons (as well as all the other components of the respiratory-vocal network), the end result of which is a coordination of syringeal and respiratory muscle activity that amazingly produces the phenomenon of song. These and other considerations of multiple descending inputs from, and outputs to, other parts of the respiratory-vocal network (e.g., DM, PBvl, etc.) suggest that RAm is a true integrator of respiratory-vocal activity. Moreover, its bilateral projections to XIIts, contralateral RAm, and more rostral components of the network, also suggest that it plays an important part in coordinating activity on the two sides of the brain during singing.[75] This would seem to be an essential role in a brain that is otherwise dominated by ipsilateral projections from the telencephalic vocal control nucleus and ipsilateral projections to each side of the bipartite but bilaterally and functionally interacting syrinx.[12,76]

An intriguing finding relating to vocal production in birds has been that neurons throughout the entire song system, including the premotor and motor pathways, carry an auditory signal related to the bird's own song (BOS).[71,77,78] Since the respiratory pattern can also be influenced by BOS in the anesthetized bird in such a way as to suggest respiratory drive appropriate to singing,[56] it is likely that RAm and its bulbospinal neurons, as well as XIIts, also receive this auditory signal. If so, this could extend the motor theory of speech perception[71,79,80] to include the respiratory patterns that are functionally associated with the production of particular speech/song sounds or phrases. As every singer knows, learning to sing entails learning to breathe.

1g. Control of the Jaw and Other Upper Vocal Tract Structures

An important question is the extent to which nuclei of the respiratory-vocal system, such as RA and RAm, are involved in the control of the activity of neurons that ultimately control structures involved in singing other than the syrinx and respiratory muscles, e.g., upper vocal tract structures such as the jaw. Beak gape, or aperture, it will be remembered, is correlated to some extent with the acoustic frequency of the notes sung, which, together with other evidence, suggests that beak movements have an important role in modulating upper vocal tract filter properties.[39–42] The questions then become: How are jaw motor neurons influenced during singing to bring about the observed relationship between beak gape, acoustic frequency, and vocal tract resonances? Does RA influence jaw motor neurons during singing and, if so, how? Are the projections of RA to RAm involved in mediating an indirect influence on jaw motor neurons? Anatomically, these questions turn out to be ones for which we do not yet have adequate answers. In the apparent absence of direct projections from RA to jaw (and lingual) motor neurons[7] (FIG. 1), we were motivated to determine whether there were indirect RA projections to these nuclei. This we did by charting the distribution of jaw premotor neurons and mapping their proximity to RA terminal fields in the brainstem (Wild, unpublished observation). A distinct cluster of jaw premotor neurons was found medioventrally adjacent to the arc of RAm, with many of the neurons having dendrites that extend into the RA terminal field that encompasses RAm. The projections of these jaw premotor neurons target the contralateral trigeminal and facial motor nuclei very specifically. Thus, RAm neurons do not appear to target the jaw motor nuclei directly, and, because of their close proximity to the jaw premotor neurons, it is difficult to determine whether they project upon them. It is possible, however, that the jaw premotor neurons are influenced by RA axons by way of their dendrites that extend into RAm, but whether RA is actually capable of driving jaw motor neurons via this route requires physiological verification. It also seems probable that RAm and RA have a similar relationship to premotor neurons for the tongue and other upper vocal tract structures, as they do to the jaw premotor neurons.

In contrast to this rather indirect route for the telencephalic control of jaw motor and premotor neurons during singing, a more direct route may be available that involves pathways that also mediate telencephalic of control of the jaw during feeding. In analogous fashion to the way in which RA sends long descending projections to XIIts and the respiratory premotor neurons, other arcopallial regions send long descending projections to other parts of the medulla that house a host of premotor neurons involved in other behaviors (FIG. 2). Specifically, the lateral region of the arcopallium is a source of descending projections to the rhombencephalic lateral reticular formation and spinal trigeminal tract nuclei and, of particular importance in the present context, to the region of jaw premotor neurons located medially adjacent to RAm.[81] This lateral arcopallial region, in turn, receives specific inputs that are derived, via at least two synapses, from nucleus rostrobasalis, the telencephalic recipient of ascending projections from the principal sensory trigeminal nucleus, and other pontine nuclei (FIG. 2). In brief, there is a trigeminal sensorimotor circuit that originates in the beak, tongue and oral cavity (and in an auditory lateral lemniscal nucleus), projects polysynaptically through the telencephalon to the arcopallium, and descends upon jaw (and possibly tongue) premotor nuclei.[81,82] Although this circuit may well be primarily involved in feeding mechanisms, it is possible that it is also involved in control of beak and possibly tongue movements during singing—simply because some of the same jaw and tongue muscles are involved in both feeding and singing. Moreover, the fact that there is a distinct (and very fast) auditory component of this circuit that originates in the intermediate lateral lemniscal nucleus,[81] could suggest that auditory (and somatosensory) feedback from singing influence jaw movements via this route (*Section 2b(iv)*). It is also noteworthy that the possibility of parts of the arcopallium other than RA being involved in various aspects of vocal control is consistent with conceptualizations of the functional organization and arcopallial projections of the LMAN*shell*, a putative component of song learning circuitry.[83]

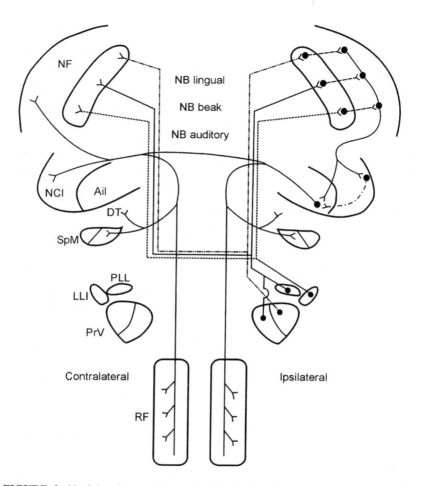

FIGURE 2. Nuclei and connections of a trigeminal and auditory sensorimotor circuit that originates in the principal sensory trigeminal nucleus (PRV) and in specific components of the lateral lemniscal nuclear complex (LLI and PLL). *Dots* represent cell bodies and *inverted arrows* represent terminations. PRV, LLI, and PLL project through the quintofrontal tract directly to nucleus rostrobasalis (NB) in the frontal telencephalon, without a thalamic relay. Via local connections with the frontal nidopallium (NF), NB then projects both to the caudolateral nidopallium (NCl) and to the lateral part of the intermediate arcopallium (Ail). From Ail projections cross to the opposite NCl and descend throughout the diencephalon and rhombencephalon. There are terminations in the dorsal thalamus (DT) and specifically in the medial spiriform nucleus (SpM), which projects to the cerebellum, and then an extensive terminal field occupies the lateral reticular formation (RF) of the pons and medulla. Specific terminations are found in the premotor cell group medial to RAm that projects contralaterally upon jaw motor neurons (not shown, Wild, unpublished observation). (Diagram taken from Wild and Farabaugh.[81])

2. SENSORY FEEDBACK

Most complex motor tasks, such as singing, are generally thought to entail some form of sensory feedback that has as its functional consequence the refinement and optimization of the motor output, or at least the continuance or completion of the very act itself. In the case of singing, because several otherwise separately functioning sensorimotor systems are involved, this feedback can conceivably take a variety of forms, including, most obviously, the auditory input that the bird's own song inevitably produces, and, least obviously, the generalized and apparently unlocalized feedback that derives from the respiratory apparatus, including the lungs, air sacs and associated muscles during breathing, and from various parts of the upper vocal tract such as the beak, tongue, larynx, and pharynx. What sensory receptors are involved in mediating feedback from these various structures? What are the neural pathways that mediate their effects? Although an attempt to answer these questions is given here, it should be recognized that we do not yet have proof that many of these receptors and their neural pathways are critically involved in the control of singing, in the same way that we know that auditory receptors and pathways are critical for singing.

2a. Auditory Feedback

A major reason for the use of songbirds in research on vocalization is that they comprise one of the few groups of animals, other than humans, that learn their songs with reference to an auditory model.[84-86] Songbirds use auditory feedback both during learning to sing as juveniles and during song production in adulthood.[84,87-91] Song is learned first by listening to conspecifics and then also to self as the bird begins to match its vocal output to a stored auditory memory. In some species, such as the zebra finch, these two phases of sensory and sensorimotor learning overlap; in others they are separated in time. But in either case auditory feedback during singing is inevitably accompanied by proprioceptive or somatosensory feedback that derives from a variety of structures used in singing. Whether and where the various sources of feedback are integrated in the brain will be considered below, but for now, the major question to be asked is how auditory feedback accesses the song system.

This question has a long history,[92] but to cut a long story short, it is now strongly suspected that nucleus interfacialis (NIf) is the principal source of auditory input to HVC.[49,93-96] But now the question becomes how auditory input accesses NIf since this nucleus, or its presumed homologue in non-songbirds,[93] has not traditionally been considered a major component of the auditory pathway through the forebrain.[97-99] Although a circuitous route of access to NIf was suggested by Vates and colleagues,[99] we suspected there might be a more direct route involving direct projections of a lateral subnucleus of nucleus ovoidalis (Ov, the principal thalamic auditory relay[93]). Unfortunately, this is very difficult to prove using the usual tract-tracing procedures. Injections of biotinylated dextran amine (BDA) into lateral Ov produce a robust terminal field in NIf (Wild, unpublished observation), but such injections invariably also retrogradely label Uva, which projects directly to NIf via axons that travel through and around the lateral part of Ov. The terminal field in NIf as a result of Ov injections could therefore be explained by uptake of tracer by Uva fibers of passage. Moreover, although injections of tracers into NIf invariably produce retrograde labeling of neurons in lateral Ov (Wild, unpublished observation), lateral parts of Ov project topographically, through NIf, to overlying more lateral parts of field L, the "auditory cortex" of the avian telencephalon.[97–99] Thus, retrograde labeling in lateral Ov as a result of NIf injections could, ipso facto, be explained by uptake of tracer by Ov fibers of passage.

A second route by which auditory feedback accesses the song system has been described as relaying through Ov to cholinergic neurons in the basal telencephalon (ventral paleostriatum), which then project, topographically, to both HVC and RA.[100,101] On the basis of finding retrogradely labeled cells in Ov following injections of tracer in the basal forebrain, Li and colleagues[101] claimed this pathway to be *the* pathway involved in vocal learning in songbirds. However, this claim does not take account of the fact that Ov projections to field L pass right through the very region, lateral to the anterior commissure, which was claimed by Li and Sakaguchi[100] and Li and colleagues[101] to be the site of origin of cholinergic projections to HVC and RA. Ov neurons could, therefore, have been inadvertently retrogradely labeled as fibers of passage. Nevertheless, Shea and Margoliash[102] have reported that glutamate, as well as electrical stimulation of the basal forebrain abolishes BOS-evoked activity in HVC, which is consistent with the findings of Li and Sakaguchi.[100] Clearly, however, further clarification of the nature and source of the afferent input to this basal forebrain nucleus is required.

A third route of possible auditory feedback is a most unusual one. It involves the ascending projections of the intermediate nucleus of the lateral lemniscus (LLI), which receives a direct projection from the cochlear nuclei. The projections of LLI reach the telencephalon directly, i.e., without a thalamic relay and terminate in a nucleus now called nucleus rostrobasalis (NB)[81] (FIG. 2). In psittaciformes, NB has been hypothesized to play an essential role in vocal learning,[9] but its role in songbird vocal learning has not been assessed, and there is no known connection of this nucleus with any of the song control nuclei in the forebrain. It therefore remains an enigma, but because NB also receives a major input from the trigeminal system, the auditory input to this nucleus could be associated with somatosensory feedback from jaw, tongue, and other head movements during singing (see *Section 2b(v)*).

2b. Nonauditory Feedback

Konishi[84] first considered the possibility that proprioceptive feedback might be used to control vocal output, either during development or after auditory feedback has contributed to and perhaps enabled the crystallization of the species typical song.[85] Although direct evidence of the specific source and nature of this feedback, or of its involvement in vocal control, has been lacking, there is now some evidence that certain forms of somatosensory feedback do play a part in adjusting output variables during singing, for example.[103] We will consider the various forms of non-auditory feedback in terms of their possible sources.

(i) Input from the Air Sacs

Because ventilation in birds involves the air sacs and their associated muscles, it is these rather than the lungs that could possess sensory receptors that inform the nervous system about subsyringeal air pressure and/or volume. To determine whether the air sacs are sensate, we injected brief pulses of air into the air sacs of northern cardinals as they sang, and simultaneously measured air sac pressure and activity in abdominal expiratory muscles (EMGs).[103] These manipulations resulted in a significant decrease in the amplitude of EMG's recorded from the expiratory muscles during the initial part of the syllable being sung at the time of air injection, with a minimum latency of about 30 msec.[103] The suggestion is that air injection elicits a decrease in abdominal expiratory muscle EMG to compensate for an increase in air sac pressure, which in turn implicates some kind of sensory receptor either in the air sac or associated muscles and a reflex arc that mediates adjustments of motor output to the muscles.

To establish the presence of an air sac receptor, we injected the vagus nerve with cholera toxin subunit B (CTB) in zebra finches and examined the air sac walls immunohistochemically.[104] We were motivated to do this because recordings of vagal afferent activity have been correlated with air sac expansion,[105] suggesting that, if the air sacs do possess pressure and/or volume receptors, they are probably innervated by the vagus nerve. Vagally innervated structures were identified at the edge of the thoracic sacs close to the openings into the lungs (ostia) that we have interpreted as a variant of the neuroepithelial bodies (NEB) that are present in the lungs and airways of many vertebrates, including birds.[106–108] One postulated role for NEBs in mammals has been as an oxygen receptor, i.e., they respond to hypoxia,[109–110] but they may also be sensitive to mechanical stimuli, such as stretch.[108] The functional nature of the receptors we identified in the zebra finch air sacs is unknown. Perhaps this could be determined by injecting a hypoxic gas mixture into the air sac during singing, but interpreting any resultant effects on expiratory muscle activity is unlikely to be straightforward, partly because the innervation and functions of NEBs are extremely complex.[108]

The receptors that sense an experimentally induced increase in air sac pressure during singing may not necessarily be located in the air sacs themselves, but in the muscles and other tissues that are stretched as a result. Unfortunately, there is no information on the presence of such receptors in songbirds. However in chickens, muscle spindles are sparse in the abdominal expiratory muscles, such as transversus.[111]

We also attempted to determine the central projections of the vagal fibers that innervate the air sacs by daubing the air sac wall with CTB. A major terminal field was found in nucleus tractus solitarius (nTS), with a particular concentration around the tract at levels just caudal to the obex.[104] The possible role of this connectivity will be discussed below.

(ii) Input from the Syrinx

The minimum latency of the reflex that brings about a reduction in expiratory muscle EMG as a result of air injected into the air sacs (30 msec[103]) is more than sufficient to involve either the spinal cord or the brainstem. That the latter is the more likely central site of a sensorimotor transform is indicated by the fact that air injected into the air sac during singing also brings about a compensatory reflex change in the tension of the syringeal adductor muscles, except that, in this case, the tension is increased rather than decreased—with the result that a constant subglottal pressure is maintained by narrowing the syringeal aperture and preventing air loss.[112] The syrinx does not, to our knowledge, receive any kind of spinal innervation, but it does receive a sensory innervation via the tracheosyringeal nerve (NXIIts[26]) (FIG. 1). The type of sensory receptor structure innervated in the syrinx has not been identified, but it is probably not muscle spindles, which appear to be absent (Wild, unpublished observation). Syringeal afferents terminate centrally in nTS in close proximity to air sac and pulmonary afferents (see below) (FIG. 1), and possibly in the spinal trigeminal nucleus (Wild, unpublished observation). The projections of the recipient parts of nTS then target several nuclei, including PAm in the ventrolateral medulla[65,66] (in songbirds, Wild, unpublished observation). In turn, PAm projects upon the syringeal motor nucleus (XIIts) and on RAm. Although speculative, by these means could be effected an increase in syringeal adductor tone and, via an inhibitory synapse, a decrease in abdominal expiratory muscle tone by way of bulbospinal RAm neurons[29,31] (Wild, unpublished observation).

(iii) Input from the Lung

Since the avian lung does not expand during inspiration, there are no pulmonary stretch receptor afferents in the vagus nerve that act to inhibit inspiration, as there are in mammals. Instead, birds have intrapulmonary CO_2 receptors that are also innervated by vagal afferents. These produce a similar inhibitory effect to mammalian lung stretch receptors by increasing their firing rate during inspiration and terminating on GABAergic neurons in nTS.[113–115] As shown for the pigeon, pulmonary afferents terminate in nTS and specifically in nucleus parasolitarius lateralis (lPs) located lateral to the tract at levels just caudal to the obex[67] (FIG. 1). In zebra finches and canaries, pulmonary afferents also terminate around the tract at these same levels (Wild, unpublished). The specific targets of lPs neurons have not specifically been determined by anterograde tracing methods in songbirds, but, on the basis of retrograde tracing, they appear to be similar to those identified by anterograde tracing methods in pigeons (Wild, unpublished observation).[65,66] In both songbirds and non-songbirds, these targets include nucleus parambigualis (PAm), which includes neurons that discharge in phase with inspiration and which project, apparently monosynaptically, upon spinal motoneurons innervating inspiratory muscles, such as the scalenes.[27,30,31] Other targets of lPs projections probably include neurons in close proximity to the inspiratory-related premotor group, but which project rostrally to terminate densely, specifically and bilaterally in nucleus uvaeformis (Uva),[31,59] a major source of input to both HVC and NIf of the vocal control circuitry (FIG. 1). A third target of lPs is the ventrolateral parabrachial nucleus (PBvl), which then projects back upon the respiratory-vocal nuclei in the medulla.[64] Thus, pulmonary afferents appear to have intimate connections with nuclei involved in the duration and timing of respiratory phase and are therefore likely to be of vital importance during normal breathing and, perhaps, during singing as well.[116] In cats somatosensory afferents in the vagus nerve are essential for phonation, signaling the CNS about the volume of air in the lungs.[117] Perhaps phonation in birds is similarly dependent on the integrity of intrapulmonary CO_2 receptor afferents in the vagus nerve. Certainly the bird needs to know how much air is available in order to regulate the timing, duration and frequency of song phrases or motifs, but it may also require information about the availability of air for the temporal control of phrase structure, in so far as minibreaths are involved.[42,116]

(iv) Input from Upper Vocal Tract Structures

Our knowledge of the roles of upper vocal tract structures, such as the trachea, larynx, tongue, and beaks, in vocalization is incomplete, and our knowledge of possible feedback from these structures is very limited.[42] Daley and Goller[118] have recently measured changes in tracheal length during singing in the zebra finch, but the small changes that took place did not appear to be implicated in changing vocal tract filter properties.

Although the larynx is not involved in phonation, it is hard to believe that it would not have some kind role to play in vocal production, because of its ability to change the shape and size of the tracheal opening, which could affect vocal tract resonance. Laryngeal muscles are innervated by the glossopharyngeal nerve, but it is not known whether they contain spindles, nor is it known whether the laryngeal mucosa has any kind of sensory receptors.

Although the phonological structure of bird song is different from that of human speech,[86] and even though birds do not have lips, teeth, or much of a deformable tongue (except in parrots), it is likely that changes in the size and/or shape of the oro-pharynx during singing play a significant role in shaping or filtering the sounds produced. Very little is yet known about this aspect of vocalization, but casual observation of a canary in full song will readily reveal the obvious importance of the gular (throat) region, which is flanked by the hyoid horns and their associated muscles.

Beak gape probably influences oro-pharyngeal shape and size, but it has the advantage of being readily measurable. It is known to play a significant part in vocal production, such that higher pitched notes are accompanied by a wider gape.[36,37,39,41] Moreover, weighting the beak during singing changes the harmonic content in canary song,[39] and fixing the beak open during singing in sparrows and zebra finches alters filter properties of the upper vocal tract.[39,41] Both these procedures could suggest that proprioceptive feedback from the jaw during singing is important for maintaining the acoustic structure of song, although the motivation for manipulating the jaw in these studies was not related to this problem.

If jaw proprioception is important for singing, it could be derived either from the craniomandibular joint, or the protractor hinge at the base of the upper beak, or from the beak muscles, which are known to contain abundant spindles. Although these are located in the jaw-closer muscles rather than the jaw openers,[44] their innervation by trigeminal afferents and their stretch-activation during beak opening could play a significant role in the fine control of gape size, via the mesencephalic trigeminal nucleus and its central projections onto jaw motor neurons.[45]

(v) Sites of Possible Integration of Auditory and Somatosensory Feedback

As mentioned above, when the bird sings, somatosensory feedback from a variety of structures of the upper vocal tract—including skin and feathers of the head and neck that move extensively during singing—is likely to be associated concomitantly with auditory feedback. Whether and where the auditory and somatosensory feedback that is produced during singing is integrated in the brain, has not been determined conclusively, although there are candidate nuclei. It is also apposite to note that there are very close associations between the auditory and somatosensory systems throughout all levels of the avian brain.[119]

One of the candidate nuclei is nucleus rostrobasalis (NB) in the telencephalon, because it receives sensory input from the beaks and oral cavity, via the principal sensory trigeminal nucleus, and a distinct auditory input from the intermediate nucleus of the lateral lemniscus[81,120] (FIG. 2). However, it is not clear that cross-modal integration takes place in this nucleus, or whether the distinct inputs remain separate until combined at a later stage of processing. All parts of NB reach the surrounding nidopallium, which then projects to the caudolateral nidopallium and to the arcopallium (FIG. 2), but the brainstem targets of the auditory-related arcopallial regions have not been determined in songbirds.[81]

Another candidate for auditory-somatosensory integration is nucleus interfacialis (NIf), especially since this nucleus, together with one of its sources of thalamic input, namely Uva, projects directly to HVC. NIf also receives a somatosensory input from Uva and the rostral Wulst,[93,121] but whether auditory and somatosensory inputs actually converge on the same NIf neurons, or whether these two kinds of inputs remain separate within the nucleus, has not been determined. Also important to determine will be which parts of the body supply the somatosensory input to NIf; so far only body, and not head (trigeminal), inputs have been recorded there.[93]

SUMMARY AND A GENERAL DIRECTION FOR FUTURE RESEARCH

The findings described in the chapters of this Section of the book derive from what is probably a small proportion of the research devoted to the remainder of the song system in the forebrain. Yet the work of Suthers and Goller and their colleagues describing the structure and function of the vocal tract, the syrinx in particular—especially of the way it forms a most flexible yet integrated respiratory-vocal organ during singing—has contributed a wealth of insights into the nature of the motor strategies used by different species of songbirds and has shown what it is that ultimately needs to be controlled by the telencephalic nuclei HVC and RA. Data from these studies have been used to construct models of the syrinx that can produce sounds that are remarkably similar to natural birdsong.[122,123] Together with increasingly exact knowledge of the morphology and connectivity of such nuclei as HVC and RA and of the nature and timing of their neuronal activities,[46,124,125] such theoretical approaches will no doubt lead to the construction of more sophisticated models that can help test predictions of how the song control system actually functions to produce the species typical song.[126,127]

Nevertheless, the ultimate success of such models will inevitably depend on the incorporation of a host of other variables related to respiration, respiratory-vocal interactions, and upper vocal tract activities about which we have as yet very limited knowledge. Between the vocal organ and the forebrain song control nuclei is a collection of brainstem nuclei, including the vocal motor nucleus itself, about which there is little information regarding their detailed contributions to singing in particular or vocalization in general. Our first examination of the relationship between XIIts and RAm[56] should make it clear to anyone that we have only just begun to scratch the surface of a most complex series of interactions between brainstem respiratory-vocal nuclei and the way these are modulated by the forebrain during singing, and by peripheral inputs that function in a feedback manner. Although further investigations of these interactions and the resolution of their underlying neural mechanisms will not be easy, they have the potential to yield important information about how, during the learning and performance of a skill such as singing, the forebrain engages and temporarily controls the vegetative, vital respiratory centers in the brainstem. Perhaps in no model system other than the songbird can this be done with respect to a learned communicative skill of such obvious relevance to humans.[86,128]

REFERENCES

1. BRENOWITZ, E.A., D. MARGOLIASH & K. NORDEEN. 1997. Introduction to birdsong and the avian song system. J. Neurobiol. **33**: 495–500.
2. WILD, J.M. 1997. Neural pathways for the control of birdsong production. J. Neurobiol. **33**: 653–670.
3. GOLLER, F. & O.N. LARSEN. 1997 In situ biomechanics of the syrinx and sound generation in pigeons. J. Exp. Biol. **200**: 2165–2176.
4. GOLLER, F. & O.N. LARSEN. 1997. A new mechanism for sound generation in songbirds. Proc. Natl. Acad. Sci. USA **94**: 14787–14791.
5. LARSEN, O.N. & F. GOLLER. 1999. Role of syringeal vibrations in bird vocalizations. Proc. R. Soc. Lond. B **266**: 1609–1615.
6. LARSEN, O.N. & F. GOLLER. 2002. Direct observation of syringeal muscle function in songbirds and a parrot. J. Exp. Biol. **205**: 25–35.
7. WILD, J.M. 1993. Descending projections of the songbird nucleus robustus archistriatalis. J. Comp. Neurol. **338**: 225–241.
8. WILD, J.M., D. LI & C. EAGLETON. 1997. Projections of the dorsomedial nucleus of the intercollicular complex (DM) in relation to respiratory-vocal nuclei in the brainstem of pigeon (*Columba livia*) and zebra finch (*Taeniopygia guttata*). J. Comp. Neurol. **377**: 392–413.
9. STRIEDTER, G.F. 1994. The vocal control pathways in budgerigars differ from those in songbirds. J. Comp. Neurol. **343**: 35–56.
10. GOLLER, F. & R.A. SUTHERS. 1996. Role of syringeal muscles in gating airflow and sound production in singing brown thrashers. J. Neurophysiol. **75**: 867–876.
11. GOLLER, F. & R.A. SUTHERS. 1996. Role of syringeal muscles in controlling the phonology of bird song. J. Neurophysiol. **76**: 287–300.
12. SUTHERS, R.A. & S.A. Zollinger. 2004. Producing song: the vocal apparatus. Ann. N.Y. Acad. Sci. **1016**: This volume.
13. VICARIO, D.S. & F. NOTTEBOHM. 1988. Organization of the zebra finch song control system: I. Representation of syringeal muscles in the hypoglossal nucleus. J. Comp. Neurol. **271**: 346–354.
14. RUAN, J. & R.A. SUTHERS. 1996. Myotopic representation of syringeal muscles in the hypoglossal nucleus of the cowbird. Soc. Neurosci. Abstr. **22**: 1402.
15. VICARIO, D.S. 1991. Organization of the zebra finch song control system: II. Functional organization of outputs from nucleus robustus archistriatalis. J. Comp. Neurol. **309**: 486–494.
16. CAMBRONERO, F. & L. PUELLES. 2000. Rostrocaudal nuclear relationships in avian medulla oblongata: a fate map with quail chick chimeras. J. Comp. Neurol. **427**: 522–545.
17. HILLEBRAND, A. 1975. An experimental study concerning the accessory nerve in the chicken and turkey. Anat. Anz. **137**: 296–302.
18. WILD, J.M. 1981. Identification and localization of the motor nuclei and sensory projections of the glossopharyngeal, vagus and hypoglossal nerves in the cockatoo (Cacatua roseicapilla), Cacatuidae. J. Comp. Neurol. **203**: 352–378.
19. LANDOLT, R. & G. ZWEERS. 1985. Anatomy of the muscle-bone apparatus of the cervical system in the mallard (*Anas platyrhyncos* L.) Neth. J. Zool. **35**: 611–670.
20. WATANABE, T. & Y. OHMORI. 1988. Location of motoneurons supplying upper neck muscles in the chicken studied by means of horseradish peroxidase. J. Comp. Neurol. **270**: 271–278.

21. HÖRSTER, W., A. FRANCHINI & S. DANIEL. 1990. Organization of neck muscle motoneurons in the cervical spinal cord of the pigeon. Neuroreport **1:** 93–96.
22. ZIJLSTRA, C. & J.L. DUBBELDAM. 1994. Organization of the motor innervation of craniocervical muscles in the mallard, Anas platyrhyncos L. J. Brain Res. **35:** 425–440.
23. KARTEN, H.J. & W. HODOS. 1967. A Stereotaxic Atlas of the Brain of the Pigeon (*Columba livia*). Johns Hopkins Press. Baltimore, MD.
24. WILD, J.M. & H.P. ZEIGLER. 1980. Central representation and somatotopic organization of the jaw muscles in the facial and trigeminal nuclei in the pigeon (*Columba livia*). J. Comp. Neurol. **192:** 175–201.
25. WILD, J.M. 1990. Peripheral and central terminations of hypoglossal afferents innervating lingual tactile mechanoreceptor complexes in Fringillidae. J. Comp. Neurol. **298:** 157–171.
26. BOTTJER, S.W. & A. ARNOLD. 1982. Afferent neurons in the hypoglossal nerve of the zebra finch (*Poephyla guttata*): localization with horseradish peroxidase. J. Comp. Neurol. **210:** 190–197.
27. FEDDE, M.R. 1987. Respiratory muscles. *In* Bird Respiration, Vol. I., T.J. Seller, Ed.: 3–37. CRC Press. Boca Raton, FL.
28. GOLLER, F. & R.A. SUTHERS. 1999. Bilaterally symmetrical respiratory activity during lateralized birdsong. J. Neurobiol. **41:** 513–523.
29. WILD, J.M. 1993. The avian nucleus retroambigualis: a nucleus for breathing, singing and calling. Brain Res. **606:** 119–124.
30. REINKE, H. & J.M. WILD. 1997. Distribution and connections of inspiratory premotor neurons in the brainstem of the pigeon (*Columba livia*). J. Comp. Neurol. **379:** 347–362.
31. REINKE, H. & J.M. WILD. 1998. Identification and connections of inspiratory premotor neurons in songbirds and budgerigar. J. Comp. Neurol. **391:** 147–163.
32. WILD, J.M., M.N. WILLIAMS & R.A. SUTHERS. 2000. Neural pathways for bilateral vocal control in songbirds. J. Comp. Neurol. **423:** 413–426.
33. GRABATIN, O. VON & M. ABS. 1986. Zur efferenten Larynxinnervierung bei der Haustaube (*Columba livia domestica* L.). Anat. Anz. **162:** 101–108.
34. DUBBELDAM, J.L. & R. BOUT. 1990. The identification of the motor nuclei innervating the tongue muscles in the mallard (*Anas platyrhyncos*); an HRP study. Neurosci. Lett. **119:** 223–237.
35. HAUSBERGER, M., J.M. BLACK & J.P. RICHARD. 1991. Bill opening and sound spectrum in barnacle goose loud calls: individuals with "wide mouths" have higher pitched voices. Anim. Behav. **42:** 319–322.
36. WESTNEAT, M.W., J.H. LONG, JR., W. HOESE & S. NOWICKI. 1993. Kinematics of birdsong: functional correlation of cranial movements and acoustic features in sparrows. J. Exp. Biol. **182:** 147–171.
37. PODOS, J.E., J.K. SHERER, S. PETERS & S. NOWICKI. 1995. Ontogeny of vocal tract movements during song production in song sparrows. Anim. Behav. **50:** 1287–1296.
38. SUTHERS, R.A., F. GOLLER, R. BERMEJO, *et al.* 1996. Relationship of beak gape to the lateralization, acoustics and motor dynamics of song in cardinals. *In* Abstracts of the Nineteenth Midwinter Meeting of the Association for Research in Otolaryngology, p158, Des Moines, IA.
39. HOESE, W., J. PODOS, N.C. BOETTICHER & S. NOWICKI. 2000. Vocal tract function in birdsong production: experimental manipulation of beak movements. J. Exp. Biol. **203:** 1845–1855.
40. WILLIAMS, H. 2001. Choreography of song, dance and beak movements in the zebra finch (Taeniopygia guttata). J. Exp. Biol. **204:** 3498–3506.
41. GOLLER, F., M.J. MALLINCKRODT & S.D. TORTI. 2003. Beak gape dynamics during song in the zebra finch. J. Neurobiol. In press.
42. GOLLER, F. & COOPER 2004. Peripheral motor dynamics of song production in the zebra finch. Ann. N.Y. Acad. Sci. **1016:** This volume.
43. DEN BOER, P.J., R.J. BOUT & J.L. DUBBELDAM. 1986. Topographical representation of the jaw muscles within the trigeminal motor nucleus. An HRP study in the mallard (*Anas platyrhyncos*). Acta Morphil. Neerl. Scand. **24:** 1–17.

44. BOUT, R.G. & J.L. DUBBELDAM. 1991. Functional morphological interpretation of the distribution of muscle spindles in the jaw muscles of the mallard (*Anas platyrhyncos*). J. Morphol. **210:** 215–226.

45. BOUT, R.G., A.J. TELLEGEN & J.L. DUBBELDAM. 1997. Central connections of the nucleus mesencephalicus nervi trigemini in the mallard (*Anas platyrhyncos* L.). Anat. Rec. **248:** 554–565.

46. SPIRO, J.E., M.B. DALVA & R. MOONEY. 1999. Long-range inhibition within the zebra finch song nucleus RA can coordinate the firing of multiple projection neurons. J. Neurophysiol. **81:** 3007–3020.

47. WILD, J.M., M.N. WILLIAMS & R.A. SUTHERS. 2001. Parvalbumin-positive projection neurons characterise the vocal premotor pathway in male, but not female, zebra finches. Brain Res. **917:** 235–252.

48. KROODSMA, D.E. & M. KONISHI. 1991. A suboscine bird (eastern phoebe, *Sayornis phoebe*) develops normal song without auditory feedback. Anim. Behav. **42:** 477–487.

49. NOTTEBOHM, F., D.B. KELLEY & J.A. PATON. 1982. Connections of vocal control nuclei in the canary telencephalon. J. Comp. Neurol. **207:** 344–357.

50. BRAUN, K., H. SCHEICH, M. SCHACHNER & C.W. HEIZMAN. 1985. Distribution of parvalbumin, cytochrome oxidase activity and ^{14}C-2-deoxyglucose uptake in the brain of the zebra finch. I. Auditory and vocal motor systems. Cell Tiss. Res. **240:** 101–115.

51. GRISHAM, W. & A.P. ARNOLD. 1994. Distribution of GABA-like immunoreactivity in the song system of the zebra finch. Brain Res. **651:** 115–122.

52. NOTTEBOHM, F., T.M. STOKES & C.M. LEONARD. 1976. Central control of song in the canary, *Serinus canaria*. J. Comp. Neurol. **165:** 457–486.

53. VATES, G.E., D.S. VICARIO & F. NOTTEBOHM. 1997. Reafferent thalamo-"cortical" loops in the song system of oscine songbirds. J. Comp. Neurol. **380:** 275–290.

54. VICARIO, D.S. 1993 A new brain stem pathway for vocal control in the zebra finch song system. NeuroReport **4:** 983–986.

55. FOSTER, E.F., R.P. MEHTA & S.W. BOTTJER. 1997 Axonal connections of the medial magnocellular nucleus of the anterior neostriatum in zebra finches. J. Comp. Neurol. **382:** 364–381.

56. STURDY, C.B., J.M. WILD & R. MOONEY. 2002. Respiratory and telencephalic modulation of vocal motor neurons in the zebra finch. J. Neurosci. **23:** 1072–1086.

57. PHILLIPS, R.E. & F.W. PEEK. 1975. Brain organization and neuromuscular control of vocalization in birds. *In* Hormones and Behaviour in Higher Vertebrates. P. Wright, P.J. Caryl & D.M. Vowles, Eds.: 243–274. Elsevier. Amsterdam.

58. VICARIO, D.S. & B. SIMPSON. 1995. Electrical stimulation in forebrain nuclei elicits learned vocal patterns in songbirds. J. Neurophysiol. **73:** 2602–2607.

59. STREIDTER, G.F. & E.T. VU. 1998. Bilateral feedback projections to the forebrain in the premotor network for singing in zebra finches. J. Neurobiol. **34:** 27–40.

60. HOLSTEGE, G. 1989. Anatomical study of the final common pathway for vocalization in the cat. J. Comp. Neurol. **284:** 242–252.

61. GERRITS, P.O. & G. HOLSTEGE. 1996. Pontine and medullary projections to the nucleus retroambiguus: a wheat germ agglutinin-horseradish peroxidase and autoradiographic tracing study in the cat. J. Comp. Neurol. **373:** 173–185.

62. VANDERHORST, G.J.M., E. TERASAWA, H.J. RALSTON II & G. HOLSTEGE. 2000. Monosynaptic projections from the lateral periaqueductal gray to the nucleus retroambiguus in the rhesus monkey: implications for vocalization and reproductive behaviour. J. Comp. Neurol. **424:** 251–268.

63. JÜRGENS, U. 2002 Neural pathways underlying vocal control. Neurosci. Biobehav. Rev. **26:** 235–258.

64. WILD, J.M., J.J.A. ARENDS & H.P. ZEIGLER. 1990. Projections of the parabrachial nucleus in the pigeon. J. Comp. Neurol. **293:** 499–523.

65. WILD, J.M., & J.J.A. ARENDS. 1987. A respiratory-vocal pathway in the brainstem of the pigeon. Brain Res. **407:** 191–194.

66. ARENDS, J.J.A., J.M. WILD & H.P. ZEIGLER. 1988. Projections of the nucleus tractus solitarius in the pigeon (*Columba livia*). J. Comp. Neurol. **278:** 405–429.

67. KATZ, D.M. & H.J. KARTEN. 1983. Visceral representation within the nucleus tractus solitarius in the pigeon (*Columba livia*). J. Comp. Neurol. **218:** 42–73.
68. WILD, J.M. 1994. The auditory-vocal-respiratory axis in birds. Brain Behav. Evol. **44:** 192-209.
69. KUBKE, M.F., R. MOONEY & J.M. WILD. 2002. Characterisation of neurons in the respiratory-vocal nucleus retroambigualis in the zebra finch. Paper presented at the first conference on the Behavioral Neurobiology of Birdsong. Hunter College. New York, NY.
70. MANOGUE, K.R. & J.A. PATON. 1982. Respiratory gating of activity in the avian vocal control system. Brain Res. **247:** 383–387.
71. WILLIAMS, H. & F. NOTTEBOHM. 1985. Auditory response in avian vocal motor neurons: A motor theory for song perception in birds. Science **229:** 279-282.
72. HARTLEY, R.S. 1990. Expiratory muscle activity during song production in the canary. Respir. Physiol. **81:** 177–187.
73. HARTLEY, R.S. & R.A. SUTHERS. 1989. Airflow and pressure during canary song: direct evidence for minibreaths. J. Comp. Physiol. A. **165:** 15–26.
74. WILD, J.M., F. GOLLER & R.A. SUTHERS. 1998. Inspiratory muscle activity during bird song. J. Neurobiol. **36:** 441–453.
75. SCHMIDT, M. *et al.* 2004. Bilateral control and interhemispheric coordination in the avian song motor system. Ann. NY Acad. Sci. **1016:** This volume.
76. SUTHERS, R.A. 1997. Peripheral control and lateralization of birdsong. J. Neurobiol. **33:** 632–652.
77. MARGOLIASH, D. 1983. Preference for autogenous song by auditory neurons in a song system nucleus of the white-crowned sparrow. J. Neurosci. **6:** 1643–1661.
78. DOUPE, A.J. & M. KONISHI. 1991. Song-selective auditory circuits in the vocal control system of the zebra finch. Proc. Natl. Acad. Sci. USA **88:** 11339–11343.
79. LIBERMAN, A.M., F.S. COOPER, D.P. SHANKWEILER & M. STUDDERT-KENNEDY. 1967. Perception of the speech code. Psych. Rev. **74:** 431–461.
80. LIBERMAN, A.M. & I.G. MATTINGLY. 1985. The motor theory of speech perception revised. Cognition **21:** 1–36.
81. WILD, J.M. & S.M. FARABAUGH. 1996. Organization of afferent and efferent projections of nucleus basalis prosencephali in a passerine (Taeneopygia guttata). J. Comp. Neurol. **365:** 306–328.
82. WILD, J.M., J.J. A. ARENDS & H.P. ZEIGLER. 1985. Telencephalic connections of the trigeminal system in the pigeon (Columba livia): a trigeminal sensorimotor circuit. J. Comp. Neurol. **234:** 441–464.
83. BOTTJER, S.W., J.D. BRADY & B. CRIBBS. 2000. Connections of a motor control region in zebra finches: relation to pathways for vocal learning. J. Comp. Neurol. **420:** 244–260.
84. KONISHI, M. 1965. The role of auditory feedback in the control of vocalization in the white-crowned sparrow. Z. Tierpsychol. **22:** 770–783.
85. KONISHI, M. 2004. The role of auditory feedback in birdsong. Ann. NY Acad. Sci. **1016:** 463–475. This volume.
86. DOUPE, A.J. & P. KUHL. 1999. Birdsong and human speech: common themes and mechanisms. Ann. Rev. Neurosci. **22:** 567–631.
87. Marler, P. 1970. A comparative approach to vocal learning: song development in white-crowned sparrows. J. Comp. Physiol. Psychol. **71:** 1–25.
88. NORDEEN, K.W. & E.J. NORDEEN. 1992. Auditory feedback is necessary for the maintenance of stereotyped song in adult zebra finches. Behav. Neurol. Biol. **57:** 58–66.
89. OKANOYA, K. & A. YAMAGUCHI. 1997. Adult Bengalese finches (*Lonchura strita*) var. domestica) require real-time auditory feedback to produce normal song syntax. J. Neurobiol. **33:** 343–356.
90. LEONARDO, A. & M. KONISHI. 1999. Decrystallization of adult birdsong by perturbation of auditory feedback. Nature **399:** 466–470.
91. BRAINARD, M.S. & A.J. DOUPE. 2000. Auditory feedback in learning and maintenance of vocal behaviour. Nature Rev. Neurosci. **1:** 31–40.
92. FORTUNE, E.S. & D. MARGOLIASH. 1995. Parallel pathways and convergence onto HVC and adjacent neostriatum of adult zebra finches (*Taeniopygia guttata*). J. Comp. Neurol. **325:** 388–404.

93. WILD, J.M. 1994. Visual and somatosensory projections to the avian song system via nucleus uvaeformis (Uva) and a comparison with the projections of a similar thalamic nucleus in a non-songbird (*Columba livia*). J. Comp. Neurol. **349:** 512–535.

94. JANATA, P. & D. MARGOLISH. 1999. Gradual emergence of song selectivity in sensorimotor structures of the male zebra finch song system. J. Neurosci. **19:** 5108–5118.

95. BOCO, T. & D. MARGOLIASH. 2001. NIf is a major source of auditory and spontaneous drive to HVc. Program No. 318.2, 2001 Abstract Viewer/Itinerary Planner. Washington, D.C. Society for Neuroscience, 2001. Online.

96. COLEMAN, M.J. & R. MOONEY. 2002. Source of auditory input to the songbird nucleus HVc revealed by pairwise recordings in NIf and HVc. Program No. 588.4, 2002 Abstract Viewer/Itinerary Planner, Washington, D.C.: Society for Neuroscience 2002, Online.

97. KARTEN, H.J. 1968. The ascending auditory pathway in the pigeon (*Columba livia*). II. Telencephalic projections of the nucleus ovoidalis thalami. Brain Res. **11:** 134–153.

98. WILD, J.M., H.J. KARTEN & B.J. FROST. 1993. Connections of the auditory forebrain in the pigeon (*Columba livia*). J. Comp. Neurol. **337:** 32–62.

99. VATES, G.E., B.M. BROOME, C.V. MELLO & F. NOTTEBOHM. 1996. Auditory pathways of caudal telencephalon and their relation to the song system of adult male zebra finches (*Taeniopygia guttata*). J. Comp. Neurol. **366:** 613–642.

100. LI, R. & H. SAKAGUCHI. 1997. Cholinergic innervation of the song control nuclei by the ventral paleostriatum in the zebra finch: a double labelling study with retrograde fluorescent tracers and choline acetyltransferase immunohistochemistry. Brain Res. **763:** 239–246.

101. LI, R., M.-X. ZUO & H. SAKAGUCHI. 1999. Auditory-vocal cholinergic pathway in zebra finch brain. Neuroreport **10:** 165–169.

102. SHEA, S.D. & D. MARGOLIASH. 2003. Basal forebrain cholinergic modulation of auditory activity in the zebra finch song system. Neuron **40:** 1213–1226.

103. SUTHERS, R.A., F. GOLLER & J.M. WILD. 2002. Somatosensory feedback modulates the respiratory motor program of crystallized birdsong. Proc. Natl. Acad. Sci. USA **99:** 5680–5685.

104. KUBKE, M.F., J.M. ROSS & J.M. WILD. Vagal innervation of the air sacs in a songbird, *Taeniopygia guttata*. J. Anat. (Lond.). In press.

105. BALLAM, G.O., T.L. CLINTON & A.L. KUNZ. 1982. Ventilatory phase duration in the chicken: Role of mechanical and CO_2 feedback. J. Appl. Physiol. **53:** 1378–1385.

106. LAUWERYNS, J.M., M. COKELAERE & P. THEUNYNCK. 1972. Neuro-epithelial bodies in the respiratory mucosa of various mammals. A light optical, histochemical and ultrastructural investigation. Z. Zellforsch. Mikrosk. Anat. **135:** 569–592.

107. BOWER, A., S. PARKER & V. MOLONEY. 1978. An autoradiographic study of the afferent innervation of the trachea, syrinx and extrapulmonary primary bronchus of *Gallus gallus domesticus*. J. Anat. **126:** 169–180.

108. ADRIAENSEN, D., I. BROUNS, J. VAN GENECHTEN & J.-P. TIMMERMANS. 2003. Functional morphology of pulmonary neuroepithelial bodies: extremely complex airway receptors. Anat. Rec. A **270A:** 25–40.

109. KEMP, P.J., A. LEWIS, M.E. HARTNESS, *et al.* 2002. Airway chemostransduction: from oxygen sensor to cellular effector. Am. J. Respir. Crit. Care Med. **166:** S17–24.

110. KEMP, P.J., G.J. SEARLE, M.E. HARTNESS, *et al.* 2003. Acute oxygen sensing in cellular models: Relevance to the physiology of pulmonary neuroepithelial and carotid bodies. Anat. Rec. **270:** 41–50.

111. DEWET, P.D., P.R. FARRELL & M.R. FEDDE. 1971. Number and morphology of muscle spindles in the transversus abdominis muscle of the chicken. Poult. Sci. **50:** 1349.

112. SUTHERS, R.A. & J.M. WILD. 2000 Real-time modulation of the syringeal motor program in response to externally imposed respiratory perturbations in adult songbirds. Soc. Neurosci. Abstr. **26:** 723.

113. GLEESON, M. 1987. The role of vagal afferents in the peripheral control of respiration in birds. *In* The Neurology of the Cardiorespiratory System. E.W. Taylor, Ed.: 51–79. Manchester University Press. Manchester.

114. GLEESON, M. & V. MOLONEY. 1989. Control of breathing. *In* Form and Function in Birds. Vol. 2. A.S. King & J. McLelland, Ed.: 439–484. Academic Press. London.
115. FORTIN, G., A.S. FOUTZ & J. CHAMPAGNAT. 1994. Respiratory rhythm generation in chick hindbrain: effects of MK-801 and vagotomy. Neuroreport **5:** 1137–1140.
116. FRANZ, M. & F. GOLLER. 2003. Respiratory patterns and oxygen consumption in singing zebra finches. J. Exp. Biol. **206:** 967–978.
117. NAKAZAWA, K., K. SHIBA, K. YOSHIDA & A. KONNO. 1997. Role of pulmonary afferent inputs in vocal on-switch in the cat. Neurosci. Res. **29:** 49–54.
118. DALEY, M. & F. GOLLER. 2004. Tracheal length changes during zebra finch song and their possible role in upper vocal tract filtering. J. Neurobiol. **59:** 319–330.
119. WILD, J.M. 1995. Convergence of somatosensory and auditory projections in the avian torus semicircularis, including the central auditory nucleus. J. Comp. Neurol. **358:** 465–486.
120. WILD, J.M., H. REINKE & S.M. FARABAUGH. 1997. A non-thalamic pathway contributes to a whole body map in the brain of the budgerigar. Brain Res. **755:** 137–141.
121. WILD, J.M. & M.N. WILLIAMS. 1999. Rostral wulst in passerine birds. II. Intratelencephalic projections to nuclei associated with the auditory and song systems. J. Comp. Neurol. **413:** 520–534.
122. GARDNER, T., G. CECCHI, M. MAGNASCO, *et al.* 2001. Simple motor gestures for birdsongs. Phys. Rev. Lett. **87:** 208101.
123. LAJE, R., T.J. GARDNER & G.B. MINDLIN. 2002. Neuromuscular control of vocalizations in birdsong: a model. Phys. Rev. E **65:** 051921.
124. YU, A.C. & D. MARGOLIASH. 1996. Temporal hierarchical control of singing in birds. Science **273:** 1871–1875.
125. HAHNLOSER, R.H.R., A.A. KOZHEVNLKOV & M.S. FEE. 2002. An ultra-sparse code underlies the generation of neural sequences in a songbird. Nature **419:** 65–70.
126. LAJE, R. & G.B. MINDLIN. 2002. Diversity within a birdsong. Phys. Rev. Lett. **89:** 288102.
127. MINDLIN, G.B., T.J. GARDNER, F. GOLLER & R.A. SUTHERS. 2003. Experimental validation of a physical model for birdsong production. Phys. Rev. E. **68:** 041908.
128. KUHL, P.K. 2003. Human speech and birdsong: communication and the social brain. Proc. Natl. Acad. Sci. USA **100:** 9645–9646.

The Role of Auditory Feedback in Birdsong

MASAKAZU KONISHI

Division of Biology, California Institute of Technology, Pasadena, California 91125, USA

ABSTRACT: Young songbirds memorize a tutor song and use the memory trace as a template to shape their own song by auditory feedback. Major issues in birdsong research include the neural sites and mechanisms for song memory and auditory feedback. The brain song control system contains neurons with both premotor and auditory function. Yet no evidence so far shows that they respond to the bird's own song during singing. Also, no neurons have been found to respond to perturbation of auditory feedback in the brain area that is thought to be involved in the feedback control of song. The phenomenon of gating in which neurons respond to playback of the bird's own song only during sleep or under anesthesia is the sole known evidence for control of auditory input to the song system. It is, however, not known whether the gating is involved in switching between the premotor and auditory function of neurons in the song control system.

KEYWORDS: songbirds; song learning; auditory feedback; gating; vocal control system

INTRODUCTION

The control of motor coordination by the central nervous system was one of the major issues in neuroethology in the 1950s when I started my thesis project under Peter Marler at the University of California, Berkeley. Central coordination was important for ethologists, because they regarded it as one of the criteria for instincts or fixed action patterns. Since both external stimuli and sensory feedback from the movement can provide cues necessary for motor coordination, removal of such cues was the main method of testing for central coordination. The late Donald Wilson,[1] who served on my thesis committee, obtained the first neurophysiological evidence for central coordination in the locust's flight system. He showed that even after systematic removal of all sources of movement-derived feedback, the basic flight motor pattern could be recorded from the motor neurons innervating the flight muscles. Like this example, many subsequent studies of central coordination were all focused on rhythmic behaviors that were relatively easy to characterize quantitatively. Central control is harder to show in movements that are more complex and are difficult

ABBREVIATIONS: HVC, high vocal center; RA, robust nucleus of acropallium; LMAN, lateral magnocellular nucleus of the anterior nidopallium; X, area X within songbird medial striatum; DLM, dorsal lateral nucleus of anterior thalamus; Nlf, interfacial nucleus of the nidopallium; DM, dorsomedial intercollicular nucleus; Uva, nucleus uvaeformis.

Address for correspondence: Division of Biology 216-76, California Institute of Technology, Pasadena, California 91125. Voice: 626-395-6815; fax: 626-449-0679.

konishi@its.caltech.edu; <http://www.biology.caltech.edu/Facultypages/konishi.html>

Ann. N.Y. Acad. Sci. 1016: 463–475 (2004). © 2004 New York Academy of Sciences.
doi: 10.1196/annals.1298.010

to describe and quantify. Nevertheless, stereotyped movements, such as courtship displays, were regarded as instincts (i.e., as centrally coordinated movement patterns without experimental proof). For the researcher interested in issues of central versus peripheral control, birdsong provided some unique opportunities for research. While it is a complex behavior, it is relatively stereotyped in form and, with the advent of sound analysis techniques, it can be objectively described (Tchernichovski et al., this volume). These characteristics made birdsong a promising subject for the analysis of the role of sensory feedback in the control of complex movements, even though the relationships between voice and muscular activities may be complex. I thought that I could use birdsong to study the role of sensory feedback in both the development and maintenance of motor coordination. The white-crowned sparrow (Zonotrichia leucophrys), which the Marler laboratory was using for the study of song learning, was particularly suitable for my project, because the song of birds raised in isolation was distinctly different from that of wild birds.[2,3] Also, young white-crowns memorize a tutor song before they can sing, as noted in other species.[4] I thought that these features of sparrow song would allow me to separate the sensory and sensorimotor phases of song learning.

The white-crowned sparrows that I had deafened before the onset of singing developed extremely abnormal songs, which clearly differed both from the songs of wild birds and those of intact isolates. It did not make any difference whether or not the birds had been tutored with a normal song or not before deafening. This example was the first to show how the development of even highly stereotyped behavior patterns may largely depend on sensory feedback. I reasoned that the deaf white-crowned sparrows developed abnormal songs because the removal of auditory feedback deprived them of access to the memorized song. I proposed that young birds use the memorized tutor song as a template to shape their own song. I first introduced the term template in my thesis[5] and later in a paper (Adret, this volume).[6] The difference in song between the deaf birds and intact isolates called for an explanation. When birds could hear themselves sing in soundproof chambers, they could compare their voice with an internal reference, which I called an innate template. Birds use it when they do not have any tutor. The deaf birds developed more abnormal songs than the isolates because the deafened birds had no access to this reference. The innate template is similar to Marler's idea that birds might rely more on sensory guidance than on motor pattern generators to shape their song.[7] White-crowned sparrows normally develop one song type, which is either an abnormal (isolate) song or a copy of the tutor song. Thus, exposure to an acceptable tutor model converts the innate template into an acquired template. Whichever template a bird may have, deafening makes it inaccessible. All subsequent studies of song development in deafened oscine songbirds reported similar results.[8–11] Although the degree and nature of the abnormalities differed between species, it was established that all oscine songbirds need auditory feedback to develop normal songs. Other models of song learning emerged to account for the development of those aspects of song acquisition that cannot be covered by the template theory, which explains only how birds imitate sounds.[12,13] Young birds not only copy tutor models but also improvise and invent news sounds during song development.[14,15] The selection model of song learning states that birds select desirable patterns from a repertoire of vocalizations that they can produce. However, no models of song learning work without auditory feedback, because deafening causes abnormal song development in all oscine songbirds studied so far. Auditory feedback requires an internal reference, which need not be a memorized tutor song but can be the bird's own voice uttered earlier.

The above conclusion about the importance of auditory feedback does not ignore the role of the central pattern generator (CPG), although what constitutes the CPG for song is unclear. Birds other than oscine passerines, parrots, and some humming-birds, must use the CPG to develop species-specific vocalizations, because they can develop normal vocalizations without auditory feedback (e.g., turkey,[16] chicken,[17] ring dove,[18] and a suboscine[19]). It is the output of the CPG that the bird controls by auditory feedback. The effects of deafening on song development appear to differ between oscine species. These variations are partly attributable to the differences in the contributions of the CPG to song. For example, the song of deaf white-crowned sparrows had little in common with the wild-type song, whereas the song of deaf juncos contained some species-specific traits, such as the trill structure.[20] American robins (*Turdus migratorius*) and black-headed grosbeaks (*Pheucticus melanocephalus*) sing syllables with a slow tempo. This trait was present in the song of deaf birds, although their syllables were very abnormal.[21] The best evidence for patterning of song by the CPG comes from the work on zebra finches (*Taeniopygia guttata*) by Price.[10] He deafened one of the experimental birds at 17 days of age. This bird produced in adulthood a song that resembled the normal song in its overall temporal pattern. The bird could have not learned this pattern either from other birds or from its singing experience prior to deafening, because zebra finches cannot sing before the axonal connections from HVC to RA are established between 25 and 30 days of age.[22] Thus, species-specific features of song in deaf birds, including the overall temporal pattern of deafened zebra finch song, is likely to derive from the innately specified properties of the CPG. The results of interspecific crossing of birds with different temporal patterns also lend support for this view. For example, hybrids between canaries (*Serinus canaria*) and greenfinches (*Chloris chloris*) delivered syllables by the rules of the maternal species, which they could not copy from their non-singing mothers.[23,24]

NEURAL REPRESENTATION OF SONG MEMORY?

The template model of song learning contains three components: vocal motor system, auditory feedback loop, and song template. There had not been any bases for speculating where and in what form these components could be found in the brain before the discovery of the song control system by Nottebohm and colleagues in 1976.[25] My laboratory was interested to know if song systems neurons might respond to sound, although there was no reason to assume encoding of song by single neurons.[26] We observed the first sign of song selectivity in the HVC of canaries.[27] A subsequent study in the white-crowned sparrow not only confirmed the initial observation but also identified some of the parameters of song for which HVC neurons were selective.[28] These studies detected song-specific neurons, which were tuned not to the species song but to the individual bird's own song (BOS), even if the song was abnormal as in the case of isolates.[28] Subsequently, song-specific responses were found in other parts of the zebra finch song system, including the hypoglossal nerves that innervate the muscles of the vocal organ.[29,30] This wide distribution of song-specific responses derives from connections that these various song areas receive directly or indirectly from HVC.[30,31] These early discoveries were exciting, because of the possibility that the song-specific neuron might represent the acquired template.

However, subsequent studies indicated that the selectivity for BOS did not emerge in HVC and LMAN neurons before the plastic song stage, in which both the structure and sequence of syllables are still variable.[32,33] Apart from this timing problem, we do not know whether and how BOS selectivity is related to the representation of tutor song. In young zebra finches singing plastic song, Solis and Doupe[34] found many LMAN and X neurons preferred BOS and tutor song to other stimuli. Of these neurons, most responded better to BOS than to the tutor song, some preferred the tutor song, and other responded equally well to both song types. Solis and Doupe[35,36] further investigated whether or not the neuronal selectivity for tutor song was attributable to its similarity to BOS by using birds that were made to develop extremely abnormal song (tsBOS) by denervation of the tracheosyringealis (ts) muscle in youth. In both LMAN and X, many neurons preferred both the tutor song and tsBOS to other stimuli, although most of them tended to respond better to tsBOS than to the tutor song. The authors did not find any neurons that responded exclusively to the tutor song. Both objective and subjective methods of comparing songs found little similarity between the tutor song and tsBOS. Therefore, the LMAN and X neurons' response to the tutor song may not be attributable to its similarity to tsBOS. However, the physical properties compared may not be the same as those to which the neurons were tuned. One must determine these properties for each song and compare how similar or different they are between the songs. This task is not simple for the complex song of zebra finches in which song-specific neurons are sensitive to both harmonic and temporal structure of individual syllables, as well as syllable sequences.[37–41] If the neurons with dual selectivity detected different sets of acoustic cues in the two songs, the finding would call for a new explanation.

Although BOS selectivity is relayed from HVC to downstream stations, its true source had not been identified until recent years. Intracelluar recordings from HVC neurons can show both their input and output. The spiking response of HVC relay neurons is exclusively sensitive to BOS but not to reverse BOS (played backwards), whereas their subthreshold responses, which copy the responses of NIf neurons, are not.[42–47] Furthermore, in a bird species that sings multiple song types, the spiking response of HVC relay neurons is tuned to a single song type, whereas their subthreshold responses are not as selective.[48] These findings show that HVC is the site for the creation of exclusive BOS selectivity, which is relayed to all song nuclei that receive direct or indirect input from HVC.

AUDITORY FEEDBACK FOR THE MAINTENANCE OF SONG

I tested whether deafness would affect the maintenance of song in adult whitecrowned sparrows.[6] The song of one of them, a wild-caught male, remained almost unchanged for 14 months after deafening. In contrast, deafening caused song to deteriorate in an adult canary.[25] Canary song was thought to be unchangeable at the time of this experiment, although the species is now regarded as an open-ended song learner, which can modify song in adulthood. However, deafening also caused the song of zebra and Bengalese finches to deteriorate[49–52] (see also chapter by Woolley). These species are supposed to be closed-ended learners. A long-term tracking of song in zebra finches appears to support this assumption.[53] A similar study for the Bengalese finch (*Lonchura striata*) will be useful. Age is another important variable in deafening experiments. Early studies showed that the effects of deafening varied with age and stage of song development.[10,54] A recent report by Lombardino and Nottebohm[53] is the most extensive study of this issue. They found that the songs of old zebra finches (2–5 years) remained unchanged for almost a year after deafening. This age dependency might account for the maintenance of song by the white-crown mentioned above. I argued that birds might learn to associate auditory and non-auditory feedback such that they may be able to use song-related non-auditory feedback to control song in the absence of auditory feedback.[6]

Non-auditory feedback includes sensory signals from the body parts that move or sense air pressure and flow during singing. Songbirds vocalize by forcing the air from the air sacs into the vocal organ, the syrinx. Birds control the air pressure in the air sacs to regulate the flow of the air in the syrinx during singing. An injection of air into the abdominal air sac of both intact and deaf birds during singing caused them to adjust the rate of airflow through the syrinx, indicating that the birds could use non-auditory sensory signals from the air passageway to regulate airflow[55] (see also Suthers, this volume).

DYNAMIC CONTROL OF AUDITORY FEEDBACK

Surgical deafening served the initial goal of determining the role of auditory feedback in the development and maintenance of song. This approach could not answer questions concerning the parameters of auditory feedback, such as the amount of delay necessary for causing changes in song. To address these questions requires non-invasive methods of controlling auditory feedback. Human subjects are given earphones for the study of delayed feedback. Although fabrication of small earphones is no longer a problem, they do not exclude the possibility of the bird hearing its own song, making them perhaps only slightly superior to free field playback techniques. Leonardo[56] developed two different computer-controlled methods to perturb auditory feedback: one detected a specific syllable and played back a recorded version of the same syllable with a delay of 50 msec and the other divided song into 100 msec bins in which recording and playback alternated, i.e., playback of whatever was recorded in the preceding bin with a delay of 100 msec. Because detection of the onset of song could not be precise, playback with the second method was more variable than that with the first method in which the computer recognized the pattern of the target syllable. So, the birds in these experiments heard playback of either a delayed version of the target syllable or a binned and delayed song superimposed on their own song. In the "single syllable" mode, one of the two birds used for this test modified only the selected syllable in less than one week. This finding indicates that the bird uses auditory feedback to control song syllable by syllable. Over several weeks, the second method caused changes that were large enough to be called "decrystallization," i.e., the bird's song was characterized by stuttering or repetitions of the same syllable, alteration of syllable structures, and randomization of syllable sequences. When delayed feedback was removed, the birds gradually re-crystallized their songs over many weeks.[57] Subsequent studies obtained similar results in zebra and Bengalese finches except that they reported immediate and transient changes in song in addition to lasting effects.[58,59] These results are consistent with those of deafening experiments, showing that normal auditory feedback is necessary for the maintenance of adult song.

THE ANTERIOR FOREBRAIN PATHWAY
AND AUDITORY FEEDBACK

Models in control theory usually have separate circuits for feedback signals. The idea that the anterior forebrain pathway might be involved in the control of song by auditory feedback is attractive. Bottjer and colleagues[60] reported that lesions of LMAN did not affect adult song but caused abnormal song development in young zebra finches. They suggested that the anterior forebrain pathway (AFP) (including HVC, X, DLM, LMAN, and RA) might carry or process auditory feedback information. Other authors subsequently reported similar results.[61,62] All of the AFP nuclei contain neurons selective for BOS.[31,33,34,63] This fact would seem to lend support for the hypothetical role of the pathway for auditory feedback control of song development.

However, recent studies provide three lines of evidence that require revisions in our view of the AFP. First, the consequences of LMAN lesions in young birds may not be a results of effects on auditory feedback but on the song motor pathway. Lesions of LMAN in young zebra finches induced a rapid (1–4 days) consolidation in the synaptic connections between HVC axons and RA neurons, resembling that which occurs more gradually over the course of normal development as the bird progresses to adulthood.[64] It might be these synaptic effects and not the presumed interference with auditory feedback that caused the abnormal song development. Second, the idea that the AFP is necessary for the plasticity of song only in youth may not hold, although the anatomical and physiological properties of the pathway may change with age. The adult X and LMAN are not silent but show neural activities that are correlated with song.[65] Severance of the hypoglossal nerve or deafening causes deterioration of song in normal adult zebra finches, but not in birds in which LMAN was previously bilaterally lesioned.[66,67] One interpretation of these findings states that the song did not change, because removal of LMAN interrupted the passage of the error signals for the feedback control of song.[67] Thus, AFP appears to be involved in the plastic control of song in adult birds. Also, LMAN is necessary for the maintenance of song in adult birds of some species.[68,69] Third, as mentioned previously, auditory responses and song selectivity are not limited to the AFP. HVC neurons projecting to RA are also sensitive to BOS.[44–47]

An "acid test" for the hypothesis that LMAN neurons convey an error signal is to observe single LMAN neurons during singing with and without delayed auditory feedback. Leonardo[56] accomplished this feat only to find that neither the rate of spikes nor their firing pattern changed between the two conditions. These results are consistent with those of an earlier report in which the pattern of multiunit activities in LMAN did not change after deafening in adult zebra finches.[65] These negative results are hard to interpret because there is more than one explanation. The original theory assumed that the AFP worked only during song development.[60] However, unpublished studies of young zebra finches found no change in multiunit activities in HVC, RA, and LMAN between normal and perturbed feedback conditions (HVC by Fee, RA by Fee and Leonardo, and RA by Leonardo). If control of voice by auditory feedback occurs "offline," no immediate change in neuronal discharge is expected. The next section discusses what is meant by "online" control of vocalization by auditory feedback.

TIMING OF VOCAL CONTROL BY AUDITORY FEEDBACK

Human examples are often cited to illustrate "online" control of voice by auditory feedback. When humans hear a rise in the fundamental frequency (F_0) of their voice, they involuntarily lower the F_0. The latency between error detection and correction is about 150 msec, which means that errors in speech sounds shorter than this duration cannot be corrected, while they are being uttered. Instead, the compensatory response works for subsequent syllables and lasts for several seconds after the cessation of modified feedback.[70] Bats are specialized in using auditory feedback in the form of echoes. How bats control vocalizations in response to echoes is best known in horseshoe bats. Their calls contain a long segment of constant frequency (CF). The "reference CF" varies little when resting horseshoe bats are emitting calls spontaneously. When flying bats detect a Doppler shift in the CF of returning echoes, they change the CF of outgoing calls such that the CF of their echoes matches with the reference frequency.[71] Three features of this Doppler shift compensation (DSC) are interesting for the present discussion. Bats show DSC only when the frequency-shifted echo returns well before the outgoing call ends.[72] However, bats do not shift frequency in the current call but in the immediately following one.[73] Also, when a large frequency shift, such as 4 kHz, occurs bats do not compensate for it in one step but in multiple steps.[73] Thus, even the species best known for auditory feedback control of vocalization, the feedback correction is not actually "online."

One possible reason for not operating feedback control faster is the temporal mismatch between neural processes for audition and vocalization, although the time difference varies with brain sites. In zebra finches, auditory feedback signals return to HVC in 65 msec, which consists of 50 msec for the latency to vocal output and 15 msec for the delay between song playback and HVC responses.[27,37] The mean duration of zebra finch song syllables is about 80 msec and the mean silent interval between them is about 35 msec.[10] If HVC is the site of comparison between premotor and auditory feedback signals, the feedback signals from a syllable returns while the next syllable is being produced. Recent models have attempted to solve the problem of temporal mismatch by finding the methods by which auditory feedback signals and vocal premotor signals can interact within HVC in the context of song learning.[74] Similarly, Mooney and colleagues[45] suggest that RA-projecting HVC neurons might send an efference copy of premotor signals for song to X-projecting HVC neurons, which produce a negative copy of the efference copy with a long delay to be compared with auditory feedback signals within HVC (Mooney, this volume). These discussions assume that auditory feedback signals reach the song system during singing. Do they?

CENTRAL AUDITORY GATING

Central auditory gating means that the flow of auditory information is blocked or regulated at locations other than the inner ear itself. This type of control is particularly important in systems in which the same neurons perform incompatible roles, such as auditory sensory and vocal motor functions. Such neurons would fire before a song syllable and then respond to the same or a later syllable. The result would be very confusing because the spikes generated in response to the song would be in a position to activate the vocal motor pathway. One way to avoid the confusion would be to close the gate for auditory input while the neuron is performing the vocal function.[30] Neurons with vocal motor and auditory dual functions occur in the bat's brainstem vocal control areas.[75] These neurons fire to produce an outgoing call and respond to its echo, which is played back from a speaker as an attenuated version of the original call. Although the above observation was made in waking bats, it is not known if and how the same neurons respond to natural echoes during echolocation, because many of these neurons are inhibited during vocalization. Are there vocal-auditory dual function neurons in the song system? Multiunit recordings in the vocal motor pathway from HVC to the syrinx indicated auditory sensitivity to BOS,[34] although these results did not show that the same neurons conveyed both vocal motor and auditory signals. RA-projecting neurons in HVC, which normally carry vocal motor signals to RA, selectively respond to BOS in anesthetized birds.[45,46] However, the best evidence came from the work of Dave and Margoliash[76] who showed that the same RA neurons fired spikes preceding each song syllable during singing and also responded to playback of BOS in sleep. However, there was no indication that these neurons responded to the natural feedback of the bird's own song. McCasland and Konishi[27] argued that auditory responses of HVC neurons in canaries were inhibited during singing because the neural activities expected from the latency of auditory responses were missing.

Evidence for auditory gating has been accumulating in recent years. Dave and colleagues[77] were the first to report that RA neurons responded to playback of BOS only in sleeping zebra finches. Nick and Konishi[78] subsequently showed that HVC neurons also responded to BOS only in sleep as judged by EEG. A recent study shows that the auditory gate is closed to all HVC neurons except one type of interneurons in waking birds.[79] Schmidt and Konishi[80] observed that HVC neurons responded to BOS only under anesthesia in contrast with Field L neurons that responded in the behaving zebra finches. This work established the central origin of gating. Gating has also been observed in NIf in waking zebra finches[81] (Hayashi and Konishi, unpublished observation), the primary auditory afferent to HVC, raising the possibility that gating occurs entirely presynaptic to HVC. The anatomical relationships between these areas suggest that NIf is the initial site of gating, because the flow of auditory and song motor information is from NIf to HVC to RA. Anatomical studies suggested that forebrain auditory areas Field L 1, 2, and 3 project to the shelf area of HVC and may even to HVC itself.[82,83] Recent physiological studies, however, show that HVC receives major auditory input from NIf. Injections of a local anesthetic into NIf abolish auditory responses in HVC but not injections in Field L.[84] Thus, within the song system, NIf may be the first site that receives auditory input.

Both NIf and HVC receive input from a thalamic nucleus Uva. Electrical stimulation of this nucleus blocked auditory responses in HVC in anesthetized birds.[30] Bilateral lesions of Uva enabled HVC neurons to respond to BOS in waking birds.[85] These lines of evidence suggest that Uva may be the source of gating signals. In additions to the above effects, lesions of Uva greatly affected the sequencing of syllables.[85,86] If Uva were an isolated nucleus, it should be the sources of gating and syllable sequencing signals. However, Uva receives input from both left and right DM in the midbrain.[87] To complicate the matter, Shea and Margoliash[88] found a new brain site from which HVC and RA receive cholinergic modulatory signals.[89] Electrical or chemical (glutamate) stimulation of VP (ventral paleostriatum) suppresses BOS responses in both HVC and RA in anesthetized zebra finches. Blocking of BOS responses in RA was always preceded by a similar shutdown in the firing of HVC neurons. However, gating of BOS response in RA cannot be explained simply by removal of HVC input to RA, because injection of carbachol into HVC stops its BOS response without affecting the BOS response of RA. It is, however, not clear whether the modulation of auditory responses in HVC and RA studied by Shea and Margoliash is the same as the modulation that is correlated with waking and sleeping. I should emphasize that we are looking for the means by which the premotor-auditory bifunctional neurons switch from one function to the other. If whichever gating discussed above involves inhibitory hyperpolarization, the neuron cannot perform its premotor function. Before we go further we should address this question by conducting intracellular recording.

FUTURE

Birdsong research is entering an exciting period in which the number of excellent investigators has reached a critical mass. Many challenges await them. We know so much about birdsong and the song control system, but important questions remain unanswered or untouched even within the scope of this article. For example, we still do not know where and how song templates, auditory feedback signals, and song motor programs are encoded. We must use all relevant methods to tackle these questions including anatomy, molecular genetics, and *in vivo* and *in vitro* electrophysiology. We have to place a greater emphasis on observing behaving birds than we used to. As I pointed out, no one has been able to detect within the song system neuronal responses to the auditory feedback of the bird's own song during singing. Is this real or just a technical problem? The solution of this relatively simple problem is important, because it concerns not only the question of online versus offline control of song by auditory feedback but also the site of the feedback-template comparator circuits, i.e., inside or outside the song control system. Finally, we should not forget comparative approaches. A comparison of an oscine and a suboscine bird clearly indicated that the presence of the song control system is correlated with song learning.[19] The physiological lateralization of HVC was shown first in the song sparrow.[90] The work on the song selectivity of HVC neurons in swamp sparrows showed that each cell was selective for only one of the multiple BOSs.[48] These important findings indicate the value and necessity of using different species.

ACKNOWLEDGMENTS

I thank Phil Zeigler and Peter Marler for their critical and caring comments on this paper. Few editors perform their duties as conscientiously as these two. Rich

Mooney and Dan Margoliash also provided valuable comments. The preparation of this article was supported by National Institutes of Health grant MH55984.

REFERENCES

1. Wilson, D.M. 1961. The central nervous control of flight in a locust. J. Exp. Biol. **38:** 471–490.
2. Marler, P. & M. Tamura. 1962. Song variation in three populations of white-crowned sparrows. Condor **64:** 368–377.
3. Marler, P. & M. Tamura. 1964. Culturally transmitted patterns of vocal behavior in sparrows. Science **146:** 1483–1486.
4. Marler, P. 1970. A comparative approach to vocal learning: song development in white-crowned sparrows. J. Comp. Physiol. Psychol. Monogr **71:** 1–25.
5. Konishi, M. 1963. The role of audition in the development and maintenance of avian vocal behavior. Ph.D. thesis, University of California, Berkeley.
6. Konishi, M. 1965. The role of auditory feedback in the control of vocalization in the white-crowned sparrow. Z. Tierpsychol. **22:** 770–783.
7. Marler, P. 1964. Inheritance and learning in the development of animal vocalizations. *In* Acoustic Behavior of Animals, R.-G. Busnell, Ed.: 228–243. Elsevier. Amsterdam.
8. Dittus, W.P.J. & R.E. Lemon. 1970. Auditory feedback in the singing of cardinals. Ibis **112:** 544–548.
9. Marler, P. & M.S. Waser. 1977. The role of auditory feedback in canary song development. J. Comp. Physiol. Psychol. **91:** 8–16.
10. Price, P.H. 1979. Developmental determinants of structure in zebra finch song. J. Comp. Physiol. Psychol. **93:** 260–277.
11. Marler, P. & V. Sherman. 1983. Song structure without auditory feedback: emendations of the auditory template hypothesis. J. Neurosci. **3:** 517–531.
12. Marler, P. 1997. Three models of song learning: evidence from behavior. J. Neurobiol. **33:** 501–516.
13. Margoliash, D. 2002. Evaluating theories of bird song learning: implications for future directions. J. Comp. Physiol. A **188:** 851–866.
14. Marler, P. & S. Peters. 1982. Subsong and plastic song: their role in the vocal learning process. *In* Acoustic Communication in Birds. Vol. 2. Song Learning and Its Consequences. D.E. Kroodsma & E.H. Miller, Eds. Academic Press. New York.
15. Marler, P. & S. Peters. 1982. Developmental overproduction and selective attrition: New processes in the epigenesis of birdsong. Dev. Psychobiol. **15:** 369–378.
16. Schleidt, W. 1961. Operative Entfernung des Gehörorgans ohne Schädigung angrenzede Labyrinthteile bei Putenküken. Experientia **17:** 464–465.
17. Konishi, M. 1963. The role of auditory feedback in the vocal behavior of the domestic fowl. Z. Tierpsychol. **20:** 349–367.
18. Nottebohm, F. & M.E. Nottebohm. 1971. Vocalizations and breeding behavior of surgically deafened ring doves (*Streptopelia risoria*). Anim. Behav. **19:** 313–327.
19. Kroodsma, D.E. & M. Konishi. 1991. A suboscine bird (eastern phoebe, *Sayornis phoebe*) develops normal song without auditory feedback. Anim. Behav. **42:** 477–484.
20. Konishi, M. 1964. Effects of deafening on song development in two species of juncos. Condor **66:** 85–102.
21. Konishi, M. 1965. Effects of deafening on song development in American robins and black-headed grosbeaks. Z. Tierpsychol. **22:** 349–367.
22. Akutagawa, E. & M. Konishi. 1985. Neuronal growth, atrophy and death in a sexually dimorphic song nucleus in the zebra finch. Nature **315:** 145–147.
23. Guettinger, H.R. 1979. The integration of learnt and genetically programmed behaviour: a study of hierarchical organization in songs of canaries, greenfinches and their hybrids. Z. Tierpyschol. **49:** 285–303.
24. Guettinger, H.R., J. Wolffgramm & F. Thimm. 1978. The relationship between species specific song programs and individual learning in song birds. Behaviour **65:** 241–262.

25. NOTTEBOHM, F., T.M. STOKES & C.M. LEONARDO. 1976. Central control of song in the canary, *Srinus canaria*. J. Comp. Neurol. **165**: 457–486.
26. KATZ, L.C. & M.E. GURNEY. 1981. Auditory responses in the zebra finch's motor system for song. Brain Res. **211**: 192–197.
27. MCCASLAND, J.S. & M. KONISHI. 1981. Interaction between auditory and motor activities in an avian song control nucleus. Proc. Natl. Acad. Sci. USA **78**: 7815–7819.
28. MARGOLIASH, D. 1983. Acoustic parameters underlying the responses of song-specific neurons in the white-crowned sparrow. J. Neurosci. **3**: 1039–1057.
29. WILLIAMS, H. & F. NOTTEBOHM. 1985. Auditory responses in avian vocal motor neurons: a motor theory for song perception in birds. Science **229**: 279–282.
30. WILLIAMS, H. 1989. Multiple representations and auditory-motor interactions in the avian song system. Ann. NY Acad. Sci. **563**: 148–164.
31. DOUPE, A.J. & M. KONISHI. 1992. Song selective auditory circuits in the vocal control system of the zebra finch. Proc. Natl. Acad. Sci. USA **88**: 11339–11343.
32. VOLMAN, S.F. 1993. Development of neural selectivity for birdsong during vocal learning. J. Neurosci. **13**: 4737–4747.
33. DOUPE, A.J. 1997. Song and order-selective neurons in the songbird anterior forebrain and their emergence during vocal development. J. Neurosci. **17**: 1147–1167.
34. SOLIS, M.M. & A.J. DOUPE. 1997. Anterior forebrain neurons develop selectivity by an intermediate stage of birdsong learning. J. Neurosci. **17**: 6447-6462.
35. SOLIS, M.M. & A.J. DOUPE. 1999. Contributions of tutor and BOS experience to neural selectivity in the songbird anterior forebrain. J. Neurosci. **19**: 4559–4584.
36. SOLIS, M.M. & A.J. DOUPE. 2000. Compromised neural selectivity for song in birds with impaired sensorimotor learning. Neuron **25**: 109–121.
37. MARGOLIASH, D. & E.S. FORTUNE. 1992. Temporal and harmonic combination-sensitive neurons in the zebra finch's HVc. J. Neurosci. **12**: 4309–4326.
38. LEWICKI, M.S. & M. KONISHI. 1995. Mechanisms underlying the sensitivity of songbird forebrain neurons to temporal order. Proc. Natl. Acad. Sci. USA **92**: 5582–5586.
39. LEWICKI, M.S. 1996. Intracellular characterization of song-specific neurons in the zebra finch forebrain. J. Neurosci. **16**: 5855–5863.
40. THEUNISSEN, F.E. & A.J. DOUPE. 1998. Temporal and spectral sensitivity of complex auditory neurons in the nucleus HVc of male zebra finches. J. Neurosci. **18**: 3786–3802.
41. THEUNISSEN, F.E., K. SEN & A.J. DOUPE. 2000. Spectral-temporal receptive fields of nonlinear auditory neurons obtained using natural sounds. J. Neurosci. **20**: 2315–2331.
42. JANATA, P. & D. MARGOLIASH. 1999. Gradual emergence of song selectivity in sensorimotor structures of the male zebra finch song system. J. Neurosci **19**: 5108–5118.
43. COLEMAN, M.J. & R. MOONEY. 2002. Source of auditory input to the songbird nucleus HVc revealed by pairwise recordings in Nif and HVc. Soc. Neurosci. Abst. 588.4.
44. MOONEY, R. 2000. Different subthreshold mechanisms underlie song selectivity in identified HVc neurons of the zebra finch. J. Neurosci. **20**: 5420–5436.
45. MOONEY, R., M.J. ROSEN & C.B. STURDY. 2002. A bird's eye view: top down intracellular analyses of auditory selectivity for learned vocalizations. J. Comp. Physiol. A **188**: 879–895.
46. ROSEN, M.J & R. MOONEY. 2000. Intrinsic and extrinsic contributions to auditory selectivity in a song nucleus critical for vocal plasticity. J. Neurosci. **20**: 5437–5448.
47. ROSEN, M.J. & R. MOONEY. 2003. Inhibitory and excitatory mechanisms underlying auditory responses to learned vocalizations in the songbird nucleus HVC. Neuron **39**: 177–194.
48. MOONEY, R., W. HOESE & S. NOWICKI. 2001. Auditory representation of the vocal repertoire in a songbird with multiple song types. Proc. Natl. Acad. Sci. USA **98**: 12778–12783.
49. NORDEEN, K.W. & E.J. NORDEEN. 1992. Auditory feedback is necessary for the maintenance of stereotyped song in adult zebra finches. Behav. Neural. Biol. **57**: 58–66.
50. OKANOYA, K. & A. YAMAGUCHI. 1997. Adult Bengalese finches (*Lonchura striata*) require real-time auditory feedback to produce normal song syntax. J. Neurobiol. **4**: 343–356.

51. WOOLLEY, S.M. & E.W. RUBEL. 1997. Bengalese finches *Lonchura striata domestica* depend upon auditory feedback for maintenance of adult song. J. Neurosci. **17:** 6380–6390.
52. WOOLLEY, S.M.N. & E.W. RUBEL. 2002. Vocal memory and learning in adult Bengalese finches with regenerated hair cells. J. Neurosci. **22:** 7774–7787.
53. LOMBARDINO, A.J. & F. NOTTEBOHM. 2000. Age at deafening affects the stability of learned song in adult male zebra finches. J. Neurosci. **20:** 5054–5064.
54. NOTTEBOHM, F. 1968. Auditory experience and song development in the chaffinch (*Fringilla coelebs*). Ibis **110:** 549–567.
55. SUTHERS, R.A. F. GOLLER & J.M. WILD. 2002. Somatosensory feedback modulates the respiratory motor program of crystallized birdsong. Proc. Natl. Acad. Sci. USA **99:** 5680–5685.
56. LEONARDO, A. 2002. Neural dynamics underlying complex behavior in a songbird. Ph.D. thesis, California Institute of Technology. Pasadena, CA.
57. LEONARDO, A. & M. KONISHI. 1999. Decrystallization of adult birdsong by perturbation of auditory feedback. Nature **399:** 466–470.
58. CYNX, J. & U. VON RAD. 2001. Immediate and transitory effects of delayed auditory feedback on bird song production. Anim. Behav. **62:** 305–312.
59. BRAINARD, M.S. & A.J. DOUPE. 2001. Alteration of auditory feedback causes both acute and lasting changes to Bengalese finch song. Soc. Neurosci. Abst. 269.6.
60. BOTTJER, S.W., E.A. MIESNER & A.P. ARNOLD. 1984. Forebrain lesions disrupt development but not maintenance of song in passerine birds. Science **224:** 901–903.
61. SOHRAJI, F., E.J. NORDEEN & K.W. NORDEEN. 1990. Selective impairment of song learning following lesions of a forebrain nucleus in the juvenile zebra finch. Behav. Neural. Biol. **53:** 51–63.
62. SCHARFF, C. & F. NOTTEBOHM. 1991. A comparative study of the behavioral deficit following lesions of various parts of the zebra finch song system: implication for vocal learning. J. Neurosci. **11:** 2896–2913.
63. VICARIO, D.S. & K.H. YOHAY. 1993. Song-selective auditory input to a forebrain vocal control nucleus in the zebra finch. J. Neurobiol. **24:** 488–505.
64. KITTELBERGER, J.M. & R. MOONEY. 1999. Lesions of an avian forebrain nucleus that disrupt song development alter synaptic connectivity and transmission in the vocal premotor pathway. J. Neurosci. **19:** 9385–9398.
65. HESSLER, N.A. & A.J. DOUPE. 1999. Singing related neural activity in a dorsal forebrain-basal ganglia circuit of adult zebra finches. J. Neurosci. **19:** 10461–10481.
66. WILLIAMS, H. & N. METHA. 1999. Changes in the adult zebra finch song require a forebrain nucleus that is not necessary for song production. J. Neurobiol. **39:** 14–28.
67. BRAINARD, M.S. & A.J. DOUPE. 2000. Interruption of a basal ganglia-forebrain circuit prevents plasticity of learned vocalizations. Nature **404:** 762–766.
68. BENTON, S., D.A. NELSON, P. MARLER & T.J. DEVOOGD. 1998. Anterior forebrain pathway is needed for stable song expression in adult male white-crowned sparrows (*Zonotrichia leucophrys*). Behav. Brain Res. **96:** 135–150.
69. KOBAYASHI, K., H. UNO & K. OKANOYA. 2001. Partial lesions in the anterior forebrain pathway affect song production in adult Bengalese finches. Neuroreport **12:** 353–358.
70. DONATH, T.M., U. NATKE & K.T. KALVERAM. 2002. Effects of frequency-shifted auditory feedback on voice F_0 contours in syllables. J. Acoust. Soc. Amer. **111:** 357–366.
71. SCHNITZLER H.U. 1968. Die Ultraschallortungslaute der Hufeisennasen-Fledermäuse (Chiroptera, Rhinolophidae) in verschiedenen Orientierungssituationen. Z. vergl. Physiol. **57:** 376–408.
72. SCHULLER, G. 1977. Echo delay and overlap with emitted orientation sounds and Doppler-shift compensation in the bat, *Rhinolophus ferrumequinum*. J. Comp. Physiol. **114:** 103–114.
73. SCHULLER, G., K. BEUTER & R. RÜBSAMEN. 1975. Dynamic properties of the compensation system for Doppler-shifts in the bat, *Rhinolophus ferrumequinum*. J. Comp. Physiol. **97:** 113–125.
74. TROYER, T.W. & A.J. DOUPE. 2000. An associational model of birdsong sensorimotor learning. 1. Efference copy and the learning of song syllables. J. Neurophysiol. **84:** 1204–1223.

75. METZNER, W. 1993. An audio-vocal interface in echolocating horseshoe bats. J. Neurosci. **13:** 1899–1915.
76. DAVE, A.S., A.C. YU & D. MARGOLIASH. 2000. Song replay during sleep and computational rules for sensorimotor vocal learning. Science **290:** 812–816
77. DAVE, A.S., A.C. YU & D. MARGOLIASH. 1998. Behavioral state modulation of auditory activity in a vocal motor system. Science **282:** 2250–2254.
78. RAUSKE, P.L., S.D. SHEA & D. MARGOLIASH. 2003. State and neuronal class-dependent reconfiguration in the avian song system. J. Neurophysiol. **89:** 1688–1701.
79. NICK, T.A. & M. KONISHI. 2001. Dynamic control of auditory activity during sleep: Correlation between song response and EEG. Proc. Natl. Acad. Sci. USA **98:** 14012–14016.
80. SCHMIDT, M.F. & M. KONISHI. 1998. Gating of auditory responses in the vocal control system of awake songbirds. Nat. Neurosci. **1:** 513–518.
81. CARDIN, J.A. & M.F. SCHMIDT. 2002. Behavioral state-dependent modulation of auditory input to HVC and NIf. Neurosci. Abstr. 588.11.
82. FORTUNE, E.S. & D. MARGOLISH. 1995. Parallel pathways and convergence onto HVc and adjacent neostriatum of adult zebra finches *(Teniopygia guttata)*. J. Comp. Neurol. **360:** 413–441.
83. VATES, G.E., B.E. BROOME, C.V. MELLO & F. NOTTEBOHM. 1996. Auditory pathways of caudal telencephalon and their relation to the song system of adult male zebra finches *(Taeniopygia guttata)*. J. Comp. Neurol. **366:** 613–642.
84. BOCO, T. & D. MARGOLIASH. 2001. NIf is a major source of auditory and spontaneous drive to HVc. Soc. Neurosci. Abstr. 381.2.
85. COLEMAN, M.J. & E.T. VU. 2001. Uva lesions affect the auditory responsiveness of HVC neurons in awake zebra finches. Soc. Neurosci. Abst. Program No. 538.12.
86. WILLIAMS, H. & D.S. VICARIO. 1993. Temporal patterning of song production: participation of nucleus uvaeformis of the thalamus. J. Neurobiol. **24:** 903–912.
87. STRIEDTER G.F. & E.T. VU. 1998. Bilateral feedback projections to the forebrain in the premotor network for singing in zebra finches. J. Neurobiol. **34:** 27–40.
88. SHEA, S.D. & D. MARGOLIASH. 2003. Basal forebrain cholinergic modulation of auditory activity in the zebra finch song system. Neuron **40:** 1213–1226.
89. LI, R. & H. SAKAGUCHI. 1997. Cholinergic innervation of the song control nuclei by the ventral paleostriatum in the zebra finch: a double labeling study with fluorescence tracers and choline acetyltransferase immunohistochemistry. Brain Res. **763:** 239–246.
90. NEALEN, P.M. & M.F. SCHMIDT. 2002. Comparative approaches to avian song system function: insight into auditory and motor processing. J. Comp. Physiol. A **188:** 929–941.

Synaptic Mechanisms for Auditory-Vocal Integration and the Correction of Vocal Errors

RICHARD MOONEY

Department of Neurobiology, Duke University Medical Center,
Durham, North Carolina 27710, USA

ABSTRACT: A central goal of neuroscience is to understand the cellular mechanisms enabling the cultural transmission of behaviors, such as speech and music. Birdsong is a rare non-human instance of a culturally transmitted vocal behavior. The songbird's brain provides a powerful system in which to study the cellular mechanisms underlying auditory-guided vocal learning. Identifying those mechanisms requires an analysis of synaptic function, because the synapse is the fundamental organizational unit of the neuronal networks that mediate behavior. Intracellular recordings provide a powerful method for simultaneously probing the activities of a single neuron and the synaptic networks in which that cell is embedded. This chapter details initial steps in the *in vivo* intracellular analysis of the synaptic connectivity of neurons important to singing and song learning. Our analysis is focused upon HVC and involves studies of interneurons as well as projection neurons of the two major output pathways of HVC. We test predictions derived from several models of how such learning may take place, including contributions from "comparator" and "corollary discharge" auditory feedback cancellation mechanisms. Our studies in anesthetized animals and brain slices provide insight into the synaptic properties of HVC that might be well suited for these mechanisms, although extrapolation to synaptic behavior in the awake, singing bird must be made with caution. We suggest that future work must extend the analysis of synaptic properties into the intact brain of the songbird, preferably as the bird learns to sing.

KEYWORDS: song system; synapse; postsynaptic potentials; intracellular recordings; excitatory; inhibitory; auditory feedback; sensorimotor integration; vocal learning; corollary discharge; cancellation

MODELS AND MECHANISMS OF SONG LEARNING

Songbirds learn to sing by using auditory feedback to match their own song to a memorized tutor model.[1,2] Because many components of the brain circuits mediating this behavior have been identified, song acquisition provides a powerful model system for studying the neural mechanisms of auditory-guided vocal learning. Song learning in birds raises two central questions: First, what is the neural substrate of the memorized tutor model (i.e., the acquired template, see Adret, this volume). Sec-

Address for correspondence: Richard Mooney, Department of Neurobiology, Box 3209, Duke University Medical Center, Durham, North Carolina 27710, USA. Voice: 919-684-5025.
mooney@neuro.duke.edu; <http://www.neuro.duke.edu/Faculty/Mooney.htm>

Ann. N.Y. Acad. Sci. 1016: 476–494 (2004). © 2004 New York Academy of Sciences.
doi: 10.1196/annals.1298.011

ond, how does the developing bird's brain use auditory feedback to acquire and maintain those features of the species-specific song transmitted by the tutor, a process which requires it to control its own vocal output during development and as an adult (see Woolley and Konishi, this volume). In this chapter we describe a number of studies designed to test, at the synaptic level, several possible models of the mechanisms mediating song learning and maintenance.

One such model is that of a comparator circuit that uses auditory information generated during production of the bird's own song (BOS) to detect differences between the currently emitted song and the stored model. These differences generate an adap-

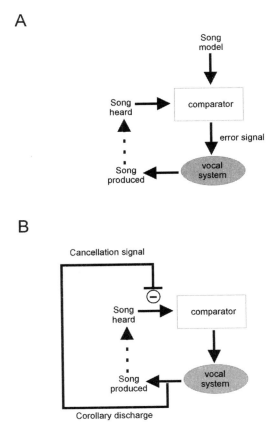

FIGURE 1. Models are shown of comparator and cancellation circuits that could underlie vocal learning through auditory feedback. (**A**) A hypothetical comparator circuit evaluates auditory feedback about the bird's own song in the context of a memorized model (or template). Differences between the actual and desired output result in an error signal that adaptively modifies the vocal system so that its output better matches the model. (**B**) Cancellation of anticipated auditory feedback could be achieved by harnessing corollary discharge from song motor circuits (the "vocal system"). The corollary discharge would ultimately inhibit auditory activity evoked by the anticipated vocal output, thus minimizing auditory desensitization and maximizing auditory sensitivity to vocal errors.

tive signal that drives the song central pattern generator (CPG) towards the memorized tutor song (FIG. 1A). Two other related problems that the songbird's brain is faced with during singing is how to discriminate self-generated sounds from those emitted by external sources, and how to prevent the auditory system from becoming desensitized to self-generated sounds during repeated bouts of singing. A neural mechanism that might play a role in solving these two problems uses corollary discharge from the song CPG to cancel out anticipated sensory feedback. This cancellation process would increase sensitivity to signals differing from the BOS, including errant self-generated vocalizations, thereby simplifying the detection of deviations from the template by the "comparator circuit." Indeed, a cancellation mechanism like this plays an important role in the communication behavior of weakly electric fish,[3] and in the maintenance of auditory sensitivity during "singing" in crickets,[4,5] and during vocalization in mammalian species, including bats and primates.[6–8] Interestingly, chronic recordings made in the song nucleus HVC also hint at cancellation of auditory responsiveness during singing.[9]

Each of these models generates certain predictions about the kinds of properties that their neural substrates might be expected to exhibit. For example, neurons in a comparator circuit might be expected to exhibit relatively broad responsiveness to auditory inputs in order to detect a wide range of vocal performances, many of which will deviate substantially from the target—the stored model. Similarly, if a cancellation mechanism is involved in song acquisition, we might expect that the neurons involved in this process will exhibit some evidence of a cancellation signal, perhaps in the form of synaptic inhibition yoked to the premotor command signal (FIG. 1B). In the expertly trained adult songbird, these cancellation signals would be optimally weighted to suppress auditory feedback arising from a correct rendition of the bird's song, only letting vocal "errors" through to modify the adaptive signal generated by the comparator. Ultimately, the cancellation signal would be subtracted from the actual auditory feedback to simplify error detection and minimize auditory desensitization in sensorimotor areas important to the error correction process.

Tests of these hypotheses must involve analyses of synaptic activity at critical points within the "song circuit." Although song learning is likely to be a distributed function within the songbird brain, the telencephalic nucleus HVC is a key place to start looking for the synaptic mechanisms governing auditory-vocal integration, song premotor-triggered auditory cancellation, and activation of error correction pathways. HVC contains two functionally distinct types of projection neurons: one class (HVC_{RA}) innervates the forebrain premotor nucleus RA, which in turn gives rise to descending projections onto the brainstem respiratory-vocal network.[10–14] During singing, HVC_{RA} neurons generate highly precise bursts of premotor activity that are thought to be essential to song patterning (see Fee and colleagues, this volume). Another class of (HVC_X) innervates a basal ganglia homologue (area X) within the AFP (see Brainard and Perkel, this volume). The output of the AFP is LMAN, whose axons innervate the same RA premotor neurons receiving direct HVC input, providing a potential cellular substrate for AFP modulation of vocal plasticity.[15,16] HVC itself receives auditory and possibly proprioceptive input, the sources of which are only partially identified (see Wild and Goller & Cooper, this volume). Inputs to HVC are likely to undergo extensive local processing, because the nucleus contains a variety of interneuron types and axons from both projection neuron types extend collaterals within the nucleus.[14] Thus, HVC sits at the apex of an auditory-vocal pathway for song, provides the synaptic organization permissive for extensive local processing, and gives rise to pathways important for song patterning and for error correction. Therefore, HVC is an obvious place to begin a search for synaptic mechanisms important to auditory-vocal interactions important to song learning, including error correction processes.

The highly selective auditory response properties of HVC neurons constitute a striking example of experience-dependent sensory tuning.[17] Both types of HVC projection neuron respond strongly and highly selectively to playback of the BOS.[14] This makes HVC the likely source of the auditory responses detected in both the posterior and anterior pathways of the song circuit, an idea that still awaits complete experimental validation. The auditory information transmitted by HVC projection neurons is also highly specific: HVC neurons are "BOS-selective," firing strongly to forward playback of the BOS, but not to temporally manipulated versions of the BOS, such as reverse song or reverse-syllable song, nor to other conspecific songs or synthetic sounds.[17–21] Moreover, BOS selectivity in HVC is important to any discussion of auditory vocal integration, because of HVC's obligatory role in song patterning.[10,22–25] An intracellular analysis of auditory-evoked activity in identified HVC neurons is likely to unearth useful clues about the functional properties of the HVC circuit and to illuminate potential cellular sites of auditory-vocal integration.

One of the primary findings of this analysis is that HVC_{RA} neurons respond to BOS playback,[14] suggesting that the same premotor neurons that pattern song also respond to the auditory feedback resulting from their premotor activity. This is an attractive idea, because it places the site of auditory feedback (and thus perhaps of error correction) directly on the song patterning side of the circuit (i.e., the posterior pathway). However, instead of displaying the broad responsiveness to be expected in components of an error detecting (comparator) mechanism, HVC_{RA} neurons discharge action potentials almost exclusively to playback of forward BOS, and not to its temporal variants.[14] At first glance, such response exclusivity would seem incompatible with the need to detect errors in vocalization. On the other hand, the exclusivity manifested in the extracellular response could reflect the outcome of several putative underlying synaptic processes, at least some of which would be compatible with the requirement of broadly tuned input to a hypothetical comparator (FIG. 2A).

One such process posits auditory afferents arising outside of HVC, which though BOS-selective also synaptically transmit information to HVC_{RA} neurons about a wide range of auditory stimuli, but at a subthreshold level. A variant of this process is a combination of non-selective extrinsic afferents to HVC_{RA} that are modulated locally by HVC neurons to add an excitatory bias to the BOS or an inhibitory bias to non-BOS stimuli, resulting in exclusive firing to the BOS. Finally, one may conceive of a "pipeline" mechanism involving auditory inputs that fire action potentials as selectively as the HVC_{RA} neurons they innervate. This last synaptic process is not compatible with the comparator input scheme, because HVC_{RA} neurons would receive narrowly tuned auditory information that would not report deviances in the vocal performance. If HVC receives a pipeline of BOS-selective information, then other areas presynaptic to HVC might be more likely places to search for the auditory input to a comparator circuit.

To determine which of these three processes applies to HVC_{RA}, we used intracellular recordings to examine their patterns of auditory-evoked synaptic activity. We found that HVC_{RA} neurons fire a very phasic burst of action potentials almost exclu-

A some possible synaptic mechanisms for BOS-selectivity

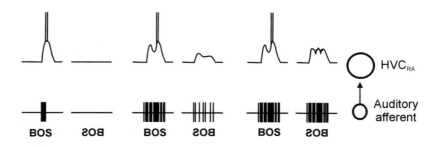

B synaptic events underlying BOS-selectivity in HVC$_{RA}$ neurons

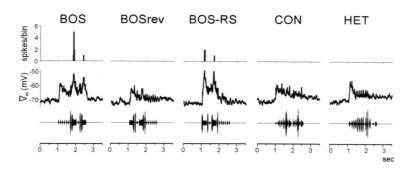

FIGURE 2. Hypothetical and observed synaptic processes underlying the genesis of narrowly tuned, BOS-selective spiking in HVC$_{RA}$ neurons. (**A**) Several models that could explain BOS-selective spiking in HVC include equally selective auditory afferents (*left*- "pipeline" model); afferents that are biased to the BOS, but that fire to other stimuli (*middle*); and unbiased afferents (*right*). In the two latter cases, additional processes, such as postsynaptic thresholding or other synaptic interactions local to HVC result in more exclusive BOS-evoked spiking. In each case, action potential activity is shown for the auditory afferent and sub- and suprathreshold activity is shown for an HVC$_{RA}$ neuron in response to both forward and reverse playback of the BOS. These two stimuli, which contain the same spectral energy but differ in their temporal organization, can be used to measure selectivity of HVC neurons.[17,19] (**B**) The actual synaptic events underlying BOS-evoked spiking in HVC$_{RA}$ neurons are consistent with the middle of the three models shown in (**A**). Only the BOS and to a lesser degree reverse syllable order BOS (BOS-RS) evoke action potentials in this neuron (*top row*: PSTHs of suprathreshold activity). However, other stimuli, including conspecific (CON) and heterospecific (HET) birds' songs and reversed BOS (BOSrev), evoke depolarizing and entirely subthreshold synaptic activity (*middle row*: median-filtered average membrane potential records). Therefore, auditory afferents to these neurons fire action potentials to these non-BOS stimuli, but display a bias to the BOS over the other stimuli. Oscillograms of the various songs are shown in the *bottom row*; neuronal responses are to 20 iterations of each stimulus.

sively to BOS playback, and then often only once per motif.[14] This pattern is strikingly similar to the discharge pattern of this same cell type recorded in the singing bird (FIG. 2B and see figure in Fee and colleagues, this volume). It is possible that the apparent equivalence of BOS-related auditory responses and song premotor activity reflects a common coding scheme that functions to simplify the process of auditory-vocal integration. Additional studies are needed to establish whether there is a similar equivalence in the song-related auditory and motor activity of individual HVC_{RA} neurons. We also found that, throughout much of their period of BOS-evoked discharge, HVC_{RA} neurons undergo a sustained subthreshold depolarization, punctuated intermittently by the much stronger depolarizations associated with the cell's phasic spiking (FIG. 2). Therefore, synaptic inputs to HVC_{RA} neurons are activated throughout the BOS, although much of this activity remains subthreshold. Furthermore, *in vivo* intracellular recordings also revealed that a wide range of non-BOS auditory stimuli (including temporally manipulated versions of the BOS, other conspecific and heterospecific songs, and noise bursts) is effective in activating synapses on HVC_{RA} neurons (FIG. 2B). Interestingly, almost all of the responses evoked by non-BOS stimuli remain subthreshold. That is, while the extracellular response appears BOS-"exclusive," the underlying subthreshold synaptic activity—which can only be detected with an intracellular electrode—is relatively broadly tuned. These broad synaptic tuning properties potentially endow HVC_{RA} neurons with the capacity to detect auditory information about vocal performances that deviate from the ideal song phenotype (i.e., the BOS)—one of the features associated with the input to our hypothetical comparator. More generally, the sharp contrast between narrow suprathreshold tuning and the much broader subthreshold tuning we have seen in HVC_{RA} neurons is also a characteristic of higher order sensory processing in other systems, including the mammalian primary visual cortex[26] and the owl auditory midbrain.[27]

The broad synaptic response patterns of HVC_{RA} neurons also may have implications for the type of auditory information that HVC can transmit to the song motor nucleus RA. Although much of the response to non-BOS stimuli remains entirely subthreshold in anesthetized animals, artificially generating a small positive offset in the cell's resting membrane potential (i.e., by injecting positive current through the recording electrode) is sufficient to enable the cell to spike to non-BOS stimuli.[14] This membrane potential effect indicates that the subthreshold response patterns of HVC_{RA} neurons are largely due to excitatory synaptic inputs. Therefore, endogenous factors that shift the resting membrane potential of HVC_{RA} neurons likely will influence whether these cells fire action potentials to auditory stimuli and thus transmit auditory information to RA. Consistent with this idea, Margoliash and his coworkers have noted a state-dependent gating of auditory responses in RA, with responses readily evoked in the sleeping bird but largely suppressed in the waking animal.[28] Furthermore, other studies have shown that gating of auditory responses also occurs at the level of HVC, at least in the zebra finch.[29] Perhaps the gating of RA's auditory responses is due to shifts in the resting membrane potential of HVC_{RA} neurons, with auditory signals propagating to RA when the HVC_{RA} neuron membrane potential is shifted to a more positive and thus permissive state. The specific factors that trigger such modulation are unknown, but are likely to involve classic neuromodulators, such as acetylcholine and norepinephrine, both of which are abundant in HVC.[30] Two key states that could augment the resting tone of HVC_{RA} neurons in the bird when it is awake are attention and song motor activity. In the future, it will be important to identify the endogenous molecules and mechanisms that mediate such modulation and to determine whether modulation of HVC_{RA} occurs when juveniles learn to sing or when adults attend to their own songs or to other singing birds.

ORIGINS OF SELECTIVE AUDITORY RESPONSIVENESS IN HVC_{RA} NEURONS

The broad subthreshold responsiveness of HVC_{RA} neurons raises questions as to the source and selectivity of their auditory afferents. One possible arrangement involves a population of broadly tuned afferents arising extrinsic to HVC. A second involves the convergence upon HVC_{RA} cells of presynaptic inputs (extrinsic or local) from multiple neurons, each of which is narrowly tuned, but to different acoustical features of the BOS and/or other stimuli. One method for distinguishing extrinsic from local contributions to song-evoked synaptic activity would be to inactivate the HVC local circuit without silencing the activity of extrinsic auditory afferents. In the inactivated HVC, intracellular recordings could be used to measure the contributions of the extrinsic inputs, as reflected by any persistent subthreshold au-

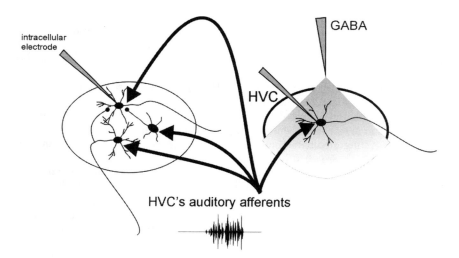

FIGURE 3. A pharmacological method for distinguishing local and extrinsic contributions to auditory responses in HVC is shown. Song-evoked synaptic activity in an HVC projection neuron is likely to reflect contributions from both extrinsic and local (intranuclear) components (*left*). Local contributions to the net synaptic activity include synapses from interneurons, and the local collaterals of other projection neurons; extrinsic contributions are from HVC's auditory afferents. Application of a concentrated GABA solution to HVC through a puffer pipette (*right*) can be used to silence local activity. Remaining auditory-evoked activity then can be attributed to the extrinsic inputs onto the impaled HVC neuron. The song stimulus is depicted as an oscillogram at the bottom of the figure.

ditory responsiveness. The comparison between song-evoked response patterns in the normal and inactivated state could also be used to infer how the local circuit contributes to the generation of BOS selectivity. To inactivate the circuit, we recorded intracellularly from identified HVC neurons, then pressure-ejected a small amount of concentrated GABA into HVC (FIG. 3). This treatment reversibly shunts the dendritic and somatic membranes of the HVC cells that the GABA contacts, preventing synaptically evoked spiking. In this state, local processing is disabled, but axons arising from outside of HVC, the terminals of which presumably lack GABA receptors, should continue to function. If local convergence of narrowly tuned inputs accounts for the broad subthreshold responses of HVC_{RA} neurons, then subthreshold responses should become more narrowly tuned (i.e., show more phasic synaptic responses to the BOS and respond to a reduced set of non-BOS stimuli) upon inactivation. In contrast, if HVC_{RA} subthreshold response patterns are dictated by extrinsic afferents, they should persist unchanged. In fact, the basic subthreshold response pattern seen in HVC_{RA} neurons prior to GABA application persisted during inactivation of the HVC local circuit, indicating to us that the extrinsic inputs into HVC are BOS selective, but also fire action potentials to a wider range of song and non-song stimuli.[31] Therefore, HVC's auditory afferents as a population are broadly responsive to different auditory stimuli, rather than being narrowly tuned. Only single unit recordings can resolve the remaining question of whether individual afferents to HVC are broadly or narrowly tuned.

NIF CONTRIBUTIONS TO BOS SELECTIVITY IN HVC

The finding that auditory afferents to HVC are BOS selective is intriguing because prior studies suggested that heightened selectivity for the BOS originated within HVC. Importantly, the pronounced BOS selectivity seen in HVC appears to be largely absent in the primary auditory telencephalic region, Field L, which is presumed to be a major source (direct or indirect) of auditory input to HVC.[19,32] Recent studies have suggested nucleus interfacialis (NIf) as the site where the auditory signal acquires BOS selectivity. NIf, which has been identified in tracing studies as a major HVC afferent, contains neurons that display BOS selectivity intermediate between that of Field L and HVC neurons.[33] These features of NIf suggested that it might be involved in the transformation of non-selective input from Field L into a moderately BOS-selective output that is further augmented by the HVC local circuit. Another possibility is that HVC receives auditory input from NIf and several other brain areas, and together these various auditory inputs give rise to the synaptic responses observed in HVC_{RA} neurons. In support of this latter view, at least one other HVC afferent, the nucleus mMAN, is known to contain neurons that are BOS selective.[34]

To determine the extent to which NIf could account for the synaptic activity of HVC_{RA} neurons and to assess any changes in auditory selectivity between these two song nuclei, we paired extracellular recordings in NIf, to measure its action potential output, with intracellular recordings from HVC_{RA} neurons, to measure their synaptic input.[35] These recordings revealed a striking concordance in the auditory properties measured at these two sites with respect to both the temporal pattern and relative strength of their auditory-evoked activities. For example, a given stimulus evoked a mean firing rate in NIf that closely paralleled the strength of the synaptic response in HVC. In addition, auditory-evoked responses in both areas were graded, with the BOS evoking the highest levels of activity, and reverse-syllable BOS, reverse BOS, and conspecific songs eliciting weaker responses. Furthermore, NIf spikes preceded synaptic activity in HVC by one to several milliseconds, and inactivating NIf with concentrated GABA abolished all spontaneous and auditory-evoked synaptic and spiking activity in HVC, suggesting to us that NIf is the dominant and perhaps sole source of ascending auditory input to HVC. Indeed, these dual recordings show that

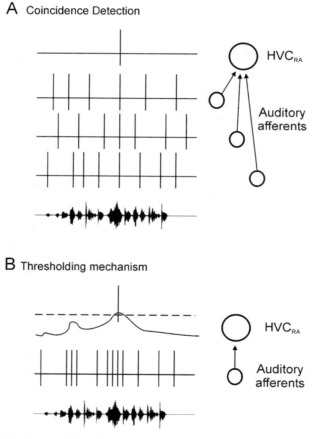

FIGURE 4. Two models depicting the generation of sparse spiking patterns in HVC_{RA} neurons in response to BOS playback. (**A**) Several neurons presynaptic to the HVC_{RA} neuron spike in a continuous fashion in response to the stimulus, but only rarely fire at the same time. The HVC_{RA} neuron only fires action potentials when it detects this coincident activity. (**B**) Another possibility is that sustained firing in the presynaptic only intermittently shifts the HVC_{RA} neuron membrane potential above spike threshold, perhaps through temporal integration by the postsynaptic cell. In both examples, the song stimulus is depicted as an oscillogram at the bottom of the panel.

HVC_{RA} neurons act largely as followers of BOS-selective input from NIf, in contrast to the idea that BOS selectivity arises or is further enhanced in HVC. One implication of these results is that the search for the origins of BOS selectivity must now extend to NIf's auditory inputs, which are reported to include Field L, clHV, and perhaps even direct projections from the auditory thalamus[36] (Wild, personal communication).

While the relative bias to the BOS does not appear to be enhanced at the NIf-HVC_{RA} synapse, this synapse does appear to be the site where an almost exclusive action potential response to self-generated vocalizations first emerges. That is, whereas NIf neurons fire to a wide range of auditory stimuli, HVC_{RA} neurons fire almost exclusively to the BOS. The mechanisms underlying this transformation in stimulus specificity remain unknown. One possibility is that subsets of NIf neurons converge on individual HVC_{RA} neurons, but only drive spiking when their activities are highly correlated, perhaps because HVC_{RA} neurons act as coincidence detectors (FIG. 4A). Another hypothesis is that the resting membrane potential of HVC_{RA} neurons and/or the strength of NIf synapses is adjusted so that only the BOS generates sufficient depolarization to exceed spike threshold (FIG. 4B). The observation that BOS-evoked spiking in an HVC_{RA} neuron becomes sustained throughout more of the stimulus when the cell's resting potential undergoes a positive DC offset (via current injection) is supportive of the thresholding model and contradicts a model where HVC spike timing is determined entirely by presynaptic cooperativity.[14] In either case, the sustained synaptic activity evoked by BOS playback is transformed into a much more intermittent, or temporally sparser, action potential output by the HVC_{RA} neuron. An added motivation to understanding how sparse spiking is generated in response to BOS playback is that a similar process likely accounts for the extremely sparse spike patterns HVC_{RA} neurons produce during singing.[23]

AUDITORY SELECTIVITY AND CANCELLATION MECHANISMS IN THE HVC_X (ANTERIOR) PATHWAY

Intracellular analyses of synaptic mechanisms in HVC_X neurons will be critical in the study of song learning. These neurons are the major and perhaps sole source of auditory input to the AFP, which is crucial to the vocal plasticity necessary to song learning.[37,38] That HVC_X neurons may make different but complementary contributions from HVC_{RA} neurons to the song learning process is suggested by the observation that though BOS playback evokes very phasic action potential responses from both projection neurons, HVC_X cells are quite distinct in their song-evoked synaptic activity from HVC_{RA} neurons. Specifically, HVC_X neurons exhibit a hyperpolarizing response in membrane potential that is sustained throughout much of the BOS, suggestive of a synaptic inhibitory process.[14,39] Such inhibition could contribute to a cancellation component of a comparator model under two conditions. First, the inhibition should be most strongly evoked by the BOS, rather than other auditory stimuli; second, the inhibition should be activated by song premotor (HVC_{RA}) neurons.

Consistent with the first condition, we found that the auditory-evoked inhibition detected as a postsynaptic hyperpolarization in HVC_X cells is greatest for the BOS, by comparison with non-preferred stimuli such as reverse BOS, other songs, or noise bursts.[14,39] In fact, the only stimulus other than the BOS that consistently evokes any hyperpolarizing response in HVC_X neurons is reverse syllable order BOS, which preserves the local temporal organization of song syllables, but does not maintain their overall sequence. The capacity of the reverse-syllable order BOS to evoke substantial inhibition suggests that the neurons driving the inhibition are tuned in part to the structure of individual syllables. Such a syllable-tuned inhibitory network could still operate to cancel out syllables that were correctly produced, even if they were not generated in the correct sequence. These findings are not readily consistent with a model where inhibition actively cancels out excitatory responses to the non-preferred stimuli, which is one way that inhibition could enhance BOS selectivity in HVC.

A second corollary prediction of a cancellation model is that inactivating the inhibition onto HVC_X neurons should unmask an even stronger BOS-evoked synaptic excitation. We investigated this possibility using concentrated GABA to inactivate the entire HVC local network, while recording intracellularly from HVC_X neurons.[31,40] This treatment completely abolished BOS-evoked hyperpolarizations in HVC_X neurons, suggesting that they originated from local circuit activity. The finding of a strong correlation between interneuron firing rates and HVC_X membrane hyperpolarizations supported this conclusion.[14] In fact, as predicted above, inactivating the local circuit did more than merely abolish the hyperpolarizing response; it unmasked BOS-evoked depolarizations in HVC_X neurons that were sustained throughout the stimulus presentation. These stronger, more sustained depolarizing responses were remarkably like those we recorded from HVC_{RA} neurons in the same animal, suggesting that the two projection neuron types receive common excitatory input, but that HVC_X cells also receive an additional inhibitory component. This finding challenges the assumption that HVC_X neurons only receive phasic excitatory synaptic activity. It suggests, instead, that the few excitatory peaks seen in control recordings are part of a more sustained synaptic excitation that is largely suppressed by inhibition.

A final important prediction of the cancellation hypothesis is that removing inhibition should increase BOS-evoked firing relatively more than firing evoked by other stimuli. That is, in the absence of inhibition, HVC_X neurons should become even more BOS selective. The results of the local inactivation experiments (involving GABA) are supportive but remain inconclusive, because GABA treatment abolished all spiking. This prevented us from testing the prediction by measuring BOS-evoked firing in HVC_X neurons. To address this question we need to selectively block inhibition onto HVC_X neurons while allowing them to continue firing action potentials. Furthermore, to avoid non-specific network effects that may accompany pharmacological disinhibition, it would be important to apply intracellular blockers to single cells rather than to the nucleus. Fortunately, this technically challenging approach was made easier by a series of *in vitro* studies that identified three major classes of inhibitory input onto HVC_X neurons.[12,41,42] The first of these inhibitory inputs is an ionotropic $GABA_A$ receptor that mediates a chloride current, while the other two are metabotropic receptors that bind glutamate (mGluR) or GABA (GABAB) to activate a G-protein–coupled inward rectifying potassium current (i.e., a GIRK). To determine which of these inhibitory processes mediates the auditory-evoked hyperpolarizing inhibition seen in HVC_X neurons, we introduced a series of compounds through the recording pipette that selectively blocked either chloride or potassium channels, or disrupted G-protein–mediated signaling. These studies demonstrated

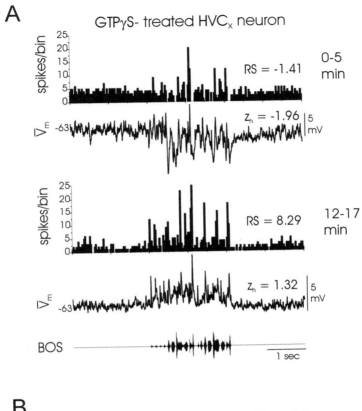

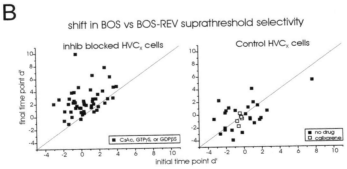

FIGURE 5. Intracellular disruption of G-protein–mediated potassium currents in HVC_X neurons augments their excitatory responses to BOS playback. (**A**) Occlusion of G-protein coupled inward rectifying potassium currents (GIRKs) with GTPγS abolishes BOS-evoked hyperpolarizations in HVC_X neurons and increases the strength of their BOS-evoked firing. The action potential PSTH (*top*) and median-filtered average membrane potential records (*bottom*) are shown either immediately after impaling the cell (0–5 min), and then again after the GIRK-mediated inhibition was occluded (12–17 min). Positive current was applied through the recording electrode to maintain the resting membrane potential at −63 mV

that GIRKs are likely to be the major source of auditory-evoked hyperpolarization in HVCx neurons.[39] When HVC_X neurons were treated with compounds that disrupt GIRK activation, the strong BOS-evoked hyperpolarizing responses rapidly waned, unmasking a sustained depolarizing response like that seen with the local circuit inactivated. Moreover, BOS-evoked firing activity of the cell was strongly and preferentially enhanced, so that disruption of the inhibitory process actually increased the suprathreshold selectivity for the BOS (FIG. 5). This observation demonstrates that the GIRK-mediated inhibition actively dampens or cancels the BOS-evoked response, a finding consistent with a cancellation process. [Note: We found that $GABA_A$-mediated chloride components are also activated by BOS playback, but do not hyperpolarize the cell, perhaps because the chloride reversal potential in HVC_X neurons is positive of the resting potential.]

THE ROLE OF SONG PREMOTOR ACTIVITY
IN THE CANCELLATION PROCESS

As noted earlier, such tuned inhibition, if effectively recruited by song premotor activity, could cancel out anticipated auditory feedback in a manner consistent with the comparator model. We therefore sought evidence that the inhibition that suppresses BOS-evoked firing in HVC_X neurons is driven by song premotor neurons (i.e., HVC_{RA}) neurons. Suggestive evidence for such an interaction between the two neuronal populations comes from simultaneous recordings from the two projection neurons types. These recordings show that BOS playback evokes opposing trajectories in their membrane potentials, almost as if the synaptic patterns in the two cell types were mirror images of each other (FIG. 6).[14] That is, when HVC_{RA} neurons are excited, HVC_X neurons are inhibited, and vice versa, resulting in alternating BOS-evoked firing patterns. Two kinds of evidence suggest that the inhibition of HVC_X neurons is driven by excitatory signals from HVC_{RA} neurons inverted through an inhibitory interneuron network. First, HVC_{RA} neurons make excitatory synapses in RA[15] and on HVC interneurons (unpublished observations). Second, interneuron firing rates positively correlate with HVC_X cell membrane potential negativity.[14]

---

throughout. The suprathreshold response strength (RS) is the difference between the mean firing rate during BOS playback (shown as an oscillogram at bottom) and the mean firing rate during a prestimulus period of similar duration, while the hyperpolarizing Z-score (Z_h) estimates the strength of the stimulus-evoked hyperpolarization. (**B**) Selectivity for forward over reverse BOS increases upon disruption of GIRK-mediated inhibition in a population of treated HVC_X neurons, as measured by d′ values at initial (x axis) and final times (y axis) during recordings in which GIRK-mediated inhibition was blocked. The d′ statistic reports the difference in RS values for forward versus reverse BOS playback divided by the standard deviation of the responses; the vertical shift in the distribution over time is due to relatively larger positive d′ values at the final time point, indicating that disrupting inhibition is accompanied by an increased bias to the forward BOS. *Left:* population data for all HVC_X neurons treated with blockers (cesium acetate (CsAc); GDPβS) or occluders (GTPγS) of GIRK-mediated inhibition. *Right:* control recordings either with no drug or with a blocker of chloride channels (calixarene). The control recordings remain evenly distributed about identity, indicating no net shift in selectivity over the recording period. (Reprinted from Rosen and Mooney[39] with permission.)

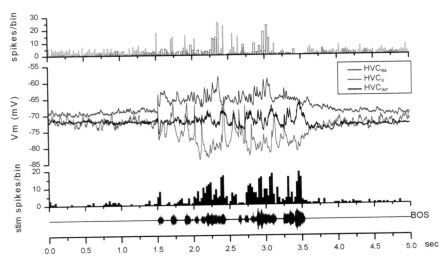

FIGURE 6. BOS playback evokes different synaptic processes and reciprocal suprathreshold activity in HVC projection neurons. The two different HVC projection neuron types fire in alternating fashion to song playback (*top*: PSTH; the BOS is shown as an oscillogram at the bottom of the figure), while HVC$_{RA}$ neurons undergo sustained depolarizing synaptic activity and HVC$_X$ neurons display sustained membrane hyperpolarizations interrupted by phasic depolarizations (*middle*: median filtered average membrane potential records). The membrane potential hyperpolarizations in HVC$_X$ neurons closely correlate with the peaks of maximum firing activity in HVC interneurons (*bottom*: PSTH), which in turn correlates closely with firing in HVC$_{RA}$ neurons. These records are consistent with the idea that HVC$_{RA}$ neurons drive feedforward inhibition in HVC$_X$ neurons through an intervening interneuron layer. Responses shown are to 20 iterations of song playback. (Reprinted from Mooney[14] with permission.)

To obtain a more detailed view of the HVC microcircuit generating these synaptic interactions, we made intracellular recordings from identified HVC neurons in brain slices.[43] We identified the synaptic connections of HVC$_{RA}$ neurons upon other HVC neurons by electrically stimulating the fiber tract that connects HVC$_{RA}$ neurons to RA. This stimulation evokes antidromic action potentials that invade the local collaterals of HVC$_{RA}$ axons, which then synaptically activate other HVC neurons. We found that such stimulation evoked short latency excitatory postsynaptic potentials (EPSPs) in HVC interneurons, and longer latency inhibitory PSPs (IPSPs) in HVC$_X$ neurons. These longer latency IPSPs were abolished by blockers of ionotropic glutamate receptors, suggesting to us that HVC$_{RA}$ neurons drive feedforward inhibition in HVC$_X$ neurons through synaptically interposed interneurons. To more directly test this idea, we made paired recordings from different HVC cell types. These recordings confirmed that HVC$_{RA}$ neurons make excitatory synapses onto interneurons, and that interneurons make inhibitory synapses onto HVC$_X$ neurons. Interestingly, the IPSPs that interneurons evoke in HVC$_X$ neurons are blocked by GABA$_A$ receptor antagonists and have onset latencies too short to be mediated by second messengers. Thus they are not the source of the GIRK-mediated inhibition evoked by song playback. One hint as to its possible source comes from the observation that, in the presence of $GABA_A$ receptor blockers, slow IPSPs are evoked in HVC_X neurons by antidromic stimulation of HVC_{RA} neurons. We do not yet know the pharmacology of these slow IPSPs, but they do not seem to be due to direct coupling between HVC_{RA} and HVC_X neurons (i.e., via metabotropic glutamate receptors), because ionotropic glutamate receptor antagonists block them (unpublished observations). One possibility is that another class of interneuron is excited by HVC_{RA} neurons and activates either mGluR- or $GABA_B$ receptors on HVC_X neurons. Another possibility is that the high instantaneous firing frequencies interneurons achieve *in vivo* result in excess transmitter release (i.e., synaptic spillover) that activates GABA receptors in addition to the $GABA_A$ variety.

In summary, we have found several synaptic features in HVC that are consistent with a hypothetical comparator model, including broadly tuned auditory input and inhibitory mechanisms that appear well suited for canceling anticipated auditory feedback. Inactivation experiments reveal that both HVC_{RA} and HVC_X neurons are innervated by extrinsic auditory inputs that respond broadly to many different auditory stimuli, not just the BOS. Broadly tuned auditory excitatory drive to the two HVC PNs likely arises from NIf, and can convey auditory information about errant as well as "correct" versions of the BOS. The synaptic architecture of HVC includes multiple forms of inhibition onto HVC_X neurons, and inhibition can be recruited by HVC_{RA} neurons, raising the possibility that singing-related activity in these HVC_{RA} neurons will be translated into inhibitory signals in HVC_X neurons. This process also could provide part of the synaptic basis for the corollary discharge that is seen in the AFP during singing. Finally, second-messenger–mediated inhibition in HVC_X neurons suppresses BOS-evoked excitation, rather than acting to enhance it, a behavior reminiscent of cancellation processes seen in other sensorimotor pathways.

PROBLEMS AND FUTURE DIRECTIONS

Despite the obvious progress represented by these findings, it is important to recognize that our current understanding of synaptic processes in HVC derives entirely from either brain slices or anesthetized whole animal preparations, and not from intracellular recordings in the singing bird. Thus it is still unknown whether song playback in the anesthetized birds activates only the auditory feedback arm of the system or instead reactivates HVC in a manner that more fully mimics its activity during singing. The intracellular recordings in singing birds that could help answer this question are likely to remain beyond our technical capacities for the near future However, intracellular or optical recording methods may eventually provide us with insights into the subthreshold activity of HVC neurons in the singing animal. In the interim, extracellular recordings from identified neurons should help to clarify the relation of real time auditory feedback to HVC and cancellation processes.

Several predictions of the comparator model could be tested using extracellular recordings from identified HVC neurons in awake songbirds. One prediction of the cancellation model is that distorted auditory feedback and/or vocal errors induced by peripheral manipulations (i.e., tracheosyringeal nerve section or injecting air into the respiratory system) should alter the activity of HVC_X neurons. Another potentially testable prediction is that interfering with GIRK signaling selectively in HVC_X neurons should destabilize vocal output, because cancellation of auditory feedback would be disrupted. A third prediction is that natural states that tonically depolarize HVC_{RA} neurons should gate auditory activity to RA. While the most obvious of these states is likely to be singing, it is also possible that attention serves to modulate the resting tone of these neurons, perhaps when the bird is in a practice rather than a performance state.[44]

Another outstanding issue is the relative importance of online auditory feedback to song learning and song maintenance.[45] In the present model, we envision that premotor-linked inhibition in HVC_X neurons would be used in real time to cancel out auditory feedback. As discussed in Konishi's article in this volume, the real-time auditory feedback model is problematic at moderate to high rates of syllable generation, because auditory feedback about a given vocal element coincides with the current motor pattern, not the earlier motor pattern that produced the vocal element itself. One way around this problem is to create short-term synaptic "memories" of the motor signal that flag which synapses are to be acted upon by the feedback signal. "Tagging" of previously active synapses has been proposed to underlie synapse specificity of certain forms of hippocampal long-term potentiation.[46] If a similar process operates in HVC to correctly assign auditory feedback to previously active synapses it likely would require extraordinarily precise temporal regulation of these tags. Another possibility is that HVC's inhibitory pathways are delay-tuned to match the corollary discharge to the appropriate auditory feedback. In this scenario, HVC_X neurons would integrate auditory feedback with the delayed and inverted representation of the song premotor signal emanating through HVC interneurons. This appears to be similar to the cancellation process, but with the outcome that the balance of motor-linked inhibition and auditory-evoked excitation in HVC_X neurons would constitute an estimate of the error signal, not simply the removal of a bias signal. This does not solve the central problem of how such an error signal then modifies the motor network, however. In addition, any model will need to incorporate the synaptic transfer function of the AFP to better understand the significance of inhibition and excitation in HVC_X neurons. By analogy to the mammalian cortical-basal ganglia pathways, HVC_X neurons may trigger LMAN activity through disinhibitory mechanisms.[47,48] In this case, the pattern of synaptic inhibition in HVC_X neurons may have special consequences for understanding the activation of circuits important to audition-dependent vocal plasticity.

A general issue that also remains unresolved is the exact pathway via which auditory information enters the song system. Our present studies suggest that NIf serves as the dominant and perhaps sole source of ascending auditory input to HVC. These studies do not address the full extent of other, perhaps weaker, ascending auditory inputs to HVC, including those from Field L and the shelf, and they also cannot address the contribution made by recurrent pathways (i.e., from mMAN). Still unresolved is the means via which auditory information enters NIf. Clearly, the lack of detailed understanding of ascending auditory projections to song nuclei stands in stark contrast to the increasingly detailed picture that is emerging of synaptic connectivity within and between the song nuclei.

Perhaps the most important aspect of the comparator circuit not touched upon here is the physical representation of the memorized model to which the BOS is being compared (see Adret, this volume). If auditory inputs to HVC convey information only about the current song as part of a comparator process, it is reasonable to assume that the representation of the model must be stored either in or beyond (i.e., postsynaptic) to HVC. Furthermore, if NIf only conveys information about the current song, then perhaps other auditory inputs to HVC, which may include mMAN, Field L, and perhaps nucleus ovoidalis (see Wild, this volume), could convey a representation of the song model to HVC. In this view, HVC would receive two distinct inputs, the first conveying information about the model, and the second conveying information about the current BOS. A further extension of the view is that these two inputs might converge on HVC neurons that also receive cancellation signals from the inhibitory network, thus providing a discrete cellular site where the three signals could be combined. Alternately, auditory representations of the model could enter at later stages of the circuit, perhaps in the AFP. Although current thinking holds that HVC serves as the only source of auditory input to the AFP, other possible points of auditory entry include the thalamic nucleus DLM or area X. Therefore, future research should try to define the number of distinct auditory inputs to HVC and to determine whether auditory information independently enters song system structures other than HVC.

A final concern is the use of song playback to probe the location of a song template. An assumption that we and others have made is that the neuronal selectivity for song playback somehow reflects the memory of that song. In the case of the BOS this idea seems reasonable, but the BOS is also a song that the bird currently performs, rather than a song that exists only in memory. This motor "confound" has made it difficult to determine the extent to which BOS selectivity purely reflects auditory memory.[49,50] Indeed, extracellular studies that have used tutor song playback to probe auditory responses in the song system have as yet failed to present convincing evidence of a tutor song bias.[49–52] In the experiments we have undertaken, the BOS rather than the tutor song has served as the probe stimulus, and thus the synaptic activity evoked by the tutor song in HVC remains unknown. One expectation of a memory is that an activity pattern resembling that evoked by the stimulus that shaped the memory should arise spontaneously, rather than depending on presentation of the stimulus itself.[53] In the songbird, future studies must determine whether tutor song memories are captured in the patterns of either auditory-evoked or spontaneous activity.[54]

REFERENCES

1. MARLER, P. & S. PETERS. 1981. Sparrows learn adult song and more from memory. Science **213:** 780–782.
2. KONISHI, M. 1965. The role of auditory feedback in the control of vocalization in the white-crowned sparrow. Z. Tierpsychologie **22:** 770–783.
3. BELL, C.C. 1981. An efference copy which is modified by reafferent input. Science **214:** 450–453.
4. POULET, J.F. & B. HEDWIG. 2002. A corollary discharge maintains auditory sensitivity during sound production. Nature **418:** 872–876.
5. POULET, J.F. & B. HEDWIG. 2003. A corollary discharge mechanism modulates central auditory processing in singing crickets. J. Neurophysiol. **89:** 1528–1540.
6. SUGA, N. & P. SCHLEGEL. 1972. Neural attenuation of responses to emitted sounds in echolocating bats. Science **177:** 82–84.
7. SUGA, N. & T. SHIMOZAWA. 1974. Site of neural attenuation of responses to self-vocalized sounds in echolocating bats. Science **183:** 1211–1213.

8. ELIADES, S.J. & X. WANG. 2003. Sensory-motor interaction in the primate auditory cortex during self-initiated vocalizations. J. Neurophysiol. **89:** 2194–2207.

9. McCASLAND, J.S. & M. KONISHI. 1981. Interaction between auditory and motor activities in an avian song control nucleus. Proc. Natl. Acad. Sci. USA **78:** 7815–7819.

10. NOTTEBOHM, F., T.M. STOKES & C.M. LEONARD. 1976. Central control of song in the canary, *Serinus canarius*. J. Comp. Neurol. **165:** 457–486.

11. FORTUNE, E.S. & D. MARGOLIASH. 1995. Parallel pathways and convergence onto HVc and adjacent neostriatum of adult zebra finches (*Taeniopygia guttata*). J. Comp. Neurol. **360:** 413–441.

12. DUTAR, P., H.M. VU & D.J. PERKEL. 1998. Multiple cell types distinguished by physiological, pharmacological, and anatomic properties in nucleus Hvc of the adult zebra finch. J. Neurophysiol. **80:** 1828–1838.

13. KUBOTA, M. & I. TANIGUCHI. 1998. Electrophysiological characteristics of classes of neuron in the HVc of the zebra finch. J. Neurophysiol. **80:** 914–923.

14. MOONEY, R. 2000. Different subthreshold mechanisms underlie song-selectivity in identified HVc neurons of the zebra finch. J. Neurosci. **20:** 5420–5436.

15. MOONEY, R. 1992. Synaptic basis for developmental plasticity in a birdsong nucleus. J. Neurosci. **12:** 2464–2477.

16. CANADY, R.A., G.D. BURD, T.J. DEVOOGD & F. NOTTEBOHM. 1988. Effect of testosterone on input received by an identified neuron type of the canary song system: a Golgi/electron microscopy/degeneration study. J. Neurosci. **8:** 3770–3784.

17. MARGOLIASH, D. 1983. Acoustic parameters underlying the responses of song-specific neurons in the white-crowned sparrow. J. Neurosci. **3:** 1039–1057.

18. MARGOLIASH, D. 1986. Preference for autogenous song by auditory neurons in a song system nucleus of the white-crowned sparrow. J. Neurosci. **6:** 1643–1661.

19. LEWICKI, M.S. & B.J. ARTHUR. 1996. Hierarchical organization of auditory temporal context sensitivity. J. Neurosci. **16:** 6987–6998.

20. VOLMAN, S.F. 1996. Quantitative assessment of song-selectivity in the zebra finch "high vocal center." J. Comp. Physiol. A Sens. Neural Behav. Physiol. **178:** 849–862.

21. THEUNISSEN, F.E. & A.J. DOUPE. 1998. Temporal and spectral sensitivity of complex auditory neurons in the nucleus HVc of male zebra finches. J. Neurosci. **18:** 3786–3802.

22. McCASLAND, J.S. 1987. Neuronal control of birdsong production. J. Neurosci. **7:** 23–39.

23. HAHNLOSER, R., A. KOZHEVNIKOV & M. FEE. 2002. An ultra-sparse code underlies the generation of neural sequences in a songbird. Nature **419:** 65–70.

24. YU, A.C. & D. MARGOLIASH. 1996. Temporal hierarchical control of singing in birds. Science **273:** 1871–1875.

25. VU, E.T., M.E. MAZUREK & Y.C. KUO. 1994. Identification of a forebrain motor programming network for the learned song of zebra finches. J. Neurosci. **14:** 6924–6934.

26. BRINGUIER, V., F. CHAVANE, L. GLAESER & Y. FREGNAC. 1999. Horizontal propagation of visual activity in the synaptic integration field of area 17 neurons. Science **283:** 695–699.

27. PENA, J.L. & M. KONISHI. 2001. Auditory spatial receptive fields created by multiplication. Science **292:** 249–252.

28. DAVE, A.S., A.C. YU & D. MARGOLIASH. 1998. Behavioral state modulation of auditory activity in a vocal motor system. Science **282:** 2250–2254.

29. SCHMIDT, M.F. & M. KONISHI. 1998. Gating of auditory responses in the vocal control system of awake songbirds. Nat. Neurosci. **1:** 513–518.

30. SAKAGUCHI, H. & N. SAITO. 1989. The acetylcholine and catecholamine contents in song control nuclei of zebra finch during song ontogeny. Brain Res. Dev. Brain Res. **47:** 313–317.

31. ROSEN, M.J. & R. MOONEY. 2000. Local and extrinsic contributions to song-selectivity in the zebra finch song nucleus HVC. Soc. Neurosci. Abstracts **26:** 2030.

32. GRACE, J.A., N. AMIN, N.C. SINGH & F.E. THEUNISSEN. 2003. Selectivity for conspecific song in the zebra finch auditory forebrain. J. Neurophysiol. **89:** 472–487.

33. JANATA, P. & D. MARGOLIASH. 1999. Gradual emergence of song selectivity in sensorimotor structures of the male zebra finch song system. J. Neurosci. **19:** 5108–5118.
34. VATES, G.E., D.S. VICARIO & F. NOTTEBOHM. 1997. Reafferent thalamo-"cortical" loops in the song system of oscine songbirds. J. Comp. Neurol. **380:** 275–290.
35. COLEMAN, M.J. & R. MOONEY. Synaptic basis for song-evoked activity in vocal patterning and plasticity pathways. In review.
36. VATES, G.E., B.M. BROOME, C.V. MELLO & F. NOTTEBOHM. 1996. Auditory pathways of caudal telencephalon and their relation to the song system of adult male zebra finches. J. Comp. Neurol. **366:** 613–642.
37. BOTTJER, S.W., E.A. MIESNER & A.P. ARNOLD. 1984. Forebrain lesions disrupt development but not maintenance of song in passerine birds. Science **224:** 901–903.
38. BRAINARD, M. & A. DOUPE. 2000. Interruption of a forebrain-basal ganglia circuit prevents plasticity of learned vocalizations. Nature **404:** 762–766.
39. ROSEN, M.J. & R. MOONEY. 2003. Inhibitory and excitatory mechanisms underlying auditory responses to learned vocalizations in the songbird nucleus HVC. Neuron **39:** 177–194.
40. ROSEN, M.J. & R. MOONEY. 2000. Intrinsic and extrinsic contributions to auditory selectivity in a song nucleus critical for vocal plasticity. J. Neurosci. **20:** 5437–5448.
41. SCHMIDT, M.F. & D.J. PERKEL. 1998. Slow synaptic inhibition in nucleus HVc of the adult zebra finch. J. Neurosci. **18:** 895–904.
42. DUTAR, P., J. PETROZZINO, H. VU, et al. 2000. Slow synaptic inhibition mediated by metabotropic glutamate receptor activation of GIRK channels. J. Neurophysiol. **84:** 2284–2290.
43. PRATHER, J.F. & R. MOONEY. 2003. Synaptic coupling of HVC neurons revealed by pairwise recordings. Soc. Neurosci. Abstracts 294.11.
44. JARVIS, E.D., C. SCHARFF, M.R. GROSSMAN, et al. 1998. For whom the bird sings: context dependent gene expression. Neuron **21:** 775–788.
45. MARGOLIASH, D. 2002. Evaluating theories of bird song learning: implications for future directions. J. Comp. Physiol. A Neuroethol. Sens. Neural. Behav. Physiol. **188:** 851–866.
46. FREY, U. & R.G. MORRIS. 1997. Synaptic tagging and long-term potentiation. Nature **385:** 533–536.
47. MOONEY, R., M.J. ROSEN & C.B. STURDY. 2002. A bird's eye view: top down intracellular analyses of auditory selectivity for learned vocalizations. J. Comp. Physiol. A Neuroethol. Sens. Neural Behav. Physiol. **188:** 879–895.
48. LUO, M. & D.J. PERKEL. 1999. A GABAergic, strongly inhibitory projection to a thalamic nucleus in the zebra finch song system. J. Neurosci. **19:** 6700–6711.
49. SOLIS, M.M. & A.J. DOUPE. 2000. Compromised neural selectivity for song in birds with impaired sensorimotor learning. Neuron **25:** 109–121.
50. SOLIS, M.M. & A.J. DOUPE. 1999. Contributions of tutor and bird's own song experience to neural selectivity in the songbird anterior forebrain. J. Neurosci. **19:** 4559–4584.
51. SOLIS, M.M. & A.J. DOUPE. 1997. Anterior forebrain neurons develop selectivity by an intermediate stage of birdsong learning. J. Neurosci. **17:** 6447–6462.
52. VOLMAN, S.F. 1993. Development of neural selectivity for birdsong during vocal learning. J. Neurosci. **13:** 4737–4747.
53. WILSON, M.A. & B.L. MCNAUGHTON. 1994. Reactivation of hippocampal ensemble memories during sleep. Science **265:** 676–679.
54. DAVE, A. & D. MARGOLIASH. 2000. Song replay during sleep and computational rules for sensorimotor vocal learning. Science **290:** 812–816.

Cellular, Circuit, and Synaptic Mechanisms in Song Learning

ALLISON J. DOUPE,[a] MICHELE M. SOLIS,[a,b] RHEA KIMPO,[a,c]
AND CHARLOTTE A. BOETTIGER[a,d]

[a]Keck Center for Integrative Neuroscience, and Departments of Physiology and
Psychiatry, University of California, San Francisco, California 94143, USA

[b]Department of Otolaryngology, University of Washington,
Seattle, Washington 98195, USA

[c]Department of Neurobiology, Stanford University,
Stanford, California 94125, USA

[d]The Gallo Center, Emeryville, California 94608, USA

ABSTRACT: Songbirds, much like humans, learn their vocal behavior, and
must be able to hear both themselves and others to do so. Studies of the brain
areas involved in singing and song learning could reveal the underlying neural
mechanisms. Here we describe experiments that explore the properties of the
songbird anterior forebrain pathway (AFP), a basal ganglia-forebrain circuit
known to be critical for song learning and for adult modification of vocal output. First, neural recordings in anesthetized, juvenile birds show that auditory
AFP neurons become selectively responsive to the song stimuli that are compared during sensorimotor learning. Individual AFP neurons develop tuning
to the bird's own song (BOS), and in many cases to the tutor song as well, even
when these stimuli are manipulated to be very different from each other. Such
dual selectivity could be useful in the BOS–tutor song comparison critical to
song learning. Second, simultaneous neural recordings from the AFP and its
target nucleus in the song motor pathway in anesthetized adult birds reveal
correlated activity that is preserved through multiple steps of the circuits for
song, including the AFP. This suggests that the AFP contains highly functionally interconnected neurons, an architecture that can preserve information
about the timing of firing of groups of neurons. Finally, in vitro studies show
that recurrent synapses between neurons in the AFP outflow nucleus, which
are expected to contribute importantly to AFP correlation, can undergo activity-dependent and timing-sensitive strengthening. This synaptic enhancement
appears to be restricted to birds in the sensory critical and early sensorimotor
phases of learning. Together, these studies show that the AFP contains cells
that reflect learning of both BOS and tutor song, as well as developmentally
regulated synaptic and circuit mechanisms well-suited to create temporally organized assemblies of such cells. Such experience-dependent sensorimotor assemblies are likely to be critical to the AFP's role in song learning. Moreover,
studies of such mechanisms in this basal ganglia circuit specialized for song

Address for correspondence: Allison J. Doupe, Keck Center for Integrative Neuroscience, and
Departments of Physiology and Psychiatry, Box 0444, HSE 802, University of California, San
Francisco, California 94143.
ajd@phy.ucsf.edu; <http://www.keck.ucsf.edu/labinfo/doupe.htm>

Ann. N.Y. Acad. Sci. 1016: 495–523 (2004). © 2004 New York Academy of Sciences.
doi: 10.1196/annals.1298.035

may shed light more generally on how basal ganglia circuits function in guiding motor learning using sensory feedback signals.

KEYWORDS: selectivity; tutor; bird's own song; template; sensorimotor; correlation; network; interconnectivity; variability; spike-timing dependence; plasticity; NMDA receptor; recurrent; critical period

Hearing is important to most animals for localization of sounds and recognition of sounds, including behaviorally important communication sounds of other individuals of the same species, such as mating and warning calls. For a subset of animals known as vocal learners, another critical function of hearing is to learn to produce sounds imitated from others. Humans are consummate vocal learners: human speech is a fantastically complex and variable communication sound, and we depend critically on hearing both of self and others for normal speech development. To understand basic brain mechanisms of vocal learning and its disorders, however, it is important to be able to study animals with related behaviors. Surprisingly, there are relatively few other mammalian vocal learners besides humans. In contrast, many thousands of songbird species, as well as the parrot and hummingbird groups, learn to make their complex vocal sounds. Their learning shows some striking parallels to human speech learning,[1] most importantly a strong dependence on hearing in early life and in adulthood: like humans, birds do not learn to vocalize normally in the absence of hearing, and as adults, show deterioration of vocal output after hearing loss.[2–5] Songbirds thus provide a promising model system for elucidating general neural mechanisms involved in vocal learning, including how the brain may evaluate auditory feedback and use it to modify vocal output, and what synaptic mechanisms could underlie this.

Experiments to investigate the neural basis of vocal learning in songbirds are aided by a wealth of information about the behavioral time course of learning,[6–8] as outlined in other articles in this volume. In brief, song learning occurs in two stages, called the sensory and sensorimotor phases (FIG. 1A). During the sensory phase, a young bird listens to and memorizes the song of an adult tutor, usually the bird's father. This memory is often called the "template." The sensorimotor phase begins later, when the young bird begins to sing; during sensorimotor learning the juvenile uses auditory feedback to compare its own immature vocalizations ("plastic song") to its memory of the tutor song, and gradually refines and adapts its vocal output until it matches the tutor song. Thus, auditory experience of both the tutor song and the bird's own song (BOS) is required during learning. In adulthood, elimination or alteration of auditory feedback of BOS induces gradual deterioration of adult song structure.[9,10] These behavioral observations suggest that there must be neural circuitry involved in memorization and evaluation of song. Specifically, after the initial storage of a song template, there must be mechanisms that compare auditory feedback from vocal output to that internal song template that generate signals to guide changes in vocal output.

One candidate circuit for processing and evaluating these song experiences is the anterior forebrain pathway (AFP), a basal ganglia-forebrain circuit found within a system of interconnected nuclei dedicated to song learning and production (FIG. 1B).[11] The AFP plays a special role during learning and song modification. Le-

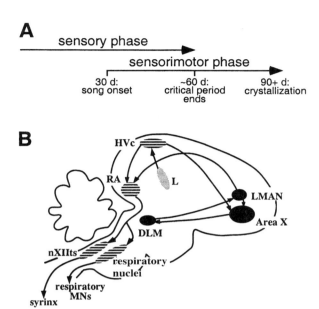

FIGURE 1. (**A**) Song learning occurs in two phases. For zebra finches, the sensory phase ends at ~60 days of age, and the sensorimotor phase begins when birds are ~30 days old and continues until they are ≥90 days of age; thus the phases of learning overlap in this species. (**B**) Anatomy of the song system, which consists of two major pathways. Motor pathway nuclei are *striped* and AFP pathway nuclei are in *black*. The motor pathway, necessary for normal song production throughout life, includes HVC, the robust nucleus of the arcopallium (RA), and the tracheosyringeal portion of the hypoglossal nucleus (nXIIts). RA also projects to nuclei involved in control of respiration. The AFP comprises Area X (X), the medial nucleus of the dorsolateral thalamus (DLM), and the lateral magnocellular nucleus of the anterior nidopallium (LMAN). The Field L complex and related areas (*stippled*) provide auditory input to the song system.

sions of the AFP severely disrupt song learning in juveniles, whereas the same lesions do not affect song in normal adult zebra finches.[12–14] However, lesions in adults prevent the degradation of adult song normally caused by perturbations of song production or feedback.[15,16] Both juvenile and adult results are consistent with the idea that the AFP participates in evaluating song feedback and computing or conveying instructive signals about the quality of song, which then drive adaptive (or in case of adult deafening, non-adaptive) changes in song[17] (see also Brainard, this volume). The output of the AFP, the lateral magnocellular nucleus of the anterior neostriatum (LMAN), projects to the motor pathway for song, which is necessary for normal song production throughout life.[11] Thus, the AFP is well positioned to influence activity in the motor pathway, and could drive changes in vocal output. We review here experiments that implicate AFP function in the sensory and sensorimotor phases of learning and describe circuit and synaptic mechanisms appropriate to shaping of neural properties by song learning.

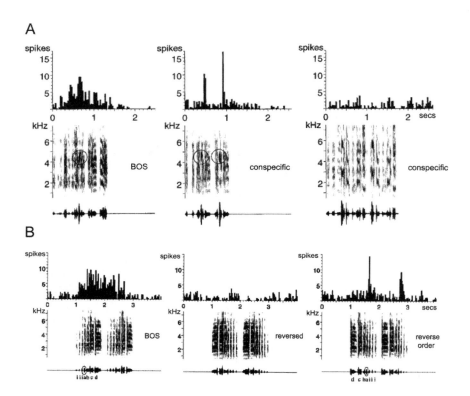

FIGURE 2. AFP neurons are song-selective. (**A**) A song-selective neuron from LMAN of an adult zebra finch. Peristimulus time histograms (PSTHs) show the greater response of a single LMAN neuron to bird's own song (BOS) than to two other conspecific songs. Song is shown underneath each PSTH as a sonogram (plot of frequency versus time, with the energy of each frequency band indicated by the darkness of the trace). Song-selective neurons respond to multiple acoustic features of the BOS: the circles in the sonograms identify a feature that is shared between BOS and the first conspecific song shown here and appears to elicit a response, but the figure also illustrates that many other features of BOS must contribute to the overall response of this neuron to BOS. (**B**) Song-selective neurons are also sensitive to temporal features of song. This single LMAN neuron responds strongly to BOS, especially the first phrase (also called motif), and very little to the fully reversed (mirror-image) song. The introductory notes (i) and syllables (a–d) of the first of the two repeated motifs of the song are labeled with lowercase letters. The BOS played in reverse order, which maintains the order within each syllable while reversing the sequence, is also a much less effective stimulus than the normal BOS, but elicits a phasic response after each occurrence of syllable a. (From Doupe *et al.*[109] *In* The Cognitive Neurosciences III, M. Gazzaniga, Ed. Reprinted with permission from MIT Press and the editor.)

SONG SELECTIVITY AND ITS EMERGENCE DURING LEARNING

As might be expected of neural circuits that may be involved in mediating song learning, neurons in the song system are responsive to sounds, and to song stimuli in particular. Such neurons were first described in HVC,[18,19] and are also seen in RA,[20,21] but their development has been especially extensively studied, in both normal and experimentally manipulated animals, in the AFP.[22–25] In adult, anesthetized zebra finches, we found that these neurons respond more strongly to BOS than to acoustically similar songs of other zebra finches (conspecific songs; FIG. 2A) or BOS played completely in reverse or with the sequence reversed (FIG. 2B).[25] In addition, like some HVC neurons, many of these neurons are "combination-sensitive" (FIG. 3): that is, they

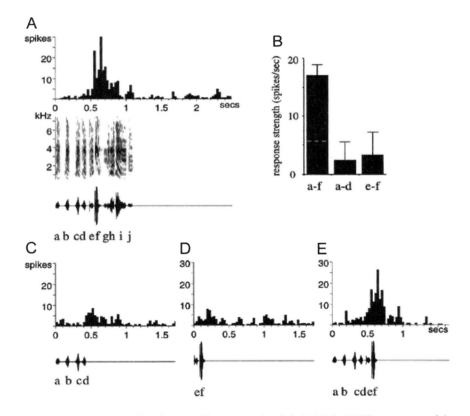

FIGURE 3. A combination-sensitive neuron in adult LMAN. (**A**) The response of the neuron to the entire BOS, whose syllables are indicated by lowercase letters below the os-cillogram. (**B**) The mean response strength (response above background; error bars indicate SEM) to each of the indicated syllable combinations. The *dashed white line* in the first bar represents the linear sum of responses to a–d and e–f. (**C–E**) PSTHs of the neuron's re-sponse to the indicated combinations of syllables. Presentation of the first four syllables alone elicits little response; the following two syllables in isolation also elicit only a weak response. In combination, however, these two stimuli (a–f) elicit a strong response that not only exceeds the sum of responses to stimuli a–d and e–f, but is as strong as the response to the entire song. (From Doupe *et al.*[109] *In* The Cognitive Neurosciences III, M. Gazzaniga, Ed. Reprinted with permission from MIT Press and the editor.)

show a highly non-linear increase in firing when the component sounds of song are combined and played in the correct sequence, compared to those sounds played alone. Neurons that are sensitive to the complex spectral and temporal properties of song could be useful for processing song stimuli during learning. Neurons in the AFP are well suited to provide feedback to the motor pathway, via their connections to RA, about how well sounds match the bird's goal.

This "song selectivity" is not present in young birds, but emerges during the course of song learning: HVC neurons in young white-crowned sparrows and AFP neurons from zebra finches early in the sensory learning phase (30 days of age) respond equally well to all song stimuli (FIG. 4A), and then over time (for instance by 60 days of age in zebra finches) increase their response to their own developing song while losing responsiveness to other stimuli (FIG. 4B).[23,25,26] There is a striking parallel to this result in human speech development: human infants initially show sensory discrimination of phonemes from all human languages tested, but gradually lose their capacity to accurately discriminate sounds that they are not experiencing, and improve their discrimination of the sounds of the language spoken around them.[27,28,53] In both cases, the initial broad sensitivity endows the young organism with the capacity to process any language or species-specific song, but this sensitivity is then narrowed and shaped by experience.

A critical question is which experience—tutor song or BOS—is responsible for the emergence of song selectivity during learning. The answer would inform our hypotheses both about AFP and song neuron function during song learning. For example, neurons tuned by BOS experience could provide information about the current state of BOS, whereas neurons tuned by tutor song could encode the tutor song memory. By 60 days of age, when zebra finches have song-selective AFP neurons,[23] they have completed the sensory phase of learning and could have neurons representing the tutor song. However, they are also in the middle of the sensorimotor phase and have been producing plastic song for about a month. Thus, the overlap between these phases of song learning creates ambiguity: experience of either the bird's own or the tutor song could have shaped the selectivity of these neurons.

FIGURE 4. AFP neurons develop selectivity for song during development. (**A**) PSTHs of auditory responses of a single LMAN neuron from a young, presinging (approximately 30 day old) zebra finch. The neuron responds to the tutor song (TUT) played in normal, forward order, but also to the tutor song fully reversed, and to a conspecific song that the bird has never heard. (**B**) In 30-day-old zebra finches, LMAN neurons exhibit equivalent response strengths (RS; mean stimulus-evoked response minus background) to tutor song (TUT), conspecific song (CON), and reverse tutor song (REV). By 60 days of age, these neurons respond significantly more to TUT than to CON or to REV. In addition, BOS also elicits a much stronger response than CON and reverse BOS (REV). In adults, LMAN neurons are extremely selective for BOS. (**C**) When a juvenile stores a good copy of the tutor song ("A") as its template ("a"), and accurately models its own song after the template, the resulting BOS ("a") will strongly resemble the tutor song. Thus, if a neuron is tuned by BOS experience only, it could also respond well to tutor song when the two songs are similar enough. This ambiguity could be resolved by making the BOS very different ("B") from the tutor song, by interfering with vocal production mechanisms; in these experiments this was done by cutting the tracheosyringeal (ts) nerves to the vocal muscles. (From Doupe et al.[109] In The Cognitive Neurosciences III, M. Gazzaniga, Ed. Reprinted with permission from MIT Press and the editor.)

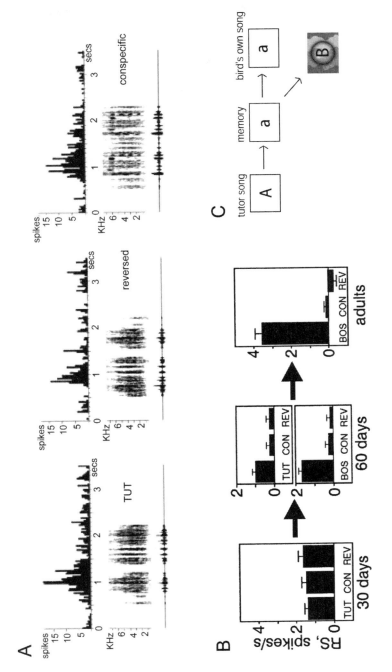

FIGURE 4. *See previous page for legend.*

As a first step towards understanding the origin of selectivity, we directly compared the neural responses to BOS and tutor song in 60-day-old birds. We found a range of preferences for one song over the other (FIG. 5A). Many neurons preferred BOS over tutor song, supporting a role for BOS experience in shaping selectivity. A few neurons preferred tutor SONG over BOS, suggesting that they were tuned by tutor song experience. Finally, many neurons responded equally well to both songs. These neurons were clearly selective, because they did not respond as well to conspecific or reversed song stimuli. Thus, such neurons might reflect experience of both BOS and tutor song.

However, there exist several important caveats with respect to the apparent shaping of AFP neurons by the two behaviorally relevant sensory experiences of tutor song and BOS. First, although BOS selectivity at first glance seems to reflect the bird's experience of its own song, it is very difficult experimentally to separate responsiveness to BOS from responsiveness to tutor, since these stimuli are often acoustically very similar. Indeed, if the bird made a perfect copy of the tutor song memory and then an accurate translation of this into its own song (FIG. 4C), neurons shaped by either BOS or tutor song should respond to both stimuli, making it impossible to tell which stimulus was initially responsible for the neural selectivity. In many birds raised by a single tutor as we do, plastic song already strongly resembles the tutor song by 60 days of age, and many neurons respond well to both BOS and tutor song. A second caveat is that even neurons that respond more strongly to BOS than to tutor song can nonetheless reflect shaping of these cells by the tutor song: if a bird memorized the tutor song poorly during sensory learning, but then faithfully modeled its own song after this inaccurate template (FIG. 4C), BOS selectivity would be a better representation of the template than the original tutor song. Finally, although we often think of song selectivity as a sensory property of neurons that reflects listening by the bird, it may be more complex and sensorimotor in nature. For

---

FIGURE 5. Preferences for BOS versus tutor song by single AFP neurons. (A) Histograms show that in 60-day-old zebra finches, there is a range of preferences among LMAN neurons. The preference for each neuron is quantified with a d' value.[25] When d'≥0.5, this indicates a strong preference for BOS over tutor song; when d'≤-0.5, this indicates a strong preference for tutor song over BOS. Neurons with d' values between -0.5 and 0.5 were considered to have equivalent responses to both song stimuli. (B) Predicted results of the manipulation of BOS. (*Left panel*) If neurons with equivalent responses to BOS and tutor song are shaped solely by BOS during development but respond to both stimuli as a result of acoustic similarities between these two songs, this type of dually responsive neuron is not expected in birds with songs unlike their tutor song, and the distribution should reveal only BOS-tuned neurons. (*Right panel*) If both BOS and tutor song independently shape different neurons in the AFP, the distribution in birds with songs very different from their tutor songs is predicted to be bimodal, as shown by the histogram. (C) The observed distribution of song preferences from ts-cut birds at 60 days of age. Neurons with equivalent responses to BOS and tutor song were maintained, even though these birds' songs did not resemble the tutor song. (D) Equivalent responses to tsBOS and tutor song. PSTHs show the responses of a single LMAN neuron to 13 presentations of each song. While this neuron responded equally well to tsBOS and tutor song, it did not respond well to other adult conspecific songs, and it had developed order selectivity for the tutor song. (From Doupe *et al.*[109] *In* The Cognitive Neurosciences III, M. Gazzaniga, Ed. Reprinted with permission from MIT Press and the editor.)

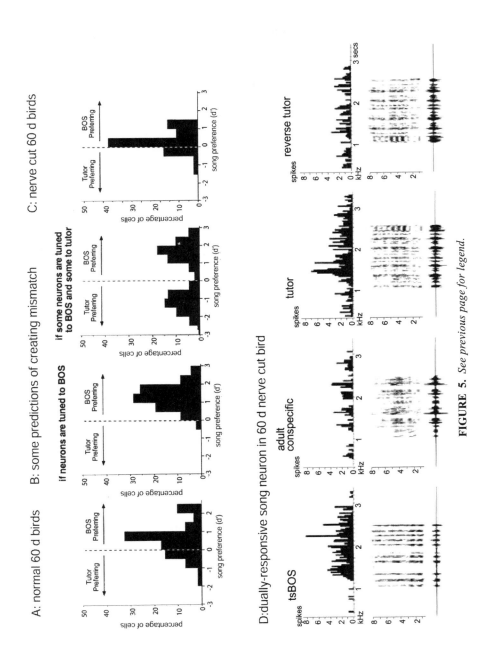

FIGURE 5. *See previous page for legend.*

instance, it could reflect matching of feedback of BOS to the song template during sensorimotor learning. Consistent with the AFP being a sensorimotor nucleus, it is increasingly clear that many song-selective neurons,[21] including those in the AFP,[29,30] are active not just during playback of sound but also during singing, with activity that appears to be premotor and related to song syllables.

These caveats, in particular the question of whether BOS indeed reflects experience (sensory or sensorimotor) of the bird's own vocalizations, can be addressed if the bird is made to sing something very different from its tutor, by a manipulation of its peripheral vocal system (FIG. 4C). Since the bird would hear the highly abnormal BOS only as a result of its own singing, neurons tuned to the abnormal song would verify that it was the experience of BOS that was critical. The same experimental manipulation would also address the complication of the acoustic similarity that normally develops between BOS and tutor song, since this similarity would be minimized by inducing juvenile zebra finches to sing abnormal songs (FIG. 4C).[24] If the neurons in normal birds that respond equally well to BOS and tutor song are actually shaped by the experience of the bird's voice but respond to both stimuli because of acoustic similarities between these songs, then this kind of neuron should not exist in birds with song unlike their tutor song (FIG. 5B, left panel). Alternatively, if these neurons reflect independent contributions of both BOS and tutor song experience to selectivity, then they should persist in birds with song unlike their tutor song, perhaps as separate neural populations (FIG. 5B, right panel).

To induce abnormal song, we bilaterally transected the tracheosyringeal portion of the hypoglossal nerve (NXIIts) prior to song onset (~25 days of age in zebra finches; FIG. 1A), thus denervating the muscles of the avian vocal organ (the syrinx). These juveniles therefore experienced a normal sensory phase with their tutor, but their entire experience of BOS was of the abnormal, nerve cut ("ts cut") song. Song analyses demonstrated that this manipulation successfully minimized both the spectral and temporal similarity between BOS and tutor song.

Using ts-cut song and tutor song as stimuli, we characterized neuronal selectivity in the AFP of ts-cut birds at 60 days of age. Some neurons responded more strongly to the unique ts-cut BOS ("tsBOS") than to tutor song, clearly demonstrating a role for BOS experience in shaping neural selectivity. Strikingly, a sizable proportion of neurons still responded equally well to both tsBOS and tutor song, despite the acoustic differences between these two songs (FIG. 5C). These neurons were not simply immature, because they exhibited selectivity for tsBOS and tutor song over conspecific and reverse song (FIG. 5D). Thus, the presence of neurons with equivalent responses to tsBOS and tutor song in these ts-cut birds suggests that both song experiences can shape the selectivity of single neurons in the AFP, creating dually selective neurons.

How might these different types of song selectivity function in song learning? Since BOS selectivity reflects the bird's current vocal output, it might provide information about the state of plastic song to a neural circuit involved in comparing BOS to a tutor song template stored in sensory coordinates. The high selectivity for BOS might also provide a kind of filter or gating function, aiding the bird in distinguishing its own vocalizations from those of others. It may also reflect in some way the pattern of motor activation during singing, as has been seen in RA.[21] The function of this selectivity could be further investigated with experiments in which AFP selectivity was broadened during song learning, perhaps with pharmacological agents.

Tutor song selectivity could encode information about the tutor song and function during sensorimotor learning as the neural reference of tutor song for birds. That is, this selectivity would result from experience of the tutor song during the sensory phase of learning. During the sensorimotor phase, the level or pattern of firing of these neurons in response to BOS would then reflect the degree to which BOS resembles the tutor song. A role for the AFP in sensory learning of the template is also supported by behavioral experiments that demonstrate a need for normal LMAN activity specifically during tutor song exposure.[31]

In addition, our experiments found that BOS selectivity often coexists with tutor song selectivity in the same individual AFP neurons. This "dual selectivity" may reflect a function for AFP neurons in the actual comparison of BOS and tutor song that is essential to learning. For example, auditory feedback from the bird's own vocalizations would elicit activity from BOS-selective cells. If this auditory feedback of the bird's own voice also matches the tutor song, then this might elicit greater or different activity in neurons that are also tuned to the tutor song than in neurons tuned to BOS or tutor song alone. Thus, the extent to which BOS resembles the tutor might be reflected in the activity of dually tuned neurons, which could then participate in the reinforcement of the motor pathway.

A further suggestion that song selectivity might not only be linked to evaluation of auditory feedback, but is actually sensitive to how well that feedback matches the target, comes from studies of adult birds that were experimentally prevented from ever producing a good copy of their tutor template. We found that when we let birds that experienced NXIIts transections prior to song onset grow to adulthood, they had abnormally low song selectivity in the AFP.[22,32] Neurons were selective enough to discriminate BOS and tutor song from conspecific and reverse songs, but the degree of selectivity was less than that found in normal adults. This result suggests that selectivity is compromised by a chronic inability of birds to match their tutor song model. If true, then these neurons are not simply reflecting sensory experience, but are influenced by the degree of matching during sensorimotor learning.

Despite the joint representation of BOS and tutor song in many AFP neurons, it seems likely that a pure sensory representation of tutor song is present somewhere in the brain. Although this could be encoded by an unidentified subset of neurons lying within other song system nuclei or even within the AFP, it seems equally plausible that such a representation lies elsewhere in the brain, perhaps in the earlier high-level auditory areas that also process songs of conspecifics.[33,34]

CORRELATION IN THE SONG SYSTEM AND ITS VARIABILITY

From the studies of song selectivity, it is clear that song-driven responses flow both down the motor pathway and the AFP (FIG. 7A).[20,35,36] Moreover, investigations of AFP activity in awake birds[29,30] revealed that this circuit fires during singing in a manner similar to the premotor activity in HVc and that this activity persists acutely after deafening. This raises the possibility that much of the AFP activity during singing originates from the song motor circuit and represents in part an "efference copy" of the premotor signals also sent to the motor output pathway. The flow of both sensory and motor information from HVc both to RA and the AFP (FIG. 7A) makes it critical to understand the timing relationship of activity in these two path-

A

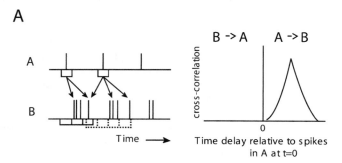

B

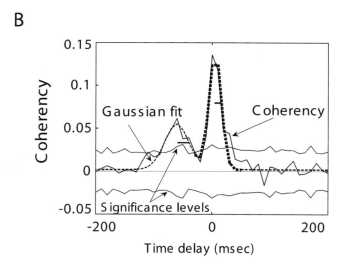

FIGURE 6. Cross-correlation between RA and LMAN. (**A**) A cross-correlation measures the interdependence between two temporal processes, in this case spike trains $r_A(t)$ and $r_B(t)$, and is given by

$$\text{Cross}(r) = \langle \frac{1}{T}\int_0^T (r_A(t)(r_B(t+\tau)))dt \rangle \ ,$$

where t is the time delay of spikes in train $r_B(t)$ relative to spikes in $r_A(t)$, T is the duration of the signal being analyzed, and $<>$ indicate that the measure is averaged across all trials. Peaks of correlation fall to the right of zero if (on average) A spikes tend to precede spikes in B (as exemplified here), and to the left of zero if spikes in B precede those in A. (**B**) The coherency function of RA activity relative to LMAN spikes shows two significant peaks (amplitude > significance level of $\pm 3\times$ Jackknife SD): LMAN-leading-RA to the right of zero, and RA-leading-LMAN to the left of zero. The raw data are shown as a *thin solid line*, and Gaussians fit to the data as *bold* (LMAN-leading-RA) and *thin* (RA-leading-LMAN) *dashed lines*.

ways and the interaction of their activity as it converges in RA. As one approach to this, we recorded activity simultaneously from LMAN and RA, and in some cases from HVc as well, in anesthetized adult zebra finches, and analyzed the cross-correlation of firing between these nuclei.[37]

A cross-correlation analysis of neural activity measures the probability of firing in one spike train as a function of the time of occurrence of firing in a second spike train, by computing the sum of the cross products of the two spike trains at different time lags (FIG. 6A). This analysis can shed light on the likelihood for instance that one set of neurons drives another—that is, correlation between LMAN and RA activity at different stages of song learning would suggest (although not prove) a functional LMAN-RA interaction; this analysis also indicates the time of occurrence of such neuronal interactions. Our correlation studies suggested functional interaction between the song motor pathway and the AFP in adult birds, even though the AFP is not required for singing in adults. Our work also provided evidence (outlined below) that there is correlation of activity between many nuclei of the song system, and surprisingly, that this correlated activity propagates through multiple stages of the song circuit, including the AFP. Such propagation of correlated activity is unusual and suggests that song neurons are strongly functionally interconnected in an architecture that can preserve information about the timing of firing of groups of neurons (FIG. 8C-2,3).

The specific measure of correlation that we used was the coherency,[38] which is calculated by normalizing the cross-covariance of two spike trains by the autocovariance of both spike trains. It is a unitless number, ranging from 1 (perfect correlation) to −1 (perfect anti-correlation). The coherency function has several advantages over the simple cross-correlation function. For one, because we derive it from the cross-covariance function, it corrects for correlated firing that simply reflects correlated changes in the mean firing rate, such as those during song-evoked activity. Second, it corrects for the temporal structure of firing within each neuron (given by the auto-covariance), such as bursting, which could contribute to correlation of activity that does not reflect true synaptic interaction between the two neurons.

We found significant correlated activity between LMAN and RA, as indicated by a positive peak in the coherency function in more than half of the LMAN-RA single unit and multiple unit pairs, both during spontaneous activity and during presentation of the bird's own song. Surprisingly, however, the majority of LMAN-RA pairs that had correlated activity had not one, but two peaks in their coherency functions (FIG. 6B). The two peaks had distinct time delays: one peak had a positive time delay, indicating an increase in RA firing probability after LMAN spikes (LMAN-leading-RA peak), while the other had a negative time delay, indicating an increase in RA firing probability before LMAN spikes (RA-leading-LMAN peak).

The LMAN-leading-RA correlation peak is consistent with the known excitatory connection from LMAN to RA (FIG. 1B).[39,40] This direct LMAN-leading-RA correlation provides support for the idea that the AFP interacts functionally with the motor pathway even in adult birds.

In contrast, the RA-leading-LMAN correlation peak was unexpected. This increase in RA firing probability before LMAN spikes could reflect RA driving LMAN activity via DLM.[41] However, the projection from RA to DLM is very weak in zebra finches[41] and seems unlikely to explain the very long time delay of the RA-leading-LMAN peak (40–50 msec). We hypothesized that the correlation represents

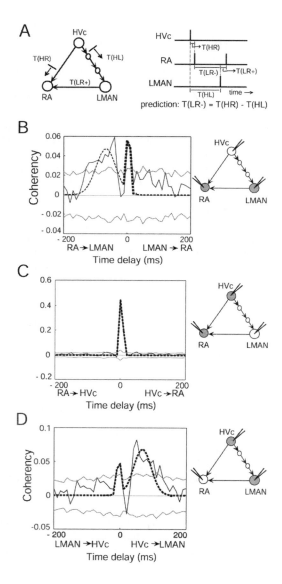

FIGURE 7. Correlation across the song system. (**A**) A common input correlation occurs when two targets receive spikes from the same source. Here, spikes in HVC drive spikes in RA, but also, although across multiple synapses, in LMAN. If these LMAN spikes remain correlated with their input, this would give rise to a correlation between RA and LMAN, with RA leading because the synaptic route between HVc and RA is shorter than that between HVc and RA is shorter than that between HVc and LMAN. (**B**) The upper panel shows a typical LMAN-RA coherency function with two well-separated peaks. The two lower panels show other coherency functions of activity recorded from the same bird (as indicated by shaded nuclei in schematics at right). The

common excitatory input to both areas from HVc, with RA receiving the input earlier than LMAN. Such a source of strong common input could result in an increase in RA firing probability before an LMAN spike (FIG. 7A).

However, this hypothesis implies a correlation that would be unusual. That is, if the RA-leading-LMAN correlation peak reflects common input to LMAN and RA from HVc, activity should also be correlated not only between HVc and RA, but also between HVc and LMAN, two areas separated by a minimum of three synapses (FIG. 7A). Significant correlation of activity between such widely separated brain areas would be surprising. Experimentally, correlation of activity between neurons that are not directly connected or do not share direct common inputs has not been observed.[42–45] This is thought to reflect the weakness and unreliability of most cortical synapses. Individual spikes only successfully cause downstream neurons to fire a small fraction of the time.[46–48] This leads to rapid dissipation of correlation after more than one or two steps in a chain.

We therefore tested directly whether HVc activity was correlated with both LMAN and RA activity by recording simultaneously from small clusters of neurons in all three nuclei. We found that in all experiments in which the LMAN-RA coherency function had two well-separated peaks (FIG. 7B), there was indeed significant coherency of activity between HVc and LMAN, as well as between HVc and RA. Moreover, the time delay of the RA-leading-LMAN peak was highly predictable from the difference in time delays of the simultaneous HVc-RA and HVc-LMAN coherency peaks.[37]

As a further and direct experimental[37] test of our hypothesis of common input to LMAN and RA, we examined the effect of disrupting HVc activity on the correlation of LMAN and RA activity. If the RA-leading-LMAN peak is due to shared input to RA and to the AFP from HVc, it should be greatly decreased by this manipulation, while the direct LMAN-leading-RA correlation should persist (as long as some spontaneous activity remains in LMAN). We recorded simultaneous multi-unit activity from HVc, LMAN, and RA of anesthetized, adult zebra finches before and during silencing of HVc activity at and around the recording site with a broad-spectrum glutamate receptor antagonist, kynurenate. During HVc inactivation the RA-leading-LMAN coherency peak decreased markedly, while the LMAN-leading-RA peak was only slightly diminished (FIG. 8A). This provides strong direct evidence that the RA-leading-LMAN peak is largely due to the common input from HVc directly to RA and indirectly to LMAN, via the AFP.

Correlation of activity is therefore well preserved across multiple synapses in the song system, particularly through the entire AFP. The strength of association between directly connected song nuclei was in the same range as those of direct corti-

---

middle panel is the coherency function of RA activity relative to HVc spikes (at time delay = 0), and has a peak with time delay > 0, indicating increased RA firing probability after HVc spikes. The bottom panel is the coherency function of LMAN activity relative to HVc spikes (at time delay = 0): this exhibits two peaks, one with a negative, and the other, a positive time delay, indicating increased LMAN firing probability before and after HVc spikes, respectively. The peak with the long negative time delay is the correlation between LMAN and HVc that is critical to the RA-leading-LMAN correlation.

cal and subcortical connections $(0.02–0.20)$.[49–52] Strikingly, however, the coherency strength between song nuclei separated by three or more synapses was also of the same order of magnitude as that of the direct connections and thus did not show the expected exponential decay across synapses.

Such resilient long-range correlations have not been experimentally observed previously, and their presence in the song system suggests that the song nuclei have a particular form of functional connectivity. That is, if neurons were connected serially and with sparse interconnectivity both within and across nuclei (FIG. 8B), the probability of detecting correlated activity between indirectly connected neurons should indeed be low. However, if neurons in a circuit have extensive intrinsic connectivity within nuclei, as well as convergence and divergence of connections across nuclei (FIG. 8C), the probability of seeing correlation across multiple synapses is much higher. In such an architecture, each cell has numerous chances to drive target neurons as well as to receive inputs, which compensates for the unreliability of individual connections and can preserve or restore a degree of correlation within each downstream nucleus. This has been demonstrated in theoretical models of such connectivity.[75,107] The correlation data thus suggest that information in the song system is processed by a highly functionally interconnected network of neurons, which could preserve the temporal relationship of firing of neuronal assemblies across multiple synaptic steps.

Anatomical and electrophysiological data support such an architecture for the song system. Many neurons within HVc and within LMAN[25,54] fire with a similar temporal profile in relation to song, and thus may be synchronized. Synchronization has been directly observed between the bursting spikes (spike rates > 100 Hz) of RA-projecting HVc neurons and HVc interneurons.[55] HVc has broad intrinsic connectivity and its projections to RA and Area X are widely divergent.[56–58] Moreover, even though there is topography of connections within the AFP,[59,60] intrinsic connections such as horizontal connections within LMAN[61] or the long-range interneu-

---

FIGURE 8. Multi-synapse correlations and functional architecture. (**A**) The schematic on the right outlines the experimental disruption of HVC activity with kynurenate while recording LMAN-RA correlations. The left panel shows the LMAN-RA coherency function before and during disruption of HVc activity. The *shaded area* represents the extent of decrease in coherency as a result of HVc inactivation. Note that there is not a significant RA-leading-LMAN peak during HVc disruption. (**B**) The average percentage of the area under the coherency curve retained during disruption of HVc activity. Error bars indicate standard error. (**C**) Examples of possible patterns of functional connectivity in the song system. Each row of circles denotes neurons within a song nucleus and each row represents a different song nucleus. The models in (1) and (3) are extreme possibilities, while that in (2) is one of a number of possible intermediate patterns. (1) Functional connectivity organized in a parallel manner with sparse connections between neurons. (2) Convergence and divergence of inputs from the first to the second step, and subsequent sparse connections, and a varying degree of short- and long-range intrinsic connectivity within nuclei (which could be direct or via interneurons). (3) Extensive convergence and divergence of functional connections between nuclei, and short and long-range intrinsic connections within each nucleus. The activity in neurons labeled 1 and 2 is more likely to be correlated in circuit patterns (2) or (3) than in (1). Convergence and divergence only at some of the levels, as in (2), would still increase the likelihood of observing correlations across a network.

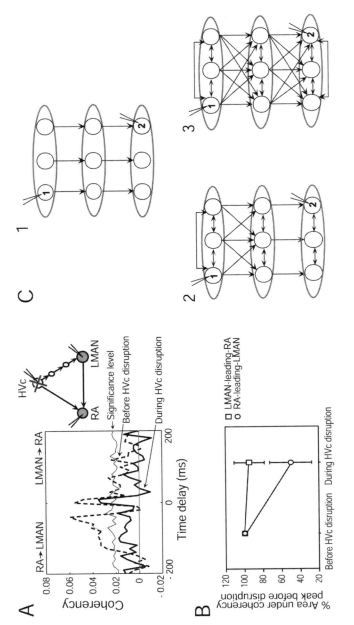

FIGURE 8. *See previous page for legend.*

rons within RA that can synchronize RA projection neuron activity,[62] may act to preserve the correlation of activity even across topographical compartments.

The extensive interconnectivity within the AFP that is suggested by the RA-leading-LMAN correlation raises the possibility that AFP signals important for vocal plasticity are encoded in the correlated firing of ensembles of AFP neurons. The degree of correlated activity in the AFP may influence the extent to which the AFP can modulate RA activity. These results also suggest that information about the overall temporal pattern of song-related activity is preserved in the form of correlated activity as it moves across processing steps. That is, waves of broadly correlated activity appear to propagate through the two song pathways, converging at RA with a time difference of approximately 60 msec. Such temporally offset waves of correlated activity could be critical for learning and generation of motor sequences, or for a delayed reinforcement signal. It will be critical in the future to compare correlation between awake and sleeping or anesthetized animals, as recent results suggest that levels of synchronization may vary greatly between awake and asleep states.[63] Indeed, the striking propagation of correlated activity across the song circuit seen in anesthetized birds could reflect information processing particularly relevant to consolidation of learned patterns of activity during sleep.[36]

Our results suggest further strong parallels between the songbird circuitry and the mammalian cortical-basal ganglia circuits with which it shares homology.[64–66] In mammals, too, there are widely divergent and convergent connections from cortical regions onto their targets in the striatum.[67–69] Although striatal projections are organized in segregated channels,[70] some striatal interneurons show synchronized firing that could act to link output channels.[71] It has been proposed that the anatomical connectivity of these pathways allows broad information sharing between subcircuits, but the extent to which subcircuits fire independently is functionally modulated, especially in learning or disease.[72–74] Our data from the song system suggest that temporally correlated patterns of activity may be important generally for behaviors mediated by cortical-basal ganglia circuits, and perhaps more tractable to analyze in the context of a specialized basal ganglia circuit.

Finally, although in these experiments most correlation functions showed two well-separated and significant peaks, occasional LMAN-RA coherency functions were well-fit by two peaks, but these peaks were either not well-separated in time and/or one of them was not significant.[37] It was always the timing and strength of the RA-leading-LMAN peak that appeared to vary in strength or timing (shifting closer to zero), while the LMAN-leading-RA peak remained significant and had a time delay similar to that in functions with two clear well-separated peaks. Similarly, the HVc-RA coherency function consistently exhibited a significant peak, while the AFP correlation varied (in parallel with the RA-leading-LMAN peak). Thus the multi-stage correlation through the AFP appears to be the more labile of the two correlations that generate the RA-leading-LMAN correlation.

Although some of this variation in the AFP correlation may reflect random sampling of different pre-existing types of connectivity in our experiments, it could also reflect active modulation of the state of connectivity within the AFP. The likely importance of horizontal interconnectivity in propagation of correlations[75] suggests that acute or long-lasting changes in the strength of this connectivity could dramatically affect information transmission in correlated circuits such as the AFP. In future experiments, it will be important to measure the correlation of AFP activity in singing birds in different states, for instance during directed or undirected singing, or in cases where the bird sings a good version of his target song compared to an imperfect version. In mammalian basal ganglia, marked changes in functional connectivity have been observed as a result of alterations in the level of dopamine.[71,72,76,108] HVc, LMAN, and Area X receive extensive dopaminergic projections from the midbrain.[64,77–79] The song system may be especially well-suited to assessing the effects of state-dependent or pathological changes in dopamine on basal ganglia circuit correlations and the functional effects of such modulation of correlation.

SYNAPTIC MECHANISMS THAT COULD UNDERLIE SONG LEARNING

Finally, learning in the song system raises the question of what cellular and molecular mechanisms of plasticity might be involved. For instance, there must be experience-driven cellular and synaptic changes that enable the bird to store a tutor song memory. Moreover, the emergence of song selectivity, such as in the LMAN studies described above, implies that neurons must dramatically change their synaptic inputs and responses so that although initially broadly responsive, the same neurons later respond only to certain sequences of sounds. Developmental investigations of these neurons point to potentially important cellular changes during learning: in particular, NMDA receptors (NMDARs) are strongly expressed in LMAN of young birds and are significantly downregulated by the end of the sensory critical period.[80] Moreover, blockade of NMDARs in LMAN during tutoring has been shown to prevent birds from producing a good copy of the tutor song,[31] consistent with LMAN contributing to tutor song memorization. These results suggest the hypothesis that NMDAR-dependent long-term plasticity is present in LMAN during sensory learning. Such plasticity could contribute to the experience-dependent shaping of auditory responses in LMAN and to the memorization of tutor song.

We investigated the hypothesis that LMAN synapses of young birds can undergo activity-dependent plasticity with an *in vitro* zebra finch brain slice preparation (FIG. 9A). Using slices from zebra finches early in sensory learning and not yet engaged in sensorimotor learning of song (20 days of age; FIG. 1A),[7,81] we made intracellular voltage recordings from LMAN principal neurons. There are two known excitatory glutamatergic inputs to these cells: afferents from the medial portion of the dorsolateral thalamus (DLM) and the recurrent axon collateral inputs that interconnect neurons within the nucleus (LMAN$_R$; FIG. 9A). We focused on the LMAN$_R$ synapses, which can be activated by stimulating the LMAN outflow tract, because they have a significantly greater NMDAR-mediated component at the cell's resting potential (V_{REST}) at 20 days than do the DLM synapses.[82–84] Moreover, these recurrent synapses are likely to be very important to the correlations described in the previous section.

Plasticity was induced by repeated (40×) delivery of single brief (100 msec) pulses of postsynaptic depolarizing current in conjunction with LMAN$_R$ stimulation. Each current injection elicited a burst of 6–10 action potentials (APs) whose duration approximated the duration of the current pulse. This pairing protocol produced a long-lasting increase of the LMAN$_R$ EPSP slope. On average, the mean LMAN$_R$

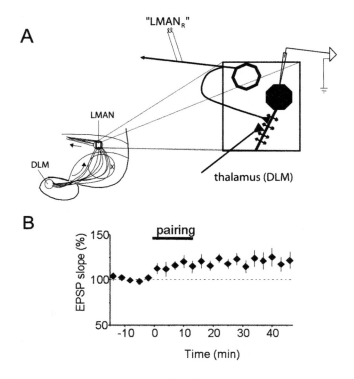

FIGURE 9. Synaptic plasticity in the LMAN slice. (**A**) Schematic of recording set-up. Slices were cut oblique to the parasagittal plane. The thalamic inputs to LMAN (DLM) come in from below, while the recurrent collaterals between LMAN neurons (LMAN$_R$) interconnect LMAN neurons within the nucleus. The LMAN$_R$ stimulating electrode was placed in the LMAN outflow tract, thus activating these recurrent axon collaterals. Electrode placement was adjusted so that the neuron being recorded was not antidromically activated. The recording electrode used to investigate LMAN synapses was also used to inject current and elicit bursting. (**B**) Summary of LMAN$_R$ data from 12 birds of approximately 20 days of age. The slope of LMAN$_R$ extracellular synaptic potentials was significantly increased 30 min after pairing stimulation of LMAN$_R$ inputs with postsynaptic depolarizing bursts. (From Doupe et al.[109] In The Cognitive Neurosciences III, M. Gazzaniga, Ed. Reprinted with permission from MIT Press and the editor.)

EPSP slope 30 min after pairing onset was increased by 21% relative to baseline (FIG. 9B), and when stable recordings could be maintained to 60 min after pairing, EPSP slopes were increased by 33% relative to baseline. Consistent with many other forms of cortical and hippocampal potentiation, the induction of LMAN$_R$ LTP depended on NMDAR activation: the presence of the NMDAR blocker DL-2-amino-5-phosphonovaleric acid (APV) during pairing blocked the increase in LMAN$_R$ responses normally observed after pairing and instead produced a small but significant depression.[61]

The changes in the LMAN$_R$ EPSP elicited by the pairing protocol also depended on the timing of the first spike elicited by the current injection relative to the onset of the EPSP (FIG. 10A). When the first spike occurred after the $LMAN_R$ EPSP onset ("spike lags"; FIG. 10A, right inset), the $LMAN_R$ pathway was potentiated. In contrast, when the first spike in the burst preceded the EPSP onset ("spike leads"; FIG. 10A, left inset), potentiation did not occur and in some cases the $LMAN_R$ EPSP was depressed. The pairing protocol induced significantly less potentiation of $LMAN_R$ responses in spike-leading versus spike-lagging experiments (FIG. 10A). Thus $LMAN_R$ LTP in 20-day-old birds exhibits timing dependence, a computationally important feature[85,86] recently described in several systems.[87–94] While the EPSP-AP burst pairing used in these experiments established this timing dependence, further experiments using a single AP will be necessary to provide a more complete description of the timing rule for $LMAN_R$ synapses. Moreover, the lack of LTP induction when the first spike of a burst preceded the EPSP, despite subsequent spikes following the EPSP, suggests that the first spike plays a critical role in determining the sign of long term plasticity in LMAN.[92]

Blockade of NMDARs in LMAN during tutoring, which impairs tutor learning,[31] would also have prevented the $LMAN_R$ LTP described in 20-day-old finches. Lack of this LTP could thus be one factor preventing the incorporation of new tutor song information in young NMDAR-blocked birds. In addition, if $LMAN_R$ LTP is critical to sensory learning, a decrease in $LMAN_R$ LTP inducibility might also occur developmentally, contributing to the normal closure of the critical period for memorization of tutor song at approximately 60 days in zebra finches (FIG. 1A).[7,8,96] To test this prediction, we paired postsynaptic bursts with $LMAN_R$ synaptic stimulation in slices from birds of 60 days of age.

The effect of the induction protocol on LMAN neurons' intrinsic synaptic inputs was strikingly different at this later age. Instead of inducing a potentiation of the $LMAN_R$ responses, a significant depression of $LMAN_R$ responses was observed at 30 min after spike-lagging pairing (average of -14%; FIG. 10B). This represented a significant decrease in the ability of the pairing protocol to induce $LMAN_R$ LTP at 60 days of age compared to that at 20 days of age. While these results do not rule out the possibility that potentiation of $LMAN_R$ responses could still be induced in older birds by a less physiological protocol, they indicate that the threshold for induction of this plasticity is substantially higher by the end of sensory learning. In addition, the change in sign of the plasticity at the $LMAN_R$ synapses suggests that functionally significant changes have taken place at these connections by 60 days of age.

Thus, long-term synaptic plasticity of intrinsic LMAN synapses can be induced by pairing stimulation of these synapses with postsynaptic bursts of APs. This supports the idea that excitatory feedback connections are key sites of synaptic plasticity within neural networks[95] and raises the possibility that the degree of correlation between principal neurons in LMAN may be shaped by plastic mechanisms. This $LMAN_R$ LTP, which depends on both NMDAR activation and the timing of the AP burst, was present at a time when sensory learning is occurring and was no longer evident by the close of the sensory critical period. This timing suggests that it may play a role in tutor song memorization and/or in the early stages of sensorimotor evaluation and refinement of song and of song-selective neurons. An advantage of the song system is that such correlations can be further tested in a straightforward manner by manipulating learning. For instance, raising zebra finches in isolation extends the normal critical period for tutor song learning.[81,96] If $LMAN_R$ LTP is critical for song memorization, it should still be present in slices from 60-day-old finches

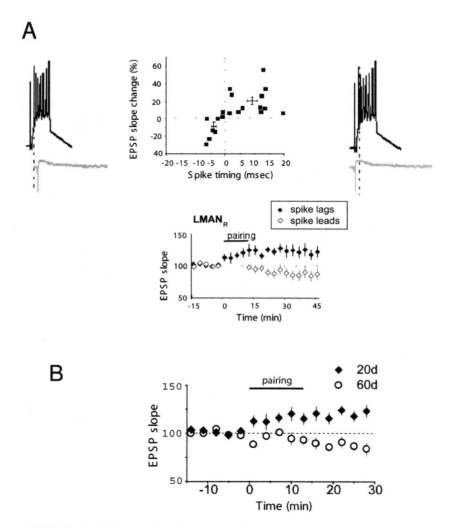

FIGURE 10. Timing- and age-dependence of LMAN$_R$ LTP. (**A**) LMAN$_R$ potentiation is dependent on the relative timing between the EPSP onset and the peak of the first spike elicited by the current injection; individual examples of postsynaptic spikes lagging (right inset) and leading (left inset) EPSPs are shown. The upper graph plots the percent change of LMAN$_R$ EPSP slope at 30' vs. spike timing relative to EPSP onset. Cross-hairs denote mean ± SEM for spike lagging & spike leading data. The lower graph plots group data showing the significant difference between LMAN$_R$ EPSPs subjected to spike-lagging (◆, N=12) vs. spike-leading (◇, N=8) pairing. (**B**) LMAN$_R$ group data reveals the significant difference between the effects of the pairing protocol on slices from 20- and 60-day-old birds. At 60 days of age, LMAN$_R$ pairing induced no significant potentiation, instead eliciting depression. (From Doupe *et al.*[109] *In* The Cognitive Neurosciences III, M. Gazzaniga, Ed. Reprinted with permission from MIT Press and the editor.)

raised in isolation. Alternatively, if LMAN$_R$ LTP is induced by early sensorimotor matching and development of song selectivity, it might still be inducible in 60-day-old birds that have memorized tutor song normally but have been prevented from hearing their own voice and refining their song (for instance by muting or otherwise preventing audible auditory feedback). Given this ability to alter the behavior very specifically, circuitry in LMAN, and the song system as a whole, may prove to be particularly advantageous for pursuing a causal link between experience-dependent changes in synaptic strength and the learning of a complex behavior.

Finally, such spike timing–dependent LMAN$_R$ plasticity provides a simple and plausible mechanism for storage and recognition of a temporal pattern, such as a song memory.[97,98] This plasticity could be useful for generating connectivity within LMAN that reflects the temporal pattern of DLM afferent activity elicited by the tutor song and thus can predict that pattern. That is, if different subsets of DLM afferents fire at different time points in response to the sound of the tutor song, LMAN$_R$ LTP would cause groups of LMAN neurons activated by DLM at one point in time to strengthen their connections onto assemblies of LMAN neurons activated by DLM at a subsequent time point (FIG. 11). In contrast, because of the spike timing-dependence of LMAN$_R$ LTP, the reciprocal LMAN$_R$ connections would weaken or remain static. These changes in synaptic strength over the course of sensory learning

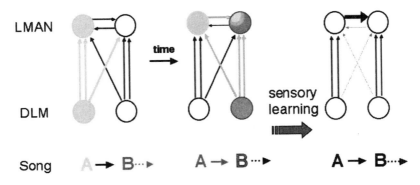

FIGURE 11. A simple model depicting a possible role for LMAN plasticity in song learning. During sensory learning, LMAN plasticity may establish a prediction within the recurrent circuitry of the temporal pattern of DLM afferent activation elicited by tutor song. A segment of tutor song "A" would elicit firing in a subset of DLM projection neurons (*left panel, light gray*), which in turn would activate a subset of LMAN neurons (*light gray*), including their recurrent projections onto other LMAN neurons. Those LMAN neurons (*light and dark gray*) activated by collateral inputs and simultaneously by DLM inputs responding to the next chunk of song "B" (*middle panel, dark gray*), would experience the conjunction required for LMAN$_R$ LTP. Over the course of sensory learning, the spike timing–dependent strengthening of LMAN$_R$ synapses would come to reflect the temporal pattern of DLM afferent activation by tutor song (*right panel*). During subsequent sensorimotor learning, the production of the correct A-B sequence could lead to firing of strong LMAN$_R$ inputs driven by A coincident with spikes driven by B, leading to enhanced LMAN neuronal activity; this could represent an instructive signal for guiding vocal motor output at RA. (From Doupe *et al.*[109] *In* The Cognitive Neurosciences III, M. Gazzaniga, Ed. Reprinted with permission from MIT Press and the editor.)

would come to represent the temporal pattern of DLM afferent activation in response to tutor song. Circuitry organized in this fashion could represent a memory of the tutor song, reminiscent of a proposed model for sequence prediction in the hippocampus.[98] During sensorimotor learning, such circuitry could then preferentially reinforce motor sequences produced by the bird that sound adequately similar to the tutor song.[99]

CONCLUSIONS

The studies here used a combination of neurophysiological studies and manipulations of both behavior and circuits to examine the function of the AFP, investigating not only normal birds at different stages of development but also animals in which the usual relationship between vocal motor output and sensory input had been in some way disrupted. The results reveal that AFP neurons develop auditory selectivity during learning for both BOS and tutor song, are densely functionally interconnected, and have synaptic mechanisms appropriate for developing temporal selectivity for song.

AFP neurons appear to reflect multiple sensory and motor aspects of song, suggesting that these processes are almost inextricably entangled, even at the level of single neurons. In this respect, birdsong is reminiscent of human speech[1]: electrical stimulation of a single language area can affect both production and perception of speech,[100] and some cortical neurons respond differently to the same word depending on whether it was spoken by the subject, or by someone else.[101] Perhaps this entanglement indicates that the primary task assigned to the song system, and to many speech areas as well, is not sensory learning, but rather the sensorimotor learning required to produce a vocal imitation. This undertaking alone may be sufficient to have created the need for the song system, and to have specialized it for sensorimotor processing, with much of the initial sensory processing and memorizing of songs taking place elsewhere in the brain. It is relevant in this regard that the AFP is a cortical-basal ganglia circuit.[65,102] Such basal ganglia circuits, which are well conserved evolutionarily, are generally implicated in motor and reinforcement learning, functions critical to sensorimotor learning of song.

The present results also stress the importance of the properties of networks, not just of single neurons, in song learning and production. There is strong functional interconnectivity between many song neurons, allowing waves of correlated activity to propagate through the system. Moreover, it is the horizontal synapses in LMAN, critical to firing of groups of neurons within the nucleus, that show spike timing–dependent plasticity restricted to early learning. Mammalian basal ganglia circuits also have strong interconnectivity that has been proposed to be functionally modulated both in learning and disease states.[74,103] In primates, striatal neurons carry sensory and motor signals as well as predictive information related to movement and reward and might participate in comparisons of motor output to internal models,[104–106] as the AFP is proposed to do. Spike timing–dependent plasticity similar to that observed here could be involved in generating such predictions. Like mammalian basal ganglia, AFP neurons could receive or even compute reinforcement signals, perhaps encoding them in part in the degree of neuronal correlation within the network, and transfer them to the motor pathway. Because the AFP is a discrete basal ganglia–

forebrain circuit specialized for one well-defined behavior, it may prove a particularly tractable system for elucidating the neural signals present in these structures, both at circuit and synaptic levels, and their function in the learning and modification of sequenced motor acts.

ACKNOWLEDGMENTS

The work described here was supported by the National Institutes of Health (MH55987 and NS34835 to A.J.D., an National Institute of General Medical Sciences training grant to R.R.K., MH11896 to C.A.B.), a National Sciences Foundation graduate fellowship (MMS), and the John Merck Fund, the National Alliance for Research on Schizophrenia and Depression, the Steven and Michele Kirsch Foundation, and the MacArthur Foundation Network on Early Experience and Brain Development (A.J.D.). M.S. Brainard provided thoughtful comments on an earlier version of the manuscript, and Paul Puri and Maureen Leung provided invaluable editorial assistance.

REFERENCES

1. DOUPE, A.J. & P.K. KUHL. 1999. Birdsong and human speech: common themes and mechanisms. Annu. Rev. Neurosci. **22:** 567–631.
2. WALDSTEIN, R.S. 1990. Effects of postlingual deafness on speech production: implications for the role of auditory feedback. J. Acoust. Soc. Am. **88:** 2099–2144.
3. KONISHI, M. 1965. The role of auditory feedback in the control of vocalization in the white-crowned sparrow. Z. Tierpsychol. **22:** 770–783.
4. NORDEEN, K.W. & E.J. NORDEEN. 1992. Auditory feedback is necessary for the maintenance of stereotyped song in adult zebra finches. Behav. Neural. Biol. **57:** 58–66.
5. PRICE, P.H. 1979. Developmental determinants of structure in zebra finch song. J. Comp. Phys. Psych. **93:** 268–277.
6. MARLER, P. 1970. A comparative approach to vocal learning: song development in white-crowned sparrows. J. Comp. Phys. Pyschol. **71:** 1–25.
7. IMMELMANN, K. 1969. Song development in the zebra finch and other estrildid finches. *In* Bird Vocalizations. R.A. Hinde, Ed.: 61–74. Cambridge University Press. London.
8. EALES, L.A. 1985. Song learning in zebra finches: some effects of song model availability on what is learnt and when. Anim. Behav. **33:** 1293–1300.
9. NORDEEN, E.J. & K.W. NORDEEN. 1992. Auditory feedback is necessary for the maintenance of stereotyped song in adult zebra finches. Behav. Neural Biol. **57:** 58–66.
10. LEONARDO, A. & M. KONISHI. 1999. Decrystallization of adult birdsong by perturbation of auditory feedback. Nature **399:** 466–470.
11. NOTTEBOHM, F., T.M. STOKES & A.P. ARNOLD. 1976. Central control of song in the canary, *Serinus canarius.* J. Comp. Neurol. **165:** 457–486.
12. BOTTJER, S.W., E.A. MIESNER & A.P. ARNOLD. 1984. Forebrain lesions disrupt development but not maintenance of song in passerine birds. Science **224:** 901–903.
13. SOHRABJI, F., E.J. NORDEEN & K.W. NORDEEN. 1990. Selective impairment of song learning following lesions of a forebrain nucleus in the juvenile zebra finch. Behav. Neural. Biol. **53:** 51–63.
14. SCHARFF, C. & F. NOTTEBOHM. 1991. A comparative study of the behavioral deficits following lesions of various parts of the zebra finch song system: implications for vocal learning. J. Neurosci. **11:** 2896–2913.
15. WILLIAMS, H. & N. MEHTA. 1999. Changes in adult zebra finch song require a forebrain nucleus that is not necessary for song production. J. Neurobiol. **39:** 14–28.
16. BRAINARD, M.S. & A.J. DOUPE. 2000. Interruption of a basal ganglia-forebrain circuit prevents plasticity of learned vocalizations. Nature **404:** 762–766.

17. BRAINARD, M.S. & A.J. DOUPE. 2000. Auditory feedback in learning and maintenance of vocal behavior. Nat. Rev. Neurosci. **1:** 31–40.
18. MCCASLAND, J.S. & M. KONISHI. 1981. Interactions between auditory and motor activities in an avian song control nucleus. Proc. Natl. Acad. Sci. USA **78:** 7815–7819.
19. MARGOLIASH, D. 1983. Acoustic parameters underlying the responses of song-specific neurons in the white-crowned sparrow. J. Neurosci. **3:** 1039–1057.
20. DOUPE, A.J. & M. KONISHI. 1991. Song-selective auditory circuits in the vocal control system of the zebra finch. Proc. Natl. Acad. Sci. USA **88:** 11339–11343.
21. DAVE, A.S. & D. MARGOLIASH. 2000. Song replay during sleep and computational rules for sensorimotor vocal learning. Science **290:** 812–816.
22. SOLIS, M. & A. DOUPE. 2000. Compromised neural selectivity for song in birds with impaired sensorimotor learning. Neuron **25:** 109–121
23. SOLIS, M.M. & A.J. DOUPE. 1997. Anterior forebrain neurons develop selectivity by an intermediate stage of birdsong learning. J. Neurosci. **17:** 6447–6462.
24. SOLIS, M.M. & A.J. DOUPE. 1999. Contributions of tutor and bird's own song experience to neural selectivity in the songbird anterior forebrain. J. Neurosci. **19:** 4559–4584.
25. DOUPE, A.J. 1997. Song- and order-selective neurons in the songbird anterior forebrain and their emergence during vocal development. J. Neurosci. **17:** 1147–1167.
26. VOLMAN, S.F. 1993. Development of neural selectivity for birdsong during vocal learning. J. Neurosci. **13:** 4737–4747.
27. KUHL, P.K. 1995. Learning and representation in speech and language. Curr. Opin. Neurobiol. **4:** 812–822.
28. WERKER, J.F. & R.C. TEES. 1984. Phonemic and phonetic factors in adult cross-language speech perception. J. Acoust. Soc. Am. **75:** 1866–1878.
29. HESSLER, N.A. & A.J. DOUPE. 1999. Social context modulates singing-related neural activity in the songbird forebrain. Nat. Neurosci. **2:** 209–211.
30. HESSLER, N.A. & A.J. DOUPE. 1999. Singing-related neural activity in a dorsal forebrain-basal ganglia circuit of adult zebra finches. J. Neurosci. **19:** 10461–10481.
31. BASHAM, M.E., E.J. NORDEEN & K.W. NORDEEN. 1996. Blockade of NMDA receptors in the anterior forebrain impairs sensory acquisition in the zebra finch. Neurobiol. Learning Mem. **66:** 295–304.
32. SOLIS, M.M., M.S. BRAINARD, N.A. HESSLER & A.J. DOUPE. 2000. Song selectivity and sensorimotor signals in vocal learning and production. Proc. Natl. Acad. Sci. USA **97:** 11836–11842.
33. MELLO, C.V., D.S. VICARIO & D.F. CLAYTON. 1992. Song presentation induces gene expression in the songbird forebrain. Proc. Natl. Acad. Sci. USA **89:** 6818–6822.
34. BOLHUIS, J.J., G.G. ZIJLSTRA, A.M. DEN BOER-VISSER & E.A. VAN DER ZEE. 2000. Localized neuronal activation in the zebra finch brain is related to the strength of song learning. Proc. Natl. Acad. Sci. USA **97:** 2282–2285.
35. VICARIO, D.S. & K.H. YOHAY. 1993. Song-selective auditory input to a forebrain vocal control nucleus in the zebra finch. J. Neurobiol. **24:** 488–505.
36. DAVE, A.S., A.C. YU & D. MARGOLIASH. 1998. Behavioral state modulation of auditory activity in a vocal motor system. Science **282:** 2250–2254.
37. KIMPO, R.R., F.E. THEUNISSEN & A.J. DOUPE. 2003. Propagation of correlated activity through multiple stages of a neural circuit. J. Neurosci. **23:** 5750–5761.
38. ROSENBERG, J.R., A.M. AMJAD, P. BREEZE, et al. 1989. The fourier approach to the identification of functional coupling between neuronal spike trains. Prog. Biophys. Molec. Biol. **53:** 1–31.
39. BOTTJER, S.W., K.A. HALSEMA, S.A. BROWN & E.A. MIESNER. 1989. Axonal connections of a forebrain nucleus involved with vocal learning in zebra finches. J. Comp. Neurol. **279:** 312–326.
40. MOONEY, R. 1992. Synaptic basis for developmental plasticity in a birdsong nucleus. J. Neurosci. **12:** 2464–2477.
41. VATES, G., D. VICARIO & F. NOTTEBOHM. 1997. Reafferent thalamo-"cortical" loops in the song system of oscine songbirds. J. Comp. Neurol. **380:** 275–290.
42. FROSTIG, R.D., Y. GOTTLIEB, E. VAADIA & M. ABELES. 1983. The effects of stimuli on the activity and functional connectivity of local neuronal groups in cat auditory cortex. Brain Res. **272:** 211–221.

43. GOCHIN, P.M., E.K. MILLER, C.G. GROSS & G.L. GERSTEIN. 1991. Functional interactions among neurons in inferior temporal cortex of the awake macaque. Exp. Brain Res. **84**: 505–516.
44. MASON, A., A. NICOLL & K. STRATFORD. 1991. Synaptic transmission between individual pyramidal neurons of the rat visual cortex *in vitro*. J. Neurosci. **11**: 72–84.
45. EGGERMONT, J.J. 1992. Neural interaction in cat primary auditory cortex. Dependence on recording depth, electrode separation, and age. J. Neurophysiol. **68**: 1216–1228.
46. SHADLEN, M.N. & W.T. NEWSOME. 1998. The variable discharge of cortical neurons: implications for connectivity, computation, and information coding. J. Neurosci. **18**: 3870–3896.
47. STEVENS, C.F. & A.M. ZADOR. 1998. Input synchrony and the irregular firing of cortical neurons. Nat. Neurosci. **1**: 210–217.
48. CHOI, S. & D.M. LOVINGER. 1997. Decreased frequency but not amplitude of quantal synaptic responses associated with expression of corticostriatal long-term depression. J. Neurosci. **17**: 8613–8620.
49. ABELES, M., E. VAADIA, H. BERGMAN, *et al.* 1993. Dynamics of neuronal interaction in the frontal cortex of behaving monkeys. Concepts Neurosci. **4**: 131.
50. VAADIA, E., I. HAALMAN, M. ABELES, *et al.* 1995. Dynamics of neuronal interactions in monkey cortex in relation to behavioural events. Nature **373**: 515–518.
51. ALONSO, J. & L.M. MARTINEZ. 1998. Functional connectivity between simple cells and complex cells in cat striate cortex. Nat. Neurosci. **1**: 395–403.
52. EGGERMONT, J.J. & G.M. SMITH. 1996. Neural connectivity only accounts for a small part of neural correlation in auditory cortex. Exp. Brain Res. **110**: 379–391.
53. EIMAS, P.D., J.L. MILLER & P.W. JUSCZYK. 1987 On infant speech perception and language acquisition. *In* Categorical Perception. S. Harnard, Ed.: 161–195. Cambridge University Press. New York.
54. SUTTER M.L. & D. MARGOLIASH. 1994. Global synchronous response to autogenous song in zebra finch HVc. J. Neurophysiol. **72**: 2105–2123.
55. HAHNLOSER, R.H., A.A. KOZHEVNIKOV & M.S. FEE. 2002. An ultra-sparse code underlies the generation of neural sequences in a songbird. Nature **419**: 65–70.
56. FORTUNE, E.S. & D. MARGOLIASH. 1995. Parallel pathways and convergence onto HVc and adjacent neostriatum of adult zebra finches (*Taeniopygia guttata*). J. Comp. Neurol. **360**: 413–441.
57. VATES, G.E. & F. NOTTEBOHM. 1995. Feedback circuitry within a song-learning pathway. Proc. Natl. Acad. Sci. USA **92**: 5139–5143.
58. FOSTER, E.F. & S.W. BOTTJER. 1998. Axonal connections of the high vocal center and surrounding cortical regions in juvenile and adult male zebra finches. J. Comp. Neurol. **397**: 118–138.
59. JOHNSON, F., M.M. SABLAN & S.W. BOTTJER. 1995. Topographic organization of a forebrain pathway involved with vocal learning in zebra finches. J. Comp. Neurol. **358**: 260–278.
60. LUO, M., L. DING & D.J. PERKEL. 2001. An avian basal ganglia pathway essential for vocal learning forms a closed topographic loop. J. Neurosci. **21**: 6836–6845.
61. BOETTIGER, C.A. & A.J. DOUPE. 2001. Developmentally restricted synaptic plasticity in a songbird nucleus required for song learning. Neuron **31**: 809–818.
62. SPIRO, J.E., M.B. DALVA & R. MOONEY. 1999. Long-range inhibition within the zebra finch song nucleus RA can coordinate the firing of multiple projection neurons. J. Neurophysiol. **81**: 3007–3020.
63. CARDIN, J.A. & M.F. SCHMIDT. 2004. Auditory responses in multiple sensorimotor song system nuclei are co-modulated by behavioral state. J. Neurophysiol. (online preprint—"Articles in Press")
64. BOTTJER, S.W. 1993. The distribution of tyrosine hydroxylase immunoreactivity in the brains of male and female zebra finches. J. Neurobiol. **24**: 51–69.
65. BOTTJER, S.W. & F. JOHNSON. 1997. Circuits, hormones, and learning: vocal behavior in songbirds. J. Neurobiol. **33**: 602–618.
66. PERKEL, D.J. & M.A. FARRIES. 2000. Complementary "bottom-up" and "top-down" approaches to basal ganglia function. Curr. Opin. Neurobiol. **10**: 725–731.
67. GRAYBIEL, A.M., T. AOSAKI, A.W. FLAHERTY & M. KIMURA. 1994. The basal ganglia and adaptive motor control. Science **265**: 1826–1831.

68. GRAYBIEL, A.M. 1998. The basal ganglia and chunking of action repertoires. Neurobiol. Learn. Mem. **70:** 119–136.
69. PARENT, A., F. SATO, Y. WU, *et al.* 2000. Organization of the basal ganglia: the importance of axonal collateralization. Trends Neurosci. **23:** S20–S27.
70. MIDDLETON, F.A. & P.L. STRICK. 2000. Basal ganglia and cerebellar loops: motor and cognitive circuits. Brain Res. Brain Res. Rev. **31:** 236–250.
71. RAZ, A., A. FEINGOLD, V. ZELANSKAYA, *et al.* 1996. Neuronal synchronization of tonically active neurons in the striatum of normal and parkinsonian primates. J. Neurophysiol. **76:** 2083–2088.
72. BERGMAN, H., A. FEINGOLD, A. NINI, *et al.* 1998. Physiological aspects of information processing in the basal ganglia of normal and parkinsonian primates. Trends Neurosci. **21:** 32–38.
73. BAR-GAD, I. & H. BERGMAN. 2001. Stepping out of the box: information processing in the neuronal networks of the basal ganglia. Curr. Opin. Neurobiol. **11:** 689–695.
74. BEVAN, M.D., P.J. MAGILL, D. TERMAN, *et al.* 2002. Move to the rhythm: oscillations in the subthalamic nucleus-external globus pallidus network. Trends Neurosci. **25:** 525–531.
75. STROEVE, S. & S. GIELEN. 2001. Correlation between uncoupled conductance-based integrate-and-fire neurons due to common and synchronous presynaptic firing. Neural Comput. **13:** 2005–2029.
76. RUSKIN, D.N., D.A. BERGSTROM, Y. KANEOKE, *et al.* 1999. Multisecond oscillations in firing rate in the basal ganglia: robust modulation by dopamine receptor activation and anesthesia. J. Neurophysiol. **81:** 2046–2055.
77. LEWIS, J.W., S.M. RYAN, A.P. ARNOLD & L.L. BUTCHER. 1981. Evidence for a catecholaminergic projection to area X in the zebra finch. J. Comp. Neurol. **196:** 347–354.
78. SOHA, J.A., T. SHIMIZU & A.J. DOUPE. 1996. Development of the catecholaminergic innervation of the song system of the male zebra finch. J. Neurobiol. **29:** 473–489.
79. APPELTANTS, D., P. ABSIL, J. BALTHAZART & G.F. BALL. 2000. Identification of the origin of catecholaminergic inputs to HVc in canaries by retrograde tract tracing combined with tyrosine hydroxylase immunocytochemistry. J. Chem. Neuroanat. **18:** 117–33.
80. AAMODT, S.M., M.R. KOZLOWSKI, E.J. NORDEEN & K.W. NORDEEN. 1992. Distribution and developmental change in [^{3}H]MK-801 binding within zebra finch song nuclei. J. Neurobiol. **23:** 997–1005.
81. EALES, L.A. 1989. The influences of visual and vocal interaction on song learning in zebra finches. Anim. Behav. **37:** 507–508.
82. BOETTIGER, C.A. & A.J. DOUPE. 1998. Intrinsic and thalamic excitatory inputs onto songbird LMAN neurons differ in their pharmacological and temporal properties. J. Neurophysiol. **79:** 2615–2628.
83. LIVINGSTON, F.S. & R. MOONEY. 1997. Development of intrinsic and synaptic properties in a forebrain nucleus essential to avian song learning. J. Neurosci. **17:** 8997–9009.
84. BOTTJER, S.W., J.D. BRADY & J.P. WALSH. 1998. Intrinsic and synaptic properties of neurons in the vocal-control nucleus IMAN in vitro slice preparations from juvenile and adult zebra finches. J. Neurobiol. **37:** 642–658.
85. ROBERTS, P.D. 1999. Computational consequences of temporally asymmetric learning rules: I. Differential Hebbian learning. J. Comput. Neurosci. **7:** 235–246.
86. SONG, S., K.D. MILLER & L.F. ABBOTT. 2000. Competitive Hebbian learning through spike-timing-dependent synaptic plasticity. Nat Neurosci. **3:** 919–926.
87. BELL, C.C., V.Z. HAN, Y. SUGAWARA & K. GRANT. 1997. Synaptic plasticity in a cerebellum-like structure depends on temporal order. Nature **387:** 278–281.
88. MAGEE, J.C. & D. JOHNSTON. 1997. A synaptically controlled, associative signal for Hebbian plasticity in hippocampal neurons. Science **275:** 209–213.
89. MARKRAM, H., J. LUBKE, M. FROTSCHER & B. SAKMANN. 1997. Regulation of synaptic efficacy by coincidence of postsynaptic APs and EPSPs. Science **275:** 213–215.
90. BI, G.Q. & M.M. POO. 1998. Synaptic modifications in cultured hippocampal neurons: dependence on spike timing, synaptic strength, and postsynaptic cell type. J. Neurosci. **18:** 10464–10472.

91. DEBANNE, D., B.H. GAHWILER & S.M. THOMPSON. 1998. Long-term synaptic plasticity between pairs of individual CA3 pyramidal cells in rat hippocampal slice cultures. J. Physiol. **507:** 237–247.
92. ZHANG, L.I., H.W. TAO, C.E. HOLT, *et al.* 1998. A critical window for cooperation and competition among developing retinotectal synapses. Nature **395:** 37–44.
93. EGGER, V., D. FELDMEYER & B. SAKMANN. 1999. Coincidence detection and changes of synaptic efficacy in spiny stellate neurons in rat barrel cortex. Nat. Neurosci. **2:** 1098–1105.
94. FELDMAN, D.E. 2000. Timing-based LTP and LTD at vertical inputs to layer II/III pyramidal cells in rat barrel cortex. Neuron **27:** 45–56.
95. HUA, S.E., J.C. HOUK & F.A. MUSSA-IVALDI. 1999. Emergence of symmetric, modular, and reciprocal connections in recurrent networks with Hebbian learning. Biol. Cybern. **81:** 211–225.
96. EALES, L.A. 1987. Song learning in female-raised zebra finches: another look at the sensitive phase. Anim. Behav. **35:** 1356–1365.
97. GERSTNER, W., R. RITZ & J.L. VAN HEMMEN. 1993. Why spikes? Hebbian learning and retrieval of time-resolved excitation patterns. Biol. Cybern. **69:** 503–515.
98. ABBOTT, L.F. & K.I. BLUM. 1996. Functional significance of long-term potentiation for sequence learning and prediction. Cereb. Cortex **6:** 406–416.
99. TROYER, T. & A.J. DOUPE. 2000. An association model of birdsong sensory motor learning I. Efference copy and the learning of song syllables. J. Neurophysiol. **84:** 1204–1223
100. OJEMANN, G.A. 1991. Cortical organization of language. J. Neurosci. **11:** 2281–2287.
101. CREUTZFELDT, O., G. OJEMANN & E. LETTICH. 1989. Neuronal activity in the human lateral temporal lobe. I. Responses to speech. Exp. Brain Res. **77:** 451–475.
102. LUO, M. & D.J. PERKEL. 1999. Long-range GABAergic projection in a circuit essential for vocal learning. J. Comp. Neurol. **403:** 68–84.
103. BERGMAN, H., A. FEINGOLD, A. NINI, *et al.* 1998. Physiological aspects of information processing in the basal ganglia of normal and parkinsonian primates. Trends Neurosci. **21:** 32–38.
104. HIKOSAKA, O., M. SAKAMOTO & S. USUI. 1989. Functional properties of monkey caudate neurons. III. Activities related to expectation of target and reward. J. Neurophysiol. **61:** 814–832.
105. HOLLERMAN, J.R., L. TREMBLAY & W. SCHULTZ. 1998. Influence of reward expectation on behavior-related neuronal activity in primate striatum. J. Neurophysiol. **80:** 947–963.
106. TREMBLAY, L., J.R. HOLLERMAN & W. SCHULTZ. 1998. Modifications of reward expectation-related neuronal activity during learning in primate striatum. J. Neurophysiol. **80:** 964–977.
107. DIESMANN, M., M. GEWALTIG & A. AERTSEN. 1999. Stable propagation of synchronous spiking in cortical neural networks. Nature **402:** 529–533
108. RAZ, A., V. FRECHTER-MAZAR, A. FEINGOLD, *et al.* 2001. Activity of pallidal and striatal tonically active neuron is correlated in MPTP-treated monkeys but not in normal monkeys. J. Neurosci. **21:** 1–5.
109. DOUPE, A.J., M.M. SOLIS, C.A. BOETTIGER & N.A. HESSLER. 2004. Birdsong: hearing in the service of vocal learning. *In* The Cognitive Neurosciences III. M.S. Gazzaniga, Ed. MIT Press. Cambridge, MA.

Hormonal Modulation of Singing

Hormonal Modulation of the Songbird Brain and Singing Behavior

CHERYL F. HARDING

Psychology Department, Hunter College and Biopsychology Doctoral Program, City University of New York, New York, New York, 10021, USA

ABSTRACT: During the past three decades research on the hormonal control of singing has fundamentally altered our basic concepts about how hormones modulate brain function and activate behavior. Exciting discoveries first documented in songbird brains have since been documented in a wide variety of vertebrate species, including humans. Circulating hormones organize sexual dimorphisms in brain structure during development, activate changes in brain structure during adulthood, and modulate the addition of new neurons in the adult brain. The brain has proved to be the primary source of estrogens in general circulation in adult male finches. Studies of the hormonal modulation of singing are complicated by multiple sites of hormone production, multiple sites of hormone action, hormone metabolism by different tissues, the involvement of a variety of hormones, and the effects of social context. This chapter provides a brief review of these topics, as well as a brief overview of techniques used to study endocrine mechanisms controlling behavior.

KEYWORDS: vocal control; hormone dependent; seasonal; androgen; estrogen

HORMONES AND BEHAVIOR: AN INTRODUCTION

The term hormone is derived from the Greek word "hormao"—to stimulate. Thus, hormones were originally defined as stimulatory chemical signals secreted by endocrine glands into the bloodstream that acted at multiple sites to integrate physiology and behavior. The definition of hormones was expanded as researchers discovered that some hormones were inhibitory, some were secreted by tissues other than endocrine glands and some acted without being secreted into the bloodstream. In most cases, hormones are potentially available to every cell, depending on their rate of metabolism and clearance. Hormones exert their biologic actions by binding to specific receptors in either the cell membrane or inside the cell to activate receptor-coupled effector mechanisms.[1] Thus, hormones only affect those tissues that contain receptors (i.e., target tissues). Hydrophilic hormones (e.g., peptide/protein hormones like those of the anterior pituitary) and a few lipophilic hormones (e.g.,

Address for correspondence: Cheryl Harding, Psychology Department, Hunter College, 695 Park Avenue, New York, NY 10021. Voice: 212-772-5047; fax: 212-650-3647.
    harding@genectr.hunter.cuny.edu
    <http://sonhouse.hunter.cuny.edu/faculty/sh/harding.html>

Ann. N.Y. Acad. Sci. 1016: 524–539 (2004). © 2004 New York Academy of Sciences.
doi: 10.1196/annals.1298.030

melatonin) act through receptors in the plasma membrane. These receptors span the plasma membrane and rapidly alter cellular function by (1) modulating ion channels, membrane potential, or intracellular electrolyte composition or by (2) stimulating protein kinases inducing phosphorylation of intracellular proteins. Most lipophilic hormones (e.g., gonadal steroids) bind to intracellular receptors that act as ligand-regulated transcription factors, binding to DNA response elements and altering the transcription of specific genes and the production of proteins, such as enzymes or receptors. Effects on gene transcription are much slower than those regulated by membrane receptors. Hormone receptors typically have a high specificity and high affinity for either a specific hormone or class of hormones. This allows low concentrations of hormone to exert major effects. For example, at its highest levels during the reproductive cycle estradiol is normally available only in picogram quantities per milliliter of plasma, yet these levels cause major behavioral and physiological changes. But when high levels of hormone are available or when synthetic hormones are administered, there can be cross-talk with other receptor systems.

Early research emphasized the differences between the endocrine system and the nervous system. Endocrine effects tend to be slower and longer lasting than those mediated by the nervous system (e.g., behavioral changes during the breeding season). Endocrine effects also tend to integrate physiology and behavior by acting on multiple sites (e.g., assuring that sexual behavior occurs close enough to ovulation to maximize chances of fertilization). Today, differences between the nervous system and the endocrine system are becoming blurred.

Neurons Produce Hormones

In male songbirds, the brain appears to be the major source of estrogens circulating throughout the body.[2] Some neurotransmitters have also been shown to function as hormones. In mammals, dopamine has been shown to act on progesterone receptors and elicit gene transcription. This is caused by cross-talk between membrane-associated dopamine receptors and intracellular steroid receptors, allowing dopamine to alter protein synthesis.[3] Similarly, some hormones have been shown to act via neurotransmitter receptors. Many steroids have the ability to activate or inhibit the $GABA_A$ receptor.[3] Hormone effects are also more rapid than traditionally thought. Preventing changes in hormone levels during behavioral interactions has been shown to alter the outcome of the interactions.[4]

METHODS IN BEHAVIORAL ENDOCRINOLOGY

Historically, because of the clear relationship between the breeding season and singing behavior, behavioral endocrinological research in songbirds focused on the effects of gonadal steroids on singing behavior. Three methods are used to determine if hormones modulate behavior: correlation, ablation, and restoration. Initial observations suggested that male singing behavior was maximal during the breeding season, correlated with increased testicular volumes. Studies showed that castration significantly reduced the frequency of male singing behavior and the complexity of songs sung. Finally, studies showed that hormone replacement with testosterone reinstated normal levels of singing behavior in castrated males.

Assay Techniques

Today, circulating hormone levels are typically measured by radioimmunoassay. This technique is very sensitive, allowing hormone levels to be measured in microliter samples of plasma or serum, or from fecal samples, permitting hormone measurements even in small songbirds. Precise amounts of antibody and radioactive hormone are added to extracted samples. The amount of radioactive hormone bound to the antibody is then compared to a standard curve to determine the amount of hormone in the sample—the more hormone in the sample, the less radioactive hormone bound since both are competing for a limited amount of antibody. The specificity of the assay is determined by the antibody. For example, many antibodies to testosterone also bind dihydrotestosterone with about 67% of the affinity with which they bind testosterone. If both hormones are in the sample, chromatography is used to separate them prior to assay, increasing both the difficulty and the cost of the assay. Chromatography is also used to allow measurement of multiple hormones from a small sample, for example, measuring androgens, estrogens, and corticoids in a 100-microliter plasma sample. Assay studies should always correct for sample loss during extraction and chromatography, present data on the specificity of the antibodies used, and provide both intra- and inter-assay coefficients of variation. Intra-assay variability should be $\leq 5\%$, while interassay variation should be $\leq 12\%$.

Hormone receptors can be measured by a variety of techniques: (1) "grind and bind" assays, (2) autoradiography, or (3) immunocytochemistry (ICC). "Grind and bind" assays homogenize the tissue of interest and then quantify receptor levels by determining the amount of radioactive hormone bound by the homogenate. The assay can either measure all receptors available, or an exchange assay can measure only those receptors occupied by endogenous hormone. Autoradiography involves exposing the tissue of interest to radioactive hormone. For *in vivo* autoradiography, radioactive hormone is administered to the animal, which is sacrificed shortly thereafter and the tissue of interest sectioned, and applied to slides. For *in vitro* autoradiography, the animal is sacrificed, the tissue sectioned, applied to slides, and then exposed to radioactive hormone. For both techniques, the slides are then incubated with photographic emulsion, which is later developed to quantify the level of hormone bound to receptors. Alternatively, receptors can be visualized by ICC, incubating the tissue with an antibody to the receptor. "Grind and bind" assays are the most sensitive, but the distribution of receptors cannot be determined. Both autoradiography and ICC show the distribution of receptors in tissue, but both techniques tend to underestimate total receptor numbers.

Hormone Administration

Today hormones are typically administered via silastic implants or osmotic minipumps. These implants offer the advantage of steady hormone release for weeks or, in the case of silastics, even longer. Silastic implants are used for lipophilic hormones like steroids, which diffuse easily through the silastic. The dose is determined by the surface area of the implant; the larger the surface area, the more hormone released per unit time. The more polar the hormone, the faster it diffuses through silastic. Thus, different hormones diffuse at different rates. This means that it is difficult to compare the effects of equivalent doses of different hormones, implants of the same size will result in different doses if the hormones' polarities differ. Osmotic minipumps are used to administer peptide hormones. These pumps release a set volume per hour, so the hormone dose depends on the concentration of hormone in the vehicle. Different size pumps are available to provide hormones for different periods of time. The release rates provided by the manufacturer are for mammals, and in most cases need to be adjusted for the higher temperatures of birds.

HISTORICAL OVERVIEW OF RESEARCH ON HORMONAL MODULATION OF SINGING

Research on the hormonal modulation of the songbird vocal control system has revolutionized the field of neuroscience, altering our basic concepts about how hormones modulate brain function and activate behavior. Singing behavior was the subject of informal observation for centuries and scientific research for many years. People quickly noted that singing appeared to be stimulated by gonadal hormones, since many species of temperate-zone birds showed striking increases in both the quality and quantity of singing behavior during the breeding season. A sexual dimorphism in singing behavior was also recognized, since in most species males sing more frequently and more complex songs than females.

Research on singing behavior entered a new era in 1976 with the discovery of some of the brain areas involved in the control of singing.[5] The hormone dependence of brain areas controlling singing behavior was quickly documented. When Arnold, Nottebohm, and Pfaff[6] investigated the distribution of androgen receptors in the zebra finch brain, they found high levels of receptors in hypothalamic and limbic areas, as expected. This receptor distribution appears to have been conserved across vertebrate species. However, they also found high levels of androgen receptors in two telencephalic (i.e., forebrain) brain areas involved in the control of singing. Such high levels of gonadal hormone receptors, sufficient to delineate the vocal control areas from surrounding brain tissue, had never been seen in such recently evolved brain areas in mammals. Clearly the vocal control nuclei are target tissues for gonadal steroids.

Organizational Hormone Effects

But the most influential publication of that year was the discovery that the gross structure of the vocal control system in male and female songbirds differed, and these structural differences correlated with differences in singing behavior.[7] Within four years, researchers documented that female songbirds could be induced to develop male-like brain structure and singing behavior by early hormone treatment.[8] This marked a major change in our understanding of the organizational effects of early hormone exposure on the brain. In 1959, Phoenix and coworkers[9] proposed that hormone effects on behavior could be divided into two types, organizational and activational. According to this schema, exposure to particular hormones during critical periods in development "organized" the nervous system, permanently altering animals' behavioral potential. Stimulation by hormones later in life activated hormone-dependent behaviors as long as the activational hormones were available. By 1976 there was plenty of evidence that early hormone exposure permanently altered animals' behavioral potential, with sexual dimorphisms in behavior being prime examples. However, thirty years ago researchers did not expect early hormone exposure to cause gross changes in neuroanatomy. Prior to Arnold and Nottebohm's seminal paper, only one hormone-induced sexual dimorphism in brain structure had been published, and that was a difference in synapse number at the electron microscope level.[10] But the structural differences in the songbird brain were so large that they could be seen with the naked eye. The other important aspect of this study was that the dimorphisms in brain structure correlated with clear dimorphisms in behavior. Since 1976, a plethora of sexual dimorphisms in brain structure in a wide variety of species have been documented, but aside from those in songbirds, few of them are so clearly related to dimorphisms in behavior. As others discuss in this volume, there are clearly exceptions to the correlations between changes in brain structure and changes in behavior, but overall, the songbird system has proven a remarkable model for examining the relationship between variations in brain structure and behavior.

Activational Hormones Affect Brain Structure

In 1981, the Nottebohm lab published two studies demonstrating that changes in circulating hormone levels in adult birds also caused striking changes in brain anatomy. Nottebohm[11] found that there were large seasonal changes in the size of two vocal control nuclei in canaries. Two of the nuclei on the motor pathway controlling singing, HVC and RA, were, respectively, 99% and 76% larger in the spring when males were singing vigorously compared to the fall when they had not been singing for several months. As expected, androgen levels were significantly higher in the spring. The second study[12] demonstrated that treating female canaries with androgen stimulated the growth of dendrites in RA. Testosterone-treated females showed a 250% increase in the dendritic fields of one type of neuron in RA compared to those in ovariectomized controls. Testosterone treatment also stimulated the females to sing. Once again, these results took the research community by surprise. Scientists knew changes in circulating hormone levels caused changes in brain neurochemistry, but they did not expect treatment with gonadal steroids to alter the structure of adult brains. Since that time, researchers have demonstrated that the alteration of brain structure is an important mechanism in hormonal activation of behavior. These changes in brain structure often occur quite rapidly, and typically precede changes in behavior.[13] But unlike the organizational structural changes underlying sexual dimorphisms, these structural changes last only as long as increased hormone levels are available.

Neurogenesis in the Adult Brain

The third discovery that fundamentally altered our vision of brain function was that new neurons are born in the adult brain and incorporated into functional circuits. When adult female canaries are treated with testosterone, the volume of HVC increases, and the birds begin to sing. Goldman and Nottebohm[14] were interested in whether neurogenesis might be involved in this phenomenon. They treated birds with ^{3}H-thymidine. When sacrificed 5 weeks later, the females had significant numbers of labeled neurons, glia, endothelia, and ventricular zone cells in and around HVC.[14] Testosterone treatment did not affect the number of labeled neurons, though it significantly increased the numbers of glia and endothelia. This initial report was greeted with much scepticism, because everyone knew that new neurons were not born in adult brains. But over the next few years, the Nottebohm lab documented that these new cells were born in the ventricular zone, migrated along radial glia into HVC where they differentiated into neurons that projected to RA or became interneurons.[15] The process of adding new neurons to HVC proved to be hormone sensitive, but rather than a direct effect on cell birth, endocrine status modulates the survival and/or recruitment of neurons incorporated into HVC as well as the lifespan of these cells.[16]

COMPLEXITY OF STUDYING THE HORMONAL MODULATION OF SINGING

Understanding the hormonal modulation of singing has been complicated by a number of factors.

Hormone Metabolism

The frequency of singing behavior changes over the year.[17] In many temperate-zone species there are multiple peaks, with singing rates rising when males first arrive in breeding areas and begin to defend territories. A second peak may occur when females return to the area. In many species, male singing rates crest as females lay their first clutch, though in some species, males stop singing once they have acquired a mate. These increases in singing are presumably driven by increased levels of gonadal steroids. In temperate-zone species, the initial increase in gonadal hormones is stimulated by the increase in daylength. Interactions with males[18,19] or females[19] can result in further increases in hormone production by the brain, pituitary, and gonads. Singing rates typically plummet at the close of the breeding season when birds enter the postnuptial molt. It is not clear if this is merely the result of decreased activity of the hypothalamic-pituitary-gonadal axis, or if other hormones may actively inhibit singing during this period. This cyclicity is not as obvious in tropical zones, where breeding may occur year-round, and the onset of breeding may be cued by factors such as rainfall or food availability.

Initial studies of the hormonal control of singing behavior focused on the effects of gonadal androgens such as testosterone, showing that testosterone injections or implants could stimulate singing in castrated males or males outside of the normal breeding season. However, researchers soon demonstrated that, as in other vertebrates, many of the effects of testosterone were caused by its metabolism to other hormones.[12,20] In all songbirds investigated thus far, the activation of singing by testosterone treatment appears to involve metabolism to estrogenic metabolites. As in other vertebrates, songbird brains contain significant quantities of aromatase, the enzyme that converts androgens to estrogens.[21] Research has shown that singing is activated by the combined actions of androgenic and estrogenic metabolites; treatments that provide only androgenic or only estrogenic metabolites do not stimulate singing.[12,20,22] As might be expected from these data, estrogenic metabolites also stimulate some of the structural changes in the brain associated with increased singing. Hormone treatments that provided both androgenic and estrogenic metabolites caused significantly greater increases in the dendritic fields of neurons in RA than treatments that provided only estrogens or only androgens that could not be converted to estrogens.[12] Blocking estrogen formation in androgen-treated males significantly decreased singing behavior, similar to the effects of castration.[23] Not only is singing itself activated by the combination of androgenic and estrogenic metabolites, but the visual displays used during singing in many species are stimulated by these metabolites as well. Thus, the courtship dance display in zebra finches and the song-spread display in red-winged blackbirds are stimulated by the combined effects of estrogenic and androgenic metabolites.[20,22]

Estrogenic metabolites also appear to be involved in sexual differentiation of the songbird brain. Early studies on sexual differentiation of zebra finch brains showed that estrogenic metabolites were much more effective in masculinizing female brains than androgenic metabolites.[8] The production of estrogens appears to play an important role in the neurochemical cascade controlling sexual differentiation of the brain across vertebrate species, even in species in which sexual differentiation is cued by environmental factors rather than by chromosomal sex.[24,25] However, as detailed In Wade and Arnold (this volume), the precise role of estrogen in sexual differentiation in songbirds remains in question, because while many studies have masculinized female brains and behavior by early estrogen treatment, no one has successfully blocked masculinization of genetic males by blocking estrogen's actions during early development, despite years of attempts. However, this strategy has worked *in vitro*.[26] Blocking estrogen synthesis in brain slices from male zebra finches in culture, blocked normal differentiation of the vocal control system. However, some aspects of masculine differentiation appear to develop independent of hormone exposure.[27]

Studies of circulating hormone levels usually focus on just one or two hormones (e.g., testosterone or testosterone and dihydrotestosterone). This means that many other metabolites are rarely studied and their effects little appreciated. For example, dehydroepiandrosterone (DHEA) was long considered a weak androgen and an unimportant precursor in androgen production. Recent research documents the ability of this hormone to increase the size of HVC and stimulate singing behavior.[28] In fact, DHEA may be stimulating singing and territorial behavior in male song sparrows outside the breeding season. Adding yet another level of complexity to the analysis of endocrine modulation of singing is the fact that patterns of hormone metabolism are labile. Hormone metabolism is affected by a variety of internal and environmental factors including changes in photoperiod, age, social interactions, and the availability of other hormones metabolized by the same enzymes.[29]

Multiple Production Sites

Hormones are produced at multiple sites. The typical paradigm for determining if gonadal hormones stimulate a behavior is the castration/hormone replacement study. But androgens can also be produced by other tissues, like the adrenal glands. Researchers working with mammals have often combined adrenalectomy with gonadectomy to remove the two most likely sources of sex steroids. But songbirds are difficult to adrenalectomize, so researchers have rarely attempted this strategy in songbirds. This means that if a behavior persists following castration, one cannot assume that it is not dependent on sex steroids, because these hormones may be produced by other tissues. In fact, one study found that castrating male zebra finches significantly increased circulating levels of estradiol.[30] This anomalous finding was ultimately explained by the unexpected discovery that the brain is the primary source of estradiol in peripheral circulation in male zebra finches.[2] Although researchers had long documented the ability of target tissues in the brain to metabolize steroids to both more active and inactive forms, researchers had not imagined that the brain might be releasing significant quantities of steroids into general circulation.

Multiple Sites of Hormone Action

Hormones act at multiple sites to influence singing behavior. Hormones may act directly on the various nuclei of the vocal control system, increasing the number of neurons in HVC during development, for example.[31] Hormones may also influence vocal control nuclei indirectly. Several of the hormone effects on the structure and function of RA have been shown to be indirect effects mediated by hormonal changes in HVC.[32,33] Many hormonal effects on singing appear to involve the catecholamine neurotransmitters, norepinephrine and dopamine. Gonadal steroids strongly modulate levels and turnover of norepinephrine and dopamine available in the vocal control system.[34] Some effects are estrogen dependent, some are androgen dependent, and both classes of steroids are necessary to restore normal catecholamine levels and turnover throughout the vocal control system. These neurotransmitters have been shown to modulate female responsiveness to male songs, the probability that males will sing to females, and song learning.[35–37] All these effects are probably related to the effects of these neurotransmitter systems on auditory processing as well as on the vocal control system. This is just one example of hormonal modulation of other neural systems that affect singing or the response to songs.

Hormones also modulate function of the syrinx, the avian vocal organ. While the brain areas controlling singing are sensitive to both estrogens and androgens, syringeal function appears to be primarily androgen sensitive. Androgens stimulate growth of syrinx, the number and the morphology of synapses, and neurotransmitter function (e.g., acetylcholine).[38–40] Thus, hormonal modulation of male singing behavior appears to follow the pattern seen in the control of male behavior in most vertebrates with brain function modulated by the combined effects of androgenic and estrogenic metabolites, while modulation of peripheral tissues involved in behavior is strongly androgen dependent.[29]

I should also note that when the same hormone affects multiple sites in the vocal control system, it often has different effects on different nuclei or it may achieve the same result through different mechanisms. For example, adult male zebra finches typically have more androgen receptors in several vocal control nuclei than females. The number of androgen receptors in lMAN and HVC in females can be significantly increased by early estrogen treatment However, the increase in androgen receptor levels is established by two different mechanisms. In lMAN, estrogen treatment preserves androgen-sensitive cells in the face of cell loss, while in HVC estrogen treatment promotes the development of androgen-sensitive cells.[31]

The Role of Other Hormones

Most studies of hormonal modulation of the vocal control system and singing have focused on the effects of gonadal steroids. However, a wide variety of other hormones appear to be involved in modulating the vocal control system and singing behavior. Voorhuis[41,42] found evidence of projections containing vasotocin innervating RA in canaries and the area around RA in both canaries and zebra finches. Despite the apparent paucity of direct vasotocin input to the vocal control system, vasotocin can both inhibit and stimulate courtship singing depending on a number of factors. I think vasotocin plays a particularly important role in controlling singing and reproductive behavior in zebra finches. This species evolved in arid areas of Australia, and their breeding is cued by the availability of water, which in the past was unpredictable. Cheng[43] hypothesized that the primary mechanism controlling reproduction in species relying on unpredictable cues should be inhibitory. The onset of stimulatory environmental conditions terminates the inhibition, allowing rapid initiation of reproduction. As the primary hormone regulating water balance in birds, vasotocin appears a likely candidate to modulate reproduction in finches. Drought conditions cause sustained vasotocin release, which in other species inhibits androgen production. Systemic infusions of nanogram levels of vasotocin inhibit singing and reproductive behavior in intact male finches fairly rapidly, presumably by inhibiting androgen production.[44] Inhibition of reproductive behavior by vasotocin may be a more general phenomenon. Large quantities of vasotocin are released when animals are stressed, and high levels may inhibit reproductive behavior. Vasotocin's extremely short half-life means that once proximal factors become more favorable, the gonads should rapidly be released from its inhibitory actions. In contrast to the systemic effects of vasotocin, infusions of very low levels (0.01 ng) into the lateral ventricle in male finches stimulate courtship singing (unpublished data). Thus, vasotocin can both inhibit and stimulate singing, depending on season, dose, route of administration, and gonadal hormone status.[44–46]

One interesting recent development was the discovery of a third form of gonadotropin-releasing hormone (GnRH) in the brains of two species of sparrows.[47] Immunoreactivity to lamprey GnRH-III was found in abundance in auditory processing areas, song production areas, and the hippocampus, as well as the hypothalamus. Just as high levels of steroid receptors are unique to the vocal control system and not found in recently evolved areas in other vertebrate brains, only in songbirds has GnRH immunoreactivity been found in such recently evolved areas of the brain. Treatment of birds with exogenous GnRH-III resulted in rapid release of LH into circulation. These data suggest that auditory processing and singing can directly affect production of LH and gonadal steroids. Given the ability of GnRH I and II to stimulate solicitation in female white-crowned sparrows,[48] and the ability of GnRH to stimulate behavior in other vertebrate groups, it is likely that this innervation may also modulate singing.

Thyroid hormones are involved in the seasonal control of reproductive behavior in songbirds[49] and have been shown to modulate apoptosis in brain areas that normally show neuron turnover.[50] HVC neurons that project to RA show variable levels of turnover in adult birds. In zebra finches, many of these neurons have thyroxine receptors. Acute treatment with thyroxine induces cell death in HVC as well as other telencephalic areas that normally show neuron turnover. Long-term treatment with thyroxine reduces the number of neurons in HVC. Thyroxine treatment appears to modulate cell death; no effects were seen on cell birth or recruitment.[50] Melatonin may also modulate singing. Melatonin and testosterone appear to function antagonistically in regulating the volume of vocal control areas, with testosterone increasing and melatonin decreasing volume.[49] The efficacy of melatonin appears to be modulated by thyroid hormones.[51]

Immunohistochemical studies have found evidence of other peptide hormones in the vocal control system, including vasoactive intestinal peptide (VIP), cholecysto-kinin, substance P, and corticotropin releasing hormone (CRH).[52] The function of these peptides in the vocal control system remains to be elucidated. VIP has been shown to stimulate prolactin release in songbirds during the breeding season,[53] so it might be involved in decreasing singing by males in species showing paternal care. CRH infusions rapidly inhibit female responses to male song through a mechanism involving endogenous opioids.[54] It is likely that these peptides also decrease singing in males. Stress reduced singing behavior in male zebra finches. However this effect appeared to be mediated by a factor that bound to brain estrogen receptors, essential-ly acting as an antiestrogen.[29]

The Importance of Context

Birds sing in many contexts. They sing during the breeding season. These songs may repel other males and defend territories and/or attract females and stimulate their ovarian development. Some species, like many American warblers, have differ-ent song types to serve these two functions.[17] In American warblers, unaccented songs appear to be used primarily in interactions between males and are sung prima-rily at dawn and dusk and during territorial interactions. Accented songs are sung more in the presence of females, during courtship, and appear to promote pair-bond maintenance. While it appears likely that endocrine factors differentially modulate these two song types, this remains to be investigated. Perhaps the balance of different hormone metabolites plays a role in this differential control.

Many species of birds sing outside the breeding season. In some species, such as great tits and willow tits, the frequency of singing behavior is correlated with maxi-mal plasma testosterone levels in the spring and smaller peaks in the fall.[17] While testosterone treatment can stimulate singing in both males and females outside of the normal breeding season, several studies have found that in some species, including mockingbirds, song sparrows, and European robins, singing in fall or winter appears to be independent of circulating levels of gonadal androgens.[19] Even castrated males continue to sing and defend territories. However, as mentioned previously, just re-moving the testes does not demonstrate that the behavior is independent of sex ste-roids, since these hormones can be produced by other tissues, including the adrenals and brain. For example, in male song sparrows castration did not reduce singing and territorial defense in the fall. However, treatment with an inhibitor of estrogen syn-thesis blocked fall singing behavior, and singing was restored by estrogen treat-ment.[55] Thus, singing outside the breeding season in this species is not independent of sex steroids as previously concluded on the basis of castration studies, but appears to rely on extragonadal steroid synthesis. Other studies have used pharmacological manipulations like hormone receptor blockers or estrogen synthesis inhibitors to demonstrate that singing is independent of endocrine status outside the breeding sea-son. While it is relatively easy to interpret studies using these drugs when they cause decreases in behavior, it is more difficult to interpret studies in which drug treatment has no effect on behavior, because only one dose is usually administered.

The effects of context have been investigated more extensively in zebra finches. Male finches sing relatively simple songs. These songs are typically classified depending on whether they are clearly directed at another bird or not. The initial classification scheme differentiated between female-directed courtship songs and undirected songs. During courtship singing, males clearly orient towards a female, and the song is often accompanied by specific patterns of feather erection and a pivoting dance display. Undirected songs are sung in a variety of social contexts, including in mixed social groups, near the nest when the female is incubating, and in complete isolation from other birds. As the name implies, males do not orient towards other birds while singing undirected songs. There are subtle acoustic differences between these two song types. Although a male's courtship and undirected songs are composed of the same elements, courtship songs contain more introductory notes, more repeated sequences, are more stereotyped, and are sung slightly faster.[56] During observations, we noticed that males also sang to other males. The hormonal basis of these three song types differs.[57] Estrogenic metabolites stimulate males to direct songs to other birds, both males and females, but undirected song does not require estrogenic activation. Estrogenic metabolites also stimulate males to sing more songs per bout when they sing to females than when they sing to other males or when they sing undirected song. Finally, estrogenic metabolites cause males to sing more rapidly when they are courting females than when they sing to other males or sing undirected song. Thus, males subtly alter their singing behavior depending on the intended recipient, and this phenomenon is hormone dependent.

Another study investigating the response of female zebra finches to playbacks of male song found very interesting contextual effects.[58] While many studies have employed estrogen-treated females to evaluate which aspects of male song stimulate copulatory displays, this study tried to stimulate female estrogen secretion by playing back male songs. The authors found that song playback could increase, decrease, or have no effect on female estrogen levels, depending on how the playback was presented. Presentation of song playbacks alone caused a decrease in female estrogen levels. Song playback only stimulated female estrogen secretion and egg laying when song was broadcast from inside a male model positioned at a distance from the female's nest and a second silent male model was positioned on the rim of the nest. When song was broadcast from the male positioned on the nest, it did not stimulate estrogen secretion. Thus, context is as important to the song recipient as to the singer.

Other studies have examined contextual effects in natural settings. One study[59] examined the relationships between song rate and 14 variables describing song structure, plasma testosterone levels, body mass, body condition, and social context in male barn swallows. Song rate was not correlated with any of the other variables. One particular song component, which the researchers called the harsh rattle, was positively related to testosterone levels, and its peak amplitude frequency varied inversely with male body mass and body condition. Several song features varied according to social context. Males sang longer and more varied songs when they had fewer or no neighbors. Presumably males in this condition are singing primarily to females. Males in highly competitive areas sang short songs, were more likely to interrupt their songs, and were more likely to include rattles in their songs. These data agree with the hypothesis that intersexual selection has resulted in longer more complex songs, while intrasexual interactions select for shorter, simpler songs.[17] Neighboring males sang more similar songs and this resulted in matched countersinging.

The authors suggest that female choice may depend on context so that matched countersinging may promote female choice for dominant males providing short, harsh aggressive displays in competitive situations, but that females prefer longer, more complex songs in less competitive situations.

Oversimplification

Most researchers assume that when they administer exogenous gonadal steroids they are mimicking the effects of increased circulating hormones during the breeding season. While treatment with exogenous androgen does increase the volumes of the vocal control nuclei in males of many temperate-zone species as expected, this hormone treatment results in differential effects in other brain areas.[60] A meta-analysis of the literature found that brain mass, telencephalon volume, and n. rotundus (a thalamic visual nucleus) volume increased from the nonbreeding season (low testosterone) to the breeding season (higher testosterone). However, treating males with exogenous testosterone caused the exact opposite, volumes of the telencephalon and nuclei outside the vocal control system were lower in androgen-treated animals than in controls. These results suggest that artificial hormone manipulations do not necessarily mimic the effects of natural variations in hormone levels and that results from experiments using hormone implants to mimic natural hormonal effects should be interpreted with caution. In part, the differences between the effects of naturally occurring increases in circulating androgens and those caused by experimental manipulation may be caused by differences in the photoperiods to which the birds were exposed. It should also be noted that birds in the laboratory are living in an impoverished environment relative to birds in the field. We gain experimental control, but we lose normal complexity.

CONCLUSIONS

Research on the hormonal control of singing has fundamentally altered basic concepts about how hormones modulate brain function and activate behavior. Circulating hormones organize sexual dimorphisms in brain structure during development, activate changes in brain structure during adulthood, and modulate the addition of new neurons in the adult brain. In part, these discoveries resulted from the specialized nature of the vocal control system. Because the vocal control nuclei are clearly delineated and because they have only one function, controlling singing behavior, it was much easier to study brain/behavior relationships in this hormone-sensitive system compared to classic hormone target tissues like the limbic system, which is involved in regulating so many different physiological processes and behavior patterns. These discoveries also resulted from the fact that the researchers involved were open to data that conflicted with current dogma about how the brain functioned. Research has now demonstrated that all of these phenomena occur in other vertebrates, including humans.

Although studies of songbird brains have revolutionized the field of neuroscience, there is still much to be learned. Most research has focused on the role of gonadal steroids in modulating singing, but we know that many other hormones also influence this behavior, including adrenal corticoids, vasotocin, GnRH, melatonin, and thyroid hormone. A bird's response to endocrine manipulations also depends on other factors, such as photoperiod and social interactions. We have learned that endocrinology is not as simple as once thought—the primary source of estradiol found in peripheral circulation in male finches is the brain, not the gonads or the adrenal glands, for example. If we administer a hormone and behavior is altered, was it a direct effect of that hormone or was the administered hormone converted to an active metabolite? Which tissue was responsible for this conversion? Similarly, we need to determine where hormones act to modulate behavior. Research to date has shown that all of the vocal control nuclei respond to androgens and estrogens. In some cases, the hormone affects the nucleus directly. In other cases, the effects are indirect, either acting via effects in another vocal control nucleus or even another brain system (e.g., dopaminergic). The effects of social context on the type of song sung, the hormonal control of different song types, and the hormonal and behavioral responses to songs sung in different contexts have just begun to be studied.

Most of the research to date has focused on relatively few species, particularly zebra finches. Zebra finches are opportunistic breeders whose endocrine control mechanisms are likely to be rather different from species whose reproduction is cued by changes in photoperiod. For example, singing in zebra finches appears to be less hormone-dependent than that in photoperiod-cued species. Although castration significantly lowers singing behavior in zebra finches, it does not eliminate it. In photoperiod-cued species, castrated males rarely, if ever sing. There is a rich diversity in songbird species that invites further exploration of the hormonal modulation of singing behavior.

ACKNOWLEDGMENTS

Support from NIH Grant GM 60654 to Hunter College and from the Research Centers in Minority Institutions Award RR-03037 from the National Center for Research Resources of the National Institutes of Health, which supports the infrastructure of the Biopsychology Program at Hunter, is gratefully acknowledged. The contents are solely the responsibility of the author and do not necessarily represent the official views of the NCRR/NIH.

REFERENCES

1. KACSOH, B. 2000. Endocrine Physiology. McGraw-Hill. New York.
2. SCHLINGER, B.A. & A.P. ARNOLD. 1992. Circulating estrogens in a male songbird originate in the brain. Proc. Natl. Acad. Sci. USA 89: 7650–7653.
3. BRANN, D.W., L.B. HENDRY & V.B. MAHESH. 1995. Emerging diversities in the mechanism of action of steroid hormones. J. Steroid Biochem. Mol. Biol. 52: 113–133.
4. NOCK, B.L. & A.I. LESHER. 1976. Hormonal mediation of the effects of defeat on agonistic responding in mice. Physiol. Behav. 17: 111–119.
5. NOTTEBOHM, F., T.M. STOKES & C.M. LEONARD. 1976. Central control of song in the canary, Serinus canarius. J. Comp. Neurol. 165: 457–486.
6. ARNOLD, A.P., F. NOTTEBOHM & D.W. PFAFF. 1976. Hormone concentrating cells in vocal control and other areas of the brain of the zebra finch (Poephila guttata). J. Comp. Neurol. 165: 487–512.
7. NOTTEBOHM, F. & A.P. ARNOLD. 1976. Sexual dimorphism in vocal control areas of the songbird brain. Science 194: 211–213.

8. GURNEY, M.E. & M. KONISHI. 1980. Hormone-induced sexual differentiation of brain and behavior in zebra finches. Science **208:** 1380–1382.
9. PHOENIX, C.H., R.W. GOY, A.A. GERALL & W.C. YOUNG. 1959. Organizing action of prenatally administered testosterone propionate on the tissues mediating mating behavior in the female guinea pig. Endocrinology **65:** 369–382.
10. RAISMAN, G. & P.M. FIELD. 1971. Sexual dimorphism in the preoptic area of the rat. Science **173:** 731–733.
11. NOTTEBOHM, F. 1981. A brain for all seasons: cyclical anatomical changes in song control nuclei of the canary brain. Science **214:** 1368–1370.
12. DEVOOGD, T. & F. NOTTEBOHM. 1981. Gonadal hormones induce dendritic growth in the adult avian brain. Science **214:** 202–204.
13. LUINE, V.N. & C.F. HARDING, EDS. 1994. Hormonal Restructuring of the Adult Brain: Basic and Clinical Perspectives. Ann. N.Y. Acad. Sci. **743.**
14. GOLDMAN, S.A. & F. NOTTEBOHM. 1983. Neuronal production, migration, and differentiation in a vocal control nucleus of the adult female canary brain. Proc. Natl. Acad. Sci. USA **80:** 2390–2394.
15. NOTTEBOHM, F. & A. ALVAREZ-BUYLLA. 1993. Neurogenesis and neuronal replacement in adult birds. *In* Neuronal Cell Death and Repair. A.C. Cuello, Ed.: 227–236. Elsevier Science Publishers. Amsterdam.
16. ALVAREZ-BUYLLA, A. & J.R. KIRN. 1997. Birth, migration, incorporation, and death of vocal control neurons in adult songbirds. J. Neurobiol. **33:** 585–601.
17. CATCHPOLE, C.K. & P.J.B. SLATER. 1995. Bird Song: Biological Themes and Variations. Cambridge University Press. Cambridge, UK.
18. HARDING, C.F. & B.K. FOLLETT. 1979. Hormone changes triggered by aggression in a natural population of blackbirds. Science **203:** 918–920.
19. HARDING, C.F. 1998. Androgens, Effects in birds. *In* Encyclopedia of Reproduction. E. Knobil & J.D. Neill, Eds.: 188–196. Academic Press. New York.
20. HARDING, C.F., K. SHERIDAN & M.J. WALTERS. 1983. Hormonal specificity and activation of sexual behavior in male zebra finches. Horm. Behav. **17:** 111–133.
21. SILVERIN, B., M. BAILLIEN, A. FOIDART & J. BALTHAZART. 2000. Distribution of aromatase activity in the brain and peripheral tissues of passerine and nonpasserine avian species. Gen. Comp. Endocrinol. **117:** 34–53.
22. HARDING, C.F., M.J. WALTERS, D. COLLADO & K. SHERIDAN. 1988. Hormonal specificity and activation of social behavior in male red-winged blackbirds. Horm. Behav. **22:** 402–418.
23. WALTERS, M.J. & C.F. HARDING. 1988. The effects of an aromatization inhibitor on the reproductive behavior of male zebra finches. Horm. Behav. **22:** 207–218.
24. ELBRECHT, A. & R.G. SMITH. 1992. Aromatase enzyme activity and sex determination in chickens. Science **255:** 467–470.
25. GUTZKE, W.H. & J.J. BULL. 1986. Steroid hormones reverse sex in turtles. Gen. Comp. Endocrinol. **64:** 368–372.
26. HOLLOWAY, C.C. & D.F. CLAYTON. 2001. Estrogen synthesis in the male brain triggers development of the avian song control pathway in vitro. Nat. Neurosci. **4:** 170–175.
27. AGATE, R.J., W. GRISHAM, J. WADE, et al. 2003. Neural, not gonadal, origin of brain sex differences in a gynandromorphic finch. Proc. Natl. Acad. Sci. USA **100:** 4873–4878.
28. SOMA, K.K., A.M. WISSMAN, E.A. BRENOWITZ & J.C. WINGFIELD. 2002. Dehydroepiandrosterone (DHEA) increases territorial song and the size of an associated brain region in a male songbird. Horm. Behav. **41:** 203–212.
29. HARDING, C.F. 1986. The role of androgen metabolism in the activation of male behavior. Ann. NY Acad. Sci. **474:** 371–378.
30. ADKINS-REGAN, E., M. ABDELNABI, M. MOBARAK & M.A. OTTINGER. 1990. Sex steroid levels in developing and adult male and female zebra finches (*Poephila guttata*). Gen. Comp. Endocrinol. **78:** 93–109.
31. NORDEEN, E., K.W. NORDEEN & A.P. ARNOLD. 1987. Sexual differentiation of androgen accumulation within the zebra finch brain through selective cell loss and addition. J. Comp. Neurol. **259:** 393–399.
32. HERRMANN, K. & A.P. ARNOLD. 1991. Lesions of HVc block the developmental masculinizing effects of estradiol in the female zebra finch song system. J. Neurobiol. **22:** 29–39.

33. BRENOWITZ, E.A. & K. LENT. 2002. Act locally and think globally: intracerebral testosterone implants induce seasonal-like growth of adult avian song control circuits. Proc. Natl. Acad. Sci. USA **99:** 12421–12426.
34. BARCLAY, S. R. & C. F. HARDING. 1990. Differential modulation of monoamine levels and turnover rates by estrogen and/or androgen in hypothalamic and vocal control nuclei of male zebra finches. Brain Res. **523:** 251–262.
35. HARDING, C.F. 2002. The effects of manipulating catecholamines on song learning. 2002. Neurobiology of Singing, Annual Symposium of Research Centers in Minority Institutions. Hunter College. New York.
36. APPELTANTS, D., C. DEL NEGRO & J. BALTHAZART. 2002. Noradrenergic control of auditory information processing in female canaries. Behav. Brain Res. **133:** 221–235.
37. BARCLAY, S. R., C.F. HARDING & S.A. WATERMAN. 1991. Correlations between catecholamine levels and sexual behavior in male zebra finches. Pharmacol. Biochem. Behav. **41:** 195–201.
38. LUINE, V.N., C.F. HARDING & W.V. BLEISCH. 1983. Specificity of gonadal hormone modulation of cholinergic enzymes in the avian syrinx. Brain Res. **279:** 339–342.
39. BLEISCH, W.V., V.N. LUINE & F. NOTTEBOHM. 1984. Modification of synapses in an androgen sensitive muscle: I. Hormonal regulation of acetylcholine receptors in the muscle of the songbird syrinx. J. Neurosci. **4:** 786–792.
40. CLOWER, R.P., B.E. NIXDORF & T.J. DEVOOGD. 1989. Synaptic plasticity in the hypoglossal nucleus of female canaries: structural correlates of season, hemisphere, and testosterone treatment. Behav. Neural Biol. **52:** 63–77.
41. KISS, J.Z., T.A.M. VOORHUIS, J.A.M. EEKLEN, et al. 1987. Organization of vasotocin-immunoreactive cells and fibers in the canary brain. J. Comp. Neurol. **263:** 347–364.
42. VOORHUIS, T.A.M & E.R. DE KLOET. 1992. Immunoreactive vasotocin in the zebra finch brain (*Taeniopygia guttata*). Dev. Brain Res. **69:** 1–10.
43. CHENG, M.-F. 1993. Vocal, auditory, and endocrine systems: three-way connectivities and implications. Poult. Sci. Rev. **5:** 37–47.
44. HARDING, C.F. & S.A. ROWE. 2003. Vasotocin treatment inhibits courtship in male zebra finches: concomitant androgen treatment inhibits this effect. Horm. Behav. **44:** 413–418.
45. VOORHUIS, T.A. M., E.R. DE KLOET & D. DE WIED. 1991. Effect of a vasotocin analog on singing behavior in the canary. Horm. Behav. **25:** 549–559.
46. MANEY, D.L., C.T. GOODE & J.C. WINGFIELD. 1997. Intraventricular infusion of arginine vasotocin induces singing in a female songbird. J. Neuroendocrinol. **9:** 487–491.
47. BENTLEY, G.E., I.T. MOORE, S.A. SOWER & J.C. WINGFIELD. 2004. Evidence for a novel gonadotropin-releasing hormone in hypothalamic and forebrain areas in songbirds. Brain Behav. Evol. **63:** 34–46.
48. MANEY, D.L., R.D. RICHARDSON & J.C. WINGFIELD. 1997. Central administration of chicken gonadotropin-releasing hormone-II enhances courtship behavior in a female sparrow. Horm. Behav. **32:** 11–18.
49. DAWSON, A., V.M. KING, G.E. BENTLEY & G.F. BALL. 2001. Photoperiodic control of seasonality in birds. J. Biol. Rhythms. **16:** 365–380.
50. TEKUMALLA, P.K., M. TONTONOZ, M.A. HESLA & N.J.R. KIRN. 2002. Effects of excess thyroid hormone on cell death, cell proliferation, and new neuron incorporation in the adult zebra finch telencephalon. J. Neurobiol. **51:** 323–341.
51. BENTLEY, G.E. 2001. Unraveling the enigma: the role of melatonin in seasonal processes in birds. Microsc. Res. Tech. **53:** 63–71.
52. HARDING, C.F. 1992. Hormonal modulation of neurotransmitter function and behavior in male songbirds. Poult. Sci. Rev. **4:** 261–273.
53. MANEY, D.L., S.J. SCHOECH, P.J. SHARP & J.C. WINGFIELD. 1999. Effects of vasoactive intestinal peptide on plasma prolactin in passerines. Gen. Comp. Endocrinol. **113:** 323–330.
54. MANEY, DL. & J. C. WINGFIELD. 1998. Neuroendocrine suppression of female courtship in a wild passerine: corticotropin-releasing factor and endogenous opioids. J. Neuroendocrinol. **10:** 593–599.
55. SOMA, K.K., A.D. TRAMONTIN & J.C. WINGFIELD. 2000. Oestrogen regulates male aggression in the non-breeding season. Proc. R. Soc. Lond. B. Biol. Sci. **267:** 1089–1096.

56. SOSSINKA, R. & J. BÖHNER. 1980. Song types in the zebra finch, (*Poephila guttata castanotis*). Z. Tierpsychol. **53:** 123–132.
57. WALTERS, M.J., D. COLLADO & C.F. HARDING. 1991. Oestrogenic modulation of singing in male zebra finches: differential effects on directed and undirected songs. Anim. Behav. **42:** 445–452.
58. TCHERNICHOVSKI, O., H. SCHWABL & F. NOTTEBOHM. 1998. Context determines the sex appeal of male zebra finch song. Anim. Behav. **55:** 1003–1010.
59. GALEOTTI, P., N. SAINO, R. SACCHI & A.P. MOLLER. 1997. Song correlates with social context, testosterone and body condition in male barn swallows. Anim. Behav. **53:** 687–700.
60. SMULDERS, T.V. 2002. Natural breeding conditions and artificial increases in testosterone have opposite effects on the brains of adult male songbirds: a meta-analysis. Horm. Behav. **41:** 156–169.

Sexual Differentiation of the Zebra Finch Song System

JULI WADE[a] AND ARTHUR P. ARNOLD[b]

[a]Departments of Psychology and Zoology, and Program in Neuroscience, Michigan State University, East Lansing, Michigan 48824-1101, USA

[b]Department of Physiological Science, and Laboratory of Neuroendocrinology of the Brain Research Institute, University of California, Los Angeles, California 90095-1606, USA

ABSTRACT: The song system of zebra finches (*Taeniopygia gutatta*) is highly sexually dimorphic. Only males sing, and the brain regions and muscles controlling song are much larger in males than in females. Development of the song system is highly sensitive to steroid hormones. However, unlike similar sexually dimorphic systems in other animal models, masculinization of song system structure and function is most likely not induced by testosterone secreted from the testes. Instead, sex-specific development of the neural song system appears to be regulated by factors intrinsic to the brain, probably by the expression of sex chromosome gene(s) that influence the levels of estradiol synthesized in the brain and/or the responses of brain tissue to estradiol. However, the existing data are complex and in some cases contradictory. More work is required to identify the critical genes and their relationships with steroid hormones.

KEYWORDS: estrogen; androgen; aromatase; gonadal hormone; sexual dimorphism

The study of the passerine song system has provided a novel perspective on sexual differentiation of the brain in vertebrates. In mammals and birds, sex differences in development of all organs are initiated by sex differences in the expression of genes encoded on the sex chromosomes, which are the only genes present in different amounts in male and female zygotes. In most mammals, for example, the gonads of males and females begin to differentiate when the Y-linked testis determining gene *Sry* begins to be expressed within the undifferentiated gonad of the male.[1] *Sry* initiates a cell-autonomous program of development in males that is different than that of females. Once the gonads form as testes or ovaries, they secrete different levels of sex steroids which act on diverse tissues to cause permanent sex differences in development.[2] Specifically, testosterone released from the testes into general circulation early in development travels to the neural and muscular substrates for a variety of sexually dimorphic behaviors, including courtship and copulation, and induces irreversible masculine differentiation. Thus, the cell-autonomous, *genetic* mechanism

Address for correspondence: Juli Wade, Michigan State University, Neuroscience Program, 108 Giltner Hall, East Lansing, MI 48824-1101. Voice: 517-432-8301; fax: 517-432-2744. wadej@msu.edu; <http://www.msu.edu/~wadej> <http://www.physci.ucla.edu/html/arnold.htm>

Ann. N.Y. Acad. Sci. 1016: 540–559 (2004). © 2004 New York Academy of Sciences. doi: 10.1196/annals.1298.015

dictating sexual differentiation of the gonads has classically been contrasted with the *gonadal hormonal* mechanism of sexual differentiation in the central nervous system and its muscular targets. However, study of the zebra finch song system suggests two major exceptions to these patterns of sexual differentiation. Some neural sexual dimorphisms may be caused by (1) hormones produced locally in the brain rather than in the gonads and (2) cell-autonomous genetic mechanisms not unlike those in the gonads.

MAMMALIAN SEXUAL DIFFERENTIATION— ROLE OF GONADAL HORMONES

Substantial support for gonadal hormonal control of neural sexual differentiation comes from studies of various mammalian species.[3] The testes of males secrete testosterone during fetal and postnatal periods, which acts on the brain (often after conversion to estradiol) to cause permanent masculine neural differentiation. Feminine development in mammals typically occurs in the relative absence of testosterone and its metabolites (although this is an oversimplification[4,5]). The permanent masculinizing effects of androgens and estrogens in males are called "organizational," and are contrasted with more transient effects of gonadal steroids later in life, which are seen as activating the neural substrate that differentiated earlier in development.[6,7] These adult "activational" effects of gonadal steroids contribute to and maintain the sex differences in various structures and behavioral repertoire.

Examples of hormonally induced sexual differentiation are common in regions of the mammalian preoptic area (POA), an area critical for the display of masculine reproductive behaviors.[3] In parallel with the sex difference in behavior, portions of the preoptic area are substantially larger or only present in males in a variety of species.[8–12] A neighboring region, the anteroventral periventricular nucleus (AVPv) is larger in females than in males. It is involved in a female-specific function—the surge of luteinizing hormone that initiates ovulation.[13] Gonadal hormones regulate the permanent differentiation of the morphology and function of both of these brain regions.[8,10,13–20] This masculinization of brain and behavior often requires the metabolizing of testosterone to estradiol in specific brain cells, a reaction catalyzed by the aromatase enzyme.[21,22] The masculinization of the mammalian POA, therefore, is typically mediated by the action of estradiol on estrogen receptors, which are expressed in brain regions that are destined to become sexually dimorphic. However, androgens themselves, acting via androgen receptors, are critical for masculinization of the penis and its associated neuromuscular systems that are necessary for successful copulation in male mammals. Although penile muscles and their motoneurons develop in both sexes prenatally, they become sexually dimorphic when androgen acts around the time of birth to prevent their regression in males.[23]

AVIAN SEXUAL DIFFERENTIATION— COPULATORY STRUCTURE AND FUNCTION

The role of steroid hormones and their receptors in avian sexual differentiation is less clear. This issue has been investigated in relatively few species, and many of the results are not consistent among avian species or similar to the mechanisms of sexual differentiation in the mammalian brain. Perhaps the most striking effect is that estradiol administration to young male Japanese quail or zebra finches feminizes copulatory behavior,[24–27] rather than masculinizing females, as occurs in mammals. As in mammalian species, a region of the medial POA in Japanese quail that is important for the activation of masculine reproductive behaviors[28,29] is significantly larger in males than in females. However, unlike most mammalian systems described above, gonadal hormones apparently do not induce sexual differentiation early in development, but testosterone in adulthood transiently masculinizes the structure of the quail POA.[24,27] Regardless of the age at which the effect occurs, testicular hormones appear critical for sexual differentiation of brain and behavior in quail.[30] In zebra finches, sex differences in the morphology of the preoptic area have not been reported and are not obvious with a standard Nissl stain (Wade and Arnold, unpublished data).

SEX DIFFERENCES IN THE ZEBRA FINCH SONG SYSTEM

Most research on the role of steroid hormones in sexual differentiation of the avian brain has been conducted in zebra finches and has focused on the structures important for learning and production of song.[31,32] Regions of the brain and muscles of the vocal organ (syrinx) are highly sexually dimorphic.[33] HVC, RA, and nXIIts are larger in volume in males than in females (FIG. 1), and area X cannot be detected in Nissl-stained female brains. HVC and RA contain more and larger neurons in males than in females, and the projection from HVC to RA is substantially more robust in males.[34] Dendritic arborization in RA is also greater in males.[35] Expression of androgen receptors is higher in males in HVC, lMAN, and area X[36–38] and in the syrinx.[39] The mass of this organ is also greater in males, as is the average size of fibers in its ventralis and dorsalis muscles.[40] These substantial sexual dimorphisms in the structure of the song circuit are correlated with sexual dimorphism in song. Under normal conditions, only males sing.

ROLE OF ESTROGENS AND ANDROGENS IN SEXUAL DIFFERENTIATION OF THE SONG SYSTEM

Estrogens

As in the mammalian forebrain, administration of estradiol to young female zebra finches (shortly after hatching) causes morphological and behavioral masculinization. It increases the volume of the forebrain song control regions, as well as the size and number of neurons in the song circuit.[41–44] Estradiol also causes axons from HVC to enter RA, which normally only happens in males.[34,45] Unlike normal females, estrogen-masculinized females sing as adults, [25,26,41,46,47] and they have a greater expression of androgen receptors in lMAN, HVC, and area X.[38,48] These results, coupled with the demonstration that estradiol is more potent than testosterone in enhancing the female song system,[43] are consistent with the idea that various as-

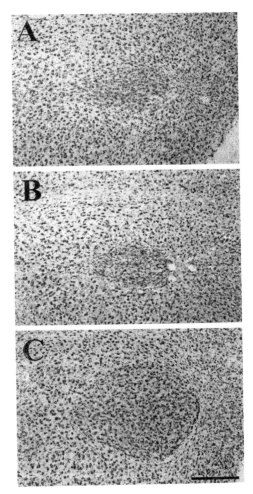

FIGURE 1. Coronal sections through RA in one-month-old zebra finches. **A,** control female; **B,** a genetic female treated embryonically with the aromatase inhibitor fadrozole that developed testicular, but not ovarian, tissue; **C,** control male. Scale bar = 150 μm. (From Wade *et al.*[56])

pects of the song system are masculinized by the same mechanism as the mammalian POA. Specifically, these data are compatible with the idea that testosterone is secreted by the testes of males and, after traveling to the brain via the circulatory system, is metabolized (aromatized) into estradiol. Increased levels of neural estrogen, rather than androgen, are subsequently responsible for masculine brain differentiation. Although the sites of this early estrogen action are not clear, HVC may be a primary target. Estradiol implanted directly in or near HVC masculinizes its soma size,[49] and, importantly, HVC must be intact for estradiol to masculinize RA and area X in females.[50] Moreover, lesioning HVC prevents the masculine pattern of increase in cell size in RA, and lesioning both HVC and lMAN causes the male RA to appear feminine in terms of cell size, number, and volume.[51] However, because estrogen acts to increase androgen receptor expression in area X at posthatching day 11,[38] before HVC innervates area X, non-HVC site(s) of estrogen action are also likely.

In three studies, interfering with the synthesis or action of estradiol partially blocked specific events in the masculine pattern of development of the song system, as would be predicted if estrogen is normally important for masculinization in males. Fadrozole, an estrogen synthesis (aromatase) inhibitor, decreases the normal masculine increase in expression of BDNF in HVC at days 30–35.[52] Moreover, when fadrozole is given to males during the first week after hatching, the masculine level of androgen receptor expression is partially blocked in HVC and area X at day 11.[38] The growth of HVC axons into RA, which occurs *in vivo* in males at about day 30, can be inhibited in slice cultures of the telencephalon with an estrogen receptor blocker or the aromatase inhibitor fadrozole.[45] As a group, these studies suggest that estrogen normally acts to cause several different events during masculinization of the male's song system.

Paradoxically, however, attempts to prevent masculinization of the song system in males by long-term treatments that block estrogen synthesis or action have produced little or no effect. Inhibiting aromatase activity with fadrozole in the first month after hatching did not prevent masculine development of the song control nuclei measured in juveniles, although fadrozole did appear to decrease the size of HVC neurons in males analyzed in adulthood.[53,54] The aromatase inhibitor vorozole given to young males at approximately the same time did not prevent masculine development of song system anatomy; it decreased the rate of singing but did not block singing altogether.[55] Similarly, treatment with fadrozole after hatching did not modify singing behavior.[54] When fadrozole was used at any of several developmental periods *in ovo*, including dipping the eggs in a fadrozole solution daily for 80% of the prehatching period, no effect was observed on masculine development of the song system.[56] Several putative antiestrogens given after hatching actually had hypermasculinizing effects, increasing the volume of the forebrain song control regions and neuron size in both sexes.[57–59] In one study, an estrogen receptor blocker inhibited myelination in RA, but the effect was not specific to or widespread in the song system; it occurred in the cerebellum and was not detected in lMAN.[60]

In contrast to its effect on the brain, but similar to those on copulatory behavior, estradiol feminizes the developing syrinx. Administering estradiol to males in the first three weeks after hatching decreases the overall mass of the syrinx to that typical of females, a decrease that is at least in part due to a change in muscle fiber size.[61] This result is consistent with estrogen's feminizing effects on the syrinx of ducks.[62] However, parallel to results on the forebrain song control regions, the aromatase inhibitor fadrozole administered during the same time period does not prevent feminization of the syrinx in females.[61]

It is difficult to reconcile the estrogenic feminization of the syrinx with estrogenic masculinization of the forebrain song circuit, but clearly the two tissues must differ in some fashion. One possibility is that the source of the estrogen that masculinizes the brain may be the telencephalon itself (see below), so it is exposed to much higher levels than the syrinx. Perhaps exposure to this increased estradiol affects morphology differently than a much lower level does. The opposite effects could also be caused by tissue-specific steroid receptor coactivators or corepressors. These factors are important in determining the positive and negative effects of estrogen receptor ligands.[63] Previous studies do not resolve this paradox, nor do they unambiguously indicate whether estradiol is critical for, or a participant in, sexual differentiation of the brain and syrinx. Before concluding that estradiol has a central role in masculinization or feminization, one would need to account for the absence of effects of blocking the synthesis or action of estrogen, and for effects opposite to those predicted. Alternatively, to argue that estrogen does not play a central role in sexual differentiation leaves unexplained a number of potent effects of this steroid on the brain and syrinx.

Androgens

When hatchling female zebra finches are given three weeks of treatment with 5α-dihydrotestostone (DHT), a nonaromatizable androgen that is thought to act exclusively via the androgen receptor, the soma size of the nXIIts motoneurons innervating the syrinx can be completely masculinized.[61] However, this masculinization process is not prevented by treating males with the androgen receptor blocker flutamide during the same time period.[61] The volume of the nXIIts brain region is not masculinized by DHT or other steroid hormones.[31,42] Posthatching DHT treatment also has modest masculinizing effects on the number and size of neurons in RA, although not all studies agree on the details.[35,64] These small or paradoxical effects suggest that androgen by itself plays a relatively minor role in masculinization. Reinforcing this idea is the finding that combined treatment of females with DHT and estradiol causes no more masculinization than estradiol alone,[44] and that aromatizable androgens are less, not more, effective than estradiol.[43]

Some recent evidence is, however, consistent with a more prominent role for androgens. When hatchling females are treated with both estrogen and the androgen receptor blocker flutamide, the masculinizing effect of estradiol is almost completely prevented.[65] One explanation is that estrogen in females triggers a cascade of cellular events leading to masculinization of the telencephalic circuit and that one or more of these events requires the action of androgen. If so, females have sufficient endogenous androgen to allow the masculinization when they are treated only with estradiol.[66–68] However, the lack of complete masculinization of females after combined androgen and estrogen exposure[44] suggests that additional mechanisms are involved. Estrogen treatment of females upregulates the expression of androgen receptors in HVC, area X, and lMAN,[38,48] and males have more androgen receptor in HVC and area X by posthatching days 9–11,[37,38] early in the formation of the song circuit. Thus, one of estrogen's effects may be to gate the ability of androgens to participate in masculinization of these brain regions after day 9.

A role for androgens is also indicated by the finding that castration at day 20 followed by treatment with flutamide decreases the volume of lMAN and area X by adulthood.[69] Paradoxically, the effect was not seen in HVC in which estradiol also induces increased androgen receptor expression.[38,48] Moreover, androgen receptors are expressed strongly by cells in the anterior telencephalic ventricular zone at posthatching day 1.[70] The ventricular zone also expresses CYP17, the enzyme required for synthesis of androgen,[71] suggesting that androgen may be synthesized in the ventricular zone itself. Specific regions of the ventricular zone of males have higher levels of cellular proliferation (compared to females) at about one month after hatching,[72] thus androgens could play a role in sexually dimorphic neurogenesis related to the song system. The link of this proliferation to the song system, however, has yet to be established.

In summary, substantial masculinization of females occurs with estradiol treatment in the first few weeks after hatching. However, the effect is not complete. Whereas some specific components of masculine development appear to require steroid hormone action (i.e., individual masculine developmental events are substantially blocked by drugs that interfere with the synthesis or action of estrogens or androgens; see above), in no case has it been possible to sex-reverse the male's song or song system development by interfering with androgen or estrogen action. Although these negative findings can be taken as evidence that nonhormonal factors might participate in sexual differentiation,[37,73] it remains possible that future experiments will find a regime of hormonal manipulation that does succeed in blocking masculinization. One therefore cannot rule out the idea. If, however, hormones are critical to the sexual differentiation process, it is more likely that their source is neural than gonadal (see below).

DOUBTS ABOUT A CRITICAL ROLE FOR GONADAL STEROIDS IN SONG SYSTEM SEXUAL DIFFERENTIATION

Several considerations undermine confidence in a theory of sexual differentiation that is initiated by sex differences in the levels of gonadal secretions. First, dimorphisms in circulating levels of gonadal steroids have not been consistently found after hatching (but have not been measured before hatching). One study found a higher level of circulating estradiol in males during the first week after hatching when plasma was sampled from jugular blood as it leaves the brain,[67] but two others sampling systemic plasma did not confirm this finding.[66,68] Circulating androgens were also generally equivalent between the sexes during development and, when sex differences were detected, the levels were higher in females, not in males.[66,67] Thus, the measurement of plasma steroid levels has not strongly supported the gonadal origin of the sexually dimorphic signal that initiates sexual differentiation. Consistent with that idea, when sexual differentiation of the song system can first be detected, just after hatching, the activity of androgen synthetic enzymes in the gonads does not appear to be sexually dimorphic.[74]

If the circulating levels of gonadal steroids are not dimorphic, a greater effect of estrogen could still be achieved in males if brain aromatase levels were higher in males than in females or if estrogen receptors were expressed at a higher level. (In these cases, the factors causing sex differences in brain metabolism or responses to estrogen would need to be defined). To date, no studies indicate that either of these genes are expressed more in males at various pre- or posthatching ages, using measures of mRNA expression, protein expression, and aromatase activity.[68,75,76] A failure to find a sex difference does not prove that no difference exists, but these studies do not support the hypothesis that dimorphisms in the level or action of estradiol are a root cause of sexual differentiation.

A critical test of the role of gonadal secretions would be to remove the gonads before they are able to secrete significant quantities of hormones. This experimental approach, which was decisive in proving the importance of testicular secretions in studies of mammalian sexual differentiation,[77] has not been possible in zebra finches earlier than one week posthatching, because of their small size. Castration of males has been accomplished in the second week after hatching,[78,79] although this age is probably too late to interfere with the earliest events in sexual differentiation. For example, HVC and area X are already sexually dimorphic by posthatching days 9–11.[37,38] Still, these castrates developed normal song, although more slowly than control birds,[78,79] suggesting that testicular secretions after day 9 are not required for masculine differentiation of song and the song circuit. Several important sexually dimorphic events occur well after this time, including the male-specific growth of axons from HVC into RA,[34] and a male-specific estradiol-dependent upregulation of BDNF in HVC,[52] both of which occur at about day 30. We can infer from these results that such masculinization as occurs after the first week posthatching does not require the presence of the testes, a conclusion supported by the finding that the growth of HVC axons into RA occurs *in vitro* in the absence of gonads.[45]

Although it has not yet been possible to raise zebra finches in the complete absence of gonadal tissue, the phenotype of the gonads in genetic female zebra finches has been switched to test the importance of ovarian and testicular secretions.[56,80–82] This experimental approach is feasible because differentiation of the ovary in birds requires estradiol.[83] Thus, when genetically female zebra finches are treated prior to or during gonadal differentiation with the estrogen synthesis (aromatase) inhibitor fadrozole, ovarian development is blocked. Such genetic females typically develop a testis on the right and an ovotestis on the left. In adulthood, these testes produce sperm, and the birds can have plasma androgen levels in the range of normal males.[80–82] However, their song control regions are not masculinized, and they do not sing.[56,84] These results were obtained even in the few females that developed only testicular tissue in the absence of ovarian tissue (FIG. 1), and in birds whose left gonad (which contains all of the ovarian tissue) was surgically removed at one week posthatching. These studies demonstrate that (1) ovarian tissue is not required for the differentiation of a feminine song system (contradicting the idea that ovarian secretions trigger feminine development in birds[27]) and (2) the presence of large amounts of testicular tissue is insufficient to cause masculine development in genetic females. Although one cannot prove that the testes in genetic females produced hormones at levels comparable to those in genetic males at all stages of development, the results raise significant doubt about a primary role for testicular and ovarian secretions in brain sexual differentiation.

In summary, if the mammalian aromatization hypothesis for brain organization applied to the zebra finch song system and gonadal hormones were critical, then the secretion of testicular androgens would be required for masculine development and would be higher in males than in females during or just prior to the period of sexual differentiation. However, the removal of testes in genetic males and the induction of testicular tissue in genetic females have little, if any, effect on song system development, and young males do not have higher levels of androgens in plasma. Alternative possibilities are that estrogens produced directly by the testes of developing males are responsible for brain masculinization, in which case plasma estradiol would be higher in males than in females, or that males have an increased capacity to respond to the circulating estrogen (increased estrogen receptor expression) or to produce estradiol in the brain from androgen released by the gonads (increased aromatase expression). However, the data are generally not consistent with any of these scenarios and lead to the conclusion that steroid hormones produced in the periphery are not critical for masculine development of the neural song system.

A ROLE FOR ESTROGENS SYNTHESIZED IN THE BRAIN ITSELF

An alternative hypothesis is that estradiol synthesized in the brain is important for masculinization. When adult male zebra finches are castrated, plasma levels of estrogen do not decline, but paradoxically can increase.[66] A similar result was found with sparrows.[85] The nongonadal source for plasma estrogen appears to be the brain itself, because levels of the estrogen-synthesizing enzyme, aromatase, are higher in the brain than in other tissues, and estradiol synthesized in brain can enter the systemic circulation.[68,86] Aromatase mRNA and protein are found at particularly high levels in numerous telencephalic regions including the neostriatum and hippocampus.[75,87,88] In zebra finches most song control nuclei have little or no aromatase, but expression of the enzyme occurs in nearby brain regions. Thus, estrogen synthesized locally could well contribute to brain masculinization.

In resting adult brain, aromatase is expressed predominantly in neurons,[88] but when primary cell cultures are prepared from neonatal telencephalon, much of the expression is in astrocytes.[89] Moreover, damage to the telencephalon causes dramatic upregulation of aromatase expression in astrocytes surrounding the wound.[90] Conceivably, the high expression of astrocytic aromatase in dissociated cell cultures may also be due to damage. Although no sex differences in aromatase activity, mRNA expression, or protein levels have been detected in zebra finches at any age, from day 11 of embryonic life to adulthood (see above), slice cultures of 25-day-old telencephalon release estrogen into culture medium. This medium contains insufficient precursors to account for the levels of estrogen produced, suggesting that estrogen is synthesized *de novo* from cholesterol in the telencephalon.[45] Moreover, male slices produce more estradiol than do female slices, which could be sufficient to cause masculine growth of HVC fibers into RA in the female slices (since coculturing with a male slice produces effects similar to estradiol treatment). This male-specific growth of fibers from HVC to RA occurs in males but not females *in vivo* at about 25–30 days of age.[34] These studies as a whole suggest that during juvenile life, male telencephalic cells may secrete estradiol at a higher level than does the female telencephalon, and that this brain-derived estradiol contributes to masculinization of the song circuit.[91]

These studies *in vitro* are the first to provide evidence that the male telencephalon produces more estrogen than the does female telencephalon. However, the events studied in tissue slices harvested from 25-day-old zebra finches occur 2–3 weeks after sex differences are first detected in HVC at posthatching day 9.[37,38] Thus, it becomes important to confirm that the telencephalons of males produce more estradiol *in vivo* than do those of females (and if so when) and to isolate the factors that regulate estrogen synthesis and cause it to be sexually dimorphic.

SEX CHROMOSOME GENES AS THE PRIMARY AGENTS OF BRAIN SEXUAL DIFFERENTIATION

As doubts arose concerning the gonadal origin of sex differences in the song system, attention turned to other factors that might initiate sexual differentiation. Possible contributors are the genes encoded on the sex chromosomes because they are the only genes that are present in different numbers in the two sexes at the time of conception,[92] and sex differences in neural expression of sex chromosome genes continue throughout life.[93] In both invertebrates and mammals,[93,94] sex chromosome genes are known to act within cells to cause sex differences in neural and non-neural phenotypes. In mammals, for example, gonadal differentiation, embryonic growth rate, differentiation of genitalia (in the marsupial wallaby), and sex differences in midbrain dopamine neurons have all been found to be mediated, not by the effect of steroids, but by differences in expression of sex chromosome genes.[92] Similarly, sexual differentiation of the brain and other tissues in *Drosophila* is attributed to sex differences in the dosage of genes encoded on the X chromosome (higher in females with two doses of X genes, lower in males with one dose of X genes).[95,96] Thus, XX and XY cells differ in their constitutive expression of X and Y genes, and these differences in numerous species control the phenotypic sex of specific cells.

In birds, males are homogametic (ZZ) and females are heterogametic (ZW). Thus, female cells express W genes not found in males, and male cells have a higher genomic dose of Z genes than female cells. The avian W and Z chromosomes share some characteristics with mammalian X and Y chromosomes. Both Z-W and X-Y chromosomes are thought to have evolved from an ancient pair of autosomes.[97,98] One chromosome of the pair (W and Y) has lost most of its genes during evolution, so that very few remain (for example, only 27 proteins are encoded by the human Y chromosome).[99] Genes on the W and Y chromosomes typically have a closely related homologous gene on the Z or X, respectively.[99,100] Thus, expression of W genes in female brain cells does not necessarily cause a sex-specific phenotype because the closely related homologous Z gene may be expressed in the male (ZZ) cells.[101] In mammalian cells, one of the two X chromosomes is often transcriptionally silenced by the process of X-inactivation, which will tend to balance the expression of X genes in XX and XY cells.[102] However, X-inactivation is incomplete, so that as many as 19% of X genes in humans escape inactivation.[103] It is not yet known whether analogous Z-inactivation occurs in birds,[104] but some Z genes are expressed at a higher level in adult male zebra finch brain than in female zebra finch brain.[101,105] To date only five W genes have been identified and about 50 Z genes in birds.[106–113] Thus, little information is available concerning avian sex chromosome genes and their patterns of expression. In zebra finches, for example, only one Z-W gene pair has been analyzed in some detail. CHD1Z and CHD1W have quite similar predicted protein sequences, and appear to have a similar pattern of expression throughout the adult brain.[101] However, the promoters of the two genes show substantial differences, and the temporal patterns of expression differ in the first week after hatching, suggesting the possibility that the Z and W forms of CHD1 might have sex-specific effects. There is, however, no known link between CHD1 and song system development.

Recent analysis of a bilateral gynandromorphic zebra finch (FIG. 2) supports the idea that the genetic sex of brain cells contributes significantly to sexual differenti-

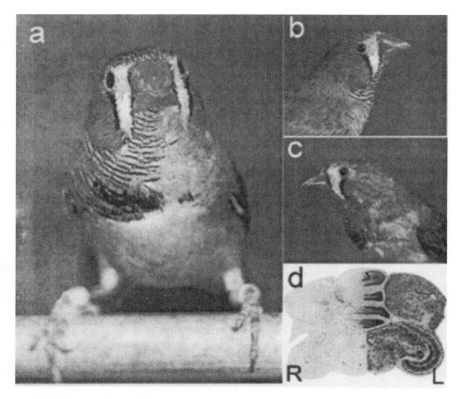

FIGURE 2. The gynandromorphic finch had male plumage (chest bar and stripes, orange cheek patch) on its right side (**a, b**), and gray female plumage on its left side (**a, c**), with a sharp line dividing the male and female plumage at the midline. A testis was found on the right and an ovary on the left (not shown). In the brain (**d**), *in situ* hybridization for the W-linked ASW mRNA, which is expressed normally only in females (dark indicates expression), shows that labeling is limited almost completely to the left side of the brain, compatible with other data suggesting that the right brain had a male (ZZ) genotype and the left brain a female (ZW) genotype. Nuclei within the song system were more masculine on the right than on the left, a lateral difference attributable to genetic differences between the sides rather than a systemic factor such as gonadal hormones. (From Agate *et al.*[105])

ation of the song system.[105] This individual had male plumage on the right side of its body and female plumage on the left. The dividing line between right and left plumage was sharp and at the midline. The right gonad was a testis and the left gonad an ovary. In the brain, expression of W genes was largely limited to the left half, with a clear separation at the midline. In addition, the right half of the brain expressed higher levels of Z-linked genes, a pattern compatible with a ZZ genotype for the right brain and ZW genotype for the left brain. Analysis of genomic DNA demonstrated higher levels of W DNA on the left than on the right, in brain and other tissues. The amount of DNA in blood cells was in the diploid range, indicating that the bird was not a sex chromosome aneuploid or triploid. In the neural song system, HVC was 82% larger on the right side than on the left, a difference far outside of the normal range of lateral differences in volume of HVC. This finding, and the fact that area X was also somewhat larger on the right than the left side, is consistent with a primary role of genes acting in HVC to stimulate of masculinization. Note that, if circulating hormones of gonadal origin had been solely responsible for sexual differentiation of the song system, in the gyandromorph the two sides of the song system should have been equivalent. If, on the other hand, factors intrinsic to the brain cells are important, the right side should have been more masculine than the left, as was observed. The results support the idea that Z and/or W genes expressed within brain cells contribute to brain sexual differentiation. However, the female (left) side of the brain was more masculine than in a normal female, and therefore was likely masculinized by one or more diffusible factors from the male side of the animal. The diffusible factor(s) could be hormones from the unilateral testis (unlikely because females with even more testicular tissue are not masculinized).[56,80] Alternatively, a ZZ genotype in male brain cells may have caused masculine neural secretion of hormones such as estradiol, which then acted to cause partial masculine brain development. Another idea is that W gene(s) expressed in female brain cells might reduce the synthesis of or sensitivity to estradiol. Interestingly, the gynandromorph had a distinct masculine behavioral phenotype. It sang a normal song, and courted and copulated with females in a normal fashion. These results suggest that the morphology of brain regions need not be completely masculinized in order to facilitate the display of masculine reproductive behaviors.

A study in Japanese quail also recently supports the idea that the genetic sex of brain cells constrains the cell's functional phenotype.[30] When genetically female hypothalamic tissue was transplanted into the body of a male, testicular growth and testosterone secretion were lower than in genetic males receiving transplants of genetically male hypothalamus. The result suggests that genetically female cells could not support the normal masculine function of the hypothalamo-pituitary-gonadal axis. A number of sexually dimorphic features (POA anatomy and neurochemistry, as well as reproductive behaviors) were also feminized in these individuals, presumably due to the relative lack of circulating testosterone.

CELLULAR MODELS OF ESTROGEN AND ANDROGEN ACTION

The cellular mechanisms mediating sexual differentiation of the telencephalic song circuit are diverse. Sex differences in cell death contribute to differentiation of lMAN and RA. Nucleus lMAN becomes sexually dimorphic because females lose more of their original RA-projecting neurons than do males.[114,115] RA is initially similar in size and structure in juvenile male and female zebra finches, and becomes dimorphic when it loses more neurons after day 15 in females than in males.[34,48,116,117] RA becomes sexually dimorphic by day 25 even if its neurons never receive their two major inputs from HVC and lMAN,[118] indicating that at least some of the sexual differentiation of RA is not secondary to sex differences in HVC and lMAN. Although males and females have the same number and size of RA neurons at day 18, they differ in the number of surviving glial cells that were born a few days earlier.[119] Therefore, trophic factors from glia might regulate the sexually dimorphic cell loss in RA. Indeed, when the potent glial mitogen fibroblast growth factor 2 is infused in the RA of juvenile females, it reduces normally occurring cell loss.[120]

In contrast to RA and lMAN, sexual differentiation of HVC and area X reflects the greater addition of new neurons in males in the posthatching period including days 20–30.[121] Estradiol treatment of females after hatching masculinizes neuron number in these nuclei. In RA, estradiol prevents cell death in males,[34,117] whereas in HVC it increases the addition of neurons born around posthatch day 15.[114,122] Estradiol acts on postmitotic neurons in HVC,[122] but probably not by preventing cell death in HVC.[123] Because HVC neurons born after hatching appear not to express estrogen receptors,[123] estradiol's action on postmitotic HVC neurons born after hatching is likely to be indirect.

In male but not in female zebra finches, BDNF expression increases in HVC between days 20 and 35. This increase is reduced by treatment of males with the estrogen synthesis (aromatase) inhibitor fadrozole and hence is attributable to a greater action of estrogen in males.[52] Premature estrogen treatment of males at days 15–25 rapidly (but transiently) increases expression of BDNF in HVC, but treatment of females at the same age does not. Thus, the male appears to have developed a greater sensitivity to estrogen by this age. The increase in BDNF suggests that some of the masculinizing actions of estradiol (e.g., cell survival, neural outgrowth) may be mediated by BDNF.[52,124]

Further suggestion of BDNF's importance in HVC comes from studies of adult female canaries, in which testosterone treatment causes growth of HVC by stimulating the addition of new neurons and other cells. One may view the HVC of an intact adult female canary as being in an unmasculinized state somewhat similar to the state of HVC just prior to sexual differentiation at about day 9 in zebra finches. From that perspective, the studies on the effects of testosterone on adult female canaries model cellular changes that may occur during the initial masculinization of HVC in males. In adult canaries, testosterone increases expression of BDNF, and the testosterone-induced growth of female HVC is blocked by antibodies to BDNF, implying that testosterone increases BDNF which increases neuronal recruitment to HVC and other forms of cellular growth.[125,126] TrkB, the high-affinity receptor for BDNF, is expressed in HVC as well.[127] The testosterone effect on BDNF appears to be mediated by vascular endothelial growth factor (VEGF).[128] Testosterone treatment increases VEGF, which triggers angiogenesis via an estrogen-sensitive increase in endothelial cell division.[102,129] Estrogen also increases the expression of the VEGF receptor, VEGF-R2, in endothelial cells, enabling them to respond to VEGF. After some delay, the endothelial cells secrete BDNF, a process that is stimulated by androgens such as DHT and testosterone, and the BDNF recruits newly born neurons to HVC.[128] Importantly, the testosterone-induced growth of female canary HVC is blocked not only by an antibody to BDNF[125] but also by an inhibitor of VEGF-R2.[128] Thus, the co-induction of BDNF and VEGF appear to be critical to the estrogen and androgen-induced masculinization of HVC in adult female canaries. A comparable process may contribute to masculinization of the developing male zebra finch's HVC.

CONCLUSIONS AND QUESTIONS FOR FUTURE RESEARCH

Sexual differentiation of the zebra finch song system appears to be initiated, at least in part, by the differential action of genes encoded on the sex chromosomes. Little is known about which genes are W- or Z-linked in birds. With the imminent sequencing of the chicken genome, more information on this linkage should soon be available. Once Z and W genes have been more thoroughly characterized, it will be important to determine which are expressed in the brain at critical times of development. Are Z genes expressed in the anlage of the song system at a higher level in males, and does this greater expression promote masculine patterns of song system development? Are W genes expressed in the cells that give rise to the song system, and do they act to prevent masculine development?

Although the literature on estrogen and androgen involvement in sexual differentiation is confusing and sometimes contradictory, several independent lines of evidence indicate that these steroids probably play a significant role. The potent masculinizing effects of estrogen in females, and the fact that in some cases aromatase inhibitors partially prevent masculinization of males,[38,45,52] all point to a masculinizing role for estrogen. However, the sexual phenotype of the song system usually correlates with genetic sex of the brain but sometimes not with the phenotypic sex of the gonads, which strongly undermines the causal relation between gonadal hormones and song system sexual differentiation. One hypothesis is that sex chromosome genes lead to sex differences in the neural synthesis of estrogen, which are detectable in slice cultures.[45] The higher levels of estrogen in male brain tissue may in turn contribute to masculinization of the song system. Because estrogen increases expression of androgen receptors in HVC, area X, and lMAN, and because HVC and area X express higher levels of androgen receptors in males than in females at the earliest stages at which these nuclei can be detected histologically, it is conceivable that androgens have greater action in males and thus contribute to subsequent masculinization. Much more information is needed to confirm this idea, however.

Another possibility is that the cellular masculinization caused by high doses of estradiol in females may not reflect a role for estradiol in the normal process of masculinization of genetic males. Some of these cellular changes might *mimic* the masculinization of males, but are normally triggered by other factors in males, for example, by genes encoded on the sex chromosomes. The clarification of these complex issues will require deeper analysis of the normal cellular events underlying the differentiation of the male and female song system, the role of W- and Z-linked genes, and the comparison with the cellular events triggered by estradiol in females.

ACKNOWLEDGMENTS

Work on zebra finches in the authors' laboratories is supported by National Institutes of Health Grants R01-MH55488 and K02-MH65907 to J.W. and R01-DC000217 to A.P.A.

REFERENCES

1. GOODFELLOW, P.N. & R. LOVELL-BADGE. 1993. SRY and sex determination in mammals. Annu. Rev. Genet. **27:** 71–92.
2. JOST, A. 1973. Becoming a male. Adv. Biosci. **10:** 3–13.
3. MEISEL, R.L. & B.D. SACHS. 1994. The physiology of male sexual behavior. *In* The Physiology of Reproduction. Second edit. E. Knobil & J.D. Neill, Eds.: 3–105. Raven Press. New York.
4. FITCH, R.H. & V.H. DENENBERG. 1998. A role for ovarian hormones in sexual differentiation of the brain. Behav. Brain Sci. **21:** 311–352.
5. NUNEZ, J.L., J. SODHI & J.M. JURASKA. 2002. Ovarian hormones after postnatal day 20 reduce neuron number in the rat primary visual cortex. J. Neurobiol. **52:** 312–321.
6. ARNOLD, A.P. & S.M. BREEDLOVE. 1985. Organizational and activational effects of sex steroids on brain and behavior: a reanalysis. Horm. Behav. **19:** 469–498.
7. PHOENIX, C.H. *et al.* 1959. Organizing action of prenatally administered testosterone propionate on the tissues mediating mating behavior in the female guinea pig. Endocrinology **65:** 369–382.
8. TOBET, S.A., D.J. ZAHNISER & M.J. BAUM. 1986. Differentiation in male ferrets of a sexually dimorphic nucleus of the preoptic/anterior hypothalamic area requires prenatal estrogen. Neuroendocrinology **44:** 299–308.
9. KINDON, H.A., M.J. BAUM & R.J. PAREDES. 1996. Medial preoptic/anterior hypothalamic lesions induce a female-typical profile of sexual partner preference in male ferrets. Horm. Behav. **30:** 514–527.
10. ULIBARRI, C. & P. YAHR. 1996. Effects of androgens and estrogens on sexual differentiation of sex behavior, scent marking, and the sexually dimorphic area of the gerbil hypothalamus. Horm. Behav. **30:** 107–130.
11. GORSKI, R.A. *et al.* 1978. Evidence for a morphological sex difference within the medial preoptic area of the rat brain. Brain Res. **148:** 333–346.
12. GORSKI, R.A. *et al.* 1980. Evidence for the existence of a sexually dimorphic nucleus in the preoptic area of the rat. J. Comp. Neurol. **193:** 529–539.
13. SIMERLY, R.B. 2002. Wired for reproduction: organization and development of sexually dimorphic circuits in the mammalian forebrain. Annu. Rev. Neurosci. **25:** 507–536.
14. DÖHLER, K.D. *et al.* 1984. Pre- and postnatal influence of testosterone propionate and diethylstilbestrol on differentiation of the sexually dimorphic nucleus of the preoptic area in male and female rats. Brain Res. **302:** 291–295.
15. DÖHLER, K.D. *et al.* 1986. Pre- and postnatal influence of an estrogen antagonist and an androgen antagonist on differentiation of the sexually dimorphic nucleus of the preoptic area in male and female rats. Neuroendocrinology **42:** 443–448.
16. RHEES, R.W., J.E. SHRYNE & R.A. GORSKI. 1990. Termination of the hormone-sensitive period for differentiation of the sexually dimorphic nucleus of the preoptic area in the male and female rats. Dev. Brain Res. **52:** 17–23.
17. RHEES, R.W., J.E. SHRYNE & R.A. GORSKI. 1990. Onset of the hormone-sensitive perinatal period for sexual differentiation of the sexually dimorphic nucleus of the preoptic area in female rats. J. Neurobiol. **21:** 781–786.
18. TARTTELIN, M.F. & R.A. GORSKI. 1988. Postnatal influence of diethylstilbestrol on the differentiation of the sexually dimorphic nucleus in the rat is as effective as perinatal treatment. Brain Res. **456:** 271–274.
19. ULIBARRI, C. & P. YAHR. 1988. Role of neonatal androgens in sexual differentiation of brain structure, scent marking, and gonadotropin secretion in gerbils. Behav. Neural Biol. **49:** 27–44.
20. HOLMAN, S.D. & A. RICE. 1996. Androgenic effects on hypothalamic asymmetry in a sexually differentiated nucleus related to vocal behavior in Mongolian gerbils. Horm. Behav. **30:** 662–672.
21. FEDER, H. 1981. Perinatal hormones and their role in the development of sexually dimorphic behaviors. *In* Neuroendocrinology of Reproduction. N.T. Adler, Ed.: 127–157. Plenum Press. New York.
22. NAFTOLIN, F. & N. MACLUSKY. 1984. Aromatization hypothesis revisited. *In* Sexual Differentiation: Basic and Clinical Aspects. M. Serio, Ed.: 79–91. Raven Press. New York.

23. BREEDLOVE, S.M., B.M. COOKE & C.L. JORDAN. 1999. The orthodox view of brain sexual differentiation. Brain Behav. Evol. **54:** 8–14.
24. PANZICA, G.C. *et al.* 1987. Sexual differentiation and hormonal control of the sexually dimorphic medial preoptic nucleus in the quail. Brain Res. **416:** 59–68.
25. ADKINS-REGAN, E. & M. ASCENZI. 1987. Social and sexual behaviour of male and female zebra finches treated with oestradiol during the nestling period. Anim. Behav. **35:** 1100–1112.
26. ADKINS-REGAN, E. *et al.* 1994. Sexual differentiation of brain and behavior in the zebra finch: critical periods for effects of early estrogen treatment. J. Neurobiol. **25:** 865–877.
27. BALTHAZART, J. & E. ADKINS-REGAN. 2002. Sexual differentiation of brain and behavior in birds. *In* Hormones, Brain and Behavior. D.W. Pfaff *et al.*, Eds.: 223–301. Academic Press. San Diego.
28. WATSON, J.T. & E. ADKINS-REGAN. 1989. Testosterone implanted in the preoptic area of male Japanese quail must be aromatized to activate copulation. Horm. Behav. **23:** 432–447.
29. WATSON, J.T. & E. ADKINS-REGAN. 1989. Activation of sexual behavior by implantation of testosterone propionate and estradiol benzoate into the preoptic area of the male Japanese quail (*Coturnix japonica*). Horm. Behav. **23:** 251–268.
30. GAHR, M. 2003. Male Japanese quails with female brains do not show male sexual behaviors. Proc. Natl. Acad. Sci. USA **100:** 7959–7964.
31. WADE, J. 2001. Zebra finch sexual differentiation: the aromatization hypothesis revisited. Microsc. Res. Tech. **54:** 354–363.
32. ARNOLD, A.P. 1992. Developmental plasticity in neural circuits controlling birdsong: sexual differentiation and the neural basis of learning. J. Neurobiol. **23:** 1506–1528.
33. NOTTEBOHM, F. & A.P. ARNOLD. 1976. Sexual dimorphism in vocal control areas of the songbird brain. Science **194:** 211–213.
34. KONISHI, M. & E. AKUTAGAWA. 1985. Neuronal growth, atrophy and death in a sexually dimorphic song nucleus in the zebra finch brain. Nature **315:** 145–147.
35. GURNEY, M.E. 1981. Hormonal control of cell form and number in the zebra finch song system. J. Neurosci. **1:** 658–673.
36. ARNOLD, A.P. 1980. Quantitative analysis of sex differences in hormone accumulation in the zebra finch brain: methodological and theoretical issues. J. Comp. Neurol. **189:** 421–436.
37. GAHR, M. & R. METZDORF. 1999. The sexually dimorphic expression of androgen receptors in the song nucleus hyperstriatalis ventrale pars caudale of the zebra finch develops independently of gonadal steroids. J. Neurosci. **19:** 2628–2636.
38. KIM, Y.-H., W.R. PERLMAN & A.P. ARNOLD. 2004. Expression of androgen receptor mRNA in zebra finch song system: developmental regulation by estrogen. J. Comp. Neurol. **469:** 535–547.
39. VENEY, S.L. & J. WADE. 2004. Steroid receptors in the adult zebra finch syrinx: a sex difference in androgen receptor mRNA, minimal expression of estrogen receptor α and aromatase. Gen. Comp. Endocrinol. **136:** 192–199.
40. WADE, J. & L. BUHLMAN. 2000. Lateralization and effects of adult androgen in a sexually dimorphic neuromuscular system controlling song in zebra finches. J. Comp. Neurol. **426:** 154–164.
41. GURNEY, M.E. & M. KONISHI. 1980. Hormone-induced sexual differentiation of brain and behavior in zebra finches. Science **208:** 1380–1383.
42. GURNEY, M.E. 1982. Behavioral correlates of sexual differentiation in the zebra finch song system. Brain Res. **231:** 153–172.
43. GRISHAM, W. & A.P. ARNOLD. 1995. A direct comparison of the masculinizing effects of testosterone, androstenedione, estrogen, and progesterone on the development of the zebra finch song system. J. Neurobiol. **26:** 163–170.
44. JACOBS, E.C., W. GRISHAM & A.P. ARNOLD. 1995. Lack of a synergistic effect between estradiol and dihydrotestosterone in the masculinization of the zebra finch song system. J. Neurobiol. **27:** 513–519.
45. HOLLOWAY, C.C. & D.F. CLAYTON. 2001. Estrogen synthesis in the male brain triggers development of the avian song control pathway *in vitro*. Nat. Neurosci. **4:** 170–175.

46. POHL-APEL, G. & R. SOSSINKA. 1984. Hormonal determination of song capacity in females of the zebra finch: critical phase of treatment. Z. Tierpsychol. **64:** 330–336.
47. SIMPSON, H.B. & D.S. VICARIO. 1991. Early estrogen treatment alone causes female zebra finches to produce learned, male-like vocalizations. J. Neurobiol. **22:** 755–776.
48. NORDEEN, K.W., E.J. NORDEEN & A.P. ARNOLD. 1986. Estrogen establishes sex differences in androgen accumulation in zebra finch brain. J. Neurosci. **6:** 734–738.
49. GRISHAM, W., G.A. MATHEWS & A.P. ARNOLD. 1994. Local intracerebral implants of estrogen masculinize some aspects of the zebra finch song system. J. Neurobiol. **25:** 185–196.
50. HERRMANN, K. & A.P. ARNOLD. 1990. Lesions of HVc block the developmental masculinizing effects of estradiol in the female zebra finch song system. J. Neurobiol. **22:** 29–39.
51. AKUTAGAWA, E. & M. KONISHI. 1994. Two separate areas of the brain differentially guide the development of a song control nucleus in the zebra finch. Proc. Natl. Acad. Sci. USA **91:** 12413–12417.
52. DITTRICH, F. *et al.* 1999. Estrogen-inducible, sex-specific expression of brain-derived neurotrophic factor mRNA in a forebrain song control nucleus of the juvenile zebra finch. Proc. Natl. Acad. Sci. USA **96:** 8241–8246.
53. WADE, J. & A.P. ARNOLD. 1994. Post-hatching inhibition of aromatase activity does not alter sexual differentiation of the zebra finch song system. Brain Res. **639:** 347–350.
54. MERTEN, M.D.P. & S. STOCKER-BUSCHINA. 1995. Fadrozole induces delayed effects on neurons in the zebra finch song system. Brain Res. **671:** 317–320.
55. BALTHAZART, J. *et al.* 1995. Effects of the aromatase inhibitor R76713 on sexual differentiation of brain and behavior in zebra finches. Behaviour **120:** 225–260.
56. WADE, J., D.A. SWENDER & T.L. MCELHINNY. 1999. Sexual differentiation of the zebra finch song system parallels genetic, not gonadal, sex. Horm. Behav. **36:** 141–152.
57. MATHEWS, G.A. & A.P. ARNOLD. 1990. Antiestrogens fail to prevent the masculine ontogeny of the zebra finch song system. Gen. Comp. Endocrinol. **80:** 48–58.
58. MATHEWS, G.A. & A.P. ARNOLD. 1991. Tamoxifen's effects on the zebra finch song system are estrogenic, not antiestrogenic. J. Neurobiol. **22:** 957–969.
59. MATHEWS, G.A., E.A. BRENOWITZ & A.P. ARNOLD. 1988. Paradoxical hypermasculinization of the zebra finch song system by an antiestrogen. Horm. Behav. **22:** 540–551.
60. GÜTTINGER, H.R. *et al.* 1993. Antioestrogen inhibits myelination in brains of juvenile zebra finches. Neuroreport **4:** 1019–1022.
61. WADE, J., L. BUHLMAN & D. SWENDER. 2002. Post-hatching hormonal modulation of a sexually dimorphic neuromuscular system controlling song in zebra finches. Brain Res. **929:** 191–201.
62. TAKAHASHI, M.M. & T. NOUMURA. 1987. Sexually dimorphic and laterally asymmetric development of the embryonic duck syrinx: effect of estrogen on *in vitro* cell proliferation and chondrogenesis. Dev. Biol. **121:** 417–422.
63. WEBB, P., P. NGUYEN & P.J. KUSHNER. 2003. Differential SERM effects on corepressor binding dictate ERα activity in vivo. J. Biol. Chem. **278:** 6912–6920.
64. SCHLINGER, B.A. & A.P. ARNOLD. 1991. Androgen effects on the development of the zebra finch song system. Brain Res. **561:** 99–105.
65. GRISHAM, W. *et al.* 2002. Antiandrogen blocks estrogen-induced masculinization of the song system in female zebra finches. J. Neurobiol. **51:** 1–8.
66. ADKINS-REGAN, E. *et al.* 1990. Sex steroid levels in developing and adult male and female zebra finches (*Poephila guttata*). Gen. Comp. Endocrinol. **78:** 93–109.
67. HUTCHISON, J.B., J.C. WINGFIELD & R.E. HUTCHISON. 1984. Sex differences in plasma concentrations of steroids during the sensitive period for brain differentiation in the zebra finch. J. Endocrinol. **103:** 363–369.
68. SCHLINGER, B.A. & A.P. ARNOLD. 1992. Plasma sex steroids and tissue aromatization in hatchling zebra finches: implications for the sexual differentiation of singing behavior. Endocrinology **130:** 289–299.
69. BOTTJER, S.W. & S.J. HEWER. 1992. Castration and antisteroid treatment impair vocal learning in male zebra finches. J. Neurobiol. **23:** 337–353.

70. PERLMAN, W.R., B. RAMACHANDRAN & A.P. ARNOLD. 2003. Expression of androgen receptor mRNA in the late embryonic and early posthatch zebra finch brain. J. Comp. Neurol. 455: 513–530.
71. LONDON, S.E., J. BOULTER & B.A. SCHLINGER. 2003. Cloning of the zebra finch androgen synthetic enzyme CYP17: a study of its neural expression throughout posthatch development. J. Comp. Neurol. 467: 496–508.
72. DEWULF, V. & S.W. BOTTJER. 2002. Age and sex differences in mitotic activity within the zebra finch telencephalon. J. Neurosci. 22: 4080–4094.
73. ARNOLD, A.P. 1997. Sexual differentiation of the zebra finch song system: positive evidence, negative evidence, null hypotheses, and a paradigm shift. J. Neurobiol. 33: 572–584.
74. FREKING, F., T. NAZAIRIANS & B.A. SCHLINGER. 2000. The expression of the sex steroid-synthesizing enzymes CYP11A1, 3β-HSD, CYP17, and CYP19 in gonads and adrenals of adult and developing zebra finches. Gen. Comp. Endocrinol. 119: 140–151.
75. VOCKEL, A., E. PRÖVE & J. BALTHAZART. 1990. Sex- and age-related differences in the activity of testosterone-metabolizing enzymes in microdissected nuclei of the zebra finch brain. Brain Res. 511: 291–302.
76. WADE, J., B.A. SCHLINGER & A.P. ARNOLD. 1995. Aromatase and 5β-reductase activity in cultures of developing zebra finch brain: an investigation of sex and regional differences. J. Neurobiol. 27: 240–251.
77. ADKINS-REGAN, E. 1981. Early organizational effects of hormones: an evolutionary perspective. In Neuroendocrinology of Reproduction: Physiology and Behavior. N.T. Adler, Ed.: 159–228. Plenum Press. New York.
78. ARNOLD, A.P. 1975. The effects of castration on song development in zebra finches (Poephila guttata). J. Exp. Zool. 191: 261–278.
79. ADKINS-REGAN, E. & M. ASCENZI. 1990. Sexual differentiation of behavior in the zebra finch: effect of early gonadectomy or androgen treatment. Horm. Behav. 24: 114–127.
80. WADE, J. & A.P. ARNOLD. 1996. Functional testicular tissue does not masculinize development of the zebra finch song system. Proc. Natl. Acad. Sci. USA 93: 5264–5268.
81. WADE, J. et al. 1996. Neither testicular androgens nor embryonic aromatase activity alters morphology of the neural song system in zebra finches. Biol. Reprod. 55: 1126–1132.
82. GONG, A. et al. 1999. Effects of embryonic treatment with fadrozole on phenotype of gonads, syrinx, and neural song system in zebra finches. Gen. Comp. Endocrinol. 115: 346–353.
83. ELBRECHT, A. & R.G. SMITH. 1992. Aromatase enzyme activity and sex determination in chickens. Science 255: 467–470.
84. SPRINGER, M.L. & J. WADE. 1997. The effects of testicular tissue and prehatching inhibition of estrogen synthesis on the development of courtship and copulatory behavior in zebra finches. Horm. Behav. 32: 46–59.
85. MARLER, P. et al. 1988. The role of sex steroids in the acquisition of birdsong. Nature 336: 770–772.
86. SCHLINGER, B.A. & A.P. ARNOLD. 1991. Brain is the major site of estrogen synthesis in a male songbird. Proc. Natl. Acad. Sci. USA 88: 4191–4194.
87. SHEN, P. et al. 1994. Isolation and characterization of a zebra finch aromatase cDNA: in situ hybridization reveals high aromatase expression in brain. Mol. Brain Res. 24: 227–237.
88. SALDANHA, C.J. et al. 2000. Distribution and regulation of telencephalic aromatase expression in the zebra finch revealed with a specific antibody. J. Comp. Neurol. 423: 619–630.
89. SCHLINGER, B.A. et al. 1994. Neuronal and non-neuronal aromatase in primary cultures of developing zebra finch telencephalon. J. Neurosci. 14: 7541–7552.
90. PETERSON, R.S., C.J. SALDANHA & B.A. SCHLINGER. 2001. Rapid upregulation of aromatase mRNA and protein following neural injury in the zebra finch (Taeniopygia guttata). J. Neuroendocrinol. 13: 317–323.

91. SCHLINGER, B.A., K.K. SOMA & S.E. LONDON. 2001. Neurosteroids and brain sexual differentiation. Trends Neurosci. **24:** 429–431.
92. ARNOLD, A.P. 2002. Concepts of genetic and hormonal induction of vertebrate sexual differentiation in the twentieth century, with special reference to the brain. *In* Hormones, Brain and Behavior. D.W. Pfaff *et al.*, Eds.: 105–135. Academic Press. San Diego.
93. XU, J., P.S. BURGOYNE & A.P. ARNOLD. 2002. Sex differences in sex chromosome gene expression in mouse brain. Hum. Mol. Genet. **11:** 1409–1419.
94. ARNOLD, A.P. & P.S. BURGOYNE. 2004. Are XX and XY brain cells intrinsically different? Trends Endocrinol. Metab. **15:** 6–11.
95. CLINE, T.W. & B.J. MEYER. 1996. Vive la différence: Males vs females in flies and worms. Ann. Rev. Genet. **30:** 637–702.
96. MARIN, I. & B.S. BAKER. 1998. The evolutionary dynamics of sex determination. Science **281:** 1990–1994.
97. DELBRIDGE, M.L. & J.A. GRAVES. 1999. Mammalian Y chromosome evolution and the male-specific functions of Y chromosome-borne genes. Rev. Reprod. **4:** 101–109.
98. FRIDOLFSSON, A.-K. *et al.* 1998. Evolution of the avian sex chromosomes from an ancestral pair of autosomes. Proc. Natl. Acad. Sci. USA **95:** 8147–8152.
99. SKALETSKY, H. *et al.* 2003. The male-specific region of the human Y chromosome is a mosaic of discrete sequence classes. Nature **423:** 825–837.
100. JEGALIAN, K. & D.C. PAGE. 1998. A proposed path by which genes common to mammalian X and Y chromosomes evolve to become X inactivated. Nature **394:** 776–780.
101. AGATE, R.J., M. CHOE & A.P. ARNOLD. 2004. Sex differences in structure and expression of the sex chromosome genes *CHD1Z* and *CHD1W* in zebra finches. Mol. Biol. Evol. **21:** 384–396.
102. LYON, M.F. 1999. X-chromosome inactivation. Curr. Biol. **9:** R235–R237.
103. CARREL, L. *et al.* 1999. A first-generation X-inactivation profile of the human X chromosome. Proc. Natl. Acad. Sci. USA **96:** 14440–14444.
104. ELLEGREN, H. 2002. Dosage compensation: Do birds do it as well? Trends Genet. **18:** 25–28.
105. AGATE, R.J. *et al.* 2003. Neural, not gonadal, origin of brain sex differences in a gynandromorphic finch. Proc. Natl. Acad. Sci. USA **100:** 4873–4878.
106. GRIFFITHS, R., S. DAAN & C. DIJKSTRA. 1996. Sex identification in birds using two CHD genes. Proc. R. Soc. Lond. B Biol. Sci. **263:** 1251–1256.
107. GRIFFITHS, R., S. DAAN & C. DIJKSTRA. 1997. Sex identification in birds using two CHD genes: erratum. R. Soc. Lond. B. Biol. Sci. **264:** 623.
108. ITOH, Y. *et al.* 2001. Chicken spindlin genes on W and Z chromosomes: transcriptional expression of both genes and dynamic behavior of spindlin in interphase and mitotic cells. Chromosome Res. **9:** 283–299.
109. ITOH, Y. *et al.* 2001. Chicken spindlin genes on W and Z chromosomes: transcriptional expression of both genes and dynamic behavior of spindlin in interphase and mitotic cells: erratum. Chromosome Res. **9:** 519.
110. HORI, T. *et al.* 2000. Wpkci, encoding an altered form of PKCI, is conserved widely on the avian W chromosome and expressed in early female embryos: implication of its role in female sex determination. Mol. Biol. Cell **11:** 3645–3660.
111. O'NEILL, M. *et al.* 2000. ASW: a gene with conserved avian W-linkage and female specific expression in chick embryonic gonad. Dev. Genes Evol. **210:** 243–249.
112. REED, K.J. & A.H. SINCLAIR. 2002. FET-1: a novel W-linked, female specific gene upregulated in the embryonic chicken ovary. Mech. Dev. **119** (Suppl. 1): S87–90.
113. SCHMID, M. *et al.* 2000. First report on chicken genes and chromosomes. Cytogenet. Cell Genet. **90:** 169–218.
114. NORDEEN, E.J. & K.W. NORDEEN. 1989. Estrogen stimulates the incorporation of new neurons into avian song nuclei during adolescence. Dev. Brain Res. **49:** 27–32.
115. NORDEEN, E.J., K.W. NORDEEN & A.P. ARNOLD. 1987. Sexual differentiation of androgen accumulation within the zebra finch brain through selective cell loss and addition. J. Comp. Neurol. **259:** 393–399.

116. KONISHI, M. & E. AKUTAGAWA. 1990. Growth and atrophy of neurons labeled at their birth in a song nucleus of the zebra finch. Proc. Natl. Acad. Sci. USA **87:** 3538–3541.
117. KONISHI, M. & E. AKUTAGAWA. 1987. Hormonal control of cell death in a sexually dimorphic song nucleus in the zebra finch. Ciba Found. Symp. **126:** 173–185.
118. BUREK, M.J., K.W. NORDEEN & E.J. NORDEEN. 1995. Initial sex differences in neuron growth and survival within an avian song nucleus develop in the absence of afferent input. J. Neurobiol. **27:** 85–96.
119. NORDEEN, E.J. & K.W. NORDEEN. 1996. Sex difference among nonneuronal cells precedes sexually dimorphic neuron growth and survival in an avian song control nucleus. J. Neurobiol. **30:** 531–542.
120. NORDEEN, E.J., L. VOELKEL & K.W. NORDEEN. 1998. Fibroblast growth factor-2 stimulates cell proliferation and decreases sexually dimorphic cell death in an avian song control nucleus. J. Neurobiol. **37:** 573–581.
121. NORDEEN, E.J. & K.W. NORDEEN. 1988. Sex and regional differences in the incorporation of neurons born during song learning in zebra finches. J. Neurosci. **8:** 2869–2874.
122. BUREK, M.J., K.W. NORDEEN & E.J. NORDEEN. 1995. Estrogen promotes neuron addition to an avian song-control nucleus by regulating post-mitotic events. Dev. Brain Res. **85:** 220–224.
123. BUREK, M.J., K.W. NORDEEN & E.J. NORDEEN. 1997. Sexually dimorphic neuron addition to an avian song-control region is not accounted for by sex differences in cell death. J. Neurobiol. **33:** 61–71.
124. AKUTAGAWA, E. & M. KONISHI. 1998. Transient expression and transport of brain-derived neurotrophic factor in the male zebra finch's song system during vocal development. Proc. Natl. Acad. Sci. USA **95:** 11429–11434.
125. RASIKA, S., A. ALVAREZ-BUYLLA & F. NOTTEBOHM. 1999. BDNF mediates the effects of testosterone on the survival of new neurons in an adult brain. Neuron **22:** 53–62.
126. RASIKA, S., F. NOTTEBOHM & A. ALVAREZ-BUYLLA. 1994. Testosterone increases the recruitment and/or survival of new high vocal center neurons in adult female canaries. Proc. Natl. Acad. Sci. USA **91:** 7854–7858.
127. WADE, J. 2000. TrkB-like immunoreactivity in the song system of developing zebra finches. J. Chem. Neuroanat. **19:** 33–39.
128. LOUISSAINT, A. et al. 2002. Coordinated interaction of neurogenesis and angiogenesis in the adult songbird brain. Neuron **34:** 945–960.
129. GOLDMAN, S.A. & F. NOTTEBOHM. 1983. Neuronal production, migration, and differentiation in a vocal control nucleus of the adult female canary brain. Proc. Natl. Acad. Sci. USA **80:** 2390–2394.

Plasticity of the Adult Avian Song Control System

ELIOT A. BRENOWITZ

Departments of Psychology and Biology, and the Virginia Merrill Bloedel Hearing Research Center, University of Washington, Seattle, Washington 98195-1525, USA

ABSTRACT: There is extensive plasticity of the song behavior of birds and the neuroendocrine circuit that regulates this behavior in adulthood. One of the most pronounced examples of plasticity, found in every species of seasonally breeding bird examined, is the occurrence of large seasonal changes in the size of song control nuclei and in their cellular attributes. This seasonal plasticity of the song circuits is primarily regulated by changes in the secretion and metabolism of gonadal testosterone (T). Both androgenic and estrogenic sex steroids contribute to seasonal growth of the song system. These steroids act directly on the forebrain song nucleus HVC, which then stimulates growth of its efferent target nuclei transsynaptically. Seasonal growth and regression of the song circuits occur rapidly and sequentially following changes in circulating T and its metabolites. As the neural song circuits change across seasons, there are changes in different aspects of song behavior, including the structural stereotypy of songs, their duration, and the rate of production. The burden of evidence supports a model in which changes in song behavior are a consequence rather than a cause of the changes in the song circuits of the brain. Seasonal plasticity of the song system may have evolved as an adaptation to reduce the energetic demands imposed by these regions of the brain outside the breeding season, when the use of song for mate attraction and territorial defense is reduced or absent. The synaptic plasticity that accompanies seasonal changes in the song system may have acted as a preadaptation that enabled the evolution of adult song learning in some species of birds.

KEYWORDS: bird; birdsong; song; songbird; song control system; plasticity; androgen; testosterone; estrogen; sex steroids; hormone; steroid; season; neurogenesis; neurotrophic,; brain-derived neurotrophic factor; learning; evolution; sparrow

INTRODUCTION

A fundamental feature of nervous systems is that they provide a basis for the plasticity of structure and function that, in turn, allows animals to adapt to changes in their environment. Seasonal changes of the environment that are critical to survival and reproduction have a profound effect on birds and essentially all other animals. It

Address for correspondence: Eliot A. Brenowitz, Department of Psychology, Box 351525, University of Washington, Seattle, WA 98195-1525. Fax: 206-685-3157.
eliotb@u.washington.edu
<http://web.psych.washington.edu/directory/?option=info&person_id=10>

Ann. N.Y. Acad. Sci. 1016: 560–585 (2004). © 2004 New York Academy of Sciences.
doi: 10.1196/annals.1298.006

is therefore not surprising that seasonal plasticity of the brain has been observed in every vertebrate taxon.[1] The avian song control system provides the best model for studying the mechanisms and functional significance of seasonal plasticity in brain and behavior, with changes that are the most pronounced yet observed in any vertebrate model: song is a learned stereotyped behavior that can be quantitatively analyzed, it is regulated by well-identified neural circuits, and sex steroids and their metabolites exert a strong influence on the morphology and physiology of these neural circuits.

Various forms of plasticity are observed in the birdsong system, including (1) ongoing neurogenesis and neuronal recruitment in forebrain song control regions,(2) pronounced seasonal changes in the structure and physiology of song nuclei, (3) social influences on seasonal growth and immediate early gene expression, and (4) changes in adult song behavior, including the learning of new songs in some species. Here I will examine the proximate mechanisms underlying seasonal plasticity, discuss potential adaptive benefits of plasticity in the song control system, and speculate on the possible relationship between brain plasticity and the evolution of adult song learning.

SONG BEHAVIOR AND LEARNING

Song is a critical aspect of reproduction in songbirds. In most species song is produced only by the male and is used to defend a territory and attract females. In several tropical species, both sexes sing, sometimes in complex vocal duets.

Song must be learned by songbirds. Young birds acquire a sensory model of song by listening to adult conspecifics and subsequently convert this memory to a motor pattern of song production in the sensorimotor phase of development. There is a progressive improvement of song structure from subsong to crystallized (i.e., stereotyped) song. Species vary widely in the timing of song learning, but two general developmental patterns exist. In "closed-ended" species, such as the zebra finch[2] and the white-crowned sparrow,[3] song learning is usually restricted to the first year of life. In "open-ended" species, such as the canary[4] and the starling,[5] substantial song learning continues at least into the second year. In the adult male canary, motor song learning is most pronounced in the nonbreeding season.[6]

SONG CONTROL SYSTEM AND INFLUENCES
OF STEROID SEX HORMONES

Our current view of the network of interconnected discrete brain regions involved in song learning and production is summarized in FIGURE 1 (see Farries; Jarvis; Wild; Reiner and colleagues, this volume). The main descending motor pathway is essential for song production. The anterior forebrain pathway (AFP) is essential for song learning and for the maintenance of crystallized song in relation to auditory feedback.[7] Parallels have been drawn between the anterior forebrain pathway in songbirds and the basal ganglia system in mammals.[8,9]

Steroid sex hormones have pronounced effects on song learning and production, and the juvenile development and adult plasticity of the song circuits[10] (see Harding;

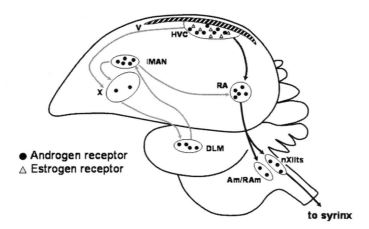

FIGURE 1. Simplified schematic sagittal view of the avian song control system showing the distribution of steroid receptors. *Black arrows* connect nuclei in the main descending
motor circuit, and *gray arrows* connect nuclei in the anterior forebrain circuit. DLM, Dorsolateral nucleus of the medial thalamus; lMAN, lateral portion of the magnocellular nucleus of the anterior nidopallium; nXIIts, the tracheosyringeal portion of the hypoglossal
nucleus; RA, the robust nucleus of the arcopallium; syrinx, vocal production organ; V, lateral ventricle; X, area X of the medial striatum.

Wade and Arnold; Ball and colleagues, this volume. Nuclear receptors for testosterone (T) and/or its androgenic metabolites (AR) are present in the song nuclei HVC,
RA, LMAN, ICo (intercollicular nucleus), and nXIIts in all species of songbird examined, and AR mRNA is present in area X.[11] Estrogen receptors (ER) occur to
varying degrees in different species in HVC and ICo.[10] In HVC, both RA- and area
X–projecting neurons contain AR,[12] and area X–projecting neurons also contain ER
(though not in the same individual cells).[13]

Males castrated as juveniles can acquire a sensory model of conspecific song and
go through the early stages of sensorimotor song learning, but cannot develop stereotyped adult song without T replacement.[14–16] Sex steroids are necessary for the
activation of song behavior in adults. Castration reduces or eliminates song, and
treatment with T or a combination of estrogenic (E) and α-reduced androgenic steroids reinstates it (see Harding, this volume).

SEASONALITY OF BREEDING AND SONG BEHAVIOR IN BIRDS

Photoperiod is the most common environmental factor that influences activation
of the avian reproductive system (Ball and colleagues, this volume). In arctic, temperate, and subtropical birds, breeding is usually restricted to spring and early summer.
Reproduction may also be seasonal in tropical species in which there are seasonal
changes in environmental factors, such as rainfall, that influence breeding.[17] Song behavior occurs most often or only in the breeding season. As will be discussed below

in detail, in both closed-ended and open-ended species that sing throughout the year, song structure also changes seasonally.[4,18,19] Open-ended learners, such as canaries, develop more new songs during the nonbreeding period of song instability.[4,20]

SEASONAL PLASTICITY IN THE BRAIN

Seasonal changes in brain structure were first reported in the song system of domestic canaries by Nottebohm.[21] The song control system provides the most pronounced example of seasonal plasticity in an adult brain and remains the leading model for study of this process.

Seasonal changes in song behavior are accompanied by changes in the morphology of song nuclei in every seasonally breeding songbird species that has been examined, including rufous-collared sparrows (*Zonotrichia capensis*) that breed seasonally in the Andes on the equator[1,17,22] (see also Ball and colleagues, this volume) (TABLE 1). The volumes of HVC, RA, X, and nXIIts increase by up to 200% during the breeding season in both open-ended and closed-ended song learners (FIG. 2). These seasonal changes are observed regardless of what cytological markers are used to define the borders of the nuclei.[1] Cellular attributes of song regions also change (TABLE 1).[6,23,24] The spontaneous neurophysiological activity of RA neurons is greater in breeding condition white-crowned sparrows (*Zonotrichia leucophrys*).[25]

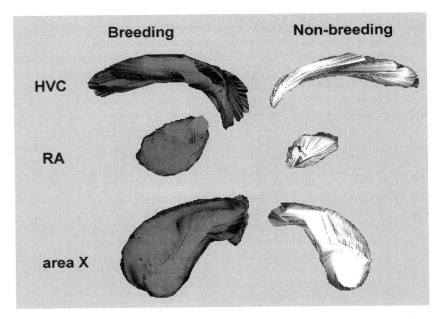

FIGURE 2. Song nuclei of spotted towhees represented three-dimensionally, from a caudal perspective. HVC, RA, and area X are each greater in three-dimensional extent in breeding-condition birds (*shown in gray*) than in non-breeding-condition birds (*shown in white*). (Adapted from Bentley and Brenowitz.[113])

TABLE 1. Attributes of song system that change seasonally

Volumes of HVC, RA, area X, and nXIIts
Neuronal number in HVC
Neuronal soma size in RA, area X, and LMAN
Neuronal density in RA and area X
Synaptic/dendritic traits in RA
Metabolic capacity of neurons in HVC, RA, and X
Spontaneous electrophysiological activity of RA neurons[a]
Incorporation of new neurons into HVC
Song stereotypy, duration, and rate of production

[a]See Park and colleagues.[25] See reviews by Tramontin and Brenowitz[1] and Ball[112] for other references.

An especially interesting form of seasonal plasticity is a dramatic change in neuron number in HVC. In wild-caught song sparrows (*Melospiza melodia*), for example, neuron number in HVC increases from about 150,000 in the fall to 250,000 during the breeding season.[18] This change in neuron number results from seasonal patterns of cell death and ongoing neurogenesis. At the end of the breeding season, circulating T levels drop and there is an increase in the death of existing HVC neurons (Kirn, this volume). There is a subsequent increase in the rate of incorporation of new neurons to HVC in nonbreeding birds, in both open-ended and closed-ended species.[26,27]

SEX STEROID INFLUENCES ON SEASONAL PLASTICITY

As described above, sex steroid hormones and their metabolites influence the development of song behavior and the song control circuits. The secretion and metabolism of gonadal steroids vary with season; plasma T levels in males are high during breeding and low after breeding. These seasonal changes in circulating hormone levels modulate song production (birds sing frequently in the breeding season and less or not at all outside of breeding) and are correlated with the morphological changes in the song control regions (which are fully grown when T levels are high, and regressed when T is low).[18]

The seasonal changes in the song nuclei are primarily regulated by changes in gonadal T and its metabolites. Smith and colleagues[28] showed that T induced volumetric and neuronal growth in HVC, RA, X, and nXIIts in castrated Gambel's white-crowned sparrows housed on either long days (LD) or short days (SD). An LD photoperiod in the absence of a T implant induced only small increases in neuron size and spacing in RA. Other studies are consistent with the conclusion that growth of the song nuclei is due primarily to increased levels of T and its metabolites in breeding birds.[29,30]

The sensitivity of song nuclei to sex steroids varies seasonally. Immunostaining for the AR in the HVC of male Gambel's white-crowned sparrows is more intense and labels more cells during the breeding season when plasma T levels are high, than in the fall when plasma T drops to basal levels.[31] The expression of AR and ER mRNA by cells in HVC is greater in breeding canaries.[32] In starlings that are photorefractory treatment with exogenous T does not increase HVC volume.[33] T does induce growth of HVC in photorefractory white-crowned sparrows,[34] however, suggesting that there are species differences in seasonal patterns of sensitivity to the trophic effects of T.

T secreted by the gonads may be metabolized in the brain to either physiologically active androgens, such as 5α-dihydrotestosterone (DHT), or estrogens, such as estradiol (E_2). This observation raises the possibility that the effects of T on seasonal growth of the song circuits may be mediated by androgens, estrogens, or both. In

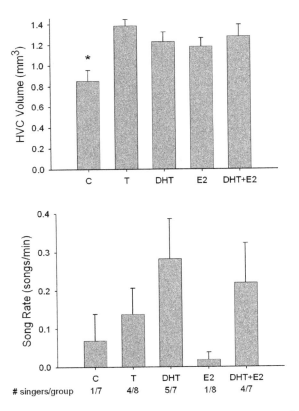

FIGURE 3. Effects of different sex steroids on the size of HVC (*top*) and on song behavior (*bottom*) in castrated male Gambel's white-crowned sparrows. Androgens and estrogens significantly increased the mean volume of HVC. * indicates that HVC in controls (C) was significantly smaller than in all steroid-treated groups. No significant differences were detected among groups that received steroid implants. *Bars* in lower panel represent means of maximum song rate. *Numbers* beneath the *x* axis represent the ratio of singing birds to all birds in each treatment group. While maximum song rate did not differ significantly among treatment groups, only one of seven E_2-treated birds sang, and that bird sang very little. Error bars represent the standard error of the mean. (Adapted from Tramontin and colleagues.[37])

adult female canaries exogenous DHT and E_2 delivered together stimulated greater dendritic growth in RA than did either metabolite alone.[35] E_2 promoted the survival of new neurons and decreased neuronal turnover in the HVC of adult male canaries.[36] To measure the relative contributions of androgens and estrogens to seasonal growth, castrated Gambel's white-crowned sparrows with regressed song nuclei were implanted with either T, DHT, E_2, or a combination of DHT+E_2.[37] All three steroid treatments increased the volumes of HVC, RA, and X when compared to controls (FIG. 3). These data demonstrate that androgen and estrogen receptor binding are each sufficient to trigger seasonal growth of the song circuits, and that T's effects may depend, in part, upon enzymatic conversion of T to active metabolites. Song production was highly variable within these treatment groups. Interestingly, only one of seven birds treated with E_2 alone was observed to sing, whereas a majority of birds with T or DHT sang. Despite the low level of song in E_2-treated birds, however, this hormone induced substantial growth of the song nuclei. This observation suggests that increased song behavior is not the primary factor driving changes in the morphology of the song circuits, as will be discussed further below.

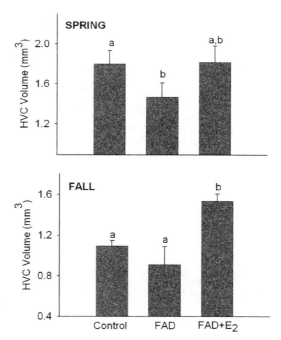

FIGURE 4. Effects of estrogen manipulations on the volume of HVC. Subjects were wild adult male song sparrows in the spring and fall. Birds were treated with vehicle (control), the aromatase inhibitor fadrozole (FAD), or fadrozole and concurrent estrogen replacement (FAD+E_2). *Letters* above bars denote groups that are significantly different (ANOVA followed by *post hoc* pairwise comparisons). In the spring, FAD-treatment reduced HVC volume, and E_2 blocked this effect. In the fall treatment with E_2 stimulated growth of HVC. (Adapted from Soma and colleagues[38])

Additional evidence in support of an estrogenic contribution to seasonal growth of the song circuits comes from a study of wild male song sparrows.[38] Territorial males were implanted in both the breeding and non-breeding seasons with osmotic pumps that released fadrozole, an inhibitor of the aromatase enzyme that catalyzes the conversion of T to E_2. In breeding males, aromatase inhibition caused the volume of HVC to decrease, and this effect was partially rescued by concurrent estrogen replacement (FIG. 4). It is noteworthy that fadrozole decreased HVC volume even though plasma T increased in breeding males due to disrupted neuroendocrine feedback. Fadrozole-treated males sang less than controls in response to song playback and a live decoy.[39] In nonbreeding males, E_2 treatment caused HVC and X to grow to maximal breeding size within two weeks. Fadrozole decreased singing behavior and E_2 treatment rescued song in the nonbreeding birds.[39] Taken together the results of Soma and colleagues[38] and Tramontin and colleagues[37] strongly suggest that both estrogenic and androgenic metabolites of gonadal T contribute to seasonal growth of the song circuits and song production.

NON-STEROIDAL CUES CONTRIBUTE TO SEASONAL PLASTICITY

The seasonal growth of the song nuclei is primarily regulated by the secretion of gonadal T and its metabolism in the brain, but non-steroidal factors such as melatonin and thyroid hormone may modulate this growth (see Ball and colleagues, this volume).[40,41] In the laboratory, social cues from sexually receptive female Gambel's white-crowned sparrows enhance the photo-induced growth of two song nuclei in their male cage-mates.[42]

SEASONAL GROWTH AND REGRESSION OF THE SONG CONTROL CIRCUITS OCCUR RAPIDLY AND SEQUENTIALLY

Seasonal changes in the song circuits seem to occur quickly following changes in photoperiod and circulating T levels. Smith and colleagues[18] measured changes in plasma T and the morphology of the song nuclei in a population of wild song sparrows at four times of the year: early spring, at the onset of breeding; late spring, at the peak of breeding; early fall, immediately after the prebasic feather molt; and late fall (December). HVC was already fully grown by early spring, and RA was intermediate in size between its regressed late fall and fully grown late spring states. These results suggested that the growth of the song system occurs rapidly and may precede the onset of breeding. To get a better sense of the time course of growth of the song system relative to the onset of breeding, Tramontin and colleagues[43] measured changes in plasma T, gonadal size, and the size of song nuclei in wild song sparrows from November to April. T levels began to increase in early February. Less than a month later, HVC and RA were fully grown, even though plasma T levels had reached only about 20% of the breeding maximum at that time, and the testes were less than 10% of typical breeding size (FIG. 5). These results indicate that growth of the song system occurs rapidly once plasma T levels first start to rise as day length increases in late winter, and precedes full seasonal reproductive development.

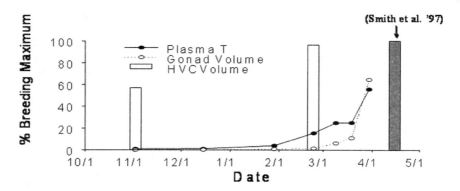

FIGURE 5. The seasonal growth of the song control system in western song sparrows precedes seasonal reproductive development. Data are expressed as a percentage of the typical level observed during the height of the breeding season in April. Mean breeding gonad volume (*open circles*) is 350 mm^3 in late April.[26] Mean breeding plasma T (*filled circles*) is approximately 5.5 ng/mL in late April.[114] HVC volume during April was measured by Smith and colleagues[18] and was approximately 1.60 mm^3. In this study, HVC (*white bars*) was fully developed by late February and was similar in volume to that reported for males during April. (Adapted from Tramontin and colleagues.[43])

The fact that the song nuclei of these sparrows grew fully when T levels were still below peak breeding levels has been interpreted as evidence that the song system can grow in response to photoperiodic cues independent of the action of T.[44] We prefer to interpret this finding as evidence that submaximal levels of circulating T are sufficient to induce growth of the song system. T levels in the study of Tramontin and colleagues[43] were just over 1 ng/mL in late February, which is consistent with the mean T level of 1.5 ng/mL observed by Smith and colleagues[18] in early spring, when HVC was fully grown. Also, as noted above, increased photoperiod has only minimal effects on growth of the song nuclei, independent of T.[28] These and other studies are consistent with the idea that the song system is stimulated to grow by the initial increases in circulating T that occur as day length increases in late winter.

The early growth of HVC and RA observed by Tramontin and colleagues[43] raised the question of just how rapidly the song circuits can grow in response to exposure to breeding photoperiod and T levels. This question was addressed in a laboratory study of Gambel's white-crowned sparrows.[45] Two groups of male white-crowns were shifted overnight from SD to LD and implanted with T at a dose sufficient to produce breeding-typical plasma levels. One group was sacrificed 7 days after the initial exposure to breeding LD+T, and the other group was sacrificed after 20 days. HVC increased its volume to breeding size within 7 days of exposure to LD+T. Neuron number in HVC increased from about 90,000 in SD control birds to 140,000 in LD+T birds by 7 days. This addition of 50,000 neurons within such a short time period represents a striking example of plasticity. HVC's efferent targets, RA and X, grew more slowly and were not significantly larger until day 20. In the field study of Soma and colleagues,[38] estradiol treatment of nonbreeding song sparrows caused X (as well as HVC) to grow to maximal breeding size within two weeks. These studies taken together indicate that the song control circuitry grows rapidly and sequentially in response to seasonal cues.

Regression of the song system at the end of the breeding season also occurs rapidly and sequentially. HVC and RA in the wild song sparrows studied by Smith and colleagues[18] were already fully regressed in the early fall, just after the prebasic feather molt. We have investigated the time course of seasonal regression of the song circuits in Gambel's white-crowned sparrows in the laboratory (Thompson and colleagues, unpublished observations). Male white-crowns were exposed to LD+T for 20 days to induce full growth of the song nuclei. The birds were castrated, their T pellets were removed, and they were shifted overnight to SD, and they were sacrificed at different times 2–20 days later. With great rapidity, HVC regressed fully to a nonbreeding volume by two days. Preliminary analysis indicates that HVC neuron number also decreased by two days, again pointing to pronounced plasticity of this nucleus to changes in circulating hormone levels. X was partially regressed by day 7, and regressed further by day 20. RA did not regress until day 20. These efferent targets therefore regress more slowly than does HVC.

SITE OF HORMONE ACTION IN SEASONAL GROWTH OF SONG CIRCUITS

Given the pronounced and rapid effects that steroid hormones have on seasonal growth of the song circuits, we may ask which nuclei within this circuit are directly targeted to initiate such growth. Some insights may be provided by the observation that HVC grows rapidly and its efferent targets RA and X grow more slowly.[45] Two hypotheses can be proposed to explain this pattern of growth. (1) As described above, steroid receptors or their mRNA are present in all of the major song nuclei (FIG. 1). It is therefore possible that steroids act directly and independently on each nucleus in the song circuits, perhaps with different time courses which could account for the differences in the time required for growth of the various nuclei. (2) Alternatively, the rapid growth of HVC and slower growth of its efferent targets may indicate that T and its metabolites initially act directly on HVC, which subsequently stimulates growth of RA and X transsynaptically.

We have conducted two types of studies to test these hypotheses. In one study we lesioned HVC on one side of the brain in Gambel's white-crowned sparrows housed on SD, and then exposed these birds to LD + systemic T implants for 30 days.[46] The unlesioned side of the brain acted as an internal control. The unilateral HVC lesions completely blocked the growth of the ipsilateral RA and X, but the contralateral RA and X, as well as the contralateral HVC, showed normal growth. In a second study we placed small T implants unilaterally in the brain near HVC or RA in male Gambel's white-crowned sparrows housed on SD for 30 days.[47] The T implant near HVC produced significant growth of the ipsilateral (but not contralateral) HVC, RA, and X, and increased neuronal number in the ipsilateral HVC. The T implant near RA, however, did not produce growth of the ipsilateral RA, HVC, or X. The failure of this latter implant to stimulate growth of RA is noteworthy given that this nucleus has abundant androgen receptors.[10] The results of these two studies indicate that T and its metabolites induce seasonal growth by acting directly on HVC, which in turn provides some permissive or trophic support of growth to its efferent targets RA and X.

The specific nature of the T-induced trophic support provided by HVC to its efferent targets is not yet clear. The release of neurotransmitter molecules across chemical synapses may have trophic effects on postsynaptic neurons.[48–50] Synaptic input from HVC may have this type of trophic effect on neurons in RA and X. Alternatively, there is evidence that presynaptic terminals from HVC may release brain-derived neurotrophic factor (BDNF) or other neurotrophins that stimulate growth of postsynaptic neurons. Neurotrophins can be transported anterogradely and taken up by postsynaptic neurons.[51,52] BDNF and other neurotrophins are present in the song system and influence the development of the song circuits in juveniles and their T-induced growth in adult females.[53–56] Singing increases BDNF mRNA in HVC, and BDNF increases neuronal recruitment in adult male canaries.[57] BDNF mRNA expression in HVC increased in male Gambel's white-crowned sparrows exposed to LD + T for 7 days compared with SD controls.[58] The steroid-stimulated seasonal growth of HVC and its efferent targets may thus also be mediated by the action of neurotrophins, perhaps interacting with chemical neurotransmission; neurotrophins are known to modulate neuronal excitability.[59]

SEASONAL CHANGES IN SONG BEHAVIOR

Seasonal changes in various aspects of song behavior accompany plasticity of the song circuits. In some species of birds, such as the spotted towhee (*Pipilo maculatus*) and sedge warbler (*Acrocephalus schoenobaenus*), song is produced only during the breeding season and is absent at other times of year. Other species, such as song sparrows, white-crowned sparrows, and canaries, sing throughout most of the year. Even in these year-round singers, however, song is produced at much higher rates during the breeding season, as a result of the higher circulating T levels then. As described above, sex steroids are necessary for the activation of song behavior.

Song structure also changes seasonally in year-round singers. Songs typically become more variable after the breeding season. The morphology of individual song syllables becomes less stereotyped in species including canaries, song sparrows, and white-crowned sparrows (FIG. 6).[18–20,45] Song sparrows sing a greater number of variations of specific song types outside the breeding season.[18] Songs also are shorter in nonbreeding song sparrows and white-crowned sparrows (FIG. 7).[18,19] Stable song produced during the breeding season, however, does not change in structure from year to year in closed-ended learners like song sparrows and white-crowned sparrows.[60,61]

Two hypotheses, which need not be mutually exclusive, can be proposed to explain why regression of the song circuits leads to increased variability of song structure outside the breeding season. (1) As the number of neurons in HVC decreases by one-third or more at the end of the breeding season, the accuracy of timing for song production is decreased. In discussing the evolutionary enlargement of the human cortex as a possible adaptation to improve the accuracy of throwing weapons at prey, Calvin[62] pointed out that due to the inherent jitter or noise introduced by ion channels, individual muscle or brain cells cannot time events with great accuracy. He suggested that a way of decreasing this cellular jitter is to assign a large number of cells to the same timing task; with an increase in the number of cells involved in timing, the timing signals can be averaged and a more accurate estimate obtained. An anal-

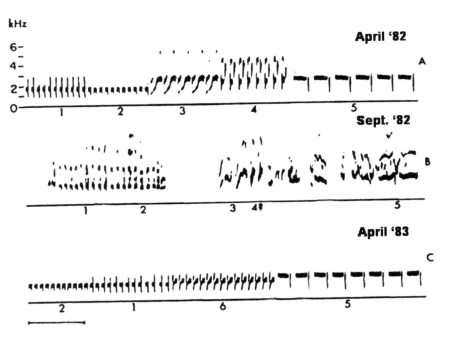

FIGURE 6. Song stereotypy changes seasonally. Spectrograms are presented of songs recorded from a single adult male canary during two successive breeding seasons (April 1982 and 1983) and the intervening non-breeding season (September 1982). During April 1982, this bird's repertoire contained highly stereotyped syllables. In September, song stereotypy was markedly decreased and syllables were poorly structured. By the following April (1983), this bird's song production was once again stable and stereotyped. Bar = 0.5 sec. (Modified, with permission, from Nottebohm and colleagues.[20])

ogous argument can be made for the song system. Some evidence suggests that neurons in HVC generate the timing signal for the motor production of song.[63,64] As neuron number in HVC decreases after the breeding season, the effective population size generating the timing signal for song is decreased and the averaged signal therefore has greater variability, which may be manifested as decreased song stereotypy.

(2) The aerobic capacity of the syringeal muscles involved in generating sound may decrease outside the breeding season, which might in turn decrease their ability to produce sustained, stereotyped song. The muscle fibers of the syrinx contain androgen receptors,[65] and the mass of the syrinx decreases when T levels drop after the breeding season.[43] In another hormone-sensitive vocal motor system, the sonic muscle of plainfin midshipman fish (*Porcithys notatus*), there is a similar seasonal change in muscle mass with changes in circulating androgens, and this is coupled with changes in the aerobic capacity of the muscle (Mommsen and Bass, cited in Walsh and colleagues[66]). If comparable changes in aerobic capacity of the syringeal muscles occur seasonally, then the regressed muscles in nonbreeding birds may not be able to sustain prolonged production of stereotyped song. If these muscles do fa-

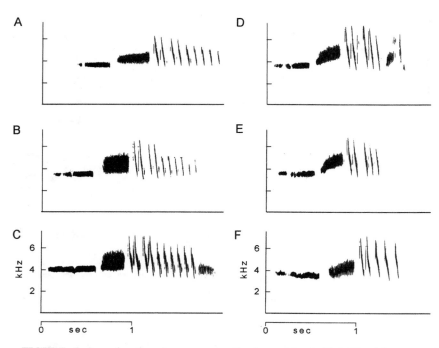

FIGURE 7. Song duration changes seasonally. Songs of male Nuttall's white-crowned sparrows recorded in the spring breeding season (**A–C**), and from sparrows at the same locality in the autumn after the breeding season (**D–F**). Note the greater duration of songs in the spring, as well as the quavering quality of the introductory whistles and the second phrases in the autumn songs. (Reprinted from Brenowitz and colleagues,[19] with permission.)

tigue more rapidly when they are regressed, then this could introduce variability in syllabic structure between successive renditions of song. Such reduced muscular aerobic capacity could also help explain the decreased duration of song in non-breeding birds.

CAUSAL RELATIONSHIPS BETWEEN SEASONAL CHANGES IN SONG BEHAVIOR AND SONG NUCLEI

Having identified neural and hormonal changes correlated with seasonal changes in singing behavior, there is a debate about the direction of the causal links involved. Are changes in song behavior a consequence or a cause of seasonal changes in the song circuits? Although it is generally assumed that causation works forward from hormonally induced changes in the song circuit to song, it has also been suggested that changes in the circuit are a consequence of the stimulating effects of song production itself (see Ball and colleagues; Cheng and Durand, this volume). One account posits that increased circulating T in the breeding season stimulates song behavior by acting on hormone-sensitive brain regions related to sexual and aggressive behavior outside the song system, rather than acting directly on the cells of the song nuclei.[44] The increased song production, in turn, is seen as inducing seasonal growth of the song nuclei by increasing the expression of the gene for BDNF, which increases neuronal recruitment in HVC.[56,57] In this scenario, the growth of the song nuclei in breeding birds is viewed as the consequence of high rates of singing at this time of year.[67]

Because it can be difficult to separate causation and correlation, the hypothesis, though appealing, is challenging to test experimentally. A fundamental limitation of this hypothesis stems from the idea that song behavior can be meaningfully dissociated from its physical substrates. Song production, for example, is the result of a constellation of events, including neuronal activity in the brain, contraction of the syringeal and respiratory muscles, pressure in the air sacs, the flow of air through the broncho-tracheal pathway, vibration of the sound-generating membranes in the syrinx, the configuration of the vocal tract, and beak movement.[68] At the risk of stating the obvious, we cannot divorce a behavior such as song production from this underlying ensemble of events. When we measure song behavior, we are indirectly measuring the outcome of this series of actions. Thus, a phenomenon such as enhanced gene expression with increased song production may reflect changes in one or more of these underlying processes, rather than being a result of changes in song behavior per se.

One way to test the idea that enhanced song production increases processes such as neuronal recruitment to HVC or seasonal growth of the song system is to devocalize birds, by cutting the tracheosyringeal nerve or lesioning the syrinx.[67,69] With such manipulations, however, the independent variable is the nerve cut or syringeal lesion, not the desired changes in song output. Identifying the direct causal basis of changes in a dependent variable such as growth of the song nuclei following manipulations therefore may be problematic. Such experimental manipulations may affect several systems, only some of which are being measured. Tracheosyringeal nerve cuts, for example, will alter syringeal function, which in turn might have unintended consequences in terms of altered feedback to brain nuclei,[70] and/or altered retrograde trophic support from syringeal muscles to nXIIts and its afferent nuclei. Syringeal lesions could alter respiration as well. Such considerations constrain our ability to attribute changes in neuronal recruitment or song nuclear volume after "devocalization" to changes in "song behavior" itself.

Similarly, the issue of seasonal growth of the song system presents particular challenges for experimental manipulations. In gonadally intact birds, many factors co-vary with each other, including circulating T and its metabolites in the brain, the morphology and physiology of the song circuits, expression of genes for BDNF and other neurotrophins, and song behavior. The level of causal complexity increases still further if, in fact, steroid hormones motivate song behavior by acting on areas of the brain outside the song system.[44] With this diverse pattern of interactions, manipulating T levels may simultaneously influence song production and neural circuits in and out of the song system. It thus becomes easy to confound correlation and causation and difficult to determine the direction of causal relationships.

There is also a practical difficulty in trying to dissociate the direct effects of sex steroids on the song circuits from such non-steroidal cues as those associated with photoperiod and social factors. Typically birds are castrated to remove the primary endogenous source of the sex steroids.[28,29,71] When partial or complete growth of the song system occurs in castrated birds exposed to long day photoperiods or social cues, one might conclude that such growth is mediated by factors other than sex steroids.[29,71] Castration, however, even when complete, does not eliminate all sex steroids. For example, the avian adrenal gland may release the androgen precursor dehydroepiandrosterone (DHEA), which in turn may be converted in the brain to active sex steroids such as T and E_2.[72,73] Castrated male song sparrows and swamp sparrows (*Melospiza georgiana*), for example, had elevated plasma levels of E_2.[15] Treatment of nonbreeding wild song sparrows with DHEA stimulated growth of HVC.[74] Furthermore, all of the essential enzymes for the *de novo* synthesis of androgens and estrogens from cholesterol have been identified in the songbird brain (Freking and Schlinger, cited in Schlinger and Brenowitz[10]; see also Wade and Arnold, this volume). It is therefore possible that physiologically active levels of sex steroid hormones may be present in the brain but undetectable in the peripheral circulation. For these reasons, it is necessary to use caution in interpreting growth of the song nuclei in castrated birds exposed to long day photoperiods and social cues.

There is also specific evidence suggesting that behavioral changes follow rather than precede changes in the song nuclei or implying that behavioral contributions to changes in the song circuits are minor compared with the effects of T and its metabolites. (1) Wild song sparrows sing at higher rates in the early fall, when juvenile males establish territories, than in the late fall. The song nuclei, however, are fully and equally regressed at both times of year.[18] This result shows that enhanced song production need not stimulate growth of the song nuclei. (2) As noted earlier, HVC grows to its full size by 7 days of LD+T in Gambel's white-crowned sparrows. Song stereotypy, however, did not increase until 20 days of treatment.[45] This observation suggests that significant growth of the song circuit must occur before song becomes more stereotyped. (3) Treatment of castrated Gambel's white-crowned sparrows with E_2 and DHT stimulated HVC and RA to grow equally. Only one of seven E_2-treated birds was observed to sing, however, and that one sang only at a very low rate, whereas most DHT-treated birds sang and did so at a high rate (FIG. 3). Song production in DHT-treated birds was considerably greater but this did not, however, produce increased growth of the song nuclei compared with the E_2-treated birds, which essentially did not sing. (4) Intracerebral T pellets implanted unilaterally near HVC in Gambel's white-crowned sparrows housed on SD are sufficient to induce growth of the ipsilateral HVC, RA, and X, but these birds were not observed to sing.[75] This result demonstrates again that sex steroids can induce growth in the absence of song production. (5) Alvarez-Borda and Nottebohm[76] compared neuronal recruitment to HVC in gonadally intact and castrated male canaries that produced comparable amounts of song in the autumn. When matched for song behavior, the intact birds had about four times as many new RA-projecting neurons and about 2.6 times as many total new HVC neurons as did the castrated birds. This result suggests that the contribution of T to the incorporation of HVC neurons is considerably greater than that of song production *per se*.

Such observations are inconsistent with the hypothesis that seasonal change in song behavior is the primary factor driving changes in the morphology and physiology of the song circuits. Instead, the burden of evidence is consistent with the idea that seasonal changes in the song nuclei are predominantly regulated by changes in gonadal T and its metabolites, and that subsequent changes in song behavior may play only a secondary or modulatory role in reinforcing the neural changes by mechanisms such as song-induced expression of BDNF. It is possible, and perhaps even likely, that there are species differences in the relative contributions to seasonal plasticity of the song circuits of sex steroids and physical actions associated with song behavior. But caution should be used in invoking species differences, however, given the complex nature of interactions between sex steroids, neural and muscular function, gene expression, and behavior.

ADAPTIVE VALUE OF SEASONAL PLASTICITY

What is the adaptive value of the extensive seasonal changes observed in the song circuits? Regrowing the song system each spring, which includes the addition of 50,000 or more neurons to HVC, must impose an energetic cost on birds. Is the cost of such yearly growth outweighed by some advantage that is gained? After all, other hormone-sensitive regions of the avian brain, such as the hippocampus, do not undergo the seasonal regression and growth characteristic of the song system.[77]

One hypothesis of the benefit of seasonal plasticity was presented by Nottebohm[21] in the original study of this phenomenon in canaries. Male canaries develop new song patterns as adults and do so in a seasonal manner. Nottebohm reasonably proposed that the synaptic plasticity associated with the seasonal changes in the song nuclei provides a neural substrate for this adult song learning. He predicted that seasonal plasticity would be restricted to open-ended song-learning species. Comparable patterns of seasonal changes in the song system, however, have been observed in every species of seasonally breeding songbird examined thus far, regardless of whether they are open-ended or closed-ended song learners. Thus, while seasonal plasticity may be necessary for adult song learning, it is not sufficient for such learning to occur and is therefore unlikely to have evolved explicitly as a mechanism for learning.

An alternative hypothesis about the adaptive value of seasonal plasticity is that rather than having evolved specifically as a mechanism for adult song learning, it is a form of performance-associated hypertrophy.[1] The sustained peak performance of a seasonally predictable behavioral task is often preceded by hypertrophy of the organs and/or tissues involved in performance of the task.[78] For example, the size of the gonads and other reproductive structures increases dramatically in preparation for the annual breeding season, and these organs regress when the breeding season is terminated. Anticipatory changes such as these are stimulated by seasonal environmental cues and mediated by neural and endocrine signaling mechanisms. The maintenance of hypertrophied organ systems and tissues is thought to be energetically expensive and so these systems regress when peak performance is not required.[79]

The principle of performance-associated hypertrophy might also pertain to seasonal plasticity of the song circuitry. This hypothesis predicts that song performance should be enhanced during the breeding season. This prediction is supported by data from canaries, white-crowned sparrows, and song sparrows. As described above, males of these species sing more stereotyped songs, and sing more frequently, during the breeding season.

Another prediction of the performance-associated hypertrophy hypothesis is that the growth of the song nuclei should precede behavioral changes. In the study of Tramontin and colleagues,[45] HVC in male Gambel's white-crowned sparrows grew fully by 7 days of exposure to LD+T, but song stereotypy only increased between 7 and 20 days.

A third prediction of the performance-associated hypertrophy hypothesis is that the energetic costs of maintaining a fully developed song system throughout the non-breeding season outweigh those associated with regrowing the song system each spring. The relative metabolic costs of maintaining and regrowing the song system each year are not yet known. Some insight into this issue, however, comes from the study of Wennstrom and colleagues.[80] They measured the activity of cytochrome oxidase (CO), an enzymatic marker of cellular metabolic capacity, in the song nuclei of Gambel's white-crowned sparrows with regressed song systems in comparison with birds who were treated with T to induce growth of the song system. T-induced growth of the song system increased CO activity considerably in HVC, RA, and X. This result suggests that the song system does impose a greater metabolic cost in its fully grown state than when regressed.

Although additional research is necessary, the existing evidence is consistent with the performance-associated hypertrophy hypothesis and suggests that seasonal plasticity of the song system may be an adaptation to reduce the energetic costs imposed by the song system in the fall and winter. Outside the breeding season, there is no need to produce frequent, stereotyped song for mate attraction and territorial defense. At the same time, birds may experience the energetic stress of migration, increased thermoregulatory demands, and decreased food availability. Songbirds are relatively small animals with large surface area to volume ratios and are therefore particularly subject to energetic constraints.[81] Given that the brain requires large amounts of energy to maintain signaling activities,[82] regression of the song system outside the breeding season reduces the energetic costs imposed by the song nuclei and this is probably advantageous for birds. On balance, the reduced energy required by a regressed song system throughout the fall and winter may outweigh the energy required to regrow it the following spring.

EVOLUTIONARY RELATIONSHIP BETWEEN SEASONAL PLASTICITY AND ADULT SONG LEARNING

Seasonal plasticity of the song system may provide insights into the evolution of adult song learning. The birdsong field has traditionally distinguished between "closed-ended" species, in which sensorimotor song learning is restricted to the first year of life, and "open-ended" or "age-independent" species, in which song learning continues into adulthood.[83,84–86] In the song learning literature there has been a largely unstated assumption that these represent two distinct strategies, perhaps reflecting a dichotomous evolutionary divergence from a common ancestral pattern (but see references 86 and 87). Various types of evidence suggest, however, that adult song plasticity may be more common than we originally thought, particularly in closed-ended species, and that closed-ended and open-ended song learning are not dichotomous but lie on a continuum. In reviewing this evidence, I will consider adulthood to begin when birds first become reproductively competent. Due to space constraints, only selected examples in support of each point can be cited.

(1) The timing of song memorization and sensorimotor development may be strongly influenced by photoperiod and the amount of song a male hears. Kroodsma and Pickert[88] showed that male marsh wrens (*Cistothorus palustris*) hatched early in the breeding season and exposed to long-day photoperiods in the laboratory complete their acquisition of song models in the hatching year. Males born late in the breeding season and exposed only to shorter photoperiods, however, retained the ability to learn songs the following spring. Due to short breeding seasons at high altitudes or northern latitudes and a parasitic reproductive pattern where young are raised in the nest of other species, wild migratory brown-headed cowbirds (*Molothrus ater*) also show evidence of prolonged sensitive periods for development of local dialect songs.[89–91] Young males hatched late in the breeding season have restricted opportunities to hear and acquire a sensory memory of local songs. The memorization phase of development continues during the next breeding season, a year after they were hatched. These sexually mature yearling males, however, do not produce their newly acquired local songs until the start of their second breeding season.

(2) The timing of song development may be influenced by social interactions. White-crowned sparrows can be induced to learn heterospecific songs, if housed with other species, and to learn the songs of live tutors first encountered beyond the close of the sensitive period for birds tutored by tape recording.[92] In migratory indigo buntings (*Passerina cyanea*), males may defer memorizing songs until the first breeding season the year after hatching, when they learn the song of a local territorial neighbor with whom they will interact aggressively.[93] These year-old bunting males appear to selectively copy the songs of adult males that either arrived early in the breeding season, whose song would thus be heard over the greatest time period, or that had relatively more blue plumage, which is typical of older birds. Similarly, young saddleback (*Philesturnus carunculatus*) males seem to delay song learning until their first breeding season, when they learn songs produced by adult males in that area, rather than in the area where the young males hatched.[94] A potential advantage of such social copying is that learning the songs of adjacent territorial males allows a young bird to engage in aggressive song-matching interactions with them. It is possible that some young males could have memorized these songs from local adults in their hatching year.[60,95] This suggestion does not seem likely, however, for males that do not return to their natal area to breed, and thus would not have opportunities to learn songs that specifically match those of neighbors in the previously unfamiliar breeding area.

(3) The selective retention and "discarding" of crystallized songs to form the adult song repertoire is influenced by social interactions. Some species produce more syllable types in the plastic song phase of sensorimotor learning than are retained in the stable adult song.[96] In field sparrows (*Spizella pusilla*), song sparrows, and other species, males seem to selectively retain previously learned song or note types that are most similar to those of conspecifics on neighboring territories, which facilitates song matching.[97–100]

(4) Some species retain the ability to memorize or improvise new song patterns well into adulthood. Adult European starlings and nightingales (*Luscinia megarhynchos*) can memorize and produce entirely new songs.[101,102] Adult song plasticity is perhaps most pronounced in species that mimic a wide range of sounds in their environment and consequently have very large repertoires, such as northern mockingbirds (*Mimus polyglottos*), brown thrashers (*Toxostoma rufum*), and lyrebirds

(*Menura superba*). In mockingbirds, adult repertoires may include 400 or more song types, and increase in size with age.[103] An adult brown thrasher may produce in excess of 1,800 different types of sounds in his song, and continually improvise new sounds.[104] In such species it is more parsimonious to hypothesize that pronounced age-related increases in song complexity are the outcome of improvisation or new auditory memorization than to assume that all of these signals were learned as juveniles.

(5) Disrupting auditory feedback can result in increased song variability in adult birds. Traditionally it was thought that closed-ended song learners do not require ongoing auditory feedback to maintain their crystallized songs, whereas adult open-ended learners do need to hear themselves to maintain song.[105–107] More recent studies, however, have shown that some closed-ended learning species do have to hear themselves in order to continue producing stereotyped songs as adults. Song begins to deteriorate within one week of deafening in Bengalese finches (*Lonchura striata domestica*), and after one to two months in zebra finches.[108,109] Leonardo and Konishi[110] showed that exposing adult zebra finches to delayed auditory feedback similarly leads to song deterioration after several weeks.

(6) Castration prevents the normal development of stable motor patterns of song. Nottebohm[111] castrated a male chaffinch (*Fringilla coelebs*) at six months of age, before it developed crystallized song. When he treated this bird with T at two years of age, it learned to copy a conspecific tutor song presented then. Song learning in gonadally intact chaffinches does not occur past the first year of life. Castration therefore extended the sensitive period for song development. Male swamp sparrows and song sparrows castrated by fours weeks posthatching acquired a sensory model of conspecific song and went through the subsong and early plastic song stages of sensorimotor learning. These castrated birds, however, continued to produce variable song until they were implanted with T, at which point they rapidly crystallized song.[15] When T pellets were removed from these castrates, they quickly reverted to producing more variable song.

(7) Seasonal plasticity of the song system induces plasticity of song behavior. As discussed above, even in closed-ended learning species like song sparrows and white-crowned sparrows, there are pronounced seasonal changes in song. Song becomes more variable in structure and shorter in duration in nonbreeding birds. Also, male white-crowned sparrows can temporarily sing song types early in adult breeding seasons that had been produced as juveniles during the plastic phase of song learning but were deleted at the time of crystallization.[60] By the peak of the breeding season, however, the adult birds revert to producing only the one song type on which they crystallized as a juvenile.

Taken together, these observations indicate that plasticity is a common feature of adult songs in both closed-ended and open-ended species. Rather than representing two distinct adaptations, juvenile and adult song learning may represent a continuum of plasticity. From such a perspective, closed-ended and open-ended song learning species can be regarded as differing in the degree of plasticity present in adult song, rather than in the presence or absence of plasticity. In closed-ended species, song becomes variable in structure outside the breeding season but then reverts to its previous stereotyped form in the following breeding season. In open-ended species, the plasticity of song structure outside the breeding season is more pronounced and can be exploited to develop entirely new song patterns. The observation that canaries develop more new songs outside the breeding season[4] is consistent with this suggestion.

An extension of this scenario is that seasonal plasticity of the song control circuits, which appears to be widespread among the songbirds and is therefore perhaps an ancestral trait, may have served as a preadaptation that enabled the evolution of adult song learning in some species. In this view, the synaptic plasticity that occurs with seasonal changes of the song system is necessary but not sufficient for adults to develop new songs. A broad comparative study of seasonal plasticity of song behavior and the song control system of a wider range of closed-ended and open-ended taxa will help to test the generality of this model and will foster a better understanding of the adaptive value(s) conferred by adult song learning.

SUMMARY AND CONCLUSIONS

Seasonal plasticity of the song control system occurs in every species of seasonally breeding songbird examined thus far, including a tropical species that breeds on the equator. FIGURE 8 presents a summary of some of the many interactions between photoperiod, hormones, brain, and behavior that characterize seasonal growth. As daylength increases beyond a threshold level in late winter, the hypothalamic-pituitary-gonadal axis is stimulated. The testes begin to recrudesce and secrete increased levels of T into the blood. T is transported to the brain, where it acts directly on cells in HVC via the androgen receptor. In addition, T is metabolized to E_2 in adjacent areas of the caudal telencephalon, and the E_2 may also act on cells in HVC. Both androgenic and estrogenic hormones act on HVC predominantly to increase neuron number and the overall volume. Growth of HVC induces the growth of its efferent targets RA and X transsynaptically, by the release of chemical neurotransmitters and/or neurotrophins. Volume increases of both RA and X largely result from increases in neuron size and spacing, but not in neuron number. As the song circuits grow and the syringeal muscles hypertrophy, songs become longer and more stereotyped in structure. There is also an increase in the rate of song production, perhaps due to the action of sex steroids on areas of the brain outside the song system that are associated with sexual and aggressive motivation. The neural activity associated with increased singing may reinforce or consolidate the growth of the song circuits by increased expression of the gene for BDNF in HVC neurons.

Regression of the song system after the breeding season may have evolved as an adaptation to reduce the energetic demands imposed by these regions of the brain at a time of year when song production is greatly reduced or absent. The neural and behavioral plasticity that occurs with seasonal changes of the song circuits may in turn have served as preadaptations for the evolution of adult song learning in some species of birds.

Many new questions have been raised for future research. Do androgenic and estrogenic metabolites of T act in a complementary manner directly on HVC to stimulate growth of the song circuits or is growth mediated predominantly by one of these two classes of metabolites? What is the nature of the transsynaptic support provided by HVC to stimulate the growth of its efferent targets RA and X? To what extent does the neural activity underlying increased song production contribute to growth of the song circuits? Can behavioral contributions to neural plasticity even be addressed in an interpretable way given the complex interactions between hormones, neural circuits, gene expression, and song behavior? Why does the song sys-

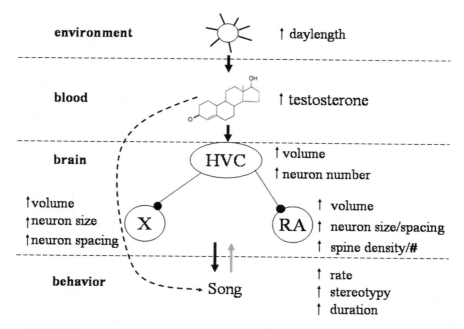

FIGURE 8. A summary of the main interactions between photoperiod, hormones, brain, and behavior that characterize seasonal growth of the song system. See text for explanation. (Modified from a figure by A.M. Wissman.)

tem undergo extensive seasonal changes whereas other hormone-sensitive brain systems remain stable throughout the year? Is there a functional relationship between seasonal plasticity of the song circuits and the ability of some species to develop new songs as adults? The pursuit of questions such as these will ensure that the song system continues to be a highly productive model for studying relationships between behavioral flexibility and plasticity of the adult brain.

ACKNOWLEDGMENTS

This research was supported by Grants MH53032 and MH 66939 from the National Institutes of Health, and by the Virginia Merrill Bloedel Hearing Research Center of the University of Washington. My thanks to Arthur Arnold, Michael Beecher, Adrian O'Loghlen, and David Perkel for comments on sections of the manuscript, and to Peter Marler and Phil Zeigler for helpful editorial comments.

REFERENCES

1. TRAMONTIN, A.D. & E.A. BRENOWITZ. 2000. Seasonal plasticity in the adult brain. Trends Neurosci. **23:** 251–258.

2. EALES, L.A. 1985. Song learning in zebra finches: some effects of song model availability on what is learnt and when. Anim. Behav. **33**: 1293–1300.
3. MARLER, P. 1970. A comparative approach to vocal learning: song development in white-crowned sparrows. J. Comp. Physiol. Psychol. Suppl. **71**: 1–25.
4. NOTTEBOHM, F. & M.E. NOTTEBOHM. 1978. Relationship between song repertoire and age in the canary, *Serinus canarius*. Z. Tierpsychol. **46**: 298–305.
5. BOHNER, J. *et al.* 1990. Song acquisition in photosensitive and photorefractory male European starlings. Horm. Behav. **24**: 582–594.
6. NOTTEBOHM, F. 1987. Plasticity in adult avian central nervous system: possible relation between hormones, learning, and brain repair. *In* Handbook of Physiology, Section 1. F. Plum, Ed.: 85–108. Williams & Wilkins. Baltimore.
7. BRAINARD, M.S. & A.J. DOUPE. 2000. Interruption of a basal ganglia-forebrain circuit prevents plasticity of learned vocalizations. Nature **404**: 762–766.
8. BOTTJER, S.W. 1993. The distribution of tyrosine hydroxylase immunoreactivity in the brains of male and female zebra finches. J. Neurobiol. **24**: 51–69.
9. PERKEL, D.J. & M.A. FARRIES. 2000. Complementary "bottom-up" and "top-down" approaches to basal ganglia function. Curr. Opin. Neurobiol. **10**: 725–731.
10. SCHLINGER, B.A. & E.A. BRENOWITZ. 2002. Neural and hormonal control of birdsong. *In* Hormones, Brain and Behavior. Vol. 2. D.W. Pfaff *et al.*, Eds.: 799–839. Academic Press. New York.
11. PERLMAN, W.R., B. RAMACHANDRAN & A.P. ARNOLD. 2003. Expression of androgen receptor mRNA in the late embryonic and early posthatch zebra finch brain. J. Comp. Neurol. **455**: 513–530.
12. SOHRABJI, F., K.W. NORDEEN & E.J. NORDEEN. 1989. Projections of androgen-accumulating neurons in a nucleus controlling avian song. Brain Res. **488**: 253–259.
13. GAHR, M. 1990. Localization of androgen receptors and estrogen receptors in the same cells of the songbird brain. Proc. Natl. Acad. Sci. USA **87**: 9445–9448.
14. ARNOLD, A.P. 1975. The effects of castration on song development in zebra finches (*Poephila guttata*). J. Exp. Zool. **191**: 261–278.
15. MARLER, P. *et al.* 1988. The role of sex steroids in the acquisition and production of birdsong. Nature **336**: 770–772.
16. BOTTJER, S.W. & S.J. HEWER. 1992. Castration and antisteroid treatment impair vocal learning in male zebra finches. J. Neurobiol. **23**: 337–353.
17. MOORE, I.T. *et al.* 2003. Seasonal plasticity in the brain of a tropical songbird. Soc. Neurosci. Abst. **29**.
18. SMITH, G.T. *et al.* 1997. Seasonal changes in testosterone, neural attributes of song control nuclei, and song structure in wild songbirds. J. Neurosci. **17**: 6001–6010.
19. BRENOWITZ, E.A. *et al.* 1998. Seasonal plasticity of the song control system in wild Nuttall's white- crowned sparrows. J. Neurobiol. **34**: 69–82.
20. NOTTEBOHM, F., M.E. NOTTEBOHM & L. CRANE. 1986. Developmental and seasonal changes in canary song and their relation to changes in the anatomy of song-control nuclei. Behav. Neural Biol. **46**: 445–471.
21. NOTTEBOHM, F. 1981. A brain for all seasons: cyclical anatomical changes in song control nuclei of the canary brain. Science **214**: 1368–1370.
22. BRENOWITZ, E.A. 1997. Comparative approaches to the avian song system. J. Neurobiol. **33**: 517–531.
23. BRENOWITZ, E.A. *et al.* 1991. Seasonal changes in avian song nuclei without seasonal changes in song repertoire. J. Neurosci. **11**: 1367–1374.
24. DEVOOGD, T.J. 1991. Endocrine modulation of the development and adult function of the avian song system. Psychoneuroendocrinol. **16**: 41–66.
25. PARK, K.H. J., E.A. BRENOWITZ & D.J. PERKEL. 2003. Testosterone and its metabolites modulate eletrophysiology of the robust nucleus of the archistriatum in a seasonal songbird. Soc. Neurosci. Abst. **29**.
26. TRAMONTIN, A.D. & E.A. BRENOWITZ. 1999. A field study of seasonal neuronal incorporation into the song control system of a songbird that lacks adult song learning. J. Neurobiol. **40**: 316–326.

27. ALVAREZ-BUYLLA, A., J.R. KIRN & F. NOTTEBOHM. 1990. Birth of projection neurons in adult avian brain may be related to perceptual or motor learning [published erratum appears in Science 250:360]. Science 249: 1444–1446.

28. SMITH, G.T., E.A. BRENOWITZ & J.C. WINGFIELD. 1997. Roles of photoperiod and testosterone in seasonal plasticity of the avian song control system. J. Neurobiol. 32: 426–442.

29. BERNARD, D.J., F.E. WILSON & G.F. BALL. 1997. Testis-dependent and -independent effects of photoperiod on volumes of song control nuclei in American tree sparrows (Spizella arborea). Brain Res. 760: 163–169.

30. GULLEDGE, C.C. & P. DEVICHE. 1997. Androgen control of vocal control region volumes in a wild migratory songbird (Junco hyemalis) is region and possibly age dependent. J. Neurobiol. 32: 391–402.

31. SOMA, K.K. et al. 1998. Seasonal changes in androgen receptor immunoreactivity in the song nucleus HVc of a wild bird. J. Comp. Neurol. 409: 224–236.

32. GAHR, M. & R. METZDORF. 1997. Distribution and dynamics in the expression of androgen and estrogen receptors in vocal control systems of songbirds. Brain Res. Bull. 44: 509–517.

33. BERNARD, D.J. & G.F. BALL. 1997. Photoperiodic condition modulates the effects of testosterone on song control nuclei volumes in male European starlings. Gen. Comp. Endocrinol. 105: 276–283.

34. WENNSTROM, K.L., B.J. REEVES & E.A. BRENOWITZ. 2001. Testosterone treatment increases the metabolic capacity of adult avian song control nuclei. J. Neurobiol. 48: 256–264.

35. DEVOOGD, T. & F. NOTTEBOHM. 1981. Gonadal hormones induce dendritic growth in the adult avian brain. Science 214: 202–204.

36. HIDALGO, A. et al. 1995. Estrogens and non-estrogenic ovarian influences combine to promote the recruitment and decrease the turnover of new neurons in the adult female canary brain. J. Neurobiol. 27: 470–487.

37. TRAMONTIN, A.D., J.C. WINGFIELD & E.A. BRENOWITZ. 2003. Androgens and estrogens induce seasonal-like growth of song nuclei in the adult songbird brain. J. Neurobiol. 57: 130–140.

38. SOMA, K.K. et al. 2004. Estrogen contributes to seasonal plasticity of the adult avian song control system. J. Neurobiol. 58: 413–422.

39. SOMA, K.K., N.A. ALDAY & B.A. SCHLINGER. 2002. 3 Beta-HSD and aromatase in songbird brain: DHEA metabolism, aggression, and song. Soc. Neurosci. Abstracts 28.

40. BENTLEY, G.E. et al. 1997. Photorefractoriness in European starlings (Sturnus vulgaris) is not dependent upon the long-day-induced rise in plasma thyroxine. Gen. Comp. Endocrinol. 107: 428–438.

41. TEKUMALLA, P.K. et al. 2002. Effects of excess thyroid hormone on cell death, cell proliferation, and new neuron incorporation in the adult zebra finch telencephalon. J. Neurobiol. 51: 323–341.

42. TRAMONTIN, A.D., J.C. WINGFIELD & E.A. BRENOWITZ. 1999. Contributions of social cues and photoperiod to seasonal plasticity in the adult avian song control system. J. Neurosci. 19: 476–483.

43. TRAMONTIN, A.D. et al. 2001. Seasonal growth of song control nuclei precedes seasonal reproductive development in wild adult song sparrows. Gen. Comp. Endocrinol. 122: 1–9.

44. BALL, G.F., L.V. RITERS & J. BALTHAZART. 2002. Neuroendocrinology of song behavior and avian brain plasticity: multiple sites of action of sex steroid hormones. Front. Neuroendocrinol. 23: 137–178.

45. TRAMONTIN, A.D., V.N. HARTMAN & E.A. BRENOWITZ. 2000. Breeding conditions induce rapid and sequential growth in adult avian song control circuits: a model of seasonal plasticity in the brain. J. Neurosci. 20: 854–861.

46. BRENOWITZ, E.A. & K. LENT. 2001. Afferent input is necessary for seasonal growth and maintenance of adult avian song control circuits. J. Neurosci. 21: 2320–2329.

47. BRENOWITZ, E.A. & K. LENT. 2002. Act locally and think globally: intracerebral test-osterone implants induce seasonal-like growth of adult avian song control circuits. Proc. Natl. Acad. Sci. USA **99**: 12421–12426.
48. BRENNEMAN, D.E., C. YU & P.G. NELSON. 1990. Multi-determinate regulation of neu-ronal survival: neuropeptides, excitatory amino acids and bioelectric activity. Int. J. Dev. Neurosci. **8**: 371–378.
49. RUBEL, E.W., R.L. HYSON & D. DURHAM. 1990. Afferent regulation of neurons in the brain stem auditory system. J. Neurobiol. **21**: 169–196.
50. GALLI-RESTA, L. et al. 1993. Afferent spontaneous electrical activity promotes the sur-vival of target cells in the developing retinotectal system of the rat. J. Neurosci. **13**: 243–250.
51. VON BARTHELD, C.S. et al. 1996. Anterograde transport of neurotrophins and axoden-dritic transfer in the developing visual system. Nature **379**: 830–833.
52. KOHARA, K. et al. 2001. Activity-dependent transfer of brain-derived neurotrophic fac-tor to postsynaptic neurons. Science **291**: 2419–2423.
53. JOHNSON, F. et al. 1997. Neurotrophins suppress apoptosis induced by deafferentation of an avian motor-cortical region. J. Neurosci. **17**: 2101–1211.
54. AKUTAGAWA, E. & M. KONISHI. 1998. Transient expression and transport of brain-derived neurotrophic factor in male zebra finch's song system during vocal develop-ment. Proc. Natl. Acad. Sci. USA **95**: 11429–11434.
55. DITTRICH, F. et al. 1999. Estrogen-inducible, sex-specific expression of brain-derived neurotrophic factor mRNA in a forebrain song control nucleus of the juvenile zebra finch. Proc. Natl. Acad. Sci. USA **96**: 8241–8246.
56. RASIKA, S., A. ALVAREZ-BUYLLA & F. NOTTEBOHM. 1999. BDNF mediates the effects of testosterone on the survival of new neurons in an adult brain. Neuron **22**: 53–62.
57. LI, X.C. et al. 2000. A relationship between behavior, neurotrophin expression, and new neuron survival. Proc. Natl. Acad. Sci. USA **97**: 8584–8589.
58. WISSMAN, A.M. & E.A. BRENOWITZ. 2003. Regulation of BDNF expression in the song system in response to seasonal cues. Soc. Neurosci. Abst. **29**.
59. SCHUMAN, E.M. 1999. Neurotrophin regulation of synaptic transmission. Curr. Opin. Neurobiol. **9**: 105–109.
60. HOUGH, G.E., II, D.A. NELSON & S.F. VOLMAN. 2000. Re-expression of songs deleted during vocal development in white-crowned sparrows, *Zonotrichia leucophrys*. Ani-mal Behav. **60**: 279–287.
61. NORDBY, J.C., S.E. CAMPBELL & M.D. BEECHER. 2002. Adult song sparrows do not alter their song repertoires. Ethology **108**: 39–50.
62. CALVIN, W.H. 1993. The unitary hypothesis: A common neural circuitry for novel manipulations, language, plan-ahead, and throwing? *In* Tools, Language, and Cogni-tion in Human Evolution. K.R. Gibson & T. Ingold, Eds.: 230–250. Cambridge Uni-versity Press. Cambridge.
63. YU, A.C. & D. MARGOLIASH. 1996. Temporal hierarchical control of singing in birds. Science **273**: 1871–1875.
64. HAHNLOSER, R.H., A.A. KOZHEVNIKOV & M.S. FEE. 2002. An ultra-sparse code under-lies the generation of neural sequences in a songbird. Nature **419**: 65–70.
65. WADE, J. & L. BUHLMAN. 2000. Lateralization and effects of adult androgen in a sexu-ally dimorphic neuromuscular system controlling song in zebra finches. J. Comp. Neurol. **426**: 154–164.
66. WALSH, P.J., T.P. MOMMSEN & A.H. BASS. 1995. Biochemical and molecular aspects of singing in batrachoidid fishes. *In* Biochemistry and Molecular Biology of Fishes. Vol. 4. P.W. Hochachka & T.P. Mommsen, Eds.: 279–289. Elsevier Science. Amster-dam.
67. SARTOR, J.J. et al. 2002. Converging evidence that song performance modulates sea-sonal changes in the avian song control system. Soc. Neurosci. Abst. **28**.
68. SUTHERS, R.A. 1997. Peripheral control and lateralization of birdsong. J. Neurobiol. **33**: 632–652.
69. WILBRECHT, L., A. CRIONAS & F. NOTTEBOHM. 2002. Experience affects recruitment of new neurons but not adult neuron number. J. Neurosci. **22**: 825–831.

70. BOTTJER, S.W. & A.P. ARNOLD. 1982. Afferent neurons in the hypoglossal nerve of the zebra finch (*Poephila guttata*): localization with horseradish peroxidase. J. Comp. Neurol. **210:** 190–197.

71. GULLEDGE, C.C. & P. DEVICHE. 1998. Photoperiod and testosterone independently affect vocal control region volumes in adolescent male songbirds. J. Neurobiol. **36:** 550–558.

72. VANSON, A., A.P. ARNOLD & B.A. SCHLINGER. 1996. 3 beta-hydroxysteroid dehydrogenase/isomerase and aromatase activity in primary cultures of developing zebra finch telencephalon: dehydroepiandrosterone as substrate for synthesis of androstenedione and estrogens. Gen. Comp. Endocrinol. **102:** 342–350.

73. SCHLINGER, B.A. *et al.* 1999. Androgen synthesis in a songbird: a study of cyp17 (17alpha-hydroxylase/C17,20-lyase) activity in the zebra finch. Gen. Comp. Endocrinol. **113:** 46–58.

74. SOMA, K.K. *et al.* 2002. Dehydroepiandrosterone (DHEA) increases territorial song and the size of an associated brain region in a male songbird. Horm. Behav. **41:** 203–212.

75. BRENOWITZ, E.A. & K. LENT. 2000. Intracerebral implants of testosterone induce seasonal-like growth of adult avian song control circuits. Soc. Neurosci. Abst. **26.**

76. ALVAREZ-BORDA, B. & F. NOTTEBOHM. 2002. Gonads and singing play separate, additive roles in new neuron recruitment in adult canary brain. J. Neurosci. **22:** 8684–8690.

77. LEE, D.W. *et al.* 2001. Hippocampal volume does not change seasonally in a non foodstoring songbird. Neurorep. **12:** 1925–1928.

78. PIERSMA, T. & A. LINDSTROM. 1997. Rapid reversible changes in organ size as a component of adaptive behavior. Trends Ecol. Evol. **12:** 134–138.

79. GAUNT, A.S. *et al.* 1990. Rapid atrophy and hypertrophy of an avian flight muscle. Auk **107:** 649–659.

80. WENNSTROM, K.L. *et al.* 2001. Testosterone treatment increases the metabolic capacity of adult avian song control nuclei. J. Neurobiol. **48:** 256–264.

81. CALDER, W.A. & J.R. KING. 1974. Thermal and caloric relations in birds. *In* Avian Biology. Vol. 4. D.S. Farner, J.R. King & K.C. Parkes, Eds.: 259–413. Academic Press. New York.

82. AMES, A., 3rd. 2000. CNS energy metabolism as related to function. Brain Res. Rev. **34:** 42–68.

83. IMMELMANN, K. 1969. Song development in the zebra finch and other estrildid finches. *In* Bird Vocalizations. R.A. Hinde, Ed.: 61–77. Cambridge UP. Cambridge.

84. SLATER, P.J. 1983. Bird song learning: theme and variations. *In* Perspectives in Ornithology. G.H. Brush & G.A. Clark, Jr., Eds.: 475–511. Cambridge University Press. Cambridge.

85. NOTTEBOHM, F. 1984. Birdsong as a model in which to study brain processes related to learning. Condor **86:** 227–236.

86. MARLER, P. & S. PETERS. 1987. A sensitive period for song acquisition in the song sparrow, *Melospiza melodia*: A case of age-limited learning. Ethology **76:** 89–100.

87. KROODSMA, D.E. & R. PICKERT. 1984. Sensitive phases for song learning: Effects of social interaction and individual variation. Animal Behav. **32:** 389–394.

88. KROODSMA, D.E. & R. PICKERT. 1980. Environmentally dependent sensitive periods for avian vocal learning. Nature **288:** 477–479.

89. O'LOGHLEN, A.L. & S.I. ROTHSTEIN. 1995. Delayed access to local songs prolongs vocal development in dialect populations of brown-headed cowbirds. Condor **97:** 402–414.

90. O'LOGHLEN, A.L. & S.I. ROTHSTEIN. 2002. Vocal development is correlated with an indicator of hatching date in brown-headed cowbirds. Condor **104:** 761–777.

91. O'LOGHLEN, A. & S.I. ROTHSTEIN. 2002. Ecological effects on song learning: Delayed development is widespread in wild populations of brown-headed cowbirds. Animal Behav. **63:** 475–486.

92. BAPTISTA, L.F. & L. PETRINOVICH. 1986. Song development in the white-crowned sparrow: Social factors and sex differences. Animal Behav. **34:** 1359–1371.

93. PAYNE, R.B. & L.L. PAYNE. 1993. Song copying and culturnal transmission in indigo buntings. Anim. Behav. **46:** 1045–1065.
94. JENKINS, P.F. 1978. Cultural transmission of song patterns and dialect development in a free-living bird population. Animal Behav. **26:** 50–78.
95. MARGOLIASH, D., C. STAICER & S.A. INOUE. 1994. The process of syllable acquisition in adult indigo buntings. Behaviour **131:** 39–64.
96. MARLER, P. & S. PETERS. 1982. Developmental overproduction and selective attrition: new processes in the epigenesis of birdsong. Dev. Psychobiol. **15:** 369–378.
97. NELSON, D.A. 1992. Song overproduction and selective attrition lead to song sharing in the field sparrow (*Spizella pusilla*). Behav. Ecol. Sociobiol. **30:** 415–424.
98. MARLER, P. 1997. Three models of song learning: evidence from behavior. J. Neurobiol. **33:** 501–516.
99. BEECHER, M.D., S.E. CAMPBELL & J.C. NORDBY. 2000. Territory tenure in song sparrows is related to song sharing with neighbours, but not to repertoire size. Animal Behav. **59:** 29–37.
100. NORDBY, J.C. *et al.* 2000. Social influences during song development in the song sparrow: A laboratory experiment simulating field conditions. Animal Behav. **59:** 1187–1197.
101. CHAIKEN, M., J. BOEHNER & P. MARLER. 1994. Repertoire turnover and the timing of song acquisition in European starlings. Behaviour **128:** 25–39.
102. GEBERZAHN, N. & H. HULTSCH. 2003. Long-time storage of song types in birds: evidence from interactive playbacks. Proc. R. Soc. Lond. B Biol. Sci. **270:** 1085–1090.
103. DERRICKSON, K.C. 1987. Yearly and situational changes in the estimate of repertoire size in northern mockingbirds. Auk **104:** 198–207.
104. KROODSMA, D.E. 1977. Vocal virtuosity in the brown thrasher. Auk **94:** 783–784.
105. KONISHI, M. & F. NOTTEBOHM. 1969. Experimental studies in the ontogeny of avian vocalizations. *In* Bird Vocalizations: Their relations to current problems in biology and psychology. Essays presented to W. H. Thorpe. R.A. Hinde, Ed. Cambridge U.P. London.
106. NOTTEBOHM, F. 1968. Auditory experience and song development in the chaffinch. Ibis **110:** 549–568.
107. NOTTEBOHM, F., T.M. STOKES & C.M. LEONARD. 1976. Central control of song in the canary, *Serinus canarius*. J. Comp. Neurol. **165:** 457–486.
108. NORDEEN, K.W. & E.J. NORDEEN. 1992. Auditory feedback is necessary for the maintenance of stereotyped song in adult zebra finches. Behav. Neural Biol. **57:** 58–66.
109. WOOLLEY, S.M. & E.W. RUBEL. 1997. Bengalese finches *Lonchura striata domestica* depend upon auditory feedback for the maintenance of adult song. J. Neurosci. **17:** 6380–6390.
110. LEONARDO, A. & M. KONISHI. 1999. Decrystallization of adult birdsong by perturbation of auditory feedback. Nature **399:** 466–470.
111. NOTTEBOHM, F. 1969. The "critical period" for song learning. Ibis **111:** 386–387.
112. BALL, G.F. 2000. Neuroendocrine basis of seasonal changes in vocal behavior among songbirds. *In* Neural Mechanisms of Communication. M. Hauser & M. Konishi, Eds.: 213–253. MIT Press. Cambridge, MA.
113. BENTLEY, G.E. & E.A. BRENOWITZ. 2002. Three-dimensional analysis of avian song control nuclei. J. Neurosci. Methods **121:** 75–80.
114. WINGFIELD, J.C. 1984. Environmental and endocrine control of reproduction in the song sparrow, Melospiza melodia. I. Temporal organization of the breeding cycle. Gen. Comp. Endocrinol. **56:** 406–416.

Seasonal Plasticity in the Song Control System

Multiple Brain Sites of Steroid Hormone Action and the Importance of Variation in Song Behavior

GREGORY F. BALL,[a] CATHERINE J. AUGER,[a] DANIEL J. BERNARD,[b] THIERRY D. CHARLIER,[c] JENNIFER J. SARTOR,[a] LAUREN V. RITERS,[d] AND JACQUES BALTHAZART[c]

[a]*Department of Psychological and Brain Sciences, Johns Hopkins University, Baltimore, Maryland 21218, USA*

[b]*Center for Biomedical Research, The Population Council and The Rockefeller University, New York, New York 10021, USA*

[c]*Center for Cellular and Molecular Neurobiology, Research Group in Behavioral Neuroendocrinology, University of Liège, 17 Place Delcour (Bat. L1), B-4020 Liège, Belgium*

[d]*Department of Zoology, University of Wisconsin, Madison, Wisconsin 53706, USA*

ABSTRACT: Birdsong, in non-tropical species, is generally more common in spring and summer when males sing to attract mates and/or defend territories. Changes in the volumes of song control nuclei, such as HVC and the robust nucleus of the arcopallium (RA), are observed seasonally. Long photoperiods in spring stimulate the recrudescence of the testes and the release of testosterone. Androgen receptors, and at times estrogen receptors, are present in HVC and RA as are co-factors that facilitate the transcriptional activity of these receptors. Thus testosterone can act directly to induce changes in nucleus volume. However, dissociations have been identified at times among long photoperiods, maximal concentrations of testosterone, large song control nuclei, and high rates of song. One explanation of these dissociations is that song behavior itself can influence neural plasticity in the song system. Testosterone can act via brain-derived neurotrophic factor (BDNF) that is also released in HVC as a result of song activity. Testosterone could enhance song nucleus volume indirectly by acting in the preoptic area, a region regulating sexual behaviors, including song, that connects to the song system through catecholaminergic cells. Seasonal neuroplasticity in the song system involves an interplay among seasonal state, testosterone action, and behavioral activity.

KEYWORDS: testosterone; photoperiod; catecholamine; European starling; seasonal reproduction

Address for correspondence: Gregory F. Ball, Department of Psychological and Brain Sciences, Johns Hopkins University, 3400 N. Charles Street, Baltimore, MD 21218-2686, USA. Voice: 410-516-7910; fax: 410-516-6008.
  gball@jhu.edu; <http://psy.jhu.edu/~ball/>

Ann. N.Y. Acad. Sci. 1016: 586–610 (2004). © 2004 New York Academy of Sciences.
doi: 10.1196/annals.1298.043

INTRODUCTION

Seasonal Plasticity in the Adult Songbird Song Control System What Is It and Why Is It Interesting?

The avian song control system has emerged as a valuable model system for the investigation of the neural bases of a complex learned behavior. Many investigators have focused on the physiological properties of cells in this circuit to elucidate the neural coding rules involved in the representation of song in the brain.[1–4] The temporal resolution of these studies is measured in seconds or milliseconds and this scale of resolution is necessary to understand the neural control of song as produced or perceived in real time. However, there is another temporal dimension to the control of song. In many songbird species, especially those that live in temperate or boreal regions of the world, song production is most common during the breeding season, which is only a few months in duration in most species and in some extreme cases may only be a few weeks.[5,6] It has been known for many years, based on field observations as well as studies of captive birds, that the reproductive state of a songbird and the associated variation in endocrine physiology can have profound effects on various aspects of song behavior.[7–9]

In this article, we selectively review studies on the neuroendocrine mechanisms involved in the seasonal regulation of song behavior and the avian song control system. We highlight recent studies of endocrine systems involved in seasonal changes in song production, with emphasis on where and how the gonadal sex steroid testosterone acts, especially with respect to the brain. We also discuss the interplay among photoperiodic cues, behavioral activation, and endocrine state on the regulation of this brain system.

Association of Seasonal Changes in the Song System with Long Photoperiods and Testosterone and Other Hormones

For investigators of the seasonal regulation of song and the song control system, the scenario most often accepted either explicitly or implicitly to account for seasonal changes is that increasing day lengths in the spring result in testicular recrudescence and associated increases in the release of the sex steroid hormone testosterone. These increases in testosterone concentration in the plasma result in increased action at neural target sites that potentiates and enhances song production.[10] With the discovery in the 1970s that key nuclei in the song control circuit exhibit binding sites for testosterone,[11,12] it was hypothesized that these nuclei were a critical target for the actions of testosterone on song behavior.[13] The subsequent discovery in canaries of marked seasonal plasticity in the song circuit that correlates positively with both song production and song learning reinforced the assumption that testosterone acts to promote various aspects of song behavior via direct effects on nuclei such as HVC and RA.[14] This view is widely held (see Brenowitz, this volume), however several observations—including some drawn from our recent work in European starlings (*Sturnus vulgaris*)—raise questions about the associated pattern of high testosterone, large song control nuclei and high rates of song production.

Evidence for Dissociations among Steroid Hormones, Brain, and Song Behavior

While the bulk of the evidence supports such associations, they are not always observed. For example a marked increase in the volumes of HVC and RA was observed not only in gonadally intact, but also in castrated American tree sparrows (*Spizella arborea*) exposed for three weeks to day lengths characteristic of the breeding season (photostimulated).[15] This finding suggests that changes in the volume of song control nuclei can occur in the absence of significant concentrations of gonadal steroids circulating in the plasma. Similarly, castration has been found to be ineffectual in regulating song control nucleus volumes in house sparrows (*Passer domesticus*).[16] Moreover, in juvenile male dark-eyed juncos with low testosterone concentrations in a photorefractory condition (i.e., a reproductive state that is non-responsive to the stimulatory effects of long days and is characteristic of the non-breeding season), exposure to long photoperiods resulted in enlarged nuclei (such as HVC, RA, and area X of the medial striatum) as compared to testosterone-treated birds on short days. These data also suggest that photoperiod can enhance the volume of song control nuclei in the absence of testosterone.[17] Interestingly, in this study administering exogenous testosterone to the birds maintained on short days did induce high rates of singing though there was a concomitant increase only in the volume of the song nucleus, RA, not HVC or area X.[17] In a subsequent study on castrated male juncos, exposure to long photoperiods induced growth in the volume of HVC that was not enhanced by the administration of exogenous testosterone, though song behavior did increase.[18]

Recent field studies of wild canaries have also shown imperfect correlations among maximal testosterone concentrations, song behavior and enlarged song control nuclei.[19] Despite marked seasonal differences in testosterone concentrations in breeding and non-breeding birds, seasonal variations in nuclear volume were not detected.[19] Testosterone concentrations can vary within the breeding period and in this study the breeding birds were not behaviorally characterized as a function of the stage of reproductive cycle. This means that fluctuations that occur within this period may account for this finding. Nonetheless, these data provide evidence that seasonal differences in plasma testosterone are not always associated with seasonal differences in song control nuclei volume. In a study of two populations of song sparrows in the state of Washington (USA) at the onset of the breeding season, the volumes of HVC and RA were already fully recrudesced when testosterone concentrations were still quite low and the gonads were only 10% of their full adult size.[20] The authors interpreted these data to mean that submaximal concentrations of testosterone are able to stimulate seasonal growth in the song control system and this conclusion certainly fits the data. A study of wild-caught great tits (*Parus major*) in Sweden also indicates that the sizes of HVC and RA were already enlarged in January,[21] well before this population breeds and presumably attains the maximal concentrations of testosterone.[22] In both of these studies, it is surprising in light of previous assumptions about how seasonally fluctuating gonadal steroids regulate target organs, that the brain sites involved in song re-develop so early in relation to the recrudescence of the testes. These findings also indicate that maximal testosterone concentrations, large song control nuclei, and high rates of song behavior are not always coincident when one collects data from field-caught birds.

Patterns of Association and Dissociation among Testosterone, Song Behavior, and the Volume of Song Control Nuclei: The Case of European Starlings

The European starling is a seasonally breeding songbird whose complex song plays an important role in mate attraction during the breeding season and which exhibits an extreme pattern of seasonal reproduction controlled by photoperiod and other supplementary cues.[23] The seasonal control of reproduction and song behavior of this species has been well characterized, making them an ideal species for investigating factors controlling seasonal neuroplasticity in the song system.[23,24]

Although reproduction in these birds is highly constrained to the late spring and early summer,[23] the production of song behavior is not constrained to the breeding

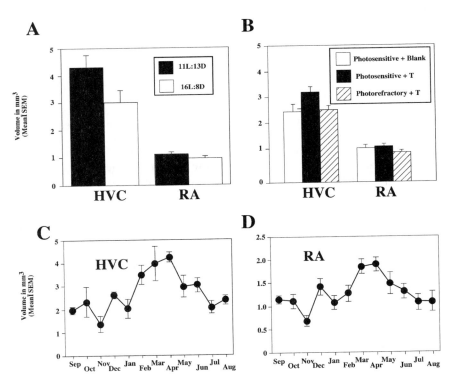

FIGURE 1. A summary of graphs from three studies supporting a role for testosterone in the regulation of the song control nuclei, such as HVC in European starlings. (**A**) Photosensitive males with large testes (on 11 h light) have larger HVC volumes than photorefractory males with tiny testes (on 16 h light).[35] (**B**) Administration of exogenous testosterone to photosensitive males maintained on short days with small gonads leads to a significant increase in HVC volume though a similar treatment is ineffective in photorefractory males maintained on long days.[36] (**C** and **D**) Pronounced seasonal changes in HVC and RA volume are observed in wild-caught male starlings maintained in outside aviaries in Belgium with the largest volumes being observed in the late winter and spring when plasma testosterone concentrations are high.[37]

season, but songs can be heard throughout the year especially in the autumn.[24,25] There is a major difference in the contextual stimuli that elicit song behavior associated with the breeding season versus that observed in the fall.[26] In the breeding season, prior to pairing, males produce high levels of song in response the presence of a female.[27,28] Song rate decreases markedly in males immediately after they pair with a female.[28] Moreover, the removal of a male's mate immediately results in an increase in singing whereas reuniting the pair suppresses song.[29] Even after pairing, males sing immediately prior to nearly every copulation.[30–32] In contrast to what occurs during the breeding season, providing fall males with a female has no appreciable effect on the rate of singing or on other associated reproductive behaviors.[26] Plasma testosterone concentrations in males is only high during the spring, not the fall,[33] and studies of the hormonal regulation of starling song indicate that testosterone specifically enhances such female-directed song and has no apparent effect on song produced in other contexts.[34] Thus, in starlings, song in the context of female attraction is linked with high testosterone concentrations.

In addition to enhancing song produced in a reproductive context, gonadal testosterone has powerful effects on the volume of song nuclei in starlings. For example, photosensitive males (i.e., males in a reproductive state responsive to long days characteristic of the late winter and early spring) with large testes display HVC volumes that are 44% larger than photorefractory males with small gonads (FIG. 1A).[35] Administering exogenous testosterone to photosensitive males maintained on short days with small gonads will also stimulate significant increases in HVC volume, though a similar treatment is ineffective in photorefractory males maintained on long days (FIG. 1B).[35,36] These two studies are consistent with the view that testosterone has powerful effects on adult neuroplasticity in the starling song control system, though the ability of testosterone to exert its effects may be modulated by seasonal state. In wild-caught Belgian starlings[37] marked seasonal changes in HVC, RA and area X volumes were detected with the largest volumes being observed in the late winter and spring (FIG. 1C).[37] Interestingly, HVC and area X volumes were already significantly increased in February prior to the onset of maximal concentrations of testosterone, which were not detected until March and April (as expected based on previous field studies of wild starlings).[33,38]

However, a study of wild-caught starlings in Baltimore showed that while the birds exhibited the expected prominent seasonal cycle in gonadal size, plasma testosterone concentrations and molt, the volumes of HVC and RA tended to peak in spring. However, no significant seasonal cycle was observed in HVC or RA in either males or females (FIG. 2). There were significant changes observed in the volume of area X but these changes were counterintuitive in that they indicated an increase in area X size in the fall-caught birds.

There are many differences between the two studies related to geography, methods of collecting and social factors that might be responsible for the difference in findings. Nevertheless these data raise a number of questions about the regulation of seasonal cycles in the song control system of starlings. If variation in testosterone was the only factor responsible for seasonal neuroplasticity, one would expect to have observed a seasonal change in volume of HVC and perhaps RA in these birds. These and subsequent data suggest an important role for factors related to behavioral and social status.

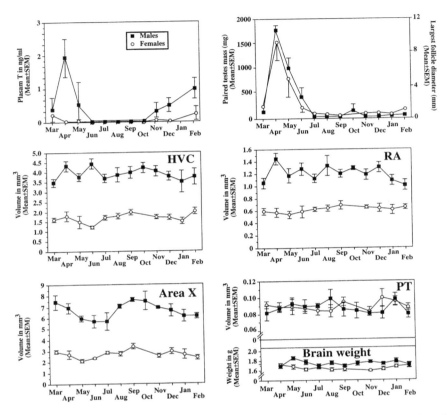

FIGURE 2. Lack of seasonal changes in the volume of song control nuclei in male and female starlings. Birds were trapped monthly on the campus of Johns Hopkins University. Although these males and females exhibited a prominent seasonal cycle in gonadal size and plasma testosterone concentrations as shown in the figure, no significant seasonal cycle was observed in HVC or RA volume. Significant changes were detected in the volume of area X but unexpectedly resulted from an increase in area X size in the fall-caught birds. No change was observed in a control brain nucleus (nucleus pretectalis, PT) nor in the total brain weight. (From Bernard,[122] with permission.)

NEUROENDOCRINE CHEMICAL NEUROANATOMY OF THE SONG SYSTEM

Expression of Steroid Receptors in the Song System

Given the existence of a well-defined song control circuitry and the evidence for a modulatory role of testosterone on singing behavior and circuit components, it was natural to ask whether testosterone is able to act directly on song control nuclei to activate song and whether testosterone acts as an androgen or an estrogen or both at these brain sites. Initial autoradiographic studies utilizing [³H]testosterone revealed

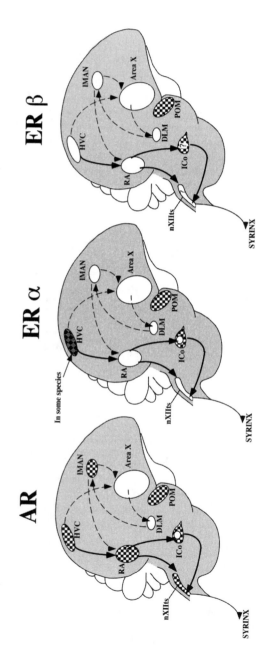

FIGURE 3. Generalized view of the songbird vocal control system schematically illustrating the distribution of androgen receptors (AR), estrogen receptors alpha (ERα), and estrogen receptors beta (ERβ) in the song control nuclei and in the medial preoptic nucleus (POM) that also participates in the activation of singing behavior. The nuclei of the forebrain pathway involved in song production (HVC, RA, ICo and nXIIts) are connected by *black arrows*. Nuclei of the anterior forebrain pathway involved in song learning during ontogeny and song maintenance in adulthood (HVC, area X, lMAN and RA) are connected by *dashed arrows*. The presence of *dark dots* in a given nucleus means that the receptor is expressed in the brain area. In the case of ERα in HVC, there is species diversity in this expression. (See text for more detail.)

uptake in several of the forebrain song control nuclei.[11,12] Subsequent studies utilizing immunocytochemistry to identify the receptor protein or *in situ* hybridization to reveal the corresponding messenger RNA have confirmed the presence of steroid-sensitive neurons in these nuclei. As illustrated in FIGURE 3, androgen receptors (AR) are present in several forebrain song nuclei and estrogen receptor (ER) α is observed in HVC in some species. The recently cloned ER β subtype has not been observed in forebrain song control regions based on a single study in starlings (FIG. 3).[39] The presence of brain areas that highly express androgen receptors in discrete nuclei in the telencephalon represents a neural specialization that distinguishes songbirds from other vertebrates.[10,40,41]

Co-Factors and Co-Repressors of Steroid Hormone Receptor Action

While the correlation of steroid activity with behavior and structure has been amply demonstrated, absent or reduced correlations have also been noted (see above). The origins of these variations in responsiveness to steroids have not been fully identified. Recent studies indicate that steroid receptor co-activators and co-repressors can markedly enhance or inhibit the transcriptional ability of nuclear steroid receptors and are therefore candidates to modify the physiological and behavioral responses to steroid hormones.[42–45] It is possible that, in specific conditions, circulating steroid hormone concentrations could be relatively high, but they would be ineffective due to insensitivity to steroid action in the target tissue. One generally thinks about a change in the availability of steroid receptors when considering target responsiveness, but the discovery of co-activators and co-repressors provides an entirely new class of proteins that could regulate the efficacy of steroid hormone action.

We decided to investigate this possibility in avian species, focusing on the molecule best characterized to this date, the steroid receptor co-activator 1 or SRC-1.[46] For technical reasons, we used Japanese quail in our initial studies. We found that SRC-1 mRNA was broadly expressed in the brain with particularly high densities of this protein in steroid-sensitive brain areas that play a key role in the control of sexual behavior, such as the medial preoptic area and the nucleus striae terminalis.[46]

Based on these results, we were able to use the information about the SRC-1 gene from the quail studies to analyze the neuroanatomical distribution of SRC-1 transcript in canaries (see FIG. 4).[47] A particularly dense expression of SRC-1 transcripts was detected in several mesencephalic catecholaminergic cell groups, such as the ventral tegmental area and the substantia nigra. SRC-1-expressing cells were also observed in the locus coeruleus and to a lesser extent in the substantia grisea centralis (homologous to the periaqueductal gray of mammals). These nuclei represent the primary sources of noradrenergic and dopaminergic inputs to the telencephalic song control nuclei. It is also known that the ventral tegmental area and substantia nigra express sex steroid hormone receptors[48] and some of the effects of steroid hormones on the song system may be mediated indirectly by an effect on these catecholaminergic cell groups.[10]

Interestingly, several of the telencephalic song control nuclei also expressed a higher density of SRC-1 transcripts than the surrounding brain regions and could therefore be easily delineated in sections processed by *in situ* hybridization histochemistry (ISH) for SRC-1. This was the case for nuclei such as HVC, area X, lMAN, and Nif. A closer observation of HVC and area X in males and females sug-

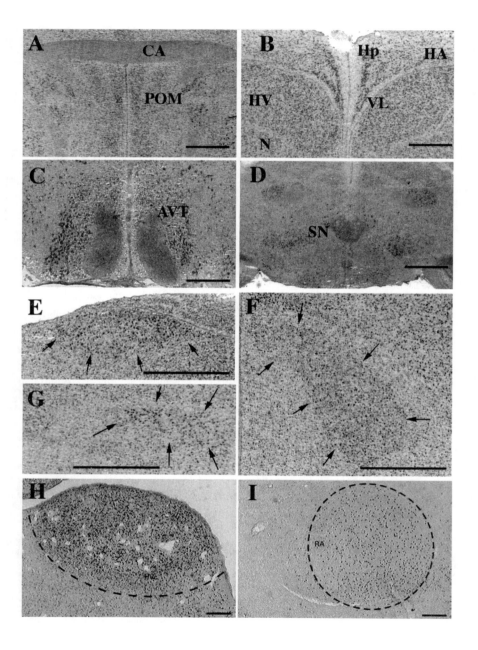

FIGURE 4. *See following page for legend.*

gested there may be a sex difference in volume defined by the high density of SRC-1 transcripts. We therefore measured the volume of HVC and area X defined based on the dense ISH signal and demonstrated that HVC volumes defined in this way are significantly larger in males than in females. Moreover, the boundaries of area X could be outlined by the dense expression of SRC-1 in males but not in females in which SRC-1 expression was equivalent within area X and in the surrounding medial striatum.[47] Recent studies in starlings[49] confirmed, for the SRC-1 protein, the distribution that had been observed by ISH. In particular, song control nuclei such as area X, HVC, and RA were found to be densely labeled and clearly distinct from the surrounding brain regions based on higher relative patterns of immunoreactivity. A similar high expression of the SRC-1 protein was also detected in the periventricular hypothalamus.[49]

SRC-1 represents only one of the many co-activators that modulate signal transduction by steroid receptors. The CREB binding protein (CBP), for example, has been shown to be essential for the full transcriptional activity of many steroid receptors (including estrogen receptors).[50,51] Interestingly, immunocytochemical studies with a specific CBP antibody demonstrated that, in starlings, this coactivator is also expressed at higher density in the telencephalic song control nuclei than in surrounding tissue.[52] This was shown to be the case in the HVC and RA, and to a lesser extent, in area X.

The limited data collected so far on the expression of steroid receptor coactivators in songbirds therefore clearly support the notion that, as in mammals, these proteins may play a significant role in the control of steroid action in the brain, in particular on the activation of song. It is firmly established at this point that the SRC-1 distribution is highly conserved in the brain of different avian species and that it resembles the distribution identified in rodents. Importantly, the distributions of co-activators and steroid receptors cannot be dissociated. SRC-1 is densely expressed in evolutionarily conserved steroid target sites in the brain, such as the preoptic area and bed nucleus striae terminalis but also in the newly evolved steroid-sensitive areas of the songbird telencephalon. There was therefore presumably some evolutionary pressure that led to the co-evolution of the distribution of these two types of proteins, suggesting that functionally they must be very closely related and that the regulation of the steroid co-factors may indeed be a promising avenue to pursue to understand variation in the effectiveness of steroid hormone action both intra-specifically and inter-specifically. Future studies on the regulation of steroid receptor co-factors in birds might explain how seasonal variation in steroid hormone action is controlled.

FIGURE 4. Photomicrographs illustrating the distribution of the steroid receptor co-activators SRC-1 and CBP in the brain of songbirds with special emphasis on song control nuclei. High densities of SRC-1 expression highlight the medial preoptic nucleus (**A**), the hippocampus (**B**), ventral tegmental area (**C**), substantia nigra (**D**), HVC (**E**), area X (**F**), and lateral nucleus of the anterior nidopallium (**G**) in male canaries. High densities of CBP-expressing cells also outline the song control nuclei HVC (**H**) and RA (**I**) in starlings. AVT, ventral tegmental area; CA, commissura anterior; HA, accessory hyperpallium; Hp, hippocampus; HV, hyperstriatum ventrale now called the mesopallium; POM, medial preoptic nucleus; SN, substantia nigra; VL, ventriculus lateralis. (From data in Charlier and colleagues[47] and Auger and colleagues.[52])

The Possible Role of Other Hormone Systems: Melatonin and Thyroid Hormones

Besides the gonadal sex steroids, there are two other hormone systems that are well known to exhibit marked seasonal changes in their release and are involved in a variety of seasonal processes in avian species: thyroid hormones, such as T3 and T4, and the pineal indoleamine hormone melatonin.[53–55] An intact thyroid is needed for transitions among seasonal states related to photoperiodic responsiveness to occur.[55] In several species it is known that thyroidectomized birds maintained on long days will not make the transition to a state known as photorefractoriness (a condition characterized by the regression of the gonads in the presence of what were previously stimulating photoperiods).[55] More generally chronically thyroidectomized starlings appear to be "blind" to photoperiod in that responses to long and short days are blunted.[56] Cellular plasticity in the gonadotrophin-releasing hormone system is regulated by thyroid hormones in seasonally breeding songbirds, so it is reasonable to hypothesize that thyroid hormones might influence seasonal changes in the song control system. However, although studies support a role for thyroid hormones in the development of the song system,[57] no role has yet been identified for these hormones in seasonal plasticity.

The pineal hormone melatonin also exhibits a well-characterized seasonal cycle in its secretion. In birds and mammals, melatonin is high when it is dark so that there is a seasonal change in the duration of periods of high melatonin secretion, with long periods of high melatonin in the fall and winter when photoperiods are short, and short periods of high melatonin secretion when photoperiods are long.[54] Although the melatonin read-out of night-length is essential for photoperiodic time measurement in mammals it is not necessary in birds.[54] However, its well known effects on seasonal processes in mammals make it a good candidate to be another hormone acting on seasonal plasticity in the song system of birds.[54] There are some hints that this is the case. Studies of castrated starlings show that male starlings maintained on long days had larger HVC volumes than males maintained on short days.[58] The administration of exogenous melatonin attenuated the increase in HVC volumes stimulated by long days and also suppressed increases in area X observed in the untreated castrates in this study.[58] The manipulations performed in this study were pharmacological in that melatonin capsules were implanted that resulted in a constant release of the hormone rather than the diurnal rhythm that occurs naturally. However, one appealing preliminary scenario is that there is an interaction between vernal increases in concentrations of testosterone in the plasma with simultaneous decreases in the duration of high concentrations of melatonin in the plasma and this antagonistic interaction fine-tunes seasonal plasticity in the song system.[59]

Melatonin Receptors in the Song System

The development of autoradiographic procedures for the reliable visualization of melatonin receptors revealed, based on initial studies in chicks, that binding sites for iodomelatonin are widely distributed throughout the visual system, including both thalamic nuclei such as the lateral geniculate nucleus, and the optic tectum, as well as telencephalic structures, such as the entopallium.[60] Subsequently, detailed autoradiographic studies were carried out in zebra finches,[61] house sparrows,[62] and European starlings.[59] The striking finding for songbirds is that the song nucleus HVC

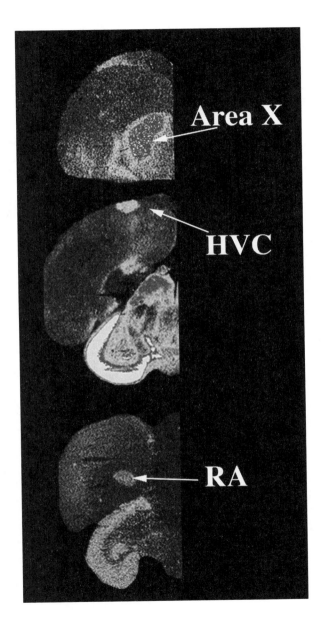

FIGURE 5. Autoradiograms based on iodomelatonin binding illustrating the distribution of melatonin binding sites in the starling song control system. Three song control nuclei (area X, HVC, and RA) can be delineated by a high density of melatonin receptors. (From data in Bentley and Ball.[123])

exhibits high receptor density in all species investigated, while RA also exhibits significant receptor binding though at lower densities than HVC (FIG. 5). Area X is more variable but this is probably due to the fact that melatonin receptors in this nucleus exhibit a marked seasonal regulation in both starlings and house sparrows.[59,62] In starlings it is clear that receptor densities are high when birds are photosensitive and photorefractory but not when photostimulated and this regulation is independent of gonadal steroid hormones.[59] Thus binding in this nucleus is regulated seasonally and it is important to take into account seasonal state when describing binding in this nucleus.

POSSIBLE ALTERNATIVE SITES OF STEROID HORMONE ACTION OUTSIDE THE SONG SYSTEM THAT AFFECT SONG BEHAVIOR

As reviewed elsewhere in this volume, research on the neurobiology of song demonstrates a clear role for the various song control nuclei in specific aspects of song behavior such as song perception (HVC[63]), song production (HVC and RA[64]), song learning (HVC, area X, lMAN[65]), auditory feedback needed for song maintenance,[66] and the context in which song is sung (area X[67,68]). Both the close relationship between T and song behavior, and the presence of androgen and/or estrogen receptors within particular nuclei of the song system indicate that T and its metabolite E_2 act within the song system to regulate aspects of song (such as learning, production, and perception). However, there are still major gaps in our understanding of the contribution of each nucleus to the control of specific functions and we know little about the neural regulation of other aspects of song production such as the motivation to sing. By the term "motivation to sing" we are referring to the fact that song behavior is very much dependent upon reproductive state, which tends to be seasonally regulated. Males in a reproductive context are much more apt to sing or to sing in a different way than males in a non-reproductive state. The decision to sing or not to sing undoubtedly involves affective as well as cognitive processes (see Cheng and Durand, this volume). The following section attempts to identify putative brain regions linking affective, cognitive, and motor processes in song.

The Preoptic Region and Motivational Control of Singing Behavior

Many lines of evidence support the idea that a nucleus in the preoptic region, the medial preoptic nucleus (POM), and possibly testosterone activity within this nucleus, plays a key role in the regulation of male sexual motivation, including song, in male songbirds. A role for this nucleus in male sexual motivation in birds has been established in a seasonally breeding non-songbird, the Japanese quail.[69] In quail the POM is larger in males with high testosterone[70,71] and the larger volume is associated with the expression of male sexual behavior.[70–72] Both androgen and estrogen receptor (both the α and β forms) proteins and the mRNA encoding these receptors have been located within the POM in male quail.[73–76] The POM is also rich in aromatase, the enzyme converting T into estrogen.[77,78] Peripheral blockade of aromatase in castrated, T-treated male quail abolishes the expression of behaviors associated with sexual motivation (i.e., the amount of time a male quail spends near or looking at a female located behind a window),[79] suggesting that estrogen is the active metabolite involved in the expression of these behaviors. Lesions to the POM in quail are followed by a significant reduction in these same behaviors[80] and castrated male quail with T implants located directly in the POM exhibit an elevation in measures of sexual arousal,[81] suggesting that the POM is the site in which the aromatization of T is critical for the regulation of behaviors associated with male sexual arousal and appetitive sexual behaviors related to the pursuit of a female.

In songbirds as in quail, the POM is rich in the enzyme aromatase (zebra finches[82] and starlings[26]), and cells within the starling POM express the mRNA for androgen receptors and for both forms of the estrogen receptor.[39] In male zebra finches castration results in a significant reduction in courtship behaviors, including song.[83] This deficit can be completely restored by treating males with aromatizable androgens, such as androstenedione,[83] whereas treatment with an aromatase antagonist completely blocks the effects of androstenedione, and estrogen treatment restores courtship behavior, including song, disrupted by the blockade of aromatase.[84] Thus the aromatization of T appears to play an important role in the regulation of behaviors reflecting male sexual arousal (i.e., courtship including song) in zebra finches as in quail.

Where in the brain aromatase is acting to support courtship behaviors is not known. Because the nuclei known to participate exclusively in song learning and production do not contain either the aromatase protein[82,85] or cells expressing aromatase mRNA,[86] courtship singing may be regulated by aromatase activity outside of these brain areas, perhaps in the aromatase-rich POM. In support of this hypothesis, lesions to the POM in reproductively active male starlings interfere with both song expression in response to the presentation of females and the gathering of green nest materials (another courtship behavior[27,87]), suggesting that the POM plays a role in male courtship behaviors including song.[88]

Together the findings from quail, zebra finches, and starlings suggest the attractive hypothesis that the role of the POM in song is exclusively related to its role in sexual motivation. Interestingly, the volume of the POM in male starlings is largest in spring, when T concentrations are highest.[26] The seasonal changes in the POM correspond to seasonal changes in the primary function of male song (i.e., the POM is largest when males use song largely to attract females and is smallest when the function of song is not related to immediate mate attraction). Additionally, the volume of the POM was positively correlated with song-bout length in these males.[26] Males sang longer songs in spring, when a longer song bout serves to attract mates and repel competitors,[89–91] providing additional evidence for a role for the POM in song behaviors exclusively observed in spring. Finally, in fall aromatase is completely undetectable in the POM of starlings, whereas in spring this nucleus contains dense aromatase immunoreactive cells, a change that is likely steroid dependent as has been shown in quail.[92] The effects of POM lesions on courtship song and the dramatic seasonal changes in POM volume and aromatase immunoreactivity implicate the POM as at least one brain area in which the aromatization of T might act to regulate the expression of male sexual arousal, including courtship song.

The evidence so far suggests that the POM interacts with the song control system to initiate song within the context of breeding. Song has generally been thought to be regulated by seasonal changes in T activity and neural plasticity within the song control system.[8,9,93,94] The close associations among seasonal changes in steroid concentrations, song activity, and the volume of song control nuclei have been taken as evidence that androgens and estrogens acting directly on cells within nuclei of the song control system are critical for the activation of song.[95] However, the exact function of T in the song system is unknown. One possibility is that T in the song system might act to fine-tune song behavior (e.g., increase song stereotypy[96] or song-bout length in spring) and T activity within brain areas known to regulate male sexual arousal, such as the POM, might be involved in the motivation to sing in a reproductive context. A growing body of data suggests that the POM regulates courtship song; however additional studies investigating POM involvement in song sung outside the context of courtship are necessary to more precisely define the role of the POM in song.

Ascending Catecholamine Projections and Song Behavior

A prominent catecholaminergic innervation of the song control system has been demonstrated in several songbird species, most notably in zebra finches, by the presence of fibers immunoreactive for the catecholamine synthesizing enzymes tyrosine hydroxylase (TH)[97,98] and/or dopamine beta-hydroxylase.[99] Similarly, immunocytochemical studies of TH in male canaries have found that the boundaries of HVC and RA can be defined in a manner in agreement with Nissl-defined boundaries by a higher density of fibers immunoreactive for TH compared to the surrounding nidopallium.[100]

High concentrations of NE and DA have accordingly been measured in the song control nuclei of zebra finches.[101–103] Autoradiographic studies have revealed binding sites for [^{3}H]RX821002, a ligand specific for α_2-adrenergic receptors, to be enriched in forebrain song control nuclei of this species.[104] In European starlings, high densities of noradrenergic receptors of the α_2 and $\beta1/\beta2$ subtypes are also present in several song control nuclei (HVC, RA, and area X)[37,105,106] (FIG. 6) and high densities of dopamine D1 receptors have been described in area X of the medial striatum in the same species.[107] In these cases, boundaries of these song control nuclei can be defined based on the high receptor densities compared to the surrounding brain area that are consistent with Nissl-defined boundaries.

Seasonal changes in the densities of α_2 receptors have been identified within HVC and RA in male European starlings. The density of α_2-adrenergic receptors within song nuclei were largest in spring when testosterone was highest and males were presumably singing at high rates to attract mates. In contrast, outside of the breeding season when song is not involved in immediate mate attraction, the density of α_2-adrenergic receptors and testosterone concentrations were lowest. These results suggest that changes in testosterone and α_2-receptor densities might regulate seasonal changes in song behavior or the context in which song is sung.[37]

Further understanding of the relationships between steroids, catecholamines, and song learning/production was until recently limited by the lack of precise knowledge concerning the anatomical organization of catecholaminergic projections to the song control nuclei. The origins of the catecholaminergic innervation of the song control nuclei have been investigated to some extent by tract-tracing in canaries. HVC receives dopaminergic inputs mainly from the mesencephalic central gray (GCt; group A11 in the nomenclature of Dahlström and Fuxe;[108] see Reiner and colleagues[109] for a review of this nomenclature use in birds) and to a lesser extent from the ventral tegmental area (AVT; group A10) and noradrenergic inputs from the complex of the lo-

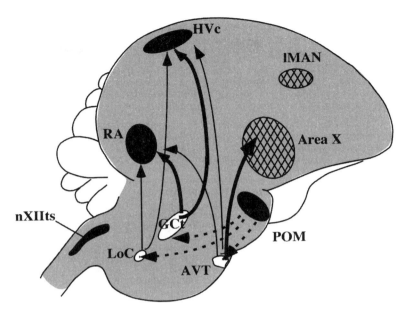

FIGURE 6. Generalized view of the songbird vocal control system schematically illustrating the catecholaminergic innervation of the song control nuclei and anatomical relationships with the medial preoptic nucleus. *Arrows* indicate the direction of the projections. (Based on data in previously published articles.[110,111,113,124])

cus coeruleus (Loc; group A6).[110] Similarly, dopaminergic inputs to RA come mostly from the A11 (mesencephalic central gray) and A10 (ventral tegmental area) cell groups and noradrenergic inputs come from the locus coeruleus and subcoeruleus (A6).[111] In contrast, area X, a key nucleus of the rostral forebrain pathway controlling song learning but not song production, seems to receive catecholaminergic inputs exclusively from AVT.[112] These data thus suggest that different populations of catecholaminergic cell groups could control the motor and anterior forebrain pathways (FIG. 6).

Recent work has identified two brain sites outside of the song control system proper where steroids could act to modify song production: the medial preoptic nucleus that regulates appetitive aspects of male sexual behavior in a variety of species and the catecholaminergic nuclei of the mesencephalon and pons that send afferent projections to the song control nuclei. If the POM is involved in the regulation of sexually motivated song, then this structure must interact with the song control system. Using biotinylated dextran amine (BDA) as a retrograde and anterograde tracer, the possible neuroanatomical connections between the POM and song control nuclei in male starlings were examined.[113] While no direct connections were identified between the POM and song control nuclei, labeled fibers were found to terminate in a region bordering dorsal-medial portions of RA. Additionally, several indirect routes via which the POM might communicate with the song control system were identified. Specifically, POM projected to the dorsomedial nucleus intercollicularis (DM), the mesencephalic central gray (GCt), the ventral tegmental area (VTA), and the locus coeruleus (LoC), structures projecting directly to nuclei involved in song production (DM→vocal-patterning and respiratory nuclei; GCt, AVT, and LoC→RA and HVC), and the context in which song is sung (AVT→area X). This work suggests that these projections could represent an anatomical substrate that coordinates the actions of POM and of song control nuclei on song production (FIG. 6).

OVERVIEW OF THE POSSIBLE FUNCTIONS OF
SEASONAL NEUROPLASTICITY IN SONGBIRDS

A key issue in the study of seasonal plasticity is its functional significance. Some workers have hypothesized that these plastic changes are related to mechanisms of song learning, and these hypotheses have been examined by Brenowitz (this volume). An alternative approach is to look at the functional significance of these changes for the reproductive success of the male.

For example, seasonal changes in some features of song performance may correlate with seasonal variation in the size of song nuclei. For example in song sparrows and white-crowned sparrows, seasonal changes in the song system are correlated with seasonal variation in song stereotypy.[96,114] Song is less stereotyped in the fall than in the spring in both of these species. In starlings, seasonal variation in song performance has still not been carefully assessed. However, as noted previously, there are clear changes in the behavioral context that elicits song based on season.[26,88] This suggests that aspects of song performance directed at females will be more pronounced in the spring than in the fall. Females prefer starlings that sing songs organized into long bouts of motifs.[90] Variation in the size of HVC and RA in adult male starlings correlates most closely with variation in bout length.[115] Male starlings have been found to sing longer songs in spring compared to fall,[26] indicating that males adjust aspects of song production seasonally so that they are most attractive to females in spring. Even in canaries there is evidence that testosterone and its metabolites selectively enhance aspects of song that females find most attractive.[116–118] Males produce rapid trills that have been termed "sexy song" by Kreutzer and colleagues[116] because they are so attractive to females. Perhaps even in canaries a seasonal increase in HVC volume is a necessary prelude for the production of song most attractive to females.

Highly complex motor output is often associated with increases in brain space. The key to seasonal variation in song system structures may well be the need for increased brain space to mediate the performance of more complex song to attract females and defend territory from other males. Our review suggests that this hypothesis may require further testing.

ALTERNATE VIEWS OF THE INTERRELATIONSHIPS AMONG
HORMONES, BRAIN, AND SONG BEHAVIOR

What are the directions of the causal links that may exist between photoperiod, testosterone, song control nucleus size, and song behavior? Is testosterone action on the song control nuclei the prerequisite for all its effects on song behavior or are there alternative organizations of the causal chain? It has generally been assumed that steroids change the morphological and neurochemical organization of song control nuclei, which in turn affects the expression of vocalizations. However the data can also be taken to suggest that a large song control nucleus is the consequence rather than the cause of high rates of vocal production. A potential mechanism that could underlie this causal interaction has been recently identified: singing activity was shown to promote the release of brain-derived neurotrophic factor (BDNF),[119] a neurotrophin that promotes growth of HVC.[120] It is also known that testosterone promotes the growth of HVC volume at least in part by acting via BDNF.[120] Therefore, in addition to the typical view that increases in the volumes of song control nuclei are followed by increases in song production, these data provide evidence for a mechanism by which song production can lead to increases in the volumes of song control nuclei. Such bidirectional interactions between brain and behavior could explain the dissociation sometimes observed between seasonal or steroid-induced changes in song control nuclei and measures of vocal behavior.

We have started testing this idea using different manipulations of song output in European starlings.[121] For example, we suppressed song behaviorally using domi-

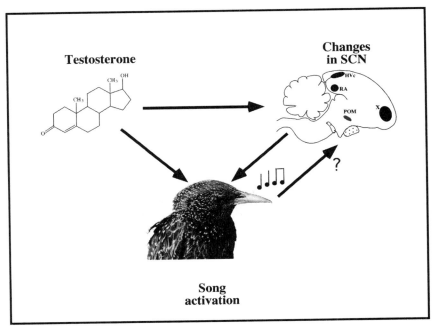

FIGURE 7. Schematic representation of potential interactions between hormones, song control nuclei (SCN), and singing activity. The effects of testosterone could be sequential on the two responses with SCN modulating song or vice versa or T effects on morphology and behavior could be relatively independent with the singing activity secondarily affecting the size of brain nuclei through the modulation of brain-derived neurotrophic factor (BDNF) production.

nance hierarchies in starlings housed in semi-natural settings and showed that song suppression in subordinate males attenuates the long day-induced HVC growth. In a second study we irreversibly devocalized castrated males by lesioning the syrinx. Birds subsequently received either T-filled (+T) or control (C) empty implants. The data indicate that devocalized+T males have smaller HVC volumes than sham-operated+T males, such that they were similar to sham+C males. Devocalized+C males had smaller HVC volumes than all other groups. The patterns of BDNF mRNA expression in HVC of these groups mirrored the volume results. Taken together, these data support the idea that seasonal adult neuroplasticity in the starling song control system is partially driven by variation in singing behavior.

A major challenge of future studies will be to discriminate between alternative hypotheses concerning how steroids and other hormones exert their effects on song system plasticity. For example, how does one explain the increase in HVC size in the late winter, before full gonadal growth has occurred, that is observed in song sparrows and great tits? Is this growth a response to very low concentrations of testosterone or do the birds start singing in the winter and activity-dependent BDNF also acts to promote the growth in nucleus volume? These hypotheses are of course not mutually exclusive (FIG. 7). To this date, most of the work trying to answer these sorts of questions has been correlational in nature and it has been very difficult to dissect the web of multiple correlations between endocrine, morphological, neurochemical, and behavioral measures. Providing detailed answers to these questions will thus represent a complicated task in part because steroids obviously must act simultaneously at multiple loci to activate a full song. Although this is a challenging problem in systems neuroscience, solving it will have many payoffs for our general understanding of the causal nexus linking hormones, brain activity, and behavior.

ACKNOWLEDGMENTS

Research from our laboratories described in this review was supported by grants from National Institutes of Health/National Institute of Neurological Disorders and Stroke (R01 NS 35467) to G.F.B.; National Institutes of Health/National Institute of Mental Health to L.V.R. (R01 MH65645); and grants from the Belgian FRFC (Fonds de la Recherche Fondamentale Collective) (2.4555.01), the French Community of Belgium (ARC 99/04-241), and the University of Liege (Fonds Spéciaux pour la Recherche) to J.B. T.D.C. is FRIA (Fonds pour la Formation à la Recherche dans l'Industrie et dans l'Agriculture) research fellow. J.J.S. was supported by Natural Sciences and Engineering Research Council, Canada and C.J.A. by an National Research Service Award fellowship National Institutes of Health/National Institute on Deafness and Other Communication Disorders (F32 DC00042).

REFERENCES

1. MARGOLIASH, D., E.S. FORTUNE, M.L. SUTTER, et al. 1994. Distributed representation in the song system of oscines: Evolutionary implications and functional consequences. Brain Behav. Evol. **44:** 247–264.
2. YU, A.C. & D. MARGOLIASH. 1996. Temporal hierarchical control of singing in birds. Science **273:** 1871–1875.

3. MOONEY, R. 2000. Different subthreshold mechanisms underlie song selectivity in identified HVc neurons of the zebra finch. J. Neurosci. **20:** 5420–5436.
4. SOLIS, M.M. & A.J. DOUPE. 2000. Compromised neural selectivity for song in birds with impaired sensorimotor learning. Neuron **25:** 109–121.
5. WINGFIELD, J.C. & D.S. FARNER. 1980. Control of seasonal reproduction in temperate-zone birds. Prog. Reprod. Biol. **5:** 62–101.
6. HAHN, T.P., T. BOSWELL, J.C. WINGFIELD & G.F. BALL. 1997. Temporal flexibility in avian reproduction. *In* Patterns and Mechanism. V.J. Nolan, E.D. Ketterson & C.F. Thompson, Eds. **14:** 39–80. Plenum Press. New York.
7. NOTTEBOHM, F. 1975. Vocal behavior in birds. *In* Avian Biology. Vol. 5. D.S. Farner & J.R. King, Eds.: 287–332. Academic Press. New York.
8. BALL, G.F. 1999. Neuroendocrine basis of seasonal changes in vocal behavior among songbirds. *In* The Design of Animal Communication. M. Hauser & M. Konishi, Eds.: 213–253. MIT Press. Cambridge, MA.
9. TRAMONTIN, A.D. & E.A. BRENOWITZ. 2000. Seasonal plasticity in the adult brain. Trends. Neurosci. **23:** 251–258.
10. BALL, G.F., L.V. RITERS & J. BALTHAZART. 2002. Neuroendocrinology of song behavior and avian brain plasticity: multiple sites of action of sex steroid hormones. Front. Neuroendocrinol. **23:** 137–178.
11. ARNOLD, A.P., F. NOTTEBOHM & D.W. PFAFF. 1976. Hormone concentrating cells in vocal control areas of the brain of the zebra finch (*Poephila guttata*). J. Comp. Neurol. **165:** 487–512.
12. ARNOLD, A.P. & A. SALTIEL. 1979. Sexual difference in pattern of hormone accumulation in the brain of a song bird. Science **205:** 702–705.
13. NOTTEBOHM, F. 1980. Brain pathways for vocal learning in birds: a review of the first 10 years. Progr. Psychobiol. Physiol. Psychol. **9:** 85–214.
14. NOTTEBOHM, F. 1981. A brain for all seasons: cyclical anatomical changes in song-control nuclei of the canary brain. Science **214:** 1368–1370.
15. BERNARD, D.J., F.E. WILSON & G.F. BALL. 1997. Testis-dependent and -independent effects of photoperiod on volumes of song control nuclei in American tree sparrows (*Spizella arborea*). Brain Res. **760:** 163–169.
16. WHITFIELD-RUCKER, M. & V.M. CASSONE. 2000. Photoperiodic regulation of the male house sparrow song control system: gonad dependent and independent mechanisms. Gen. Comp. Endocrinol. **118:** 173–183.
17. GULLEDGE, C.C. & P. DEVICHE. 1998. Photoperiod and testosterone independently affect vocal control region volumes in adolescent male songbirds. J. Neurobiol. **36:** 550–558.
18. DLONIAK, S.M. & P. DEVICHE. 2001. Effects of testosterone and photoperiodic condition on song production and vocal control region volumes in adult male dark-eyed juncos (*Junco hyemalis*). Horm. Behav. **39:** 95–105.
19. LEITNER, S., C. VOIGT, L.M. GARCIA-SEGURA, *et al.* 2001. Seasonal activation and inactivation of song motor memories in wild canaries is not reflected in neuroanatomical changes of forebrain song areas. Horm. Behav. **40:** 160–168.
20. TRAMONTIN, A.D., N. PERFITO, J.C. WINGFIELD & E.A. BRENOWITZ. 2001. Seasonal growth of song control nuclei precedes seasonal reproductive development in wild adult song sparrows. Gen. Comp. Endocrinol. **122:** 1–9.
21. SILVER, D.W., B. SILVERIN & G.F. BALL. 2003. Seasonal changes and sex differences in the song control system of free-living Great tits. Soc. Neurosci. Abstr. 200.10.
22. Van Duyse, E., R. Pinxten & M. Eens. 2003. Seasonal fluctuations in plasma testosterone levels and diurnal song activity in free-living male great tits. Gen. Comp. Endocrinol. **134:** 1–9.
23. BALL, G.F. & G.E. BENTLEY. 2000. Neuroendocrine mechanisms mediating the photoperiodic and social regulation of seasonal reproduction in birds. *In* Reproduction in Context: Social and Environmental Influences on Reproductive Physiology and Behavior. K. Wallen & J.E. Schneider, Eds.: 129–158. MIT Press. Cambridge, MA.
24. EENS, M. 1997. Understanding the complex song of the European starling: An integrated ethological approach. Adv. Study Anim. Behav. **26:** 355–434.
25. FEARE, C.J. 1984. The Starling. Oxford Press. Oxford.

26. RITERS, L.V., M. EENS, R. PINXTEN, *et al.* 2000. Seasonal changes in courtship song and the medial preoptic area in male European starlings (*Sturnus vulgaris*). Horm. Behav. **38:** 250–261.
27. EENS, M., R. PINXTEN & F.R. VERHEYEN. 1993. Function of the song and song repertoire in the European starling (*Sturnus vulgaris*): an aviary experiment. Behaviour **125:** 51–66.
28. EENS, M., R. PINXTEN & F.R. VERHEYEN. 1994. Variation in singing activity during the breeding cycle of the European starling *Sturnus vulgaris*. Belg. J. Zool. **124:** 167–174.
29. CUTHILL, I. & A.M. HINDMARSH. 1985. Increase in starling song activity with removal of mate. Anim. Behav. **33:** 326–328.
30. EENS, M. & R. PINXTEN. 1990. Extra-pair courtship in the starling, *Sturnus vulgaris*. Ibis **132:** 618–619.
31. EENS, M. & R. PINXTEN. 1995. Inter-sexual conflicts over copulations in the European starling: evidence for the female mate-guarding hypothesis. Behav. Ecol. Sociobiol. **36:** 71–81.
32. PINXTEN, R. & M. EENS. 1997. Copulation and mate-guarding patterns in polygynous European starlings. Anim. Behav. **54:** 1141–1147.
33. BALL, G.F. & J.C. WINGFIELD. 1987. Changes in plasma levels of luteinizing hormone and sex steroid hormones in relation to multiple-broodedness and nest-site density in male starlings. Physiol. Zool. **60:** 191–199.
34. PINXTEN, R., E. DE RIDDER, J. BALTHAZART & M. EENS. 2002. Context-dependent effects of castration and testosterone treatment on song in male European starlings. Horm. Behav. **42:** 307–318.
35. BERNARD, D.J. & G.F. BALL. 1995. Two histological markers reveal a similar photoperiodic difference in the volume of the high vocal center in male European starlings. J. Comp. Neurol. **360:** 726–734.
36. BERNARD, D.J. & G.F. BALL. 1997. Photoperiodic condition modulates the effects of testosterone on song control nuclei volumes in male European starlings. Gen. Comp. Endocrinol. **105:** 276–283.
37. RITERS, L.V., M. EENS, R. PINXTEN & G.F. BALL. 2002. Seasonal changes in the densities of alpha2-noradrenergic receptors are inversely related to changes in testosterone and the volumes of song control nuclei in male European starlings. J. Comp. Neurol. **444:** 63–74.
38. DAWSON, A. 1983. Plasma gonadal steroid levels in wild starlings (*Sturnus vulgaris*) during the annual cycle and in relation to the stages of breeding. Gen. Comp. Endocrinol. **49:** 286–294.
39. BERNARD, D.J., G.E. BENTLEY, J. BALTHAZART, *et al.* 1999. Androgen receptor, estrogen receptor alpha, and estrogen receptor beta show distinct patterns of expression in forebrain song control nuclei of European starlings. Endocrinology **140:** 4633–4643.
40. KELLEY, D.B. & D.W. PFAFF. 1978. Generalizations from comparative studies on neuroanatomical and endocrine mechanisms of sexual behaviour. *In* Biological Determinants of Sexual Behaviour. J.B. Hutchison, Ed.: 225–254. John Wiley & Sons. Chichester.
41. MORRELL, J.I. & D.W. PFAFF. 1978. A neuroendocrine approach to brain function: localization of sex steroid concentrating cells in vertebrate brains. Am. Zool. **18:** 447–460.
42. MCKENNA, N.J., R.B. LANZ & B.W. O'MALLEY. 1999. Nuclear receptor coregulators: cellular and molecular biology. Endocr. Rev. **20:** 321–344.
43. MCKENNA, N.J. & B.W. O'MALLEY. 2002. Minireview: nuclear receptor coactivators - An update. Endocrinology **143:** 2461–2465.
44. AUGER, A.P., M.J. TETEL & M.M. MCCARTHY. 2000. Steroid receptor coactivator-1 (SRC-1) mediates the development of sex-specific brain morphology and behavior. Proc. Natl. Acad. Sci. USA **97:** 7551–7555.
45. MOLENDA, H.A., A.L. GRIFFIN, A.P. AUGER, *et al.* 2002. Nuclear receptor coactivators modulate hormone-dependent gene expression in brain and female reproductive behavior in rats. Endocrinology **143:** 436–444.
46. CHARLIER, T.D., B. LAKAYE, G.F. BALL & J. BALTHAZART. 2002. Steroid receptor coactivator SRC-1 exhibits high expression in steroid-sensitive brain areas regulating reproductive behaviors in the quail brain. Neuroendocrinology **76:** 297–315.

47. CHARLIER, T.D., J. BALTHAZART & G.F. BALL. 2003. Sex differences in the distribution of the steroid receptor coactivator SRC-1 in the song control nuclei of male and female canaries. Brain Res. **959:** 263–274.

48. MANEY, D.L., D.J. BERNARD & G.F. BALL. 2001. Gonadal steroid receptor mRNA in catecholaminergic nuclei of the canary brainstem. Neurosci. Lett. **311:** 189–192.

49. AUGER, C.J. & G.F. BALL. 2002. Expression of steroid receptor coactivator-1 (SRC-1) in the brain of two species of songbird. Horm. Behav. **41:** 455.

50. RATAJCZAK, T. 2001. Protein coregulators that mediate estrogen receptor function. Reprod. Fertil. Dev. **13:** 221–229.

51. DUTERTRE, M. & C.L. SMITH. 2003. Ligand-independent interactions of p160/steroid receptor coactivators and CREB-binding protein (CBP) with estrogen receptor-alpha: regulation by phosphorylation in the A/B region depends on other receptor domains. Mol. Endocrinol. **17:** 1296–1314.

52. AUGER, C.J., G.E. BENTLEY, A.P. AUGER, *et al.* 2002. Expression of cAMP response element binding protein-binding protein in the song control system and hypothalamus of adult European starlings (*Sturnus vulgaris*). J. Neuroendocrinol. **14:** 805–813.

53. NICHOLLS, T.J., A.R. GOLDSMITH & A. DAWSON. 1988. Photorefractoriness in birds and comparison with mammals. Physiol. Rev. **68:** 133–176.

54. GWINNER, E. & M. HAU. 2000. The pineal gland, circadian rhythms and photoperiodism. *In* Sturkies Avian Physiology, 5th edit. G.C. Whittow, Ed.: 557–568. Academic Press. San Diego, CA.

55. DAWSON, A., V.M. KING, G.E. BENTLEY & G.F. BALL. 2001. Photoperiodic control of seasonality in birds. J. Biol. Rhythms **16:** 365–380.

56. BENTLEY, G.E., A. DAWSON & A.R. GOLDSMITH. 2000. Lack of gonadotrophin-releasing hormone (GnRH) response to decreasing photoperiod in thyroidectomised male starlings (*Sturnus vulgaris*). J. Exp. Zool. **287:** 74–79.

57. TEKUMALLA, P.K., M. TONTONOZ, M.A. HESLA & J.R. KIRN. 2002. Effects of excess thyroid hormone on cell death, cell proliferation, and new neuron incorporation in the adult zebra finch telencephalon. J. Neurobiol. **51:** 323–341.

58. BENTLEY, G.E., T.J. VAN'T HOF & G.F. BALL. 1999. Seasonal neuroplasticity in the songbird telencephalon: a role for melatonin. Proc. Natl. Acad. Sci. USA **96:** 4674–4679.

59. BENTLEY, G.E. & G.F. BALL. 2001. Steroid-melatonin interactions and seasonal regulation of the song control system. *In* Avian Endocrinology. A. Dawson & C.M. Chaturvedi, Eds. Narosa Publishing House. New Delhi, India.

60. RIVKEES, S.A., V.M. CASSONE, D.R. WEAVER & S.M. REPPERT. 1989. Melatonin receptors in chick brain: characterization and localization. Endocrinology **125:** 363–368.

61. GAHR, M. & E. KOSAR. 1996. Identification, distribution, and developmental changes of a melatonin binding site in the song control system of the zebra finch. J. Comp. Neurol. **367:** 308–318.

62. WHITFIELD-RUCKER, M.G. & V.M. CASSONE. 1996. Melatonin binding in the house sparrow song control system: sexual dimorphism and the effect of photoperiod. Horm. Behav. **30:** 528–537.

63. BRENOWITZ, E.A. 1991. Altered perception of species-specific song by female birds after lesions of a forebrain nucleus. Science **251:** 303–305.

64. NOTTEBOHM, F., T. STOKES & M. LEONARD. 1976. Central control of song in the canary, *Serinus canarius*. J. Comp. Neurol. **165:** 457–486.

65. BOTTJER, S.W. & F. JOHNSON. 1997. Circuits, hormones, and learning: vocal behavior in songbirds. J. Neurobiol. **33:** 602–618.

66. BRAINARD, M.S. & A.J. DOUPE. 2000. Interruption of a basal ganglia-forebrain circuit prevents plasticity of learned vocalizations. Nature **404:** 762–766.

67. HESSLER, N.A. & A.J. DOUPE. 1999. Social context modulates singing-related neural activity in the songbird forebrain. Nat. Neurosci. **2:** 209–211.

68. JARVIS, E.D., C. SCHARFF, M.R. GROSSMAN, *et al.* 1998. For whom the bird sings: context-dependent gene expression. Neuron **21:** 775–788.

69. BALTHAZART, J. & G.F. BALL. 1998. The Japanese quail as a model system for the investigation of steroid-catecholamine interactions mediating appetitive and consummatory aspects of male sexual behavior. Ann. Rev. Sex Res. **9:** 96–176.

70. PANZICA, G.C., C. VIGLIETTI-PANZICA, F. SANCHEZ, *et al.* 1991. Effects of testosterone on a selected neuronal population within the preoptic sexually dimorphic nucleus of the Japanese quail. J. Comp. Neurol. **303:** 443–456.

71. PANZICA, G.C., C. VIGLIETTI-PANZICA & J. BALTHAZART. 1996. The sexually dimorphic medial preoptic nucleus of quail: a key brain area mediating steroid action on male sexual behavior. Front. Neuroendocrinol. **17:** 51–125.

72. THOMPSON, R.R. & E. ADKINS-REGAN. 1994. Photoperiod affects the morphology of a sexually dimorphic nucleus within the preoptic area of male Japanese quail. Brain Res. **667:** 201–208.

73. BALTHAZART, J., A. FOIDART, E.M. WILSON & G.F. BALL. 1992. Immunocytochemical localization of androgen receptors in the male songbird and quail brain. J. Comp. Neurol. **317:** 407–420.

74. BALTHAZART, J., M. GAHR & C. SURLEMONT. 1989. Distribution of estrogen receptors in the brain of the Japanese quail: an immunocytochemical study. Brain Res. **501:** 205–214.

75. FOIDART, A., B. LAKAYE, T. GRISAR, *et al.* 1999. Estrogen receptor-beta in quail: Cloning, tissue expression and neuroanatomical distribution. J. Neurobiol. **40:** 327–342.

76. BALL, G.F., D.J. BERNARD, A. FOIDART, *et al.* 1999. Steroid sensitive sites in the avian brain: does the distribution of the estrogen receptor alpha and beta types provide insight into their function? Brain Behav. Evol. **54:** 28–40.

77. BALTHAZART, J., A. FOIDART, C. SURLEMONT, *et al.* 1990. Distribution of aromatase in the brain of the Japanese quail, ring dove, and zebra finch: an immunocytochemical study. J. Comp. Neurol. **301:** 276–288.

78. FOIDART, A., J. REID, P. ABSIL, *et al.* 1995. Critical re-examination of the distribution of aromatase-immunoreactive cells in the quail forebrain using antibodies raised against human placental aromatase and against the recombinant quail, mouse or human enzyme. J. Chem. Neuroanat. **8:** 267–282.

79. BALTHAZART, J., C. CASTAGNA & G.F. BALL. 1997. Aromatase inhibition blocks the activation and sexual differentiation of appetitive male sexual behavior in Japanese quail. Behav. Neurosci. **111:** 381–397.

80. BALTHAZART, J., P. ABSIL, M. GÉRARD, *et al.* 1998. Appetitive and consummatory male sexual behavior in Japanese quail are differentially regulated by subregions of the preoptic medial nucleus. J. Neurosci. **18:** 6512–6527.

81. RITERS, L.V., P. ABSIL & J. BALTHAZART. 1998. Effects of brain testosterone implants on appetitive and consummatory components of male sexual behavior in Japanese quail. Brain Res. Bull. **47:** 69–79.

82. BALTHAZART, J., P. ABSIL, A. FOIDART, *et al.* 1996. Distribution of aromatase-immunoreactive cells in the forebrain of zebra finches (*Taeniopygia guttata*): implications for the neural action of steroids and nuclear definition in the avian hypothalamus. J. Neurobiol. **31:** 129–148.

83. HARDING, C.F., K. SHERIDAN & M.J. WALTERS. 1983. Hormonal specificity and activation of sexual behavior in male zebra finches. Horm. Behav. **17:** 111–133.

84. WALTERS, M.J. & C.F. HARDING. 1988. The effects of an aromatization inhibitor on the reproductive behavior of male zebra finches. Horm. Behav. **22:** 207–218.

85. SALDANHA, C.J., M.J. TUERK, Y.H. KIM, *et al.* 2000. Distribution and regulation of telencephalic aromatase expression in the zebra finch revealed with a specific antibody. J. Comp. Neurol. **423:** 619–630.

86. SHEN, P., B.A. SCHLINGER, A.T. CAMPAGNONI & A.P. ARNOLD. 1995. An atlas of aromatase mRNA expression in the zebra finch brain. J. Comp. Neurol. **360:** 172–184.

87. GWINNER, H. 1997. The function of green plants in nests of European starlings (*Sturnus vulgaris*). Behaviour **134:** 337–351.

88. RITERS, L.V. & G.F. BALL. 1999. Lesions to the medial preoptic area affect singing in the male European starling (*Sturnus vulgaris*). Horm. Behav. **36:** 276–286.

89. EENS, M., R. PINXTEN & R.F. VERHEYEN. 1991. Male song as a cue for mate choice in the European starling. Behaviour **116:** 210–238.

90. GENTNER, T.Q. & S.H. HULSE. 2000. Female European starling preference and choice for variation in conspecific male song. Anim. Behav. **59:** 443–458.

91. MOUNTJOY, D.J. & R.E. LEMON. 1995. Female choice for complex song in the European starling. Behav. Ecol. Sociobiol. **38:** 65–71.

92. BALTHAZART, J., O. TLEMÇANI & N. HARADA. 1996. Localization of testosterone-sensitive and sexually dimorphic aromatase-immunoreactive cells in the quail preoptic area. J. Chem. Neuroanat. **11:** 147–171.
93. NOTTEBOHM, F., M.E. NOTTEBOHM, L.A. CRANE & J.C. WINGFIELD. 1987. Seasonal changes in gonadal hormone levels of adult male canaries and their relation to song. Behav. Neural Biol. **47:** 197–211.
94. SMITH, G.T., E.A. BRENOWITZ & J.C. WINGFIELD. 1997. Roles of photoperiod and testosterone in seasonal plasticity of the avian song control system. J. Neurobiol. **32:** 426–442.
95. ARNOLD, A.P. 1981. Logical levels of steroid hormone action in the control of vertebrate behavior. Am. Zool. **21:** 233–242.
96. SMITH, G.T., E.A. BRENOWITZ, M.D. BEECHER & J.C. WINGFIELD. 1997. Seasonal changes in testosterone, neural attributes of song control nuclei, and song structure in wild songbirds. J. Neurosci. **17:** 6001–6010.
97. BOTTJER, S.W. 1993. The distribution of tyrosine hydroxylase immunoreactivity in the brains of male and female zebra finches. J. Neurobiol. **24:** 51–69.
98. SOHA, J.A., T. SHIMIZU & A.J. DOUPE. 1996. Development of the catecholaminergic innervation of the song system of the male zebra finch. J. Neurobiol. **29:** 473–489.
99. MELLO, C.V., R. PINAUD & S. RIBEIRO. 1998. Noradrenergic system of the zebra finch brain: Immunocytochemical study of dopamine-beta-hydroxylase. J. Comp. Neurol. **400:** 207–228.
100. APPELTANTS, D., G.F. BALL & J. BALTHAZART. 2001. The distribution of tyrosine hydroxylase in the canary brain: demonstration of a specific and sexually dimorphic catecholaminergic innervation of the telencephalic song control nuclei. Cell Tissue Res. **304:** 237–259.
101. BARCLAY, S.R. & C.F. HARDING. 1988. Androstenedione modulation of monoamine levels and turnover in hypothalamic and vocal control nuclei in the male zebra finch: Steroid effects on brain monoamines. Brain Res. **459:** 333-343.
102. BARCLAY, S.R. & C.F. HARDING. 1990. Differential modulation of monoamine levels and turnover rates by estrogen and/or androgen in hypothalamic and vocal control nuclei of male zebra finches. Brain Res. **523:** 251–262.
103. SAKAGUCHI, H. & N. SAITO. 1989. The acetylcholine and catecholamine contents in song control nuclei of zebra finch during song ontogeny. Dev. Brain Res. **47:** 313–317.
104. RITERS, L.V. & G.F. BALL. 2002. Sex differences in the densities of alpha2-adrenergic receptors in the song control system, but not the medial preoptic nucleus in zebra finches. J. Chem. Neuroanat. **23:** 269–277.
105. BALL, G.F. 1994. Neurochemical specializations associated with vocal learning and production in songbirds and budgerigars. Brain Behav. Evol. **44:** 234–246.
106. BALL, G.F., J.M. CASTO & D.J. BERNARD. 1994. Sex differences in the volume of avian song control nuclei: comparative studies and the issue of brain nucleus delineation. Psychoneuroendocrinol. **19:** 485–504.
107. CASTO, J.M. & G.F. BALL. 1994. Characterization and localization of D1 dopamine receptors in the sexually dimorphic vocal control nucleus, area X, and the basal ganglia of European starlings. J. Neurobiol. **25:** 767–780.
108. DAHLSTRÖM, A. & K. FUXE. 1964. Evidence for the existence of monoamine-containing neurons in the central nervous system. I. Demonstration of monoamines in the cell bodies of brain stem neurones. Acta Physiol. Scand. **62:** 1–55.
109. REINER, A., E.J. KARLE, K.D. ANDERSON & L. MEDINA. 1994. Catecholaminergic perikarya and fibers in the avian nervous system. In Phylogeny and Development of Catecholamine Systems in the CNS of Vertebrates. W.J.A.J. Smeets & A. Reiner, Eds.: 135–181. Cambridge University Press. Cambridge.
110. APPELTANTS, D., P. ABSIL, J. BALTHAZART & G.F. BALL. 2000. Identification of the origin of catecholaminergic inputs to HVc in canaries by retrograde tract tracing combined with tyrosine hydroxylase immunocytochemistry. J. Chem. Neuroanat. **18:** 117–133.
111. APPELTANTS, D., G.F. BALL & J. BALTHAZART. 2002. The origin of catecholaminergic inputs to the song control nucleus RA in canaries. Neuroreport **13:** 649–653.

112. LEWIS, J.W., S.M. RYAN, A.P. ARNOLD & L.L. BUTCHER. 1981. Evidence for cate-cholamine projection to area X in the zebra finch. J. Comp. Neurol. **196:** 347–354.
113. RITERS, L.V. & S.J. ALGER. 2004. Neuroanatomical evidence for indirect connections between the medial preoptic nucleus and the song control system: possible neural substrates for sexually motivated song. Cell Tissue Res. **316:** 35–44.
114. SMITH, G.T., E.A. BRENOWITZ, J.C. WINGFIELD & L.F. BAPTISTA. 1995. Seasonal changes in song nuclei and song behavior in Gambels white-crowned sparrows. J. Neurobiol. **28:** 114–125.
115. BERNARD, D.J., M. EENS & G.F. BALL. 1996. Age- and behavior-related variation in volumes of song control nuclei in male European starlings. J. Neurobiol. **30:** 329–339.
116. VALLET, E. & M. KREUTZER. 1995. Female canaries are sexually responsive to special song phrases. Anim. Behav. **49:** 1603–1610.
117. VALLET, E., I. BEME & M. KREUTZER. 1998. Two-note syllables in canary songs elicit high levels of sexual displays. Anim. Behav. **55:** 291–297.
118. VALLET, E., M. KREUTZER & M. GAHR. 1996. Testosterone induces sexual release quality in the song of female canaries. Ethology **102:** 617–628.
119. LI, X.C., E.D. JARVIS, B. ALVAREZ-BORDA, *et al.* 2000. A relationship between behavior, neurotrophin expression, and new neuron survival. Proc. Natl. Acad. Sci. USA **97:** 8584–8589.
120. RASIKA, S., A. ALVAREZ-BUYLLA & F. NOTTEBOHM. 1999. BDNF mediates the effects of testosterone on the survival of new neurons in an adult brain. Neuron **22:** 53–62.
121. SARTOR, J.J., T. CHARLIER, C.L. PYTTE, *et al.* 2002. Converging evidence that song performance modulates seasonal changes in the avian song control system. Soc. Neurosci. Abstr. 2002 CD-ROM: Program No.781.10.
122. BERNARD, D.J. 1995. The effects of testosterone, photoperiod, and season on plasticity in the song control system of European starlings (*Sturnus vulgaris*). Ph.D. Dissertation. Johns Hopkins University. Baltimore, MD.
123. BENTLEY, G.E. & G.F. BALL. 2000. Photoperiod-dependent and -independent regulation of melatonin receptors in the forebrain of songbirds. J. Neuroendocrinol. **12:** 745–752.
124. ABSIL, P., L.V. RITERS & J. BALTHAZART. 2001. Preoptic aromatase cells project to the mesencephalic central gray in the male Japanese quail (*Coturnix japonica*). Horm. Behav. **40:** 369–383.

Song and the Limbic Brain

A New Function for the Bird's Own Song

MEI-FANG CHENG[a] AND SARAH E. DURAND[b]

[a]Department of Psychology, Rutgers University, Newark, New Jersey 07102, USA

[b]Department of Natural and Applied Science, LaGuardia Community College, City University of New York, New York, New York 11101, USA

ABSTRACT: The neurobiological investigation of the avian song system has largely focused on the unique neural features of vocal control systems that contribute to learned motor patterns in songbirds. The role of emotion has been disregarded in developing a theory of song learning and performance. Here we review emerging evidence in support of Darwin's observation that vocal communication is emotional expression. We propose that neural pathways mediating emotional state remained integrated with the vocal control system as forebrain vocal control pathways evolved to support learned communication patterns. Vocalizations are therefore both a motor component of an emotional state and can influence emotional state via sensory feedback during vocal production. By acknowledging the importance of emotion in vocal communication, we are proposing that the song system and limbic brain are functionally linked in the production and reception of song.

KEYWORDS: song; vocalization; limbic brain; emotion; self-stimulation

INTRODUCTION: SONG AND EMOTION

Darwin's observation that vocalization is a form of emotional expression has never been disputed and song has long been understood as the expression of emotion, motivation, or intent.[1,2] But among neuroethologists, questions concerning the role of emotion in vocal communication have been superseded by questions that concern sensory-motor integration: What acoustic features are acquired by auditory learning and how are these features reproduced by the motor pathways of the vocal system? To address these questions, focus has been turned upon those features of forebrain vocal control systems that contribute to the acquisition and production of acquired motor patterns. Although this approach to song has been extremely fruitful in revealing the nature of sensory-motor interactions and their neurochemical regulation, the reduction of song to a set of modifiable motor patterns limits a broader appreciation of the relationship between brain and behavior. To quote West and King:[3] "animals do not perceive or communicate for the sake of perceiving or pro-

Address for correspondence: Mei-Fang Cheng, Department of Psychology, Rutgers University, 101 Warren Street, Newark, New Jersey 07102, USA. Voice: 973-353-5440, x226; fax: 973-353-1171.

mcheng@axon.rutgers.edu; <http://psychology.rutgers.edu/~mfc/>

Ann. N.Y. Acad. Sci. 1016: 611–627 (2004). © 2004 New York Academy of Sciences.
doi: 10.1196/annals.1298.019

ducing a display, but for the sake of managing a social environment." This understanding should inform an examination of the neural and neuroendocrine systems that underlie song. The relationship between forebrain vocal systems and neural systems that regulate emotional state begs examination.

We define emotion as an all-inclusive state, mediated by endocrine, autonomic, and skeletomotor responses organized by pathways through the amygdala and hypothalamus. If vocal behavior is recognized as an interdependent skeletomotor component of emotional state, then its dependence upon internal stimuli (neuroendocrine and autonomic activity) for expression can be appreciated; singing is a motivated behavior. Vocalizations, in turn, can affect neuroendocrine and autonomic function by sensory feedback induced during vocal performance. The interactive relationship between neural circuitry that mediates affect and sensorimotor circuitry that mediates vocal behavior has begun to be revealed in work with ring doves, a "non-vocal" learner discussed in the next section. To date, most research on the affective component of learned song has focused on one-way regulation of telencephalic vocal control circuits by steroids and neuromodulators of ascending brainstem systems (Harding, this volume).[4,5]

Vocalization has obvious social consequences, because information about the performer's motivation increases the ability of the receiver to predict the performer's future actions. Predictability is also to the performer's advantage, given that performer and receiver are usually members of a social group whose cohesion depends upon cooperative interactions.[6] To the extent that individually specific variations in past behavior can be associated with specific vocal features, predictive value increases with the familiarity of the voice. In vocal learning species, there appears to be powerful motivation for an individual to acquire the vocal patterns of its social group,[7,8] a behavior manifest in the occurrence of avian dialects.[9] Familiar voices appear to trigger vocal responses and "call-response" interactions[10,11] that further facilitate predictable outcomes of subsequent actions by coordinating the behavior of the participants.[12] Examples include counter-singing across a territorial boundary (whether this be learned or unlearned song), duetting between members of a mated pair of birds or vocal greeting ceremonies during incubation exchange among colonial breeders. We propose here that vocal interactions generate in the participants a shared emotional state—emotional sharing—that coordinates their motivation and facilitates the achievement of a common goal.[13] Evidence for this is presented below.

To date we have little knowledge of the neural mechanisms in oscine songbirds that mediate the critical role of emotional context in determining which auditory stimuli in the social environment are learned.[14] Neural pathways that mediate emotional memory appear to be integral to vocal production, even in the absence of vocal learning. For example, a male gull will perform a "long-call" (an "innate" song with associated gestures) when he hears the voice of his mate but not the voice of a neighboring female, although he has interacted extensively with the latter in pair-wise displays across a mutually defined boundary.[10,11] A close association between vocal and motivational systems is apparent even under experimental conditions that artificially remove the social interactions that drive vocal communication: An isolated juvenile finch can be conditioned to peck a key that triggers the playback of a tutor song[15,16] (Tchernichovski et al., this volume); therefore, pecking the key can be classified as a motor response conditioned by positive reinforcement. For song playback to act as positive reinforcement it must be rewarding. What is the similarity between key pecking for auditory stimulation of song and pressing a bar to electrically stimulate reward pathways in the brain?

If the sound of a familiar voice is rewarding and vocal learning is a motivated behavior, then the goal of vocal practice can be postulated as the reward of attaining a familiar voice. From this perspective, we can address the surprising phenomenon that unrestricted access to a tutor song reduces the fidelity of its imitation:[16] when the reward of the familiar voice is readily available by pecking a key (i.e., the learner has unrestricted access to the model) then the ready availability of the reward could be associated with a concomitant reduction in the motivation to achieve it through practice. Vocal practice in itself could be intrinsically rewarding behavior. The persistent vocal performance that characterizes subsong and plastic song during vocal learning is a form of self-stimulation. Each vocalization produced during the motor acquisition of song generates a sensory experience that could feed back onto pathways that regulate motivation. It can be reasoned that this proprioceptive and auditory feedback is inherently rewarding or vocal practice would not be pursued.

THE SELF-STIMULATION HYPOTHESIS AND EMOTIONAL SHARING

While vocalizations are traditionally recognized as products of a particular motivational (physiological) state, the concept of self-stimulation hypothesizes that repeated performance of a vocalization can alter motivational state by modulating neuroendocrine function. This hypothesis can explain results acquired from studies of dove reproductive behavior, research that has been pursued for several decades.[13,17] The songs of ring doves (family Columbiformes) are stereotyped and individually unique two-note vocalizations ("coos") characterized by a well-defined syntactic structure and associated non-vocal gestures. Although coos have been termed "calls" in the past (and there are true calls in the repertoire of this species), coos are better defined as songs because their syntactical structure and role in social interactions are comparable to the structure and function of learned oscine song.[18]

Dove courtship is initiated by male song. Like oscine song, columbiform coo songs are accompanied by stereotyped non-vocal gestures—visual displays—that include bowing, high stepping, and turning. Should the female remain in the male's vicinity as he performs these displays and the accompanying vocal performance (termed "bow coo" in this behavioral context), the male then performs a different set of gestures to accompany the song. These non-vocal gestures include tipping forward the head and chest towards a point on the substrate and rapidly flipping the closed wings, gestures that are accompanied by changes in the timbre of the coo, which is termed a "nest coo" in this case. (FIG. 1). If the female is motivated to sing her own nest coo in response to the male's courtship song, she may perform the song at a different site, whereupon the male joins her. The female's own vocal performance, constituting repetitive singing of 2–20 songs/min in bouts upwards of 2–8 minutes, triggers a cascade of neuroendocrine responses that generate a physiological state commensurate with that of the courting male: gametic maturation and the motivation to build a nest.[17,19]

Lesions of the posterior medial hypothalamus (PMH) were performed as part of an early attempt to determine the neural pathways that mediated the female's response to male courtship. These PHM lesions blocked performance of nest coo song, its associated gestures (tip and wing-flip), and the female solicitation posture.[20] What neural pathways were implicated in this result? The PMH projects massively upon the midbrain nucleus intercollicularis (ICo),[21,22] a neuronal population within the midbrain torus. Recent results from anterograde and retrograde tracing studies[23]

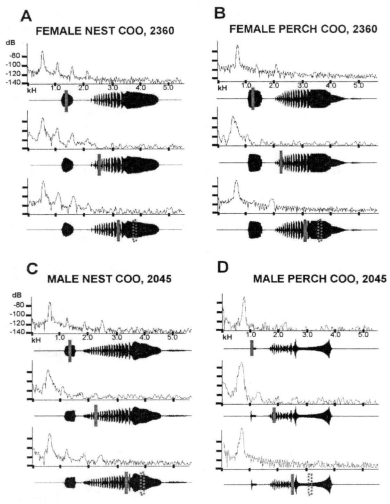

FIGURE 1. Coo songs of male and female ring doves. **A–D:** Coo spectra (Fourier transforms) of a nest coo and a perch coo (undirected song) from, respectively, a female (**A,B**) and male (**C,D**) dove recorded during courtship within a sound-isolation chamber. Three spectra are illustrated from each coo song and were generated from three 30 ms time bins. The temporal location of each bin is identified by a bar within the accompanying coo oscillogram (the spectrograph of a fourth bin, dotted outline, was similar to bin 3 and omitted here). Note drop in harmonic amplitudes in perch coo spectrograms relative to nest coo spectrograms.

suggest that the ICo region that receives PMH input includes the dorsomedial nucleus of ICo (DM), identified by Arends and colleagues[24] (see their Figure 8) in pigeons and proposed as the songbird DM homologue by Wild and colleagues.[25] The DM of oscine vocal control pathways[26,27] has comparable connections in oscines and columbiformes[25] and, like PMH, concentrates estrogen.[28] ICo is a principal target of ascending somatosensory and proprioceptive input and projects onto brainstem respiratory and vocal nuclei.[25,29] Electrical stimulation of ICo, a region described by the authors as "lying rostromedial to the nucleus mesencephalicus lateralis pars dorsalis (MLd)," has elicited vocalizations in pigeons,[30] whereas bilateral lesions of the anterior ICo produced muting in domestic chicks.[31] Thus, lesions of PMH that eliminated the nest coo vocalization may have acted by eliminating critical excitatory input to the midbrain vocal control nucleus ICo.

That lesions of PMH blocked follicular development was not surprising given the well-established role of the hypothalamus regulating the pituitary-gonadal axis. However, we were surprised to find that follicular growth was blocked by procedures that devocalized the female, either by hypoglossal nerve section[32] or by lesioning the medial portion of ICo (mICo.)[33] We concluded from these results that performance by the female dove of her own coo song, rather than male courtship, per se, stimulates her follicular growth. These studies provided the first evidence for the self-stimulation hypothesis in doves.

To test the hypothesis, we compared the effectiveness of stimulating follicular development with male coos, coos of other females, and the female's own coos. Female subjects were isolated and devocalized for the experiment.[34] Playback of the female's own songs was the most effective stimulus for her follicular development, but playback of other female song was also more effective than playback of male song (FIG. 2). (Note that the female nest coo carries information that other females in the colony are responsive to male courtship, a fact that could serve to coordinate egg laying.) However, in a second test we found that male coo playback was most effective in stimulating follicular development in intact unpaired females housed in the colony and in the presence of a nest bowl. Playback of a female's own coo, though less effective, was again more effective than playback of coos from other females.[35] The apparent discrepancy between the results of these two experiments was clarified by the observation that females hearing male coo playback in the second experiment sang nest coo more frequently than females hearing their own recorded coo songs. Therefore, it was concluded that performing her song was a more effective stimulus of follicular maturation than hearing its playback alone. In sum, the results of both experiments were supportive of the self-stimulation hypothesis.

Two variables distinguished the playback condition from the normal reproductive situation. Under normal conditions (1) vocal performance is temporally controlled by the subject and (2) performance is associated with proprioceptive feedback. To assess the relative contribution of proprioceptive versus auditory feedbacks, we paired deafened females with normal males and monitored the frequency of female song for 60 min/day over 26 days in treated and sham (deafened) control groups. Of the deafened females, 50% ($N=12$) experienced significant delay in the onset of nest cooing and ovulation relative to sham-deafened females. The other 50% failed to nest coo and did not show any follicular development.[35] Thus, in addition to its auditory feedback, proprioceptive feedback from performance of nest coos could also contribute to follicular development.

Playback Study 1: Females in sound isolation chambers. Mean increment in follicle size (diameter in mm) of devocalized and sham females hearing playback of their own vs other types of coos.

Groups	Number of Ss	Mean
Dev + male coos	10	2.1 (±2.3)*
Dev + female's own coos	10	6.8 (± 0.9)
Dev + other female coos	10	4.7 (± 1.8)
Dev + no playback	10	1.7 (± 0.1)*
Sham + no playback	10	6.5 (± 1.1)

Playback Study 2: Females in colony room. Mean increment in follicle size (diameter in mm) of intact females hearing playback of their own vs other types of coos

Groups	Number of Ss	Mean
Intact + male coos	9	7.8 (± 1.9)
Intact + female's own coos	7	2.7 (± 1.8)
Intact + other female coos	9	1.9 (± 0.5)
Intact + no playback	6	0.8 (± 0.7)*
Intact + paired	11	9.8 (± 1.9)**

FIGURE 2. Effects of coo stimulation on follicular growth: Playback studies. (*Top*): Playback of female nest coos to devocalized female in sound isolation chamber in the presence of the male facilitates follicular growth. This is not the case with the male nest coo. *Changes in follicular diameter in playback female coos is significantly higher than playback of male coos or females who received no playback (t-test, $P < 0.01$). (Data from Cheng, 1986) (*Bottom*): Playback of male nest coos facilitates follicular growth more than playback of female nest coos.*Changes in follicular diameter in each playback group is significantly higher than those in females who received no playback (control). Schaffe test, $P < 0.01$. **Changes in follicular diameter of the playback group are less than those of the paired group (one way analysis of variance $P < 0.01$). (Data from Cheng, et al., 1988) (From Cheng, 2003; copyright 2003 by Elsevier)

AN AUDITORY-VOCAL CIRCUIT THROUGH THE HYPOTHALAMUS

By what pathways could proprioceptive and auditory feedback from nest coo performance produce endocrine effects? We traced auditory pathways through the midbrain and thalamus and uncovered two previously unrecognized auditory streams into the anterior and posterior medial hypothalamus that originated from the shell of the thalamic auditory relay nucleus (nucleus ovoidalis or Ov).[36–38] This finding established a connection through the Ov shell between ascending auditory pathways and endocrine control centers. Anterograde tracing from a midbrain region interposed between the auditory midbrain (commonly referred to as MLd) and ICo revealed a discrete ascending projection that specifically targeted the shell of Ov. We designated the source of Ov shell projections as the medial margin of the central nucleus (ICM).[36,37] An ICo region just medial to ICM was subsequently also implicat-

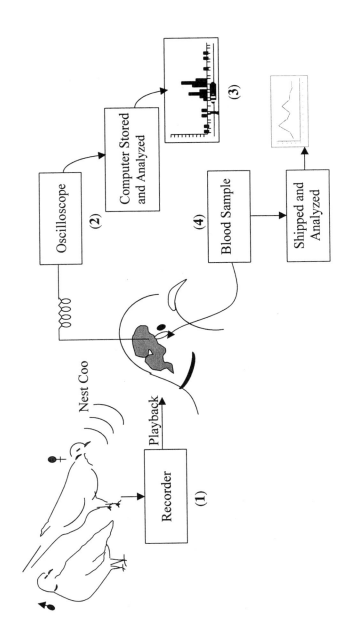

FIGURE 3. A demonstration of neuroendocrine and physiological mechanisms underlying vocal self-stimulation. A diagram depicting the various parts (auditory stimulation, recording and blood sampling) of the experimental procedure employed in one online experimental setup. (1) Before neural recording, tapes of various coo signals including female nest coo were prepared from breeding pairs. (2) Recording electrode was placed in the preoptic hypothalamic regions of female ring doves. (3) Units that burst in response to nest coo signal was monitored by the oscilloscope, stored and analyzed. (4) While recording and auditory stimulation were in session, blood samples were drawn from the pituitary veins, stored and shipped to another lab for the RIA of luteinizing hormone (LH) outputs. (Reproduced from Cheng 2003; copyright 2003 by Elsevier, Academic Press.).

ed in the midbrain pathway into the Ov shell.[38] A region corresponding to "ICM" has now been identified by other researchers as distinct from surrounding regions with respect to its neurochemistry and afferent connectivity and has been designated by them as the caudomedial shell nucleus of the torus semicircularis (CM).[39,40] CM receives input from the auditory brainstem cochlear nuclei as well as proprioceptive (somatosensory) input from the ascending dorsal column system. The medial ICo (mICo) in our earlier studies included CM.

The thalamic subnucleus in receipt of CM input, the Ov shell, was found to differ with respect to its connections and immunohistochemistry from core populations of the thalamus auditory relay nucleus, the Ov core.[36] Furthermore, CM and the Ov shell are the components of the ascending auditory system that receive descending input from a principal integration center of telencephalic auditory streams, the intermediate arcopallium.[41,42] Thus, both CM and the Ov shell are potential sites where input from the multimodal arcopallium[43,44] can modify ascending auditory input arising principally from the nucleus angularis and proprioceptive input from the head and wings.[40]

The two streams of descending auditory input from the Ov shell into the hypothalamus terminated in the preoptic area and anterior-medial hypothalamus (POA/AMH) and, more massively, in the PMH.[36] The POA/AMH region was also found to receive a projection from the mICo, which is located posterior to DM and anterior to CM. The POA/AMH is the site of gonadotrophin-releasing hormone (chicken[c]GnRH I) neurons;[38,45,46] i.e., the triggers of gonadotrophin release from the pituitary that stimulate follicular development. Antidromic stimulation from both the PMH and POA/AMH effectively blocked Ov shell spikes; i.e., shell hypothalamic projections were confirmed with collision extinction experiments.[47] In sum, a putative feedback circuit onto the vocal midbrain (ICo) was established whereby auditory and proprioceptive sensory feedback from vocal production (via CM and the Ov shell) could modulate neuroendocrine function (via Ov to POA/AMH) and further stimulate vocalization (via PMH to ICo).

To confirm these functions of the meso-diencephalic circuit just outlined, physiological data were needed. To provide such data, anesthetized doves were exposed to auditory stimulation while extracellular potentials were recorded from the POA/AMH or from the PMH. Concurrently, blood samples were drawn from the venous outflow of the pituitary gland.[48] FIGURE 3 provides a schematic layout of the experiment designed to demonstrate a direct linkage between the neuronal processing of vocal-auditory input and the contingent luteinizing hormone release response. In total, we recorded 935 units from 36 birds. The vast majority of these units were not responsive to sound stimulation. Only 20.8% of the recorded units were coo responsive. There were slightly more excitatory units than inhibitory units (52%). Interestingly, the majority of excitatory units (75.2%) were found in the POA-AMH regions where concentrations of active form of GnRH (cGnRH-1) neurons were observed.[38,46]

FIGURE 4 shows a female-nest-coo–specific unit in the preoptic area that responded specifically to the female nest coo in that it showed no response to reversed female nest coo, male nest coo, or white noise. These units typically were silent or showed slow and irregular firing when not stimulated. The spike train of the female-nest-coo–specific units consisted of two bursts of four to seven spikes each separated by a silent period of 200–600 msec. The firing pattern of female-nest-coo–specific

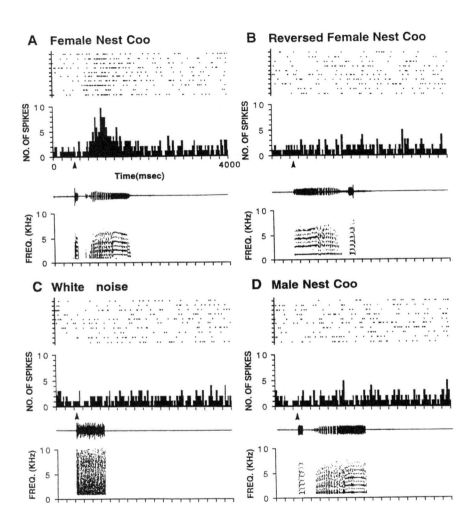

FIGURE 4. Female-nest-coo-specific units in the preoptic area of the hypothalamus. Response of unit 960108 in the preoptic area of a female ring dove to different acoustic stimuli. (**A**) The female nest coo as the stimulus; the activity of the unit increases significantly. *Top*, Dot raster plot showing 10 sweeps of the unit's response. Each dot represents one spike. *Middle*, Histogram of the unit's response. *Bottom*, Computer amplitude display and spectrogram of the female nest coo. (**B**) Reversed female nest coo as the stimulus; no change in neuronal activity can be detected in the number of spikes over time or in the histogram representation. (**C**) White noise as the stimulus: no change in neuronal activity. (**D**) Male nest coo as the stimulus; no change in neuronal activity. A *closed triangle* denotes the onset of the stimulus. (Reproduced from Cheng *et al.*, 1998; copyright 1998 by the Society for Neuroscience)

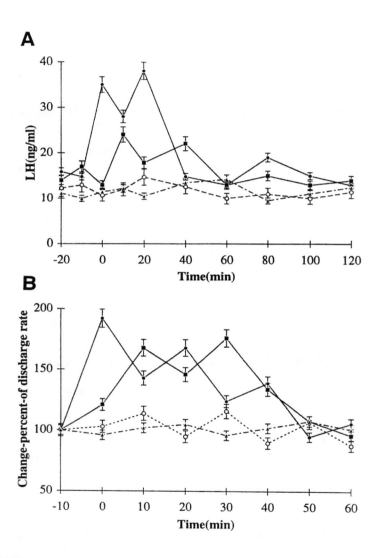

FIGURE 5. Effects of nest coo stimulation on neuronal response of anterior medial hypothalamus units and pituitary LH levels in female ring doves. LH levels were significantly higher for the female birds ($n = 3$) hearing female nest coo play backs (*closed circles*) than for those receiving no playback (*closed triangles*) at time points 0, 10 and 20min, in which $0 = 40$ min after the onset of female nest coo stimulation ($t = 3.08$; $P<0.01$) (Reproduced from Cheng *et al.*, 1998; copyright 1998 by the Society for Neuroscience.)

units corresponds temporally to the two-note coo shown in FIGURE 3 (box 3). As to the LH release in response to different sound stimulation, the RIA LH assay showed a significant elevation in doves hearing female nest coo but not in doves hearing reversed female nest coo, other coo or white noise. These LH levels were three times higher than those in doves hearing male nest coo (FIG. 5). The close proximity of female-nest-coo–sensitive neurons to cGnRH-1 neurons suggests that these coo-responsive units are part of or in contact with the GnRH network.

Do GnRH neurons respond to the intensity of coo-responsive neurons in incremental manner? Analysis of the sum total of all discharges (excitatory and inhibitory) arriving at the POA-AMH area showed no difference between birds hearing male coos or those hearing female nest coos. These observations suggest that GnRH network is not governed by the overall intensity of the arriving stimuli but rather by the feature recognition of the unique discharge pattern of female-nest-coo–specific units. This non-linear response of GnRH neurons is a perfect match with the pattern of follicular growth: follicle size takes on an exponential growth at certain threshold level of female nest-cooing.[49] In sum, the single unit recording and the LH data validate at the cellular level our earlier behavioral observation that a female's own nest-cooing stimulates her hypothalamus-pituitary-ovarian system.

These data suggested the following sequence of physiological events: Coo songs of other breeding females can initiate a rise in gonadotrophin levels via Ov shell auditory-vocal input to the POA/AMH, triggering a gradual rise in circulating estrogen and sensitizing the female to male courtship stimuli. Given sufficient levels of such auditory-vocal stimulation (the male is persistent in his courtship), there is sufficient feedback drive into the midbrain ICo to stimulate song in the female. The resulting convergent audio-proprioceptive feedback increases activity in the CM-Ov shell pathway and excitatory drive into ICo, directly via ascending somatosensory input and via the feedback loop through the Ov shell and PMH, which increases excitatory drive onto ICo via descending projections from PMH into ICo/DM. As follicles mature, levels of circulating estrogen increase, which could further stimulate the estrogen-concentrating neurons of ICo, the Ov shell, and hypothalamus[28] and increase the rate of song production. Combined actions of estrogen and progesterone from a mature follicle also act to motivate the female to join the male in nest construction.[19,50]

In conclusion, the hypothalamus plays a critical role in both "endocrine" and "vocal" aspects of self-stimulation through POA/AMH and PMH respectively. We propose therefore that the CM-Ov shell-Hypothalamus pathway provides the neural circuits for nest coo effects: audio-proprioceptive input → CM (ICo) → Ov shell → (1) posterior medial hypothalamus → ICo → vocal output and (2) preoptic-anterior medial hypothalamus → pituitary → endocrine change.

RECEIVER SELF-STIMULATION: POTENTIAL RELEVANCE TO VOCAL LEARNING

The concept of receiver self-stimulation can be applied to observations of vocal-learning species with respect to both behavior and brain studies. Observations obtained from a small colonial parrot, the budgerigar (*Melopsittacus undulatus*), have particular relevance to the ring dove story. The forebrain vocal control pathways of budgerigars are organized similarly to those of oscine songbirds.[51] Pairs of budgerigars, small parrots that learn and improvise complex vocalizations, rarely breed when isolated from the colony.[52] However, auditory access to conspecific "warble song" of other males' triggers a male to also perform this vocalization. Gonadal maturation occurs only after a male commences to sing.[53,54] Thus, budgerigar reproductive behavior appears to present an example of receiver self-stimulation; the receiver being a mature male who receives stimulation in the form of learned vocalizations from other members of his social group. Self-stimulation, which is triggered by the receipt of auditory input from members of his social group, is then obtained by performance of his own warble song. Self-stimulation establishes the neuroendocrine status that supports reproductive competence. It is noteworthy that warble song, like passerine song and unlearned coo songs, incorporates stereotyped non-vocal gestures. Warble is delivered in conjunction with rhythmic head-bobbing and short bursts of flight; thus, both auditory and proprioceptive feedback from motor systems other than the respiratory-vocal system is implicated in the sensory feedback of self-stimulation.

In cowbirds, a vocal-learning songbird, females perform wing strokes during a male's serenade in response to acoustic structures in the male's performance that are most effective at eliciting her copulatory postures.[14] Males respond to the wing strokes by altering their songs to include more of these vocal patterns. Is there a role for proprioceptive feedback in the female cowbird? It is possible that performance of wing strokes could have a stimulatory effect on the female's motivation to copulate: Proprioceptive feedback from wing strokes, non-vocal gestures, would have access at the level of the auditory midbrain[40] to the midbrain-thalamo-hypothalamic circuit described for doves. Pallial connections of this circuit include neural substrates that subserve formation of emotional memory, given projections from the Ov shell into the avian amygdala, ventral striatopallidum, and caudomedial neostriatum.[36,43,56,57]

The effectiveness of a vocal signal to generate a memory trace may depend upon the ability of the signal to engage the limbic brain; i.e., neural pathways through the amygdala and hypothalamus. Anterograde and retrograde tracing across doves, chicks, and songbirds label Ov shell projections into limbic structures of the pallium (the avian amygdala and associated ventral striatopallidum) and into pallial regions implicated in memory formation (the caudomedial nidopallium and intermediate mesopallium, formerly IMHV).[36,43,56,57] In addition to neural pathways that link audiosomatic input with pallial emotional centers in the pallium, neural connections between the Ov shell and forebrain vocal control system of oscine songbirds have been explicitly identified.[56] These currently identified pathways between the Ov shell and vocal learning system are indirect. However, there is evidence for a direct Ov shell projection into the songbird vocal control nucleus, n. interface, and its homologue in columbiformes that awaits confirmation.[29,36,58] In sum, the same auditory population that links vocal behavior with the neuroendocrine system at the level diencephalon could also serve to link limbic and audio-vocal activity at the level of the telencephalon.

Vocalizations that trigger a receiver to vocalize in return, receiver self-stimulation, would therefore generate combined audio-somatic feedback into limbic and mnemonic brain structures. This hypothesis provides a framework for examining how and why particular vocal structures are retained in memory and subsequently performed to the exclusion of others. Given that the hypothesis rests upon neuroanatomical data indicating physical associations between neural structures that mediate vocal learning and neural structures that mediate internal state, it is noteworthy that neurochemical associations also exist between auditory populations of the Ov shell, the limbic brain, and forebrain vocal control nuclei. Immunocytochemistry for the neuropeptide methionine enkephalin has revealed immunoreactivity throughout the vocal system of oscine songbirds and budgerigars and within shell, but not core, populations of Ov and its targets in the hypothalamus and limbic pallium.[37,59–62] Furthermore, scattered neurons within enkephalin-rich regions of the ventral striato-pallidum that receive shell input[36,37] have been backfilled from vocal control nuclei[51] and the enkephalin-immunoreactive fiber fields present here are continuous with those of vocal control nuclei.[62] Thus, with respect to both physiology and anatomy, there is provocative but as yet unconfirmed evidence to suggest that neural systems that support vocal learning are integrated with motivational systems of the forebrain.

RECEIVER SELF-STIMULATION: GENERAL APPLICABILITY TO VOCAL INTERACTIONS

The theory may also have implications for analysis of auditory-vocal interactions outside of reproduction and song.[13] As noted above, projections from the thalamic auditory shell target limbic structures in the brain that include the extended amygdala (nucleus taenia and the adjacent ventral striatum) as well as pallial structures that subserve imprinting and auditory memory. Given these connections, consider the vocal interaction between a lost chick and her hen. The hen's absence induces separation stress in the chick, presumably via pathways through the avian amygdala.[13] The amygdala has access to the midbrain vocal center via its projections to the hypothalamus,[57] the putative channel whereby anxiety induces vocalizations. In parallel with the induction of separation peeps, activity within descending amygdalar projections to the hypothalamus would trigger a neuroendocrine response: release of corticosterone. Auditory stimulation from the chick's peeps could activate thalamic shell projections to the amygdala in the hen, a brain region that has been demonstrated to respond to species-specific fight-or-flight stimuli. Thus, the motivation to seek interaction that is experienced by the chick is transferred to the hen—emotional sharing—an emotional state that evokes the hen's own vocalizations. What is the role of vocal self-stimulation in maintaining the peep vocalizations of the chick, thereby increasing the likelihood of their reaching the hen? Evidence suggests that peep vocalizations are rewarding to produce under conditions of stress, given they are sustained in the absence of auditory-vocal input from the hen.[13] Self-stimulation of reward pathways would have high adaptive value in this context, given the dependence of the chick upon the hen for its survival.

CONCLUSION

To manage their social environment, birds sing learned or unlearned songs. Yet the neural basis for the motivation of song has received relatively little attention. By investigating the integration of communication and motivation we will serve to broaden our understanding of both song function and song learning.

In doves, vocal self-stimulation not only stimulates the female to ovulate but also serves to stimulate the female's male partner to initiate nest construction, presumably by auditory stimulation of a comparable pathway into the male hypothalamus that regulates reproductive behavior. Linkage between audio-vocal pathways and the limbic brain constrains communication to exert an effect upon both performer and receiver. The integration of audio-vocal and neuroendocrine circuitry in doves is accomplished via pathways through discrete populations of the thalamic auditory relay, the shell of the nucleus ovoidalis (Ov shell). We have argued that the Ov shell probably serves a similar function in vocal learning species: it has connections with both the limbic brain and vocal control pathways and shares with these two neural subsystems common neurochemical features.

We contend that the social function of song requires the integration of sensory-motor pathways with limbic association areas. Although direct evidence for such integration comes from ring doves, there is emerging evidence for a conserved system of connections that could permit emotional responses to modify sensorimotor activity in telencephalic vocal control nuclei by pathways unique to shell populations of the thalamic auditory relay nucleus. An examination of the neural systems that drive the motivation to sing, which would expand the neuroethology of song to include the limbic brain, could ultimately enhance the applicability of song learning as a model for the affective control of speech.

ACKNOWLEDGMENTS

This work was supported by National Institute of Mental Health Grant NS35924 and a Rutgers Busch Biomedical Research Grant (M.F.C.).

REFERENCES

1. WHITE, G. 1789. The Natural History of Seborne. Dent. London.
2. HOWARD, H.E. 1920. Territory in Bird Life. John Murray. London.
3. WEST, M. & A.P. KING. 1996. Eco-gen-actics: a systems approach to the ontogeny of avian communication. *In* Ecology and Evolution of Acoustic Communication in Birds. D.E. Kroodsma & E.H. Miller, Eds: 20–38. Cornell University Press. Ithaca, NY.
4. DAVE, A.S, A.C. YU & D. MARGOLIASH. 1998. Behavioral state modulation of auditory activity in a vocal motor system. Science **282:** 2250–2254.
5. LIVINGSTON, F.S & R. MOONEY. 2001. Androgens and isolation from adult tutors differentially affect the development of songbird neurons critical to vocal plasticity. J. Neurophysiol. **85:** 34–42.
6. SMITH, W.J. 1977. The Behavior of Communicating. Harvard University Press. Cambridge, MA.
7. BROWN, E. 1985. The role of song and vocal imitation among common crows (*Corvus brachyrhynchos*). Z. Tierpsychol. **68:** 115–136.
8. FARABAUGH S.M, A. LINZENBOLD & R.J. DOOLING. 1994. Vocal plasticity in (*Melopsittacus undulatus*): evidence for social factors in the learning of contact calls. J. Comp. Psychol. **108:** 81–92.
9. PAYNE, R.B. 1996. Song traditions in indigo buntings: origin, improvisation, dispersal and extinction in cultural evolution. *In* Ecology and Evolution of Acoustic Communication in Birds D.E. Kroodsma & E.H. Miller, Eds.: 198–220. Cornell University Press. Ithaca, NY.

10. BEER, C.G. 1970. Individual recognition of voice in the social behavior of birds. *In* Advances in the Study of Behavior. D.S. Lehrman, R.A. Hinde & E. Shaw, Eds.: 27–74. Academic Press. New York.

11. BEER, C.G. 1980. The communication behavior of gulls and other seabirds. *In* Behavior of Marine Animals. J. Burger, B.L. Olla & H.E. Winn, Eds. **4:** 169–205. Plenum Press. New York.

12. SMITH, W.J. 1996. Using interactive playback to study how songs and singing contribute to communication about behavior. *In* Ecology and Evolution of Acoustic Communication in Birds. D.E. Kroodsma & E.H. Miller, Eds.: 375–397. Cornell University Press. Ithaca, NY.

13. CHENG, M.F. 2003. Vocal self-stimulation: from the ring dove story to emotion-based vocal communication. *In* Advances in the Study of Behavior. P.J. Slater, J.S. Rosenblatt, C.T. Snowden & T.J. Roper, Eds. **30:** 309–353. Academic Press. New York.

14. WEST, M.J., N. STROUD & A.P. KING. 1983. Mimicry of human voice by European starlings: the role of social interaction. Wilson Bull. **95:** 640–643.

15. ADRET, P. 1993. Operant conditioning, song learning and imprinting to taped song in the zebra finch. Anim. Behav. **46:** 49159

16. TCHERNICHOVSKI, O., T. LINTS, P.P. MITRA & F. NOTTEBOHM. 1999. Vocal imitation in zebra finches is inversely related to model abundance. Proc. Natl. Acad. Sci. USA **96:** 12901–12904.

17. CHENG, M.F. 1992. For whom does the female dove coo? A case for the role of vocal self stimulation. Anim. Behav. **43:** 1035–1044.

18. BAPTISTA, L.F. 1996. Nature and nurture in avian vocal development. *In* Ecology and Evolution of Acoustic Communication in Birds. D.E. Kroodsma & E.H. Miller, Eds.: 39–60. Cornell University Press. Ithaca, NY.

19. CHENG, M.F. 1979. Progress and prospect in ring dove research. *In* Advances in the Study of Behavior. J. Rosenblatt, R.A. Hind, C.G. Beer & M.C. Busnel Eds. **9:** 97–124. Academic Press. New York.

20. GIBSON, M. & M.F. CHENG. 1977. The neural mediation of estrogen dependent courtship behavior in the female ring dove. J. Comp. Physiol. Psychol. **93:** 855–867.

21. BERK, M.L. & A.B. BUTLER. 1981. Efferent projections of the medial preoptic nucleus and medial hypothalamus in the pigeon. J. Comp. Neurol. **203:** 379–399.

22. CHENG, M.F., T.R. AKESSON & N. DELANEROLLE. 1987. Retrograde HRP demonstration of afferent projections to the midbrain and nest calls in the ring dove. Brain Res. Bull. **18:** 45–48.

23. CHEN, G., E. BONDER & M.F. CHENG. 2003. Lesion-induced newborn neurons send projections to the midbrain vocal center in ring doves. Collected abstracts of the 33rd Annual Meeting of the Society for Neuroscience (New Orleans, LA): no. 541.9

24. ARENDS, J.J.A., J.M. WILD & H.P. ZIEGLER. 1988. Projections of the nucleus of the tractus solitarius in the pigeon (*Columba livia*). J. Comp. Neurol. **278:** 405–429.

25. WILD, J.M., D. LI & C. EAGLETON. 1997. Projections of the dorsomedial nucleus of the intercollicular complex (DM) in relation to respiratory-vocal nuclei in the brainstem of pigeon (*Columba livia*) and zebra finch (*Taeniopygia guttata*). J. Comp. Neurol. **377:** 392–413.

26. NOTTEBOHM, F., T.M. STOKES & C.M. LEONARD. 1976. Central control of song in the canary, *Serinus canarius*. J. Comp. Neurol. **165:** 457–486.

27. PATON, J.A., K.R. MANOGUE & F. NOTTEBOHM. 1981. Bilateral organization of the vocal control pathway in the budgerigar (*Melopsittacus undulatus*). J. Neurosci. **1:** 1279–1288.

28. MARTINEZ-VARGAS, M.C., W.E. STUMP & M. SAR. 1976. Anatomical distribution of estrogen target cells in the avian CNS: A comparison with the mammalian CNS. J. Comp. Neurol. **167:** 83–104.

29. WILD, J.M. 1989. Avian somatosensory system: II. Ascending projections of the dorsal column and external cuneate nuclei in the pigeon. J. Comp. Neurol. **287:** 1–18.

30. JAHNKE, H.J. & M. ABS. 1982. Vocalization after electrostimulation of the brain of pigeons in relation to heart- and breathing-rates. Behav. Brain Res. **5:** 65–72.

31. DE LANEROLLE, N. & R.J. ANDREW. 1975. Midbrain structures controlling vocalization in the domestic chick. Brain Behav. Evol. **10:** 354–376.

32. COHEN, J. & M.F. CHENG. 1979. Role of vocalization in the reproductive cycle of ring doves (*Streptopelia risoria*): effects of hypoglossal nerve section on the reproductive behavior and physiology of the female. Horm. Behav. **13:** 113–127.
33. COHEN, J. & M.F. CHENG. 1981. The role of the midbrain in courtship behavior of the female ring dove (*Streptopelia risoria*): evidence from radiofrequency lesion and hormone implant studies. Brain Res. **207:** 279–301.
34. CHENG, M.F. 1986. Female cooing promotes ovarian development in ring doves. Physiol. Behav. **37:** 371–374.
35. CHENG, M.F., C. DESIDERIO, M. HAVENS & A. JOHNSON. 1988. Behavioral stimulation of ovarian growth. Horm. Behav. **22:** 388–401.
36. DURAND, S.E., J.M. TEPPER & M.F. CHENG. 1992. The shell region of the nucleus ovoidalis: A subdivision of the avian auditory thalamus. J. Comp. Neurol. **323:** 495–518.
37. DURAND, S.E., M.X. ZUO., S.L. ZHOU & M. CHENG. 1993. Avian auditory pathways show met-enkephalin-like immunoreactivity. NeuroReport **4:** 727–730.
38. CHENG, M.F. & M. ZUO. 1994. Proposed pathways for vocal self-stimulation: met-enkephalinergic projections linking the midbrain vocal nucleus, auditory-responsive thalamic regions and neurosecretory hypothalamus. J. Neurobiol. **25:** 361–379.
39. PUELLES, L., C. ROBLES, T. MARTINEZ-DE-LA TORRE & S. MARTINEZ. 1994. New subdivision schema for the avian torus semicircular: neurochemical maps in the chick. J. Comp. Neurol. **340:** 98–152.
40. WILD, J.M. 1995. Convergence of somatosensory and auditory projections in the avian torus semicircularis, including the central auditory nucleus. J. Comp. Neurol. **358:** 465–486.
41. WILD, J.M., B.J. FROST & H.J. KARTEN. 1993. Connections of the auditory forebrain in the pigeon *(Columba livia)*. J. Comp. Neurol. **337:** 32–62.
42. MELLO, C.V., G.E. VATES, S. OKUHATA & F. NOTTEBOHM.1998. Descending auditory pathways in the adult male zebra finch (*Taeniopygia guttata*). J. Comp. Neurol. **395:** 137–160.
43. METZGER, M., S. JIANG & K. BRAUN. 1998. Organization of the dorsocaudal neostriatal complex: a retrograde and anterograde tracing study in the domestic chick with special emphasis on pathways relevant to imprinting. J. Comp. Neurol. **395:** 380–404.
44. HUSBAND S.A. & T. SHIMIZU. 1999. Efferent projections of the ectostriatum in the pigeon *(Columba livia)*. J. Comp. Neurol. **406:** 329–345.
45. KUENZEL, W.J. & S. BLAHSER. 1991. The distribution of gonadotropin-releasing hormone (GnRH) neurons and fibers throughout the chick brain (*Gallus domesticus*). Cell Tissue Res. **264:** 481–496.
46. SILVER, R., C. RAMOS, H. MACHCA & B. SILVERIN. 1992. Immunocytochemical distribution of GnRH in the brain of adult and posthatching great tit (*Parus major*) and ring dove (*Streptopelia risoria*). Ornis Scan **23:** 222–232.
47. CHENG, M.F. & J.P. PENG. 1997. Reciprocal talk between the auditory thalamus and the hypothalamus: an antidromic study. NeuroReport **8:** 653–658.
48. CHENG, M.F., J.P. PENG & P. JOHNSON. 1998. Hypothalamic neurons preferentially respond to female nest coo stimulation: demonstration of direct acoustic stimulation of luteinizing hormone release. J. Neurosci. **18:** 5477.
49. CHENG, M.F. 1993. Vocal, auditory and endocrine systems: 3-way connectivities and implications. Poultry Sci. Rev. **5:** 37–47.
50. CHENG, M.F. & R. SILVER 1975. Estrogen-progesterone regulation of nest-building and incubation behavior in ovariectomized ring doves. J. Comp. Physiol. Psychol. **88:** 256–263.
51. DURAND, S.E., J.T. HEATON, S.K. AMATEAU & S.E. BRAUTH. 1997. Vocal control pathways through the anterior forebrain of a parrot. J.Comp. Neurol. **377:** 179–206.
52. FARABAUGH, S.M. & R.J. DOOLING. 1996. Vocal communication in budgerigars. *In* Ecology and Evolution of Acoustic Communication in Birds. D.E. Kroodsma & E.H. Miller, Eds.: 368–385. Cornell University Press. Ithaca, NY.
53. BROCKWAY, B.F. 1964. Social influences on reproductive physiology and ethology of budgerigars (*Melopsittacus undulatus*). Anim. Behav. **12:** 493–501.

54. BROCKWAY, B.F. 1969 Roles of budgerigar vocalization in the integration of breeding behavior. *In* Bird Vocalizations. R.A. Hind, Ed.: 131–158. Cambridge University Press. London.

55. WEST, M.J. & A.P. KING. 1988. Female visual displays affect the development of male song in the cowbird. Nature **334:** 244–246.

56. VATES, G.E., B.M. BROOME, C.V. MELLO & F. NOTTEBOHM. 1996. Auditory pathways of caudal telencephalon and their relation to the song system of adult male zebra finches (*Taenopygia guttata*). J. Comp. Neurol. **366:** 613–642.

57. CHENG, M.F., M. CHAIKEN, M. ZUO & H. MILLER. 1999. Nucleus taenia of the amygdale of birds: anatomical and functional studies in ring doves and European starlings. Brain Behav. Evol. **53:** 243–270.

58. WILD, J.M. 1994. Visual and somatosensory inputs to the avian song system via nucleus uvaeformis (Uva) and a comparison with the projections of a similar thalamic nucleus in a nonsongbird, *Columbia livia*. J. Comp. Neurol. **349:** 512–535.

59. RYAN, S.M., A.P. ARNOLD & R.P. ELDE. 1981. Enkephalin-like immunoreactivity in vocal control regions of the zebra finch brain. Brain Res. **229:** 236–240.

60. BALL, G.F., P.L FARIS., B.K. HARTMEN & J.C. WINGFIELD. 1988. Immunohistochemical localization of neuropeptides in the vocal control regions of two songbird species. J. Comp. Neurol. **268:** 171–180.

61. BOTTJER, S.W. & A. ALEXANDER. 1995. Localization of met-enkephalin and vasoactive intestinal polypeptide in the brains of male zebra finches. Brain Behav. Evol. **45:** 153–177.

62. DURAND, S.E., W. LIANG & S.E. BRAUTH. 1998. Methionine enkephalin immunoreactivity in the brain of the budgerigar: similarities and differences with respect to oscine songbirds. J. Comp. Neurol. **393:** 145–168.

The Road We Travelled

Discovery, Choreography, and Significance of Brain Replaceable Neurons

FERNANDO NOTTEBOHM

The Rockefeller University, Field Research Center, Millbrook, New York 12545, USA

ABSTRACT: Neurons are constantly added to the telencephalon of songbirds. In the high vocal center (HVC), where this has been studied, new neurons replace older ones that died. Peaks in replacement are seasonal and affect some neuronal classes but not others. Peaks in replacement coincide with peaks in information acquisition. The new neurons are produced by division of cells in the wall of the lateral ventricle. Where studied closely, the neuronal stem cells proved to be radial glia. Life expectancy of the new neurons ranges from weeks to months. New neuron survival is regulated by vacancies, hormones, and activity. The immediate agent of new neuron survival is, in some cases, brain-derived neurotrophic factor (BDNF). The effect of BDNF is maximal 14–20 days after the cells are born, when they are establishing their connections. These observations are now being extended to other vertebrates and may apply, to varying degrees, to all of them. The function of neuronal replacement in healthy adult brain remains unclear. If synaptic number and efficacy sufficed as mechanisms for long-term memory storage and could be adjusted again and again to incorporate new memories, then neuronal replacement would seem unnecessary. Since it occurs, it seems reasonable to suppose that replacement serves to maintain learning potential in a way that could not be done just by synaptic change. Long-term memories may be encoded by long-term changes in gene expression akin to a last step in cell differentiation. If so, neuronal replacement may be the adult brain's way of striking a balance between limited memory space and the need to acquire new memories. The testing of this hypothesis remains in the future. This chapter tells how neuronal replacement was discovered in the adult songbird brain.

KEYWORDS: birdsong; vocal learning; laterality; sexual dimorphism; adult neurogenesis; neuronal replacement; long term memory

The discovery that some brain cells are constantly replaced in an adult vertebrate brain came as a surprise because it was widely believed that central nervous system neurogenesis stopped soon after birth and that the same complement of neurons, perhaps with some losses, was present throughout life. An account of this discovery be-

Address for correspondence: Fernando Nottebohm, The Rockefeller University, Field Research Center, Tyrrel Road, Millbrook, NY 12545, USA.
nottebo@mail.rockefeller.edu
<http://www.rockefeller.edu/labheads/nottebohm/nottebohm-lab.html>

Ann. N.Y. Acad. Sci. 1016: 628–658 (2004). © 2004 New York Academy of Sciences.
doi: 10.1196/annals.1298.027

longs in this book because it was made in the song system of birds and may help explain some aspects of vocal learning.

The story starts with the classical studies of Thorpe, Marler, and Konishi. In 1958, W.H. Thorpe of the University of Cambridge published "The learning of song patterns by birds, with special reference to the song of the chaffinch, *Fringilla coelebs*."[1] In that study, Thorpe showed that young chaffinches acquired their song by imitating the song of adults of their own kind, for which they seemed to have a preference. Imitation of the model occurred during a sensitive period that normally ended at sexual maturity. However, if conspecific models were not available by then, song could still be altered in future years. Thorpe interpreted his observations as evidence for the existence of an innate "blueprint" that guided song development.

Peter Marler was involved as a doctoral student and research assistant with much of Thorpe's work on song learning. Marler became very interested in the natural history of song dialects in birds, and he continued that work when he settled in the late fifties at the University of California in Berkeley. The laboratory that Marler founded then focused on vocal learning in birds. Many of us that have worked on this topic— Baker, Dooling, Konishi, Kroodsma, Nowicki, Searcy, and myself, among others— apprenticed in Marler's laboratory.

Marler and his colleagues used California's white-crowned sparrows, *Zonotrichia leucophrys*, and other songbirds to confirm and extend Thorpe's observations, adding new experimental refinements, better quantification, and controls, and exploring new conceptual issues.[2–14] Marler[15] concluded from all these studies that oscine songbirds had an inherited program typical of each species that could be thought of as an "instinct to learn." This instinct defined the "when," "what," and "how" of learning, so only the details of the imitated pattern were left to external sources of information. There are similarities between Thorpe's "blueprint" for song learning and Marler's "instinct to learn," (see Adret, this volume), but Marler put more work into fleshing out this concept and provided many more details.

Mark Konishi did his doctoral work in Marler's laboratory. Konishi[16,17] investigated how auditory experience exerted its effect on song development (see Konishi, this volume). Using the technique of cochlear removal developed by Schwartz-kopf,[18] Konishi[16] noticed that the marked effect of early deafening on song learning in white-crowned sparrows was the same whether the operation occurred before or after exposure to a model song, provided that the model had not yet been imitated. This result suggested that the auditory model did not have a direct effect on vocal output but, rather, guided learning through a two-step process: (1) first the auditory memory of the model was acquired, (2) as vocal development proceeded, vocal output was modified until the auditory feedback generated matched the auditory model, which acted as a template. Konishi's insight went well with the observation, later emphasized by Marler,[5] that several months can elapse from the time a model is heard until it is imitated—i.e., acquisition of the template and its imitation are two separate processes that can also be separated in time.

Konishi[16] made another tantalizing observation. The song of intact white-crowned sparrows reared as isolates included tonal whistles also present in wild-type song but typically absent from the song of early-deafened individuals. Thus, access to auditory feedback helped a young bird steer song development in the direction of wild-type song even when this bird had never heard an external model. This type of vocal ontogeny differs radically from that of non-vocal learners, such as domestic fowl (*Gallus domesticus,*)[17] ring-doves (*Streptopelia risoria*),[19] and eastern phoebes (*Sayornis phoebe*),[20] that produce normal adult vocalizations even when deafened very early in ontogeny.

Many of the seminal insights of Thorpe, Marler and Konishi were already in place or being finalized by the time I started my doctorate in Marler's laboratory in 1962. In the fall of 1963 I left for Cambridge, U.K. to spend a year in Thorpe's laboratory. It was during that year that I started to experiment with syringeal denervation. Konishi[16] thought that the stability of learned song that he observed in white-crowned sparrows deafened as adults might be maintained by proprioceptive feedback, though it was not known whether the syrinx had sensory nerves. I expected that if the syrinx were denervated in an adult that had been previously deafened, the bird would still have a voice but that many of the learned sounds would disappear. I speculated that under these conditions proprioceptive information that normally accompanied song would be altered. If proprioception played a role in the song stability of deafened adults, then denervation of the syrinx (FIG. 1) should lead not just to song that was aberrant in its motor execution, but also that was unstable. As I set to test this prediction, I encountered a roadblock. When both halves of the syrinx of an adult male chaffinch were denervated by section of the right and left tracheosyringeal nerves, the birds, when alarmed had difficulty breathing—in fact, if the disturbing stimulus was not promptly stopped, they suffocated. I then denervated the syrinx unilaterally. Breathing now was unimpeded, but in addition I encountered a paradox. Though both halves of the syrinx were anatomically similar, denervation of the left half eliminated most of the elements of a chaffinch's learned song but denervation of the right half had little or no effect (FIG. 2). I called this phenomenon left hypoglossal dominance or "the vocal left."[21-23] Now I had something to work with!

Left hypoglossal dominance is also present in the canary[24,25] and white-crowned sparrow,[24] so it is not a one-species fluke. As I returned from England, where wild-born chaffinches had been kindly provided by Thorpe's laboratory, I switched my research on laterality to **canaries**, which were easy to breed in captivity and therefore better suited for laboratory work. Peter Marler kindly gave me the birds I needed, which came from his colony of Belgian Waterslagers.

The discovery of left hypoglossal dominance in chaffinches, canaries, and white-crowned sparrows delighted me because it suggested that the song of at least some oscine songbirds might blend three very human traits: vocal learning, handedness, and hemispheric dominance. If some songbirds had left hypoglossal dominance for the production of learned song, might they also show left hemispheric dominance for this same behavior and if so, which parts of the brain were responsible for the acquisition and production of learned song? Philosophers and evolutionary biologists have struggled for a long time with the origins of vocal learning in humans. Could it be that birds would shed independent light on this key evolutionary step? I now had a strong incentive to delve into the songbird brain.

Soon after I moved (at Peter Marler's invitation) to Rockefeller University in 1967, I teamed up with a brilliant comparative neuroanatomist, Christiana Leonard, and a very gifted technician, Tegner Stokes. Our first task was to produce a stereotaxic atlas of the canary brain.[26] We were guided in this work by the recently published pigeon atlas of Karten and Hodos.[27] Our next task was to identify the motor neurons that innervate the muscles of the syrinx. We found them in the hypoglossal nucleus of the medulla. Then we placed electrolytic lesions in the vicinity of the

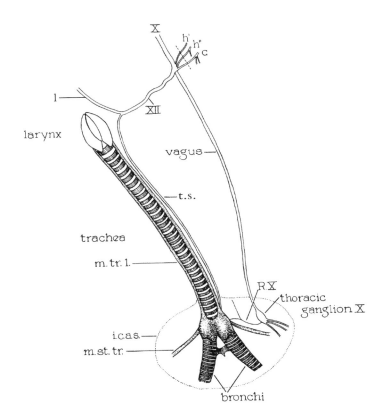

FIGURE 1. (A) Schematic ventral view of the syrinx, trachea and larynx of a male chaffinch (*Fringilla coelebs*), and attendant musculature and innervation. All anatomical details are very similar in canaries and **zebra finches**. The syrinx is the vocal organ of birds, at the confluence of both bronchi and the trachea. It is surrounded by an air space, the interclavicular air sac (i.c.a.s.). Each syringeal half has its own air flow, sound source, muscular control, and innervation. Each tracheosyringeal branch of the hypoglossal nerve innervates just the muscles of the ipsilateral, syringeal half; this drawing shows just the left side innervation; a very slender vagal branch reaches the syrinx, but its role is unknown. Unilateral syringeal denervation can be achieved by cutting all three roots (h', h'', and c) of one hypoglossal (XII) nerve or just by cutting the tracheosyringeal (ts) branch on one side. The anatomy and pattern of innervation of the songbird syrinx allow it to function as two separate sound sources.[22,104] The involvement of the larynx in phonation has not been described; the extent of its opening probably affects sound loudness and the emphasis or suppression of different harmonics, as described for bill movements.[105] **(B)** A longitudinal section of the syrinx of an adult male canary shows the point of constriction, on each side, where the external labium (l.e.) extends towards the rostral end of the internal tympaniform membrane (t.i.); sound is thought to be generated by the periodic oscillations of the external labium.[106,107] The bronchidesmus, a membrane, anchors the syrinx to the dorsal wall of the interclavicular air sac (i.c.a.s.). Notice the somewhat heavier muscle mass on the left syringeal half. Abbreviations: R.B and L.B., right and left bronchi; X, tenth cranial nerve; RX, recurrens branch of the vagus, that reaches the syrinx; m. st.tr., sternotrachealis muscle; m.tr.l., tracheolateralis muscle; lingual, branch of the hypoglossus nerve that innervates the tongue

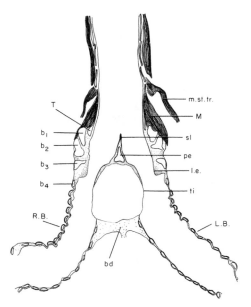

FIGURE 1B. *Continued.*
(not shown). The syrinx also has several bony components: the tympanum (T), bronchial
half-rings 1–4, and the pessulus (pe); the pessulus is crested by the semi-lunar membrane
(sl). (The drawings, with modifications, come from Nottebohm.[23] Used with permission.)

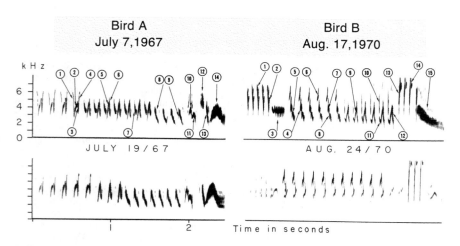

FIGURE 2. The song of two intact adult male chaffinches, A and B. Both birds were
recorded again after denervation of the left (Bird A) or right (Bird B) syringeal halves. The
elements of pre-operative song, defined as frequency upsweeps, down sweeps or buzzes,
were numbered. In bird A, only three out of fourteen elements (numbers 1, 7, and 12) were
lost after section of the right tracheo-syringeal nerve. In bird B, only three elements out of
fifteen (numbers 6, 13 and 14) survived section of the left tracheosyringeal nerve. These re-

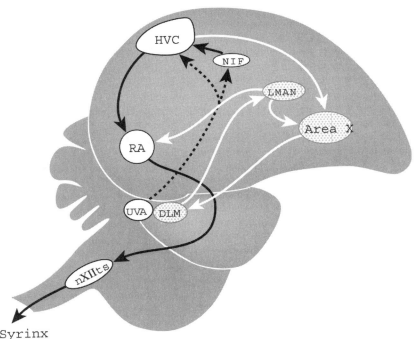

To Syrinx

FIGURE 3. Schematic view of the song system in a parasaggital section of the adult songbird brain. The anatomical relations shown apply equally to adult male canaries and zebra finches, the two species that have received the greatest anatomical and neurophysiological attention. The details shown here are not complete. A posterior pathway, responsible for the production of learned song, leads from the nucleus interface (NIf) to the high vocal center (HVC), from HVC to the robust nucleus of the archipallium (RA), and from there to a number of mid-brain and medullary nuclei that control structures involved with phonation and respiration—including the caudal half of the hypoglossal nucleus, which houses the motor neurons that innervate the muscles of the syrinx. An anterior pathway necessary for song learning but not song production goes from HVC to Area X, then to the medial portion of the dorsolateral thalamic nucleus (DLM) and from there to the lateral magnocellular nucleus of the anterior nidopallium (LMAN); LMAN sends a projection back to Area X and another one to RA; other feedback loops are not shown. Interestingly, nucleus uvaeformis (Uva) of the thalamus, which projects to NIf and HVC, is capable of driving the firing of HVC neurons. All the projections shown here are ipsilateral. (This drawing is based on anatomical information from Nottebohm and colleagues,[29,108] Okuhata and Saito,[109] Bottjer and colleagues,[110] Vates and Nottebohm,[111] Nixdorf-Bergweiler and colleagues,[112] and Vates and colleagues[113] and on neurophysiological observations from McCasland,[114] Williams,[115] Yu and Margoliash,[116] and Hahnloser and colleagues.[88])

sults suggest that a majority of the elements of adult chaffinch song is under left hypoglossal control, while the remainder of elements (usually simple in structure and high pitched) is under control of the left syringeal innervation. Lost elements were replaced by silence or by altered sounds. The horizontal axis indicates time in seconds, the vertical one frequency in kiloHerz. Dates stand for when the preoperative and postoperative recordings were made. (Reproduced from Nottebohm,[22] with permission.)

forebrain's known auditory projection, Field L of Rose,[28] and noticed which of these lesions had an effect on song and how these regions were connected, directly or indirectly, to the hypoglossal motor neurons that innervated the syrinx. That is how the discrete nuclei that we now call the high vocal center (HVC), the robust nucleus of the arcopallium (RA), and Area X of lobus parolfactorius were discovered. We saw that HVC projected to RA which, in turn projected to nXIIts; in addition, HVC projected to Area X. All these projections were ipsilateral.[29] That was our first glimpse of the song system. Several subsequent studies added more anatomical details (FIG. 3).

Lesions of the left HVC and of the left RA of adult male canaries had a greater effect on the quality of post-operative song than similar lesions on the right side; complete lesions of the left HVC were particularly devastating in that, without muting the bird, they erased all traces of learned song.[29,30] If HVC was destroyed bilaterally the bird would still adopt a singing posture and efforts to sing persisted, but with exception of a few clicking sounds the song was silent; there was no recovery from this condition.[30] It seemed, from the above results that the HVC of adult canaries did not initiate song, yet the left HVC played a dominant role in the production of its learned contents. To my surprise, this dominance could be reversed. Following the elimination of the left HVC of an adult male canary, song quality was back to normal one year later, this time under right side control[30] (FIG. 4). We now had three useful handles on the neurobiology of learned canary song: (1) a well-defined path-

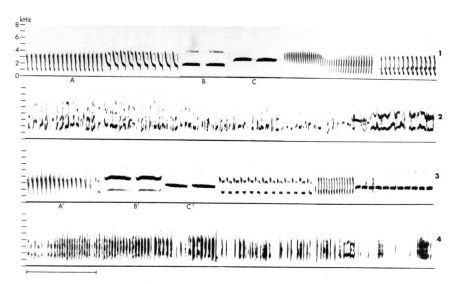

FIGURE 4. Effects on the song of an adult male canary of an electrolytic lesion that fully destroyed the left HVC.[30] (1) Fragment of preoperative song. (2) Song recorded 7 days after lesion of left HVC. (3) Song recorded 7 months after left HVC lesion. (4) Song recorded 4 days after section of right tracheosyringeal nerve. Letters A, B, and C identify preoperative syllables; A′, B′, and C′ identify the somewhat altered postoperative version of these same syllables. No syllable survived section of the right tracheosyringeal nerve. (Reproduced from Nottebohm,[30] with permission.)

way whose principal role was the production of learned vocal patterns; (2) functional lateralization; and (3) adult plasticity that allowed for laterality reversal and recovery of function. There is even now, at the time of this writing, no other known system that shows this combination of attributes.

There are in canaries no obvious, systematic differences in the size of the right and left HVC and RA,[31] so the functional asymmetry that normally occurs does not seem to be dictated by asymmetrical pathway limitations. Indeed, the very fact that following lesion of the dominant side the previously subordinate one takes over suggests that in terms of their potential both sides are similar.[30,32]

The next significant insight occurred when Art Arnold and I noticed—he in **zebra finches** (*Taeniopygia guttata*), I in canaries—that the nuclei of the song system were much larger in males than in females.[33] Gross sexual dimorphism in a specific CNS pathway had not been observed before. We already knew that several of the nuclei of the adult song system concentrated testosterone and its metabolites.[34,35] Given this ability to concentrate hormones, the song system's sexual dimorphism could result from sexual differences in the hormone levels present at any one time or from differences in development that occurred earlier in ontogeny. Both these possibilities proved to be correct.

Adult female canaries sing relatively little and when they sing their song tends to be simpler and less stereotyped than that of males. However, after systemic treatment with testosterone, adult female canaries sing much more[36–39] and their song syllables become more stereotyped, though their diversity does not increase. This change in behavior is accompanied by gross anatomical changes. Song nuclei HVC and RA are 90% and 50% larger, respectively, one month after onset of hormone treatment than in untreated controls. At that time, though, these two song nuclei remain in females still half as large as those of males.[40] Full masculinization of the song system can only be achieved by hormone treatment early in juvenile life.[41,42]

The observation of hormone-induced changes in the size of the female song control nuclei, led, then, to the next question: Did the size of the song control nuclei of adult males change seasonally, as the birds went in and out of reproductive state? The answer was yes. The size of HVC and RA became considerably smaller after the end of the breeding season, then bounced back. This was the first report of seasonal changes in brain structure.[43]

The marked sexual dimorphism in the size of song nuclei can be related to sexual differences in singing behavior. Male **canaries** and **zebra finches** sing a lot, but female canaries sing little and female zebra finches never sing. In addition, the song of male canaries has a greater diversity of syllable types than that of females. Perhaps our observations of song system sexual dimorphism could be explained as a simple principle of brain economy: the amount of brain space allotted by each sex to a learned behavior is proportional to the relative complexity of that behavior in males and females. This, of course, raises the question of whether male canaries, which show marked individual variability in their number of song syllable types, might show a corresponding difference in the size of song nuclei. The answer to this question is intriguing. There is a significant relation between the size of HVC and the number of different song syllable types, but this relation seems to be a permissive one. Adult canaries that have a large syllable repertoire also tend to have a large HVC and birds with a small HVC tend to have small song repertoires. However, a bird can have a large HVC and a small repertoire, a case, perhaps of unfulfilled learn-

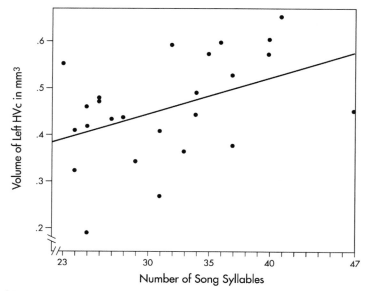

FIGURE 5. Regression of a number of different song syllables on the volume of left HVC for 25 adult male canaries.[31] Song recordings were made during March and April when the birds, in full breeding condition, sang adult stereotyped song; samples of song of 600 or more sec were used for the syllable counts. Brains obtained in mid summer, after the birds had bred. There were no significant age difference in HVC volume. Though at that time the testis of some of the birds had already regressed, there was no significant correlation between testis volume and HVC volume. Only left HVC volumes are plotted here; there was no consistent right-left asymmetry in the volume of HVC. (Reproduced from Nottebohm,[31] with permission.)

ing potential (FIG. 5). I called the relation between complexity of learned song and amount of space devoted to it "brain space for a learned task"[44] and, as described above, this brain space can change seasonally. Subsequent studies have found this relation between song complexity and HVC volume very robust. It holds when comparing different populations of a same species[45] or different congeners,[46] or when comparing a large group of different oscine songbirds.[47]

How do hormones and season affect the size of adult HVC and RA? Tim De-Voogd and I used Golgi-stained material to show that the dendrites of the most numerous type of RA neuron are significantly longer in adult male canaries than in adult females of the same age.[48] These differences, though, are less dependent on genetic sex than on circulating hormone levels. When adult female canaries were treated with testosterone levels as found in spring-time males, they started, as expected, start to sing like males. In these birds the dendrites of the cells we studied grew and many new synapses were formed.[49–51] For a while this seemed like the obvious explanation for the seasonal and hormone-induced changes in the volume of song nuclei, because as dendrites grew cells would be spaced further apart. However, it puzzled me that whereas the RA of testosterone-treated adult female canaries grew

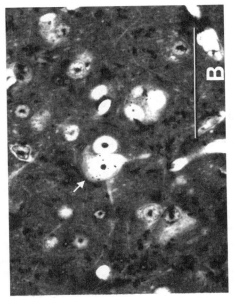

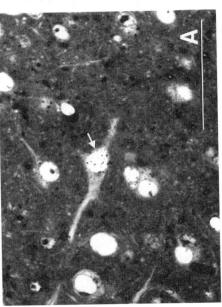

FIGURE 6. (A and B) Two examples of cresyl violet–stained, araldite-embedded, 1 μm–thick sections of the HVC of an adult canary killed one month after the last of a series of systemic injections of ^{3}H-thymidine. As some of the unstable tritium (^{3}H) atoms give up their excess energy (beta rays), it exposes silver grains in the overlying photographic emulsion, which then look like pepper grains. Two of the cells shown (*arrows*) have a clear neuronal profile and 10 or more exposed grains overlying their nucleus. The thinness of the sections made it unlikely that the radiation came from pieces of other, unseen, adjacent cells. Electron microscopy analysis of these same sections yielded further evidence of the neuronal identity of the labeled cells. (Reproduced from Goldman and Nottebohm,[52] with permission.)

by 50%, the HVC of these birds grew by 90%. Might there be in HVC still another process at work? Could it be that more cells were added? Might neurons come and go as hormone levels changed?

Steve Goldman and Sue Kasparian[52] tested the latter possibility by injecting testosterone-treated adult female canaries with the birth-date marker ^{3}H-thymidine. As a cell prepares to divide, ^{3}H-thymidine becomes part of newly synthesized DNA. To our delight, there were many HVC neuron-like cells autoradiographically labeled with tritium (^{3}H) when the birds were killed 30 days later (FIG. 6). Interestingly, too, these cells were present regardless of whether or not the birds had been treated with testosterone, but were not present if the birds were killed one or two days after ^{3}H-thymidine injection. At those short survivals, though, we could see many labeled cells on the wall of the lateral ventricle overlying HVC. We inferred that, as during embryogeny, new neurons were born on the walls of the lateral ventricle and, from there, migrated into HVC, where they settled and differentiated. As a double check on the neuronal identity of these cells, Steve Goldman and later Gail Burd looked at some of these cells electron microscopically. What they saw was compatible with our earlier identification of them as neurons.[52,53]

We had learned, by then, about Joseph Altman's earlier reports, in the 1960s, of post-natal neurogenesis in the brain of rats and cats[54–57] and of the resistance these reports had met. The Altman studies, like ours, used ^{3}H-thymidine to document the presence of newly born cells. Subsequent studies by Kaplan had also used electron microscopy to show that at least some new cells born in adulthood were neurons.[58] Yet questions remained as to what was reliable proof of neuronal identity and adult birth: Could synapses be formed on glia? Was a neuron-like cell necessarily a neuron? Was the nuclear presence of ^{3}H-thymidine definitive proof of time of birth? Where could new neurons possibly come from? The resistance to adult neurogenesis was, perhaps, understandable, in view of the long-held dogma that no neurons were formed in adulthood.

Given the persistent scepticism that continued to surround claims of adult neurogenesis in warm-blooded vertebrates, our first priority now was to test whether the cells we called new HVC neurons were in fact working neurons and were connected to existing circuits. John Paton undertook this task. We knew that if we injected a male or female canary with ^{3}H-thymidine twice a day for 2 weeks, approximately 10% of the neurons in HVC would be labeled 30 days after the last injection. At that time the bird was anesthetized and Paton entered HVC with a hollow glass electrode filled with the marker horseradish peroxidase (HRP). As the electrode advanced, Paton knew when a neuron was penetrated because of the change in electrical potential. Once the electrode was inside a cell, the bird was exposed to sound stimulation. Katz and Gurney,[59] working in the Konishi laboratory at Caltech, had shown earlier that neurons in HVC fired in response to auditory stimulation and so did some of Paton's cells. The same electrode that Paton used to impale the cells and record changes in potential and responses to sound was then used to fill the cells with HRP. After the bird was killed, the brains were sliced at 120-μm intervals. Immunocytochemistry was used to visualize the HRP-filled cells. Typically, one to three HRP-filled cells were recovered per HVC. These cells showed as much detail, including dendritic spines, as if they had been stained with the Golgi method (FIG. 7). After the HRP-filled cells were drawn, the 120 μm–thick sections were thin sliced at 6-μm intervals. These thinner slices were used for autoradiography. Seventy-seven

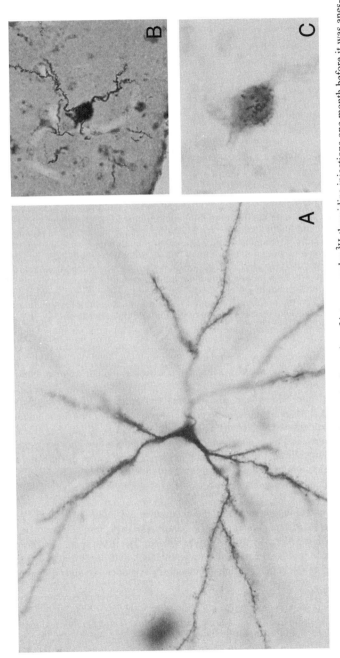

FIGURE 7. (A) HVC neuron of an adult canary that received a series of intra-muscular ³H-thymidine injections one month before it was anesthetized. This cell was then impaled by a hollow glass electrode and produced action potentials in response to sound stimulation. After the electrophysiological recordings were made, the same electrode was used to fill the cell with HRP. The bird was then killed, its brain sectioned at intervals of 100 μm and the resulting HVC sections were cleared in glycerine, so that this cell could be seen and photographed. Notice the well developed and typically neuronal dendritic tree and dendritic spines. (B) The same cell was then sectioned at 6 μm intervals. In this section we see the cell's soma. (C) Same as in **B** but focusing on the overlying photographic emulsion. The diameter of this cell's soma is approximately 9 μm. The 30 or so exposed silver grains clustering over the cell's nucleus suggest that this cell was born a month earlier, while the bird received ³H-thymidine. This was the first direct evidence that a vertebrate brain cell that looked and behaved like a neuron was born in adulthood and had become connected to existing circuits. (Adapted from Paton and Nottebohm,⁶⁰ with permission.)

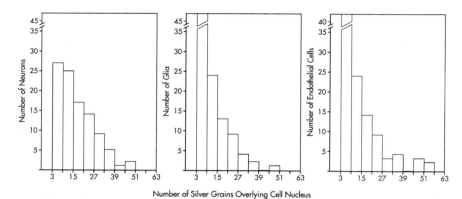

Number of Silver Grains Overlying Cell Nucleus

FIGURE 8. Histogram showing the relative frequency with which various numbers of exposed silver grains occurred over the nuclei of 100 labeled neurons (*left*), 100 labeled glia (*middle*), and 100 labeled endothelial cells (*right*). The sample of labeled cells was obtained from the HVC and adjacent neostriatum of an adult canary treated with ^{3}H-thymidine one month earlier; the tissue was sectioned at 6 μm intervals, stained with cresyl violet, and exposed for autoradiography for 10 days. The criterion for labelling was three silver grains, which corresponds here to 10× background. However, in all three cell classes a majority of labeled cells had nine or more exposed silver grains. The short exposure time was chosen to reduce the instances in which the number of exposed silver grains over the nucleus was too high to count or too high to allow for identification of the underlying cell. (Reproduced from Nottebohm,[61] with permission.)

HRP-filled cells with neuronal neurophysiological profiles and clear neuronal anatomy were recovered from HVC. Seven of these, the expected 10%, were well labeled with ^{3}H-thymidine. Four of the latter seven had given vigorous electrophysiological responses to sound. The simplest interpretation of these results was that the cells we called new HVC neurons were, indeed, neurons and that at least some of them were connected to existing circuits.[60] I have dwelt on this particular experiment because it provided the first direct evidence that some cells born in adulthood became working neurons. This was the evidence that had not been available in Altman's work and whose absence accounted, probably, for the resistance it had encountered.

Another important question was whether the amount of ^{3}H label we saw in neurons of ^{3}H-thymidine–treated birds warranted the conclusion that these cells had been born at the time the birth marker was given. It was known that thymidine was incorporated into existing cells not just during the stage of DNA synthesis that precedes mitosis but also during DNA repair, which is an ongoing process in living tissues.

FIGURE 9. (**A**) Nucleus HVC of an adult male canary backfilled by fluorogold injected into RA. Backfilled axons and cell bodies are clearly visible. (**B** and **C**) Two examples on HVC neurons backfilled with fluorogold from RA and also labeled with ^{3}H-thymidine (black grains over soma). These observations provided evidence that a majority of the neurons added to the adult HVC projected to RA. (Reproduced from Kirn and colleagues,[63] with permission.)

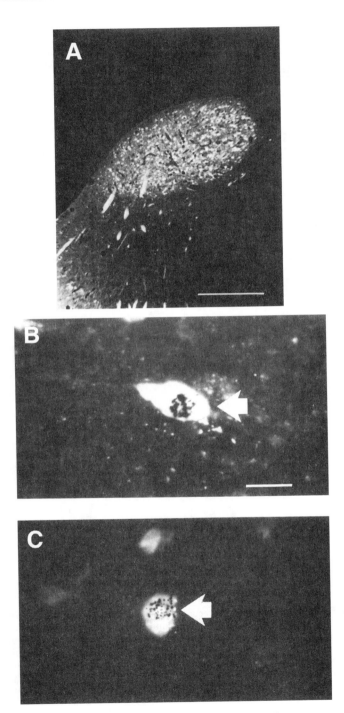

FIGURE 9. *See previous page for legend.*

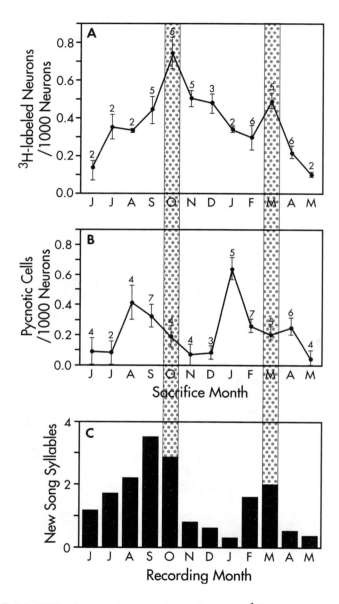

FIGURE 10. (A) Twelve-month record of mean number of ^{3}H-labeled neurons (±SEM) per 1,000 HVC neurons and per day of ^{3}H-thymidine treatment in adult male canaries that received eight successive intramuscular injections of ^{3}H-thymidine at 12-h intervals and were killed 27 days after the last injection. The number of birds in each monthly sample is indicated above the SEM bar. The letter in the horizontal axis stands for the month of the year when the birds were killed, starting with June (J) on the extreme left. (B) Pycnotic cells per 1,000 labeled neurons were counted in the same birds as in **A** plus in 10 more added to make up for the fact that pycnotic cells occur at very low densities and thus require more

Might we be dealing with a situation in which, for some reason, in some cells DNA incorporation was exacerbated without this being part of a mitotic event? Our answer to this question was simple. We showed that the extent of autoradiographic label in the ^{3}H-labeled neurons we saw in the adult canary HVC was similar to that in other kinds of ^{3}H-labeled cells, such as glia and endothelia, also found in the same animals[61] (FIG. 8). Since it was generally accepted that glia and endothelia continue to be produced in adulthood, the most parsimonious interpretation was that in all three kinds of cells ^{3}H-thymidine had been incorporated into DNA during the S-phase that precedes mitosis and that this was the main source of autoradiographic labeling.

Now that we were confident that new neurons were added to nucleus HVC, what kind of neuron were they? Initially, we thought that the new neurons were predominantly interneurons because very few were backfilled when HRP was injected into either of HVC's target nuclei, RA or Area X.[62] However, this result was misleading and was probably affected by the fact that HRP is not a universal agent for backfilling neurons. When, in a later study we used fluorogold instead of HRP we found, to our surprise, that a majority of the new neurons added to HVC projected from HVC to RA, i.e., were projection neurons; these cells were backfilled by injections of fluorogold into RA (FIG. 9), but not into Area X;[63] the remainder of new HVC neurons, we suspect, are interneurons because they can not be backfilled by tracer injections into RA or Area X. Moreover, as later studies showed, these new neurons that cannot be back-filled from RA have other properties that set them apart from HVC's RA-projecting new neurons.[64]

Next came evidence that the neurons added to adult HVC persisted for a number of months and then disappeared. Addition and disappearance occurs even at times of year when total HVC numbers remain constant. Apparently the neurons added to adult HVC hold their job for a limited time and are then replaced by new ones. Evidence for this "replacement" is numerical. We do not know if the new neuron is employed in the same position and capacity as the one it replaces. The notion of "throwaway" neurons, i.e., neurons used for a while and then discarded, is still a novel one.[65]

Soon thereafter we put together seasonal data collected over a number of years. Adult male canaries change their song every year by adding new syllable types and discarding others.[66] This process of recruiting new syllable types, which occurs during all months of the year, shows a major peak in September, after the end of the breeding season, and a less pronounced one in February-March.[67] Recruitment of new HVC neurons also occurs spontaneously throughout the year, but shows seasonal peaks in October and March. These peaks are preceded, two months earlier, by peaks of cell death[68] (FIG. 10). The peaks in syllable addition are sandwiched be-

---

individuals to yield a reliable mean. (C) Mean number of new syllable types that appeared every month in the song of six male canaries in their second year of life. (Adapted from Nottebohm and colleagues[78]). For a syllable to be counted it had to be different from all others produced by the bird at that time and recur with sufficient stereotypy as to make its identification unambiguous, though these syllables are not, at that time, fully stereotyped. The shaded bars linking (A–C) are meant to make it easier to compare the temporal relation between peaks of cell death (pycnotic cells), new cell recruitment, and first appearance of new song syllables. (Reproduced from Kirn and colleagues,[68] with permission.)

tween the peaks in cell death and cell recruitment. This temporal relation suggests that the learning of new song syllables is enabled by a cell death–mediated weakening in the motor control of the pre-existing syllables, which as a result become more variable and thus provide the raw material and opportunity for new learning. As new syllables emerge from this variability, the peak in new neuron arrivals is associated with a restoration of stereotypy; thereafter new syllable learning wanes. Presumably the new neurons receive instruction in song after or while they connect with the existing circuitry.

Soon after neuronal recruitment was discovered in adult HVC,[52] it became clear that it also occurred throughout most of the songbird telencephalon.[61] If, as evidence

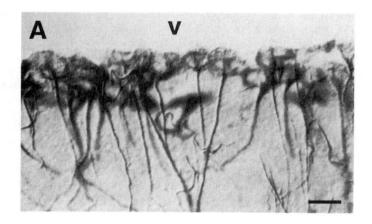

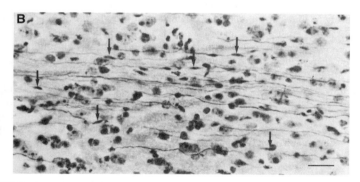

FIGURE 11. (A) Radial glia in adult canary brain stained with an anti-vimentin antibody. The body of the cells, with clear nuclei, is in the ventricular zone that forms the wall of the lateral ventricle (V). These cells project a single, unbranching process into the underlying brain parenchyma. Calibration bar: 10 μm. (Reproduced from Alvarez-Buylla and colleagues,[69] with permission.). (B) Section of forebrain showing radial fibers stained brown by an anti-vimentin antibody in association with small elongated cells closely apposed to the fibers and showing the same orientation. These elongated cells were suspected, at the time, of being young migrating neurons. (Reproduced from Alvarez-Buylla and colleagues,[70] with permission.)

suggested, new neurons were part of a choreography of constant replacement, we needed a mechanism that showed how it occurred and that was applicable to much of the forebrain. Dan Buskirk provided the crucial component of this mechanism by producing a monoclonal antibody that revealed cells with a small body lodged in the wall of the lateral ventricle. These cells had long, unbranching processes that penetrated the adjacent parenchyma (FIG. 11A) and at times could be seen reaching the pial surface. This typical anatomy was well known to embryologists. These cells were called radial glia and they had not been observed before in adult brain. They were very plentiful in the brain of our adult canaries. Arturo Alvarez-Buylla characterized the antibody that had revealed these cells and showed it to be positive to vimentin, an intermediate filament protein also found in astrocytes.[69]

Soon after radial glia were first visualized in our adult birds, we noticed that small elongated cells of uncertain identity, closely apposed to the radial fibers and showing their same orientation were particularly common close to the lateral ventricle and in parts of the telencephalon rich in radial glia fibers. It was tempting to imagine that these young elongated cells (FIG. 11B), which had not been previously described in adult brain, were young migrating neurons.[70] To test this possibility, adult canaries received two systemic injections of ^{3}H-thymidine 12 h apart and were then killed after 1 h or 1, 3, 6, 15, 20, 30, or 40 days later. At 1 h and 1 day survivals there were many ^{3}H-labeled cells on the walls of the lateral ventricle but none of the small elongated cells that we suspected of being young migrating neurons was labeled nor were there any labeled differentiated neurons. A small number of the small, elongated cells was labeled, however, 3 day after injection and all of them were close to the lateral ventricle. On subsequent days these small, elongated, ^{3}H-labeled cells were found further and further away from the lateral ventricle, giving the impression of a migrating wave. Some of these cells had reached the farthest corners of the telencephalon by day 20, which was also when we saw in that material the first, differentiated (post-migratory) ^{3}H-labeled neuron. Between days 20 and 40 the number of labeled elongated cells decreased, while that of labeled neurons increased (FIG. 12). We inferred from these results[71] that our time series showed the migration and eventual settling and differentiation of a wave of young neurons that had been born in the adult canary brain on a particular day. We noticed, too, that the maximal number of cells thought to be young migrating neurons seen on a particular day (day 20 after ^{3}H-thymidine injection) was three times higher than the number of labeled neurons seen on day 40. Apparently, as during embryogeny, a majority of the migrating neurons or newly differentiated neurons are culled, so that by day 40 only one-third of the initial cohort survives.[71]

The next step was to identify the cells that gave birth to new neurons. We noticed that labeled ventricular zone cells were not evenly distributed throughout the walls of the lateral ventricle, but were particularly abundant in the dorsal and ventral reaches of the lateral ventricular wall, which we called "hot spots." We dissociated the cells in these hot spots one hour after a systemic ^{3}H-thymidine injection. At that time, the majority of the individually dissociated ^{3}H-labeled cells were positive to vimentin and had long, un-dividing processes, i.e., a majority of the dividing cells were radial glia. We suggested, from this observation, that new neurons were formed when radial glia divided and, presumably, one of the daughter cells assumed the identity of a young migrating neuron.[72] This view was confirmed later by more detailed work in adult birds[73] and in mouse embryos.[74] More recently Alvarez-Buylla

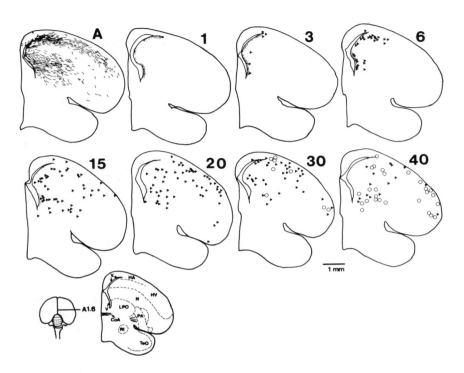

FIGURE 12. (A) Distribution of radial glia fibers in a transverse section of adult canary brain cut in the plane of the canary atlas[26] at the level of the anterior commissure (*inset*). The number on the other sections indicates survival time, in days, after the second of two intramuscular doses, 12 h apart, of ^{3}H-thymidine. At the earliest survivals there are many ^{3}H-labeled cells (indicated as *dots*) in the wall of the lateral ventricle, where new neurons are thought to be born. On day 3 one sees the first small, elongated, ^{3}H-labeled cells (*filled triangles*) close to the wall of the lateral ventricle, presumed to be young migratory neurons born after label injection and starting to move away from their birth site. Thereafter, the number of these cells increases. The first ^{3}H-labeled cells with a post-migratory neuronal phenotype (*open circles*) were seen on day 20 and their number much increased thereafter. (Reproduced from Alvarez-Buylla and Nottebohm,[71] with permission.)

and coworkers found that in adult mammals too the brain's neuronal progenitors are glia—astrocytes in the case of the subventricular zone cells that give rise to new ol-factory bulb neurons[75] and radial glia in the case of the cells that give rise to hippoc-ampal granule cells.[76] The accepted view at this time is that there is in the adult vertebrate brain a subset of glial cells—as defined by ultrastructure and molecular markers—that gives rise to neurons and that these cells are, therefore, neuronal stem cells.

Depending on where in the brain one looks, the process from birth of a young neuron to its post-migratory differentiation can take from eight days, which is the case for new cells in HVC,[77] to 20–40 days elsewhere in telencephalon.[71] This timing is of general interest when looking for evidence of new neuron production in adult brain. It is possible that in larger brains, such as those of primates, where the distance from point of origin to final destination might be greater, the time spent in migration is longer than in songbirds, so comparisons between birds and mammals should take this possible timing difference into account.

Now that all the cellular players are in place, I will review the experiments that show how neuronal replacement is orchestrated. We know that canary song is a seasonal behavior,[67,78] that HVC size in adult male canaries changes seasonally,[43] and that testosterone can double HVC size in adult female canaries.[40] It seemed likely, from this, that testosterone levels would play a role in neuronal replacement and Rasika, a doctoral student in my laboratory, set out to investigate this possibility using ^{3}H-thymidine as the birth-date marker. She noticed that the number of cells dividing in the ventricular wall above the HVC (the presumptive, but not proven, origin of new HVC neurons) of adult female canaries two days after onset of testosterone treatment was the same as in controls. However, if the females that received ^{3}H-thymidine were killed 60 days later and treated with physiological doses of testosterone during their last 40 days, then the number of ^{3}H-labeled neurons tripled compared to controls.[79] Apparently testosterone or its metabolites promoted new neuron survival.

Some years later Rasika found evidence that the testosterone effect on new neuron survival was mediated by brain-derived neurotrophic factor, BDNF, as suggested by the following four kinds of evidence. (1) The HVC of male and female canaries has the TrkB receptor, which is specific to BDNF. (2) Systemic testosterone treatment of adult female canaries increases the levels of BDNF protein in their HVC. (3) In the absence of testosterone, BDNF infusion into the HVC of adult females triples new neuron survival. (4) Infusion of an antibody that binds to BDNF into the HVC of testosterone-treated females, thus preventing BDNF from binding to its receptor, blocks testosterone's effect on new neuron survival.[80]

Rasika's experiments left a question unanswered. Did testosterone exert its effect on HVC's BDNF levels directly or by inducing higher singing levels? We knew that the act of singing could induce the expression of selected genes in HVC;[81] perhaps this applied to BDNF expression as well. Xiao-Ching Li provided a first answer. She showed that BDNF expression in HVC is proportional to the amount of singing. Moreover, males treated with the birth date marker BrdU and allowed to sing as much as they wanted had twice as many new neurons in HVC as males prevented from singing during their last eight days (days 31–38 post BrdU injection) of life.[82] Interesting as these results were, however, they did not tell us whether singing, in the absence of testosterone, might affect BDNF production and neuronal survival, an issue addressed by the next experiment.

We knew that testosterone levels were very low in early fall in adult male canaries, though these birds sang a lot at that time.[83] We presumed that castration of those males would not affect their singing and so these birds might be able to tell us whether under those circumstances singing, in the absence of gonadal hormones, affected new neuron survival. Benjamin Alvarez-Borda did these experiments and showed that the number of new HVC neurons was lower in the castrates than in the non-castrates, even though both groups of birds sang, as expected, similar amounts of song. However, when the castrates were ranked by their amount of singing, then again

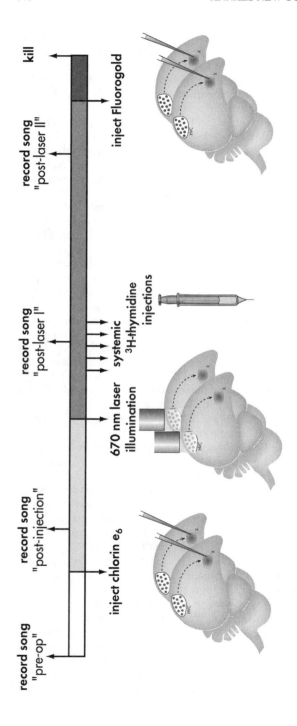

FIGURE 13. Method used for selective killing of a particular type of projection cell and evaluating the effect of this removal on song quality and new cell numbers. Song was recorded at the beginning of the experiments involving adult zebra finches. After bilateral injection of chlorin e_6–conjugated nanospheres into area X (as depicted) or RA, song was recorded again to assure that no behavioral changes had occurred due to potential tissue damage at the injection site. After allowing sufficient time for retrograde transport of the chlorin e_6, HVC was non-invasively illuminated with 674 nm laser light, photoactivating the production of oxygen singlets in the cells that had been backfilled by the nanospheres and thus producing their death. To monitor subsequent neurogenesis, ^{3}H-thymidine was injected intramuscularly five times over a 10-day period, starting with the second day after the laser illumination. During a survival period of 3 months, newly generated neurons were incorporated into HVC. During this time, short-term and long-term effects of the induced neuronal death on song were monitored through song recordings. To test whether some of the new neurons projected to the original nanosphere injection site, fluorogold was injected 5 days before perfusion into the same target site. There were no new area X-projecting neurons, but many new RA-projecting neurons. (Reproduced from Scharff and colleagues,[86] with permission.)

there was a relation between amount of singing and new neuron survival.[64] These results and the earlier work by Rasika and colleagues[80] suggest that singing and blood testosterone levels affect new neuron survival in an additive manner.[64] It is possible that both these effects are mediated by BDNF, but direct evidence for this is not yet available for singing. Intriguingly, a positive effect of BDNF on the survival of new HVC neurons occurs only during a restricted time window 14–20 days after the new cells are born.[83]

We know, by now, that the great majority, if not all, of the HVC cells that project to RA in the canary brain, regardless of whether they are born in nestlings or in adults, is eventually replaced.[84] Apparently this is a population of cells that is constantly turning over. We know too, that the rate of turnover varies with times of year. For example, cells born in late summer/early fall and that presumably partake in song learning at that time, are still around next spring, when the song learned eight months earlier is used during the breeding season. By contrast, half of the neurons added to HVC in the spring has disappeared by four months later.[85] Presumably seasonal changes in testosterone levels and in amount of singing account, in part at least, for this effect of season on new neuron survival. However, there is one more variable, referred to earlier,[68] that affects the choreography of neuronal replacement and that I have not discussed yet. That variable is cell death and its consequence, vacancies.

We knew that some brain cells continued to be produced and replaced in adult brain, but we did not know if the death of some cells promoted the survival of others. If adult neurogenesis is, as we believe, part of a process of replacement, might it be that the type of cell that continues to be produced and recruited into adult circuits depends on the type of cells that died? If that were so, then the fact that RA-projecting but not Area X-projecting neurons continue to be added to the adult HVC might result from the fact that in our birds cells of one type, but not of the other, died and thus created a specific type of vacancy. The concept of vacancy is metaphorical, of course, and we shall leave it, for the time being, that way.

Constance Scharff, John Kirn, and Jeff Macklis explored the relation between death and replacement.[86] Using technology recently developed by Macklis at Harvard, Scharff and Kirn selectively removed RA-projecting neurons from the HVC of adult male zebra finches (FIG. 13). The method used destroyed a specific type of cell without leaving behind scar tissue. Elimination of RA-projecting cells resulted in a marked increase in the recruitment of new cells of this kind. However, elimination of HVC's Area X–projecting cells in adult male zebra finches was not followed by increased recruitment of new cells. Apparently, the brain of songbirds has a program for the constant replacement of some cells, but not of all cells and the effect of "vacancies" in up-regulating new neuron survival may be specific to a relatively small class of replaceable neurons. If this is true of neuronal replacement in general, then we will have to learn a good deal more before it becomes possible to orchestrate, at will, the replacement of any central nervous system neuron that dies. We do not know how the effect of vacancies on new neuron survival comes about. Maybe this effect is mediated by "empty space" (e.g., synaptic space) left behind by a neuron that dies, or by an excess of unused neurotrophin, or by chemical signals produced by dying cells, to name a few possibilities.

The experiment of Scharff and colleagues[86] had another, remarkable consequence. Some of the male zebra finches that lost bilaterally many of their RA-projecting neurons, also lost their learned song. In two of these birds, over a period of weeks, as the lost cells were replaced, the learned song was reinstated. This was of great interest to us. Zebra finches, like chaffinches and white-crowned sparrows, learn the motor pattern of their song during a sensitive period that precedes full sexual maturity.[87] Was reinstatement of the learned song after elimination of RA-projecting neurons a case of re-learning of the motor program? If so, it would be dependent on auditory feedback, just as the original learning, but we do not yet know if this is the case. Regardless of how the recovery comes about, the initial loss and subsequent recovery of the behavior suggests that HVC's replaceable RA-projecting cells play a role in the production of learned song. This view is in line with the electrophysiological evidence provided by Michale Fee and colleagues at Bell Laboratories[88] (see also Fee and colleagues, this volume).

Taken together, the observations of Kirn,[68] Rasika,[79,80] Li,[82] Scharff,[86] and Alvarez-Borda[64,83] suggest the following choreography for neuronal replacement in HVC. A drop in testosterone levels and singing that occurs in mid-summer towards the end of the breeding season induces a drop in the levels of BDNF present in HVC, which leads to the death of many of HVC's replaceable neurons. The death of these cells creates vacancies. The new neurons that are constantly added to HVC sense the existence of these vacancies and this increases their survival. For this survival to occur, though, the new cells or others nearby must engage in moderate to high levels of circuit activity (singing), thereby increasing BDNF expression and the amount of BDNF protein present in HVC. A rise in the level of testosterone or of its metabolites also enhances new cell survival. This cycle of events is summarized in FIGURE 14. It is possible that trophic substances other than BDNF are also involved and so our list of factors promoting new neuron survival could grow longer. Regulation of new neuron survival by extent of circuit use may be a general mechanism for ensuring that neuronal replacement is closely attuned to environmental change and hence to the brain's and the individual's needs.

Silastic implants filled with testosterone can be used to maintain the typically high, spring testosterone levels throughout the summer and early fall. When this treatment is applied to adult male canaries, relatively few HVC neurons are added in late summer/early fall, perhaps because high testosterone levels prevent the death of existing neurons that normally occurs at the end of the breeding season and so there are fewer vacancies to promote the survival of new neurons.[89]

Direct evidence for neuronal replacement is available only for the HVC neurons that project to RA. However, cells of this kind do not account for all the new neurons added to the adult HVC; it seems likely that at least one other type of HVC neuron, presumed to be an interneuron[64] continues to be recruited during adulthood and new neurons are added also to Area X. If we assume that 20 or so nuclei are involved with the acquisition and production of song (including nuclei also involved with respiration) and if we assume that each of these nuclei has two neuron types and that neurons produced in adulthood are of the replaceable kind, then only three neuron types out of an estimated 40 (7.5%) is in the replaceable category. We do not know, at this time, whether this percentage is representative of other functional systems and whether, therefore, it would apply to the whole brain. Evidence from mammals suggests that the percentage of replaceable neurons in them is smaller than in birds. We do not yet know why a subset of neurons falls into the replaceable class, but this is now a key research question.

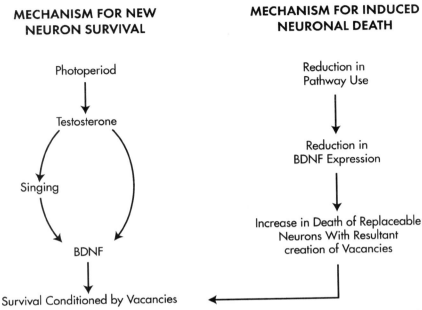

MECHANISM FOR NEW NEURON SURVIVAL

Photoperiod

Testosterone

Singing

BDNF

Survival Conditioned by Vacancies

MECHANISM FOR INDUCED NEURONAL DEATH

Reduction in Pathway Use

Reduction in BDNF Expression

Increase in Death of Replaceable Neurons With Resultant creation of Vacancies

FIGURE 14. Chain of events that promote (*left*) or suppress (*right*) new neuron survival in the HVC of adult songbirds. Although the role of BDNF in promoting new neuron survival has been shown, other neurotrophins may also act in this manner. *Arrows* indicate the temporal order in which events are driven. Notice that the events that induce neuronal death, with the consequent creation of "vacancies," will also affect the survival of new neurons. (Reproduced from Nottebohm,[103] with permission.)

Early on it became clear that while some birds learn new songs only once, before sexual maturity[1,2,9,14,87] others continue to learn new songs as adults and can change their song from one year to the next.[66,67,78] I thought that eventually our understanding of how the song system works must meet a stringent test: Could we turn a sensitive period learner, such as the chaffinch[1] or zebra finch,[87] into an open-ended learner, such as the canary.[66,78] This goal has not yet been achieved. However, it has been possible to delay in the chaffinch and zebra finch the closure of the sensitive period for song learning. The behavioral studies of W.H. Thorpe[1] and Lucy Eales[90,91] suggest that this can be achieved by withholding exposure to a wild-type model. Linda Wilbrecht may have uncovered the mechanism that maintains the sensitive period open. In socially reared male zebra finches the number of new HVC neurons born 30 days earlier and still present at the time the animal is killed decreases from day 50 until day 120 after hatching.[92] These birds produce stable adult song by day 90. However, young zebra finches kept singly are still able to imitate the song of a live model presented after day 90.[90,91] In these isolates the number of new neurons labeled with a birth-date marker and still present in HVC 30 days later when the bird is killed at the age of 120 days is twice as high as in the colony-reared individuals.[93] We speculate that though isolates develop a song that becomes relatively stable by day 90, they are not committed to this song; it seems as if this holding back is reflected in the turnover of existing neurons that continues at relatively high levels. This turnover does not affect the total number of HVC neurons, which is the same in the socially reared and isolate individuals.

The above study fits well with observations from two other laboratories. When adult Bengalese finches (*Lonchura domestica*) and zebra finches are deafened at a comparable age (6 months), song deterioration in the former proceeds much more rapidly than in the latter. This effect might be related to the fact that new neuron addition is twice as high, at that time, in the HVC of the Bengalese finches as in that of the zebra finches.[94] Presumably, the neurons added after deafening are "uneducated" while the ones they replace are "educated," leading to an erosion of the learned skill. In zebra finches, song deterioration following deafening occurs faster in young than in older adults[95] and in these birds addition of new HVC neurons is higher in young adults than in older adults.[96]

Taken together, several of the song system studies reviewed here[68,86,92,93,97] (see also Wilbrecht and Kirn, this volume) suggest that the addition of new HVC neurons is related to the learning of new songs. This relation between learning and the addition of new neurons is reinforced by two other studies focusing on parts of the brain other than the song system. A study of free-ranging black-capped chickadees (*Parus atricapillus*) showed that in these food-storing birds seasonal peaks in hippocampal new-neuron addition occur at times of year when these birds are pressed to learn much new spatial information.[98,99] In the other study, which used zebra finches, the number of new neurons in caudal telencephalon was shown to increase when adults were moved from cages in which they lived as male/female pairs into others where they encountered a more complex social group, where they presumably had to learn to identify many new individuals and forge new social relations.[100] The sum of these studies (see also Nottebohm[61]) suggests that the recruitment and replacement of neurons is widespread in the adult songbird brain and that its occurrence is related to the acquisition of new information. This may turn out to be a basic and important aspect of how the brain functions.

However, correlations should be treated with care. The song sparrow (*Melospiza melodia*) learns its song during its first year of life, yet shows, as adult, seasonal changes in the recruitment of new HVC neurons. As in canaries, a greater number of new neurons is added in the fall than in the spring. This remarkable study by Tramontin and Brenowitz[101] was conducted with free-ranging individuals. It is not known whether these birds would keep their learned song if they were deafened. If they did not, then, as in young adult zebra finches,[95] the cells added in adulthood might have to relearn the pattern already mastered by the cells they replace. The logic or selective advantage of such an arrangement is not obvious at this time. Perhaps the songs of all song learners, whether of the sensitive period or open-ended kind, become better with age in ways that we do not yet appreciate and this improvement depends on neuronal replacement. It is possible, though, that neurons play roles in the adult brain that we do not yet suspect and that would necessitate periodic replacement even when this offers no learning advantages and poses an extra learning load. If so, then it would be fascinating to know why this role is present in HVC's RA-projecting cells, which are periodically replaced, and not in the X-projecting cells, which are not replaced.[86]

My account stops here. It described a process of discovery—the road we travelled—that started in the late 1950s and 25–30 years later brought us, quite unexpectedly, to the realization that new neurons are constantly added to the adult brain, where they replace older neurons that died. We now realize that there are in the adult vertebrate brain a majority of neurons born during embryonic development or very early in post-natal life that are never replaced, and other, ephemeral neurons, that are replaced several times during a normal life-span. The presence of ephemeral neurons suggests that existing notions of learning and brain function are incomplete.[61] If synapses were able to acquire and store, through their modification in number, specificity, and efficacy all the changes needed to learn and forget, then neuronal replacement would seem unnecessary. Since neuronal replacement occurs and does not seem to be linked in any obvious way to wear and tear or to disease, it must serve a unique function in the healthy brain that cannot be easily achieved by other means. I speculate that this function is the acquisition of long-term memory through irreversible changes in cell configuration and connectivity, possibly mediated by irreversible changes in gene expression[61,102,103] as are thought to occur in cell differentiation. If this is a secure way to lay down long-term memories, then it also creates a problem, because as more and more neurons become learned entities, there may not be enough pupils left to acquire new knowledge. Neuronal replacement may take care of this dilemma as a process that balances the need to learn and the need to forget. I suspect that if and when neuronal replacement slows down and comes to a halt, then the aging of the whole brain reaches an irreversible point. The song system of birds, which alerted us to this phenomenon, may also provide clues on how to bring it under control.

ACKNOWLEDGMENTS

The work I review was funded since 1970 by National Institutes of Mental Health grant 18343. I am extremely grateful for this support, which started when there were only the faintest of glimmers of the many things to come and when the relation between birdsong and mental health could only be imagined. This work was also supported for many years by the late Herbert Singer, who in addition made very generous provisions in his will for its continued funding. It was supported, too by the Mary Flagler Cary Charitable Trust, under the guidance of my good friend Ned Ames. Another handsome source of support came from Mr. Howard Phipps, whose love for birds and nature includes a strong curiosity for how things work. I was helped too, by many wonderful colleagues, including my erstwhile mentor Peter Marler and my good friend Mark Konishi, and by an outstanding group of doctoral and post-doctoral students whose names appear in the references. I was much helped, as well, by my gifted secretary, Patricia Tellerday, and by a devoted and skilled group of animal caretakers that included Daun Jackson, Sharon Sepe, and Helen Ecklund. To all of these people, my unlimited gratitude. Yet all I did would not have been done had it not been for the love, company, patience, encouragement, hands-on help, and ideas of my wonderful wife, Marta Elena Seeber de Nottebohm, who also edited most of the things I wrote. My final thanks goes to Rockefeller University, which has supported me in innumerable ways since 1967 and provided a secure intellectual haven during the many years of this adventure.

REFERENCES

1. THORPE, W.H. 1958. The learning of song patterns by birds, with especial reference to the song of the chaffinch, *Fringilla coelebs*. Ibis **100:** 535–570.
2. MARLER, P. 1970. A comparative approach to vocal learning: song learning in white-crowned sparrows. J. Comp. Physiol. Psychol. **71:**1–25.
3. MARLER, P. & S. PETERS. 1977. Selective vocal learning in a sparrow. Science **198:** 519–521.
4. MARLER, P. & S. PETERS. 1981. Sparrows learn adult song and more from memory. Science **213:** 780–782.
5. MARLER, P. & S. PETERS. 1982. Long-term storage of bird songs prior to production. Anim. Behav. **30:** 479–482.
6. MARLER, P. & S. PETERS. 1982. Developmental overproduction and selective attrition: New Processes in the epigenesis of birdsong. Dev. Psychobiol. **15:** 369–378.
7. MARLER, P. & S. PETERS. 1982. Structural changes in song ontogeny in the swamp sparrow, *Melospiza georgiana*. Auk **99:** 446–458.
8. MARLER, P. & S. PETERS. 1982. Subsong and plastic song: Their role in the vocal learning process. *In* Acoustic Communication in Birds. Vol. 2, D.E. Kroodsma & E.H. Miller, Eds.: 25–50. Academic Press. New York.
9. MARLER P. & S. PETERS. 1987. A sensitive period for song acquisition in the song sparrow, *Melospiza melodia*, a case of age-limited learning. Ethology **76:** 89–100.
10. MARLER P. & S. PETERS. 1988. The role of song phonology and syntax in vocal learning preferences in the song sparrow, *Melospiza melodia*. Ethology **77:** 125–149.
11. MARLER, P. & V. SHERMAN. 1983. Song structure without auditory feedback: emendations of the auditory template hypothesis. J. Neurosci. **3:** 517–531.
12. MARLER, P. & V. SHERMAN. 1985. Innate differences in singing behaviour of sparrows reared in isolation from adult conspecific song. Anim. Behav. **33:** 57–71.
13. MARLER, P. & M. TAMURA. 1962. Song "dialects" in three populations of white-crowned sparrows. Condor **64:** 368–377.
14. MARLER, P. & M. TAMURA. 1964. Culturally transmitted patterns of vocal behaviour in sparrows. Science **146:** 1483–1486.
15. MARLER, P. 1991. The Instinct to Learn. *In* The Epigenesis of Mind: Essays on Biology and Cognition. S. Carey & R. Gelman, Eds.: 37–65. Lawrence Erlbaum Assoc. Hillsdale, NJ.
16. KONISHI, M. 1965. The role of auditory feedback in the control of vocalization in the white-crowned sparrow. Zeitschr. Tierpsychologie **22:** 770–783
17. KONISHI, M. 1963. The role of auditory feedback in the vocal behavior of the domestic fowl. Zeitschr. Tierpsychologie **20:** 349–367.
18. SCHWARTZKOPF, J. 1949. Über Sitz und Leistung von Gehör und Vibrationssinn bei Vögeln. Z vergl. Physiol. **31:** 527–608.
19. NOTTEBOHM, F. & M. NOTTEBOHM. 1971. Vocalizations and breeding behavior of surgically deafened ring doves, *Streptopelia risoria*. Anim. Behav. **19:** 313–327.
20. KROODSMA, D.E. & M. KONISHI. 1991. A suboscine bird (eastern phoebe, *Sayornis phoebe*) develops normal song without auditory feedback. Anim. Behav. **42:** 477–487.
21. NOTTEBOHM, F. 1970. Ontogeny of bird song. Science **167:** 950–956.
22. NOTTEBOHM, F. 1971. Neural lateralization of vocal control in a passerine bird. I. Song. J. Exp. Zool. **177:** 229–262.
23. NOTTEBOHM, F. 1972. Neural lateralization of vocal control in a passerine bird. II. Subsong, calls and a theory of vocal learning. J. Exp. Zool. **179:** 35–49.
24. NOTTEBOHM F. & M. NOTTEBOHM. 1976. Left hypoglossal dominance in the control of canary and white-crowned sparrow song. J. Comp. Physiol. A **108:** 171–192.
25. HARTLEY, S.R. & R. SUTHERS. 1990. Lateralization of syringeal function during song production in the canary. J. Neurobiol. **21:** 1236–1248.
26. STOKES, T.C., C.M. LEONARD & F. NOTTEBOHM. 1974. A stereotaxic atlas of the telencephalon, diencephalon and mesencephalon of the canary, *Serinus canaria*. J. Comp. Neurol. **156:** 337–374.

27. KARTEN, H.J. & W. HODOS. 1967. A stereotaxic atlas of the brain of the pigeon (*Columba livia*). Johns Hopkins Press. Baltimore, MD.
28. ROSE, M. 1914. Über die cytoarchitectonische Gliederung des Vorderhirns der Vögel. J. Psychol. Neurol. (Leipzig) **21:** 278–352.
29. NOTTEBOHM, F., T.M. STOKES & C.M. LEONARD. 1976. Central control of song in the canary, *Serinus canaria*. J. Comp. Neurol. **165:** 457–486.
30. NOTTEBOHM, F. 1977. Asymmetries in neural control of vocalization in the canary. *In* Lateralization in the Nervous System. S.R. Harnad *et al.* Eds.: 23–44. Academic Press. New York.
31. NOTTEBOHM, F., S. KASPARIAN & C. PANDAZIS. 1981. Brain space for a learned task. Brain Res. **213:** 99–109.
32. NOTTEBOHM, F., E. MANNING & M.E. NOTTEBOHM. 1979. Reversal of hypoglossal dominance in canaries following syringeal denervation. J. Comp. Physiol. A **134:** 227–240.
33. NOTTEBOHM F. & A.P. ARNOLD 1976. Sexual dimorphism in vocal control areas of the songbird brain. Science **194:** 211–213.
34. ZIGMOND, R., F. NOTTEBOHM & D.W. PFAFF. 1973. Androgen-concentrating cells in the midbrain of a songbird. Science **179:** 1005–1007.
35. ARNOLD, A.P., F. NOTTEBOHM & D.W. PFAFF. 1976. Hormone concentrating cells in vocal control and other areas of the brain of the zebra finch, *Poephila guttata*. J. Comp. Neurol. **165:** 487–512.
36. BALDWIN, F.M., H.S. GOLDIN & M. METFESSEL. 1940. Effects of testosterone proprionate on female Roller Canaries under complete song isolation. Proc. Soc. Exp. Biol Med. **44:** 373–375
37. HERRICK, E.H. & J.O. HARRIS. 1957. Singing female canaries. Science **125:** 1299–1300.
38. LEONARD, S.L. 1939. Induction of singing in female canaries by injections of male hormone. Proc. Soc. Exp. Biol. **41:** 229–230.
39. SHOEMAKER, H.H. 1939. Effect of testosterone propionate on the behavior of the female canary. Proc. Soc. Exp. Biol. **41:** 299–302.
40. NOTTEBOHM, F. 1980. Testosterone triggers growth of brain vocal control nuclei in adult female canaries. Brain Res. **189:** 429–443.
41. GURNEY, M.E. & M. KONISHI. 1980. Hormone induced sexual differentiation of brain and behavior in zebra finches. Science **208:** 1380–1383.
42. GURNEY, M.E. 1981. Hormonal control of cell form and number in the zebra finch song system. J. Neurosci. **1:** 658–673.
43. NOTTEBOHM, F. 1981. A brain for all seasons: cyclical anatomical changes in song control nuclei of the canary brain. Science **214:** 1368–1370.
44. NOTTEBOHM, F., S. KASPARIAN & C. PANDAZIS. 1981. Brain space for a learned task. Brain Res. **213:** 99–109.
45. CANADY, R.A., D.E. KROODSMA & F. NOTTEBOHM. 1984. Population differences in complexity of a learned skill are correlated with brain space involved. Proc. Natl. Acad. Sci. USA **81:** 6232–6234.
46. SZEKELY, T., C.K. CATCHPOLE, T.J. DEVOOGD, *et al.* 1996. Evolutionary changes in a song control area of the brain (HVC) are associated with evolutionary changes in song repertoire among European warblers (*Sylviidae*). Proc. R. Soc. Lond. B **263:** 607–610.
47. DEVOOGD, T.J., J.R. KREBS, S.D. HEALY & A. PURVIS. 1993. Relations between song repertoire size and the volume of brain nuclei related to song: comparative evolutionary analysis amongst oscine birds. Proc. R. Soc. Lond. B **254:** 75–82.
48. DEVOOGD, T.J. & F. NOTTEBOHM. 1981. Sex differences in dendritic morphology of a song control nucleus in the canary: a quantitative Golgi study. J. Comp. Neurol. **196:** 309–316.
49. DEVOOGD, T.J. & F. NOTTEBOHM. 1981. Gonadal hormones induce dendritic growth in the adult brain. Science **214:** 202–204.
50. DEVOOGD, T.J., B. NIXDORF & F. NOTTEBOHM. 1985. Synaptogenesis and changes in synaptic morphology related to acquisition of a new behavior. Brain Res. **329:** 304–308.

51. CANADY, R.A., G.D. BURD, T.J. DEVOOGD, *et al.* 1988. Effect of testosterone on input received by an identified neuron type of the canary song system: a Golgi/EM/degeneration study. J. Neurosci. **8:** 3770–3784.
52. GOLDMAN, S.A. & F. NOTTEBOHM. 1983. Neuronal production, migration and differentiation in a vocal control nucleus of the adult female canary brain. Proc. Natl. Acad. Sci. USA **80:** 2390–2394.
53. BURD, G.D. & F. NOTTEBOHM. 1985. Ultrastructural characterization of synaptic terminals formed on newly generated neurons in a song control nucleus of the adult canary forebrain. J. Comp. Neurol. **240:** 143–152.
54. ALTMAN, J. 1962. Are new neurons formed in the brains of adult mammals? Science **135:** 1127–1128.
55. ALTMAN, J. 1963. Autoradiographic investigation of cell proliferation in the brain of rats and cats. Anat. Rec. **145:** 573–591.
56. ALTMAN, J. 1970. Post-natal neurogenesis and the problem of neural plasticity. *In* Developmental Neurobiology. W.A. Himwich Ed.: 192–237. Thomas. Springfield, IL.
57. ALTMAN, J. & G.D. DAS. 1965. Autoradiographic and histological evidence of postnatal hippocampal neurogenesis in rats. J. Comp. Neurol. **124:** 319–336.
58. KAPLAN, M.S. & J.W. HINDS. 1977. Neurogenesis in the adult rat: electron microscopic analysis of light radioautographs. Science **197:** 1092–1094.
59. KATZ. L.C. & M.E. GURNEY. 1981. Auditory responses in the zebra finch's motor system for song. Brain. Res. **221:** 192–197.
60. PATON, J.A. & F. NOTTEBOHM. 1984. Neurons generated in adult brain are recruited into functional circuits. Science **225:** 1046–1048.
61. NOTTEBOHM, F. 1985. Neuronal replacement in adulthood. Ann. NY Acad. Sci. **457:** 143–161.
62. PATON, J.A., B.E. O'LOUGHLIN & F. NOTTEBOHM. 1985. Cells born in adult canary forebrain are local interneurons. J. Neurosci. **5:** 3088–3093.
63. KIRN, J.R., A. ALVAREZ-BUYLLA & F. NOTTEBOHM. 1991. Production and survival of projection neurons in the forebrain vocal center of adult male canaries. J. Neurosci. **11:** 1756–1762.
64. ALVAREZ-BORDA, B. & F. NOTTEBOHM. 2002. Gonads and singing play separate, additive roles in new neuron recruitment in adult canary brain. J. Neurosci. **22:** 8684–8690.
65. KIRN, J.R. & F. NOTTEBOHM. 1993. Direct evidence for loss and replacement of projection neurons in adult canary brain. J. Neurosci. **13:** 1654–1663.
66. NOTTEBOHM, F. & M.E. NOTTEBOHM. 1978. Relationship between song repertoire and age in the canary, *Serinus canaria.* Z. Tierpsychol. **46:** 298–305.
67. NOTTEBOHM, F., M.E. NOTTEBOHM, L.A. CRANE & J.C. WINGFIELD. 1987. Seasonal changes in gonadal hormone levels in adult male canaries and their relation to song. Behav. Neur. Biol. **47:** 197–211.
68. KIRN, J., B. O'LOUGHLIN, S. KASPARIAN & F. NOTTEBOHM. 1994. Cell death and neuronal recruitment in the high vocal center of adult male canaries are temporally related to changes in song. Proc. Natl. Acad. Sci. USA **91:** 7844–7848.
69. ALVAREZ-BUYLLA, A., D.R. BUSKIRK & F. NOTTEBOHM. 1987. Monoclonal antibody reveals radial glia in adult avian brain. J. Comp. Neurol. **264:** 159–170.
70. ALVAREZ-BUYLLA, A., M. THEELEN & F. NOTTEBOHM. 1988. Mapping of radial glia and of a new cell type in adult canary brain. J. Neurosci. **8:** 2707–2712.
71. ALVAREZ-BUYLLA A. & F. NOTTEBOHM. 1988. Migration of young neurons in adult avian brain. Nature **335:** 353–354.
72. ALVAREZ-BUYLLA A, M. THEELEN & F. NOTTEBOHM. 1990. Proliferation "hot spots" in adult avian ventricular zone reveal radial cell division. Neuron **5:** 101–109.
73. ALVAREZ-BUYLLA, A., J.M. GARCIA-VERDUGO, A.S. MATEO & H. MERCHANT-LARIOS. 1998. Primary neural precursors and intermitotic nuclear migration in the ventricular zone of adult canaries. J. Neurosci. **18:** 1020–1037.
74. NOCTOR, C.S., A.C. FLINT, T.A. WEISSMAN, *et al.* 2001. Neurons derived from radial glial cells establish radial units in neocortex. Nature **409:** 714–720.

75. DOETSCH, F., I. CAILLE, D.A. LIM, et al. 1999. Subventricular zone astrocytes are neural stem cells in the adult mammalian brain. Cell 97: 703–716.
76. ALVAREZ-BUYLLA, A., B. SERI & F. DOETSCH. 2002. Identification of neural stem cells in the adult vertebrate brain. Brain Res. Bull. 57: 751–758.
77. KIRN, J.R., Y. FISHMAN, K. SASPORTAS, et al. 1999. Fate of new neurons in adult canary High Vocal Center during the first 30 days after their formation. J. Comp. Neurol. 411: 487–494.
78. NOTTEBOHM, F., M.E. NOTTEBOHM & L. CRANE. 1986. Developmental and seasonal changes in canary song and their relation to changes in the anatomy of song control nuclei. Behav. Neur. Biol. 46: 445–471.
79. RASIKA, S., F. NOTTEBOHM & A. ALVAREZ-BUYLLA. 1994. Testosterone increases the recruitment and/or survival of new high vocal center neurons in adult female canaries. Proc. Natl. Acad. Sci. USA 91: 7854–7858.
80. RASIKA, A., A. ALVAREZ-BUYLLA & F. NOTTEBOHM. 1999. BDNF mediates the effects of testosterone on the survival of new neurons in an adult brain. Neuron 22: 53–62.
81. JARVIS, E.D. & F. NOTTEBOHM. 1997. Motor-driven gene expression. Proc. Natl. Acad. Sci. USA 94: 4097–4102.
82. LI, X-C., E.D. JARVIS, B. ALVAREZ-BORDA, et al. 2000. A relationship between behavior, neurotrophin expression and new neuron survival. Proc. Natl. Acad. Sci. USA 97: 8584–8589.
83. ALVAREZ BORDA, B. & F. NOTTEBOHM. 2004. Timing of BDNF exposure affects life expectancy of new neurons. Proc. Natl. Acad. Sci. USA. 101: 3957–3961.
84. ALVAREZ BORDA, B., 2002. On New Neurons in Canary Brains. Doctoral dissertation. The Rockefeller University.
85. NOTTEBOHM, F., B. O'LOUGHLIN, K. GOULD, et al. 1994. The life span of new neurons in a song control nucleus of the canary brain depends on time of year when these cells are born. Proc. Natl. Acad. Sci. USA 91: 7849–7853.
86. SCHARFF, C., J. KIRN, M. GROSSMAN, et al. 2000. Targeted neuronal death affects neuronal replacement and vocal behavior in adult songbirds. Neuron 25: 481–492.
87. IMMELMANN, K. 1969. Song development in the zebra finch and other estrildid finches. In Bird Vocalizations. R.A. Hinde, Ed.: 64–74. Cambridge University Press, Cambridge, UK.
88. HAHNLOSER, R.H.R., A.A. KOSZHEVNIKOV & M.S. FEE. 2002. An ultra-sparse code underlies the generation of neural sequences in a songbird. Nature 419: 65–70.
89. RASIKA, S. 1998. A steroid-neurotrophin pathway for the seasonal regulation of neuronal replacement in the adult canary brain. Doctoral dissertation, The Rockefeller University. New York.
90. EALES, L.A. 1985. Song learning in zebra finches: some effects of song model availability on what is learnt and when. Anim. Behav. 33: 1293–1300.
91. EALES, L.A. 1987. Song learning in female-raised zebra finches: another look at the sensitive phase. Anim. Behav. 35: 1356–1365
92. WILBRECHT L., A. CRIONAS & F. NOTTEBOHM. 2002. Experience affects recruitment of new neurons but not adult neuron number. J. Neurosci. 22: 825–831.
93. WILBRECHT, L. 2003. The Recruitment of New Neurons to the Song System during the Sensitive Period for Song Learning in the Zebra Finch. Doctoral dissertation. Rockefeller University. New York.
94. SCOTT, L.L., E.J. NORDEEN & K.W. NORDEEN. 2000. The relationship between rates of HVC neuron addition and vocal plasticity in adult songbirds. J. Neurobiol. 43: 79–88
95. LOMBARDINO, A.J. & F. NOTTEBOHM. 2000. Age at deafening affects the stability of learned song in adult male zebra finches. J. Neurosci. 20: 5054–5064.
96. WANG, N, P. HURLEY, C. PYTTE & J.R. KIRN. 2002. Vocal control neuron incorporation decreases with age in the adult zebra finch. J. Neurosci. 22: 10864–10870.
97. ALVAREZ-BUYLLA, A., J.R. KIRN & F. NOTTEBOHM. 1990. Birth of projection neurons in adult avian brain may be related to perceptual or motor learning. Science 249: 1444–1446.
98. BARNEA, A. & F. NOTTEBOHM. 1994. Seasonal recruitment of new neurons in the hippocampus of adult, free-ranging black-capped chickadees. Proc. Natl. Acad. Sci. USA 91: 11217–11221.

99. BARNEA, A. & F. NOTTEBOHM. 1996. Recruitment and replacement of hippocampus neurons in young and adult chickadees: an addition to the theory of hippocampal learning. Proc. Natl. Acad. Sci. USA **93:** 714–718.
100. LIPKIND, D., F. NOTTEBOHM, R. RADO & A. BARNEA. 2002. Social change affects the survival of new neurons in the forebrain of adult songbirds. Behav. Brain Res. **133:** 31–43.
101. TRAMONTIN, A.D & E.A. BRENOWITZ. 1999. A field study of seasonal neuronal incorporation into the song control system of a songbird that lacks adult song learning. J. Neurobiol. **40:** 316–326.
102. NOTTEBOHM, F. 2002. Neuronal replacement in adult brain. Brain Res. Bull. **57:** 737–749.
103. NOTTEBOHM, F. 2002. Why are some neurons replaced in adult brain? J. Neurosci. **22:** 624–628.
104. GREENWALT, C.H. 1968. Bird Song: Acoustics and Physiology. Smithsonian Institution Press. Washington, DC.
105. HOESE, W.J., J. PODOS, N.C. BOETTICHER & S. NOWICKI. 2000. Vocal tract function in birdsong production: experimental manipulation of beak movements. J. Exp. Biol. **203:** 1845–1855.
106. GOLLER, F. & O.N. LARSEN. 1997. A new mechanism of sound generation in songbirds. Proc. Natl. Acad. Sci. USA **94:** 14787–14791.
107. FEE, M.S., B. SHRAIMAN, B. PESARAN & P.P. MITRA. 1998. The role of non-linear dynamics of the syrinx in the vocalizations of a songbird. Nature **395:** 67–71.
108. NOTTEBOHM, F., D.B. KELLEY & J.A. PATON. 1982. Connections of vocal control nuclei in the canary telencephalon. J. Comp. Neurol **207:** 344–357.
109. OKUHATA, S. & N. SAITO. 1987. Synaptic connections of thalamo-cerebral vocal nuclei of the canary. Brain Res. Bull. **18:** 35–44.
110. BOTTJER, S.W., K.A. HALSEMA & S.A. BROWN. 1989. Axonal connections of a forebrain nucleus involved with vocal learning in zebra finches. J. Comp. Neurol. **279:** 312–326.
111. VATES, G.E. & F. NOTTEBOHM. 1995. Feedback circuitry within a song-learning pathway. Proc. Natl. Acad. Sci. USA **92:** 5139–5143.
112. NIXDORF-BERGWEILER, B.E., M.B. LIPS & U. HEINEMANN. 1995. Electrophysiological and morphological evidence for a new projection of lMAN-neurons towards Area X. NeuroReport **6:** 1729–1732.
113. VATES, G.E., D.S. VICARIO & F. NOTTEBOHM. 1997. Reafferent thalamo-"cortical" loops in the song system of oscine songbirds. J. Comp. Neurol. **380:** 275–290.
114. McCASLAND, J.S. 1987. Neuronal control of bird song production. J. Neurosci. **7:** 23–39.
115. WILLIAMS, H. 1989. Multiple representations and auditory-motor interactions in the avian song system. Ann. NY Acad. Sci. **563:** 148–164.
116. YU, A.C. & D. MARGOLIASH. 1996. Temporal hierarchical control of singing in birds. Science **273:** 1871–1875.

Neuron Addition and Loss in the Song System

Regulation and Function

LINDA WILBRECHT[a] AND JOHN R. KIRN[b]

[a]Svoboda Laboratory, Cold Spring Harbor Laboratory,
Cold Spring Harbor, New York 11724, USA

[b]Department of Biology and the Neuroscience and Behavior Program, Wesleyan
University, Middletown, Connecticut 06459, USA

ABSTRACT: Neurons continue to be produced and replaced throughout life in
songbirds. Proliferation in the walls of the lateral ventricles gives rise to neurons that migrate long distances to populate many diverse telencephalic regions, including nuclei dedicated to the perception and production of song, a
learned behavior. Many projection neurons are incorporated into the efferent
motor pathway for song control. Replacement of these neurons is regulated, in
part, by neuron death. Underlying mechanisms include gonadal steroids and
BDNF, but are likely to involve other trophic factors as well. The functional
significance of neuronal replacement remains unclear. However, recent experiments suggest a link between cell turnover and one or more specific attributes
of song learning and production. Several hypotheses are critically examined,
including the possibility that neuronal replacement provides motor flexibility
to allow for error correction—a capacity needed for juvenile and adult song
learning, but also likely to be important for the maintenance of song stereotypy.
We highlight important gaps in our knowledge and discuss future directions
that may bring us closer to solving the riddle of why neurons are produced and
replaced in adulthood.

KEYWORDS: adult neurogenesis; cell death; birdsong; motor learning

INTRODUCTION

It is now well established that new neurons are born and continue to be added to
the adult brain. In humans and other mammals this process appears to be limited to
the hippocampus, olfactory bulb, and, perhaps, cerebral cortex.[1,2] In contrast, neurons formed in the juvenile and adult avian brain are incorporated throughout much
of the telencephalon where they replace other neurons that have died (FIG. 1).[3–7] The
mechanisms that control post-hatching neurogenesis and the functions that it serves
are not well understood. While new neurons are probably added to the telencephalon
of all birds,[10,11] songbirds possess some unique features. They have the rare ability
to learn vocalizations, their brains contain discrete and easily identifiable nuclei that

Address for correspondence: John Kirn, Biology Department, Wesleyan University, 237
Church St., Middletown, CT 06459. Voice: 860-685-3494.
  jrkirn@wesleyan.edu; <http://www.wesleyan.edu/bio/kirn/kirn.html>

Ann. N.Y. Acad. Sci. 1016: 659–683 (2004). © 2004 New York Academy of Sciences.
doi: 10.1196/annals.1298.024

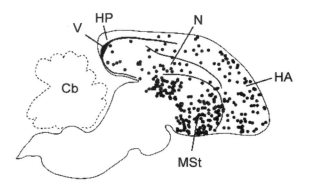

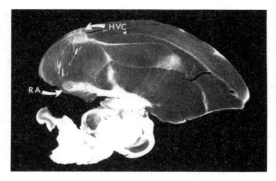

FIGURE 1. (*Top*) Reconstruction of incorporation sites for new neurons in adult canary brain in sagittal view. Rostral is to the right. Each dot represents a single [³H]-labeled neuron in a canary that had received two injections of [³H]-thymidine/day for 14 days, 1 month prior to sacrifice. Modified from Alvarez-Buylla and colleagues.[5] (*Bottom*) Darkfield sagittal view of an unstained section from canary brain showing motor control regions HVC and RA. Many new neurons send axons (white streaks) 2–3 mm from HVC to RA. Rostral is to the right. From Kirn and colleagues.[8] ABBREVIATIONS: HA, hyperpallium accessorium; HP, hippocampus; HVC, high vocal center; RA, robust nucleus of the arcopallium; Mst, medial striatum; N, nidopallium; V, ventricle; CB, cerebellum. Subtelencephalic regions do not receive new neurons in adulthood. Nomenclature based on Reiner and colleagues.[9]

are dedicated to the production and perception of vocalizations, and some of these regions receive new neurons throughout life. This unprecedented neural plasticity in a warm-blooded vertebrate makes the avian brain a valuable model that both challenges existing concepts of brain function and may provide insights relevant for advancing methods of brain repair. In this article we review recent work on the control and possible functions of post-natal song system neuron addition and replacement. With respect to function, we speculate unapologetically, in the hope of stimulating further thinking and research. For additional perspectives see recent reviews[7,12,13] and the review by Nottebohm in this volume.

SONG DEVELOPMENT AND MAINTENANCE

There are hundreds of different songbird species and they vary in the number of songs they sing, song complexity, the age at which they acquire songs, and the frequency and context in which they sing, among other things. Our studies have been commonly performed on the zebra finch and the canary, both of which copy songs

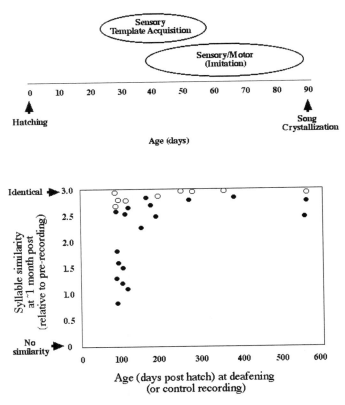

FIGURE 2. Time course for song learning in the zebra finch (*top*). The sensory phase (template acquisition), when males memorize the songs of adult conspecifics, begins early and overlaps with the sensory/motor phase, where the template is used to guide vocal imitation. The sensitive phase for song learning is completed by 90 days of age, and song remains largely unchanged thereafter.[19,20] However, even song maintenance may be an active process relying on auditory feedback, and this reliance wanes with increasing age or practice (*bottom*). Shown are changes in song syllable morphology between songs recorded before and 1 month after deafening (*filled circles*) or over a similar interval in hearing male zebra finches (*open circles*) as a function of bird age. Note that in young adults (100–200 days posthatch) deafening has a much more dramatic impact on song compared to birds deafened at older ages. From Brainard and Doupe.[36] It should be noted that deafening at any age probably leads to the eventual deterioration in song structure, but the latency increases and the magnitude of deterioration decreases as adults' age.[35]

they have heard from adult conspecifics, though they learn and produce songs on very different schedules. Once an appropriate tutor is selected, it is assumed that the learning process first involves formation of an auditory memory or "template" of the song or songs that they will imitate (see Adret, this volume),[14] and that this takes place during a "sensitive period" for song learning. The time delay between template acquisition (sensory phase) and the first attempts at vocal imitation (sensorimotor phase) varies from species to species. In the zebra finch, attempts at imitation can occur in juveniles as soon as a few hours after song model presentation.[15] In juvenile canaries, songs heard in the first summer are imitated in the following fall and spring.[16–18]

The sensitive period for song learning is thought to end when songs become stereotyped or "crystallized." Despite the fact that zebra finches can imitate some sounds a few hours after presentation, the natural course of song learning in this species takes some two months, and song becomes stereotyped 90 days after hatching (FIG. 2). In the canary, song becomes stereotyped 6 months to a year after hatching, during the first breeding season.[17,18] Zebra finches learn a song once during this initial 90 days after hatching and then continue to sing it in a highly stereotyped manner throughout their lifetime,[19,20] while canaries modify their song patterns seasonally as adults.[18,21] Thus, the zebra finch represents an example of an "age-limited" learner while the canary is an example of an "open-ended" learner.

Adult male canaries can have 30–40 or more distinct syllables in their repertoire.[18,22] Between year 1 and 2 in laboratory-housed birds, approximately one-third of the syllables are dropped and replaced by new ones, one-third are modified, and the remainder are unchanged.[18] Although there is clear evidence that adult canaries change their songs, and can copy the songs of other males,[23] the extent to which seasonal song modifications reflect the learning of new songs from conspecifics, improvisation, or the selection of different subsets of syllables yearly from a "library" of songs learned during development[14,21,24] is unknown. This is an important issue because the neural mechanisms underlying these different scenarios may vary in significant ways.

In some species, song maintenance may be as active a process as song learning. Song learning requires intact hearing, which is used not only to acquire a model but also to monitor and guide vocal output.[25–27] However, even after song crystallization and throughout adulthood, deafening or distorting auditory feedback in hearing birds results in deterioration of song structure[28–32] (also see articles by Konishi, Margoliash, and Brainard, this volume), suggesting that comparisons between expected and received auditory feedback from song are also important for the maintenance of stereotyped song. Mismatches between expected and received auditory feedback may create error signals (or the withholding of reinforcement signals)[33] used to make adjustments to motor commands. Thus, even song stereotypy may rely on motor flexibility. Recent work has shown that, as in human speech,[34] the reliance of adult song on auditory feedback wanes with increasing age, suggesting that the motor program for song becomes increasingly stable with age, singing experience, or both (FIG. 2).[35,36] The possibility that post-crystallization singing experience contributes to age-related increases in motor program stability is intriguing because it would indicate that even in so-called age-limited learners, song development is a lifelong process.[35]

Although song stereotypy after crystallization is high even in young adults, there may be subtle improvements in song fidelity with age or cumulative singing experience. For example, it has been reported that with increasing age, individual song notes and syllables become less "noisy" and variable in fine structural detail and are delivered more rapidly by zebra finches.[36] Another source of fine-grained variability within stereotyped song, but which has not been explored as a function of bird age, is note duration within a song bout. Zebra finches will sing their song from one to several times in rapid succession, known as a song "bout." It has been shown that within bouts, same syllable duration increases with repetition, followed by a "resetting" of duration back to a value similar to when the syllable is sung for the first time in a bout.[37] Perhaps reproducing notes with precisely the same duration within a bout is a difficult skill that improves with protracted (lifelong?) practice.

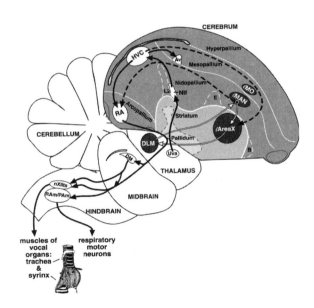

FIGURE 3. Diagram of the major brain regions involved in song learning and production. The pathway necessary for the production of learned song is demarcated by *solid black lines*. The anterior forebrain pathway, necessary for song learning, is shown with *dashed and white lines*. Within the song system, only HVC and Area X receive new neurons throughout life. ABBREVIATIONS: nAM, nucleus ambiguus; AV, nucleus avalanche; B, basolateral nucleus; DLM, medial portion of the dorsolateral nucleus of the thalamus; E, entopallial nucleus; HVC, high vocal center; L2, field L; lMAN, lateral subdivision of the magnocellular nucleus of the anterior nidopallium; LMO, lateral oval nucleus of the mesopallium; NIf, interfacial nucleus of the nidopallium; RA, robust nucleus of the arcopallium; Ram, nucleus retroambigualis; Uva, nucleus uvaeformis; X, Area X; nXIIts, tracheosyringeal part of the nucleus nervi hypoglossi. Nomenclature based on Reiner and colleagues.[9]

NEUROGENESIS AND THE AVIAN SONG SYSTEM: WHERE, WHEN, AND HOW?

The dynamic nature of song learning and song maintenance suggests a high degree of plasticity in the neurons that make up the song system. No one expected how dramatic this plasticity might be until Steve Goldman and Fernando Nottebohm[3] discovered that neurons in the song system are constantly dying and being replaced (see Nottebohm, this volume). By studying the replacement of neurons in the context of the song system, we hope to learn more about how complex behaviors like song can be learned, and why some neurons are biologically "destined" to live transiently, while others persist for a lifetime.

The most detailed information about neuron addition and loss has been obtained from studies of zebra finches and canaries. Area X and HVC are the only vocal control regions known to exhibit large scale neuron addition both after hatching and throughout adulthood.[4] HVC, part of the posterior (sensorimotor) pathway, is necessary for song production at all ages, while Area X and the anterior forebrain path-

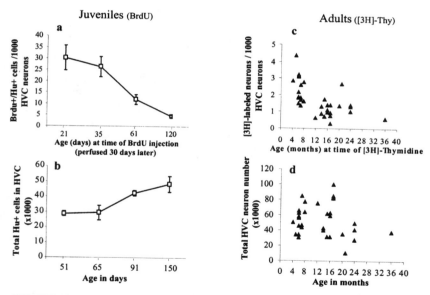

FIGURE 4. Neurons labeled with the cell birth marker BrdU are added to HVC in juvenile zebra finches (a) as the total number of neurons, Hu+ cells, grows to adult levels (b). After day 150 the number of new neurons [identified using [³H]-thymidine and retrograde labeling from RA (not shown) or Nissl stain] added to HVC declines with age (c) but total HVC neuron number does not (d). Neuronal replacement probably occurs throughout life, however, the juvenile stage is dominated by net addition whereas addition and loss are more closely matched in adulthood. Values in left panels are means ± SEM and the data are from Wilbrecht and colleagues.[95] In panels to the right, each symbol represents 1 bird and the data are from Wang and colleagues.[51] The use of different methods of quantification in the two studies prevents direct numerical comparisons. Nevertheless, it is clear from these data that HVC neuron recruitment is higher during song acquisition than after song crystallization and that in adulthood, neuron recruitment continues to decrease with increasing age.

way are critical for the acquisition of song in juveniles,[27,38–40] but appear to play only a more subtle role in song maintenance in adults (FIG. 3, also see Brainard, this volume).[41,42] A third region, the caudomedial nidopallium (NCM), an auditory region that has indirect projections to the vocal control system,[43] also receives new neurons in adulthood.[44,45]

Relatively little is known about neuron addition to Area X or NCM,[44–46] however, because HVC is necessary for song production and plays a role in perception[4,38,47] neuronal recruitment in this nucleus has been extensively studied. In both canaries and zebra finches, HVC is not fully developed at hatching but adds substantial numbers of new neurons during juvenile life as shown in FIGURE 4. In zebra finches, proliferation in the walls of the lateral ventricles is higher in juveniles than in adults, although it is not known whether this is true specifically for the production of HVC neurons.[48] Therefore it is unclear whether the high incorporation rates during this time are due to cell production or survival. Once HVC has reached adult size in both species, total HVC neuron number does not increase further with increasing age, yet new HVC neurons continue to be produced and replaced throughout life.[8,49–51]

Thus, in both species, neuron addition to HVC occurs at the very time song is initially learned and in both species neuron addition is accompanied by neuron loss. Pyknotic, degenerating cells have been found in HVC at all ages examined.[52–55] It is possible that addition and loss occur throughout post-hatching life but that during the juvenile growth phase neuron addition surpasses loss and once adult neuron numbers have been attained, these two processes are more closely matched. The balancing act between net addition and loss may also be regulated seasonally in adults of some species. In western song sparrows, total HVC neuron number in the fall is only about two-thirds the number found in spring.[56] Therefore, in some birds, the scale appears to alternate between net cell addition and loss at various times throughout life.

HVC has two types of projection neurons. Neurons projecting to Area X (HVC-X) are produced before hatching and are not replaced in adulthood.[49,57–59] The other major projection is to RA, and most HVC neurons produced and replaced post-natally are of this type (FIG. 5). Indirect evidence suggests that interneurons are also replaced throughout life (see Nottebohm, this volume).[49,50,60] Thus, many adult-formed HVC neurons perform the remarkable feat of migrating from their birth place in the walls of the lateral ventricles to HVC and then sending an axon 2–3 mm to their target cells in RA. Adult-formed HVC neurons respond with action potentials to acoustic stimulation,[61] demonstrating that they become functionally incorporated. HVC-RA projection neurons are known to have highly selective auditory response properties[62] and exhibit discrete and selective bursts of premotor activity during singing[63] (see articles by Fee and colleagues as well as by Konishi and by Margoliash, this volume). In the zebra finch, as few as 20–40 HVC-RA projecting neurons participate in each 6-msec portion of song.[63] Therefore, the death and replacement of HVC-RA projecting neurons could dramatically alter song. While these attributes may be conducive to changes in song motor programs associated with learning (see later), they also pose potential problems for conserving information in a system with constant cell replacement.

Cell death probably plays a pivotal role in the regulation of neuronal recruitment and replacement. In canaries, seasonal peaks in HVC neuron recruitment are preced-

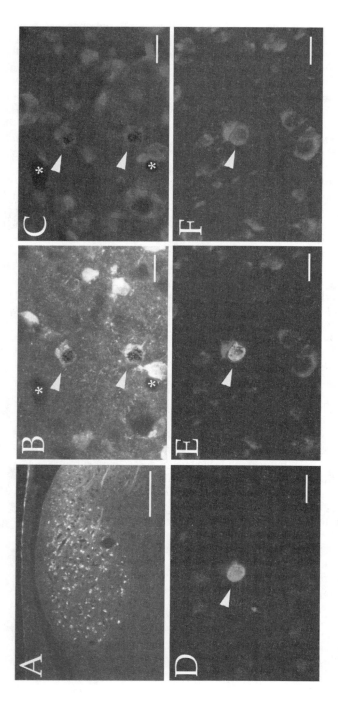

FIGURE 5. (**A**) Low magnification fluorescence (UV) photomicrograph of zebra finch HVC after retrograde labeling with fluoro-gold (FG) injections into RA. (**B**) Higher power view of two HVC-RA neurons formed in adulthood (*arrows*). These neurons have autoradiographically developed silver grains overlying their nucleus and FG in their cytoplasm. (**C**) Same view as in **B**, showing all cells counterstained with fluorescent cresyl violet and viewed under rhodamine fluorescence. *Arrows* point to the [³H]-labeled neurons shown in **B**. *Asterisks* in **B** and **C** label blood vessels. (**D**–**F**) BrdU-labeled cell nucleus viewed with a FITC filter (**D**), with dual FITC-rhodamine filter to reveal BrdU and Hu (**E**), and rhodamine filter showing only HV (**F**). Cytoplasmic staining with the neuronal marker Hu surrounds the BrdU-labeled cell nucleus. Scale bars: (**A**) 100 μm, (**B**–**F**) 10 μm. (Reproduced from Wang and colleagues.[51])

ed by peaks in cell death,[53] and the selective killing of RA-projecting HVC neurons by laser ablation leads to an increase in the incorporation of new neurons of the same kind.[59] It follows by extension that for replaceable neuron types, the number of healthy neurons present constrains the number of new cells that can be added.

What Fraction of HVC Neurons Is Involved in Cell Turnover and How Long Do Replaceable Neurons Live?

In the canary, 50–60% of all HVC neurons project to RA, roughly 20% project to Area X and much of the remainder are interneurons.[8,49,58,64] Replaceable RA-projecting neurons represent a large fraction of the pathway connecting HVC to RA. Roughly 50% of this pathway can be replaced over 6 months from spring to fall in adult canaries.[65] We do not know whether there is complete replacement in 12 months, nor do we know when the cells that die were formed after hatching. However, these results suggest that a large fraction of the dominant cell type in HVC undergoes loss and replacement.

The lifespan of neurons formed after hatching can vary from days to months. Some cells die while migrating.[66] The journey from the ventricular zone to HVC can take as little as one week and among those cells that reach HVC, many more die between the ages of 2 and 3 weeks, at the time when their axons first reach RA.[58,67,68] New HVC neurons that survive to one month of age have lifespans of 4–8 months or longer.[8,31,51,69]

Trophic Factors and the Control of Neuronal Replacement

To date, no factors have been found to be essential for adult neurogenesis. However, in recent years, significant progress has been made in understanding how cell turnover is modulated. In many seasonally breeding songbirds, HVC volume increases in tandem with rising testosterone levels (T) (see Brenowitz, this volume).[70] In the male canary, HVC neuron incorporation rates are highest in the fall, after T has been low for some time but is beginning to rise again. In May, when T is high and has been for some time, cell incorporation is low.[53,69] These results suggest a trophic effect of androgens on neuron recruitment that is conditional on available space in HVC. A working hypothesis is that a period of low T is associated with the death of many HVC neurons and this, in turn, makes room for a wave of new neuron addition. T then promotes the survival of incoming neurons until available circuit space is occupied again (see Nottebohm, this volume).[53,59,71]

Most work on the causal relationship between steroids and adult neurogenesis has been done on female canaries. Testosterone and its metabolite estradiol promote the incorporation of HVC neurons in adult female canaries.[71–73] This is also true of juvenile female finches.[74] In turn, brain-derived neurotrophic factor (BDNF) may act downstream of T. Both BDNF and tyrosine kinase (TrkB) receptors are present in HVC and T treatment increases BDNF protein content in adult female HVC. Exposing female HVC to exogenous BDNF increases new neuron number and infusion of BDNF antibodies into HVC blocks T's stimulatory effect on neuron incorporation.[72] These findings suggest a strong link between gonadal steroids, BDNF, and neuronal incorporation. Steroids probably do not influence proliferation[75] and so it is likely that differential cell survival accounts for these results.

The relative contributions of androgens and estrogens to steroid effects on neuronal replacement have not been systematically explored. BDNF expression is also under the control of estradiol[76] and so many of the effects ascribed to T could be dependent on the aromatization of T into estradiol. However, at least some aspects of overall HVC growth can be achieved with the nonaromitizable androgen dihydrotestosterone,[77] and so both androgens and estrogens may be involved. Interestingly, another effect of androgen treatment is a dramatic increase in endothelial cell division and angiogenesis in HVC.[3,78] Endothelial cells have the capacity to produce BDNF in a T-dependent manner[78] and so perhaps the trophic effects of steroids on HVC neuron addition are mediated by both neuronal and endothelial BDNF production. BDNF expression is also proportional to the amount of singing in adult male canaries.[79] It is possible that T independently promotes BDNF expression and singing. Alternatively, song-related sensory or motor activity could have independent effects on BDNF. Although this issue remains unresolved, results from a recent study suggest that singing and T act independently and in an additive way to promote new HVC neuron survival.[80] It would be interesting to know whether T and singing differentially affect BDNF expression by endothelial cells and neurons.

Several other factors have been identified that may be involved in regulating neuronal replacement. Excess thyroxine increases HVC cell death in zebra finches[55] and may suppress mitotic activity in canaries[81] and excess melatonin decreases HVC volume,[82] raising the possibility that these hormones normally curtail HVC growth, neuron addition, or survival. The gene for insulin-like growth factor 2 (IGF-2) is expressed by HVC-X neurons and the IGF-2 protein is accumulated by the HVC-RA cells.[83] IGF-2 is also expressed by radial cells and IGF-1 is expressed by astrocytes.[84] This is a particularly interesting finding since radial cells are the likely stem cells for adult-formed neurons.[85–88] HVC-X cells also produce retinoic acid, a factor known to have trophic activity.[89] A particularly interesting recent observation is that caspase-3, a protease with a well-established role in apoptosis,[90,91] is activated by song presentation and may be involved in song learning and long-term memory more generally.[92,93] Since one proposed function of neuronal replacement is new song learning (see the following discussion), caspase-3 could prove to be an important player in the regulation of both processes. Collectively, these findings suggest a strong link between steroids, BDNF, and neuron incorporation and suggest a number of new and exciting avenues for research on the regulation of neuronal turnover.

The Functions of Neuron Replacement in the Song System

The most intriguing puzzle may be why neuronal replacement occurs at all. We are so focused on the historical view that each neuron is precious that we often don't ask the opposite question: Why are neurons one of the few cell types that does not undergo replacement as a general rule? Any comprehensive answer to this riddle has to explain why neuronal replacement is as selective as it appears to be, how the brain can do this without going "off line," and what a new neuron can do better than an older one. Studies of the function of new neurons in the song system initially focused on their potential role in song learning. However, more recent work has provided correlational evidence suggesting a role for new neurons in lifelong song production and song maintenance. Here we discuss some potential hypotheses regarding the function(s) of postnatal neurogenesis and neuronal replacement.

Neuronal Replacement Is an Epiphenomenon

One could argue that the recruitment of new neurons to HVC during juvenile life serves only to populate the brain with sufficient neurons to control the later expression of adult song. In turn, ongoing adult neurogenesis could simply be a hold-over from development that serves no particular function, against which there simply hasn't been sufficient counterselective pressure. Once adult neuron numbers have been achieved in zebra finches, relatively few new neurons are added per day compared to the case in juveniles, and these numbers may be low enough that they have no effect on brain or behavior. This explanation for the postnatal persistence of neurogenesis must be considered, but it leaves many questions unanswered. In juveniles, why is the HVC-RA pathway put in place during, rather than before song motor development? In adults, why do many of these cells persist for months and why do they then die? Why do only some neurons get replaced? If adult neurogenesis was simply a hold-over from development with no particular function, why would cell incorporation or survival be influenced seasonally and by experience? Also, if 50% or more of the HVC-RA projection neurons are replaced over the course of one year, it seems more likely that neuronal replacement in adult brains serves some biological function.

Neuronal Replacement Is Associated with Song Learning

A hypothesis first put forward and later refined by Nottebohm[7,94] proposes that as a cell ages it becomes progressively less plastic in a manner analogous to cellular differentiation and commitment during development. If true, it follows that an evolutionarily adaptive strategy would be to build increasingly larger brains, thus providing a surplus of cells for adaptive plasticity in long-lived animals. However, an alternative strategy to achieve the same goal, particularly for animals that place a premium on minimizing body weight, such as birds, would be to have a smaller brain and to discard and replace old neurons that have limited potential for acquiring new information or that encode information that is no longer relevant to the animal.[7,94] Thus, one would predict that neuronal replacement should be highest at times when birds are learning new song, and the recruitment of new HVC neurons should be different in species with different learning trajectories. Indeed, in zebra finches, more new HVC neurons are added during the sensitive phase for song learning than after song is crystallized (FIG. 6).[60,95] Moreover, in zebra finches individual differences in the total number of HVC neurons by the time song has fully developed are positively correlated with the degree to which birds had imitated their tutor's song.[96] After song crystallization new neurons continue to be added to the zebra finch HVC but at lower levels. In adult canaries, new HVC neurons are added at the highest rate during the fall when song modifications are greatest (FIG. 6).[53] Another peak in new neuron recruitment is seen in the early spring, when there is a second, more modest peak in song modification. New neuron recruitment is notably lower in the summer and mid-winter months when song is modified little.

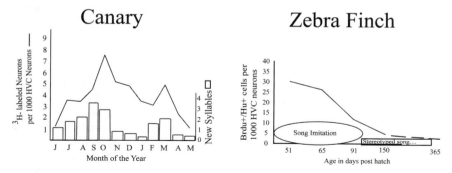

FIGURE 6. Schematic of new neuron recruitment in the canary and zebra finch. More new neurons are found in HVC during the periods where song is being learned or modified. This is age-limited in zebra finches, and open-ended and seasonal in canaries. Data for canaries are from Kirn and colleagues.[53] Data for zebra finches spanning days 51–150 are from Wilbrecht and colleagues[95] and days 150–365 are roughly extrapolated from Wang and colleagues[51] taking into account differences in number of injection days. The use of different methods in the experiments precludes direct species comparisons of neuron recruitment rates. However, in adult canaries between 1–2years old, HVC neuron recruitment rates at times of year when song is relatively stereotyped are similar to those for 8–13-month-old zebra finch males.[50]

These data suggest that higher levels of new neuron recruitment and replacement to HVC are correlated with song modification. This seems an initially satisfying hypothesis, but it does not explain why new neurons would continue to be added in zebra finches when song is stereotyped. It also does not explain data from field studies of the western song sparrow, which like the zebra finch learns songs only in its first year of life, but which annually recruits more HVC neurons in the fall than in the spring, like the canary.[56] Song sparrows sing more variable song in the fall than in the spring suggesting that in this species, and perhaps all species, song instability, rather than song learning, may be a better correlate of new HVC neuron recruitment levels. Of course, song should become less stereotyped as it goes through changes directed by learning. In this sense new neurons may provide the raw variability in song upon which a new song can be sculpted.

To further explore the relationship between new neuron recruitment and song learning, experiments have been done to see if blocking imitation during the sensitive period for song learning disrupts the recruitment of new neurons to the zebra finch HVC. When 26-day-old birds were deafened, lesioned bilaterally in nucleus LMAN, or had their syrinx denervated bilaterally, they all were unable to imitate their tutor's song by day 90. However poor their ability to imitate, they nonetheless recruited a normal number of HVC neurons between day 61–day 91[95,97] (FIG. 7, left). This suggested that there was little relation between the song imitation process and new neuron recruitment to HVC. However, one group that sustained only a unilateral denervation of the syrinx at day 26 recruited nearly twice the number of new HVC neurons on the intact side as controls over the same day 61–day 91 period[95,97] (FIG. 7, right). Interestingly, these birds were capable of making an imitation of their

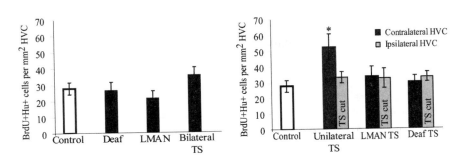

FIGURE 7. (*Left*) New neuron recruitment into the zebra finch HVC after imitation was blocked by various surgeries at day 26. BrdU was given on days 61–65 and birds were killed on day 91. All of the experimental birds represented in *black* made poor imitations of their tutor's song at day 90, yet they had normal levels of new neuron recruitment. (*Right*) Under the same conditions as in the left panel, the intact side HVC of unilateral tracheosyringeal (TS) nerve cut birds had nearly twice the number of new neurons as control HVCs, and they made successful imitation of their father's song. When unilateral TS cuts were combined with bilateral LMAN lesions or deafening, also at day 26, this effect at day 90 disappeared. Error bars=SEM. Data are from Wilbrecht and colleagues.[95,97]

father's song. When the unilateral denervation was combined with bilateral LMAN lesions or deafening, the effect on new neuron recruitment disappeared (FIG. 7, right), suggesting that the unilateral increase in new neurons was caused not only by unilateral denervation, but by "learning" a song with only one syringeal muscle. These data suggest that experience (namely the process of imitating song under the abnormal conditions of unilateral syringeal control) can affect neuronal recruitment to HVC. As the effect of unilateral denervation was only seen at the latest stages of song learning[95] (data not shown), it could be that imitation under these difficult circumstances prolonged the song learning process, maintaining the recruitment of new neurons at a higher, more juvenile level permissive for behavioral plasticity. It is known that the sensitive period for song learning can be extended by isolating zebra finches from other birds.[20,98] Interestingly, the normal rate of decline of new neuron recruitment to HVC is attenuated in isolated zebra finches.[99] Collectively, these results suggest that new neuron addition to HVC may largely be permissive for song plasticity, while the process of song imitation has subtle effects on neuronal recruitment and replacement that we do not yet fully understand.

In summary, the causal relationship between neuronal replacement, song learning, and stereotyped song production in adults is also still ambiguous. Correlations between seasonal song modification and neuronal replacement led to the hypothesis of a causal relationship between neuronal replacement and new song learning.[10,50,53,58] However, as we mentioned above, seasonal changes in HVC neuron addition can occur in the absence of new song learning.[56] Moreover, neuronal replacement continues long after song crystallization in the zebra finch.[31,51,60] Thus, studies of neuronal replacement in both juveniles and adults cast doubt on the simple equation of new neurons and new song learning.

Neuronal Replacement as a Mechanism Providing Motor Flexibility for Both Song Learning and Song Maintenance

A modified version of the learning hypothesis is that neuronal replacement provides flexibility to the motor pathway, enabling it to respond adaptively to mismatches between expected and received auditory feedback from singing. Perhaps neurons receive selective feedback signals just after they have been active indicating their participation in an error or a more optimized sound. These signals could promote the death or long-term survival of a neuron (respectively), and thereby act as a mechanism that sculpts the motor output pathway and song. In this model new neurons are essential raw material for motor plasticity. Their individual role in song and their survival could simply rely on the optimality of their random connections to other cells, rather than on any other intrinsic aspect of their newness. Alternatively, by virtue of their newness and potentially greater capacity for anatomical plasticity, young neurons may play a more active role in determining their own survival and the functional properties of the circuits to which they are added. Instructional signals might be provided by modulatory neurotransmitters such as dopamine, which has been shown to increase under novel or unexpected outcomes.[100,101] HVC is rich in tyrosine hydroxylase (TH), an enzyme involved in the synthesis of dopamine, and TH immunostaining intensifies in zebra finches at ages when song learning occurs.[102]

Error correction systems are likely necessary for song learning and also song maintenance. If new neuron addition and survival are regulated by song error correction, this would account for the overall reduction in neuron incorporation between the initial song-learning phase in juvenile zebra finches and the song-maintenance phase of adult zebra finches and explain why neuronal replacement persists postcrystallization when song is stable in this species. It could also explain why neuronal recruitment is high during the seasonal variation in stereotypy both for new song (canary) as well as for a previously learned song in adults (western song sparrow). Moreover, this scenario is consistent with the finding that in adult zebra finches, an age-related decline in neuron incorporation occurs specifically over the period when reliance of song on auditory feedback wanes (FIG. 4, right; compare to FIG. 2).[35,36]

Perhaps the "building" of optimal (error free) circuitry for song motor control is a lifelong process that is regulated by singing history (FIG. 8). A bird that has sung more in his life will have had a greater opportunity to build a long-lived and optimal collection of neurons in HVC. Thus with time and practice a greater cohort of "correctly" firing neurons would be assembled leading to more reliable output and thus decreased reliance on auditory "instruction" for appropriate activity patterns. As these cells accumulate with age, motor program stability would increase, and the neuronal replacement process would decrease.

While a role for neuronal replacement in error correction is intriguing, some data do not fit well with this model. When a deaf bird sings there are likely to be gross error signals related to the absence of song feedback and so one might expect neuronal replacement to increase in deaf birds. However, deafening does not affect HVC neuron incorporation in juveniles,[95] while deafening in adulthood leads to a decrease, rather than an increase in neuron incorporation.[31] Age, social housing conditions, and singing rate all could have contributed to this difference in data on new neurons in deaf birds and we suggest experiments to resolve this below.

Neuronal Replacement Is a Mechanism for Renewal of Damage-Prone Neurons

We have yet to consider that neuronal replacement may be unrelated to learning or error correction, but still serve motor functions associated with the act of singing. One potential function of adult neurogenesis is to replace premotor HVC neurons that become damaged by use. Physiological recording experiments in singing birds show that RA-projecting HVC neurons fire at high rates for brief intervals during singing.[63] Perhaps the high metabolic demands associated with these response properties result in short lifespans. If neurogenesis serves to replenish damage-prone neurons, then one would expect a correlation between rates of turnover and amount of singing. Singing rate in zebra finches peaks during the plastic phase of song learning in juveniles, declining to lower levels in adulthood, and this correlates with HVC neuron incorporation rates.[60,95,103] Even in adults, the age-related decline in HVC neuron recruitment correlates with both a decrease in the reliance of song on auditory feedback as well as an overall decrease in singing rates.[103] Suppression of singing in adult canaries results in decreased survival of new HVC neurons[79] and naturally

FIGURE 8. A metaphor illustrating the potential role of neuronal replacement in error correction. Songbirds may audition new neurons based on a cell's ability to contribute to song development and maintenance. Neurons with response properties consistent with optimal song structure are cast while those that do not fit the part are rejected, prompting more neurons to be auditioned. The assembly of the entire cast may be a lifelong process but one that diminishes with age and experience as ever fewer roles in the musical remain unfilled.

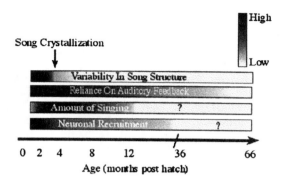

FIGURE 9. A summary integrating previous behavioral work with neuronal replacement rates in the zebra finch. Song crystallization occurs at roughly 90 days after hatching. Prior to this age, song structure and amplitude are highly variable. After crystallization, song structure remains highly stereotyped throughout adulthood. However, even after song structure becomes stable, song stereotypy relies on the bird's ability to compare expected with received auditory feedback and respond with adaptive adjustments to motor output. In short, song stereotypy may require motor flexibility. With increasing age, the motor program for song becomes increasingly stable and less reliant on auditory feedback. Amount of singing also decreases from a peak during the plastic song stage to 12 months of age. It is not known whether there are further decreases in singing rate after 12 months of age. HVC neuronal recruitment rates are highest prior to song crystallization but neuronal replacement continues to 36 months of age and perhaps throughout life. However, the recruitment of new neurons, including those inserted into the premotor HVC-RA pathway, decreases with age, in parallel with decreases in amount of singing and reliance of song acoustic structure on auditory feedback. See text for specific citations.

occurring individual differences in the amount of singing are positively correlated with HVC neuron incorporation.[80] These results are all consistent with the proposal that singing regulates new neuron incorporation, perhaps to replace damage-prone premotor neurons. However, other work suggests that this hypothesis alone is insufficient. Singing in canaries and western song sparrows is highest in the spring mating season, a time when HVC neuron incorporation is much lower than in the fall, when amount of song is reduced.[50,56] If, however, one focuses on the survivorship of new neurons once they are incorporated into HVC, lifespans of neurons formed in spring, at least in canaries, are shorter than those of neurons born in the fall,[69] which would be consistent with this model.

Dissociating Learning, Error Correction, and Motor Activity

Collectively, there are some data to suggest that HVC neuronal recruitment or replacement may (1) be specifically linked with song learning, (2) enable adaptive adjustments to song by error correction in a more general sense, and (3) serve a singing-related function not directly linked to learning but, perhaps, to the replacement of damage-prone neurons (FIG. 9). Yet for each of these hypotheses the data are inconsistent. In future work, several issues should be considered. First, the timing of cell birth dating relative to experimental manipulations, the length and number of survival times can impact adult-formed neuron numbers in ways that are critical for assessing specifically how neuronal replacement is affected and its functional significance.[31,45,95] Second, social housing conditions, which have varied across experiments, are known to influence HVC neuron addition.[44] In group-housed birds, manipulations, such as deafening may alter social dynamics that influence amount of singing, resulting in either higher than normal levels of cell recruitment in hearing birds, or lower than normal rates in deaf birds. If true, such effects would not be readily observed when birds are housed in more impoverished social environments. There may also be limits to how much experience can influence cell recruitment rates. Variation in social complexity may set cell recruitment rates at levels against which the propensity for further increases or decreases is affected. An impoverished social environment may be better for identifying factors that increase, rather than decrease cell recruitment while the opposite may be true when birds are housed in a complex social environment. Third, song learning, the maintenance of stereotypy by error correction, and amount of singing may not be independent factors. For example, one could argue that so long as a bird relies on auditory feedback for song maintenance, every time it sings it is learning something by a template-matching process. Manipulations intended to alter one song attribute may inadvertently alter others, making distinctions between hypotheses (2) and (3) difficult. For example, preliminary data suggest that deafening in adulthood decreases the amount of singing.[104] In turn, a deaf bird must sing to generate error signals. Fourth, the more a bird has sung in its life the more optimized and stable the HVC-RA cell population may be, potentially resulting in a weaker or absent correlation between experimental manipulations and cell recruitment.

However, with appropriate experimental design, these variables can be systematically explored. For example, in order to appraise fully the relative contributions of error signals and song-related motor activity to neuronal replacement, hearing and deaf birds could be matched for lifelong singing rate and age and then compared with respect to neuron recruitment. More extensive examinations of how social complexity affects neuron recruitment are also needed. Controlling for these variables could provide a better appraisal of the potential role of neuronal replacement both during song learning by juveniles as well as song maintenance by adults.

Neuronal Replacement and Perception

Thus far, the models presented have focused on neuronal replacement and motor or sensory-motor function. However, new neurons are found in the auditory area NCM.[44,45] Moreover, neurons in Area X and HVC show both auditory and motor-related activity[62,105–107] (see Konishi and Mooney this volume), and lesions to Area X, HVC and surrounding tissue disrupt auditory discrimination.[47,108,109] All of these facts raise the possibility that new neurons may be involved in perceptual functions. Indeed, physiological recordings of adult-formed HVC neurons show that they respond to sound.[61]

There is evidence that neuronal replacement may be correlated with the richness of the auditory environment. When compared to birds housed singly or in pairs, birds housed in complex social groups recruit more neurons to HVC, Area X, and NCM.[44] Given these data, we must consider the possibility that the effects of deafening on new neuron recruitment to HVC discussed previously are due to a change in perception of the songs of other birds. Interestingly, in juvenile swamp sparrows, total HVC neuron number increases more during the auditory template-formation phase than during the sensorimotor phase of song learning.[110] However without cell birth markers it is impossible to say whether greater or equivalent levels of neuronal *replacement* occur during the motor phase of song learning when HVC size is more stable. Nevertheless, a role for neuronal replacement in perceptual learning provides yet another potential explanation for why neuronal replacement continues even when a bird's own song is stable. Work on the auditory area NCM, as well as HVC and Area X, should shed greater light on the potential relationship between neuronal replacement and perception.

SUMMARY AND FUTURE DIRECTIONS

Over the past decade, substantial advances have been made in understanding the trophic factors involved in the control of adult-formed neuron incorporation and survival. There is strong evidence that gonadal steroids and BDNF are involved, and recent work suggests a role for other molecules as well. Recent behavioral and neurobiological work has broadened the list of potential functions of vocal control neuron addition and replacement. New neuron recruitment levels in HVC can be correlated with song learning, the achievement of song stereotypy, and the amount of singing, which may not be independent variables. Even in age-limited learners, such as zebra finches, replacement may play a role in song maintenance. Future work should systematically examine the relative contributions of each of these song attributes in the control of cell replacement.

None of the proposed functions of neuronal replacement explains why some neuron populations turnover while others do not. Within the efferent pathway for song control, replaceable HVC neurons project to a brain region (RA) that does not undergo cell turnover. Conversely, within the anterior forebrain pathway, permanent HVC neurons project to a region (Area X) that does! There may be important reasons why both major pathways from HVC have permanent and replaceable elements. Circuit analyses relating neurophysiological properties to morphology and connectivity will likely provide important clues as to why this is so.

Neuronal replacement may be conducive to changes in song, however, preserving information while inserting neurons into preexisting circuits remains a fundamental problem. An intriguing possibility is that this occurs "off line" while birds are sleeping. Song-related neurophysiological activity patterns occur during sleep in zebra finches.[111,112] Perhaps one function of this activity is to entrain new neurons.

Correlational studies exploring natural variation in song attributes and neuronal replacement have provided valuable contributions in formulating hypotheses about the behavioral relevance of neuronal turnover. These types of studies are especially valuable when they demonstrate dissociations between neuronal turnover rates and proposed functions.[56] However, the ultimate test for any hypothesis must involve manipulating the variables of interest and seeing what happens. A preliminary step in this direction has been to determine the outcome of targeted killing of HVC cells. While the main focus of this work was to test the relationship between cell death and neuronal replacement, behavioral analyses were also conducted. Targeted laser ablation of RA-projecting neurons resulted in a transient disruption in song structure followed by recovery that was accompanied by increases in neuronal replacement.[59] In some birds, recovered song bore a strong resemblance to preoperative song, although this was not always true. These birds were housed singly and it would be interesting to know whether the presence of potential tutors would have led to new song learning. While not without some weaknesses, a complimentary approach could be to examine the behavioral effects of attenuating cell recruitment by antimitotic treatments, as has been done in mice.[113]

Future work characterizing the morphology and physiological response properties of adult-formed neurons with retroviral techniques[114–117] is also likely to improve our understanding of neuronal replacement. Retroviruses carrying the reporter gene for green fluorescent protein (GFP)[118] could be especially useful because the fluorescence requires no processing for visualization and so it can be used to visually target cells for physiology in tissue slices or, in the case of HVC, perhaps *in vivo* due to its superficial location. Using retroviruses, we could ask: Are there morphological and physiological subtypes of adult-formed HVC interneurons and RA-projection neurons that differ with respect to their lifespan, time of year when they are born, or sensitivity to environmental and behavioral change? How do adult-formed neurons change as they age and as a function of experience? Are young neurons actually more plastic than older ones?

Behavioral studies will continue to provide valuable information on the processes of song learning and maintenance essential for understanding the functions of post hatching neurogenesis. Careful studies of song development in some age-limited learners have revealed that young birds overproduce notes that are then culled during the establishment of crystallized song and yet, some of the deleted material can reemerge in adulthood.[14,24] Similar longitudinal studies in open-ended learners would begin to address the question of whether new songs are learned each year or whether adult changes in song reflect a process where a different subset of sounds is selected each year from a larger reservoir learned early in life. This important work would not only address issues regarding assumptions about when song is learned but also the question of when and even whether syllables are ever truly forgotten. Perhaps the latter could be addressed with operant techniques where rates of acquisition of a song discrimination task using apparently forgotten song elements are compared to acquisition rates using unfamiliar song. Even if a new song is learned yearly and then forgotten, questions still remain about whether the new song material arises by improvisation or by copying song from conspecifics. The answers to these questions could have considerable impact on current models of the functions of neuronal replacement. The notion that song stereotypy requires flexibility and error correction—a form of plasticity that continues long after song crystallization—raises new possibilities for the functions of adult neurogenesis. At the very least, there is now both behavioral and neurobiological evidence that even in age-limited learners, an adult is not an adult is not an adult. Adult zebra finches and other age-limited learners may continue to perfect their songs in subtle ways throughout life. The extent to which this means refinement in stereotypy or changes in the dependence of song structure on auditory feedback without changes in stereotypy remains to be seen. If the former is true, an ultimate test of its functional significance would be to see whether such subtle changes in song structure influence female mate choice and reproductive success. We are rapidly coming to a stage where each of the formerly distinct research areas using songbirds as a "model system" impacts all others.

ACKNOWLEDGMENTS

We thank Phil Zeigler for organizing the birdsong conference, inviting us to participate, gently prodding us to complete our review on schedule, and for his editorial suggestions. We are grateful to Fernando Nottebohm for his support, enthusiasm, and unquenchable scientific curiosity. We also thank the National Institutes of Health and National Science Foundation for their support.

REFERENCES

1. GAGE, F.H. 2002. Neurogenesis in the adult brain. J. Neurosci. **22:** 612–613.
2. GOULD, E. & C.G. GROSS. 2002. Neurogenesis in adult mammals: some progress and problems. J. Neurosci. **22:** 619–623.
3. GOLDMAN, S.A. & F. NOTTEBOHM. 1983. Neuronal production, migration, and differentiation in a vocal control nucleus of the adult female canary brain. Proc. Natl. Acad. Sci. USA **80:** 2390–2394.
4. ALVAREZ-BUYLLA, A. & J.R. KIRN. 1997. Birth, migration, incorporation, and death of vocal control neurons in adult songbirds. J. Neurobiol. **33:** 585–601.
5. ALVAREZ-BUYLLA, A., C.-Y. LING & W.S. YU. 1994. Contribution of neurons born during embryonic, juvenile, and adult life to the brain of adult canaries: regional specificity and delayed birth of neurons in the song-control nuclei. J. Comp. Neurol. **347:** 233–248.
6. GOLDMAN, S.A. 1998. Adult neurogenesis: from canaries to the clinic. J. Neurobiol. **36:** 267–286.
7. NOTTEBOHM, F. 2002. Why are some neurons replaced in adult brain? J. Neurosci. **22:** 624–628.
8. KIRN, J.R., A. ALVAREZ-BUYLLA & F. NOTTEBOHM. 1991. Production and survival of projection neurons in a forebrain vocal center of adult male canaries. J. Neurosci. **11:** 1756–1762.
9. REINER, A.B.L., A. BUTLER, A. CSILLAG, *et al.* 2004. Revised nomenclature for avian telencephalon and some related brainstem nuclei. J. Comp. Neurol. In press.
10. NOTTEBOHM, F. 1985. Neuronal replacement in adulthood. Ann. N.Y. Acad. Sci. **457:** 143–161.
11. LING, C. *et al.* 1997. Neurogenesis in juvenile and adult ring doves. J. Comp. Neurol. **379:** 300–312.
12. BANTA LAVENEX, P., P. LAVENEX & N.S. CLAYTON. 2001. Comparative studies of postnatal neurogenesis and learning: a critical review. Avian Poultry Biol. Rev. **12:** 103–125.
13. GAHR, M. *et al.* 2002. What is the adaptive role of neurogenesis in adult birds? Prog. Brain Res. **138:** 233–254.
14. MARLER, P. 1997. Three models of song learning: evidence from behavior. J. Neurobiol. **33:** 501–516.
15. TCHERNICHOVSKI, O. *et al.* 2001. Dynamics of the vocal imitation process: how a zebra finch learns its song. Science **291:** 2564–2569.
16. WASER, M.S. & P. MARLER. 1977. Song learning in canaries. J. Comp. Physiol. Psychol. **91:** 1–7.
17. WEICHEL, K. *et al.* 1986. Sex differences in plasma steroid concentrations and singing behaviour during ontogeny in canaries (*Serinus canaria*). Ethology **73:** 281–294.
18. NOTTEBOHM, F., M.E. NOTTEBOHM & L. CRANE. 1986. Developmental and seasonal changes in canary song and their relation to changes in the anatomy of song-control nuclei. Behav. Neural Biol. **46:** 445–471.
19. IMMELMANN, K. 1969. Song development in the zebra finch and other estrildid finches. *In* Bird Vocalizations. R.A. Hinde, Ed.: 61–74. Cambridge University Press. London.
20. EALES, L.A. 1985. Song learning in zebra finches: some effects of song model availability on what is learnt and when. Anim. Behav. **33:** 1293–1300.

21. LEITNER, S. *et al.* 2001. Seasonal activation and inactivation of song motor memories in wild canaries is not reflected in neuroanatomical changes of forebrain song areas. Horm. Behav. **40:** 160–168.
22. GUTTINGER, H.R. 1985. Consequences of domestication on the song structures in the canary. Behavior **94:** 254–278.
23. GUTTINGER, H.R. 1979. The integration of learned and genetically programmed behavior: study of hierarchical organization in songs of canaries, greenfinches and their hybrids. Z. Tierpsychol. **49:** 285–303.
24. HOUGH, G.E., 2ND, D.A. NELSON & S.F. VOLMAN. 2000. Re-expression of songs deleted during vocal development in white-crowned sparrows, *Zonotrichia leucophrys.* Anim. Behav. **60:** 279–287.
25. PRICE, P.H. 1979. Developmental determinants of structure in zebra finch song. J. Comp. Physiol. Psychol. **93:** 260–277.
26. BUREK, M.J., K.W. NORDEEN & E.J. NORDEEN. 1991. Neuron loss and addition in developing zebra finch song nuclei are independent of auditory experience during song learning. J. Neurobiol. **22:** 215–223.
27. SCHARFF, C. & F. NOTTEBOHM. 1991. A comparative study of the behavioral deficits following lesions of various parts of the zebra finch song system: implications for vocal learning. J. Neurosci. **11:** 2896–2913.
28. NORDEEN, K.W. & E.J. NORDEEN. 1992. Auditory feedback is necessary for the maintenance of stereotyped song in adult zebra finches. Behav. Neural Biol. **57:** 58–66.
29. WOOLLEY, S.M. & E.W. RUBEL. 1997. Bengalese finches *Lonchura Striata domestica* depend upon auditory feedback for the maintenance of adult song. J. Neurosci. **17:** 6380–6390.
30. OKANOYA, K. & A. YAMAGUCHI. 1997. Adult Bengalese finches (*Lonchura striata* var. *domestica*) require real-time auditory feedback to produce normal song syntax. J. Neurobiol. **33:** 343–356.
31. WANG, N., R. AVIRAM & J.R. KIRN. 1999. Deafening alters neuron turnover within the telencephalic motor pathway for song control in adult zebra finches. J. Neurosci. **19:** 10554–10561.
32. LEONARDO, A. & M. KONISHI. 1999. Decrystallization of adult birdsong by perturbation of auditory feedback. Nature **399:** 466–470.
33. MARGOLIASH, D. 2002. Evaluating theories of bird song learning: implications for future directions. J. Comp. Physiol. A Neuroethol. Sens. Neural Behav. Physiol. **188:** 851–866.
34. WALDSTEIN, R.S. 1990. Effects of postlingual deafness on speech production: implications for the role of auditory feedback. J. Acoust. Soc. Am. **88:** 2099–2114.
35. LOMBARDINO, A.J. & F. NOTTEBOHM. 2000. Age at deafening affects the stability of learned song in adult male zebra finches. J. Neurosci. **20:** 5054–5064.
36. BRAINARD, M.S. & A.J. DOUPE. 2001. Postlearning consolidation of birdsong: stabilizing effects of age and anterior forebrain lesions. J. Neurosci. **21:** 2501–2517.
37. CHI, Z. & D. MARGOLIASH. 2001. Temporal precision and temporal drift in brain and behavior of zebra finch song. Neuron **32:** 899–910.
38. NOTTEBOHM, F., T.M. STOKES & C.M. LEONARD. 1976. Central control of song in the canary, *Serinus canarius.* J. Comp. Neurol. **165:** 457–486.
39. BOTTJER, S.W., E.A. MIESNER & A.P. ARNOLD. 1984. Forebrain lesions disrupt development but not maintenance of song in passerine birds. Science **224:** 901–902.
40. SOHRABJI, F., E.J. NORDEEN & K.W. NORDEEN. 1990. Selective impairment of song learning following lesions of a forebrain nucleus in juvenile zebra finch. Behav. Neural Biol. **53:** 51–63.
41. WILLIAMS, H. & N. MEHTA. 1999. Changes in adult zebra finch song require a forebrain nucleus that is not necessary for song production. J. Neurobiol. **39:** 14–28.
42. BRAINARD, M.S. & A.J. DOUPE. 2000. Interruption of a basal ganglia-forebrain circuit prevents plasticity of learned vocalizations. Nature **404:** 762–766.
43. MELLO, C.V. 2002. Mapping vocal communication pathways in birds with inducible gene expression. J. Comp. Physiol. A Neuroethol. Sens. Neural Behav. Physiol. **188:** 943–959.

44. LIPKIND, D. *et al.* 2002. Social change affects the survival of new neurons in the fore-brain of adult songbirds. Behav. Brain Res. **133:** 31–43.
45. ALVAREZ-BORDA, B. 2002. On new neurons in canary brains. Ph.D. dissertation. The Rockefeller University.
46. SOHRABJI, F., E.J. NORDEEN & K.W. NORDEEN. 1993. Characterization of neurons born and incorporated into a vocal control nucleus during avian song learning. Brain Res. **620:** 335–338.
47. BRENOWITZ, E.A. 1991. Altered perception of species-specific song by female birds after lesions of a forebrain nucleus. Science **251:** 303–305.
48. DEWULF, V. & S.W. BOTTJER. 2002. Age and sex differences in mitotic activity within the zebra finch telencephalon. J. Neurosci. **22:** 4080–4094.
49. ALVAREZ-BUYLLA, A., M. THEELEN & F. NOTTEBOHM. 1988. Birth of projection neu-rons in the higher vocal center of the canary forebrain before, during, and after song learning. Proc. Natl. Acad. Sci. USA **85:** 8722–8726.
50. ALVAREZ-BUYLLA, A., J.R. KIRN & F. NOTTEBOHM. 1990. Birth of projection neurons in adult avian brain may be related to perceptual or motor learning. Science **249:** 1444–1446.
51. WANG, N. *et al.* 2002. Vocal control neuron incorporation decreases with age in the adult zebra finch. J. Neurosci. **22:** 10864–10870.
52. KIRN, J.R. & T.J. DEVOOGD. 1989. Genesis and death of vocal control neurons during sexual differentiation in the zebra finch. J. Neurosci. **9:** 3176–3187.
53. KIRN, J.R. *et al.* 1994. Cell death and neuronal recruitment in the high vocal center of adult male canaries are temporally related to changes in song. Proc. Natl. Acad. Sci. USA **91:** 7844–7848.
54. BUREK, M.J., K.W. NORDEEN & E.J. NORDEEN. 1997. Sexually dimorphic neuron addi-tion to an avian song-control region is not accounted for by sex differences in cell death. J. Neurobiol. **33:** 61–71.
55. TEKUMALLA, P.K. *et al.* 2002. Effects of excess thyroid hormone on cell death, cell pro-liferation, and new neuron incorporation in the adult zebra finch telencephalon. J. Neurobiol. **51:** 323–341.
56. TRAMONTIN, A.D. & E.A. BRENOWITZ. 1999. A field study of seasonal neuronal incor-poration into the song control system of a songbird that lacks adult song learning. J. Neurobiol. **40:** 316–326.
57. GAHR, M. 1990. Delineation of a brain nucleus: comparisons of cytochemical, hod-ological, and cytoarchitectural views of the song control nucleus HVC of the adult canary. J. Comp. Neurol. **294:** 30–36.
58. KIRN, J.R. *et al.* 1999. The fate of new neurons in adult canary high vocal center during the first 30 days after their formation. J. Comp. Neurol. **411:** 487–494.
59. SCHARFF, C. *et al.* 2000. Targeted neuronal death affects neuronal replacement and vocal behavior in adult songbirds. Neuron **25:** 481–492.
60. NORDEEN, K.W. & E.J. NORDEEN. 1988. Projection neurons within a vocal motor path-way are born during song learning in zebra finches. Nature **334:** 149–151.
61. PATON, J.A. & F. NOTTEBOHM. 1984. Neurons generated in the adult brain are recruited into functional circuits. Science **225:** 1046–1048.
62. MOONEY, R., M.J. ROSEN & C.B. STURDY. 2002. A bird's eye view: top down intracel-lular analyses of auditory selectivity for learned vocalizations. J. Comp. Physiol. A Neuroethol. Sens. Neural. Behav. Physiol. **188:** 879–895.
63. HAHNLOSER, R.H., A.A. KOZHEVNIKOV & M.S. FEE. 2002. An ultra-sparse code under-lies the generation of neural sequences in a songbird. Nature **419:** 65–70.
64. NOTTEBOHM, F. *et al.* 1990. Song learning in birds: the relation between perception and production. Phil. Trans. R. Soc. Lond. B **329:** 115–124.
65. KIRN, J.R. & F. NOTTEBOHM. 1993. Direct evidence for loss and replacement of projec-tion neurons in adult canary brain. J. Neurosci. **13:** 1654–1663.
66. ALVAREZ-BUYLLA, A. & F. NOTTEBOHM. 1988. Migration of young neurons in adult avian brain. Nature **335:** 353–354.
67. BUREK, M.J., K.W. NORDEEN & E.J. NORDEEN. 1994. Ontogeny of sex differences among newly-generated neurons of the juvenile avian brain. Dev. Brain Res. **78:** 57–64.

68. BARAMI, K. *et al.* 1995. Hu protein as an early marker of neuronal phenotypic differentiation by subependymal zone cells of the adult songbird forebrain. J. Neurobiol. **28:** 82–101.
69. NOTTEBOHM, F. *et al.* 1994. The life span of new neurons in a song control nucleus of the adult canary brain depends on time of year when these cells are born. Proc. Natl. Acad. Sci. USA **91:** 7849–7853.
70. BALL, G.F., L.V. RITERS & J. BALTHAZART. 2002. Neuroendocrinology of song behavior and avian brain plasticity: multiple sites of action of sex steroid hormones. Front. Neuroendocrinol. **23:** 137–178.
71. RASIKA, S., F. NOTTEBOHM & A. ALVAREZ-BUYLLA. 1994. Testosterone increases the recruitment and/or survival of new high vocal center neurons in adult female canaries. Proc. Natl. Acad. Sci. USA **91:** 7854–7858.
72. RASIKA, S., A. ALVAREZ-BUYLLA & F. NOTTEBOHM. 1999. BDNF mediates the effects of testosterone on the survival of new neurons in an adult brain. Neuron **22:** 53–62.
73. HIDALGO, A. *et al.* 1995. Estrogens and non-estrogenic ovarian influences combine to promote the recruitment and decrease the turnover of new neurons in the adult female canary brain. J. Neurobiol. **27:** 470–487.
74. BUREK, M.J., K.W. NORDEEN & E.J. NORDEEN. 1995. Estrogen promotes neuron addition to an avian song-control nucleus by regulating post-mitotic events. Dev. Brain Res. **85:** 220–224.
75. BROWN, S.D., F. JOHNSON & S.W. BOTTJER. 1993. Neurogenesis in adult canary telencephalon is independent of gonadal hormone levels. J. Neurosci. **13:** 2024–2032.
76. DITTRICH, F. *et al.* 1999. Estrogen-inducible, sex-specific expression of brain-derived neurotrophic factor mRNA in a forebrain song control nucleus of the juvenile zebra finch. Proc. Natl. Acad. Sci. USA **96:** 8241–8246.
77. TRAMONTIN, A.D., J.C. WINGFIELD & E.A. BRENOWITZ. 2003. Androgens and estrogens induce seasonal-like growth of song nuclei in the adult songbird brain. J. Neurobiol. **57:** 130–140.
78. LOUISSAINT, A., Jr. *et al.* 2002. Coordinated interaction of neurogenesis and angiogenesis in the adult songbird brain. Neuron **34:** 945–960.
79. LI, X.C. *et al.* 2000. A relationship between behavior, neurotrophin expression, and new neuron survival. Proc. Natl. Acad. Sci. USA **97:** 8584–8589.
80. ALVAREZ-BORDA, B. & F. NOTTEBOHM. 2002. Gonads and singing play separate, additive roles in new neuron recruitment in adult canary brain. J. Neurosci. **22:** 8684–8690.
81. ARAI, O. & N. SAITO. 1995. Thyroxine reduces the production rate of BrdU-labeled cells in the ventricular zone of the adult canary brain. Neurosci. Lett. **198:** 135–138.
82. BENTLEY, G.E., T.J. VAN'T HOF & G.F. BALL. 1999. Seasonal neuroplasticity in the songbird telencephalon: a role for melatonin. Proc. Natl. Acad. Sci. USA **96:** 4674–4679.
83. HOLZENBERGER, M. *et al.* 1997. Selective expression of insulin-like growth factor II in the songbird brain. J. Neurosci. **17:** 6974–6987.
84. JIANG, J. *et al.* 1998. Insulin-like growth factor-1 is a radial cell-associated neurotrophin that promotes neuronal recruitment from the adult songbird ependyma/subependyma. J. Neurobiol. **36:** 1–15.
85. ALVAREZ-BUYLLA, A., M. THEELEN & F. NOTTEBOHM. 1990. Proliferation "hot spots" in adult avian ventricular zone reveal radial cell division. Neuron **5:** 101–109.
86. GOLDMAN, S.A. *et al.* 1996. Ependymal/subependymal zone cells of postnatal and adult songbird brain generate both neurons and nonneuronal siblings *in vitro* and *in vivo.* J. Neurobiol. **30:** 505–520.
87. ALVAREZ-BUYLLA, A. & S. TEMPLE. 1998. Stem cells in the developing and adult nervous system. J. Neurobiol. **36:** 105–110.
88. DOETSCH, F. & C. SCHARFF. 2001. Challenges for brain repair: insights from adult neurogenesis in birds and mammals. Brain Behav. Evol. **58:** 306–322.
89. DENISENKO-NEHRBASS, N.I. *et al.* 2000. Site-specific retinoic acid production in the brain of adult songbirds. Neuron **27:** 359–370.
90. THORNBERRY, N.A. & Y. LAZEBNIK. 1998. Caspases: enemies within. Science **281:** 1312–1316.

91. NICHOLSON, D.W. & N.A. THORNBERRY. 2003. Apoptosis. Life and death decisions. Science **299:** 214–215.
92. HUESMANN, G. & D.F. CLAYTON. 2002. Is it memory or is it death? Rapid non-lethal caspase-3 activation during acoustic memory trace formation. Soc. Neurosci. Abst. 382.3
93. DASH, P.K., S. BLUM & A.N. MOORE. 2000. Caspase activity plays an essential role in long-term memory. Neuroreport **11:** 2811–2816.
94. NOTTEBOHM, F. 1989. From bird song to neurogenesis. Sci. Am. **260:** 74–79.
95. WILBRECHT, L., A. CRIONAS & F. NOTTEBOHM. 2002. Experience affects recruitment of new neurons but not adult neuron number. J. Neurosci. **22:** 825–831.
96. WARD, B.C., E.J. NORDEEN & K.W. NORDEEN. 1998. Individual variation in neuron number predicts differences in the propensity for avian vocal imitation. Proc. Natl. Acad. Sci. USA **95:** 1277–1282.
97. WILBRECHT, L., T. PETERSEN & F. NOTTEBOHM. 2002. Bilateral LMAN lesions cancel differences in HVC neuronal recruitment induced by unilateral syringeal denervation. Lateral magnocellular nucleus of the anterior neostriatum. J. Comp. Physiol. A Neuroethol. Sens. Neural Behav. Physiol. **188:** 909–915.
98. MORRISON, R.G. & F. NOTTEBOHM. 1993. Role of a telencephalic nucleus in the delayed song learning of socially isolated zebra finches. J. Neurobiol. **24:** 1045–1064.
99. WILBRECHT, L. 2003. The Recruitment of New Neurons to HVC during the Sensitive Period for Song Learning in the Zebra Finch. Doctoral dissertation. Rockefeller University. New York.
100. WAELTI, P., A. DICKINSON & W. SCHULTZ. 2001. Dopamine responses comply with basic assumptions of formal learning theory. Nature **412:** 43–48.
101. SCHULTZ, W. 2002. Getting formal with dopamine and reward. Neuron **36:** 241–263.
102. SOHA, J.A., T. SHIMIZU & A.J. DOUPE. 1996. Development of the catecholaminergic innervation of the song system of the male zebra finch. J. Neurobiol. **29:** 473–489.
103. JOHNSON, F., K. SODERSTROM & O. WHITNEY. 2002. Quantifying song bout production during zebra finch sensory-motor learning suggests a sensitive period for vocal practice. Behav. Brain Res. **131:** 57–65.
104. PYTTE C.L., M. GERSON & J.R. KIRN. 2003. Singing may contribute to age-related changes in song motor program stability and neuron replacement. Soc. Neurosci. Abstr. 942.6.
105. KATZ, L.C. & M.E. GURNEY. 1981. Auditory responses in the zebra finch's motor system for song. Brain Res. **221:** 192–197.
106. BANKES, S.C. & D. MARGOLIASH. 1993. Parametric modeling of the temporal dynamics of neuronal responses using connectionist architectures. J. Neurophysiol. **69:** 980–991.
107. SOLIS, M.M. et al. 2000. Song selectivity and sensorimotor signals in vocal learning and production. Proc. Natl. Acad. Sci. USA **97:** 11836–11842.
108. SCHARFF, C., F. NOTTEBOHM & J. CYNX. 1998. Conspecific and heterospecific song discrimination in male zebra finches with lesions in the anterior forebrain pathway. J. Neurobiol. **36:** 81–90.
109. GENTNER, T.Q. et al. 2000. Individual vocal recognition and the effect of partial lesions to HVc on discrimination, learning, and categorization of conspecific song in adult songbirds. J. Neurobiol. **42:** 117–133.
110. NORDEEN, K.W., P. MARLER & E.J. NORDEEN. 1989. Addition of song-related neurons in swamp sparrows coincides with memorization, not production, of learned songs. J. Neurobiol. **20:** 651–661.
111. DAVE, A.S. & D. MARGOLIASH. 2000. Song replay during sleep and computational rules for sensorimotor vocal learning. Science **290:** 812–816.
112. MARGOLIASH, D. 2001. Do sleeping birds sing? Population coding and learning in the bird song system. Prog. Brain Res. **130:** 319–331.
113. SHORS, T.J. et al. 2001. Neurogenesis in the adult is involved in the formation of trace memories. Nature **410:** 372–376.
114. CEPKO, C.L. et al. 1998. Lineage analysis using retroviral vectors. Methods **14:** 393–406.

115. GOLDMAN, S.A. *et al.* 1996. Ependymal/subependymal zone cells of postnatal and adult songbird brain generate both neurons and nonneuronal siblings *in vitro* and *in vivo*. J. Neurobiol. **30:** 505–520.
116. CARLETON, A. *et al.* 2003. Becoming a new neuron in the adult olfactory bulb. Nat. Neurosci. **6:** 507–518.
117. VAN PRAAG, H. *et al.* 2002. Functional neurogenesis in the adult hippocampus. Nature **415:** 1030–1034.
118. OKADA, A. *et al.* 1999. Imaging cells in the developing nervous system with retrovirus expressing modified green fluorescent protein. Exp. Neurol. **156:** 394–406.

Hormone-Dependent Neural Plasticity in the Juvenile and Adult Song System

What Makes a Successful Male?

MANFRED GAHR

Department of Developmental and Behavioural Neuroscience, Institute of Neuroscience, Faculty of Earth and Life Sciences, Vrije Universiteit Amsterdam, 1081 HV Amsterdam, The Netherlands

ABSTRACT: The sexual quality of adult song is the result of genetic and epigenetic mechanisms shaping the neural song system throughout life. Genetic brain-intrinsic mechanisms determine the neuron pools that develop into forebrain song control areas independent of gonadal steroid hormones, androgens and estrogens. One fate of these neurons is the potential to express sex steroid receptors, such as androgen and estrogen receptors. Genetic brain-intrinsic mechanisms, too, determine the activity of hypothalamic-pituitary-gonad (HPG) axis, i.e., the working range and responsiveness of HPG axis to produce gonadal hormones. The epigenetic action of gonadal steroid hormones (androgens and estrogens) on determined vocal neurons is required to maintain and increase the pool of determined vocal neurons and to complete the connections of the vocal system, i.e., to make it function motorically. The subsequent influence of environmental information, including both external (socio-sexual and physical) and internal (body physiology) signals, specify the further neural phenotype of vocal areas either through acting on the HPG axis and differential release of gonadal hormones or through non-gonadal hormone systems, both of which have target neurons in the functional vocal system. Despite the clear evidence of hormone dependency of the development of both the adult song phenotype and song system phenotype, their causal relation is complex.

KEYWORDS: neural plasticity; hormones; hypothalamic-pituitary-gonad axis

INTRODUCTION

The function of the song of male birds is closely linked to reproductive success and the result of sexual selection.[1] The two main functions of song in male birds are mate attraction and territory defense against other males.[2] Individual variation in song characteristics does affect reproductive success through mate choice and male-male competition, the two mechanisms of sexual selection.[3] Current theory predicts that when senders and receivers have different evolutionary interests, as in sexual

Address for correspondence: Manfred Gahr, Department of Developmental and Behavioural Neuroscience, Institute of Neuroscience, Faculty of Earth and Life Sciences, Vrije Universiteit Amsterdam, 1087 De Boelelaan, 1081 HV Amsterdam, The Netherlands.
Gahr@bio.vu.nl; <http://www.bio.vu.nl/vakgroepen/od/onb/gahr.html>

Ann. N.Y. Acad. Sci. 1016: 684–703 (2004). © 2004 New York Academy of Sciences.
doi: 10.1196/annals.1298.025

selection, signals must be costly (i.e., subject to some constraint) to constitute stable, honest indicators of quality.[4] Individual variation in the expression of these signals will therefore depend on the condition of the adult male.[5] The song of songbirds requires auditory-motor learning.[6] Although the amount of motor learning from external models might considerably vary between species, such learning appears a general feature of male songbirds while the features to be learned are likely species specific.[7–11] Experimental works strongly suggest that the integrity of the forebrain vocal system is necessary for the learning and production of learned vocalizations.[12–19] Thus, a successful (selected by a female) male needs at least to develop a forebrain song system, needs to modify the system through learning, and, finally, needs to adapt the system to its physiological condition, which in turn depends on its genetic background and its environment. Since the behavior that makes a male successful takes place in adulthood, while song development and learning are either restricted to or, at least start during, ontogeny,[9,10] we have to consider the quality of male vocal signaling as a result of life history. In a recent review of honesty signaling of bird song, Gil and Gahr[20] proposed the neuroendocrine control of song development and production as a major cost.

The action of gonadal steroid hormones (androgens and estrogens) specifies the sexual differentiation of brain and behavior upon brain-intrinsic genetic mechanisms.[21–24] In this process, the hormones first specify the global development of sexually determined brain areas, such as the song system, frequently called organizational action, and subsequently modify more detailed phenotypes, frequently called activational action.[25] Although the differences between both are quantitative rather than qualitative, we shall use these terms. One major cellular mechanism of steroid action is the change of protein synthesis via activating their cognate receptors, which are ligand-dependent transcription factors.[26] Although gonadal steroids act on neurons *in vitro* via a wide range of non-genomic mechanisms not involving their cognate receptors,[27] there are only a few examples involving such mechanisms in sexual differentiation.[27] Genetic and environment-driven mechanisms that control the expression of androgen and estrogen receptors and those that control the cerebral availability of active androgens and estrogens appear crucial for sexual differentiation of brain and behavior throughout life.

In relation to the life history process of adult sexual behavior, we discuss the genetic mechanisms of song system development while distinguishing between such mechanisms that determine (1) hormone-sensitive song areas and (2) the activity of the hypothalamus-pituitary-gonadal axis that delivers neuroactive steroids or its precursors. Subsequently, we investigate (3) the epigenetic action of gonadal steroid hormones to achieve a functional song system and (4) the role of gonadal and non-gonadal endocrine signaling on plasticity of the functional song system. Last (5), we discuss the (controversial evidence of) causal relations between hormone-dependent song and song system phenotypes.

HORMONE-RESPONSIVE SONG AREAS ARE DETERMINED BY BRAIN-INTRINSIC MECHANISMS

One hallmark of the song system is the anatomical and neurochemical feature of the forebrain vocal areas, in particular the expression of androgen receptors and estrogen receptors of forebrain vocal areas. All these areas, either permanently or transiently, express androgen receptors.[28-38] Estrogen receptors occur in a subpopulation of HVC neurons, albeit in a species-specific manner while all other forebrain vocal areas don't express these receptors.[39,40] This pattern is specific for oscines and not present in sub-oscine passerines or non-oscines, with exception of hummingbirds.[35,37,40] In the following, we study the expression pattern of androgen receptors in the developing HVC of the zebra finch to argue for sex hormone–independent establishment of this pattern.

The forebrain areas of the zebra finch are first detectable between posthatching (P) day P5 to P10. In the zebra finch, the size, neuron number, androgen receptor expression of the HVC is already sexually dimorphic on P9[21] (FIG. 1). No androgen receptors or estrogen receptors are expressed in this area before P9,[21] although androgen and estrogen receptors are found in various neural tissues outside HVC before.[33,41-43] Slice cultures of the caudale neostriatum, where HVC develops, of P5 males and females in hormone-free conditions show that the sexually dimorphic expression of androgen receptor mRNA in HVC is independent of the direct action of steroids on this nucleus or any of its immediate presynaptic or postsynaptic partners.[21] Therefore, gonadal steroids do not appear to be directly involved in the initial sex difference in the expression pattern of androgen receptors, neuron number, and size of the HVC. Similar, works with quail-chicken brain chimeras suggest brain-intrinsic determination of sex hormone expressing neuron pools.[44] The brain-autono-

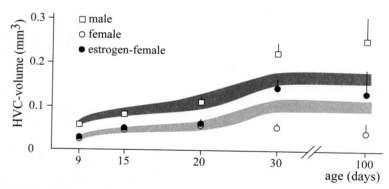

FIGURE 1. Estrogen-dependent and gonadal steroid-independent development of the HVC volume of juvenile male and female zebra finches. The HVC was defined by the distribution of androgen receptor mRNA in the caudale neostriatum, which is first detectable at P9. For each time point the male HVC is larger compared with the female HVC. The male HVC increased significantly from P9 to P15 to P20 to P30 to P100. The *dark gray band* indicates the expected growth of the HVC based on its genetically determined size at P9 and the subsequent extension of the forebrain. The male HVC grows linearly with the caudale forebrain until P20, but grows faster than the forebrain after P20. In females, the HVC volume increases from P9 to P15 to P20 but does not undergo significant increase or decrease afterward. The female HVC grows less than expected after P20 (*light gray band*). In estrogen-treated females, the HVC volume increases significantly after P20 compared with normal females and compared with the expected values (*light gray band*). Thus epigenetic factors, such as estrogens, induce a 30–40% increase of the HVC size after P20, whereas 60–70% of the maximal HVC size is defined by steroid-independent mechanisms. (From Gahr and Metzdorf,[21] with permission.)

mous mechanisms that determine forebrain vocal neurons, such as expression of homeotic genes and morphogens, are unknown. However, two possibilities for a steroid-dependent development of AR expression pattern in HVC remain, a sex steroid–dependent non-genomic priming of putative HVC cells before or during migration to later produce androgen receptors and a sex steroid–dependent trophic or transsynaptic signaling from non-telencephalic areas to HVC before P5. The recent finding of a gynandromorphic zebra finch supports the above argument of brain-autonomous determination of vocal neuron pools such as HVC independent of the general hormonal milieu.[23] During later development, the amount of secreted gonadal steroids together with autologous and heterologous regulation of receptor expression[31,45,46] might explain large individual and periodical differences in the abundance of the androgen and estrogen receptors in vocal areas.[33,36,38]

BRAIN-AUTONOMOUS, SEX-SPECIFIC PRIMING OF THE HPG AXIS, THE SEX HORMONE DELIVERING SYSTEM

The hypothalamus-pituitary-gonadal (HPG) axis controls the production level of gonadal steroids. The HPG axis appears at least functional at hatching.[47] The main gonadal steroid secreted by the male testis is the androgen testosterone and that of the female ovary is the estrogen 17β-estradiol. Although there is no information concerning the priming of the HPG axis in songbirds, research on Japanese quails suggest a brain-intrinsic mechanism.[24] In gallinaceous birds such as quails and chicken, female brain sex is thought to develop due to estrogen-dependent demasculinization of a default male brain phenotype.[48,49] To test this concept of gonad-dependent brain sex, male-to-female (MF), female-to-male (FM), male-to male (MM), and female-to-female (FF) isotopic isochronic transplantation of the brain primordium rostral to the otic capsules were performed at the second embryonic day in Japanese quails.[24] In these brain chimeras, the forebrain including the hypothalamus originates from the donor. MM, FF, and MF chimeras showed sexual behavior according to the host genetic sex. FM males showed no mounting and only rudimentary crowing behavior. While chimeras of each type showed host-typical production of steroid hormones during embryonic life, only FM chimeras were hypogonadal and had atypical low levels of circulating testosterone in adulthood. In relation, features of the medial preoptic nucleus, a sexually dimorphic brain area, were not male-like in FM males.[24] These data suggest that brain sexual development depends on brain-intrinsic genetic mechanisms that organize the sex-typical production of gonadal hormones in adulthood. It further supports the notion of a brain-intrinsic, sexual development of the song control area HVC of the zebra finch[21,23] (see above). It remains to be seen to what extent the genetic mechanisms determine the large individual differences in the production of gonadal hormones of adult male birds, i.e., its working range and responsiveness to the external environment and overall body condition.

GONADAL HORMONES ARE THE MAIN PLAYER TO MODULATE "EARLY" SEXUAL DIFFERENTIATION OF VOCAL AREAS

A second hallmark of the song system is its hodological features, brain-intrinsic feedback loops between vocal areas and sensory inputs from primary sensory systems,[13,50,51] both of which are likely necessities for vocal learning.[6,18] Juvenile songbirds do not utter song precursors, so-called subsongs, until a species-specific ontogenetic time-window. In the zebra finch, this time-window coincides with the formation of the HVC-to-RA synapses, which is delayed relative to the interconnection of the other neuron pools determined to become vocal areas.[52–55] We assume that this hodological property causes the transition from the non-functional to the functional song system concerning its motor function. In animals, which naturally or experimentally lack this connection, many HVC and RA neurons die and the survivors do not develop the neuronal phenotypes that are typical for HVC and RA of adult singing songbirds.[52,56–58]

That gonadal steroids influence the fate of determined vocal neurons to reach this functional state is best evidenced by the sex-specific development of the HVC and RA in some songbird species. In juvenile female zebra finches and starlings, estrogen treatment shifts the differentiation of these areas (measured in terms of area volume and neuron size) in male direction.[21,59–63] These anatomical features nevertheless remain different from the male phenotypes, reflecting the above discussed genetic brain-autonomous sex differences.[21] Gene expression of male (but not female) HVC neurons is sensitive to estrogens as early as P15[64] and estrogen treatment partially masculinizes the volume (and probably neuron numbers) of female HVC between posthatching day 20 and 30[21] (Fig. 1). The formation of HVC-to-RA synapses is inducible if estrogen treatment occurs in the first weeks posthatching.[52] In vitro experiments with brain slice cultures of both male and female forebrains support the estrogen dependency of the RA-to-HVC connection.[65] This work, the results of intracerebral implantation of estrogens near HVC,[66] and HVC lesions[67] point to the HVC as the origin of estrogen-dependent differentiation of forebrain vocal areas. Estrogen receptors occur in low abundance in the HVC area during posthatching life.[68] These data suggest the following scenario of estrogen-dependent functional development of the song system: Estrogens, likely derived from testosterone in the forebrain,[65,69] support the survival and differentiation of HVC neurons during the time period of motoric silence (i.e., until day 28–35[55]). In parallel, estrogen might directly or indirectly, through the increased number of surviving and differentiating neurons, stimulate the recruitment of late-born neurons into HVC.[70] Subsequently, estrogens directly induce the HVC-to-RA synapse formation. Alternatively, the latter might be the consequence of the estrogen-dependent previous survival, recruitment, and maturation of HVC and RA neurons. In case of elevated levels of intracerebral estrogens, the HVC-to-RA connection makes the vocal system functional, which leads to abrupt changes of its neuronal phenotypes as indicated by the upregulation of brain-derived neurotrophic factor (BDNF)[64] and the song-system-nuclear-antigen.[71] In case of low levels of intracerebral estrogens, HVC neurons shall enter a cell-death fate at a certain time point, in the latest after 35 days of posthatching life,[72] which coincides with the loss of estrogen receptors in the HVC region.[68]

A further potential source of hormone-dependent variance of early differentiation of forebrain vocal neuron pools is the feedback of the motoric endpoint of the song system, the syrinx (the sound producing organ) and its hypoglossal motoneurons upon forebrain vocal areas. The hypoglossal motoneurons are among the first neurons of the brain to express androgen receptors, which occurs around embryonic (E)7.[41] The syrinx becomes androgen sensitive around E10.[41] This expression precedes that of the forebrain vocal areas by about two weeks. Large amounts of sex hormones originating from the mother and deposited in the yolk during egg formation are likely to influence the development of behaviors of birds.[73–76] Thus embryonic hormone production (pre- and posthatching) and/or maternal sex hormones might influence the development of the syrinx and its motoneurons, which in turn could feedback on the forebrain vocal areas via retrograde signaling.

Cutting the nervus hypoglossus pars tracheosyringealis shortly after hatching experimentally tested this idea.[77] Although the hypoglossal motoneurons degenerate in this procedure as expected, there is little impact on the differentiation of its afferent RA neurons. Further, estrogens masculinize the fate of RA of such denervated female zebra finches.[77] This in vivo experiments suffer, however, from the caveat that RA reside next to nXIIts a second major androgen-sensitive target, brainstem respiratory pre-motor neurons[78] that are difficult to eliminate experimentally. Effects of maternal gonadal hormones on adult sexual signaling[75] are, nevertheless, likely due to long-term changes of overall body physiology and/or the function of the HPG axis rather than direct effects on vocal areas.

The early presence of androgen receptors and estrogen receptors indicates,[21,32] as detailed above, that the fate of vocal areas to achieve the functional state is heavily influenced by gonadal hormones acting on the forebrain. The external (socio-sexual and physical) and internal environment could change the sexual differentiation by either acting directly on vocal neurons and/or brain areas that deliver neuroactive steroids or, as generally thought, indirectly via changing the activity of the HPG axis and thus the abundance of gonadal hormones. In the first case, the physical and socio-sexual environments need to signal to vocal areas, i.e., vocal neurons need to have sensory properties or receptors for endocrine signals that reflect the environment.

Receptors for non-gonadal endocrine signals such as leptins (nutritional), glucocorticoids (stress), cytokines (immunosystem), and melatonin (photoperiod), are, however, unknown in the non-functional song system. Melatonin binding sites start to be abundant in vocal areas around P40[79] and we so far failed to localize substantial expression of stress hormone receptors in the young song areas (Gahr and Metzdorf, unpublished observations). Sensory input, in particular auditory input, modulates the later differentiation of vocal areas but has no impact on its basic development.[80–82] We therefore suggest that the gonadal hormones are the main epigenetic players for sexual differentiation of the vocal circuit to achieve its functional state. The impact of environmental challenges during early ontogeny on adult song signaling[83–85] and vocal area size[86] is, likely, indirect through priming of the HPG axis, which specifies the level of secretion of androgens and estrogens in adulthood.

SEXUAL DIFFERENTIATION OF THE FUNCTIONAL VOCAL CIRCUIT IS SENSITIVE TO MULTIPLE ENDOCRINE SIGNALS

In the time period immediately after achieving a functional state, vocal neurons start to express many if not all neurochemical features of adults. Vocal neurons continue to contain receptors for gonadal hormones,[28–40] but start to express as well receptors for non-gonadal hormones, the pineal hormone melatonin,[79,87,88] for stress hormones such mineralocorticoids and glucocorticoids (Gahr and Metzdorf, unpublished), and for cytokines.[89] These neurochemical phenotypes suggest, that, in addition to being dependent on auditory feedback,[6,82] further vocal development is probably under the control of multiple endocrine signals that directly act on vocal neurons, bypassing the gonadal system. Such mechanisms might explain the impact of the socio-sexual environment on song development and performance.[90,91] This mechanism does not exclude indirect effects of the external (socio-sexual and physical) and internal (body physiology) environment on sexual signaling through action on the HPG axis, as discussed above for the earlier period, in which gonadal hormones are the dominant players. Since various entities of the body physiology such as the immune system are, in turn, sensitive to gonadal hormones,[92] we need to consider rather complex mechanisms underlying indirect and direct affects of gonadal steroids on song development and the adult overt phenotype.

We next discuss the impact of gonadal hormones (testosterone and estrogen) and of the pineal hormone melatonin on sexually attractive song pattern of adults in two case studies. The case of testosterone-dependent song pattern of adult canaries is reminiscent of the organizational action of hormones while that of melatonin-dependent song pattern of the adult zebra finches provides an example of activational hormone action.

Testosterone-Dependent Song Pattern of Adult Canaries

Androgens and estrogens directly or indirectly affect the neuron numbers, neuron morphology including size and synapses, metabolic activity, and protein and gene expression of vocal neuron populations of adult songbirds (for review see ref. 93). As neural bases for a direct action of sex hormones, androgen receptors are abundant in most vocal areas throughout life[28–38] (FIG. 2). Even Area X neurons express either in some individuals or under certain conditions (which we do not know) androgen receptors (Metzdorf and Gahr, unpublished data) (FIG. 2). Estrogen receptors are found only in HVC[40] and occur there mainly in Area X–projecting neurons.[94,95] Further, androgen and estrogen receptors occur, too, in the areas that send catecholaminergic fibers to the forebrain vocal areas.[96] In the following we like to point out that androgens and estrogens target different neural phenotypes, which correlates with androgen- and estrogen-specific song phenotypes.

Testosterone and its estrogenic metabolites are necessary for the development of stable songs typical of reproductively active male songbirds.[97–103] In the canary such songs are composed of syllables that are repeated identically several times (so-called tours) before switching to the next syllable.[104] Syllables are stereotyped sequences of one to three frequency modulations interrupted by short silent intervals.[104] Canaries need to learn parts of the syllable repertoire while the temporal organization of the song is innate.[7,8] Female canaries respond with increased nest-building activity to songs that are composed of large syllable repertoires.[105] Further, females respond to songs that contain tours with high repetition rates with increased numbers of courtship solicitation displays.[106–108] Thus, both innate and learned song pattern of the canary as well as of other species[109,110] are under sexual selection.

Fusani and colleagues[111] induced singing in adult female canaries through testosterone treatment, but inhibited in one group of such females the aromatization of testosterone into estrogens with an aromatase inhibitor (FIG. 3). Although songbirds have low levels of circulating estrogen, large amounts of estrogen can be produced in the brain from circulating testosterone.[69] Further, testosterone-induced develop-

A AR- and ERmRNA expression in the areas of the vocal control pathway

Brain Areas	AR (%)	ER (%)
HVC	100 (Z,C)	100 (Z,C)
RA	100 (Z,C)	0
mMAN	100 (Z,C)	0
lMAN	100 (Z,C)	0
NIF	25 (Z), 20 (C)	0
Area X	5 (Z)	0
DLM	20 (Z), 25 (C)	0
UVA	?	0
AVT	20 (Z)	0
nXII	100 (Z,C)	0
RAM	100 (Z,C)	0
rVRG	100 (Z,C)	0

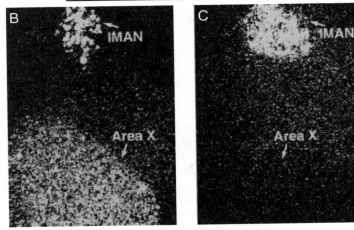

FIGURE 2. (A) The table shows the frequency with which we find androgen receptors (AR) and estrogen receptors (ER) in areas of the song system of adult male zebra finches (Z, $N = 40$) and canaries (C, $N = 25$). Neurons of all forebrain vocal areas have the potential to express androgen receptor mRNA. Area X neurons express in a few adult male zebra finches androgen receptors (**B**) while in most cases this mRNA is absent (**C**). Shown are dark-field photomicrographs of parasagittal sections of the lMAN and Area X. *Arrowheads* indicate the position of lMAN and Area X. Bar is 100 μm. (Gahr and Metzdorf, unpublished data.)

ment of male-like song in female canaries is accompanied by an increase in the expression and enzymatic activity of aromatase in the telencephalon near HVC.[112] After 3 to 4 weeks of testosterone treatment, females develop a male-like song, with the exception that such females sing few different syllables. In correlation with the male-like songs (long tours), the HVC size of singing females is similarly increased and different from untreated non-singing control females[111] (FIG. 3). The estrogen-deprived singing females differ, however, in that they produce tours with lower repetition rates compared to the non-deprived singing females.[111] This difference correlates with the decreased expression of BDNF, while another gene ATPsynthase,

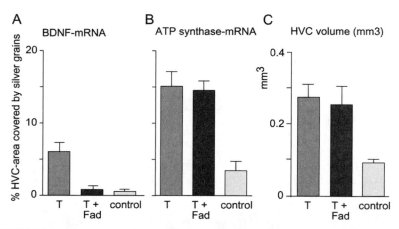

FIGURE 3. The expression level of BDNF-mRNA (**A**) is higher in testosterone-treated (T) females than in testosterone-treated females, in which estrogen formation (T+Fad) is inhibited, and than in control females. In contrast, the expression level of ATPsynthase-mRNA (**B**) and the size of HVC (**C**) is increased in both T and T+Fad females compared to control females but do not differ between T and T+Fad females. (From Fusani and colleagues,[111] with permission.)

involved in cellular metabolism, is expressed similarly in both groups (FIG. 3). The data suggest that certain neural phenotypes of vocal neurons are under androgenic control (HVC size, ATPsynthase expression) while others (BDNF expression) are under estrogenic control.[111] Similarly, BDNF expression is upregulated by estrogens in zebra finches.[64] The song activity of both groups of testosterone-induced singing females was similar, suggesting that the difference in BDNF expression level is not due to the singing activity, as proposed previously for male canaries.[113] The cellular mechanisms of song neurons sensitive to BDNF are currently not known, but members of the neurotrophin gene family, such as BDNF, are well known to affect the differentiation and functions of central neurons.[114,115] Although these works do not suggest that the BDNF level is the cause for the observed behavioral differences between the above experimental singers, they do suggest that hormone-dependent overall HVC morphology (reflected in HVC-volume) is necessary for the production of certain song pattern while others require hormone-dependent neurotransmission.

The syllable numbers of singing testosterone-treated females are, with some exceptions, very low.[103,111] As a consequence, the impact of sex hormones on syllable learning is difficult to study in these animals. It is evident that hormone-dependent protein synthesis of vocal neurons might facilitate or restrain or at least modify development of both innate and learned song pattern,[88,102,116] i.e., make vocal learning in general a matter of sexual selection.

Melatonin-Dependent Song Pattern of Adult Zebra Finches

Photoperiod has been identified as a factor for the differentiation of the volume of vocal areas[117–119] and melatonin was indicated as the mediating endocrine signal.[117] In difference to these works, we point in the following to melatonin as a sig-

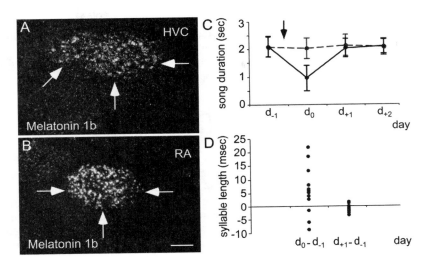

FIGURE 4. Neurons of the HVC (**A**) and RA (**B**) express the melatonin-1b (Mel-1b) receptor. Shown are dark-field photomicrographs of parasagittal sections. *Arrowheads* indicate the position of HVC and RA. Bar is 100 μm. In **C**, the song length before and after (*arrow*) application of a Mel-1b antagonist (*squares*) or a control vehicle (*circles*) is shown (mean ± SD). The song length is transiently reduced. In **D**, the difference between the lengths of the syllables at the day before and after (d_{-1}–d_0) and between the day before and the next day after (d_{-1}–d_{+1}) application of the inhibitor is shown. Syllable length except the length of introductory notes did change at d_0 compared to d_{-1} but was back to normal at d_{+1}. The plot includes syllables of two males. (From Jansen and colleagues,[120] with permission.)

nal that has rather activational function, modifying song pattern on a short-time scale.

In adult male zebra finches, HVC and RA express only the melatonin-1b receptor (Mel-1b)[120] (FIG. 4). Melatonin levels are high during the night and very low during the day.[121] Systemic application of a Mel-1b antagonist at the beginning of the night shortens the length of songs uttered the next day (FIG. 4). In these songs, syllables at the end of the strophes are frequently omitted and/or the length of those syllables is modified. RA and HVC are likely to control the song pattern of zebra finches.[122–124] These gene expression, electrophysiological, and behavioral data together suggest that the "melatonin–Mel-1b receptor" pathway of song control areas plays a crucial role in the production of the stereotyped individual song pattern. The nightly melatonin surge appears to prime the song control circuit to maintain its stereotyped neural activity during daytime singing episodes. This priming might involve the nightly episodes of spontaneous activity of RA neurons that are thought to shape motor output of the day-time singing period.[125,126]

Male zebra finches use their individual song to maintain contact with other zebra finches or their mates, but the song is also an integral feature of the male courtship behavior and female mate selection.[127–129] Effects on the song of adult zebra finches that depend on gonadal production of sex hormones are rather slow and long-lasting.[98,99] By contrast, the fast and transient effects of melatonin on the song pattern could mediate day-to-day changes in the socio-sexual and physical environment and thus guarantee honest signal value of the songs. The interpretation of these results in light of sexual selection theories, such as honest signaling, remains however speculative due to the lack of detailed knowledge concerning the control of melatonin production of birds other than the photoperiod.

CAUSAL RELATIONS BETWEEN HORMONE-DEPENDENT BEHAVIORAL AND NEURAL PHENOTYPES?

Since hormones affect, on one hand, song development and production and, on the other hand, the neuronal phenotypes of forebrain vocal areas, it is thought that gonadal hormones causally link individual neural variability to individual song learning and production. Considering the pattern of activity of HVC and RA neurons during singing,[122–124] this assumption appears warranted but suffers from the type of brain-behavior correlations performed. The correlations are widely done between the gross anatomical features of vocal areas, such as volume or neuron numbers, and song features, such as repertoire size, comparing either singers in a particular physiological condition within a species, among seasons, between sexes, or among species (see refs. 130–133 for review).

Although singing is frequently restricted to males, species do vary in the extent to which females are vocal. Accordingly, HVC and RA are larger in males than in females, and the extent of this difference is correlated with the extent of sexual dimorphism in singing behavior and repertoire size in some species (see refs. 131 and 132 for review). This trend does, however, include some important noise, such as large HVC sexual differences in species with similar song repertoires in both sexes, for example, the bush shrike (*Laniarius funebris*).[131] In this dueting species the size of the forebrain vocal control areas HVC and RA and its neuron numbers are about twice as large in males compared to females. Further, neuron soma size is similar between males and females in the song motor nucleus nXIIts and in the RA, but sexually dimorphic in the HVC. However, song types are of similar complexity in both sexes and repertoire size in captive shrikes does not differ between males and females. This suggests that the sex difference in the size of vocal control areas, its neuron numbers, and neuron size does not explain sex-typical vocal behavior in the shrike.

In several species, seasonal changes in singing behavior parallel changes in HVC size.[133] This pattern is, however, not universal and some species do not show such a correlation: In the rufous-sided towhee (*Pipilo erythrophthalmus*), HVC volume changes seasonally without seasonal changes in the song.[134] Male canaries (*Serinus canaria*) appear to lose song units (syllables) after the breeding season and learn new ones until the next breeding season.[135] Testosterone-dependent neuroanatomical changes, neuron death, and addition of new neurons in the song control nuclei HVC and RA are thought to be responsible for the seasonal changes in their song temporal pattern and learned song repertoire.[136–139] In a longitudinal field study of individual free-living (wild) canaries, a different mode of seasonal behavioral plasticity, seasonal activation, and inactivation of auditory-motor memories was obvious[140] (FIG. 5). The song repertoire composition of wild canaries changes seasonally: about 25% of the syllables are sung seasonally, the remainder occurs year-round, despite

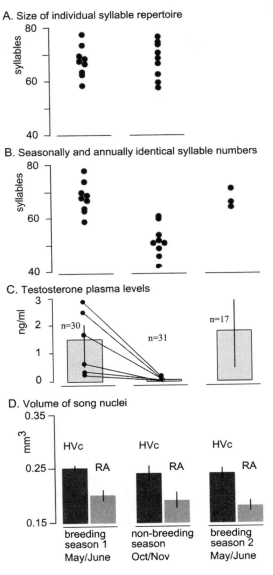

FIGURE 5. Seasonal and annual changes in the total number of song syllables (**A**), the number of permanent song syllables (**B**), testosterone plasma levels (**C**), and the size of the forebrain vocal areas HVC and RA (**D**) of individual free-living wild male canaries. The size of the syllable repertoire and the size of the vocal control areas remained unchanged whereas a remarkable seasonal change occurred in the plasma testosterone (T) level and in the repertoire composition. However, the individuals recovered many syllables that were seasonally lost on an annual basis. Volumes are medians and quartiles. T levels are medians and quartiles of the entire breeding or non-breeding seasons. Connected dots in (**C**) indicate seasonal changes in the T levels of the same individuals. (From Leitner and colleagues,[140] with permission.)

seasonal changes in the temporal patterns of song. In the breeding season, males sing an increased number of fast frequency-modulated syllables, which are sexually attractive for females, in correlation with seasonally increased testosterone levels (FIG. 5). About half of the syllables that were lost after one breeding season reappear in the following breeding season. Furthermore, some identical syllable sequences are reactivated on an annual basis. The seasonal plasticity in vocal behavior of wild canaries occurred despite gross anatomical and ultrastructural stability of the forebrain song control areas HVC and RA.[140]

Although, some studies suggest a link between hormone-dependent song features, such as song repertoire size, and hormone-dependent neuroanatomy, such as HVC size, the above examples, the example of androgen- and estrogen-dependent song pattern of female canaries, and the example of melatonin-dependent song pattern suggest that the picture is far more complex. It is particularly worrisome that even intra-species comparisons, that circumvent the problem of identifying comparable song units, do not show a unified picture. The work of Fusani[111] and Jansen[120] suggest one possible explanation: The size of vocal areas does not always correlate with all cellular phenotypes, such as expression level of certain genes or firing rate of vocal neurons, and does not correlate with all behavioral phenotypes. This suggests that neuronal phenotypes that are much closer to neurotransmission than area size and neuron numbers are likely to correlate with the overt song phenotype.

SUMMARY

These data suggest the following mechanisms for determination and specification of the of the song system that is required to produce sexual signals, i.e., to be a member of the reproductive pool (FIG. 6). Genetic brain-intrinsic mechanisms determine the neuron pools that develop into forebrain song control areas independent of sex steroids (FIG. 6, "1"). One fate of these neurons is the potential to express sex steroid receptors such as androgen and estrogen receptors. Genetic brain-intrinsic mechanisms determine the activity of hypothalamic-pituitary-gonad (HPG) axis, i.e., the working range and responsiveness of HPG axis to produce gonadal hormones (FIG. 6, "2"). The epigenetic action of gonadal steroid hormones, androgens and estrogens, on determined vocal neurons is required to maintain and increase the pool of determined vocal neurons and to complete the connections of the vocal system, i.e., to make it function motorically (FIG. 6, "3"). The net outcome of these developmental mechanisms, that run independent of auditory input, are forebrain areas that are hodologically, anatomically, and neurochemically distinct from surrounding tissues and distinct from homologous brain regions of non-oscines, that show a high degree of individual differences, such as brain area sizes and neuron numbers, and that are determined to unfold specific neuronal phenotypes under the subsequent influence of environmental information. These environmental information, including both external (socio-sexual and physical) and internal (body physiology) signals, specifies the further neural phenotype of vocal areas either through acting on the HPG axis and differential release of gonadal hormones (FIG. 6, "4") or through non-gonadal hormone systems, both of which have target neurons in the functional vocal system (FIG. 6, "5"). The discussion of the role of sensory input for the specification of the song system is discussed in detail by Brainard in this volume. Despite the clear evi-

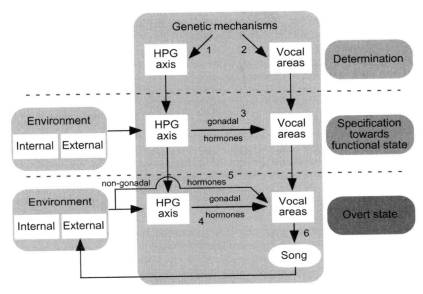

FIGURE 6. A scenario of sexual differentiation of the adult song pattern.

dence of hormone dependency of the development of both the adult song phenotype and song system phenotype, their causal relation is complex (FIG. 6, "6").

ACKNOWLEDGMENT

I thank Anton Pieneman for help with the artwork.

REFERENCES

1. SEARCY, W.A. & K. YASUKAWA. 1996. Song and female choice. *In* Ecology and Evolution of Acoustic Communication in Birds. D.E. Kroodsma & E.H. Miller, Eds: 454–473. Cornell University Press. New York.
2. CATCHPOLE, C.K. & P.J.B. SLATER. 1995. Bird Song: Biological Themes and Variations. Cambridge University Press.
3. ANDERSSON, M. 1994. Sexual Selection. Princeton University Press. Princeton, NJ.
4. GRAFEN, A. 1990. Biological signals as handicaps. J. Theor. Biol. **144:** 517–546.
5. ROWE, L. & D. HOULE. 1996. The lek paradox and the capture of genetic variance by condition dependent traits. Proc. R. Soc. London B. Biol. Sci. **263:** 1215–1421.
6. KONISHI, M. 1965. The role of auditory feedback in the control of vocalization in the white-crowned sparrow. Z. Tierpsychol. **22:** 770–783.
7. GÜTTTINGER, H.R. 1979. The integration of learnt and genetically programmed behaviour: a study of hierarchical organization in songs of canaries, greenfinches and their hybrids. Z. Tierpsychol. **49:** 285–303.

8. GÜTTINGER, H.R. 1981. Self-differentiation of song organization rules by deaf canaries. Z. Tierpsychol **56:** 323–340.
9. MARLER, P. 1991. Song-learning behavior: the interface with neuroethology. Trends Neurosci. **14:** 199–206.
10. MARLER, P. 1997. Three models of song learning: evidence from behavior. J. Neurobiol. **33:** 501–516.
11. LEITNER, S. *et al.* 2002. Song and the song control pathway in the brain can develop independently of exposure to song in the sedge warbler. Proc. Royal Soc. London B **269:** 2519–2524.
12. NOTTEBOHM, F., T.M. STOKES & C.M. LEONARD. 1976. Central control of song in the canary, *Serinus canaria.* J. Comp. Neurol. **165:** 457–486.
13. BOTTJER, S.W., E.A MIESNER & A.P ARNOLD. 1984. Forebrain lesions disrupt development but not maintenance of song in passerine birds. Science **224:** 901–902.
14. SCHARFF, C. & F. NOTTEBOHM. 1991. A comparative study of the behavioral deficits following lesions of various parts of the zebra finch song system: implications for vocal learning. J. Neurosci. **11:** 2896–2913.
15. BENTON, S. *et al.* 1998. Anterior forebrain pathway is needed for stable song expression in adult white-crowned sparrow (*Zonotrichia leucophrys*). Behav. Brain. Res. **96:** 135–150.
16. LEONARDO, A. & M. KONISHI. 1999. Decrystallization of adult birdsong by perturbation of auditory feedback. Nature **399:** 466–470.
17. SCHARFF, C., J.R. KIRN, M. GROSSMAN, *et al.* 2000. Targeted neuronal death affects neuronal replacement and vocal behavior in adult songbirds. Neuron **25:** 481–492.
18. BRAINARD, M.S. & A.J. DOUPE. 2000. Interruption of a basal ganglia-forebrain circuit prevents plasticity of learned vocalizations. Nature **113:** 762–726.
19. HALLE, F. *et al.* 2003. Effects of unilateral lesions of HVC on song patterns of males domesticated canaries. J. Neurobiol. **56:** 303–314.
20. GIL, D. & M. GAHR. 2002. The honesty of bird song: multiple constraints for multiple traits. Trends Ecol. Evol. **17:** 133–140.
21. GAHR, M. & R. METZDORF. 1999. The sexually dimorphic expression of androgen receptors in the song nucleus hyperstriatalis ventrale pars caudale of the zebra finch develops independently of gonadal steroids. J. Neurosci. **19:** 2628–2636.
22. CARRUTH, L.L. *et al.* 2002. Sex chromosome genes directly affect brain sexual differentiation. Nat. Neurosci. **5:** 933–934.
23. AGATE, R.J. *et al.* 2003. Neural, not gonadal, origin of brain sex differences in a gynandromorphic finch. Proc. Natl. Acad. Sci. USA **100:** 4873–4878.
24. GAHR, M. 2003. Male Japanese quails with female brains do not show male sexual behaviors. Proc. Natl. Acad. Sci. USA **100:** 7959–7964.
25. ARNOLD, A.P. & R.A. GORSKI. 1984. Gonadal steroid induction of structural sex differences in the central nervous system. Annu. Rev. Neurosci. **7:** 413–442.
26. CARSON-JURICA, M.A., W.T. SCHRADER & B.W. O'MALLEY. 1990. Steroid receptor family: structure and functions. Endocr. Rev. **11:** 201–220.
27. BEYER, C. *et al.* 2002. Cell-type specificity of non-classical estrogen signaling in the developing midbrain. J. Steroid Biochem. Mol. Biol. **81:** 319–325.
28. ARNOLD, A.P., F. NOTTEBOHM & D.W. PFAFF. 1976. Hormone concentrating cells in vocal control and other areas of the brain of the zebra finch (*Poephila guttata*). J. Comp. Neurol. **165:** 487–511.
29. GAHR, M. 1990. Localization of androgen receptors and estrogen receptors in the same cells of the songbird brain. Proc. Natl. Acad. Sci. USA **87:** 9445–9448.
30. BALTHAZART, J. *et al.* 1992. Immunocytochemical localization of androgen receptors in the male songbird and quail brain. J. Comp. Neurol. **317:** 407–420.
31. NASTIUK, K.L. & D.F. CLAYTON. 1995. The canary androgen receptor mRNA is localized in the song control nuclei of the brain and is rapidly regulated by testosterone. J. Neurobiol. **26:** 213–224.
32. GAHR, M., R. METZDORF & S. ASCHENBRENNER. 1996. The ontogeny of the canary HVC revealed by the expression of androgen and oestrogen receptors. NeuroReport **8:** 311–315.

33. GAHR, M. & R. METZDORF. 1997. Distribution and dynamics in the expression of androgen and estrogen receptors in vocal control systems of songbirds. Brain Res. Bull. **44:** 509–517.
34. BERNARD, D.J, G.E. BENTLEY, J. BALTHAZART, *et al.* 1999. Androgen receptor, estrogen receptor alpha, and estrogen receptor beta show distinct patterns of expression in forebrain song control nuclei of European starlings. Endocrinology **140:** 4633–4643.
35. METZDORF, R., M. GAHR & L. FUSANI. 1999. Distribution of aromatase, estrogen receptor, and androgen receptor mRNA in the forebrain of songbirds and nonsongbirds. J. Comp. Neurol. **407:** 115–129.
36. SOMA, K.K. *et al.* 1999. Seasonal changes in androgen receptor immunoreactivity in the song nucleus HVC of a wild bird. J. Comp. Neurol. **409:** 224–236.
37. GAHR, M. 2000. Neural song control system of hummingbirds: comparison to swifts, vocal learning (songbirds) and nonlearning (suboscines) passerines, and vocal learning (budgerigars) and nonlearning (dove, owl, gull quail, chicken) nonpasserines. J. Comp. Neurol. **426:** 182–196.
38. FUSANI, L., T. VAN'T HOF, J.B. HUTCHISON & M.J. GAHR. 2000. Seasonal expression of androgen receptors, oestrogen receptors and aromatase in the canary brain in relation to circulating androgens and oestrogens. J. Neurobiol. **43:** 254–268.
39. GAHR, M. *et al.* 1987. Immunocytochemical localization of estrogen-binding neurons in the songbird brain. Brain Res. **402:** 173–177.
40. GAHR, M., H.R. GÜTTINGER & D.E. KROODSMA. 1993. Estrogen receptors in the avian brain: survey reveals general distribution and forebrain areas unique to songbirds. J. Comp. Neurol. **327:** 112–122.
41. GODSAVE, S.F. *et al.* 2002. Androgen receptors in the embryonic zebra finch hindbrain suggest a function for maternal androgens in perihatching survival. J. Comp. Neurol. **453:** 57–70.
42. PERLMAN, W.R. *et al.* 2003. Expression of androgen receptor mRNA in the late embryonic and early posthatch zebra finch brain. J. Comp. Neurol. **455:** 513–530.
43. PERLMAN, W.R. & A.P. ARNOLD. 2003. Expression of estrogen receptor and aromatase mRNAs in embryonic and posthatch zebra finch brain. J. Neurobiol. **55:** 204–219.
44. GAHR, M. & E. BALABAN. 1996. The development of a species difference in the local distribution of brain estrogen receptive cells. Dev. Brain Res. **92:** 182–189.
45. LISCIOTTO, C.A. & J.I. MORELL. 1993. Circulating gonadal steroid hormones regulate estrogen receptor mRNA in the male rat forebrain. Brain Res. **20:** 79–90.
46. BURGESS, L.H. & R.J. HANDA. 1993. Hormonal regulation of androgen receptor mRNA in the brain and anterior pituitary gland of the male rat. Mol. Brain Res. **19:** 31–38.
47. SCHLINGER, B.A & A.P. ARNOLD. 1992. Plasma sex steroids and tissue aromatization in hatchling zebra finches: implications for the sexual differentiation of singing behavior. Endocrinol. **130:** 289–299.
48. WILSON, J.A. & B. GLICK. 1970. Am. J. Physiol. **218:** 951–955.
49. ADKINS, E.K. & N.T. ADLER. 1972 J. Comp. Physiol. Psychol. **81:** 27–36.
50. VATES, G.E. *et al.* 1997. Reafferent thalamo-cortical loops in the song system of oscine songbirds. J. Comp. Neurol. **380:** 275–290.
51. WILD, J.M. 1997. Neural pathways for the control of birdsong production. J. Neurobiol. **33:** 653–670.
52. KONISHI, M.& E. AKUTAGAWA. 1985. Neuronal growth, atrophy and death in a sexually dimorphic song nucleus in the zebra finch brain. Nature **315:** 145–147.
53. MOONEY, R. 1992. Synaptic basis for developmental plasticity in a birdsong nucleus. J. Neurosci. **12:** 2464–2477.
54. MOONEY, R. & M. RAO. 1994. Waiting periods versus early innervation: the development of axonal connections on the zebra finch song system. J. Neurosci. **14:** 6532–6543.
55. IMMELMANN, K. 1969. Song development in the zebra finch and other estrildid finches. *In* Bird Vocalizations. R.A. Hind, Ed.: 61–74. Cambridge University Press.
56. KONISHI, M. & E. AKUTAGAWA. 1987. Hormonal control of cell death in a sexually dimorphic song nucleus in the zebra finch. *In* Selective Neuronal Death. Ciba Foundation Symposium 126. pp. 173–185. Wiley. New York.

57. SAKAGUCHI, H. & N. SAITO. 1989. The acetylcholine and catecholamine contents in song control nuclei of zebra finch during song ontogeny. Dev. Brain. Res. **47:** 313–317.

58. SKAGUCHI, H. 1996. Sex differences in the developmental changes of GABAergic neurons in zebra finch song control nuclei. Exp. Brain Res. **108:** 62–68.

59. GURNEY, M.E. & M. KONISHI. 1980. Hormone-induced sexual differentiation of brain and behavior in zebra finches. Science **208:** 1380–1383.

60. GURNEY, M.E. 1981. Hormonal control of cell form and number in the zebra finch song system. J. Neurosci. **1:** 658–673.

61. POHL-APEL, G. 1985. The correlation between the degree of brain masculinization and song quality in estradiol treated female zebra finches. Brain Res. **336:** 381–383.

62. SIMPSON, H.B. & D.S. VICARIO. 1991. Early estrogen treatment alone causes female zebra finches to produce learned, male-like vocalization. J. Neurobiol. **22:** 755–776.

63. CASTO, J.M. & G.F. BALL. 1996. Early administration of 17beta-estradiol partially masculinizes song control regions and alpha2-adrenergic receptor distribution in European starlings (*Sturnus vulgaris*). Horm. Behav. **30:** 387–406.

64. DITTRICH, F., Y. FENG, R. METZDORF & M. GAHR. 1999. Estrogen-inducible, sex- of brain-derived neurotrophic factor mRNA in a forebrain song control nucleus of the juvenile zebra finch. Proc. Natl. Acad. Sci. USA **96:** 8221–8246.

65. HOLLOWAY, C.C. & D.F. CLAYTON. 2001. Estrogen synthesis in the male brain triggers development of the avian song control pathway in-vitro. Nat. Neurosci. **4:** 170–175.

66. GRISHAM, W., G.A. MATHEWS & A.P. ARNOLD. 1994. Local intracerebral implants of estrogen masculinize some aspects of the zebra finch song system. J. Neurobiol. **25:** 185–196.

67. HERRMANN, K. & A.P. ARNOLD. 1991. Lesions of HVC block the developmental masculinizing effects of estradiol in the female zebra finch song system. J. Neurobiol. **22:** 29–39.

68. GAHR, M. & M. KONISIHI. 1988. Developmental changes in estrogen-sensitive neurons in the forebrain of the zebra finch. Proc. Natl. Acad. Sci USA **85:** 7380–7383.

69. SCHLINGER, B. & A.P. ARNOLD. 1991. Brain is the major site of estrogen synthesis in a male songbird. Proc. Natl. Acad. Sci. USA **88:** 2191–2194.

70. KIRN, J.R. & T.J. DEVOOGD. 1989. Genesis and death of vocal control neurons during sexual differentiation in the zebra finch. J. Neurosci. **9:** 3176–3187.

71. AKUTAGAWA, E. & M. KONISHI. 2001. A monoclonal antibody specific to a song system nuclear antigen in estrildine finches. Neuron **31:** 545–556.

72. KONISHI, M. & E. AKUTAGAWA. 1988. A critical period for estrogen action on neurons of the song control system in the zebra finch. Proc. Natl. Acad. Sci. USA **85:** 7006–7007.

73. SCHWABL, H. 1993. Yolk is a source of maternal testosterone for developing birds. Proc. Natl. Acad. Sci. USA **90:** 11446–11450.

74. SCHWABL, H. 1996. Maternal testosterone in the avian egg enhances postnatal growth. Comp Biochem Physiol A Physiol **114:** 271–276.

75. GIL, D., J. GRAVES, N. HAZON & A. WELLS. 1999. Male attractiveness and differential testosterone investment in zebra finch eggs. Science **286:** 126–128.

76. EISING, C.M., C. EIKENAAR, H. SCHWABL & T.G. GROOTHUIS. 2001. Maternal androgens in black-headed gull (*Larus ridibundus*) eggs: consequences for chick development. Proc. R. Soc. Lond. B Biol. Sci. **268:** 839–846.

77. LOHMANN, R. & M. GAHR. 2000. Muscle-dependent and hormone-dependent differentiation of the vocal control premotor nucleus robustus archistriatalis and the motornucleus hypoglossus pars tracheosyringealis of the zebra finch. J. Neurobiol. **42:** 220–231.

78. GAHR, M. & J.M. WILD. 1997. Localization of androgen receptor mRNA-containing cells in avian respiratory-vocal nuclei: an in situ hybridization study. J. Neurobiol. **33:** 865–876.

79. GAHR, M. & E. KOSAR. 1996. Identification, distribution, and developmental changes of a melatonin binding site in the song control system of the zebra finch. J. Comp. Neurol. **367:** 308–318.

80. BUREK, M.J. *et al.* 1991 Neuron loss and addition in developing zebra finch song nuclei are independent of auditory experience during song learning. Neurobiol. **22:** 215–223.

81. BRENOWITZ, E.A. *et al.* 1995. Brain space for learned song in birds develops independently of song learning. J. Neurosci. **15:** 6281–6286.
82. IYENGAR, S. & S.W. BOTTJER. 2002. The role of auditory experience in the formation of neural circuits underlying vocal learning in zebra finches. J. Neurosci. **22:** 946–958.
83. NOWICKI, S. *et al.* 1998. Song learning, early nutrition and sexual selection in songbirds. Am. Zool. **38:** 179–190.
84. NOWICKI, S. *et al.* 2000. Nestling growth and song repertoire size in the Great Reed Warblers: evidence for song learning as an indicator mechanism in female choice. Proc. R. Soc. Lond. Ser. B Biol. Sci. **267:** 2219–2424.
85. SPENCER, K.A. *et al.* 2003. Song as an honest signal of developmental stress in the zebra finch (*Taeniopygia guttata*). Horm. Behav. **44:** 132–139.
86. WARD, B.C. *et al.* 2001. Anatomical and ontogenetic factors producing variation in HVc neuron number in zebra finches. Brain Res. **904:** 318–326.
87. WHITFIELD-RUCKER, M.G. & V.M. CASSONE. 1996. Melatonin binding in the house sparrow song control system: sexual dimorphism and the effect of photoperiod. Horm. Behav. **30:** 528–537.
88. BENTLEY, G.E. & G.F. BALL. 2000. Photoperiod-dependent and -independent regulation of melatonin receptors in the forebrain of songbirds. J. Neuroendocrinol. **12:** 745–752.
89. LOUISSAINt, A. Jr. *et al.* 2002. Coordinated interaction of neurogenesis and angiogenesis in the adult songbird brain. Neuron **34:** 945–960.
90. TCHERNICHOVSKI, O. & F. NOTTEBOHM. 1998. Social inhibition of song imitation among sibling male zebra finches. Proc. Natl. Acad. Sci. USA **95:** 8951–8956.
91. TRAMONTIN, A.D. *et al.* 1999. Contributions of social cues and photoperiod to seasonal plasticity in the adult avian song control system. J. Neurosci. **19:** 476–483.
92. TANRIVERDI, F. *et al.* 2003. The hypothalamic-pituitary-gonadal axis: immune function and autoimmunity. J. Endocrinol. **176:** 293–304.
93. BALL, G.F. *et al.* 2002. Neuroendocrinology of song behavior and avian brain plasticity: multiple sites of action of sex steroid hormones. Front. Neuroendocrinol. **23:** 137–178.
94. GAHR, M. 1990. Delineation of a brain nucleus: comparison of cytochemical, hodological, and cytoarchitectural views of the song control nucleus HVc of the adult canary. J. Comp. Neurol. **294:** 30–36.
95. JOHNSON, F. & S.W. BOTTJER. 1995. Differential estrogen accumulation among populations of projection neurons in the higher vocal center of male canaries. J. Neurobiol. **26:** 87–108.
96. MANEY, D.L. *et al.* 2001. Gonadal steroid receptor mRNA in catecholaminergic nuclei of the canary brainstem. Neurosci. Lett. **311:** 189–192.
97. LEONARD, S.L. 1939. Induction of singing in female canaries by injections of male hormone. Proc. Soc. Exp. Biol. **21:** 229–230.
98. PRÖVE, E. 1974. Der Einfluss von Kastration und Testosteronsubstitution auf das Sexualverhalten maennlicher Zebrafinken (*Taeniopygia guttata castanotis* Gould). J. Ornithol. **115:** 338-347.
99. ARNOLD, A.P. 1975. The effects of castration and androgen replacement on song, courtship and aggression in zebra finches. J. Exp. Zool. **191:** 301–325.
100. MARLER, P., S. PETERS, G.F. BALL, *et al.* 1988. The role of sex steroids in the acquisition and production of birdsong. Nature **336:** 369–378.
101. HEID, P., H.R. GÜTTINGER & E. PRÖVE. 1985. The influence of castration and testosterone replacement on the song architecture of canaries (*Serinus canaria*). Z. Tierpsychol. **69:** 224–236.
102. BOTTJER, S.W. & S.J. HEWER. 1992. Castration and antisteroid treatment impair vocal learning in male zebra finches. J. Neurobiol. **23:** 337–618.
103. HARTLEY, R.S. & R.A. SUTHERS. 1990. Lateralization of syringeal function during song production in the canary. J. Neurobiol. **21:** 1236–1248.
104. GÜTTINGER, H.R. 1985. Consequences of domestication on the song structures in the canary. Behaviour **94:** 254–278.
105. KROODSMA, D.E. 1976. Reproductive development in a female songbird: differential stimulation by quality of male song. Science **192:** 574–575.

106. KREUTZER, M. & E. VALLET. 1991. Differences in the response of captive female canaries to variation in conspecific and heterospecific songs. Behaviour 117: 106–116.
107. VALLET, E. & M. KREUTZER. 1995. Female canaries are sexually responsive to special song phrases. Anim. Behav. 49: 1603–1610.
108. DRAGANOIU, T., L. NAGLE & M. KREUTZER. 2002. Directional female preference for an exaggerated male trait in canary (Serinus canaria) song. Proc. R. Soc. Lond. Ser. B Biol. Sci. 269: 2525–2531.
109. Hasselquist, D. et al. 1996. Correlation between male song repertoire, extra-pair paternity and offspring survival in the great reed warbler. Nature 381: 229–232.
110. NOWICKI, S. et al. 2002. Quality of song learning affects female response to male bird song. Proc. R. Soc. Lond. Ser. B Biol. Sci. 269: 1949–1954.
111. FUSANI, L. et al. 2003. Aromatase inhibition affects testosterone-induced masculinization of song and the neural song system in female canaries. J. Neurobiol. 54: 370–379.
112. FUSANI, L., J.B. HUTCHISON & M. GAHR. 2001. Testosterone regulates the activity and expression of aromatase in the canary neostriatum. J. Neurobiol. 49: 1–8.
113. RASIKA, S., A. ALVAREZ-BUYLLA & F. NOTTEBOHM. 1999. BDNF mediates the effects of testosterone on the survival of new neurons in an adult brain. Neuron 22: 53–62.
114. BONHOEFFER, T. 1996. Neurotrophins and activity-dependent development of the neocortex. Curr. Opin. Neurobiol 6: 119–126.
115. MARTY, S., M.P. BERZAGHI & B. BERINGER. 1997. Neurotrophins and activity-dependent plasticity of cortical interneurons. Trends Neurosci. 20: 198–202.
116. GÜTTINGER, H.R., H. FUCHS & G. SCHWAGER. 1990. Das Gesangslernen und seine Beziehung zur Gehirnentwicklung beim Kanarienvogel (Serinus canaria). Die Vogelwarte 35: 287–300.
117. BENTLEY, G.E., T.J. VAN'T HOF & G.F. BALL. 1999. Seasonal neuroplasticity in the songbird telencephalon: a role for melatonin. Proc. Natl. Acad. Sci. USA 96: 4674–4679.
118. GULLEDGE, C.C. & P. DEVICHE. 1998. Photoperiod and testosterone independently affect vocal control region volumes in adolescent male songbirds. J. Neurobiol. 36: 550–558.
119. DEVICHE, P. & C.C. GULLEDGE. 2000. Vocal control region sizes of an adult female songbird change seasonally in the absence of detectable circulating testosterone concentrations. J. Neurobiol. 42: 202–211.
120. JANSEN, R., R. METZDORF, M. ROEST, et al. Melatonin-dependent song pattern of adult male zebra finches. Submitted for publication.
121. VAN'T HOF, T.J. & E. GWINNER. 1996. Development of post-hatching melatonin rhythm in zebra finches (Poephila guttata). Experientia 52: 249–252.
122. VU, E., E. MAZUREK & K. KUO. 1994. Identification of a forebrain motor programming network for the learned song of zebra finches. J. Neurosci. 14: 6924–6934.
123. YU, A.C., A.S. DAVE & D. MARGOLIASH. 1996. Temporal hierarchical control of singing in birds. Science 273: 1871–1875.
124. HAHNLOSER, R.H.R., A.A. KOZHEVNIKOV & M.S. FEE. 2002. An ultra-sparse code underlies the generation of neural sequences in a songbird. Nature 219: 65–70.
125. DAVE, A.S., A.C. YU & D. MARGOLIASH. 1998. Behavioral state modulation of auditory activity in a vocal motor system. Science 282: 2250–2254.
126. DAVE, A.S. & D. MARGOLIASH. 2000. Song replay during sleep and computational rules for sensorimotor vocal learning. Science 290: 812–816.
127. SOSSINKA, R. & J. BÖHNER. 1980. Song types in the zebra finch Poephila guttata castanotis. Z. Tierpsychol. 53: 123–128.
128. CLAYTON, N.C. & E. PROVE. 1989. Song discrimination in female zebra finches and Bengalese finches. Anim. Behav. 8: 352–354.
129. NEUBAUER, R.L. 1999. Super normal length preferences of female zebra finches (Taeniopygia guttata) and a theory of the evolution of bird song. Evol. Ecol. 13: 365–380.
130. DEVOOGD, T.J. et al. 1993. Relations between song repertoire size and the volume of brain nuclei related to song: comparative evolutionary analyses amongst oscine birds. Proc. R. Soc. London B. Biol. Sci. 254: 75–82.

131. GAHR, M., E. SONNENSCHEIN & W. WICKLER. 1998. Sex differences in the size of the neural song control regions in a dueting songbird with similar song repertoire size of males and females. J. Neurosci. **18:** 1124–1131.

132. MACDOUGALL-SHACKELTON, S.A. & G.F. BALL. 1999. Comparative studies of sex differences in the song control system of songbirds. Trends Neurosci. **22:** 432–436.

133. TRAMONTIN, A.D. & E.A. BRENOWITZ. 2000. Seasonal plasticity in the adult brain. Trends Neurosci. **23:** 251–258.

134. BRENOWITZ, E.A., B. NAFIS, J.C. WINGFIELD & D.E. KROODSMA. 1991. Seasonal changes in avian song nuclei without seasonal changes in song repertoire. J. Neurosci. **11:** 1367–1374.

135. NOTTEBOHM, F., M.E. NOTTEBOHM & L.A. CRANE. 1986. Development and seasonal changes in canary song and their relation to changes in the anatomy of song control nuclei. Behav. Neur. Biol. **46:** 445–471.

136. NOTTEBOHM, F. 1981. A brain for all seasons: cyclical anatomical changes in song control nuclei of the canary brain. Science **214:** 1368–1370.

137. ALVAREZ-BUYLLA, A. & J. KIRN. 1997. Birth. migration, incorporation and death of vocal control neurons in adult songbirds. J. Neurosci. **33:** 585–601.

138. RASIKA, S., F. NOTTEBOHM & A. ALVAREZ-BUYLLA. 1994. Testosterone increases the recruitment and/or survival of new high vocal center neurons in adult female canaries. Proc. Natl. Acad. Sci. USA **91:** 7854–7858.

139. KIRN, J.R., B. O'LOUGHLIN, S. KASPARIAN & F. NOTTEBOHM. 1994. Cell death and neuronal recruitment in the high vocal center of adult male canaries are temporally related to changes in song. Proc. Natl. Acad. Sci. USA **91:** 7844–7848.

140. LEITNER, S., C. VOIGT, L.M. GARCIA-SEGURA, et al. 2001. Seasonal activation and inactivation of song motor memories in free living canaries is not reflected in neuroanatomical changes of forebrain song areas. Horm. Behav. **40:** 160–168.

Song Function and the Evolution of Female Preferences

Why Birds Sing, Why Brains Matter

STEPHEN NOWICKI[a] AND WILLIAM A. SEARCY[b]

[a]*Department of Biology, Duke University, Durham, North Carolina 27708, USA*

[b]*Department of Biology, University of Miami, Coral Gables, Florida 33124, USA*

ABSTRACT: Analyzing the function of song and its evolution as a communication signal provides an essential backdrop for understanding the physiological and neural mechanisms responsible for song learning, perception, and production. The reverse also is true—understanding the mechanisms underlying song learning provides insight into how song has evolved as a communication signal. Song has two primary functions: to repel other males from a defended space and to attract females and stimulate their courtship. The developmental stress hypothesis we present here builds on studies of the development of the song system to suggest how learned features of song, including complexity and local dialect structure, can serve as indicators of male quality useful to females in mate choice. The link between song and male quality depends on the fact that brain structures underlying song learning largely develop during the first few months post-hatching and that during this same period, songbirds are likely to be subject to nutritional and other developmental stresses. Individuals faring well in the face of stress are able to invest more resources to brain development and are expected to be correspondingly better at song learning. Learned features of song thus become reliable indicators of male quality, with reliability maintained by the developmental costs of song. Data from both field and laboratory studies are now beginning to provide broad support for the developmental stress hypothesis, illustrating the utility of connecting mechanistic and evolutionary analyses of song learning.

KEYWORDS: female choice; sexual selection; song development; nutritional stress; indicator mechanism; reliable signaling

INTRODUCTION

Syrinx, according to Greek mythology, was a nymph who chanced to attract the unwanted attentions of Pan, the amorous god of fields, flocks, and fertility. Syrinx fled from Pan, but he pursued her relentlessly, eventually trapping the unfortunate nymph at the marshy edge of a stream. There, in a final effort to preserve her chastity, Syrinx was transformed into a reed, which Pan took and turned into a flute—the pan-

Address for correspondence: Stephen Nowicki, Department of Biology, Duke University, Durham, North Carolina 27708, USA. Voice: 919-684-6950; fax: 919-660-7293.
snowicki@acpub.duke.edu; <http://www.biology.duke.edu/nowicki/about.html>

Ann. N.Y. Acad. Sci. 1016: 704–723 (2004). © 2004 New York Academy of Sciences.
doi: 10.1196/annals.1298.012

pipe—that he played ever after in her memory. Some thousands of years after this myth originated, comparative anatomists thought it fitting to name the vocal apparatus of birds in honor of the nymph Syrinx, given the extraordinarily musical and flute-like sounds this organ can produce.

The choice of the name "syrinx" for the avian sound-producing organ is apt for another reason, having to do with Pan's intentions rather than Syrinx's fate, and specifically with the similarity between Pan's motivation and that of a singing male bird. For all the beauty of bird song and the intricacies of its production, the function of song nonetheless boils down to sex. A male bird's song attracts females and stimulates them to mate. Song also is directed at other males, but the point of the effort typically is to gain exclusive access to an area so that females will settle there for nesting. Either way, song has evolved in the context of singers being selected to increase their individual reproductive success.

Understanding the function of song is important even for the most reductionist analyses because function defines the context in which the mechanisms responsible for the development, production, and perception of song have evolved. We therefore begin this chapter by providing an overview of how song functions as a communication signal. The transfer of insight between ultimate and proximate levels of analysis is, however, a two-way street. A second aim of this essay is to suggest that the question of why female birds respond preferentially to certain features of male song (a persistent problem for behavioral ecologists) might be clarified by considering the brain mechanisms responsible for song learning and production, especially their development. Thus, the remainder of this chapter focuses on implications of these developmental mechanisms for female preferences based on song. Here, we outline an hypothesis that we think can explain how song functions as an indicator of male quality, based on developmental trade-offs affecting brain growth and learning abilities, and we review data from our own work and that of others that addresses predictions of this hypothesis.

THE FUNCTIONS OF BIRD SONG

Does Song Repel Males?

In most species, the peak of singing activity is associated with breeding.[1,2] During this time, males often sing for hours on end without obviously interacting with other birds, and it is difficult to know whether females, other males, or both are the intended audience. However, if two males interact aggressively, as for example when a neighbor crosses an established territory boundary, they often increase their rate of singing or start singing if they were previously silent.[3] If song is played from a loudspeaker within the boundaries of a male's territory, the territory owner again often increases its singing rate, while approaching and searching for the apparent intruder. Further, when males interact, they often respond to each other using stylized patterns of singing behavior, such as overlapping each others' songs,[4–6] changing the rate at which they switch between song types,[7,8] or matching songs with similar song types.[9–11] This association between patterns of singing and territorial aggression suggests that song must act as a signal to other males in the context of territory defense.

More direct evidence that song functions in territorial defense comes from experimental approaches such as muting. Muting can be accomplished by either syringeal denervation[12] or puncture of the interclavicular air sac,[13] and tests whether an inability to sing hampers defense. The most thorough study of this type was done by McDonald,[14] working with Scott's seaside sparrow (*Ammodramus maritimus*). Males muted by airsac puncture lost all or part of their territories, while the territories of control males increased in size. Both airsac puncture and syringeal denervation are potentially debilitating,[15] but MacDonald[14] found that her muted males showed activity levels just as high as those of the controls, indicating that it was the inability to sing rather than an overall decline in vigor that was responsible for the difficulties the muted males experienced in holding territory.

If loss of song diminishes a male's ability to defend its territory, can song alone be shown to maintain territory? To answer this question, researchers have removed males from their territories and replaced them with loudspeakers from which male song was broadcast at regular intervals. The results of these studies—done with thrush nightingales (*Luscinia luscinia*),[16] great tits (*Parus major*),[17] red-winged blackbirds,[18] white-throated sparrows (*Zonotrichia albicollis*),[19] and song sparrows (*Melospiza melodia*)[20]—show that territories from which song is broadcast take longer to be reoccupied than territories that remain silent.

Does Song Attract and Stimulate Females?

Observations of singing behavior also suggest that song functions in communicating to females. Peaks in the frequency of male song typically occur during the period when a male is attempting to attract a female to his territory[1] or, slightly later, during the period when females are producing fertile eggs.[2] If a female is removed from a territory, the territorial male's song rate increases, only to decline again when his mate is returned.[21,22]

These kinds of behavioral correlations are consistent with the view that song functions as a mate attraction signal, but again it is necessary to demonstrate directly that song influences female behavior. Eriksson and Wallin[23] provided the first such demonstration. They set up nest boxes in a mixed population of pied and collared flycatchers (*Ficedula hypoleuca* and *F. albicollis*), outfitting each box with a stuffed male decoy but providing only half the boxes with loudspeakers playing male songs. Most females caught inspecting nest boxes were found at boxes with song, supporting the function of song as a mate attraction signal. Similar experiments with starlings (*Sturnus vulgaris*)[24] and house wrens (*Troglodytes aedon*)[25] have confirmed this result.

Beginning with the pioneering work of Lehrman on doves,[26,27] the effect of song on female reproductive behavior has been demonstrated in a number of bird species. For example, Hinde and Steele[28] demonstrated that captive female canaries (*Serinus canaria*) increase their nest building activity when exposed to conspecific song, while Wright and Cuthill[29] showed that wild starling females laid their clutch earlier the more their mate sang. A striking short-term effect of song on female behavior is that it provokes in many passerines a distinctive and stereotypic precopulatory display, in which the female crouches and raise her tail in preparation for copulation, often while shivering her wings and making precopulatory calls. A patient observer will observe this response in the field, but the display also can be elicited in captive females of many species by exposing them to recorded song.[30,31] This fact both provides further evidence that song functions in female mate choice and led to the development of what is now a widely used laboratory method—the "solicitation assay"—for determining what features of song are preferred by females.

SONG AS AN INDICATOR MECHANISM IN MATE CHOICE

The term "indicator" refers to a signal that correlates reliably with the condition or viability of the signaler, with the correlation between signal expression and individual quality being maintained by some cost associated with the signal. If a signal is a reliable indicator, it may be used by an individual of the opposite sex to identify a high quality mate.[32] The idea that an indicator trait must have some underlying cost is critical to understanding how indicators work in mate choice. Females, as the sex investing more in reproduction, are expected to be choosier than males about the quality of their mates. Males, as the sex more eager to mate, are expected to exaggerate their quality whenever it is possible to do so. Females therefore should respond to signals of male quality only if the reliability of the signal, that is the correlation between signal properties and male quality, is somehow ensured. Signal costs can ensure reliability if the costs fall differentially on low quality males, so that optimal signaling levels (where costs balance benefits) are lower for low quality than for high quality males. Signal costs that can maintain reliability may include the time and energy expended during signaling, but they also may include the costs associated with developing the trait or display.[33–37]

Indicator traits may provide information related to both "indirect" and "direct" benefits a female might receive by mating with a particular male. If the expression of a trait is somehow linked to a male's genetic quality, for example because he has "good genes" that allow him to avoid parasites and thus have more resources to produce a high-quality signal, then the female may obtain "indirect benefits" that affect her fitness through improved viability of her offspring.[38] A female also may benefit from mating with a phenotypically superior male because such males provide better territories, better parental care, or other "direct benefits" that improve the female's own survival and fecundity.[38] Note that the expression of an indicator trait can be influenced by both environmental and genetic factors, and thus indicators can potentially signal both phenotypic and genotypic quality. Theoretical models demonstrate that female preferences can evolve either when females obtain only direct benefits by mating with phenotypically superior males[38–42] or when they obtain indirect benefits by mating with genotypically superior males.[43–45]

The emblematic example of an indicator trait is the elaborate train of the male peacock (*Pavo cristatus*). Females prefer to mate with males having larger tails, specifically those that have more "eyespots" in the train. Producing and maintaining such large tails is costly, however, and not all males are able to produce equally large trains. Males with large trains have offspring with better growth and survival,[46] so females receive an indirect benefit from preferring these males. In another well-known example, male house finches (*Carpodacus mexicanus*) have red coloration on the feathers of their head and breast, but there is considerable variation among individual males in the extent to which this color is expressed and female house finches prefer males with bright plumage.[47–49] Plumage brightness is strongly influenced by the amount and type of carotenoids present in the diet at the time of the post-winter molt and thus can serve as a reliable indicator of male condition.[50] Brighter males provide better parental care, which is a direct benefit to the females that choose them as mates.[48] Brighter males also have a higher overwinter survival, suggesting that brightness may be an indicator of viability. Brightness of fathers is positively correlated with brightness of sons, consistent with the idea that females also obtain indirect benefits for their offspring by mating with brighter males.[48]

The fact that a male bird's song may influence a female's choice of mates suggests that song may function, like the peacock's tail and the house finch's red coloration, as an indicator of male quality.[32,51,52] This suggestion, however, raises a difficulty in that many of the features of song on which female birds base their preferences have no obvious costs.

SONG FEATURES THAT INFLUENCE FEMALE CHOICE

As a prelude to addressing how song can serve as an honest indicator of male quality, we next ask what features of song appear to be important in female choice. Not surprisingly, not all species exhibit preferences for the same song features, and certain female preferences may be idiosyncratic to particular species. However, three broad categories of features seem to have the most consistent effects: song output, song complexity, and local song structure. A fourth category, vocal performance, is only now beginning to emerge as a feature of song important to female mate choice. For each of these categories, we first point out key studies illustrating the preference and we then ask what, if any, cost might be associated with the song feature that could maintain its reliability as a signal of male quality.

Song Output

In many species, females prefer males that have a higher song output, that is, that simply sing more. In some species (e.g., European starlings) males that sing longer song bouts pair earlier, obtain more mates in the field, and are preferred by females in laboratory solicitation assays.[53] Male blue tits (*Parus caeruleus*) singing longer songs are more successful in obtaining extra-pair fertilizations and are less likely to lose paternity to other males.[54] Female white-throated sparrows also respond more to longer songs in the lab.[55] In other species, females have been shown to prefer males that sing at a faster rate. Female pied flycatchers pair more quickly in the field with males that have faster song rates[56,57] and female zebra finches (*Taenopygia guttata*) respond more to higher song rates in laboratory tests.[58]

It is easy to understand how song output can be a costly signal of male quality. Although the energetic costs of producing song appear to be low,[59,60] singing costs something in time if not in energy, regardless of what is sung. Presumably, males in better condition can afford to devote more time and effort to singing than can males in poorer condition. Male condition, in turn, may correlate with direct benefits a female obtains, if males in good condition have superior territories or provide better parental care, or may correlate with indirect benefits to the extent that condition reflects "good genes" affecting offspring viability.

Song Complexity

One of the most commonly demonstrated song preferences is a preference for more complex song repertoires. Complexity can be measured either as the number of discrete song types a male can produce or, in the case of species having more continuous songs, as the number of syllable types in a male's repertoire. For example, male sedge warblers (*Acrocephalus schoenobanus*) with larger syllable type repertoires have been shown in field studies to obtain mates at an earlier date,[61,62] while male great reed warblers (*A. arundinaceus*) with larger syllable repertoires obtain more extra-pair fertilizations.[63] Great reed warblers males with larger syllable repertoires also attract more social mates,[64] as do male red-winged blackbirds (*Agelaius phoeniceus*) with larger song type repertoires.[65] In the laboratory, females have been shown to perform more courtship displays in response to larger song type repertoires in song sparrows[31,66] and great tits,[67] and in response to larger syllable repertoires in sedge warblers[68] and great reed warblers.[69] Unlike song output, song complexity is hard to explain as a reliable indicator of quality because it is not apparent why complex songs would be more costly to produce than simple ones.

Local Song Structure

A third aspect of song that affects female preferences is whether songs are local or foreign in origin. In white-crowned sparrows (*Zonotrichia leucophrys*)[70] and corn buntings (*Miliaria calandra*),[71] geographic variation in song is pronounced over very short distances with distinct boundaries occurring between "dialect" regions. In most species, however, variation is more gradual with differences only apparent over broad geographic ranges.[72] In either case, females generally discriminate against songs recorded from foreign populations and prefer songs sung by males from their own local population.[73]

The differences between songs from two geographic locales can be subtle[74] and it is unclear how producing songs typical of one locale can be more costly than producing songs typical of another. One oft-cited hypothesis for the evolution of local song preferences is that females benefit by mating with locally born males by obtaining genes that are particularly well adapted to local conditions.[75,76] There is scant direct support for local genetic adaptation in birds, however. Further, females seem to prefer local song even in species in which males learn song after dispersal, in which case song is not indicative of a males natal population.[77,78] Equally problematic is the fact that, in species with gradual geographic variation, typical dispersal distances may make it unlikely that a female would ever hear a song outside the range that she accepts as equally attractive to local song.[72] Thus, the genetic adaptation hypothesis does not appear to be a general explanation for the evolution of female preferences for local song.

Vocal Performance

Performance features are attributes of song that affect how difficult a song is to produce. Physical and physiological constraints must exist that limit the sounds that birds are able to produce, and performance features are song traits that exhibit how closely a male is able to push those limits. There is now growing evidence that how well a male produces these sounds, or whether he produces them at all, serves as a measure of male quality.[79,80] Examples of female preferences based on vocal performance include a preference in canaries for a particular class of complex syllables,[81] a preference in dusky warblers (*Phylloscopus fuscatus*) for songs maintaining a consistently high amplitude across elements,[82] and a preference in swamp sparrows (*Melospiza georgiana*) for songs having both a rapid trill rate and a wide frequency bandwidth.[83] In the last case, the biomechanical basis of the performance limitation is particularly well understood. When producing a high frequency sound, songbirds must open their beaks widely, shortening the vocal tract and raising its resonance frequency. Conversely, to produce a low frequency sound the beak must be relatively closed, lengthening the tract and lowering its resonance frequency.[84,85] Because trilled swamp sparrow songs are composed of rapid frequency-modulated notes, there is a performance trade-off between how fast a bird can repeat syllables in a trill (trill rate) and how broad a range of frequencies each repeated syllable encompasses (frequency bandwidth).[86] In simple terms, the trade-off is a consequence of the fact that it is difficult for birds to open and close their beaks both widely and rapidly. Ballentine and colleagues[83] demonstrated that female swamp sparrows respond preferentially to songs that lie near the upper limit of the bandwidth–trill rate tradeoff relative to songs that lie farther from that limit, consistent with the hypothesis that females use vocal performance to assess males in this species.

To the extent that vocal performance is like any other "performance" measure, for example the performance of a lizard running on a treadmill, then song may correlate with other aspects of male phenotype that directly affect female reproductive success, or aspects of male genotype that reflect heritable factors affecting performance. This idea, however, begs the question of how song performance is linked to other aspects of phenotype or genotype.

THE "DEVELOPMENTAL STRESS HYPOTHESIS"

Theory holds that signals can be reliable indicators of quality if they are costly,[35] yet many of the features of song on which female birds base their preferences appear to be cheap to produce. To resolve this apparent paradox, Nowicki and colleagues[87] proposed what they originally named the "nutritional stress hypothesis." This hypothesis postulates that learned features of song can serve as reliable indicators of male quality because the brain structures underlying song learning and production develop during a period early in life when young birds are likely to be susceptible to developmental stress, largely due to undernutrition. Individuals may differ both in the magnitude of the stress they experience and in their developmental response to a given level of stress. In either case, individuals faring well in the face of this potential stress will be better able to invest resources necessary for development in general and for brain development in particular. Variation in brain development, in turn, will translate into variation in song learning abilities among males. By choosing males based on song features that reflect the outcome of song learning, females obtain mates that have fared better in the face of developmental stresses experienced early in life. The reliability of song as an indicator of male quality, then, is maintained by the cost of developing the neural substrate for song learning.

Buchanan and colleagues[88] have argued that stressors other than undernutrition also may affect brain development and thus have suggested renaming this hypothesis the "developmental stress hypothesis." For example, parasites attack young birds of most species, with a variety of detrimental effects.[89,90] In some respects, the effects are parallel to those of undernutrition, in that parasites can potentially drain away resources from the host and cause the host to mount energetically costly defenses.[91] Indeed, in a recent study of sedge warblers, Buchanan and colleagues[92] found a negative relationship between parasite load and aspects of song, including repertoire size, consistent with the hypothesis that parasite-induced stress lowers condition in males, which in turn affects their singing behavior. Similarly, unpredictable food supplies may also have stressful effects on development.[88] Social interactions may impose developmental costs through the activation of hormonal stress pathways. Thus, a number of stressors experienced early in life may act synergistically to adversely affect song system development and song learning. In any case, the amount of stress experienced by an individual and that individual's response to the stress it experiences should be reflected in brain development and song learning. In this way, the expression of song features may correlate with male quality, with the reliability of the signal maintained by the fact that brains are costly to build.

Song learning may be a particularly good indicator of the effects of post-hatch developmental stress because the song system develops later than other parts of the nervous system (FIG. 1).[87,93,94] The general pattern, based largely on work with ze-

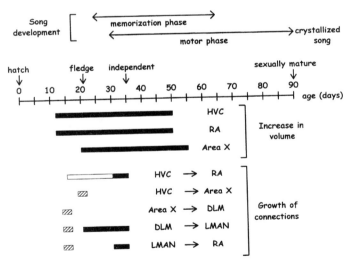

FIGURE 1. Time line of zebra finch life history events, song learning, and development of the song system. The memorization phase spans approximately 25 to 65 days of age, and the motor phase begins at about 30 days of age and continues until crystallized song production.[131,132] Zebra finches fledge at about 20 days of age[131] and are not fully independent from parental care until approximately 35 days of age.[52] *Black bars* indicate reported periods of volume increase for brain nuclei and growth of connections between nuclei. *Shaded bars* indicate earliest time for which functional connections between nuclei have been reported. The *open bar* shows that HVC neurons project to RA between 15 and 30 days of age, but do not make functional connections until day 30. See other references in text. (From Nowicki and colleagues,[87] reproduced with permission.)

bra finches, is that the song system undergoes considerable growth, from approximately 10 to 50 days post-hatching.[95–99] In the zebra finch, neurogenesis leads to a significant increase in the number of neurons in HVC between 10 and 50 days and in Area X between 20 and 50 days.[95,97] RA volume in the zebra finch increases between 10 and 50 days of age due to an increase in neuron size, greater spacing between neurons and an increase in synaptic density.[95,96] Most neurons in the canary HVC also are added after hatching.[100,101] In this species, the increase in size of HVC and RA begins later than in zebra finches, around 30 days of age; RA doubles in size by 60 days with correspondingly large increases in the size of HVC, although HVC continues to grow incrementally for another several months.[102] The progression is similar in swamp sparrows[103] with the majority of growth of HVC, RA, and Area X completed by 61 days post-hatch.

Even more critical from a functional point of view, synaptic connections between song system nuclei also continue to develop in the first several weeks after hatching (FIG. 1). In the zebra finch, for example, HVC neurons project to RA between 15 and 30 days of age and then hold at the border[99] until they rapidly innervate RA between 30 and 35 days of age.[96] Although HVC connections to Area X in the canary are almost all completed in the embryo stage, some connections also are established after hatching.[100] Area X connections to DLM in the zebra finch appear to be established in the first 15 days post-hatch.[98] DLM axons appear to innervate LMAN by 15 days of age as well in the zebra finch, but there is "exuberant" growth from DLM to LMAN between 20 and 35 days of age.[98] Finally, in the zebra finch, some LMAN projections may reach RA as early as day 15, but they are readily detected after day 30.[99]

At the same time these critical events in song system development are occurring, young songbirds are particularly susceptible to developmental stress. A typical songbird nestling reaches 90% of its adult weight within the first 10 days of life.[104] Growth rates depend on the amount of food delivered by parents, and starvation is common.[105,106] Even after fledging, young songbirds depend on their parents to deliver food for several days or even weeks as their own foraging skills improve.[107] In general, the growth and survival of young songbirds is clearly tied to the level of nutrition provided by parents during the nestling and fledgling stages.[108,109]

The deleterious effects of early nutritional and other developmental stressors on brain development are well-established in mammals.[110–112] Development may be more buffered against resource deprivation in birds than in mammals, but the rapid development of structures in the avian brain may be particularly vulnerable to undernutrition.[113] To the extent that developmental stress does affect brain development in young songbirds, variation in the development of brain structures responsible for song learning and production will lead to variation in song learning abilities among males. Females mating with males that have learned better will be choosing mates that fared better in the face of stresses experienced early in life and who thus have otherwise superior phenotypes, and to the extent that response to stress involves heritable factors, superior genotypes as well. Both how much and how well song is learned may be equally useful cues for females to use when assessing males. Indeed, the common preference of females for local versus foreign songs may reflect the perception that they are less well learned.[72,114] The "developmental stress hypothesis" thus accounts for the widespread preferences both for more complex songs and for more local-sounding songs, with signal reliability being maintained by developmental costs in each case.

TESTING PREDICTIONS

The developmental stress hypothesis makes a number of straightforward predictions that we can use to test the validity of this idea. First, developmental stress experienced in the nestling and fledgling stages of a bird's life should have a lasting effect on brain structures involved in song memory and production. Second, early stress should affect features of the songs of adult males that females attend to in mate choice. Third, developmental stress should affect other aspects of male phenotype that are important to a female when choosing a mate. This last is necessary if song traits are to be honest indicators of aspects of male phenotype of interest to females. Below, we address each of these predictions in turn.

Prediction 1: Stress Affects Brain Development

Nowicki and colleagues[115] hand-raised two groups of swamp sparrow nestlings, a control group fed *ad libitum* and an experimental group fed only 70% of the volume of food given the controls. The groups were otherwise raised under identical conditions. The nutritional restriction was maintained for 14–18 days, but the major difference in amount of food available to the two groups only lasted 7–10 days because birds began to feed themselves after they fledged. At 14 months, during what would be their first breeding season, birds were perfused and their brains measured. The nutritional manipulation had a clear effect on the song system, with the controls having significantly greater volumes for both HVC and RA than the stressed group (FIG. 2). Of course, these differences could be accounted for by an overall size difference in the brains of the two groups and indeed the telencephalon as a whole also was significantly larger for the control group. However, the ratio of RA:telencephalon also was significantly greater in the controls than the experimentals, demonstrating that this nucleus was disproportionately affected by stress during development.

Thus, in swamp sparrows, a brief exposure to nutritional stress occurring within the first couple of weeks after hatching has a measurable and lasting effect on the brain and on the song system. Developmental programs may be able to compensate for limitations by redirecting resources from less critical phenotypic component in order to buffer more essential components such as the brain, by delaying the rate of maturation, or through compensatory growth later on in life.[113] The result of Nowicki and colleagues[115] shows that such strategies do not completely compensate for the effects of early stress on brain development.

Prediction 2: Stress Affects Features of Song Important to Females

Two studies have tested this prediction with correlative field data. Doutrelant and colleagues[116] found a positive correlation between repertoire size and tarsus length in adult blue tits, with the latter measure known to reflect early nutrition. In a more direct test, Nowicki and colleagues[117] found that nestling feather growth, also known to be influenced by nutritional stress, was positively correlated with syllable repertoire size of adults in great reed warblers (FIG. 3). Female great reed warblers are known to prefer males with large repertoires,[64,69] so this result supports the idea that developmental stress affects song parameters important to females.

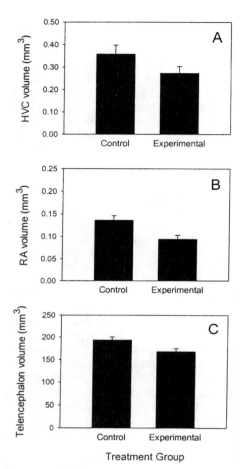

FIGURE 2. Effects of early nutritional stress on volume of brain areas in adult male swamp sparrows. (**A**) Nucleus HVC ($P=0.028$); (**B**) nucleus RA ($P=0.011$); (**C**) telencephalon ($P=0.028$). $N=8$ control, 7 experimental birds in all cases. Volume data were averaged across left and right hemispheres for each individual in the analysis. (From Nowicki and colleagues,[115] reproduced with permission.)

Several recent experimental tests also test this prediction. In the experiment with swamp sparrows described above, Nowicki and colleagues[115] measured the effects of early nutritional stress on several aspects of adult song. Song repertoire sizes did not differ between the stressed experimental males and the well-fed controls. Experimentals and controls did differ, however, in the accuracy with which they copied the songs they heard when young, as measured by calculating spectrogram cross correlations between learned notes and tutor notes. No test has yet been made of whether female swamp sparrows prefer accurately copied songs, but Nowicki and colleagues[114] tested this prediction in a close relative, the song sparrow. Male song sparrows were taken as nestlings and hand-reared, either with or without nutritional restriction, and tutored during their sensitive phase with songs recorded in their natal locality. The songs produced by these males as adults were assessed for accuracy of learning, based on the proportion of notes that were copied from the tutor songs and the mean spectrogram cross correlations between the learned notes and the tutor

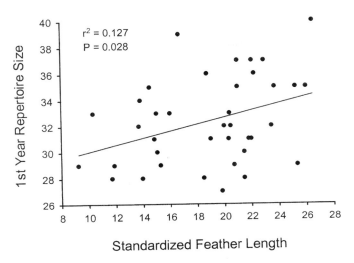

FIGURE 3. The relationship between standardized nestling primary feather length and subsequent first-year repertoire size of individual male great reed warblers, demonstrating a relationship between measures of growth and development and subsequent repertoire complexity in a field population. $N=38$, $r^2=0.127$, $P=0.028$. (From Nowicki and colleagues,[117] reproduced with permission.)

notes. Females from the same locality were then tested for response to sets of these songs that differed in learning accuracy (FIG. 4). In one test, females responded with significantly more courtship displays to well-learned songs, when the well-learned songs differed from the poorly learned songs in both the proportion of copied notes and copy accuracy. In a second test, the proportion of copied notes was held constant, and females still showed a preference for well-learned songs that differed only in copy accuracy from the poorly learned songs. These results, then, provide evidence for a female preference in song sparrows based on a song trait known to be influenced by early nutritional stress in the congeneric swamp sparrow.

Buchanan and colleagues[88] stressed fledgling starlings for 80 days starting at 35–50 days post-hatching—a time when some song control nuclei, notably RA, are expected to increase in size—by removing food unpredictably from the experimental group for four hours each day. When song traits were measured at the start of the next breeding season, previously stressed birds had lower song output by a number of measures, including time spent singing, number of song bouts, and mean song bout duration. The last measure is particularly interesting, as bout duration is correlates with syllable repertoire size in starlings, and female starlings prefer males with longer song bouts and higher repertoire sizes.[53,118]

Spencer and colleagues[119] stressed zebra finches between 5 and 30 days, by two methods. In one, the parents were given restricted access to food; in the other, the young birds were directly fed corticosterone, a hormone that mediates stress in birds. Both treatments affected the subsequent adult songs of the stressed birds with respect to song duration, number of syllables per song, and maximum frequency. Clay-

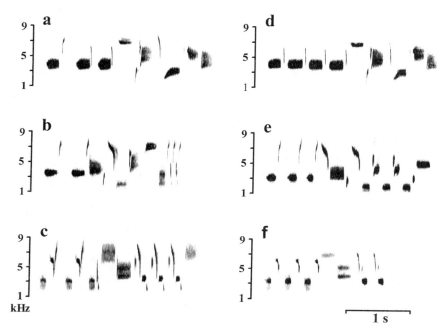

FIGURE 4. Examples of model song sparrow songs (**a, b, c**) used to tutor young males in the laboratory and learned songs (**d, e, f**) subsequently produced by these males, used to test preferences of females for quality of song learning.[114] Learned song **d** best matches model song **a** and includes a high proportion of notes that have been accurately copied. Learned song **e** best matches model song **b** and includes a lower proportion of notes that have been less accurately copied. Learned song **f** best matches model song **c** and includes a high proportion of copied notes, but these notes are inaccurately copied. Note that songs having a high proportion of copied notes may include notes that have been copied from several different models; such an example is not shown here. (From Nowicki and colleagues,[114] reproduced with permission.)

ton and Pröve1[20] had previously shown that female zebra finches discriminate in courtship based on two of these song parameters, song duration and number of syllables per song. The zebra finch results are thus in accord with the other studies showing that females attend to song features affected by early stress.

Prediction 3: Stress Affects Male Phenotypic Quality

We have tested this prediction in song sparrows,[121] using nutritional treatments slightly more severe but parallel to those shown to affect song learning in swamp sparrows.[115] The controls had significantly higher growth rates and at the end of treatment (at 18 days) were approximately 7% larger in tarsus length, 10% larger in primary length, and 40% larger in mass. As adults, the controls remained significantly larger in body size, as measured by a principal component measure combining

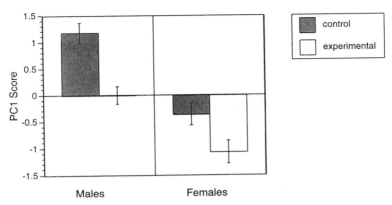

FIGURE 5. Adult body size of song sparrows as measured by the PC1 scores combining six post-mortem skeletal measurements, illustrating the lasting phenotypic effect of limited exposure to nutritional stress experienced when young. The scores are shown as the means of the brood/sex means (± SE). Both treatment and sex effects are significant. (From Searcy and colleagues,[121] reproduced with permission.)

post-mortem measurements of six skeletal characters (FIG. 5). Individual bone lengths in the controls were about 2–3% larger than in the stressed birds. Early nutrition has also been shown to affect adult size in zebra finches[122] and ring-necked pheasants (*Phasianus colchicus*).[123]

Body size is known to affect fitness in birds. Large individuals, for example, often have a survival advantage during adverse weather,[124–126] and in some species female birds prefer large over small males as mates.[54,127] Since early nutrition affects both song and adult size, female might use song to assess size in potential mates. It seems more likely, however, that females would assess size visually, and use song to assess more subtle aspects of phenotypic quality. Birds whose growth rates are nutritionally restricted for some period are often able to catch up later, at least in part, using compensatory strategies such as delayed maturation and accelerated growth.[113] The nutritionally restricted birds in our song sparrow study, for example, reduced their size disadvantage relative to the controls after the end of the diet manipulation by means of a slight delay in maturation and a large reduction in the magnitude of post-fledging weight recession. Compensatory strategies such as these, however, entail a variety of costs in terms of the quality of development.[128] Experimental evidence exists showing that compensation for depressed growth does produce costs, including adult obesity in rats (*Rattus norvegicus*),[129] depressed locomotory performance in Coho salmon (*Oncorhynchus kisutch*),[130] and shorter lifespan in zebra finches.[122]

Another negative phenotypic consequence of early nutritional stress is poor development of the immune system. Again, such a cost might be incurred either as a direct effect of a nutritional deficit or as an effect of attempts to catch up in growth after the period of poor nutrition has ended. Buchanan and colleagues[88] found that nutritional stress in young starlings depressed humoral immune response relative to controls during the period of stress, but they did not assess whether immune response continued to be depressed later in life. Our experiment with nutrition in song sparrows produced evidence that early stress has a negative effect on humoral immune response that persists into adulthood (Hasselquist, Nowicki, Duckworth and Searcy, unpublished data).

CONCLUSIONS

Studies of the function of song by behavioral ecologists and of the mechanisms of song development and production by neurobiologists should inform and guide each other. A review of the evidence from behavioral ecology demonstrates that the primary functions of bird song are in male-male competition for territory and in the attraction of females for mating. These general functions, and their variations across species, should help us interpret why the mechanisms of song development and production work the way they do. At the same time, whatever is learned about mechanisms can be used to illuminate and deepen hypotheses on the evolution of song as a communication signal. The developmental stress hypothesis illustrates the way in which knowledge of mechanisms informs a functional hypothesis.

The developmental stress hypothesis is primarily an idea about the hidden costs of the song traits used by females to choose mates. Theoretical analyses of the evolution of animal communication have shown that mating signals should be costly if they are to be reliable. Studies of behavior have determined what aspects of song are important to females in mate choice. With the exception of song output, preferred song traits have little or nothing in the way of immediate production costs, suggesting that the important costs must be developmental. Knowledge of the brain structures that support song in songbirds and of the timing of the development of these structures, suggests when and how stresses might operate to influence song development. The evidence available to date confirms key predictions of the developmental stress hypothesis: there are effects of early stress on the development of the song control system in the brain, and on at least some of the song traits on which female birds base their mating preferences, and these same preferences affect other aspects of the phenotype that might in turn affect the direct and indirect benefits females receive from mating with particular males. The developmental stress hypothesis thus has been successful, both in receiving empirical support from new data, and, perhaps more importantly, in suggesting new avenues for investigation.

REFERENCES

1. CATCHPOLE, C.K. 1973. The functions of advertising song in the sedge warbler (*Acrocephalus schoenobaenus*) and reed warbler (*A. scripaceus*). Behaviour **46:** 300–320.
2. SLAGSVOLD, T. 1977. Bird song activity in relation to breeding cycle, spring weather, and environmental phenology. Ornis Scand. **8:** 197–222.
3. TODT, D. & M. NAGUIB. 2000. Vocal interactions in birds: the use of song as a model in communication. Adv. Study Behav. **29:** 247–296.
4. HULTSCH, H. & D. TODT. 1982. Temporal performance roles during vocal interactions in nightingales (*Luscinia megarhynchos*). Behav. Ecol. Sociobiol. **11:** 253–260.
5. MCGREGOR, P.K., T. DABELSTEEN, M. SHEPHERD, *et al.* 1992. The signal value of matched singing in great tits: evidence from interactive playback experiments. Anim. Behav. **43:** 987–998.

6. DABELSTEEN, T., P.K. MCGREGOR, M. SHEPHERD, et al. 1996. Is the signal value of overlapping different from that of alternating during matched singing in Great Tits? J. Avian Biol. **27:** 189–194.

7. FALLS, J.B. & L.G. D'AGINCOURT. 1982. Why do meadowlarks switch song types? Can. J. Zool. **60:** 3400–3408.

8. SEARCY, W. A., S. NOWICKI & C. HOGAN. 2000. Song type variants and aggressive context. Behav. Ecol. Sociobiol. **48:** 358–363.

9. LEMON, R.E. 1968. The relation between organization and function of song in cardinals. Behaviour **32:** 158–178.

10. KREBS, J.R., R. ASHCROFT & K. V. ORSDOL. 1981. Song matching in the great tit *Parus major* L. Anim. Behav. **29:** 918–923.

11. STODDARD, P.K., M.D. BEECHER, S.E. CAMPBELL, et al. 1992. Song-type matching in the song sparrow. Can. J. Zool. **70:** 1440–1444.

12. PEEK, F.W. 1972. An experimental study of the territorial function of vocal and visual display in the male red-winged blackbird (*Agelaius phoeniceus*). Anim. Behav. **20:** 112–118.

13. SMITH, D.G. 1979. Male singing ability and territory integrity in red-winged blackbirds (*Agelaius phoeniceus*). Behaviour **68:** 193–206.

14. MCDONALD, M.V. 1989. Function of song in Scott's seaside sparrow, A*mmodramus maritimus pennisulae*. Anim. Behav. **38:** 468–485.

15. NOTTEBOHM, F. 1971. Neural lateralization of vocal control in a passerine bird. I. Song. J. Exp. Zool. **177:** 229–262.

16. GÖRANSSON, G., G. HÖGSTEDT, J. KARLSSON, et al. 1974. Sångens roll för revirhållandet hos näktergal *Luscinia luscinia*—några experiment me play-back-teknik. Vår Fågelvärld **33:** 201–209.

17. KREBS, J.R. 1977. Song and territory in the great tit *Parus major*. *In* Evolutionary Ecology. B. Stonehouse & C. Perrins, Eds: 47–62. University Park Press. Baltimore.

18. YASUKAWA, K. 1981. Song repertoires in the red-winged blackbird (*Agelaius phoeniceus*): a test of the Beau Geste hypothesis. Anim. Behav. **29:** 114–125.

19. FALLS, J.B. 1988. Does song deter intrusion in white-throated sparrows (*Zonotrichia albicollis*)? Can. J. Zool. **66:** 206–211.

20. NOWICKI, S., W.A. SEARCY & M. HUGHES. 1998. The territory defenses function of song in song sparrows: a test with the speaker occupation design. Behaviour **135:** 615–628.

21. KREBS, J.R., M. AVERY & R.J. COWIE. 1981. Effect of removal of mate on the singing behavior of great tits. Anim. Behav. **29:** 635–637.

22. OTTER, K. & L. RATCLIFFE. 1993. Changes in singing behavior of male black-capped chickadees (*Parus atricapillus*) following mate removal. Behav. Ecol. Sociobiol. 409–414.

23. ERIKSSON, D. & L. WALLIN. 1986. Male bird song attracts females: a field experiment. Behav. Ecol. Sociobiol. **19:** 297–299.

24. MOUNTJOY, D.J. & R.E. LEMON. 1991. Song as an attractant for male and female European starlings and the influence of song complexity on their response. Behav. Ecol. Sociobiol. **28:** 97–100.

25. JOHNSON, L.S. & W.A. SEARCY. 1996. Female attraction to male song in house wrens (*Troglodytes aedon*). Behaviour **133:** 357–366.

26. LEHRMAN, D.S. 1958. Effect of female sex hormones on incubation behavior in the ring dove (*Streptopelia risoria*). J. Comp. Physiol. Psychol. **51:** 142–145.

27. LEHRMAN, D.S. 1964. Control of behavior cycles in reproduction. *In* Social Behavior and Organization among Vertebrates. W. Etkin, Ed: 143–166. University of Chicago Press. Chicago.

28. HINDE, R.A. & E. STEELE. 1976. The effect of male song on an oestrogen dependent behaviour in the female canary *Serinus canarius*. Horm. Behav. **7:** 293–304.

29. WRIGHT, J. & I. CUTHILL. 1992. Monogamy in the European starling. Behaviour **120:** 262–285.

30. KING, A.P. & M.J. WEST. 1977. Species identification in the North American cowbird: appropriate responses to abnormal song. Science **195:** 1002–1004.

31. SEARCY, W.A. & P. MARLER. 1981. A test for responsiveness to song structure and programming in female sparrows. Science **213:** 926–928.
32. ANDERSSON, M. 1994. Sexual Selection. Princeton University Press. Princeton, NJ.
33. ZAHAVI, A. 1975. Mate selection—a selection for a handicap. J. Theor. Biol. **53:** 205–214.
34. ENQUIST, M. 1985. Communication during aggressive interactions with particular reference to variation in choice of behaviour. Anim. Behav. **33:** 1152–1161.
35. GRAFEN, A. 1990. Biological signals as handicaps. J. Theor. Biol. **144:** 517–546.
36. JOHNSTONE, R.A. & A. GRAFEN. 1993. Dishonesty and the handicap principle. Anim. Behav. **46:** 759–764.
37. VEHRENCAMP, S.L. 2000. Handicap, index, and conventional signal elements of bird song. *In* Animal Signals. Y. Espmark, T. Amundsen & G. Rosenqvist, Eds. Tapir Academic. Trondheim.
38. KIRKPATRICK, M. & M.J. RYAN. 1991. The evolution of mating preferences and the paradox of the lek. Nature **350:** 33–38.
39. GRAFEN, A. 1990. Sexual selection unhandicapped by the Fisher process. J. Theor. Biol. **144:** 473–516.
40. HOELZER, G.A. 1989. The good parent process of sexual selection. Anim. Behav. **38:** 1067–1078.
41. HEYWOOD, J.S. 1989. Sexual selection by the handicap mechanism. Evolution **43:** 1387–1397.
42. PRICE, T.D., D. SCHLUTER & N.E. HECKMAN. 1993. Sexual selection when the female directly benefits. Biol. J. Linn. Soc. **48:** 187–211.
43. ANDERSSON, M. 1986. Evolution of condition-dependent sex ornaments and mating preferences: sexual selection based on viability differences. Evolution **40:** 804–816.
44. POMIANKOWSKI, A. 1987. Sexual selection: the handicap principle does work—sometimes. Proc. R. Soc. Lond. B **231:** 123–145.
45. IWASA, Y., A. POMIANKOWSKI & S. NEE. 1991. The evolution of costly mate preferences. II. The "handicap" principle. Evolution **45:** 1431–1442.
46. PETRIE, M. 1994. Improved growth and survival of offspring of peacocks with more elaborate trains. Nature **371:** 598–599.
47. HILL, G.E. 1990. Female house finches prefer colorful males: Sexual selection for a condition-dependent trait. Anim. Behav. **40:** 563–572.
48. HILL, G.E. 1991. Plumage colouration is a sexually selected indicator mechanism. Nature **350:** 337–339.
49. HILL, G.E. 2003. A Red Bird in a Brown Bag: The function and evolution of colorful plumage in the house finch. Oxford University Press. Oxford.
50. HILL, G.E. 1992. Proximate basis of variation in carotenoid pigmentation in male house finches. Auk **109:** 1–12.
51. SEARCY, W.A. & M. ANDERSSON. 1986. Sexual selection and the evolution of song. Ann. Rev. Ecol. Syst. **17:** 507–533.
52. CATCHPOLE, C.K. & P.J.B. SLATER 1995. Bird Song: Biological themes and variations. Cambridge University Press. Cambridge.
53. EENS, M., R. PINXTEN & R.F. VERHEYEN. 1991. Male song as a cue for mate choice in the European starling. Behaviour **116:** 210–238.
54. KEMPENAERS, B., G.R. VERHEYEN & A.A. DHONDT. 1997. Extrapair paternity in the blue tit (*Parus caeruleus*): female choice, male characteristics, and offspring quality. Behav. Ecol. **8:** 481–492.
55. WASSERMAN, F.E. & J.A. CIGLIANO. 1991. Song output and stimulation of the female in white-throated sparrows. Behav. Ecol. Sociobiol. **29:** 55–59.
56. GOTTLANDER, K. 1987. Variation in the song rate of the male pied flycatcher *Ficedula hypoleuca*: causes and consequences. Anim. Behav. **35:** 1037–1043.
57. ALATALO, R.V., C. GLYNN & A. LUNDBERG. 1990. Singing rate and female attraction in the pied flycatcher: an experiment. Anim. Behav. **39:** 601–603.
58. COLLINS, S.A., C. HUBBARD & A.M. HOUTMAN. 1994. Female mate choice in the zebra finch—the effect of male beak colour and male song. Behav. Ecol. Sociobiol. **35:** 21–25.

59. OBERWEGER, K. & F. GOLLER. 2001. The metabolic cost of birdsong production. J. Exp. Biol. **204:** 3379–3388.
60. EBERHARDT, L.S. 1994. Oxygen consumption during singing by male carolina wrens (*Thryothorus ludovicianus*). Auk **111:** 124–130.
61. BUCHANAN, K.L. & C.K. CATCHPOLE. 1997. Female choice in the sedge warbler, *Acrocephalus schoenobaenus*: multiple cues from song and territory. Proc. R. Soc. Lond. B **264:** 521–526.
62. CATCHPOLE, C.K. 1980. Sexual selection and the evolution of complex songs among European warblers of the genus *Acrocephalus*. Behaviour **74:** 149–166.
63. HASSELQUIST, D., S. BENSCH & T. V. SCHANTZ. 1996. Correlation between male song repertoire, extra pair paternity and offspring survival in the great reed warbler. Nature **381:** 229–232.
64. HASSELQUIST, D. 1998. Polygyny in great reed warblers: a long-term study of factors contributing to male fitness. Ecology **79:** 2376–2390.
65. YASUKAWA, K., J.L. BLANK & C.B. PATTERSON. 1980. Song repertoires and sexual selection in the red-winged blackbird. Behav. Ecol. Sociobiol. **7:** 233–238.
66. SEARCY, W.A. 1984. Song repertoire size and female preferences in song sparrows. Behav. Ecol. Sociobiol. **14:** 281–286.
67. BAKER, M.C., T.K. BJERKE, H.U. LAMPE, *et al.* 1986. Sexual response of female great tits to variation in size of males' song repertoires. Amer. Nat. **128:** 491–498.
68. CATCHPOLE, C.K., J. DITTAMI & B. LEISLER. 1984. Differential responses to male song in female songbirds implanted with oestradiol. Nature **312:** 563–564.
69. CATCHPOLE, C.K., B. LEISLER & J. DITTAMI. 1986. Sexual differences in the responses of captive great reed warblers (*Acrocephalus arundinaceus*) to variation in song structure and repertoire size. Ethology **73:** 69–77.
70. MARLER, P. & M. TAMURA. 1964. Culturally transmitted patterns of vocal behavior in sparrows. Science **146:** 293–296.
71. MCGREGOR, P.K. 1980. Song dialects in the corn bunting (*Emberiza calandra*). Z. Tierpsychol. **54:** 285–297.
72. SEARCY, W.A., S. NOWICKI, M. HUGHES, *et al.* 2002. Geographic song discrimination in relation to dispersal distances in song sparrows. Amer. Nat. **159:** 221–230.
73. SEARCY, W.A. 1992. Measuring responses of female birds to male song. *In* Playback and Studies of Animal Communication. P.K. McGregor, Ed: 175–189. Plenum. New York.
74. SEARCY, W.A., S. NOWICKI & S. PETERS. 2003. Phonology and geographic song discrimination in song sparrows. Ethology **109:** 23–35.
75. NOTTEBOHM, F. 1972. The origins of vocal learning. Amer. Nat. **106:** 116–140.
76. BAKER, M.C. & M.A. CUNNINGHAM. 1985. The biology of bird-song dialects. Behav. Brain Sci. **8:** 85–100.
77. BAKER, M.C., K.J. SPITLER-NABORS & D.C. BRADLEY. 1981. Early experience determines song dialect responsiveness of female sparrows. Science **214:** 819–821.
78. BAPTISTA, L.F. & M.L. MORTON. 1988. Song learning in montane white-crowned sparrows: from whom and when? Anim. Behav. **36:** 1753–1764.
79. SUTHERS, R.A. & F. GOLLER. 1997. Motor correlates of vocal diversity in songbirds. *In* Current Ornithology. J.V Nolan, Ed: 235–288. Plenum Press. New York.
80. VALLET, E., I. BEME & M. KREUTZER. 1998. Two-note syllables in canary songs elicit high levels of sexual display. Anim. Behav. **55:** 291–297.
81. VALLET, E. & M. KREUTZER. 1995. Female canaries are sexually responsive to special song phrases. Anim. Behav. **49:** 1603–1610.
82. FORSTMEIER, W., B. KEMPENAERS, A. MEYER, *et al.* 2002. A novel song parameter correlates with extra-pair paternity and reflects male longevity. Proc. R. Soc. Lond. B **269:** 1479–1485.
83. BALLENTINE, B., J. HYMAN & S. NOWICKI. 2004. Singing performance influences female response to male bird song: an experimental test. Behav. Ecol. **15:** 163–168.
84. WESTNEAT, M.W., J.H.J. LONG, W. HOESE, *et al.* 1993. Kinematics of birdsong: functional correlation of cranial movements and acoustic features in sparrows. J. Exp. Biol. **182:** 147–171.

85. HOESE, W.J., J. PODOS, C. BOETTICHER NICHOLAS, et al. 2000. Vocal tract function in birdsong production: Experimental manipulation of beak movements. J. Exp. Biol. 203: 1845–1855.
86. PODOS, J. 1997. A performance constraint on the evolution of trilled vocalizations in a songbird family (Passeriformes: Emberizidae). Evolution 51: 537–551.
87. NOWICKI, S., S. PETERS & J. PODOS. 1998. Song learning, early nutrition and sexual selection in songbirds. Amer. Zool. 38: 179–190.
88. BUCHANAN, K.L., K.A. SPENCER, A.R. GOLDSMITH, et al. 2003. Song as an honest signal of past developmental stress in the European starling (Sturnus vulgaris). Proc. R. Soc. Lond. B 270: 1149–1156.
89. LOYE, J.E. & M. ZUK 1991. Bird-Parasite Interactions: Ecology, evolution, and behaviour. Oxford University Press. Oxford.
90. CLAYTON, D.H. & J. MOORE. 1997. Host-Parasite Evolution: General principles and avian models. Oxford University Press. Oxford.
91. SHELDON, B.C. & S. VERHULST. 1996. Ecological immunity: costly parasite defenses and trade-offs in evolutionary ecology. Trends Ecol. Evol. 11: 317–321.
92. BUCHANAN, K.L., C.K. CATCHPOLE, J.W. LEWIS, et al. 1999. Song as an indicator of parasitism in the sedge warbler. Anim. Behav. 57: 307–314.
93. ALVAREZ-BUYLLA, A., C. LING & W.S. YU. 1994. Contribution of neurons born during embryonic, juvenile and adult life to the brain of adult canaries: regional specificity and delayed birth of neurons in the song-control nuclei. J. Comp. Neurol. 347: 233–248.
94. DEVOOGD, T.J. 1994. The neural basis for the acquisition and production of bird song. In Causal Mechanisms in Behavioural Development. J.A. Hogan & J.J. Bolhuis, Eds: 49–81. Cambridge University Press. Cambridge.
95. BOTTJER, S.W., S.L. GLAESSNER & A.P. ARNOLD. 1985. Ontogeny of brain nuclei controlling song learning and behavior in zebra finches. J. Neurosci. 5: 1556–1562.
96. KONISHI, M. & E. AKUTAGAWA. 1985. Neuronal growth, atrophy and death in a sexually dimorphic song nucleus in the zebra finch brain. Nature 315: 145–147.
97. NORDEEN, E.J. & K.W. NORDEEN. 1988. Sex and regional differences in the incorporation of neurons born during song learning in zebra finches. J. Neurosci. 8: 2869–2874.
98. JOHNSON, F. & S.W. BOTTJER. 1992. Growth and regression of thalamic efferents in the song-control system of male zebra finches. J. Comp. Neurol. 326: 442–450.
99. MOONEY, R. & M. RAO. 1994. Waiting periods versus early innervation: the development of axonal connections in the zebra finch song system. J. Neurosci. 14: 6532–6543.
100. ALVAREZ-BUYLLA, A., M. THEELEN & F. NOTTEBOHM. 1988. Birth of projection neurons in the higher vocal center of the canary forebrain before during and after song learning. Proc. Natl. Acad. Sci. USA 85: 8722–8726.
101. ALVAREZ-BUYLLA, A., C. LING & F. NOTTEBOHM. 1992. High vocal center growth and its relation to neurogenesis, neuronal replacement and song acquisition in juvenile canaries. J. Neurobiol. 23: 396–406.
102. NOTTEBOHM, F., M.E. NOTTEBOHM & L. CRANE. 1986. Developmental and seasonal changes in canary song and their relationship to changes in the anatomy of song-control nuclei. Behav. Neural Biol. 46: 445–471.
103. NORDEEN, K.W., P. MARLER & E.J. NORDEEN. 1989. Addition of song-related neurons in swamp sparrows coincides with memorization, not production, of learned songs. J. Neurobiol. 20: 651–661.
104. RICKLEFS, R.E. 1968. Patterns of growth in birds. Ibis 110: 419–451.
105. RICKLEFS, R.E. 1983. Avian postnatal development. In Avian Biology. D.S. Farner, J.R. King & K.C. Parkes, Eds: 1–83. Academic Press. New York.
106. O'CONNOR, R.J. 1984. The Growth and Development of Birds. Wiley & Sons. New York.
107. SULLIVAN, K.A. 1988. Age-specific profitability and prey choice. Anim. Behav. 36: 613–615.
108. LACK, D. 1966. Population Studies of Birds. Oxford University Press. Oxford.

109. RINGSBY, T.H., B.E. SAETHER & E.J. SOLBERG. 1998. Factors affecting juvenile survival in house sparrow *Passer domesticus*. J. Avian Biol. **29:** 241–247.
110. DOBBING, J. 1981. Nutritional growth restriction and the nervous system. *In* The Molecular Basis of Neuropathology. R.H.S. Thompson & A.N. Davison, Eds. Arnold. London.
111. SMART, J.L. 1986. Undernutrition, learning and memory: review of experimental studies. *In* Proceedings of the 13th Congress of Nutrition. T.G. Taylor & N.K. Jenkins, Eds: 74–78. Libbey. London.
112. LEVITSKY, D.A. & B.J. STRUPP. 1995. Malnutrition and the brain: changing concepts, changing concerns. J. Nutrition **125:** 2212S–2220S.
113. SCHEW, W.A. & R.E. RICKLEFS. 1998. Developmental plasticity. *In* Avian Growth and Development. J.M. Starck & R.E. Ricklefs, Eds: 288–304. Oxford University Press. New York.
114. NOWICKI, S., W.A. SEARCY & S. PETERS. 2002. Quality of song learning affects female response to male bird song. Proc. R. Soc. Lond. B **269:** 1949–1954.
115. NOWICKI, S., W.A. SEARCY & S. PETERS. 2002. Brain development, song learning and mate choice in birds: a review and experimental test of the "nutritional stress hypothesis." J. Comp. Physiol. A **188:** 1003–1014.
116. DOUTRELANT, C., J. BLONDEL, P. PERRET, *et al.* 2000. Blue tit song repertoire size, male quality and interspecific competition. J. Avian Biol. **31:** 360–366.
117. NOWICKI, S., D. HASSELQUIST, S. BENSCH, *et al.* 2000. Nestling growth and song repertoire size in great reed warblers: evidence for song learning as an indicator mechanism in mate choice. Proc. R. Soc. Lond. B **267:** 2419–2424.
118. MOUNTJOY, D.J. & R.E. LEMON. 1996. Female choice for complex song in the European starling: a field experiment. Behav. Ecol. Sociobiol. **38:** 65–-71.
119. SPENCER, K.A., K.L. BUCHANAN, A.R. GOLDSMITH, *et al.* 2003. Song as an honest signal of developmental stress in the zebra finch (*Taeniopygia guttata*). Horm. Behav. **44:** 132–139.
120. CLAYTON, N. & E. PRÖVE. 1989. Song discrimination in female zebra finches and Bengalese finches. Anim. Behav. **38:** 352–354.
121. SEARCY, W.A., S. PETERS & S. NOWICKI. 2004. Effects of early nutrition on growth rate and adult size in song sparrows. J. Avian Biol. In press.
122. BIRKHEAD, T.R., F. FLETCHER & E.J. PELLATT. 1999. Nestling diet, secondary sexual traits and fitness in the zebra finch. Proc. R. Soc. Lond. B **266:** 385–390.
123. OHLSSON, T.H.G.S. 2001. Early nutrition causes persistent effects on pheasant morphology. Physiol. Biochem. Zool. **74:** 212–218.
124. BUMPUS, H.C. 1899. The elimination of the unfit as illustrated by the introduced sparrow, *Passer domesticus*. Biol. Lect. Woods Hole Mar. Biol. Station **6:** 209–226.
125. BOAG, P.T. & P.R. GRANT. 1981. Intense natural selection in a population of Darwin's finches (Geospizinae) in the Galapagos. Science **214:** 82–85.
126. PUGESEK, B.H. & A. TOMER. 1996. The Bumpus house sparrow data: a reanalysis using structural equation models. Evol. Ecol. **10:** 387–404.
127. WEATHERHEAD, P.J. & P.T. BOAG. 1995. Pair and extra-pair mating success relative to male quality in red-winged blackbirds. Behav. Ecol. Sociobiol. **37:** 81–91.
128. METCALFE, N. & P. MONAGHAN. 2001. Compensation for a bad start: grow now, pay later? Trends Ecol. Evol. **16:** 254–260.
129. WATERLAND, R. & C. GARZA. 1999. Potential mechanisms of metabolic imprinting that lead to chronic disease. Am. J. Clin. Nutr. **69:** 179–197.
130. FARRELL, A., W. BENNETT & R. DEVLIN. 1997. Growth-enhanced transgenic salmon can be inferior swimmers. Can. J. Zool. **75:** 335–337.
131. IMMELMANN, K. 1969. Song development in the zebra finch and other estrilid finches. *In* Bird Vocalizations. R. A. Hinde, Ed: 61–74. Cambridge University Press. Cambridge.
132. SLATER, P.J.B., L.A. EALES & N.S. CLAYTON. 1988. Song learning in zebra finches (*Taeniopygia guttata*): Progress and prospects. Adv. Study Behav. **18:** 1–34.

The Bengalese Finch

A Window on the Behavioral Neurobiology of Birdsong Syntax

KAZUO OKANOYA[a,b]

[a]Faculty of Letters, Chiba University

[b]Precursory Research for Embryonic Science and Technology (PRESTO), Japan Science and Technology Agency

ABSTRACT: The Bengalese finch *Lonchura striata* var. *domestica* is a domesticated strain of a wild species, the white-rumped munia *Lonchura striata* of Southeast Asia. Bengalese finches have been domesticated in Japan for 240 years. Comparing their song syntax with that of their wild ancestors, we found that the domesticated strain has highly complex, conspicuous songs with finite-state syntax, while the wild ancestor sang very stereotyped linear songs. To examine the functional utility of the song complexity, we compared serum levels of estradiol and measured the amount of nesting materials carried into the nest by female birds that were stimulated with either the complex "domesticated" song or the simple wild-type song. In the females stimulated with complex songs the estradiol levels were significantly higher and the amount of nesting material carried was significantly greater. We then performed brain lesions in the song system to identify the neural substrates that are responsible for these differences in song behavior. In Bengalese finches lesions of NIf, a higher order song control nucleus, resulted in simplification of the complex song syntax. That is, the complex "domesticated" syntax changed into the simple wild-type syntax. Based on these data, we hypothesize that mutations in the song control nuclei have occurred that enabled complex song syntax and became fixed into the population of domesticated Bengalese finches through a process of indirect sexual selection.

KEYWORDS: estrildid finches; domestication: song complexity; finite-state syntax; female choice; neuro-ecology

INTRODUCTION: BIRDSONG AND FOUR QUESTIONS

Tinbergen's four questions[1] define the ideal aims of classical ethology. He pointed out that when studying behavior, we should ask questions from mechanistic, developmental, functional, and evolutionary viewpoints. However, as ethological study advanced, the four questions were divided into two major areas of inquiry,

Address for correspondence: Kazuo Okanoya, Faculty of Letters, Chiba University, 1-33 Yayoi-cho, Inage-ku, Chiba 263-8522 Japan. Voice: 81-43-290-3757.
okanoya@cogsci.L.chiba-u.ac.jp
<http://bengalese.s.chiba-u.ac.jp/okanoyaLab/e/Information/index.html>

Ann. N.Y. Acad. Sci. 1016: 724–735 (2004). © 2004 New York Academy of Sciences.
doi: 10.1196/annals.1298.026

namely, neuroethology and behavioral ecology.[2] One consequence of this trend has been the neglect of important questions about the relationship between ecological adaptation and associated changes in the central nervous system. However, the study of birdsong has made a more integrative approach possible, simultaneously addressing proximate and ultimate causes of behavior.[3,4] Here we present an example of such integration.

SEQUENTIAL AND SYNTACTICAL CONTROLS

Birdsong has been regarded as a biological model of human language, especially because of the similarity in developmental processes.[5,6] Birdsong shares another exciting aspect with human language: its syntactical organization.[7,8] Human language is an hierarchically organized syntactical behavior.[9] Phonemes are formed into a word, words into a sentence, and sentences into a speech. When each word is integrated into a sentence, a mental grammar combines them into a syntactical organization. By this combinatory action, a finite word set can generate an infinite number of meanings. Such combinatory productivity of new meanings is lacking in birdsong: birdsong functions in mate attraction and/or territorial defense,[10] but changing the order of song notes does not change the meaning.

Syntactical control of birdsong should nevertheless provide important insights into neural control of syntactical behavior[11–13] and the evolutionary emergence of syntax.[14,15] However, most studies dealing with birdsong syntax actually deal with sequential control of song elements. Sequential control is a part of syntactical control, but it lacks the interesting feature of syntax, namely, the rule-based production of new sequences. I suggest that Bengalese finch songs can provide a new perspective on the study of birdsong.

We may divide birdsongs into two types. When one song note is followed by another song note in deterministic fashion in a single song, or the order of song notes are fixed in each song of a multirepertoire bird, such songs may be identified as "linear" song. The most widely used oscine song system models (the zebra finch, white-crowned sparrow, song sparrow, and swamp sparrow) could all be identified as having linear song syntax.[16] When there are some variations introduced in the ordering of song notes, such a song should be called as a non-deterministic song. Species with non-deterministic song repertoires include the nightingale,[17] starling,[18] willow warbler,[19] and Bengalese finch.[20]

Among these species, Bengalese finches are unique in that their songs are characterized by finite-state syntax. Finite-state syntax refers to a simple form of syntax in which finite numbers of state are interconnected by arrows and a string of letters is produced when state transition occurs. In Bengalese finches, 2 to 5 song notes are chunked together, each of these chunks are emitted at a particular state transition, and the pattern of chunk production follows finite-state syntax. More simply, finite-state syntax can be expressed as a Markov model of note-to-note transitions, in which transition probabilities of certain combinations of notes are high, while that between some note and others are low, reflecting chunking, recursive loop, and complex state transitions of the song production.[20,21] Given such complexity Bengalese finch song may be useful to answer questions about both proximate and ultimate aspects of behavior.[22]

PROXIMATE AND ULTIMATE VALUE OF
BENGALESE FINCH SONG SYNTAX

On the proximate side, we have found that Bengalese finches are critically dependent on auditory input for real-time control of songs and show complex finite-state syntax in their singing patterns.[23,24] Furthermore, Bengalese finches adjust sound pressure level of ongoing singing to the background noise level.[25] When exposed to helium air that changes the velocity of sound and alters resonating property of vocal apparatus, Bengalese finches change finite-state syntax during and after such treatment.[26] These data suggest that Bengalese finches are actively listening their own vocalizations while singing and branching patterns of finite-state syntax is also con-

FIGURE 1. A white-rumped munia (*left*) and a Bengalese finch. (Photo by Maki Ikebuchi).

trolled by the real-time auditory feedback. Bengalese finches are therefore of interest as a model system in which to study neural mechanisms of feedback control.[27]

On the ultimate side, behavioral comparisons between Bengalese finches and white-rumped munias (FIG. 1) are of interest because this bird, considered to be the ancestor of Bengalese finches,[28] sings linear songs without finite-state syntax.[20] White-rumped munia of southeast Asia were imported to Japan 240 years ago[29] and then domesticated in Japan. Several factors might have affected the song syntax of white-rumped munias under natural conditions and under the domesticated environment. Thus, from such comparisons we hope to define evolutionary forces that transformed linear syntax into finite-state syntax. We pursued this aim in a series of field and laboratory studies.

NEURO-ECOLOGY OF BIRDSONG SYNTAX

We first made field observations of white-rumped munias and found that contact calls of white-rumped munias were the same as those of Bengalese finches.[30] We then imported some white-rumped munias to Japan and began comparing their songs with those of Bengalese finches.[20] Recently, by using molecular techniques, we have established that the white-rumped munia and the Bengalese finch are indeed the same species (Yodogawa and colleagues, unpublished data). Through these studies, we hoped that the comparison between wild and domesticated strains might reveal a process of behavioral evolution that is also tractable from a neuroethological perspective. It may provide us with a unique opportunity for truly fruitful "neuro-ecology."

The results of our laboratory studies are summarized below. First, we compared syntactical complexity in domesticated and wild strains of white-rumped munias.[20] Next, we showed that song complexity is an important parameter for females when selecting a potential mate.[32,33] Finally, we used a lesion study to implicate a higher-order song control nucleus in the generation of song complexity in Bengalese finches.[21]

EXPERIMENTAL STUDIES

Comparisons of Song Parameters

Bengalese finches *Lonchura striata* var. *domestica* are the domesticated strain of the wild white-rumped munia *Lonchura striata*, a species imported into Japan about 240 years ago, and subsequently domesticated. Japanese aviculturists selected white-rumped munias for their parental abilities and for white mutations, but there are no records in the avicultural literature indicating that Bengalese finches were selected for their songs.[34] Casual interviews with modern aviculturists in Japan and in Europe also supported this notion.[29] It is unlikely that songs of Bengalese finches experienced artificial selection.

To begin asking evolutionary questions about song complexity we first compared song syntax of the white-rumped munia and the Bengalese finch.[20] FIGURE 2 shows examples of transition diagrams obtained from a white-rumped munia (*upper*) and a

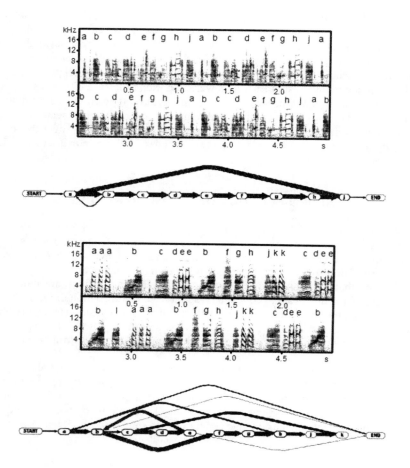

FIGURE 2. Example of sonograms and transition diagrams of a white-rumped munia song (*upper*) and a Bengalese finch song (*lower*). Re-plotted from Honda and Okanoya.[20] Diagrams based on second-order Markovian model.

Bengalese finch (*lower*). While the average number of notes used in a song by white-rumped munias and Bengalese finches was not significantly different, the average song linearity, an index of song simplicity, was significantly lower in Bengalese finches (0.33) than in white-rumped munias (0.61). The overall amplitude of songs is also significantly higher for the Bengalese finches.[20] Bengalese finches were singing, on average, 14 dB louder than the white-rumped munias.

Thus, Bengalese finch song has become much louder and much more complex than white-rumped munias during the past 240 years, an interval roughly equivalent to 500 generations for Bengalese finches. We suspect the song characteristics (amplitude and complexity) enhanced in Bengalese finches are both traits that can be a handicap in the wild. That is, louder song would be easier to be located by predators and elaborated song syntax would require more cognitive cost, which would also result in predation.[35] These possibilities should be tested in the wild. Whether or not the differences between wild and domesticated strains may be attributed to cultural or genetic factors could be clarified by cross-fostering experiments.[36]

Function of Song Complexity

Bengalese finches have been bred under domesticated environment. Under such conditions, sexual selection should only function indirectly, because birds are paired artificially. Although active choice on female's side might not function directly, indirect female choice will result in reproductive efficiency in the female who was coupled with desirable mate. Since white-rumped munias were selected mainly for their parenting behavior,[34] reproductively efficient pairs might be the pair in which the male was singing a complex syntactical song.

To examine the functional implications of song complexity we manipulated song complexity directly.[32,33] Song recordings obtained from a male Bengalese finch were analyzed, and four distinctive song phrases were identified. In this bird's song, these four phrases were organized so that phrases A or B were repeated several times, and phrases C or D followed this repetition, but these phrases were never repeated consecutively. After C or D was sung once, phrases A or B were again repeated. We wrote software that produced either this sequence of song phrases (the complex syntax song), or only repeated phrase B (the simple syntax song). Phrase B included most of the song notes that made up phrases A, C, and D.

Three groups of female Bengalese finches were studied. Each group consisted of four finches, separately caged, and kept together in a sound isolation box. In each cage, one hundred nesting strings were presented every day in a string dispenser. The

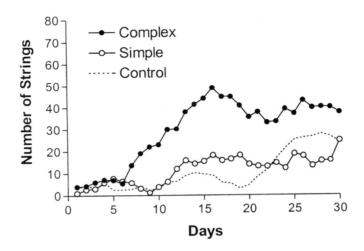

FIGURE 3. Median number of strings carried by each of the complex, simple, and control groups.

first group was stimulated with the complex syntax song, the second group with the simple syntax song, and the third group was not stimulated. The levels of serum estradiol adjusted by the level prior to the experiment were compared among the groups and the number of strings carried into the pot nest was counted.

Estradiol level was twice as high in the females stimulated with the complex song, but only minimally higher in the females stimulated with the simple song. The maximum number of strings carried into the nest was significantly higher in the complex song group than in the non-stimulated (control) group and the number of days required to reach the maximum number of strings was also significantly smaller in the complex song group than in the simple song group (FIG. 3). Thus, the complex song was more effective in stimulating female Bengalese finches to come into reproductive condition. Artificial pairing under domesticated environment could result in enhancement of particular male trait through indirect selection. To prove this is in fact the case, we will need to gather evidence from broader measures of reproductive behavior.

Mechanism of Song Complexity

What mechanisms make the complex song of Bengalese finches possible? Central and peripheral mechanisms for birdsong production have been well studied.[37,38] Song is produced by the combined activity of respiratory and syringeal mechanisms, and a resonating apparatus consisting of the trachea, the tongue, and the beak. The neural pathway that directly controls syringeal activity is well described and sometimes called the posterior pathway.[38] The syringeal muscles are directly controlled by the tracheo-syringeal branch of the hypoglossal nerve NXIIts. This nucleus is innervated both by the telencephalic motor nucleus (RA) and by a mesencephalic motor nucleus, the dorsomedialis (DM). Going upstream, RA is then innervated by the telencephalic sensory/motor integration nucleus (HVC). This nucleus receives auditory input from the primary auditory center, Field L, and from surrounding higher auditory structures. Among them, NIf sends auditory/motor input to HVC.

Since NIf is a higher order nucleus than HVC, we hypothesized that it was mediating a song feature of more complexity—such as organization of the song syntax.[38] However, bilateral lesions of NIf in zebra finches produced no detectable effects, other than some transient deterioration of song structure.[39] It is possible that zebra finch song, which involves a repeated sequence of syllable types in an identical order,[16] might be too simple to display NIf lesion effects. If NIf is in fact governing a higher order aspect of song organization, its function might be evident only in songs with a syntactical organization higher than the level of song phrase.

We therefore repeated NIf lesion studies on Bengalese finch song, which consists of several different phrases organized into variable sequences. The effects proved to be a joint function of song complexity and the bilateral extent of the lesion. Unilateral lesions or those of adjacent structures had no effects on song syntax. Of the three cases of complete bilateral lesion, however, effects upon song were seen only in two birds that were singing complex, multi-phrased songs. In these birds, bilateral NIf lesion eliminated phrase level complexity, reducing the multi-phrased organization of the song to a single phrase (FIG. 4). In the remaining bird, which was singing a simple single-phrase song, there were no effects of bilateral NIf lesions. Thus we conclude that NIf is responsible for phrase-to-phrase transitions.[21]

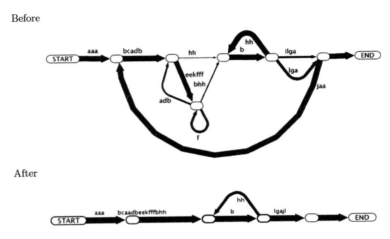

FIGURE 4. Changes in song syntax of a Bengalese finch following NIf lesion. Pre-operatively, song had a complex transition pattern as in most Bengalese finches (*upper*) while post-operative song lost complex transitions (*lower*). The post-operative song syntax is more similar to that of white-rumped munias. Re-plotted from Hosino and Okanoya.[20] Diagrams constructed by third-order Markovian model optimized by a genetic algorithm.

Moreover, we noticed that the post-operative song of the bilaterally lesioned bird is more like that of a white-rumped munia than a Bengalese finch. Most of the recursive loops and song element repetitions were eliminated by this operation and the syntax was very linear. NIf is thus responsible of the unique feature of Bengalese finch song syntax. Whether white-rumped munias do not have a recursive program in their NIf or they simply did not have such structures in their song culture should be identified in a future research. Ongoing cross-fostering experiments in fact suggest that there may be several syntactical and phonological aspects of Bengalese finch songs that white-rumped munias are not adapted to learn well (Takahashi and Okanoya, unpublished data).

GENERAL DISCUSSION

Song Complexity and Female Choice

The most remarkable difference we found between the white-rumped munia and its domesticated strain, the Bengalese finch, is that the domesticated strain sang songs with more complex note-to-note transitions than the wild strain. Previous studies had shown that female Bengalese finches gave more copulation displays to the playback of a six-element song over a four-element song.[40] Similarly, female Bengalese finches perch-hopped more often when stimulated with a song with more elements rather than a song with a few elements.[41] These results suggested that females might favor more variety in the number of song element types. However, we did not find significant differences in the number of song elements between wild and domestic birds. In the study by Clayton and Prove,[40] the degree of complexity of the stimulus songs in the temporal domain was not reported, as was the case with the study by Nakamura and colleagues.[41] Since these authors were using tape-recorded songs, temporal-domain dynamics were not introduced. Thus until now, how song complexity in the temporal domain might influence female birds in Bengalese finches was not known. Although there are several studies relating "song complexity" and female choice,[40–44] most of these studies viewed variations in note type as "complexity."

In our present research, song complexity in Bengalese finches was introduced as dynamic variations in time series rather than variations in note types.[32,33] We found that in females stimulated with complex song E2 levels were elevated twice as much compared to the basal level and these birds carried more strings to the nest than other groups. Song complexity thus brought females into reproductive condition more quickly (see Nowicki and Searcy, this volume)

Neural Control of Song Complexity

We showed that lesions of the higher vocal-auditory integration nucleus NIf disrupted phrase-level variability in those Bengalese finches that sang multistate songs.[21] When the same operation was performed on birds whose song was simpler, we did not find any effects on song syntax. The results on the simpler Bengalese singers are reminiscent of negative results reported by Vu and colleagues[39] on zebra finches. Based on this limited data set, we postulate that NIf may control higher-order or phrase-to-phrase song transition. In addition, NIf-lesioned birds did not change the pattern of note-to-note transitions within their song phrases, suggesting that NIf is responsible only for phrase level transitions and not for note level transitions.

When HVC was partially lesioned in Bengalese finches, there are very small, but reproducible effects on note-to-note transitions within song phrases.[45,46] Taken together, these observations suggest that NIf may govern phrase-to-phrase (or chunk-to-chunk) transitions while HVC may govern element chunking in Bengalese finch songs. Finite-state syntax in Bengalese finches thus may involve contributions from both NIf and HVC.

Evolutionary Schema for Finite-State Syntax in Bengalese Finches

Based on these discussions, we propose the following scenario to explain ultimate and proximate causes of song complexity in Bengalese finches. We assume that there is some rate of mutation occurring in NIf that enables finite-state song syntax in white-rumped munias. However, syntactically complex songs impose a greater cognitive load and singing such songs might increase predation in a natural environment. Upon domestication, however, such mutation is not eliminated from the population because cognitively demanding song would do no harm. Rather, since the females' perceptual system evolved under such predation pressure, females would prefer song complexity because an individual's ability to sing a complex song yet survive in a harsh environment would guarantee that individuals with these songs should have a reproductive advantage.

We suggest that a female bias to prefer syntactical complexity led to selection for this mutation in the population of domesticated Bengalese finches. When female preference in a natural environment guides the direction of evolution and then domestication eliminates natural constraints, the directed feature will continued to evolve until certain limits and that is what we see in domesticated Bengalese finches.

CONCLUSION

Obviously, further work is necessary to prove this scenario. One obvious question is the influence of genetic factors in determining song complexity. This should be sorted out by cross-fostering experiments between Bengalese finches and white-rumped munias. A second question is: Why does NIf seem to be critical only in Bengalese finches with complex song syntax? For what functions has NIf evolved in the male songbird brain? Although it is one of the most conspicuous sex-linked brain structures on oscine brain, we know too little about the physiology and anatomy of this nucleus to answer questions about its function. Finally, a more comprehensive analysis of female song preferences in this species should be carried out in a semi-natural environment. Nevertheless, even this brief review suggests that proximate and ultimate analyses of song syntax in Bengalese finches should provide a worth-while and rewarding task for integrative behavioral neurobiology.

ACKNOWLEDGMENTS

Work reported here was supported by PRESTO, Japan Science and Technology Agency. I am indebted to Peter Marler and Phil Zeigler for their very helpful and patient advice in revising the manuscript. Most studies introduced here were joint endeavors with students and research associates in the Okanoya Laboratory, Chiba University. I thank Masaru Wada and Ryoko Otsuka for performing the radioimmu-noassay and Miki Takahashi, Maki Ikebuchi, and Hiroko Yamada for preparing figures.

REFERENCES

1. TINBERGEN, N. 1963. On aims and methods of ethology. Z. Tierpsychol. **20:** 410–433.
2. WILSON, E.O. 1975. Sociobiology: the New Synthesis. Harvard University Press. Cambridge, MA.
3. BAPTISTA, L.F. 1995. A guide to the study of estrildids. Estrildian **3:** 13–24.
4. BAPTISTA, L.F. & S.L.L. GAUNT. 1994. Advances in studies of avian sound communication. Condor **96:** 817–830.
5. MARLER, P. 1970. Birdsong and speech development: could there be parallels? Am. Sci. **58:** 669–673.
6. DOUPE, A.J. & P.K. KUHL. 1999. Birdsong and human speech. Annu. Rev. Neurosci. **22:** 567–631.
7. SOHA, J. & P. MARLER. 2001. Vocal syntax development in the white-crowned sparrow (*Zonotrichia leucophrys*). J. Comp. Psychol. **115:** 172–180.
8. BALABAN, E. 1988. Bird song syntax: learned intraspecific variation is meaningful. Proc. Natl. Acad. Sci. USA **85:** 3657–3660.
9. JACKENDOFF, R. 2002. Foundations of Language: Brain, Meaning, Grammar, Evolution. Oxford University Press. Oxford.
10. CATCHPOLE, C.K. & P.J.B. SLATER. 1995. Bird Song: Biological Themes and Variations. Cambridge University Press. Cambridge.

11. HAHNLOSER R.H.R., A.A. KOZHEVNIKOV & M.S. FEE. 2002. An ultra-sparse code underlies the generation of neural sequences in a songbird. Nature **419:** 65–70.
12. VU, E.T., M.E. MAZUREK & Y.C. KUO. 1994. Identification of a forebrain motor programming network for the learned song of zebra finches. J. Neurosci. **14:** 6923–6934.
13. YU, A.C. & D. MARGOLIASH. 1996. Temporal hierarchical control of singing in birds. Science **273:** 1871–1875.
14. PACKERT, M., J. MARTENS, J. KOSUCH, *et al.* 2003. Phylogenetic signal in the song of crests and kinglets (Aves: Regulus). Evolution **57:** 616–629.
15. PODOS, J., S. NOWICKI & S. PETERS. 1999. Permissiveness in the learning and development of song syntax in swamp sparrows. Anim. Behav. **58:** 93–103.
16. ZANN, R.A. 1996. The Zebra Finch. Oxford University Press. Oxford.
17. TODT, D. & H. HULTSCH. 1996. Acquisition and performance of song repertoires: ways of coping with diversity and versatility. *In* Ecology and Evolution of Acoustic Communication in Birds. D.E. Kroodsma & E.H. Miller, Eds.: 79–96. Cornell University Press. Ithaca, NY.
18. EENS, M. 1997. Understanding the complex song of European starling: an integrated ethological approach. Adv. Study Behav. **26:** 355–434.
19. GIL, D. & P.J.B. SLATER. 2000. Song organisation and singing patterns of the willow warbler, *Phylloscopus trochilus*. Behaviour **137:** 759–782.
20. HONDA, E. & K. OKANOYA. 1999. Acoustical and syntactical comparisons between songs of the white-backed munia *Lonchura striata* and its domesticated strain, the Bengalese finch *Lonchura striata* var. *domestica*. Zool. Sci. **16:** 319–326.
21. HOSINO, T. & K. OKANOYA. 2000. Lesion of a higher-order song nucleus disrupts phrase level complexity in Bengalese finches. NeuroReport **11:** 2091–2095.
22. OKANOYA, K. 1997. Voco-auditory behavior in the Bengalese finch: a comparison with the zebra finch. Biomed. Res. **18:** 53–70.
23. OKANOYA, K. & A. YAMAGUCHI. 1997. Adult Bengalese finches require real-time auditory feedback to produce normal song syntax. J. Neurobiol. **33:** 343–356.
24. WOOLLEY, S.M.N. & E.W. RUBEL. 1997. Bengalese finches *Lonchura striata domestica* depend upon auditory feedback for the maintenance of adult song. J. Neurosci. **15:** 6380–6390.
25. KOBAYASI, K.I. & K. OKANOYA. 2003. Context-dependent song amplitude control in Bengalese finches. NeuroReport **14:** 521–524.
26. YAMADA, H. & K. OKANOYA. 2003. Song syntax changes in Bengalese finches singing in a helium atmosphere. NeuroReport **14:** 1725–1729.
27. BRAINARD, M.S. & A.J. DOUPE. 2000. Auditory feedback in learning and maintenance of vocal behaviour. Nat. Rev. Neurosci. **1:** 31–40.
28. BUCHAN, J. 1976. The Bengalese Finch. Isles d'Avon. Bristol.
29. WASHIO, K. 1996. Enigma of Bengalese finches. (In Japanese). Kindai Bungei-sha, Tokyo.
30. OKANOYA, K., T. YONEDA & S. ISEKI. 1995. Distance calls of the wild white-backed munia in Kijoka, Okinawa, Jap. J. Ornithol. **44:** 231–233.
31. BOLHUIS, J.J. & E.M. MACPHAIL. 2001. A critique of the neuroecology of learning and memory. Trends Cog. Sci. **5:** 426–433.
32. OKANOYA, K. & A. TAKASHIMA. 1997. Auditory preference of the female as a factor directing the evolution of Bengalese finch songs. Trans. Tech. Comm. Psychol. Physiol. Acoust. **27:** 1–6.
33. OKANOYA, K., A. TAKASHIMA, A. OKUHARA, *et al.* Syntactical complexity of male songs stimulates reproductive development in female Bengalese finches. Zool. Sci. Submitted for publication.
34. TAKA-TSUKASA, N. 1917. Kahidori. (In Japanese). Shokabo, Tokyo.
35. NAKAMURA, K. & K. OKANOYA. 2000. Measuring the cognitive cost of voco-auditory behavior: a case of Bengalese finch song. Trans. Tech. Comm. Psychol. Physiol. Accoust. **30:** 1–6.
36. OKANOYA, K. 2002. Sexual selection as a vehicle of syntax. *In* Transitions to Language. A. Wray, Ed.: 46–63. Oxford University Press. Oxford.

37. MARGOLIASH, D. 1997. Functional organization of forebrain pathways for song production and perception. J. Neurobiol. **33:** 671–693.
38. SUTHERS, R.A. 1997. Peripheral control and lateralization of birdsong. J. Neurobiol. **33:** 632–652.
39. VU, E.T., M.E. MAZUREK & Y.C. KUO. 1995. Hierarchical organization of brain areas mediating zebra finch learned vocalizations. Abstr. Neuroscience Soc.
40. CLAYTON, N.S. & E. PROVE. 1989. Song discrimination in female zebra finches and Bengalese finches. Anim. Behav. **38:** 352–362.
41. NAKAMURA, T., K. MATSUNO & S. SUGA. 1985. Reproductive response of female common finches to the different quality of male songs. Yamanashi Univ. Res. Rep. **35:** 66–70.
42. CATCHPOLE, C.K. & B. LEISLER. 1996. Female aquatic warblers *Acrocephalus paludicola* are attracted by playback of longer and more complicated songs. Behav. **133:** 1153–1164.
43. EENS, M., R. PINXTEN & R.F. VERHEYEN. 1991. Male song as a cue for mate choice in the European starling. Behavior **116:** 211–238.
44. KROODSMA, D.E. 1976. Reproductive development in a female songbird: differential stimulation by quality of male song. Science **192:** 574–575.
45. UNO, H. & K. OKANOYA. 1998. Neural basis for song production in Bengalese finches: effects of partial lesions on the higher vocal center. Tech. Report. IEICE SP97:137.
46. UNO, H. & K. OKANOYA. Partial lesions of HVC alter song element chunking in Bengalese finches. Neurosci. Res. Submitted for publication.

Origin of the Anterior Forebrain Pathway

DAVID J. PERKEL

Departments of Biology and Otolaryngology, University of Washington, Seattle, Washington 98195-6515, USA

ABSTRACT: The brain nuclei and pathways comprising the song system of oscine songbirds bear many similarities with circuits in other bird species and in mammals. This suggests that the song system evolved as a specialization of pre-existing circuits and may retain fundamental properties in common with those of other taxa. Here we review evidence for these similarities, including electrophysiological, morphological, and neurochemical data for identifying specific cell types. In addition, we discuss connectional data, addressing similarities in axonal projections among nuclei across taxa. We focus primarily on the anterior forebrain pathway, a circuit essential for song learning and vocal plasticity, because the evidence is strongest that this circuit is homologous to mammalian circuits. These fundamental similarities highlight the importance of comparative approaches; for example, understanding the role the anterior forebrain pathway plays in song plasticity may shed light on general principles of basal ganglia function. In addition, understanding specializations of such circuits in songbirds may illuminate specific innovations critical for vocal learning.

KEYWORDS: striatum; basal ganglia; comparative neurobiology; evolution

WHAT IS SPECIAL ABOUT THE SONG SYSTEM?

One of the principal attractions of the song system as an experimental model system is the fact that it is made up of discrete nuclei, many of which are readily identifiable in Nissl-stained tissue or even in unstained, living brain slices. Ample evidence now supports the notion that these nuclei are devoted to song perception, learning and generation. Their absence in avian species that do not learn their vocalizatio—for example, pigeons and chickens—suggests that the evolution of these structures was probably an essential step in the evolution of song learning. It seems natural to ask how these nuclei evolved and which of their features are critical to their function in song learning. In attempting to answer both of these questions , it is necessary to determine in what respects the properties of these neural structures differ from those of neighboring forebrain structures. Answering a complementary

Address for correspondence: David J. Perkel, Departments of Biology and Otolaryngology, Box 356515, University of Washington, Seattle, WA 98195-6515. Voice: 206-221-2477; fax: 206-543-5152.

perkel@u.washington.edu; <http://faculty.washington.edu/perkel>

Ann. N.Y. Acad. Sci. 1016: 736–748 (2004). © 2004 New York Academy of Sciences.
doi: 10.1196/annals.1298.039

question—What characters have been retained in the song nuclei during their evolution?—will shed light on features that are generally essential for motor learning that is guided by sensory feedback.

Because connections between the song-system nuclei and the surrounding forebrain are sparse, previous discussions of the evolutionary origin of, or comparative approaches to, the song system[1,2] (Jarvis, this volume) have tended, at least implicitly, to focus on the song system as autonomous and self-contained. Viewing the song system in this manner has encouraged a tendency to think about the song system as if it arose *de novo*. Such a view is never explicitly stated because it is incompatible with what we know of brain evolution. However, it seems possible that this implicit understanding has tended to delay acceptance of an alternative view, that each nucleus arose from, and shares many features with, the neural tissue in which it is embedded. This latter perspective may provide a much simpler and coherent account of song-system evolution [3] (Farries, this volume). Its central hypothesis holds that the song system evolved from preexisting structures and circuits common to all birds. Furthermore, although the song-system nuclei are clearly specialized in many ways, including their morphology and hodology, they also closely resemble the surrounding tissue in which they are embedded and from which they are derived. Here we provide some background and a review of data providing a preliminary test of this hypothesis. We focus here primarily on the anterior forebrain pathway (AFP) because more data are available for this component of the system. We argue that the AFP has features closely resembling those of similar structures in other bird species, including non-oscine birds.

A further generalization of this view involves considering the song system in the context of vertebrate brain evolution. Increasingly, it is recognized that the majority of vertebrate brain organization is highly conserved. As discussed by Reiner *et al.* (this volume) and by Farries (this volume), even telencephalic organization, although superficially very different between birds and mammals, shows strong molecular, connectional, developmental, and other similarities. A second thread running through this chapter deals with comparisons between the AFP and mammalian cortico–basal ganglia–thalamocortical circuits. Such comparisons reveal strong similarities that offer considerable advantages for song-system researchers. For example, the abundant work on mammalian basal ganglia structure and function, driven in part by devastating clinical disorders such as Parkinson's disease and Huntington's disease, has guided and accelerated song-system research. But the benefits may eventually flow in the other direction as well. We suggest that because song is a relatively well understood, naturally learned behavior with a discrete neural substrate, understanding the role of the AFP in song learning has the potential to reveal general principles of basal ganglia function that apply to all vertebrates.

THE AFP WITHIN THE LARGER SONG-SYSTEM CIRCUIT— BRIEF HISTORY OF THE DISCOVERY OF NUCLEI AND CONNECTIONS OF THE AFP

The song system can be divided into three main components: auditory, motor, and plasticity. Nottebohm and colleagues[4] first identified the song nuclei HVC (used as a proper name; see Reiner *et al.*, this volume for a discussion of nomenclature), robust nucleus of the arcopallium (RA), and the hypoglossal nucleus, which form a descending motor pathway essential for song production. While it was initially thought that auditory information reached HVC directly via field L, it now seems clear that much of this information is carried to HVC via the interfacial nucleus of the nidopallium (NIf), which makes a strong direct projection to HVC [5-7] (see chapters in Part III. Hearing the Song, this volume). The initial identification of HVC [4] also revealed a projection from HVC to a large nucleus in the anterior forebrain, which Nottebohm and colleagues named Area X. Subsequent work, including lesion and tracing studies,[8,9] identified the medial portion of the dorsolateral nucleus of the anterior thalamus (DLM), the lateral magnocellular nucleus of the anterior nidopallium (LMAN), and the medial magnocellular nucleus of the anterior nidopallium (MMAN) and worked out much of the core forebrain portions of the song-system circuit we now recognize (Farries, this volume). A key insight was that the projection from HVC to Area X was the beginning of a circuit that reaches RA indirectly, via DLM and LMAN. Lesion studies[8,10,11] showed that the AFP, while not essential for production of learned song, is crucial for song learning (see Brainard; Bottjer; Nordeen and Nordeen, this volume). Refinement of the circuit diagram has continued, and we now recognize a number of additional connections. Furthermore, the projection forming the first step of the AFP, from HVC to Area X, is not topographically organized, but subsequent steps are organized in a topographic fashion.[12,13] When Vates *et al.*[14] and Nixdorf-Bergweiler *et al.*[15] showed, by different methods, that LMAN neurons that project to RA also send axon collaterals to Area X, it became clear that the AFP was not simply an indirect pathway from HVC to RA, but also a recurrent network. Although it is not clear precisely what functional role this recurrence plays, such connections are likely capable of more complex information processing than a simpler direct connection. Moreover, the projections through this recurrent loop, traversing Area X, DLM, and LMAN and returning to Area X, maintain topographic position in register throughout the loop, resulting in a number of parallel microcircuits.[12,13,16] Because the output from LMAN to RA is also topographically organized, and because RA itself has a myotopic organization related to the syringeal and respiratory muscles,[17] Luo *et al.*[13] raised the possibility that the AFP has a motor-related organization, even though it appears not to have a primarily motor role.

Each of the nuclei of the song system is embedded in grey matter and is distinguished from that surrounding neural tissue primarily by such cytoarchitectonic features as higher cell density, larger neuronal somata, or darker Nissl staining of individual neurons. In addition, levels of expression of a wide variety of neurochemical markers differ between areas within and surrounding song-system nuclei (see, for example, Jarvis, this volume). These borders almost always coincide with the Nissl-defined nuclear borders.[8] It is thus clear that the song-system nuclei differ in important quantitative ways from their immediate surroundings. However, since these nuclei are directly adjacent to the tissue in which they are embedded, with no structural borders separating them, it seems reasonable to consider them as part of their surrounding structures. Of the three main components of the song system—the auditory pathway, the posterior motor pathway, and the anterior forebrain pathway— we focus here on the anterior forebrain pathway because we have a better current understanding of the evolutionary nature of these structures.

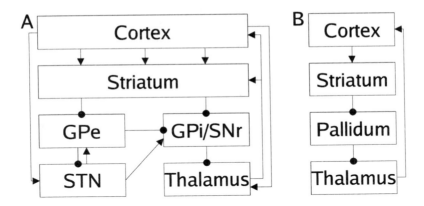

FIGURE 1. (**A**) Schematic description of mammalian basal ganglia pathways. *Arrows* indicate glutamatergic excitatory connections; *filled circles,* GABAergic inhibitory connections. Redrawn after Smith et al.[23] (**B**) Highly simplified view of the so-called direct pathway of the basal ganglia, to which we here compare the anterior forebrain pathway of the song system.

THE AVIAN AND MAMMALIAN BASAL GANGLIA—
EVIDENCE FOR HOMOLOGY

Some years prior to the identification of the posterior pathway, Karten and colleagues investigated the connections of the avian basal ganglia (then known as the paleostriatal complex).[19,20] That work focused on pigeons, which are not songbirds, do not learn their vocalizations, and do not have song nuclei. The work provided evidence suggesting that the avian paleostriatal complex (now termed the lateral striatum, medial striatum and globus pallidus) is homologous with components of the mammalian basal ganglia in mammals; the basal ganglia are grey-matter regions lying below the cortex and at the base of the telencephalon (FIG. 1; see also chapters by Farries and by Reiner et al., this volume). The main basal ganglia structures are the striatum, the globus pallidus, the substantia nigra and the subthalamic nucleus. In primates, the striatum has two major subdivisions, known as the caudate nucleus and the putamen, and the globus pallidus is divided into an internal and an external segment.[21–23]

The striatum is the major input structure of the basal ganglia; it receives excitatory connections from many regions of cerebral cortex and dense dopaminergic projections from the substantia nigra, pars compacta (SN_C), in the midbrain. The majority of neurons in the striatum possess small- to medium-sized somata and densely spiny dendrites. These so-called medium-spiny neurons (MSNs) are all GABAergic, and they all send axonal projections to other structures. In addition, the striatum is known to contain at least three classes of interneurons, each with distinct electrophysiological, morphological, and neurochemical properties. MSNs can be divided grossly into two major classes, based on their projections and on the presence of peptide co-transmitters. One class expresses the peptide substance P (SP) and projects to the internal segment of the globus pallidus and to the substantia nigra pars reticulata (SN_R). The other class of MSNs expresses the peptide enkephalin (ENK) and projects to the external segment of the globus pallidus (GP_E). Neurons of the GP_E extend GABAergic projections to the subthalamic nucleus, which sends glutamatergic projections to the GP_I. Neurons of the GP_I send GABAergic projections to the thalamus and brainstem. Thalamic nuclei that receive pallidal input project back to regions of cortex that originated these corticostriatal projections. Each projection of this cortico–basal ganglia–thalamocortical loop is organized topographically, such that information concerning, for example, motor control of different parts of the body is handled in parallel.

Subsequent to the initial tract-tracing studies of Karten,[19,20] Reiner and colleagues, using a variety of approaches, including tracing, immunostaining, in situ hybridization, confirmed, for pigeons, close parallels of the avian basal ganglia with their mammalian counterparts. They identified projections from overlying pallium to the structures now called the medial and lateral striatum. They found that lateral striatum projects to the globus pallidus, which projects in turn to the thalamus and brainstem. In addition, Jiao et al.[24] reported reciprocal connections between the GP and the avian subthalamic nucleus (formerly called the anterior nucleus of the ansa lenticularis). Additional evidence comes from recent studies of the expression patterns of a small number of transcription factors that serve as markers and in some cases specifiers for early telencephalic territories. For example, Puelles et al.[25] studied the expression pattern in developing chick brain of the transcription factors Dlx-2, Pax-6, Nkx-2.1 and found striatal and pallidal territories corresponding to primordial striatum and pallidum, respectively. Additionally, overlying these basal ganglia structures was a region expressing transcription factors essential for specifying pallial structures such as cortex, claustrum, and amygdala. Taken together, these observations support the identification of striatal and pallidal components of the avian basal ganglia, as well as an overlying pallial structure[26] (see Reiner et al., this volume).

ORGANIZATION OF BASAL GANGLIA CIRCUITRY WITHIN THE SONGBIRD FOREBRAIN

Area X, the first nucleus of the anterior forebrain pathway, lies entirely within the medial striatum, suggesting that it should have striatal features, including GABAergic inhibitory projection neurons, heavy dopaminergic innervation, and outputs to the globus pallidus. Indeed, Lewis et al.,[27] Bottjer,[28] and Soha et al.[29] recognized the predicted dopaminergic innervation early on. They examined the catecholaminergic inputs to Area X and identified a dopaminergic input to Area X from the ventral tegmental area of the midbrain. Casto and Ball[30] found high levels of D1 dopamine receptor binding in Area X, further supporting this view. However, other striatal features of this nucleus were not investigated for some time. Moreover, the possibility of a GABAergic, inhibitory projection within the AFP was not imagined in the literature on the song system, though it was clearly predicted by this view of Area X as being part of the basal ganglia.

From a comparative perspective then, one might argue that HVC and LMAN represent overlying pallial structures, analogous and possibly homologous to cortex.

Furthermore, Area X would represent basal ganglia structures, and in this context it makes some sense that Area X should project to the thalamus. However, in mammals, the basal ganglia pathway from cortex to thalamus traverses at least two relay stations, striatum and pallidum, while Area X is only a single structure. This difference raises the possibility that Area X is not simply "striatal," with the potential implication that the AFP is fundamentally different from a standard basal ganglia circuit in its connections, cellular architecture, and neurotransmitter phenotype, as well as in other features. This prompted us to test whether Area X shares one of the signature features of striatal neurons—one that is relatively rare in the vertebrate brain: long-range GABAergic projection neurons. Grisham and Arnold[31] had shown GABA immunoreactivity in Area X and DLM, as well as in a number of other areas of the songbird brain. Unfortunately, they were unable to attain the cellular resolution needed to determine whether the projection neurons of Area X contain GABA. Luo and Perkel[32] addressed this question by using immunostaining for glutamic acid decarboxylase (GAD), the rate-limiting enzyme in the synthetic pathway for GABA, and a marker for GABAergic neurons. They first found that most Area X neurons are GAD positive, though some have substantially more intense staining than others. They combined this technique with anterograde and retrograde tracing and with lesions to demonstrate that the cell bodies and terminals of the Area X neurons projecting to DLM express GAD. Moreover, the strong GAD-like immunoreactivity in DLM was eliminated after lesions of Area X, suggesting that Area X provides most, if not all, of the GABAergic input to DLM.

Luo and Perkel[33] went on to study this connection using electrophysiological methods in brain slices containing DLM and the axon pathway arriving from Area X. They found that afferents from Area X form powerful GABAergic synapses on DLM neurons, that these synapses use $GABA_A$ receptors, and that the intrinsic properties of DLM neurons closely resemble those of mammalian thalamic neurons. These results confirmed that Area X provides a GABAergic, inhibitory input to DLM. Moreover, they highlighted an additional approach, heretofore unused in the AFP, that could be used to test for similarities between the AFP and mammalian basal ganglia pathways: cellular electrophysiology. Although some cellular work has been carried out on mammalian pallidothalamic connections,[34] it appears that our understanding of the Area X–DLM synapse in songbirds is at least equal to the current understanding of comparable synapses in mammals.

These experiments indicate that Area X has the additional key striatal feature of GABAergic, inhibitory projection neurons. However, as mentioned above, two observations complicate a simple one-to-one comparison of Area X to the striatum. First, Area X projects to the thalamus, which mammalian striatum is not thought to do. Second, only a minority of the constituent neurons of Area X, i.e., large, sparsely spaced ones with aspiny dendrites, project to DLM.[9,32] These observations suggest that there may be important differences in the organization of basal ganglia circuits in birds and mammals.

IS AREA X A STRIATOPALLIDAL NUCLEUS?

One way to account for these observations is to suggest that Area X might have both pallidal and striatal features. If the small, densely packed, weakly GAD-immunoreactive neurons in Area X are striatal and the sparsely spaced projection neurons are pallidal, Area X would have both striatal and pallidal aspects. The hypothesis is readily testable because the cellular properties of mammalian striatal neurons are relatively well characterized.

Some data already supported this hypothesis; the numerous small neurons of Area X showed at least a low level of GAD expression.[32] Farries and Perkel[35] provided a more direct test, however, by making whole-cell recordings from neurons in Area X in brain slices. They characterized the intrinsic electrophysiological properties of the neurons and also examined the cellular morphology by filling neurons. They recorded from four classes of neuron, each corresponding to a striatal neuron class: spiny neurons were most numerous, and three rarer classes corresponded to striatal interneuron classes.[36] (It is important to note that in Area X, the spiny neurons do not project to DLM.[9,32] In addition, a fifth neuron class was recorded, not corresponding to any type of mammalian striatal neuron. This cell type, with a large soma and aspiny dendrites, is spontaneously active and can be driven to fire at very high rates with current injection and was thus called the aspiny fast-firing (AF) cell type. This cell shares many features with pallidal neurons in mammals. This finding provided direct support for the idea that Area X contains a mixture of striatal and pallidal neurons. Moreover, these neurons have dendritic morphology similar to that of the Area X projection neurons, suggesting that they may project to DLM. Experiments designed to test directly whether the AF cell type of Area X projects to DLM have produced results suggesting that only AF cells project to DLM, but that perhaps not all AF cells project (Farries, Ding, and Perkel, unpublished observations). Recently, Reiner et al.[46] provided neurochemical evidence that the neurons of area X that project to DLM are pallidal; they express the neurotensin-related peptide LANT-6, a marker of pallidal neurons in mammals. Clearly, more work is necessary to determine the microcircuitry of Area X, and whether all types of connections expected from the mammalian plan are present. However, the currently available data are consistent with the idea that Area X represents an agglomeration of striatum and pallidum (FIG. 2).

IS THE AFP UNIQUE IN FORMING A THREE-STATION BASAL GANGLIA CIRCUIT?

If the AFP represents a basal ganglia circuit, it differs from those already identified in mammals and birds in having only three stations: HVC/LMAN as the pallial station; Area X as the basal ganglia station; and DLM as the thalamic station. As we have seen, several lines of evidence suggest that both striatal and pallidal cellular components are intermingled in Area X. But a key question remains. Is this organization unique to the song system, an evolutionary innovation arising with the arrival of vocal learning in songbirds, or rather a neural arrangement more common than has been previously realized in bird, or even mammal brains? Four lines of evidence suggest that three-station basal ganglia circuits may not be unique to the songbird AFP and may in fact be a common feature of vertebrates.

First, if the AFP represents an evolutionary innovation of songbirds in which striatal and pallidal neurons are intermingled, then one would predict that other regions of the basal ganglia would differ in not having pallidal cells intermingled with striatal cells. Farries and Perkel[37] carried out whole-cell recordings from neurons in the basal ganglia of male zebra finches outside of Area X. The electrophysiological and morphological features of the neurons recorded revealed several cell types within the basal ganglia. The majority of cells had features of the principal neuron of the mammalian striatum, the so-called medium spiny neuron. In addition, three classes of neurons could be distinguished, each corresponding to a class of mammalian striatal interneuron. Finally, a separate class of cell was observed, resembling mammalian pallidal neurons in both electrophysiological and morphological properties. These data suggest that at least a substantial portion of the zebra finch "medial striatum" has pallidal cells intermingled with striatal cell types. Thus, Area X may not differ in a qualitative way from the surrounding striatal tissue, at least in its cellular composition.

A second line of evidence comes from studies of connections of structures in non-song-system structures in songbirds. Bottjer and colleagues have shown a number of pathways parallel to song-system circuits[38] (see also chapter by Bottjer, this volume). These connections link regions immediately surrounding the nuclei of the song system and suggest that the song system may have evolved in songbirds from preexisting circuits in ancestral birds.

Third, several studies suggest a high degree of conservation in electrophysiological and morphological properties of neurons in the brain structures of both oscine and non-oscine birds. Reiner et al.[39] made in vivo intracellular recordings from pallial neurons in pigeons that project to the basal ganglia. They found that these neu-

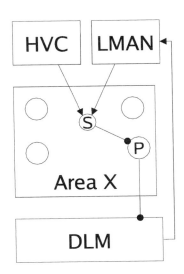

FIGURE 2. A current view of the microcircuitry of Area X, indicating a mixture of striatal and pallidal cell types. HVC and LMAN are pallidal nuclei that make glutamatergic projections to spiny neurons (S).[47,48] Spiny neurons contact pallidal neurons (P) that project to the thalamic nucleus DLM, where they make GABAergic, inhibitory connections.[46,47] *Open circles* represent the three classes of Area X interneuron.[35] DLM neurons make glutamatergic, excitatory connections on LMAN neurons.[49–51]

rons have some properties similar to those of mammalian corticostriatal projection neurons. For example, like their mammalian counterparts, these neurons have slow axonal conduction velocity, a signature pattern of inward rectification, and spontaneous oscillations (approximately 1 Hz) between depolarized and hyperpolarized states. In mammals, these are known as "up" and "down" states,[40] and the excitatory connections they make onto striatal spiny neurons confer a similar pattern on the recipient cells. While recording from the cells, they also filled them with biocytin and later analyzed their dendritic morphology. This revealed an important difference— these projection neurons lack the striking apical dendrite that is typical of the pyramidal neurons of mammalian cortical structures. In addition, preliminary electrophysiological studies of the functional and morphological cell types in the basal ganglia of the domestic chicken suggest that the cellular composition of the medial striatum is similar to that of the zebra finch.[41]

A final piece of evidence of similarity between oscine and non-oscine birds derives from comparing connections. Because of their role in filial imprinting and in passive-avoidance learning (for review, see refs. 42 and 43), the connections of chicken basal ganglia have been carefully studied.The medial striatum (previously known as the lobus parolfactorius or LPO) receives afferents from the overlying nidopallium.[44] Those regions, in turn, receive inputs from dorsal thalamic regions.[45] These connections form two parts of what might be a three-station basal-ganglia loop in chickens. Together, these data support the idea that the AFP is a songbird basal ganglia pathway. Further work will be required to characterize microcircuitry among the neuron types within each nucleus in the circuit (see, for example, ref. 46). Such studies will address to what degree the AFP maintains a four-cell "direct" basal ganglia pathway (pallium to spiny neuron to pallidal neuron to thalamus to pallium), through a three-station loop. They may also uncover either fundamental differences in connectivity from that of mammals, or important quantitative variations that may contribute to functional divergence between the taxa.

IMPLICATIONS OF A CLEARLY IDENTIFIED BASAL GANGLIA PATHWAY IN SONGBIRDS

Acceleration of Song-System Research

This view of the AFP as a basal ganglia pathway that shares many features with its mammalian counterpart has several important implications for both avian and mammalian researchers. For students of the song system, an immediate benefit is the ability to make and test predictions guided by the substantial, detailed information available on the mammalian basal-ganglia structures and pathways. This will doubtless accelerate progress in describing the basic features of the song system, an essential step toward building a detailed understanding of how the system functions. Some of the most important descriptive questions along these lines include: What are the main microcircuits of Area X? Which neurotransmitters and receptors mediate these circuits? What are the physiological actions of dopamine on neurons other than Area X spiny neurons and on synapses other than the glutamatergic afferents to Area X? What other neuromodulators are present and what are their actions? What forms of synaptic plasticity exist in Area X and how could they affect song learning?

In addition to "guiding" descriptive studies, viewing the AFP as a basal ganglia circuit will help mechanistic and functional studies. For example, it will be crucial to determine the effect of depleting dopamine on song learning and performance. Moreover, the role of cholinergic function will also be important to investigate, based on the dramatic role this neurotransmitter system plays in mammals.

Better Communication

Two aspects of recent progress should serve to improve communication and foster collaboration between song-system researchers and students of mammalian basal ganglia. First, the recent effort to modernize the avian brain nomenclature[26] (see also Reiner *et al.*, this volume) will help avoid erroneous assumptions about the bird brain. Among these is the belief that most of the bird forebrain is striatal and therefore has little, if any, tissue corresponding to cortex and that the medial striatum (formerly called the lobus parolfactorius) is primarily concerned with olfaction. Second, enough progress has been made in describing the avian forebrain plan and, in particular, the detailed makeup of the AFP, that it is now fairly easy to convince neuroscientists who study mammalian brains that the AFP is a basal ganglia pathway. Since we also have strong behavioral data indicating that the AFP is essential for song learning in juveniles as well as adult song plasticity (see Brainard, this volume), there is, in some sense, more specific information available about the function of the AFP in a natural learning process than there is for the mammalian striatum, with the exception of the role of ventral striatum in adaptations caused by drugs of abuse.

Potential Benefits for Mammalian Basal Ganglia Research

Although much is known about the role of the mammalian basal ganglia in behaviors and pathologies, specific, testable hypotheses about how neuronal circuits can explain these processes are difficult because the basal ganglia are involved in so many types of behaviors. The song system offers advantages for illuminating general principles of basal ganglia function because of the well-characterized, naturally learned behavior, the discrete nature of the nuclei, and the apparent segregation of function into pathways for song production and song learning.

FUTURE DIRECTIONS

Thus far, the major benefits of viewing the song system in the context of broader vertebrate brain organization have been in the domain of improving descriptive studies. Work toward identifying cell types, determining properties of connections, and identifying neurotransmitter and transmitter-receptor types has been accelerated by considering the songbird brain in this light. There is little doubt, given the extremely detailed knowledge available concerning the mammalian brain—especially the basal ganglia—that we will see rapid and significant advances in the understanding of, in ever more detail, the basic structural and functional properties of the song system. In the basal ganglia of songbirds, some key questions that we hope will be answered include: To what degree are there direct and "indirect" pathways? What, if any, role does the subthalamic nucleus play in the anterior forebrain pathway? Are any additional projections that might be predicted based on mammalian work present in the song system? To what degree does the intrinsic connectivity of Area X match that of the mammalian basal ganglia, with segregated striatal and pallidal territories? Such questions also extend outside the basal ganglia, and we will see additional advances as possible homologies between avian and mammalian pallial structures become clearer.

In addition, we expect that more mechanistic studies will benefit from seeing the song system as part of the rest of the brain. *In vivo* recording during song playback and song production has already begun to clarify the functional role of both the motor pathway and the anterior forebrain pathway. But many more questions remain that can be addressed by recording in behaving animals. In addition, perturbations of neural activity during behavior will test specific hypotheses generated by recording. Furthermore, neurochemical measurements and manipulations (e.g., of catecholamines) will clarify the role of neuromodulation in the song system. It will be crucial ultimately to relate all of these data, at the biophysical, cellular, circuit and systems levels, to behavior. A main advantage of studying the song system, the ability to link neural features to song learning, perception and production, will prove key as we move forward. At each step, better understanding of the structural and functional features of the system will allow formation and testing of better hypotheses about the evolutionary origin of the song system.

REFERENCES

1. NOTTEBOHM, F. 1980. Brain pathways for vocal learning in birds: a review of the first 10 years. Prog. Psychobiol. Physiol. Psychol. **9:** 85–124.
2. BRENOWITZ, E.A. 1997. Comparative approaches to the avian song system. J. Neurobiol. **33:** 517–531.
3. FARRIES, M.A. 2001. The oscine song system considered in the context of the avian brain: lessons learned from comparative neurobiology. Brain Behav. Evol. **58:** 80–100.
4. NOTTEBOHM, F., T.M. STOKES & C.M. LEONARD. 1976. Central control of song in the canary, *Serinus canarius*. J. Comp. Neurol. **165:** 457–486.
5. FORTUNE, E.S. & D. MARGOLIASH. 1995. Parallel pathways and convergence onto HVc and adjacent neostriatum of adult zebra finches (*Taeniopygia guttata*). J. Comp. Neurol. **360:** 413–441.
6. VATES, G.E. *et al.* 1996. Auditory pathways of caudal telencephalon and their relation to the song system of adult male zebra finches. J. Comp. Neurol. **366:** 613–642.
7. JANATA, P. & D. MARGOLIASH. 1999. Gradual emergence of song selectivity in sensorimotor structures of the male zebra finch song system. J. Neurosci. **19:** 5108–5118.
8. BOTTJER, S.W., E.A. MIESNER & A.P. ARNOLD. 1984. Forebrain lesions disrupt development but not maintenance of song in passerine birds. Science **224:** 901–903.
9. BOTTJER, S.W. *et al.* 1989. Axonal connections of a forebrain nucleus involved with vocal learning in zebra finches. J. Comp. Neurol. **279:** 312–326.
10. SOHRABJI, F., E.J. NORDEEN & K.W. NORDEEN. 1990. Selective impairment of song learning following lesions of a forebrain nucleus in juvenile zebra finches. Behav. Neural Biol. **53:** 51–631.
11. SCHARFF, C. & F. NOTTEBOHM. 1991. A comparative study of the behavior deficits following lesions of various parts of the zebra finch song system: implications for vocal learning. J. Neurosci. **11:** 2896–2913.
12. JOHNSON, F., M.M. SABLAN & S.W. BOTTJER. 1995. Topographic organization of a forebrain pathway involved with vocal learning in zebra finches. J. Comp. Neurol. **358:** 260–278.

13. LUO, M., L. DING & D.J. PERKEL. 2001. An avian basal ganglia pathway essential for vocal learning forms a closed topographic loop. J. Neurosci. **21:** 6836–6845.
14. VATES, G.E. & F. NOTTEBOHM. 1995. Feedback circuitry within a song-learning pathway. Proc. Natl. Acad. Sci. USA **92:** 5139–5143.
15. NIXDORF-BERGWEILER, B., M.B. LIPS & U. HEINEMANN. 1995. Electrophysiological and morphological evidence for a new projection of L-MAN neurons towards area X. Neuroreport **6:** 1729–1732.
16. IYENGAR, S., S.S. VISWANATHAN & S.W. BOTTJER. 1999. Development of topography within song control circuitry of zebra finches during the sensitive period for song learning. J. Neurosci. **19:** 6037–6057.
17. VICARIO, D.S. 1991. Organization of the zebra finch song control system: II. Functional organization of outputs from nucleus *robustus archistriatalis*. J. Comp. Neurol. **309:** 486–494.
18. BOTTJER, S.W. & F. JOHNSON. 1997. How should brain nuclei be delineated? They don't need to be! Trends Neurosci. **20:** 344–345; author reply, 345–346.
19. KARTEN, H.J. 1969. The organization of the avian telencephalon and some speculations on the phylogeny of the amniote telencephalon. *In* Comparative and Evolutionary Aspects of the Vertebrate Central Nervous System. C. Noback & J. Petras, Eds. Ann. N.Y. Acad. Sci. **167:** 146–179.
20. KARTEN, H.J. & J.L. DUBBELDAM. 1973. The organization and projections of the paleostriatal complex in the pigeon (*Columba livia*). J. Comp. Neurol. **148:** 61–90.
21. ALEXANDER, G.E. & M.D. CRUTCHER. 1990. Functional architecture of basal ganglia circuits: neural substrates of parallel processing. Trends Neurosci. **13:** 266–271.
22. PARENT, A. & L.-N. HAZRATI. 1995. Functional anatomy of the basal ganglia. I. The cortico-basal ganglia thalamo-cortical loop. Brain Res. Brain Res. Rev. **20:** 91–127.
23. SMITH, Y. *et al.* 1998. Microcircuitry of the direct and indirect pathways of the basal ganglia. Neuroscience **86:** 353–387.
24. JIAO, Y. *et al.* 2000. Identification of the anterior nucleus of the ansa lenticularis in birds as the homolog of the mammalian subthalamic nucleus. J. Neurosci. **20:** 6998–7010.
25. PUELLES, L. *et al.* 2000. Pallial and subpallial derivatives in the embryonic chick and mouse telencephalon, traced by the expression of the genes Dlx-2, Emx-1, Nkx- 2.1, Pax-6, and Tbr-1. J. Comp Neurol. **424:** 409–438.
26. REINER, A. *et al.* 2004. Revised nomenclature for avian telencephalon and some related brainstem nuclei. J. Comp. Neurol. **473:** 377–414.
27. LEWIS, J.W. *et al.* 1981. Evidence for a catecholaminergic projection to area X in the zebra finch. J. Comp. Neurol. **196:** 347–354.
28. BOTTJER, S.W. 1993. The distribution of tyrosine hydroxylase immunoreactivity in the brains of male and female zebra finches. J. Neurobiol. **24:** 51–69.
29. SOHA, J., T. SHIMIZU & A.J. DOUPE. 1996. Development of the catecholaminergic innervation of the song system of the male zebra finch. J. Neurobiol. **29:** 473–489.
30. CASTO, J.M. & G.F. BALL. 1994. Characterization and localization of D1 dopamine receptors in the sexually dimorphic vocal control nucleus, area X, and the basal ganglia of European starlings. J. Neurobiol. **25:** 767–780.
31. GRISHAM, W. & A.P. ARNOLD. 1994. Distribution of GABA-like immunoreactivity in the song system of the zebra finch. Brain Res. **651:** 115–122.
32. LUO, M. & D.J. PERKEL. 1999. Long-range GABAergic projection in a circuit essential for vocal learning. J. Comp. Neurol. **403:** 68–84.
33. LUO, M. & D.J. PERKEL. 1999. A GABAergic, strongly inhibitory projection to a thalamic nucleus in the zebra finch song system. J. Neurosci. **19:** 6700–6711.
34. DENIAU, J.M. & G. CHEVALIER. 1985. Disinhibition as a basic process in the expression of striatal functions. II. The striatonigral influence on thalamocortical cells of the ventromedial thalamic nucleus. Brain Res. **334:** 227–233.
35. FARRIES, M.A. & D.J. PERKEL. 2002. A telencephalic nucleus essential for song learning contains neurons with physiological characteristics of both striatum and globus pallidus. J. Neurosci. **22:** 3776–3787.
36. KAWAGUCHI, Y. 1993. Physiological, morphological, and histochemical characterization of three classes of interneurons in rat neostriatum. J. Neurosci. **13:** 4908–4923.

37. FARRIES, M.A. & D.J. PERKEL. 2000. Electrophysiological properties of avian basal ganglia neurons recorded in vitro. J. Neurophysiol. **84:** 2502–2513.
38. BOTTJER, S.W. & F. JOHNSON. 1997. Circuits, hormones, and learning: vocal behavior in songbirds. J. Neurobiol. **33:** 602–618.
39. REINER, A., E.A. STERN & C.J. WILSON. 2001. Physiology and morphology of intra-telencephalically projecting corticostriatal-type neurons in pigeons as revealed by intracellular recording and cell filling. Brain Behav. Evol. **58:** 101–114.
40. COWAN, R.L. & C.J. WILSON. 1994. Spontaneous firing patterns and axonal projections of single corticostriatal neurons in the rat medial agranular cortex. J. Neurophysiol. **71:** 17–32.
41. FARRIES, M.A. & D.J. PERKEL. 2002. Pallidum-like elements in the avian "striatum" outside of specialized vocal structures project directly to the thalamus. Soc. Neurosci. Abstr. 680.18.
42. HORN, G. 1998. Visual imprinting and the neural mechanisms of recognition memory. Trends Neurosci. **21:** 300–305.
43. ROSE, S.P.R. & M.G. STEWART. 1999. Cellular correlates of stages of memory formation in the chick following passive avoidance training. Behav. Brain Res. **98:** 237–243.
44. METZGER, M., S. JIANG & K. BRAUN. 1998. Organization of the dorsocaudal neostriatal complex: a retrograde and anterograde tracing study in the domestic chick with special emphasis on pathways relevant to imprinting. J. Comp. Neurol. **395:** 380–404.
45. MONTAGNESE, C.M., S.E. MEZEY & A. CSILLAG. 2003. Efferent connections of the dorsomedial thalamic nuclei of the domestic chick (*Gallus domesticus*). J. Comp. Neurol. **459:** 301–326.
46. REINER, A. *et al.* 2004. An immunohistochemical and pathway tracing study of the striatopallidal organization of area X in the male zebra finch. J. Comp. Neurol. **469:** 239–261.
47. FARRIES, M.A., L. DING & D.J. PERKEL. 2000. Physiological properties of synapses in area X of the zebra finch. Soc. Neurosci. Abstr. **26:** 758.6.
48. DING, L., D.J. PERKEL & M.A. FARRIES. 2003. Presynaptic depression of glutamatergic synaptic transmission by D1-like dopamine receptor activation in the avian basal ganglia. J. Neurosci. **23:** 6086–6095.
49. LIVINGSTON, F.S. & R. MOONEY. 1997. Development of intrinsic and synaptic properties in a forebrain nucleus essential to avian song learning. J. Neurosci. **17:** 8997–9009.
50. BOETTIGER, C.A. & A.J. DOUPE. 1998. Intrinsic and thalamic excitatory inputs onto songbird LMAN neurons differ in their pharmacological and temporal properties. J. Neurophysiol. **79:** 2615–2628.
51. BOTTJER, S.W., J.D. BRADY & J.P. WALSH. 1998. Intrinsic and synaptic properties of neurons in the vocal-control nucleus lMAN from in vitro slice preparations of juvenile and adult zebra finches. J. Neurobiol. **37:** 642–658.

Learned Birdsong and the Neurobiology of Human Language

ERICH D. JARVIS

Department of Neurobiology, Duke University Medical Center,
Durham, North Carolina 27710, USA

ABSTRACT: Vocal learning, the substrate for human language, is a rare trait found to date in only three distantly related groups of mammals (humans, bats, and cetaceans) and three distantly related groups of birds (parrots, humming-birds, and songbirds). Brain pathways for vocal learning have been studied in the three bird groups and in humans. Here I present a hypothesis on the rela-tionships and evolution of brain pathways for vocal learning among birds and humans. The three vocal learning bird groups each appear to have seven sim-ilar but not identical cerebral vocal nuclei distributed into two vocal pathways, one posterior and one anterior. Humans also appear to have a posterior vocal pathway, which includes projections from the face motor cortex to brainstem vocal lower motor neurons, and an anterior vocal pathway, which includes a strip of premotor cortex, the anterior basal ganglia, and the anterior thalamus. These vocal pathways are not found in vocal non-learning birds or mammals, but are similar to brain pathways used for other types of learning. Thus, I ar-gue that if vocal learning evolved independently among birds and humans, then it did so under strong genetic constraints of a pre-existing basic neural network of the vertebrate brain.

KEYWORDS: speech; song; warble; Broca's area; Wernicke's area; dorsal lat-eral prefrontal cortex; auditory pathway; epigenetic constraints

VOCAL LEARNERS

Vocal learning is the ability to acquire vocalizations through imitation rather than instinct. It is distinct from auditory learning, which is the ability to make associa-tions with sounds heard. An example of auditory learning is demonstrated when a dog learns to associate the words "sit" (English), "sientese" (Spanish), or "osuwali" (Japanese) with the act of sitting. The dog understands the word, but cannot imitate the sound of the word. However, auditory learning is not solely defined in the con-text of one species learning to grasp the meaning of sounds of another species. For example, a young vervet monkey will make innate alarm calls to all large animals. Auditory learning is exhibited when the young animals apparently learns from adult conspecifics to refine the production of their alarm calls only to predators.[1] Vocal learners, such as humans, parrots, and some songbirds, are able to imitate non-innate

Address for correspondence: Erich D. Jarvis, Department of Neurobiology, Duke University Medical Center, Box 3209, Durham, NC 27710, USA. Voice: 919-681-1680; fax: 919-681-0877. jarvis@neuro.duke.edu; <http://www.jarvislab.net/>

Ann. N.Y. Acad. Sci. 1016: 749–777 (2004). © 2004 New York Academy of Sciences.
doi: 10.1196/annals.1298.038

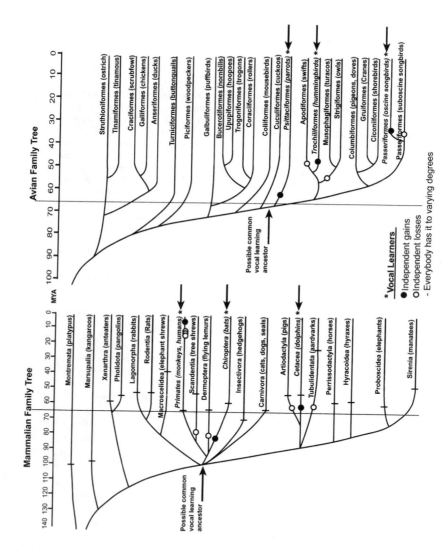

FIGURE 1. *See following page for legend.*

sounds such as sit, sientese, or osuwali. Most vocal learners, however, imitate sounds of their own species that have been passed on through cultural transmission.[2] Vocal learning depends upon auditory learning, but auditory learning does not depend on vocal learning. Vocal learners must hear the sounds they will later imitate. They must also use auditory feedback to correct their vocal output,[3] apparently forming auditory memories of whether or not they matched the sounds that they are trying to imitate.

Given the above definitions, most, if not all, vertebrates are capable of auditory learning, but few are capable of vocal learning. The latter has been experimentally found to date only in three distantly related groups of mammals (humans, bats, and cetaceans) and three distantly related groups of birds (parrots, hummingbirds, and songbirds) (FIG. 1).[4,5] Not all species in these groups have vocal learning abilities to the same degree. For example, humans, the most prolific vocal learners, can learn to produce a seemingly infinite number of combinations of learned vocalizations. While not as prolific, some parrots, corvid songbirds, starlings, and mockingbirds can produce hundreds if not thousands of calls and/or learned warble/song combinations. Finally, less prolific vocal learners, such as some very stereotyped songbirds and hummingbirds produce only one distinct song type with little variation.[6–8]

Each of the vocal learning avian and mammalian groups has close vocal non-learning relatives (FIG. 1). Thus, it has been argued that vocal learning has evolved independently of a common ancestor in the three vocal learning bird groups[4] and presumably in the three vocal learning mammalian groups. The question thus arises is whether there is something special about the brains of these animals that can imitate sounds.

FIGURE 1. Family trees of living mammalian and avian orders. The mammalian tree is derived from the morphological analysis by Novacek;[182,183] *horizontal lines* indicate extant of geologic evidence from fossils. The avian tree is derived from DNA-DNA hybridization analysis by Sibley and Alquist (page 838).[184] The Latin name of each order is given along with examples of common species. Passeriformes are divided into its two suborders, suboscine and oscine songbirds. The *vertical line* down the trees indicates the cretaceous-tertiary boundary, the time of the dinosaur extinction; MYA=millions of years ago. *Open* and *closed circles* show the minimal ancestral nodes where vocal learning could have either evolved independently or been lost independently. Independent losses would have at least required one common vocal learning ancestor, located by the *right-facing arrows*. Within primates, there would have to have been least seven independent losses (tree shrews, prosimians, new and old world monkeys, apes, and chimps) followed by the regaining of vocal learning in humans (assuming that all non-human primates are vocal non-learners). Both trees are modified here from the original sources[182–184] such that they include updated information and are stylistically more comparable. The trees are not meant to present the final dogma of mammalian and avian evolution, as there are many differences of opinion among scientists. Rather, the trees presented here are those that lead to more conservative interpretations of the evolution of vocal learning. For example, one alternative view of avian evolution posted on <http://tolweb.org/tree?group=Neornithes&contgroup=Aves> as of 2/15/2004 would have resulted in the interpretation of 16 independent losses of vocal learning instead of three.

CONSENSUS BIRD BRAIN SYSTEM FOR LEARNED VOCALIZING

Cerebral Vocal Nuclei in Vocal Learning Birds

A combination of methods, which include tract tracing, Nissl staining of brain sections, lesioning of specific brain regions, electrophysiological recordings, and vocalizing-driven gene expression, has revealed that songbirds, parrots, and hummingbirds each have seven cerebral or telencephalic vocal brain nuclei that are active when they are producing learned vocalizations (FIG. 2A–C; abbreviations in TABLE 1).[5,9-12] These brain nuclei have been given different names in each bird group because of the possibility that each group evolved them independently of a common ancestor with such nuclei.[5,13] Three of the nuclei are in nearly identical brain locations in each bird group, forming a column across three brain subdivisions (FIG. 2A–C, dark grey): (1) a nucleus in the anterior striatum (parrot MMSt, hummingbird VAS, and songbird Area X); (2) one in the anterior nidopallium (parrot NAOc, hummingbird VAN, and songbird MAN); and (3) one in the anterior mesopallium (parrot MOc, hummingbird VAM, and songbird MOc-like). The other four nuclei are located more posteriorly, in different locations relative to each other for each bird group, but within comparable areas of the same cerebral subdivisions (FIG. 2A–C, white): (4) a prominent nucleus that bulges from the nidopallium into the overlying ventricle (parrot NLC, hummingbird VLN, and songbird HVC); (5) a robust appearing nucleus within the arcopallium (parrot AAC, hummingbird VA, and songbird RA); (6) a small nucleus in the nidopallium (parrot lAN, hummingbird VMN, and songbird NIf); and (7) a small nucleus near the latter in the mesopallium (parrot lAM, hummingbird VMM, and songbird Av). To date, none of these seven vocal nuclei have been found in the cerebrums of vocal non-learning birds.[14-16]

The neural connectivity between most of the seven cerebral vocal nuclei has been determined in both songbirds and parrots,[13,17,18] and some connections have been determined in hummingbirds.[16] In all three bird groups, the posterior nuclei (numbers 4 and 5 above) appear to be part of a posterior vocal pathway that is connected with vocal motor neurons of the brainstem. This pathway includes a projection from a nidopallial vocal nucleus (HVC, NLC, VLN) to the arcopallial vocal nucleus (RA, AAC dorsal part, VA), and from there to midbrain (DM) and medulla (nXIIts) vocal motor neurons (FIG. 2A–C, black arrows). DM and nXIIts are also present in vocal non-learning birds and are known to control production of innate vocalizations.[19] However, vocal non-learning birds apparently do not contain projections from the arcopallium to DM and nXIIts.[20] The connectivity of the other two cerebral posterior vocal nuclei (numbers 6 and 7 above) in hummingbirds is not known, and in parrots has not been well studied.[12] In songbirds, one of these nuclei (NIf) projects to HVC and the other (Av) receives a projection from HVC (see Figure 2 of Reiner et al., this volume,[34] pp. 90,91).[21]

In songbirds and parrots, the nuclei located anteriorly are part of what is called an anterior forebrain pathway loop, where the pallial vocal nucleus (MAN, NAO) projects to the striatal vocal nucleus (Area X, MMSt), the striatal vocal nucleus in turn projects to a nucleus in DLM of the dorsal thalamus (DLM, DMM), and the dorsal thalamus nucleus in turn projects back to the pallial vocal nucleus (MAN, NAO) (FIG. 2A,C, white arrows).[17,18] In the songbird DLM, the anterior part has been proposed to be the vocal part of this nucleus.[22] The parrot pallial MO vocal nucleus also projects to the striatal vocal nucleus (MMSt).[17] Connectivity of the songbird MO analogue has not yet been determined.

TABLE 1. Abbreviations used in text

AAC	central nucleus of the anterior arcopallium	AACd	central nucleus of the anterior arcopallium, dorsal part
AACv	central nucleus of the anterior arcopallium, ventral part	Ai	intermediate arcopallium
ACM	caudal medial arcopallium	aDLPFC	dorsal lateral prefrontal cortex
aCC	anterior cingulate cortex	aCd	anterior caudate
aINS	anterior insula cortex	Am	nucleus ambiguous
aPt	anterior putamen	aT	anterior thalamus
Area X	area X of the striatum	Av	avalanch
CMM	caudal medial mesopallium	CM	caudal mesopallium
CSt	caudal striatum	DLM	medial nucleus of dorsolateral thalamus
DM	dorsal medial nucleus of the midbrain	DMM	magnocellular nucleus of the dorsomedial thalamus
FMC	face motor cortex	HVC	(a letter-based name)
MMSt	magnocellular nucleus of the anterior striatum	L2	field L2
MLd	mesencephalic lateral dorsal nucleus	MAN	magnocellular nucleus of anterior nidopallium
NCM	caudal medial nidopallium	MOc	oval nucleus of the mesopallium complex
NIDL	Intermediate dorsal lateral nidopallium	NAOc	oval nucleus of the anterior nidopallium complex
NLC	central nucleus of the lateral nidopallium	NDC	caudal dorsal nidopallium
Ov	nucleus oviodalis	NIf	Interfacial nucleus of the nidopallium
preSMA	pre-supplementary motor area	nXIIts	tracheosyringeal subdivision of the hypoglossal nucleus
RA	robust nucleus of the arcopallium	PAG	periaqueductal grey
VA	vocal nucleus of the arcopallium	St	striatum
VAM	vocal nucleus of the anterior mesopallium	Uva	nucleus uvaeformis
VAS	vocal nucleus of the anterior striatum	VA/VL	ventral anterior/ventral lateral nuclei of the mammalian thalamus.
VAN	vocal nucleus of the anterior nidopallium	VLN	vocal nucleus of the lateral nidopalllium

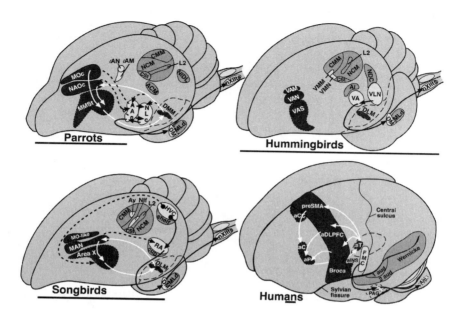

FIGURE 2. Proposed comparable vocal and auditory brain areas among vocal learning birds and humans: (**A**) parrot, (**B**) hummingbird, (**C**) songbird, and (**D**) human. Left hemispheres are shown, as this is the dominant side for human language. *White regions* and *black arrows* indicate proposed posterior vocal pathways; *dark grey regions* and *white arrows* indicate proposed anterior vocal pathways; *dashed lines* show connections between the two vocal pathways; *light grey* indicates auditory regions. For simplification, not all connections are shown. The globus pallidus in the human brain, also not shown, is presumably part of the anterior pathway as in non-vocal pathways of mammals. Basal ganglia, thalamic, and midbrain (for the human brain) regions are drawn with *dashed-line* boundaries to indicate that they are deeper in the brain relative to the anatomical structures above them. The anatomical boundaries drawn for the proposed human brain regions involved in vocal and auditory processing should be interpreted conservatively and for heuristic purposes only. Human brain lesions and brain imaging studies do not allow one to determine functional anatomical boundaries with high resolution. Scale bar: ~7 mm. Abbreviations are in TABLE 1.

The major differences among avian vocal learning groups, I argue, are in the connections between the posterior and anterior vocal pathways.[12] Each group appears to have differences in the inputs and outputs between the two pathways. In songbirds, the anterior vocal pathway receives input into Area X of the striatum from HVC of the nidopallium; the posterior pathway's HVC receives input from the medial portion of the anterior pathway via mMAN, and the posterior's RA receives input from the lateral portion of the anterior pathway via lMAN (FIG. 2A, 3A).[23] In contrast, in parrots, the anterior pathway receives input into its two pallial nuclei (NAO and MO) from the ventral part of arcopallial nucleus, called AACv; the posterior pathway's NLC and AACv and AACd (the dorsal part) appear to receive input from the same region of the anterior pathway's NAO and from DMM of the dorsal thalamus (FIG. 2B, 3B).[17] One important distinction is that the parrot posterior pathway vocal nuclei do not appear to send projections to the striatal nucleus of the anterior pathway.

Cerebral Auditory Nuclei in All Birds

Vocal learning (FIG. 2A–C) and vocal non-learning birds, I argue, share similar auditory pathways. These similarities include projections from ear hair cells to cochlear ganglia neurons, to auditory pontine nuclei (CN, LL), to midbrain (MLd) and thalamic (Ov) nuclei, and to primary (L2) and secondary (L2, L3, NCM, and CM) pallial areas (see Figure 2 of Reiner et al., this volume,[34] pp. 90,91).[24–28] Also found in both vocal learning and non-learning birds are auditory regions in the arcopallium (vocal learners: songbird RA cup, parrot ACM, hummingbird Ai; vocal non-learner: pigeon AIVM) and in the striatum (CSt) (FIG. 2A–C).[5,12,26,29] The auditory arcopallial nuclei receive input from the auditory nidopallium areas. Due to lack of detailed study on the connectivity of CSt (formally known as PC or caudal PA) in different species, it is not yet possible to make reliable comparisons for the striatal auditory region.

The source of auditory input into the vocal pathways of vocal learning birds is also unclear. Various routes have been proposed. These include the HVC shelf into HVC, the RA cup into RA, Ov or CM into NIf, and from NIf dendrites in L2, in songbirds.[27,29–31] In parrots, these include the NLC shell into NLC, and nucleus basorostralis, L1 and L3 into the comparable NIf-like nucleus lAN.[13,17,32] More study is necessary to determine whether any of these regions/nuclei truly brings auditory input into the vocal pathways. The location of the vocal nuclei relative to the auditory regions suggests that there will be some differences among vocal learning groups. In songbirds, the posterior vocal nuclei are embedded in the auditory regions; in hummingbirds, they are situated more lateral, but still adjacent to the auditory regions; in parrots, they are situated far laterally and physically separate from the auditory regions (FIG. 2A–C). At a minimum, the axons connecting the vocal and auditory systems would have to take different routes in the different vocal learners.

Much like generating a consensus DNA sequence from comparing comparable genes of different species, this comparative analysis suggests that a consensus bird brain system for learned vocalizing consists of seven cerebral vocal nuclei, with at least one nucleus located in each major brain subdivision except for the hyperpallium and pallidum, with the seven nuclei distributed into two pathways: (1) a posterior pathway that projects onto lower motor neurons and (2) an anterior pathway that forms a pallial-basal ganglia-thalamic-pallial loop.

COMPARATIVE BIRD AND MAMMAL CONNECTIVITY

Posterior and Anterior Motor Pathways

A recent forum on avian neuroanatomy led comparative neurobiologists to propose nomenclature changes in describing the avian brain and its homologies with the mammalian brain (see Reiner et al., this volume[34])[33,35] This new understanding of avian brain organization makes possible better-informed comparisons of vocal

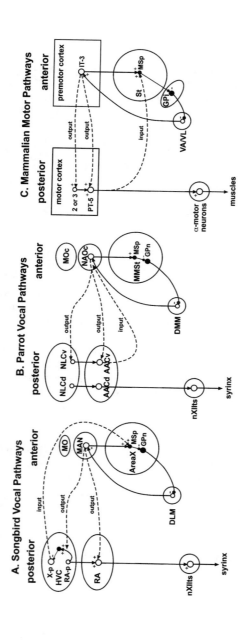

FIGURE 3. Comparative and simplified connectivity of posterior and anterior vocal pathways in (**A**) songbirds, (**B**) parrots, and (**C**) mammals. *Dashed lines:* connections between posterior and anterior pathways; inputs and outputs are labeled relative to anterior pathways. Output from songbird MAN to HVC and RA is not from the same neurons; medial MAN neurons project to HVC, lateral MAN neurons project to RA. ○, excitatory neurons; ●, inhibitory neurons; +, excitatory glutamate neurotransmitter release; −, inhibitory GABA release. MSp, medium spiny neuron. GPn, globus pallidus-like neuron in songbird Area X and parrot MMSt. Only the direct pathway through the mammalian basal ganglia (St to GPi) is shown as this is the one most similar to Area X connectivity (MSp to GPn).[56] X-p, X-projecting neuron of HVC. RA-p, RA-projecting neuron of HVC. PT-5, pyramidal tract neuron of motor cortex layer 5. IT-3, Intratelencephalic projecting neuron of layer 3. Connections that need validation for this model to be correct are whether collaterals of the same neurons of mMAN project to mArea X and to HVC, as opposed to different neurons, whether input from HVC into Area X is onto the Area X MSp neurons, whether the microcircuitry in parrot MMSt is the same as in songbirds, whether the collaterals of single IT-3 neurons of mammal cortex send branches to both layers 3 and 5 of motor cortex or just to one layer per IT-3 neuron. Abbreviations are in TABLE 1.

learning brain pathways in birds with the pathways in mammals. However, a caveat limiting such comparisons is that ethical and practical issues prevent tract-tracing experiments in humans and cetaceans. In bats, the vocal learning brain areas are not known. Thus, the connectivity of vocal learning pathways is not known for any mammal. Studies have been performed on the cerebrums of non-vocal learning mammals, such as cats, rats, and macaque monkeys. Therefore, I make connectivity comparisons between vocal learning pathways in vocal learning birds with non-vocal pathways in vocal non-learning mammals.

I argue that the songbird and parrot posterior vocal pathways are similar in connectivity to mammalian motor corticospinal pathways (FIG. 3). As has been proposed generally for the arcopallium by Karten and Shimizu,[36] I more specifically suggest that projecting neurons of songbird RA and parrot AACd are similar to what has been called pyramidal tract (PT) neurons of lower layer 5 of mammalian motor cortex.[37–40] The latter send long axonal projections out of the cerebrum through pyramidal tracts to synapse onto brainstem and spinal cord α-motor neurons that control muscle contraction and relaxation. As has been proposed generally for the nidopallium by Karten and Shimizu,[36] I more specifically suggest that the projection neurons of parrot NLC and the RA-projecting neurons of songbird HVC are similar to layer 2 and 3 neurons of mammalian motor cortex, which send intrapallial projections to layer 5 (FIG. 3).[41,42] I suggest that songbird Av of the mesopallium is also similar to layers 2 and 3 in that Av has an intrapallial connection from another motor pallial nucleus (HVC; see Figure 2 of Reiner et al., this volume,[34] pp. 90,91). Mammalian parallels to songbird NIf are less clear. In mammals, primary sensory input from the thalamus projects to layer 4 of cortex; motor feedback from the thalamus projects to layer 5 (in primary motor cortex) or layer 3 (in frontal cortex).[43,44] NIf is directly adjacent to L2 and like L2 it is similar to mammalian layer 4 neurons receiving thalamic input from UVa, but like the mammalian thalamic input to layer 3, UVa has motor-associated activity, firing during vocalizing.[45]

In humans, the only connectivity determined in a cerebral vocal brain area that I am aware of has been conducted by Kuypers.[46] Using silver staining of degenerated axons in patients that had vascular strokes to brain areas that included but were not limited to face motor cortex, he found that this area of cortex projects to nucleus ambiguous (also spelled ambiguus) and the hypoglossal nucleus. He reproduced similar lesions in macaque monkeys and chimpanzees (vocal non-learners) and found that their face motor cortex projects minimally, if at all, to nucleus ambiguous, but it does project massively to the hypoglossal nucleus and to all other brainstem cranial motor nuclei as found in humans.[47] Nucleus ambiguous in mammals controls muscles of the vocal organ (the larynx)[48,49] much like nXIIts does in birds (the syrinx). The hypoglossal nucleus in mammals and the non-tracheosyringeal part of nXII in birds controls muscles of the tongue.[19] In this manner, the pallial nuclei combined of the songbird and parrot posterior vocal pathways are more similar to the human face motor cortex than to any other part of the human pallium.

Others and I have argued that the songbird and parrot anterior vocal pathways are similar in connectivity to mammalian cortical-basal ganglia-thalamic-cortical loops (FIG. 3).[17,50–52] Going further, I argue that projection neurons of songbird MAN and parrot NAO[17,53,54] are similar to what has been called intratelencephalic (IT) neurons of layer 3 and upper layer 5 of mammalian premotor cortex, which send two collateral projections, one to medium spiny neurons of the striatum ventral to it and the other to other cortical regions, including motor cortex (FIG. 3).[40,55] Unlike mammals, the spiny neurons in both songbird Area X, and presumably parrot MMSt, project to pallidal-like cells within the vocal nuclei Area X and MMSt instead of to a separate structure consisting only of pallidal cells.[17,52,56] This striatal-pallidal cell intermingling may be a general trait of the anterior avian striatum. The projection of the pallidal-like cells of songbird Area X and parrot MMSt are similar to the pallidal projection neurons of the internal globus pallidus (GPi) of mammals, which project to the ventral lateral (VL) and ventral anterior (VA) nuclei of the dorsal thalamus (FIG. 3).[57] Like songbird DLM and parrot DMM projection's to lMAN and NAO, mammalian VL/VA projects back to layer 3 neurons of the premotor areas, closing parallel loops.[43,57,58]

Because connections between the posterior and anterior vocal pathways differ between songbirds and parrots, comparisons between them and mammals will also differ. I argue that input into mammalian anterior pathways is from collaterals of PT-layer 5 neurons of motor cortex, one projecting to the brainstem and spinal cord and the other projecting into the striatum (FIG. 3C).[40,59] This is different from the songbird where a specific cell type of HVC, called X-projecting neuron, projects to the striatum separately from those (neurons of RA) that project to the medulla. Parrot vocal connectivity is even more different from the mammalian, where AAC of the arcopallium has two anatomically separate neuron populations, AACd projecting to the medulla and AACv projecting to anterior pallial vocal nuclei NAO and MO.[60] I argue that output of mammalian anterior pathways are the collaterals of the above-mentioned IT-layer 3 and IT-upper layer 5 neurons that project to other cortical regions (FIG. 3C).[40]

Auditory Pathways

A comparative analysis of the literature[27,28,61] reveals that birds, reptiles, and mammals have relatively similar auditory pathways (FIG. 4). All three groups have ear hair cells that synapse onto sensory neurons, which project to cochlea and lemniscal nuclei of the brainstem, which in turn project to midbrain (avian MLd, reptile torus, mammalian inferior colliculus) and thalamic (avian Ov, reptile reunions, mammalian medial geniculate) auditory nuclei. The thalamic nuclei in turn project to primary auditory cell populations in the pallium (avian L2, reptile caudal pallium, mammalian layer 4 of primary auditory cortex). For connectivity in the cerebrum, the only detailed information we have is for mammals and birds. It has been proposed that avian L1 and L3 neurons are similar to mammalian layers 2 and 3 of primary auditory cortex, the latter of which receive input, like L2, from layer 4.[26,62] I suggest that avian NCM and CM are also similar to layers 2 and 3 in that they form reciprocal intrapallial connections with each other and receive some input from L2. Neurons of the songbird RA cup, parrot ACM, and pigeon AIVM of the arcopallium are similar to mammalian layers 5 and 6, which send auditory feedback projections to the shell regions of thalamic and midbrain auditory nuclei.[28,29,63-65] I further suggest that avian CSt is similar to an auditory region in the mammalian striatum. Similar to birds (FIG. 2A–C), this mammalian brain region is located caudally in the striatum, is smaller in dimension to the anterior motor striatal regions, and may receive connections from the pallium/cortex.[5,27,66,67] The connectivity of this region has not been verified in birds or mammals.

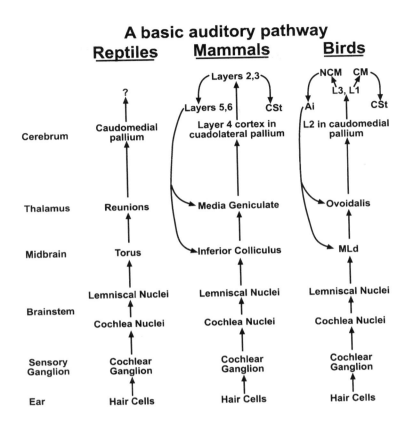

FIGURE 4. Comparative and simplified connectivity among auditory pathways in reptiles, mammals, and birds, placed in order from left to right of the most recently evolved. The connectivity from CM to CSt in birds needs verification by retrograde tracing. Abbreviations are in TABLE 1.

Taken together, the above analysis suggests that there are gross similarities between the connectivity of the consensus bird brain system for learned vocalizing and the non-vocal motor pathways (a posterior-like pathway) and cortical-basal-ganglia-thalamic-cortical loops (an anterior-like pathway) of mammals (FIG. 3A–C). It also suggests that the auditory pathways of birds, reptiles, and mammals may be homologous (FIG. 4). Differences between birds and mammals in connectivity of each of these pathways appear to be in the details, particularly at the level of the pallium. With this knowledge as a base, we can use vocal learning birds to gain some insight into the neurobiology of vocal learning pathways in humans. I first compare brain regions where lesions result in somewhat comparable behavioral deficits.

COMPARATIVE BIRD AND HUMAN LESIONS

Comparable Vocal Deficits

There are some gross similarities in behavioral deficits following lesions in specific brain areas of vocal learning birds (experimentally placed) and humans (due to stroke or trauma). For example, lesions to songbird HVC and RA,[9,68] particularly those placed on the left side in canaries, cause deficits similar to those found after damage to human face motor cortex, this being muteness for learned vocalizations, i.e., for speech (FIG. 5A,B).[69–71] Innate sounds, such as crying and screaming, can

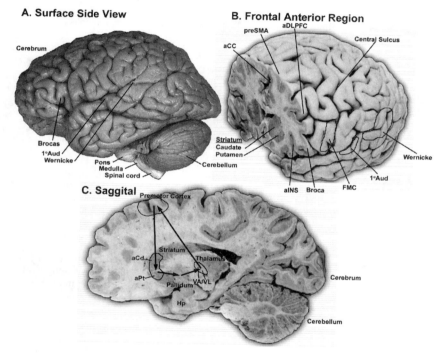

FIGURE 5. Human brain areas where damage results in speaking and/or hearing deficits. (**A**) Surface view of the left side of a human brain. (**B**) Frontal section cut through the prefrontal areas that show verbal aphasias and brain activation when speaking. Also highlighted are the face motor cortex (FMC) and auditory areas. (**C**) Saggital section highlighting anterior, cortical, basal ganglia, and thalamic areas that when damaged appear to lead to aphasia deficits. The *arrows* indicate proposed connectivity based upon that found in non-human mammals. The exact anatomical boundaries drawn for the proposed brain regions involved in vocal and auditory processing should be interpreted conservatively and for heuristic purposes only. Human brain lesions and brain imaging studies do not allow one to determine functional anatomical boundaries with high resolution. The image in **A** is from John W. Sundsten of the Digital Anatomist Project <http://www9.biostr.washington.edu/da.html>; Those in **B** and **C**, are from S. Mark Williams at the Duke University Medical Center. All images are used with permission. ABBREVIATIONS are in TABLE 1.

still be produced, however. When the lesions are unilateral, both birds and patients often recover some vocal behavior, because the opposite hemisphere appears to take over some function; likewise, recovery is better when the canary is a juvenile or the patient a child.[72–74] Partial lesions to parrot NLC causes partial deficits in producing the correct acoustic structure of learned vocalizations, including for learned speech.[75] The symptoms are similar to that of dysarthia in humans after recovery from damage to the face motor cortex. Lesions to the face motor cortex in chimpanzees and other non-human primates do not affect their ability to produce vocalizations.[47,70,76] I am not aware of the effects of such forebrain lesions on vocal behavior being tested in vocal non-learning birds. Lesions to avian nXIIts and mammalian nucleus ambiguous, and large lesions to the midbrain that include bird DM and mammalian (including human) central grey, result in the inability to vocalize (muteness) in both vocal learners and non-learners.[9,48,77–80] One difference between the avian posterior vocal pathways and the face motor cortex in humans is that lesions to songbird NIf or parrot lAN of the posterior pathway do not prevent production of learned vocalizations or cause dysarthic-like vocalizations, but lead to production of more varied syntax[81] or impaired vocal imitation.[82]

Lesions to songbird MAN[23,83,84] cause deficits that are most similar to those found after damage to anterior part of the human premotor cortex, this being prevention of vocal learning and/or inducing sequencing problems (FIG. 5B). In birds and humans, such lesions do not prevent the ability to produce learned song or speech. In humans, these deficits are called verbal aphasias and verbal amusias.[85] Damage to the left side often leads to verbal aphasias, whereas damage to the right often leads to verbal amusias.[86] My analysis of the literature (only example references listed)[69,85,87–95] indicates that these brain areas include a lateral-to-medial strip of premotor cortex from the anterior insula (aINS), Broca's area, the anterior dorsal lateral prefrontal cortex (aDLPFC), the pre-supplementary motor area (preSMA), and the anterior cingulate (aCC) (FIG. 5B). The deficits in humans, however, are more complex. Specifically, lesions to songbird lMAN[83,96] and lesions to the human insula and Broca's[85,91,94] leads to poor imitation, i.e., disrupted vocal learning, with spared maintenance of stereotyped song or speech. However, in addition, lesions to Broca's and/or DLPFC[85] lead to poor syntax production in construction of phonemes into words and words into sentences. Lesions to DLPFC also result in uncontrolled echolalia imitation, whereas lesions to pre-SMA and anterior cingulate[69,88–90,92] result in spontaneous speech arrest, lack of spontaneous speech, and/or loss of emotional tone in speech, but with imitation preserved. Lesions to songbird mMAN lead to a decreased ability in vocal learning (i.e., vocal imitation) and some disruption of syntax,[23] as do lesions to Broca's. It is not clear whether lesions to mMAN lead to singing arrest or reduced emotional tone in singing similar to the effects produced by lesions of the medial anterior premotor cortex in humans.

Lesions to songbird Area X and to the human anterior striatum (the head of the caudate and putamen, FIG. 5C) do not prevent the ability to produce already learned speech, but do result in disruption of vocal learning and disruption of some syntax in birds[83,97,98] or verbal aphasias and amusias in humans.[91,93,99–104] More specifically, songbirds have trouble crystallizing onto correct acoustic structure of syllables and syntax heard, and as adults they stutter on syllables that were repeated in tandem before the lesions.[83,97,98] In humans, the aphasias from subcortical lesions can be a combination of types found with premotor cortical lesions,[91] perhaps because, as is the case in non-human mammals, large cortical areas send connections that converge onto relatively smaller striatal areas.[105] Not many cases have been reported of lesions to the human globus pallidus leading to aphasias,[106] but the fact that this can occur, suggests some link with a striatal vocal area in humans.

Similar to a preliminary report on songbird DLM,[107] damage to anterior portions of the human thalamus (VA, VL) leads to verbal aphasias (FIG. 5C).[108] In humans, there is temporary muteness followed by aphasia deficits that are sometimes greater than those accompanying lesions to the anterior striatum or premotor cortical areas. This greater deficit may occur because there is further convergence of inputs from the striatum into the thalamus.[105] The interpretation of thalamic lesions in humans, however, is not without significant controversy,[85] perhaps because of small but important differences in lesion locations between patients among studies. The thalamus concentrates many functions into small adjacent nuclei, and thus, a relatively small variance in the location of a lesion may lead to a large difference in the brain function affected.

Comparable Auditory Deficits

Not many studies have investigated the effects of lesions to auditory cerebral areas of birds,[109–111] and therefore, only relatively rough comparisons can be made with humans and vocal non-learning mammals with such lesions. Lesions to Bengalese finch female NCM and zebra finch female CM appear to result in a significant decline in the ability to form long-term auditory discrimination memories of songs heard.[111,112] This deficit has some similarity to that which results from lesions to secondary auditory cortex in mammals, where animals have more difficulty forming discriminative memories of complex sounds. In humans, bilateral combined damage to primary auditory cortex and Wernicke's area (FIG. 5B) leads to full auditory agnosia, the inability to consciously recognize any sounds (speech, musical instruments, natural noises, etc.); it does not prevent unconscious perception of sounds.[85] If the lesion is more restricted to primary auditory cortex, a patient may suffer an inability to process rapid sequencing of sounds. If restricted to Wernicke's, the patient may suffer word-deafness, the inability to identify the sounds of speech (left side) with a preserved ability to identify nonverbal sounds, or tone-deafness (right side), called auditory aphasias or amusias, respectively. It is difficult to ascertain how non-human animals, including birds, perceive sensory stimuli, and therefore it is difficult to make comparisons with humans in regard to perceptual auditory deficits.

The lesions mentioned above that affect vocal and auditory behaviors in vocal learning birds and in humans can affect more than one modality. For example, lesions to lMAN in songbirds[113,114] and to Broca's and anterior striatum in humans[85,115] lead to decreased abilities in song/speech perception and discrimination. Lesions to auditory cortices in humans lead to fluent aphasia: patients unconsciously produce long stretches of nonsensical words and sentences (and were once characterized as crazy people).[85] It is not known if lesions to pallial auditory areas of vocal learning songbirds will result in fluent aphasic singing: long sequences of nonsensical song syllables and motifs. However, it is known that in parrots, lesions to pallial auditory areas do not affect the acoustic structure of already learned vocalizations.[109] This is similar to the consequences of auditory cortex lesions in humans, where acoustic structure of phonemes and words are not affected.

Taken together, the evidence from behavioral speech/language deficits in humans resulting from damage to known brain areas is consistent with the presence of a posterior-like motor pathway and an anterior-like vocal learning pathway that are similar to the vocal pathways in vocal learning birds. There also appears to be a separate pathway for basic auditory processing and auditory learning in humans, as seen in vocal learning birds. The relative locations of the brain regions in humans appear to be comparable to the relative location of the three pathways in birds. The clearest difference between birds and humans appears to be the greater complexity of the deficits found after lesions in humans. I now ask whether comparisons of patterns of brain activation support the similarities between birds and humans derived from lesion results.

COMPARATIVE BIRD AND HUMAN BRAIN ACTIVATION

Activation by Vocalizing

We can define brain activation as a relatively rapid neural change (milliseconds to minutes) that occurs during production of a behavior and/or processing of a sensory stimulus. Thus, activation includes changes in electrophysiological activity (recorded in both birds and humans, during surgery of patients for the latter), electrical stimulation (birds and humans), motor- and sensory-driven gene expression (birds and non-human mammals), and imaging of activated brain regions (in humans). Not all types of activation occur in the same brain areas and not all approaches are simple to perform. For example, expression of the most commonly studied activity-dependent gene in birds, ZENK, is associated with increased electrophysiological activity in neurons of all cerebral brain subdivisions except for those in the pallidum and in primary sensory receiving areas of the pallium (FIG. 6; e.g., L2).[116,117] Accumulated ZENK expression levels occur in certain brain areas after a bird sings its learned songs for 10–30 minutes (FIG. 6). However, measurement of gene expression changes in humans after speaking is not possible, and thus, other methods to quantify activity changes in specific brain areas must be used. Two alternatives are functional magnetic resonance imaging (fMRI) and positron emission tomography (PET) scanning. FMRI measures increased blood flow to activated brain areas, whereas PET measures increased glucose usage. It is difficult to image fMRI signals when speaking, as movement of the face causes image distortions. It is easier to do so with PET, as the signal is examined after the person speaks. A general problem with activation and vocal communication studies is that many do not separate neural changes due to vocalizing versus hearing. When an individual vocalizes, he/she hears himself and thus activation in a given brain region, when compared to the silent condition, could be due to either vocalizing and/or hearing. Separation requires comparison of the vocalizing condition with additional control conditions where an individual hears the same sounds while not vocalizing, or vocalizes while deaf.[118]

In vocal learning birds, activation studies have revealed that all seven comparable cerebral nuclei display ZENK expression that is vocalizing-driven and not hearing-driven;[5,12,51,118] this is in part how some of the nuclei were initially identified (FIG. 6). In deafened songbirds, these nuclei still display vocalizing-driven ZENK expression when the birds sing.[118] Likewise, premotor neural firing has been found in HVC, RA, NIf, lAreaX, and lMAN when songbirds sing.[10,11,119,120] In deafened birds, similar singing-associated activity still occurs when a bird sings, at least for lMAN.[11] The firing in HVC and RA correlates with specific features of produced songs (sequencing of syllables and syllable structure, respectively), whereas firing in lAreaX and lMAN is much more varied and no specific correlating feature has yet been found. However, firing and gene expression in lAreaX, lMAN, as well as RA differ depending upon the social context in which singing occurs (see Brainard, this volume).[51,121,122] Singing directed to another bird results in lower activation in these nuclei relative to singing in an undirected manner. On the other hand, HVC appears to be active at a similar firing rate and pattern whenever the bird sings.[51,123] No difference has been observed between right (the dominant) and left HVC activity during singing in zebra finches, but in song sparrows activity in the left and right HVC is associated with production of specific sequences of song syllables.[124] Stimulation with electrical pulses to HVC during singing temporarily disrupts song output, i.e., song arrest.[125]

If we compare the songbird HVC data, the brain area in humans that appears to be always activated with any speech task, as measured by PET or fMRI signals, is the face motor cortex.[126,127] Similar to other songbird vocal nuclei, other human brain areas appear to be activated or not depending upon the context in which speech is produced. Production of verbs and complex sentences can be accompanied by activation in all or a subregion of the strip of cortex anterior to the face motor cortex: the anterior insula, Broca's, DLPFC, pre-SMA, and anterior cingulate.[126–133] Activation in Broca's, DLPFC, and pre-SMA appears to be higher when speech tasks are more complex, including learning to vocalize new words or sentences, sequencing words into complex syntax, producing non-stereotyped sentences, and thinking about speaking.[129,134–136] The left brain vocal areas show more activity than their right counterparts during speaking.[127–129,132] Only one electrophysiological recording study that I am aware of has been conducted on these regions, where premotor speech-related neural activity was found to occur in Broca's area.[137] Stimulation studies have shown that low threshold electrical stimulation to the face motor cortex, Broca's, or the anterior supplementary areas will cause speech arrest or generation of phonemes or words.[92,138–140] For other cortical areas anterior or posterior to these, higher stimulation is often required to elicit similar results.

In non-cortical areas, activation has been found in the anterior striatum[141–143] and the thalamus[141] during speaking. Low threshold electrical stimulation to specific ventral lateral and anterior thalamic nuclei, particularly in the left hemisphere, leads to a variety of speech responses, including word repetition, speech arrest, speech acceleration, spontaneous speech, anomia, and verbal aphasia (but also auditory aphasia).[144] I have only found one study that has shown activation in the globus pallidus during speaking.[130] In non-human mammals and birds, specific comparable nuclei of the midbrain (avian DM and part of mammalian periaqueductal grey (PAG)) and medulla (avian nXII, mammalian ambiguous, and other nuclei) display premotor vocalizing neural firing[49,145–147] and/or vocalizing-driven gene expression.[5,12,51]

Activation by Hearing

In vocal learning and vocal non-learning birds, hearing songs or other ethologically relevant sounds results in increased neural firing and/or hearing-driven gene expression in midbrain (MLd), thalamic (Ov), and caudal cerebral (L2, L3, L1, NCM, CM, CSt, and Ai) auditory areas that have helped identify some of these regions as part of an auditory pathway (FIG. 6).[5,12,51,123,148–152] Activation in the secondary auditory pallial areas NCM and CM in songbirds is higher when they hear species-specific sounds and during auditory learning.[151,153–157] However, when a bird hears himself vocalize, the gene activation in these secondary pallial areas is less pronounced than when he hears other birds vocalize.[51] Similarly, in both humans and non-human mammals, hearing vocalizations activates midbrain (inferior colliculus), thalamic (medial geniculate), and cerebral (primary auditory and Wernicke's area in humans) regions that are part of the known mammalian auditory pathway.[128,132,135,158–160] Similar to avian NCM and CM, activation in Wernicke's area of humans and a Wernicke's-like area of non-human primates is higher during hearing of species-specific vocalizations, and is less prominent when an animal or patient hears himself speak.[161–163]

There is some overlap with cerebral areas that show neural firing during vocalizing or hearing, and this depends upon the species. In awake male zebra finches, firing is minimal in vocal nuclei when a bird hears playbacks of song, but greater when he is anesthetized or asleep and presented with playbacks of his own song.[122,124,164] In song sparrows, the reverse occurs: robust firing is observed in HVC when an awake bird hears playbacks of his own song, and this response is diminished when he is anesthetized.[124] In both species, the level or number of neurons firing in vocal nuclei during hearing is lower than that during singing. In humans, the face motor cortex, Broca's and/or the DLPFC often show increased activation when a person hears speech or is asked to perform a task that requires thinking in silent speech.[127–134] The magnitude of activation is usually lower during hearing than that seen during actual speaking. The anterior insula, Broca's, and DLPFC can also be activated by other factors, such as by engaging working memory,[165,166] which is a short-term memory that is formed before committing it to long-term storage. A potential flaw of some of these studies is that they incorporate into their design a person hearing instructions in speech, or reading, which is often accompanied by subvocalizing or thinking in silent speech, or by actually speaking. Thus, the non-language task is accompanied by a language task, confounding variables. Further, other studies describe activation in language/speech areas during a non-language/speech task, but actually measure regions adjacent (more anterior or posterior) to those activated by speaking. Thus, presently it is not clear whether areas specifically activated by hearing and speaking can be activated in tasks that do not require language processing, language production, or thinking in silent speech.

Taken together, although there are differences between the results, tasks, and methods used to study brain activation during vocalizing in birds and humans, and although there are discrepancies among studies, the comparative data are consistent with the idea that songbird HVC and RA are more similar in their activation properties to face motor cortex than to any other human brain area and that songbird MAN, Area X, and the anterior part of DLM are more similar in their properties to parts of

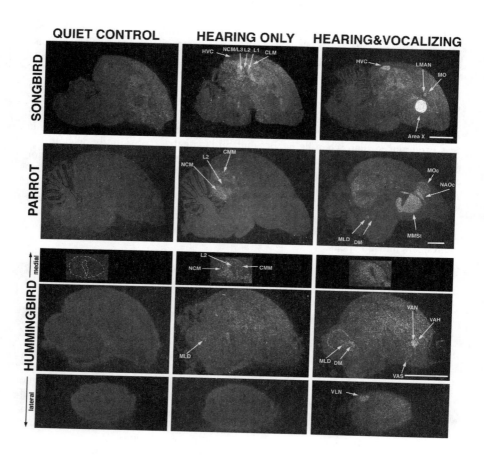

FIGURE 6. Some of the brain areas that show hearing and vocalizing-driven ZENK gene expression in vocal learning birds: songbirds (canary), parrots (budgerigar), and hummingbirds (sombre). Each image is a sagittal section each from a different bird of a different behavioral condition for 30 minutes; white label is ZENK mRNA gene expression, accumulated from over 30-minutes; grey background is cresyl violet stained cells. Quiet control animals did not hear songs or sing for an extended period of time. Hearing only animals heard playbacks of their species-specific songs. Hearing & Vocalizing animals heard similar playbacks and sang. The quiet control canary was actively moving around, causing ZENK expression in areas around vocal nuclei. It is not possible to have all activated brain regions in one section. In parrots, the HVC analogue, NLC (not shown), is situated more laterally, and it is also in hummingbirds (VLN shown). The auditory activated areas NCM and CMM in hummingbirds are shown without the rest of the brain. In the vocalizing canary, MO is not distinctly revealed by ZENK, whereas it is in zebra finches.[51] The MO analogue in hummingbirds, VAH, is flat and small. Area X, MMSt, and VAS of songbirds, parrots and hummingbirds respectively are all in the same area of the striatum, but have different vocalizing-driven gene expression levels and different shapes. Songbird images are from ref. 118, parrot from ref. 12, and hummingbird from ref. 5. Scale bar 1mm.

the human premotor cortex, anterior striatum, and ventral lateral/anterior thalamus, respectively.

A MODEL OF BRAIN PATHWAYS FOR HUMAN LANGAUGE

On the basis of the comparative analyses presented in the previous pages, I will make some predictions about the organization of brain pathways for human language. I argue that, similar to the vocal learning birds, humans have at least three basic cerebral pathways used for learned vocal communication: (1) a posterior vocal pathway, (2) an anterior vocal pathway, and (3) an auditory pathway (FIG. 2D). I suggest that the human posterior vocal pathway consists of the six-layered face motor cortex, with layer 5 neurons sending projections down to the vocal part of the brainstem central grey and to nucleus ambiguous, controlling the production of speaking and singing. I suggest that the human anterior vocal pathway consists of a cortical-basal-ganglia-thalamic-cortical loop, connecting a strip of premotor cortex, which I tentatively call the language strip (to include part of the anterior insula, Broca's, DLPFC, pre-SMA, and anterior cingulate), to the anterior striatum, to the ventral lateral and/or anterior nuclei of the dorsal thalamus, back to the same strip of cortex (FIG. 2D). If the human vocal pathways are similar to mammalian non-vocal pathways (FIG. 3C), then the human anterior vocal pathway would receive input from the posterior vocal pathway via axonal collaterals from PT-layer 5 neurons of the face motor cortex projecting into the anterior striatum; the human posterior vocal pathway would receive input to the face motor cortex from axonal collaterals of IT-layer 3 or upper layer 5 neurons of the language strip. The major difference between vocal learning and vocal non-learning mammals would be the absence in non-learners of these two types of pathways controlling nucleus ambiguous. The major similarity would be the presence of posterior and anterior motor pathways that control other learned sensorimotor behaviors.

I propose that the human auditory pathway follows the basic mammalian system (FIG. 4). Having a cerebral auditory area would explain why non-human mammals, including a dog, exhibit auditory learning, including learning to understand the meaning of human speech, although presumably with less facility than a human. I have no proposal yet as to how auditory information enters posterior and anterior vocal pathways of humans, as there is no consensus connectivity that can yet be deciphered from the vocal learning birds. The arcuate fibers that traverse a caudal-rostral direction in the human brain have been proposed to carry information from Wernicke's to Broca's,[167] but this has not been demonstrated experimentally.

I suggest that major differences between vocal learning birds and humans are ones of general brain organization and degree. In terms of organization, the avian pallium is nuclear and the mammalian pallium is layered. In terms of degree, according to my hypothesis, the human brain has relatively much more pallial tissue dedicated to vocal behavior than do vocal learning birds. In addition, the human brain is many orders of magnitude bigger than any known vocal learning bird. Humans apparently have more complex syntax, more learned rules in their speech production and perception, and much bigger bodies to control than do any vocal learning bird. Vocal learning bird species, however, are not uniform in their abilities. Some have more complex syntax and continued adult learning whereas others do not. These differences may be controlled by variance in the relative sizes of vocal nuclei and/or the amount of expression of specific genes.[168,169] Nevertheless, the vocal brain similarities among three vocal learning bird groups are striking and the similarities with humans are intriguing, leading one to wonder how such similarities in distantly related groups could have evolved.

EVOLUTIONARY HYPOTHESES

Three Alternative Hypotheses for Evolution of Brain Pathways for Vocal Learning

Given that auditory pathways in avian, mammalian, and reptilian species are similar, whether or not a given species is a vocal learner, I suggest that the auditory pathway in vocal learning birds and in humans was inherited from their common stem-amniote ancestor, thought to have lived ~320 million years ago.[170] For the evolution of vocal learning brain pathways among birds and in humans, I propose three alternative possibilities[5]: (1) the vocal system in the three vocal learning bird groups and the proposed comparable system in humans all evolved independently; (2) there was a vocal system in the common ancestor of vocal learning birds with seven cerebral nuclei, and a similar system in the common ancestor of vocal learning mammals, that were then lost multiple independent times in closely related bird and mammalian groups; or (3) most, if not all birds, mammals, and perhaps reptiles have vocal learning to various degrees, and songbirds, parrots, hummingbirds, and humans (and perhaps bats and cetaceans) independently amplified the associated brain structures for their more highly developed vocal learning behaviors.

If hypothesis 1 were true, then the evolution of brain pathways for vocal learning may be under strong epigenetic (outside the genome) constraints. The evolution of wings provides an analogy. Wings evolved independently at least four times, in birds, bats, pterosaurs (ancient flying dinosaurs), and insects. In each case, they evolved at the sides of the body, usually one on each side, and not one on the head, the other on the tail, or elsewhere. One hypothesis is that wings evolved in similar ways because of a strong epigenetic constraint, the environmental force of the center of gravity/mass on the body, dictating the most energetically efficient manner for flight.[171] If hypothesis 2 were true, then maintenance of vocal learning may be under an environmental/social epigenetic constraint that selects against vocal learning. If hypothesis 3 were true, it would mean that many birds and mammals, and maybe reptiles, have at least primordial brain structures for vocal learning. I believe that a combination of all three hypotheses is true, where both genetic and epigenetic constraints have influenced the evolution of vocal learning.

Genetic Constraints

Because the connections of the anterior and posterior vocal pathways in vocal learning birds bear some resemblance to those of non-vocal pathways in both birds and mammals, pre-existing connectivity was presumably a genetic constraint for the evolution of vocal learning.[17,22,160,172] In this manner, I argue that a mutational event that caused descending projections of avian arcopallium neurons to synapse onto nXIIts or mammalian layer 5 neurons of the face motor cortex to synapse onto nucleus ambiguous may be the only major change that is needed to initiate a vocal learning pathway. Thereafter, other vocal brain regions could develop out of adjacent motor brain regions with pre-existing connectivity. Such a mutational event would be expected to occur in genes that regulate synaptic connectivity of upper pallial motor neurons to lower α-motor neurons. This hypothesis requires that avian non-vocal motor learning systems have up to seven nuclei distributed into two pathways in at least six brain subdivisions (the mesopallium, nidopallium, arcopallium, striatum, pallidal-like cells in the striatum, and dorsal thalamus). It would also require that mammalian non-vocal motor learning systems have brain regions distributed in two pathways involving at least four brain subdivisions (the six layers of the cortex, the striatum, the pallidum, and the dorsal thalamus). Not apparent in this view, is the question of whether there is a genetic constraint for auditory information entering vocal learning pathways. Sensory processing neurons projecting into cerebral motor pathways do exist for non-vocal functions of the cerebrum, but I have not been able to extract a consensus-connectivity at this time.

Epigenetic Constraints

Is there an environmental or social factor that selects for or against vocal learning? If selection for vocal learning requires a relatively simple mutational event, then why is it not more common? My graduate student, Adriana Ferreira, and I have brainstormed on possible answers to these questions. We have come up with six possible epigenetic factors for selection for vocal learning, some of which have been previously proposed:[173,174] (1) individual identification; (2) semantic communication; (3) territory defense; (4) mate attraction; (5) complex syntax; and (6) rapid adaptation to sound propagation in different environments. We believe that the first three factors cannot explain selection for vocal learning. As no two individuals look alike, so too no two individuals within a population appear to sound alike, allowing vocal non-learners to identify individual conspecifics by voice. Many vocal non-learners use calls to communicate semantic information, such as "an eagle above," "a snake on the ground," or "a food source,"[175] whereas most vocal learners use their learned vocalizations in more affective, emotional context. Yet, many vocal non-learners use their innate calls and crows to attract mates and defend territories. We believe that factors 5 and 6 in combination with factor 4 can explain selection for vocal learning. Vocal learners, but not vocal non-learners, have the ability to produce more varied syntax, either during vocal development and/or after reaching adulthood in some species. Females of some songbird species appear to prefer more varied syntax.[6,174,176] Therefore, birds with the ability to produce more vocal variety are likely to be selected for this trait. For sound transmission, vocal non-learners produce their vocalizations best in specific habitats,[177–180] which makes their vocal behaviors less adaptable to changes in environments. For example, a pigeon's low frequency vocalizations travel best near the ground, while an eastern phoebe's higher pitched vocalizations travel better higher in the air. In contrast, vocal learners have the ability to change voice characteristics, either during the lifetime of an individual or through several generations, presumably allowing better group communication in different environments.

We believe that predation is a strong selection factor against vocal learning and this may be why it is so rare. If more varied syntax is attractive to mates, it may also be more attractive to predators. As innate vocalizations tend to be more constant, they are habituated to more easily, potentially becoming part of the background noise. Therefore, in order for a predator not to habituate to the sounds of his prey, he would have to evolve a neural mechanism to overcome the natural habituation at times when he is hungry. Some findings support the prey side of this view: Okanoya has shown that Bengalese finches that have been bred in captivity without predators for the last 250 years and without human selection for singing behavior, show more varied syntax than their white-backed munia conspecifics still living in the wild from which they derive.[174] Zebra finches bred in captivity show more variation on the songs learned among adults of a colony than do their wild-type conspecifics.[181] For both species, females prefer the more complex songs, including the wild munia finches preferring the more varied songs of the domesticated Bengalese finches.[174,176] Given these findings, we would expect to find more syntax complexity selected for in the wild than currently exists. We argue, as does Okonoya,[174] that it is predatory pressure selecting against it.

CONCLUSION

In this chapter, I have presented the sketches of a hypothesis about the evolution of vocal learning and human language. The analysis demonstrates the value of using a comparative approach to generate insight into the neurobiology of human language. Except for the proposed connectivity of the human vocal brain pathways, various parts of the hypothesis are testable. I suspect that with additional experimentation some of the details will need revision, but that the general principles will hold.

ACKNOWLEDGMENTS

This work was funded by National Science Foundation Grant IBN0084357 and the Alan T. Waterman Award. I thank Tony Zimmerman at Duke University for assistance in editing and critical reading of the manuscript.

REFERENCES

1. SEYFARTH, R.M., D.L. CHENEY & P. MARLER. 1980. Vervet monkey alarm calls: Semantic communication in a free-ranging primate. Anim. Behav. **28:** 1070–1094.
2. MARLER, P. 1967. Animal communication signals. Science **157:** 769–774.
3. KONISHI, M. 1965. The role of auditory feedback in the control of vocalization in the white-crowned sparrow. Z. Tierpsychol. **22:** 770–783.
4. NOTTEBOHM, F. 1972. The origins of vocal learning. Am. Nat. **106:** 116–140.
5. JARVIS, E.D. et al. 2000. Behaviourally driven gene expression reveals song nuclei in hummingbird brain. Nature **406:** 628–632.
6. CATCHPOLE, C.K. & P.J.B. SLATER. 1995. Bird Song: Biological Themes and Variations. Cambridge University Press. Cambridge, England.
7. FARABAUGH, S.M. & R.J. DOOLING. 1996. Acoustic communication in parrots: Laboratory and field studies of budgerigars, *Melopsittacus undulatus. In* Ecology and Evolution of Acoustic Communication in Birds. D.E. Kroodsma & E.H. Miller, Eds.: 97–117. Cornell University Press. Ithaca, NY.

8. FERREIRA, A. *et al.* Vocal communication in hummingbirds II: songs of the sombre hummingbird (Trochilinae) and the rufous-breasted hermit (Phaethornithinae). Ethology. Submitted.

9. NOTTEBOHM, F., T.M. STOKES & C.M. LEONARD. 1976. Central control of song in the canary, *Serinus canarius*. J. Comp. Neurol. **165:** 457–486.

10. YU, A.C. & D. MARGOLIASH. 1996. Temporal hierarchical control of singing in birds. Science **273:** 1871–1875.

11. HESSLER, N.A. & A.J. DOUPE. 1999. Singing-related neural activity in a dorsal forebrain-basal ganglia circuit of adult zebra finches. J. Neurosci. **19:** 10461–10481.

12. JARVIS, E.D. & C.V. MELLO. 2000. Molecular mapping of brain areas involved in parrot vocal communication. J. Comp. Neurol. **419:** 1–31.

13. STRIEDTER, G.F. 1994. The vocal control pathways in budgerigars differ from those in songbirds. J. Comp. Neurol. **343:** 35–56.

14. NOTTEBOHM, F. 1980. Brain pathways for vocal learning in birds: A review of the first 10 years. Prog. Psychobiol. Physiol. Psychol. **9:** 85–124.

15. KROODSMA, D.E. & M. KONISHI. 1991. A suboscine bird (eastern phoebe, *Sayornis phoebe*) develops normal song without auditory feedback. Anim. Behav. **42:** 477–487.

16. GAHR, M. 2000. Neural song control system of hummingbirds: comparison to swifts, vocal learning (songbirds) and nonlearning (suboscines) passerines, and vocal learning (budgerigars) and nonlearning (dove, owl, gull, quail, chicken) nonpasserines. J. Comp. Neurol. **426:** 182–196.

17. DURAND, S.E. *et al.* 1997. Vocal control pathways through the anterior forebrain of a parrot (*Melopsittacus undulatus*). J. Comp. Neurol. **377:** 179–206.

18. VATES, G.E., D.S. VICARIO & F. NOTTEBOHM. 1997. Reafferent thalamo-"cortical" loops in the song system of oscine songbirds. J. Comp. Neurol. **380:** 275–290.

19. WILD, J.M. 1997. Neural pathways for the control of birdsong production. J. Neurobiol. **33:** 653–670.

20. WILD, J.M., D. LI & C. EAGLETON. 1997. Projections of the dorsomedial nucleus of the intercollicular complex (DM) in relation to respiratory-vocal nuclei in the brainstem of pigeon (*Columba livia*) and zebra finch (*Taeniopygia guttata*). J. Comp. Neurol. **377:** 392–413.

21. NOTTEBOHM, F., D.B. KELLEY & J.A. PATON. 1982. Connections of vocal control nuclei in the canary telencephalon. J. Comp. Neurol. **207:** 344–357.

22. WADA, K. *et al.* Differential expression of glutamate receptors in avian neural pathways for learned vocalization. J. Comp. Neurol. Submitted for publication.

23. FOSTER, E.F. & S.W. BOTTJER. 2001. Lesions of a telencephalic nucleus in male zebra finches: Influences on vocal behavior in juveniles and adults. J. Neurobiol. **46:** 142–165.

24. BRAUTH, S.E. *et al.* 1987. Auditory pathways in the budgerigar. I. Thalamo-telencephalic projections. Brain Behav. Evol. **30:** 174–199.

25. BRAUTH, S.E. & C.M. MCHALE. 1988. Auditory pathways in the budgerigar. II. Intratelencephalic pathways. Brain Behav. Evol. **32:** 193–207.

26. WILD, J.M., H.J. KARTEN & B.J. FROST. 1993. Connections of the auditory forebrain in the pigeon (*Columba livia*). J. Comp. Neurol. **337:** 32–62.

27. VATES, G.E. *et al.* 1996. Auditory pathways of caudal telencephalon and their relation to the song system of adult zebra finches. J. Comp. Neurol. **366:** 613–642.

28. CARR, C.E. & R.A. CODE. 2000. The central auditory system of reptiles and birds. *In* Comparative Hearing: Birds and reptiles, Vol. 13. R.J. Dooling, R.R. Fay & A.N. Popper, Eds.: 197–248. Springer. New York.

29. MELLO, C.V. *et al.* 1998. Descending auditory pathways in the adult male zebra finch (*Taeniopygia guttata*). J. Comp. Neurol. **395:** 137–160.

30. WILD, J.M. 1994. Visual and somatosensory inputs to the avian song system via nucleus uvaeformis (Uva) and a comparison with the projections of a similar thalamic nucleus in a nonsongbird, *Columba livia*. J. Comp. Neurol. **349:** 512–535.

31. FORTUNE, E.S. & D. MARGOLIASH. 1995. Parallel pathways converge onto HVc and adjacent neostriatum of adult male zebra finches (*Taeniopygia guttata*). J. Comp. Neurol. **360:** 413–441.

32. FARABAUGH, S.M. & J.M. WILD. 1997. Reciprocal connections between primary and secondary auditory pathways in the telencephalon of the budgerigar (*Melopsittacus undulatus*). Brain Res. **747:** 18–25.
33. REINER, A. *et al.* 2004. Revised nomenclature for avian telencephalon and some related brainstem nuclei. J. Comp. Neurol. **473:** 377–414.
34. REINER, A. *et al.* 2004. Songbirds and the revised avian brain nomenclature. Ann. N.Y. Acad. Sci. **1016:** 77–108. This volume.
35. JARVIS, E.D. *et al.* A paradigm shift in understanding the organization, evolution and function of the avian brain. Submitted.
36. KARTEN, H.J. & T. SHIMIZU. 1989. The origins of neocortex: connections and lamination as distinct events in evolution. J. Cogn. Neurosci. **1:** 291–301.
37. MATSUMURA, M. & K. KUBOTA. 1979. Cortical projection to hand-arm motor area from post-arcuate area in macaque monkeys: a histological study of retrograde transport of horseradish peroxidase. Neurosci. Lett. **11:** 241–246.
38. GLICKSTEIN, M., J.G. MAY, 3RD & B.E. MERCIER. 1985. Corticopontine projection in the macaque: the distribution of labelled cortical cells after large injections of horseradish peroxidase in the pontine nuclei. J. Comp. Neurol. **235:** 343–359.
39. KEIZER, K. & H.G. KUYPERS. 1989. Distribution of corticospinal neurons with collaterals to the lower brain stem reticular formation in monkey (*Macaca fascicularis*). Exp. Brain Res. **74:** 311–318.
40. REINER, A. *et al.* 2003. Differential morphology of pyramidal tract-type and intratelencephalically projecting-type corticostriatal neurons and their intrastriatal terminals in rats. J. Comp. Neurol. **457:** 420–440.
41. ARONIADOU, V.A. & A. KELLER. 1993. The patterns and synaptic properties of horizontal intracortical connections in the rat motor cortex. J. Neurophysiol. **70:** 1553–1569.
42. CAPADAY, C. *et al.* 1998. Intracortical connections between motor cortical zones controlling antagonistic muscles in the cat: a combined anatomical and physiological study. Exp. Brain Res. **120:** 223–232.
43. JACOBSON, S. & J.Q. TROJANOWSKI. 1975. Corticothalamic neurons and thalamocortical terminal fields: an investigation in rat using horseradish peroxidase and autoradiography. Brain Res. **85:** 385–401.
44. FITZPATRICK, D. 1996. The functional organization of local circuits in visual cortex: insights from the study of tree shrew striate cortex. Cerebral Cortex **6:** 329–341.
45. WILLIAMS, H. & D.S. VICARIO. 1993. Temporal patterning of song production: participation of nucleus uvaeformis of the thalamus. J. Neurobiol. **24:** 903–912.
46. KUYPERS, H.G.J.M. 1958. Corticobulbar connexions to the pons and lower brain-stem in man. Brain **81:** 364–388.
47. KUYPERS, H.G.J.M. 1958. Some projections from the peri-central cortex to the pons and lower brain stem in monkey and chimpanzee. J. Comp. Neurol. **100:** 221–255.
48. JURGENS, U. 1998. Neuronal control of mammalian vocalization, with special reference to the squirrel monkey. Naturwissenschaften **85:** 376–388.
49. ZHANG, S.P., R. BANDLER & P.J. DAVIS. 1995. Brain stem integration of vocalization: role of the nucleus retroambigualis. J. Neurophysiol. **74:** 2500–2512.
50. BOTTJER, S.W. & F. JOHNSON. 1997. Circuits, hormones, and learning: vocal behavior in songbirds. J. Neurobiol. **33:** 602–618.
51. JARVIS, E.D. *et al.* 1998. For whom the bird sings: context-dependent gene expression. Neuron **21:** 775–788.
52. PERKEL, D. & M. FARRIES. 2000. Complementary "bottom-up" and "top-down" approaches to basal ganglia function. Curr. Opin. Neurobiol. **10:** 725–731.
53. VATES, G.E. & F. NOTTEBOHM. 1995. Feedback circuitry within a song-learning pathway. Proc. Natl. Acad. Sci. USA **92:** 5139–5143.
54. FOSTER, E.F., R.P. MEHTA & S.W. BOTTJER. 1997. Axonal connections of the medial magnocellular nucleus of the anterior neostriatum in zebra finches. J. Comp. Neurol. **382:** 364–381.
55. AVENDANO, C., A.J. ISLA & E. RAUSELL. 1992. Area 3a in the cat. II. Projections to the motor cortex and their relations to other corticocortical connections. J. Comp. Neurol. **321:** 373–386.

56. REINER, A. *et al.* 2004. An immunohistochemical and pathway tracing study of the striatopallidal organization of Area X in the zebra finch. J. Comp. Neurol. **469:** 239–261.

57. ALEXANDER, G.E., M.R. DELONG & P.L. STRICK. 1986. Parallel organization of functionally segregated circuits linking basal ganglia and cortex. Ann. Rev. Neurosci. **9:** 357–381.

58. LUO, M., L. DING & D.J. PERKEL. 2001. An avian basal ganglia pathway essential for vocal learning forms a closed topographic loop. J. Neurosci. **21:** 6836–6845.

59. ALEXANDER, G.E. & M.D. CRUTCHER. 1990. Functional architecture of basal ganglia circuits: neural substrates of parallel processing. Trends Neurosci. **13:** 266–271.

60. ALVAREZ-BUYLLA, A. & J.R. KIRN. 1997. Birth, migration, incorporation, and death of vocal control neurons in adult songbirds. J. Neurobiol. **33:** 585–601.

61. WEBSTER, D.B., A.N. POPPER & R.R. FAY, EDS. 1992. The Mammalian Auditory Pathway: Neuroanatomy. Springer-Verlag. New York.

62. KARTEN, H.J. 1991. Homology and evolutionary origins of the "neocortex." Brain Behav. Evol. **38:** 264–272.

63. HUFFMAN, R.F. & O.W. HENSON, JR. 1990. The descending auditory pathway and acousticomotor systems: connections with the inferior colliculus. Brain Res. Brain Res. Rev. **15:** 295–323.

64. PRIETO, J.J. & J.A. WINER. 1999. Layer VI in cat primary auditory cortex: Golgi study and sublaminar origins of projection neurons. J. Comp. Neurol. **404:** 332–358.

65. WINER, J.A. & J.J. PRIETO. 2001. Layer V in cat primary auditory cortex (AI): cellular architecture and identification of projection neurons. J. Comp. Neurol. **434:** 379–412.

66. BONKE, B.A., D. BONKE & H. SCHEICH. 1979. Connectivity of the auditory forebrain nuclei in the guinea fowl (*Numida meleagris*). Cell Tissue Res. **200:** 101–121.

67. MCGEORGE, A.J. & R.L.M. FAULL. 1989. The organization of the projection from the cerebral cortex to the striatum in the rat. Neuroscience **29:** 503–537.

68. SIMPSON, H.B. & D.S. VICARIO. 1990. Brain pathways for learned and unlearned vocalizations differ in zebra finches. J. Neurosci. **10:** 1541–1556.

69. VALENSTEIN, E. 1975. Nonlanguage disorders of speech reflect complex neurologic apparatus. Geriatrics **30:** 117–121.

70. JURGENS, U., A. KIRZINGER & D. VON CRAMON. 1982. The effects of deep-reaching lesions in the cortical face area on phonation. A combined case report and experimental monkey study. Cortex **18:** 125–139.

71. JURGENS, U. 1995. Neuronal control of vocal production in non-human and human primates. *In* Current Topics in Primate Vocal Communication. E. Zimmermann, J.D. Newman & U. Jurgens, Eds.: 199–206. Plenum Press. New York.

72. NOTTEBOHM, F. 1977. Asymmetries in neural control of vocalizations in the canary. *In* Lateralization in the Nervous System. G. Krauthamer, Ed.: 23–44. Academic Press. New York.

73. REY, M. *et al.* 1988. Hemispheric lateralization of motor and speech functions after early brain lesion: study of 73 epileptic patients with intracarotid amytal test. Neuropsychologia **26:** 167–172.

74. HERTZ-PANNIER, L. *et al.* 2002. Late plasticity for language in a child's non-dominant hemisphere: a pre- and post-surgery fMRI study. Brain **125:** 361–372.

75. LAVENEX, P.B. 2000. Lesions in the budgerigar vocal control nucleus NLc affect production, but not memory, of English words and natural vocalizations. J. Comp. Neurol. **421:** 437–460.

76. KIRZINGER, A. & U. JURGENS. 1982. Cortical lesion effects and vocalization in the squirrel monkey. Brain Res. **233:** 299–315.

77. BROWN, J. 1965. Loss of vocalizations caused by lesions in the nucleus mesencephalicus lateralis of the Redwinged Blackbird. Am. Zool. **5:** 693.

78. SELLER, T. 1981. Midbrain vocalization centers in birds. Trends Neurosci. **12:** 301–303.

79. JURGENS, U. 1994. The role of the periaqueductal grey in vocal behaviour. Behav. Brain Res. **62:** 107–117.

80. ESPOSITO, A. *et al.* 1999. Complete mutism after midbrain periaqueductal gray lesion. Neuroreport **10:** 681–685.

81. HOSINO, T. & K. OKANOYA. 2000. Lesion of a higher-order song nucleus disrupts phrase level complexity in Bengalese finches. Neuroreport **11:** 2091–2095.
82. PLUMMER, T.K. & G.F. STRIEDTER. 2002. Brain lesions that impair vocal imitation in adult budgerigars. J. Neurobiol. **53:** 413–428.
83. SCHARFF, C. & F. NOTTEBOHM. 1991. A comparative study of the behavioral deficits following lesions of various parts of the zebra finch song system: implications for vocal learning. J. Neurosci. **11:** 2896–2913.
84. NOTTEBOHM, F. *et al.* 1990. Song learning in birds: the relation between perception and production. Phil. Trans. Royal Soc. Lond. B Biol. Sci. **329:** 115–124.
85. BENSON, D.F. & A. ARDILA. 1996. Aphasia: A Clinical Perspective. Oxford University Press. New York.
86. BERMAN, I.W. 1981. Musical functioning, speech lateralization and the amusias. South African Med. J. **59:** 78–81.
87. BROCA, P. 1861. Nouvelle observation d'aphemie produite par une lesion de la moitie posterierure des deuxieme et troisieme circonvolutions frontales. Bull. Soc. Anatomy Paris **4:** 398–407.
88. NIELSEN, J.M. & L.L. JACOBS. 1951. Bilateral lesions of the anterior cingulated gyri. Bull. Los Angeles Neurological Soc. **16:** 231–234.
89. BARRIS, R.W., M.D. SCHUMAN & H.R. SCHUMAN. 1953. Bilateral anterior cingulated gyrus lesions: Syndrome of the anterior cingulate gyri. Neurology **3:** 44–52.
90. RUBENS, A.B. 1975. Aphasia with infarction in the territory of the anterior cerebral artery. Cortex **11:** 239–250.
91. MOHR, J.P. 1976. Broca's area and Broca's aphasia. *In* Studies in Neurolinguistics. Vol. 1. H.A. Whitaker, Ed.: 201–235. Academic Press. New York.
92. JONAS, S. 1981. The supplementary motor region and speech emission. J. Commun. Disorders **14:** 349–373.
93. CUMMINGS, J.L. 1993. Frontal-subcortical circuits and human behavior. Arch. Neurol. **50:** 873–880.
94. DRONKERS, N.F. 1996. A new brain region for coordinating speech articulation. Nature **384:** 159–161.
95. GRODZINSKY, Y. 2000. The neurology of syntax: language use without Broca's area. Behav. Brain Sci. **23:** 1–21; discussion 21–71.
96. BOTTJER, S.W., E.A. MIESNER & A.P. ARNOLD. 1984. Forebrain lesions disrupt development but not maintenance of song in passerine birds. Science **224:** 901–903.
97. SOHRABJI, F., E.J. NORDEEN & K.W. NORDEEN. 1990. Selective impairment of song learning following lesions of a forebrain nucleus in the juvenile zebra finch. Behav. Neural Biol. **53:** 51–63.
98. KOBAYASHI, K., H. UNO & K. OKANOYA. 2001. Partial lesions in the anterior forebrain pathway affect song production in adult Bengalese finches. Neuroreport **12:** 353–358.
99. BECHTEREVA, N.P. *et al.* 1979. Neurophysiological codes of words in subcortical structures of the human brain. Brain Language **7:** 143–163.
100. LEICESTER, J. 1980. Central deafness and subcortical motor aphasia. Brain Language **10:** 224–242.
101. DAMASIO, A.R. *et al.* 1982. Aphasia with nonhemorrhagic lesions in the basal ganglia and internal capsule. Arch. Neurol. **39:** 15–24.
102. ALEXANDER, M.P., M.A. NAESER & C.L. PALUMBO. 1987. Correlations of subcortical CT lesion sites and aphasia profiles. Brain **110:** 961–991.
103. SPEEDIE, L.J. *et al.* 1993. Disruption of automatic speech following a right basal ganglia lesion. Neurology **43:** 1768–1774.
104. LIEBERMAN, P. 2000. Human Language and Our Reptilian Brain: The Subcortical Bases of Speech, Syntax, and Thought. Harvard University Press. Cambridge.
105. BEISER, D.G., S.E. HUA & J.C. HOUK. 1997. Network models of the basal ganglia. Curr. Opin. Neurobiol. **7:** 185–190.
106. STRUB, R.L. 1989. Frontal lobe syndrome in a patient with bilateral globus pallidus lesions. Arch. Neurol. **46:** 1024–1027.
107. HALSEMA, K.A. & S.W. BOTTJER. 1991. Lesioning afferent input to a forebrain nucleus disrupts vocal learning in zebra finches. Soc. Neurosci. Abstracts **17:** 1052.

108. GRAFF-RADFORD, N.R. *et al.* 1985. Nonhaemorrhagic thalamic infarction. Clinical, neuropsychological and electrophysiological findings in four anatomical groups defined by computerized tomography. Brain **108:** 485–516.
109. HALL, W.S., S.E. BRAUTH & J.T. HEATON. 1994. Comparison of the effects of lesions in nucleus basalis and field "L" on vocal learning and performance in the budgerigar (*Melopsittacus undulatus*). Brain Behav. Evol. **44:** 133–148.
110. BRAUTH, S.E. *et al.* 1994. Functional anatomy of forebrain auditory pathways in the budgerigar (*Melopsittacus undulatus*). Brain Behav. Evol. **44:** 210–233.
111. MACDOUGALL-SHACKLETON, S.A., S.H. HULSE & G.F. BALL. 1998. Neural bases of song preferences in female zebra finches (*Taeniopygia guttata*). Neuroreport **9:** 3047–3052.
112. IKEBUCHI, M. & K. OKANOYA. Brain site for female choice coincides with the locus of gene expression in a songbird. Submitted for publication.
113. SCHARFF, C., F. NOTTEBOHM & J. CYNX. 1998. Conspecific and heterospecific song discrimination in male zebra finches with lesions in the anterior forebrain pathway. J. Neurobiol. **36:** 81–90.
114. BURT, J. *et al.* 2000. Lesions of the anterior forebrain song control pathway in female canaries affect song perception in an operant task. J. Neurobiol. **42:** 1–13.
115. FREEDMAN, M., M.P. ALEXANDER & M.A. NAESER. 1984. Anatomic basis of transcortical motor aphasia. Neurology **34:** 409–417.
116. MELLO, C.V. & D.F. CLAYTON. 1995. Differential induction of the ZENK gene in the avian forebrain and song control circuit after metrazole-induced depolarization. J. Neurobiol. **26:** 145–161.
117. JARVIS, E.D. 2004. Brains and birdsong. *In* Nature's Music: The Science of Birdsong. P. Marler & H. Slabbekoorn, Eds. Elsevier-Academic Press. In press.
118. JARVIS, E.D. & F. NOTTEBOHM. 1997. Motor-driven gene expression. Proc. Natl. Acad. Sci. USA **94:** 4097–4102.
119. MCCASLAND, J.S. 1987. Neuronal control of bird song production. J. Neurosci. **7:** 23–39.
120. HAHNLOSER, R.H.R., A.A. KOZHEVNIKOV & M.S. FEE. 2002. An ultra-sparse code underlies the generation of neural sequences in a songbird. Nature **419:** 65–70.
121. HESSLER, N.A. & A.J. DOUPE. 1999. Social context modulates singing-related neural activity in the songbird forebrain. Nature Neurosci. **2:** 209–211.
122. DAVE, A. & D. MARGOLIASH. 2000. Song replay during sleep and computational rules for sensorimotor vocal learning. Science **290:** 812–816.
123. JARVIS, E.D. *et al.* 2002. A framework for integrating the songbird brain. J. Comp. Physiol. A Neuroethol. Sens. Neural Behav. Physiol. **188:** 961–980.
124. NEALEN, P. M. & M. F. SCHMIDT. 2002. Comparative approaches to avian song system function: insights into auditory and motor processing. J. Comp. Physiol. A Neuroethol. Sens. Neural Behav. Physiol. **188:** 929–941.
125. VU, E.T., M.F. SCHMIDT & M.E. MAZUREK. 1998. Interhemispheric coordination of premotor neural activity during singing in adult zebra finches. J. Neurosci. **18:** 9088–9098.
126. PETERSEN, S.E. *et al.* 1988. Positron emission tomographic studies of the cortical anatomy of single-word processing. Nature **331:** 585–589.
127. ROSEN, H.J. *et al.* 2000. Comparison of brain activation during word retrieval done silently and aloud using fMRI. Brain Cogn. **42:** 201–217.
128. PRICE, C.J. *et al.* 1996. Hearing and saying. The functional neuro-anatomy of auditory word processing. Brain **119:** 919–931.
129. POEPPEL, D. 1996. A critical review of PET studies of phonological processing. Brain Lang. **55:** 317–385.
130. WISE, R.J. *et al.* 1999. Brain regions involved in articulation. Lancet **353:** 1057–1061.
131. CROSSON, B. *et al.* 1999. Activity in the paracingulate and cingulate sulci during word generation: an fMRI study of functional anatomy. Cerebral Cortex **9:** 307–316.
132. PAPATHANASSIOU, D. *et al.* 2000. A common language network for comprehension and production: a contribution to the definition of language epicenters with PET. Neuroimage **11:** 347–357.
133. PALMER, E.D. *et al.* 2001. An event-related fMRI study of overt and covert word stem completion. Neuroimage **14:** 182–193.

134. HINKE, R. et al. 1993. Functional magnetic resonance imaging of Broca's area during internal speech. Neuroreport 4: 675–678.
135. BOOKHEIMER, S.Y. et al. 2000. Activation of language cortex with automatic speech tasks. Neurology 55: 1151–1157.
136. BUCKNER, R.L., W.M. KELLEY & S.E. PETERSEN. 1999. Frontal cortex contributes to human memory formation. Nat. Neurosci. 2: 311–314.
137. FRIED, I., G.A. OJEMANN & E.E. FETZ. 1981. Language-related potentials specific to human language cortex. Science 212: 353–356.
138. FRIED, I. et al. 1991. Functional organization of human supplementary motor cortex studied by electrical stimulation. J. Neurosci. 11: 3656–3666.
139. OJEMANN, G.A. 1991. Cortical organization of language. J. Neurosci. 11: 2281–2287.
140. OJEMANN, G.A. 2003. The neurobiology of language and verbal memory: observations from awake neurosurgery. Int. J. Psychophysiol. 48: 141–146.
141. WALLESCH, C.W. et al. 1985. Observations on regional cerebral blood flow in cortical and subcortical structures during language production in normal man. Brain Lang. 25: 224–233.
142. KLEIN, D. et al. 1994. Left putaminal activation when speaking a second language: evidence from PET. Neuroreport 5: 2295–2297.
143. WILDGRUBER, D., H. ACKERMANN & W. GRODD. 2001. Differential contributions of motor cortex, basal ganglia, and cerebellum to speech motor control: effects of syllable repetition rate evaluated by fMRI. Neuroimage 13: 101–109.
144. JOHNSON, M.D. & G.A. OJEMANN. 2000. The role of the human thalamus in language and memory: evidence from electrophysiological studies. Brain Cogn. 42: 218–230.
145. LARSON, C.R. 1991. On the relation of PAG neurons to laryngeal and respiratory muscles during vocalization in the monkey. Brain Res. 552: 77–86.
146. DUSTERHOFT, F., U. HAUSLER & U. JURGENS. 2004. Neuronal activity in the periaqueductal gray and bordering structures during vocal communication in the squirrel monkey. Neuroscience 123: 53–60.
147. LARSON, C.R., Y. YAJIMA & P. KO. 1994. Modification in activity of medullary respiratory-related neurons for vocalization and swallowing. J. Neurophysiol. 71: 2294–2304.
148. BIEDERMAN-THORSON, M. 1970. Auditory responses of units in the ovoid nucleus and cerebrum (field L) of the ring dove. Brain Res. 24: 247–256.
149. MELLO, C.V. & D.F. CLAYTON. 1994. Song-induced ZENK gene expression in auditory pathways of songbird brain and its relation to the song control system. J. Neurosci. 14: 6652–6666.
150. COHEN, Y.E. & E.I. KNUDSEN. 1994. Auditory tuning for spatial cues in the barn owl basal ganglia. J. Neurophysiol. 72: 285–298.
151. CHEW, S.J. et al. 1995. Decrements in auditory responses to a repeated conspecific song are long-lasting and require two periods of protein synthesis in the songbird forebrain. Proc. Natl. Acad. Sci. USA 92: 3406–3410.
152. COHEN, Y.E. & E. I. KNUDSEN. 1996. Representation of frequency in the primary auditory field of the barn owl forebrain. J. Neurophysiol. 76: 3682–3692.
153. MELLO, C.V., D.S. VICARIO & D.F. CLAYTON. 1992. Song presentation induces gene expression in the songbird forebrain. Proc. Natl. Acad. Sci. USA 89: 6818–6822.
154. MELLO, C.V., F. NOTTEBOHM & D. CLAYTON. 1995. Repeated exposure to one song leads to a rapid and persistent decline in an immediate early gene's response to that song in zebra finch telencephalon. J. Neurosci. 15: 6919–6925.
155. JARVIS, E.D., C.V. MELLO & F. NOTTEBOHM. 1995. Associative learning and stimulus novelty influence the song-induced expression of an immediate early gene in the canary forebrain. Learn Mem. 2: 62–80.
156. BOLHUIS, J.J. et al. 2001. Localized immediate early gene expression related to the strength of song learning in socially reared zebra finches. Eur. J. Neurosci. 13: 2165–2170.
157. GENTNER, T.Q. & D. MARGOLIASH. 2003. Neuronal populations and single cells representing learned auditory objects. Nature 424: 669–674.
158. ROUILLER, E.M. et al. 1992. Mapping of c-fos expression elicited by pure tones stimulation in the auditory pathways of the rat, with emphasis on the cochlear nucleus. Neurosci. Lett. 144: 19–24.

159. FRIAUF, E. 1992. Tonotopic order in the adult and developing auditory system of the rat as shown by c-fos immunocytochemistry. Eur. J. Neurosci. **4:** 798–812.
160. LIEBERMAN, P. 2002. On the nature and evolution of the neural bases of human language. Am. J. Phys. Anthropol. Suppl. **35:** 36–62.
161. MULLER-PREUSS, P. & D. PLOOG. 1981. Inhibition of auditory cortical neurons during phonation. Brain Res. **215:** 61–76.
162. CREUTZFELDT, O., G. OJEMANN & E. LETTICH. 1989. Neuronal activity in the human lateral temporal lobe. I. Responses to speech. Exp. Brain Res. **77:** 451–475.
163. CREUTZFELDT, O., G. OJEMANN & E. LETTICH. 1989. Neuronal activity in the human lateral temporal lobe. II. Responses to the subjects own voice. Exp. Brain Res. **77:** 476–489.
164. CARDIN, J.A. & M.F. SCHMIDT. 2003. Song system auditory responses are stable and highly tuned during sedation, rapidly modulated and unselective during wakefulness, and suppressed by arousal. J. Neurophysiol. **90:** 2884–2899.
165. MACLEOD, A.K. *et al.* 1998. Right anterior prefrontal cortex activation during semantic monitoring and working memory. Neuroimage **7:** 41–48.
166. ZHANG, J.X., H.C. LEUNG & M.K. JOHNSON. 2003. Frontal activations associated with accessing and evaluating information in working memory: an fMRI study. Neuroimage **20:** 1531–1539.
167. GESCHWIND, N. 1979. Specializations of the human brain. Sci. Am. **241:** 180–199.
168. DEVOOGD, T.J. *et al.* 1993. Relations between song repertoire size and the volume of brain nuclei related to song: comparative evolutionary analyses amongst oscine birds. Proc. R. Soc. London B **254:** 75–82.
169. WADA, K. & E.D. JARVIS. Genes and Syntax. Manuscript in preparation.
170. EVANS, S.E. 2000. General discussion II: amniote evolution. *In* Evolutionary Developmental Biology of the Cerebral Cortex. Vol. 228. G.R. Bock & G. Cardew, Eds.: 109–113. John Wiley & Sons. Chichester.
171. TARSITANO, S.F. *et al.* 2000. On the evolution of feathers from an aerodynamic and constructional view point. Am. Zool. **40:** 676–686.
172. FARRIES, M.A. 2001. The oscine song system considered in the context of the avian brain: lessons learned from comparative neurobiology. Brain Behav Evol. **58:** 80–100.
173. MORTON, E. 1975. Ecological sources of selection on avian sounds. Am. Natural. **109:** 17–34.
174. OKANOYA, K. 2002. Sexual display as a syntactical vehicle: the evolution of syntax in birdsong and human language through sexual selection. *In* The Transition to Language. A. Wray, Ed.: 46–63. Oxford University Press. Oxford.
175. MARLER, P., A. DUFTY & R. PICKERT. 1986. Vocal communication in the domestic chicken: I. Does a sender communicate information about the quality of a food referent to a receiver? Anim. Behav. **34:** 188–193.
176. TCHERNICHOVSKI, O., H. SCHWABL & F. NOTTEBOHM. 1998. Context determines the sex appeal of male zebra finch song. Anim. Behav. **55:** 1003–1010.
177. MARTEN, K., D. QUINE & P. MARLER. 1977. Sound transmission and its significance for animal vocalization II. Tropical Forest Habitats. Behav. Ecol. Sociobiol. **2:** 291–302.
178. MARTEN, K. & P. MARLER. 1977. Sound transmission and its significance for animal vocalization I. Temperate habitats. Behav. Ecol. Sociobiol. **2:** 271–290.
179. WILEY, R.H. 1978. Physical constrains on acoustic communication in the atmosphere: implications for the evolution of animal vocalisations. Behav. Ecol. Sociobiol. **3:** 69–94.
180. MCCRACKEN, K.G. & F.H. SHELDON. 1997. Avian vocalizations and phylogenetic signal. Proc. Natl. Acad. Sci. USA **94:** 3833–3836.
181. ZANN, R.A. 1996. Chapter 10: Vocalizations. *In* The Zebra Finch: A Synthesis of Field and Laboratory Studies.: 196–247. Oxford University Press. New York.
182. NOVACEK, M.J. 1992. Mammalian phylogeny: shaking the tree. Nature **356:** 121–125.
183. NOVACEK, M.J. 2001. Mammalian phylogeny: genes and supertrees. Curr. Biol. **11:** R573–575.
184. SIBLEY, C.G. & J.E. AHLQUIST. 1990. Phylogeny and Classification of Birds: A Study in Molecular Evolution. Yale University Press. New Haven, CT.

Where Is the Bird?

TIMOTHY J. DEVOOGD

Department of Psychology, Uris Hall, Cornell University, Ithaca, New York 14853, USA

ABSTRACT: **Patterns of song perception, learning, and expression differ across species, sexes, and individuals. We can understand the neurobiology of song better by paying attention to these differences. I focus selectively on a few of the studies done in my lab over in recent years to illustrate this.**

KEYWORDS: **evolution; female choice; phylogenetic analysis; dendritic spines; Acrocephalus warbler; heritability**

Although many of the papers in this volume are attempts to generalize their research results as broadly as possible, I would like to ask where the bird is in all this. I mean by this that patterns of song perception, learning, and expression differ across species, sexes, and individuals. We can understand the neurobiology of song better by paying attention to these differences. I will focus selectively on a few of the studies done in my lab over in recent years to illustrate this. More complete reviews both of our own work and of more general song system neurobiology can be found elsewhere.[1,2]

RELATIONS BETWEEN SONG AND THE SONG SYSTEM ACROSS MALES

First, as even a casual observer of songbirds knows, species differ dramatically in all possible features of song—from the timing of learning, to contexts for its use, to the acoustic structure of individual sound elements, to the pattern in which elements are assembled into a song. Of particular interest is the observation that aspects of song are learned—and in this feature as in the ones mentioned above, there is immense variation across songbird species. For example, the songs of a nightingale and a black-capped chickadee differ immensely in the amount of learning that they incorporate. We have found that these differences are correlated with variation in gross morphology of the song system. Across a group of 41 very diverse species, the relative volume of HVC was positively correlated with the number of different songs typically produced by males in the species.[3] These findings suggest that essential functions of the song system evolved early in the songbird phylogeny and have persisted in many of the families of this group. However, only limited inferences can be drawn from studying such a wide phylogeny. The structure of song differs so widely

Address for correspondence: Timothy J. DeVoogd, Department of Psychology, Uris Hall, Cornell University, Ithaca, New York 14853, USA. Voice: 607-255-6430; fax: 607-255-8433.
tjd5@cornell.edu; <http://comp9.psych.cornell.edu/people/Faculty/tjd5.html>

Ann. N.Y. Acad. Sci. 1016: 778–786 (2004). © 2004 New York Academy of Sciences.
doi: 10.1196/annals.1298.033

that quantification with the same metrics is often impossible. Different avian families have experienced such prolonged and divergent selective pressures that the distribution of function within the song system may have diverged. Thus, to understand structure-function relations in more detail, it is necessary to study more closely related taxa.

Even within avian families, there can be immense variation in song complexity. This can be observed within reed warblers, several closely related genera that are part of the sylviidae family. These species live in similar habitats, eat similar diets, and look very much alike. Marsh warbler (*Acrocephalus palustris*) songs consist of up to 100 different syllables.[4] In contrast, grasshopper warbler (*Locustella naevia*) songs consist of a single two-note syllable repeated scores to hundreds of times. Even this simple song contains features that are learned from models in a juvenile sensitive period.[5] HVC is several times larger in the marsh warbler than in the grasshopper warbler (FIG. 1). Across eight such warbler species, the relative volume of HVC is significantly related to the number of different song syllables typically found in a male's repertoire, once degree of relatedness is factored into the statistics (FIG. 2).[6]

We and other labs have found that the relations between gross morphology of the song system and aspects of singing can even be found across individuals within a species. Nottebohm and colleagues first observed that the number of syllables in the repertoire of male canaries is positively correlated with the volumes of HVC and of RA.[7] This observation extends to female canaries: the number of syllables they produce when induced to sing with testosterone implants is correlated with the volume of HVC.[8] There is no significant relation between HVC volume and size of the repertoire of song types sung by marsh wrens (*Cistothorus palustris*) that had been exposed to a restricted number of song types during rearing. However, if raised hearing a more normal number of song models, HVC volume and adult repertoire are correlated.[9] Even in laboratory-housed zebra finches, the number of notes comprising the stereotyped song varies between normal individuals. We have found that this variation in the overall content of song is positively correlated with the volume of the bird's HVC.[10] Ward and colleagues[11] have found a significant correlation between the number of learned elements in the zebra finch's song and HVC volume. This brain-behavior relation is present in wild birds too. In sedge warblers (*A. schoenobaenus*), HVC volume is significantly correlated with syllable repertoires recorded in individuals singing on their territories.[12] Thus, as Nottebohm observed in the early 1980s, learning literally requires brain space, and more learning requires more space. Together, these data suggest that learning makes use of the amount of substrate that is available, not that learning induces measurable changes in the overall volume of HVC.

These correlations should be viewed cautiously on the anatomical side. Clearly, volume is only an estimate of features like number of neurons or amount of neuropil that are in fact directly related to function. Furthermore, HVC by itself does not learn or produce a song. It is part of sensory and motor circuits that contain many brain regions, and it is the connectivity and interactions between these components that determines outcome. Indeed, in the study relating zebra finch song and song system anatomy, we found that the volumes of Area X and l-MAN also predict repertoire size. Interestingly, reduced size in Area X was associated with a larger repertoire. A statistical model in which HVC volume was a positive factor and Area X volume a

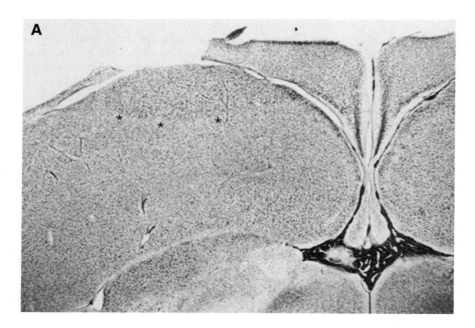

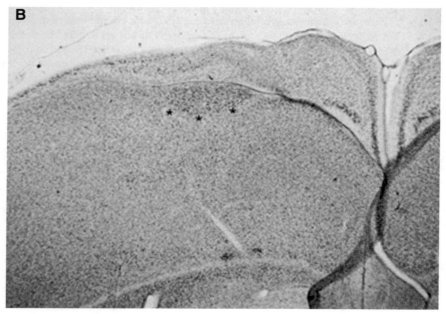

FIGURE 1. HVC is substantially larger in a marsh warbler (**A**) (which sings a large repertoire) than in a closely related grasshopper warbler (which sings a very small repertoire).

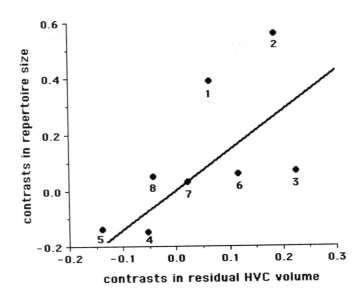

FIGURE 2. Across eight closely related warbler species, contrasts in the relative volume of HVC are positively correlated with contrasts in syllable repertoire, once degree of relatedness is factored out.[6]

negative factor accounted for nearly 90% of the variance in syllable repertoire.[10] A reanalysis of our comparative reed warbler data also indicates that including Area X volume together with HVC volume produces a stronger correlation with repertoire size. Across these species, as among the zebra finches, a smaller Area X is associated with a larger repertoire.[13] Perhaps Area X inhibits shifting from one motor pattern to another when the motor patterns of song are learned.

Correlations between song complexity and song system anatomy should be viewed cautiously on the behavioral side as well. It would be easy to conclude from these studies that a function of HVC is to encode vocal motor variety, permitting a male to learn and produce as many syllables as his HVC will accommodate. However, different aspects of song are correlated with each other, and our ability to readily measure one aspect like repertoire size does not mean that this is the factor that has been shaped by selection and learning. In our work on wild sedge warblers, we also measured song length and the number of unique syllables per song bout, and these values also were significantly related to HVC volume.[12] In our work with zebra finches, HVC volume was correlated with the length of song phrases as well as with the number of unique syllables.[10] Ultimately, resolving what the singer (and the song system) is designed to achieve may come from studying the receiver: if a male sings to a female, her reaction to songs may give the best indication of the song qualities that his song system is being optimized to produce.

In recent years, we have begun to look for cellular correlates of song learning, both in males in which the consequence of not learning is typically an inability to produce a complex song, and in females in which it is still unclear whether song learning contributes to later song recognition and selection. In both sets of experiments, we have examined zebra finches that grew up with restrictions on their opportunity for song learning. We have chosen to do this by removing adult males from a colony before the chicks reached the sensitive period for song learning. While this eliminates some kinds of social interaction as well as exposure to stereotyped song, it seems the least disruptive means of depriving the young birds of song models.

Several components of the song system are affected by this treatment in male zebra finches. At 5 weeks, early in the sensitive period, neurons in l-MAN have elaborate dendrites with large numbers of dendritic spines. In normally reared birds, the number of spines per unit length decreases by more than 50% over the next two months.[14] However, rearing the birds in aviaries from which adult males have been removed, results in preserving high numbers of dendritic spines on these neurons, at least for an additional 3 weeks.[15] This is consistent with this rearing treatment prolonging the period during which song elements can still be learned from a tutor.[16,17] Perhaps large numbers of spines can reinforce many sorts of motor programs within RA, whereas practicing a particular song reinforces and preserves only a subset of these.

In adult birds, spine density in HVC is related to the complexity of an individual male's song. For example, adult male marsh wrens that had experienced 45 different song types and acquired songs with similar numbers of song types have higher spine densities on HVC neurons than do adult males that heard only five song types and formed a similarly simple song.[18] The two groups did not differ in spine density in RA. In zebra finches, removing adult males from the colony results in young males forming an abnormally simple "isolate" song. When mature, these males also have fewer dendritic spines on neurons in HVC than do normally reared males.[19] In contrast, sedge warblers raised with either complex or simple models for song do not differ in HVC spine density. However, in spite of the differences in rearing, these warblers also did not differ in the complexity of their adult song repertoires. Birds reared hearing a simple song appear to have improvised a repertoire at least as large as that of the birds reared with more complex song.[20] Thus, the density of spine synapses in HVC seems to be related to the complexity of the song that a bird produces, and not to the complexity of the songs that he had experienced. These data imply that song learning acts at the level of individual synapses in HVC, not noticeably at the level of region size or number of cells within a region. One of the implications of this is that a larger HVC can accommodate more of the synapses and temporal modules that might be needed for a complex repertoire than can a smaller HVC.

RELATIONS BETWEEN SONG AND THE SONG SYSTEM ACROSS FEMALES

Song is interactive. In many species, males sing to attract or maintain pair bonds with females. And in many species, females not only discriminate conspecific song from heterospecific song, they use song to discriminate between individual conspecific males. For example, female great reed warblers (*A. arundinaceus*) pair with and have extra-pair copulations with the males they encounter whose songs are most elaborate.[21,22] In such lineages, males will have experienced a selective advantage if they have been able to produce the sort of song that is most exciting to females. Motor processing within males can only really be understood in the context of female perception. More precisely, variation in the content of a male's song is only meaningful to the extent that it can be perceived by females. However, much less is known about how females perceive song than about how males produce it. A huge advance in studying the problem of perception has come with the discovery of novel brain areas that are activated similarly in both sexes by song perception.[23-25] In one of these areas, NCM, different song syllables evoke distinct patterns of immediate early gene activation,[26] consistent with NCM being involved in song discrimination.

Preliminary data from several experiments suggest that relations between the anatomy of NCM and aspects of song perception in females are parallel to the brain-behavior relations described above for males. We have presented conspecific song to female African Marsh (*A. baeticatus*) and Cape Reed (*A. gracilirostris*) warblers, two species of reed warblers from southern Africa. While closely related and similar in appearance, habitat, and diet, the two species differ widely in the structure of male song. After returning from migration, male African Marsh warblers sing prolonged elaborate songs with scores of different syllables, while trying to establish a territory and attract a female. In contrast, Cape Reed males have prolonged pair bonds and territories and sing a much less elaborate song, in which variety comes more slowly. Hearing conspecific song evokes much higher levels of expression of ZENK protein in NCM in the African Marsh females than in the Cape Reed females. Thus females of the species that customarily listens to a more complex repertoire and must respond to it quickly show a greater amount of activation than females of the species that normally listens to a less complex repertoire.[27]

Initial observation in zebra finches indicates that learning contributes to a female's ability to discriminate between male songs. Normally reared females readily choose to approach normal song over isolate song. However, females raised in colonies without adult males (i.e., without exposure to song) are as likely to choose the isolate as the normal song.[28] Such females have fewer dendritic spines on neurons in NCM than do normally reared females.[19] Perhaps females learn about song by modifying synapses within a brain region that will be activated by song perception when they are adult.

RELATIONS BETWEEN SONG AND THE SONG SYSTEM OVER GENERATIONS

The song system is present throughout the oscine phylogeny (the "songbirds") but not present in their closest relatives, the suboscines. Thus the nuclei and their interrelations develop in response to genetic instructions that differ from those present in the suboscines. Similarly, genetic differences must underlie the major differences in neural representation of the song system between families of oscines—the structures are relatively large throughout the Muscicapidae and quite small throughout the Paridae. As indicated above and elsewhere in this volume, females in many oscine species use song features in selecting mates. In *Acrocephalus* species, females appear to select males whose songs have many syllables (or other song features highly correlated with syllable number), a trait that usually is enhanced by learning. Over many generations, sexual selection like this can lead to increased expression of the trait in the species and so shape evolution, but only if the selected trait is heritable. Or more specifically, capacity for learning should increase over evolutionary time if females select males with high levels of a heritable trait that depends on learning. While these theories have been developed over several decades, until recently, few experimental data have been available for assessing them.

The volumes of the nuclei comprising the song system vary between individual males. We have studied this variation in zebra finch families.[29] Two findings stand out. First, within individuals, variation in the volume of a song system nucleus is significantly correlated with variation in the volumes of the nuclei to which that nucleus is monosynaptically connected, as well as with the volume of the telencephalon as a whole. Thus, if an individual has a large HVC, he will tend to have a large RA and Area X as well as a relatively large telencephalon. Second, variation in the volumes of the caudal song system nuclei HVC, RA, and nXIIts is strongly heritable, whereas variation in the volumes of the rostral nuclei is only weakly heritable. Thus, fathers with a large HVC are likely to have sons with a large HVC.

These relations indicate that genetic variation contributes to individual differences in volumes of song system nuclei. Sexual selection for a complex song is likely to select for these genes, resulting in an increase in their representation and probably their effect as well. In evolutionary theory, sexual selection usually is associated with a benefit to the female's reproductive fitness, either related to a direct quality of the male, or an indirect feature that will be of benefit to the progeny. What could song tell a female about a male? Theories include information about his health, his age, his social experience, and his condition. To these, we can now add another. Elaborate song could tell a female that the male has a large HVC and so is likely to have a large telencephalon. It could also tell her that these traits are likely to be passed on to their sons.

Taken together, our findings suggest that if you want to increase the capacity for vocal learning in a species, you have to increase the volume of song system nuclei, especially HVC. If you increase the size of HVC, it is likely that RA and Area X will increase in size as well. However, our data suggest that increased volume in Area X is negatively correlated with song complexity, perhaps due to inhibition or gating motor programs encoded in HVC and RA. In a sense, this constraint against easy modification of the song system could keep a male honest—his song reflects qualities of his song system and his brain, and he cannot change the song without changes in his song system and, ultimately, more widely in his brain.

Our data on females suggest that the female side of the story may be just as interesting as that of the male, both in terms of perception and discrimination, and in terms of the evolutionary course that has given her these capacities. While much less is known of female abilities than of male abilities, it is likely that females have neural circuits dedicated to song perception. Neurons in these circuits are plastic and their anatomy is affected by auditory experience. This experiential tuning of perception then enhances the female's ability for fine discrimination. We do not know if this circuitry and the female's capacity for tuning and for complex discrimination differ between individuals. Data from our lab and others indicate that these features differ between species, which would suggest that they are genetically specified and may be subject to selective pressures as song production has been in males.

The identity of the bird is central to understanding the neurobiology of the song system. A zebra finch is not a prototypic songbird. Males and females have different evolutionary goals in their use of song, and have neural circuitry likely to emphasize production and perception, respectively. In fact, different individuals of the same sex have differences in the neurobiology of their song systems that are reflected in individual differences in the amount or quality of song learning that is possible. Such differences are not annoyances in the path to a clear description of how the system works. Rather, they are the results of a grand evolutionary experiment, and provide an opportunity to understand the ultimate function of the song system as well as how it has been optimized for diverse goals across species, between sexes, and from one individual to another.

ACKNOWLEDGMENTS

Supported by National Science Foundation—Division of Integrative Biology and Neuroscience (grant 0090963). Thanks to Zach Buchan, Michelle Tomaszycki, and Jordan Moore for suggestions and comments.

REFERENCES

1. DeVoogd, T.J. & C.H.A. Lauay. 2001. Emerging psychobiology of the avian song system. *In* Handbook of Behavioral Neurobiology, E. Blass, Ed.: 356–392. Kluwer Academic/Plenum. New York, NY.
2. DeVoogd, T.J. 2004. Neural constraints on the complexity of avian song. Brain Behav. Evol. **63:** 221–232.
3. DeVoogd, T.J., J.R. Krebs, S.D. Healy & A. Purvis. 1993. Evolutionary correlation between repertoire size and a brain nucleus amongst passerine birds. Proc. R. Soc. London B **254:** 75–82.
4. Dowsett-Lemaire, F. 1979. The imitative range of the song of the marsh warbler *Acrocephalus palustris*, with special reference to imitations of African birds. Ibis **121:** 453–468.
5. Becker, P.H. 1990. Der Gesang des Feldschwirls (*Locustella naevia*) bei Lernentzug. Vogelwarte **35:** 257–267.
6. Szekely, T., C.K. Catchpole, A. DeVoogd, *et al.* 1996. Evolutionary changes in a song control area of the brain (HVC) are associated with evolutionary changes in song repertoire among European warblers (Sylviidae). Proc. R Soc. London B. **263:** 607–610.
7. Nottebohm, F., S. Kasparian & C. Pandazis. 1981. Brain space for a learned task. Brain Res. **213:** 99–109.
8. Nottebohm, F. 1980. Brain correlates of a learned motor skill. Verh. Dtsch. Zool. Ges. **73:** 262–267.
9. Brenowitz, E.A., K. Lent & D.E. Kroodsma. 1995. Brain space for learned song in birds develops independently of song learning. J. Neurosci. **15:** 6281–6286.
10. Airey, D.C. & T.J. DeVoogd. 2000. Variation in song complexity and HVC volume are significantly related in zebra finches. Neuroreport **10:** 2339–2344.
11. Ward, B.C., E.J. Nordeen & K.W. Nordeen. 1998. Individual variation in neuron number predicts differences in the propensity for avian vocal imitation. Proc. Natl. Acad. Sci. USA **95:** 1277–1282.
12. Airey, D.C., K.L. Buchanan, T. Szekely, *et al.* 2000. Song complexity, sexual selection and a song control nucleus (HVC) in the brains of European sedge warblers. J. Neurobiol. **44:** 1–6.
13. Székely, T. & T.J. DeVoogd. Unpublished observations.
14. Nixdorf-Bergweiler, B.E., E. Wallhausser-Franke & T.J. DeVoogd. 1995. Regressive development in neuronal structure during song learning in birds. J. Neurobiol. **27:** 204–215.

15. WALLHAUSSER-FRANKE, E., B.E. NIXDORF-BERGWEILER & T.J. DEVOOGD. 1995. Song isolation is associated with maintaining high spine frequencies on zebra finch lMAN neurons. Neurobiol. Learn. Mem. **64:** 25–35.
16. MORRISON, R.G. & F. NOTTEBOHM. 1993. Role of a telencephalic nucleus in the delayed song learning of socially isolated zebra finches. J. Neurobiol. **24:** 1045–1064.
17. JONES, A.E., C. TEN CATE & P.J.B. SLATER. 1996 Early experience and plasticity of song in adult male zebra finches. J. Comp. Psychol. **110:** 354–369.
18. AIREY, D.C., D.E. KROODSMA & T.J. DEVOOGD. 2000. Learning a larger song repertoire increases spine density in a songbird telencephalic control nucleus. Neurobiol. Learn. Mem. **73:** 274–281.
19. LAUAY, C.H.A., R.W. KOMOROSKI & T.J. DEVOOGD. Dendritic spine frequency in the song system is decreased in female zebra finches as well as in males if they are prevented from hearing song. J. Comp. Neurol. Submitted for publication.
20. LEITNER, S., B. LEISLER, T.J. DEVOOGD & C.K. CATCHPOLE. 2002. The size of a major song control nucleus (HVC) in the brains of European sedge warblers has a strong genetic component. Proc. R. Soc. London B **269:** 2519–2524.
21. BENSCH, S. & D. HASSELQUIST. 1992. Evidence for active female choice in a polygynous warbler. Anim. Behav. **44:** 301–311.
22. HASSELQUIST, D., S. BENSCH & T. VON-SCHANTZ. 1996. Correlation between male song repertoire, extra-pair paternity and offspring survival in the great reed warbler. Nature **381:** 229–232.
23. MELLO, C.V., D.S. VICARIO & D.F. CLAYTON. 1992. Song presentation induces gene expression in the songbird forebrain. Proc. Natl. Acad. Sci. USA **89:** 6818–6822.
24. MELLO, C.V. & D.F. CLAYTON. 1994. Song-induced ZENK gene expression in auditory pathways of songbird brain and its relation to the song control system. J. Neurosci. **14:** 6652–6666.
25. JARVIS, E.D. & F. NOTTEBOHM. 1997. Motor-driven gene expression. Proc. Natl. Acad. Sci. USA **94:** 4097–4102.
26. REBEIRO, S., G.A. CECCHI, M.O. MAGNASCO & C.V. MELLO. 1998. Toward a song code: Evidence for a syllabic representation in the canary brain. Neuron **21:** 359–371.
27. SUNDBERG, K.A., S.W. NEWMAN, J. BÜKI & T.J. DEVOOGD. 2001. Female songbirds that differ in song experience or quality of song discrimination also differ in their IEG response to hearing song. Soc. Neurosci. Abs.
28. LAUAY, C., N. GERLACH, E. ADKINS-REGAN & T.J. DEVOOGD. 2004. Female zebra finches require early song exposure to prefer high quality song as adults. Anim. Behav. (In press.)
29. AIREY, D.C., H. CASTILLO-JUAREZ, G. CASELLA, *et al.* 2000. Variation in the volume of zebra finch song control nuclei is heritable: developmental and evolutionary implications. Proc. R. Soc. London B **267:** 2099–2104.

Index of Contributors